THE ENGLISH AND SCOTTISH
POPULAR BALLADS

F. J. Child

THE
ENGLISH AND SCOTTISH
POPULAR BALLADS

EDITED BY

FRANCIS JAMES CHILD

IN FIVE VOLUMES

VOLUME I

CORRECTED SECOND EDITION
PREPARED BY
MARK F. HEIMAN
LAURA SAXTON HEIMAN

LOOMIS HOUSE PRESS

Loomis House Press
503 Washington Street
Northfield, Minnesota, USA
http://www.loomishousepress.com/

This edition contains an article by Francis Child
entitled "Ballad Poetry" from *Johnson's New Universal Cyclopædia*,
Vol. 1. Ed. Frederic A. P. Barnard, et al. New York: A. J. Johnson & Son, 1877. p. 365–68.

Publishers Cataloging-in-Publication Data

Child, Francis James, 1825–1896
 The English and Scottish popular ballads / edited by
Francis James Child ; prepared by Mark F. Heiman, Laura
Saxton Heiman. — Corrected 2nd ed.
 p. cm.
 ISBN 0-9707020-1-9 (paper) — ISBN 0-9707020-2-7 (cloth)
 1. Ballads, English — England — Texts.
 2. Ballads, Scots — Scotland — Texts.
 3. Ballads, English — Bibliography.
 4. Ballads, Scots — Bibliography.
 5. Narrative poetry, Scottish.
 6. Narrative poetry, English.
 7. Folk songs, English.
 8. Folk songs, Scots.
 I. Title. II. Heiman, Mark F. III. Heiman, Laura Saxton.
 PR1181. C5 2001
 821.04

Printed in the United States of America

FREDERICK J. FURNIVALL, ESQ.

OF LONDON

MY DEAR FURNIVALL:

Without the Percy MS. no one would pretend to make a collection of the English Ballads, and but for you that manuscript would still, I think, be beyond reach of man, yet exposed to destructive chances. Through your exertions and personal sacrifices, directly, the famous and precious folio has been printed; and, indirectly, in consequence of the same, it has been transferred to a place where it is safe, and open to inspection. This is only one of a hundred reasons which I have for asking you to accept the dedication of this book from

Your grateful friend and fellow-student,

F J. CHILD.

Cambridge, Mass., December 1, 1882.

PREFACE TO THE NEW EDITION

It is not without trepidation that we undertake to improve upon one of the foundational works of ballad studies in the English language. Since its initial publication between 1883 and 1898, *The English and Scottish Popular Ballads* has been recognized as the first comprehensive study of ballad texts, and has served as a starting point for ballad studies ever since. It seems appropriate that, just over a century since its initial publication, Francis James Child's life work should be made available again for a new generation of ballad scholars and students. Spurred, perhaps, by the publication of *Popular Ballads* at the end of the nineteenth century, the twentieth century has witnessed a renaissance of the ballad: the work of the great ballad collectors in the first half of the century, both in Great Britain and America, and the publication of numerous collections and recordings; the maturation of ballad study as an academic field, and the articles, books, and inevitable battles which arose within that field; and the (re)entry of traditional ballads into the popular culture and imagination through the folk revival of the 60's and 70's—a movement which continues to influence modern music and literature.

In preparing this new edition, we have not attempted to update or annotate the text in light of modern ballad scholarship. Rather, this work may regarded as the text which might have resulted had Child lived to oversee the production of a second edition of *The English and Scottish Popular Ballads*. During the sixteen years over which the original edition was released, Child's research continued unabated, and he frequently encountered new variants and supporting material for ballads which had already been committed to print. As a result, the original five volumes contain appendices comprising more than two hundred and fifty pages of cumulative additions and corrections.

This new edition inserts all of the additional material in the appropriate locations and applies all of the corrections to the text as specified by the author, making this material readily accessible to the reader for the first time. Ballad variants with letters assigned have been inserted in the appropriate locations, and other variants not assigned a letter designation have been included in an appendix to each ballad ("Additional Copies"), following the pattern established by Child. Punctuation has been slightly regularized, and references to books and other major works have been italicized according to modern conventions, to aid the reader in navigating the profusion of citations. No other editorial changes have been made. The text has been completely re-set, which, combined with the additions, creates a new pagination. The original page numbers have been indicated in the margins of the text as an aid in following references to the first edition. All internal cross-references have been updated to reflect the new page numbers.

Perhaps the most significant departure from the original edition is the inclusion of a small number of tunes in the body of the text. One of the most frequent criticisms made of the ballad scholars of the nineteenth century concerns their treatment of ballads as a literary form divorced from musical or performance considerations, an omission explored and corrected by later scholars such as Bertrand Bronson. Child was not unaware of the musical tradition—as the "Index of Published Airs" and the fifty-five tunes in the appendices to Volume V attest—but he was a man of his time, and the texts were his central concern. In preparing this new edition, we felt that it would benefit both scholars and casual readers to, where possible, reunite texts and tunes. We have included only tunes which originally accompanied the texts that Child cites, supplementing the original fifty-five with tunes collected by Bronson in *The Traditional Tunes of the Child Ballads*. In consideration for those who might wish to experience these ballads by singing them, we have provided conjectural text underlays for all of the melodies. These have no basis in the manuscript sources, but are based on Bronson's careful phrase markings and on attention to scansion and singability. Nonetheless, the connection between texts and tunes remains imperfect, in many cases because the aggregate text provided by Child differs from the particular text with which the tune is associated. In all cases we have indicated which source of a given variant provided the tune, so that the original text can be reconstructed by recourse to the appropriate end notes.

Finally, this volume includes, in place of the introduction left unbegun at the time of Child's death, his rarely seen article entitled "Ballad Poetry," from 1877. Written for a popular audience immediately before he began work on the first volume of this collection, this article cannot substitute for the over arching introduction that Child wished to prepare when the collection was complete, but it does provide a window on the state of ballad scholarship at the time and on Child's own assumptions about the field and the work he was undertaking. For the modern student of ballads, it provides a valuable context for this collection, but should, of course, be supplemented with reading of more recent scholarship.

George Kittredge's biography of Child, and the original "Advertisements" to the two parts of each volume have been retained unchanged from the original edition.

For those new to this collection, a brief overview of the scope and structure of Child's work may be helpful.

As a result of failed attempts to obtain evidence of a living tradition of ballad performance, Child regarded the ballad as a lost art, and consequently felt it was possible to assemble "every valuable copy of every known ballad," primarily from manuscript and printed

sources, to produce a collection modelled on Sven Gruntvig's edition of the Danish ballads. The result was this compilation of three hundred and five ballads, most with multiple variants. The numbers assigned to each ballad are still used today to refer to variants of ballads in this collection: e.g. Child 10 for versions of "The Twa Sisters."

Each ballad chapter is headed by a list of all of the variants (**A**, **B**, etc.) and their sources, followed by an introduction to the ballad. This introduction typically consists of a brief discussion of the textual sources for the ballad, followed by a summary of the ballad story, with variations noted. From this follows what is usually the most substantial portion of the introduction: a detailed survey of similar stories and story elements in the literatures of the (mostly) Western world, with extensive notes and references. Some passages and footnotes conclude with a parenthetical name or initials (e.g. "R. Kohler" or "G.L.K."); these indicate that the preceding information was supplied in large part by the referenced source. Ballads from collections in other languages are frequently referred to, using capital letters to distinguish variants. At the end of the introduction are sometimes historical or textual notes on the ballad in question, concluding with a listing of translations of the ballad into other languages.

In many cases, the discussion devoted to the ballad texts themselves is surprisingly brief, and many questions about the meaning and context of the ballad are left unaddressed. These introductions are invaluable for describing the historical and cultural antecedents of the ballad stories, however, and certainly repay the effort required to approach them.

Following the introduction are the ballad texts, headed by the letter assigned to each variant. Some variants are compounded from multiple sources which Child deemed similar enough to represent a single text. These sources are listed at the beginning of each variant, and designated by lowercase letters (a, b, etc.). The texts as they stand often do not represent any one source, but are "ideal" texts created by combining the best or most complete elements from several source texts, with punctuation and capitalization normalized and some spelling corrections made. The texts are also divided into numbered stanzas, even when this is not done in the original sources. Rows of dots (. . .) are used to indicate lines which are clearly missing from the text, and rows of asterisks are used to indicate places where Child felt that portions of the story had been lost, possibly as a result of missing stanzas.

After the last variant text, end notes explain how the given texts vary from each of the original sources; for instance, the notation "**K. b.** *Omits* 4" indicates that source **b** of variant **K** does not include the stanza given in the text as number four. The end notes also include valuable notations and comments about the text that appear in the original sources.

Some ballads include appendices, which highlight other texts that are related to the ballad in question, or include additional variants that are incomplete or uncataloged. Each of these has its own set of end notes.

The entire collection concludes, in Volume V, with an extensive set of reference materials including a glossary, lists of sources, indices, and bibliographies.

We hope that this edition of Child—the first new edition in more than forty years, and the first ever non-facsimile edition—will be of value both to scholars and to casual students of balladry, traditional music, and folklore. We are extremely grateful for all of the encouragement and assistance we have been given as we undertook this project, and are glad for the opportunity to give something back to the ballad community.

MARK F. HEIMAN
LAURA SAXTON HEIMAN
November 1, 2001
Northfield, Minnesota

ADVERTISEMENT TO PART I

NUMBERS 1–28

It was my wish not to begin to print *The English and Scottish Popular Ballads* until this unrestricted title should be justified by my having at command every valuable copy of every known ballad. A continuous effort to accomplish this object has been making for some nine or ten years, and many have joined in it. By correspondence, and by all extensive diffusion of printed circulars, I have tried to stimulate collection from tradition in Scotland, Canada, and the United States, and no becoming means has been left unemployed to obtain possession of unsunned treasures locked up in writing. The gathering from tradition has been, as ought perhaps to have been foreseen at this late day, meagre, and generally of indifferent quality. Materials in the hands of former editors have, in some cases, been lost beyond recovery, and very probably have lighted fires, like that large cantle of the Percy manuscript, *maxime deflendus!* Access to several manuscript collections has not yet been secured. But what is still lacking is believed to bear no great proportion to what is in hand, and may soon come in, besides: meanwhile, the uncertainties of the world forbid a longer delay to publish so much as has been got together.

Of hitherto unused materials, much the most important is a large collection of ballads made by Motherwell. For leave to take a copy of this I am deeply indebted to the present possessor, Mr Malcolm Colquhoun Thomson, of Glasgow, who even allowed the manuscript to be sent to London, and to be retained several months, for my accommodation. Mr J. Wylie Guild, of Glasgow, also permitted the use of a note-book of Motherwell's which supplements the great manuscript, and this my unwearied friend, Mr James Barclay Murdoch, to whose solicitation I owe both, himself transcribed with the most scrupulous accuracy. No other good office, asked or unasked, has Mr Murdoch spared.

Next in extent to the Motherwell collections come those of the late Mr Kinloch. These he freely placed at my disposal, and Mr William Macmath, of Edinburgh, made during Mr Kinloch's life an exquisite copy of the larger part of them, enriched with notes from Mr Kinloch's papers, and sent it to me across the water. After Mr Kinloch's death his collections were acquired by Harvard College Library, still through the agency of Mr Macmath, who has from the beginning rendered a highly valued assistance, not less by his suggestions and communications than by his zealous mediation.

No Scottish ballads are superior in kind to those recited in the last century by Mrs Brown, of Falkland. Of these there are, or were, three sets. One formerly owned by Robert Jamieson, the fullest of the three, was lent me, to keep as long as I required, by my honored friend the late Mr David Laing, who also secured for me copies of several ballads of Mrs Brown which are found in an Abbotsford manuscript, and gave me a transcript of the Glenriddell manuscript. The two others were written down for William Tytler and Alexander Fraser Tytler respectively, the former of these consisting of a portion of the Jamieson texts revised. These having for some time been lost sight of, Miss Mary Fraser Tytler, with a graciousness which I have reason to believe hereditary in the name, made search for them, recovered the one which had been obtained by Lord Woodhouselee, and copied it for me with her own hand. The same lady furnished me with another collection which had been made by a member of the family.

For later transcriptions from Scottish tradition I am indebted to Mr J. F. Campbell of Islay, whose edition and rendering of the racy West

Highland Tales is marked by the rarest appreciation of the popular genius; to Mrs A. F. Murison, formerly of Old Deer, who undertook a quest for ballads in her native place on my behalf; to Mr Alexander Laing, of Newburgh-upon-Tay; to Mr James Gibb, of Joppa, who has given me a full score; to Mr David Louden, of Morham, Haddington; to the late Dr John Hill Burton and Miss Ella Burton; to Dr Thomas Davidson.

The late Mr Robert White, of Newcastle-upon-Tyne, allowed me to look through his collections in 1873, and subsequently made me a copy of such things as I needed, and his ready kindness has been continued by Mrs Andrews, his sister, and by Miss Andrews, his niece, who has taken a great deal of trouble on my account.

In the south of the mother-island my reliance has, of necessity, been chiefly upon libraries. The British Museum possesses, besides early copies of some of the older ballads, the Percy MS., Herd's MSS and Buchan's, and the Roxburgh broadsides. The library of the University of Cambridge affords one or two things of first-rate importance, and for these I am beholden to the accomplished librarian, Mr Henry Bradshaw, and to Professor Skeat. I have also to thank the Rev. F. Gunton, Dean, and the other authorities of Magdalen College, Cambridge, for permitting collations of Pepys ballads, most obligingly made for me by Mr Arthur S. B. Miller. Many things were required from the Bodleian library, and these were looked out for me, and scrupulously copied or collated, by Mr George Parker.

Texts of traditional ballads have been communicated to me in America by Mr W. W. Newell, of New York, who is soon to give us an interesting collection of Children's Games traditional in America; by Dr Huntington, Bishop of Central New York; Mr G. C. Mahon, of Ann Arbor, Michigan; Miss Margaret Reburn, of New Albion, Iowa; Miss Perine, of Baltimore; Mrs Augustus Lowell, Mrs L. F. Wesselhoeft, Mrs Edward Atkinson, of Boston; Mrs Cushing, of Cambridge; Miss Ellen Marston, of New Bedford; Mrs Moncrieff, of London, Ontario.

Acknowledgments not well despatched in a phrase are due to many others who have promoted my objects: to Mr Furnivall, for doing for me everything which I could have done for myself had I lived in England; to that master of old songs and music, Mr William Chappell, very specially; to Mr J. Payne Collier; Mr Norval Clyne, of Aberdeen; Mr Alexander Young, of Glasgow; Mr Arthur Laurenson, of Lerwick, Shetland; Mr J. Burrell Curtis, of Edinburgh; Dr Vigfusson, of Oxford; Professor Edward Arber, of Birmingham; the Rev. J. Percival, Mr Francis Fry, Mr J. F. Nicholls, of Bristol; Professor George Stephens, of Copenhagen; Mr R. Bergström, of the Royal Library, Stockholm; Mr W. R. S. Ralston, Mr William Henry Husk, Miss Lucy Toulmin Smith, Mr A. F. Murison, of London; Professor Sophocles; Mr W. G. Medlicott, of Longmeadow; to Mr M. Heilprin, of New York, Mme de Maltchycé, of Boston, and Rabbi Dr Cohn, for indispensable translations from Polish and Hungarian; to Mr James Russell Lowell, Minister of the United States at London; to Professor Charles Eliot Norton, for such "pains and benefits" as I could ask only of a life-long friend.

In the editing of these ballads I have closely followed the plan of Grundtvig's *Old Popular Ballads of Denmark*, a work which will be prized highest by those who have used it most, and which leaves nothing to be desired but its completion. The author is as much at home in English as in Danish tradition, and whenever he takes up a ballad which is common to both nations nothing remains to be done but to supply what has come to light since the time of his writing. But besides the assistance which I have derived from his book, I have enjoyed the advantage of Professor Grundtvig's criticism and advice, and have received from him unprinted Danish texts, and other aid in many ways.

Such further explanations as to the plan and conduct of the work as may be desirable can be more conveniently given by and by. I may say here that textual points which may seem to be neglected will be considered in an intended Glossary, with which will be given a full account of Sources, and such indexes of Titles and Matters as will make it easy to find everything that the book may contain.

With renewed thanks to all helpers, and helpers' helpers, I would invoke the largest coöperation for the correction of errors and the supplying of deficiencies. To forestall a misunderstanding which has often occurred, I beg to say that every traditional version of a popular ballad is desired, no matter how many texts of the same may have been printed already.

F. J. CHILD.

[DECEMBER, 1882.]

ADVERTISEMENT TO PART II

NUMBERS 29–53

I have again to express my obligations and my gratitude to many who have aided in the collecting and editing of these Ballads.

To Sir Hugh Hume Campbell, for the use of two considerable manuscript volumes of Scottish Ballads.

To Mr Allardyce, of Edinburgh, for a copy of the Skene Ballads, and for a generous permission to print such as I required, in advance of a possible publication on his part.

To Mr Mansfield, of Edinburgh, for the use of the Pitcairn manuscripts.

To Mrs Robertson, for the use of Note-Books of the late Dr Joseph Robertson, and to Mr Murdoch, of Glasgow, Mr Lugton, of Kelso, Mrs Alexander Forbes, of Edinburgh, and Messrs G. L. Kittredge and G. M. Richardson, former students of Harvard College, for various communications.

To Dr Reinhold Köhler's unrivalled knowledge of popular fiction, and his equal liberality, I am indebted for valuable notes, which will be found in the Additions at the end of this volume.

The help of my friend Dr Theodor Vetter has enabled me to explore portions of the Slavic ballad-field which otherwise must have been neglected.

Professors D. Silvan Evans, John Rhys, Paul Meyer, and T. Frederick Crane have lent me a ready assistance in literary emergencies.

The interest and coöperation of Mr Furnivall and Mr Macmath have been continued to me without stint or weariness.

It is impossible, while recalling and acknowledging acts of courtesy, good will, and friendship, not to allude, with one word of deep personal grief, to the irreparable loss which all who are concerned with the study of popular tradition have experienced in the death of Svend Grundtvig.

F. J. C.

JUNE 1884.

CONTENTS

FRANCIS JAMES CHILD

FRANCIS JAMES CHILD was born in Boston on the first day of February, 1825. He was the third in a family of eight children. His father was a sailmaker, "one of that class of intelligent and independent mechanics," writes Professor Norton, "which has had a large share in determining the character of our democratic community, as of old the same class had in Athens and in Florence." The boy attended the public schools, as a matter of course; and, his parents having no thought of sending him to college, he went, in due time, not to the Latin School, but to the English High School of his native town. At that time the head master of the Boston Latin School was Mr Epes Sargent Dixwell, who is still living, at a ripe old age, one of the most respected citizens of Cambridge. Mr Dixwell had a keen eye for scholarly possibilities in boys, and, falling in with young Francis Child, was immediately struck with his extraordinary mental ability. At his suggestion, the boy was transferred to the Latin School, where he entered upon the regular preparation for admission to Harvard College. His delight in his new studies was unbounded, and the freshness of it never faded from his memory. "He speedily caught up with the boys who had already made considerable progress in Greek and Latin, and soon took the first place here, as he had done in the schools which he had previously attended." Mr Dixwell strongly advised his father to permit him to continue his studies, and made arrangements by which his college expenses should be provided for. The money Professor Child repaid, with interest, as soon as his means allowed. His gratitude to Mr Dixwell and the friendship between them lasted through his life.

In 1842 Mr Child entered Harvard College. The intellectual condition of the college at that time and the undergraduate career of Mr Child have been admirably described by his classmate

and lifelong friend, Professor Norton, in a passage which must be quoted in full:[*]—

"Harvard was then still a comparatively small institution, with no claims to the title of University; but she had her traditions of good learning as an inspiration for the studious youth, and still better she had teachers who were examples of devotion to intellectual pursuits, and who cared for those ends the attainment of which makes life worth living. Josiah Quincy was approaching the close of his term of service as President of the College, and stood before the eyes of the students as the type of a great public servant, embodying the spirit of patriotism, of integrity, and of fidelity in the discharge of whatever duty he might be called to perform. Among the Professors were Walker, Felton, Peirce, Channing, Beck, and Longfellow, men of utmost variety of temperament, but each an instructor who secured the respect no less than the gratitude of his pupils.

"The class to which Child belonged numbered hardly over sixty. The prescribed course of study which was then the rule brought all the members of the class together in recitations and lectures, and every man soon knew the relative standing of each of his fellows. Child at once took the lead and kept it. His excellence was not confined to any one special branch of study; he was equally superior in all. He was the best in the classics, he was Peirce's favorite in mathematics, he wrote better English than any of his classmates. His intellectual interests were wider than theirs, he was a great reader, and his tastes in reading were mature. He read for amusement

[*]   C. E. Norton, 'Francis James Child,' in the *Proceedings of the American Academy of Arts and Sciences*, XXXII, 334, 335; reprinted, with some additions, in the *Harvard Graduates' Magazine*, VI, 161–169 (Boston, 1897). I have used this biographical sketch freely in my brief account of Professor Child's boyhood.

as well as for learning, but he did not waste his time or dissipate his mental energies over worthless or pernicious books. He made good use of the social no less than of the intellectual opportunities which college life affords, and became as great a favorite with his classmates as he had been with his schoolfellows.

"The close of his college course was marked by the exceptional distinction of his being chosen by his classmates as their Orator, and by his having the first part at Commencement as the highest scholar in the class. His class oration was remarkable for its maturity of thought and of style. Its manliness of spirit, its simple directness of presentation of the true objects of life, and of the motives by which the educated man, whatever might be his chosen career, should be inspired, together with the serious and eloquent earnestness with which it was delivered, gave to his discourse peculiar impressiveness and effect."

Graduating with the degree of Bachelor of Arts in 1846, Mr Child immediately entered the service of the college, in which he continued till the day of his death. From 1846 to 1848 he was tutor in mathematics. In 1848 he was transferred, at his own request, to a tutorship in history and political economy, to which were annexed certain duties of instruction in English. In 1849 he obtained leave of absence for travel and study in Europe. He remained in Europe for about two years, returning, late in 1851, to receive an appointment to the Boylston Professorship of Rhetoric and Oratory, then falling vacant by the resignation of Professor Edward T. Channing.

The tutorships which Mr Child had held were not entirely in accordance with his tastes, which had always led him in the direction of literary and linguistic study. The faculty of the college was small, however, and it was not always possible to assign an instructor to the department that would have been most to his mind. But the governors of the institution were glad to secure the services of so promising a scholar; and Mr Child, whose preference for an academic career was decided, had felt that it was wise to accept such positions as the college could offer, leaving exacter adjustments to time and circumstances. Meantime he had devoted his whole leisure to the pursuit of his favorite

studies. His first fruits were a volume entitled Four Old Plays,[*] published in 1848, when he was but twenty-three years old. This was a remarkably competent performance. The texts are edited with judgment and accuracy; the introduction shows literary discrimination as well as sound scholarship, and the glossary and brief notes are thoroughly good. There are no signs of immaturity in the book, and it is still valued by students of our early drama.

The leave of absence granted to Mr Child in 1849 came at a most favorable moment. His health had suffered from close application to work, and a change of climate had been advised by his physicians. His intellectual and scholarly development, too, had reached that stage in which foreign study and travel were certain to be most stimulating and fruitful. He was amazingly apt, and two years of opportunity meant much more to him than to most men. He returned to take up the duties of his new office a trained and mature scholar, at home in the best methods and traditions of German universities, yet with no sacrifice of his individuality and intellectual independence.

While in Germany Mr Child studied at Berlin and Göttingen, giving his time mostly to Germanic philology, then cultivated with extraordinary vigor and success. The hour was singularly propitious. In the three or four decades preceding Mr Child's residence in Europe, Germanic philology (in the wider sense) had passed from the stage of "romantic" dilettantism into the condition of a well-organized and strenuous scientific discipline, but the freshness and vivacity of the first half of the century had not vanished. Scholars, however severe, looked through the form and strove to comprehend the spirit. The ideals of erudition and of a large humanity were not even suspected of incompatibility. The imagination was still invoked as the guide and illuminator of

---

[*]   Four Old Plays | Three Interludes: Thersytes Jack Jugler | and Heywoods Pardoner and Frere: | and Jocasta a Tragedy | by Gascoigne and | Kinwelmarsh | with an | Introduction and Notes | Cambridge | George Nichols | MDCCCXLVIII. The editor's name does not appear in the title-page, but the Preface is signed with the initials F. J. C. Jocasta was printed from Steevens's copy of the first edition of Gascoigne's *Posies*, which had come into Mr Child's possession.

learning. The bond between antiquity and mediævalism and between the Middle Ages and our own century was never lost from sight. It was certainly fortunate for American scholarship that at precisely this juncture a young man of Mr Child's ardent love of learning, strong individuality, and broad intellectual sympathies was brought into close contact with all that was most quickening in German university life. He attended lectures on classical antiquity and philosophy, as well as on Germanic philology; but it was not so much by direct instruction that he profited as by the inspiration which he derived from the spirit and the ideals of foreign scholars, young and old. His own greatest contribution to learning, *The English and Scottish Popular Ballads*, may even, in a very real sense, be regarded as the fruit of these years in Germany. Throughout his life he kept a picture of William and James Grimm on the mantel over his study fireplace.

Mr Child wrote no "dissertation," and returned to Cambridge without having attempted to secure a doctor's degree. Never eager for such distinctions, he had been unwilling to subject himself to the restrictions on his plan of study which candidacy for the doctorate would have imposed. Three years after, however, in 1854, he was surprised and gratified to receive from the University of Göttingen the degree of Doctor of Philosophy, accompanied by a special tribute of respect from that institution. Subsequently he received the degree of LL.D. from Harvard (in 1884) and that of L.H.D. from Columbia (in 1887); but the Göttingen Ph.D., coming as it did at the outset of his career, was in a high degree auspicious.

The Boylston Professorship of Rhetoric and Oratory, to which, as has been already mentioned, Mr Child succeeded on his return to America toward the end of 1851, was no sinecure. In addition to academic instruction of the ordinary kind, the duties of the chair included the superintendence and criticism of a great quantity of written work, in the nature of essays and set compositions prepared by students of all degrees of ability. For twenty-five years Mr Child performed these duties with characteristic punctuality and devotion, though with increasing distaste for the drudgery which they

involved. Meantime a great change had come over Harvard: it had developed from a provincial college into a national seminary of learning, and the introduction of the "elective system"—corresponding to the "Lernfreiheit" of Germany—had enabled it to become a university in the proper sense of the word. One result of the important reform just referred to was the establishment of a Professorship of English, entirely distinct from the old chair of Rhetoric. This took place on May 8, 1876, and on the 20th of the next month Mr Child was transferred to the new professorship. His duties as an instructor were now thoroughly congenial, and he continued to perform them with unabated vigor to the end. In the onerous details of administrative and advisory work, inseparable, according to our exacting American system, from the position of a university professor, he was equally faithful and untiring. For thirty years he acted as secretary of the Library Council, and in all that time he was absent from but three meetings. As chairman of the Department of English and of the Division of Modern Languages, and as a member of many important committees, he was ever prodigal of time and effort. How steadily he attended to the regular duties of the class-room, his pupils, for fifty years, are the best witnesses. They, too, will best understand the satisfaction he felt that, in the fiftieth year of his teaching, he was not absent from a single lecture. No man was ever less a formalist; yet the most formal of natures could not, in the strictest observance of punctilio, have surpassed the regularity with which he discharged, as it were spontaneously, the multifarious duties of his position.

Throughout his service as professor of rhetoric, Mr Child, hampered though he was by the requirements of his laborious office, had pursued with unquenchable ardor the study of the English language and literature, particularly in their older forms, and in these subjects he had become an authority of the first rank long before the establishment of the English chair enabled him to arrange his university teaching in accordance with his tastes. Soon after he returned from Germany he undertook the general editorial supervision of a series of the 'British Poets,' published at Boston in 1853 and several following years, and extending to some hundred and fifty volumes. Out of this grew, in one way or another, his three most important contributions to learning: his edition of Spenser, his Observations on the Language of Chaucer and Gower, and his *English and Scottish Popular Ballads*.

Mr Child's Spenser appeared in 1855.[*] Originally intended, as he says in the preface, as little more than a reprint of the edition published in 1839 under the superintendence of Mr George Hillard, the book grew upon his hands until it had become something quite different from its predecessor. Securing access to old copies of most of Spenser's poems, Mr Child subjected the text to a careful revision, which left little to be done in this regard. His Life of Spenser was far better than any previous biography, and his notes, though brief, were marked by a philological exactness to which former editions could not pretend. Altogether, though meant for the general reader and therefore sparingly annotated, Mr Child's volumes remain, after forty years, the best edition of Spenser in existence.

The plan of the 'British Poets' originally contemplated an edition of Chaucer, which Mr Child was to prepare. Becoming convinced, however, that the time was not ripe for such a work, he abandoned this project, and to the end of his life he never found time to resume it. Thomas Wright's print of the *Canterbury Tales*[†] from the Harleian MS. 7334 had, however, put into his hands a reasonably faithful reproduction of an old text, and he turned his attention to a minute study of Chaucer's language. The outcome was the publication, in the *Memoirs of the American Academy of Arts and Sciences* for 1863, of the great treatise to which Mr Child gave the modest title of Observations on the Language of Chaucer's *Canterbury Tales*. It is difficult, at the present day, to imagine the state of Chaucer philology at the moment when this paper appeared. Scarcely anything, we may say,

was known of Chaucer's grammar and metre in a sure and scientific way. Indeed, the difficulties to be solved had not even been clearly formulated. Further, the accessible mass of evidence on Anglo-Saxon and Middle English was, in comparison with the stores now at the easy command of every tyro, almost insignificant. Yet, in this brief treatise, Mr Child not only defined the problems, but provided for most of them a solution which the researches of younger scholars have only served to substantiate. He also gave a perfect model of the method proper to such inquiries—a method simple, laborious, and exact. The Observations were subsequently rearranged and condensed, with Professor Child's permission, by Mr A. J. Ellis for his work *On Early English Pronunciation*; but only those who have studied them in their original form can appreciate their merit fully. "It ought never to be forgotten," writes Professor Skeat, "that the only full and almost complete solution of the question of the right scansion of Chaucer's *Canterbury Tales* is due to what Mr Ellis rightly terms 'the wonderful industry, acuteness, and accuracy of Professor Child.'" Had he produced nothing else, this work, with its pendant, the Observations on Gower,[‡] would have assured him a high place among those very few scholars who have permanently settled important problems of linguistic science.

Mr Child's crowning work, however, was the edition of the *English and Scottish Popular Ballads*, which the reader now has before him. The history of this is the history of more than half a lifetime.

The idea of the present work grew out of Mr Child's editorial labors on the series of the 'British Poets,' already referred to. For this he pre-

---

[*]   *The Poetical Works of Edmund Spenser*. The text carefully revised, and illustrated with notes, original and selected, by Francis J. Child. Boston: Little, Brown, and Company. 1855. 5 vols.

[†]   *The Canterbury Tales of Geoffrey Chaucer*. A new text, with illustrative notes. Edited by Thomas Wright. London, printed for the Percy Society, 1847–51. 3 vols.

[‡]   The paper entitled Observations on the Language of Chaucer was laid before the American Academy of Arts and Sciences on June 3, 1862, and was published in the *Memoirs of the Academy*, Vol. VIII, pt. ii, 445–502 (Boston, 1863). The second paper, entitled Observations on the Language of Gower's *Confessio Amantis*, was laid before the Academy on January 9, 1866, and appeared in *Memoirs*, IX, ii, 265–315 (Boston, 1873). A few copies of each paper were struck off separately, but these are now very hard to find. Mr Ellis's rearrangement and amalgamation of the two papers, which is by no means a good substitute for the papers themselves, may be found in Part I of his *Early English Pronunciation*, London, 1869, pp. 343–97.

pared a collection in eight small volumes (1857–58) called *English and Scottish Ballads*.[*] This was marked by the beginnings of that method of comparative study which is carried out to its ultimate issues in the volumes of the present collection. The book circulated widely, and was at once admitted to supersede all previous attempts in the same field. To Mr Child, however, it was but the starting-point for further researches. He soon formed the plan of a much more extensive collection on an altogether different model. This was to include every obtainable version of every extant English or Scottish ballad, with the fullest possible discussion of related songs or stories in the "popular" literature of all nations. To this enterprise he resolved, if need were, to devote the rest of his life. His first care was to secure trustworthy texts. In his earlier collection he had been forced to depend almost entirely on printed books. No progress, he was convinced, could be made till recourse could be had to manuscripts, and in particular to the Percy MS. Accordingly he directed his most earnest efforts to securing the publication of the entire contents of the famous folio. The Percy MS. was at Ecton Hall, in the possession of the Bishop's descendants, who would permit no one even to examine it. Two attempts were made by Dr Furnivall, at Mr Child's instance, to induce the owners to allow the manuscript to be printed,—one as early as 1860 or 1861, the other in 1864,—but without avail. A third attempt was more successful, and in 1867–68 the long-secluded folio was made the common property of scholars in an edition prepared by Professor Hales and Dr Furnivall.[†]

The publication of the Percy MS. not only put a large amount of trustworthy material at the disposal of Mr Child; it exposed the full enormity of Bishop Percy's sins against popular tradition. Some shadow of suspicion inevitably

fell on all other ballad collections. It was more than ever clear to Mr Child that he could not safely take anything at second hand, and he determined not to print a line of his projected work till he had exhausted every effort to get hold of whatever manuscript material might be in existence. His efforts in this direction continued through many years. A number of manuscripts were in private hands; of some the whereabouts was not known; of others the existence was not suspected. But Mr Child was untiring. He was cordially assisted by various scholars, antiquaries, and private gentlemen, to whose coöperation ample testimony is borne in the Advertisements prefixed to the volumes in the present work. Some manuscripts were secured for the Library of Harvard University— notably Bishop Percy's Papers, the Kinloch MSS, and the Harris MS.,[‡]—and of others careful copies were made, which became the property of the same library. In all these operations the indispensable good offices of Mr William Macmath, of Edinburgh, deserve particular mention. For a long series of years his services were always at Mr Child's disposal. His self-sacrifice and generosity appear to have been equalled only by his perseverance and wonderful accuracy. But for him the manuscript basis of *The English and Scottish Popular Ballads* would have been far less strong than it is.

Gradually, then, the manuscript materials came in, until at last, in 1882, Mr Child felt justified in beginning to print. Other important documents were, however, discovered or made accessible as time went on. Especially noteworthy was the great find at Abbotsford (see the Advertisement to Part VIII). In 1877 Dr David Laing procured, "not without difficulty," leave to prepare for Mr Child a copy of the single manuscript of ballads then known to remain in the library at Abbotsford. This MS., entitled "Scottish Songs," was so inconsiderable, in proportion to the accumulations which Sir Walter Scott had made in preparing his *Border Minstrelsy*, that further search seemed to be imperatively necessary. In 1890 permission to make

---

[*]   *English and Scottish Ballads*. Selected and edited by Francis James Child. Boston, 1857–58.

[†]   How inseparable were the services of Dr Furnivall and those of Professor Child in securing this devoutly wished consummation may be seen by comparing Dr Furnivall's Forewords (I, ix, x), in which he gives much of the credit to Mr Child, with Mr Child's Dedication (in vol. I of the present collection), in which he gives the credit to Dr Furnivall.

[‡]   Since Mr Child's death the important "Buchan original MS" has been secured for the Child Memorial Library of the University,—a collection endowed by friends and pupils of the dead master.

such a search, and to use the results, was given by the Honorable Mrs Maxwell-Scott. The investigation, made by Mr Macmath, yielded a rich harvest of ballads, which were utilized in Parts VII–IX. To dwell upon the details would be endless. The reader may see a list of the manuscript sources following the Glossary in the fifth volume; and, if he will observe how scattered they were, he will have no difficulty in believing that it required years, labor, and much delicate negotiation to bring them all together. One manuscript remained undiscoverable, William Tytler's Brown MS., but there is no reason to believe that this contained anything of consequence that is not otherwise known.[*]

Meanwhile, concurrently with the toil of amassing, collating, and arranging texts, went on the far more arduous labor of comparative study of the ballads of all nations; for, in accordance with Mr Child's plan it was requisite to determine, in the fullest manner, the history and foreign relations of every piece included in his collection. To this end he devoted much time and unwearied diligence to forming, in the Library of the University, a special collection of "Folk-lore," particularly, of ballads, romances, and *Märchen*. This priceless collection, the formation of which must be looked on as one of Mr Child's most striking services to the university, numbers some 7000 volumes. But these figures by no means represent the richness of the Library, in the departments concerned, or the services of Mr Child in this particular. Mediæval literature in all its phases was his province, and thousands of volumes classified in other departments of the University Library bear testimony to his vigilance in ordering books, and his astonishing bibliographical knowledge. Very few books are cited in the present collection which are not to be found on the shelves of this Library.

In addition, Mr Child made an effort to stimulate the collection of such remains of the traditional ballad as still live on the lips of the people in this country and in the British Islands. The harvest was, in his opinion, rather scanty; yet, if all the versions thus recovered from tradition were enumerated, the number would not be found inconsiderable. Enough was done, at all events, to make it clear that little or nothing of value remains to be recovered in this way.

To readers familiar with such studies, no comment is necessary, and to those who are unfamiliar with them, no form of statement can convey even a faint impression of the industry, the learning, the acumen, and the literary skill which these processes required. In writing the history of a single ballad, Mr Child was sometimes forced to examine hundreds of books in perhaps a dozen different languages. But his industry was unflagging, his sagacity was scarcely ever at fault, and his linguistic and literary knowledge seemed to have no bounds. He spared no pains to perfect his work in every detail, and his success was commensurate with his efforts. In the Advertisement to the Ninth Part (1894), he was able to report that the three hundred and five numbers of his collection comprised the whole extant mass of this traditional material, with the possible exception of a single ballad.[†]

In June, 1896, Mr Child concluded his fiftieth year of service as a teacher in Harvard College. He was at this time hard at work on the Tenth and final Part, which was to contain a glossary, various indexes, a bibliography, and an elaborate introduction on the general subject. For years he had allowed himself scarcely any respite from work, and, in spite of the uncertain condition of his health,—or perhaps in consequence of it, he continued to work at high pressure throughout the summer. At the end of August he discovered that he was seriously ill. He died at Boston on the 11th day of September. He had finished his great work except for the introduction and the general bibliography. The bibliography was in preparation by another hand and has since been completed. The introduction, however, no other scholar had the hardihood to undertake. A few pages of manuscript,—the last thing written by his pen,—almost illegible, were found among his papers to show that he had actually begun the composition of this essay, and many sheets of excerpts testified to the time he had spent in refreshing his memory as to the opinions of his

---

[*]   See Volume V, Sources of Texts.

[†]   This is 'Young Betrice,' No 5 in William Tytler's lost Brown MS., which "may possibly be a version of 'Hugh Spencer's Feats in France'" (see No. 99, No. 158).

predecessors, but he had left no collectanea that could be utilized in supplying the Introduction itself. He was accustomed to carry much of his material in his memory till the moment of composition arrived, and this habit accounts for the fact that there are no jottings of opinions and no sketch of precisely what line of argument he intended to take.

Mr Child's sudden death was felt as a bitter personal loss, not only by an unusually large circle of attached friends in both hemispheres, but by very many scholars who knew him through his works alone. He was one of the few learned men to whom the old title of "Master" was justly due and freely accorded. With astonishing erudition, which nothing seemed to have escaped, he united an infectious enthusiasm and a power of lucid and fruitful exposition that made him one of the greatest of teachers, and a warmth and openness of heart that won the affection of all who knew him. In most men, however complex their characters, one can distinguish the qualities of the heart, in some degree, from the qualities of the head. In Professor Child no such distinction was possible, for all the elements of his many-sided nature were fused in his marked and powerful individuality. In his case, the scholar and the man cannot be separated. His life and his learning were one; his work was the expression of himself.

As an investigator Professor Child was at once the inspiration and the despair of his disciples. Nothing could surpass the scientific exactness of his methods and the unwearied diligence with which he conducted his researches. No possible source of information could elude him; no book or manuscript was too voluminous or too unpromising for him to examine on the chance of its containing some fact that might correct or supplement his material, even in the minutest point. Yet these qualities of enthusiastic accuracy and thoroughness, admirable as they undoubtedly were, by no means dominated him. They were always at the command of the higher qualities of his genius,—sagacity, acumen, and a kind of sympathetic and imaginative power in which he stood almost alone among recent scholars. No detail of language or tradition or archæology was to him a mere lifeless fact; it was transmuted into something vital,

and became a part of that universal humanity which always moved him wherever he found it, whether in the pages of a mediæval chronicle, or in the stammering accents of a late and vulgarly distorted ballad, or in the faces of the street boys who begged roses from his garden. No man ever felt a keener interest in his kind, and no scholar ever brought this interest into more vivifying contact with the technicalities of his special studies. The exuberance of this large humanity pervades his edition of the English and Scottish ballads. Even in his last years, when the languor of uncertain health sometimes got the better, for a season, of the spirit with which he commonly worked, some fresh bit of genuine poetry in a ballad, some fine trait of pure nature in a stray folk-tale, would, in an instant, bring back the full flush of that enthusiasm which he must have felt when the possibilities of his achievement first presented themselves to his mind in early manhood. For such a nature there was no old age.

From this ready sympathy came that rare faculty—seldom possessed by scholars—which made Professor Child peculiarly fit for his greatest task. Few persons understand the difficulties of ballad investigation. In no field of literature have the forger and the manipulator worked with greater vigor and success. From Percy's day to our own it has been thought an innocent device to publish a bit of one's own versifying, now and then, as an "old ballad" or an "ancient song." Often, too, a late stall-copy of a ballad, getting into oral circulation, has been innocently furnished to collectors as traditional matter. Mere learning will not guide an editor through these perplexities. What is needed is, in addition, a complete understanding of the "popular" genius, a sympathetic recognition of the traits that characterize oral literature wherever and in whatever degree they exist. This faculty, which even the folk has not retained, and which collectors living in ballad-singing and tale-telling times have often failed to acquire, was vouchsafed by nature herself to this sedentary scholar. In reality a kind of instinct, it had been so cultivated by long and loving study of the traditional literature of all nations that it had become wonderfully swift in its operations and almost infallible. A forged or retouched piece could not deceive him for a moment; he detected the slightest jar in the genuine ballad tone. He speaks in one place of certain writers "who would have been all the better historians for a little reading of romances." He was himself the better interpreter of the poetry of art for this keen sympathy with the poetry of nature.

Constant association with the spirit of the folk did its part in maintaining, under the stress of unremitting study and research, that freshness and buoyancy of mind which was the wonder of all who met Professor Child for the first time, and the perpetual delight of his friends and associates. It is impossible to describe the charm of his familiar conversation. There was endless variety without effort. His peculiar humor, taking shape in a thousand felicities of thought and phrase that fell casually and as it were inevitably from his lips, exhilarated without reaction or fatigue. His lightest words were full of fruitful suggestion. Sudden strains of melancholy or high seriousness were followed, in a moment, by flashes of gaiety almost boyish. And pervading it all one felt the attraction of his personality and the goodness of his heart.

Professor Child's humor was not only one of his most striking characteristics as a man; it was of constant service to his scholarly researches. Keenly alive to any incongruity in thought or fact, and the least self-conscious of men, he scrutinized his own nascent theories with the same humorous shrewdness with which he looked at the ideas of others. It is impossible to think of him as the sponsor of some hypotheses which men of equal eminence have advanced and defended with passion; and, even if his goodness of nature had not prevented it, his sense of the ridiculous would not have suffered him to engage in the absurdities of philological polemics. In the interpretation of literature, his humor stood him in good stead, keeping his native sensibility under due control, so that it never degenerated into sentimentalism. It made him a marvelous interpreter of Chaucer, whose spirit he had caught to a degree attained by no other scholar or critic.

To younger scholars Professor Child was an influence at once stimulating and benignant. To confer with him was always to be stirred to greater effort, but, at the same time, the serenity of his devotion to learning chastened the petulance of immature ambition in others. The talk might be quite concrete, even definitely practical,—it might deal with indifferent matters; but, in some way, there was an irradiation of the master's nature that dispelled all unworthy feelings. In the presence of his noble modesty the bustle of self-assertion was quieted and the petty spirit of pedantic wrangling could not assert itself. However severe his criticism, there were no personalities in it. He could not be other than outspoken,—concealment and shuffling were abhorrent to him,—yet such was his kindliness that his frankest judgments never wounded; even his reproofs left no sting. With his large charity was associated, as its necessary complement in a strong character, a capacity for righteous indignation. "He is almost the only man I know," said one in his lifetime, "who *thinks no evil*." There could be no truer word. Yet when he was confronted with injury or oppression, none could stand against the anger of this just man. His unselfishness did not suffer him to see offences against himself, but wrong done to another roused him in an instant to protesting action.

Professor Child's publications, despite their magnitude and importance, are no adequate measure either of his acquirements or of his influence. He printed nothing about Shakspere, for example, yet he was the peer of any Shaksperian, past or present, in knowledge and interpretative power. As a Chaucer scholar he had no superior, in this country or in Europe: his published work was confined, as we have seen, to questions of language, but no one had a wider or closer acquaintance with the whole subject. An edition of Chaucer from his hand would have been priceless. His acquaintance with letters was not confined to special authors or centuries. He was at home in modern European literature and profoundly versed in that of the Middle Ages. In his immediate territory,— English,—his knowledge, linguistic and literary, covered all periods, and was alike exact and thorough. His taste and judgment were exquisite, and he enlightened every subject which he touched. As a writer, he was master of a singularly felicitous style, full of individuality and charm. Had his time not been occupied in other ways, he would have made the most delightful of essayists.

Fortunately, Professor Child's courses of instruction in the university—particularly those on Chaucer and Shakspere—gave him an opportunity to impart to a constantly increasing circle of pupils the choicest fruits of his life of thought and study. In his later years he had the satisfaction to see grow up about him a school of young specialists who can have no higher ambition than to be worthy of their master. But his teaching was not limited to these,—it included all sorts and conditions of college students; and none, not even the idle and incompetent, could fail to catch something of his spirit. One thing may be safely asserted: no university teacher was ever more beloved.

And with this may fitly close too slight a tribute to the memory of a great scholar and a good man. Many things remain unsaid. His gracious family life, his civic virtues, his patriotism, his bounty to the poor,—all must be passed by with a bare mention, which yet will signify much to those who knew him. In all ways he lived worthily, and he died having attained worthy ends.

G. L. KITTREDGE.

BALLAD POETRY

The word *ballad* signifies in English a narrative song, a short tale in lyric verse, which sense it has come to have, probably through the English, in some other languages. It means, by derivation, a dance-song, but though dancing was formerly, and in some places still is, performed to song instead of instrumental music, the application of the word in English is quite accidental. The *popular* ballad, for which our language has no unequivocal name, is a distinct and very important species of poetry. Its historical and natural place is anterior to the appearance of the poetry of art, to which it has formed a step among every people that has produced an original literature, and by which it has been regularly displaced, and, in some cases, all but extinguished. Whenever a people in the course of its development reaches a certain intellectual and moral stage, it will feel an impulse to express itself in literature, and the form of expression to which it is first impelled is, as is well known, not prose but verse, and in fact narrative verse. The condition of society in which a truly national popular poetry appears, explains the character of such poetry. It is a condition in which the people are not divided by political organization and book-culture into markedly distinct classes, in which consequently there is such community of ideas and feelings that the whole people form an individual. Such poetry, accordingly, while it is in its essence an expression of our common human nature, and so of universal and indestructible interest, will in each case be differenced by circumstances and idiosyncrasy. On the other hand, it will always be an expression of the mind and heart of the people as an individual, and never of the personality of individual men. The fundamental characteristic of popular ballads is therefore the absence of subjectivity and of self-consciousness. Though they do not

"write themselves," as William Grimm has said, though a man and not a people has composed them, still the author counts for nothing, and it is not by mere accident, but with the best reason, that they have come down to us anonymous. Hence, too, they are extremely difficult to imitate by the highly-civilized modern man, and most of the attempts to reproduce this kind of poetry have been ridiculous failures.

The primitive ballad then is popular, not in the sense of something arising from and suited to the lower orders of a people. As yet, no sharp distinction of high and low exists, in respect to knowledge, desires, and tastes. An increased civilization, and especially the introduction of book-culture, gradually gives rise to such a division: the poetry of art appears; the popular poetry is no longer relished by a portion of the people, and is abandoned to an uncultivated or not over-cultivated class—a constantly diminishing number. But whatever may be the estimation in which it may be held by particular classes or at particular epochs, it cannot lose its value. Being founded on what is permanent and universal in the heart of man, and now by printing put beyond the danger of perishing, it will survive the fluctuations of taste, and may from time to time serve, as it notoriously did in England and Germany a hundred years ago, to recall a literature from false and artificial courses to nature and truth.

Of the Europeans nations, the Spaniards and those of Scandinavian-German stock have best preserved their early popular poetry. We have early notices of the poetry of the Germans. Their ballads, mythical or historical, are several times spoken of by Tacitus, who says that these were their only annals. The earth-born Tuiscio and his son Mannus were celebrated in the one, and the hero Arminius in the other. The historian of the Goths, Jornandes, writing in the sixth century, says that these people were accustomed to sing the exploits of their fathers to the harp, and seems to have taken not a little of his history from such songs. The like is true of Paulus Diaconus, the Lombard historian, who wrote in the eighth century, and mentions songs about Alboin (who died in 563) as existing among all the nations of German speech. Charlemagne had the old traditional songs of his people collected and committed to writing, and even made them one of the subjects of school instruction. Side by side with heroic ballads, social, convivial, and funeral songs (which may, to be sure, have been pretty much the same thing) seem to have been in use from the earliest recorded times. To all this popular poetry, by reason of its heathen derivation and character, the Christian clergy opposed themselves with the most determined hostility. Not succeeding in extirpating it by the use of the spiritual and legal means at their command, the German churchmen of the ninth century conceived the idea of crowding it out by substituting poetry of a Christian subject and tone—an expedient which has been tried more than once since then. Though popular song lived on in obscure places, the foreground of history is filled for six hundred years with religious and courtly poetry and with the chivalrous and native epic. Nothing is left of the old heroic songs but a fragment of the Hildebrandslied, from the eighth century (best known in a modernized form of the fifteenth century); and of the Christianized song we have also but a single specimen, the Ludwigslied of the year 881. The former is in the ancient alliterative metre, the latter in the then newly-introduced rhymed stanza. During the fifteenth and the early part of the sixteenth centuries a second growth of the genuine popular song appears, some of it springing, doubtless, out of shoots from the old stock which had lived through this long interval, some of it fresh product of the age. These ballads were popular in the large and strict sense; that is, they were the creation and the manifestation of the whole people, great and humble, who were still one in all essentials, having the same belief, the same ignorance and the same tastes, and living in much closer relations than now. The diffusion of knowledge and the stimulation of thought through the art of printing, the religious and intellectual consequences of the Reformation, the intrusion of cold reflection into a world of sense and fancy, broke up the national unity. The educated classes took a direction of their own, and left, what had been a common treasure, to the people in the lower sense, the ignorant or unschooled mass. German ballads have been collected in considerable numbers. The sources have been "flying-leaves," manuscripts, printed song-books (mostly of the sixteenth century), and oral tradition. In interest they are decidedly inferior to the Scandinavian and English.

Christianity and foreign culture, which in different ways have been equally destructive in their effects upon ancient national poetry, were introduced into the Scandinavian countries much later than into Germany and England. In the Scandinavian countries, too, the peasantry long maintained a much higher position. They were not an oppressed and ignorant class, but free men, who shared fully in the indigenous culture, and so were well fitted to keep and transmit their poetical heritage. While, therefore, the heroic ballads of Germany and England have been lost—those of England utterly, those of Germany being preserved only in epic conglomerates like the Nibelungenlied—and while the mythical cycle in both countries is but feebly, if at all, represented, Scandinavia has kept a great deal of both. The story of Thor's Hammer forms the subject of a ballad still known in all the Scandinavian countries; a volume of ballads concerning Sigurd has been gathered from tradition in the Faroe Isles within this century, and several ballads of this cycle and of that of Dietrich of Bern are found in Danish manuscript ballad-books. Svend Grundtvig, the editor of the still unfinished but truly magnificent collection of the old Danish ballads has arranged them in four classes: first, the Heroic; second, the Trylleviser, or ballads of giants, dwarfs, nixes, elves, mountain spirits, enchantment, spells, and ghosts; third, the Historic; and fourth, ballads of Chivalry. The historic ballads (intending their original, not their actual, form) most fall within the period from 1150 to 1300; the chivalrous are later, and the two other classes belong to a still earlier term, which may extend over the first half of the twelfth century, and into, or perhaps through, the eleventh; that is, to the epoch of the introduction of Christianity. Ballads are best preserved by oral tradition in Norway and the Faroe Isles, but not at all, there, in old manuscripts; Sweden has a few manuscripts, and Denmark a great number, written mostly by noble ladies living on their estates, and giving the ballads as they were sung three or four hundred years ago, as well in the lord's castle as in the peasant's hut. The Danish ballads were collected in a printed form earlier than any others except the Spanish. Vedel published a hundred in 1591; another collection, called Tragica, or old Danish historic love-ballads, appeared at Copenhagen in 1657; and in 1695 Syv republished Vedel's ballads, with the addition of another hundred.

The English have preserved but a moderate number of very early ballads, and the date of many of these it is impossible to fix. There are some narrative poems in Anglo-Saxon which, without stretch of language, might be called ballads. The Norman Conquest, and the predominance of the French language for more than two hundred years, had of course momentous literary consequences, but there is no reason why the production of the native ballad should have stopped. The story of the Saxon outlaw Hereward, which begins with the second year after the Conquest, and has been handed down to us in Latin prose of the twelfth century, is full of such adventures as form the themes of ballads, and very likely was made up from popular songs. Such ballads, if they existed, are lost, but ballads concerning outlaws are among the earliest and best ones of the English. In place of Hereward of the Conqueror's time, and Fulk Fitz-Warin of John's time (whose history was also extremely popular), we have Robin Hood of uncertain time. Songs of Robin Hood and of Randolph, earl of Chester (probably the third earl, who died in 1232), we know, from Piers Ploughman, were current among the lower orders at the middle of the fourteenth century, and one Robin Hood ballad exists in a manuscript which may be as old as the first quarter of the next century. Another occurs in a manuscript dated at about

1500, others in the Percy manuscript. The Little Gest of Robin Hood, which is a miniature epic made up of half a dozen ballads, was printed by Wynken de Worde, "probably," says Ritson, "in 1489." We may reasonably place the origin of the Robin Hood ballads as early as the thirteenth century. To the thirteenth century may belong Hugh of Lincoln, which is founded on an incident that occurred in 1255. An Anglo-Norman ballad on the same subject twice refers to a King Henry, and is therefore put within the reign of Henry III, which ended 1276. Sir Patrick Spens, if the occasion of the ballad has been rightly understood, dates from 1281. After this there are only one or two ballads with dates till we come to the Battle of Otterbourn, 1388, from which time we have a succession of ballads founded on ascertained events, down to the middle of the eighteenth century. Ballads like those of Grundtvig's second class exist in a small number; one of them in a manuscript of the middle of the fifteenth century. The little that we have of ballads of the Arthur cycle, and many of the best of all kinds, we owe to the Percy manuscript, written just before 1650. A few ballads besides those named have been gleaned from manuscripts and early prints, but a large part of our whole stock has been recovered within the last hundred years from the oral tradition of Scotland. The first impulse to the collecting of this poetry was given by the publication of Percy's "Reliques" in 1765. The "Reliques" inspired Bürger and Herder, through whom, and especially through Herder's "Volkslieder" (1778–79), that interest in the literature of the people was awakened in Germany which has spread over the whole of Europe, and has led to the collecting and study of the traditional songs and tales of all the European, and some of the Asiatic, African, and American races.

The Spanish alone of the Latin nations can boast a ballad poetry of great compass and antiquity. Following the law of analogy where documents are wanting, the origin of these ballads would be put between the years 1000 and 1200, the period when the Spanish nationality and language had been developed to that degree which invariably incites and leads to expression in epic song. Some sort of popular poetry about the Cid (whose time is 1040–99) is known to have been sung as early as 1147; the poem of the Cid itself is placed about 1200. During the century that follows we find occasional mention of ballad-singers, but no ballads. As in Germany, the popular poetry, after the first bloom of the national genius, was supplanted by art-poetry, among the higher classes, and it passed out of notice for two or three hundred years. A reaction set in in the sixteenth century. This was the glorious period of Spanish history, and the return to the national poetry was a natural consequence of the powerful stirring of the national mind. Omitting "flying leaves" or broadsides, and a few ballads in the "Cancionero, General" of 1511, the earliest collection of Spanish ballads is an undated "Cancionero de Romances," printed at Antwerp about 1546; and this, it must be observed, is the first ballad-book printed in any language, and was gathered in part from the memory of the people. Other similar collections followed, from which was made in 1600 the great "Romancero General." Towards the end of the seventeenth century the national ballads declined in favor, with a decline of national spirit, but since the beginning of the present century they have been restored to a high estimation at home, and have gained the admiration of the world. The oldest ballads are those which relate to the history and traditions of Spain, and recount the exploits of Bernardo del Carpio, Fernan Gonzalez, the Seven Lords of Lara, and the Cid. Then comes a variety of romantic and chivalrous ballads, and then ballads of the Carlovingian cycle. These oldest and most characteristic of the Spanish ballads have been excellently edited by Wolf and Hofmann, and the entire body of this literature, amounting to more than 1900 pieces, is included in the "Romancero General," edited by Duran in 1849–51, a work which surpasses every other in the same line, except the Danish collection of Grundtvig. The collections of ballads in the other Latin languages will be found below. The most important are the Portuguese "Romanceiro," by Almeida-Garrett, 1863; the Piedmontese ballads, by Nigra, 1858–63, and the "Songs and Tales of the Italian People," by Comparetti and D'Ancona, begun in 1870, both first-rate

works; Arbaud's, Puymaigre's, and Bujeaud's French collections.

The ballads of other European nations are scarcely less interesting than those which have been noticed, and those of races which possess little or no other literature are peculiarly instructive, by reason of the light which they throw on the history of national poetry; for instance, the songs of the Slavic races, and, most of all, of the Servians. The Slavic songs as a class are distinguished from the Teutonic by the absence of the sentiment of *romantic* love and of *chivalrous* heroism. In their form, too, they are much less dramatic, and even the division of epic from lyric songs is not easy. Many songs begin with a few narrative verses, and then become entirely lyric, and the narrative part is almost always descriptive. The Servians—especially those of Turkish Servia, Bosnia, and Montenegro, who have not been much affected by civilization—afford a capital example of a race that has not outlived the ballad era. Vuk has collected five or six hundred of their songs, one third of them epic, and every one of them from the mouths of the people. A few of these are, in their actual form, as old as the fifteenth century, some belong to a remoter time, and indeed many retain marks of an ante-Christian origin. So far, the Servians are like the German nations: the distinction is that the fountain of popular poetry still flows, and that heroic poems have been produced among the Servians in this century which are essentially similar to the older ones, and not at all inferior. We find the national poetry, there, in a condition closely resembling that in which it was among the races of Northern and Eastern Europe many hundred years ago. New songs appear with new occasions, but do not supersede the ancient ones. The heroic ballads are chanted at taverns, in the public squares, in the halls of chiefs, to the accompaniment of a simple instrument. Sometimes they are only recited, and in this way are taught by the old to the young. All classes know them: the peasant, the merchant, the hayduk (the klepht of the modern Greek, a sort of Robin Hood), as well as the professional bard. No class scorns to sing them—not even the clergy or the chiefs.

One or two general remarks are required to prevent misconceptions and to supply omissions. From what has been said, it may be seen or inferred that the popular ballad is not originally the product or the property of the lower orders of the people. Nothing, in fact, is more obvious than that many of the ballads of the now most refined nations had their origin in that class whose acts and fortunes they depict—the upper class—though the growth of civilization has driven them from the memory of the highly-polished and instructed, and has left them as an exclusive possession to the uneducated. The genuine popular ballad had its rise in a time when the distinctions since brought about by education and other circumstances had practically no existence. The vulgar ballads of our day, the "broadsides" which were printed in such huge numbers in England and elsewhere in the sixteenth century or later, belong to a different genus; they are products of a low kind of *art*, and most of them are, from a literary point of view, thoroughly despicable and worthless.

Next it must be observed that ballads which have been handed down by long-repeated tradition have always departed considerably from their original form. If the transmission has been purely through the mouths of unlearned people, there is less probability of wilful change, but once in the hands of professional singers, there is no amount of change which they may not undergo. Last of all comes the modern editor, whose so called improvements are more to be feared than the mischances of a thousand years. A very old ballad will often be found to have resolved itself in the course of what may be called its propagation into several distinct shapes, and each of these again to have received distinct modifications. When the fashion of verse has altered, we shall find a change of form as great as that in the Hildebrandslied, from alliteration without stanza to stanza with rhyme. In all cases the language drifts insensibly from ancient forms, though not at the same rate with the language of every-day life. The professional ballad-singer or minstrel, whose sole object is to please the audience before him, will alter, omit, or add, without scruple, and nothing is more common than to find different ballads blended together.

There remains the very curious question of the origin of the resemblances which are found in the ballads of different nations, the recurrence of the same incidents or even of the same story, among races distinct in blood and history, and geographically far separated. The Scottish ballad of May Colvin, for instance—the German Ulinger—is also found in the Swedish, Dutch, Spanish, Portuguese, Italian, French, Servian, Bohemian, Wendish, Esthonian, Breton, and perhaps other languages. Some have thought that to explain this phenomenon we must go back almost to the cradle of mankind, to a primeval common ancestry of all or most of the nations among whom it appears. But so august an hypothesis is scarcely necessary. The incidents of many ballads are such as might occur anywhere and at any time; and with regard to agreements that cannot be explained in this way, we have only to remember that tales and songs were the chief social amusement of all classes of people in all the nations of Europe during the Middle Ages, and that new stories would be eagerly sought for by those whose business it was to furnish this amusement, and be rapidly spread among the fraternity. A great effect was undoubtedly produced by the Crusades, which both brought the chief European nations into closer intercourse and made them acquainted with the East, thus facilitating the interchange of stories and greatly enlarging the stock.

The most important collections of ballads are—

English.—"Reliques of Ancient English Poetry," by Thomas Percy, fourth improved ed., London, 1794, and often since; "Ancient and Modern Scottish Songs," by David Herd, second ed., 2 vols., Edinburgh, 1776; "Minstrelsy of the Scottish Border," by Sir Walter Scott, 3 vols., Edinburgh, 1802–3, and often since; "Popular Ballads and Songs," by Robert Jamieson, 2 vols., Edinburgh, 1806; "Ancient Scottish Ballads," by George R. Kinloch, Edinburgh, 1827; "Minstrelsy, Ancient and Modern," by William Motherwell, Glasgow, 1827; "English and Scottish Ballads," by F. J. Child, 8 vols., Boston, 1860, which contains all but two or three of the ancient ballads, and a full list of collections;

"Bishop Percy's Folio Manuscript," by J. W. Hales and F. J. Furnivall, 3 vols., London, 1867–68.

Scandinavian.—"Danmarks Gamle Folkeviser" ("The Ancient Ballads of Denmark"), by Svend Grundtvig, 3 vols., and part of a fourth, Copenhagen, 1853–72—by far the greatest work in this class of literature; "Ancient Danish Ballads," translated from the originals by R. C. Alex. Prior, 3 vols., London, 1860; "Norske Folkeviser" ("Norwegian Ballads"), by M. B. Landstad, Christiania, 1853; "Gamle Norske Folkeviser" ("Ancient Norwegian Ballads"), by Sophus Bugge, Christiania, 1858; "Svenska Folk-Visor" ("Swedish Ballads"), by Geijer and Afzelius, 3 vols., Stockholm, 1814–16; "Svenska Fornsänger." by A. I. Arwidsson, 3 vols., Stockholm, 1834–42; Rosa Warren's "Dänische Volkslieder," Hamburg, 1858, "Norwegische, etc. Volkslieder," Hamburg, 1866, "Schwedische Volkslieder," Hamburg, 1857; "Færöiske Kvæder" ("Ballads of the Faroe Isles"), by V. U. Hammershaimb, 2 parts, Copenhagen, 1851–55; "Islenzk Fornkvæði," by Grundtvig and Sigurðsson, 3 parts, Copenhagen, 1854–59.

High German.—"Des Knaben Wunderhorn," Arnim and Brentano, 3 vols., Heidelberg, 1806–08, 4 vols., Berlin, 1853–54; "Alte teutsche Volkslieder in der Mundart des Kuhländchens," Vienna and Hamburg, 1817; "Oesterreichische Volkslieder," Ziska and Schottky, Pesth, 1819; "Die Volkslieder der Deutschen," F. K. von Erlach, 5 vols. Mannheim 1834–36; "Schlesische Volkslieder," Hoffmann von Fallersleben and Richter, Leipsic, 1842; "Alte hochund nieder-deutsche Volkslieder," L. Uland, 2 vols. Stuttgart, 1844–45; "Deutsche Volkslieder," F. L. Mittler, Marburg and Leipsic, 1855; "Fränkische Volkslieder," F. M. von Ditfurth, 2 parts, Leipsic, 1855; "Deutscher Liederhort," L. Erk, Berlin, 1856; "Die historischen Volkslieder der Deutschen," R. von Liliencron, 4 vols., Leipsic, 1865–69.

Low-German, Netherlandish.—"Letterkundig overzigt en proeven van de Nederlandsche Volkszangen," J. C. W. le Jeune, Amsterdam, 1828; Uhland, as before; "Oude Vlaemsche Liederen," J. F. Willems, Ghent, 1848; "Niederländsche Volkslieder," Hoffmann von Fallersleben, second ed., Hannover, 1856; "Chants Populaires des Flamands de France," E. de Coussemaker, Ghent, 1856.

Spanish and Portuguese.—"Tesoro de los Romanceros," etc., Eug. de Ochoa, Paris, 1838, Barcelona, 1840; "Romancero Castellano," G. B. Depping and A. A. Galiano, 2 vols., Leipsic, 1844; "Romancero General" (vols. x. and xvi. of "Biblioteca de autores Españoles"), Madrid, 1849–51; "Observaciones sobra la poesia popular," etc., M. Milá y Fontanals, Barcelona, 1853; "Primavera y Flor de Romances," F. J. Wolf and C. Hoffmann, 2 vols., Berlin, 1856; "Romanzen Asturiens," u. s. w., José Amador de los Rios, in "Jahrbuch für romanische- u. englische Literatur," iii., 268, 1861; "Cancionero Popular," E. Lafuente y Alcantara, 2 vols., Madrid, 1866; "Cansons de la Terra, Cants populars Catalans." F. Pelay Bríz y Candi Candi, 3 vols., Barcelona, 1866–71; "Romanceiro," Almeida-Garrett, 3 vols., Lisbon, 1863; Th. Braga, "Cancioneiro Popular," Coimbra, 1867; "Romanceiro, Geral," Coimbra, 1867; "Cantos Populares do Archipelago Açoriano," Porto, 1869; "Ancient Spanish Ballads," J. G. Lockhart, London, 1823; "Portugiesische Volkslieder u. Romanzen," C. F. Bellermann, Leipsic, 1864; "Romanzero der Spanier u. Portugieser," Stuttgart, 1866.

Italian.—"Canti popolari Toscani, Corsi, Illirici, Greci," N. Tommaséo, 4 vols., Venice, 1841–42, second ed. of vol. i., 1848; "Canti pop. inediti Umbri, etc.," O. Marcoaldi, Genoa, 1856; "Canzoni pop. del Piemonte," C. Nigra in the "Rivista Contemporanea" of Turin, 1858–63; "Saggio di canti pop. Veronesi," E. S. Righi, Verona, 1863; "Volkslieder aus Venetien, gesammelt von G. Widter," 1864; "Canti pop. Siciliani," G. Pitrè, vol. i., Palermo, 1870, vol. ii., 1871; "Canti e Racconti del Popolo Italiano," D. Comparetti and A. d'Ancona, Turin and Florence, vol. i., 1870; vol. ii., 1871; vol. iii., 1872.

French.—"Instructions relatives aux Poésies Populaires de le France," J. J. Ampère, Paris, 1853; "Etude sur la poésie populaire en Normandi," Eug. de Beaurepair, Avranches, 1856; "Chants populaires du pays castrais," A. Combes, Castres, 1862; "Chants pop. de la Provence," Damase Arbaud, 2 vols., Aix, 1862–64; "Romancero de Champagne," P. Tarbé, 5 vols., Reims, 1863–64; "Chants pop. recueillis dans le pays messin," Compte de Puymaigre, Metz, 1865; "Chants et chansons pop. des provinces de l'ouest, Poitou, etc.," J. Bujeaud, 2 vols., Niort, 1866; "Des chansons pop. chez les anciens et chez les Français," C. Nisard, 2 vols., Paris, 1867; "Recueil de chants historiques français," Leroux de Lincy, 2 vols., Paris, 1841–42.

Rouman and Wallachian.—"Ballade," B. Alexandri, 2 vols., Jassy, 1853–54; and "Poesiĕ-Populare ale Românilor," Bucharest, 1866; "Ballades et chants pop. de la Roumanie, recueillis et traduits par Alexandri," Paris, 1855; "Rouman Anthology, National Ballads of Moldavia," etc., H. Stanley, Hertford, 1856; (Alexandri's) "Rumänische Volkspoesie," deutsch v. W. v. Kotzebue, Berlin, 1857; "Poesia Popurala, Balade," Marienescu, Pesth, 1859; "Romänische Volkslieder," Schuller, Hermannstadt, 1859.

Romaic.—"Chants populaires de la Grèce moderne," C. Fauriel, 2 vols., Paris, 1824–25; the same in German, by W. Müller, Leipsic, 1825; "Neugriechische Volksgesänge," J. M. Firmenich, Berlin, 1840; "Canti popolari Toscani, Corsi, Illirici, Greci," N. Tommaséo, 4 vols., Venice, 1841–42; "Neugriechische Volks- u. Freiheitslieder," D. H. Sanders, Leipsic, 1842; "Das Volksleben der Neugriechen," etc., D. H. Sanders, Mannheim, 1844; "Die neugriechischen Volkslieder," Th. Kind, Leipsic, 1849; "Chants du Peuple en Grèce," Compte de Marcellus, 2 vols., Paris, 1851; "Άισματα δημοτικὰ της Ἑλλάδος" (Popular Songs of Greece), Spyr. Zambelios, Corcyra, 1852; "Carmina popularia Græciæ recentioris," A. Passow, Leipsic, 1860; "Anthologie neugriechischer Volkslieder," Th. Kind, Leipsic, 1861.

Slavic, Eastern Branch.—I. *a, Russian.*— "Piesni russkago naroda" (Songs of the Russian People), J. Sakharof, 5 parts, St. Petersburg, 1838–39; "Piesni sobranniya, P. V. Kirieevskim" (Songs collected by P. V. Kirievsky), 8 parts, Moscow, 1850–68; "Piesni, etc." ("Songs collected by P. N. Rybnikof"), 5 vols., Moscow, 1861–70; "Russkiya Narodniya Piesni" (Russian Popular Songs), collected and arranged by P. V. Shein, vol. i., Moscow, 1870; "Stimmen des russischen Volks in Liedern," P. v. Götze, Stuttgart 1828; "Die Balalaika" (Russian Popular Songs, in German translation), J. Altmann, Berlin, 1863; "The Songs of the Russian People, as illustrative of Slavonic Mythology and Russian Social Life," by W. R. S. Ralston, London, 1872.

b, Malorussian, Ruthenian.—"Malorossiiskiya Piesni" (Little-Russian Songs), M. Maximovitch, Moscow, 1827; "Pieśni Ludu ruskiego w Galicyi" (Songs of the Russian People in Galicia), Z. Pauli, Lemberg, 1839–40; "Sbornik ukrainskikh Piesen" (Collection of Songs of the Ukraine), M. Maximovitch, Kief, 1849; "Pisni, Dumki," etc. ("Songs, Thoughts, and Jests of the Russian People in Podolia, Ukraine, and Little-Russia"), A. Kotzipinsky, Kief, 1862; "Volkslieder der Polen" (i.e., of the Ruthenian people in Poland), gesammelt u. übersetzt von W. P., Leipsic, 1833; "Die poetische Ukraine," F. Bodenstedt, Stuttgart, 1845.—II. *Illyrico-Servian.*—1, *a, Servian.*—"Narodne srpske Pjesme" ("Songs of the Servian People"), Vuk Stephanovitch Karadshitch, third ed., 6 vols., Vienna, 1841–66; "Volkslieder der Serben," Talvj (Mrs Robinson), second ed., 2 vols., Leipsic, 1853; "Die Gesänge der Serben," 2 parts, S. Kapper, Leipsic, 1852; "Poésies populaires Serbes," A. Dozon, Paris, 1859. *b, Bosnian.*— "Srpske Narodne Pjesme iz Bozne" ("Songs of the Servian People in Bosnia"), J. V. Petranovitch, Sarajevo, 1867. *c, Montenegrin.*— "Pjevanija Tzernogorska," etc. ("Popular Poetry of Montenegro and Herzegovina"), collected by Tshubar Tshoikovitch, ed. by J. Milovuk, Ofen, 1833; another collection, ed. by himself, Leipsic, 1839. *d, Dalmatian.*—"Razgovor ugodni" ("Entertaining Conversations"), by A. Cacich Miossich, Venice, 1759, Agram, 1862; "Viaggio in Dalmazia," Alberto Fortis, 2 vols., Venice, 1774. 2, *Croatian.*—"Narodne Pjesme" etc. ("Popular Songs of the Croats, Dalmatians, Bosnians, and Servians"), Leopold Zupan, Agram, 1848. 3, *Slovenian* (Slaves of Carniola and Carinthia), "Slovenske Pesmi krajnskiga naroda" ("Songs of the Slovenzi in Carniola") [Achazel and Korytko], Laibach, 1839–44; "Narodne Pèsni ilirske," etc., Stanko Vraz, Part I., Agram, 1839; "Volkslieder aus Krain," übersetzt von Anastasius Grün, Leipsic, 1850. 4, *Bulgarian.*— "Bulgarske Narodne Pèsni," D. and K. Miladinof, Agram, 1867. *Western Branch*, I. Czekho-Slovakian,—1, *a, Bohemian and Moravian.*— "Pjsnĕ národnj w Čechách" ("Songs of the People in Bohemia"), J. Erben, 3 parts, Prague, 1842–45; "Morawské národnj Pjsnĕ" ("Songs of the Moravian People"), F. Suschil, Brünn, 1835, 1840, also 1853–57; "Böhmische Rosen," Ida v.

Düringsfeld, Breslau, 1851; "Böhmische Granaten, Czechische Volkslieder," M. Waldau, 2 vols., Prague, 1858–60. *b, Slovak.*—"Slowanské Naródnj Pjsně," F. L. Czelakowsky (including, besides Slovak songs, Slovenian, Bohemian, etc.), 3 parts, Prague, 1822–27, and 1839–44; "Národnjé zpiewanky čili pjesně swietské Slowáků w Uhrach" ("Songs of the Slovaks in Hungary"), J. Kollar, 2 parts, Buda, 1823–27, 1834–35. 2, *Polish.*—"Pieśni polskie i ruskie Ludu galicyjskiego," ("Songs of the Polish and Russian people in Galicia"), W. z. Oleska, Lemberg, 1833; "Pieśni Ludu bialo-chrobatów, mazurów, i russinów z nad Bugu" ("Songs of the White Chrobatians, Massovians, and Russinians on the Bug"), K. W. Woicicki, Warsaw, 1836; "Pieśni Ludu polskiego w Galicyi" ("Songs of the Polish People in Galicia"), Z. Pauli, Lemberg, 1838; Pieśni Ludu polskiego," P. Kolberg, Warsaw, 1857; "Pieśni Ludu polskiego w Górnym Szlasku" ("Songs of the Polish People in Silesia"), Juliusz Roger, Wrocław, 1863. 3, *Sorabian-Wendish.*—"Volkslieder der Wenden in der Ober- u. Nieder-Lausitz," L. Haupt and J. E. Schmaler, Grimma, 1841–43. General Works.—"Historical View of the Languages and Literature of the Slavic Nations," etc., Talvj (Mrs Robinson), New York, 1850; "Slawische Volkslieder" (Russian, Bohemian, Slovak, Bulgarian), J. Wenzig, Halle, 1830; "Slawische Balalaika" (Russian, Little Russian, Carniolan, Polish), W. v. Waldbrühl, Leipsic, 1843.

Lithuanian.—"Littauische Volkslieder," collected and translated by G. H. F. Nesselmann, Berlin, 1859; "Litthauische Volkslieder u. Sagen," Wm. Jordan, Berlin, 1844.

Breton.—"Barzaz-Breiz, Chants populaires de la Bretagne," Th. Hersart de la Villemarqué, fourth ed., 2 vols., Paris; 1846; "Volkslieder aus der Bretagne," A. Keller u. E. Seckendorff, Tübingen, 1841; "Bretonische Volk-slieder," M. Hartmann u. L. Pfau, Cologne, 1859; "Chants populaires de la Basse-Bretagne," F. M. Luzel, Vol. i., L'Orient, 1868.

Of non-Indo-European races the more important collections are—

Finnish.—"Finnische Runen" (Finnish and German), by H. R. von Schröter, edited by G. H. v. Schröter, Stuttgart, 1834; "Suomen Kansan wanhoja Runoja" ("Ancient Songs of the Finnish People"), Oscar Topelius, 3 parts,

Turussa, 1822–26; "Kanteletar," etc., "The Harp, or Ancient Songs and Hymns of the Finnish People," E. Lönnroth, 2 vols., Helsingfors, 1840. *Esthonian.*—"Ehstnische Volkslieder," original and translation, H. Neus, Reval, 1850–52. *Hungarian.*—"Népdalok és Mondák" ("Songs and Tales"), J. Erdélyi, 3 vols., Pesth, 1842–48; "Ausgewählte ungarische Volkslieder," translated and edited by, K. M. Kertbeny, Darmstadt, 1851. *Turkish.*—"Proben der Volkslitteratur der türkischen Stämme Süd-Siberiens" ("Specimens of the Popular Literature of the Turkish Races of South Siberia"), W. Radlof, 3 vols., St. Petersburg, 1866–70.

Of comprehensive works and collections the most noticeable are—"Stimmen der Völker in Liedern," J. G. v. Herder, 1778, ed. by J. v. Müller, Tübingen, 1807; Talvj (Mrs Robinson), "Versuch einer geschichtlichen Charakteristik der Volkslieder germanischen Nationen," etc., Leipsic, 1840; "Hausschatz der Volkspoesie," O. L. B. Wolff, Leipsic, 1853; "Volksdichtungen nord- u. südeuropäischer Völker alter u. neuer Zeit," J. M. Firmenich, 1867.

—F. J. CHILD.

Johnson's New Universal Cyclopædia, Vol. 1. Ed. Frederic A. P. Barnard, et al. New York: A. J. Johnson & Son, 1877, p. 365–68.

The English and Scottish
Popular Ballads

1

RIDDLES WISELY EXPOUNDED

A. a. 'A Noble Riddle Wisely Expounded; or, The Maid's Answer to the Knight's Three Questions,' 4to, Rawlinson, 566, fol. 193, Bodleian Library; Wood, E. 25, fol. 15, Bod. Lib. **b.** Pepys, III, 19, No 17, Magdalen College, Cambridge. **c.** Douce, II, fol. 168 b, Bod. Lib. **d.** 'A Riddle Wittily Expounded,' *Pills to Purge Melancholy*, IV, 129, ed. 1719. "II, 129, ed. 1712."

B. 'The Three Sisters.' *Some Ancient Christmas Carols . . . together with two Ancient Ballads, etc.* By Davies Gilbert, 2d ed., p. 65.

C. 'The Unco Knicht's Wowing,' Motherwell's MS., p. 647.

D. Motherwell's MS., p. 142.

E. *Nursery Rhymes and Country Songs*, p. 31.

THE FOUR COPIES of **A** differ but very slightly: **a, b, c** are broadsides, and **d** is evidently of that derivation. **a** and **b** are of the 17th century. There is another broadside in the Euing collection, formerly Halliwell's, No 253. The version in *The Borderer's Table Book*, VII, 83, was compounded by Dixon from others previously printed.

Riddles, as is well known, play an important part in popular story, and that from very remote times. No one needs to be reminded of Samson, Œdipus, Apollonius of Tyre. Riddle-tales, which, if not so old as the oldest of these, may be carried in all likelihood some centuries beyond our era, still live in Asiatic and European tradition, and have their representatives in popular ballads. The largest class of these tales is that in which one party has to guess another's riddles, or two rivals compete in giving or guessing, under penalty in either instance of forfeiting life[*] or some other heavy wager; an example of which is the English ballad, modern in form, of 'King John and the

Abbot of Canterbury.' In a second class, a suitor can win a lady's hand only by guessing riddles, as in our 'Captain Wedderburn's Courtship' and 'Proud Lady Margaret.' There is sometimes a penalty of loss of life for the unsuccessful, but not in these ballads. Thirdly, there is the tale (perhaps an offshoot of an early form of the first) of The Clever Lass, who wins a husband, and sometimes a crown, by guessing riddles, solving difficult but practicable problems, or matching and evading impossibilities; and of this class versions **A** and **B** of the present ballad and **A–H** of the following are specimens.

Ballads like our 1, **A, B,** 2, **A–H,** are very common in **German**. Of the former variety are the following:

A. 'Räthsellied,' Büsching, *Wöchentliche Nachrichten*, 1, 65, from the neighborhood of Stuttgart. The same, Erlach, III, 37; *Wunderhorn*, IV, 139; *Liederhort*, p. 338, No 153; Erk u. Irmer, H. 5, p. 32, No 29; Mittler, No 1307 (omits the last stanza); Zuccalmaglio, II, 574, No 317 [with change in st. 11]; Mündel, *Elsässische Volkslieder*, p. 27, No 24. A knight meets a maid on the road, dismounts, and says, "I will ask you a riddle; if you guess it, you shall be my wife." She answers, "Your riddle shall soon be guessed; I will do my best to be your wife;" guesses eight pairs of riddles, is taken up behind

---

[*] A grim kemp, an unco knicht, asks nine riddles of a young man; all are guessed; wherefore the kemp says it shall go well with him. Kristensen, *Skattegraveren*, II, 97ff, 154f, Nos 457, 458, 724; V, 49, No 454. Also, Kristensen, *Jyske Folkeminder*, X, 2, 'Svend Bondes Spørgsmaal,' **B**.

him, and they ride off. **B.** 'Räthsel um Räthsel,' *Wunderhorn*, II, 407 [429, 418] = Erlach, I, 439. Zuccalmaglio, II, 572, No 316, rearranges, but adds nothing. Mittler, No 1306, inserts three stanzas (7, 9, 10). This version begins: "Maid, I will give you some riddles, and if you guess them will marry you." There are ten pairs, and, these guessed, the man says, "I can't give you [2] riddles: let's marry;" to which she gives no coy assent: but this conclusion is said not to be genuine (Liederhort, p. 341, note). **C.** 'Räthsellied,' Erk, *Neue Sammlung*, Heft 3, p. 64, No 57, and *Liederhort*, 340, No 153[a], two Brandenburg versions, nearly agreeing, one with six, the other with five, pairs of riddles. A proper conclusion not having been obtained, the former was completed by the two last stanzas of **B**, which are suspicious. **C** begins like **B. D.** 'Räthselfragen,' Peter, *Volksthümliches aus Österreichisch-Schlesien*, I, 272, No 83. A knight rides by where two maids are sitting, one of whom salutes him, the other not. He says to the former, "I will put you three questions, and if you can answer them will marry you." He asks three, then six more, then three, and then two, and, all being answered, bids her, since she is so witty, build a house on a needle's point, and put in as many windows as there are stars in the sky; which she parries with, "When all streams flow together, and all trees shall fruit, and all thorns bear roses, then come for your answer." **E.** 'Räthsellied,' Tschischka u. Schottky, *Oesterreichische Volkslieder*, 2d ed., p. 28, begins like **B**, **C**, has only three pairs of riddles, and ends with the same task of building a house on a needle's point. **F.** 'Räthsellied,' Hocker, *Volkslieder von der Mosel*, in Wolf's *Zeits. für deutsche Myth.*, I, 251, from Trier, begins with the usual promise, has five pairs of riddles, and no conclusion. **G.** 'Räthsel,' Ditfurth, *Fränkische Volkslieder*, II, 110, No 146, has the same beginning, six pairs of riddles, and no conclusion. **H.** J. H. Schmitz, *Sitten u. s. w. des Eifler Volkes*, I, 159; five pairs of riddles and no conclusion. (Köhler.) **I.** Alfred Müller, *Volkslieder aus dem Erzgebirge*, p. 69; four pairs of riddles, and no conclusion. **J.** Lemke, *Volksthümliches in Ostpreussen*, p. 152; seven riddles guessed, "nun bin ich Deine Frau."

Some of the riddles occur in nearly all the versions, some in only one or two, and there is now and then a variation also in the answers. Those which are most frequent are:

Which is the maid without a tress? **A–D, G.**
And which is the tower without a crest? **A–D, F, G.**
  (Maid-child in the cradle; tower of Babel.)
Which is the water without any sand? **A, B, C, F, G.**
And which is the king without any land? **A, B, C, F, G.**
  (Water in the eyes; king in cards.)
Where is no dust in all the road? **A–G.**
Where is no leaf in all the wood? **A–G.**
  (The milky way, or a river; a fir-wood.)
Which is the fire that never burnt? **A, C–G.**
And which is the sword without a point? **C–G.**
  (A painted fire; a broken sword.)
Which is the house without a mouse? **C–G.**
Which is the beggar without a louse? **C–G.**
  (A snail's house; a painted beggar.)[*]

---

[*]   **D** 4, What is green as clover? What is white as milk? comes near to English **A** 15, **C** 13, **D** 5, What is greener than grass? **C** 11, **D** 2, What is whiter than milk? We have again, What is greener than grass? in 'Capt. Wedderburn's Courtship,' **A** 12; What is whiter than snow? What is greener than clover? in 'Räthselfragen,' Firmenich, *Germaniens Völkerstimmen*, III, 634; in 'Kranzsingen,' Erk's *Liederhort*, p. 342, 3; 'Traugemundslied,' 11; 'Ein Spiel von den Freiheit,' *Fastnachtspiele aus dem* 15n *Jahrhundert*, II, 555; *Altdeutsche Wälder*, III, 138. So, What is whiter than a swan? in many of the versions of Svend Vonved, Grundtvig, III, 786; IV, 742–3–7–8; Afzelius, II, 139, etc.; and Sin is blacker than a sloe, or coal (cf. **C** 15, Sin is heavier nor the lead), Grundtvig, I, 240, 247; IV, 748, 9; Afzelius, II, 139. The road without dust and the tree without leaves are in 'Ein Spiel von den Freiheit,' p. 557; and in Meier, *Deutsche Kinder-Reime*, p. 84, no doubt a fragment of a ballad, as also the verses in Firmenich. The question in German, **A** 4, Welches ist das trefflichste Holz? (die Rebe) is in the Anglo-Saxon prose Salomon and Saturn: Kemble, *Sal. and Sat.* 188, No 40; 204; see also 287, 10. Riddle verses with little or no story (sometimes fragments of ballads like **D**) are frequent. The Traugemundslied, Uhland, I, 3, and the Spiel von den Freiheit, *Fastnachtspiele*, II, 553, have only as much story as will serve as an excuse for long strings of riddles. Shorter pieces of the kind are (Italian) Casetti e Imbriani, *C. p. delle Provincie meridionali*, I, 197f. (Servian) 'The Maid and the Fish,' Vuk, I, 196, No 285, Talvj, II, 175, Goetze, *Serbische V. L.*, p. 75, Bowring, *Servian Popular Poetry*. p. 184; (Polish) Wojcicki, I, 203; (Wendish) Haupt and Schmaler, I, 177, No 150, II, 69, No 74; (Russian) Wenzig, *Bibliothek Slav. Poesie*, p. 174; (Esthonian) Neus, *Ehstnische V. L.*, 390ff, and *Fosterländskt Album*, I, 13, Prior, *Ancient Danish Ballads*, II, 341.

Russian. A ballad from Shein, *Russkiya Narodnuiya Pyesni*, Plyasovuiya, Dance Songs, Nos 88, 87; 89, p. 233f, translated in Ralston's *Songs of the Russian People*, p. 356, from Buslaef's *Historical Sketches of National Literature and Art*, I, 31, resembles very closely German **A**. A merchant's son drives by a garden where a girl is gathering flowers. He salutes her; she returns her thanks. Then the ballad proceeds:

'Shall I ask thee riddles, beauteous maiden?
Six wise riddles shall I ask thee?'
'Ask them, ask them, merchant's son,
Prithee ask the six wise riddles.'
'Well then, maiden, what is higher than the forest?
Also, what is brighter than the light?
Also, maiden, what is thicker than the forest?
Also, maiden, what is there that's rootless?
Also, maiden, what is never silent?
Also, what is there past finding out?'
'I will answer, merchant's son, will answer,
All the six wise riddles will I answer.
Higher than the forest is the moon;
Brighter than the light the ruddy sun;
Thicker than the forest are the stars;
Rootless is, O merchant's son, a stone;
Never silent, merchant's son, the sea;
And God's will is past all finding out.'
'Thou hast guessed, O maiden fair, guessed rightly,
All the six wise riddles hast thou answered;
Therefore now to me shalt thou be wedded,
Therefore, maiden, shalt thou be the merchant's
    wife.'[*]

So a Kosak: "I give thee this riddle: if thou guess it, thou shalt be mine; if thou guess it not, ill shall it go with thee." The riddle, seven-fold, is guessed. Metlinskiy, *Narodnyya yuzhnorusskiya Pyesni*, pp 363f. Cf. Snegiref, *Russkie prostonarodnye Prazdniki*, II, 101f. Also Romanov, I, 420, No 163 (White Russian).

Little-Russian. Three lads give a girl riddles. 'If you guess right, shall you be ours?' Golovatsky, II, 83, 19. Two other pieces in the same, III, 180, 55. (W. W.)

A king's daughter, or other maid, makes the reading of her riddles a condition of marriage in several Polish tales; it may be further stipulated

that a riddle shall be also given which the woman cannot guess, or that those who fail shall forfeit their life. Karłowicz in Wisła, III, 258, 270, where are cited, besides a MS. communication, *Zbiór wiadomoči do antropologii krajowej*, V, 194, VII, 12; Gliński, *Bajarz Polski*, III, No 1; Kolberg, *Krakowskie*, IV, 204.

Among the Gaels, both Scotch and Irish, a ballad of the same description is extremely well known. Apparently only the questions are preserved in verse, and the connection with the story made by a prose comment. Of these questions there is an Irish form, dated 1738, which purports to be copied from a manuscript of the twelfth century. Fionn would marry no lady whom he could pose. Graidhne, "daughter of the king of the fifth of Ullin," answered everything he asked, and became his wife. Altogether there are thirty-two questions in the several versions. Among them are: What is blacker than the raven? (There is death.) What is whiter than the snow? (There is the truth.) 'Fionn's Questions,' Campbell's *Popular Tales of the West Highlands*, III, 36; 'Fionn's Conversation with Ailbhe,' *Heroic Gaelic Ballads*, by the same, pp. 150, 151.

The familiar ballad-knight of **A**, **B** is converted in **C** into an "unco knicht," who is the devil, a departure from the proper story which is found also in 2 I. The conclusion of **C**,

As soon as she the fiend did name,
He flew awa in a blazing flame,

reminds us of the behavior of trolls and nixes under like circumstances, but here the naming amounts to a detection of the Unco Knicht's quiddity, acts as an exorcism, and simply obliges the fiend to go off in his real character. **D** belongs with **C**: it was given by the reciter as a colloquy between the devil and a maiden.

The earlier affinities of this ballad can be better shown in connection with No 2.

Translated, after **B** and **A**, in Grundtvig's *Engelske og skotske Folkeviser*, p. 181: Herder, *Volkslieder*, I, 95, after **A** d.

---

[*] 'Capt. Wedderburn's Courtship,' 12: What's higher than the tree? (heaven). Wojcicki, *Pieśni*, I, 203, l. 11, 206, l. 3; What grows without a root? (a stone).

A

a. Broadside in the Rawlinson collection, 4to, 566, fol. 193, Wood, E. 25, fol. 15. **b.** Pepys, III, 19, No 17. **c.** Douce, II, fol. 168 b. **d.** *Pills to Purge Melancholy*, IV, 130, ed. 1719.

A. d. D'Urfey, 1719–20, IV, pp. 129–32 (emended)

1 THERE was a lady of the North Country,
  Lay the bent to the bonny broom
And she had lovely daughters three.
  Fa la la la, fa la la la ra re

2 There was a knight of noble worth
  Which also lived in the North.

3 The knight, of courage stout and brave,
  A wife he did desire to have.

4 He knocked at the ladie's gate
  One evening when it was late.

5 The eldest sister let him in,
  And pin'd the door with a silver pin.

6 The second sister she made his bed,
  And laid soft pillows under his head.

7 The youngest daughter that same night,
  She went to bed to this young knight.

8 And in the morning, when it was day,
  These words unto him she did say:

9 'Now you have had your will,' quoth she,
  'I pray, sir knight, will you marry me?'

10 The young brave knight to her replyed,
  'Thy suit, fair maid, shall not be deny'd.

[4] 11 'If thou canst answer me questions three,
  This very day will I marry thee.'

12 'Kind sir, in love, O then,' quoth she,
  'Tell me what your [three] questions be.'

13 'O what is longer than the way,
  Or what is deeper than the sea?

14 'Or what is louder than the horn,
  Or what is sharper than a thorn?

15 'Or what is greener than the grass,
  Or what is worse then a woman was?'

16 'O love is longer than the way,
  And hell is deeper than the sea.

17 'And thunder is louder than the horn,
  And hunger is sharper than a thorn.

18 'And poyson is greener than the grass,
  And the Devil is worse than woman was.'

19 When she these questions answered had,
  The knight became exceeding glad.

20 And having [truly] try'd her wit,
  He much commended her for it.

21 And after, as it is verifi'd,
  He made of her his lovely bride.

22 So now, fair maidens all, adieu,
  This song I dedicate to you.

23 I wish that you may constant prove
  Vnto the man that you do love.

B

Gilbert's *Christmas Carols*, 2d ed., p. 65, from the
editor's recollection. West of England.

There were three Sis - ters fair and bright, Jen - ni - fer gen - tle and Rose - ma - ree,

And they__ three loved one val - iant Knight, As the dew flies ov - er the Mul - ber - ry tree.

1 THERE were three sisters fair and bright,
   Jennifer gentle and rosemaree
And they three loved one valiant knight.
   As the dew flies over the mulberry tree

2 The eldest sister let him in,
   And barred the door with a silver pin.

3 The second sister made his bed,
   And placed soft pillows under his head.

4 The youngest sister, fair and bright,
   Was resolved for to wed with this valiant
      knight.

5 'And if you can answer questions three,
   O then, fair maid, I will marry with thee.

6 'What is louder than an horn,
   And what is sharper than a thorn?'

7 'Thunder is louder than an horn,
   And hunger is sharper than a thorn.'

8 'What is broader than the way,
   And what is deeper than the sea?'

9 'Love is broader than the way,
   And hell is deeper than the sea.'

*   *   *   *   *

10 .   .   .   .   .
   'And now, fair maid, I will marry with thee.'

C

Motherwell's MS., p. 647. From the recitation of Mrs Storie.

1 THERE was a knicht riding frae the east,
   Sing the Cather banks, the bonnie brume
Wha had been wooing at monie a place.
   And ye may beguile a young thing sune

2 He came unto a widow's door,
   And speird whare her three dochters were.

3 The auldest ane's to a washing gane,
   The second's to a baking gane.

4 The youngest ane's to a wedding gane,
   And it will be nicht or she be hame.

5 He sat him doun upon a stane,
   Till thir three lasses came tripping hame.

6 The auldest ane's to the bed making,
   And the second ane's to the sheet spreading.

7 The youngest ane was bauld and bricht,
   And she was to lye with this unco knicht.

8 'Gin ye will answer me questions ten,
   The morn ye sall be made my ain.

9 'O what is heigher nor the tree?
   And what is deeper nor the sea?

10 'Or what is heavier nor the lead?
   And what is better nor the breid?

11 'O what is whiter nor the milk?
   Or what is safter nor the silk?

12 'Or what is sharper nor a thorn?
   Or what is louder nor a horn?

13 'Or what is greener nor the grass?
   Or what is waur nor a woman was?'

14 'O heaven is higher nor the tree,
   And hell is deeper nor the sea.

15 'O sin is heavier nor the lead,
   The blessing's better nor the bread.

16 'The snaw is whiter nor the milk,
   And the down is safter nor the silk.

17 'Hunger is sharper nor a thorn,
   And shame is louder nor a horn.

18 'The pies are greener nor the grass,
   And Clootie's waur nor a woman was.'

19 As sune as she the fiend did name,
   He flew awa in a blazing flame.

D

Motherwell's MS., p. 142.

1 'O WHAT is higher than the trees?
   Gar lay the bent to the bonny broom
  And what is deeper than the seas?
   And you may beguile a fair maid soon

2 'O what is whiter than the milk?
   Or what is softer than the silk?

3 'O what is sharper than the thorn?
   O what is louder than the horn?

4 'O what is longer than the way?
   And what is colder than the clay?

5 'O what is greener than the grass?
   And what is worse than woman was?'

6 'O heaven's higher than the trees,
   And hell is deeper than the seas.

7 'And snow is whiter than the milk,
   And love is softer than the silk.

8 'O hunger's sharper than the thorn,
   And thunder's louder than the horn.

9 'O wind is longer than the way,
   And death is colder than the clay.

10 'O poison's greener than the grass,
   And the Devil's worse than eer woman was.'

E

From Miss M. H. Mason's *Nursery Rhymes and Country Songs*, p. 31; sung in Northumberland.

There was a la - dy__ in the West, Lay the bank with the bon - ny broom,

She had three daugh - ters of__ the best, Fa lang the dil - lo,__

Fa lang the dil - lo, dil - lo,__ dee.

Mason, 1878, p. 31. Also in Broadwood and Maitland, 1893, pp. 6–7.

1 There was a lady in the West,
   Lay the bank with the bonny broom
She had three daughters of the best.
   Fa lang the dillo
   Fa lang the dillo dillo dee

2 There came a stranger to the gate,
   And he three days and nights did wait.

3 The eldest daughter did ope the door,
   The second set him on the floor.

4 The third daughter she brought a chair,
   And placed it that he might sit there.

(To first daughter.)
5 'Now answer me these questions three,
   Or you shall surely go with me.

(To second daughter.)
6 'Now answer me these questions six,
   Or you shall surely be Old Nick's.

(To all three.)
7 'Now answer me these questions nine,
   Or you shall surely all be mine.

8 'What is greener than the grass?
   What is smoother than crystal glass?

9 'What is louder than a horn?
   What is sharper than a thorn?

10 'What is brighter than the light?
   What is darker than the night?

11 'What is keener than an axe?
   What is softer than melting wax?

12 'What is rounder than a ring?'
   'To you we thus our answers bring.

13 'Envy is greener than the grass,
   Flattery smoother than crystal glass.

14 'Rumour is louder than a horn,
   Hunger is sharper than a thorn.

15 'Truth is brighter than the light,
   Falsehood is darker than the night.

16 'Revenge is keener than an axe,
   Love is softer than melting wax.

17 'The world is rounder than a ring,
   To you we thus our answers bring.

18 'Thus you have our answers nine,
   And we never shall be thine.'

A. **a**. *Title*. A Noble Riddle wisely Expounded: or,
The Maids answer to the Knights Three Ques-
tions.
She with her excellent wit and civil carriage,
Won a young Knight to joyn with him in mar-
riage;
This gallant couple now is man and wife,
And she with him doth lead a pleasant Life.
Tune of Lay the bent to the bonny broom.

WOODCUT OF THE KNIGHT.

WOODCUT OF THE MAID.

c. Knights questions. Wed a knight . . . with her in
marriage.
[6] **a**. Printed for F. Coles, T. Vere, I. Wright, and I.
Clarke.
b. Printed for W. Thackeray, E. M. and A. M.
c. Licens'd according to Order. London. Printed
by Tho. Norris, at the L[o]oking glass on Lon-
don-bridge. And sold by J. Walter, in High Hol-
born.
*In Rawlinson and Wood the first seven lines are in
Roman and Italic type; the remainder being in black
letter and Roman. The Pepys copy has one line of
the ballad in black letter and one line in Roman
type. The Douce edition is in Roman and Italic.*
A. 1^1. **c**, i' th' North: **d**, in the.
3^1. **c**, This knight.
5^1. **a**, **b**, **c**, **d**, The youngest sister.
7^1. **b**, **d**, The youngest that same. **c**, that very
same.
7^2. **a**, with this young knight.
9^2. **d**, sir knight, you marry me.
*After 10, there is a wood-cut of the knight and the
maid in* **a**; *in* **b** *two cuts of the knight.*

11^2. **a**, I'll marry. **d**, I will.
12^1. **c** *omits* in love. 12^2. **b**, **c**, **d**, three questions.
14^1. **d**, a horn.
After 15: **a**, Here follows the Damosels answer to
the Knight's Three Questions: **c**, The Damsel's
Answers To The Knight's Questions: **d**, The
Damsel's Answer to the Three Questions.
17, 18. **b**, **c**, **d**, thunder's, hunger's, son's, devil's.
18^2. **d**, the woman.
19^1. **c**, those.
20. **a**, **b** *omit* truly.
21^1. **b**, **c**, **d**, as 't is.

B. *The burden is printed by Gilbert, in the text* "Jennifer
gentle and Rosemaree." *He appears to take Jenni-
fer and Rosemaree to be names of the sisters. As
printed under the music, the burden runs,*

Juniper, Gentle and Rosemary.

*No doubt, juniper and rosemary, simply, are
meant; Gentle might possibly be for gentian. In* 2
H *the burden is,*

Parsley, sage, rosemary and thyme:

curiously varied in **I** *thus:*

Every rose grows merry wi thyme:

and in **G**,

Sober and grave grows merry in time.

C. 18. "Vergris *in another set*." M.

D. *MS. before st.* 1, "The Devil speaks;" *before st.* 6,
"The maiden speaks."

APPENDIX

Additional Copies

Rawlinson MS. D. 328, fol. 174 b., Bodleian Library.

I was unaware of the existence of this very important copy until it was pointed out to me by my friend Professor Theodor Vetter, of Zürich, to whom I have been in other ways greatly indebted. It is from a book acquired by Walter Pollard, of Plymouth, in the 23d year of Henry VI, 1444–5, and the handwriting is thought to authorize the conclusion that the verses were copied into the book not long after. The parties are the fiend and a maid, as in C, D, which are hereby evinced to be earlier than A, B. The "good ending" of A, B, is manifestly a modern perversion, and the reply to the last question in A, D, 'The Devil is worse than eer woman was,' gains greatly in point when we understand who the so-called knight really is. We observe that in the fifteenth century version, 12, the fiend threatens rather than promises that the maid shall be his: and so in E.

Inter diabolus et virgo.

1 Wol ȝe here a wonder thynge
   Betwyxt a mayd and þe fovle fende?

2 Thys spake þe fend to þe mayd:
   'Beleue on me, mayd, to day.

3 'Mayd, mote y thi leman be,
   Wyssedom y wolle teche the:

4 'All þe wyssedom off the world,
   Hyf þou wolt be true and forward holde.

5 'What ys hyer þan ys [þe] tre?
   What ys dypper þan ys the see?

6 'What ys scharpper þan ys þe þorne?
   What ys loder þan ys þe horne?

7 'What [ys] longger þan ys þe way?
   What is rader þan ys þe day?

8 'What [ys] bether than is þe bred?
   What ys scharpper than ys þe dede?

9 'What ys grenner þan ys þe wode?
   What ys swetter þan ys þe note?

10 'What ys swifter þan ys the wynd?
   What ys recher þan ys þe kynge?

11 'What ys ȝeluer þan ys þe wex?
   What [ys] softer þan ys þe flex?

12 'But þou now answery me,
   Thu schalt for soþe my leman be.'

13 'Ihesu, for þy myld myȝth,
   As thu art kynge and knyȝt,

14 'Lene me wisdome to answere here ryȝth,
   And schylde me fram the fovle wyȝth!

15 'Hewene ys heyer than ys the tre,
   Helle ys dypper þan ys the see.

16 'Hongyr ys scharpper than [ys] þe thorne,
   Tonder ys lodder than ys þe horne.

17 'Loukynge ys longer than ys þe way,
   Syn ys rader þan ys the day.

18 'Godys flesse ys betur þan ys the brede,
   Payne ys strenger þan ys þe dede.

19 'Gras ys grenner þan ys þe wode,
   Loue ys swetter þan ys the notte.

20 'Þowt ys swifter þan ys the wynde,
   Ihesus ys recher þan ys the kynge.

21 'Safer is ȝeluer than ys the wexs,
   Selke ys softer þan ys the flex.

22 'Now, thu fende, styl thu be;
   Nelle ich speke no more with the!'

———•———

2^2. Be leue.
3^1. the leman. 3^2. theche.
13^2. kny3t *seems to be altered to* knyt.
14^2. fold: *Cf.* 1^2.
19^2. lowe.

Pollarde *is written in the left margin of* 22^1. *and*
WALTERVS POLLARD *below the last line of the*
piece.

['Inter Diabolus et Virgo' is printed by Dr Furni-
vall in *Englische Studien,* XXIII, 444, 445,
March, 1897.]

———◆———

Findlay's MSS, I, 151, from J. Milne.

'What's greener than the grass?
　What's higher than the clouds?
What is worse than women's tongues?
　What's deeper than the floods?'

'Hollin's greener than the grass,
　Heaven's higher than the clouds,
The devil's worse than women's tongues,
　Hell's deeper than the floods.'

2

THE ELFIN KNIGHT

A. 'A proper new ballad entituled The Wind hath blown my Plaid away, or, A Discourse betwixt a young [Wo]man and the Elphin Knight;' a broadside in black letter in the Pepysian library, bound up at the end of a copy of Blind Harry's 'Wallace,' Edin. 1673.

B. 'A proper new ballad entitled The Wind hath blawn my Plaid awa,' etc. Webster, A Collection of Curious Old Ballads, p. 3.

C. 'The Elfin Knicht,' Kinloch's Anc. Scott. Ballads, p. 145.

D. 'The Fairy Knight,' Buchan, II, 296.

E. Motherwell's MS., p. 492.

F. 'Lord John,' Kinloch MSS, I, 75.

G. 'The Cambrick Shirt,' Gammer Gurton's Garland, p. 3, ed. 1810.

H. 'The Deil's Courtship,' Motherwell's MS., p. 92.

I. 'The Deil's Courting,' Motherwell's MS., p. 103.

J. Communicated by Rev. Dr Huntington, Bishop of Central New York, as sung at Hadley, Mass.

K. Halliwell's Nursery Rhymes of England, p. 109, No 171, 6th ed.

L. Notes and Queries, 1st S., VII, 8.

M. Notes and Queries, 4th Series, III, 605.

PINKERTON gave the first information concerning **A**, in Ancient Scotish Poems . . . from the MS. collections of Sir Richard Maitland, etc., II, 496, and he there printed the first and last stanzas of the broadside. Motherwell printed the whole in the appendix to his Minstrelsy, No I. What stands as the last stanza in the broadside is now prefixed to the ballad, as having been the original burden. It is the only example, so far as I remember, which our ballads afford of a burden of this kind, one that is of greater extent than the stanza with which it was sung, though this kind of burden seems to have been common enough with old songs and carols.[*]

The "old copy in black letter" used for **B** was close to **A**, if not identical, and has the burden-stem at the end like **A**. 'The Jockey's Lamentation,' Pills to Purge Melancholy, v, 317, has the burden,

'T is oer the hills and far away [thrice],
The wind hath blown my plaid away.

The 'Bridal Sark,' Cromek's Remains of Nithsdale and Galloway Song, p. 108, and 'The Bridegroom Darg,' p. 113, are of modern manufacture and impostures; at least, they seem to have imposed upon Cromek.

The last two stanzas of **F** are also in Kinloch MSS, V, 275, with one trivial variation, and the burden, 'And then, etc.'

Sir Walter Scott had a copy beginning, 'There lived a wife in the wilds of Kent:' Sharpe's Ballad Book, 1880, p. 147f.

A like ballad is very common in **German**. A man would take, or keep, a woman for his love or his wife [servant, in one case], if she would spin brown silk from oaten straw. She will do this if he will make clothes for her of the linden-leaf. Then she must bring him shears from the middle of the Rhine. But first he must build her a bridge from a single twig, etc., etc. To this effect, with some variations in the tasks set, in **A**, 'Eitle Dinge,' Rhaw, Bicinia (1545), Uhland, I, 14, No 4 A, Böhme, p. 376, No 293. **B**. 'Van ideln unmöglichen Dingen,' Neocorus († c. 1630), Chronik des Landes Ditmarschen, ed.

Dahlmann, p. 180 = Uhland, p. 15, No 4 B, Müllenhoff, p. 473, Böhme, p. 376, No 294. **C.** *Wunderhorn*, II, 410 [431] = Erlach, I, 441, slightly altered in Kretzschmer [Zuccalmaglio], II, 620. **D.** 'Unmöglichkeiten,' Schmeller, *Die Mundarten Bayerns*, p. 556. **E.** *Schlesische Volkslieder*, p. 115, No 93. **F.** 'Liebes-Neekerei,' Meier, *Schwäbische V. L.*, p. 114, No 39. **G.** 'Liebesspielereien,' Ditfurth, *Fränkische V. L.*, II, 109, No 144. **H.** 'Von eitel unmöglichen Dingen,' Erk's *Liederhort*, p. 337, No 152^b. **I.** 'Unmögliches Begehren,' V. L. aus Oesterreich, *Deutsches Museum*, 1862, II, 806, No 16. **J.** 'Unmögliche Dinge,' Peter, *Volksthümliches aus Österreichisch-Schlesien*, I, 270, No 82. In **K,** 'Wettgesang,' Meinert, p. 80, and **L,** *Liederhort*, p. 334, No 152, there is a simple contest of wits

---

* All that was required for the burden, Mr Chappell kindly writes me, was to support the voice by harmonious notes under the melody; it was not sung *after* each half of stanza, or after the stanza, and it was heard separately only when the voices singing the air stopped. Even the Danish ballads exhibit but a few cases of these "burden-stems," as Grundtvig calls them: see *Danmarks gamle Folkeviser*, II, 221, B 1; 295, B 1; 393, A 1: III, 197, D; 470, A. Such burden-stems are, however, very common in Icelandic ballads. They are, for the most part, of a different metre from the ballad, and very often not of the same number of lines as the ballad stanza. A *part* of the burden stem would seem to be taken for the refrain; as *Íslenzk Fornkvæði*, I, 30, of four verses, 1, 2, 4; 129, of two, the last half of the first and all the second; 194, of four, the last; 225, of five, the last two; II, 52, of five, the second and last two. Another ballad with a burden-stem is a version of 'Klosterrovet,' **C**, MSS of 1610, and later, communicated to me by Svend Grundtvig.

In later times the Danish stev-stamme was made to conform to the metre of the ballad, and sung as the first stanza, the last line perhaps forming the burden. Compare the stev-stamme, Grundtvig, III, 470, with the first stanza of the ballad at p. 475. If not so changed, says Grundtvig, it dropped away. Lyngbye, at the end of his *Færöiske Qvæder*, gives the music of a ballad which he had heard sung. The whole stem is sung first, and then repeated as a burden at the end of every verse. The modern way, judging by Berggreen, *Folke-Sange og Melodier*, 3d ed., I, 352, 358, is simply to sing the whole stem after each verse, and so says Grundtvig, III, 200, D. The whole stem is appended to the last stanza (where, as usual, the burden, which had been omitted after stanza 1, is again expressed) in the Færöe ballad in Grundtvig, III, 199, exactly as in our broadside, or in Motherwell's *Minstrelsy*, Appendix, p. iii. I must avow myself to be very much in the dark as to the exact relation of stem and burden.

between a youth and a maid, and in **M**, Erk, *Neue Sammlung*, H. 2, No 11, p. 16, and **N**, 'Wunderbare Aufgaben,' Pröhle, *Weltliche u. geistliche Volkslieder*, p. 36, No 22 B, the wit-contest is added to the very insipid ballad of 'Gemalte Rosen.' **O.** 'Ehestandsaussichten' [Norrenberg], *Des Dülkener Fiedlers Liederbuch*, 1875, p. 88, No 99. (Köhler.) **P, Q,** Hruschka u. Toischer, *Deutsche Volkslieder aus Böhmen*, p. 171, No 124, a, b.

'Store Fordringer,' Kristensen, *Jydske Folkeviser*, I, 221, No 82; *Skattegraveren*, II, 8, No 6; *Jyske Folkeminder*, X, 342, No 85 (with the stupid painted roses); *Jyske Folkeminder*, XI, 175, No 66 (three copies), 294, No 4; 'Umulige Fordringer,' Kristensen, *Efterslæt til Skattegraveren*, p. 20, No 16; and 'Opsang,' Lindeman, *Norske Fjeldmelodier*, No 35 (Text Bilag, p. 6), closely resemble German **M, N**. In the Stev, or alternate song, in Landstad, p. 375, two singers vie one with another in propounding impossible tasks.

A **Wendish** ballad, Haupt and Schmaler, I, 178, No 151, and a Slovak, Čelakowsky, II, 68, No 12 (the latter translated by Wenzig, *Slawische Volkslieder*, p. 86, *Westslawischer Märchenschatz*, p. 221, and *Bibliothek Slavischer Poesien*, p. 126), have lost nearly all their story, and, like German **K, L**, may be called mere wit-contests.

Polish. Five examples of wit-contests in verse, the motive of love or marriage having probably dropped out are cited by Karłowicz, *Wisła*, III, 267ff: Kolberg, *Krakowskie*, II, 149, and *Mazowsze*, II, 149, No 332, *Zbiór wiad. do antrop.*, X, 297, No 217, and two not before printed. Moravian examples from Sušil, p. 692f, No 809, p. 701ff, No 815: make me a shirt without needle or thread, twist me silk out of oaten straw; count me the stars, build me a ladder to go up to them; drain the Red Sea, make me a bucket that will hold it; etc. Zapolski, *White Russian Weddings and Wedding-Songs*, p. 35, No 19. *Wisła*, as before, III, 532ff.

Polish tales of The Clever Wench are numerous: *Wisła*, III, 270ff.

Italian. 'I tre Tamburi,' Ferraro, *C. P. del Basso Monferrato*, p. 52; 'Il Compito,' Romaic, Tommaseo, III, 13 (already cited by Nigra).

French. 'Les Conditions impossibles,' Beauquier, *Chansons p. recueillies en Franche-Comté,* p. 133.

Servian ballads. Karadžić, *Sr. n. pj.* I, 164, No 240, 'The Spinster and the Tsar;' I, 165, No 242, 'The Spinster and the Goldsmith.' Cf. I, 166, No 243. Also, Karadžić, *Sr. n. pj. iz Herz.,* p. 217, No 191; Petranović, I, 13, No 16 (where the girl's father sets the tasks), and p. 218, No 238; Rajković, p. 209, No 237.

Bulgarian. *Collection of the Bulgarian Ministry of Public Instruction,* III, 31, 3; III, 28, 4. Cf. Verković, p. 52, 43; Bezsonov, II, 74, 105; Miladinof, p. 471, 536.

Russian ballad of Impossibilities propounded reciprocally by youth and maid (including a shirt): Shein, *Russkiya N. P.,* Plyasovuiya, Nos 85, 86, p. 231f. An episode in the old Russian legend of Prince Peter of Murom and his wife Fevronija, three versions: Kušelev-Bezborodko, *Monuments of the older Russian Literature,* I, 29ff. (W. W.)

White Russian. Šejn, *Materialy,* I, i, 494, No 608 (shirt, etc.).

Croatian, Marjanović, 'Dar i uzdarje,' p. 200, No 46.

Jagie, in *Archiv für slavische Philologie,* 'Aus dem südslavischen Marchenschatz,' V, 47–50, adds five Slavic stories of the wench whose ready wit helps her to a good marriage, and Köhler, in notes to Jagie, pp. 50ff, cites, in addition to nearly all those which I have mentioned, one Slavic, one German, five Italian, one French, one Irish, one Norwegian, besides very numerous tales in which there is a partial agreement. Wollner, in Leskien and Brugman's *Litauische Volkslieder und Märchen,* p. 573, cites Slavic parallels to No 34, of which the following, not previously noted, and no doubt others, are apposite to this ballad: Afanasief, VI, 177, No 42, a, b; Trudy, II, 611–614, No 84, 614–616, No 85; Dragomanof, p. 347, No 29; Sadok Baràcz, p. 33; Kolberg, *Lud,* VIII, 206; Kulda, II, 68.

The Graidhne whom we have seen winning Fionn for husband by guessing his riddles, p. 3, afterwards became enamored of Diarmaid, Fionn's nephew, in consequence of her accidentally seeing a beauty spot on Diarmaid's forehead. This had the power of infecting with love any woman whose eye should light upon it:

wherefore Diarmaid used to wear his cap well down. Graidhne tried to make Diarmaid run away with her. But he said, "I will not go with thee. I will not take thee in softness, and I will not take thee in hardness; I will not take thee without, and I will not take thee within; I will not take thee on horseback, and I will not take thee on foot." Then he went and built himself a house where he thought he should be out of her way. But Graidhne found him out. She took up a position between the two sides of the door, on a buck goat, and called to him to go with her. For, said she, "I am not without, I am not within; I am not on foot, and I am not on a horse; and thou must go with me." After this Diarmaid had no choice. 'Diarmaid and Grainne,' *Tales of the West Highlands,* III, 39–49; 'How Fingal got Graine to be his wife, and she went away with Diarmaid,' *Heroic Gaelic Ballads,* p. 153; 'The Death of Diarmaid,' *ib.,* p. 154. The last two were written down c. 1774.

In all stories of the kind, the person upon whom a task is imposed stands acquitted, if another of no less difficulty is devised which must be performed first. This preliminary may be something that is essential for the execution of the other, as in the German ballads, or equally well something that has no kind of relation to the original requisition, as in the English ballads.[*]

An early form of such a story is preserved in *Gesta Romanorum,* c. 64, Oesterley, p. 374. It were much to be wished that search were made for a better copy, for, as it stands, this tale is to be interpreted only by the English ballad. The old English version, Madden, XLIII, p. 142, is even worse mutilated than the Latin. A king, who was stronger, wiser, and handsomer than any man, delayed, like the Marquis of Saluzzo, to take a wife. His friends urged him to marry, and he replied to their expostulations, "You know I am rich enough and powerful enough; find me a maid who is good looking and sensible, and I will take her to wife, though she be poor." A maid was found who was eminently good looking and sensible, and of royal blood

---

[*] Questions and tasks offset by other questions and requisitions appear in the Babylonian Talmud. See Singer, *Sagengeschichtliche Parallelen aus dem babylonischen Talmud, Zeitschrift des Vereins für Volkskunde,* II, 296.

besides. The king wished to make trial of her sagacity, and sent her a bit of linen three inches square, with a promise to marry her if she would make him a shirt of this, of proper length and width.[*] The lady stipulated that the king should send her "a vessel in which she could work," and she would make the shirt: "michi vas concedat in quo operari potero, et camisiam satis longam ei promitto." So the king sent "vas debitum et preciosum," the shirt was made, and the king married her.[†] It may be doubted whether the sagacious maid did not, in the unmutilated story, deal with the problem as is done in a Transylvanian tale, Haltrich, *Deutsche Volksmärchen, u. s. w.*, No 45, p. 245, where the king requires the maid to make a shirt and drawers of two threads. The maid, in this instance, sends the king a couple of broomsticks, requiring that he should first make her a loom and bobbin-wheel out of them.

The tale just cited, 'Der Burghüter und seine kluge Tochter,' is one of several which have been obtained from tradition in this century, that link the ballads of The Clever Lass with [9] oriental stories of great age. The material points are these. A king requires the people of a parish to answer three questions, or he will be the destruction of them all: What is the finest sound, the finest song, the finest stone? A poor warder is instructed by his daughter to reply, the ring of bells, the song of the angels, the philosopher's stone. "Right," says the king, "but that never came out of your head. Confess who told you, or a dungeon is your doom." The man owns that he has a clever daughter, who had told him what to say. The king, to prove her sagacity further, requires her to make a shirt and drawers of two threads, and she responds in the manner just indicated. He next sends her by her father an earthen pot with the bottom out, and tells her to sew in a bottom so that no seam or stitch can be seen. She sends her father back with a request that the king should first turn the pot inside out, for cobblers always sew on the inside, not on the out. The king next demanded that the girl should come to him, neither driving, nor walking, nor riding; neither dressed nor naked; neither out of the road nor in the road; and bring him something that was a gift and no gift. She put two wasps between two plates, stripped, enveloped herself in a fishing-net, put her goat into the rut in the road, and, with one foot on the goat's back, the other stepping along the rut, made her way to the king. There she lifted up one of the plates, and the wasps flew away: so she had brought the king a present and yet no present. The king thought he could never find a shrewder woman, and married her.

Of the same tenor are a tale in Zingerle's *Tyrolese Kinder u. Hausmärchen*, 'Was ist das Schönste, Stärkste und Reichste?' No 27, p. 162, and another in the Colshorns' *Hanoverian Märchen u. Sagen*, 'Die kluge Dirne,' No 26, p. 79. Here a rich and a poor peasant [a farmer and his bailiff] have a case in court, and wrangle till the magistrate, in his weariness, says he will give them three questions, and whichever answers right shall win. The questions in the former tale are: What is the most beautiful, what the strongest, what the richest thing in the world? In the other, What is fatter than fat? How heavy is the moon? How far is it to heaven? The answers suggested by the poor peasant's daughter are: Spring is the most beautiful of things, the ground the strongest, autumn the richest. And the bailiff's daughter answers: The ground is fatter than fat, for out of it comes all that's fat, and this all goes back

---

[*] Of the custom of a maid's making a shirt for her betrothed, see L. Pineau in *Revue des Traditions Populaires*, XI, 68. A man's asking a maid to sew him a shirt is equivalent to asking for her love, and her consent to sew the shirt to an acceptance of the suitor. See, for examples, Grundtvig, III, 918. When the Elf in 'Elveskud,' **D** 9, Grundtvig, II, 116, offers to give Ole a shirt of silk, it is meant as a love-token; Ole replies that his true love had already given him one. The shirt demanded by the Elfin Knight may be fairly understood to have this significance, as Grundtvig has suggested. So, possibly, in 'Clerk Colvill,' No 42, **A** 5, considering the relation of 'Clerk Colvill' and 'Elveskud.' We have silken sarks sewn by a lady's hand in several other ballads which pass as simple credentials; as in 'Johnie Scot,' No 99, **A** 12, 13, **D** 6, **E** 2, **H** 4, 5; etc. Here they may have been given originally in trothplight: but not in 'Child Maurice,' No 83, **D** 7, **F** 9.

[†] Grundtvig has noticed the resemblance of G. R. 64 and the ballad.—Much of what follows is derived from the admirable Benfey's papers, 'Die kluge Dirne, Die indischen Märchen von den klugen Räthsellösern, und ihre Verbreitung über Asien und Europa,' Ausland, 1859, p. 457, 486, 511, 567, 589, in Nos 20, 21, 22, 24, 25.

again; the moon has four quarters, and four quarters make a pound; heaven is only one day's journey, for we read in the Bible, "Today shalt thou be with me in Paradise." The judge sees that these replies are beyond the wit of the respondents, and they own to having been prompted by a daughter at home. The judge then says that if the girl will come to him neither dressed nor naked, etc., he will marry her; and so the shrewd wench becomes a magistrate's wife.

'Die kluge Bauerntochter,' in the Grimms' *K. u. H. märchen*, No 94, and 'Die kluge Hirtentochter,' in Pröhle's *Märchen für die Jugend*, No 49, p. 181, afford another variety of these tales. A peasant, against the advice of his daughter, carries the king a golden mortar, as he had found it, without any pestle. The king shuts him up in prison till he shall produce the pestle [Grimms]. The man does nothing but cry, "Oh, that I had listened to my daughter!" The king sends for him, and, learning what the girl's counsel had been, says he will give her a riddle, and if she can make it out will marry her. She must come to him neither clothed nor naked, neither riding nor driving, etc. The girl wraps herself in a fishing-net [Grimms, in bark, Pröhle], satisfies the other stipulations also, and becomes a queen.[*]

Another story of the kind, and very well preserved, is No 25 of Karadžič's *Volksmärchen der Serben*, 'Von dem. Mädchen das an Weisheit den Kaiser übertraf,' p. 157. A poor man had a wise daughter. An emperor gave him thirty eggs, and said his daughter must hatch chickens from these, or it would go hard with her. The girl perceived that the eggs had been boiled. She boiled some beans, and told her father to be ploughing along the road, and when the emperor came in sight, to sow them and cry, "God grant my boiled beans may come up!" The emperor, hearing these ejaculations,

stopped, and said, "My poor fellow, how *can* boiled beans grow?" The father answered, according to instructions, "As well as chickens can hatch from boiled eggs." Then the emperor gave the old man a bundle of linen, and bade him make of it, on pain of death, sails and everything else requisite for a ship. The girl gave her father a piece of wood, and sent him back to the emperor with the message that she would perform what he had ordered, if he would first make her a distaff, spindle, and loom out of the wood. The emperor was astonished at the girl's readiness, and gave the old man a glass, with which he was to drain the sea. The girl dispatched her father to the emperor again with a pound of tow, and asked him to stop the mouths of all the rivers that flow into the sea; then she would drain it dry. Hereupon the emperor ordered the girl herself before him, and put her the question, "What is heard furthest?" "Please your Majesty," she answered, "thunder and lies." The emperor then, clutching his beard, turned to his assembled counsellors, and said, "Guess how much my beard is worth." One said so much, another so much. But the girl said, "Nay, the emperor's beard is worth three rains in summer." The emperor took her to wife.

With these traditional tales we may put the story of wise Petronelle and Alphonso, king of Spain, told after a chronicle, with his usual prolixity, by Gower, *Confessio Amantis*, Pauli, I, 145ff. The king valued himself highly for his wit, and was envious of a knight who hitherto had answered all his questions. Determined to confound his humbler rival, he devised three which he thought unanswerable, sent for the knight, and gave him a fortnight to consider his replies, which failing, he would lose his goods and head. The knight can make nothing of these questions, which are, What is that which needs help least and gets most? What is worth most and costs least? What costs most and is worth least? The girl, who is but fourteen years old, observing her father's heavy cheer, asks him the reason, and obtains his permission to go to court with him and answer the questions. He was to say to the king that he had deputed her to answer, to make trial of her wits. The answer to the first question is the earth, and

---

[*] Ragnar Loðrók (*Saga*, c. 4, Rafn, *Fornaldar Sögur*, I, 245), as pointed out by the Grimms, notes to No 94, requires Kraka (Aslaug) to come to him clothed and not clothed, fasting and not fasting, alone and not without a companion. She puts on a fishing-net, bites a leek, and takes her dog with her. References for the very frequent occurrence of this feature may be found in Oesterley's note to *Gesta Romanorum*, No 124, at p. 732.

agrees in the details with the solution of the query, What is fatter than fat? in the Tyrolese and the Hanoverian tale. Humility is the answer to the second, and pride the third answer. The king admires the young maid, and says he would marry her if her father were noble; but she may ask a boon. She begs for her father an earldom which had lately escheated; and, this granted, she reminds the king of what he had said; her father is now noble. The king marries her.

In all these seven tales a daughter gets her father out of trouble by the exercise of a superior understanding, and marries an emperor, a king, or at least far above her station. The Grimms' story has the feature, not found in the others, that the father had been thrown into prison. Still another variety of these stories, inferior, but preserving essential traits, is given by Schleicher, *Litauische Märchen*, p. 3, 'Vom schlauen Mädchen.'

A Turkish tale from South Siberia will take us a step further, 'Die beiden Fürsten,' Radloff, *Proben der Volkslitteratur der türkischen Stämme Süd-Sibiriens*, I, 197. A prince had a feeble-minded son, for whom he wished to get a wife. He found a girl gathering fire-wood with others, and, on asking her questions, had reason to be pleased with her superior discretion. He sent an ox to the girl's father, with a message that on the third day he would pay him a visit, and if by that time he had not made the ox drop a calf and give milk, he would lose his head. The old man and his wife fell to weeping. The daughter bade them be of good cheer, killed the ox, and [11] gave it to her parents to eat. On the third day she stationed herself on the road by which the prince would come, and was gathering herbs. The prince asked what this was for. The girl said, "Because my father is in the pangs of child-birth, and I am going to spread these herbs under him." "Why," said the prince, "it is not the way, that men should bear children." "But if a man can't bear children," answered the girl, "how can an ox have a calf?" The prince was pleased, but said nothing. He went away, and sent his messenger again with three stones in a bag. He would come on the third day, and if the stones were not then made into boots, the old man would lose his head. On the third day

the prince came, with all his grandees. The girl was by the roadside, collecting sand in a bag. "What are you going to do with that sand?" asked the prince. "Make thread," said she. "But who ever made thread out of sand?" "And who ever made boots out of stones?" she rejoined. The prince laughed in his sleeve, prepared a great wedding, and married the girl to his son. Soon after, another prince wrote him a letter, saying, "Do not let us be fighting and killing, but let us guess riddles. If you guess all mine, I will be your subject; if you fail, I will take all your having." They were a whole year at the riddles. The other prince "knew three words more," and threw ours into a deep dungeon. From the depths of this dungeon he contrived to send a profoundly enigmatic dispatch to his daughter-in-law, who understood everything, disguised herself as one of his friends, and proposed to the victor to guess riddles again. The clever daughter-in-law "knew seven words more" than he, took her father-in-law out of the dungeon, threw his rival in, and had all the people and property of the vanquished prince for her own.

This Siberian tale links securely those which precede it with a remarkable group of stories, covering by representatives still extant, or which may be shown to have existed, a large part of Asia and of Europe. This group includes, besides a Wallachian and a Magyar tale from recent popular tradition, one Sanskrit form; two Tibetan, derived from Sanskrit; one Mongol, from Tibetan; three Arabic and one Persian, which also had their source in Sanskrit; two Middle-Greek, derived from Arabic, one of which is lost; and two old Russian, from lost Middle-Greek versions.[*]

The gist of these narratives is that one king propounds tasks to another; in the earlier ones, with the intent to discover whether his brother monarch enjoys the aid of such counsellors as will make an attack on him dangerous; in the later, with a demand that he shall acquit himself satisfactorily, or suffer a forfeit: and the king is delivered from a serious strait, by the sagacity either of a minister (whom he had ordered to be put to death, but who was still living in prison, or at least seclusion) or of the daughter of his minister, who came to her father's assistance.

Which is the prior of these two last inventions it would not be easy to say. These tasks are always such as require ingenuity of one kind or another, whether in devising practical experiments, in contriving subterfuges, in solving riddles, or even in constructing compliments.*

One of the Tibetan tales, which, though dating from the beginning of our era, will very easily be recognized in the Siberian tradition of this century, is to this effect. King Rabssaldschal had a rich minister, who desired a suitable wife for his youngest son. A Brahman, his trusty friend, undertook to find one. In the course of his search, which extended through many countries, the Brahman saw one day a company of five hundred maidens, who were making garlands to offer to Buddha. One of these attracted his notice by her behavior, and impressed him favorably by replies to questions which he put.† The Brahman made proposals to her father in behalf of the minister's son. These were accepted, and the minister went with a great

---

* Benfey, *Das Ausland*, 1859, p. 459. The versions referred to are; *Shukasaptati* (Seventy Tales of a Parrot), 48th and 49th night; the Buddhist *Kanjur*, Vinaya, III, fol. 71–83, and Dsanglun, oder der Weise u. der Thor, also from the *Kanjur*, translated by I. J. Schmidt, c. 23; the Mongol translation of Dsanglun [see Popow, *Mongolische Chrestomathie*, p. 19, Schiefner's preface to Radloff, I, XI, XII]; an imperfect Singhalese version in Spence Hardy's *Manual of Buddhism*, p. 220, 'The History of Wisákhá;' 'Geschichte des weisen Heykar,' 1001 *Nacht*, Habicht, v. d. Hagen u. Schall, XIII, 71, ed. 1840; 'Histoire de Sinkarib et de ses deux Visirs,' *Cabinet des Fées*, XXXIX, 266 (Persian); two old Russian translations of Greek tales derived from Arabic, Pypin, 'in the Papers of the Second Division of the Imperial Acad. of Sciences, St Petersburg, 1858, IV, 63–85;' Planudes, *Life of Æsop*; A. and A. Schott, *Walachische Mährchen*, p. 125, No 9, 'Vom weissen und vom rothen Kaiser;' Erdélyi, *Népdalok és Mondák*, III, 262, No 8, 'The Little Boy with the Secret and his Little Sword.' To these is to be added, 'L'Histoire de Moradbak,' Caylus, Nouveaux Contes Orientaux, *Œuvres Badines*, VII, 289ff, *Cabinet des Fées*, XXV, 9–406 (from the Turkish?). In the opinion of Benfey, it is in the highest degree likely, though not demonstrable, that the Indian tale antedates our era by several centuries. Ausland, p. 511; see also pp. 487, 459.
* Ingenuity is one of the six transcendental virtues of Mahāyāna Buddhism. Schlagintweit, *Buddhism in Tibet*, p. 36.
† The resemblance to the Siberian tale is here especially striking.

---

train to fetch home the bride. On the way back his life was twice saved by taking her advice, and when she was domiciliated, she so surpassed her sisters-in-law in housekeeping talents and virtues that everything was put under her direction. Discord arose between the king of the country she had left and Rabssaldschal, under whom she was now living. The former wished to make trial whether the latter had an able and keen-witted minister or not, and sent him two mares, dam and filly, exactly alike in appearance, with the demand that he should distinguish them. Neither king nor counsellor could discern any difference; but when the minister's daughter heard of their difficulty, she said, "Nothing is easier. Tie the two together and put grass before them; the mother will push the best before the foal." This was done; the king decided accordingly, and the hostile ambassador owned that he was right. Soon after, the foreign prince sent two snakes, of the same size and form, and demanded which was male, which female. The king and his advisers were again in a quandary. The minister resorted to his daughter-in-law. She said, "Lay them both on cotton-wool: the female will lie quiet, the male not; for it is of the feminine nature to love the soft and the comfortable, which the masculine cannot tolerate." They followed these directions; the king gave his verdict, the ambassador acquiesced, the minister received splendid presents. For a final trial the unfriendly king sent a long stick of wood, of equal thickness, with no knots or marks, and asked which was the under and which the upper end. No one could say. The minister referred the question to his daughter. She answered, "Put the stick into water: the root end will sink a little, the upper end float." The experiment was tried; the king said to the ambassador, "This is the upper end, this the root end," to which he assented, and great presents were again given to the minister. The adverse monarch was convinced that his only safe course was peace and conciliation, and sent his ambassador back once more with an offering of precious jewels and of amity for the future. This termination was highly gratifying to Rabssaldschal, who said to his minister, How could you see through all these things? The minister said, It was not I, but my clever daughter-in-law. When the king learned this, he raised the young woman to the rank of his younger sister.[*]

The wise daughter is not found in the Sanskrit tale,[†] which also differs from the Buddhist versions in this: that in the Sanskrit the minister had become an object of displeasure to the king, and in consequence had long been lying in prison when the crisis occurred which rendered him indispensable, a circumstance which is repeated in the tale of The Wise Heykar (*Arabian Nights*, Breslau transl., XIII, 73 ff, *Cabinet des Fées*, XXXIX, 266 ff) and in the *Life of Æsop*. But The Clever Wench reappears in another tale in the same Sanskrit collection (with that express title), and gives her aid to her father, a priest, who has been threatened with banishment by his king if he does not clear up a dark matter within five days. She may also be recognized in Moradbak, in Von der Hagen's *1001 Tag*, VIII, 199 ff, and even in the minister's wife in the story of The Wise Heykar.

[13]   The tasks of discriminating dam and filly and the root end from the tip end of a stick, which occur both in the Tibetan tales and the Shukasaptati, are found again, with unimportant changes, in the Wallachian popular story, and the Hungarian, which in general resemble the Arabic. Some of those in the Arabian tale and in the *Life of Æsop* are of the same nature as the wit-trials in the Servian and German popular tales, the story in the *Gesta Romanorum*, and the German and English ballads. The wise Heykar, e.g., is required to sew together a burst mill-

stone. He hands the king a pebble, requesting him first to make an awl, a file, and scissors out of that. The king of Egypt tells Æsop, the king of Babylon's champion sage, that when his mares hear the stallions neigh in Babylon, they cast their foal. Æsop's slaves are told to catch a cat, and are set to scourging it before the Egyptian public. Great offense is given, on account of the sacred character of the animal, and complaint is made to the king, who sends for Æsop in a rage. Æsop says his king has suffered an injury from this cat, for the night before the cat had killed a fine fighting-cock of his. "Fie, Æsop!" says the king of Egypt; "how could the cat go from Egypt to Babylon in one night?" "Why not," replies Æsop, "as well as mares in Egypt hear the stallions neigh in Babylon and cast their foal?"

The tales in the Shukasaptati and in the Dsanglun represent the object of the sending of the tasks to be to ascertain whether the king retains the capable minister through whom he has acquired supremacy. According to the Arabian tale, and those derived from it, tribute is to be paid by the king whose riddles are guessed, or by him who fails to guess. This form of story, though it is a secondary one, is yet by no means late, as is shown by the anecdote in Plutarch, *Septem Sapientum Convivium* (6), itself probably a fragment of such a story, in which the king of the Æthiops gives a task to Amasis, king of Egypt, with a stake of many towns and cities. This task is the favorite one of draining [drinking] all the water in the sea, which we have had in the Servian tale (it also is in the *Life of Æsop*), and Bias gives the customary advice for dealing with it.[‡]

From the number of these wise virgins should not be excluded the king's daughter in the *Gesta Romanorum* who guesses rightly among the riddles of the three caskets and marries the emperor's son, though Bassanio has extinguished her just fame: Madden's *Old English Versions*, p. 238, No 66; Collier, *Shakspere's Library*, II, 102.

Another Clever Wench is found in Hurwitz's *Hebrew Tales*, New York, 1847, p. 154, Nos 61, 62; or *Sagen der Hebräer aus dem Englischen, u. s. w.*, Leipzig, 1828, p. 129, Nos 56, 57.

---

[*]   The story of the two mares is No 48 of R. Schmidt's translation of the *Çukasaptati*, p. 68 ff; that of the staff of which the two ends were to be distinguished, No 49, p. 70 f. The Clever Wench (daughter of a minister) appears in No 52, p. 73 ff, with some diversities from the tale noted at p. 18. More as to the Clever Wench in R. Köhler's notes to L. Gonzenbach's *Sicilianische Märchen*, now published by J. Bolte in *Zeitschrift des Vereins für Volkskunde*, VI, 59. [See also Radloff, *Proben der Volkslitteratur der nördlichen türkischen Stämme*, VI, 191–202.]

[†]   The Shukasaptati, in the form in which we have them, are supposed to date from about the 6th century, and are regarded as abridgments of longer tales. The Vinaya probably took a permanent shape as early as the beginning of the Christian era. As already remarked, there is scarcely a doubt that the Indian story is some centuries older still.

The first three or four stanzas of **A–E** form the beginning of 'Lady Isabel and the Elf-Knight,' and are especially appropriate to that ballad, but not to this. The two last stanzas of **A, B,** make no kind of sense here, and these at least, probably the opening verses as well, must belong to some other and lost ballad. An elf setting tasks, or even giving riddles, is unknown, I believe, in Northern tradition, and in no form of this story, except the English, is a preternatural personage of any kind the hero. Still it is better to urge nothing more than that the elf is an intruder in this particular ballad, for riddle-craft is practised by a variety of preternatural beings: notoriously by Odin, Thor, the giant Vafþrúðnir, and the dwarf Alwíss in the Edda, and again by a German "berggeist" (Ey, *Harzmärchenbuch,* p. 64, 'Die verwünschte Prinzessin'), a Greek dragon (Hahn, *Griechische u. Albanesische Märchen,* II, 210), the Russian rusalka, the Servian vila,* the Indian rakshas. For example: a rusalka (water-nymph) pursues a pretty girl, and says, I will give you three riddles: if you guess them, I will let you go home to your father; if you do not, I shall take you with me. What grows without a root? What runs without any object? What blooms without any flower? She answers, Stones grow without a root; water runs without any object; the fern blooms without any flower. These answers seem satisfactory, as riddles go, but the ballad concludes (with an injustice due to corruption?), "The girl did not guess the riddles: the rusalka tickled her to death." (Wojcicki *Pieśni,* I, 205; Snegiref, IV. 8; Trudy, III, 190, No 7.)[†] A rakshas (ogre) says he will spare a man's life if he can answer four questions, and shall devour him if he cannot. What is cruel? What is most to the advantage of a householder? What is love? What best accomplishes difficult things? These questions the man answers, and confirms his answers by tales, and gains the rakshas' good will. (Jacob, *Hindoo Tales, or the Adventures of Ten Princes, a translation of the Sanskrit Dasakumaracharitam,* p. 260 ff.)

In the third or "Forest" book of the Mahābhārata, chapters 311–313, is a story that bears marks of being an ancient part of the compilation. Yudhishthira and his four younger brothers are distressed with thirst. The eldest sends these one after another in quest of water. Each reaches a lake and hears a voice of a sprite in the air, "I have the first claim on this lake. Do not drink till you have answered my questions," drinks notwithstanding, and falls as if dead. At last Yudhishthira goes himself, answers the questions, and is offered boons by the sprite. He is very modest, and asks the life of one of his two half-brothers only, not that of either of his full brothers. Whereupon the sprite rewards his virtue by bringing all four to life.

[‡] Amasis in return (8) puts some of the questions which we are apt to think of as peculiarly mediaeval: What is oldest? What is most beautiful, biggest, wisest, strongest? etc. Two of these we have had in Zingerle's story. They are answered in a commonplace way by the Æthiop, with more refinement by Thales. Seven similar questions were propounded by David to his sons, to determine who was worthiest to succeed him, and answered by Solomon, according to an Arabian writer of the 14th century: Rosenöl, I, 167. Amasis also sent a victim to Bias (2), and asked him to cut out the best and worst of the flesh. Bias cut out the tongue. Here the two anticipate the Anglo-Saxon Salomon and Saturn: "Tell me what is best and worst among men." "I tell thee word is best and worst:" Kemble, p. 188, No 37; Adrian and Ritheus, p. 204, No 43; and *Bedæ Collectanea,* p. 326. This is made into a very long story in the *Life of Æsop,* 11. See other examples in Knust, *Mittheilungen aus dem Eskurial,* p. 326f, note b, and Nachtrag, p. 647; Oesterley's *Kirchhof,* v, 94, note to 3, 129; and Landsberger, *Die Fabeln des Sophos,* cx, ff. We may add that Plutarch's question, Which was first, the bird or the egg? (*Quaest. Conviv.* l. 2, q. 3), comes up again in The Demaundes Joyous, No 41, Kemble's *Salomon and Saturn,* p. 290.

A fragment of a riddle given by a wise man to the gods is preserved in a cuneiform inscription: [What is that] which is in the house? which roars like a bull? which growls like a bear? which enters into the heart of a man? etc. The answer is evidently air, wind. George Smith, *The Chaldean Account of Genesis,* 1876, p. 156: cited by J. Karlowicz, Wisla, III, 273.

* Afanasief, *Poetic Views of the Slavonians about Nature,* I, 25. The poludnitsa, seems to belong to the same class: Afanasief, III, 76; Ralston, *Songs of the Russian People,* p. 147.

† The Baba-Yaga, a malignant female spirit, has the ways of the Rusalka and the Vila, and so the Wendish Pszepolnica, the 'Mittagsfrau,' and the Serpolnica: Afanasief, II, 333; Veckenstedt, *Wendische Sagen,* p. 107, No 14, p. 108f, No 19, p. 109f, No 4. The Red Etin puts questions, too, in the Scottish tale, Chambers, *Popular Rhymes,* 1870, p. 92. There is certainly no occasion to scruple about elf or elf-knight.

The riddles and questions are spun out at great length, and many are palpable interpolations. A few examples may be given. What is weightier (more reverend) than the earth? One's mother. What is loftier than the heavens? One's father. What is fleeter than the wind? The mind. What are more numerous than the blades of grass? Thoughts. What does not close its eyes while asleep? A fish. What is that which does not move after birth? An egg. What is that which is without heart? A stone. And so on. A paraphrase of parts of these chapters is given by Ed. Arnold, *Indian Idylls*, Boston, 1883, pp. 212–235.

Similarly, in the Kathā-sarit-sāgara, chapter v, a man escapes death by resolving an ogre's riddle. See Tawney's translation, I, 26, and especially the note, where Benfey is cited as comparing Mahā-bhārata, XIII, 5883 ff. (C. R. Lanman.)

The auld man in I is simply the "unco knicht" of 1 C, D, over again. He has clearly displaced the elf-knight, for the elf's attributes of hill-haunting and magical music remain, only they have been transferred to the lady. That the devil should supplant the knight, unco or familiar, is natural enough. He may come in as the substitute of the elfin knight because the devil is the regular successor to any heathen sprite, or as the embodiment of craft and duplicity, and to give us the pleasure of seeing him outwitted. We find the devil giving riddles, as they are called (tasks), in the Grimms' *K. u. H. märchen*, No 125 (see also the note in vol. III); Pröhle's *K. u. V. märchen*, No 19; Vernaleken, *Oesterreichische K. u. H. märchen*, No 37. He also appears as a riddle-monger in one of the best stories in the *Golden Legend*. A bishop, who was especially devoted to St Andrew, was tempted by Satan under the semblance of a beautiful woman, and was all but lost, when a loud knocking was heard at the door. A pilgrim demanded admittance. The lady, being asked her pleasure about this, recommended that three questions should be put to the stranger, to show whether he were fit to appear in such presence. Two questions having been answered unexceptionably, the fiend proposed a third, which was meant to be a clincher: How far is it from earth to heaven? "Go back to him that sent you," said the pilgrim (none other than St Andrew) to the messenger, "and say that he himself knows best, for he measured the distance when he fell." *Antiquus hostis de medio evanuit.* Much the same is related in the legend of St Bartholomew, and, in a Slovenian ballad, of St Ulrich, who interposes to save the Pope from espousing Satan in disguise.[*]

J, **K**, **L**, have completely lost sight of the original story.

Translated, after **A**, **C**, and **D**, in Grundt-vig's *Engelske og skotske Folkeviser*, p. 251; R. Warrens, *Schottische Lieder der Vorzeit*, p. 8; Knortz, *Lieder u. Romanzen Alt-Englands*, No 54.

---

[*] The legend of St Andrew in *Legenda Aurea*, Grässe, cap. III, 9, p. 19 ff; also in the *Fornsvenskt Legendarium*, I, 143 ff; Zambrini, *Leggende Inedite*, ii, 94 ff; Pitrè, *Canti pop. Siciliani*, ii, 232 ff; Horstmann, Altenglische Legenden, Neue Folge, 1881, p. 8.; Gering, *Íslendzk Æventyri*, I, 95, No 24, 'Af biskupi ok puka,' and Köhler's references, II, 80 f. (Köhler): that of St Bartholomew, Grässe, p. 545, cap. cxxiii, 5, and in a German Passional, Mone's *Anzeiger*, 1839, viii, col. 319 f: that of St Ulrich in Achazel and Korytko, i, 76, 'Svéti Ureh,' translated by A. Grün, *Volkslieder aus Krain*, p. 136 ff. The third question and answer are in all the same. St Serf also has the credit of having baffled the devil by answering occult questions in divinity: Wintown's *Scottish Chronicle*, I, 131, v, 1238 ff, first pointed out by Motherwell, *Minstrelsy*, p. lxxiv, who besides cites the legend of St Andrew.

A

A broadside in black letter, "printed, I suppose," says Pinkerton, "about 1670," bound up with five other pieces at the end of a copy of Blind Harry's 'Wallace,' Edin. 1673, in the Pepysian Library.

My plaid awa, my plaid awa,
And ore the hill and far awa,
And far awa to Norrowa,
My plaid shall not be blown awa.

1 The elphin knight sits on yon hill,
  Ba, ba, ba, lilli ba
He blaws his horn both lowd and shril.
  The wind hath blown my plaid awa

2 He blowes it east, he blowes it west,
He blowes it where he lyketh best.

3 'I wish that horn were in my kist,
Yea, and the knight in my armes two.'

4 She had no sooner these words said,
When that the knight came to her bed.

5 'Thou art over young a maid,' quoth he,
'Married with me thou il wouldst be.'

6 'I have a sister younger than I,
And she was married yesterday.'

7 'Married with me if thou wouldst be,
A courtesie thou must do to me.

8 'For thou must shape a sark to me,
Without any cut or heme,' quoth he.

9 'Thou must shape it knife-and-sheerlesse,
And also sue it needle-threedlesse.'

10 'If that piece of courtesie I do to thee,
Another thou must do to me.

11 'I have an aiker of good ley-land,
Which lyeth low by yon sea-strand.

12 'For thou must eare it with thy horn,
So thou must sow it with thy corn.

13 'And bigg a cart of stone and lyme,
Robin Redbreast he must trail it hame.

14 'Thou must barn it in a mouse-holl,
And thrash it into thy shoes soll.

15 'And thou must winnow it in thy looff,
And also seek it in thy glove.

16 'For thou must bring it over the sea,
And thou must bring it dry home to me.

17 'When thou hast gotten thy turns well done,
Then come to me and get thy sark then.'

18 'I'l not quite my plaid for my life;
It haps my seven bairns and my wife.'
  The wind shall not blow my plaid awa

19 'My maidenhead I'l then keep stir,
Let the elphin knight do what he will.'
  The wind's not blown my plaid awa

B

A *Collection of Curious Old Ballads*, etc., p. 3. Partly from an old copy in black letter, and partly from the recitation of an old lady.

My plaid awa, my plaid awa,
And owre the hills and far awa,
And far awa to Norrowa,
My plaid shall not be blawn awa.

1 The Elphin knight sits on yon hill,
  Ba, ba, ba, lillie ba
He blaws his horn baith loud and shrill.
  The wind hath blawn my plaid awa

2 He blaws it east, he blaws it west,
   He blaws it where he liketh best.

3 'I wish that horn were in my kist,
   Yea, and the knight in my arms niest.'

4 She had no sooner these words said,
   Than the knight came to her bed.

5 'Thou art oer young a maid,' quoth he,
   'Married with me that thou wouldst be.'

6 'I have a sister, younger than I,
   And she was married yesterday.'

[16] 7 'Married with me if thou wouldst be,
   A curtisie thou must do to me.

8 'It's ye maun mak a sark to me,
   Without any cut or seam,' quoth he.

9 'And ye maun shape it, knife-, sheerless,
   And also sew it needle-, threedless.'

10 'If that piece of courtisie I do to thee,
   Another thou must do to me.

11 'I have an aiker of good ley land,
   Which lyeth low by yon sea strand.

12 'It's ye maun till 't wi your touting horn,
   And ye maun saw 't wi the pepper corn.

13 'And ye maun harrow 't wi a thorn,
   And hae your wark done ere the morn.

14 'And ye maun shear it wi your knife,
   And no lose a stack o 't for your life.

15 'And ye maun stack it in a mouse hole,
   And ye maun thrash it in your shoe sole.

16 'And ye maun dight it in your loof,
   And also sack it in your glove.

17 'And thou must bring it over the sea,
   Fair and clean and dry to me.

18 'And when that ye have done your wark,
   Come back to me, and ye'll get your sark.'

19 'I'll not quite my plaid for my life;
   It haps my seven bairns and my wife.'

20 'My maidenhead I'll then keep still,
   Let the elphin knight do what he will.'

C

Kinloch's A. S. Ballads, p. 145. From the recitation
of M. Kinnear, a native of Mearnsshire, 23 Aug., 1826.

1 THERE stands a knicht at the tap o yon hill,
   Oure the hills and far awa
   He has blawn his horn loud and shill.
   The cauld wind's blawn my plaid awa

2 'If I had the horn that I hear blawn,
   And the knicht that blaws that horn!'

3 She had na sooner thae words said,
   Than the elfin knicht cam to her side.

4 'Are na ye oure young a may
   Wi onie young man doun to lie?'

5 'I have a sister younger than I,
   And she was married yesterday.'

6 'Married wi me ye sall neer be nane
   Till ye mak to me a sark but a seam.

7 'And ye maun shape it knife-, sheer-less,
   And ye maun sew it needle-, threed-less.

8 'And ye maun wash it in yon cistran,
   Whare water never stood nor ran.

9 'And ye maun dry it on yon hawthorn,
   Whare the sun neer shon sin man was born.'

10 'Gin that courtesie I do for thee,
   Ye maun do this for me.

11 'Ye'll get an acre o gude red-land
   Atween the saut sea and the sand.

12 'I want that land for to be corn,
    And ye maun aer it wi your horn.

13 'And ye maun saw it without a seed,
    And ye maun harrow it wi a threed.

14 'And ye maun shear it wi your knife,
    And na tyne a pickle o't for your life.

15 'And ye maun moue it in yon mouse-hole
    And ye maun thrash it in your shoe-sole.

16 'And ye maun fan it wi your luves,
    And ye maun sack it in your gloves.

17 'And ye maun bring it oure the sea,
    Fair and clean and dry to me.

18 'And whan that your wark is weill deen,
    Yese get your sark without a seam.'

D

Buchan's *Ballads of the North of Scotland*, II, 296.

17]

1 The Elfin knight stands on yon hill,
    Blaw, blaw, blaw winds, blaw
Blawing his horn loud and shrill.
    And the wind has blawin my plaid awa

2 'If I had yon horn in my kist,
    And the bonny laddie here that I luve best!

3 'I hae a sister eleven years auld,
    And she to the young men's bed has made
      bauld.

4 'And I mysell am only nine,
    And oh! sae fain, luve, as I woud be thine.'

5 'Ye maun make me a fine Holland sark,
    Without ony stitching or needle wark.

6 'And ye maun wash it in yonder well,
    Where the dew never wat, nor the rain ever
      fell.

7 'And ye maun dry it upon a thorn
    That never budded sin Adam was born.'

8 'Now sin ye've askd some things o me,
    It's right I ask as mony o thee.

9 'My father he askd me an acre o land,
    Between the saut sea and the strand.

10 'And ye maun plow 't wi your blawing horn,
    And ye maun saw 't wi pepper corn.

11 'And ye maun harrow 't wi a single tyne,
    And ye mane shear 't wi a sheep's shank bane.

12 'And ye maun big it in the sea,
    And bring the stathle dry to me.

13 'And ye maun barn 't in yon mouse hole,
    And ye maun thrash 't in your shee sole.

14 'And ye maun sack it in your gluve,
    And ye maun winno 't in your leuve.

15 'And ye maun dry 't without candle or coal,
    And grind it without quirn or mill.

16 'Ye'll big a cart o stane and lime,
    Gar Robin Redbreast trail it syne.

17 'When ye've dune, and finishd your wark,
    Ye'll come to me, luve, and get your sark.'

E

Motherwell's MS., p. 492.

1 THE Elfin Knight sits on yon hill,
    Ba ba lilly ba
  Blowing his horn loud and shill.
    And the wind has blawn my plaid awa

2 'I love to hear that horn blaw;
    I wish him [here] owns it and a'.'

3 That word it was no sooner spoken,
    Than Elfin Knight in her arms was gotten.

4 'You must mak to me a sark,
    Without threed, sheers or needle wark.'

F

Kinloch MSS, I, 75. From Mary Barr.

1 'DID ye ever travel twixt Berwick and Lyne?
    Sober and grave grows merry in time
  There ye'll meet wi a handsome young dame,
    Ance she was a true love o mine.

2 'Tell her to sew me a holland sark,
    And sew it all without needle-wark:
      And syne we'll be true lovers again.

3 'Tell her to wash it at yon spring-well,
    Where neer wind blew, nor yet rain fell.

4 'Tell her to dry it on yon hawthorn,
    That neer sprang up sin Adam was born.

5 'Tell her to iron it wi a hot iron,
    And plait it a' in ae plait round.'

6 'Did ye ever travel twixt Bềrwick and Lyne?
    There ye'll meet wi a handsome young man,
      Ance he was a true lover o mine.

7 'Tell him to plough me an acre o land   [18]
    Betwixt the sea-side bot and the sea-sand,
      And syne we'll be true lovers again.

8 'Tell him to saw it wi ae peck o corn,
    And harrow it a' wi ae harrow tine.

9 'Tell him to shear it wi ae hook-tooth,
    And carry it hame just into his loof.

10 'Tell him to stack it in yon mouse-hole,
    And thrash it a' just wi his shoe-sole.

11 'Tell him to dry it on yon ribless kiln,
    And grind it a' in yon waterless miln.

12 'Tell this young man, whan he's finished his
        wark,
    He may come to me, and hese get his sark.'

G

Gammer Gurton's Garland, p. 3, ed. 1810.

1 'CAN you make me a cambrick shirt,
    Parsley, sage, rosemary and thyme
  Without any seam or needle work?
    And you shall be a true lover of mine

2 'Can you wash it in yonder well,
    Where never sprung water nor rain ever fell?

3 'Can you dry it on yonder thorn,
    Which never bore blossom since Adam was
        born?

4 'Now you have askd me questions three,
    I hope you'll answer as many for me.

5 'Can you find me an acre of land
    Between the salt water and the sea sand?

6 'Can you plow it with a ram's horn,
    And sow it all over with one pepper corn?

7 'Can you reap it with a sickle of leather,
    And bind it up with a peacock's feather?

8 'When you have done, and finishd your work,
    Then come to me for your cambrick shirt.'

H

Motherwell's MS., p. 92.

1 'COME, pretty Nelly, and sit thee down by me,
   Every rose grows merry wi thyme
And I will ask thee questions three,
   And then thou wilt be a true lover of mine.

2 'Thou must buy me a cambrick smock
Without any stitch of needlework.

3 'Thou must wash it in yonder strand,
Where wood never grew and water neer ran.

4 'Thou must dry it on yonder thorn,
Where the sun never shined on since Adam
   was formed.'

5 'Thou hast asked me questions three;
Sit down till I ask as many of thee.

6 'Thou must buy me an acre of land
Betwixt the salt water, love, and the sea-sand.

7 'Thou must plow it wi a ram's horn,
And sow it all over wi one pile o corn.

8 'Thou must shear it wi a strap o leather,
And tie it all up in a peacock feather.

9 'Thou must stack it in the sea,
And bring the stale o 't hame dry to me.

10 'When my love's done, and finished his work,
Let him come to me for his cambric smock.'

I

Motherwell's MS., p. 103. From the recitation of
John McWhinnie, collier, Newtown Green, Ayr.

1 A LADY wonned on yonder hill,
   Hee ba and balou ba
And she had musick at her will.
   And the wind has blown my plaid awa

2 Up and cam an auld, auld man,
Wi his blue bonnet in his han.

3 'I will ask ye questions three;
Resolve them, or ye'll gang wi me.

4 'Ye maun mak to me a sark,
It maun be free o woman's wark.

5 'Ye maun shape it knife- sheerless,
And ye maun sew it needle- threedless.

6 'Ye maun wash it in yonder well,
Whare rain nor dew has ever fell.

7 'Ye maun dry it on yonder thorn,
Where leaf neer grew since man was born.'

8 'I will ask ye questions three;
Resolve them, or ye'll neer get me.

9 'I hae a rig o bonnie land
Atween the saut sea and the sand.

10 'Ye maun plow it wi ae horse bane,
And harrow it wi ae harrow pin.

11 'Ye maun shear 't wi a whang o leather,
And ye maun bind 't bot strap or tether.

12 'Ye maun stack it in the sea,
And bring the stale hame dry to me.

13 'Ye maun mak a cart o stane,
And yoke the wren and bring it hame.

14 'Ye maun thresh 't atween your lufes,
And ye maun sack 't atween your thies.'

15 'My curse on those wha learnëd thee;
This night I weend ye'd gane wi me.'

J

Communicated by Rev. F. D. Huntington, Bishop
of Western New York, as sung to him by his father in
1828, at Hadley, Mass.; derived from a rough, roystering
"character" in the town.

1 Now you are a-going to Cape Ann,
　Follomingkathellomeday
Remember me to the self-same man.
　Ummatiddle, ummatiddle, ummatallyho, tal-
　　lyho, follomingkathellomeday

2 Tell him to buy me an acre of land
Between the salt-water and the sea-sand.

3 Tell him to plough it with a ram's horn,
Tell him to sow it with one peppercorn.

4 Tell him to reap it with a penknife,
And tell him to cart it with two mice.

5 Tell him to cart it to yonder new barn
That never was built since Adam was born.

6 Tell him to thrash it with a goose quill,
Tell him to fan it with an egg-shell.

7 Tell the fool, when he's done his work,
To come to me, and he shall have his shirt.

K

Halliwell's *Nursery Rhymes of England*, 6th ed., p. 109, No 171.

1 MY FATHER left me three acres of land,
　Sing ivy, sing ivy
My father left me three acres of land.
　Sing holly, go whistle and ivy

2 I ploughed it with a ram's horn,
And sowed it all over with one pepper corn.

3 I harrowed it with a bramble bush,
And reaped it with my little penknife.

4 I got the mice to carry it to the barn,
And thrashed it with a goose's quill.

5 I got the cat to carry it to the mill;
The miller he swore he would have her paw,
And the cat she swore she would scratch his
　　face.

L

Notes and Queries, 1st S., VII, 8. Signed D.

1 MY FATHER gave me an acre of land,
　Sing ivy, sing ivy
My father gave me an acre of land.
　Sing green bush, holly and ivy

2 I ploughd it with a ram's horn.

3 I harrowd it with a bramble.

4 I sowd it with a pepper corn.

5 I reapd it with my penknife.

6 I carried it to the mill upon the cat's back.

7 I made a cake for all the king's men.

[20]

M

Similar to **F–H**: *Notes and Queries*, 4th Series, III, 605, communicated by W. F., Glasgow, from a manuscript collection; Findlay's MSS, I, 21, from the recitation of Jeany Meldrum, Framedrum, Forfarshire.

1 As I went up to the top o yon hill,
  Every rose springs merry in' t' time
I met a fair maid, an her name it was Nell.
  An she langed to be a true lover o mine

2 'Ye'll get to me a cambric sark,
  An sew it all over without thread or needle.
  Before that ye be, etc.

3 'Ye'll wash it doun in yonder well,
  Where water neer ran an dew never fell.

4 'Ye'll bleach it doun by yonder green,
  Where grass never grew an wind never blew.

5 'Ye'll dry it doun on yonder thorn,
  That never bore blossom sin Adam was born.'

6 'Four questions ye have asked at me,
  An as mony mair ye'll answer me.

7 'Ye'll get to me an acre o land
  Atween the saut water an the sea sand.

8 'Ye'll plow it wi a ram's horn,
  An sow it all over wi one peppercorn.

9 'Ye'll shear it wi a peacock's feather,
  An bind it all up wi the sting o an adder.

10 'Ye'll stook it in yonder saut sea,
  An bring the dry sheaves a' back to me.

11 'An when ye've done and finished your wark,
  Ye'll come to me, an ye'se get your sark.'
  An then shall ye be true lover o mine

———◆———

A. *The verses here prefixed to the ballad are appended to the last stanza in the broadside. For* Norrowa, *v. 3,* Pinkerton *has* To-morrow. 9^1, needle and sheerlesse.

B. 'A Proper New Ballad entitled The Wind hath blawn my Plaid awa, or a Discourse between a Young Woman and the Elphin Knight. To be sung with its own proper tune.'
  "This ballad is printed partly from an old copy in black letter, and partly from the recitation of an old lady, which appears to be the Scottish version, and is here chiefly adhered to."

  Dr Davidson informs me that the introductory stanza, or burden-stem, exists in the form:

    Her plaidie awa, her plaidie awa,
    The win blew the bonnie lassie's plaidie
      awa.

C. This version is in Kinloch MSS, VII, 163. 3 *is wanting.*

    6 Married ye sall never get nane

    Till ye mak a shirt without a seam.

    7 And ye maun sew it seamless,
      And ye maun do it wi needle, threedless.

10. *wanting.* 12^1. I hae a bit o land to be corn.
14 *is wanting.* 16. loof—glove.
17 *is wanting.*
3, 10, 14, 17, are evidently supplied from some
  form of **B.**

D. 3^2. hae made.
  9^1. askd *should perhaps be* left, *or* gave, *as in* K1, L1.

E. Burden^2, *in* MS., 1, blown her; 2, 3, blawn her; 4,
  blawn my.
  2^1, blow; 2^2, and a.

H. 1^1. He speaks, *in the margin of* MS.
  Burden^1, time *in margin.*
  5^1. Maid speaks, *in margin.*

I. *Not divided regularly into stanzas in the* MS.
  4^2. needlework *in margin.*
  10^1. shin? *in margin.*

L. *After* 6: "Then follows some more which I forget,
  but I think it ends thus."

———◆———

APPENDIX

Additional Copies

Communicated by the Rev. S. Baring-Gould. "From the north of Cornwall, near Camelford. This used to be sung as a sort of game in farm-houses, between a young man who went outside the room and a girl who sat on the settle or a chair, and a sort of chorus of farm lads and lasses. Now quite discontinued." The dead lover represents the auld man in I.

1 A FAIR pretty maiden she sat on her bed,
   The wind is blowing in forest and town
She sighed and she said, O my love he is dead!
   And the wind it shaketh the acorns down

2 The maiden she sighed; 'I would,' said she,
   'That again my lover might be with me!'

3 Before ever a word the maid she spake,
   But she for fear did shiver and shake.

4 There stood at her side her lover dead;
   'Take me by the hand, sweet love,' he said.

5 .   .   .   .   .   .
       .   .   .   .   .   .

6 'Thou must buy me, my lady, a cambrick shirt,
   Whilst every grove rings with a merry antine
And stitch it without any needle-work.
   O and thus shalt thou be a true love of mine

7 'And thou must wash it in yonder well,
   Whilst, etc.
Where never a drop of water in fell.
   O and thus, etc.

8 'And thou must hang it upon a white thorn
That never has blossomed since Adam was
       born.

9 'And when that these tasks are finished and
       done
   I'll take thee and marry thee under the sun.'

10 'Before ever I do these two and three,
   I will set of tasks as many to thee.

11 'Thou must buy for me an acre of land
   Between the salt ocean and the yellow sand.

12 'Thou must plough it oer with a horse's horn,
   And sow it over with one peppercorn.

13 'Thou must reap it too with a piece of leather,
   And bind it up with a peacock's feather.

14 'And when that these tasks are finished and
       done,
   O then will I marry thee under the sun.'

15 'Now thou hast answered me well,' he said,
   The wind, etc.
   'Or thou must have gone away with the dead.'
   And the wind, etc.

16 .   .   .   .   .   .
       .   .   .   .   .   .

———◆———

Communicated by Mr Walker, of Aberdeen, as
sung, 1893, by John Walker, Portlethen; learned by him
from his father, above fifty years before.

1 THERE was a knight on the head o yon hill
  Blowing his horn lood and shrill.
    Blow, blow, blow the wind, blow

2 'Ye'se get to me a camrick sark
  Without ae steek o needlework.

3 'An ye will wash it in a wall
  Where rain never fell nor water sprang.

4 'An ye sall dry it on a thorn
  That never wis sprung sin Adam was born.'

5 'Ye'se gie me an acre o red lan
  Atween the see an the watery san.

6 'An ye will plough it wi yer horn,
  An sa it a' wi ae pick o corn.

7 '.   .   .   .
  An cut it doon wi a sheepshank bone.

8 'An ye will big it in the sea,
  An bring the foonshief dry to me.

9 'An when ye have done and finished yer wark,
  Come in, Jock Sheep, an ye'll get yer sark.'

As delivered, 5–8 precede 2–4.

'Scarborough Fair,' taken down by H. M. Bower,
December, 1891, from William Moat, a Whitby fisher-
man. *English County Songs,* by Lucy E. Broadwood and J.
A. Fuller Maitland, 1893, p. 12.

1 'Is ANY of you going to Scarborough Fair?
  Remember me to a lad as lives there;
  Remember me to a lad as lives there;
    For once he was a true lover of mine.
    (*Second line always twice.*)

2 'Tell him to bring me an acre of land
  Betwixt the wild ocean and yonder sea sand;
    And then he shall be a true lover of mine.

3 'Tell him to plough it with one ram's horn,
  And sow it all over with one pepper corn;
    And then he shall be a true lover of mine.

4 'Tell him to reap it with sickle of leather,
  And bind it together with one peacock-feather
    And then he shall be a true lover of mine.

5 'And now I have answered your questions three,
  I hope you'll answer as many for me;
     And then thou shalt be a true lover of mine.'

6 'Is any of you going to Scarborough Fair?
  Remember me to a lass as lives there;
     For once she was a true lover of mine.

7 'Tell her to make me a cambric shirt,
  Without any needles or thread, or owt through't;
     And then she shall be a true lover of mine.

8 'Tell her to wash it by yonder wall,
  Where water neer sprung, nor a drop o rain fall;
     And then she shall be a true lover of mine.

9 'Tell her to dry it on yonder thorn,
  Where blossom neer grew sin Adam was born;
     And then she shall be a true lover of mine.

10 'And now I have answered your questions three,
   And I hope you'll answer as many for me;
      And then thou shalt be a true lover of mine.'

Rev. S. Baring-Gould gives me these variations,
from the West of England:

'O TELL her to bleach it on yonder fresh grass,
Where never a foot or a hoof did pass.'

'O tell him to thresh it in yonder barn,
That hangs to the sky by a thread of yarn.'
                    (Dartmoor.)

'Pray take it up in a bottomless sack,
   And every leaf grows merry in time
And bear it to the mill on a butterfly's back.
   O thus you shall be a true lover of mine.'
                    (Cornwall.)

Mr Frank Kidson has given a copy of 'Scarborough
Fair,' with some better readings, as sung "in Whitby
streets twenty or thirty years ago," in *Traditional Tunes*,
p. 43, 1891.

"O, where are you go-ing?" "To Scar-borough fair," Sav-ou-ry sage,— Rose-ma-ry and thyme;
"Re-mem-ber me to a lass who lives there, For once she was— a true love of mine.

1 'O, where are you going?' 'To Scarborough fair,'
  Savoury sage, rosemary, and thyme;
  'Remember me to a lass who lives there,
     For once she was a true love of mine.

2 'And tell her to make me a cambric shirt,
  Savoury sage, rosemary, and thyme;
  Without any seam or needlework.
     And then she shall be a true love of mine.

3 'And tell her to wash it in yonder dry well,
  Where no water sprung, nor a drop of rain fell.

4 'Tell her to dry it on yonder thorn,
  Which never bore blossom since Adam was
     born.

5 'O, will you find me an acre of land,
  Savoury sage, rosemary, and thyme;
  Between the sea foam, the sea sand,
     Or never be a true lover of mine.

6 'O, will you plough it with a ram's horn,
   And sow it all over with one peppercorn.

7 'O, will you reap it with a sickle of leather,
   And tie it all up with a peacock's feather.

8 'And when you have done and finished your
      work,
   Savoury sage, rosemary, and thyme;
   You may come to me for your cambric shirt,
   And then you shall be a true lover of mine.'

At p. 172, the first stanza of another version is given, with Rue, parsley, rosemary and thyme *for the first line of the burden.*

The Journal of American Folk-Lore, VII, 228f, gives the following version, contributed by Miss Gertrude Decrow of Boston, in whose family the song has been traditional.

1 As I walked out in yonder dell,
   Let ev'ry rose grow merry in time
   I met a fair damsel, her name it was Nell,
   I said, 'Will you be a true lover of mine?

2 'I want you to make me a cambric shirt
   Without any seam or needlework,
      And then you shall be, etc.

3 'I want you to wash it on yonder hill,
   Where dew never was nor rain never fell.

4 'I want you to dry it on yonder thorn,
   Where tree never blossomed since Adam was
      born.'

5 'And since you have asked three questions of
      me,
   Let ev'ry rose grow merry in time
   Now and I will ask as many of thee,
      And then I will be a true lover of thine.

6 'I want you to buy me an acre of land
   Between the salt sea and the sea-sand,
      And then, etc.

7 'I want you to plough it with an ox's horn,
   And plant it all over with one kernel of corn.

8 'I want you to hoe it with a peacock's feather,
   And thrash it all out with the sting of an adder,
      And then,' etc.

A variety of **F, G**, Bruce and Stokoe, *Northumbrian*
Minstrelsy, p. 79; *The Denham Tracts*, II, 358, from D. D.
Dixon's tractate on The Vale of Whittingham, Newcas-
tle-upon-Tyne, 1887. 'Whittingham Fair,' popular in
the north and west of the county of Northumberland;
usually sung as a nursery-ballad.

Are you go-ing to Whit-ting-ham fair, Par - sley, sage,__ rose - ma - ry and thyme;

Re - mem-ber me__ to one who lives there,__ For once she was a true love__ of mine.

1 'ARE you going to Whittingham fair?
   Parsley, sage, rosemary, and thyme
Remember me to one who lives there;
For once she was a true-love of mine.

2 'Tell her to make me a cambric shirt,
   Without any seam or needlework.

3 'Tell her to wash it in yonder well,
   Where never spring-water nor rain ever fell.

4 'Tell her to dry it on yonder thorn,
   Which never bore blossom since Adam was
      born.'

5 'Now he has asked me questions three,
   Parsley, sage, rosemary, and thyme
I hope he will answer as many for me;
For once he was a true-love of mine.

6 'Tell him to find me an acre of land
   Betwixt the salt water and the sea-sand.

7 'Tell him to plough it with a ram's horn,
   And sow it all over with one pepper-corn.

8 'Tell him to reap it with a sickle of leather,
   And bind it up with a peacock's feather.

9 'When he has done, and finished his work,
   O tell him to come, and he'll have his shirt.'

In *The Monthly Chronicle of North Country Lore and
Legend*, III, 7, 'Whittingham Fair' is given by Mr Stokoe
with a few variations.

1. *Second line of refrain*,
   For once she was a true lover of mine.
2, 4. *Second line of refrain*,
   Then she shall be a true lover.
3. *Second line of refrain*,
   And she shall be a true lover.
5. *Second line of refrain*,
   Before he shall be a true lover.

6. *Second line of refrain*,
   Then he shall be a true lover.
7, 8, 9. *Second line of refrain*,
   And he shall be a true lover.
6^1. to buy. 8^1. to sheer 't.
After 8: Tell him to thrash it on yonder wall,
   And never let one corn of it fall.
   Then he shall be a true lover of mine.

Another variety of **F**, **G**, communicated by Mr
Frank Kidson, Leeds, 1884; from tradition.

1 'Oн where are you going?' 'To Scarbro fair.'
    Savoury, sage, rosemary and thyme
    'Remember me to a lass who lives there;
      For once she was a true lover of mine.

2 'And tell her to make me a cambric shirt,
    Without a needle or thread or ought else;
      And then she shall be a true lover of mine.

3 'And tell her to wash it in yonder well,
    Where water neer sprung nor a drop of rain
      fell;
      And then, etc.

4 'And tell her to hang it on yonder stone,
    Where moss never grew since Adam was born.

5 'And when she has finished and done, her I'll
    repay,
    She can come unto me and married we'll be.'

6 'Oh where are you going?' 'To Scarbro fair.'
    'Remember me to a lad who lives there;
      For once he was a true lover of mine.

7 'And tell him to buy me an acre of land
    Between the wide ocean and the sea-sand
      And then he, etc.

8 'And tell him to plough it with a ram's horn,
    And sow it all over with one pepper-corn.

9 'And tell him to reap't with a sickle of leather,
    And bind it up with a peacock's feather.

10 'And when he has finished, and done his work,
    He can come unto me for his cambric shirt.'

Variations in a fragment of the same, remembered by
another person: F. Kidson.

1[1] Oh are you going to . . .

    7 Tell her . . . .
      Sow it all over with sand.

    9 Reap it with . . . .
      And tie it . . . .
      And then she shall be . .

3 (after 9):

    And tell her to wash it in yonder dry well,
    Where no water sprung nor a drop of rain fell,
    And tell her to wash it in yonder dry well,
    Or never be a true lover of mine.

*At p. 229 of the same are these stanzas from a version
contributed by Mrs Sarah Bridge Farmer, as
learned from an elderly lady born in Beverly, Mas-
sachusetts.*

    Can't you show me the way to Cape Ann?
      Parsley and sage, rosemary and thyme
    Remember me to a young woman that's there,
      In token she's been a true lover of mine.

("The requirements which follow are identical
with those of the previous version. There is an
additional stanza:"—)

    And when he has done, and finished his work,
    If he'll come unto me, he shall have his shirt,
      And then he shall be, etc.

3

THE FAUSE KNIGHT UPON THE ROAD

A. 'The Fause Knight upon the Road,' Mother-well's *Minstrelsy*, Introduction, p. lxxiv.
B. 'The False Knight,' Motherwell's *Minstrelsy*, Appendix, Musick, p. xxiv.

C. 'The False Knight,' communicated by Mr Mac-math, of Edinburgh.

THIS singular ballad is known only through Motherwell. The opening stanza of a second version is given by the editor of the music, Mr Blaikie, in the Appendix to the *Minstrelsy*. The idea at the bottom of the piece is that the devil will carry off the wee boy if he can nonplus him. So, in certain humorous stories, a fool wins a princess by dumfounding her: e.g., Halli-well's *Popular Rhymes and Nursery Tales*, p. 32; Von der Hagen's *Gesammtabenteuer*, No 63, III, 179; Asbjørnsen og Moe, *Norske Folke-Eventyr*, No 4; Köhler, *Germania*, XIV, 271; Leskien u. Brugman, *Litauische Volkslieder und Märchen*, p. 469, No 33, and Wollner's note, p. 573. But here the boy always gets the last word. (See fur-ther on, under 'Captain Wedderburn's Court-ship.')*

An extremely curious Swedish ballad of the same description, from the Lappfiord, Finland, with the substitution of an old crone, possibly a witch, and clearly no better than one of the wicked, for the false knight, is given by Oskar Rancken in *Några Prof af Folksång och Saga i det svenska Österbotten*, p. 25, No 10. It is a point in

both that the replicant is a wee boy (gossen, som liten var).

1 'Why are you driving over my field?' said the   [2
    carlin:
    'Because the way lies over it,' answered the boy,
        who was a little fellow.

2 'I will cut [hew] your traces,' said etc.:
    'Yes, you hew, and I'll build,' answered etc.

3 'I wish you were in the wild wood:'
    'Yes, you in, and I outside.'

4 'I wish you were in the highest tree-top:'
    'Yes, you up in the top, and I at the roots.'

5 'I wish you were in the wild sea:'
    'Yes, you in the sea, and I in a boat.'

6 'I'll bore a hole in your boat:'
    'Yes, you bore, and I'll plug.'

7 'I wish you were in hell:'
    'Yes, you in, and I outside.'

8 'I wish you were in heaven:'
    'Yes, I in, and you outside.'

'Kall og svein ungi,' Hammershaimb, *Færøsk Anthologi*, p. 283, No 36 (three versions), is another piece of this kind. The boat is in all the copies, Scotish, Swedish, and Færöe.

* There is a related tradition of foiling mischievous sprites and ghosts by getting the last word, or prolonging talk till the time when they must go, especially the noon-sprite: Wisła, III, 275f, and notes 44–6; also, 269f. The Wends have the proverbial phrase, to ask as many ques-tions as a noon-sprite. The Poles have many stories of beings that take service without wages, on condition of no fault being found, and make off instantly upon the terms being broken.

M. Gaidoz, *Mélusine*, IV, 207, cites a passage from Plutarch's life of Numa, c. 15, which is curiously like this ballad. The question being what is the proper expiatory sacrifice when divine displeasure has been indicated by thunderbolts, Zeus instructs Numa that it must be made with heads. Onions'? interposes Numa. With men's—says Zeus. Hairs? suggests Numa. With LIVE—says Zeus. Sardines? puts in Nama.

The last verses of 'Tsanno d'Oymé,' Daymard, *Vieux Chants pop. recueillis en Quercy*, p. 70, are after the fashion of this ballad.

'Tsano d'Oymé, atal fuessés négado!'
'Lou fil del rey, et bous né fuessés l'aygo!'

'Tsano d'Oymé, atal fuessés brullado!'
'Lou fil del rey, et bous fuessés las clappos!'

Chambers, in his *Popular Rhymes of Scotland*, p. 66 of the new edition, gives, without a word of explanation, a piece, 'Harpkin,' which seems to have been of the same character, but now sounds only like a "flyting."[*] The first stanza would lead us to expect that Harpkin is to be a form of the Elfin Knight of the preceding ballad, but Fin is seen to be the uncanny one of the two by the light of the other ballads. Finn (Fin) is an ancestor of Woden, a dwarf in Völuspá 16 (19), and also a trold (otherwise a giant), who is induced by a saint to build a church: Thiele, *Danske Folkesagn*, I, 45, Grimm, *Mythologie*, p. 455.[†] The name is therefore diabolic by many antecedents.

HARPKIN.

1   Harpkin gaed up to the hill,
      And blew his horn loud and shrill,
         And by came Fin.

2   'What for stand you there?' quo Fin:
      'Spying the weather,' quo Harpkin.

3   'What for had you your staff on your shouther?'
         quo Fin:
      'To haud the cauld frae me,' quo Harpkin.

4   'Little cauld will that haud frae you,' quo Fin:
      'As little will it win through me,' quo Harpkin.

5   'I came by your door,' quo Fin:
      'It lay in your road,' quo Harpkin.

6   'Your dog barkit at me,' quo Fin:
      'It's his use and custom,' quo Harpkin.

7   'I flang a stane at him,' quo Fin:
      'I'd rather it had been a bane,' quo Harpkin.

8   'Your wife's lichter,' quo Fin:
      'She'll clim the brae the brichter,' quo Harpkin.

9   'Of a braw lad bairn,' quo Fin:

---

[*]   At the last moment I come upon this: "The only safeguard against the malice of witches is 'to flight wi dem,' that is, draw them into a controversy and scold them roundly:" (Mrs Saxby, in an interesting contribution of folk-lore from Unst, Shetland, in *The Leisure Hour*, for March 27, 1880, p. 199.)

Mr George Lyman Kittredge has called my attention to Apollonius of Tyana's encounter with an *empusa* between the Caucasus and the Indus. Knowing what the spectre was, Apollonius began to revile it, and told his attendants to do the same, for that was the resource, in such cases, against an attack. The empusa went off with a shriek. Philostratus's *Life of Apollonius*, II, 4. Mr Kittredge referred me later to what is said by Col. Yule (who also cites Philostratus), *Marco Polo*, I, 183, that the wise, according to Mas'udi, revile ghúls, and the ghúls vanish. Mr Kittredge also cites Luther's experience: how, when he could not be rid of the Devil by the use of holy writ and serious words, "so hätte er ihn oft mit spitzigen Worten und lächerlichen Possen vertrieben; . . . quia est superbus spiritus, et non potest ferre contemptum sui." Tischreden, in Auswahl, Berlin, 1877, pp 152–154.

Sprites of the more respectable orders will quit the company of men if scolded: Walter Mapes, *De Nugis Curialium*, ed. Wright, p. 81, Alpenburg, *Deutsche Alpensagen*, p. 312, No 330. So Thetis, according to Sophocles, left Peleus when he reviled her: *Scholia in Apollonii Argonautica*, IV, 816. (Mannhardt, *Wald- und Feldkulte*, II, 60, 68.) See, further, on reproaching or insulting elves and the like, Liebrecht, *Zur Volkskunde*, pp. 54–56: Cassel, *Der Schwan*, 1863, p. 14. (F. Liebrecht); Bladé, *Contes populaires de la Gascogne*, II, 8, 9. (G. L. K.)

Also this: "Die Windsbraut soll man brav schelten, sich selber aber bekreuzigen, dann weicht sie. Sie ist des Teufels Braut. Wo eine Windsbraut auffährt, ist eine Hexe aufgesprungen." Birlinger u. Buck, *Volksthümliches aus Schwaben*, I, 192, No 304. (G. L. K.)

[†]   Finnur is a trold in a corresponding Icelandic story, Árnason, *Íslenzkar Þjóðsögur*, I, 58. (G. L. K.)

See, for Finn and Finns, Karl Blind in *The Contemporary Review*, XL, 402ff, 1881; also, 'The Great Silkie of Sule Skerry,' No 113 in this collection.

'There'll be the mair men for the king's wars,'
　　quo Harpkin.

10 'There's a strae at your beard,' quo Fin:
　　'I'd rather it had been a thrave,' quo Harpkin.

11 'The ox is eating at it,' quo Fin:
　　'If the ox were i the water,' quo Harpkin.

12 'And the water were frozen,' quo Fin:
　　'And the smith and his fore-hammer at it,' quo
　　Harpkin.

13 'And the smith were dead,' quo Fin:
　　'And another in his stead,' quo Harpkin.

14 'Giff, gaff,' quo Fin:
　　'Your mou's fou o draff,' quo Harpkin.

The peit (peat) in st. 3, below, as I am informed by Dr Davidson, is the wee boy's contribution to the school firing.

A

Motherwell's *Minstrelsy*, Introduction, p. lxxiv. From Galloway.

1 'O WHARE are ye gaun?
　　Quo the fause knicht upon the road:
　'I'm gaun to the scule,'
　　Quo the wee boy, and still he stude.

2 'What is that upon your back?' quo etc.
　'Atweel it is my bukes,' quo etc.

3 'What's that ye've got in your arm?'
　'Atweel it is my peit.'

4 'Wha's aucht they sheep?'
　'They are mine and my mither's.'

5 'How monie O them are mine?'
　'A' they that hae blue tails.'

6 'I wiss ye were on yon tree:'
　'And a gude ladder under me.'

7 'And the ladder for to break:'
　'And you for to fa down.'

8 'I wiss ye were in yon sie:'
　'And a gade bottom under me.'

9 'And the bottom for to break:'
　'And ye to be drowned.'

B

Motherwell's *Minstrelsy*, Appendix, p. xxiv, No xxxii.

O whare are ye gaun, quo' the false___ knight, And___ false___ false___ was his rede,

I'm gaun to the scule, says the pret-ty lit-tle boy, And___ still___ still___ he stude.

Motherwell, 1827, Appendix No. 32 and p. xxiv.

'O WHARE are ye gaun?' quo the false knight,
And false, false was his rede:
'I'm gaun to the scule,' says the pretty little boy,
And still, still he stude.

C

Obtained by Mr Macmath from the recitation of his aunt, Miss Jane Webster, formerly of Airds of Kells, Stewartry of Kirkcudbright, Galloway, who learned it many years ago from the wife of Peter McGuire, then cotman at Airds.

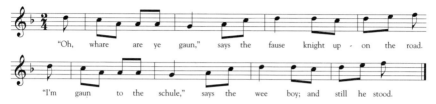

1 'O WHARE are ye gaun?'
  Says the false knight upon the road:
 'I am gaun to the schule,'
  Says the wee boy, and still he stood.

2 'What's that ye hae on your back?'
 'It's my dinner and my book.'

3 'Wha's aught the sheep on yonder hill,'
 'They are my papa's and mine.'

4 'How many of them's mine?'
 'A' them that has blue tails.'

5 'I wish you were in yonder well:'
 'And you were down in hell.'

LADY ISABEL AND THE ELF-KNIGHT

A. a. 'The Gowans sae gay,' Buchan's *Ballads of the North of Scotland*, I, 22. **b.** 'Aye as the Gowans grow gay,' Motherwell's MS., p. 563.
B. 'The Water o Wearie's Well.' **a.** Buchan's MSS, II, fol. 80. **b.** Buchan's *B. N. S.*, II, 201. **c.** Motherwell's MS., p. 561. **d.** 'Wearie's Wells,' Harris MS., No 19.
C. a. 'May Colven,' Herd's MSS, I, 166. **b.** 'May Colvin,' Herd's *Scottish Songs*, 1776, I, 93. **c.** 'May Colvin, or, False Sir John,' Motherwell's *Minstrelsy*, p. 67.

D. a. 'May Collin,' Sharpe's *Ballad Book*, No 17, p. 45. **b.** 'Fause Sir John and May Colvin,' Buchan, *B. N. S.*, II, 45. **c.** 'May Collean,' Motherwell's *Minstrelsy*, Appendix, p. xxi. **d.** 'The historical ballad of May Culzean,' an undated stall-copy.
E. 'The Outlandish Knight,' Dixon, *Ancient Poems, Ballads, etc.*, p. 74 = Bell, *Ancient Poems, Ballads, etc.*, p. 61.
F. 'The False Knight Outwitted,' *Roxburghe Ballads*, British Museum, III, 449.
G. 'The Knight and the Chief's Daughter,' British Museum, MS. Addit. 20094.

OF all ballads this has perhaps obtained the widest circulation. It is nearly as well known to the southern as to the northern nations of Europe. It has an extraordinary currency in Poland. The Germans, Low and High, and the Scandinavians, preserve it, in a full and evidently ancient form, even in the tradition of this generation. Among the Latin nations it has, indeed, shrunk to very meagre proportions, [23] and though the best English forms are not without ancient and distinctive marks, most of these have been eliminated, and the better ballads are very brief.

A has but thirteen two-line stanzas. An elf-knight, by blowing his horn, inspires Lady Isabel with love-longing. He appears on her first breathing a wish for him, and induces her to ride with him to the greenwood.* Arrived at the wood, he bids her alight, for she is come to the place where she is to die. He had slain seven kings' daughters there, and she should be the eighth. She persuades him to sit down, with

his head on her knee, lulls him asleep with a charm, binds him with his own sword-belt, and stabs him with his own dagger, saying, If seven kings' daughters you have slain, lie here a husband to them all.

B, in fourteen four-line stanzas, begins unintelligibly with a bird coming out of a bush for water, and a king's daughter sighing, "Wae's this heart o mine." A personage not characterized, but evidently of the same nature as the elf-knight in **A**, lulls everybody but this king's daughter asleep with his harp,[†] then mounts her behind him, and rides to a piece of water called Wearie's Well. He makes her wade in up to her chin; then tells her that he has drowned seven kings' daughters here, and she is to be the eighth. She asks him for one kiss before she dies, and, as he bends over to give it, pitches him from his saddle into the water, with the words, Since ye have drowned seven here, I'll make you bridegroom to them all.[‡]

C was first published by David Herd, in the second edition of his *Scottish Songs*, 1776, and

---

* 'The Elfin Knight' begins very much like **A**, but perhaps has borrowed its opening stanzas from this ballad. See page 19.

† The second stanza, which describes the harping, occurs again in 'Glenkindie' (st. 6).

afterwards by Motherwell, "collated" with a copy obtained from recitation. D,[*] E, F are all broadside or stall copies, and in broadside style. C, D, E, F have nearly the same story. False Sir John, a knight from the south country [west country, north lands], entices May Colven, C, D [a king's daughter, C 16, E 16; a knight's daughter, Polly, F 4, 9], to ride off with him, employing, in D, a charm which he has stuck in her sleeve. At the knight's suggestion, E, F, she takes a good sum of money with her, D, E, F. They come to a lonely rocky place by the sea [river-side, F], and the knight bids her alight: he has drowned seven ladies here [eight D, six E, F], and she shall be the next. But first she is to strip off her rich clothes, as being too good to rot in the sea. She begs him to avert his eyes, for decency's sake, and, getting behind him, throws him into the water. In F he is absurdly sent for a sickle, to crop the nettles on the river brim, and is pushed in while thus occupied.

---

‡   Perhaps the change from wood, **A**, to water, **B–F**, was made under the influence of some Merman ballad, or by admixture with such a ballad; e.g., 'Nøkkens Svig,' Grundtvig, No 39. In this (**A**) the nix entices a king's daughter away from a dance, sets her on his horse, and rides with her over the heath to a wild water, into which she sinks. It is also quite among possibilities that there was originally an English nix ballad, in which the king's daughter saved herself by some artifice, not, of course, such as is employed in **B–F**, but like that in **A**, or otherwise. Maid Heiemo, in Landstad, No 39, kills a nix with "one of her small knives." Had she put him to sleep with a charm, and killed him with *his own* knife, as Lady Isabel does, there would have been nothing to shock credibility in the story.

Aytoun, *Ballads of Scotland*, I, 219, 2d ed., hastily pronounces Buchan's ballad not authentic, "being made up of stanzas borrowed from versions of 'Burd Helen' ['Child Waters']." There are, indeed, three successive steps into the water in both ballads, but Aytoun should have bethought himself how natural and how common it is for a passage to slip from one ballad into another, when the circumstances of the story are the same; and in some such cases no one can say where the verses that are common originally belonged. Here, indeed, as Grundtvig remarks, IV, 7, note*, it may well be that the verses in question belonged originally to 'Burd Helen,' and were adopted (but in the processes of tradition) into 'The Water of Wearie's Well;' for it must be admitted that the transaction in the water is not a happy conception in the latter, since it shocks probability that the woman should be able to swim ashore, and the man not.

He cries for help, and makes fair promises, [24] C, E, but the maid rides away, with a bitter jest [on his steed, D, leading his steed, E, F], and reaches her father's house before daybreak. The groom inquires in D about the strange horse, and is told that it is a found one. The parrot asks what she has been doing, and is silenced with a bribe; and when the father demands why he was chatting so early, says he was calling to his mistress to take away the cat. Here C, E, F stop, but D goes on to relate that the maid at once tells her parents what has happened, and that the father rides off at dawn, under her conduct, to find Sir John. They carry off the corpse, which lay on the sands below the rocks, and bury it, for fear of discovery.

There is in Hone's *Table Book*, III, 130, ed. 1841, a *rifacimento* by Dixon of the common English broadside in what passes for old-ballad style. This has been repeated in Richardson's *Borderer's Table Book*, VI, 367; in Dixon's *Scottish Traditional Versions of Ancient Ballads*, p. 101; and, with alterations, additions, and omissions, in Sheldon's *Minstrelsy of the English Border*, p. 194.

A copy in Christie's *Traditional Ballad Airs*, II, 236, 'May Colvine and Fause Sir John' (of which no account is given), is a free compilation from **D b**, **D a**, and **C c**.

Jamieson (1814) had never met with this ballad in Scotland, at least in anything like a perfect state; but he says that a tale to the same effect, intermixed with scraps of verse, was familiar to him when a boy, and that he afterwards found it, "in much the same state, in the

---

*   "This ballad appears modern, from a great many expressions, but yet I am certain that it is old: the present copy came from the housekeeper at Methven." Note by Sharpe, in Laing's ed. of the *Ballad Book*, 1880, p. 130, xvii. Motherwell, in his *Minstrelsy*, p. lxx, n. 24, says that he had seen a stall ballad as early as 1749, entitled 'The Western Tragedy,' which perfectly agreed with Sharpe's copy. But in his *Note-Book*, p. 5 (about 1826–7), Motherwell says, "The best copy of May Colean with which I have met occurs in a stall copy printed about thirty years ago [should we then read 1799 instead of 1749?], under the title of 'The Western Tragedy.' I have subsequently seen a posterior reprint of this stall copy under this title, 'The Historical Ballad of May Collean.' In Mr Sharpe's *Ballad Book*, the same copy, wanting only one stanza, is given."

Highlands, in Lochaber and Ardnamurchan."
According to the tradition reported by Jamie-
son, the murderer had seduced the younger sis-
ter of his wife, and was seeking to prevent
discovery, a difference in the story which might
lead us to doubt the accuracy of Jamieson's rec-
ollection. (*Illustrations of Northern Antiquities*, p.
348.)[*]

Stories like that of this ballad will inevitably
be attached, and perhaps more or less adapted,
to localities where they become known. May
Collean, says Chambers, *Scottish Ballads*, p. 232,
note, "finds locality in that wild portion of the
coast of Carrick (Ayrshire) which intervenes
betwixt Girvan and Ballantrae. Carlton Castle,
about two miles to the south of Girvan (a tall
old ruin, situated on the brink of a bank which
overhangs the sea, and which gives title to Sir
John Cathcart, Bart, of Carlton), is affirmed by
the country people, who still remember the
story with great freshness, to have been the res-
idence of 'the fause Sir John;' while a tall rocky
eminence called Gamesloup, overhanging the
sea about two miles still further south, and over
which the road passes in a style terrible to all
travellers, is pointed out as the place where he
was in the habit of drowning his wives, and
where he was finally drowned himself. The peo-
ple, who look upon the ballad as a regular and
proper record of an unquestionable fact, farther
affirm that May Collean was a daughter of the
family of Kennedy of Colzean," etc. Binyan's
(Bunion) Bay, in **D**, is, according to Buchan,
the old name of the mouth of the river Ugie.[†]

Far better preserved than the English, and
marked with very ancient and impressive traits,
is the **Dutch** ballad 'Halewijn,' which, not
many years ago, was extensively sung in Bra-

bant and Flanders, and is still popular as a
broadside, both oral tradition and printed cop-
ies exhibiting manifold variations. A version of
this ballad (**A**) was communicated by Willems
to Mone's *Anzeiger* in 1836, col. 448ff, thirty-
eight two-line stanzas, and afterwards appeared
in Willems's *Oude vlæmsche Liederen* (1848),
No 49, p. 116, with some changes in the text
and some various readings. Uhland, 1, 153, 74
D, gave the *Anzeiger* text, with one correction.
So Hoffmann, *Niederländische Volkslieder*, 2d
ed., No 9, p. 39, but substituting for stanzas 19,
20 four stanzas from the margin of O. *v. L.*, and
making other slighter changes. Bæcker, *Chants
historiques de la Flandre*, No 9, p. 61, repeats
Willems's second text, with one careless omis-
sion and one transposition. Coussemaker,
Chants populaires des Flamands de France, No 45,
p. 142, professes to give the text of *Oude vlæm-
sche Liederen*, and does so nearly. Snellært,
Oude en nieuwe Liedjes, 2d ed., 1864, No 55, p.
58, inserts seven stanzas in the place of 33, 34
of O. *v. L.*, and two after 35, making forty-five
two- (or three-) line stanzas instead of thirty-
eight. These additions are also found in an
excessively corrupt form of the ballad (**B**), [25
Hoffmann, No 10, p. 43, in which the stanzas
have been uniformly extended to three verses,
to suit the air, which required the repetition of
the second line of the original stanza.[‡] The
Flemish ballad is given by Fétis, *Histoire
Générale de la Musique*, V, 59, "d'après un texte
ancien qui a deux strophes de plus que celui de
Willems." (G. L. K.)

Heer Halewijn (**A**), like the English elf-
knight, sang such a song that those who heard
it longed to be with him. A king's daughter
asked her father if she might go to Halewijn.
No, he said; those who go that way never come
back [sixteen have lost their lives, **B**]. So said
mother and sister, but her brother's answer was,
I care not where you go, so long as you keep
your honor. She dressed herself splendidly, took
the best horse from her father's stable, and rode
to the wood, where she found Halewijn waiting

---

[*]   The Gaelic tale referred to by Jamieson may be seen,
as Mr Macmath has pointed out to me, in Rev. Alex-
ander Stewart's *'Twixt Ben Nevis and Glencoe*, Edinburgh,
1885, p. 205ff. Dr Stewart gives nine stanzas of a Gaelic
ballad, and furnishes an English rendering. The story has
no connection with that of this ballad.

[†]   May Colvin in Ireland has undergone a similar
attachment. According to a Connemara story given
briefly in *Once a Week*, II, 53f, July 2, 1864, one Captain
Webb was wont to ill-use young women, and then strip
them and throw them into the Murthering Hole, not far
from Maarn. At last a girl induced him to turn his back,
and then thrust him into the Hole. (P. Z. Round)

[‡]   *Een Liedeken van den Heere van Haelewyn*, with
trifling verbal differences from Hoffmann's text, is in
Oude Liedekens in Bladeren, L. van Paemel, No 25. The
copy in *Nederlandsch Liederboek*, Gent, 1892, II, 1, No 44,
'Van Heer Halewijn,' is Willems's.

for her.* They then rode on further, till they came to a gallows, on which many women were hanging. Halewijn says, Since you are the fairest maid, choose your death [**B** 20 offers the choice between hanging and the sword]. She calmly chooses the sword. "Only take off your coat first, for a maid's blood spirts a great way, and it would be a pity to spatter you." His head was off before his coat, but the tongue still spake. This dialogue ensues:

'Go yonder into the corn,
And blow upon my horn,
That all my friends you may warn.'

'Into the corn I will not go,
And on your horn I will not blow:
A murderer's bidding I will not do.'

'Go yonder under the gallows-tree,
And fetch a pot of salve for me,
And rub my red neck lustily.'

'Under the gallows I will not go,
Nor will I rub your red neck, no,
A murderer's bidding I will not do.'

She takes the head by the hair and washes it in a spring, and rides back through the wood. Half-way through she meets Halewijn's mother, who asks after her son; and she tells her that he is gone hunting, that he will never be seen again, that he is dead, and she has his head in her lap. When she came to her father's gate, she blew the horn like any man.

And when the father heard the strain,
He was glad she had come back again.
Thereupon they held a feast,
The head was on the table placed.

---

* According to the variation given by Willems, and adopted by Hoffmann, Halewijn's *son* came to meet her, tied her horse to a tree, and bade her to sit down by him and loose her hair. For every hair she undid she dropped a tear. But it will presently be seen not only that the time has not come for them to sit down, but that Halewijn's bidding her undo her hair (to no purpose) is a perversion of her offering to "red" *his*, to get him into her power, an offer which she makes in the German and Scandinavian ballads, where also there is good reason for her tears, but none as yet here.

Snellaert's copy and the modern three-line ballad have a meeting with father, brother, sister, and mother successively. The maid's answer to each of the first three is that Halewijn is amusing himself with sixteen maids, or to that effect, but to the mother that he is dead, and she has his head in her lap. The mother angrily replies, in **B**, that if she had given this information earlier she would not have got so far on her way home. The maid retorts, Wicked woman, you are lucky not to have been served as your son; then rides, "like Judith wise," straight to her father's palace, where she blows the horn blithely, and is received with honor and love by the whole court.[†]

Another Flemish version (**C**) has been lately published under the title, 'Roland,' by which only, we are informed, is this particular form known in Bruges and many parts of Flanders:[‡] *Chants populaires recueillis à Bruges* [26] par Adolphe Lootens et J. M. E. Feys, No 37, p. 60, 183 vv, in sixty-three stanzas, of two, three, four, or five lines. This text dates from the last century, and is given with the most exact fidelity to tradition. It agrees with **A** as to some main points, but differs not a little as to others. The story sets out thus:

It was a bold Roland,
He loved a lass from England
He wist not how to get her,
With reading or with writing,
With brawling or with fighting.

---

† J. W. Wolf, *Deutsche Märchen u. Sagen*, No 29, p. 143, gives the story according to **B**, apparently from a ballad like Snellært's. So Luise v. Ploennies, *Reiseerinnerungen aus Belgien*, p. 38.

Halewyn makes his appearance again in the Flemish ballad, 'Halewyn en het kleyne Kind,' Coussemaker, No 46, p. 149 = *Poésies populaires de la France*, vol. 1. Other copies in Lootens et Feys, No 45, p. 85 (see p. 296); *Volkskunde*, II, 194, 'Van Mijnheerken van Bruindergestem.' A boy of seven years has shot one of Halewyn's rabbits, and is for this condemned to be hanged on the highest tree in the park. The father makes great offers for his ransom, but in vain. On the first step of the ladder the child looks back for his mother, on the second for his father, on the third for his brother, on the fourth for his sister, each of whom successively arrives and is told that delay would have cost him his life. It will presently be seen that there is a resemblance here to German ballads (**G–X, Z**).

Roland has lost Halewyn's art of singing. Louise asks her father if she may go to Roland, to the fair, as all her friends do. Her father refuses: Roland is "een stoute kalant," a bad fellow that betrays pretty maids; he stands with a drawn sword in his hand, and all his soldiers in armor. The daughter says she has seen Roland more than once, and that the tale about the drawn sword and soldiers is not true. This scene is exactly repeated with mother and brother. Louise then tries her shrift-father. He is easier, and does not care where she goes, provided she keeps her honor and does not shame her parents. She tells father, mother, and brother that she has leave from her confessor, makes her toilet as in **A**, takes the finest horse in the stable, and rides to the wood. There she successively meets Roland's father, mother, and brother, each of whom asks her where she is going, and whether she has any right to the crown she wears. To all she replies, Whether I have or not, be off; I know you not. She does not encounter Roland in the wood, they do not ride together, and there is no gallows-field. She enters Roland's house, where he is lying abed. He bids her gather three rose-wreaths "at his hands" and three at his feet; but when she approaches the foot of the bed he rises, and offers her the choice to lose her honor or kneel before the sword. She chooses the sword, advises him to spare his coat, and, while he is taking it off, strikes off his head, all as in **A**. The head speaks: Go under the gallows (of which we have heard nothing hitherto), fetch a pot of salve, rub it on my wounds, and they shall

straight be well. She declines to follow a murderer's rede, or to learn magic. The head bids her go under the blue stone and fetch a pot of maidens-grease, which also will heal the wounds. This again she refuses to do, in the same terms; then seizes the head by the hair, washes it in a spring, and rides off with it through the wood, duly meeting Roland's father, mother, and brother once more, all of whom challenge her, and to all of whom she answers,

> Roland your son is long ago dead;
> God has his soul and I his head;
> For in my lap here I have his head,
> And with the blood my apron is red.

When she came back to the city the drums and the trumpets struck up.[*] She stuck the head out of the window, and cried, "Now I am Roland's bride!" She drew it in, and cried, "Now I am a heroine!"

Another Dutch (Frisian) version (**D**), spirited, but with gaps, is given by Dykstra and van der Meulen, *In Doaze fol alde Snypsnaren*, Frjentsjer, 1882, p. 118, 'Jan Alberts,' 66vv (Köhler). Jan Alberts sings a song, and those that hear it know it not. It is heard by a king's daughter, who asks her mother's leave to go out for a walk, and is told that it is all one where she goes or stays, if she keeps her honor. Her father says the same, when she applies for his leave. She goes to her bedroom and dresses herself finely, dons a gold crown, puts her head out of the window, and cries, Now am I Jan Alberts' bride. Jan Alberts takes her on his horse; they ride fast and long, with nothing to eat or drink for three days. She then asks Jan why he gives her nothing, and he answers that he shall ride to the high tree where hang fourteen fair maids. Arrived there, he gives her the choice of tree, sword, or water. She chooses the sword, bids him spare his coat, for a pure maid's blood goes far, and before his coat is half off his head lies behind him. The head cries, Behind the bush is a pot of grease; smear my neck with it. She will

---

‡ "La chanson de Halewyn, telle à peu près que la donnent Willems, Snellaert et de Coussemaker, se vend encore sur le marché de Bruges. Quoiqu'elle ports pour titre *Halewyn*, jamais notre pièce n'a été connue ici sous ce nom. Le nom de Halewijn, Alewijn ou Alwin . . . est réservé au héros de la pièce suivante" [Mi Adel en Hir Alewijn]. Lootens et Feys, p. 66. "Il est à regretter que Willems et de Coussemaker n'aient pas jugé à propos de donner cette pièce telle que le people l'a conservée; on serait sans aucun doute en possession de variantes remarquables, et les lacunes qui existent dans notre version n'eussent pas manqué d'être com blées. Il est bon d'insister sur la remarque faite à la suite de la chanson, qu'à Bruges et dans beaucoup de localités de la Flandre, elle n'est connue que sous le titre de *Roland*. Ajoutons que notre texte appartient an dernier siècle." L. et F., 295.

---

* So in 'Liebe ohne Stand,' one of the mixed forms of the German ballad, *Wunderhorn*, Erk i, 41, Crecelius, i, 36,
> Und als es nun kam an den dritten Tag,
> Da gingen die Pfeiffen and Trommeln an.

not smear from a murderer's pot, nor blow in a murderer's horn. She mounts his horse, and rides far and long. Jan Alberts' mother comes to meet her, and asks after him. She says he is not far off, and is sporting with fourteen maids. Had you told me this before, I would have laid you in the water, says the mother. The maid rides on till she comes to her father's gate. Then she cries to her father to open, for his youngest daughter is without. The father not bestirring himself, she swims the moat, and, the door not being open, goes through the glass. The next day she dries her clothes.

Danish. Eleven versions of this ballad are known in Danish, seven of which are given in *Danmarks gamle Folkeviser*, No 183, 'Kvindemorderen,' **A–G**. Four more, **H–L**, are furnished by Kristensen, *Jyske Folkeviser*, I, Nos 46, 47, 91; II, No 85. **A**, in forty-one two-line stanzas (previously printed in Grundtvig's *Engelske og skotske Folkeviser*, p. 233), is from a 16th century MS.; **B**, thirty stanzas, **C**, twenty-four, **D**, thirty-seven, from MSS of the 17th century; **E**, fifty-seven, from a broadside of the end of the 18th; **F**, thirty, from one of the beginning of the 19th; and **G–L**, thirty-five, twenty-three, thirty-one, twenty-six, thirty-eight stanzas, from recent oral tradition.[*]

The four older versions, and also **E**, open with some lines that occur at the beginning of other ballads.[†] In **A** and **E**, and, we may add, **G**, the maid is allured by the promise of being taken to a paradise exempt from death and sorrow; **C**, **D**, **F** promise a train of handmaids and splendid presents. All the versions agree very

well as to the kernel of the story. A false knight prevails upon a lady to elope with him, and they ride to a wood [they simply meet in a wood, **H**, **K**]. He sets to work digging a grave, which she says is too long for his [her] dog and too narrow for his [her] horse [all but **F**, **H**]. She is told that the grave is for her. He has taken away the life [and honor, **B**, **C**, **I**] of eight maids, and she shall be the ninth. The eight maids become nine kings' daughters in **E**, ten in **F**, nineteen in **G**, and in **E** and **F** the hard choice is offered of death by sword, tree, or stream. In **A**, **E**, **I**, **L** the knight bids the lady get her gold together before she sets out with him, and in **D**, **H**, **K**, **L** he points out a little knoll under which he keeps the gold of his previous victims. The maid now induces the knight to lie down with his head in her lap, professing a fond desire to render him the most homely of services[‡] [not in **C**, **G**, **I**, **K**]. He makes an express condition in **E**, **F**, **G**, **H**, **L** that she shall not betray him in his sleep, and she calls Heaven to witness that she will not. In **G** she sings him to sleep. He slept a sleep that was not sweet. She binds him hand and foot, then cries, Wake up! I will not betray you in sleep.[§] Eight you have killed; yourself shall be the ninth. Entreaties and fair promises and pretences that he had been in jest, and desire for shrift, are in vain. Woman-fashion she drew his sword, but man-fashion she cut him down. She went home a maid.

E, **F**, **G**, however, do not end so simply. On her way home through the wood [**E**], she comes upon a maid who is working gold, and who says, The last time I saw that horse my brother rode it. She answers, Your brother is dead, and will do no more murdering for gold; then turns her horse, and sets the sister's bower on fire. Next she encounters seven robbers on the heath, who recognize the horse as their master's, and are informed of his death and of the end of his

---

[*]   Add these Danish copies: Kristensen, *Skattegraveren*, I, 210ff, Nos 1198, 1199. (Some stanzas of 'Kvindemorderen' are inserted in No 932, III, 177.) 'Kvindemorderen,' two fragments; Kristensen, *Folkeminder*, XI, 62, No 33.

[†]   E.g., the wonderland in **A** 2–6, and the strict watch kept over the lady in 7–10 are repeated in 'Ribold og Guldborg,' Grundtvig, 82, **B** 2–7, 8–11, and in 'Den trofaste Jomfru,' ib. 249, **A** 3–6, 7–10. The watching in **A**, **B**, **C** and the proffered gifts of **C**, **D**, **F** are found in 'Nøkkens Svig,' Grundtvig, 39, **A**, **B**, 12–18. The disguise in **A** 11–14, the rest in the wood with the knight's head in the lady's lap, **A** 16, 27, **B** 11, 21, **D** 14, 24, **E** 11, 21, etc., recur in Ribold, **B** 12–14, **L** 9, 10, **M** 19, 20, **N** 11, 13, **P** 12, 13. These resemblances, naturally, are not limited to the Danish copies.

[‡]   So the princess in Asbjørnsen og Moe, *N. Folkeeventyr*, p. 153. Cf. Campbell's *Tales of the West Highlands*, III, 209; IV, 282, 283; MacInnes, *Folk and Hero Tales* [Gaelic], p. 301, a Highland St George: see p. 62, note.

[§]   The binding and waking, with these words, are found also in a made-up text of 'Frændehævn,' Grundtvig, No 4, **C** 51–53, but certainly borrowed from some copy of 'Kvindemorderen.'

crimes. They ask about the fire. She says it is an old pig-sty. She rides on, and they call to her that she is losing her horse's gold shoe. But nothing can stop her; she bids them pick it up and drink it in wine; and so comes home to her father's. F has nothing of the sister; in place of seven robbers there are nine of the robber's brothers, and the maid sets their house on fire. G indulges in absurd extravagances: the heroine meets the robber's sister with twelve fierce dogs, and then his twelve swains, and cuts down both dogs and swains.

The names in the Danish ballads are, A, Ulver and Vænelil; B, Olmor, or Oldemor, and Vindelraad; C, Hollemen and Vendelraad; D, Romor, Reimord, or Reimvord, and the maid unnamed; F, Herr Peder and Liden Kirsten; H–L, Ribold, Rıgbold [I, Rimmelil] and Guldborg.

Four **Swedish** versions are known, all from tradition of this century. A, 'Den Falske Riddaren,' twenty-three two-line stanzas, Arwidsson, 44 B, I, 301. B, 'Röfvaren Brun,' fifteen [28] stanzas, Afzelius, 83, III, 97. C, twenty-seven stanzas, Arwidsson, 44 A, I, 298. D, 'Röfvaren Rymer,' sixteen stanzas, Afzelius, 82, III, 94. A, B, D have resemblances, at the beginning, to the Ribold ballads, like the Danish A, B, E, G, while the beginning of C is like the Danish C, D, F. A has the gravedigging; there have been eight maids before; the knight lays his head in the lady's lap for the same reason as in most of the Danish ballads, and under the same assurance that he shall not be betrayed in sleep; he is bound, and conscientiously waked before his head is struck off; and the lady rides home to her father's. There have been eight previous victims in C, and they king's daughters; in B, eleven (maids); D says not how many, but, according to an explanation of the woman that sang it, there were seven princesses. C, D, like Danish E, F, G, make the maid encounter some of the robber's family on the way home. By a misconception, as we perceive by the Dutch ballad, she is represented as blowing the robber's horn. Seven sisters come at the familiar sound to bury the murdered girl and share the booty, but find that they have their brother to bury.

The woman has no name in any of the Swedish ballads. A calls the robber "an outlandish man" (en man ifrån fremmande land),

B, simple Brun, C, a knight, and D, Riddaren Rymer, or Herr Rymer.

A Swedish ballad given in Grundtvig, D. g. F. IV, 818f, F, and here referred to under 'Hind Etin' as Swedish C, has resemblances with 'Kvindemorderen;' see Bugge, Arkiv för nordisk Filologi, VII, 120–36, 1891. Fru Malin is combing her hair al fresco, when a suitor enters her premises; he remarks that a crown would sit well on her head. The lady skips off to her chamber, and exclaims, Christ grant he may wish to be mine! The suitor follows her, and asks, Where is the fair dame who wishes to be mine? But when Fru Malin comes to table she is in trouble, and the suitor puts her several leading questions. She is sad, not for any of several reasons suggested, but for the bridge under which her seven sisters (syskon) lie. 'Sorrow not,' he says, 'we shall build the bridge so broad and long that four-and-twenty horses may go over at a time.' They pass through a wood; on the bridge her horse stumbles, and she is thrown into the water. She cries for help; she will give him her gold crown. He cares nothing for the crown, and never will help her out. Bugge maintains that this ballad is not, as Grundtvig considered it, a compound of 'Nökkens Svig' and 'Harpens Kraft,' but an independent ballad, 'The Bride Drowned,' of a set to which belong 'Der Wasserman,' Haupt and Schmaler, I, 62, No 34, and many German ballads: see Grundtvig, IV, 810f, and below, p. 492f.

Of Norwegian versions, but two have been printed: A, 'Svein Norðmann,' twenty two-line stanzas, Landstad, 69, p. 567; B, 'Rullemann og Hildeborg,' thirty stanzas, Landstad, 70, p. 571, both from recent recitation. Bugge has communicated eight others to Grundtvig. Both A and B have the paradise at the beginning, which is found in Danish A, E, G, and Swedish D. In both the lady gets her gold together while the swain is saddling his horse. They come to a grave already dug, which in B is said to be made so very wide because Rulleman has already laid nine maidens in it. The stanza in A which should give the number is lost, but the reciter or singer put it at seven or nine. The maid gets the robber into her power by the usual artifice, with a slight variation in B. According to A, she rides straight home to her father. B, like

Danish **F**, has an encounter with her false lover's [five] brothers. They ask, Where is Rullemann, thy truelove? She answers, He is lying down, in the green mead, and bloody is his bridal bed.

Of the unprinted versions obtained by Professor Bugge, two indicate that the murderer's sleep was induced by a spell, as in English **A**. **F** 9 has,

> Long time stood Gullbjör; to herself she thought,
> May none of my *runes* avail me ought?

And **H** 18, as also a variant to **B** 20, says it was a rune-slumber that came over him. Only **G**, **H**, **I**, **K** give the number of the murdered women: in **G**, **H**, eight, in **I**, nine, in **K**, five.

The names are, in **A**, Svein Norðmann and Guðbjörg; **B**, Rulleman and Hildeborg [or Signe]; **C**, **D**, **E**, **F**, Svein Nórmann and Gullbjör [Gunnbjör]; **G**, Rullemann and Kjersti; **H**, Rullball and Signelill; **I**, Alemarken and Valerós; **K**, Rulemann and a fair maid.

Such information as has transpired concerning **Icelandic** versions of this ballad is furnished by Grundtvig, IV, 4. The Icelandic form, though curtailed and much injured, has shown tenacity enough to preserve itself in a series of closely agreeing copies from the 17th century down. The eldest, from a manuscript of 1665, runs thus:[*]

1 Ása went along the street, she heard a sweet sound.

2 Ása went into the house, she saw the villain bound.

3 'Little Ása, loose me! I will not beguile thee.'

4 'I dare not loose thee, I know not whether thou'lt beguile me.'

5 'God almighty take note who deceives the other!'

6 She loosed the bands from his hand, the fetter from his foot.

7 'Nine lands have I visited, ten women I've beguiled;

8 'Thou art now the eleventh, I'll not let thee slip.'   [29]

A copy, from the beginning of the 18th century, has, in stanza 2, "Ása went into the *wood*," a recent copy, "over the fields;" and stanza 3, in the former, with but slight differences in all the modern copies, reads,

> 'Welcome art thou, Ása maid! thou wilt mean to loose me.'

Some recent copies (there is one in Berggreen, *Danske Folkesange*, 2d ed., 1, 162) allow the maid to escape, adding,

9 'Wait for me a little space, whilst I go into the green wood.'

10 He waited for her a long time, but she never came back to him.

11 Ása took her white steed, of all women she rode most.

12 Ása went into a holy cell, never did she harm to man.

This is certainly one of the most important of the **German** ballads, and additions are constantly making to a large number of known versions. Excepting two broadsides of about 1560, and two copies from recitation printed in 1778, all these, twenty-six in number, have been obtained from tradition since 1800.[†] They are as follows: **A a**, 'Gert Olbert,' 'De Mörners Sang,' in Low German, as written down by William Grimm, in the early years of this century, 61vv, Reifferscheid, p. 161, II. **A b**, "from the Münster region," communicated to Uhland by the Baroness Annette von Droste-Hüllshof, 46vv, Uhland, 1, 151, No 74 C; repeated in Mittler, No 79. **A c**, a fragment from the same source as the preceding, and written down at the beginning of this century, 35vv, Reiffersc-

---

[*]   'Ásu kvaedi' in *Íslenzk Fornkvædi*, II, 226, No 60, **A–M**: this copy **D** (**E–M**). Published in 1885.

[†]   All the German versions appear to have been *originally* in the two-line stanza.

heid, p. 161, 1. **B**, 'Es wollt sich ein Markgraf ausreiten,' from Bökendorf, Westphalia, as taken down by W. Grimm, in 1813, 41 vv, Reifferscheid, p. 116. **C a**, 'Die Gerettete,' "from the Lower Rhine," twenty-six two-line stanzas, Zuccalmaglio, No 28, p. 66; Mittler, No 85. **C b**, eleven two-line stanzas, Montanus (=Zuccalmaglio) *Die deutschen Volksfeste*, p. 45. **D**, 'Von einem wackern Mägdlein, Odilia geheissen,' etc., from the Rhine, 34 vv [Longard], No 24, p. 48. **E**, 'Schondilie,' Menzenberg and Breitbach, 59 vv, Simrock, No 7, p. 19; Mittler, No 86. **F**, 'Jungfrau Linnich,' communicated by Zuccalmaglio as from the Rhine region, Berg and Mark, fourteen two-line stanzas, Erlach, IV, 598, and Kretzschmer (nearly), No 92, p. 164; Mittler, No 87. **G a**, 'Ulinger,' 120 vv, Nuremberg broadside "of about 1555" (Böhme) in *Wunderhorn*, ed. 1857, IV, 101, Böhme, No 13ª, p. 56. **G b c**, Basel broadsides, "of about 1570" (Böhme), and of 1605, in Uhland, No 74 A, 1, 141; Mittler, No 77. **H**, 'Adelger,' 120 vv, an Augsburg broadside, "of about 1560" (Böhme), Uhland, No 74 B, 1, 146; Böhme, No 13ᵇ, p. 58; Mittler, No 76. **I**, 'Der Brautmörder,' in the dialect of the Kuhländchen (Northeast Moravia and Austrian Silesia), 87 vv, Meinert, p. 61; Mittler, No 80. **J**, 'Annele,' Swabian, from Hirrlingen and Obernau, 80 vv, Meier, *Schwäbische V. L.*, No 168, p. 298. **K**, another Swabian version, from Hirrlingen, Immenried, and many other localities, 80 vv, Scherer, *Jungbrunnen*, No 5 B, p. 25. **L a**, from the Swabian-Würtemberg border, 81 vv, Birlinger, *Schwäbisch-Augsburgisches Wörterbuch*, p. 458. **L b**, [Birlinger], *Schwäbische V. L.*, p. 159, from Immenried, nearly word for word the same. **M**, 'Der falsche Sänger,' 40 vv, Meier, No 167, p. 296. **N**, 'Es reitets ein Ritter durch Haber und Klee,' 43 vv, a fifth Swabian version, from Hirrlingen, Meier, p. 302. **O**, 'Alte Ballade die in Entlebuch noch gesungen wird,' twenty-three double stanzas, in the local dialect, *Schweizerblätter von Henne und Reithard*, 1833, 11ʳ Jahrgang, 210–12; repeated in Lütolf, *Sagen, Bräuche u. Legenden, u. s. w.*, p. 71, No 29, 'Schön Anneli.' **P**, 'Das Guggibader-Lied,' twenty-one treble stanzas (23?), in the Aargau dialect, Rochholz, *Schweizersagen aus dem Aargau*, 1, 24; repeated in Kurz, *Aeltere Dichter, u. s.*

w., *der Schweizer*, I, 117.[*] **Q**, 'Es sitzt gut Ritter auf und ritt,' a copy taken down in 1815 by J. Grimm, from the recitation of a lady who had heard it as a child in German Bohemia, 74 vv, Reifferscheid, p. 162. **R**, 'Bie wrüe işt auv der ritterşmàn,' in the dialect of Gottschee, Carniola, 86 vv, Schröer, *Sitzungsberichte der Wiener Ak., phil-hist. Cl.*, LX, 462. **S**, 'Das Lied von dem falschen Rittersmann,' 60 vv, from Styria, Rosegger and Heuberger, *Volkslieder aus Steiermark*, No 19, p. 17. **T**, 'Ulrich und Ännchen,'[†] 49 vv, Herder's *Volkslieder*, 1778, 1, 79; Mittler, No 78. **U**, 'Schön Ulrich und Roth-Aennchen,' 46 vv, in *Taschenbuch für Dichter und Dichterfreunde*, Abth. viii, 126, 1778, Upper Lusatia (slightly altered by the contributor, Meissner); Mittler, No 84. A copy from Kapsdorf, in Hoffmann and Richter's *Schlesische V. L.*, No 13, p. 27, is the same, differing by only three words. **V**, 'Schön-Aennelein,' 54 vv, from the eastern part of Brandenburg, Erk u. Irmer, 6th Heft, p. 64, No 56 (stanzas 4–8 from the preceding). **W**, 'Schön Ullerich und Hanselein,' twenty-nine two-line stanzas, from the neighborhood of Breslau, in Gräter's *Idunna und Hermode*, No 35, Aug. 29, 1812, following p. 140. The same in *Schlesische V. L.*, No 12, p. 23, 'Schön Ulrich u. Rautendelein,' with a stanza (12) inserted; and Mittler, No 81. **X**, 'Der Albrecht u. der Hanselein,' 42 vv, from Natangen, East Prussia, in *Neue preussische Provinzial-Blätter*, 2d series, III, 158, No 8. **Y**, 'Ulrich u. Annle,' nineteen two-line stanzas, a second Kuhländchen version, Meinert, p. 66; Mittler, No 83. **Z a**, 'Von einem frechen Räuber, Herr Ulrich geheissen,' nineteen two-line stanzas, from the Rhine [Longard], No 23, p. 46. **Z b**, 'Ulrich,' as sung on the Lower Rhine, the same ballad, with unimportant verbal differences, and the insertion of one stanza (7, the editor's?), Zuccalmaglio, No 15, p. 39; Mittler, No 82. **AA**. Spee, *Volksthümliches vom Niederrhein*, Köln, 1875, Zweites Heft. p. 3, 'Schöndili,' 50 vv. (Köhler.) **BB**. Alfred Müller,

---

[*]   'Schön Anneli,' Töbler, *Schweizerische Volkslieder*, II, 170, No 6, is an edited copy, mainly **O**, with use of **P**. See p. 51f below.

[†]   The copies with this title in Simrock, No 6, p. 15, and in Scherer's *Jungbrunnen*, No 5 A, and his *Deutsche V. L.*, 1851, p. 349, are compounded from various texts.

Volkslieder aus dem Erzgebirge, p. 92, 'Schön Ulrich' [und Trautendelein], 36vv. (Köhler.) Like **T**, without the song. **CC**. A. Schlossar, *Deutsche Volkslieder aus Steiermark*, 1881, p. 338, No 309, 'Der Ritter und die Maid.' (Köhler: not yet seen by me.) **DD**. Curt Mündel, *Elsässische Volkslieder*, p. 12, No 10, a fragment of fifteen verses; 'Als die wunderschöne Anna auf dem Brautstuhle sass,' Wolfram, p. 66f, No 39 a; and No 39 b, which is even worse preserved; 'Die wunderschöne Anna auf dem Rheinsteine,' K. Becker, *Rheinischer Volksliederborn*, p. 20, No 17. 'Die schöne Anna,' Böckel, *Deutsche Volkslieder aus Oberhessen*, p. 86, No 103, 'Als die wunderschöne Anna,' Lewalter, *Deutsche V. l. in Niederhessen gesammelt*, 1^s Heft, No 24, p. 51, and also No 25, are fragmentary pieces. **EE**, Hruschka u. Toischer, *Deutsche Volkslieder aus Böhmen*, p. 126, No 35. Like **Q**. **FF**. 'Schön Hannchen,' Frischbier und Sembrzycki, *Hundert Ostpreussische Volkslieder*, 1893, p. 35, No 22, from Angerburg, 51vv. **GG, HH**, 'Der Ritter im Walde,' Herrmann u. Pogatschnigg, *Deutsche V.-L. aus Kärnten*, Salon-Ausgabe, p. 33; 'Es ritt ein Räuber wohl über den Rhein,' Wolfram, *Nassauische Volkslieder*, p. 61, No 33. [*]

The German ballads, as Grundtvig has pointed out, divide into three well-marked classes. The first class, embracing the versions **A–F, AA** (7), and coming nearest to English and Dutch tradition, has been found along the lower half of the Rhine and in Westphalia, or in Northwest Germany; the second, including **G–S, EE** (14), is met with in Swabia, Switzerland, Bohemia, Moravia, Styria, Carniola, or in South Germany; the third, **T–Z, BB, DD, FF, GG, HH** (12), in East Prussia, the eastern part of Brandenburg and of Saxony, Silesia, and, again, Moravia, or, roughly speaking, in North and East Germany; but, besides the Moravian, there is also of this third class one version, in two copies, from the Rhine.

---

[*] Böhme, in his edition of Erk's *Deutscher Liederhort*, I, 118–146, 1893, prints twenty German versions under numbers 41, 42. Of these 41^i, 42^k, 42^l are of oral derivation, and 42^h is from Erk's papers. Böhme notes two other copies taken down from singing, and one in MS., which he does not give. Judging by what has been given, what has been withheld must be of trifling value.

(I.) **A** runs thus. She that would ride out with Gert Olbert must dress in silk and gold. When fair Helena had so attired herself, she called from her window, Gert Olbert, come and fetch the bride. He took her by her silken gown and swung her on behind him, and they rode three days and nights. Helena then said, We must eat and drink; but Gert Olbert said, We must go on further. They rode over the green heath, and Helena once more tenderly asked for refreshment. Under yon fir [linden], said Gert Olbert, and kept on till they came to a green spot, where nine maids were hanging. Then it was, Wilt thou choose the fir-tree, the running stream, or the naked sword? She chose the sword, but begged him to take off his silken coat, "for a maid's blood spirts far, and I should be sorry to spatter it." While he was engaged in drawing off his coat, she cut off his head. But still the false tongue spoke. It bade her blow in his horn; then she would have company enough. She was not so simple as to do this. She rode three days and nights, and blew the horn when she reached her father's castle. Then all the murderers came running, like hounds after a hare. Frau Clara [Jutte] called out, Where is my son? Under the fir-tree, sporting with nine maids; he meant me to be the tenth, said Helena.

B is the same story told of a margrave and Fair Annie, but some important early stanzas are lost, and the final ones have suffered injury; for the ballad ends with this conceit, "She put the horn to her mouth, and blew the margrave quite out of her heart." Here, by a transference exceedingly common in tradition, it is the man, and not the maid, that "would ride in velvet and silk and red gold."

C a has the names Odilia and Hilsinger, a trooper (reiter). Odilia was early left an orphan, and as she grew up "she grew into the trooper's [31] bosom." He offered her seven pounds of gold to be his, and "she thought seven pounds of gold a good thing." We now fall into the track of **A**. Odilia dresses herself like a bride, and calls to the trooper to come and get her. They ride first to a high hill, where she asks to eat and drink, and then go on to a linden-tree, on which seven maids are hanging. The choice of three deaths is offered, the sword chosen, he is entreated to spare his coat, she seizes his sword and hews off his head. The false tongue suggests blowing the horn. Odilia thinks "much biding or blowing is not good." She rides away, and presently meets the trooper's "little foot-page" (bot), who fancies she has Hilsinger's horse and sword. "He sleeps," she says, "with seven maids, and thought I was to be the eighth." This copy concludes with a manifestly spurious stanza. **C** **b** agrees with **C a** for ten stanzas, as to the matter, and so far seems to be **C a** improved by Zuccalmaglio, with such substitutions as a princely castle for "seven pounds of gold." The last stanza (11),

> Und als die Sternlein am Himmel klar,
> Ottilia die achte der Todten war,

was, no doubt, suggested by the last of **F**, another of Zuccalmaglio's versions, and, if genuine, would belong to a ballad of the third class.

D has the name Odilia for the maid, but the knight, or trooper, has become expressly a robber (ritter, reiter, räuber). They ride to a green heath, where there is a cool spring. Odilia asks for and gets a draught of water, and is told that at the linden-tree there will be eating and drinking for them. And when they come to the linden, there hang six, seven maids! All proceeds as before. The talking head is lost. Odilia meets the robber's mother, and makes the usual reply.[*]

E resembles **C** closely. Odilia becomes Schondilg (Schön Odilie), Räuber returns to Ritter, or Reiter, and the servant-maid bribe of seven pounds of gold rises to ten tons.[†] Schondilg's toilet, preparatory to going off (6–8), is described with a minuteness that we find only in the Dutch ballad (12–16). After this, there is no important variation. She meets the

---

[*] Both **D** and **E** have attached to them this final stanza:

> 'Odilia, why are thy shoes so red?'
> 'It is three doves that I shot dead.'

This is a well-known commonplace in tragic ballads; and Grundtvig suggests that this stanza was the occasion of the story taking the turn which we find in ballads of the third class.

trooper's three brothers, and makes the same replies to them as to the mother in **D**.

F. The personages here are Linnich (i.e., Nellie) and a knight from England. The first twelve stanzas do not diverge from **C, D, E**. In stanza 13 we find the knight directing the lady to strip off her silk gown and gold necklace, as in the English **C, D, E**; but certainly this inversion of the procedure which obtains in German **C, D, E** is an accident arising from confused recollection. The 14th and last stanza similarly misunderstands the maid's feigned anxiety about the knight's fine coat, and brings the ballad to a false close, resembling the termination of those of the third class, still more those of certain mixed forms to be spoken of presently.

AA closely resembles **A**. Schöndili's parents died when she was a child. Schön-Albert, knowing this, rides to her. She attires herself in silk, with a gold crown on her hair, and he swings her on to his horse. They ride three days and nights, with nothing to eat or drink. She asks whether it is not meal-time; he replies that they are coming to a linden, where they will eat and drink. Seven women are hanging on the tree. He gives her the wale of tree, river, and sword. She chooses the sword; would be loath to spot his coat; whips off his head before the coat is half off. The head says there is a pipe in the saddle; she thinks no good can come of playing a murderer's pipe. She meets first the father, then the mother; they think that must be Schön-Albert's horse. That may be, she says; I have not seen him since yesterday. She sets the pipe to her mouth, when she reaches her father's gate, and the murderers come like hares on the wind.

(II.) The second series, **G–S**, has three or four traits that are not found in the foregoing ballads. **G**, which, as well as **H**, was in print more than two hundred years before any other copy is known to have been taken down,

---

[†] One scarcely knows whether this bribe is an imperfect reminiscence of splendid promises which the knight makes, e.g., in the Danish ballads, or a shifting from the maid to the knight of the gold which the elsewhere opulent or well-to-do maid gets together while the knight is preparing to set forth; or simply one of those extravagances which so often make their appearance in later versions of ballads.

begins, like the Dutch Halewijn, with a knight (Ulinger) singing so sweetly that a maid (Fridburg) is filled with desire to go off with him. He promises to teach her his art. This magical song is wanting only in **R**, of class II, and the promise to teach it only in **Q**, **R**. She attires herself splendidly; he swings her on to his horse behind him, and they ride to a wood. When they came to the wood there was no one there but a white dove on a hazel-bush, that sang, Listen, Fridburg: Ulinger has hanged eleven[*] maids; the twelfth is in his clutches. Fridburg asked what the dove was saying. Ulinger replied, It takes me for another; it lies in its red bill; and rode on till it suited him to alight. He spread his cloak on the grass, and asked her to sit down:

Er sprach sie solt ihm lausen,
Sein gelbes Haar zerzausen.[†]

Looking up into her eyes, he saw tears, and asked why she was weeping. Was it for her sorry husband? Not for her sorry husband, she said. But here some stanzas, which belong to another ballad,[‡] have crept in, and she is, with no reason, made to ride further on. She comes to a lofty fir, and eleven maids hanging on it. She wrings her hands and tears her hair, and implores Ulinger to let her be hanged in her clothes as she is.

'Ask me not that, Fridburg,' he said;
'Ask me not that, thou good young maid;
Thy scarlet mantle and kirtle black
Will well become my young sister's back.'

Then she begs to be allowed three cries.

---

[*] The number eleven is remarkably constant in the German ballads, being found in **G**, **H**, **J–L**, **N–W**; it is also the number in Swedish **B**. Eight is the favorite number in the North, and occurs in Danish **A–D**, **H–L**, Swedish **A**, **C**, Norwegian **G**, **H**; again in German **I**. German **M**, **X**, Danish **F**, have ten; German **A**, **B**, Danish **A** Norwegian **I**, have nine; German **C**, **D**, seven; Danish **G** has nineteen. French **A**, **B** have fourteen, fifteen, Italian ballads still higher numbers: **A**, **B**, **C**, thirty-six, **D**, fifty-two, **E**, thirty-three, **F**, three hundred and three.
[†] This stroke of realism fails only in **M**, **N**, **R**, of this second class.
[‡] Apparently to a Ribold ballad, of which no other trace has been found in German. See further on in this volume.

'So much I may allow thee well,
Thou art so deep within the dell;
So deep within the dell we lie,
No man can ever hear thy cry.'

She cries, "Help, Jesu!" "Help, Mary!" "Help, dear brother!"

'For if thou come not straight,
For my life 'twill be too late!'

Her brother seems to hear his sister's voice "in every sense."

He let his falcon fly,
Rode off with hounds in full cry;
With all the haste he could
He sped to the dusky wood.

'What dost thou here, my Ulinger?
What dost thou here, my master dear?'
'Twisting a withe, and that is all,
To make a halter for my foal.'

'Twisting a withe, and that is all,
To make a halter for thy foal!
I swear by my troth thus shall it be,
Thyself shalt be the foal for me.'

'Then this I beg, my Fridburger,
Then this I beg, my master dear,
That thou wilt let me hang
In my clothes as now I stand.'

'Ask me not that, thou Ulinger,
Ask me not that, false perjurer;
Thy scarlet mantle and jerkin black
Will well become my scullion's back.'

His shield before his breast he slung,
Behind him his fair sister swung,
And so he hied away
Where his father's kingdom lay.

H, the nearly contemporaneous Augsburg broadside, differs from **G** in only one important particular. The "reuter" is Adelger, the lady unnamed. A stanza is lost between 6 and 7, which should contain the warning of the dove, and so is Adelger's version of what the bird had said. The important feature in **H**, not present in **G**, is that the halt is made near a spring, about which blood is streaming, "der war mit blut umbrunnen." This adds a horror to this powerful scene which well suits with it. When the maid begins to weep, Adelger asks whether her tears are for her father's land, or because she dislikes him so much. It is for neither reason, but because on yon fir she sees eleven maids hanging. He confirms her fears:

[33]
'Ah, thou fair young lady fine,
O palsgravine, O empress mine,
Adelger's killed his eleven before,
Thou'lt be the twelfth, of that be sure.'*

The last two lines seem, by their form, to be the dove's warning that has dropped out between stanzas 6 and 7. The maid's clothes in **H** are destined to be the perquisite of Adelger's mother, and the brother says that Adelger's are to go to his shield-bearer. The unhappy maid cries but twice, to the Virgin and to her brother. When surprised by the brother, Adelger feigns to be twisting a withe for his falcon.

I begins, like **G**, **H**, with the knight's seductive song. Instead of the dove directly warning the maid, it upbraids the man: "Whither now, thou Ollegehr?[†] Eight hast thou murdered already; and now for the ninth!" The maid asks what the dove means, and is told to ride on, and not mind the dove, who takes him for another man. There are eight maids in the fir. The cries are to Jesus, Mary, and her brothers, one of whom hastens to the rescue. He is struck with the beauty of his sister's attire,—her velvet dress, her virginal crown, "which you shall wear many a year yet." So saying, he draws his sword, and whips off his "brother-in-law's" head, with this epicedium:

---

* 13 'Ach du schöne junkfraw fein,
        Du pfalzgrävin, du kaiserin!
        Der Adelger hat sich vorailf getödt,
        Du wirst die zwölft, das sei dir gsait.

  15 'So bitt mich nit, du junkfraw fein,
        So bitt mich nit, du herzigs ein!'

The *liebkosung* of this murder-reeking Adelger, o'ersized with coagulate gore, is admirably horrible.
† Nimmersatt (All-begehrend) as interpreted by Meinert, not Adelger.

'Lie there, thou head, and bleed,
Thou never didst good deed.

'Lie there, thou head, and rot,
No man shall mourn thy lot.

'No one shall ever be sorry for thee
But the small birds on the greenwood tree.'[‡]

In **J**, again, the knight comes riding through the reeds, and sings such a song that Brown Annele, lying under the casement, exclaims, "Could I but sing like him, I would give my troth and my honor!" There are, by mistake, two[§] doves in stanza 4, that warn Annele not to be beguiled, but this error is set right in the next stanza. When she asks what the dove is cooing, the answer is, "It is cooing about its red foot; it went barefoot all winter." We have here again, as in **H**, the spring in the wood, "mit Blute umrunnen," and the lady asks again the meaning of the bloody spring. The knight replies, in a stanza which seems both corrupted and out of place, "This is where the eleven pure virgins perished." Then follow the same incidents as in **G–I**. He says she must hang with the eleven in the fir, and be queen over all. Her cries are for her father, for Our Lady, and for her brother, who is a hunter in the forest. The hunter makes all haste to his sister, twists a withe, and hangs the knight without a word between them, then takes his sister by the hand and conducts her home, with the advice never more to trust a knight: for all which she returns her devout thanks.[**]

---

‡   Verses which recur, nearly, not only in **Y** 17–19, **W** 27, 28, but elsewhere, as in a copy of 'Graf Friedrich,' Erk's *Liederhort*, p. 41, No 15, st. 19.
§   There is no sense in two doves. The single dove one may suppose to be the spirit of the last victim. We shall find the eleven appearing as doves in **Q**. There is no occasion to regard the dove here as a Waldminne (Vilmar, *Handbüchlein für Freunde des deutschen Volkslieds*, p. 57). Cf. the nightingale (and two nightingales) in the Danish 'Redselille og Medelvold:' see 'Leesome Brand,' further on in this volume.
**   This ballad has become, in Tübingen, a children's game, called 'Bertha im Wald.' The three cries are preserved in verse, and very nearly as in **J**, **M**. The game concludes by the robber smothering Bertha. Meier, *Deutsche Kinder-Reime*, No 439.

K and L are of the same length and the same tenor as J. There are no names in L; in K both Annele and Ulrich, but the latter is very likely to have been inserted by the editor. K, L have only one dove, and in neither does the lady ask the meaning of the dove's song. The knight simply says, "Be still; thou liest in thy throat!" Both have the bloody spring, but out of place, for it is very improperly spoken of by the knight as the spot he is making for:

'Wir wollen ein wenig weiter vorwärts faren,
Bis zu einem kühlen Waldbrunnen,
Der ist mit Blut überronnen.'*
            L 26–28, 17–19.

The three cries are for father, mother, brother. In K the brother fights with "Ulrich" two hours and a half before he can master him, then despatches him with his two-edged sword, and hangs him in a withe. He fires his rifle in L, to announce his coming, and hears his sister's laugh; then stabs the knight through the heart. The moral of J is repeated in both: Stay at home, and trust no knight.

M smacks decidedly of the bänkelsänger, and has an appropriate moral at the tail: *animi index cauda!* The characters are a cavalier and a girl, both nameless, and a brother. The girl, hearing the knight sing "ein Liedchen von dreierlei Stimmen," which should seem to signify a three-part song, says, "Ah, could I sing like him, I would straightway give him my honor." They ride to the wood, and come upon a hazel-bush with *three* doves, one of which informs the maid that she will be betrayed, the second that she will die that day, and the third that she will be buried in the wood. The second and third doves, as being false prophets, and for other reasons, may safely be pronounced intruders. All is now lost till we come to the cries, which are addressed to father, mother,

and brother. The brother stabs the traitor to the heart.[†]

N is as short as M, and, like it, has no names, but has all the principal points: the fascinating song, the dove on the bush, eleven maids in the fir, the three cries, and the rescue by the huntsman-brother, who cocks his gun and shoots the knight. The reciter of this ballad gave the editor to understand that if the robber had succeeded in his twelfth murder, he would have attained such powers that nobody after that could harm him.[‡]

O is a fairly well-preserved ballad, resembling G–J as to the course of the story. Anneli, lying under the casement, hears the knight singing as he rides through the reeds. The elaborate toilet is omitted, as in I, J. The knight makes haste to the dark wood. They come to a cold spring, "mit Bluot war er überrunnen;" then to a hazel, behind which a dove coos ominously. Anneli says, Listen. The dove coos you are a false man, that will not spare my life. No, says the knight, that is not it; the dove is cooing

---

* K, or the editor, seeks to avoid the difficulty by taking the last line from the knight, and reading, "Mit Blut war er umronnen," an emendation not according with the simplicity of ballads. Another Swabian copy, Meier, p. 301, note, strophe 6, has:

'Wir müssen zu selbigem Brennen
Wo Wasser und Blut heraus ronnen.'

---

† The last verses are these, and not very much worse than the rest:

Mein Bruder ist ein Jägersmann,
Der alle Thierlein schiessen kann;
Er hatt' ein zweischneidiges Schwerte,
Und stach es dem Falschen ins Herze.

Ihr Mädchen alle insgemein,
Lasst euch doch diess zur Warnung sein,
Und geht doch mit keinem so falschen
In einen so finstern Walde.

My brother is a hunting man,
And all the small game shoot he can;
He had a sword with edges two,
And ran the heart of the false man through

Ye maidens now in general,
Let this be warning to you all;
With man so false you never should
Go to so very dark a wood.

‡ So in Rochholz, *Schweizer Sagen*, No 14, i, 23, a man who had killed eleven maids would, if he could have made up the number twelve, have been able to pass through walls and mouseholes. Again, a certain robber in Jutland, who had devoured eight children's hearts, would have acquired the power of flying could he but have secured one more. Grundtvig, *D. g. F.* iv, 16, note.

about its blue foot, for its fate is to freeze in winter. The cloak is thrown on the grass, the eleven maids in the fir are descried, and Anneli is told she must hang highest, and be empress over all. He concedes her as many cries as she likes, for only the wood-birds will hear. She calls on God, the Virgin, and her brother. The brother thinks he hears his sister's voice, calls to his groom to saddle, comes upon the knight while he is twisting a withe for his horse, as he says, ties him to the end of the withe, and makes him pay for all he has perpetrated in the wood. He then swings Anneli behind him, and rides home with her.

[35]   P, the other Swiss ballad, has been retouched, and more than retouched in places, by a modern pen. Still the substance of the story, and, on the whole, the popular tone, is preserved. Fair Anneli, in the miller's house, hears the knight singing as he rides through the rushes, and runs down-stairs and calls to him: she would go off with him if she could sing like that, and her clothes are fit for any young lady. The knight promises that he will teach her his song if she will go with him, and bids her put these fine clothes on. They ride to the wood. A dove calls from the hazel, "He will betray thee." Anneli asks what the dove is saying, and is answered much as in J and O, that it is talking about its frost-bitten feet and claws. The knight tears through the wood, to the great peril of Anneli's gown and limbs, and when he has come to the right place, spreads his cloak on the grass, and makes the usual request. She weeps when she sees eleven maids in the fir-tree, and receives the customary consolation:

'Weep not too sore, my Anneli,
'T is true thou art doomed the twelfth to be;
Up to the highest tip must thou go,
And a margravine be to all below;
Must be an empress over the rest,
And hang the highest of all as the best.'

The request to be allowed three cries is lost. The knight tells her to cry as much as she pleases, he knows no one will come; the wild birds will not hear, and the doves are hushed. She cries to father, mother, and brother. The brother, who is sitting over his wine at the inn,

hears, saddles his best horse, rides furiously, and comes first to a spring filled with locks of maid's hair and red with maid's blood; then to a bush, where the knight (Rüdeli, Rudolph) is twisting his withe. He bids his sister be silent, for the withe is not for her; the villain is twisting it for his own neck, and shall be dragged at the tail of his horse.

Q resembles the Swabian ballads, and presents only these variations from the regular story. The dove adds to the warning. "Fair maid, be not beguiled," what we find nowhere else, "Yonder I see a cool spring, around which blood is running." The knight, to remove the maid's anxiety, says, "Let it talk; it does not know me; I am no such murderer." The end is excessively feeble. When the brother, a hunter as before, reaches his sister, "a robber runs away," and then the brother takes her by the hand, conducts her to her father's land, and enjoins her to stay at home and spin silk. There are no names.

There is one feature entirely peculiar to R. The knight carries off the maid, as before, but when they come to the hazel bush there are eleven doves that sing this "new song:"

'Be not beguiled, maiden,
The knight is beguiling thee:

'We are eleven already,
Thou shalt be the twelfth.'

The eleven doves are of course the spirits of the eleven preceding victims. The maid's inquiry as to what they mean is lost. The knight's evasion is not ingenious, but more likely to allay suspicion than simply saying, "I am no such murderer." He says, "Fear not: the doves are singing a song that is common in these parts." When they come to the spring "where blood and water are running," and the maid asks what strange spring is this, the knight answers in the same way, and perhaps could not do better: "Fear not: there is in these parts a spring that runs blood and water." This spring is misplaced, for it occurs before they enter the wood. The last scene in the ballad is incomplete, and goes no further than the brother's exclamation when he comes in upon the knight: "Stop, young knight!

Spare my sister's life." The parties in **R** are nameless.

So again in **S**, which also has neither the knight's enchanting song nor the bloody spring. There are two doves, as in **J**, stanza 4. The cries are addressed to mother, father, brother, as in **N**, and, as in **N**, again, the brother cocks his gun, and shoots the knight down;[*] then calmly leads his sister home, with the warning against knights.

(III.) **T**, the first of the third series, has marked signs of deterioration. Ulrich does not enchant Ännchen by his song, and promise to teach it to her; he offers to teach her "bird-song." They *walk* out together, apparently, and come to a hazel, with no dove; neither is there any spring. Annie sits down on the grass; Ulrich lays his head in her lap; she weeps, and he asks why. It is for eleven maids in the fir-tree, as so often before. Ulrich's style has become much tamer:

'Ah, Annie, Annie, dear to me,
How soon shalt thou the twelfth one be!'

She begs for three cries, and calls to her father, to God, to her youngest brother. The last is sitting over the wine and hears. He demands of Ulrich where she is, and is told, Upon yon linden, spinning silk. Then ensues this dialogue: Why are your shoes blood-red? Why not? I have shot a dove. That dove my mother bare under her breast. Annie is laid in the grave, and angels sing over her; Ulrich is broken on the wheel, and round him the ravens cry.

There is no remnant or reminiscence of the magical singing in **U**. Schön Ulrich and Roth Ännchen go on a walk, and come first to a fir-tree, then a green mead. The next scene is exactly as in **T**. Ulrich says the eleven maids were his wives, and that he had thrust his sword through their hearts. Annie asks for three *sighs*, and directs them to God, to Jesus, and to her youngest brother. He is sitting over his wine, when the sigh comes into the window, and Ulrich simultaneously in at the door. The remainder is very much as in **T**.

V differs from **U** only in the names, which are Schön-Heinrich and Schön-Ännelein, and in the "sighs" returning to cries, which invoke God, father, and brother.

W begins with a rivalry between Ulrich and Hanselein[†] for the hand of Rautendelein (Rautendchen). Ulrich is successful. She packs up her jewels, and he takes her to a wood, where she sees eleven maids hanging. He assures her she shall presently be the twelfth. It is then they sit down, and she leans her head on his breast and weeps, "because," as she says, "I must die." His remark upon this, if there was any, is lost. Hoffmann inserts a stanza from another Silesian copy, in which Ulrich says, Rather than spare thy life, I will run an iron stake through thee. She asks for three cries, and he says, Four, if you want. She prefers four, and calls to her father, mother, sister, brother. The brother, as he sits over the wine, hears the cry, and almost instantly Ulrich comes in at the door. He pretends to have killed a dove; the brother knows what dove, and hews off Ulrich's head, with a speech like that in **I**. Still, as Rautendchen is brought to the grave, with toll of bells, so Ulrich is mounted on the wheel, where ravens shriek over him.

X. Albrecht and Hänselein woo Alalein. She is promised to Albrecht, but Hänsel gets her. He takes her to a green mead, spreads his mantle on the grass, and she sits down. His lying in her lap and her discovery of the awful tree are lost. She weeps, and he tells her she shall be "his eleventh." Her cries are condensed into one stanza:

[†]   A variety of **W**, cited in *Schlesische Volkslieder*, p. 26, has,

'Ach Ulbrich, Ulbrich, Halsemann, Halsemann,
Lass du mich nur drei Gale schrei'n!'

Grundtvig, assuming that the name is Ulbrich Halsemann, would account for the second and superfluous character here [found also in **W**] by a divarication of Ulrich Halsemann into Ulrich and Halsemann (Hanslein). Ansar, "bisher unverständlicher Vorname des Ritters Uleraich" in **Y** (Meinert), would equally well yield Hanslein. Might not Halsemann possibly be an equivalent of Halsherr? Cf. Bugge, Helge-Digtene i den Ældre Edda, deres Hjem og Forbindelser (second series of his *Studier over de nordiske Gude- og Heltesagn*), Kjøbenhavn, 1896, p. 271.

---

[*]   What will those who are so troubled about cork-heeled shoon in 'Sir Patrick Spens' say to the firearms in **L, N, S**?

'Gott Vater, Sohn, Herr Jesu Christ,
Mein jüngster Bruder, wo Du bist!'

Her brother rides in the direction of the voice, and meets Hänselein in the wood, who says Alalein is sitting with princes and counts. The conclusion is as in **T, U, V.**

Y has Ansar Uleraich wooing a king's daughter, Annle, to the eighth year. He takes her to a fir-wood, then to a fir, a stump of a tree, a spring; in each case bidding her sit down. At [37] the spring he asks her if she wishes to be drowned, and, upon her saying no, cuts off her head. He has not walked half a mile before he meets her brother. The brother inquires where Ulrich has left his sister, and the reply is, "By the green Rhine." The conclusion is as in **W.** Ulrich loses his head, and the brother pronounces the imprecation which is found there and in **I.***

Z, which takes us back from Eastern Germany to the Rhine, combines features from all the three groups. Ulrich fascinates a king's daughter by his song. She collects her gold and jewels, as in **W,** and goes to a wood, where a dove warns her that she will be betrayed. Ulrich appropriates her valuables, and they wander about till they come to the Rhine. There he takes her into a wood, and gives her a choice between hanging and drowning, and, she declining both, says she shall die by his sword. But first she is allowed three cries,—to God, her parents, her youngest brother. The youngest brother demands of Ulrich where he has left his sister. "Look in my pocket, and you shall find fourteen tongues, and the last cut [reddest] of all is your sister's." The words were scarcely out of his mouth before Ulrich's sword had taken off his head.

DD presents a fragmentary version of the story. As Anna sits by the Rhine combing her hair, Heinrich comes along on his horse, sees her weep, and asks why. It is not for gold and not for goods, but because she is to die that day. Heinrich draws his sword, runs her through, and rides home. He is asked why his sword is

red, and says he has killed two doves. They say the dove must be Anna.

In **FF,** Hannchen walks in the wood, and Ulrich advances to meet her. The birds are all singing, and the maid asks why. 'Every bird has its song,' says Ulrich; 'go you your gait.' He takes her under a briar where there is a pretty damsel (who is quite superfluous). Hannchen lays her head in the damsel's lap and begins to weep. The damsel asks whether her weeping is for her father's gear, or because Ulrich is not good enough for her. It is not for her father's gear, and Ulrich is good enough. 'Is it, then,' says the damsel or Ulrich, 'for the stakes on which the eleven maidens are hanging? Rely upon it, you shall be the twelfth.' She begs for three cries, which are addressed to God, her parents, and her brothers. The brothers hear, hasten to the wood, and encounter Ulrich, who pretends to know nothing of their sister. His shoes are red with blood. 'Why not?' says Ulrich, 'I have shot a dove.' They know who the dove is. Hannchen is borne to the churchyard, Ulrich is strung up on the gallows. No 23 of the same collection is **X.**

The three classes of the German ballad, it will be observed, have for their principal distinction that in I the maid saves her own life by an artifice, and takes the life of her treacherous suitor; in II, she is rescued by her brother, who also kills the traitor; in III, she dies by the villain's hand, and he by her brother's, or by a public execution. There are certain subordinate traits which are constant, or nearly so, in each class. In I, **A–F,** a choice of deaths is invariably offered; the maid gets the advantage of the murderer by persuading him to take off his coat [distorted in **F,** which has lost its conclusion]; and, on her way home, she falls in with one or more of the robber's family, mother, brothers, servant, who interrogate her [except **F,** which, as just said, is a fragment]. Class II has several marks of its own. All the thirteen ballads [**G–S**], except the last, represent the knight as fascinating the maid by his singing; in all but **Q** she is warned of her danger by a dove,[†] or more than one; in all but the much-abridged **M, N,**

---

* And in 'Der Mutter Fluch,' Meinert, p. 246, a ballad with which **Y** agrees in the first two and last four stanzas.

[†] There is a dove in **Z,** but **Z,** as has been said, presents traits of all three classes.

the knight spreads his cloak on the grass, they sit down, and, excepting **M, N, R**, the unromantic service is repeated which she undertakes in Danish **A, B, D, E, F, H, L**, Swedish **A**, Norwegian **A, B**. The bloody spring occurs in some form, though often not quite intelligible, in **H, J, K, L, O, P, Q, R** (also in **D, Y**). All but the much-abridged **M, N** have the question, What are you weeping for? your father's land, humbled pride, lost honor? etc.; but this question recurs in **T, U, V, W**. The cries for help are a feature of both the second and the third class, and are wanting only in **Y**. Class III differs from I, and resembles II, in having the cries for help, and, in the less impaired forms, **T–W**, the knight spreads his cloak, lies down with his head in the lady's lap, and asks the cause of her tears. Beyond this, and the changed catastrophe, the ballads of Class III are distinguished by what they have lost.

Forms in which the story of this is mixed with that of some other German ballad remain to be noticed.

A. A ballad first published in Nicolai's *Almanach*, ii, 100, No 21 (1778), and since reprinted, under the titles, 'Liebe ohne Stand,' 'Der Ritter und die Königstochter,' etc., but never with absolute fidelity, in *Wunderhorn* (1819), i, 37 (= Erlach, ii, 120), Kretzschmer, No 72, i, 129; Mittler, No 89; Erk, *Neue Sammlung*, iii, 18, No 14; also, with a few changes, by Zuccalmaglio, No. 95, p. 199, as 'aus Schwaben;' by Erk, *Liederhort*, No 28, p. 90, as "corrected from oral tradition;" and as "from oral tradition," in Erk's *Wunderhorn* (1857), i, 39. Independent versions are given by Mittler, No 90, p. 88, from Oberhessen; Pröhle, *Weltliche u. geistliche Volkslieder*, No 5, p. 10, from the Harz; Reifferscheid, No 18, p. 36, from Bokendorf; 'Der Reiter u. die Kaisertochter,' K. Becker, *Rheinischer Volksliederborn*, p. 15, No 12. Erk refers to still another copy, five stanzas longer than Nicolai's, from Hesse-Darmstadt, *Neue Sammlung*, iii, 19, note.

What other ballad is here combined with Ulinger, it is impossible to make out. The substance of the narrative is that a knight rides singing through the reeds, and is heard by a king's daughter, who forthwith desires to go with him. They ride till the horse is hungry

[tired]; he spreads his cloak on the grass, and makes, *sans façon*, his usual request. The king's daughter sheds many tears, and he asks why. "Had I followed my father's counsel, I might have been empress." The knight cuts off her head at the word, and says, Had you held your tongue, you would have kept your head. He throws the body behind a tree, with Lie there and rot; my young heart must mourn [no knight, a knight, shall mourn over thee]. Another stanza or two, found in some versions, need not be particularly noticed.

'Stolz Sieburg,' Simrock, No 8, p. 21, from the Rhine, Mittler, No 88, is another and somewhat more rational form of the same story. To the question whether she is weeping for Gut, Muth, Ehre, the king's daughter answers:

'Ich wein um meine Ehre,
Ich wollt gern wieder umkehren.'

For this Stolz Sieburg strikes off her head, with a speech like that which we have just had, and throws it into a spring; then resolves to hang himself.[*]

A variety of **A** is printed in *Altpreussische Monatschrift*, N. F., XXVIII, 632, 1892, without indication of local derivation, 'Der Ritter und die Königstochter.' The knight takes measures (not very summary ones) to drown himself.

A **Dutch** version of this ballad, Le Jeune, No 92, p. 292; Willems, No 72, p. 186; Hoff-

[*]   'Da lyge, feyns Lybchen, unndt fawle,
        Meyn jungk Herze muss trawren.'
        Nicolai, vv 35, 36,

        'Da liege, du Häuptchen, und faule,
        Kein Reuter wird dir nachtrauern.'
        Simrock, vv 35, 36,

are evidently derived from the apostrophe to the murderer's head in **I, W, Y**.

Stolz Syburg is the hero of a very different ballad, from the Münster region, Reifferscheid, No 16, p. 32 (also No 17, and Simrock, No 9, p. 23, 'Stolz Heinrich'). And from this the name, in consequence of a remote resemblance in the story, may have been taken up by the Rhine ballad, though it has contributed nothing more. Margaret, a king's daughter, is wiled away by a splendid description of Stolz Syburg's opulence. When they have gone a long way, he tells her that he has nothing but a barren heath. She stabs herself at his feet.

mann, No 29, p. 92, has less of the Halewyn in it, and more motive than the German, though less romance. "If you might have been an empress," says the knight, "I, a margrave's son, will marry you to-morrow." "I would rather lose my head than be your wife," replies the lady; upon which he cuts off her head and throws it into a fountain, saying, Lie there, smiling mouth! Many a thousand pound have you cost me, and many pence of red gold. Your head is clean cut off.

B. The Ulinger story is also found combined with that of the beautiful ballad, 'Wassermanns Braut.'* (1.) In a Transylvanian ballad, 'Brautmörder,' Schuster, *Siebenbürgisch-sächsische Volkslieder*, p. 57, No 54 A, 38vv, with variations, and p. 59, B, a fragment of 10vv; (A in a translation, Böhme, No 14, p. 61.) A king from the Rhine sues seven years for a king's daughter, and does not prevail till the eighth. She begs her mother not to consent, for she has seen it in the sun that she shall not long be her daughter, in the moon that she shall drown before the year is out, in the bright stars that her blood shall be dispersed far and wide. He takes her by the hand, and leads her through a green wood, at the end of which a grave is already made. He pushes her into the grave, and drives a stake through her heart. The princess' brother asks what has become of his sister. "I left her on the Rhine, drinking mead and wine." "Why are your skirts so bloody?" "I have shot a turtle-dove." "That turtle-dove was, mayhap, my sister." They spit him on a red-hot stake, and roast him like a fish. Lines 1–4 of this ballad correspond to 1–4 of Y (which last agree with 1–4 of Meinert's 'Wassermanns Braut'); 17, 18, to Y 5, 6; 25–34 to 21–30; and we find in verse 22 the stake through the heart which Hoffmann has interpolated in W, stanza 12.

(2.) A Silesian copy of 'Wassermanns [39] Braut,' contributed by Hoffman to *Deutsches Museum*, 1852, II, 164, represents the bride, after she has fallen into the water and has been

recovered by the nix, as asking for three cries, and goes on from this point like the Ulrich ballad W, the conclusion being that the sister is drowned before the brother comes to her aid.[†]

'Nun schürz dich, Gredlein,' "Forster's Frische Liedlein, No 66," Böhme, No 53, Uhland, No 256 A, which is of the date 1549, and therefore older than the Nuremberg and Augsburg broadsides, has derived stanzas 7–9 from an Ulinger ballad, unless this passage is to be regarded as common property. Some copies of the ballad commonly called 'Müllertücke' have also adopted verses from Ulinger, especially that in Meier's *Schwäbische Volkslieder*, No 233, p. 403.

A form of ballad resembling English C–F, but with some important differences, is extraordinarily diffused in **Poland**. There are also two versions of the general type of English **A**, or, better, of the first class of the German ballads. The first, **A a**, Pauli, *Pieśni ludu Polskiego w Galicyi*, p. 90, No 5, and Kolberg, *Pieśni ludu Polskiego*, No 5, **bbb**, p. 70, runs thus. There was a man who went about the world wiling away young girls from father and mother. He had already done this with eight; he was now carrying off the ninth. He took her to a frightful wood; then bade her look in the direction of her house. She asked, "What is that white thing that I see on yon fir?" "There are already eight of them," he said, "and you shall be the ninth; never shall you go back to your father and mother. Take off that gown, Maria." Maria was looking at his sword. "Don't touch, Maria, for you will wound your pretty little hands." "Don't mind my hands, John," she replied, "but rather see what a bold heart I have;" and instantly John's head flew off. Then follows a single

[†] The remarkable Norwegian ballad of the 'Wassermanns Braut' group, The Nix and Heiemo, Landstad, No 39, p. 350, has not been unaffected by the one we are now occupied with. There is even a verbal contact between stanza 19,

'Heiemo tenkte með sjave seg:
Tru mine smá *knivar* 'ki hjelper meg?'

and Norwegian **F**, stanza 9, cited by Grundtvig, IV, 4,

Lengji stó Gullbjör, hó tenkte mæ seg:
'Kann inkje mí' *rúninne* hjelpe meg?'

---

* 'Wassermans Braut,' Meinert, p. 77; 'Die unglückliche Braut,' Hoffmann u. Richter, *Schlesische V. L.*, p. 6, No. 2; 'Königs Töchterlein,' Erk u. Irmer, vi, 6, No 4; 'Der Wassermann,' Erk's *Liederhort*, p. 50, No 17. ('Die Nixenbraut,' "Norddeutschland," Zuccalmaglio, p. 192, No 92, seems to be Meinert's copy written over.)

stanza, which seems to be addressed to John's mother, after the manner of the German **A**, etc.: "See, dear mother! I am thy daughter-in-law, who have just put that traitor out of the world." There is a moral for conclusion, which is certainly a later addition.

Kozłowski, *Lud*, p. 54, No 15, furnishes **A b**, a second and inferior but still important form of **A** (Masovian). Ligar (afterwards Jasia, Golo) bids Kasia take all she has. She has already done this, and is ready to range the world with him. Suddenly she asks, after they have been some time on their way, What is that yonder so green? Jasia replies, Our house, to which we are going. They go on further, and Kasia again inquires abruptly, What is that yonder so white? "That is my eight wives, and you shall be the ninth: you are to die, and will be the tenth." "Where is the gold, the maidens' gold?" "In the linden, Kasia, in the linden; plenty of it." "Let me not die so wretchedly; let me draw your sword for once." She drew the sword, and with one stroke Jasia's head was off.

The other ballads may be arranged as follows, having regard chiefly to the catastrophe. B, Kolberg, No 5, **oo**: C, **rr**: D, **ccc**: E, **dd**: F, **uu**: G, **ww**: H, **t**: I, **u**: J, **gg**: K, **mm**: L, *Wacław z Oleska*, p. 483, 2, Kolberg, **p**: L*, Kozłowski, *Lud*, p. 33, No IV: M, Wojcicki, I, 234, Kolberg, **r**: N, Wojcicki, I, 82, Kolberg, **s**: O, Kolberg, **d**: P, *ib.* **f**: Q, **pp**: R, Wojcicki, I, 78, Kolberg, **e**: S, Kolberg, **l**: T, *ib.* **n**: U, Pauli, *Pjeśni ludu Polskiego w Galicyi*, p. 92, No 6, Kolberg, **q**: V, Kolberg, **y**: W, Wojcicki, II, 298, J. Lipiński, *Piosnki ludu Wielkopolskiego*, p. 34, Kolberg, **ee**; X, Kolberg, **a**: Y, *ib.* **z**: Z, **aa**: AA, **qq**: BB, **w**; CC, **ddd**: DD, **m**: EE, **c**: FF, **o**: GG, **ll**: HH, **ss**: II, **ii**: JJ, **ff**: KK, **tt**: LL, **i**: MM, **g***. In **B–K** the woman comes off alive from her adventure: in **O–CC**, she loses her life: in **L–N** there is a jumble of both conclusions: **DD–MM** are incomplete.[*] To the preceding should also be added **NN**,

Piosnki wieśniacze znad Dźwiny, p. 41, No 51; **OO**, Roger, p. 78, No 138; **PP**, Roger, p. 69, No 125; **QQ**, ib., p. 79, No 140; **RR**, p. 81, No 142; **SS**, p. 79, No 139. The last three are imperfect, and **QQ**, **RR**, have a beginning which belongs elsewhere.

The story of the larger part of these ballads, conveyed as briefly as possible, is this: John, who is watering horses, urges Catherine,[†] who is drawing water, to elope with him. He bids her take silver and gold enough, that the horse may have something to carry. Catherine says her mother will not allow her to enter the new chamber. Tell her that you have a headache, says John, and she will consent. Catherine feigns a headache, is put into the new chamber, [40] and absconds with John while her mother is asleep.[‡] At a certain stage, more commonly at successive stages,—on the high road, **K, P, S, DD, II, LL**, in a dark wood, **D, P, T, X, Z, DD, EE, NN, PP** (which is corrupt here), **SS**, at a spring, **D, K, S, T, V, W, X, Y, Z, EE, II, LL**, etc., to a deep stream, **NN, OO, QQ, SS**; it is red sea in **RR**, as in **J**—he bids her take off, or himself takes from her, her "rich attire," **D, P, T, V, W, X, Y, Z, DD, EE, OO**, her satin gown, **D, T, X, DD, EE**, her French or Turkish costume, **K, P, II**, robes of silver, **K**, shoes, **Z, CC, FF**, silk stockings, **T**, corals, **D, X, CC, EE**, pearls, **T**, rings, **K, O–T, X, Z, CC–FF, II, LL**. In many of the ballads he tells her to go back to her mother, **B–G, K, L*, M, N, Q, S, U, X, Y, EE, HH–LL, NN** (twice), **RR**, sometimes after pillaging her, sometimes without mention of this. Catherine generally replies that she did not come away to have to go back, **B, C, D, G, L*, M, S, U, X, Y, EE, HH, JJ, KK, LL**. John seizes her by the hands and sides and throws her into a deep river [pool, water, sea], from a bridge in **OO, QQ**. Her apron [tress, **AA, II**, both apron and tress, **O**, petticoat, **KK**] is caught on a stake

---

[*] Kolberg's **b, h, k, v, x, bb, cc, hh, kk, ll, nn, xx, yy, zz**, consist of only one or two initial stanzas, containing no important variation. His **aaa**, a fragment of six stanzas, Pauli, p. 147, No 6, Wojcicki, II, 169, though it begins like the rest, sounds like a different ballad.

The ballad in Wojcicki, I, 38, is allied with the one we are engaged with, and the two fragments on p. 36, p. 37 with both this and that.

[†] Anne in **R, LL**, and Kolberg's **h**: Mary in **I, U, II**: Ursula, **N**: both Catherine and Alice, **AA**. John is found in all but **N**, where there is a nameless seigneur. Jasia and Kasia in **NN–SS**.

[‡] They are expressly said to go off in a carriage in **I, O, Q, T, BB, DD, FF**. Still, in **I**, John says, "Let the black horse have something to carry under us." In **O, T, FF**, the horses have a presentiment of evil to their mistress, and refuse to stir.

or stump of a tree, **B, C, G, H, I, O, P, R, T, U, V, W, Y, BB, DD, EE, II, JJ, KK** [in a bush **D**]. John cuts it away with axe or sword, **G, I, O, R, T, BB, II, JJ**. She swims to a stake, to which she clings, and John hews her in three, **QQ**. She cries to him for help. He replies, "I did not throw you in to help you out,"* **B, C, F, P, U, V, W, X, Z, EE, II, OO**. Catherine is drawn ashore in a fisherman's net [swims ashore **I, J, GG**].

Catherine comes out from the water alive in **B–N**. The brother who plays so important a part in the second class of German ballads, appears also in a few of the Polish versions, **B, C, D**, and **L*, O, P, Q, X**, but is a mere shadow. In **B** 21, 22, and **C** 16, 17, the brother, who is "on the mountain," and may be supposed to hear the girl's cry, slides down a silken cord, which proves too short, and the girl "adds her tress"![†] He asks the fishermen to throw their

---

* One version of 'The Two Sisters,' **Q**, has the same answer;

    9 'I did not put you in with the design
        Just for to pull you out again.'

This might be called a formula in Polish ballads: something of the kind occurs three times in **X**, four times in **B**, five times in **P**; in other ballads also. In **Q** 25, Catherine clutches the river bank, and John pushes away her hands. Compare 'The Two Sisters,' **F** 9, further on in this volume.

    In a Ruthenian ballad a girl who runs away from her mother with a lover tells her brothers, who have come in search of her, I did not leave home to go back again with you: Golovatsky, Part I, p. 77, No 32; Part III, 1, p. 17, No 4, p. 18, No 5. So, "I have not poisoned you to help you," Part I, p. 206, No 32, p. 207, No 33.

† In the tale of the Sea-horse, Schiefner, Awarische Texte, *Memoirs of the St Petersburg Academy*, vol. xix, No 6, p. 11 f, a sixty-ell rope being required to rescue a prince from a well into which he had been thrown, and no rope forthcoming, the daughter of a sea-king makes a rope of the required length with her hair, and with this the prince is drawn out. Dr Reinhold Köhler, who pointed out this incident to me, refers in his notes to the texts, at p. vii f, to the song of Südäi Märgän, Radloff, II, 627–31, where Südäi Märgän's wife, having to rescue her husband from a pit, tries first his horse's tail, and finds it too short, then her hair, which proves also a little short. A maid is then found whose hair is a hundred fathoms long, and her hair being tied on to the horse's tail, and horse, wife, and maid pulling together, the hero is drawn out. For climbing up by a maid's hair, see, further, Köhler's note to Gonzenbach, No 53, II, 236.

nets for her. She is rescued, goes to church, takes an humble place behind the door, and, when her eyes fall on the young girls, melts into tears. Her apron catches in a bush in **D**: she plucks a leaf, and sends it down the stream to her mother's house. The mother says to the father, "Do you not see how Catherine is perishing?" The leaf is next sent down stream to her sister's house, who says to her brother, "Do you not see how Catherine is perishing?"[‡] He rides up a high mountain, and slides down his silken cord. Though one or two stanzas are lost, or not given, the termination was probably the same as in **B, C**. In **L*** 15, **O** 12, the brother, on a high mountain, hears the cry for help, and slides down to his sister on a silken cord, but does nothing. **X** does not account for the brother's appearance: he informs the fishermen of what has happened, and they draw Catherine out, evidently dead. The brother hears the cry from the top of a wall in **P** 21, 22; slides down his cord; the sister adds her tress; he directs the fishermen to draw her out; she is dead. Instead of the brother on the wall, we have a mason in **Q** 27 [perhaps "the brother on the wall" in **P** *is* a mason]. It is simply said that "he added" a silken cord: the fishermen drew out Catherine dead. The conclusion is equally, or more, impotent in all the versions in which the girl escapes from drowning. In **G, I, J, QQ, SS**, she seats herself on a stone, and apostrophizes her hair, saying [in **G, J**], "Dry, my locks, dry, for you have had much pleasure in the river!" She goes to church, takes an humble place, and weeps, in **E, F, G**, as in **B, C, D**. John goes scot-free in all these.[§] Not so in the more vigorous ballads of tragic termination. Fierce [41] pursuit is made for him. He is cut to pieces, or torn to pieces, **O, P, S, T, Y**; broken on the wheel, **L, U, V, W**; cut *and* broken in **OO**; cleft in two, **BB**; broken small as barley-corns, or quartered, by horses, **L*, Z**; committed to a dungeon, to await, as we may hope, one of these penalties, **Q, R**. The bells toll for Cathe-

---

‡ A message is sent to a father by a daughter in the same way, in Chodzko, *Les Chants historiques de l'Ukraine*, p. 75; cf. p. 92, of the same. Tristram sends messages to Isonde by linden shavings inscribed with runes: *Sir Tristrem*, ed. Kölbing, p. 56, st. 187; *Tristrams Saga*, cap. 54, p. 68, ed. Kölbing; Gottfried von Strassburg, vv 14427–441.

rine [the organs play for her], and she is laid in the grave, **O–W, Y, Z, L, L***.

There are, besides, in various ballads of this second class, special resemblances to other European forms. The man (to whom rank of any sort is assigned only in **N***) comes from a distant country, or from over the border, in **O, Q, R, T, DD, GG**, as in English **D, E**. The maid is at a window in **M, W**, as in German **G, J, M, O, P, Q**, etc. In **Q** 2, John, who has come from over the border, persuades the maid to go with him by telling her that in his country "the mountains are golden, the mountains are of gold, the ways of silk," reminding us of the wonderland in Danish **A, E**, etc.[†] After the pair have stolen away, they go one hundred and thirty miles, **O, DD, FF**; thrice nine miles, **Q**; nine and a half miles, **T**; cross one field and another, **M, R**; travel all night, **GG**; and nei-

ther says a word to the other. We shall find this trait further on in French **B, D**, Italian **B, C, D, F, G**. The choice of deaths which we find in German **A–F** appears in **J**. Here, after passing through a silent wood, they arrive at the border of the (red) *sea*. She sits down on a stone, he on a rotten tree. He asks, By which death will you die: by my right hand, or by drowning in this *river*? They come to a dark wood in **AA**; he seats himself on a beech-trunk, she near a stream. He asks, Will you throw yourself into the river, or go home to your mother? So **H**, and **R** nearly.[‡] She prefers death to returning. Previous victims are mentioned in **T, DD, HH**. When she calls from the river for help, he answers, **T** 22, You fancy you are the only one there; six have gone before, and you are the seventh: **HH** 16, Swim the river; go down to the bottom; six maids are there already, and you shall be the seventh [four, fifth]: **DD** 13, Swim, swim away, to the other side; there you will see my seventh wife.[§]

PP closely resembles German ballads of the third class. Katie shouts three times: at her first cry the grass curls up; at the second the river overflows; the third wakes her mother, who rouses her sons, saying, Katie is calling in the wood. They find John with a bloody sword; he says he has killed a dove. They answer, No dove, but our sister, and maltreat him till he tells what he has done with his victim: "I have hidden her under the yew-bush; now put me on the wheel."

In Wisła, IV, 393–424, Mr John Karłowicz has given the results of a study of this Polish ballad, which may be briefly summarized:

Ten unprinted versions are there added to the large number already published, making about ninety copies, if fragments are counted. Copies not already noted are, besides these ten, the following. Kolberg, Krakowskie, II, 111, 168, Nos 208, 336; Kieleckie, II, 148, No 453; Łęczyckie, p. 131, No 223; Lubelskie, I, 289ff, Nos 473, 474; Poznanskie, IV, 63, No 131; Mazowsze, III, 274, No 386, IV, 320, No 346.

---

§   **L, L*, M, N**, as already said, confuse the two catastrophes. John says, in **N**, "Do you see that broad river? I will measure its depth by throwing you in." We may assume that he was as good as his word. But Ursula made her way home through woods and forests, weeping her eyes out on the way. Kind souls dug a grave for her. The conclusion of **M** is absurd, but need not be particularized. **G** has a passage of the sternest theology. While Catherine is struggling in the water, her father comes by. She cries to him to save her. He says, "My dear Catherine, you have loved pleasure too much. Lord Jesus grant you drown!" Her mother appears, and makes the same reply to her daughter's appeal. There are stall-copy terminal morals to many of the ballads.

*   **N** 1, "A lord came riding from his estate to a neighbor."

†   Golovatsky, at **I**, 116, No 29, has a ballad, found elsewhere without the feature here to be noticed, in which a Cossack, who is watering his horse while a maid is drawing water, describes his home as a Wonderland, like John in Polish **Q**. "Come to the Ukraine with the Cossacks," he says. "Our land is not like this: with us the mountains are golden, the water is mead, the grass is silk; with us the willows bear pears and the girls go in gold." She yields; they go over one mountain and another, and when they have crossed the third the Cossack lets his horse graze. The maid falls to weeping, and asks the Cossack, Where are your golden mountains, where the water that is mead, the grass that is silk? He answers, No girl of sense and reason engages herself to a young Cossack. So in Zegota Pauli, *P. l. ruskiego*, II, 29, No 26 = Golovatsky, I, 117, No 30, where the maid rejoins to the glowing description, I have ranged the world: golden mountains I never saw; everywhere mountains are of stone, and everywhere rivers are of water; very like the girl in Grundtvig, 82 **B**, st. 7; 183 **A** 6, **E** 5, 6.

‡   The place is high above the water in **R** 10, 11, as in English **D** 9, 29, **C** 4.
§   **BB** 6, "My mother said that I had seen you; she will *watch me closely*," may be an accidental coincidence with Danish **A** 7–9, **B** 6–8, etc.

Zbiór wiadomości do antropologii krajowej, II, 78, Nos 89, 90; IV, 129; X, 123. Wisła, II, 132, 159. *Prace filologiczne*, II, 568. Kętrzyński, *O Mazurach*, p. 35, No 1. Zawiliński, *Z powieści i pieśni górali beskidowych*, p. 88, No 66. Wasilewski, Jagodne, etc., No 120. Fedorowski, *Lud okolic Żarek, etc.*, p. 102, No 49.[*]

Most of the ten versions printed in Wisła agree with others previously published; in some there are novel details. In No 3, p. 398, Kasia, thrown into the water by her lover, is rescued by her brother. In No 10, p. 404, Jás, when drowning the girl, tells her that he has drowned four already, and she shall be the fifth; her brother comes sliding down a silken rope; fishermen take the girl out dead. There are still only two of all the Polish versions in which Catharine kills John, **A a, b**. The name Ligar, in the latter, points clearly, Mr Karłowicz remarks, to the U-linger, Ad-elger, Ol-legehr of the German versions, and he is convinced that the ballad came into Poland from Germany, although the girl is not drowned in the German ballad, as in the Polish, English, and French.

John, who is commonly the hero in the Polish ballad, is at the beginning of many copies declared to have sung, and the words have no apparent sense. But we observe that in the versions of western Europe the hero plays on the horn, sings a seductive song, promises to teach the girl to sing, etc.; the unmeaning Polish phrase is therefore a survival.

In many of the German versions a bird warns the maid of her danger. This feature is found once only in Polish: in Zawiliński (No 69 A of Karłowicz).

There is a **Little-Russian** ballad which begins like the Polish 'Jás i Kasia,' but ends with the girl being tied to a tree and burned, instead of being drowned: Wisła, IV, 423, from *Zbiór wiadom. do antrop.*, III, 150, No 17. Traces of the incident of the burning are also found in Polish and Moravian songs: Wisła, pp. 418–22, and in a White Russian ballad, Šejn, *Materialy*, I, 1, 492, No 606. It is probable that there were two independent ballads, and that these have been confounded.

A **Russian** version in Trudy, V, 425, No 816, while corrupted, resembles the first German class. On the oaken bridge stood Galya, there Galya stood and drew water, she drew water and spoke with Marko. "O Marko mine, what dost thou say to me? Come wander with me, youth; let us wander on foot through the dark night." One field traversed, a second they crossed, and in the third lay down on the grass to sleep. The rain began to sprinkle, the fierce rain to fall, and Marko began to slumber. "O Marko mine, sleep not while with me; bare your sword and fight with me." Young Galya vanquished Marko; she conquered Marko, and rode, she mounted and rode over the level field. Galya arrives at the new gate; there stands Marko's mother, more beautiful than gold. "Young Galya, what can I say? Have you seen Marko near my house?" "Oh, hush, mother; weep not, mourn not. Thy Marko has married in the field; he has taken to himself a fine young lady, a grave in the meadow."

In Trudy, V, 335, No 660, a man beguiles a girl with tales of a land where the rivers are of honey, where pears grow on willows, and maidens are clothed in gold, as in German **Q 2**. In one version of this ballad a cuckoo flies up and bids the maid not listen to the Cossack's tales: "I have flown all over the world, and I have never seen golden mountains, nor eaten pears from willow-trees, nor beheld maidens clad in gold."

In Trudy, V, 226, No 454, a maid going to the ford for water meets Marko, and suggests that he should propose for her; if her mother will not consent, they will *roam*. They cross one field and two, and lie down on the grass in a third. He is falling asleep, when she wakes him with a cry that they are pursued. Marko is overtaken and his head cut off. No 548, p. 278, is nearly the same. No 690, p. 352, resembles in part No 454, and partly Golovatsky, I, 116.

Other Slavic forms of this ballad resemble more or less the third German class. A **Wendish** version from Upper Lusatia, Haupt and Schmaler, Part I, No 1, p. 27, makes Hilžička (Lizzie) go out before dawn to cut grass. Hołdrašk suddenly appears, and says she must pay

---

[*] At p. 777 of Sušil's *Moravian Songs* there are two other version not previously mentioned, the second of them manifestly derived from Poland.

him some forfeit for trespassing in his wood. She has nothing but her sickle, her silver finger-ring, and, when these are rejected, her wreath, and that, she says, he shall not have if she dies for it. Hołdrašk, who avows that he has had a fancy for her seven years (cf. German **Y**, and the Transylvanian mixed form **B**), gives her her choice, to be cut to pieces by his sword, or trampled to death by his horse. Which way pleases him, she says, only she begs for three cries. All three are for her brothers. They ride round the wood twice, seeing nobody; the third time Hołdrašk comes up to them. Then follows the dialogue about the bloody sword and the dove. When asked where he has left Hilžička, Hołdrašk is silent. The elder brother seizes him, the younger dispatches him with his sword.

Several **Bohemian** ballads are very similar. **A**, translated in Waldau's *Böhmische Granaten*, ii, 25;[*] **B**, Sušil, *Moravské Národní Písně*, No 189, p. 191, 'Vrah,' 'The Murderer;' **C**, Sušil, p. 193; **D**, Erben, *Prostonárodni české Písně a Říkadla*, p. 480, No 16, 'Zabité děvče,' 'The Murdered Maid;' **E**, p. 479, No 15, 'Zabitá sestra,' 'The Murdered Sister.'

A. While Katie is cutting grass, early in the morning, Indriasch presents himself, and demands some for his horse. She says, You must dismount, if your horse is to have grass. "If I do, I will take away your wreath." "Then God will not grant you his blessing." He springs from his 2| horse, and while he gives it grass with one hand snatches at the wreath with the other. "Will you die, or surrender your wreath?" Take my life, she says, but allow me three cries. Two cries reached no human ear, but the third cry her mother heard, and called to her sons to saddle, for Katie was calling in the wood, and was in trouble. They rode over stock and stone, and came to a brook where Indriasch was washing his hands. The same dialogue ensues as in the Wendish ballad. The brothers hewed the murderer into fragments. **B**, while very similar to **A**, has a double set of names, beginning with black George,—not the Servian, but "king of Hungary,"—and ending with Indriasch. The

maid is once called Annie, otherwise Katie. At her first call the grass becomes green; at the second the mountain bows; the third the mother hears. **C** has marvels of its own. Anna entreats John to allow her to call to her mother. "Call, call," he says, "you will not reach her with your call; in this dark wood, even the birds will not hear you." At her first call a pine-tree in the forest breaks; at the second the river overflows; at the third her mother rises from the grave. She calls to her sons to go to Anna's rescue, and *they* rise from their graves. The miscreant John confesses that he has buried their sister in the wood. They strike off his head, and put a hat on the head, with an inscription in gold letters, to inform people what his offence has been. There is a gap after the seventh stanza of **D**, which leaves the two following stanzas unintelligible by themselves: 8, Choose one of the two, and trust nobody; 9, She made her choice, and shouted three times towards the mountains. At the first cry the mountain became green; at the second the mountain bowed backwards; the third the mother heard. She sent her sons off; they found their neighbor John, who had cut off their sister's head. The law-abiding, and therefore modern, young men say that John shall go to prison and never come out alive. In **E** the man, a young hunter, says, Call *five* times; not even a wood-bird will hear you. Nothing is said of the first call; the second is heard by the younger brother, who tells the elder that their sister must be in trouble. The hunter has a bloody rifle in his hand: how he is disposed of we are not told. All these ballads but **C** begin with the maid cutting grass, and all of them have the dove that is "no dove, but our sister."

Fragments of this ballad are found, **F**, in Sušil, p. 112, No 113, 'Nevěsta nest' astnice,' 'The Unhappy Bride;' **G**, p. 171, No 171, 'Zbojce,' 'The Murderer;' and there is a variation from **B** at p. 192, note 3, which is worth remarking, **H**. **F**, sts 11–14: "Get together what belongs to you; we will go to a foreign land;" and when they came to the turf, "Look my head through."[†] Every hair she laid aside she wet with a tear. And when they came into the dark of the wood he cut her into nine [three] pieces. **G**. Katie meets John in a meadow; they sit down on the grass. "Look my head through."

---

[*] The second, and more valuable, volume of Waldau's B. G. I have found it impossible to obtain. Reifferscheid cites the ballad at p. 166.

She weeps, for she says there is a black fate impending over her; "a black one for me, a red one for thee." He gets angry, cuts off her head, and throws her into the river, for which he is hanged. **H**. He sprang from his horse, robbed the maid, and laughed. He set her on the grass, and bade her look his head through. Every hair she examined she dropped a tear for. "Why do you weep, Katie? Is it for your crants?" "I am not weeping for my crants, nor am I afraid of your sword. Let me call three times, that my father and mother may hear." Compare German **H** 16, 11; **Q** 8–10, etc., etc.

A **Servian** ballad has fainter but unmistakable traces of the same tradition: Vuk, *Srpske Narodne Pjesme*, I, 282, No 385, ed. 1841; translated by Goetze, *Serbische V. L.*, p. 99, by Talvj, *V. L. der Serben*, 2d ed., II, 172, by Kapper, *Gesänge der Serben*, II, 318. Mara is warned by her mother not to dance with Thomas. She disobeys. Thomas, while dancing, gives a sign to his servants to bring horses. The two ride off, and when they come to the end of a field Thomas says, Seest thou you withered maple? There thou shalt hang, ravens eat out thine eyes, eagles beat thee with their wings. Mara shrieks, Ah me! so be it with every girl that does not take her mother's advice.*

---

† "Cette action, si peu séante pour nous, est accomplie dans maint conte grec, allemand, etc., par des jeunes filles sur leurs amants, sur des dragons par les princesses qu'ils ont enlevées, et, même dans une légende bulgare en vers, saint Georges reçoit le même service de la demoiselle exposée an dragon, dont il va la délivrer." Dozon, *Contes albanais*, p. 27, note. In the Bulgarian legend referred to, *Bùlgarski narodni pěsni*, by the brothers Miladinof, p. 31, the saint having dozed off during the operation, the young maid sheds tears, and a burning drop falls on the face of George, and wakes him. This recalls the Magyar ballad, Molnár Anna, see p. 67. A Cretan legend of St George has the same trait: Jeannaraki, p. 2, v. 41. Even a dead lover recalled to the earth by his mistress, in ballads of the Lenore class, asks the same service: Golovatsky, II, 708, No 12; Sušil, p. 111, No 112, 'Umrlec,' 'The Dead Man.' The scene between St George and the maiden is woven into a Greek tale, 'Der Goldäpfelbaum und die Höllenfahrt,' Hahn, No 70, II, 55. See, also, George's legend in Bezsonof, *Kalyeki Perekhozhie*, I, 506, 509, 520, Nos 117, 118, 120.
* A few silly verses follow in the original, in which Thomas treats what he had said as a jest. These are properly rejected by Talvj as a spurious appendage.

Two **Ruthenian** ballads belong with these Slavic parallels: **A**, Zegota Pauli, *P. l. ruskiego*, II, 21 = Golovatsky, III, 1, 149, No 21; **B**, Golovatsky, III, 1, 172, No 46. **A**. A man induces a girl to go off with him in the night. They wander over one land and another, and then feel need of rest. Why does your head ache? he asks of her. Are you homesick? "My head does not ache; I am not homesick." He takes her by the white sides and throws her into the deep Donau, saying, Swim with the stream; we shall not live together. She swims over the yellow sand, crying, Was I not fair, or was it my fate? and he dryly answers, Fair; it was thy fate. In **B** it is a Jew's daughter that is wiled away. They go in one wagon; another is laden with boxes [of valuables?] and pillows, a third with gold pennies. She asks, Where is your house? Over those hills, he answers. He takes her over a high bridge, and throws her into the Donau, with, Swim, since you were not acquainted with our way, our faith! Six additional copies (in two of which the girl is a Jewess), Kolberg, *Pokucie*, II, 20–25, Nos 21–26.

White Russian versions of the ballad of the Jewess are found in Šejn, I, 1, 490f, Nos 604, 605; Romanov, I, II, 199, No 46.

French. This ballad is well known in France, and is generally found in a form resembling the English; that is to say, the scene of the attempted murder is the sea or a river (as in no other but the Polish), and the lady delivers herself by an artifice. One French version nearly approaches Polish **O–CC**.

A. 'Renauld et ses quatorze Femmes,' 44vv, Puymaigre, *Chants populaires recueillis dans le pays messin*, No 31, I, 140; 'Renaud et ses Femmes,' *Revue des Traditions Populaires*, VI, 34. Renauld carried off the king's daughter. When they were gone half-way, she called to him that she was dying of hunger (cf. German **A–F**). Eat your hand, he answered, for you will never eat bread again. When they had come to the middle of the wood, she called out that she was dying of thirst. Drink your blood, he said, for you will never drink wine again. When they came to the edge of the wood, he said, Do you see that river? Fourteen dames have been drowned there, and you shall be the fifteenth. When they came to the riverbank, he bade her put off her cloak, her shift. It is not for knights, she said, to see ladies in such plight; they should bandage their eyes with a handkerchief. This Renauld did, and the fair one threw him into the river. He laid hold of a branch; she cut it off with his sword (cf. the Polish ballad, where the catastrophe, and consequently this act, is reversed). "What will they say if you go back without your lover?" "I will tell them that I did for you what you meant to do for me."* "Reach me your hand; I will marry you Sunday."

"Marry, marry a fish, Renauld,
The fourteen women down below."

B. 'De Dion et de la Fille du Roi,' from Auvergne, Ampère, *Instructions, etc.*, 40 vv, p. 40, stanzas 15–24, the first fourteen constituting another ballad.[†] The pair went five or six leagues without exchanging a word; only the fair one said, I am so hungry I could eat my fist. Eat it, replied Dion, for you never again will eat bread. Then they went five or six leagues in silence, save that she said, I am so thirsty I could drink my blood. "Drink it, for you never will drink wine. Over there is a pond in which fifteen ladies have had a bath, have drowned themselves, and you will make sixteen." Arrived at the pond, he orders her to take off her clothes. She tells him to put his sword under his feet, his cloak before his face, and turn to the pond; and, when he has done so, pushes him in. Here are my keys! he cries. "I don't want them; I will find locksmiths." "What will your friends say?" "I will tell them I did by you as you would have done by me."

---

* 'De achte de soll Helena sin'
De achte de most he sölwer sin.'
German **A b** 13.
[†] Another version of this double ballad, but much corrupted in the second part, was known to Gérard de Nerval. See *Les Filles du Feu, Œuvres Complètes*, v, 132.
In *Poésies pop. de la France*, MS., VI, 278, Poésies pop. de la Corrèze, a ballad called 'Chanson du brave Altizar' is mentioned as a variant of 'Dion et la Fille da Roi,' and, fol. 321 of the same volume, a version from Mortain, *Basse Normandie*, is said to have been communicated, which, however, I have not found.
Another variety of **A** in *Revue des Traditions populaires*, II, 293, communicated by A. Gittée, *Chanson wallonne, de Bliquy, environs d'Ath*.

C. 'Veux-tu venir, bell' Jeanneton,' 32 vv, from Poitou and Aunis, Bujeaud, II, 232. When [43] they reach the water, the fair one asks for a drink. The man says, incoherently enough, Before drinking of this white wine I mean to drink your blood. The stanza that should tell how many have been drowned before is lost. Jeanneton, having been ordered to strip, pushes the "beau galant" into the sea, while, at her request, he is pulling off her stockings. He catches at a branch; she cuts it off, and will not hear to his entreaties.

D. 'En revenant de la jolie Rochelle,' twelve two-line stanzas, Gagnon, *Chansons populaires du Canada*, p. 155. A cavalier meets three fair maids, mounts the fairest behind him, and rides a hundred leagues without speaking to her, at the end of which she asks to drink. He takes her to a spring, but when there she does not care to drink. The rest of the ballad is pointless, and shows that the original story has been completely forgotten. Also in *Poésies populaires de la France*, IV, fol. 332, Chanson de l'Aunis, Charente Inférieur; but even more of the story is lost.

E. 'Belle, allons nous épromener,' from the Lyonnais, 28 vv, Champfleury, *Chansons des Provinces*, p. 172 = Guillon, *Chansons pop. de l'Ain*, p. 85 is like **C**, but still more defective. The pair go to walk by "la mer courante." There is no order for the lady to strip: on the contrary, she cries, Déshabillez-moi, déchaussez-moi! and, while the man is drawing off her shoe, "la belle avance un coup de pied, le beau galant tombe dans l'eau."

F. 'Allons, mie, nous promener,' 32 vv, *Poésies populaires de la France*, MS., III, fol. 84, No 16, is like **C**. The lady asks the man to pull off her shoes before he kills her. The man clutches a branch; the woman cuts it away.

G. 'Le Traître Noyé,' *Chants pop. du Velay et du Forez*, Romania, x, 199, is like **E**, **F**.

H. 'La Fillette et le Chevalier,' Victor Smith, Chants pop. du Velay et du Forez, *Romania*, x, 198, resembles the common Polish ballad. Pierre rouses his love early in the morning, to take a ride with him. He mounts her on his horse, and when they come to a lonesome wood bids her alight, for it is the last of her days. He plunges his sword into her heart, and throws her into a river. Her father and mother come searching for her, and are informed of her fate by a shepherdess, who had witnessed the murder. The youngest of her three brothers plunges into the water, exclaiming, Who threw you in? An angel descends and tells him it was her lover. A less romantic version, described in a note, treats of a valet who is tired of an amour with a servant-girl. He is judicially condemned to be hanged or burned.

I. 'Monsieur de Savigna,' Decombe, Chansons pop. d'Ille-et-Vilaine, p. 264, No 92. The ballad begins like A, B, but the conclusion is inverted. The fair one is thrown into a pond; M. Savigna cuts away with his sword the plant she seizes when she comes up from the bottom the fourth time; she asks, If you ever go back, where will you say you left me? and he answers, In the big wood full of robbers.

'La Fille de Saint-Martin de l'Ile,' Bujeaud, II, 226, has the conclusion of the third class of German ballads. A mother incites her son to make away with his wife. He carries her off on his horse to a wheat-field [wood], and kills her with sword and dagger. Returning, he meets his wife's brother, who asks why his shoes are covered with blood. He says he has been killing rabbits. The brother replies, I see by your paleness that you have been killing my sister. So Gérard de Nerval, Les Filles du Feu, OEuvres Com., v, 134; La Bohème galante (1866), p. 79: 'Rosine,' Chants pop. du Velay, etc., Romania, x, 197; and 'Le Mari Assassin,' Chanson du pays de Caux, Revue des Traditions Populaires, IV, 133.

'Le Voleur des Crêpes,' Sébillot, Contes pop. de la Haute-Bretagne, I, 341, No 62 is more like the German first class. A robber has his hand cut off by a girl. Later he marries her. The day after the marriage they go on horseback to see his relations. On coming to a wood he says, Do you remember the night when you cut off my hand? It is now my turn. He orders her to strip, threatening her with his dagger. When she is in her shift, she begs him to turn away his eyes, seizes the dagger, and cuts his throat.

'Lou Cros dé Proucinello,' Daymard, Vieux Chants p. recueillis en Quercy, p. 130, has at the end two traits of this ballad. A young man carries off a girl whom he has been in love with

seven years; he throws her into a ravine; as she falls, she catches at a tree; he cuts it away; she cries, What shall I do with my pretty gowns? and is answered, Give them to me for another mistress. Cf. also Daymard, p. 128.

The ballad is known over all **North Italy,** and always nearly in one shape.

A. 'Monchisa,' sixty-four short verses, Bernoni, Canti popolari veneziani, Puntata v, No 2. A count's son asks Monchesa, a knight's daughter, in marriage in the evening, espouses her in the morning, and immediately carries her off. When they are "half-way," she heaves a sigh, which she says is for father and mother, whom she shall no more see. The count points out his castle; he has taken thirty-six maids there, robbed them of their honor, and cut off their heads. "So will I do with you when we are there." The lady says no word till she is asked why she is silent; then requests the count to lend her his sword; she wishes to cut a branch to shade her horse. The moment she gets the sword in her hand, she plunges it into his heart; then throws the body into a ditch. On her way back, she meets her brother, whom she tells that she is looking after the assassins who have killed her husband. He fears it was she; this she denies, but afterwards says she must go to Rome to confess a great sin. There she obtains prompt absolution.

B. 'La Figlia del Conte,' Adolf Wolf, Volks-[144 lieder aus Venetien, No 73, a, 34vv, b, 48vv. Here it is the daughter of a count that marries Malpreso, the son of a knight. He takes her to France immediately. She goes sixty miles (b) without speaking. She confesses to her brother what she has done.

C. Righi, Canti popolari veronesi, 58vv, No 94*, p. 30. The count's son marries Mampresa, a knight's daughter. For thirty-six miles she does not speak; after five more she sighs. She denies to her brother having killed her husband, but still says she must go to the pope to confess an old sin; then owns what she has done.

D. 'La Monferrina,' 48vv, Nigra, Canzoni popolari del Piemonte, in Rivista Contemporanea, XXIV, 76. The lady is a Monferrina, daughter of a knight. After the marriage they travel fifty miles without speaking to one another. Fifty-two Monferrine have lost their heads; the bridegroom does not say why. She goes to the Pope to confess.

Nigra, *Canti popolari del Piemonte*, 1888, p. 90ff, No 13, 'Un' Eroina,' gives five unpublished versions (B–F), 'La Monferrina,' D, being A of this large and beautiful collection.

E. 'La Vendicatrice,' an incomplete copy from Alexandria, 18vv only, Marcoaldi, *Canti popolari*, No 12, p. 166, like D, as far as it goes. Thirty-three have been beheaded before.

F. 'La Inglese,' 40vv, Ferraro, *Canti popolari di Ferrara, Cento e Pontelagoscuro*, No 2, p. 14. The count's son marries an English girl, daughter of a knight. She never speaks for more than three hundred miles; after two hundred more she sighs. She denies having killed her husband; has not a heart of that kind.

G. 'La Liberatrice,' 24vv, Ferraro, *Canti popolari monferrini*, No 3, p. 4. Gianfleisa is the lady's name. When invited to go off, she says, If you wish me to go, lend me a horse. Not a word is spoken for five hundred miles. The man (Gilardu) points out his castle, and says that no one he has taken there has ever come back. Gianfleisa goes home without meeting anybody.

'Laura,' Ferraro, *C. p. di Pontelagoscuro, Rivista di Filologia romanza*, II, 197, and *C. p. di Ferrara, etc.*, p. 86, is a mixture of this ballad with another. Cf. 'La Maledetta,' Ferraro, *C. p. monferrini*, No 27, p. 35.

A ballad in Casetti e Imbriani, *C. p. delle Provincie meridionali*, II, 1, begins like 'La Contadina alla Fonte' (see p. 521), and ends like 'La Monferrina Incontaminata.' Of the same class as the last is Nannarelli, *Studio comparativo sui Canti popolari di Arlena*, p. 51, No 50 (Köhler), which is like 'La Monferrina incontaminata.'*

Several other French and Italian ballads have common points with Renauld, Monchisa, etc., and for this have sometimes been improp-

erly grouped with them: e.g., 'La Fille des Sables,' Bujeaud, II, 177ff. A girl sitting by the water-side hears a sailor sing, and asks him to teach her the song. He says, Come aboard, and I will. He pushes off, and by and by she begins to weep.† She says, My father is calling me to supper. "You will sup with me." "My mother is calling me to bed." "You will sleep with me." They go a hundred leagues, and not a word said, and at last reach his father's castle. When she is undressing, her lace gets into a knot. He suggests that his sword would cut it. She plunges the sword into her heart. So 'Du Beau Marinier,' Beaurepaire, p. 57f, and *Poésies populaires de la France*, MS., III, fol. 59, No 4; 'L'Épée Libératrice,' V. Smith, Chansons du Velay, etc., *Romania*, VII, 69, nearly; also 'Il Corsaro,' Nigra, *Rivista Contemporanea*, XXIV, p. 86ff, No 14, p. 106ff, with the addition of another version; 'El Mariner' and 'Giovanina,' Villanis, Canzoni p. Zaratine, in *Archivio*, XI, 33, 34, Nos 2, 3. In 'La Monferrina Incontaminata,' Ferraro, *C. p. m.*, No 2, p. 3; Nigra, 'La Fuga,' No 15, pp. 111ff; Finamore, in *Archivio*, I, 87, 'La Fandell' e lu Cavaljiere' (mixed); a French knight invites a girl to go off with him, and mounts her behind him. They ride five hundred miles without speaking,‡ then reach an inn, after which the story is the same. So Bernoni, Puntata IX, No 2. 'La Fille du Patissier,' Paymaigre, No 30, p. 93, has the same conclusion. All these, except 'La Fille des Sables,' make the girl ask for the sword herself, and in all it is herself that she kills.

---

† So far there is agreement in 'La Fille du Prince,' Paymaigre, No 32, p. 106; *Poésies pop. de la France*, MS., III, fol. 133.

‡ It is a commonplace for a pair on horseback to go a long way without speaking. So Pidal, pp. 114, 115, 130, 133, 135, 159:

> Siete leguas anduvieron
> sin hablar una palabra.

See also Munthe, *Folkpoesi från Asturien*, p. 118f, VII, A, 76f, B, 70f. ('Don Bueso,' Duran, I, lxv, no hablara la niña.) Dead lover and maid in Bartoš, *Nové Národne písně moravské*, p. 150. Lagus, *Nyländska Folkvisor*, 'Kung Valdemo' (= Ribold), No 1, a, 28, b, 18, 'Kämpen Grimborg,' No 3, a, 21, b, 19.

---

* To these should be added: Canti popolari Emiliani by Maria Carmi, *Archivio*, XII, 178, No 2; 'La bella Inglese,' Salvadori, in *Giornale di Filologia Romanza*, II, 201; 'Un' eroina,' A. Giannini, Canzoni del Contado di Massa Lunense, No 1, *Archivio*, VIII, 273; ['Montiglia'], ['Inglesa'], Bolognini, *Annuario degli Alpinisti Tridentini*, XIII, Usi e Costumi del Trentino, 1888, p. 37f; Giannini, *Canti p. della Montagna Lucchese*, 1889, p. 143, 'La Liberatrice;' Finamore, Storie p. abruzzesi, in *Archivio*, I, 207, 'Lu Pringepe de Meláne.'

The **Spanish** preserves this ballad in a single form, the earliest printed in any language, preceding, by a few years, even the German broadsides **G, H.**

'Romance de Rico Franco,' 36vv, "Cancionero de Romances, s. a., fol. 191: Canc. de Rom., ed. de 1550, fol. 202: ed. de 1555, fol. 296;" Wolf and Hofmann, *Primavera*, No 119, II, 22: Duran, No 296, I, 160: Grimm, p. 252: Depping and Galiano, 1844, II, 167: Ochoa, p. 7: 'La Princesa Isabel,' Pidal, *Romancero Asturiano*, p. 350 (sung by children as an accompaniment to a game). The king's huntsmen got no game, and lost the falcons. They betook them[45] selves to the castle of Maynes, where was a beautiful damsel, sought by seven counts and three kings. Rico Franco of Aragon carried her off by force. Nothing is said of a rest in a wood, or elsewhere; but that something has dropped out here is shown by the corresponding Portuguese ballad. The lady wept. Rico Franco comforted her thus: If you are weeping for father and mother, you shall never see them more; and if for your brothers, I have killed them all three. I am not weeping for them, she said, but because I know not what my fate is to be. Lend me your knife to cut the fringes from my mantle, for they are no longer fit to wear. This Rico Franco did, and the damsel thrust the knife into his breast. Thus she avenged father, mother, and brothers.

Nos 38–41, 'Venganza de Honor,' No 42, 'La Hija de la Viudina,' Pidal, *Asturian Romances*, have the incident of the girl's killing with his own sword or dagger a caballero who offers her violence. The weapon is dropped in the course of a struggle in all but No 40; in this the damsel says, Give me your sword, and see how I would wear it.

A **Portuguese** ballad has recently been obtained from tradition in the island of St. George, Azores, which resembles the Spanish closely, but is even curter: **A**, 'Romance de Dom Franco,' 30vv; **B**, 'Dona Inez,' a fragment of 18vv; Braga, *Cantos populares do Archipelago açoriano*, No 48, p. 316, No 49, p. 317: Hartung's *Romanceiro*, II, 61, 63; **C**, **D**, in Alvaro Rodrigues de Azevedo, *Romanceiro do Archipelago da Madeira*, p. 57, 'Estoria do Bravo-Franco,' p. 60, 'Gallo-frango;' **E**, 'O caso de D. Ignez,'

Braga, *Ampliações so Romanceiro das Ilhas dos Açores, Revista Lusitana*, I, 103. Dona Inez was so precious in the eyes of her parents that they gave her neither to duke nor marquis. A knight who was passing [the Duke of Turkey, **B**] took a fancy to her, and stole her away. When they came to the middle of the mountain ridge on which Dona Inez lived, the knight stopped to rest, and she began to weep. From this point Portuguese **A**, and **B** so far as it is preserved, agree very nearly with the Spanish.[*]

Certain **Breton** ballads have points of contact with the Halewyn-Ulinger class, but, like the French and Italian ballads mentioned on the preceding page, have more important divergences, and especially the characteristic distinction that the woman kills herself to preserve her honor. 1. 'Jeanne Le Roux,' Luzel, I, 324ff, in two versions; *Poésies pop. de la France*, MS., III, fol. 182. The sieur La Tremblaie attempts the abduction of Jeanne from the church immediately after her marriage ceremony. As he is about to compel her to get up on the crupper of his horse, she asks for a knife to cut her bridal girdle, which had been drawn too tight. He gives her the choice of three, and she stabs herself in the heart. La Tremblaie *remarks*, I have carried off eighteen young brides, and Jeanne is the nineteenth, words evidently taken from the mouth of a Halewyn, and not belonging here. 2. Le Marquis de Coatredrez, Luzel, I, 336ff, meets a young girl on the road, going to the pardon of Guéodet, and forces her on to his horse. On the way and at his house she vainly implores help. He takes her to the garden to gather flowers. She asks for his knife to shorten the stems, and kills herself. Early in the morning the door of the château is broken in by Kerninon, foster-brother of the victim, who forces Coatredrez to fight, and runs him through. 3. 'Rozmelchon,' Luzel, I, 308ff, in three versions, and, 4, 'La Filleule de du Guesclin,' Villemarqué, *Barzaz-Breiz*, 6th ed., 212ff, are very like 2. The wicked Rozmelchon is

---

[*] The Asturian romance communicated in two copies by Amador de los Rios to *Jahrbuch für rom. u. eng. Literatur*, III, 285, No 2, and the Portuguese 'Romance de Romeirinha,' Braga, *Romanceiro*, No 9, p. 24, 'A Romeira,' Almeida-Garrett, III, 11, are not parallels, though they have been cited as such.

burned in his château in Luzel's first copy; the other two do not bring him to punishment. Villemarqué's villain is an Englishman, and has his head cloven by du Guesclin. 5. 'Marivonnic,' Luzel, I, 350ff; Quellien, *Chansons et Danses des Bretons*, 1889, p. 99, a pretty young girl, is carried off by an English vessel, the captain of which shows himself not a whit behind the feudal seigneurs in ferocity. The young girl throws herself into the water.

Magyar. Five versions from recent traditions, all of them interesting, are given in Arany and Gyulai's collection of Hungarian popular poetry, 'Molnár Anna,' I, 137ff, Nos 1–5.* —**A**, p. 141, No 3. A man, nameless here, but called in the other versions Martin Ajgó, or Martin Sajgó, invites Anna Miller to go off with him. She refuses; she has a young child and a kind husband. "Come," he says; "I have six palaces, and will put you in the seventh," and persists so long that he prevails at last. They went a long way, till they came to the middle of a green wood. He asked her to sit down in the shade of a branchy tree (so all); he would lie in her lap, and she was to look into his head (a point found in all the copies). But look not up into the tree, he said. He went to sleep (so **B, D**); she looked up into the tree, and saw six fair maids hanging there (so all but **E**). She thought to herself, He will make me the seventh! (also **B, D**). A tear fell on the face of the "brave sir," and waked him. You have looked up into the tree, he said. "No, but three orphans passed, and I thought of my child." He bade her go up into the tree. She was not used to go first, she said. He led the way. She seized the opportunity, tore his sword from its sheath (so **C**), and hewed off his head. She then wrapped herself in his cloak, sprang upon his horse, and returned home, where (in all the copies, as in this) she effected a reconcilement with her husband. **B**, p. 138, No 2, agrees

closely with the foregoing. Martin Ajgó calls to Anna Miller to come with him a long way into the wilderness (so **D, E**). He boasts of no palaces in this version. He calls Anna a long time, tempts her a long time, drags her onto his horse, and carries her off. The scene under the tree is repeated. Anna pretends (so **D, E**) that the tear which drops on Martin's face is dew from the tree, and he retorts, How can it be dew from the tree, when the time is high noon? His sword falls out of its sheath as he is mounting the tree, and he asks her to hand it to him. She throws it up (so **E**), and it cuts his throat in two. Rightly served, Martin Ajgó, she says: why did you lure me from home? **C**, p. 144, No 4. Martin Sajgó tells Anna Miller that he has six stone castles, and is building a seventh. It is not said that he goes to sleep. As in **A**, Anna pulls his sword from the scabbard. **D**, p. 146, No 5. Here reappears the very important feature of the wonderland: "Come, let us go, Anna Miller, a long journey into the wilderness, to a place that flows with milk and honey." Anna insists, as before, that Martin shall go up the tree first. He puts down his sword; she seizes it, and strikes off his head with one blow. **E**, p. 137, No 1, is somewhat defective, but agrees essentially with the others. Martin Ajgó calls Anna; she will not come; he carries her off. He lets his sword fall as he is climbing, and asks Anna to hand it up to him. She throws it up, as in **B**, and it cuts his back in two.

Neus, in his *Ehstnische Volkslieder*, maintains the affinity of 'Kallewisohnes Tod,' No 2, p. 5, with the Ulinger ballads, and even of his Holepi with the Dutch Halewyn. The resemblance is of the most distant, and what there is must be regarded as casual. The same of the Finnish 'Kojoins Sohn,' Schröter, *Finnische Runen*, p. 114, 115; 'Kojosen Poika,' Lönnrot, *Kanteletar*, p. 279.

A story from Neumünster about one Görtmicheel, a famous robber, in Müllenhoff, p. 37, No 2, blends features of 'Hind Etin,' or 'The Maid and the Dwarf-King,' No 41, with others found in the Magyar ballad. A handsome wench, who had been lost seven years, suddenly reappeared at the home of her parents. She said that she was not at liberty to explain where she had been, but her mother induced her to reveal

---

* *Magyar Népköltési Gyüjtemény. Uj Folyam, szerkesztik és kiadják Arany László és Gyulai Pál.* Collection of Magyar Popular Poetry, New Series, Pest, 1872, 2 vols. Aigner has blended Nos 4 and 3 (**C, A**) in 'Martin und Aennchen,' *Ungarische Volksdichtungen*, p. 170, and has translated No 1 (**E**), at p. 120, 'Molnár Anna,' in each case obscuring or omitting one or two traits which are important for a comparative view.

this to a stone near the side-door, and taking her station behind the door heard all. She had been carried off by a robber; had lived with him seven years, and borne him seven children. The robber, who had otherwise treated her well, had refused to let her visit her home, but finally had granted her this permission upon her promising to say nothing about him. When the time arrived for her daughter to go back, the mother gave her a bag of peas, which she was to drop one by one along the way. She was kindly received, but presently the robber thought there was something strange in her ways. He laid his head in her lap, inviting her to perform the service so common in like cases. While she was doing this, she could not but think how the robber had loved her and how he was about to be betrayed by her, and her remorseful tears dropped on his face. "So you have told of me!" cried the astute robber, springing up. He cut off the children's heads and strung them on a willow-twig before her eyes, and was now coming to her, when people arrived, under the mother's conduct, who put a stop to his further revenge, and took their own. See the note, Müllenhoff, p. 592f.

In places where a ballad has once been known, the story will often be remembered after the verses have been wholly or partly forgotten, and the ballad will be resolved into a prose tale, retaining, perhaps, some scraps of verse, and not infrequently taking up new matter, or blending with other traditions. Naturally enough, a ballad and an equivalent tale sometimes exist side by side. It has already been mentioned that Jamieson, who had not found this ballad in Scotland, had often come upon the story in the form of a tale interspersed with verse. Birlinger at one time (1860) had not been able to obtain the ballad in the Swabian Oberland (where it has since been found in several forms), but only a story agreeing essentially with the second class of German ballads. According to this tradition, a robber, who was at the same time a portentous magician, enticed the twelve daughters of a miller, one after another, into a wood, and hanged eleven of them on a tree, but was arrested by a hunter, the brother of the twelve, before he could dispatch the last, and was handed over to justice.

The object of the murders was to obtain blood for magical purposes. This story had, so to speak, naturalized itself in the locality, and the [47] place where the robber's house had been and that where the tree had stood were pointed out. The hunter-brother was by some conceived of as the Wild Huntsman, and came to the rescue through the air with a fearful baying of dogs. (Birlinger in Volksthümliches aus Schwaben, I, 368, No 592, and Germania, 1st Ser., v, 372.)

The story of the German ballad **P** has attached itself to localities in the neighborhood of Weissenbach, Aargau, and is told with modifications that connect it with the history of the Guggi-, or Schongauer-, bad. A rich man by lewd living had become a leper. The devil put it into his head that he could be cured by bathing in the blood of twelve [seven] pure maidens. He seized eleven at a swoop, while they were on their way to church, and hanged them, and the next day enticed away a miller's daughter, who was delivered from death as in the ballad. A medicinal spring rose near the fatal tree. (Rochholz, I, 22.) No pure version of this ballad has been obtained in the Harz region, though a mixed form has already been spoken of; but 'Der Reiter in Seiden,' Pröhle, Märchen für die Jugend, No 32, p. 136, which comes from the western Harz, or from some place further north, on the line between Kyffhäuser and Hamburg, is, roughly speaking, only 'Gert Olbert' turned into prose, with a verse or two remaining. 'Der betrogene Betrüger,' from Mühlbach, Müller's Siebenbürgische Sagen, No 418, p. 309, has for its hero a handsome young man, addicted to women, who obtains from the devil the power of making them follow his piping, on the terms that every twelfth soul is to be the devil's share. He had taken eleven to a wood, and hanged them on a tree after he had satisfied his desire. The brother of a twelfth substituted himself for his sister, dressed in her clothes, snatched the rope from the miscreant, and ran him up on the nearest bough; upon which a voice was heard in the wind, that cried The twelfth soul is mine. Grundtvig, in his Engelske og skotske Folkeviser, p. 249, gives his recollections of a story that he had heard in his youth which has a catastrophe resembling that of English **C–F**. A charcoal burner had a way of taking up women beside him on his wagon, and driving them into a wood, where he forced them to take off their clothes, then killed them, and sunk them with heavy stones in a deep moss. At last a girl whom he had carried off in this way got the advantage of him by inducing him to turn away while she was undressing, and then pushing him into the moss. Something similar is found in the conclusion of a robber story in Grundtvig's *Danske Folkeminder*, 1861, No 30, p. 108, and in a modern Danish ballad cited in *Danmarks gamle Folkeviser*, iv, 24, note.**

Another Transylvanian tale, Schuster, p. 433, has a fountain, a thirsty bride, and doves (two or three) that sing to her, traits which have perhaps been derived from some Ulinger ballad; but the fountain is of an entirely different character, and the doves serve a different purpose. The tale is a variety of 'Fitchers Vogel,' Grimms, No 46, and belongs to the class of stories to which 'Bluebeard,' from its extensive popularity, has given name. The magician of 'Fitcher's Vogel' and of 'Bluebeard' becomes, or remains, a preternatural being (a hill-man) further north, as in Grundtvig's *Gamle danske Minder*, 1857, No 312, p. 182. There is a manifest affinity between these three species of tales and our ballad (also between the German and Danish tales and the Scandinavian ballad of 'Rosmer'), but the precise nature of this affinity it is impossible to expound. 'Bluebeard,' 'La Barbe Bleue,' Perrault, *Histoires on Contes du temps passé*, 1697, p. 57 (Lefèvre), has a special resemblance to the German ballads of the second class in the four calls to sister Anne, which represent the cries to father, mother, and brother, and agrees with these ballads as to the means by which the death of the malefactor is brought about.

Looking back now over the whole field covered by this ballad, we observe that the framework of the story is essentially the same in English, Dutch, Danish, Swedish, Norwegian; in the first class of the German ballads; in Polish **A**; in French, Italian, Spanish, Portuguese, and Magyar. The woman delivers herself from death by some artifice,[*] and retaliates upon the man the destruction he had intended for her. The second form of the German ballad attributes the deliverance of the woman to her

brother, and also the punishment of the murderer. The third form of the German ballad makes the woman lose her life, and her murderer, for the most part, to suffer the penalty of the law, though in some cases the brother takes immediate vengeance. Polish **B–K** may be ranked with the second German class, and **O–CC** still better with the third; but the brother appears in only a few of these, and, when he appears, counts for nothing. The Wendish and the Bohemian ballad have the incident of fraternal vengeance, though otherwise less like the German. The Servian ballad, a slight thing at best, is still less like, but ranks with the third German class. The oldest Icelandic copy is altogether anomalous, and also incomplete, but seems to imply the death of the woman: later copies suffer the woman to escape, without vengeance upon the murderer.

It is quite beyond question that the third class of German ballad is a derivation from the second,[†] Of the versions **T–Z**, **Z** alone has preserved clear traits of the marvellous. A king's daughter is enticed from home by Ulrich's singing, and is warned of her impending fate by the dove, as in Class II. The other ballads have the usual marks of degeneracy, a dropping or obscuring of marvellous and romantic incidents, and a declension in the rank and style of the characters. **T**, to be sure, has a hazel, and **Y** a tree-stump and a spring, and in **T** Ulrich offers to teach Ännchen bird-song, but these traits have lost all significance. Knight and lady sink to ordinary man and maid; for though in **Y** the woman is called a king's daughter, the opening stanzas of **Y** are borrowed from a different ballad. Ulrich retains so much of the knight that he rides to Ännchen's house, in the first stanza of **T**, but he apparently goes on foot with her to the wood, and this is the rule in all the other ballads of this class. As Ulrich has lost his

---

[*] Very little remains of the artifice in Polish **A**. The idea seems to be that the girl pretends to be curious about the sword in order to get it into her hands. But the whole story is told in ten stanzas.

[†] I accept and repeat Grundtvig's views as to the relation of the three forms of the story. And with regard to the history of the ballad generally, this is but one of many cases in which much or most of the work had been done to my hand in *Danmarks gamle Folkeviser*.

horse, so the brother, in **T, U, V, X**, has lost his sword, or the use of it, and in all these (also, superfluously, in **W**) Ulrich, like a common felon as he was, is broken on the wheel.

That the woman should save her life by her own craft and courage is certainly a more primitive conception than that she should depend upon her brother, and the priority of this arrangement of the plot is supported, if not independently proved, by the concurrence, as to this point, of so many copies among so many nations, as also by the accordance of various popular tales. The second German form must therefore, so far forth, be regarded as a modification of the first. Among the several devices, again, which the woman employs in order to get the murderer into her power, the original would seem to be her inducing him to lay his head in her lap, which gives her the opportunity (by the use of charms or runes, in English **A**, Danish **G**, Norwegian **F, H**, and one form of **B**) to put him into a deep sleep. The success of this trick no doubt implies considerable simplicity on the part of the victim of it; not more, however, than is elsewhere witnessed in preternatural beings, whose wits are frequently represented as no match for human shrewdness. Some of the Scandinavian ballads are not liable to the full force of this objection, whatever that may be, for they make the knight express a suspicion of treachery, and the lady solemnly asseverate that she will not kill [fool, beguile] him in his sleep. And so, when he is fast bound, she cries out, Wake up, for I will not kill thee *in thy sleep!* This last circumstance is wanting in hardly any of the Scandinavian ballads, whereas the previous compact is found only in Danish **E, F, G, H, L**, Swedish **A**, Norwegian **A**, and the Icelandic ballad. Not occurring in any of the older Danish copies, it may be that [49] the compact is an after-thought, and was inserted to qualify the improbability. But the lady's equivocation is quite of a piece with Memering's oath in 'Ravengaard and Memering,' Grundtvig, No 13, and King Dietrich's in the Dietrichsaga, Unger, c. 222, p. 206.[*]

English **A** and all the Danish, Swedish, and Norwegian ballads employ the stratagem of lulling the man to sleep, but these are not the only ballads in which the man lays his head in the woman's lap. This trait is observed in nearly all German ballads of the second and third class, in all the well-preserved ones, and also in the Magyar ballad. With regard to the German ballads, however, it is purposeless (for it does not advance the action of the drama in the least), and must be regarded as a relic of an earlier form.[†] English **B–F** and all the French ballads dispose of the traitor by a watery death. The scene is shifted from a wood to a sea-coast, pool, or river bank, perhaps to suit the locality to which the ballad had wandered. In English **B**, where, apparently under the influence of other ballads,[‡] the lady is forced to wade into water up to her chin, the knight is pushed off his horse when bending over to give a last kiss for which he had been asked; in English **C–F** and French **A, B**, the man is induced to turn his face to save the woman's modesty; in French **C–E** he is made to pull off her stockings or shoes, and then, while off his guard, pitched into a sea or river. This expedient is sufficiently trivial; but still more so, and grazing on the farcical, is that which is made use of in the Dutch ballad and those of the German first class, the woman's persuading the man to take off his fine coat lest it should be spattered with her blood, and cutting off his head with his own sword while he is thus occupied. The Spanish and Portuguese ballads make the lady borrow the knight's knife to remove some of the trimming of her dress, and in the Italian she borrows his sword to cut a bough to shade her horse; for in Italian the halt in the wood is completely forgotten, and the last half of the action takes place on horseback. All these contrivances

---

[*]   Memering was required by his adversary to swear that he knew not of the sword Adelring, and took his oath that he knew of nothing but the hilt being above ground, which was accepted as satisfactory. Presently he pulls Adelring out of the ground, into which he had thrust the blade, and, being accused of perjury, triumphantly rejoins that he had sworn that he knew of nothing but the hilt *being above ground*. Dietrich does the same in his duel with Sigurd Swain.

[†]   Magyar **A** is entirely peculiar. Apparently the man lays his head in the woman's lap that he may know, by the falling of her tears, when she has disobeyed his command not to look into the tree. This is like 'Bluebeard,' and rather subtle for a ballad.

[‡]   'Child Waters,' 'The Fair Flower of Northumberland.'

plainly have less claim to be regarded as primary than that of binding the murderer after he has been put to sleep.

The knight in English **A** is called an Elf, and as such is furnished with an enchanting horn, which is replaced by a harp of similar properties in **B**, where, however, the male personage has neither name nor any kind of designation. The elf-horn of English **A** is again represented by the seductive song of the Dutch ballad and of German **G–R** and **Z**. Though the lady is not lured away in the Scandinavian ballads by irresistible music,[*] Danish **A**, **E**, Norwegian **A**, 13, and Swedish **D** present to her the prospect of being taken to an elf-land, or elysium, and there are traces of this in Danish **G** and **D** also, and in Polish **Q**. The tongue that talks after the head is off, in the Dutch ballad and in German **A**, **B**, **C**, **E**, is another mark of an unearthly being. Halewyn, Ulver, Gert Olbert, like the English knight, are clearly supernatural, though of a nondescript type. The elf in English **A** is not to be interpreted too strictly, for the specific elf is not of a sanguinary turn, as these so conspicuously are. He is comparatively innocuous, like the hill-man Young Akin, in another English ballad, who likewise entices away a woman by magical music, but only to make her his wife. But the elf-knight and the rest seem to delight in bloodshed for its own sake; for, as Grundtvig has pointed out, there is no other apparent motive for murder in English **A**, **B**, the Norwegian ballads, Danish **A**, Swedish **A**, **B**, or German **A–E**.[†] This is true again, for one reason or another, of others of the German ballads, of the French, of most of the Italian, and of the Hungarian ballads.

The nearest approach to the Elf-knight, Halewyn, etc., is perhaps Quintalin, in the saga of Samson the Fair. He was son of the miller Galin. Nobody knew who his mother was, but many were of the mind that Galin might have had him of a "goddess," an elf or troll woman, who lived under the mill force. He was a thief, and lay in the woods; was versed in many knave's tricks, and had also acquired agreeable arts. He was a great master of the harp, and would decoy women into the woods with his playing, keep them as long as he liked, and send them home pregnant to their fathers or husbands. A king's daughter, Valentina, is drawn on by his music deep into the woods, but is rescued by a friendly power. Some parts of her dress and ornaments, which she had laid off in her rapid following up of the harping, are afterwards found, with a great quantity of precious things, in the subaqueous cave of Quintalin's mother, who is a complete counterpart to Grendel's, and was probably borrowed from Beówulf.[‡] This demi-elf Quintalin is a tame personage by the side of Grendel or of Halewyn. Halewyn does not devour his victims, like Grendel: Quintalin does not even murder his. He allures women with his music to make them serve his lust. We may infer that he would plunder them, for he is a notorious thief. Even two of the oldest Danish ballads, **B**, **C**, and again Danish **I** and Swedish **C**, make the treacherous knight as lecherous as bloody, and so with German **J**, **K**, **L**, **O**, **P**, **Q**, **R**, **S**, and Italian **A**, **B**, **C**, **E**, **F**. This trait is wanting in Danish **D**, where, though traces of the originally demonic nature of the knight remain, the muckle gold of the maids already appears as the motive for the murders. In the later Danish **E– H**, **K**, **L**, and Swedish **C**, **D**, the original elf or demon has sunk to a remorseless robber, generally with brothers, sisters, or underlings for accomplices.[§] This is preëminently his character in English **C–F**, in nearly all the forty Polish

---

[*]   The murderer has a horn in Swedish **C**, **D**, as also in the Dutch Halewyn and the German **A**, **B**, **C**, **E**, and the horn may be of magical power, but it is not distinctly described as such.

[†]   The scenery of the halting-place in the wood—the bloody streams in Danish **A**, **B**, **D**, **H**, **L**, **K**, the blood-girt spring in German **H**, **J**, **K**, **L**, **O**, **P**, **Q**—is also, to say the least, suggestive of something horribly uncanny. These are undoubtedly ancient features, though the spring, as the Danish editor observes, has no longer any significance in the German ballads, because in all of them the previous victims are said to have been *hanged*.

[‡]   The saga in Björner's *Nordiska Kämpa Dater*, c. 5–7.

[§]   Danish **E**, **I**, **L**, and even **A**, make the knight suggest to the lady that she should get her gold together while he is saddling his horse; but this is a commonplace found in other cases of elopement, and *by itself* warrants no conclusion as to the knight's rapacity. See 'Samson,' Grundtvig, No 6, **C** 5; 'Ribold og Guldborg,' No 82, **C** 13, **E** 14, etc.; 'Redselille og Medelvold,' No 271, **A** 21, **B** 20; 272, Bilag 3, st. 8; 270, 18, etc.

ballads, and in the two principal ballads of the German second class, **G, H,** though English **D,** German **H,** and Polish **Q** retain a trace of the supernatural: the first in the charm by means of which the knight compels the maid to quit her parents, the second in the bloody spring, and the last in the golden mountains. There is nothing that unequivocally marks the robber in the other German ballads of the second class and in those of the third. The question 'Weinst du um deines Vaters Gut?' in **I–L, O–S, T–W,** is hardly decisive, and only in **W** and **Z** is it expressly said that the maid had taken valuable things with her (as in Swedish **D,** Norwegian **A, B,** English **D–F**). **J–L, O–S,** give us to understand that the lady had lost her honor,[*] but in all the rest, except the anomalous **Z,** the motive for murder is insufficient.[†]

The woman in these ballads is for the most part nameless, or bears a stock name to which no importance can be attached. Not so with the names of the knight. Most of these are [51] peculiar, and the Northern ones, though superficially of some variety, have yet likeness enough to tempt one to seek for a common original. Grundtvig, with considerable diffidence, suggests Oldemor as a possible ground-

form. He conceives that the R of some of the Scandinavian names may be a relic of a foregoing Herr. The initial H would easily come or go. Given such a name as Hollemen (Danish **C**), we might expect it to give place to Halewyn, which is both a family and a local name in Flanders, if the ballad should pass into the Low Countries from Denmark, a derivation that Grundtvig is far from asserting. So Ulinger, a local appellation, might be substituted for the Ulver of Danish **A.** Grundtvig, it must be borne in mind, declines to be responsible for the historical correctness of this genealogy, and would be still less willing to undertake an explanation of the name Oldemor.

In place of Oldemor, Professor Sophus Bugge, in a recent article, marked by his characteristic sharp-sightedness and ingenuity, has proposed Hollevern, Holevern, or Olevern as the base-form of all the Northern names for the bloody knight, and he finds in this name a main support for the entirely novel and somewhat startling hypothesis that the ballad we are dealing with is a wild shoot from the story of Judith and Holofernes.[‡] His argument, given as briefly as possible, is as follows.

That the Bible story was generally known in the Middle Ages no one would question. It was treated in a literary way by an Anglo-Saxon poet, who was acquainted with the scriptural narrative, and in a popular way by poets who had no direct acquaintance with the original.[§] The source of the story in the ballad must in any case be a tradition many times removed from the biblical story; that much should be changed, much dropped, and much added is only what would be expected.

Beginning the comparison with 'Judith' with this caution, it is first submitted that Holofernes can be recognized in most of the Scandinavian and German names of the knight. The v of the proposed base-form is preserved in Ulver, Halewyn, and probably in the English Elf-knight. It is easy to explain a v's

---

[*]　So perhaps a Polish ballad in Wójcicki, I, 38, akin to the other John and Katie ballads.

[†]　It is well known that in the Middle Ages the blood of children or of virgins was reputed a specific for leprosy (see, e.g., Cassel in the *Weimar Jahrbücher,* I, 408.) Some have thought to find in this fact an explanation of the murders in these ballads and in the Bluebeard stories, and, according to Rochholz, this theory has been adopted into popular tradition in the Aargau. So far as this cycle of ballads is concerned, there is as much ground for holding that the blood was wanted to cure leprosy as for believing that the gold was wanted for *aurum potabile.* As to this use of blood, cf. H. von Wlislocki, *Volksthümliches zum Armen Heinrich, Ztschr. f. deutsche Philologie;* 1890, XXIII, 217ff; *Notes and Queries,* 7th Series, VIII, 363. (G. L. K.) See also G. Rua, *Novelle del "Mambriano,"* pp. 84, 88ff. The story about Constantine's leprosy (*Reali di Francia,* lib. I, c. 1) occurs also in Higden's *Polychronicon,* Lumby, V, 122ff, and in Gower, *Confessio Amantis,* bk. II, Pauli, I, 266ff. See also Ben Jonson, *Discoveries,* ed. Schelling, p. 35 (G. L. K. and W. P. Few). [See Prym u. Socin, *Kurdische Sammlungen,* pp. 35, 36. H. von Wlislocki, M. u. S. der Bukowinaer u. Siebenbürger Armenier, pp. 60, 61. The latter gives a number of references for the story about Constantine. Cf. also Dames, Balochi Tales, No 2, in *Folk-Lore,* III, 518.]

[‡]　Det philologisk-historiske Samfunds Mindeskrift i Anledning af dets femogtyveaarige Virksomhed, 1854–79, Bidrag til den nordiske Balladedigtnings Historie, p. 75ff.

[§]　Bugge cites the Old German Judith, Müllenhoff u. Scherer, *Denkmäler,* 2d ed., No 37, p. 105, to show how the Bible story became modified under a popular treatment.

passing over to g, as in Ulinger, Adelger, and especially under the influence of the very common names in –ger. Again, v might easily become b, as in Olbert, or m, as in Hollemen, Olmor; and the initial R of Rulleman, Romor, etc., may have been carried over from a prefixed Herr.[*]

The original name of the heroine has been lost, and yet it is to be noticed that Gert Olbert's mother, in German **A**, is called Fru Jutte.

The heroine in this same ballad is named Helena (Linnich in **F**); in others (German **C**, **D**, **E**), Odilia. These are names of saints, and this circumstance may tend to show that the woman in the ballad was originally conceived of as rather a saint than a secular character, though in the course of time the story has so changed that the devout widow who sought out her country's enemy in his own camp has been transformed into a young maid who is enticed from home by a treacherous suitor.

It is an original trait in the ballad that the murderer, as is expressly said in many copies, is from a foreign land. According to an English version (**E**), he comes from the north, as Holofernes does, "venit Assur ex montibus ab aquilone" (Jud. xvi, 5).

The germ of this outlandish knight's bloodthirstiness is found in the truculent part that Holofernes plays in the Bible, his threats and devastations. That the false suitor appears without companions is in keeping with the ballad style of representation; yet we might find suggestions of the Assyrian's army in the swains, the brothers, the stable-boy, whom the maid falls in with on her way home.

The splendid promises made in many of the ballads might have been developed from the passage where Holofernes, whose bed is described as wrought with purple, gold, and precious stones, says to Judith, Thou shalt be great in the house of Nebuchadnezzar, and thy name shall be named in all the earth (xi, 21).

In many forms of the ballad, especially the Dutch and the German, the maid adorns herself splendidly, as Judith does: she even wears some sort of crown in Dutch **A** 16, German **D** 8, as Judith does in x, 3, xvi, 10 (mitram).

In the English **D**, **E**, **F**, the oldest Danish, **A**, and the Polish versions, the maid, like Judith, leaves her home in the night.

The Piedmontese casté, Italian **E** 1 [there is a castle in nearly all the Italian ballads, and also in Dutch **B**], may remind us of Holofernes' castra.

The knight's carrying off the maid, lifting her on to his horse in many copies, may well come from a misunderstanding of elevaverunt in Judith x, 20: Et cum in faciem ejus intendisset, adoravit eum, prosternens se super terram. Et elevaverunt eam servi Holofernis, jubente domino suo.[†]

In German **A** Gert Olbert and Helena are said to ride three days and nights, and in Danish **D** the ride is for three days; and we may remember that Judith killed Holofernes the fourth day after her arrival in his camp.

The place in which the pair alight is, according to German **G** 20, a deep dale, and this agrees with the site of Holofernes' camp in the valley of Bethulia. There is a spring or stream in many of the ballads, and also a spring in the camp, in which Judith bathes (xii, 7).

Most forms of the ballad make the knight, after the halt, inform the maid that she is to die, as many maids have before her in the same place; e.g., German **G** 7:

'Der Ulinger hat eylff Jungfrawen gehangen, Die zwölfft hat er gefangen.' [‡]

---

[*] Holofern might doubtless pass into Halewyn, but there is not the slightest need of Holofern to *account* for Halewyn. Halewyn, besides being a well-known local and family appellation, is found in two other Dutch ballads, one of which (Lootens and Feys, p. 66, No 38; Hoffmann, p. 46, No 11) has no kind of connection with the present, and is no more likely to have derived the name from this than this from that. It shall not be denied that Adelger, Hilsinger, Rullemann, Reimvord might have sprung from or have been suggested by Holofern, under the influence of familiar terminations, but it may be remarked that Hildebrand, Ravengaard, Valdemar, Rosmer, if they had occurred in any version, would have occasioned no greater difficulty.

[†] The Old German poem makes Holofernes kindle with desire for Judith the moment he sees her, and he bids his men bring her to his tent. They lift her up and bring her in.

[‡] It should be observed that these words are from the dove's warning.

This corresponds with the passage in Judith's song (xvi, 6), Dixit se . . . infantes meos dare in prædam et virgenes in captivitatem: but it is reasonable to suppose that the ballad follows some version of the Bible words that varied much from the original.

The incident of the maid's lousing and tousing her betrayer's hair, while he lies with his head in her lap, may have come from Judith seizing Holofernes by the hair before she kills him, but the story of Samson and Delilah may have had influence here.

According to many German versions, the murderer grants the maid three cries before she dies. She invokes Jesus, Mary, and her brother. Or she utters three sighs, the first to God the Father, the second to Jesus, the third to her brother. These cries or sighs seem to take the place of Judith's prayer, Confirma me, Domine Deus Israel (xiii, 7), and it may also be well to remember that Holofernes granted Judith, on her request, permission to go out in the night to pray.

The Dutch, Low-German, Scandinavian, and other versions agree in making the woman kill the knight with his own sword, as in Judith. The Dutch and Low-German [also Danish F, Swedish A] have preserved an original trait in making the maid hew off the murderer's head. English and French versions dispose of the knight differently: the maid pushes him into sea or river. Perhaps, in some older form of the story, after the head was cut off, the *trunk* was pushed into the water: cf. Judith xiii, 10: Abscidit caput ejus et . . . evolvit corpus ejus truncum. The words apprehendit comam capitis [53] ejus (xiii, 9) have their parallel in Dutch A, 33: "Zy nam het hoofd al by het haer." The Dutch ballad makes the maid carry the head with her.

"Singing and ringing" she rode through the wood: Judith sings a song of praise to the Lord after her return home.

In English C–F, May Colven comes home before dawn, as Judith does. The Dutch A says, When to her father's gate she came, she blew the horn like a man. Compare Judith xiii, 13: Et dixit Judith a longe custodibus murorum, Aperite portas!

The Dutch text goes on to say that when the father heard the horn he was delighted at his daughter's return: and Judith v, 14, Et factum est, cum audissent viri vocem ejus, vocaverunt presbyteros civitatis.

The conclusion of Dutch A is that there was a banquet held, and the head was set on the table. So Judith causes Holofernes' head to be hung up on the city wall, and after the enemy have been driven off, the Jews hold a feast.

The Icelandic version, though elsewhere much mutilated, has a concluding stanza which certainly belongs to the ballad:

> Ása went into a holy cell,
> Never did she harm to man.

This agrees with the view taken of the heroine of the ballad as a saint, and with the Bible account that Judith lived a chaste widow after her husband's demise.

Danish D is unique in one point. The robber has shown the maid a little knoll, in which the "much gold" of the women he has murdered lies. When she has killed him, the maid says, "I shall have the much gold," and takes as much as she can carry off. Compare with this Holofernes putting Judith into his treasury (xii, 1),[*] her carrying off the conopœum (xiii, 10), and her receiving from the people all Holofernes' gold, silver, clothes, jewels, and furniture, as her share of the plunder of the Assyrian camp (xv, 14). It is, perhaps, a perversion of this circumstance that the robber in German G, H, is refused permission to keep his costly clothes.

English D seems also to have preserved a portion of the primitive story, when it makes the maid tell her parents in the morning all that has happened, whereupon they go with her to the sea-shore to find the robber's body. The foundation for this is surely the Bible account that Judith makes known her act to the elders of the city, and that the Jews go out in the morning and fall on the enemy's camp, in which Holofernes' body is lying. In Swedish C the robber's sisters mourn over his body, and in Judith xiv, 18 the Assyrians break out into loud cries when they learn of Holofernes' death.

---

[*] Simply because he had no other apartment at his disposition. Shall we add, the Polish mother putting her daughter into the "new room," in which she kept her valuables?

In all this it is simply contended that the story of Judith is the remote source of the ballad, and it is conceded that many of the correspondences which have been cited may be accidental. Neither the Latin text of Judith nor any other written treatment of the story of Judith is supposed to have been known to the author of the ballad. The knowledge of its biblical origin being lost, the story would develop itself in its own way, according to the fashion of oral tradition. And so the pious widow into whose hands God gave over his enemies is converted into a fair maid who is enticed by a false knight into a wood, and who kills him in defence of her own life.

A similar transformation can be shown elsewhere in popular poetry. The little Katie of certain northern ballads (see Grundtvig, No 101) is a maid among other maids who prefers death to dishonor; but was originally Saint Catherine, daughter of the king of Egypt, who suffered martyrdom for the faith under the Emperor Maxentius. All the versions of the Halewyn ballad which we possess, even the purest, may be far removed from the primitive, both as to story and as to metrical form. New features would be taken up, and old ones would disappear. One copy has preserved genuine particulars, which another has lost, but Dutch tradition has kept the capital features best of all.[*]

Professor Bugge's argument has been given with an approach to fulness out of a desire to do entire justice to the distinguished author's case, though most of the correspondences adduced by him fail to produce any effect upon my mind.

The case is materially strengthened by the Dutch text C ('Roland'), which was not accessible at the time Bugge's paper was written. The name Roland is not so close to Holofern as Halewyn, but is still within the range of con-

ceivable metamorphosis. The points of coincidence between Dutch C and the story of Judith are these: The woman, first making an elaborate toilet,[†] goes out to seek the man, who is spoken of as surrounded with soldiers; she is challenged on the way; finds Roland lying on his bed, which he proposes she shall share (or lose her life);[‡] she cuts off his head, which, after her return home, she exposes from her window.[§]

If this was the original form of the Dutch ballad, and the Dutch ballad is the source from which all the other ballads have come, by processes of dropping, taking up, and transforming, then we may feel compelled to admit that this ballad might be a wild shoot from the story of Judith. Any one who bears in mind the strange changes which stories undergo will hesitate to pronounce this impossible. What poor Ophelia says of us human creatures is even truer of ballads: "We know what we are, but know not what we may be."

But when we consider how much would have to be dropped, how much to be taken up, and how much to be transformed, before the Hebrew "gest" could be converted into the European ballad, we naturally look for a less difficult hypothesis. It is a supposition attended with less difficulty that an independent European tradition existed of a half-human, half-

---

[*] Bugge holds that the ballad was derived by the Scandinavians from the Germans, more precisely by the Danes from a Low German form. This, he says, would follow from what he has maintained above, and he finds support for his view in many particular traits of Norse copies. Thus, one of the Norwegian names for the murderer is Alemarken. The first three syllables are very near to the Danish Oldemor; but -ken seems to be the German diminutive suffix, and can only be explained by the ballad having come from Germany.

[†] This toilet derives importance solely from the agreement with Judith x, 3: for the rest it is entirely in the ballad style. Compare the toilets in 'Hafsfrun,' Afzelius, No 92, III, 148, Arwidsson, No 150, II, 320, Wigström, *Folkdiktning*, No 2, p. 11, Landstad, No 55, p. 494: 'Guldsmedens Datter,' Grundtvig, No. 245, IV, 481ff, Wigström, *ib.*, No 18, p. 37, Landstad, No 43, p. 437: Torkilds Riim, Lyngbye, *Færøiske Qvæder*, 534, 535, Afzelius, III, 202: 'Stolts Karin,' Arwidsson, No 63, I, 388; 'Liti Kerstis hevn,' Landstad, No 67, p. 559 = 'Lord Thomas and Fair Annet': in many of which there is a gold crown. There is a man's toilet in Grundtvig, No 207, IV, 201.

[‡] Bugge would naturally have seen the Assyrian scouts that Judith falls in with (x, 11) in Roland's father, mother, and brother, all of whom hail the maid as she is making for Roland's quarters (C 30–38); still more "Holofernes jacebat in lecto" (xiii, 4), in "Roland die op zijn bedde lag," C 39.

[§] Judith xiv, 1: "Suspendite caput hoc super muros nostros." The cutting off and bringing home of the head, as need hardly be said, is not of itself remarkable, being found everywhere from David to Beówulf, and from Beówulf to 'Sir Andrew Barton.'

demonic being, who possessed an irresistible power of decoying away young maids, and was wont to kill them after he got them into his hands, but who at last found one who was more than his match, and lost his own life through her craft and courage. A modification of this story is afforded by the large class of Bluebeard tales. The Quintalin story seems to be another variety, with a substitution of lust for blood-thirst. The Dutch ballad may have been *affected* by some lost ballad of Holofern, and may have taken up some of its features, at least that of carrying home Halewyn's [Roland's] head, which is found in no other version.[*]

A a is translated by Grundtvig in *Engelske og skotske Folkeviser*, No 37, p. 230: **B b** in the same, No 36, p. 227: **C a, b, D a, b**, blended, No 35, p. 221. **A**, by Rosa Warrens, *Schottische V. l. der Vorzeit*, No 1, p. 1: Gerhard, p. 15. **C b**, by Rosa Warrens, No 34, p. 148: Wolf, *Halle der Völker*, 1, 38, Hausschatz, 225. **C, D**, etc., as in Allingham, p. 244, by Knortz, *Lied. u. Rom. Alt-Englands*, No 4, p. 14.

---

[*]   Dutch **B**, which, as before said, has been completely rewritten, makes the comparison with Holofernes:

> 34 'Ik heb van't leven hem beroofd,
> in mynen schoot heb ik zyn hoofd,
> hy is als Holofernes gelooft.'

> 37 Zy reed dan voort als Judith wys,
> zoo regt nae haer vaders paleis,
> daer zy wierd ingehaeld met eer en prys.

A

a. Buchan's *Ballads of the North of Scotland*, 1, 22. **b.** Motherwell's MS., p. 563.

1 FAIR lady Isabel sits in her bower sewing,
   Aye as the gowans grow gay
There she heard an elf-knight blawing his horn.
   The first morning in May

2 'If I had yon horn that I hear blawing,
   And yon elf-knight to sleep in my bosom.'

3 This maiden had scarcely these words spoken,
   Till in at her window the elf-knight has luppen.

4 'It's a very strange matter, fair maiden,' said he,
   'I canna blaw my horn but ye call on me.

5 'But will ye go to yon greenwood side?
   If ye canna gang, I will cause you to ride.'

6 He leapt on a horse, and she on another,
   And they rode on to the greenwood together.

7 'Light down, light down, lady Isabel,' said he,
   'We are come to the place where ye are to die.

8 'Hae mercy, hae mercy, kind sir, on me,
   Till ance my dear father and mother I see.'

9 'Seven king's-daughters here hae I slain,
   And ye shall be the eight o them.'

10 'O sit down a while, lay your head on my knee,
   That we may hae some rest before that I die.'

11 She stroakd him sae fast, the nearer he did creep,
   Wi a sma charm she lulld him fast asleep.

12 Wi his ain sword-belt sae fast as she ban him,
   Wi his ain dag-durk sae sair as she dang him.

13 'If seven king's-daughters here ye hae slain,
   Lye ye here, a husband to them a'.'

B

a. Buchan's MSS, ɪɪ, fol. 80. **b.** Buchan's *Ballads of the North of Scotland*, ɪɪ, 201. **c.** Motherwell's MS., p. 561. **d.** Harris MS., No 19.

1 THERE came a bird out o a bush,
   On water for to dine,
   An sighing sair, says the king's daughter,
   'O wae's this heart o mine!'

2 He's taen a harp into his hand,
   He's harped them all asleep,
   Except it was the king's daughter,
   Who one wink couldna get.

3 He's luppen on his berry-brown steed,
   Taen 'er on behind himsell,
   Then baith rede down to that water
   That they ca Wearie's Well.

4 'Wide in, wide in, my lady fair,
   No harm shall thee befall;
   Oft times I've watered my steed
   Wi the waters o Wearie's Well.'

5 The first step that she stepped in,
   She stepped to the knee;
   And sighend says this lady fair,
   'This water's nae for me.'

6 'Wide in, wide in, my lady fair,
   No harm shall thee befall;
   Oft times I've watered my steed
   Wi the water o Wearie's Well.'

7 The next step that she stepped in,
   She stepped to the middle;
   'O,' sighend says this lady fair,
   'I've wat my gowden girdle.'

8 'Wide in, wide in, my lady fair,   [56]
   No harm shall thee befall;
   Oft times have I watered my steed
   Wi the water o Wearie's Well.'

9 The next step that she stepped in,
   She stepped to the chin;
   'O,' sighend says this lady fair,
   'They sud gar twa loves twin.'

10 'Seven king's-daughters I've drownd there,
   In the water o Wearie's Well,
   And I'll make you the eight o them,
   And ring the common bell.'

11 'Since I am standing here,' she says,
   'This dowie death to die,
   One kiss o your comely mouth
   I'm sure wad comfort me.'

12 He louted him oer his saddle bow,
   To kiss her cheek and chin;
   She's taen him in her arms twa,
   An thrown him headlong in.

13 'Since seven king's daughters ye've drowned there,
   In the water o Wearie's Well,
   I'll make you bridegroom to them a',
   An ring the bell mysell.'

14 And aye she warsled, and aye she swam,
   And she swam to dry lan;
   She thanked God most cheerfully
   The dangers she oercame.

C

a. Herd's MSS, 1, 166. **b.** Herd's *Ancient and Modern Scottish Songs*, 1776, 1, 93. **c.** Motherwell's *Minstrelsy*, p. 67, = **b** "collated with a copy obtained from recitation."

1 FALSE Sir John a wooing came
    To a maid of beauty fair;
  May Colven was this lady's name,
    Her father's only heir.

2 He wood her butt, he wood her ben,
    He wood her in the ha,
  Until he got this lady's consent
    To mount and ride awa.

3 He went down to her father's bower,
    Where all the steeds did stand,
  And he's taken one of the best steeds
    That was in her father's land.

4 He's got on and she's got on,
    And fast as they could flee,
  Until they came to a lonesome part,
    A rock by the side of the sea.

5 'Loup off the steed,' says false Sir John,
    'Your bridal bed you see;
  For I have drowned seven young ladies,
    The eight one you shall be.

6 'Cast off, cast off, my May Colven,
    All and your silken gown,
  For it's oer good and oer costly
    To rot in the salt sea foam.

7 'Cast off, cast off, my May Colven,
    All and your embroiderd shoen,
  For they're oer good and oer costly
    To rot in the salt sea foam.'

8 'O turn you about, O false Sir John,
    And look to the leaf of the tree,
  For it never became a gentleman
    A naked woman to see.'

9 He turnd himself straight round about,
    To look to the leaf of the tree;
  So swift as May Colven was
    To throw him in the sea.

10 'O help, O help, my May Colven,
    O help, or else I'll drown;
   I'll take you home to your father's bower,
    And set you down safe and sound.'

11 'No help, no help, O false Sir John,
    No help, nor pity thee;
   Tho seven king's-daughters you have drownd,
    But the eight shall not be me.'

12 So she went on her father's steed,
    As swift as she could flee,
   And she came home to her father's bower
    Before it was break of day.

13 Up then and spoke the pretty parrot: [57]
    'May Colven, where have you been?
   What has become of false Sir John,
    That woo'd you so late the streen?

14 'He woo'd you butt, he woo'd you ben,
    He woo'd you in the ha,
   Until he got your own consent
    For to mount and gang awa.'

15 'O hold your tongue, my pretty parrot,
    Lay not the blame upon me;
   Your cup shall be of the flowered gold,
    Your cage of the root of the tree.'

16 Up then spake the king himself,
    In the bed-chamber where he lay:
   'What ails the pretty parrot,
    That prattles so long or day?'

17 'There came a cat to my cage door, It almost a
          worried me,
   And I was calling on May Colven
    To take the cat from me.'

D

a. Sharpe's *Ballad Book* (1823), No 17, p. 45. **b.** Buchan's *Ballads of the North of Scotland*, II, 45. **c.** Motherwell's *Minstrelsy*, Appendix, p. 21, No. XXIV, one stanza. **d.** A stall-copy lent me by Mrs Alexander Forbes, Liberton, Edinburgh. (See p. 39, note.)

O heard ye e'er o' a blood-y knight That liv'd in the west— Coun-trie? For he has stown seven la-dies— fair And drown'd them a' in the sea. For he has stown se-ven la-dies fair And drown'd them a' in the sea.

D. c. Motherwell, 1827, Appendix No 24.

1 O HEARD ye of a bloody knight,
   Lived in the south country?
For he has betrayed eight ladies fair
   And drowned them in the sea.

2 Then next he went to May Collin,
   She was her father's heir,
The greatest beauty in the land,
   I solemnly declare.

3 'I am a knight of wealth and might,
   Of townlands twenty-three;
And you'll be lady of them all,
   If you will go with me.'

4 'Excuse me, then, Sir John,' she says
   'To wed I am too young;
Without I have my parents' leave,
   With you I darena gang.'

5 'Your parents' leave you soon shall have,
   In that they will agree;
For I have made a solemn vow
   This night you'll go with me.'

6 From below his arm he pulled a charm,
   And stuck it in her sleeve,
And he has made her go with him,
   Without her parents' leave.

7 Of gold and silver she has got
   With her twelve hundred pound,
And the swiftest steed her father had
   She has taen to ride upon.

8 So privily they went along,
   They made no stop or stay,
Till they came to the fatal place
   That they call Bunion Bay.

9 It being in a lonely place,
   And no house there was nigh,
The fatal rocks were long and steep,
   And none could hear her cry.

10 'Light down,' he said, 'fair May Collin,
    Light down and speak with me,
For here I've drowned eight ladies fair,
    And the ninth one you shall be.'

11 'Is this your bowers and lofty towers,
    So beautiful and gay?
Or is it for my gold,' she said,
    'You take my life away?'

12 'Strip off,' he says, 'thy jewels fine,
    So costly and so brave,
For they are too costly and too fine
    To throw in the sea wave.'

13 'Take all I have my life to save,
   O good Sir John, I pray;
   Let it neer be said you killed a maid
   Upon her wedding day.'

14 'Strip off,' he says, 'thy Holland smock,
   That's bordered with the lawn,
   For it's too costly and too fine
   To rot in the sea sand.'

[58] 15 'O turn about, Sir John,' she said,
   'Your back about to me,
   For it never was comely for a man
   A naked woman to see.'

16 But as he turned him round about,
   She threw him in the sea,
   Saying, 'Lie you there, you false Sir John,
   Where you thought to lay me.

17 'O lie you there, you traitor false,
   Where you thought to lay me,
   For though you stripped me to the skin,
   Your clothes you've got with thee.'

18 Her jewels fine she did put on,
   So costly, rich and brave,
   And then with speed she mounts his steed,
   So well she did behave.

19 That lady fair being void of fear,
   Her steed being swift and free,
   And she has reached her father's gate
   Before the clock struck three.

20 Then first she called the stable groom,
   He was her waiting man;
   Soon as he heard his lady's voice
   He stood with cap in hand.

21 'Where have you been, fair May Collin?
   Who owns this dapple grey?'
   'It is a found one,' she replied,
   'That I got on the way.'

22 Then out bespoke the wily parrot
   Unto fair May Collin:
   'What have you done with false Sir John,
   That went with you yestreen?'

23 'O hold your tongue, my pretty parrot,
   And talk no more to me,
   And where you had a meal a day
   O now you shall have three.'

24 Then up bespoke her father dear,
   From his chamber where he lay:
   'What aileth thee, my pretty Poll,
   That you chat so long or day?'

25 'The cat she came to my cage-door,
   The thief I could not see,
   And I called to fair May Collin,
   To take the cat from me.'

26 Then first she told her father dear
   The deed that she had done,
   And next she told her mother dear
   Concerning false Sir John.

27 'If this be true, fair May Collin,
   That you have told to me,
   Before I either eat or drink
   This false Sir John I'll see.'

28 Away they went with one consent,
   At dawning of the day,
   Until they came to Carline Sands,
   And there his body lay.

29 His body tall, by that great fall,
   By the waves tossed to and fro,
   The diamond ring that he had on
   Was broke in pieces two.

30 And they have taken up his corpse
   To yonder pleasant green,
   And there they have buried false Sir John,
   For fear he should be seen.

E

J. H. Dixon, *Ancient Poems, Ballads, and Songs of the Peasantry of England*, p. 74. Given from singing and recitation in *Shropshire Folk-Lore*, edited by Charlotte Sophia Burne, 1883–86, p. 548.

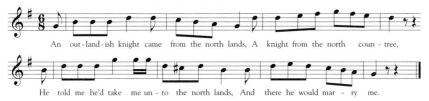

An out-land-ish knight came from the north lands, A knight from the north coun-tree,

He told me he'd take me un-to the north lands, And there he would mar-ry me.

Burne, 1883, p. 652; text, pp. 549–50. Sung by Jane Butler, Edgmond, Shropshire, 1870–80.

1 AN outlandish knight came from the north
    lands,
  And he came a-wooing to me;
He told me he'd take me unto the north lands,
  And there he would marry me.

2 'Come, fetch me some of your father's gold,
  And some of your mother's fee,
And two of the best nags out of the stable,
  Where they stand thirty and three.'

3 She fetched him some of her father's gold,
  And some of her mother's fee,
And two of the best nags out of the stable,
  Where they stood thirty and three.

4 She mounted her on her milk-white steed,
  He on the dapple grey;
They rode till they came unto the sea-side,
  Three hours before it was day.

5 'Light off, light off thy milk-white steed,
  And deliver it unto me;
Six pretty maids have I drowned here,
  And thou the seventh shalt be.

6 'Pull off, pull off thy silken gown,
  And deliver it unto me;
Methinks it looks too rich and too gay
  To rot in the salt sea.

7 'Pull off, pull off thy silken stays,
  And deliver them unto me;
Methinks they are too fine and gay
  To rot in the salt sea.

8 'Pull off, pull off thy Holland smock,
  And deliver it unto me;
Methinks it looks too rich and gay
  To rot in the salt sea.'

9 'If I must pull off my Holland smock,
  Pray turn thy back unto me;
For it is not fitting that such a ruffian
  A naked woman should see.'

10 He turned his back towards her
  And viewed the leaves so green;
She catched him round the middle so small,
  And tumbled him into the stream.

11 He dropped high and he dropped low,
  Until he came to the side;
'Catch hold of my hand, my pretty maiden,
  And I will make you my bride.'

12 'Lie there, lie there, you false-hearted man,
  Lie there instead of me;
Six pretty maids have you drowned here,
  And the seventh has drowned thee.'

13 She mounted on her milk-white steed,
  And led the dapple grey;
She rode till she came to her own father's hall,
  Three hours before it was day.

14 The parrot being in the window so high,
  Hearing the lady, did say,
'I'm afraid that some ruffian has led you astray,
  That you have tarried so long away.'

15 'Don't prittle nor prattle, my pretty parrot,
    Nor tell no tales of me;
  Thy cage shall be made of the glittering gold,
    Although it is made of a tree.'

16 The king being in the chamber so high,
    And hearing the parrot, did say,
  'What ails you, what ails you, my pretty parrot,
    That you prattle so long before day?'

17 'It's no laughing matter,' the parrot did say,
    'That so loudly I call unto thee,
  For the cats have got into the window so high,
    And I'm afraid they will have me.'

18 'Well turned, well turned, my pretty parrot,
    Well turned, well turned for me;
  Thy cage shall be made of the glittering gold,
    And the door of the best ivory.'

F

Roxburghe Ballads, III, 449.

1 'Go fetch me some of your father's gold,
    And some of your mother's fee,
  And I'll carry you into the north land,
    And there I'll marry thee.'

2 She fetchd him some of her father's gold,
    And some of her mother's fee;
  She carried him into the stable,
    Where horses stood thirty and three.

3 She leapd on a milk-white steed,
    And he on a dapple-grey;
  They rode til they came to a fair river's side,
    Three hours before it was day.

4 'O light, O light, you lady gay,
    O light with speed, I say,
  For six knight's daughters have I drowned here,
    And you the seventh must be.'

[60] 5 'Go fetch the sickle, to crop the nettle
    That grows so near the brim,
  For fear it should tangle my golden locks,
    Or freckle my milk-white skin.'

6 He fetchd the sickle, to crop the nettle
    That grows so near the brim,
  And with all the strength that pretty Polly had
    She pushd the false knight in.

7 'Swim on, swim on, thou false knight,
    And there bewail thy doom,
  For I don't think thy cloathing too good
    To lie in a watry tomb.'

8 She leaped on her milk-white steed,
    She led the dapple grey;
  She rid till she came to her father's house,
    Three hours before it was day.

9 'Who knocked so loudly at the ring?'
    The parrot he did say;
  'O where have you been, my pretty Polly,
    All this long summer's day?'

10 'O hold your tongue, parrot,
    Tell you no tales of me;
  Your cage shall be made of beaten gold,
    Which is now made of a tree.'

11 O then bespoke her father dear,
    As he on his bed did lay:
  'O what is the matter, my parrot,
    That you speak before it is day?'

12 'The cat's at my cage, master,
    And sorely frighted me,
  And I calld down my Polly
    To take the cat away.'

G

British Museum, MS. Addit. 20094. 'The Knight and the Chief's Daughter,' communicated to Mr T. Crofton Croker in 1829, as remembered by Mr W. Pigott Rogers, and believed by Mr Rogers to have been learned by him from an Irish nursery-maid.

1 'Now steal me some of your father's gold,
    And some of your mother's fee,
And steal the best steed in your father's stable,
    Where there lie thirty three.'

2 She stole him some of her father's gold,
    And some of her mother's fee,
And she stole the best steed from her father's
        stable,
    Where there lay thirty three.

3 And she rode on the milk-white steed,
    And he on the barb so grey,
Until they came to the green, green wood,
    Three hours before it was day.

4 'Alight, alight, my pretty colleen,
    Alight immediately,
For six knight's daughters I drowned here,
    And thou the seventh shall be.'

5 'Oh hold your tongue, you false knight villain,
    Oh hold your tongue,' said she;
''Twas you that promised to marry me,
    For some of my father's fee.'

6 'Strip off, strip off your jewels so rare,
    And give them all to me;
I think them too rich and too costly by far
    To rot in the sand with thee.'

7 'Oh turn away, thou false knight villain,
    Oh turn away from me;
Oh turn away, with your back to the cliff,
    And your face to the willow-tree.'

8 He turned about, with his back to the cliff,
    And his face to the willow-tree;
So sudden she took him up in her arms,
    And threw him into the sea.

9 'Lie there, lie there, thou false knight villain,
    Lie there instead of me;
'Twas you that promised to marry me,
    For some of my father's fee.'

10 'Oh take me by the arm, my dear,
    And hold me by the hand,
And you shall be my gay lady,
    And the queen of all Scotland.'

11 'I'll not take you by the arm, my dear,
    Nor hold you by the hand;
And I won't be your gay lady,
    And the queen of all Scotland.'

12 And she rode on the milk-white steed,
    And led the barb so grey,
Until she came back to her father's castle,
    One hour before it was day.

13 And out then spoke her parrot so green,
    From the cage wherein she lay:
Where have you now been, my pretty colleen,
    This long, long summer's day?

14 'Oh hold your tongue, my favourite bird,
    And tell no tales on me;
Your cage I will make of the beaten gold,
    And hang in the willow-tree.'

15 Out then spoke her father dear,
    From the chamber where he lay:
Oh what hath befallen my favourite bird,
    That she calls so loud for day?

16 ''Tis nothing at all, good lord,' she said,
    ''Tis nothing at all indeed;
It was only the cat came to my cage-door,
    And I called my pretty colleen.'

A. *Burden. Song xix of Forbes's 'Cantus,' Aberdeen, 1682, 3d ed., has, as pointed out by Motherwell, Minstrelsy, p. lx, nearly the same burden:* The gowans are gay, The first morning of May. *And again, a song in the* Tea Table Miscellany, *as remarked by Buchan,* There gowans are gay, The first morning of May: *p. 404 of the 12th ed., London, 1763. In John Squair's MS., fol. 22, Laing collection, library of the University of Edinburgh, handwriting about 1700. (W. Macmath.)*

b. *No doubt furnished to Motherwell by Buchan, as a considerable number of ballads in this part of his MS. seem to have been.*

3^2. Then in. 8^1. kind sir, said she.
10^2. That we may some rest before I die.
11^1. the near. 13^2. to them ilk ane.

1 *is given by Motherwell,* Minstrelsy, *p. lx, but apparently to improve metre and secure rhyme, thus:*

> Lady Isabel sits in her bouir sewing,
> She heard an elf-knight his horn blowing.

B b. *Buchan's printed copy differs from the manuscript very slightly, except in spelling.*
4^3, 6^3. Aft times hae I.
5^3. And sighing sair says. 7^3, 9^3. And sighing says.
14^2. Till she swam. 14^3. Then thanked. 14^4. she'd.

A copy in Walks near Edinburgh, *by Margaret Warrender, 1890, p. 104, differs from* **B b** *in only a few words, as any ordinary recollection would. As:*

4^3,6^3, 8^3. my guid steed.
9^4. it will gar our loves to twine.
10^4. An I'll ring for you the bell.
11^3. Grant me ae kiss o your fause, fause mouth (*improbable reading*).
14^2. she won. 14^3. most heartily.

c. *Like* **A b,** *derived by Motherwell from Buchan.*
4^1, 6^1, 8^1. wade in, wade in.
14^3. And thanked.

Dixon, Scottish Traditional Versions of Ancient Ballads, *p. 63, printing* **B** *from the manuscript, makes one or two trivial changes.*
d *is only this fragment.*

> 4^3 Mony a time I rade wi my brown foal
> The water o Wearie's Wells.

> 'Leave aff, leave aff your gey mantle,
> It's a' gowd but the hem;

> Leave aff, leave [aff], it's far owre gude
> To weet i the saut see faem.'

> 5 She wade in, an he rade in,
> Till it took her to the knee;
> Wi sighin said that lady gay
> 'Sic wadin's no for me.'

> *   *   *   *

> 9 He rade in, and she wade in,
> Till it took her to the chin;
> Wi sighin said that ladie gay
> 'I'll wade nae farer in.'

> 10^3 'Sax king's dochters I hae drowned,
> An the seventh you sall be.'

> *   *   *   *

> 13 'Lie you there, you fause young man,
> Where you thought to lay me.'   [61

C b. *The printed copy follows the manuscript with only very trifling variations:* Colvin *for* Colven; 13^1, up then spak; 16^4, ere day; 17^2, almost worried.
c. $2^{1,2}$. he's courted. 2^3. Till once he got.
Between 2 and 3 is inserted:

> She's gane to her father's coffers,
> Where all his money lay,
> And she's taken the red, and she's left the
>   white,
> And so lightly as she tripped away.

> 3^1 She's gane down to her father's stable,
> 3 And she's taken the best, and she's left the
>   warst.

> 4 He rode on, and she rode on,
> They rode a long summer's day,
> Until they came to a broad river,
> An arm of a lonesome sea.

> $5^{3,4}$ 'For it's seven king's daughters I have
>   drowned here,
> And the eighth I'll out make with thee.'

> $6^{1,2}$ 'Cast off, cast off your silks so fine,
> And lay them on a stone.'

> $7^{1,2,3}$ 'Cast off, cast off your holland smock,
> And lay it on this stone,
> For it's too fine.' . .

> $9^{3,4}$ She's twined her arms about his waist,
> And thrown him into

$10^{1,2}$ 'O hold a grip of me, May Colvin,
　　For fear that I should'

^{3} father's gates　^{4} and safely I'll set you down.

11 'O lie you there, thou false Sir John,
　　O lie you there,' said she,
　'For you lie not in a caulder bed
　　Than the ane you intended for me.'

12^3. father's gates.　^{4}. At the breaking of the day.
13^4. yestreen.
Between 13 and 14 is inserted:

　　Up then spake the pretty parrot,
　　　In the bonnie cage where it lay:
　　'O what hae ye done with the false Sir John,
　　　That he behind you does stay?'

$15^{3,4}$ 'Your cage will be made of the beaten gold,
　　And the spakes of ivorie.'

$17^{1,2}$ 'It was a cat cam . . .
　　I thought 't would have' . . .

D a. *Derived* "from the housekeeper at Methven."
　Sharpe's Ballad Book, ed. 1880, *p.* 130.
　2^1. Colin.
b. *Buchan's copy makes many slight changes which are*
　not noticed here.
　1^2. west countrie.
After 1 is inserted:

　　All ladies of a gude account
　　　As ever yet were known;
　　This traitor was a baron knight,
　　　They calld him fause Sir John.

After 2:

　　'Thou art the darling of my heart,
　　　I say, fair May Colvin,
　　So far excells thy beauties great
　　　That ever I hae seen.'

3^2. Hae towers, towns twenty three.
7^2. five hunder. 7^3. The best an steed.
8^1. fatal end. 8^4. Binyan's Bay.
12^2. rich and rare. 12^4. sea ware.
After 12:

　　Then aff she's taen her jewels fine,
　　　And thus she made her moan:
　　'Hae mercy on a virgin young,
　　　I pray you, gude Sir John.'

'Cast aff, cast aff, fair May Colvin,
　Your gown and petticoat,
　For they're too costly and too fine
　To rot by the sea rock.'

13^4. Before her. 14^4. to toss. 18^3. her steed.
23^3. What hast thou made o fause.
28^3. Charlestown sands. *Sharpe thinks Carline*
　Sands means Carlinseugh Sands on the coast of [62]
　Forfarshire.
After 30:

　　Ye ladies a', wherever you be,
　　　That read this mournful song,
　　I pray you mind on May Colvin,
　　　And think on fause Sir John.

　　Aff they've taen his jewels fine,
　　　To keep in memory;
　　And sae I end my mournful sang
　　　And fatal tragedy.

c. *Motherwell's one stanza is:*

　　O heard ye eer o a bloody knight
　　　That livd in the west countrie?
　　For he has stown seven ladies fair,
　　　And drownd them a' in the sea.

d. $1^{1,2}$. Have ye not heard of fause Sir John,
　　Wha livd in the west country?

After 2 a stanza nearly as in **b.**
5 *wanting.*
6^1. But he's taen a charm frae aff his arm.
6^3. follow him.
7^2. five hundred. 7^3. the bravest horse.
8^1. So merrily.
8^4. Which is called Benan Bay.
9, 11, *wanting.*
12^1. Cast aff, cast aff. 12^4. To sink.
13. *Nearly as in* **b.**

　14. 'Cast aff thy coats and gay mantle,
　　　And smock o Holland lawn,
　　For thei'r owre costly and owre guid
　　　To rot in the sea san.'

　15. 'Then turn thee round, I pray, Sir John,
　　　See the leaf flee owre the tree,
　　For it never befitted a book-learned man
　　　A naked lady to see.'

Sir John being a Dominican friar, according to the histori-
cal preface.

18. As fause Sir John did turn him round,
    To see the leaf flee owre the [tree],
    She grasped him in her arms sma,
    And flung him in the sea.

17. 'Now lie ye there, ye wild Sir John,
    Whar ye thought to lay me;
    Ye wad hae drownd me as naked's I was
        born,
    But ye's get your claes frae me!'

18. Her jewels, costly, rich and rare,
    She straight puts on again;
    She lightly springs upon her horse,
    And leads his by the rein.

21³. O that's a foundling.

22. Then out and spake the green parrot,
    He says, Fair May Culzean,
    O what hae ye done wi yon brave knight?

23. 'Haud your tongue, my pretty parrot,
    An I 'se be kind to thee;
    For where ye got ae handfu o groats,
    My parrot shall get three.'

25. 'There came a cat into my cage,
    Had nearly worried me,
    And I was calling on May Culzean
    To come and set me free.'

27 *wanting.* 28³. Carleton sands.

29². Was dashed. 29³. The golden ring.

E. *A copy of 'The Outlandish Knight,' with unimportant verbal variations, is given in* English County Songs, *by Lucy E. Broadwood and J. A. Fuller Maitland, p. 164.*
3². of the. 17². But so.

F. *In the catalogue of the British Museum,* "London? 1710?"

APPENDIX

Additional Copies

Mr W. H. Babcock has recently printed the following version, as sung in a Virginian family from "the corner between the Potomac and the Blue Ridge:" *The Folk-Lore Journal*, VII, 28.

WILSON.

1 Wilson, sitting in his room one day,
    With his true-love on his knee,
Just as happy as happy could be, be, be,
    Just as happy as happy could be,

2 'Do you want for fee?' said she,
    'Or do you want for gold?
Or do you want a handsome ladye,
    More handsomer than me?'

3 'I do want for fee,' said he,
    'And I do want for gold;
But I don't want a handsomer ladye,
    More handsomer than thee.

4 ' Go get some of your father's fee,
    And some of your father's gold,
And two of the finest horses he has,
    And married we will be, be, be,
    And married we will be.'

5 She mounted on the milk-white steed,
    And he the iron-grey,
And when they got to the broad waterside
    It was six hours and a half till day.

6 'Get down, get down! my pretty fair maid,
    Get down, get down!' said he;
'For it's nine of the kings daughters I've
        drowned here,
    And the tenth one you shall be.

7 'Take off, take off that costly silk,
    For it is a costly thing;
  It cost your father too much bright gold
    To drown your fair body in.

8 'In stooping down to cut the cords round,
    Sing, Turn your back on me;'
  And with all the strength this lady had,
    She pushed him right into the sea.

9 'Help me out! my pretty fair miss,
    'O help me out!' said he,
  'And we'll go down to the Catholic church,
    And married we will be.'

10 'Lie there, lie there! you false-hearted man,
    Lie there, lie there!' said she,
  'For it's nine of the king's daughters you've
      drowned here,
    But the tenth one's drowned thee.'

11 She mounted on the milk-white steed,
    And led the iron-grey,
  And when she got to her own father's house
    It was three hours and a half till day.

12 While she was walking in the room,
    Which caused the parrot to wake,
  Said he, What's the matter, my pretty fair miss,
    That you're up so long, before day?

13 'Hush up, hush up! my pretty little parrot,
    Don't tell no tales on me;
  Your cage shall be lined with sweet may gold,
    And the doors of ivorie.'

14 While they were talking all of this,
    Which caused the old man to wake,
  Said, What's the matter, my pretty little parrot,
    That you chatter so long before day?

15 'The cat she sprung against my cage,
    And surely frightened me,
  And I called for the pretty fair miss
    To drive the cat away.'

————

1 *lacks the third verse.*
2[1,2], 3[1,2], 4[1,2] fee and gold *should be exchanged.*
12[2], 14[2] wake *should perhaps be* say.

————

The copy of 'May Collin' which follows is quite the best of the series **C–G**. It is written on the same sheet of paper as the "copy of some antiquity" used by Scott in making up his 'Gay Goss Hawk' (ed. 1802, II, 7). The sheet is perhaps as old as any in the volume in which it occurs, but may possibly not be the original. 'May Collin' is not in the same hand as the other ballad. Both hands are of the 18th century.

According to the preface to a stall-copy spoken of by Motherwell, *Minstrelsy*, p. lxx, 24, "the treacherous and murder-minting lover was an ecclesiastic of the monastery of Maybole," and the preface to **D d** makes him a Dominican friar. So, if we were to accept these guides, the 'Sir' would be the old ecclesiastical title and equivalent to the 'Mess' of the copy now to be given.

'May Collin,' "Scotch Ballads, Materials for Border
Minstrelsy," No 146, Abbotsford.

1 MAY COLLIN   .   .   .
      .   .   was her father's heir,
  And she fell in love with a falsh priest,
    And she rued it ever mair.

2 He followd her butt, he followd her benn,
    He followd her through the hall,
  Till she had neither tongue nor teeth
    Nor lips to say him naw.

3 'We'll take the steed out where he is,
    The gold where eer it be,
  And we'll away to some unco land,
    And married we shall be.'

4 They had not riden a mile, a mile,
    A mile but barely three,
  Till they came to a rank river,
    Was raging like the sea.

5 'Light off, light off now, May Collin,
   It's here that you must die;
   Here I have drownd seven king's daughters,
   The eight now you must be.

6 'Cast off, cast off now, May Collin,
   Your gown that's of the green;
   For it's oer good and oer costly
   To rot in the sea-stream.

7 'Cast off, cast off now, May Collin,
   Your coat that's of the black;
   For it's oer good and oer costly
   To rot in the sea-wreck.

8 'Cast off, cast off now, May Collin,
   Your stays that are well laced;
   For thei'r oer good and costly
   In the sea's ground to waste.

9 'Cast [off, cast off now, May Collin,]
   Your sark that's of the holland;
   For [it's oer good and oer costly]
   To rot in the sea-bottom.'

10 'Turn you about now, falsh Mess John,
    To the green leaf of the tree;
    It does not fit a mansworn man
    A naked woman to see.'

11 He turnd him quickly round about,
    To the green leaf of the tree;
    She took him hastly in her arms
    And flung him in the sea.

12 'Now lye you there, you falsh Mess John,
    My mallasin go with thee!
    You thought to drown me naked and bare,
    But take your cloaths with thee,
    And if there be seven king's daughters there
    Bear you them company.'

13 She lap on her milk steed
    And fast she bent the way,
    And she was at her father's yate
    Three long hours or day.

14 Up and speaks the wylie parrot,
    So wylily and slee:
    'Where is the man now, May Collin,
    That gaed away wie thee?'

15 'Hold your tongue, my wylie parrot,
    And tell no tales of me,
    And where I gave a pickle befor
    It's now I'll give you three.'

—————

1[1,2]. *One line:* May Collin was her father's heir.
7[4]. on the. 8[4]. ina? *indistinct.* 12[5]. 7.

—————

In *Traditionary Stories of Old Families*, by Andrew Picken, 1833, I, 289, 'The Three Maids of Loudon,' occur the following stanzas (W. Macmath).

Seven pretty sisters dwelt in a bower,
   With a hey-down, and a ho-down
And they twined the silk, and they workd the
      flower.
   Sing, a hey-down and a ho-down

And they began for seven years' wark,
   With a hey-down and a ho-down
All for to make their dear loves a sark.
   With a hey down and a ho-down

O three long years were passd and gone,
And they had not finishd a sleeve but one.

'O we'll to the woods, and we'll pull a rose,'
And up they sprang all at this propose.

5

GIL BRENTON

A. a. 'Gil Brenton,' Jamieson Brown MS., p. 34. **b.**
'Chil Brenton,' William Tytler Brown MS., No 3.
B. 'Cospatrick,' Scott's *Minstrelsy*, II, 117 (1802).
C. 'We were sisters, we were seven,' Cromek's
Remains of Nithsdale and Galloway Song, p. 207.
D. 'Lord Dingwall,' Buchan's *Ballads of the North of
Scotland*, I, 204.

E. Elizabeth Cochrane's Song-Book, No 112.
F. a. 'Lord Brangwill,' Motherwell's MSS, p. 219.
b. 'Lord Bengwill,' Motherwell's *Minstrelsy*,
Appendix, p. xvi.
G. 'Bothwell,' Herd's *Ancient and Modern Scots
Songs*, p. 244.
H. Kinloch MSS, v, 335.

EIGHT copies of this ballad are extant, four
of them hitherto unpublished. **A a**, No 16 in
the Jamieson-Brown MS., is one of twenty bal-
lads written down from the recitation of Mrs
Brown of Falkland, by her nephew, Robert
Scott, in 1783, or shortly before. From these
twenty thirteen were selected, and, having first
been revised by Mrs Brown, were sent, with two
others, to William Tytler in the year just men-
tioned. William Tytler's MS. has disappeared,
but a list of the ballads which it contained, with
the first stanza of each, is given by Dr Ander-
son, in Nichols's *Illustrations of the Literary His-
tory of the Eighteenth Century*, VII, 176. **B** is the
'Cospatrick' of the *Border Minstrelsy*, described
by Scott as taken down from the recitation of a
lady (said by Lockhart to be Miss Christian
Rutherford, his mother's half-sister) "with some
stanzas transferred from Herd's copy, and some
readings adopted from a copy in Mrs Brown's
manuscript under the title of Child Brenton,"
that is, from **A b**. **C** purports to be one of a con-
siderable number of pieces, "copied from the
recital of a peasant-woman of Galloway,
upwards of ninety years of age." Though over-
laid with verses of Cunningham's making (of
which forty or fifty may be excided in one mass)
and though retouched almost everywhere, both
the groundwork of the story and some genuine
lines remain unimpaired. The omission of most

of the passage referred to, and the restoration of
the stanza form, will give us, perhaps, a thing of
shreds and patches, but still a ballad as near to
genuine as some in Percy's *Reliques* or even
Scott's *Minstrelsy*. **D** and **F** are (the former pre-
sumably, the second certainly) from recitation
of the first quarter of this century. **E** is one of [63]
the few ballads in Elizabeth Cochrane's song-
book, and probably of the first half of the last
century. **G**, the earliest printed form of the bal-
lad, appeared in Herd's first collection, in the
year 1769. **H** was taken down from recitation
by the late Dr Hill Burton in his youth.

A, **B**, and **C** agree in these points: A bride,
not being a maid, looks forward with alarm to
her wedding night, and induces her bower-
woman to take her place for the nonce. The
imposture is detected by the bridegroom,
through the agency of magical blankets, sheets,
and pillows, **A**; or of blankets, bed, sheet, and
sword, **B**; or simply of the Billie Blin, **C**. (The
sword is probably an editorial insertion; and
Jamieson, *Illustrations of Northern Antiquities*, p.
843, doubts, but without sufficient reason, the
Billie Blin.) The bridegroom has recourse to his
mother, who demands an explanation of the
bride, and elicits a confession that she had once
upon a time encountered a young man in a
wood, who subjected her to violence. Before
they parted, he gave her certain tokens, which

he enjoined her to be very careful of, a lock of his hair, a string of beads, a gold ring, and a knife. **B** omits the knife, and **C** the beads. The mother goes back to her son, and asks what he had done with the tokens she had charged him never to part with. He owns that he had presented them to a lady, one whom he would now give all his possessions to have for his wife. The lady of the greenwood is identified by the tokens.

A, **C**, and **D** make the mother set a golden chair for the bride, in which none but a maid can sit, **D** [no leal maid will sit till bidden, **C**]. In **D** the chair is declined; in **C**, taken without bidding; in **A** the significance of the chair has been lost. **E**, **F**, **G** employ no kind of test of maidenhood,—the bride frankly avows that she is with child to another man; and **D**, as well as **E**, **F**, **G**, omits the substitution of the chambermaid. The tokens in **D** are a chain, a ring, and three locks of hair; in **E**, gloves and a ring; in **F**, **G**, green gloves, a ring, and three locks [plaits] of hair. Only the ring remains in **H**.

"This ballad," says Motherwell (1827), "is very popular, and is known to reciters under a variety of names. I have heard it called Lord Bangwell, Bengwill, Dingwall, Brengwill, etc., and The Seven Sisters, or the Leaves of Lind." He adds: "There is an unedited ballad in Scotland, which is a nearer approximation to the Danish song inasmuch as the substitution of the maiden sister for the real bride constitutes a prominent feature of the tale."[*] (*Minstrelsy*, Introduction, lxix[21] and xc.)

Scott remarks that Cospatrick[†] "was the designation of the Earl of Dunbar, in the days of Wallace and Bruce." Mr Macmath informs me

that it is in use at the present day in the families of the Earl of Home and of Dunbar of Mochrum, Bart, who, among others, claim descent from the ancient earls of Dunbar and March. The story of the ballad might, of course, attach itself to any person prominent in the region where the ballad was known.

Swedish. Three Swedish versions of this ballad were given by Afzelius: **A**, 'Riddar Olle' in 50 two-line stanzas, II, 217; **B**, 19 two-line stanzas, II, 59; **C**, 19 two-line stanzas, II, 56: No 33, I, 175–182 of Bergström's edition. 'Riddar Olof,' Lagus, *Nyländska Folkvisor*, I, 63, No 16, *a*, *b*, are imperfect copies. Besides these, there are two fragments in Cavallius and Stephens's unprinted collection: **D**, 6 stanzas; **E**, 7 stanzas, the latter printed in Grundtvig, V, 307.[‡] All these were obtained from recitation in the [64] present century. **A** comes nearest to our **A**, **B**. Like Scottish **B**, it seems to have been compounded from several copies. Sir Olof betrothed Ingalilla, and carried her home for the spousal, wearing a red gold crown and a wan cheek. Ingalilla gave birth to twin-boys. Olof had a maid who resembled Ingalilla completely, and who, upon Ingalilla's entreaty, consented to play the part of bride on the morrow. Dressed in Ingalilla's clothes, blue kirtle, green jacket, etc., and wearing five gold rings and a gold crown, the maid rode to church, with Ingalilla at her back, and her beauty was admired by all as she came and went. But outside of the church were a good many musicians; and one of these piped out, "God-a-mercy, Ingalilla, no maid art thou!" Ingalilla threw into the piper's hand something which made him change his tune. He was an old drunken fellow, and no one need mind what he sang. After five days of drinking, they took the bride

---

[*]   In his note-book, p. 117, Motherwell writes, with less than his usual discretion: "The ballad of Bothwell, Cospatric, or Gil Brenton, appears to be copied from an account of the birth of Makbeth given by Wintown." The substance of this account is, that Macbeth's mother had a habit of repairing to the woods for wholesome air, and that, during one of her rambles, she fell in with a fair man, really the Devil, who passed the day with her, and got on her a son.

"And of that dede in taknyng
He gave his lemman there a ryng,
And bad hyr that scho suld kepe that wele,
And held for hys luve that jwele."
Cronykil, Book VI, ch. xviii, 57–90.

[†]   Scott says: "Cospatrick, Comes Patricius;" but Cos-(Gos-)patrick is apparently Servant of Patrick, like Gilpatrick (Kil-patrick). Mr Macmath suggests to me that Gil Brenton may have originally been Gil-brandon, which seems very likely. See *Notes and Queries*, 5th S., x, 443.

[‡]   A fragment in Rancken's 'Några Prof af Folksång,' p. 14f, belongs not to 'Riddar Olle,' as there said, but to 'Herr Aster och Fröken Sissa,' though the burden is 'Riddar Olof.' Other verses, at p. 16, might belong to either. 'Riddar Ola,' E. Wigström's *Folkdiktning*, p. 37, No 18, belongs with the Danish 'Guldsmedens Datter,' Grundtvig, No 245.

to her chamber, not without force. Ingalilla bore the light before her, and helped put her to bed; then lay down herself. Olof had over him a fur rug, which could talk as well as he, and it called out,

'Hear me, Sir Olof, hear what I say;
Thou hast taken a strumpet, and missed a may.'

And Olof,

'Hear, little Inga, sweetheart,' he said
'What didst thou get for thy maidenhead?'*

Inga explained. Her father was a strange sort of man, and built her bower by the sea-strand where all the king's courtiers took ship. Nine had broken in, and one had robbed her of her honor. He had given her an embroidered sark, a blue kirtle, green jacket, black mantle, gloves, five gold rings, a red gold crown, a golden harp, and a silver-mounted knife which she now wishes in the youngster's body. The conclusion is abruptly told in two stanzas. Olof bids Inga not to talk so, for he is father of her children. He embraces her and gives her a queen's crown and name. **B** has the same story, omitting the incident of the musician. **C** has preserved this circumstance, but has lost both the substitution of the waiting-woman for the bride and the magical coverlet. **D** has also lost these important features of the original story; **E** has retained them.

Danish. 'Brud ikke Mø,' Grundtvig, No 274, v, 304; 'Den rette Brudgom' (Samson and Vendelru), Kristensen, *Jyske Folkeminder*, X, 363, No 97. There are two old versions (more properly only one, so close is the agreement), and a third from recent tradition. This last, Grundtvig's **C**, from Jutland, 1856, seems to be of Swedish origin, and, like Swedish **C**, **D**, wants the talking coverlet, though it has kept the other material feature, that of the substitution. **A** is found in two manuscripts, one of the

sixteenth and the other of the seventeenth century. **B** is the well-known 'Ingefred og Gudrune,' or 'Herr Samsings Nattergale,' Syv, IV, No 62, *Danske Viser*, No 194, translated in Jamieson's *Illustrations*, p. 340, and by Prior, III, 347. A later form of **B**, from recent recitation, 1868, is given in Kristensen's *Jydske Folkeviser*, I, No 53.

The story in **A** runs thus: Sølverlad and Vendelrod [Ingefred and Gudrune] were sitting together, and Vendelrod wept sorely. Sølverlad asked her sister the reason, and was told there was cause. Would she be bride one night? Vendelrod would give her wedding clothes and all her outfit. But Sølverlad asked for bridegroom too, and Vendelrod would not give up her bridegroom, happen what might. She went to church and was married to Samsing. On the way from church they met a spaeman [**B**, shepherd], who warned Vendelrod that Samsing had some nightingales that could tell him whether he had married a maid or no. The sisters turned aside and changed clothes, but could not [65] change cheeks! Sølverlad was conducted to Samsing's house and placed on the bride bench. An unlucky jester called out, "Methinks this is not Vendelrod!" but a gold ring adroitly thrown into his bosom opened his eyes still wider, and made him pretend he had meant nothing. The supposed bride is put to bed. Samsing invokes his nightingales: "Have I a maid or no?" They reply, it is a maid that lies in the bed, but Vendelrod stands on the floor. Samsing asks Vendelrod why she avoided her bed, and she answers: her father lived on the strand; her bower was broken into by a large company of men, and one of them robbed her of her honor. In this case there are no tokens for evidence. Samsing owns immediately that he and his men had broken into the bower, and Vendelrod's agony is over.

Some of the usual tokens, gold harp, sark, shoes, and silver-mounted knife, are found in the later **C**. Danish **D** is but a single initial stanza.

Besides Sølverlad and Vendelrod, there is a considerable number of Danish ballads characterized by the feature that a bride is not a maid, and most or all of these have similarities to 'Gil Brenton.' 'Hr. Find og Vendelrod,' Grundtvig,

---

* The inquiry seems to refer to the morning gift. "Die Morgengabe ist ein Geschenk des Mannes als Zeichen der Liebe (in signum amoris), für die Uebergabe der vollen Schönheit (in honore pulchritudinis) und der Jungfräulichkeit (pretium virginitatis)." Weinhold, *Die deutschen Frauen in dem Mittelalter*, S. 270

No 275, has even the talking blanket (sometimes misunderstood to be a bed-*board*). In this piece there is no substitution. Vendelrod gives birth to children, and the news makes Find jump over the table. Still he puts the question mildly, who is the father, and recognizes that he is the man, upon hearing the story of the bower on the strand, and seeing half a gold ring which Vendelrod had received "for her honor."

In 'Ingelilles Bryllup,' Grundtvig, No 276, Blidelild is induced to take Ingelild's place by the promise that she shall marry Ingelild's brother. Hr. Magnus asks her why she is so sad, and says he knows she is not a maid. Blidelild says, "Since you know so much, I will tell you more," and relates Ingelild's adventure,—how she had gone out to the river, and nine knights came riding by, etc. [so A; in B and C we have the bower on the strand, as before]. Hr. Magnus avows that he was the ninth, who stayed when eight rode away. Blidelild begs that he will allow her to go and look for some lost rings, and uses the opportunity to send back Ingelild in her stead.

Various other Scandinavian ballads have more or less of the story of those which have been mentioned. In the Danish 'Brud i Vaande,' Grundtvig, No 277, a bride is taken with untimely pains while being "brought home." The question asked in several of the Scottish ballads, whether the saddle is uncomfortable, occurs in A, B; the bower that was forced by eight swains and a knight in A, C, D, F; the gifts in A, B, F; and an express acknowledgment of the act of violence by the bridegroom in A, B, D. We find all of these traits except the first in the corresponding Swedish ballad 'Herr Äster och Fröken Sissa,' Afzelius, No 38, new ed., No 32,[1]; the saddle and broken bower in Swedish D, Grundtvig, No 277, Bilag 1; only the saddle in Swedish F, Grundtvig, No. 277, Bilag 3, and C, Arwidsson, No 132; the saddle and gifts in Icelandic A, B, C, D, E, Grundtvig, No 277, Bilag 5, 6, 7, 8.

'Peder og Malfred,' Grundtvig, No 278 (= 'Herr Peders Hustru,' Kristensen, *Jyske Folkeminder*, X, p. 365), in four versions, the oldest from a manuscript of 1630, represents Sir Peter as riding away from home about a month after his marriage, and meeting a woman who informs him that there is a birth in his house. He returns, and asks who is the father. Sir Peter satisfies himself that he is the man by identifying the gifts, in A, B, C, D; and in A, B we have also the bower by the strand.[*]

In 'Oluf og Ellinsborg,' Grundtvig, No 279, A, B, C, one of the queen's ladies is habitually sad, and is pressed by her lover to account for this. She endeavors to put him off with fictitious reasons, but finally nerves herself to tell the truth: she was walking by herself in her orchard, when five knights came riding by, and one was the cause of her grief. Oluf owns it was all his doing. A Swedish ballad, remarkably close to the Danish, from a manuscript of the date 1572 (the oldest Danish version is also from a manuscript of the 16th century), is 'Riddar Lage och [66] Stolts Elensborg,' Arwidsson, No 56.

'Iver Hr. Jonsøn,' Grundtvig, No 280, in five versions, the oldest of the 16th century, exhibits a lady as fearing the arrival of her lover's ship, and sending her mother to meet him, while she takes to her bed. Immediately upon her betrothed's entering her chamber, she abruptly discloses the cause of her trouble. Eight men had broken into her bower on the strand, and the ninth deprived her of her honor. Iver Hr. Jonsøn, with as little delay, confesses that he was the culprit, and makes prompt arrangements for the wedding.

There is another series of ballads, represented by 'Leesome Brand' in English, and by 'Redselille og Medelvold' in Danish, which

---

[*] A ballad from Normandy, published by Legrand, *Romania*, X, 367, III, which I am surprised to find that I have not mentioned, is a very interesting variety of 'Gil Brenton,' more particularly of the Danish 'Peder og Malfred.' It has the attempt at substitution (a sister); the wife acknowledges that she had been forced (par ses laquais les bras il me bandit); the husband reveals, and proves, that he was the ravisher. The beginning of the Norman ballad, which is lost, would probably have had the feature of the information given the husband by the shepherdess. Another French ballad, corrupted (environs de Redon, Ille-et-Vilaine), has this and the attempt to pass off the sister; the husband kills his wife. Music is ordered in the last stanza. Rolland, IV, 70. An Italian and a Breton ballad which begin like the Danish, but proceed differently, are spoken of under 'Fair Janet,' No 64 in this collection. See now Nigra's 'Fidanzata infedele' in his collection, No 34, p. 197.

describe a young woman, who is on the point of becoming a mother, as compelled to go off on horseback with her lover, and suffering from the ride. We find the question, whether the saddle is too narrow or the way too long, in the Danish 'Bolde Hr. Nilaus' Løn,' Grundtvig, 270, 'Redselille og Medelvold,' Grundtvig, 271 C, D, E, I, K, L, M, P, Q, V, Y, and the Norwegian versions, A, D, E, F, of 'Sønnens Sorg,' Grundtvig, 272, Bilag 1, 4, 5, 6.[*] The gifts also occur in Grundtvig's 271 A, Z, and Norwegian D, Bilag 9.

Perhaps no set of incidents is repeated so often in northern ballads as the forcing of the bower on the strand, the giving of keepsakes, the self-identification of the ravisher through these, and his full and hearty reparation. All or some of these traits are found in many ballads besides those belonging to the groups here spoken of: as 'Hildebrand og Hilde,' E, I, Grundtvig, No 83, and Norwegian A, III, 857; 'Guldsmedens Datter,' Grundtvig, 245, and its Swedish counterpart at p. 481 of the preface to the same, and in Eva Wigström's *Folkdiktning*, p. 37, No 18; 'Liden Kirstins Dans,' Grundtvig, 263 (translated by Prior, 112), and Norwegian B, C, Bilag 2, 3; 'Jomfruens Harpeslæt,' Grundtvig, 265 (translated by Jamieson, *Illustrations*, p. 382, Prior, 123, Buchanan, p. 6), and Swedish D, Bilag 2, Swedish A, Afzelius, 81. So Landstad, 42, 45; Arwidsson, 141; Grundtvig, 37 G, 38 A, D, and other versions of both; Kristensen, I, No 95, II, No 28 A, C. 'Bitte Mette,' Kristensen, *Jyske Folkeminder*, V, 57, No 7, affords another version.

A very pretty Norwegian tale has for the talisman a stepping-stone at the side of the bed: Asbjørnsen og Moe, No 29, 'Vesle Aase Gaasepige,' Dasent, 2d ed., p. 478. An English prince had pictures taken of all the handsomest princesses, to pick his bride by. When the chosen one arrived, Aase the goose-girl informed her that the stone at the bedside knew everything and told the prince; so if she felt uneasy on any account, she must not step on it. The princess begged Aase to take her place till the prince was fast asleep, and then they would change. When Aase came and put her foot on the stone, the prince asked, "Who is it that is stepping into my bed?" "A maid clean and pure," answered the stone. By and by the princess came and took Aase's place. When they were getting up in the morning, the prince asked again, "Who is it stepping out of my bed?" "One that has had three children," said the stone. The prince sent his first choice away, and tried a second. Aase faithfully warned her, and she had cause for heeding the advice. When Aase stepped in, the stone said it was a maid clean and pure; when the princess stepped out, the stone said it was one that had had six children. The prince was longer in hitting on a third choice. Aase took the bride's place once more, but this time the prince put a ring on her finger, which was so tight that she could not get it off, for he saw that all was not right. In the morning, when he asked, "Who is stepping out of my bed?" the stone answered, "One that has had nine children." Then the prince asked the stone to clear up the mystery, and it revealed how the princesses had put little Aase in their place. The prince went straight to Aase to see if she had the ring. She had tied a rag over her finger, pretending she had cut it; but the prince soon had the rag off, recognized his ring, and Aase got the prince, for the good reason that so it was to be.

The artifice of substituting waiting-woman for bride has been thought to be derived from [67] the romance of Tristan, in which Brangwain [Brengain, Brangæne] sacrifices herself for Isold: Scott's 'Sir Tristrem,' ii, 54; Gottfried v. Strassburg, xviii, ed. Bechstein. Grundtvig truly remarks that a borrowing by the romance from the popular ballad is as probable a supposition as the converse; and that, even should we grant the name of the hero of the ballad to be a reminiscence of that of Isold's attendant (e.g. Brangwill of Brangwain), nothing follows as to the priority of the romance in respect to this passage. A similar artifice is employed in the ballad of 'Torkild Trundeson,' *Danske Viser*, 200 (translated by Prior, 100); Afzelius, II, 86, from the Danish; Arwidsson, 36; *Íslenzk Fornkvæði*, II, 281, No 612, A 42f, B 42, C 29. The resemblance is close to 'Ingelilles Bryllup,' C,

---

[*]   And again, "is it the saddle, your horse, or your true-love?" almost exactly as in our **B, E, F**, Grundtvig, 40 C, **E, F**, Afzelius, 91, Landstad, 45, 52. So the Scottish ballad, 'The Cruel Brother,' **B** 15f.

Grundtvig, 276. See also, further on, 'The Twa Knights.' For other cases of this substitution see Legrand, *Recueil de Contes populaires grecs*, p. 257, 'La Princesse et sa Nourrice;' Köhler, *Romania*, XI, 581–84, 'Le conte de la reine qui tua son sénéchal; '*Neh-Manzer, ou Les Neuf Loges, conte, traduit du persan par M. Lescallier*, Gènes, 1808, p. 55, 'Histoire du devin Afezzell.' (Köhler.) The last I have not seen.

The Billie Blin presents himself in at least four Scottish ballads: 'Gil Brenton,' **C**; 'Willie's Lady;' one version of 'Young Beichan;' two of 'The Knight and Shepherd's Daughter;' and also in the English ballad of 'King Arthur and the King of Cornwall,' here under the slightly disfigured name of Burlow Beanie.[*] In all he is a serviceable household demon; of a decidedly benignant disposition in the first four, and, though a loathly fiend with seven heads in the last, very obedient and useful when once thoroughly subdued. He is clearly of the same nature as the Dutch *belewitte* and German *bilwiz*, characterized by Grimm as a friendly domestic genius, *penas, guote holde*;[†] and the names are actually associated in a passage cited by Grimm from Voet: "De illis quos nostrates appellant *beeldwit et blinde belien*, a quibus nocturna visa videri atque ex iis arcana revelari putant."[‡] Though the etymology of these words is not unencumbered with difficulty, *bil* seems to point to a just and kindly-tempered being. Bilvís, in the seventh book of *Saxo Grammati-*

cus, is an aged counsellor whose bent is to make peace, while his brother Bölvís, a blind man, is a strife-breeder and mischief-maker.[§] The same opposition of Bil and Böl apparently occurs in the Edda, Grímnismál, 47[4], where Bil-eygr and Böl-eygr (Bal-eygr) are appellatives of Odin, which may signify mild-eyed and evil-eyed. Bölvís is found again in the Hrómund's saga, under the description of 'Blind the Bad,' and 'the Carl Blind whose name was Bavís.' But much of this saga is taken from the story of Helgi Hundingslayer; and Blind the Bad in the saga is only Sæmund's Blindr inn bölvísi,—the blind man whose baleful wit sees through the disguise of Helgi, and all but betrays the rash hero to his enemies; that is, Odin in his malicious mood (Bölverkr), who will presently be seen in the ballad of 'Earl Brand' masking as Old Carl Hood, "aye for ill and never for good." Originally and properly, perhaps, only the bad member of this mythical pair is blind; but it would not be at all strange that later tradition, which confuses and degrades so much in the old mythology, should transfer blindness to the good-natured one, and give rise to the anomalous Billie Blind. See Grimm, *Deutsche Mythologie*, 1879, I, 391 ff; Uhland, *Zur Geschichte der Dichtung u. Sage*, III, 132 ff, VII, 229; Schmeller, *Bayerisches Wörterbuch*, II, 1037 ff, ed. 1877; Van den Bergh, *Woordenboek der nederlandsche Mythologie*, 12.

It has been suggested to me that "the Haleigh throw" in **E** 6 is a corruption of the High Leith Row, a street in Edinburgh. I have not as yet been able to obtain information of such a street.

D is translated by Grundtvig, *Engelske og skotske Folkeviser*, No 40, p. 262.

---

[*] The auld belly-blind man in 'Earl Richard,' 44[3], 45[1], Kinloch's A. S. *Ballads*, p. 15, retains the bare name; and Belly Blind, or Billie Blin, is a Scotch name for the game of Blindman's-buff.

[†] What is said of the *bilwiz* must be understood of the original conception. Grimm notes that this sprite, and others, lose their friendly character in later days and come to be regarded as purely malicious. See also E. Mogk in Paul's *Grundriss der germ. Philologie*, I, 1019.

[‡] Gisbertus Voetius, De Miraculis, *Disput.*, II, 1018. Cited also by Schmeller, *Bayerisches Wörterbuch*, from J. Prætorius's *Alectryomantia*, p. 3.

[§] Merlin, in Layamon, v. 17130ff (as pointed out by Grundtvig, I, 274), says that his mind is balewise, "mi gæst is bæliwis," and that he is not disposed to gladness, mirth, or good words.

A

a. Jamieson-Brown MS., No 16, p. 34. **b.** William
Tytler's Brown MS., No 3. From the recitation of Mrs
Brown of Falkland, 1783, Aberdeenshire.

Chil' Bren-ton has sent o'er the____ fame, Chil' Bren-ton's brought his__ la-dy hame;

An' sev-en score o'__ ships came her wi', The la-dy by the_ green-wood____ tree.

A. b. Ritson-Tytler-Brown MS., pp. 22–30; copied by Joseph Ritson, c. 1792–1794. See Bronson, I, 102, for
a conjectural reading of this tune.

1 GIL BRENTON has sent oer the fame,
    He's woo'd a wife an brought her hame.

2 Full sevenscore o ships came her wi,
    The lady by the greenwood tree.

3 There was twal an twal wi beer an wine,
    An twal an twal wi muscadine:

4 An twall an twall wi bouted flowr,
    An twall an twall wi paramour:

5 An twall an twall wi baken bread,
    An twall an twall wi the goud sae red.

6 Sweet Willy was a widow's son,
    An at her stirrup-foot he did run.

7 An she was dressd i the finest pa,
    But ay she loot the tears down fa.

8 An she was deckd wi the fairest flowrs,
    But ay she loot the tears down pour.

9 'O is there water i your shee?
    Or does the win blaw i your glee?

10 'Or are you mourning i your meed
    That eer you left your mither gueede?

11 'Or are ye mourning i your tide
    That ever ye was Gil Brenton's bride?'

12 'The[re] is nae water i my shee,
    Nor does the win blaw i my glee:

13 'Nor am I mourning i my tide
    That eer I was Gil Brenton's bride:

14 'But I am mourning i my meed
    That ever I left my mither gueede.

15 'But, bonny boy, tell to me
    What is the customs o your country.'

16 'The customs o't, my dame,' he says,
    'Will ill a gentle lady please.

17 'Seven king's daughters has our king wedded,
    An seven king's daughters has our king bedded.

18 'But he's cutted the paps frae their breast-bane,
    An sent them mourning hame again.

19 'But whan you come to the palace yate,
    His mither a golden chair will set.

20 'An be you maid or be you nane,
    O sit you there till the day be dane.

21 'An gin you're sure that you are a maid,
    Ye may gang safely to his bed.

22 'But gin o that you be na sure,
    Then hire some woman o youre bowr.'

23 O whan she came to the palace yate,
    His mither a golden chair did set.

24 An was she maid or was she nane,
    She sat in it till the day was dane.

25 An she's calld on her bowr woman,
    That waiting was her bowr within.

26 'Five hundred pound, maid, I'll gi to the,
    An sleep this night wi the king for me.'

27 Whan bells was rung, an mass was sung,
   An a' man unto bed was gone,

28 Gil Brenton an the bonny maid
   Intill ae chamber they were laid.

29 'O speak to me, blankets, an speak to me, sheets,
   An speak to me, cods, that under me sleeps;

30 'Is this a maid that I ha wedded?
   Is this a maid that I ha bedded?'

31 'It's nae a maid that you ha wedded,
   But it's a maid that you ha bedded.

32 'Your lady's in her bigly bowr,
   An for you she drees mony sharp showr.'

33 O he has taen him thro the ha,
   And on his mither he did ca.

34 'I am the most unhappy man
   That ever was in christend lan.

35 'I woo'd a maiden meek an mild,
   An I've marryed a woman great wi child.'

36 'O stay, my son, intill this ha,
   An sport you wi your merry men a'.

37 'An I'll gang to yon painted bowr,
   An see how 't fares wi yon base whore.'

38 The auld queen she was stark an strang;
   She gard the door flee aff the ban.

39 The auld queen she was stark an steer;
   She gard the door lye i the fleer.

40 'O is your bairn to laird or loon?
   Or is it to your father's groom?'

41 'My bairn's na to laird or loon,
   Nor is it to my father's groom.

42 'But hear me, mither, on my knee,
   An my hard wierd I'll tell to thee.

43 'O we were sisters, sisters seven,
   We was the fairest under heaven.

44 'We had nae mair for our seven years wark
   But to shape an sue the king's son a sark.

45 'O it fell on a Saturday's afternoon,
   Whan a' our langsome wark was dane,

46 'We keist the cavils us amang,
   To see which shoud to the greenwood gang.

47 'Ohone, alas! for I was youngest,
   An ay my wierd it was the hardest.

48 'The cavil it did on me fa,
   Which was the cause of a' my wae.

49 'For to the greenwood I must gae,
   To pu the nut but an the slae;

50 'To pu the red rose an the thyme,
   To strew my mother's bowr and mine.

51 'I had na pu'd a flowr but ane,
   Till by there came a jelly hind greeme,

52 'Wi high-colld hose an laigh-colld shoone,
   An he 'peard to be some kingis son.

53 'An be I maid or be I nane,
   He kept me there till the day was dane.

54 'An be I maid or be I nae,
   He kept me there till the close of day.

55 'He gae me a lock of yellow hair,
   An bade me keep it for ever mair.

56 'He gae me a carket o gude black beads,
   An bade me keep them against my needs.

57 'He gae to me a gay gold ring,
   An bade me ke[e]p it aboon a' thing.

58 'He gae to me a little pen-kniffe,
   An bade me keep it as my life.'

59 'What did you wi these tokens rare
   That ye got frae that young man there?'

60 'O bring that coffer hear to me,
   And a' the tokens ye sal see.'

61 An ay she rauked, an ay she flang,
   Till a' the tokens came till her han.

62 'O stay here, daughter, your bowr within,
   Till I gae parley wi my son.'

63 O she has taen her thro the ha,
   An on her son began to ca.

64 'What did you wi that gay gold ring
   I bade you keep aboon a' thing?

65 'What did you wi that little pen-kniffe
   I bade you keep while you had life?

66 'What did you wi that yallow hair
   I bade you keep for ever mair?

67 'What did you wi that good black beeds
   I bade you keep against your needs?'

68 'I gae them to a lady gay
   I met i the greenwood on a day.

69 'An I would gi a' my father's lan,
   I had that lady my yates within.

70 'I would gi a' my ha's an towrs,
   I had that bright burd i my bowrs.'

71 'O son, keep still your father's lan; [70]
   You hae that lady your yates within.

72 'An keep you still your ha's an towrs
   You hae that bright burd i your bowrs.'

73 Now or a month was come an gone,
   This lady bare a bonny young son.

74 An it was well written on his breast-bane
   'Gil Brenton is my father's name.'

B

Scott's *Minstrelsy*, ii, 117, ed. 1802. Ed. 1830, iii, 263.
Partly from the recitation of Miss Christian Rutherford.

1 COSPATRICK has sent oer the faem,
   Cospatrick brought his ladye hame.

2 And fourscore ships have come her wi,
   The ladye by the grenewood tree.

3 There were twal and twal wi baken bread,
   And twal and twal wi gowd sae reid:

4 And twal and twal wi bouted flour,
   And twal and twal wi the paramour.

5 Sweet Willy was a widow's son,
   And at her stirrup he did run.

6 And she was clad in the finest pall,
   But aye she let the tears down fall.

7 'O is your saddle set awrye?
   Or rides your steed for you owre high?

8 'Or are you mourning in your tide
   That you suld be Cospatrick's bride?'

9 'I am not mourning at this tide
   That I suld be Cospatrick's bride;

10 'But I am sorrowing in my mood
   That I suld leave my mother good.

11 'But, gentle boy, come tell to me,
   What is the custom of thy countrye?'

12 'The custom thereof, my dame,' he says,
   'Will ill a gentle laydye please.

13 'Seven king's daughters has our lord wedded,
   And seven king's daughters has our lord bedded;

14 'But he's cutted their breasts frae their breast
   bane,
   And sent them mourning hame again.

15 'Yet, gin you're sure that you're a maid,
   Ye may gae safely to his bed;

16 'But gif o that ye be na sure,
   Then hire some damsell o your bour.'

17 The ladye's calld her bour-maiden,
That waiting was into her train;

18 'Five thousand merks I will gie thee,
To sleep this night with my lord for me.'

19 When bells were rung, and mass was sayne,
And a' men unto bed were gane,

20 Cospatrick and the bonny maid,
Into ae chamber they were laid.

21 'Now, speak to me, blankets, and speak to me,
bed,
And speak, thou sheet, inchanted web;

22 'And speak up, my bonny brown sword, that
winna lie,
Is this a true maiden that lies by me?'

23 'It is not a maid that you hae wedded,
But it is a maid that you hae bedded.

24 'It is a liel maiden that lies by thee,
But not the maiden that it should be.'

25 O wrathfully he left the bed,
And wrathfully his claiths on did.

26 And he has taen him thro the ha,
And on his mother he did ca.

[71] 27 'I am the most unhappy man
That ever was in christen land!

28 'I courted a maiden meik and mild,
And I hae gotten naething but a woman wi
child.'

29 'O stay, my son, into this ha,
And sport ye wi your merrymen a';

30 'And I will to the secret bour,
To see how it fares wi your paramour.'

31 The carline she was stark and sture;
She aff the hinges dang the dure.

32 'O is your bairn to laird or loun?
Or is it to your father's groom?'

33 'O hear me, mother, on my knee,
Till my sad story I tell to thee.

34 'O we were sisters, sisters seven,
We were the fairest under heaven.

35 'It fell on a summer's afternoon,
When a' our toilsome task was done,

36 'We cast the kavils us amang,
To see which suld to the grene-wood gang.

37 'O hon, alas! for I was youngest,
And aye my wierd it was the hardest.

38 'The kavil it on me did fa,
Whilk was the cause of a' my woe.

39 'For to the grene-wood I maun gae,
To pu the red rose and the slae;

40 'To pu the red rose and the thyme,
To deck my mother's bour and mine.

41 'I hadna pu'd a flower but ane,
When by there came a gallant hende,

42 'Wi high-colld hose and laigh-colld shoon,
And he seemd to be sum king's son.

43 'And be I maid or be I nae,
He kept me there till the close o day.

44 'And be I maid or be I nane,
He kept me there till the day was done.

45 'He gae me a lock o his yellow hair,
And bade me keep it ever mair.

46 'He gae me a carknet o bonny beads,
And bade me keep it against my needs.

47 'He gae to me a gay gold ring,
And bade me keep it abune a' thing.'

48 'What did ye wi the tokens rare
That ye gat frae that gallant there?

49 'O bring that coffer unto me,
And a' the tokens ye sall see.'

50 'Now stay, daughter, your hour within,
  While I gae parley wi my son.'

51 O she has taen her thro the ha,
  And on her son began to ca.

52 'What did you wi the bonny beads
  I bade ye keep against your needs?

53 'What did you wi the gay gowd ring
  I bade ye keep abune a' thing?'

54 'I gae them a' to a ladye gay
  I met in grene-wood on a day.

55 'But I wad gie a' my halls and tours,
  I had that ladye within my bours.

56 'But I wad gie my very life,
  I had that ladye to my wife.'

57 'Now keep, my son, your ha's and tours;
  Ye have that bright burd in your bours.

58 'And keep, my son, your very life;
  Ye have that ladye to your wife.'

59 Now or a month was cum and gane,
  The ladye bore a bonny son.

60 And 't was weel written on his breast-bane,
  'Cospatrick is my father's name.'

61 'O rowe my ladye in satin and silk,
  And wash my son in the morning milk.'

C

Cromek's *Remains of Nithsdale and Galloway Song*,
p. 207. "From the recital of a peasant-woman of Gallo-
way, upwards of ninety years of age."

1 WE were sisters, we were seven,
  We were the fairest under heaven.

2 And it was a' our seven years wark
  To sew our father's seven sarks.

3 And whan our seven years wark was done,
  We laid it out upo the green.

4 We coost the lotties us amang,
  Wha wad to the greenwood gang,

5 To pu the lily but and the rose,
  To strew witha' our sisters' bowers.

6 . . . . . I was youngest,
  . . . . . my weer was hardest.

7 And to the greenwood I bud gae,
  .   .   .   .   .

8 There I met a handsome childe,
  .   .   .   .   .

9 High-coled stockings and laigh-coled shoon,
  He bore him like a king's son.

10 An was I weel, or was I wae,
  He keepit me a' the simmer day.

11 An though I for my hame-gaun sich[t],
  He keepit me a' the simmer night.

12 He gae to me a gay gold ring,
  And bade me keep it aboon a' thing.

13 He gae to me a cuttie knife,
  And bade me keep it as my life:

14 Three lauchters o his yellow hair,
  For fear we wad neer meet mair.
    *   *   *   *   *

15 Next there came shippes three,
  To carry a' my bridal fee.

16 Gowd were the beaks, the sails were silk,
  Wrought wi maids' hands like milk.

17 They came toom and light to me,
  But heavie went they waie frae me.

18 They were fu o baken bread,
  They were fu of wine sae red.

19 My dowry went a' by the sea,
   But I gaed by the grenewode tree.

20 An I sighed and made great mane,
   As thro the grenewode we rade our lane.

21 An I ay siched an wiped my ee,
   That eer the grenewode I did see.

22 'Is there water in your glove,
      Or win into your shoe?
   O[r] am I oer low a foot-page
      To rin by you, ladie?'

23 'O there's nae water in my glove,
      Nor win into my shoe;
   But I am maning for my mither
      Wha's far awa frae me.'
   *   *   *   *   *

24 'Gin ye be a maiden fair,
   Meikle gude ye will get there.

25 'If ye be a maiden but,
   Meikle sorrow will ye get.

26 'For seven king's daughters he hath wedded,
   But never wi ane o them has bedded.

27 'He cuts the breasts frae their breast-bane,
   An sends them back unto their dame.

28 'He sets their backs unto the saddle,
   An sends them back unto their father.

29 'But be ye maiden or be ye nane,
   To the gowden chair ye draw right soon.

30 'But be ye leman or be ye maiden,
   Sit nae down till ye be bidden.'

31 Was she maiden or was she nane,
   To the gowden chair she drew right soon.

32 Was she leman or was she maiden,
   She sat down ere she was bidden.

[73] 33 Out then spake the lord's mother;
   Says, 'This is not a maiden fair.

34 'In that chair nae leal maiden
   Eer sits down till they be bidden.'

35 The Billie Blin then outspake he,
   As he stood by the fair ladie.

36 'The bonnie may is tired wi riding,
   Gaurd her sit down ere she was bidden.'
   *   *   *   *   *
37 But on her waiting-maid she ca'd
      'Fair ladie, what's your will wi me?'
   'O ye maun gie yere maidenheid
      This night to an unco lord for me.'

38 'I hae been east, I hae been west,
      I hae been far beyond the sea,
   But ay, by grenewode or by bower,
      I hae keepit my virginitie.

39 'But will it for my ladie plead,
   I'll gie 't this night to an unco lord.'
   *   *   *   *   *
40 When bells were rung an vespers sung,
   An men in sleep were locked soun,

41 Childe Branton and the waiting-maid
   Into the bridal bed were laid.

42 'O lie thee down, my fair ladie,
   Here are a' things meet for thee;

43 'Here's a bolster for yere head,
   Here is sheets an comelie weids.'
   *   *   *   *   *
44 'Now tell to me, ye Billie Blin,
   If this fair dame be a leal maiden.'

45 'I wat she is as leal a wight
   As the moon shines on in a simmer night.

46 'I wat she is as leal a may
   As the sun shines on in a simmer day.

47 'But your bonnie bride's in her bower,
   Dreeing the mither's trying hour.'

48 Then out o his bridal bed he sprang,
   An into his mither's bower he ran.

49 'O mither kind, O mither dear,
   This is nae a maiden fair.

50 'The maiden I took to my bride
   Has a bairn atween her sides.

51 'The maiden I took to my bower
    Is dreeing the mither's trying hour.'

52 Then to the chamber his mother flew,
    And to the wa the door she threw.

53 She stapt at neither bolt nor ban,
    Till to that ladie's bed she wan.

54 Says, 'Ladie fair, sae meek an mild,
    Wha is the father o yere child?

55 'O mither dear,' said that ladie,
    'I canna tell gif I sud die.

56 'We were sisters, we were seven,
    We were the fairest under heaven.

57 'And it was a' our seven years wark
    To sew our father's seven sarks.

58 'And whan our seven years wark was done,
    We laid it out upon the green.

59 'We coost the lotties us amang,
    Wha wad to the greenwode gang;

60 'To pu the lily but an the rose,
    To strew witha' our sisters' bowers.

61 . . . . . 'I was youngest,
    . . . . . my weer was hardest.

62 'And to the greenwode I bu[d] gae.
.   .   .   .   .

63 'There I met a handsome childe,
.   .   .   .   .

64 'Wi laigh-coled stockings and high-coled shoon,
    He seemed to be some king's son.

65 'And was I weel or was I wae,
    He keepit me a' the simmer day.

66 'Though for my hame-gaun I oft sicht,
    He keepit me a' the simmer night.

67 'He gae to me a gay gold ring,
    An bade me keep it aboon a' thing;

68 'Three lauchters o his yellow hair,
    For fear that we suld neer meet mair.

69 'O mither, if ye'll believe nae me,
    Break up the coffer, an there ye'll see.'

70 An ay she coost, an ay she flang,
    Till her ain gowd ring came in her hand.

71 And scarce aught i the coffer she left,
    Till she gat the knife wi the siller heft,

72 Three lauchters o his yellow hair,
    Knotted wi ribbons dink and rare.

73 She cried to her son, 'Where is the ring
    Your father gave me at our wooing,
    An I gae you at your hunting?

74 'What did ye wi the cuttie knife,
    I bade ye keep it as yere life?'

75 'O haud yere tongue, my mither dear;
    I gae them to a lady fair.

76 'I wad gie a' my lands and rents,
    I had that ladie within my brents.

77 'I wad gie a' my lands an towers,
    I had that ladie within my bowers.'

78 'Keep still yere lands, keep still yere rents;
    Ye hae that ladie within yere brents.

79 'Keep still yere lands, keep still yere towers;
    Ye hae that lady within your bowers.'

80 Then to his ladie fast ran he,
    An low he kneeled on his knee.

81 'O tauk ye up my son,' said he,
    'An, mither, tent my fair ladie.

82 'O wash him purely i the milk,
    And lay him saftly in the silk.

83 'An ye maun bed her very soft,
    For I maun kiss her wondrous oft.'

84 It was weel written on his breast-bane
    Childe Branton was the father's name.

85 It was weel written on his right hand
    He was the heir o his daddie's land.

D

Buchan's *Ancient Ballads and Songs of the North of Scotland*, 1, 204.

1 WE were sisters, sisters seven,
    Bowing down, bowing down
The fairest women under heaven.
    And aye the birks a-bowing

2 They kiest kevels them amang,
    Wha woud to the grenewood gang.

3 The kevels they gied thro the ha,
    And on the youngest it did fa.

4 Now she must to the grenewood gang,
    To pu the nuts in grenewood hang.

5 She hadna tarried an hour but ane
    Till she met wi a highlan groom.

6 He keeped her sae late and lang
    Till the evening set and birds they sang.

7 He gae to her at their parting
    A chain o gold and gay gold ring;

8 And three locks o his yellow hair;
    Bade her keep them for evermair.

9 When six lang months were come and gane.
    A courtier to this lady came.

10 Lord Dingwall courted this lady gay,
    And so he set their wedding-day.

11 A little boy to the ha was sent,
    To bring her horse was his intent.

12 As she was riding the way along,
    She began to make a heavy moan.

[75] 13 'What ails you, lady,' the boy said,
    'That ye seem sae dissatisfied?

14 'Are the bridle reins for you too strong?
    Or the stirrups for you too long?'

15 'But, little boy, will ye tell me
    The fashions that are in your countrie?'

16 'The fashions in our ha I'll tell,
    And o them a' I'll warn you well.

17 'When ye come in upon the floor,
    His mither will meet you wi a golden chair.

18 'But be ye maid or be ye nane,
    Unto the high seat make ye boun.

19 'Lord Dingwall aft has been beguild
    By girls whom young men hae defiled.

20 'He's cutted the paps frae their breast-bane,
    And sent them back to their ain hame.'

21 When she came in upon the floor,
    His mother met her wi a golden chair.

22 But to the high seat she made her boun:
    She knew that maiden she was nane.

23 When night was come, they went to bed,
    And ower her breast his arm he laid.

24 He quickly jumped upon the floor,
    And said, 'I've got a vile rank whore.'

25 Unto his mother he made his moan,
    Says, 'Mother dear, I am undone.

26 'Ye've aft tald, when I brought them hame,
    Whether they were maid or nane.

27 'I thought I'd gotten a maiden bright;
    I've gotten but a waefu wight.

28 'I thought I'd gotten a maiden clear,
    But gotten but a vile rank whore.'

29 'When she came in upon the floor,
    I met her wi a golden chair.

30 'But to the high seat she made her boun,
    Because a maiden she was nane.'

31 'I wonder wha's tauld that gay ladie
    The fashion into our countrie.'

32 'It is your little boy I blame,
　Whom ye did send to bring her hame.'

33 Then to the lady she did go,
　And said, 'O Lady, let me know

34 'Who has defiled your fair bodie:
　Ye're the first that has beguiled me.'

35 'O we were sisters, sisters seven,
　The fairest women under heaven.

36 'And we kiest kevels us amang,
　Wha woud to the grenewood gang;

37 'For to pu the finest flowers,
　To put around our summer bowers.

38 'I was the youngest o them a';
　The hardest fortune did me befa.

39 'Unto the grenewood I did gang,
　And pu'd the nuts as they down hang.

40 'I hadna stayd an hour but ane
　Till I met wi a highlan groom.

41 'He keeped me sae late and lang
　Till the evening set and birds they sang.

42 'He gae to me at our parting
　A chain of gold and gay gold ring;

43 'And three locks o his yellow hair;
　Bade me keep them for evermair.

44 'Then for to show I make nae lie,
　Look ye my trunk, and ye will see.'

45 Unto the trunk then she did go,
　To see if that were true or no.

46 And aye she sought, and aye she flang,
　Till these four things came to her hand.

47 Then she did to her ain son go,
　And said, 'My son, ye'll let me know,

48 'Ye will tell to me this thing:
　What did you wi my wedding-ring?'

49 'Mother dear, I'll tell nae lie:　　　[76]
　I gave it to a gay ladie.

50 'I would gie a' my ha's and towers,
　I had this bird within my bowers.'

51 'Keep well, keep well your lands and strands;
　Ye hae that bird within your hands.

52 'Now, my son, to your bower ye'll go:
　Comfort your ladie, she's full o woe.'

53 Now when nine months were come and gane,
　The lady she brought hame a son.

54 It was written on his breast-bane
　Lord Dingwall was his father's name.

55 He's taen his young son in his arms,
　And aye he praisd his lovely charms.

56 And he has gien him kisses three,
　And doubled them ower to his ladie.

E

Elizabeth Cochrane's Song-Book, p. 146, No 112.

1 LORD BENWALL he's a hunting gone;
　Hey down, etc.
He's taken with him all his merry men.
　Hey, etc.

2 As he was walking late alone,
　He spyed a lady both brisk and young.

3 He keeped her so long and long,
　From the evening late till the morning came.

4 All that he gave her at their parting
　Was a pair of gloves and a gay gold ring.

5 Lord Benwall he's a wooing gone,
　And he's taken with him all his merry men.

6 As he was walking the Haleigh throw,
   He spy'd seven ladyes all in a row.

7 He cast a lot among them all;
   Upon the youngest the lot did fall.

8 He wedded her and brought her home,
   And by the way she made great moan.

9 'What aileth my dearest and dayly flower?
   What ails my dear, to make such moan?

10 'Does the steed carry you too high?
   Or does thy pillow sit awry?

11 'Or does the wind blow in thy glove?
   Or is thy heart after another love?'

12 'The steed does not carry me too high,
   Nor does my pillow sit awry.

13 'Nor does the wind blow in my glove,
   Nor is my heart after another love.'

14 When they were doun to supper set,
   The weary pain took her by the back.

15 'What ails my dearest and dayly flower?
   What ails my dearest, to make such moan?'

16 'I am with child, and it's not to thee,
   And oh and alas, what shall I doe!'

17 'I thought I had got a maid so mild;
   But I have got a woman big with child.

18 'I thought I had got a dayly flower;
   I have gotten but a common whore.'
   *   *   *   *   *
19 'Rise up, Lord Benwall, go to your hall,
   And cherrish up your merry men all.'
   *   *   *   *   *

20 'As I was walking once late alone,
   I spy'd a lord, both brisk and young.

21 'He keeped me so long and long,
   From the evening late till the morning came.

22 'All that he gave me at our parting
   Was a pair of gloves and a gay gold ring.

23 'If you will not believe what I tell to thee,
   There's the key of my coffer, you may go and
   see.'

24 His mother went, and threw and flang,   [7:
   Till to her hand the ring it came.

25 'Lord Benwall, wilt thou tell to me
   Where is the ring I gave to thee?'

26 'Now I would give all my lands and tower,
   To have that lady in my bower.

27 'I would give all my lands and rents,
   To have that lady in my tents.'

28 'You need not give all your lands and tower,
   For you have that lady in your power.

29 'You need not give all your lands and rents,
   For you have that lady in your tents.'

30 Now it was written on the child's breast-bone
   Lord Benwall's sirname and his name.

31 It was written on the child's right hand
   That he should be heir of Lord Benwall's land.

32 'Canst cloath my lady in the silk,
   And feed my young son with the milk.'

F

a. Motherwell's MS., p 219. From the recitation of
Mrs Thomson, February, 1825. **b.** Motherwell's *Min-
strelsy*, Appendix, p. xvi, the first stanza only.

Se - ven   la - dies liv'd in   a   bower   Hey____ down   and____ ho____ down,

And aye the   young - est   was the   flower,   Hey____ down   and____ ho____ down.

F. b. Motherwell, 1827, Appendix No 5. Singer unknown. Collected by Andrew Blaikie, Paisley.

1 THERE were three sisters in a bouir,
  Eh down and Oh down
And the youngest o them was the fairest flour.
  Eh down and O down

2 And we began our seven years wark,
  To sew our brither John a sark.

3 When seven years was come and gane,
  There was nae a sleeve in it but ane.

4 But we coost kevils us amang
  Wha wud to the green-wood gang.

5 But tho we had coosten neer sae lang,
  The lot it fell on me aye to gang.

6 I was the youngest, and I was the fairest,
  And alace! my wierd it was aye the sairest.

7 .   .   .   .   .
  Till I had to the woods to gae.

8 To pull the cherrie and the slae,
  And to seek our ae brither, we had nae mae.

9 But as I was walking the leas o Lyne,
  I met a youth gallant and fine;

10 Wi milk white stockings and coal black shoon;
  He seemed to be some gay lord's son.

11 But he keepit me there sae lang, sae lang,
  Till the maids in the morning were singing
    their sang.

12 Would I wee or would I way,
  He keepit me the lang simmer day.

13 Would I way or would I wight,
  He keepit me the simmer night.

14 But guess what was at our parting?
  A pair o grass green gloves and a gay gold ring.

15 He gave me three plaits o his yellow hair,
  In token that we might meet mair.

16 But when nine months were come and gane,
  This gallant lord cam back again.

17 He's wed this lady, and taen her wi him
  But as they were riding the leas o Lyne,

18 This lady was not able to ride,

  .   .   .   .   .

19 'O does thy saddle set thee aside?
  Or does thy steed ony wrang way ride?

20 'Or thinkst thou me too low a groom?

  .   .   .   .   .

21 'Or hast thou musing in thy mind
  For the leaving of thy mother kind?'

22 'My saddle it sets not me aside,   [78]
  Nor does my steed ony wrang way ride.

23 'Nor think I thee too low a groom

  .   .   .   .   .

24 'But I hae musing in my mind
  For the leaving of my mother kind.'

25 'I'll bring thee to a mother of mine,
  As good a mother as eer was thine.'

26 'A better mother she may be,
   But an unco woman she'll prove to me.'

27 But when lords and ladies at supper sat,
   Her pains they struck her in the back.

28 When lords and ladies were laid in bed,
   Her pains they struck her in the side.

29 'Rise up, rise up, now, Lord Brangwill,
   For I'm wi child and you do not know 't.'

30 He took up his foot and gave her sic a bang
   Till owre the bed the red blood sprang.

31 He is up to his mother's ha,
   Calling her as hard as he could ca.

32 'I went through moss and I went through mure,
   Thinking to get some lily flouir.

33 .   .   .   .   .
   'But to my house I have brocht a hure.

34 'I thocht to have got a lady baith meek and
        mild,
   But I've got a woman that's big wi child.'

35 'O rest you here, Lord Brangwill,' she said,
   'Till I relieve your lady that lyes so low.'

36 'O daughter dear, will you tell to me
   Who is the father of your babie?'

37 'Yes, mother dear, I will tell thee
   Who is the father of my babie.

38 'As I was walking the leas o Lyne,
   I met a youth gallant and fine;

39 'With milk-white stockings and coal-black
        shoon;
   He seemd to be sum gay lord's son.

40 'He keepit me sae lang, sae lang,
   Till the maids in the morning were singing
        their sang.

41 'Would I wee or would I way,
   He keepit me the lang simmer day.

42 'Would I way or would I wight,
   He keepit me the simmer night.

43 'But guess ye what was at our parting?
   A pair of grass green gloves and a gay gold ring.

44 'He gave me three plaits o his yellow hair,
   In token that we might meet mair.'

45 'O dochter dear, will ye show me
   These tokens that he gave to thee?'

46 'Altho my back should break in three,
   Unto my coffer I must be.'

47 'Thy back it shall not break in three,
   For I'll bring thy coffer to thy knee.'

48 Aye she coost, and aye she flang,
   Till these three tokens came to her hand.

49 Then she is up to her son's ha,
   Calling him hard as she could ca.

50 'O son, O son, will you tell me
   .   .   .   .   .

51 'What ye did wi the grass green gloves and gay
        gold ring
   That ye gat at your own birth-een?'

52 'I gave them to as pretty a may
   As ever I saw in a simmer day.

53 'I wud rather than a' my lands sae broad
   That I had her as sure as eer I had.

54 'I would rather than a' my lands sae free
   I had her here this night wi me.'

55 'I wish you good o your lands sae broad,
   For ye have her as sure as eer ye had.

56 'I wish ye good o your lands sae free,
   For ye have her here this night wi thee.'

57 'Gar wash my auld son in the milk,
   Gar deck my lady's bed wi silk.'

58 He gave his auld son kisses three,
   But he doubled them a' to his gay ladye.

G

Herd's *Ancient and Modern Scots Songs*, 1769, p. 244; ed. 1776, I, 83.

1 As BOTHWELL was walking in the lowlands
  alane,
   Hey down and a down
He met six ladies sae gallant and fine.
   Hey down and a down

2 He cast his lot amang them a',
  And on the youngest his lot did fa.

3 He's brought her frae her mother's bower,
  Unto his strongest castle and tower.

4 But ay she cried and made great moan,
  And ay the tear came trickling down.

5 'Come up, come up,' said the foremost man,
  'I think our bride comes slowly on.'

6 'O lady, sits your saddle awry,
  Or is your steed for you owre high?'

7 'My saddle is not set awry,
  Nor carries me my steed owre high;

8 'But I am weary of my life,
  Since I maun be Lord Bothwell's wife.'

9 He's blawn his horn sae sharp and shrill,
  Up start the deer on evry hill.

10 He's blawn his horn sae lang and loud,
  Up start the deer in gude green-wood.

11 His lady mother lookit owre the castle wa,
  And she saw them riding ane and a'.

12 She's calld upon her maids by seven,
  To mak his bed baith saft and even.

13 She's calld upon her cooks by nine,
  To make their dinner fair and fine.

14 When day was gane, and night was come,
  'What ails my love on me to frown?

15 'Or does the wind blow in your glove?
  Or runs your mind on another love?'

16 'Nor blows the wind within my glove,
  Nor runs my mind on another love

17 'But I nor maid nor maiden am,
  For I'm wi bairn to another man.'

18 'I thought I'd a maiden sae meek and sae mild,
  But I've nought but a woman wi child.'

19 His mother's taen her up to a tower,
  And lockit her in her secret bower.

20 'Now, daughter mine, come tell to me,
  Wha's bairn this is that you are wi.'

21 'O mother dear, I canna learn
  Wha is the faither of my bairn.

22 'But as I walkd in the lowlands my lane,
  I met a gentleman gallant and fine.

23 'He keepit me there sae late and sae lang,
  Frae the evning late till the morning dawn.

24 'And a' that he gied me to my propine
  Was a pair of green gloves and a gay gold ring;

25 'Three lauchters of his yellow hair,
  In case that we shoud meet nae mair.'

26 His lady mother went down the stair:
  .   .   .   .   .

27 'Now son, now son, come tell to me,
  Where's the green gloves I gave to thee?'

28 'I gied to a lady sae fair and so fine   [80]
  The green gloves and a gay gold ring.

29 'But I wad gie my castles and towers,
  I had that lady within my bowers.

30 'But I wad gie my very life,
  I had that lady to be my wife.'

31 'Now keep, now keep your castles and towers,
  You have that lady within your bowers.

32 'Now keep, now keep your very life,
   You have that lady to be your wife.'

33 'O row my lady in sattin and silk,
   And wash my son in the morning milk.'

H

Kinloch MSS, v, 335, in the handwriting of Dr
John Hill Burton.

1 WE were seven sisters in a bower,
   Adown adown, and adown and adown
The flower of a' fair Scotland ower.
   Adown adown, and adown and adown

2 We were sisters, sisters seven,
   The fairest women under heaven.

3 There fell a dispute us amang,
   Wha would to the greenwood gang.

4 They kiest the kevels them amang,
   O wha would to the greenwood gang.

5 The kevels they gied thro the ha,
   And on the youngest it did fa.

6 The kevel fell into her hand,
   To greenwood she was forced to gang.

7 She hedna pued a flower but ane,
   When by there came an earl's son.

8 'And was he well or was he wae,
   He keepet me that summer's day.'

9 And was he weel or was he weight,
   He keepet her that summer's night.

10 And he gave her a gay goud ring
   His mother got at her wedding.

*   *   *   *   *

11 'Oh is yer stirrup set too high?
   Or is your saddle set awry?

12 'Oh is yer stirrup set too side?
   Or what's the reason ye canna ride?'

*   *   *   *   *

13 When all were at the table set,
   Then not a bit could this lady eat.

14 When all made merry at the f[e]ast,
   This lady wished she were at her rest.

*   *   *   *   *

A. a. *In the MS. two lines are written continuously, and
   two of these double lines numbered as one stanza.*
   19^1, 23^1, 69^2, 71^2, *perhaps* gate, gates *in MS.*
   54^1, MS. be a nae. 56^1. casket *in MS.?*
b. 1.

   Chil Brenton has sent oer the faem,
   Chil Brenton's brought his lady hame.

B. *Printed by Scott in four-line stanzas.*
   7, 55, 56, 58, 61, *seem to be the stanzas transferred
   from Herd, but only the last without change.*
   33^2. tell thee, *ed.* 1802; tell to thee, *ed.* 1833.
   51^1. Oh, *ed.* 1802; O, *ed.* 1833.

   *The three stanzas which follow were communicated to
   Scott by Major Henry Hutton, Royal Artillery,*

   *24th December, 1802 (Letters, I, No 77), as rec-
   ollected by his father and the family.* "Scotch Bal-
   lads, Materials for Border Minstrelsy," No 18.
   Instead of 3, 4:

   There's five o them with meal and malt,
   And other five wi beef and salt;
   There's five o them wi well-bak'd bread,
   And other five wi goud so red.

   There's five o them wi the ladies bright,
   There's other five o belted knights;
   There's five o them wi a good black neat,
   And other five wi bleating sheep.

   "And before the two last stanzas, introduce"

O there was seald on his breast-bane,
  'Cospatric is his father's name;'
O there was seald on his right hand
  He should inherit his father's land.

so *is written over the second and in* 1^2.
C. *The stanzas are not divided in Cromek. Between* 14
  and 15 *the following nineteen couplets have been*
  omitted.

First blew the sweet, the simmer wind,
Then autumn wi her breath sae kind,
Before that eer the guid knight came
The tokens of his luve to claim.
Then fell the brown an yellow leaf
Afore the knight o luve shawed prief
Three morns the winter's rime did fa,
When loud at our yett my luve did ca.
'Ye hae daughters, ye hae seven,
Ye hae the fairest under heaven.
I am the lord o lands wide,
Ane o them maun be my bride.
I am lord of a baronie,
Ane o them maun be wi me.
O cherry lips are sweet to pree,
A rosie cheek's meet for the ee;
Lang brown locks a heart can bind,
Bonny black een in luve are kind;
Sma white arms for clasping's meet,
Whan laid atween the bridalsheets;
A kindlie heart is best of a',
An debonnairest in the ha.
Ane by ane thae things are sweet,
Ane by ane in luve they're meet;
But when they a' in ae maid bide,
She is fittest for a bride.
Sae be it weel or be it wae,
The youngest maun be my ladie;
Sae be it gude, sae be it meet,
She maun warm my bridal-sheet.

Little kend he, whan aff he rode,
I was his tokend luve in the wood;
Or when he gied me the wedding-token,
He was sealing the vows he thought were
    broken.

First came a page on a milk-white steed,
Wi golden trappings on his head:
A' gowden was the saddle lap,
And gowden was the page's cap.

15–21 *have been allowed to stand principally on*
  account of 18.

There is small risk in pronouncing 24, 25, 42, 43, 80,
  81 *spurious, and Cunningham surpasses his usual*
  mawkishness in 83.
E *is written in four-line stanzas.*
  19. mother, *in the margin.*
  20. lady, *in the margin.*
F. a. 7^2. MS. Till [Still?].

  7^2 *and* 8, 17 *and* 18^1, 20^1 *and* 21, 23^1 *and* 24, 32
  and 33^2, 50^1 *and* 51, *are respectively written as a*
  stanza in the MS.

  12^1, 41^1. *Motherwell conjectures*
    Would I wait, or would I away.

  13^1, 42^1. *Motherwell conjectures*
    Would I away, or would I wait.

  14^2, 42^2. MS. green sleeves: *but see* 51^1, *and also* **E**
    22^1, **G** 24^2 28^2.
  29^2, *above* you do not know't *is written* know not
    who till, *apparently a conjecture of Motherwell's.*

  30^2, *sometimes recited*
    Till owre the bed this lady he flang.

  53^1. MS. abroad.

b.   1. Seven ladies livd in a bower,
        Hey down and ho down
        And aye the youngest was the flower.
        Hey down and ho down

G. *The stanzas are, not divided in Herd.*
H. 4 *is crossed through in the* MS., *but no reason given.*

6

WILLIE'S LADY

a. 'Willie's Lady,' Fraser-Tytler MS.
b. 'Sweet Willy,' Jamieson-Brown MS., No 15, p. 33.

a, 'Willie's Lady,' was No 1 in the manuscript of fifteen ballads furnished William Tytler by Mrs Brown in 1783, and having been written down a little later than **b** may be regarded as a revised copy. This manuscript, as remarked under No 5, is not now in the possession of the Fraser-Tytler family, having often been most liberally lent, and, probably, at last not returned. But a transcript had been made by the grandfather of the present family of two of the pieces contained in it, and 'Willie's Lady' is one of these two.

[82] Lewis had access to William Tytler's copy, and, having regulated the rhymes, filled out a gap, dropped the passage about the girdle, and made other changes to his taste, printed the ballad in 1801 as No 56 of his *Tales of Wonder*. The next year Scott gave the "ancient copy, never before published," "in its native simplicity, as taken from Mrs Brown of Faulkland's MS.,"—William Tytler's,—in *Minstrelsy of the Scottish Border*, II, 27, but not with literal accuracy. Jamieson, in 1806, gave 'Sweet Willy,' almost exactly according to the text of his Brown manuscript, in an appendix to the second volume of his collection, p. 367, and at p. 175 of the same volume, a reconstruction of the ballad which might have been spared.

b lacks altogether the passage which makes proffer of the cup, **a**, stanzas 5–11, and substitutes at that place the girdle of **a** 21–28. The woodbine in **a** 36, 41, is also wanting, and the concluding stanza. A deficiency both in matter and rhyme at **a** 32 is supplied by **b** 25, 26, but not happily:

'An do you to your mither then,
An bid her come to your boy's christnen;

'For dear's the boy he's been to you:
Then notice well what she shall do.'

Again, the transition in **a**, from st. 33 to st. 34, is abrupt even for a ballad, and **b** introduces here four stanzas narrating the execution of the Billy Blind's injunctions, and ending,

And notic'd well what she did say,

whereby we are prepared for the witch's exclamations.[*]

Danish versions of this ballad are numerous: A–I, 'Hustru og Mands Moder' ['Fostermoder,' 'Stifmoder'], Grundtvig, No 84, II, 404ff: J–T, 'Hustru og Mands Moder,' Kristensen, II, 111ff, No 35; *Skattegraveren*, I, 73, No 436, VII, 97, No 651: U–X, 'Barselkvinden,' Kristensen, I, 201ff, No 74; II, 10, No 7. (The tale, p. 83 b, is reprinted by inadvertence, I, 73, No 234.); three fragments, Kristensen, *Folkeminder*, XI, 42, No 23: Y, 'Hustru og Slegfred,' Grundtvig, No 85, II, 448ff: in all twenty-five, but many of Kristensen's copies are fragments. Grundtvig's 84 **A, B,** and 85 **a** are from manuscripts of the sixteenth century. 84 **F–I** and several repeti-

---

[*] The Jamieson-Brown copy contains seventy-eight verses; Scott's and the Tytler copy, eighty-eight. Dr Anderson's, Nichols's *Illustrations*, VII, 176, counts seventy-six instead of eighty-eight; but, judging by the description which Anderson has given of the Alexander-Fraser-Tytler-Brown MS., at p. 179, he is not exact. Still, so large a discrepancy is hard to explain.

tions of 85 are of the seventeenth. Grundtvig's 84 **C, D, E**, and all Kristensen's versions, are from recent oral tradition. Some of these, though taken down since 1870, are wonderfully well preserved.

The Danish ballads divide into two classes, principally distinguished by their employing or not employing of the artifice of wax children. (There is but one of these in **N, R**, Kristensen's **E, I**, II, 116, 122, and in the oldest Swedish ballad, as in the Scottish: but children in Scandinavian ballads are mostly born in pairs.) Of the former class, to which our only known copy belongs, are **F–I, N–T, X** (Grundtvig, 84 **F–I**, Kristensen, II, No 35, **E–L**, I, No 74 D). **N** and **I** furnish, perhaps, the most consistent story, which, in the former, runs thus: Sir Peter married Ellen (elsewhere Mettelille, Kirstin, Tidelil, Ingerlil), and gave her in charge to his mother, a formidable witch, and, as appears from **F**, violently opposed to the match. The first night of her marriage Ellen conceived twins. She wrapped up her head in her cloak and paid a visit to her mother-in-law, to ask how long women go with child. The answer was,

'Forty weeks went Mary with Christ,
And so each Danish woman must.

'Forty weeks I went with mine,
But eight years shalt thou go with thine.'

The forty weeks had passed, and Ellen began to long for relief. Sir Peter besought aid of his sister Ingerlin. If I help your young bride, she said, I must be traitor to my mother. Sir Peter insisted, and Ingerlin moulded a fine child of wax,[*] wrapped it in linen, and exhibited it to her mother, who, supposing that her arts had been baffled, burst out into exclamations of astonishment. She had thought she could twist a rope out of flying sand, lay sun and moon flat on the earth with a single word, turn the whole world round about! She had thought all the house was spell-bound, except the spot where the young wife's chest stood, the chest of red rowan, which nothing can bewitch! The chest

was instantly taken away, and Ellen's bed moved to the place it had occupied; and no sooner was this done than Ellen gave birth to two children.[†]

In the ballads of the other class, the young wife, grown desperate after eight years of suffering, asks to be taken back to her maiden home. Her husband's mother raises objections: the horses are in the meadow, the coachman is in bed. Then, she says, I will go on my bare feet. The moment her husband learns her wish, the carriage is at the door, but by the arts of the mother it goes to pieces on the way, and the journey has to be finished on horseback. The joy of her parents at seeing their daughter approaching was quenched on a nearer view: she looked more dead than quick. She called her family about her and distributed her effects. A great wail went up in the house when two sons were cut from the mother's side. (**C, J, K, L, W**: Grundtvig, 84 **C**; Kristensen, II, No 35 **A, B, C**; I, No 74 **C**.)

The first son stood up and brushed his hair:
'Most surely am I in my ninth year.'

The second stood up both fair and red:
'Most sure we'll avenge our dear mother dead.'[‡]

Several of the most important ballads of the first class have taken up a part of the story of those of the second class, to the detriment of consistency. **F, G, H, O, P** (Grundtvig, 84 **F, G, H**, Kristensen, II, No 35 **F, G**), make the wife quit her husband's house for her father's, not only without reason, but against reason. If the woman is to die, it is natural enough that she should wish to die with the friends of her early days, and away from her uncongenial mother-in-law; but there is no kind of occasion for transferring the scene of the trick with the wax children to her father's house; and, on the other hand, it is altogether strange that her husband's mother and the rowan-tree chest (which some-

---

[*] The sister does this in **F–I** and **S**: in **O, P**, the husband "has" it done.

[†] On hindering childbirth, see notes by R. Köhler to Laura Gonzenbach's *Sicilianische Märchen*, now published by J. Bolte, *Zeitschrift des Vereins für Volkskunde*, VI, 63.

[‡] Grundtvig, 84 **D, E**; Kristensen, I, No 74 **A, B, C**; II, No 35 **A, B, C**.

times appears to be the property of the mother, sometimes that of the wife) should go with her.

Y, 'Hustru og Slegfred,' Grundtvig, 85, agrees with the second class up to the point when the wife is put to bed at her mother's house, but with the important variation that the spell is the work of a former mistress of the husband; instead of his mother, as in most of the ballads, or of the wife's foster-mother, as in C, D, J, K, M (Grundtvig, 84 C, D, Kristensen, II, No 35 A, B, D), or of the wife's stepmother as in A only. The conclusion of 'Hustru og Slegfred' is rather flat. The wife, as she lies in bed, bids all her household hold up their hands and pray for her relief, which occurs on the same day. The news is sent to her husband, who rejoins his wife, is shown his children, praises God, and burns his mistress. Burning is also the fate of the mother-in-law in B, I, O, P, whereas in F she dies of chagrin, and in G bursts into a hundred flinders (flentsteene).

This ballad, in the mixed form of O, P (Kristensen, II, 35 F, G), has been resolved into a tale in Denmark, a few lines of verse being retained. Recourse is had by the spellbound wife to a cunning woman in the village, who informs her that in her house there is a place in which a rowan-tree chest has stood, and that she can get relief there. The cunning woman subsequently pointing out the exact spot, two boys are born, who are seven years old, and can both walk and talk. Word is sent the witch that her son's wife has been delivered of two sons, and that she herself shall be burned the day following. The witch says, "I have been able to twine a string out of running water. If I have not succeeded in bewitching the woman, she must have found the place where the damned rowan chest stood." (Grundtvig, III, 858, No 84 b.)

Three Swedish versions of the ballad have been printed. A, B, from tradition of this century, are given by Arwidsson, II, 252ff, 'Liten Kerstins Förtrollning,' No 134. These resemble the Danish ballads of the second class closely. Liten Kerstin goes to her mother's house, gives birth to two children, and dies. In A the children are a son and daughter. The son stands up, combs his hair, and says, "I am forty weeks on in my ninth year." He can run errands in the village, and the daughter sew red silk. In B both

[84]

children are boys. One combs his hair, and says, "Our grandmother shall be put on two wheels." The other draws his sword, and says, "Our mother is dead, our grandmother to blame. I hope our mother is with God. Our grandmother shall be laid on seven wheels." The other copy, C, mentioned by Grundtvig as being in Cavallius and Stephens' manuscript collection, has been printed in the Svenska Fornminnesföreningens Tidskrift, vol. ii, p. 72ff, 1873–74. It dates from the close of the sixteenth century, and resembles the mixed ballads of the Danish first class, combining the flitting to the father's house with the artifice of the wax children. The conclusion of this ballad has suffered greatly. After the two sons are born, we are told that Kirstin, before unmentioned, goes to the chest and makes a wax child. If the chest were moved, Elin would be free of her child. And then the boy stands up and brushes his hair, and says he has come to his eighth year.

Three stanzas and some of the incidents of a Norwegian version of this ballad have been communicated to Grundtvig, III, 858f, No 84 c, by Professor Sophus Bugge. The only place which was unaffected by a spell was where Signelíti's bride-chest stood, and the chest being removed, the birth took place. The witch was a step-mother, as in Danish A.

There are two familiar cases of malicious arrest of childbirth in classic mythology,— those of Latona and Alcmene. The wrath of Juno was the cause in both, and perhaps the myth of Alcmene is only a repetition of an older story, with change of name. The pangs of Latona were prolonged through nine days and nights, at the end of which time Ilithyia came to her relief, induced by a bribe. (Hymn to the Delian Apollo, 91ff.) Homer, Il. xix, 119, says only that Hera stopped the delivery of Alcmene and kept back Ilithyia. Antoninus Liberalis, in the second century of our era, in one of his abstracts from the Metamorphoses of Nicander, a poem of the second century B.C., or earlier, has this account: that when Alcmene was going with Hercules, the Fates and Ilithyia, to please Juno, kept her in her pains by sitting down and folding their hands; and that Galinthias, a playmate and companion of Alcmene, fearing that the suffering would drive her mad, ran out and announced the birth of a boy, upon which the Fates were seized with such consternation that they let go their hands, and Hercules immediately came into the world. (Antoninus Lib., *Metam.* c. xxix.) Ovid, *Metamorphoses*, ix, 281–315, is more circumstantial. After seven days and nights of torture, Lucina came, but, being bribed by Juno, instead of giving the aid for which she was invoked, sat down on the altar before Alcmene's door, with the right knee crossed over the left, and fingers interlocked, mumbling charms which checked the processes of birth. Galanthis, a servant girl *media de plebe*, was shrewd enough to suspect that Juno had some part in this mischief; and besides, as she went in and out of the house, she always saw Lucina sitting on the altar, with her hands clasped over her knees. At last, by a happy thought, she called out, "Whoever you are, wish my mistress joy; she is lighter, and has her wish." Lucina jumped up and unclasped her hands, and the birth followed instantly. Pausanias, ix, 11, tells a similar but briefer story, in which Historis, daughter of Tiresias, takes the place of Galanthis. The same artifice is tried, and succeeds, in a case of birth, delayed by a man's clasping his hands round his knees, in Asbjørnsen, *Norske Huldre-Eventyr*, I, 20, 2d ed. See, for the whole matter, 'Ilithyia oder die Hexe,' in C. A. Böttiger's *Kleine Schriften*, 1, 76ff.

Apuleius, in his *Metamorphoses*, mentions a case of suspended childbirth, which, curiously enough, had lasted eight years,[*] as in the Danish and Swedish ballads. The witch is a mistress of her victim's husband, as in Grundtvig, 85, and as in a story cited by Scott from Heywood's 'Hierarchy of the Blessed Angels,' p. 474. "There is a curious tale about a Count of Westeravia [Vestravia, in diocesi Argentoratensi], whom a deserted concubine bewitched upon his marriage, so as to preclude all hopes of his becoming a father. The spell continued to operate for three years, till one day, the count happening to meet with his former mistress, she maliciously asked him about the increase of his

family. The count, conceiving some suspicion from her manner, craftily answered that God had blessed him with three fine children; on which she exclaimed, like Willie's mother in the ballad, 'May Heaven confound the old hag by whose counsel I threw an enchanted pitcher into the draw-well of your palace!' The spell being found and destroyed, the count became the father of a numerous family."

A story closely resembling Heywood's is told in the *Zimmerische Chronik*, ed. Barack, IV, 262–64, 1882, of Heinrich von Dierstein; also by Liebrecht in *Germania* XIV, 404. (Köhler.) As the author of the chronicle remarks, the tale (Heywood's) is in the *Malleus Maleficarum* (1620, I, 158f).

A story like that of the ballad is told as a fact that took place in Arran within this century. A young man forsook his sweetheart and married another girl. When the wife's time came, she suffered excessively. A packman who was passing suspected the cause, went straight to the old love, and told her that a fine child was born; when up she sprang, and pulled out a large nail from the beam of the roof, calling out to her mother, "Muckle good your craft has done!" The wife was forthwith delivered. (Napier, in *The Folklore Record*, II, 117.)

In the **Sicilian** tales, collected by Laura Gonzenbach, Nos 12 and 15, we have the spell of folded hands placed between the knees to prevent birth, and in No 54 hands raised to the head.[†] In all these examples the spell is finally broken by telling the witch a piece of false news, which causes her to forget herself and take away her hands. (*Sicilianische Märchen aus dem Volksmund gesammelt*, Leipzig, 1870.) Other cases resembling No 54 in Pitrè, *Fiabe, Novelle, etc.*, I, 173, No 18; Comparetti, *Novelline popolari*, No 33, p. 139. (Köhler.)

We find in a **Roumanian** tale, contributed to *Das Ausland* for 1857, p. 1029, by F. Obert, and epitomized by Grundtvig, III, 859, No 84 d, a wife condemned by her offended husband to go with child till he lays his hand upon her. It is

---

[*] Eadem amatoris sui uxorem, quod in eam dicacule probrum dixerat, jam in sarcina prægnationis, obsæpto utero et repigrato fetu, perpetua prægnatione damnavit, et, ut cuncti numerant, jam octo annorum onere misella illa velut elephantum paritura distenditur. 1, 9.

[†] We may suppose with closed fingers, or clasping the head, though this is not said. Antique vases depict one or two Ilithyias as standing by with hands elevated and *open*, during the birth of Athene from the head of Zeus. Welcker, *Kleine Schriften*, iii, 191, note 12. (Köhler.)

twenty years before she obtains grace, and the son whom she then bears immediately slays his father. A **Wallachian** form of this story (*Walachische Mährchen* von Arthur u. Albert Schott, No 23) omits the revenge by the new-born child, and ends happily.

Birth is sought to be maliciously impeded in Swabia by crooking together the little fingers. Lammert, *Volksmedizin in Bayern, etc.*, p. 165. (Köhler.)

With respect to the knots in st. 34, it is to be observed that the tying of knots (as also the fastening of locks), either during the marriage ceremony or at the approach of parturition was, and is still, believed to, be effectual for preventing conception or childbirth. The minister of the parish of Logierait, Perthshire, testifies, about the year 1793, that immediately before the celebration of a marriage it is the custom to loosen carefully every knot about bride and bridegroom,—garters, shoe-strings, etc. The knots are tied again before they leave the church. (*Statistical Account of Scotland*, v, 83.) So among the Laps and Norwegians, when a child is to be born, all the knots in the woman's clothes, or even all the knots in the house, must be untied, because of their impeding delivery. (Liebrecht, *Zur Volkskunde*, p. 322, who also cites the *Statistical Account of Scotland*.) Also "Bei der Entbindung . . . muss man alle Schlösser im Hause an Thüren und Kisten aufmachen: so gebiert die Frau leichter." Wuttke, *Der deutsche Volksaberglaube*, p. 355, No 574, ed. 1869. (G. L. K.)

Willie's Lady is translated by Schubart, p. 74, Talvj, p. 555, and by Gerhard, p. 139. Grundtvig, 84 **H** (= Syv, 90, *Danske Viser*, 43), is translated by Jamieson, *Illustrations of Northern Antiquities*, p. 344, and by Prior, No 89.

A

a. A copy, by Miss Mary Fraser Tytler, of a transcript made by her grandfather from William Tytler's manuscript. **b.** Jamieson-Brown MS., No 15, p. 33.

[O..]   Wil - lie's taen___ him o'er the___ fame, He's woo'd a wife, and brought her___ hame;

A. b. Ritson-Tytler-Brown MS., pp. 1–5. Sung by Mrs Brown, Falkland, Aberdeenshire; copied by Joseph Ritson, c. 1792–1794.

1 WILLIE has taen him oer the fame,
  He's woo'd a wife and brought her hame.

2 He's woo'd her for her yellow hair,
  But his mother wrought her mickle care.

3 And mickle dolour gard her dree,
  For lighter she can never be.

4 But in her bower she sits wi pain,
  And Willie mourns oer her in vain.

5 And to his mother he has gone,
  That vile rank witch of vilest kind.

6 He says: 'My ladie has a cup,
  Wi gowd and silver set about.

7 'This goodlie gift shall be your ain,
  And let her be lighter o her young bairn.'

8 'Of her young bairn she'll neer be lighter,
  Nor in her bower to shine the brighter.

9 'But she shall die and turn to clay,
  And you shall wed another may.'

10 'Another may I'll never wed,
  Another may I'll neer bring home.'

11 But sighing says that weary wight,
  'I wish my life were at an end.'

12 'Ye doe [ye] unto your mother again,
  That vile rank witch of vilest kind.

13 'And say your ladie has a steed,
   The like o 'm 's no in the lands of Leed.

14 'For he [i]s golden shod before,
   And he [i]s golden shod behind.

15 'And at ilka tet of that horse's main,
   There's a golden chess and a bell ringing.

16 'This goodlie gift shall be your ain,
   And let me be lighter of my young bairn.'

17 'O her young bairn she'll neer be lighter,
   Nor in her bower to shine the brighter.

18 'But she shall die and turn to clay,
   And ye shall wed another may.'

19 'Another may I ['ll] never wed,
   Another may I ['ll] neer bring hame.'

20 But sighing said that weary wight,
   'I wish my life were at an end.'

21 'Ye doe [ye] unto your mother again,
   That vile rank witch of vilest kind.

22 'And say your ladie has a girdle,
   It's red gowd unto the middle.

23 'And ay at every silver hem,
   Hangs fifty silver bells and ten.

24 'That goodlie gift has be her ain,
   And let me be lighter of my young bairn.'

25 'O her young bairn she's neer be lighter,
   Nor in her bower to shine the brighter.

26 'But she shall die and turn to clay,
   And you shall wed another may.'

27 'Another may I'll never wed,
   Another may I'll neer bring hame.'

28 But sighing says that weary wight,
   'I wish my life were at an end.'

29 Then out and spake the Belly Blind;
   He spake aye in good time.

30 'Ye doe ye to the market place,
   And there ye buy a loaf o wax.

31 'Ye shape it bairn and bairnly like,
   And in twa glassen een ye pit;

32 'And bid her come to your boy's christening;
   Then notice weel what she shall do.

33 'And do you stand a little fore bye,
   And listen weel what she shall say.'

34 'Oh wha has loosed the nine witch knots   [87]
   That was amo that ladie's locks?

35 'And wha has taen out the kaims of care
   That hangs amo that ladie's hair?

36 'And wha's taen down the bush o woodbine
   That hang atween her bower and mine?

37 'And wha has killd the master kid
   That ran beneath that ladie's bed?

38 'And wha has loosed her left-foot shee,
   And lotten that ladie lighter be?'

39 O Willie has loosed the nine witch knots
   That was amo that ladie's locks.

40 And Willie's taen out the kaims o care
   That hang amo that ladie's hair.

41 And Willie's taen down the bush o woodbine
   That hang atween her bower and thine.

42 And Willie has killed the master kid
   That ran beneath that ladie's bed.

43 And Willie has loosed her left-foot shee,
   And letten his ladie lighter be.

44 And now he's gotten a bonny young son,
   And mickle grace be him upon.

a. *The stanzas are not regularly divided in the MS., nor were they so divided by Scott.*

41^2. hung (?) beneath: *but see* 36^2.

Scott's principal variations are:

12^1. Yet gae ye.

14^1. For he is silver shod.

15. At every tuft of that horse main
    There's a golden chess and a bell to ring.

21^1. Yet gae ye. ^{2}. o rankest kind.

22^2. It's a' red gowd to.

24^1. This gudely gift sall be.

26^1. For she.

28^2. my days.

30^1. Yet gae ye. ^{2}. there do buy.

31^1. Do shape. ^{2}. you'll put.

32^1. And bid her your boy's christening to.

33^1. a little away. ^{2}. To notice weel what she may saye.

35^2. That were amang.

38^2. And let.

39^1. Syne Willie.

40^2. That were into.

41^1, 42^1, 43^1. And he.

41^2. Hung atween her bour and the witch carline.

44^2. a bonny son.

b. *Divided in Jamieson's MS. into stanzas of four verses, two verses being written in one line: but Jamieson's* 8 = **a** 14–16.

1^1. Sweet Willy's taen.

5–11, *wanting. Instead of the cup, the girdle occurs here:* = **a** 21–28.

12^1. He did him till. ^{2}. wilest kin.

13^1. An said, My lady.

$14^{1,2}$. he is.

16^2. An lat her be lighter o her young bairn.

18^1. go to clay.

a 21^1 = **b** 5^1. Now to his mither he has gane. ^{2}. kin.

a 22^1 = **b** 6^1. He say[s] my lady. ^{2}. It's a' red.

a 23^1 = **b** 7^1. at ilka. ^{2}. Hings.

a 24^1 = **b** 8^1. gift sall be your ain. ^{2}. lat her . . . o her.

a 29 = **b** 22. Then out it spake the belly blin;
    She spake ay in a good time.

a 32 = **b** 25, 26.

> An do you to your mither then, An bid her
>   come to your boy's christnen;
> For dear's the boy he's been to you: Then
>   notice well what she shall do.

Between **a** 33 *and* **a** 34 *occurs in* **b** (28–31):

> He did him to the market place, An there
>   he bought a loaf o wax.
> He shap'd it bairn and bairnly like, An in't
>   twa glazen een he pat.
> He did him till his mither then, An bade
>   him (*sic*) to his boy's christnen.
> An he did stan a little forebye, An notic'd
>   well what she did say.

a 35^2 = **b** 33^2. hang amo.

36. *wanting in* **b**.

37^2. aneath.

39^2 = **b** 36^2. hang amo his.

40^1. kemb o care. ^{2}. his lady's.

41. wanting in **b**.

42^2 = **b** 38^2. ran aneath his.

44. *wanting in* **b**.

b 22^2 *makes the Billy Blind feminine. This is not so in* **a**, *or in any other ballad, and may be only an error of the transcriber, who has not always written carefully.*

7

EARL BRAND

A. a. b. 'Earl Bran,' Mr Robert White's papers. **c.** 'The Brave Earl Brand and the King of England's Daughter,' Bell, *Ancient Poems, etc.*, p. 122. **d.** Fragmentary verses remembered by Mr R. White's sister.
B. 'The Douglas Tragedy,' Scott's *Minstrelsy*, III, 246, ed. 1803.
C. 'Lord Douglas,' Motherwell's MS., p. 502.
D. 'Lady Margaret,' Kinloch MSS, I, 327.
E. 'The Douglas Tragedy,' Motherwell's *Minstrelsy*, p. 180.

F. 'The Child of Ell,' Percy MS., p. 57; Hales and Furnivall, I, 133.
G. 'Gude Earl Brand and Auld Carle Hude,' the *Paisley Magazine*, 1828, p. 321, communicated by W. Motherwell.
H. 'Auld Carle Hood, or, Earl Brand,' Campbell MSS, II, 32.
I. 'The Douglas Tragedy,' 'Lord Douglas' Tragedy,' from an old-looking stall-copy, without place or date.

'Earl Brand' has preserved most of the incidents of a very ancient story with a faithfulness unequalled by any ballad that has been recovered from English oral tradition.[*] Before the publication of 'Earl Brand,' **A c**, our known inheritance in this particular was limited to the beautiful but very imperfect fragment called by Scott 'The Douglas Tragedy,' **B**; half a dozen stanzas of another version of the same in Motherwell's *Minstrelsy*, **E**; so much of Percy's 'Child of Elle' as was genuine, which, upon the printing of his manuscript, turned out to be one fifth, **F**; and two versions of Erlinton, **A**, **C**.[†] What now can be added is but little: two transcripts of 'Earl Brand,' one of which, **A a**, has suffered less from literary revision than the only copy hitherto printed, **A c**; a third version of 'The Douglas Tragedy,' from Motherwell's manuscript, **C**; a fourth from Kinloch's manuscripts, **D**; and another of 'Erlinton,' **B**. Even 'Earl Brand' has lost a circumstance that forms the turning-point in Scandinavian ballads, and this capital defect attends all our other versions, though traces which remain in 'Erlinton' make it nearly certain that our ballads originally agreed in all important particulars with those which are to this day recited in the north of Europe.

The corresponding **Scandinavian** ballad is 'Ribold and Guldborg,' and it is a jewel that any clime might envy. Up to the time of Grundtvig's edition, in *Danmarks gamle Folkeviser*, No 82, though four versions had been printed, the only current copy for a hundred and fifty years had been Syv's No 88, based on a broadside of the date 1648, but compounded from several sources; and it was in this form that the ballad became known to the English through Jamieson's translation. Grundtvig has now published twenty-seven versions of 'Ribold og Guldborg' (II, 347ff, nineteen; 675ff, four; III, 849ff, four:[‡]

[*] This ballad was first given to the world by Motherwell, in the single volume of the *Paisley Magazine*, a now somewhat scarce book. I am indebted for the information and for a transcript to Mr Murdoch, of Glasgow, and for a second copy to Mr Macmath, of Edinburgh.
[†] 'Erlinton,' though not existing in a two-line stanza, follows immediately after 'Earl Brand.' The copy of 'The Douglas Tragedy' in Smith's *Scottish Minstrel*, III, 86, is merely Scott's, with changes to facilitate singing.

[‡] B*, III, 853, a fragment of five stanzas, has been dropped by Grundtvig from No 82, and assigned to No 249. See *D. g. F.* IV, 494.

[89] of all which only two are fragments), and nine of 'Hildebrand og Hilde,' No 83, which is the same story set in a dramatic frame-work (II, 393ff, seven; 680f, one; III, 857, one, a fragment). Three more Danish versions of 'Ribold og Guldborg' are furnished by Kristensen, *Gamle jydske Folkeviser*, I, No 37, II, No 84 **A**, **B** (**C***, **D***, **E***); Kristensen, *Jyske Folkeminder*, X, 33, 'Nævnet til døde, No 15, **A–I**. 'Hr. Ribolt,' Kristensen, *Skattegraveren*, VI, 17, No 257; *Skattegraveren*, VI, 17, No 257, 'Nævnet til døde,' Kristensen, *Efterslæt til Skattegraveren*, p. 81, No 76; *Folkeminder*, XI, 36, No 22, **A–D**, is a good copy of 'Ribold og Guldborg.' It has the testaments at the end, like several others (see p. 197). To these we may add the last half, sts 15–30, of 'Den farlige Jomfru,' Grundtvig, 184 **G**. 'Stolt Hedelil,' Kristensen, *Skattegraveren*, I, 68, No 231, is another version of 'Hildebrand og Hilde,' closely resembling G. So is 'Den mislykkede flugt,' the same, VIII, 17, No 24, with the proper tragic conclusion. Both are inferior copies. Of Grundtvig's texts, 82 **A** is of the sixteenth century; **B–H** are of the seventeenth; the remainder and Kristensen's three from recent tradition. Six versions of 'Hildebrand og Hilde,' **A–F**, are of the seventeenth century; one is of the eighteenth, **G**; and the remaining two are from oral tradition of our day.

The first six of Grundtvig's versions of 'Ribold and Guldborg,' **A–F**, are all from manuscripts, and all of a pure traditional character, untampered with by "collators." G and H are mixed texts: they have **F** for their basis, but have admitted stanzas from other sources. Most of the versions from recitation are wonderful examples and proofs of the fidelity with which simple people "report and hold" old tales: for, as the editor has shown, verses which never had been printed, but which are found in old manuscripts, are now met with in recited copies; and these recited copies, again, have verses that occur in no Danish print or manuscript, but which nevertheless are found in Norwegian and Swedish recitations, and, what is more striking, in Icelandic tradition of two hundred years' standing.

The story in the older Danish ballads runs thus. Ribold, a king's son, sought Guldborg's love in secret. He said he would carry her to a land where death and sorrow came not, where all the birds were cuckoos, and all the grass was leeks, and all the streams ran wine. Guldborg, not indisposed, asked how she should evade the watch kept over her by all her family and by her betrothed. Ribold disguised her in his cloak and armor, **B**, **E**, **F**, and rode off, with Guldborg behind him. On the heath they meet a rich earl [a crafty man, **C**; her betrothed, **D**], who asks, Whither away, with your stolen maid? [little page, **B**, **F**.] Ribold replies that it is his youngest sister, whom he has taken from a cloister, **A**, **E** [sick sister, **C**; brother, **B**, **F**; page, **D**]. This shift avails nothing; no more does a bribe which he offers for keeping his secret. Report is at once made to her father that Guldborg has eloped with Ribold. Guldborg perceives that they are pursued, and is alarmed. Ribold reassures her, and prepares to meet his foes. He bids Guldborg hold his horse, **B**, **C**, **E**, and, whatever may happen, not to call him by name: "Though thou see me bleed, name me not to death; though thou see me fall, name me not at all!" Ribold cuts down six or seven of her brothers and her father, besides others of her kin; the youngest brother only is left, and Guldborg in an agony calls upon Ribold to spare him, to carry tidings to her mother. No sooner was his name pronounced than Ribold received a mortal wound. He sheathed his sword, and said, Come, wilt thou ride with me? Wilt thou go home to thy mother again, or wilt thou follow so sad a swain? And she answered, I will not go home to my mother again; I will follow thee, my heart's dearest man. They rode through the wood, and not a word came from the mouth of either. Guldborg asked, Why art thou not as glad as before? And Ribold answered, Thy brother's sword has been in my heart. They reached his house. He called to one to take his horse, to another to bring a priest, and said his brother should have Guldborg. But she would not give her faith to two brothers. Ribold died that night, **C**. Three dead came from Ribold's bower: Ribold and his lief, and his mother, who died of grief! In **A** Guldborg slays herself, and dies in her lover's arms.

'Hildebrand and Hilde,' **A**, **B**, **C**, **D**, opens with the heroine in a queen's service, sewing her seam wildly, putting silk for gold and gold for silk. The queen calls her to account. Hilde begs her mistress to listen to her tale of sorrow. She was a king's daughter. Twelve knights had been appointed to be her guard, and one had beguiled her, Hildebrand, son of the king of England. They went off together, and were surprised by her brothers [father, **B, C, D**]. Hildebrand bade her be of good cheer; but she must not call him by name if she saw him bleed or fall, **A, B, D**. A heap of knights soon lay at his feet. Hilde forgot herself, and called out, Hildebrand, spare my youngest brother! Hildebrand that instant received a mortal wound, and fell. The younger brother tied her to his horse, and dragged her home. They shut her up at first in a strong tower, built for the purpose, **A, B** [Swedish **A**, a dark house], and afterwards sold her into servitude for a church bell. Her mother's heart broke at the bell's first stroke, and Hilde, with the last word of her tale, fell dead in the queen's arms.

The most important deviation of the later versions from the old is exhibited by **S** and **T**, and would probably be observed in **Q, R**, as well, were these complete. **S, T** are either a mixture of 'Ribold and Guldborg' with 'Hildebrand and Hilde,' or forms transitional between the two. In these Ribold does not live to reach his home, and Guldborg, unable to return to hers, offers herself to a queen, to spin silk and weave gold [braid hair and work gold]. But she cannot sew for grief. The queen smacks her on the cheek for neglecting her needle. Poor Guldborg utters a protest, but gives no explanation, and the next morning is found dead. Singularly enough, the name of the hero in **Q, R, S, T**, is also an intermediate form. Ribold is the name in all the old Danish copies except **C**, and that has Ride-bolt. Danish **I, K, X, Z**, all the Icelandic copies, and Swedish **D**, have either Ribold or some unimportant variation. **Q, R, S**, have Ride-brand [**T**, Rederbrand]. All copies of Grundtvig 83, except Danish **G**, Swedish **C**, which do not give the hero's name, have Hildebrand; so also 82 **N, O, P, V**, and Kristensen's, I, No 37. The name of the woman is nearly constant both in 82 and 83.

The paradise promised Guldborg in all the old versions of 82 [*] disappears from the recited copies, except **K, M**. It certainly did not origi-

nally belong to 'Ribold and Guldborg,' or to another Danish ballad in which it occurs ('Den trofaste Jomfru,' Grundtvig, 249 **A**), but rather to ballads like 'Kvindemorderen,' Grundtvig, 183 **A**, or 'Líti Kersti,' Landstad, 44, where a supernatural being, a demon or a hillman, seeks to entice away a mortal maid. See No 4, p. 43. In 82 **L, N, U, V, Y, Æ, Ø**, and Kristensen's copies, the lovers are not encountered by anybody who reports their flight. Most of the later versions, **K, L, M, N, P, U, V, Y, Æ, Ø**, and Kristensen's three, make them halt in a wood, where Ribold goes to sleep in Guldborg's lap, and is roused by her when she perceives that they are pursued. So Norwegian **B**, Swedish **A**, **B, C**, and 'Hildebrand and Hilde' **B. M, Q, R, S, T, Z**, have not a specific prohibition of *dead-naming*, but even these enjoin silence. 83 **C** is the only ballad in which there is a fight and no prohibition of either kind, but it is clear from the course of the story that the stanza containing the usual injunction has simply dropped out. **P** is distinguished from all other forms of the story by the heroine's killing herself before her dying lover reaches his house.

The four first copies of 'Hildebrand and Hilde,' as has been seen, have the story of Ribold and Guldborg with some slight differences and some abridgment. There is no elopement in **B**: the lovers are surprised in the princess' bower. When Hilde has finished her tale, in **A**, the queen declares that Hildebrand was her son. In **B** she interrupts the narrative by announcing her discovery that Hildebrand was her brother. **C** and **D** have nothing of the sort. There is no fight in **E–H**. **E** has taken up the commonplace of the bower on the strand which was forced by nine men.[†] Hildebrand is again the son of the queen, and, coming in just as Hilde has expired, exclaims that he will have no other love, sets his sword against a stone, and runs upon it. **H** has the same catastrophe. **F** [91]

* Though the paradise has not been transmitted in any known copy of 'Earl Brand,' it appears very distinctly in the opening stanza of 'Leesome Brand' **A**. This last has several stanzas towards the close (33–35) which seem to belong to 'Earl Brand,' and perhaps derived these, the "unco land," and even its name, by the familiar process of intermixture of traditions.

† See No 5, pp. 90ff.

represents the father as simply showing great indignation and cruelty on finding out that one of the guardian knights had beguiled his daughter, and presently selling her for a new church bell. The knight turns out here again to be the queen's son; the queen says he shall betroth Hille, and Hille faints for joy. **G** agrees with **B** as to the surprise in the bower. The knight's head is hewn off on the spot. The queen gives Hilde her youngest son for a husband, and Hilde avows that she is consoled. **I** agrees with **E** so far as it goes, but is a short fragment.

There are three **Icelandic** versions of this ballad, 'Ribbalds kvæði,' *Íslenzk Fornkvæði*, No 16, all of the seventeenth century. They all come reasonably close to the Danish as to the story, and particularly **A**. Ribbald, with no prologue, invites Gullbrún "to ride." He sets her on a white horse; of all women she rode best. They have gone but a little way, when they see a pilgrim riding towards them, who hails Ribbald with, Welcome, with thy stolen maid! Ribbald pretends that the maid is his sister, but the pilgrim knows very well it is Gullbrún. She offers her cloak to him not to tell her father, but the pilgrim goes straight to the king, and says, Thy daughter is off! The king orders his harp to be brought, for no purpose but to dash it on the floor once and twice, and break out the strings. He then orders his horse. Gullbrún sees her father come riding under a hill-side, then her eleven brothers, then seven brothers-in-law. She begs Ribbald to spare her youngest brother's life, that he may carry the news to her mother. He replies, I will tie my horse by the reins; you take up your sewing! then three times forbids her to name him during the fight. He slew her father first, next the eleven brothers, then the other seven, all which filled her with compunction, and she cried out, Ribbald, still thy brand! On the instant Ribbald received many wounds. He wiped his bloody sword, saying, This is what you deserve, Gullbrún, but love is your shield; then set her on her horse, and rode to his brother's door. He called out, Here is a wife for you! But Gullbrún said, Never wilt I be given to two brothers. Soon after Ribbald gave up the ghost. There was more mourning than mirth; three bodies went to the grave

in one coffin, Ribbald, his lady, and his mother, who died of grief.

B and **C** have lost something at the beginning, **C** starting at the same point as our 'Douglas Tragedy.' The king pursues Ribbald by water. Gullbrún (**B**) stands in a tower and sees him land. Ribbald gives Gullbrún to his brother, as in **A**: she lives in sorrow, and dies a maid.

Norwegian. ('Ribold and Guldborg.') **A**, 'Rikeball og stolt Guðbjörg,' Landstad, 33; **B**, 'Veneros og stolt Ölleber,' Landstad, 34; **C**, **D**, **E**, **F**, in part described and cited, with six other copies, Grundtvig, III, p. 853f. The last half of Landstad No 23, stanzas 17–34, and stanzas 18–25 of Landstad 28 **B**, also belong here. **A** agrees with the older Danish versions, even to the extent of the paradise. **B** has been greatly injured. Upon the lady's warning Veneros of the approach of her father, he puts her up in an oak-tree for safety. He warns her not to call him by name, and she says she will rather die first; but her firmness is not put to the test in this ballad, some verses having dropped out just at this point. Veneros is advised to surrender, but dispatches his assailants by eighteen thousands (like Lille brór, in Landstad, 23), and by way of conclusion hews the false Pál greive, who had reported his elopement to Ölleber's father, into as many pieces. He then takes Ölleber on his horse, they ride away and are married. Such peculiarities in the other copies as are important to us will be noticed further on.

('Hildebrand and Hilde.') **A**, one of two Norwegian copies communicated by Professor Bugge to Grundtvig, III, 857f, agrees well with Danish **E**, but has the happy conclusion of Danish **F**, **G**, **I**. The heroine is sold for *nine* bells. **B**, the other, omits the bower-breaking of **A** and Danish **E**, and ends with marriage.

The **Swedish** forms of 'Ribold and Guldborg' are: **A**, 'Hillebrand,' Afzelius, No 2; **B**, 'Herr Redebold,' and **C**, 'Kung Vallemo,' Afzelius, No 80; new ed., No 2, 1, 2, 3; 'Ellibrand och Fröken Gyllenborg,' Lagus, *Nyländska Folkvisor*, I, 1, No 1, a, b. ("Name not my name," a 20, b 12.); **D**, 'Ribbolt,' Arwidsson, No 78; **E**, 'Herr Redebold' **F**, 'Herting Liljebrand,' and **G**, 'Herr Balder,' in Cavallius and Stephens' manuscript collection; **H**, 'Kung Walmon,' E. Wigström's *Folkdiktning*, No 15, p. 33; **I**. 'Hildebrand,' Wigström, *Folkdiktning*, II, 13. **J.** 'Fröken Gyllenborg,' the same, p. 24; **K**, 'Kung Vallemo ock liten Kerstin,' Bergström ock Nordlander, *Nyare Bidrag*, o. s. v., p. 101. **A, B, C, H**, are not markedly different from the ordinary Danish ballad, and this is true also, says Grundtvig, of the unprinted versions, **E, F, G**. **D** and **G** are of the seventeenth century, the others from recent tradition. Ribold is pictured in **D** as a bold prince, equally versed in runes and arts as in manly exercises. He visits Giötha by night: they slumber sweet, but wake in blood. She binds up his wounds with rich kerchiefs. He rides home to his father's, and sits down on a bench. The king bids his servants see what is the matter, and adds, Be he sick or be he hurt, he got it at Giötha-Lilla's. They report the prince stabbed with sharp pikes within, and bound with silk kerchiefs without. Ribold bids them bury him in the mould, and not blame Giötha-Lilla; "for my horse was fleet, and I was late, and he hurtled me 'gainst an apple-tree" (so Hillebrand in **A**). **E** represents the heroine as surviving her lover, and united to a young king, but always grieving for Redebold.

'Hildebrand and Hilde' exists in Swedish in three versions: **A**, a broadside of the last part of the seventeenth century, now printed in the new edition of Afzelius, p. 142ff of the notes (the last nine stanzas before, in *Danske Viser*, III, 438f); **B**, Afzelius, No 32, new ed. No 26, **C**, Arwidsson, No 107, both taken down in this century. In **A** and **B** Hillebrand, son of the king of England, carries off Hilla; they halt in a grove; she wakes him from his sleep when she hears her father and seven brothers coming; he enjoins her not to call him by name, which still she does upon her father's being slain [or when only her youngest brother is left], and Hillebrand thereupon receives mortal wounds. He wipes his sword, saying, This is what you would deserve, were you not Hilla. The youngest brother ties Hilla to his horse, drags her home, and confines her in a dark house, which swarms with snakes and dragons (**A** only). They sell her for a new church bell, and her mother's heart breaks at the first sound. Hilla falls dead at the queen's knee. **C** has lost the dead-naming, and ends with the queen's promising to be Hilla's best friend.

A detailed comparison of the English ballads, and especially of 'Earl Brand,' with the Scandinavian (such as Grundtvig has made, III, 855f) shows an unusual and very interesting agreement. The name Earl Brand, to begin with, is in all probability a modification of the Hildebrand found in Danish 82 **N, O, P, V, C***, in all versions of Danish 83, and in the corresponding Swedish **A**. Ell, too, in Percy's fragment, which may have been Ellë earlier, points to Hilde, or something like it, and Erl-inton might easily be corrupted from such a form as the Alibrand of Norwegian **B** (Grundtvig, III, 858). Hildebrand is the son of the king of England in Danish 83 **A–E**, and the lady in 'Earl Brand' is the same king's daughter, an interchange such as is constantly occurring in tradition. Stanza 2 can hardly be the rightful property of 'Earl Brand.' Something very similar is met with in 'Leesome Brand,' and is not much in place there. For 'old Carl Hood,' of whom more presently, Danish 82 **X** and Norwegian **A, C** have an old man, Danish **C** a crafty man, **T** a false younker, and Norwegian **B** and three others "false Pál greive." The lady's urging Earl Brand to slay the old carl, and the answer, that it would be sair to kill a gray-haired man, sts 8, 9, are almost literally repeated in Norwegian **A**, Landstad, No 33. The knight does slay the old man in Danish **X** and Norwegian **C**, and slays the court page in Danish **Z**, and false Pál greive in Norwegian **B**,—in this last *after* the battle. The question, "Where have ye stolen this lady away?" in st. 11, occurs in Danish 82 **A, D, E, K, P, R, S, T, Z**, in Norwegian **B** and Icelandic **B**, and something very similar in many other copies. The reply, "She is my sick sister, whom I have brought from Winchester" [nunnery], is found almost literally in Danish **C**, **X, Z**: "It is my sick sister; I took her yesterday from the cloister." [Danish **E**, it is my youngest sister from the cloister; she is sick: Danish **A**, youngest sister from cloister: Danish **R** and [93] Norwegian **B**, sister from cloister: Danish **S, T** sister's daughter from cloister: Norwegian **F**, sister from Holstein: Danish **P**, Icelandic **A**, Norwegian **A**, sister.] The old man, crafty man, rich earl, in the Scandinavian ballads, commonly answers that he knows Guldborg very well; but in Danish **D**, where Ribold says it is a court page he has hired, we have something like sts 14, 15: "Why has he such silk-braided hair?" On finding themselves discovered, the lovers, in the Scandinavian ballad, attempt to purchase silence with a bribe: Danish **A–I, M**, Icelandic and Norwegian **A, B**. This is not expressly done in 'Earl Brand,' but the same seems to be meant in st. 10 by "I'll gie him a pound." St. 17 is fairly paralleled by Danish **S**, 18, 19: "Where is Guldborg, thy daughter? Walking in the garden, gathering roses;" and st. 18, by Norwegian **B**, 15: "You may search without and search within, and see whether Ölleber you can find." The announcement in st. 19 is made in almost all the Scandinavian ballads, in words equivalent to "Ribold is off with thy daughter," and then follows the arming for the pursuit. The lady looks over her shoulder[*] and sees her father coming, as in st. 21, in Danish 82 **A, F, H, I, Q, R, T, X, Z**, and Norwegian **A**.

The scene of the fight is better preserved in the Scottish ballads than in 'Earl Brand,' though none of these have the cardinal incident of the death-naming. All the Scottish versions, **B–F**, and also 'Erlinton,' **A, B**, make the lady hold the knight's horse: so Danish 82 **B, C, E, I, Æ, D***, Icelandic **C**, Norwegian and Swedish **A**, and Danish 83 **D**. Of the knight's injunction, "Name me not to death, though thou see me bleed," which, as has been noted, is kept by nearly every Danish ballad (and by the Icelandic, the Norwegian, and by Swedish 'Ribold and Guldborg,' **A, B, C, H**, Swedish

---

[*]   Looking over the shoulder is a recurring element in this and other ballads; A 21, B 4; 103, E 1, G 14, I 3; Nos 53, A 21; 156, A 20, E 20, F 24; 167, A 7; 169, A 11, B 13; 176, 37; 185, 35; 188, A 32; 191, C 13, E 18, H 10, I 9; 192, A 8, B 4, D 6; 198, A 5; 209, I 24.

In G, 156 A, E, F, 167 A, 169 A, B, 209 I, the person looking over the left shoulder is angry, vexed, or grieved; in the other cases, no particular state of feeling is to be remarked. Undoubtedly the look over the left shoulder had originally more significance, since, under certain conditions, it gave the power of seeing spectres, or future events (but looking over the right shoulder had much the same effect). See A. Kuhn, *Sagen, u. s. w., aus Westfalen*, I, 187, No 206, and his references; and especially Bolte, in *Zeitschrift des Vereins für Volkskunde*, VI, 205–07 (using R. Köhler's notes). After sowing hempseed in the Hallowe'en rite, you look over your left shoulder to see your destined lass or lad. See note to Burns's Hallowe'en, st. 16.

'Hildebrand and Hilde,' **A, B**), there is left in English only this faint trace, in 'Erlinton,' **A, B**: "See ye dinna change your cheer until ye see my body bleed." It is the wish to save the life of her youngest brother that causes the lady to call her lover by name in the larger number of Scandinavian ballads, and she adds, "that he may carry the tidings to my mother," in Danish 82 **A, B, C, E, F, G, H, M, X**, 83 **B, C, D**. Grief for her father's death is the impulse in Danish 82 **I, N, O, Q, R, S, Y, Z, Æ, Ø, A*, C*, D*, E***, Swedish **A, B, C, H**. English **A** says nothing of father or brother; but in **B, C, D, E**, it is the father's death that causes the exclamation. All the assailants are slain in 'Erlinton' **A, B**, except an aged knight [the auldest man], and he is spared, to carry the tidings home. 'Erlinton' **C**, however, agrees with the oldest Danish copies in making the youngest brother the motive of the lady's intervention. It is the fifteenth, and last, of the assailants that gives Earl Brand his death-wound; in Danish **H**, the youngest brother, whom he has been entreated to spare; and so, apparently, in Danish **C** and Norwegian **A**.

The question, "Will you go with me or return to your mother?" which we find in English **B, C, D**, is met with also in many Danish versions, 82 **B, H, K, L, M, N, P, U, Z, Æ, Ø, C***, and Swedish **A, B, C**. The dying man asks to have his bed made in English **B, C**, as in Danish 82 **B C, K, L, N, U, X, Æ, Ø, C*, D***, Norwegian **A**, Swedish **A, B, C, H**, and desires that the lady may marry his brother in English **A**, as in nearly all the Danish versions, Icelandic **A, B, C**, Norwegian **C, D, E**, Swedish **C**. He declares her a maiden true in 'Earl Brand,' **A** c 33, and affirms the same with more particularity in Danish 82 **B, C, E, F, G, M, Ø**, Icelandic **B, C**, Norwegian **A, C, E**, Swedish **C**. The growth of the rose and brier [bush and brier] from the lovers' grave in English **B, C**, is not met with in any version of 'Ribold and Guldborg' proper, but 'Den farlige Jomfru' **G**, Grundtvig, 184, the last half of which, as already remarked, is a fragment of a Ribold ballad, has a linden in place of the rose and brier.

No complete ballad of the Ribold class is known to have survived in **German**, but a few verses have been interpolated by tradition in the earliest copy of the Ulinger ballad (vv 47–56), which may almost with certainty be assigned to one of the other description. They disturb the narrative where they are, and a ready occasion for their slipping in was afforded by the scene being exactly the same in both ballads: a knight and a lady, with whom he had eloped, resting in a wood.* See No 4, p. 49 of this volume.

We find in a pretty **Neapolitan-Albanian** ballad, which, with others, is regarded by the editors as a fragment of a connected poem, several of the features of these northern ones. A youth asks a damsel in marriage, but is not favored by her mother, father, or brother. He wins over first the mother and then the father by handsome presents, but his gifts, though accepted, do not conciliate the brother. He carries off the lady on horseback, and is attacked by the brother, four uncles, and seven cousins. He is killed and falls from his horse; with him the lady falls dead also, and both are covered up with stones. In the spring the youth comes up a cypress, the damsel comes up a vine, and encloses the cypress in her arms. (*Rapsodie d'un poema albanese raccolte nelle colonie del Napoletano, de Rada and de' Coronei*, Florence, 1866, lib. ii., canto viii.)

These ballads would seem to belong among the numerous ramifications of the Hilde saga. Of these, the second lay of Helgi Hundingslayer, in Sæmund's Edda, and 'Waltharius,' the beautiful poem of Ekkehard, are most like the ballads.† Leaving 'Waltharius' till we come to 'Erlinton,' we may notice that Sigrún, in the Helgi lay, though promised by her father to another man, Hödbrodd, son of Granmar, preferred Helgi. She sought him out, and told him frankly her predicament: she feared, she said, the wrath of her friends, for breaking her father's promise. Helgi accepted her affection, and bade her not care for the displeasure of her

relatives. A great battle ensued between Helgi and the sons of Granmar, who were aided by Sigrún's father and brothers. All her kinsmen were slain except one brother, Dag. He bound himself to peace with Helgi, but, notwithstanding, made sacrifices to Odin to obtain the loan of his spear, and with it slew Helgi. We have, therefore, in so much of the lay of Helgi Hundingslayer, the groundwork of the story of the ballads: a woman, who, as in many of the Ribold ballads, has been betrothed to a man she does not care for, gives herself to another; there is a fight, in which a great number of her kinsmen fall; one brother survives, who is the death of the man she loves. The lay of Helgi Hiörvard's son, whose story has much in common with that of his namesake, affords two resemblances of detail not found in the lay of the Hundingslayer. Helgi Hiörvard's son, while his life-blood is ebbing, expresses himself in almost the words of the dying Ribold: "The sword has come very near my heart." He then, like Ribold

---

* Compare vv 49–56, "Wilt thou ride to them, or wilt thou fight with them, or wilt thou stand by thy love, sword in hand?" "I will not ride to them, I will not fight with them [i.e., begin the fight], but I will stand by my love, sword in hand," with Norwegian **A**, 29, 30: "Shall we ride to the wood, or shall we bide like men?" "We will not ride to the wood, but we will bide like men." And also with Danish Æ, sts 14, 15.

† The chief branches, besides the Helgi lay and Walter, are the saga in Snorri's Edda, Skáldskaparmal, § 50; that in Saxo Grammaticus, Stephanius, ed. 1644, pp. 88–90; Sörla yyáttr, in *Fornaldar Sögur*, I, 391 ff; the Shetland ballad printed in Low's *Tour through the Islands of Orkney and Shetland*, 108 ff, and in Barry's *History of the Orkney Islands*, 2d ed., 489 ff, and paraphrased in Hibbert's *Description of the Shetland Islands*, 561 ff; the Thidrik saga, §§ 233–239, Unger; Gudrun, v–viii. The names of father, daughter, and lover in these are: (1) Högni,—, Högni, Högin-, Högni,—, [Artus], Hagen; (2) [Sigrún], Hilde-gunde, Hildr, Hilda, Hildr, Hildina, Hildr, Hilde; (3) Helgi, [Walter], Hedin, Hithin-, Hedin,—, [Herburt]. Hetel. Hagan, in 'Waltharius,' may be said to take the place of the father, who is wanting; and this is in a measure true also of Hedin, Helgi's half-brother, in the lay of Helgi Hiörvard's son. See the excellent discussion of the saga by Klee, *Zur Hildesage*, Leipzig, 1873.

The Swedish ballad, 'Herr Hjelmer,' **A**, Arwidsson, I, 155, No 21; **B**, **C**, Afzelius, II, 178, 226, No 74 (Helmer); **D**, **E**. Wigström, *Folkdiktning*, p. 25, No 10 (Hjelman), has several points of agreement with Ribold and the Hilde saga. The hero kills six of seven brothers [also the father, in **A**], spares the seventh on oath of fidelity, and is treacherously slain by him. The youngest brother carries her lover's head to his sister, and is invited to drink by her (in three of the four copies), and slain while so engaged; reminding us of Hildina in the Shetland ballad. Danish 'Herr Hjælm,' Grundtvig, *Danske Folkeminder*, 1861, p. 81, agrees with the Swedish, except that there are only three brothers.

and Earl Brand, declares his wish that his wife should marry his brother, and she, like Guldborg, declines a second union.[*]

[95] There is also a passage in the earlier history of Helgi Hundingslayer of which traces appear to be preserved in ballads, and before all in the English ballad 'Earl Brand,' A. Hunding and Helgi's family were at feud. Helgi introduced himself into Hunding's court as a spy, and when he was retiring sent word to Hunding's son that he had been there disguised as a son of Hagal, Helgi's foster-father. Hunding sent men to take him, and Helgi, to escape them, was forced to assume woman's clothes and grind at the mill. While Hunding's men are making search, a mysterious blind man, surnamed the bale-wise, or evil-witted (Blindr inn bölvísi), calls out, Sharp are the eyes of Hagal's maid; it is no churl's blood that stands at the mill; the stones are riving, the meal-trough is springing; a hard lot has befallen a war-king when a chieftain must grind strange barley; fitter for that hand is the sword-hilt than the mill-handle. Hagal pretends that the fierce-eyed maid is a virago whom Helgi had taken captive, and in the end Helgi escapes. This malicious personage reappears in the Hrómund saga as "Blind the Bad" and "the Carl Blind, surnamed Bavís," and is found elsewhere. His likeness to "old Carl Hood," who "comes for ill, but never for good," and who gives information of Earl Brand's flight with the king's daughter, does not require to be insisted on. Both are identical, we can scarcely doubt, with the blind [one-eyed] old man of many tales, who goes about in various disguises, sometimes as beggar, with his hood or hat slouched over his face,—that is Odin, the Síðhöttr or Deep-hood of Sæmund, who in the saga of Hálf and his champions is called simple Hood, as here, and expressly said to be Odin.[†] Odin, though not a thoroughly malignant divinity, had his dark side, and one of his titles in Sæmund's Edda is Bölverkr, *maleficus*. He first caused war by casting his spear among men, and Dag, after he has killed Helgi, says

Odin was the author of all the mischief, for he brought strife among kinsmen.[‡]

The disastrous effects of "naming" in a great emergency appear in other northern traditions, though not so frequently as one would expect.[§] A diverting Swedish saga, which has been much quoted, relates how St. Olof bargained with a troll for the building of a huge church, the pay to be the sun and moon, or St. Olof himself. The holy man was equally amazed and embarrassed at seeing the building run up by the troll with great rapidity, but during a ramble among the hills had the good luck to discover that the troll's name was Wind and Weather, after which all was easy. For while the troll was on the roof of the church, Olof called out to him,

'Wind and Weather, hi!
You've set the spire awry;'

and the troll, thus called by his name, lost his strength, fell off, and was dashed into a hundred pieces, all flint stones. (Iduna, Part 3, p. 60f, note. Other forms of the same story in Afzelius,

---

[†]   Höttr, er Óðinn var reyndar, Hood, who was Odin really, *Fornaldar Sögur*, II, p. 25. Klee observes, p. 10f, that Högni [Hagen] is the evil genius of the Hildesage. Sometimes he is the heroine's father; in 'Waltharius,' strangely enough, the hero's old friend (and even there a one-eyed man.) Klee treats the introduction of a rival lover (as in the Shetland ballad and Gudrun) as a departure from the older story. But we have the rival in Helgi Hundingslayer. The proper marplot in this lay is Blind the Ill-witted (Odin), whose part is sustained in 'Earl Brand' by the malicious Hood, in several Norwegian ballads by a very enigmatical "false Pál greive," in two other Norwegian ballads and one Danish by an old man, and, what is most remarkable, in the Shetland ballad by the rejected lover of Hildina (the Sir Nilaus of Danish **D**, Hertug Nilssón of some Norwegian copies), who bears the name Hiluge, interpreted with great probability by Conrad Hofmann (*Munich Sitzungsberichte*, 1867, II, 209, note), Illhugi, der Bössinnige, evil-minded (Icelandic íllhugaðr, íllúðigr.)

[‡]   Inimicitias Othinus serit, Saxo, p. 142, ed. 1644. See Grimm, *Deutsche Mythologie*, I, 120, note 2, III, 56, new ed, for Odin's bad points, though some of Grimm's interpretations might now be objected to.

[§]   I have omitted to mention the effect of *naming* on 'Clootie' in No 1, C 19:

As sune as she the fiend did name,
He flew awa in a blazing flame.

---

[*]   Helgakviða Hjörvarðssonar, ed. Grundtvig, 42–44, Ribold og Guldborg, **A** 33, 34, **B** 46, **D** 46, 47, **E** 42, **Q** 24. The observation is Professor Bugge's. See his discussion of the Scandinavian and the English ballads, *Helge-Digtene i den Ældre Edda*, pp. 283 ff.

Sago-Häfder, III, 100f; Faye, Norske Folke-Sagn, p. 14, 2d ed.; Hofberg, Nerikes Gamla Minnen, p. 234.)

It is a Norwegian belief that when a nix assumes the human shape in order to carry some one off, it will be his death if the selected victim recognizes him and names him, and in this way a woman escaped in a ballad. She called out, So you are the Nix, that pestilent beast, and the nix "disappeared in red blood." (Faye, as above, p. 49, note.) A nix is baffled in the same way in a Færoe and an Icelandic ballad cited by Grundtvig, II, 57.

The marvellous horse Blak agrees to carry Waldemar [Hildebrand] over a great piece of water for the rescue of his daughter [sister], stipulating, however, that his name shall not be uttered. The rider forgets himself in a panic, calls to the horse by his name, and is thrown off into the water. The horse, whose powers had been supernatural, and who had been *running* over the water as if it were land, has now only ordinary strength, and is forced to swim. He brings the lady back on the same terms, which she keeps, but when he reaches the land he is bleeding at every hair, and falls dead. (Landstad, 58; Grundtvig, 62; Afzelius, 59, preface; Kristensen, I, No 66.)

Klaufi, a berserker, while under the operation of his peculiar fury, loses his strength, and can no longer wield the weapon he was fighting with, upon Gríss's crying out, "Klaufi, Klaufi, be not so mad!" (Svarfdæla Saga, p. 147, and again p. 156f.) So the blood-thirst of the avenger's sword in the magnificent Danish ballad 'Hævnersværdet' is restrained by naming. (Grundtvig, No 25, st. 35.) Again, men engaged in *hamfarir*, that is in roving about in the shape of beasts, their proper bodies remaining lifeless the while, must not be called by name, for this might compel them to return at once to their own shape, or possibly prevent their ever doing so. (Kristni Saga, ed. 1773, p. 149. R. T. King, in *Notes and Queries*, 2d Ser., II, 506.) Grundtvig remarks that this belief is akin to what is related in Fáfnismál (prose interpolation after st. 1), that Sigurd concealed his name by reason of a belief in old times that a dying man's word had great power, if he cursed his foe by name. (D. g. F., II, 340.)

Böðvar Bjarki, fighting with great effect as a huge bear for Hrólfr Kraki, is obliged to return to his ordinary shape in consequence of Hjalti, who misses the hero from the fight, mentioning his name: Saga Hrólfs Kraka, c. 50, Fornaldar Sögur, I, 101 ff. In Hjalmters ok Ölvers Saga, c. 20, F. S. III, 506f, Hörðr bids his comrades not call him by name while he is fighting, in form of a sword-fish, with a walrus, else he shall die. A prince, under the form of an ox, fighting with a six-headed giant, loses much of his strength, and is nigh being conquered, because a lad has, contrary to his prohibition, called him by name. Asbjørnsen og Moe, Norske Folke-Eventyr, 2d ed., p. 419. All these are cited by Moe, in Nordisk Tidskrift, 1879, p. 286f. Certain kindly domestic spirits renounce relations with men, even matrimonial, if their name becomes known: Mannhardt, Wald- und Feldkulte, I, 103.

The Alpthier loses its power to harm and appears in its proper shape, as this or that person, if called by name: Wuttke, Der deutsche Volksaberglaube der Gegenwart, 2d ed., p. 257. Were-wolves appear in their proper human shape on being addressed by their name: Wilhelm Hertz, Der Werwolf, pp. 61, 84, Ulrich Jahn, Volkssagen aus Pommern u. Rügen, pp. 386–7. An enchanted prince is freed when his name is pronounced: Meier, No 53, p. 188 and n., p. 311. "There was in the engagement a man [on the side of Hades] who could not be vanquished unless his name could be discovered:" Myvyrian Archaiology of Wales, I, 167, as quoted by Rhys, Celtic Mythology, Hibbert Lectures, p. 244. For the whole subject, see K. Nyrop, Navnets Magt, 1887, and especially sections 4, 5, pp. 46–70. As to reluctance to have one's name known, and the advantage such knowledge gives an adversary, see E. Clodd, in The Folk Lore Journal, VII, 154ff and, in continuation, Folk-Lore, I, 272. See also W. R. Paton, Holy Names of the Eleusinian Priests, International Folk-lore Congress, 1891, Papers and Transactions, p. 202ff.

The berserkr Glammaðr could pick off any man with his pike, if only he knew his name. Saga Egils ok Ásmundar, Rafn, Fornaldar Sögur, III, 387, Ásmundarson, F. s. Norðrlanda, III, 292. (G. L. K.)

The demonic Gelô informs certain saints who force her "to tell them how other people's children [may] be defended from her attacks," that if they "can write her twelve names and a half she shall never be able to come within seventy-five stadia and a half:" Thomas Wright, *Essays on Subjects connected with the Literature, etc., of the Middle Ages,* 1846, I, 294 (referring to Leo Allatius, De Græcorum hodie quorundam opinationibus). The passage in question is to be found at p. 127 of Leo Allatius, De templis Græcorum recentioribus, ad Ioannem Morinum; De Narthece ecclesiæ veteris; nec non De Græcorum hodie quorundam opinationibus, ad Paullum Zacchiam. *Coloniæ Agrippinæ,* 1645. (G. L. K.)

The beautiful fancy of plants springing from the graves of star-crossed lovers, and signifying by the intertwining of stems or leaves, or in other analogous ways, that an earthly passion has not been extinguished by death, presents itself, as is well known, very frequently in popular poetry. Though the graves be made far apart, even on opposite sides of the church, or one to the north and one to the south outside of the church,[*] or one without kirk wall and one in the choir, however separated, the vines or trees seek one another out, and mingle their branches or their foliage:

"Even from the tomb the voice of Nature cries,
Even in our ashes live their wonted fires!"

The principal ballads which exhibit this conception in one or another form are the following:

In English, 'The Douglas Tragedy,' 'Fair Margaret and Sweet William,' 'Lord Thomas and Fair Annet,' 'Fair Janet,' 'Prince Robert,' 'Lord Lovel.' The plants in all these are either a brier and a rose, or a brier and a birk.

Swedish. Arwidsson, No 73: the graves are made east and west of the church, a linden grows from each, the trees meet over the church roof. So E. Wigström, *Folkdiktning,* No 20, p. 42. Arwidsson 74 **A**: Rosea Lilla and the duke are buried south and north in the church-

yard. A rose from her grave covers his with its leaves. The duke is then laid in her grave, from which a linden springs. 74 **B**: the rose as before, and a linden from the duke's grave. Arwidsson, 72, 68, Afzelius, No 19 (new ed., 18), 23 (new ed., 21, 1, 2): a common grave, with a linden, two trees, or lilies, and, in the last, roses also growing from the mouths of both lovers. In one version the linden leaves bear the inscription, My father shall answer to me at doomsday. Two copies of 'Rosen lilla' in Lagus, *Nyländska Folkvisor,* I, 37, No 10. Cf. Kristensen, *Jyske Folkeminder,* XI, 293.

Norwegian. Landstad, 65: the lovers are laid north and south of the church; lilies grow over the church roof.

Danish. *Danske Viser,* 124, 153, two roses. Kristensen, II, No 60, two lilies, interlocking over church wall and ridge. 61 **B, C** (= Afzelius, 19), separate graves; **B**, a lily from each grave; **C**, a flower from each breast. Grundtvig, 184 **G,** 271 **N,** a linden; *Danske Folkeminder,* 1861, p. 81, two lilies. Kristensen, *Jyske Folkeminder,* X, 215, No 52, **C** 9, two lilies; p. 318, No 78, 9, 10, graves south and north, two lilies. 'Hertug Frydenborg,' *Danmarks g. Folkeviser,* No 305, V, II, 216. **A a, b, h, n, o; B b, c; E, k, l; F b, c, e, f;** with diversities, the plant nearly always lilies. (A few of these, from Kristensen, have been already cited.)

German. 'Der Ritter u. die Maid,' (1) Nicolai, I, No 2, = Kretzschmer, I, 54; (2) Uhland, 97 **A,** Simrock, 12; (3) Erk's *Liederhort,* 26; Hoffmann u. Richter, 4: the lovers are buried together, and there grow from their grave (1) three pinks, (2) three lilies, (3) two lilies. *Wunderhorn,* 1857, I, 53, Mittler, No 91: the maid buried in the church-yard, the knight under the gallows. A lily grows from his grave, with an inscription, Beid wären beisammen im Himmel. Ditfurth, II, 7: two lilies spring from her (or their) grave, bearing a similar inscription. In Haupt and Schmaler, *Volkslieder der Wenden,* I, 136, from the German, rue is *planted* on the maid's grave, in accordance with the last words of the knight, and the same inscription appears on one of the leaves.

'Graf Friedrich,' Uhland, 122, *Wunderhorn,* II, 293, Mittler, 108, Erk's *Liederhort,* 15 a: Graf Friedrich's bride is by accident mortally

---

[*]   In England the north side of the burial-ground is appropriated to unbaptized children, suicides, etc. Brand's *Antiquities,* ed. Hazlitt, II, 214–218.

wounded while he is bringing her home. Her father kills him, and he is dragged at a horse's heels. Three lilies spring from his grave, with an inscription, Er wär bei Gott geblieben. He is then buried with his bride, the transfer being attended with other miraculous manifestations. Other versions, Hoffmann u. Richter, 19, = Mittler, 112, = Liederhort, 15; Mittler, 113, 114; also Meinert, 23, = Mittler, 109, etc.: the lilies in most of these growing from the bride's grave, with words attesting the knight's innocence.

Lilies with inscriptions also in Wunderhorn, II, p. 251, = Mittler, 128, 'Alle bei Gott die sich lieben;' Mittler, 130; Ditfurth, II, 4, 9; Scherer, Jungbrunnen, 9 A, 25; Pogatschnigg und Hermann, 1458. Three lilies from a maid's grave: 'Die schwazbraune Hexe' ('Es blies ein Jäger'), Nicolai, I, 8; Wunderhorn, I, 36; Gräter's Bragur, I, 280; Uhland, 103; Liederhort, 9; Simrock, 93; Fiedler, p. 158; Ditfurth, II, 33, 34; Reifferscheid, 15, etc. Three roses, Hoffmann u. Richter, 171, p. 194; three pinks, ib., 172; rose, pink, lily, Alemannia, IV, 35. Three lilies from a man's grave: 'Der Todwunde:' Schade, Bergreien, 10, = Uhland, 93 A, = Liederhort, 34 g, = Mittler, 47, etc.

A Middle High German poem from a MS. of the end of the 14th century, printed in Haupt's Zeitschrift, VI, makes a vine rise from the common grave of Pyramus and Thisbe and descend into it again: p. 517. (Köhler.)

J. Grimm notes several instances of this marvel (not from ballads), Ueber Frauennamen aus Blumen, Kleinere Schriften, II, 379f, note **.

Armenian. The ashes of two lovers who have been literally consumed by a mutual passion are deposited by sympathetic hands in one grave. Two rose bushes rise from the grave and seek to intertwine, but a thorn interposes and makes the union forever impossible. (The thorn is creed. The young man was a Tatar, and his religion had been an insuperable obstacle in the eyes of the maid's father.) Baron von Haxthausen, Transkaukasia, I, 315f. (Köhler.)

Spanish. Milá, Romancerillo Catalan, 2d ed., No 206. D, p. 164: olivera y oliverá, which, when grown tall, join.

Portuguese. 'Conde Nillo,' 'Conde Niño,' Almeida-Garrett, III, No 18, at p. 21; Braga, Rom. Geral., No 14, at p. 38, = Hartung, I, 217:

the infanta is buried at the foot of the high altar, Conde Nillo near the church door; a cypress and an orange [pines]. Almeida-Garrett, III, No 20, at p. 38: a sombre clump of pines over the knight, reeds from the princess's grave, which, though cut down, shoot again, and are heard sighing in the night. Braga, Archip. Açor., 'Filha Maria,' 'Dom Doardos,' 'A Ermida no Mar,' Nos 32, 33, 34, Hartung, I, 220–224; Estacio da Veiga, 'Dom Diniz,' p. 64–67, = Hartung, I, 217, 2: tree and pines, olive and pines, clove-tree and pine, roses and canes: in all, new miracles follow the cutting down. So also Almeida-Garrett, No 6, I, 167. Roméro, II, 157, two pines. Roméro, Cantos pop. do Brazil, No 4, 'D. Duarte e Donzilha,' I, 9: sicupira and collar.

Roumanian. Alecsandri, 7, Stanley, p. 16, 'Ring and Handkerchief,' translated by Stanley, p. 193, Murray, p. 56, also in Marienescu, Balade, p. 50: cited in Mélusine, IV. 142: a fir and a vine, which meet over the church.

French. Beaurepaire, Poésie pop. en Normandie, p. 51: a thorn and an olive are planted over the graves; the thorn embraces the olive. 'Les deux Amoureux,' Daymard, Vieux Chants p. rec. en Quercy, p. 122, lavender and tree.

Romaic. Passow, Nos 414, 415, 456, 469; Zambelios, p. 754, No 41; Tommaseo, Canti Popolari, III, 135; Chasiotis, p. 103, No 22: a cypress from the man's grave, a reed from the maid's (or from a common tomb); reversed in Passow, Nos 418, 470, and Schmidt, Griechische Märchen, u. s. w., No 59, p. 203. Sakellarios, p. 25, No 9, cypress and apple-tree; p. 38, No 13, cypress and lemon-tree. (F. Liebrecht, Zur Volkskunde, pp. 166, 168, 182, 183.) See Ζωγραφεῖος Ἀγών, p. 170, No 321. [Georgeakis et Pineau, Folk-lore de Lesbos, pp. 208, 221.] Chasiotis, p. 169, No 5, lemon and cypress; Aravandinos, p. 284f, Nos 471, 472, cypress and reed.

Servian. Talvj, V. L. der Serben, II, p. 85: a fir and a rose; the rose twines round the fir. Karadshitch, I, 345, vv 225ff, two pines, which intertwine. In I 309, No 421, they plant a rose over the maid, a vine over the man, which embrace as if they were Jani and Milenko. The ballad has features of the Earl Brand class. (I, 239, No 341 = Talvj, II, 85.) Vuk, I, No 342, II, No 30; youth, pine, maid, grape-vine. Krasić, p.

105, No 21, p. 114, No 26; vine and pine, vine twines round pine.

Wend. Haupt and Schmaler, *V. L. der Wenden*, II, No 48; Haupt and Schmaler, II, 310, No 81: a maid, who kills herself on account of the death of her lover, orders two grape vines *to be planted* over their graves: the vines intertwine.

Breton. Luzel, I, p. 423: a fleur-de-lis springs from a common tomb, and is always in flower, however often it is plucked. Villemarqué, *Barzaz Breiz*, 'Le Seigneur Nann et La Fée,' see p. 507, note, of this volume. *Mélusine*, III, 453f: A tree springs from over the young man's heart (but this is an insertion, and not quite beyond suspicion), a rose from the maid's. There is another version of the ballad at p. 182f, in which une fleur dorée grows over the man's grave, nothing being said of his mistress's grave, or even of her death. Luzel, *Soniou*, I, 272–3: a tree from the young man's grave, a rose from the maid's.

Gaelic. Of Naisi (Naois) and Deirdre. King Conor caused them to be buried far apart, but for some days the graves would be found open in the morning and the lovers found together. The king ordered stakes of yew to be driven through the bodies, so that they might be kept asunder. Yew trees grew from the stakes, and so high as to embrace each other over the cathedral of Armagh. *Transactions of the Gaelic Society of Dublin*, I, 133, 1808.

In a Scotch-Gaelic version recently obtained, after Naois is put into his grave, Deirdre jumps in, lies down by his side and dies. The bad king orders her body to be taken out and buried on the other side of a loch. Firs shoot out of the two graves and unite over the loch. The king has the trees cut down twice, but the third time his wife makes him desist from his vengeance on the dead. The original in *Transactions of the Gaelic Society of Inverness*, XIII, 257; a translation in *The Celtic Magazine*, XIII, 138. (All of these cited by Gaidoz, *Mélusine*, IV, 12, and 62, note.)

Italian. Nigara, No 18, 'Le due Tombe,' p. 125ff. **A.** The lovers are buried apart, one in the church, one outside, a pomegranate springs from the man's grave, an almond-tree from the maid's; they grow large enough to shade three cities! **B.** A pomegranate is planted on the man's grave, a hazel on the maid's; they shade the city, and interlock. **C.** An almond-tree is planted on the maid's grave, and is cut down. **D.** The lovers are buried as in **A** (and **C**), an almond-tree grows from the grave of the man, a jessamine from the maid's. See also No 19, 'Fior di Tomba,' where, however, there is but one grave, which is to contain the maid's parents as well as her lover. The same phenomenon in the fragments **E**, **F**. 'Il Castello d'Oviglio,' Ferraro, *Canti p. monferrini*, No 45, p. 64, is another version of this ballad. A pomegranate springs up at the maid's feet, and shades three cities. Cf. 'La Mort des deux Amants,' Rolland, I, 247, No 125.

Italo-Albanian. De Rada, *Rapsodie d'un poema albanese, etc.*, p. 47: the youth comes up (nacque) a cypress; the maid a white vine, which clings around the tree. Camarda, *Appendice al saggio di grammatologia comparata*, 'Angelina,' p. 112, the same; but inappropriately, as Liebrecht has remarked, fidelity in love being wanting in this case. De Grazia, *Canti pop. albanesi*, p. 102, No 11. Also in Vigo, *Canti p. siciliani*, 1857, p. 345, V, and the edition of 1870–74, p. 698: cited in *Mélusine*, IV, 87.

Magyar. The lovers are buried before and behind the altar; white and red lilies spring from the tombs; mother or father destroys or attempts to destroy the plants: Aigner, *Ungarische Volksdichtungen*, 2d ed., at p. 92, p. 138, 131f. Again, at p. 160, of the 'Two Princes' (Hero and Leander): here a white and a red tulip are *planted* over the graves, in a garden, and it is expressly said that the souls of the enamored pair passed into the tulips. In the first piece the miracle occurs twice. The lovers had thrown themselves into a deep lake; plants rose above the surface of the water and intertwined (p. 91); the bodies were brought up by divers and buried in the church, where the marvel was repeated. In *Ungarische Revue*, 1883, pp. 756–59, these three and one more.

Magyar-Croat. Kurelac, p. 147, No 444, grape-vine and rose; No 445, youth behind the church, maid before, grape-vine and rose; p. 154, No 454, rosemary and a white flower (aleluja?). (W. W.)

Turkish. Sora Chenim went down into the grave of Täji Pascha, which opened to receive her. The "black heathen" ordered one of his slaves to slay him and bury him between the two. "Da wuchs Täji Pascha als eine Pappel aus dem Boden hervor, Sora Chenim wuchs als ein Rosenstrauch hervor. Zwischen diesen Beiden wuchs der schwarze Heide als ein Dornbusch hervor," etc. Radloff, *Proben der Volkslitteratur der nördlichen türkischen Stämme*, VI, 246.

Afghan. Audam and Doorkhaunee, a poem "read, repeated, and sung, through all parts of the country," Elphinstone's *Account of the Kingdom of Caubul*, 1815, p. 185f: two trees spring from their remains, and the branches mingle over their tomb. First cited by Talvj, *Versuch*, p. 140.

Kurd. Mem and Zin, a poem of Ahméd Xáni, died 1652–3: two rose bushes spring from their graves and interlock. *Bulletin de la classe des sciences historiques, etc., de l'acad. impér. des sciences de St. Pét.*, tome xv, No 11, p. 170.

Russian. Hilferding, *Onezhskya Byliny*, col. 154, No 31, silver willow over Basil, and cypress over Sophia, which intertwine; col. 696, No 134, cypress and golden willow; col. 1242, No 285, golden willow and cypress. Bezsonof, *Kalyeki Perekhozhie*, I, 697–700, Nos 167,168 (Ruibnikof): Vasily is laid on the right, Sophia on the left; golden willow and cypress. The hostile mother pulls up, breaks down, the willow; cuts down, pulls up, the cypress. Trudy, V, 711, No 309, **A**, man buried under church, wife under belfry; green maple and white birch., **B–J**, other copies with variations. V, 1208, No 50, a Cossack blossoms into a thorn, a maid into an elder; his mother goes to pull up the thorn, hers to pluck up the elder. "Lo, this is, no thorn! it is my son!" "Lo, this is no elder! it is my daughter!"

White-Russian. He is buried in church, she in ditch; plane and linden (planted); plane embraces linden; MS. He is buried in church, she near church; oak, birch (planted); trees touch; *Zbiór wiado. do antropol.*, XIII, 102f. (J. Karłowicz, in *Mélusine*, V, 39ff.)

Little Russian (Carpathian Russians in Hungary), Golovatsky, II, 710, No 13: John on one side of the church, Annie on the other; rosemary on his grave, a lily on hers, growing so high as to meet over the church. Annie's mother cuts them down. John speaks from the grave: Wicked mother, thou wouldst not let us live together; let us rest together. Golovatsky, I, 186, No 8: a maple from the man's grave, white birch from the woman's, which mingle their leaves. Plane-trees of the two sexes; cited by J. Karlowicz, *ib.*, 87f. Ruthenian (mother attempting to poison her son's wife poisons both wife and son), Herrmann, *Ethnologische Mittheilungen*, 205f; buried on different sides of the church, plants meet over the roof of the church, the mother tries to cut them down, and while so engaged is turned into a pillar. Kolberg, *Pokucie*, p. 41: they are buried apart; plane grows over his grave, two birches over hers; branches do *not* interlace. Holovatzky, III, 254: burial apart in a church; rosemary and lily from graves. Var.: rose and sage, rosemary; flowers interlace.

Bulgarian, Miladinof, *Bùlgarski narodni pĕsni*, p. 455, No 497, translated by Krauss, *Sagen u. Märchen der Südslaven*, II, 427; the youth as rose-tree, the maid as grape-vine. Cited by G. Meyer in *Mélusine*, IV, 87. Miladinof, p. 375, No 288, rose and vine. A poplar from the maid's grave, a pine from her lover's: *Collection of the Bulgarian Ministry of Instruction*, I, 35. (W. W.)

Slovenian. Štúr, *O národních Písních a Povĕstech Plemen slovanských*, p. 51: the lovers are buried east and west, a rose springs from the man's grave, a lily from the maid's, which mingle their growth.

Chinese. Hanpang has a young and pretty wife named Ho, whom he tenderly loves. The king, becoming enamored of her, puts her husband in prison, where he kills himself. Ho throws herself from a high place, leaving a letter to the king, in which she begs that she may be buried in the same tomb as her husband; but the king orders them to be put in separate graves. In the night cedars spring up from their tombs, which thrive so extraordinarily that in ten days their branches and their roots are interlocked. A. de Gubernatis, *La Mythologie des Plantes*, II, 53, from Schlegel, *Uranographie chinoise*, p. 679. (Already cited by Braga.)

The idea of the love-animated plants has been thought to be derived from the romance of Tristan, where it also occurs; agreeably to a general principle, somewhat hastily assumed, that when romances and popular ballads have anything in common, priority belongs to the romances. The question as to precedence in this instance is an open one, for the fundamental conception is not less a favorite with ancient Greek than with mediæval imagination.

Tristan and Isolde had unwittingly drunk of a magical potion which had the power to induce an indestructible and ever-increasing love. Tristan died of a wound received in one of his adventures, and Isolde of a broken heart, because, though summoned to his aid, she arrived too late for him to profit by her medical skill. They were buried in the same church. According to the French prose romance, a green brier issued from Tristan's tomb, mounted to the roof, and, descending to Isolde's tomb, made its way within. King Marc caused the brier to be cut down three several times, but the morning after it was as flourishing as before.[*]

Eilhart von Oberge, vv 9509–21 (ed. Lichtenstein, Quellen u. Forschungen, xix, 429) and the German prose romance (Büsching u. von der Hagen, Buch der Liebe, c. 60), Ulrich von Thürheim, vv 3546–50, and Heinrich von Freiberg, vv 6819–41 (in von der Hagen's ed. of G. v. Strassburg's Tristan) make King Marc plant, the first two a grape-vine over Tristan and a rose over Isolde, the others, wrongly, the rose over Tristan and the vine over Isolde. These plants, according to Heinrich, struck their roots into the hearts of the lovers below, while their branches embraced above. Icelandic ballads and an Icelandic saga represent Tristan's wife as forbidding the lovers to be buried in the same grave, and ordering them to be buried on opposite sides of the church. Trees spring from their bodies and meet over the church roof. (Íslenzk Fornkvæði, 23 A, B, C, D; Saga af Tristram ok Ísönd, Brynjulfson, p. 199; Tristrams Saga ok Ísondar, Kölbing, p. 112). The later Titurel imitates the conclusion of Tristan. (Der jüngere Titurel, ed. Hahn, sts 5789, 5790.)

---

[*] Et de la tombe de monseigneur Tristan yssoit une ronce belle et verte et bien feuilleue, qui alloit par dessus la chapelle, et descendoit le bout de la ronce sur la tombe de la royne Yseult, et entroit dedans. La virent les gens du pays et la comptèrent au roy Marc. Le roy la fist couper par troys foys, et quant il l'avoit le jour fait couper, le lendemain estoit aussi belle comme avoit aultre fois esté. Fol. cxxiv, as cited by Braga, Rom. Ger., p. 185.

Among the miracles of the Virgin there are several which are closely akin to the prodigies already noted. A lily is found growing from the mouth of a clerk, who, though not leading an exemplary life, had every day said his ave before the image of Mary: Unger, Mariu Saga, No 50; Berceo, No 3; Miracles de N.-D. de Chartres, p. lxiii, No 29, and p. 239; Marien-legenden (Stuttgart, 1846), No xi and p. 269. A rose springs from the grave and roots in the heart of a [9◦] knight who had spared the honor of a maid because her name was Mary: Unger, No clvi, Hagen's Gesammtabenteuer, lxxiii. Roses inscribed Maria grow from the mouth, eyes, and ears of a monk: Unger, cxxxvii; and a lily grows over a monk's grave, springing from his mouth, every leaf of which bears Ave Maria in golden letters: Unger, cxxxviii; Gesammtabenteuer, lxxxviii; Libro de Exenplos, Romania, 1878, p. 509, 43, 44; etc., etc.

No one can fail to be reminded of the purple, lily-shaped flower, inscribed with the mournful AI AI, that rose from the blood of Hyacinthus, and of the other from the blood of Ajax, with the same letters, "his name and eke his plaint," hæc nominis, illa querellæ. (Ovid, Met. x, 210 ff; xiii, 394 ff.) The northern lindens have their counterpart in the elms from the grave of Protesilaus, and in the trees into which Philemon and Baucis were transformed. See, upon the whole subject, the essay of Koberstein in the Weimar Jahrbuch, i, 73 ff, with Köhler's supplement, p. 479 ff; Grimm, Deutsche Mythologie, ii, 689 f, and iii, 246.

"The ballad of the 'Douglas Tragedy,'" says Scott, "is one of the few to which popular tradition has ascribed complete locality. The farm of Blackhouse, in Selkirkshire, is said to have been the scene of this melancholy event. There are the remains of a very ancient tower, adjacent to the farm-house, in a wild and solitary glen, upon a torrent named Douglas burn, which joins the Yarrow after passing a craggy rock called the Douglas craig. . . . From this ancient tower Lady Margaret is said to have been carried by her lover. Seven large stones, erected upon the neighboring heights of Blackhouse, are shown, as marking the spot where the seven brethren were slain; and the Douglas burn is averred to have been the stream at which the lovers stopped to drink: so minute is tradition in ascertaining the scene of a tragical tale, which, considering the rude state of former times, had probably foundation in some real event."

The localities of the Danish story were ascertained, to her entire satisfaction, by Anne Krabbe in 1605–6, and are given again in Resen's *Atlas Danicus*, 1677. See Grundtvig, II, 342 f.

B, Scott's 'Douglas Tragedy,' is translated by Grundtvig, *Engelske og skotske Folkeviser*, No 11;

Afzelius, III, 86; Schubart, p. 169; Talvj, p. 565; Wolff, *Halle*, I, 76, Hausschatz, p. 201; Rosa Warrens, No 23; Gerhard, p. 28; Loève-Veimars, p. 292.

'Ribold og Guldborg,' Danish **B**, is translated by Buchanan, p. 16 (loosely); **G** by Jamieson, *Illustrations*, p. 317, and Prior, II, 400; **T** by Prior, II, 407; Swedish **A**, *Foreign Quarterly Review*, XXV, 41. 'Hildebrand og Hilde,' Danish **A, B, F, H,** by Prior, II, 411–20.

A

a, b, from the papers of the late Robert White, Esq., of Newcastle-on-Tyne: c, R. Bell, *Ancient Poems, Ballads, etc.* (1857), p. 122: d, fragmentary lines as remembered by Mrs Andrews, Mr White's sister, from her mother's singing.

R. White MSS. (Child MSS., HCL 25241.51F, p. 49). Sung by Mrs Andrews, Northumberland.

1 Oh did ye ever hear o brave Earl Bran?
 Ay lally, o lilly lally
He courted the king's daughter of fair England.
 All i the night sae early

2 She was scarcely fifteen years of age
Till sae boldly she came to his bedside.

3 'O Earl Bran, fain wad I see
A pack of hounds let loose on the lea.'

4 'O lady, I have no steeds but one,
And thou shalt ride, and I will run.'

5 'O Earl Bran, my father has two,
And thou shall have the best o them a.'

6 They have ridden oer moss and moor,
And they met neither rich nor poor.

7 Until they met with old Carl Hood;
He comes for ill, but never for good.

8 'Earl Bran, if ye love me,   [100]
Seize this old carl, and gar him die.'

9 'O lady fair, it wad be sair,
To slay an old man that has grey hair.'

10 'O lady fair, I'll no do sae;
I'll gie him a pound, and let him gae.'

11 'O where hae ye ridden this lee lang day?
Or where hae ye stolen this lady away?'

12 'I have not ridden this lee lang day,
Nor yet have I stolen this lady away.

13 'She is my only, my sick sister,
Whom I have brought from Winchester.'

14 'If she be sick, and like to dead,
Why wears she the ribbon sae red?

15 'If she be sick, and like to die,
Then why wears she the gold on high?'

16 When he came to this lady's gate,
   Sae rudely as he rapped at it.

17 'O where's the lady o this ha?'
   'She's out with her maids to play at the ba.'

18 'Ha, ha, ha! ye are a' mistaen:
   Gae count your maidens oer again.

19 'I saw her far beyond the moor,
   Away to be the Earl o Bran's whore.'

20 The father armed fifteen of his best men,
   To bring his daughter back again.

21 Oer her left shoulder the lady looked then:
   'O Earl Bran, we both are tane.'

22 'If they come on me ane by ane,
   Ye may stand by and see them slain.

23 'But if they come on me one and all,
   Ye may stand by and see me fall.'

24 They have come on him ane by ane,
   And he has killed them all but ane.

25 And that ane came behind his back,
   And he's gien him a deadly whack.

26 But for a' sae wounded as Earl Bran was,
   He has set his lady on her horse.

27 They rode till they came to the water o Doune,
   And then he alighted to wash his wounds.

28 'O Earl Bran, I see your heart's blood!'
   ' 'T is but the gleat o my scarlet hood.'

29 They rode till they came to his mother's gate,
   And sae rudely as he rapped at it.

30 'O my son's slain, my son's put down,
   And a' for the sake of an English loun.'

31 'O say not sae, my dear mother,
   But marry her to my youngest brother.

   *   *   *   *   *

32 'This has not been the death o ane,
   But it's been that of fair seventeen.'

   *   *   *   *   *

B

Scott's *Minstrelsy*, III, 246, ed. 1803; III, 6, ed. 1833:
the copy principally used supplied by Mr Sharpe, the
three last stanzas from a penny pamphlet and from tra-
dition.

'Rise up, rise up, now, Lord Doug-las,' she says,— 'And put on your ar-mour so— bright;—

Let it ne-ver be said— that a daught-er of— thine—Was mar-ried to a lord— un-der night.

Scott, 1833–34, III, pp. 1–3.

1 'RISE up, rise up, now, Lord Douglas,' she says,
   'And put on your armour so bright;
   Let it never be said that a daughter of thine
   Was married to a lord under night.

2 'Rise up, rise up, my seven bold sons,
   And put on your armour so bright,
   And take better care of your youngest sister,
   For your eldest's awa the last night.'

3 He's mounted her on a milk-white steed,
   And himself on a dapple grey,
   With a bugelet horn hung down by his side,
   And lightly they rode away.

4 Lord William lookit oer his left shoulder,
   To see what he could see,
   And there he spy'd her seven brethren bold,
   Come riding over the lee.

01]

5 'Light down, light down, Lady Margret,' he said,
　　'And hold my steed in your hand,
　Until that against your seven brethren bold,
　　And your father, I mak a stand.'

6 She held his steed in her milk-white hand,
　　And never shed one tear,
　Until that she saw her seven brethren fa,
　　And her father hard fighting, who lovd her
　　　so dear.

7 'O hold your hand, Lord William!' she said,
　　'For your strokes they are wondrous sair;
　True lovers I can get many a ane,
　　But a father I can never get mair.'

8 O she's taen out her handkerchief,
　　It was o the holland sae fine,
　And aye she dighted her father's bloody wounds,
　　That were redder than the wine.

9 'O chuse, O chuse, Lady Margret,' he said,
　　'O whether will ye gang or bide?'
　'I'll gang, I'll gang, Lord William,' she said,
　　'For ye have left me no other guide.'

10 He's lifted her on a milk-white steed,
　　And himself on a dapple grey,
　With a bugelet horn hung down by his side,
　　And slowly they baith rade away.

11 O they rade on, and on they rade,
　　And a' by the light of the moon,
　Until they came to yon wan water,
　　And there they lighted down.

12 They lighted down to tak a drink
　　Of the spring that ran sae clear,
　And down the stream ran his gude heart's blood,
　　And sair she gan to fear.

13 'Hold up, hold up, Lord William,' she says,
　　'For I fear that you are slain;'
　''T is naething but the shadow of my scarlet
　　　cloak,
　　That shines in the water sae plain.'

14 O they rade on, and on they rade,
　　And a' by the light of the moon,
　Until they cam to his mother's ha door,
　　And there they lighted down.

15 'Get up, get up, lady mother,' he says,
　　'Get up, and let me in!
　Get up, get up, lady mother,' he says,
　　'For this night my fair lady I've win.

16 'O mak my bed, lady mother,' he says,
　　'O mak it braid and deep,
　And lay Lady Margret close at my back,
　　And the sounder I will sleep.'

17 Lord William was dead lang ere midnight,
　　Lady Margret lang ere day,
　And all true lovers that go thegither,
　　May they have mair luck than they!

18 Lord William was buried in St. Mary's kirk,
　　Lady Margret in Mary's quire;
　Out o the lady's grave grew a bonny red rose,
　　And out o the knight's a briar.

19 And they twa met, and they twa plat,
　　And fain they wad be near;
　And a' the warld might ken right weel
　　They were twa lovers dear.

20 But bye and rade the Black Douglas,
　　And wow but he was rough!
　For he pulld up the bonny brier,
　　And flang't in St. Mary's Loch.

C

Motherwell's MS., p. 502. From the recitation of
Mrs Notman.

1 'RISE up, rise up, my seven brave sons,
　　And dress in your armour so bright;
　Earl Douglas will hae Lady Margaret awa
　　Before that it be light.

2 'Arise, arise, my seven brave sons,
　　And dress in your armour so bright;
　It shall never be said that a daughter of mine
　　Shall go with an earl or a knight.'

3 'O will ye stand, fair Margaret,' he says,
    'And hold my milk-white steed,
  Till I fight your father and seven brethren,
    In yonder pleasant mead?'

[102] 4 She stood and held his milk-white steed,
    She stood trembling with fear,
  Until she saw her seven brethren fall,
    And her father that loved her dear.

5 'Hold your hand, Earl Douglas,' she says,
    'Your strokes are wonderous sair;
  I may get sweethearts again enew,
    But a father I'll ne'er get mair.'

6 She took out a handkerchief
    Was made o' the cambrick fine,
  And aye she wiped her father's bloody wounds,
    And the blood sprang up like wine.

7 'Will ye go, fair Margaret?' he said,
    'Will ye now go, or bide?'
  'Yes, I'll go, sweet William,' she said,
    'For ye've left me never a guide.

8 'If I were to go to my mother's house,
    A welcome guest I would be;
  But for the bloody deed that's done this day
    I'll rather go with thee.'

9 He lifted her on a milk-white steed
    And himself on a dapple gray;
  They drew their hats out over their face,
    And they both went weeping away.

10 They rode, they rode, and they better rode,
    Till they came to yon water wan;
  They lighted down to gie their horse a drink
    Out of the running stream.

11 'I am afraid, Earl Douglas.' she said,
    'I am afraid ye are slain;
  I think I see your bonny heart's blood
    Running down the water wan.'

12 'Oh no, oh no, fair Margaret,' he said,
    'Oh no, I am not slain;
  It is but the scad of my scarlet cloak
    Runs down the water wan.'

13 He mounted her on a milk-white steed
    And himself on a dapple gray,
  And they have reached Earl Douglas' gates
    Before the break of day.

14 'O rise, dear mother, and make my bed,
    And make it braid and wide,
  And lay me down to take my rest,
    And at my back my bride.'

15 She has risen and made his bed,
    She made it braid and wide;
  She laid him down to take his rest,
    And at his back his bride.

16 Lord William died ere it was day,
    Lady Margaret on the morrow;
  Lord William died through loss of blood and
      wounds,
    Fair Margaret died with sorrow.

17 The one was buried in Mary's kirk,
    The other in Mary's quire;
  The one sprung up a bonnie bush,
    And the other a bonny brier.

18 These twa grew, and these twa threw,
    Till they came to the top,
  And when they could na farther gae,
    They coost the lovers' knot.

D

Kinloch MSS, I, 327.

1 'SLEEPST thou or wakst thou, Lord Montgomerie,
    Sleepst thou or wakst thou, I say?
  Rise up, make a match for your eldest daughter,
    For the youngest I carry away.'

2 'Rise up, rise up, my seven bold sons,
    Dress yourselves in the armour sae fine;
  For it ne'er shall be said that a churlish knight
    Eer married a daughter of mine.'

*   *   *   *   *

3 'Loup aff, loup aff, Lady Margaret,' he said.
   'And hold my steed in your hand,
And I will go fight your seven brethren,
   And your father, where they stand.'

4 Sometimes she gaed, sometimes she stood,
   But never dropt a tear,
Until she saw her brethren all slain,
   And her father who lovd her so dear.

5 'Hold thy hand, sweet William,' she says,
   'Thy blows are wondrous sore;
Sweethearts I may have many a one,
   But a father I'll never have more.'

6 O she's taken her napkin frae her pocket,
   Was made o the holland fine,
And ay as she dichted her father's bloody
     wounds,
   They sprang as red as the wine.

7 'Two chooses, two chooses, Lady Margret,' he
     says,
   'Two chooses I'll make thee;
Whether to go back to your mother again,
   Or go along with me.'

8 'For to go home to my mother again,
   An unwelcome guest I'd be;
But since my fate has ordered it so,
   I'll go along with thee.'

9 He has mounted her on a milk-white steed,
   Himself on the dapple gray,
And blawn his horn baith loud and shill,
   And it sounded far on their way.

10 They rode oer hill, they rode oer dale,
   They rode oer mountains so high,
Until they came to that beautiful place
   Where Sir William's mother did lie.

11 'Rise up, rise up, lady mother,' he said,
   'Rise up, and make much o your own;
Rise up, rise up, lady mother,' he said,
   'For his bride's just new come home.'

12 Sir William he died in the middle o the night,
   Lady Margaret died on the morrow
Sir William he died of pure pure love,
   Lady Margaret of grief and sorrow.

E

Motherwell's *Minstrelsy*, p. 180. From recitation.

1 He has lookit over his left shoulder,
   And through his bonnie bridle rein,
And he spy'd her father and her seven bold
     brethren,
   Come riding down the glen.

2 'O hold my horse, Lady Margret,' he said,
   O hold my horse by the bonnie bridle rein,
Till I fight your father and seven bold brethren,
   As they come riding down the glen.'

3 Some time she rade, and some time she gaed,
   Till she that place did near,
And there she spy'd her seven bold brethren
     slain,
   And her father who loved her so dear.

4 'O hold your hand, sweet William,' she said,
   'Your bull baits are wondrous sair;
Sweet-hearts I may get many a one,
   But a father I will never get mair.'

5 She has taken a napkin from off her neck,
   That was of the cambrick so fine,
And aye as she wiped her father's bloody
     wounds,
   The blood ran red as the wine.

*   *   *   *   *

6 He set her upon the milk-white steed,
   Himself upon the brown;
He took a horn out of his pocket,
   And they both went weeping along.

F

Percy MS., p. 57; ed. Hales and Furnivall, I, 133.

1 .   .   .   .   .   .

    Sayes 'Christ thee saue, good Child of Ell!
    Christ saue thee and thy steede!

2 'My father sayes he will [eat] noe meate,
    Nor his drinke shall doe him noe good,
    Till he haue slaine the Child of Ell,
    And haue seene his harts blood.'

3 'I wold I were in my sadle sett,
    And a mile out of the towne;
    I did not care for your father
    And all his merry men!

[104]

4 'I wold I were in my sadle sett,
    And a little space him froe;
    I did not care for your father
    And all that long him to!'

5 He leaned ore his saddle bow
    To kisse this lady good;
    The teares *that* went them *two* betweene
    Were blend water and blood.

6 He sett himselfe on one good steed,
    This lady on a palfray,
    And sett his litle horne to his mouth,
    And roundlie he rode away.

7 He had not ridden past a mile,
    A mile out of the towne,

   .   .   .   .   .

   .   .   .   .   .

8 Her father was readye with her *seuen* brether,
    He said, 'Sett thou my daughter downe!
    For it ill beseemes thee, thou false churles
      sonne,
    To carry her forth of this towne!'

9 'But lowd thou lyest, Sir Iohn the knight,
    Thou now doest lye of me;
    A knight me gott, and a lady me bore;
    Soe neuer did none by thee.

10 'But light now downe, my lady gay,
    Light downe and hold my horsse,
    Whilest I and your father and your brether
    Doe play vs at this crosse.

11 'But light now downe, my owne trew loue,
    And meeklye hold my steede,
    Whilest your father [and your *seuen* brether]
      bold

*   *   *   *   *

G

The Paisley Magazine, June 2, 1828, p. 321, commu-
nicated by William Motherwell. "Sung to a long, drawl-
ing, monotonous tune."

*   *   *   *   *

1 'GUDE Earl Brand, I long to see
    Faldee faldee fal deediddle a dee
    All your grey hounds running over the lea.'
    And the brave knights in the valley

2 'Gude lady fair, I have not a steed but one,
    But you shall ride and I shall run.'

3 They're ower moss and they're ower mure,
    And they saw neither rich nor pure.

4 Until that they came to auld Karl Hude;
    He's aye for ill and never for gude.

5 'Gude Earl Brand, if ye love me,
    Kill auld Karl Hude, and gar him die.'

6 'O fair ladie, we'll do better than sae:
    Gie him a penny, and let him gae.'

7 'Gude Earl Brand, whare hae ye been,
    Or whare hae ye stown this lady sheen?'

8 'She's not my lady, but my sick sister,
   And she's been at the wells of Meen.'

9 'If she was sick, and very sair,
   She wadna wear the red gold on her hair.

10 'Or if she were sick, and like to be dead,
    She wadna wear the ribbons red.'

11 He cam till he cam to her father's gate,
    And he has rappit furious thereat.

12 'Where is the lady o this hall?'
    'She's out wi her maidens, playing at the ball.'

13 'If you'll get me fyfteen wale wight men,
    Sae fast as I'll fetch her back again.'

14 She's lookit ower her left collar-bane:
    'O gude Earl Brand, we baith are taen.'

15 'Light down, light down, and hold my steed;
    Change never your cheer till ye see me dead.

16 'If they come on me man by man,
    I'll be very laith for to be taen.

17 'But if they come on me one and all,
    The sooner you will see me fall.'

18 O he has killd them all but one,
    And wha was that but auld Karl Hude.

19 And he has come on him behind,
    And put in him the deadly wound.

20 O he has set his lady on,
    And he's come whistling all along.

21 'Gude Earl Brand, I see blood:'
    'It's but the shade o my scarlet robe.'

22 They cam till they cam to the water aflood;
    He's lighted down and he's wushen aff the
    blood.

23 His mother walks the floor alone:
    'O yonder does come my poor son.

24 'He is both murderd and undone,
    And all for the sake o an English loon.'

25 'Say not sae, my dearest mother,
    Marry her on my eldest brother.'

26 She set her fit up to the wa,
    Faldee faldee fal deediddle adee
    She's fallen down dead amang them a'.
    And the brave knights o the valley

H

Campbell MSS, II, 32.

1 DID you ever hear of good Earl Brand,
   Aye lally an lilly lally
   And the king's daughter of fair Scotland?
   And the braw knights o Airly

2 She was scarce fifteen years of age
   When she came to Earl Brand's bed.
   Wi the braw knights o Airly

3 'O Earl Brand, I fain wad see
   Our grey hounds run over the lea.'
   Mang the braw bents o Airly

4 'O,' says Earl Brand, 'I've nae steads but one,
   And you shall ride and I shall run.'
   Oer the braw heights o Airly

5 'O,' says the lady, 'I hae three,
   And ye shall hae yeer choice for me.'
   Of the braw steeds o Airly

6 So they lap on, and on they rade,
   Till they came to auld Carle Hood.
   Oer the braw hills o Airly

7 Carl Hood's aye for ill, and he's no for good,
   He's aye for ill, and he's no for good.
   Mang the braw hills o Airly

8 'Where hae ye been hunting a' day,
   And where have ye stolen this fair may?'
   I' the braw nights sae airly

9 'She is my sick sister dear,
  New comd home from another sister.'
    I the braw nights sae early

10 'O,' says the lady, 'if ye love me,
   Gie him a penny fee and let him gae.'
     I the braw nights sae early

11 He's gane home to her father's bower,
  .   .   .   .   .
      .   .   .   .   .

12 'Where is the lady o this ha?'
   'She's out wi the young maids, playing at the ba.'
     I the braw nights so early

13 'No,' says another, 'she's riding oer the moor,
   And a' to be Earl Brand's whore.'
     I the braw nights so early

14 The king mounted fifteen weel armed men,
   A' to get Earl Brand taen.
     I the braw hills so early

15 The lady looked over her white horse mane:
   'O Earl Brand, we will be taen.'
     In the braw hills so early

16 He says, If they come one by one,
   Ye'll no see me so soon taen.
     In the braw hills so early

17 So they came every one but one,
   And he has killd them a' but ane.
     In the braw hills so early

18 And that one came behind his back,
   And gave Earl Brand a deadly stroke.
     In the braw hills of Airly

19 For as sair wounded as he was,
   He lifted the lady on her horse.
     In the braw nights so early

20 'O Earl Brand, I see thy heart's bluid.'
   'It's but the shadow of my scarlet robe.'
     I the braw nights so early

21 He came to his mother's home;
  .   .   .   .   .
      .   .   .   .   .

22 She looked out and cryd her son was gone,
   And a' for the sake [of] an English loon.
  .   .   .   .   .

23 'What will I do wi your lady fair?'
   'Marry her to my eldest brother.'
     The brawest knight i Airly

I

A stall-copy lent me by Mrs Alexander Forbes, Lib-
erton, Edinburgh.

1 'RISE up, rise up, Lord Douglas,' she said,
  'And draw to your arms so bright;
  Let it never be said a daughter of yours
    Shall go with a lord or a knight.

2 'Rise up, rise up, my seven bold sons,
  And draw to your armour so bright;
  Let it never be said a sister of yours
    Shall go with a lord or a knight.'

3 He looked over his left shoulder,
  To see what he could see,
  And there he spy'd her seven brethren bold,
  And her father that lov'd her tenderly.

4 'Light down, light down, Lady Margret,' he said,
  'And hold my steed in thy hand,
  That I may go fight with your seven brethren
    bold,
  And your father who's just at hand.'

5 O there she stood, and better she stood,
  And never did shed a tear,
  Till once she saw her seven brethren slain,
  And her father she lovd so dear.

6 'Hold, hold your hand, William,' she said,
  'For thy strokes are wondrous sore;
  For sweethearts I may get many a one,
  But a father I neer will get more.'

7 She took out a handkerchief of holland so fine
   And wip'd her father's bloody wound,
   Which ran more clear than the red wine,
   And forked on the cold ground.

8 'O chuse you, chuse you, Margret,' he said.
   'Whether you will go or bide!'
   'I must go with you, Lord William,' she said,
   'Since you've left me no other guide.'

9 He lifted her on a milk-white steed,
   And himself on a dapple grey,
   With a blue gilded horn hanging by his side,
   And they slowly both rode away.

10 Away they rode, and better they rode,
   Till they came to yonder sand,
   Till once they came to yon river side,
   And there they lighted down.

11 They lighted down to take a drink
   Of the spring that ran so clear,
   And there she spy'd his bonny heart's blood,
   A running down the stream.

12 'Hold up, hold up, Lord William,' she says,
   'For I fear that you are slain;'
   ' 'T is nought but the shade of my scarlet clothes,
   That is sparkling down the stream.'

13 He lifted her on a milk-white steed,
   And himself on a dapple grey,
   With a blue gilded horn hanging by his side,
   And slowly they rode away.

14 Ay they rode, and better they rode,
   Till they came to his mother's bower;
   Till once they came to his mother's bower,
   And down they lighted there.

15 'O mother, mother, make my bed,
   And make it saft and fine,
   And lay my lady close at my back,
   That I may sleep most sound.'

16 Lord William he died eer middle o the night,
   Lady Margret long before the morrow;
   Lord William he died for pure true love,
   And Lady Margret died for sorrow.

17 Lord William was bury'd in Lady Mary's kirk,
   The other in Saint Mary's quire;
   Out of William's grave sprang a red rose,
   And out of Margret's a briar.

18 And ay they grew, and ay they threw,
   As they wad fain been near;
   And by this you may ken right well
   They were twa lovers dear.

A. **a, b.** *Obtained from recitation "many years ago, wrote Mr White in 1873, by James Telfer, of Laughtree Liddesdale, in some part of the neighboring country: the copy has the date,* 1818. **c** *is said by the editor to have been taken down from the recitation of an old fiddler in Northumberland, but when and by whom he does not tell us. The three are clearly more or less "corrected" copies of the same original,* **c** *having suffered most from arbitrary changes. Alterations for rhyme's sake, or for propriety's, that are written above the lines or in the margin of* **a** *2, 5, 8, 19, are adopted in* **c** *without advertisement.*

Burden. **b.** I the brave night sae early: **c.** I the brave nights so early: **d.** I (*or* O) the life o the one, the randy.

2^1. **c.** Brand, *and always in* **c.** 1^2. **a.** daughters. **b.** He's courted.

2^1. **c.** years that tide; that tide *is written over of age in* **a.** 2^2. **c.** When sae.
4^2. **c.** But thou.
5^2. **b.** best o these. **c.** best of tho. of tho *is written over o them a in* **a.**
6^2. **b, c.** have met.
7^1. **c.** Till at last they met. 7^2. **c.** He's aye for ill and never.
8^1. **b.** O Earl Bran. **c.** Now Earl Brand. Now *in the margin of* **a.** 8^2. **b, c.** Slay this.
9^2. **b.** man that wears. **c.** carl that wears. carl . . wears *written over* man . . *has in* **a.**
10. **b.** O lady fair, I'll no do that,
   I'll pay him penny, let him be jobbing at.
  c. My own lady fair, I'll not do that,
   I'll pay him his fee
11^2. **b.** where have stoln this fair. **c.** And where have ye stown this fair.
13. **b.** She is my sick sister,

Which I newly brought from Winchester.
c. For she is, I trow, my sick sister,
    Whom I have been bringing fra Winches-
ter.
14^1. **c.** nigh to dead. ^{2}. **b, c.** What makes her wear.
15^1. **c.** If she's been. ^{2}. **b, c.** What makes her wear
the gold sae high.
16^1. **c.** When came the carl to the lady's yett
^{2}. **b.** rapped at. **c.** He rudely, rudely rapped
thereat.
17^2. **b.** maids playen. **c.** a playing. **d.** She's out
with the fair maids playing at the ball.

[105] 18^1. **b.** mistkane (?): ^{2}. **b, c.** Ye may count.
    b^2. young Earl.
19. **c.** I met her far beyond the lea
    With the young. Earl Brand, his leman to
be:
In **a** lea *is written over* moor, *and* With the
young, *etc., stands as a "correction."*
20. **b.** Her father, *etc.,*
    And they have riden after them.
  c. Her father of his best men armed fifteen,
    And they're ridden after them bidene.
21^1. **b, c.** The lady looket [looked] over [owre] her
left shoulder then.
22^1. **b, c.** If they come on me one by one,
  b. Ye may stand by and see them fall.
  c. You may stand by till the fights be done.
  d. Then I will slay them every one.
23^1. **b.** all in all. **d.** all and all.
    ^{2}. **d.** Then you will see me the sooner fall.
24^2. **b.** has slain.
24. **c.** They came upon him one by one,
    Till fourteen battles he has won.
    And fourteen men he has them slain,
    Each after each upon the plain.
25. **c.** But the fifteenth man behind stole round,
    And dealt him a deep and a deadly
wound.
26. **c.** Though he was wounded to the deid,
    He set his lady on her steed.
27^1. **c.** river Donne: ^{2}. **b.** And he lighted down. **c.**
And there they lighted to wash his wound.
28^2. **b.** It's but the glent.
  c. It's nothing but the glent and my scarlet
hood.
29^1. **c.** yett.
29^2. **b.** Sae ruddly as he rappet at.
  c. So faint and feebly he rapped thereat.
30^1. **b.** O my son's slain and cut down.
  c. O my son's slain, he is falling to swoon.
32. **b.** . . . death of only one,
    But it's been the death of fair seventeen.
Instead of 32, **c** *has:*

To a maiden true he'll give his hand,
To the king's daughter o fair England,
To a prize that was won by a slain brother's brand.

B. "The copy principally used in this edition of the
ballad was supplied by Mr Sharpe." *Scott.* "The
Douglas Tragedy was taught me by a nursery-
maid, and was so great a favorite that I commit-
ted it to paper I as soon as I was able to write."
Sharpe's Letters, *ed. Allardyce, I, 135, August 5,
1802. Sharpe was born in 1781.*

3. *A stanza resembling this is found in Beaumont and
Fletcher's 'Knight of the Burning Pestle' (1611),
Dyce,* II, *172, but may belong to some other ballad,
as* 'The Knight and Shepherd's Daughter:'

    He set her on a milk-white steed,
      And himself upon a grey;
    He never turned his face again,
      But he bore her quite away.

8^4. ware. 18^1. Marie. 20^4. flang'd.
C. 12^3. MS. scâd.
D. 10. *The following stanza, superscribed* "Mrs Lin-
dores, Kelso," *was found among Mr Kinloch's
papers (Kinloch MSS, VII, 95 and 255), and was
inserted at* I, *330, of the Kinloch MSS. It may be a
first recollection of* **D** 10, *but is more likely to be
another version:*

    'We raid over hill and we raid over dale,
      And we raid over mountains sae high,
    Until we cam in sicht o yon bonnie castle
      bowr
    Whare Sir William Arthur did lie.'

E. 5–6. "Two stanzas are here omitted, in which Lord
William offers her the choice of returning to her
mother, or of accompanying him; and the ballad
concludes with this [the 6th] stanza, which is
twice repeated in singing." *Motherwell's preface.*
F. 3^4. MS. merrymen.
    6^2. of one palfray.
  7, 8 *are written in one stanza. Half a page, or about
nine stanzas, is gone after st.* 11.
H. 21^1. *to her.* 21^1, 22 *are written as one stanza.*
I. *The printed copy used by Scott was* 'Lord Douglas'
Tragedy,' *the first of four pieces in a stall-pamphlet,*
"licensed and entered, 1792:" "Scotch Ballads,
Materials for Border Minstrelsy," *No* 1. **I** *is
another edition of the same. The variations from* **I**
are as follows:

1^1. says. 2^2. your arms. 3^4. father who. 4^3. seven *wanting*. 4^4. just now. 5^3. once that. 6^1. Hold your hand. 7^2. wounds. 7^4. forkd in the. 8^1. Lady Margret. 9^3, 13^3. blue gilded, *as in* **I**, *for* bugelet: hanging down. 9^4, 13^4. slowly they both.

10^3. yon clear river-side. 11^3. his pretty. 12^3. 'Tis nothing. 15^2. soft. 16^2. long ere day. 16^4. died *wanting*. 17^1. St *for* Lady. 17^3. sprung. 18^2. be near. 18^3. ye: weil.

———◆———

APPENDIX

Additional Copies

'The Earl o Bran,' "Scotch Ballads, Materials for Border Minstrelsy," No 22 b, Abbotsford; in the hand-writing of Richard Heber.

1 DID ye ever hear o guid Earl o Bran
   An the queen's daughter o the south-lan?

2 She was na fifteen years o age
   Till she came to the Earl's bed-side.

3 'O guid Earl o Bran, I fain wad see
   My grey hounds run over the lea.'

4 'O kind lady, I have no steeds but one,
   But ye shall ride, an I shall run.'

5 'O guid Earl o Bran, but I have tua,
   An ye shall hae yere wael o those.'

6 The're ovr moss an the're over muir,
   An they saw neither rich nor poor.

7 Till they came to ald Carl Hood,
   He's ay for ill, but he's never for good.

8 'O guid Earl o Bran, if ye loe me,
   Kill Carl Hood an gar him die.'

9 'O kind lady, we had better spare;
   I never killd ane that wore grey hair.

10 'We'll gie him a penny-fie an let him gae,
    An then he'll carry nae tiddings away.'

11 'Where hae been riding this lang simmer-day?
    Or where hae stolen this lady away?'

12 'O I hae not riden this lang simmer-day,
    Nor hae I stolen this lady away.

13 'For she is my sick sister
    I got at the Wamshester.'

14 'If she were sick an like to die,
    She wad na be wearing the gold sae high.'

15 Ald Carl Hood is over the know,
    Where they rode one mile, he ran four.

16 Till he came to her mother's yett's,
    An I wat he rapped rudely at.

17 'Where is the lady o this ha?'
    'She's out wie her maidens, playing at the ba.'

18 'O na! fy na!
    For I met her fifteen miles awa.

19 'She's over moss, an she's over muir,
    An a' to be the Earl o Bran's whore.'

20 Some rode wie sticks, an some wie rungs,
    An a' to get the Earl o Bran slain.

21 That lady lookd over her left shoulder-bane:
    'O guid Earl o Bran, we'll a' be taen!
    For yond 'r a' my father's men.

22 'But if ye'll take my claiths, I'll take thine,
    An I'll fight a' my father's men.'

23 'It's no the custom in our land
   For ladies to fight an knights to stand.

24 'If they come on me ane by ane,
   I'll smash them a' doun bane by bane.

25 'If they come on me ane and a',
   Ye soon will see my body fa.'

26 He has luppen from his steed,
   An he has gein her that to had.

27 An bad her never change her cheer
   Untill she saw his body bleed.

28 They came on him ane by ane,
   An he smashed them doun a' bane by bane.

29 He sat him doun on the green grass,
   For I wat a wearit man he was.

30 But ald Carl Hood came him behind,
   An I wat he gae him a deadly wound.

31 He's awa to his lady then,
   He kissed her, an set her on her steed again.

32 He rode whistlin out the way,
   An a' to hearten his lady gay.

33 'Till he came to the water-flood:
   'O guid Earl o Bran, I see blood!'

34 'O it is but my scarlet hood,
   That shines upon the water-flood.'

35 They came on 'till his mother's yett,
   An I wat he rappit poorly at.

36 His mother she's come to the door:
   'O son, ye've gotten yere dead wie an English
      whore!'

37 'She was never a whore to me;
   Sae let my brother her husband be.'

38 Sae ald Carl Hood was not the dead o ane,
   But he was the dead o hale seeventeen.

———•———

Note at the end: I have not written the chorus, but Mr
   Leyden, having it by him, knows how to insert
   it.

———•———

"Scotch Ballads, Materials for Border Minstrelsy,"
No 22 d. In the handwriting of William Laidlaw. Scott
has written at the head, Earl Bran, another copy.

1 EARL BRAN's a wooing gane;
   Ae lalie, O lilly lalie
   He woo'd a lady, an was bringing her hame.
   O the gae knights o Airly

2 .   .   .   .   .
   They met neither wi rich nor poor.

3 Till they met wi an auld palmer Hood,
   Was ay for ill, an never for good.

4 'O yonder is an auld palmer Heed:
   Tak your sword an kill him dead.'

5 'Gude forbid, O ladie fair,
   That I kill an auld man an grey hair.

6 'We'll gie him a   an forbid him to tell;'
   The gae him a   an forbad him to tell.

7 The auld man than he's away hame,
   He telld o Jane whan he gaed hame.

8 'I thought I saw her on yon moss,
   Riding on a milk-white horse.

9 'I thought I saw her on yon muir;
   By this time she's Earl Bran's whore.'

10 Her father he's ca'd on his men:
   'Gae follow, an fetch her again.'

11 She's lookit oer her left shoulder:
   'O yonder is my father's men!

12 'O yonder is my father's men:
   Take my cleadin, an I'll take thine.'

13 'O that was never law in land,
   For a ladie to feiht an a knight to stand.

14 'But if yer father's men come ane an ane,
   Stand ye by, an ye'll see them slain.

15 'If they come twae an twae,
   Stand ye by, an ye'll see them gae.

16 'And if they come three an three,
   Stand ye by, an ye'll see them die.'

17 Her father's men came ane an ane,
   She stood by   .   .   .

18 Than they cam by twae an twae,

   .   .   .   .   .

19 Than they cam by three an three,

   .   .   .   .   .

20 But ahint him cam the auld palmer Hood,
   An ran him outthro the heart's blood.

21 'I think I see your heart's blood:'
   'It's but the glistering o your scarlet hood.'

   *   *   *   *   *

———◆———

7¹. MS., he's *, *and, in the margin,* * away has been
   gane. *Over* away hame *is written* thre them (=
   þhrae, frae, them), *or, perhaps,* thre than.
20¹. MS., palmer weed. *cf.* 3¹, 4¹. 20². outr thro.

8

ERLINTON

A. 'Erlinton,' Scott's Minstrelsy, III, 235, ed. 1803.
B. 'True Tammas,' Mr R. White's papers.

C. 'Robin Hood and the Tanner's Daughter,' Gutch's Robin Hood, II, 345.

'ERLINTON' (A) first appeared in the Minstrelsy of the Scottish Border, the text formed "from the collation of two copies obtained from recitation." B is a manuscript copy, furnished by the late Mr Robert White of Newcastle, and was probably taken down from recitation by Mr James Telfer early in the century. C, in which Robin Hood has taken the place of a hero who had at least connections out of Great Britain, was first printed in Gutch's Robin Hood, from a manuscript of Mr Payne Collier, supposed to have been written about 1650.

This ballad has only with much hesitation been separated from the foregoing. In this as in that, a man induces a maid to go off with him; he is set upon by a party of fifteen in A, B, as in 7 A; and he spares the life of one of his assailants [an old man, A, B, the younger brother, C]. Some agreements as to details with Scandinavian Ribold ballads have already been noticed, and it has been observed that while there is no vestige of the dead-naming in 'Earl Brand,' there is an obvious trace of it in 'Erlinton' A, B. 'Erlinton' A, B has also one other correspondence not found in 'Earl Brand,'—the strict watch kept over the lady (st. 2). Even the bigly bower, expressly built to confine her in, is very likely a reminiscence or a displacement of the tower in which Hilde is shut up, after her elopement, in some of the Scandinavian ballads (Danish 83 A, B; Swedish A, dark house). But notwithstanding these resemblances to the Ribold story, there is a difference in the larger part of the details, and all the 'Erlinton' ballads have a fortunate conclusion, which also does

not seem forced, as it does in Arwidsson, 107, the only instance, perhaps, in which a fortunate conclusion in a Ribold ballad is of the least account; for Grundtvig's F, G are manifestly copies that have been tampered with, and Landstad 34 is greatly confused at the close. It may be an absolute accident, but 'Erlinton' A, B has at least one point of contact with the story of Walter of Aquitania which is not found in 'Earl Brand.' This story requires to be given in brief on account of its kinship to both.

Walter, with his betrothed Hildegunde, fly from the court of Attila, at which they have both lived as hostages since their childhood, taking with them two boxes of jewels. Gunther, king of Worms, learns that a knight and lady, with a richly-laden horse, have passed the Rhine, and sets out in pursuit, with twelve of his best fighting men, resolved to capture the treasure. The fugitives, after a very long ride, make a halt in a forest, and Walter goes to sleep with his head on Hildegunde's knees. The lady meanwhile keeps watch, and rouses her lover when she perceives by the dust they raise that horsemen are approaching. Gunther sends one of his knights with a message demanding the surrender of the treasure. Walter scornfully refuses, but expresses a willingness to make the king a present of a hundred bracelets, or rings, of red gold, in token of his respect. The messenger is sent back with directions to take the treasure by force, if it should be refused again. Walter, having vainly offered a present of two hundred bracelets to avoid a conflict, is attacked by the knight, whom he slays. Ten others go the way of this first, and only the king and one of his troop, Hagen, a very distinguished knight and an old comrade of Walter, remain. These now attack Walter; the combat is long and fierce; all three are seriously wounded, and finally so exhausted as to be forced to cease fighting. Walter and Hagen enter into a friendly talk while refreshing themselves with wine, and in the end Gunther[*] is put on a horse and conducted home by Hagen, while Walter and Hildegunde continue their journey to Aquitania. There they were married and ruled thirty happy years. ('Waltharius,' ed. R. Peiper, 1873.)

The particular resemblances of 'Erlinton' **A**, **B** to 'Walter' are that the assailants are "bold knights," or "bravest outlaws," not the lady's kinsmen; that there are two parleys before the fight; and that the hero survives the fight and goes off with his love. The utmost that could be insisted on is that some features of the story of Walter have been blended in the course of tradition with the kindred story of Ribold. 'Erlin-

ton' **C** is much less like 'Walter,' and more like 'Ribold.'

The 'Sultan's Fair Daughter,' translated by Aigner, *Ungarische Volksdichtungen*, p. 93, 2d ed., has perhaps derived something from the Walter story. Two Magyars escape from the Sultan's prison by the aid of his daughter, under promise of taking her to Hungary. She often looks backwards, fearing pursuit. At last a large band overtake them. One of the Magyars guards the lady; the other assaults the Turks, of whom he leaves only one alive, to carry back information. One of the two has a love at home; the other takes the Sultan's daughter.[†]

There is possibly a souvenir of Walter in Sušil, p. 105, No 107. A man and a woman are riding on one horse in the mountains. He asks her to sing. Her song is heard by robbers, who come, intending to kill him and carry her off. He bids her go under a maple-tree, kills twelve, and spares one, to carry the booty home.

'Erlinton' is translated by Rosa Warrens, *Schottische Volkslieder*, No 24, and by Karl Knortz, *Schottische Balladen*, No 12.

---

[*] Gunther, as well remarked by Klee, 'Zur Hildesage,' p. 19, cannot have belonged originally to the Hildegunde saga. No sufficient motive is furnished for introducing him. In the Polish version of the story there is only one pursuer, Arinoldus, whom Walter slays. Rischka, *Verhältniss der polnischen Sage von Walgierz Wdaly zu. den deutschen Sagen von W. v. Aquitanien*, p. 8 ff.

[†] For the Magyar ballads of Szilágyi and Hagymási, see Herrmann, *Ethnologische Mittheilungen*, cols 65–66; also col. 215. (A Transylvanian-Saxon ballad, a Roumanian tale, and a Transylvanian-Gipsy ballad, which follow, are of more or less questionable authenticity: Herrmann, col. 216.)

A

Scott's *Minstrelsy*, III, 235, ed. 1803; ed. 1833, II, 353. Made up from two copies obtained from recitation.

1 ERLINTON had a fair daughter;
　　I wat he weird her in a great sin;
For he has built a bigly bower,
　　An a' to put that lady in.

2 An he has warnd her sisters six,
　　An sae has he her brethren se'en,
Outher to watch her a' the night,
　　Or else to seek her morn an een.

3 She hadna been i that bigly bower
　　Na not a night but barely ane,
Till there was Willie, her ain true love,
　　Chappd at the door, cryin 'Peace within!'

4 'O whae is this at my bower door,
　　That chaps sae late, nor kens the gin?'
'O it is Willie, your ain true love,
　　I pray you rise an let me in!'

5 'But in my bower there is a wake,
　　An at the wake there is a wane;
But I'll come to the green-wood the morn,
　　Whar blooms the brier, by mornin dawn.'

6 Then she's gane to her bed again,
　　Where she has layen till the cock crew thrice,
Then she said to her sisters a',
　　'Maidens, 't is time for us to rise.'

7 She pat on her back her silken gown,
  An on her breast a siller pin,
  An she's tane a sister in ilka hand,
  An to the green-wood she is gane.

8 She hadna walkd in the green-wood
  Na not a mile but barely ane,
  Till there was Willie, her ain true love,
  Whae frae her sisters has her taen.

9 He took her sisters by the hand,
  He kissd them baith, an sent them hame,
  [108]   An he's taen his true love him behind,
  And through the green-wood they are gane.

10 They hadna ridden in the bonnie green-wood
   Na not a mile but barely ane,
   When there came fifteen o the boldest knights
   That ever bare flesh, blood, or bane.

11 The foremost was an aged knight,
   He wore the grey hair on his chin:
   Says, 'Yield to me thy lady bright,
   An thou shalt walk the woods within.'

12 'For me to yield my lady bright
   To such an aged knight as thee,
   People wad think I war gane mad,
   Or a' the courage flown frae me.'

13 But up then spake the second knight,
   I wat he spake right boustouslie:
   'Yield me thy life, or thy lady bright,
   Or here the tane of us shall die.'

14 'My lady is my warld's meed;
   My life I winna yield to nane;
   But if ye be men of your manhead,
   Ye'll only fight me ane by ane.'

15 He lighted aff his milk-white steed,
   An gae his lady him by the head,
   Sayn, 'See ye dinna change your cheer,
   Untill ye see my body bleed.'

16 He set his back unto an aik,
   He set his feet against a stane,
   An he has fought these fifteen men,
   An killd them a' but barely ane.

17 .   .   .   .   .
      .   .   .   .   .
   For he has left that aged knight,
   An a' to carry the tidings hame.

18 When he gaed to his lady fair,
   I wat he kissd her tenderlie:
   'Thou art mine ain love, I have thee bought;
   Now we shall walk the green-wood free.'

B

MS. of Robert White, Esq., of Newcastle, from
James Telfer's collection.

1 THERE was a knight, an he had a daughter,
  An he wad wed her, wi muckle sin;
  Sae he has biggit a bonnie bower, love,
  An a' to keep his fair daughter in.

2 But she hadna been in the bonnie bower, love,
  And no twa hours but barely ane,
  Till up started Tammas, her ain true lover,
  And O sae fain as he wad been in.

3 'For a' sae weel as I like ye, Tammas,
  An for a' sae weel as I like the gin,
  I wadna for ten thousand pounds, love,
  Na no this night wad I let thee in.'

4 'But yonder is a bonnie greenwud,
  An in the greenwud there is a wauk,
  An I'll be there an sune the morn, love,
  It's a' for my true love's sake.

5 'On my right hand I'll have a glove, love,
  An on my left ane I'll have nane;
  I'll have wi' me my sisters six, love,
  An we will wauk the wuds our lane.'

6 They hadna waukd in the bonnie greenwud,
  Na no an hour but barely ane,
  Till up start Tammas, her ain true lover,
  He's taen her sisters her frae mang.

7 An he has kissed her sisters six, love,
   An he has sent them hame again,
But he has keepit his ain true lover,
   Saying, 'We will wauk the wuds our lane.'

8 They hadna waukd in the bonnie greenwud
   Na no an hour but barely ane,
Till up start fifteen o the bravest outlaws
   That ever bure either breath or bane.

9 An up bespake the foremost man, love,
   An O but he spake angrily:
'Either your life—or your lady fair, sir,
   This night shall wauk the wuds wi me.'

10 'My lady fair, O I like her weel, sir,
   An O my life, but it lies me near!
But before I lose my lady fair, sir,
   I'll rather lose my life sae dear.'

11 Then up bespak the second man, love,
   An aye he spake mair angrily,
Saying, 'Baith your life, and your lady fair, sir,
This night shall wauk the wuds wi me.'

12 'My lady fair, O I like her weel, sir,
   An O my life, but it lies me near!
But before I lose my lady fair, sir,
   I'll rather lose my life sae dear.

13 'But if ye'll be men to your manhood,
   As that I will be unto mine,
I'll fight ye every ane man by man,
   Till the last drop's blude I hae be slain.

14 'O sit ye down, my dearest dearie,
   Sit down and hold my noble steed,
And see that ye never change your cheer
   Until ye see my body bleed.'

15 He's feughten a' the fifteen outlaws,
   The fifteen outlaws every ane,
He's left naething but the auldest man
   To go and carry the tidings hame.

16 An he has gane to his dearest dear,
   An he has kissed her, cheek and chin,
Saying, 'Thou art mine ain, I have bought thee
   dear,
   An we will wauk the wuds our lane.'

C

Gutch's *Robin Hood*, II, 345, from a MS. of Mr Payne
Collier's, supposed to have been written about 1650.

1 As Robin Hood sat by a tree,
   He espied a prettie may,
And when she chanced him to see,
   She turnd her head away.

2 'O feare me not, thou prettie mayde,
   And doe not flie from mee;
I am the kindest man,' he said,
   'That ever eye did see.'

3 Then to her he did doffe his cap,
   And to her lowted low;
'To meete with thee I hold it good hap,
   If thou wilt not say noe.'

4 Then he put his hand around her waste,
   Soe small, so tight, and trim,
And after sought her lip to taste,
   And she to kissed him.

5 'Where dost thou dwell, my prettie maide?
   I prithee tell to me;'
'I am a tanner's daughter,' she said,
   'John Hobbes of Barneslee.'

6 'And whither goest thou, pretty maide?
   Shall I be thy true love?'
'If thou art not afeard,' she said,
   'My true love thou shalt prove.'

7 'What should I feare?' then he replied;
   'I am thy true love now;'
'I have two brethren, and their pride
   Would scorn such one as thou.'

8 'That will we try,' quoth Robin Hood;
   'I was not made their scorne;
Ile shed my blood to doe the[e] good,
   As sure as they were borne.'

9 'My brothers are proude and fierce and strong;'
   'I am,' said he, 'the same,
   And if they offer thee to wrong,
   Theyle finde Ile play their game.

10 'Through the free forrest I can run,
   The king may not controll;
   They are but barking tanners' sons,
   To me they shall pay toll.

11 'And if not mine be sheepe and kine,
   I have cattle on my land;
   On venison eche day I may dine,
   Whiles they have none in hand.'

12 These wordes had Robin Hood scarce spoke,
   When they two men did see,
   Come riding till their horses smoke:
   'My brothers both,' cried shee.

[110] 13 Each had a good sword by his side,
   And furiouslie they rode
   To where they Robin Hood espied,
   That with the maiden stood.

14 'Flee hence, flee hence, away with speede!'
   Cried she to Robin Hood,
   'For if thou stay, thoult surely bleede
   I could not see thy blood.'

15 'With us, false maiden, come away,
   And leave that outlawe bolde;
   Why fledst thou from thy home this day,
   And left thy father olde?'

16 Robin stept backe but paces five,
   Unto a sturdie tree;
   'Ile fight whiles I am left alive;
   Stay thou, sweete maide, with mee.'

17 He stood before, she stoode behinde,
   The brothers two drewe nie;
   'Our sister now to us resign,
   Or thou full sure shalt die.'

18 Then cried the maide, 'My brethren deare,
   With ye Ile freely wend,
   But harm not this young forrester,
   Noe ill doth he pretend.'

19 'Stande up, sweete maide, I plight my troth;
   Fall thou not on thy knee;
   Ile force thy cruell brothers both
   To bend the knee to thee.

20 'Stand thou behinde this sturdie oke,
   I soone will quell their pride;
   Thoult see my sword with furie smoke,
   And in their hearts' blood died.'

21 He set his backe against a tree,
   His foote against a stone;
   The first blow that he gave so free
   Cleft one man to the bone.

22 The tanners bold they fought right well,
   And it was one to two;
   But Robin did them both refell,
   All in the damsell's viewe.

23 The red blood ran from Robins brow,
   All downe unto his knee;
   'O holde your handes, my brethren now,
   I will goe backe with yee.'

24 'Stand backe, stand backe, my pretty maide,
   Stand backe and let me fight;
   By sweete St. James be no[t] afraide
   But I will it requite.'

25 Then Robin did his sword uplift,
   And let it fall againe;
   The oldest brothers head it cleft,
   Right through unto his braine.

26 'O hold thy hand, bolde forrester,
   Or ill may thee betide;
   Slay not my youngest brother here,
   He is my father's pride.'

27 'Away, for I would scorne to owe,
   My life to the[e], false maide!'
   The youngest cried, and aimd a blow
   That lit on Robin's head.

28 Then Robin leand against the tree,
   His life nie gone did seeme;
   His eyes did swim, he could not see
   The maiden start betweene.

29 It was not long ere Robin Hood
   Could welde his sword so bright;
   Upon his feete he firmly stood,
   And did renew the fight.

30 Untill the tanner scarce could heave
   His weapon in the aire;
   But Robin would not him bereave
   Of life, and left him there.

31 Then to the greenewood did he fly,
   And with him went the maide;
   For him she vowd that she would dye,
   He'd live for her, he said.

A. 4². *Ed. 1833 has or kens.*
B. 1². *If* A *1² be right, gross injustice is done the father by changing* I wat he weird her *into* he wad wed her. *One of the two is a singular corruption.*

There is another copy of B *among Mr White's papers, with the title 'Sir Thamas,' which I have no doubt has been "revised," whether by Telfer, or by Mr White himself, it is impossible to say. The principal variations are here given, that others may be satisfied.*

1². wed her mang his ain kin. 1⁴. this fair.
2³. Till up cam Thamas her only true love.
3². O tirl nae langer at the pin. 3³. I wadna for a hundred pounds, love. 3⁴. can I.
4³. fu soon. 4⁴. And by oursels we twa can talk.
5¹,². I'll hae a glove on my right hand, love, And on my left I shall hae nane.
6²⁻⁴. Beyond an hour, or scarcely twa, When up rode Thamas, her only true love, And he has tane her frae mang them a'.
7¹. He kissed her sisters, a' the six, love. 7³. his winsome true love. 7⁴. That they might walk.
8¹. didna walk.
8²⁻⁴.Beyond two hours, or barely three, Till up cam seven* stalwart outlaws, The bauldest fellows that ane could see.
9³.We'll take your life, for this lady fair, sir.
10¹.My lady's fair, I like her weel, sir.
11²,³. And he spak still mair furiously; 'Flee, or we'll kill ye, because your lady.

---

*   "The original ballad had fifteen. Seven would do as well, and the latter number would seem more nearly to resemble the truth."

12. 'My lady fair, I shall part na frae thee,
    And for my life, I did never fear;
    Sae before I lose my winsome lady,
    My life I'll venture for ane sae dear.
13. 'But if ye're a' true to your manhood,
    As I shall try to be true to mine,
    I'll fight ye a', come man by man then,
    Till the last drop o my bloud I tine.'
14². my bridled steed. 14³. And mind ye never change your colour.
15. He fought against the seven outlaws,
    And he has beat them a' himsel;
    But he left the auldest man amang them
    That he might gae and the tidings tell.
16. Then he has gane to his dearest dearie,
    And he has kissed her oer and oer;
    'Though thou art mine, I hae bought thee dearly,
    Now we shall sunder never more.'

C. 1¹. Robinhood, *and so always.*
   31.   *After this:* Finis, T. Fleming.

C, *as well as No 137, 'Robin Hood and the Pedlars,' are found in a manuscript pretended to be of about 1650, but are written in a forged hand of this century. I do not feel certain that the ballads themselves, bad as they are, are forgeries, and accordingly give the variations of Gutch's Robin Hood from the manuscript, not regarding spelling.*

3³. hold good. 3⁴. thou will. 7¹. thus he. 10¹. Thorough: I run. 11¹. [kine?] 16³. while. 19¹. Ile. 21³. he lent. 24³. be not. 25³. eldest. 28¹. leant. 29². wield. *No* "Finis" *at the end.*

APPENDIX

Additional Copies

The two copies from which (with some editorial garnish and filling out) **A** was compounded were: **a**. "Scotch Ballads, Materials for Border Minstrelsy," No 20, obtained from Nelly Laidlaw, and in the handwriting of William Laidlaw; **b**. 'Earlington's Daughter,' the same collection, No 11, in the handwriting of James Hogg. The differences are purely verbal, and both copies may probably have been derived from the same reciter; still, since only seven or eight verses in sixty-eight agree, both will be given entire, instead of a list of the variations.

a.

1 LORD ERLINTON had ae daughter,
    I trow he's weird her a grit sin;
For he has bugn a bigly bower,
    An a' to pit his ae daughter in.
        An he has buggin, etc.

2 An he has warn her sisters six,
    Her sisters six an her brethren se'en,
Thei'r either to watch her a' the night,
    Or than to gang i the mornin soon.

3 She had na been i that bigly bower
    Not ae night but only ane
Untill that Willie, her true-love,
    Chappit at the bower-door, no at the gin.

4 'Whae's this, whae's this chaps at my bower-door,
    At my bower-door, no at the gin?'
'O it is Willie, thy ain true-love;
    O will ye rise an let me in?'

5 'In my bower, Willie, there is a wane,
    An in the wane there is a wake;
But I will come to the green woods
    The morn, for my ain true-love's sake.'

6 This lady she's lain down again,
    An she has lain till the cock crew thrice;
She said unto her sisters baith,
    Lasses, it's time at we soud rise.

7 She's putten on her breast a silver tee,
    An on her back a silken gown;
She's taen a sister in ilka hand,
    An away to the bonnie green wood she's gane.

8 They hadna gane a mile in that bonnie green wood,
    They had na gane a mile but only ane,
Till they met wi Willie, her ain true-love,
    An thrae her sisters he has her taen.

9 He's taen her sisters ilk by the hand,
    He's kissd them baith, an he's sent them hame;
He's muntit his ladie him high behind,
    An thro the bonnie green wood thei'r gane.

10 They'd ridden a mile i that bonnie green wood,
    They hadna ridden but only ane,
When there cam fifteen o the baldest knights
    That ever boor flesh, bluid an bane.

11 Than up bespak the foremost knight,
    He woor the gray hair on his chin;
'Yield me yer life or your lady fair,
    An ye sal walk the green woods within.'

12 'For to gie my wife to thee,
    I wad be very laith,' said he;
'For than the folk wad think I was gane mad,
    Or that the senses war taen frae me.'

13 Up than bespak the niest foremost knight,
    I trow he spak right boustrouslie;
'Yield me yer life or your ladie fair,
    An ye sall walk the green woods wi me.'

14 'My wife, she is my warld's meed,
    My life, it lyes me very near;
But if ye be man o your manhood
    I serve will while my clays are near.'

15 He's luppen off his milk-white steed,
 He's gien his lady him by the head:
  'See that ye never change yer cheer
  Till ance ye see my body bleed.'

16 An he's killd a' the fifteen knights,
 He's killed them a' but only ane;
  A' but the auld grey-headed knight,
  He bade him carry the tiddins hame.

17 He's gane to his lady again,
 I trow he's kissd her, baith cheek an chin;
  'Now ye'r my ain, I have ye win,
  An we will walk the green woods within.'

2^3. Their *struck out.*

9^3. muntit *struck out, and* set *written above.*

12^3. than *struck out.*

14^4. while, are, *struck out, and* till, be, *written above.*

16^4. tiddins: one d *struck out. These changes would seem to be somebody's editorial improvements.* Wi me *in* 13^4 *sacrifices sense to rhyme. We are to understand in* $11^{3,4}$, $13^{3,4}$ *that Willie is to die if he will not give up the lady, but if he will resign her he may live, and walk the wood at his pleasure.* 14^4 *is corrupt in both texts.*

b.

1 O EARLINGTON, he has ae daughter,
 And I wot he has ward her in a great sin;
  He has buggin to her a bigly bowr,
  And a' to put his daughter in.

2 O he has warnd her sisters six,
 Her sisters six and her brethren seven,
  Either to watch her a' the night,
  Or else to search her soon at morn.

3 They had na been a night in that bigly bowr,
 'T is not a night but barely ane,
  Till there was Willie, her ain true-love,
  Rappd at the door, and knew not the gin.

4 'Whoe's this, whoe's this raps at my bowr-door,
 Raps at my bowr-door, and knows not the
   gin?'
 'O it is Willie, thy ain true-love;
  I pray thee rise and let me in.'

5 'O in my bower, Willie, there is a wake,
 And in the wake there is a wan;
  But I'll come to the green wood the morn,
  To the green wood for thy name's sake.'

6 O she has gaen to her bed again,
 And a wait she has lain till the cock crew
   thrice;
 Then she said to her sisters baith,
  Lasses, 't is time for us to rise.

7 She's puten on her back a silken gown,
 And on her breast a silver tie;
  She's taen a sister in ilka hand,
  And thro the green wood they are gane.

8 They had na walkt a mile in that good green
   wood,
 'T is not a mile but barely ane,
  Till there was Willie, her ain true-love,
  And from her sisters he has her taen.

9 He's taen her sisters by the hand,
 He kist them baith, he sent them hame;
  He's taen his lady him behind,
  And thro the green wood they are gane.

10 They had na ridden a mile in the good green
   wood,
 'T is not a mile but barely ane,
  Till there was fifteen of the boldest knights
  That ever bore flesh, blood or bane.

11 The foremost of them was an aged knight,
 He wore the gray hair on his chin:
  'Yield me thy life or thy lady bright,
  And thou shalt walk these woods within.'

12 ''T is for to give my lady fair
 To such an aged knight as thee,
  People wad think I were gane mad,
  Or else the senses taen frae me.'

13 Up then spake the second of them,
   And he spake ay right bousterously;
   'Yield me thy life or thy lady bright,
   And thou shalt walk these woods within.'

14 'My wife, she is my warld's meed,
   My life it lies me very near;
   But if you'll be man of your manheed,
   I'll serve you till my days be near.'

15 He's lighted of his milk-white steed,
   He's given his lady him by the head:
   'And see ye dinna change your cheer
   Till you do see my body bleed.'

16 O he has killd these fifteen lords,
   And he has killd them a' but ane,
   And he has left that old aged knight,
   And a' to carry the tidings hame.

17 O he's gane to his lady again,
   And a wait he has kist her, baith cheek and
       chin:
   'Thou art my ain love, I have thee bought,
   And thou shalt walk these woods within.'

————•————

5. wake *should be* wane *and* wan wake, *as in* **a**.

9

THE FAIR FLOWER OF NORTHUMBERLAND

A. a. Deloney's 'Jack of Newbury,' reprint of 1859, p. 61. **b.** 'The Ungrateful Knight and the Fair Flower of Northumberland,' Ritson's *Ancient Songs*, 1790, p. 169.
B. a. Kinloch MSS, v, 49. **b.** 'The Provost's Dochter,' Kinloch's *Ancient Scottish Ballads*, p. 131; as prepared by Kinloch for printing, in Kinloch MSS, VII, 105.

C. 'The Betrayed Lady.' **a.** Buchan's MSS, II, 166. **b.** Buchan's *Ballads of the North of Scotland*, II, 208.
D. Motherwell's MS., p. 102.
E. 'The Flower of Northumberland,' Mr Robert White's papers.
F. 'The Fair Flower of Northumberland,' Gibb MS., No 8.
G. 'The Heiress of Northumberland,' from C. K. Sharpe's first collection, p. 7.

THE earliest copy of this ballad is introduced as 'The Maidens' Song,'[*] in Deloney's *Pleasant History of John Winchcomb, in his younger yeares called Jacke of Newberie*, a book written as early as 1597. Mr Halliwell reprinted the "9th" edition, of the date 1633,[†] in 1869, and the ballad is found at p. 61 of the reprint (**A**). The copy in Ritson's *Ancient Songs*, 1790, p. 169, has a few variations, which are probably to be explained by Ritson having used some other edition of Deloney. Ritson's text is used in *The Borderer's Table Book*, VI, 25, and was taken thence into Sheldon's *Minstrelsy of the English Border*, with some arbitrary alterations. The ballad was formerly popular in Scotland. Kinloch and Buchan printed **B** and **C** with some slight changes; the texts are now given as they stand in the manuscripts. **E**, a traditional version from the English border, has unfortunately been improved by some literary pen.

An English lady is prevailed upon to release a Scot from prison, and to fly with him, on the promise of being made his wife, and (**A**) lady of castles and towers. She takes much gold with her (**A**), and a swift steed (two, **A**). According

to **A** they come to a rough river; the lady is alarmed, but swims it, and is wet from top to toe. On coming within sight of Edinburgh, the faithless knight bids her choose whether she will be his paramour or go back: he has wife and children. She begs him to draw his sword and end her shame: he takes her horse away, and leaves her. Two English knights come by, who restore her to her father. The dismissal takes place at the Scottish cross and moor in **B**; at a moor and a moss, **C**; at Scotland bridge, **D**; at a fair Scottish cross, **E**. She offers to be servant in his kitchen rather than go back, **B, C, E**; begs him to throw her into the water, **D**; from his castle wall, **E**. He fees an old man to take her home on an old horse, **B, E**.

We do not find the whole of this story repeated among other European nations, but there are interesting agreements in parts with Scandinavian, Polish, and German ballads.

There is some resemblance in the first half to a pretty ballad of the northern nations which treats in a brief way the theme of our exquisite romance of 'The Nutbrown Maid:' **Danish**, 'Den Trofaste Jomfru,' Grundtvig, No 249, IV, 494, nine copies, **A–I**, the first three from 16th or 17th century manuscripts, the others from tradition of this century, as are also the follow-

---
[*]   "Two of them singing the dittie," says Deloney, "and all the rest bearing the burden."
[†]   The earliest edition now known to exist is of 1619.

ing: **K–M**, 'Den Fredløse,' Kristensen, II, 191, No 57: **Swedish**, 'De sju Gullbergen,' **A**, Afzelius, No 79, III, 71, new ed., No 64, I, 322; **B**, **C**, Grundtvig, IV, 507f: **Norwegian A**, 'Herre Per og stolt Margit,' Landstad, No 74, p. 590; **B**, 'Herr' Nikelus,' Landstad, No 75, p. 594.[*] All tell very much the same tale. A knight carries off a maid on his horse, making her magnificent promises, among which are eight gold castles, Dan. **C**, **D**, **E**, **H**, **I**; one, **K**, **L**, **M**; eight, Norw. **A**; nine, Norw. **B**; seven, Swed. **B**; seven gold mountains, Swed. **A**, perhaps, by mistake of ber*gen* for bor*gar*.[†] She gets her gold together while he is saddling his horse, Dan. **A**, **C**, **D**, **F**, **H**, **M**; Swed. **A**; Norw. **A**, **B**. They come to a sea-strand or other water, it is many miles to the nearest land, Dan. **B**, **D**, Swed. **A**, **C**; the lady wishes she were at home, Dan. **E**, **F**, Swed. **B**, **C**. He swims the horse across, Dan. **A**, **B**, **D**, **E**, **F**, **H**, **K**, **L**, **M**; Swed. **A**, **B**, **C** [part of the way, having started in a boat, Norw. **A**, **B**]. The maid wrings her clothes, Dan. **A**, **D**, **K**, **L**; Swed. **A**; Norw. **A**, **B**. She asks, Where are the gold castles which you promised? Dan. **C** 7, **D** 14, **K** 9, **L** 7, **M** 8; Norw. **A** 22, **B** 16.[‡] He tells her that he has no gold castle but this green turf, Dan. **C** 8; he needs none but the black ground and thick wood, Dan. **K** 10: he is a penniless, banished man. She offers him her gold to buy him a charter of peace. In all, except Dan. **A**, **B**, **C**, and the incomplete Dan. **I**, Norw. **B**, he goes on to say that he has plighted faith to another woman, and she meekly replies, Then I will be your servant. He continues the trial no further, reveals himself as of wealth and rank, says that she shall have ladies to wait on her, and makes her his queen. The knight is king of England in Dan. **B**, **H**, King Henry, simply, in Dan. **F**. The gold castles prove to be realities:

there is in Dan. **E** even one more than was promised.[§]

The **Polish** ballads of the class of 'Lady Isabel and the Elf Knight' (see p. 56f) have thus much in common with 'The Fair Flower of Northumberland:' a maid is induced to go off with a man on horseback, and takes gold with her; after going a certain distance, he bids her return home; in **AA**, **H**, **R**, he gives her her choice whether to return or to jump into the river; she prefers death (cf. **D** 3, 5, p. 158); in all they finally come to a river, or other water, into which he throws her.[**]

The **Servian** hero Marko Kraljević is guilty of the same ingratitude. The daughter of the Moorish king releases him from a long captivity and makes him rich gifts. He promises to marry her and they go off together. During a halt the princess embraces him, and he finds her black face and white teeth so repulsive that he strikes off her head. He seeks to atone for his sin by pious foundations. Servian, Vuk, II, 376, No 64 [Bowring, p. 86]; Croat, Bogišić, p. 16; Bulgarian, Miladinof, No 54, Kačanovskij, No 132. (W. W.)

There is a **German** ballad which has some slight connection with all the foregoing, and a very slight story it is altogether: 'Stolz Heinrich,' Simrock, No 9, p. 23, 'Stolz Syburg,' Reifferscheid, No 16, p. 32, No 17, p. 34, from the Lower Rhine and Münster; made over, in Kretzschmer, I, 187, No 106. Heinrich, or Syburg, wooes a king's daughter in a distant land. He asks her to go with him, and says he has seven mills in his country. "Tell me what they grind," says Margaret, "and I will go with you." The mills grind sugar and cinnamon, mace and cloves. They come to a green heath.

---

[*] Some of these ballads begin with stanzas which are found also in Kvindemorderen and Ribold ballads (our No 4, No 7), where also a young woman is carried off furtively by a man. This is only what is to be expected.

[†] By mistake, most probably. But in one of the Polish ballads, cited a little further on, **Q** (Kolberg, P. 1. Pol*skiego*, 5 **pp**), the maid is told, "In my country the mountains are golden, the mountains are of gold."

[‡] So 'Lady Isabel and the Elf-Knight,' **D** 11:
'Is this your bowers and lofty towers?'

[§] There is a similarity, which is perhaps not accidental, between these Scandinavian ballads and 'Child Waters.' Child Waters makes Ellen swim a piece of water, shows her his hall—"of red gold shines the tower"— where the fairest lady is his paramour, subjects her to menial services, and finally, her patience withstanding all trials, marries her.

[**] They pass the water in **Q** only, and that in a boat. She is thrown in from a bridge in **V**, **W**, the bridge of Cracow in **C**: cf. Scotland bridge, **D** 2 of this ballad. By a curious accident, it is at a wayside crucifix that the man begins his change of demeanor in Polish **CC** 2 (Kolberg, **ddd**), as in **B** 5, **E** 7, of this ballad, it is at a Scottish cross.

Margaret thinks she sees the mills gleaming: he tells her that a green heath is all he has. "Then God have mercy that I have come so far," she says; draws a sword; kneels before him, and stabs herself.

The ballad of 'Young Andrew,' further on, has points in common with 'The Fair Flower of Northumberland.'

C is translated by Rosa Warrens, *Schottische Lieder der Vorzeit*, No 31, p. 137.

A

a. Deloney's *Pleasant History of John Winchcomb*, 9th ed., London, 1633, reprinted by Halliwell, p. 61. **b.** Ritson's *Ancient Songs*, 1790, p. 169.

1 It was a knight in Scotland borne
  Follow, my love, come over the strand
 Was taken prisoner, and left forlorne,
  Even by the good Earle of Northumberland.

2 Then was he cast in prison strong,
  Where he could not walke nor lie along,
   Even by the goode Earle of Northumberland.

3 And as in sorrow thus he lay,
  The Earle's sweete daughter walkt that way,
   And she the faire flower of Northumberland.

4 And passing by, like an angell bright,
  The prisoner had of her a sight,
   And she the faire flower of Northumberland.

5 And loud to her this knight did crie,
  The salt teares standing in his eye,
   And she the faire flower of Northumberland.

6 'Faire lady,' he said, 'take pity on me,
  And let me not in prison dye,
   And you the faire flower of Northumberland.'

7 'Faire Sir, how should I take pity on thee,
  Thou being a foe to our countrey,
   And I the faire flower of Northumberland.'

8 'Faire lady, I am no foe,' he said,
  'Through thy sweet love heere was I stayd,
   For thee, the faire flower of Northumberland.'

9 'Why shouldst thou come heere for love of me,
  Having wife and children in thy countrie?
   And I the faire flower of Northumberland.'

10 'I sweare by the blessed Trinitie,
   I have no wife nor children, I,
    Nor dwelling at home in merrie Scotland.

11 'If curteously you will set me free,   [114]
   I vow that I will marrie thee,
    So soone as I come in faire Scotland.

12 'Thou shalt be a lady of castles and towers,
   And sit like a queene in princely bowers,
    When I am at home in faire Scotland.'

13 Then parted hence this lady gay,
   And got her father's ring away,
    To helpe this sad knight into faire Scotland.

14 Likewise much gold she got by sleight,
   And all to helpe this forlorne knight
    To wend from her father to faire Scotland.

15 Two gallant steedes, both good and able,
   She likewise tooke out of the stable,
    To ride with this knight into faire Scotland.

16 And to the jaylor she sent this ring,
   The knight from prison forth to bring,
    To wend with her into faire Scotland.

17 This token set the prisoner free,
   Who straight went to this faire lady,
    To wend with her into faire Scotland.

18 A gallant steede he did bestride,
   And with the lady away did ride,
    And she the faire flower of Northumberland.

19 They rode till they came to a water cleare:
   'Good Sir, how should I follow you heere,
      And I the faire flower of Northumberland?

20 'The water is rough and wonderfull deepe,
   An[d] on my saddle I shall not keepe,
      And I the faire flower of Northumberland.'

21 'Feare not the foord, faire lady,' quoth he,
   'For long I cannot stay for thee,
      And thou the faire flower of Northumberland.'

22 The lady prickt her wanton steed,
   And over the river swom with speede,
      And she the faire flower of Northumberland.

23 From top to toe all wet was shee:
   This have I done for love of thee,
      And I the faire flower of Northumberland.'

24 Thus rode she all one winter's night,
   Till Edenborow they saw in sight,
      The chiefest towne in all Scotland.

25 'Now chuse,' quoth he, 'thou wanton flower,
   Whe'r thou wilt be my paramour,
      Or get thee home to Northumberland.

26 'For I have wife, and children five,
   In Edenborow they be alive;
      Then get thee home to faire England.

27 'This favour shalt thou have to boote,
   Ile have thy horse, go thou on foote,
      Go, get thee home to Northumberland.'

28 'O false and faithlesse knight,' quoth shee,
   'And canst thou deale so bad with me,
      And I the faire flower of Northumberland?

29 'Dishonour not a ladie's name,
   But draw thy sword and end my shame,
      And I the faire flower of Northumberland.'

30 He tooke her from her stately steed,
   And left her there in extreme need,
      And she the faire flower of Northumberland.

31 Then sate she downe full heavily;
   At length two knights came riding by,
      Two gallant knights of faire England.

32 She fell downe humbly on her knee,
   Saying, 'Courteous knights, take pittie on me,
      And I the faire flower of Northumberland.

33 'I have offended my father deere,
   And by a false knight that brought me heere,
      From the good Earle of Northumberland.'

34 They tooke her up behind them then,
   And brought her to her father's againe,
      And he the good Earle of Northumberland.

35 All you faire maidens be warned by me,
   Scots were never true, nor never will be,
      To lord, nor lady, nor faire England.

B

a. Kinloch MSS, v, 49, in the handwriting of J.
Beattie. b. Kinloch's *Ancient Scottish Ballads*, p. 134,
from the recitation of Miss E. Beattie.

The Pro-vost's docht-er went out a walk-ing— A may's love whiles__ is eas-ie won!

She heard a puir pri-so-ner mak-ing his meane;— And__ she was the fair flow'r o' North-umber-land.

B. b. Kinloch, 1827, pp. 131–34

1 THE provost's daughter went out a walking,
  A may's love whiles is easy won
  She heard a poor prisoner making his moan,
  And she was the fair flower of Northumberland.

2 'If any lady would borrow me
  Out into the prison strong,
  I would make her a lady of high degree,
  For I ain a great lord in fair Scotland.'

3 She's done her to her father's bed-stock,
  A may's love whiles is easy won
  She's stolen the keys o many braw lock,
  And she's loosd him out o the prison strong.

4 She's done her to her father's stable,
  A may's love whiles is easy won
  She's taen out a steed that was both swift and able,
  To carry them both to fair Scotland.

5 O when they came to the Scottish cross,
  A may's love whiles is easy won
  'Ye brazen-faced whore, light off o my horse,
  And go get you back to Northumberland!'

6 O when they came to the Scottish moor,
  A may's love whiles is easy won
  'Get off o my horse, you're a brazen-faced whore,
  So go get you back to Northumberland!'

7 'O pity on me, O pity,' said she,
  'O that my love was so easy won!
  Have pity on me as I had upon thee,
  When I loosd you out of the prison strong.'

8 'O how can I have pity on thee?
  O why was your love so easy won!
  When I have a wife and children three
  More worthy than a' Northumberland.'

9 'Cook in your kitchen I will be,
  O that my love was so easy won!
  And serve your lady most reverently,
  For I darena go back to Northumberland.'

10 'Cook in my kitchen you shall not be,
  Why was your love so easy won!
  For I will have no such servants as thee,
  So get you back to Northumberland.'

11 But laith was he the lassie to tyne,
  A may's love whiles is easy won
  He's hired an old horse and feed an old man,
  To carry her back to Northumberland.

12 O when she came her father before,
  A may's love whiles is easy won
  She fell down on her knees so low
  For she was the fair flower of Northumberland.

13 'O daughter, O daughter, why was ye so bold,
  Or why was your love so easy won,
  To be a Scottish whore in your fifteen year old?
  And you the fair flower of Northumberland!'

14 Her mother she gently on her did smile,
  O that her love was so easy won!
  'She is not the first that the Scotts have beguild,
  But she's still the fair flower of Northumberland.

15 'She shanna want gold, she shanna want fee,
  Altho that her love was so easy won,
  She shanna want gold to gain a man wi,
  And she's still the fair flower of Northumber-
    land.'

C

a. Buchan's MSS, ii, 166. **b.** Buchan's *Ballads of the North of Scotland*, ii, 208.

1 As I went by a jail-house door,
  Maid's love whiles is easy won
I saw a prisoner standing there,
  'I wish I were home in fair Scotland.'

2 'Fair maid, will you pity me?
  Ye'll steal the keys, let me gae free:
  I'll make you my lady in fair Scotland.'

3 'I'm sure you have no need of me,
  For ye have a wife and bairns three,
  That lives at home in fair Scotland.'

[116] 4 He swore by him that was crownd with thorn,
  That he never had a wife since the day he was
      born,
  But livd a free lord in fair Scotland.

5 She went unto her father's bed-head,
  She's stown the key o mony a lock,
  She's let him out o prison strong.

6 She's went to her father's stable,
  She's stown a steed baith wight and able,
  To carry them on to fair Scotland.

7 They rode till they came to a muir,
  He bade her light aff, they'd call her a whore,
  If she didna return to Northumberland.

8 They rode till they came to a moss,
  He bade her light aff her father's best horse,
  And return her again to Northumberland.

9 'I'm sure I have no need of thee,
  When I have a wife and bairns three,
  That lives at home in fair Scotland.'

10 'I'll be cook in your kitchen,
  And serve your lady handsomelie,
  For I darena gae back to Northumberland.'

11 'Ye cannot be cook in my kitchen,
  My lady cannot fa sic servants as thee,
  So ye'll return again to Northumberland.'

12 When she went thro her father's ha,
  She looted her low amongst them a',
  She was the fair flower o Northumberland.

13 Out spake her father, he spake bold,
  'How could ye be a whore in fifteen years old,
  And you the flower of Northumberland?'

14 Out spake her mother, she spake wi a smile,
  'She's nae the first his coat did beguile,
  Ye're welcome again to Northumberland.'

D

Motherwell's MS., p. 102.

1 SHE's gane down to her father's stable,
  O my dear, and my love that she wan
She's taen out a black steed baith sturdy and
      able,
  And she's away to fair Scotland.

2 When they came to Scotland bridge,
  'Light off, you whore, from my black steed,
  And go your ways back to Northumberland.'

3 'O take me by the body so meek,
  And throw me in the water so deep,
  For I daurna gae back to Northumberland.'

4 'I'll no take thee by the body so meek,
  Nor throw thee in the water so deep;
  Thou may go thy ways back to Northumber-
      land.'

5 'Take me by the body so small,
  And throw me in yon bonny mill-dam,
  For I daurna gae back to Northumberland.'

E

"Written down from memory by Robert Hutton,
Shepherd, Peel, Liddesdale." Mr R. White's papers.

1 A BAILIFF's fair daughter, she lived by the Aln,
  A young maid's love is easily won
  She heard a poor prisoner making his moan,
  And she was the flower of Northumberland.

2 'If ye could love me, as I do love thee,
  A young maid's love is hard to win
  I'll make you a lady of high degree,
  When once we go down to fair Scotland.'

3 To think of the prisoner her heart was sore,
  A young maid's love is easily won
  Her love it was much, but her pity was more,
  And she, etc.

4 She stole from her father's pillow the key,
  And out of the dungeon she soon set him free,
  And she, etc.

7] 5 She led him into her father's stable,
  And they've taken a steed both gallant and
      able,
    To carry them down to fair Scotland.

6 When they first took the way, it was darling
      and dear;
  As forward they fared, all changed was his
      cheer,
    And she, etc.

7 They rode till they came to a fair Scottish corse;
  Says he, 'Now, pray madam, dismount from my
      horse,
    And go get you back to Northumberland.

8 'It befits not to ride with a leman light,
  When awaits my returning my own lady bright,
    My own wedded wife in fair Scotland.'

9 The words that he said on her fond heart smote,
  She knew not in sooth if she lived or not,
    And she, etc.

10 She looked to his face, and it kythed so unkind
  That her fast coming tears soon rendered her
      blind,
    And she, etc.

11 'Have pity on me as I had it on thee,
  O why was my love so easily won!
  A slave in your kitchen I'm willing to be,
  But I may not go back to Northumberland.

12 'Or carry me up by the middle sae sma,
  O why was my love so easily won!
  And fling me headlong from your high castle wa,
  For I dare not go back to Northumberland.'

13 Her wailing, her woe, for nothing they went,
  A young maid's love is easily won
  His bosom was stone and he would not relent,
  And she, etc.

14 He turned him around and he thought of a
      plan,
  He bought an old horse and he hired an old
      man,
    To carry her back to Northumberland.

15 A heavy heart makes a weary way,
  She reached her home in the evening gray,
    And she, etc.

16 And all as she stood at her father's tower-gate,
  More loud beat her heart than her knock
      thereat,
    And she, etc.

17 Down came her step-dame, so rugged and doure,
  O why was your love so easily won!
  'In Scotland go back to your false paramour,
  For you shall not stay here in Northumber-
      land.'

18 Down came her father, he saw her and smiled,
  A young maid's love is easily won
  'You are not the first that false Scots have
      beguiled,
    And ye're aye welcome back to Northumber-
      land.

19 'You shall not want houses, you shall not want
      land,
  You shall not want gold for to gain a husband,
    And ye're aye welcome back to Northumber-
      land.'

F

Gibb MS., No 8: 'The Fair Flower o Northumber-
land,' from Jeannie Stirling, a young girl, as learned
from her grandmother.

*   *   *   *   *

1 SHE stole the keys from her father's bed-head,
   O but her love it was easy won!
 She opened the gates, she opened them wide,
   She let him out o the prison strong.

2 She went into her father's stable
   O but her love it was easy won!
 She stole a steed that was both stout and
       strong,
   To carry him hame frae Northumberland.

*   *   *   *   *

3 'I'll be cook in your kitchen,
   Noo sure my love has been easy won!
 I'll serve your own lady with hat an with hand,
   For I daurna gae back to Northumberland.'

4 'I need nae cook in my kitchin,
   O but your love it was easy won!
 Ye'll serve not my lady with hat or with hand,
   For ye maun gae back to Northumberland.'

5 When she gaed hame, how her father did ban!
   'O but your love it was easy won!
 A fair Scottish girl, not sixteen years old,
   Was once the fair flower o Northumberland!'

G

'The Heiress of Northumberland,' from C. K.
Sharpe's first collection, p. 7.

'Why, fair maid, have pi - ty on me,' Wa - ly's my love wi the life that she wan
'For I__ am bound in pri - son strong, And un - der the heir o North - um - ber - land.'

1 'WHY, fair maid, have pity on me,'
   Waly's my love wi the life that she wan
 'For I am bound in prison strong,
   And under the heir o Northumberland.'

2 'How can I have pity on thee,'
   Waly's my love, etc.
 'When thou hast a wife and children three,
   All dwelling at home in fair Scotland?'

3 Now he has sworn a solemn oath,
   And it was by eternity,
 That wife and children he had none,
   All dwelling at home in fair Scotland.

4 Now she's gone to her father's bedstock,
   Waly's my love, etc.
 And has stolen the key of the dungeon-lock,
   And she the great heir o Northumberland.

5 And she's gone to her father's chest,
   She has stolen away a suit of the best,
   Altho she was heir o Northumberland.

6 Now she's gone to her father's coffer,
   And has taen out gold nane kens how meickle,
   Altho she, etc.

7 She's gane to her father's stable,
   And taen out a steed baith lusty and able,
   For a' she was heir, etc.

8 The rade till they cam to Crafurdmoor,
   He bade her light down for an English whore,
      Altho she, etc.

9 The rade till the came to the water o Clyde,
   He bade her light down, nae farer she should
      ride,
   'For now I am at hame in fair Scotland.'

10 'Yonder view my castle,' said he;
   'There I hae a wife and children three,
      All dwelling at home,' etc.

11 'O take me by the middle sae sma
   And thro me oer your castle-wa,
   For I darena gang hame to Northumberland.'

12 When she came to her father's yett,
   She durst hardly rapp thereat,
      Altho she was, etc.

13 Out then spoke her stepmother sour,
   She bad her pack off for an impudent whore,
   'For thou shalt not be heir o Northumber-
      land.'

14 Out then spock her bastard brother;
   'She'll hae nae mair grace than God has gien
      her,
   And she shall be heir o Northumberland.'

15 Out and spoke her father sae mild,
   'She's no the first maid a false Scot has beguild,
   And she shall be,' etc.

———◆———

A. a. 2. *Halliwell's Deloney, in the first line of the bur-
   den, has* leape over, *but not elsewhere.*
   9². in the. 25². Where.
b. 3². walks. 3. she is.
   5¹. aloud.
   13³. *omits* sad.
   15³. the knight.
   16². forth did.
   24³. The fairest.
   27¹. thou shalt.
   32². knight.
   35². never were.
B. b. 2². this prison.
   4³. *omits* that was.
   6³. ye brazen-fac'd.
   11³. He hired.
   12³. fell at his feet.
   13¹. *omits* so.
   14¹. mother on her sae gentlie smild, *etc.*
C. 5¹. Bed-head *should certainly be* bed-stock: *cf.* **B** 3¹.
a. 8². Her bade. 8³. return him.
b. 5¹. into.
   13². at fifteen.
D. *In a copy sent by Motherwell to C. K. Sharpe with a
   letter, October 8, 1825, this version is said to have
   been obtained from Mrs Nicol, of Paisley.*

2. *Thus in Motherwell's* Minstrelsy, Appendix, *p.
xv:*

   When they came to Scotland brig,
      O my dear, my love that she wan!
   'Light off, ye hure, from my black steed,
      And hie ye awa to Northumberland.'

E. "The Flower of Northumberland. Written down
   from memory by Robert Hutton, Shepperd,
   Peel, Liddesdale, and sent by James Telfor to his
   friend Robert White, Newcastle on Tyne. 20
   copies printed." *Mr White's note.*

G. *Sir W. Scott, commenting on this copy (to which he by
   mistake gives the title of The Stirrup of Northum-
   berland), says:* "An edition considerably varied
   both from Ritson's and the present I have heard
   sung by the Miss Tytlers of Woodhouselee. The
   tune is a very pretty lilt." *Sharpe's Ballad Book,
   ed. 1880, p. 142.*

At the end of the ballad we are told: Tradition's story
   is that the hero of this song was one of the Earls
   of Douglass, who was taken captive and put in
   prison by Percy, Earl of Northumberland.

10

THE TWA SISTERS

A. a. 'The Miller and the King's Daughter,' broadside of 1656, *Notes and Queries*, 1st S., v, 591. b. *Wit Restor'd*, 1658, "p. 51," in the reprint of 1817, p. 153. c. 'The Miller and the King's Daughters,' *Wit and Drollery*, ed. 1682, p. 87. d. 'The Miller and the King's Daughter,' Jamieson's *Popular Ballads*, 1, 315.

B. a. 'The Twa Sisters,' Jamieson-Brown MS., p. 39. b. 'The Cruel Sister,' Wm. Tytler's Brown MS., No 15. c. 'The Cruel Sister,' Abbotsford MS., "Scottish Songs," fol. 21. d. 'The Twa Sisters,' Jamieson's *Popular Ballads*, 1, 48.

C. 'The Cruel Sister,' Scott's *Minstrelsy*, 11, 143 (1802).

D. 'The Bonnie Milldams of Binnorie,' Kinloch MSS, 11, 49.

E. 'The Twa Sisters,' Sharpe's *Ballad Book*, No x, p. 30.

F. 'The Bonny Bows o London,' Motherwell's MS., p. 383.

G. Motherwell's MS., p. 104.

H. Motherwell's MS., p. 147.

I. 'Bonnie Milldams o Binnorie,' Kinloch MSS, v, 425.

J. 'The Miller's Melody,' *Notes and Queries*, 4th S., v, 23.

K. 'Binnorie,' Kinloch's papers.

L. a. 'The Miller's Melody,' *Notes and Queries*, 1st S., v, 316. b. 'The Drowned Lady,' *The Scouring of the White Horse*, p. 161.

M. 'Binorie, O an Binorie,' Murison MS., p. 79.

N. 'Binnorie,' [Pinkerton's] *Scottish Tragic Ballads*, p. 72.

O. 'The Bonny Bows o London.' a. Buchan's *Ballads of the North of Scotland*, 11, 128. b. Christie's *Traditional Ballad Airs*, 1, 42.

P. a. 'The Twa Sisters,' Motherwell's MS., p. 245. b. 'The Swan swims bonnie O,' Motherwell's *Minstrelsy*, Appendix, p. xx.

Q. 'The Twa Sisters,' communicated by J. F. Campbell, Esq.

R. a. 'The Three Sisters,' *Notes and Queries*, 1st S., vi, 102. b. 'Bodown,' communicated by J. F. Campbell, Esq. c. 'The Barkshire Tragedy,' *The Scouring of the White Horse*, p. 158.

S. Kinloch MSS, vi, 89.

T. 'Sister, dear Sister,' Allingham's *Ballad Book*, p. xxxiii.

U. From Long Island, N. Y., communicated by Mr W. W. Newell.

V. 'Benorie,' Campbell MSS, II, 88.

W. 'Norham, down by Norham,' communicated by Mr Thomas Lugton, of Kelso.

X. 'Binnorie,' Dr Joseph Robertson's Note-Book, January 1, 1830, p. 7, one stanza.

Y. Communicated to Percy by Rev. P. Parsons, April 7, 1770.

Z. 'The Twa Sisters,' derived from ladies in New York.

THIS is one of the very few old ballads which are not extinct as tradition in the British Isles. Even drawing-room versions are spoken of as current, "generally traced to some old nurse, who sang them to the young ladies."* It has [119] been found in England, Scotland, Wales, and

Ireland, and was very early in print. Dr Rimbault possessed and published a broadside of the date 1656† (A a), and the same copy is included in the miscellany called *Wit Restor'd*, 1658. Both of these name "Mr Smith" as the author; that is, Dr James Smith, a well-known writer of humorous verses, to whom the larger part of the pieces in *Wit Restor'd* has been attributed. If the

---

* Campbell's *Popular Tales of the West Highlands*, iv, 126, 1862.

ballad were ever in Smith's hands, he might possibly have inserted the three burlesque stanzas, 11–13; but similar verses are found in another copy (**L a**), and might easily be extemporized by any singer of sufficiently bad taste. *Wit and Drollery*, the edition of 1682, has an almost identical copy of the ballad, and this is repeated in Dryden's *Miscellany*, edition of 1716, Part III, p. 316. In 1781 Pinkerton inserted in his *Tragic Ballads* one with the title 'Binnorie,' purporting to be from Scottish tradition. Of twenty-eight couplets, barely seven are genuine. Scott printed in 1802 a copy (**C**) compounded from one "in Mrs Brown's MS." (**B b**) and a fragment of fourteen stanzas which had been transcribed from recitation by Miss Charlotte Brooke, adopting a burden found in neither.* Jamieson followed, four years after, with a tolerably faithful, though not, as he says, *verbatim*, publication of his copy of Mrs Brown's ballad, somewhat marred, too, by acknowledged interpolations. This text of Mrs Brown's is now correctly given, with the whole or fragments of eleven others, hitherto unpublished.

The ballad is as popular with the Scandinavians as with their Saxon cousins. Grundtvig, 'Den talende Strengeleg,' No 95, gives nine **Danish** versions and one stanza of a tenth; seven, **A–E**, in II, 507 ff, the remainder, **H–K**,

---

† Jamieson, in his *Popular Ballads*, I, 315, prints the ballad, with five inconsiderable variations from the broadside, as from *Musarum Deliciæ*, 2d edition, 1656. The careful reprint of this book, and of the same edition, in "Facetiæ," etc., 1817, does not contain this piece, and the first edition, of 1655, differed in no respect as to contents, according to the editor of "Facetiæ." Still it is hardly credible that Jamieson has blundered, and we may suppose that copies, ostensibly of the same edition, varied as to contents, a thing common enough with old books.

* Cunningham has re-written Scott's version, *Songs of Scotland*, II, 109, 'The Two Fair Sisters.' He says, "I was once deeply touched with the singing of this romantic and mournful song. . . . I have ventured to print it in the manner I heard it sung." There is, to be sure, no reason why he should not have heard his own song sung, *once*, and still less why he should not have been deeply touched with his own pathos. Cunningham adds one genuine stanza, resembling the first of **G, J, P**:

Two fair sisters lived in a bower,
  Hey ho my nonnie O
There came a knight to be their wooer.
  While the swan swims bonnie O

---

in III, 875 ff. One more, **L**, is added by Kristensen, No 96, I, 253. Of these, only **E** had been previously printed. All are from tradition of this century. A Danish fragment of nine stanzas appears in Kristensen's *Skattegraveren*, IV, 161, No 509; also 'De talende Strenge,' Kristensen, *Jyske Folkeminder*, X, 68, 375, No 19, **A–E**.

There are two **Icelandic** versions, **A** from the 17th, **B** from the 19th, century, printed in *Íslenzk Fornkvæði*, No 13, 'Hörpu kvæði.'

Of twelve **Norwegian** versions, **A**, by Moe, "is printed in *Norske Universitets og Skole-Annaler* for 1850, p. 287," and in Moe's *Samlede Skrifter*, II, 118, 'Dæ bur ein Mann hær utmæ Aa;' **B**, by Lindeman, *Annaler*, as before, "p. 496," and in his *Norske Fjeldmelodier*, vol. I, Tekst-Bilag, p. 4, No 14, 'Dei tvæ, Systa;' **C**, by Landstad, 'Dei tvo systar,' No 53, p. 480; **D–L** are described by Professor Bugge in Grundtvig, III, 877 f; **M** "is printed in *Illustreret Nyhedsblads Nytaarsgave* for 1860, p. 77, Christiania."

Four **Färöe** versions are known: **A**, 'Hörpuríma,' "in Svabo's MS., No 16, I, 291," incorrectly printed by Afzelius, I, 86, and accurately, from a copy furnished by Grundtvig, in Bergström's edition of Afzelius, II, 69; **B**, a compound of two versions taken down by Pastor Lyngbye and by Pastor Schröter, in *Nyeste Skilderie af Kjøbenhavn*, 1821, col. 997 ff; **C**, a transcript from recitation by Hammershaimb (Grundtvig); **D**, "in *Fugloyjarbók*, No 31."†

Swedish versions are: **A**, 'Den underbara Harpan,' Afzelius, No 17, I, 81, new ed No 16, I, I, 72: **B**, 'De två Systrarne,' Afzelius No 69, III, 16, new ed., No 16, 2, I, 74: **C, D, E**, unprinted copies in Cavallius and Stephens's collection: **F**, 'De två Systrarne,' Arwidsson, No 99, II, 139: **G**, 'Systermordet,' **E**. Wigström, *Skånska Visor*, p. 4, and the same, *Folkdiktning*, etc., No 7, p. 19: **H**, Rancken, *Några Prof af* [120] *Folksång*, No 3, p. 10. Afzelius, moreover, gives variations from four other copies which he had collected, III, 20 ff, new ed., II, 74 ff; and Rancken from three others. Both of the editors of the new Afzelius have recently obtained excellent copies from singers. The ballad has

---

† Seven versions are now known, and one is printed, from the manuscript collection of Färöe ballads made by Svend Grundtvig and Jørgen Bloch, in Hammershaimb, *Færøsk Anthologi*, No 7, p. 23, ' Harpu rima.'

also been found in Finnish, Bergström's Afze-lius, II, 79. Three copies of the Swedish ballad are printed by Wahlfisk, *Bidrag till Södermanlands äldere Kulturhistoria*, No VI, p. 33f. Also, 'De två systrarna,' Lagus, *Nyländska Folkvisor*, I, 27, No 7, *a, b*; the latter imperfect.[*]

There is a remarkable agreement between the Norse and English ballads till we approach the conclusion of the story, with a natural diversity as to some of the minuter details.

The sisters are king's daughters in English **A, B, C, H, O** (?), **P, Q, R a**, and in Swedish **B** and two others of Afzelius's versions. They are an earl's daughters in Swedish **F**, and sink to farmer's daughters in English **R b, c**,[†] Swedish **A, G,** Norwegian **C**.

It is a thing made much of in most of the Norse ballads that the younger sister is fair and the older dark; the younger is bright as the sun, as white as ermine or as milk, the elder black as soot, black as the earth, Icelandic **A**, Swedish **A, B, G,** Danish **A, D,** etc.; and this difference is often made the ground for very unhandsome taunts, which qualify our compassion for the younger; such as Wash all day, and you will be no whiter than God made you, Wash as white as you please, you will never get a lover, Färöe **A, B,** Norwegian **A, C**, etc. This contrast may possibly be implied in "the youngest was the fairest flower," English **F, G, Q** ["sweetest," **D**], but is expressed only in **M**, "Ye was fair and I was din" (dun), and in **P a**, "The old was black and the young ane fair."

The scene of action is a seashore in Icelandic and Färöe **A, B,** Norwegian **A,** Swedish **A, B, G, H,** and in all the Danish complete copies: a seashore, or a place where ships come in, in English **A, B a, D–I, Q, R a, T**, but in all save the last of these (the last is only one stanza) we have the absurdity of a body drowned in navigable water being discovered floating down a mill-stream.[‡] **B c** has "the deep mill-dam;" **C** "the river-strand," perhaps one of Scott's changes; **M**, "the dams;" **L, O, P, R b c,** a river, Tweed mill-dam, or the water of Tweed. Norwegian **B** has a river.

The pretence for the older sister's taking the younger down to the water is in English **A–E, G, H, I, O, Q**, to see their father's ships come in; in Icelandic **B** to wash their silks;[§] in most of the Norse ballads to wash themselves, so that, as the elder says, 'we may be alike white," Danish **C–H,** Norwegian **A, C,** Swedish **F, G,** Färöe **A, B**. Malice prepense is attributed to the elder in Swedish **B, F,** Norwegian **C,** Danish **E, F, G**: but in Färöe **A, B,** Norwegian **A, B,** and perhaps some other cases, a previous evil intent is not certain, and the provocations of the younger sister may excuse the elder so far.

The younger is pushed from a stone upon which she sits, stands, or steps, in English **B, C, E–H, M, O, Q,** Icelandic **A, B,** Färöe **A, B,** Norwegian **A, B, C,** Danish **A–E, H, L,** Swedish **G, H,** and Rancken's other copies.

The drowning scene is the same in all the ballads, except as to one point. The younger sister, to save her life, offers or consents to renounce her lover in the larger number, as English **B–E, G, H, I, M, P, Q,** Danish **A–D, F, G, I,** Swedish **A–D, G, H**; and in Icelandic **B** and "all the Färöe" ballads she finally yields, after first saying that her lover must dispose of himself. But Swedish **F**, with more spirit, makes the girl, after promising everything else, reply

'Help then who can, help God above!
But ne'er shalt thou get my dear true-love.'

In this refusal concur Icelandic **A**, Danish **E**, **H**, **L**, and all the Norwegian versions except **L**.

Swedish **A**, **G**, and Rancken's versions (or two of them) make the younger sister, when she sees that she must drown, send greetings to her father, mother, true-love [also brother, sister, Rancken], and add in each case that she is drinking, or dancing, her bridal in the flood, that her bridal-bed is made on the white-sand, etc.

The body of the drowned girl is discovered, in nearly all the English ballads, by some member of the miller's household, and is taken out of the water by the miller. In **L b**, which, however, is imperfect at the beginning, a harper finds the body. In the Icelandic ballads it is found on the seashore by the lover; in all the Norwegian but **M** by two fishermen, as also in Swedish **D** [fishermen in Swedish **B**]; in all the Färöe versions and Norwegian **M** by two "pilgrims;"[*] in Danish **A–F**, **L**, and Swedish **C** by two musicians, Danish **H**, Swedish **A**, **G**, one. Danish **G**, which is corrupted at the close, has three musicians, but these simply witness and report the drowning.

According to all complete and uncorrupted forms of the ballad, either some part of the body of the drowned girl is taken to furnish a musical instrument, a harp or a viol,[†] or the instrument is wholly made from the body. This is done in the Norse ballads by those who first find the body, save in Swedish **B**, where fishermen draw the body ashore, and a passing "speleman"

makes the instrument. In English it is done by the miller, **A**; by a harper, **B**, **C**, **G**, **L b** (the *king's* harper in **B**); by a fiddler, **D**, **E**, **I**, **L a** (?), **O**, **P** (the *king's* fiddler, **O** (?), **P**); by both a fiddler and the king's harper, **H**; in **F** by the father's herdsman, who happens to be a fiddler.

Perhaps the original conception was the simple and beautiful one which we find in English **B** and both the Icelandic ballads, that the king's harper, or the girl's lover, takes three locks of her yellow hair to string his harp with. So we find three tets of hair in **D**, **E**, **I**, and three links in **F**, **P**, used, or directed to be used, to string the fiddle or the fiddle-bow, and the same, apparently, with Danish **A**. Infelicitous additions were, perhaps, successively made; as a harp-frame from the breast-bone in English **C**, and fiddle-pins formed of the finger-joints, English **F**, **O**, Danish **B**, **C**, **E**, **F**, **L**. Then we have all three: the frame of the instrument formed from the breast (or trunk), the screws from the finger-joints, the strings from the hair, Swedish **A**, **B**, **G**, Norwegian **A**, **C**, **M**. And so one thing and another is added, or substituted, as fiddle-bows of the arms or legs, Swedish **C**, **D**, Danish **H**, English **L a**; a harp-frame from the arms, Norwegian **B**, Färöe **A**; a fiddle-frame from the skull, Swedish **C**, or from the back-bone, English **L b**; a *plectrum* from the arm, Färöe **B**; strings from the veins, English **A**; a bridge from the nose, English **A**, **L a**; "hørpønota" from the teeth, Norwegian **B**; till we end with the buffoonery of English **A** and **L a**.

Swedish **H** has nothing about the finding of the body. Music is wanted for the bridal, and a man from another village, who undertakes to furnish it, looks three days for a proper tree to make a harp of. The singer of this version supplied the information, lost from the ballad, that the drowned sister had floated ashore and grown up into a linden, and that this was the very tree which was chosen for the harp. (See, further on, a Lithuanian, a Slovak, and an Esthonian ballad.)

All the Norse ballads make the harp or fiddle to be taken to a wedding, which chances to be that of the elder sister with the drowned girl's betrothed.[‡] Unfortunately, many of the English versions are so injured towards the [122] close that the full story cannot be made out.

---

[*]   There are, besides the two fishermen, in Norwegian **A**, two "twaddere," i.e., landloupers, possibly (Bugge) a corruption of the word rendered pilgrims, Färöe vallarar, Swedish vallare. The vallarar in these ballads are perhaps more respectable than those whose acquaintance we shall make through the Norse versions of 'Babylon,' and may be allowed to be harmless vagrants, seeing that they are ranked with "staff-earls" in *Norges Gamle Love*, cited by Cleasby and Vigfusson at 'vallari.'

[†]   A harp in the Icelandic and Norwegian ballads, Färöe **A**, **B**, **C**, Swedish **A**, **B**, **D**, **G**, **H**; a harp in English **B**, **C**, **G**, **J**. A harp is not named in any of the Danish versions, but a fiddle is mentioned in **C**, **E**, **H**, is plainly meant in **A**, and may always be intended; or perhaps *two* fiddles in all but **H** (which has only one fiddler), and the corrupted **G**. **D** begins with two fiddlers, but concludes with only one. We have a fiddle in Swedish **C**, and in English **A**, **D**, **E**, **F**, **I**, **J**, **K**, **L**, **O**, **P**; both harp and fiddle in **H**.

There is no wedding-feast preserved in any of them. The instrument, in **A, B, C, H**, is taken into the king's presence. The viol in **A** and the harp in **H** are expressly said to speak. The harp is laid upon a stone in **C, J**, and plays "its lone;" the fiddle plays of itself in **L b.*** **B** makes the harper play, and **D, F, K, O**, which say the fiddle played, probably mean that there was a fiddler, and so perhaps with all the Norse versions; but this is not very material, since in either case the instrument speaks "with most miraculous organ."

There are three strings made from the girl's hair in Icelandic **A, B**, English **B** [veins, English **A**], and the three tets or links in English **D, E, F, I, P** were no doubt taken to make three strings originally. Corresponding to this are three enunciations of the instrument in English **A, B, C**, Icelandic **A**, Färöe **A,**[†] **B**, Swedish **A, B, C, E, G, H**, Danish **A, D, F, I**. These are reduced to two in Icelandic **B**, Danish **B, C, H, L**, Swedish **D**, and even to one in English **D, F, I, K, O**, but some of these have suffered injury towards the conclusion. The number is increased to four in Norwegian **B**, to five in Norwegian **A, D**, and even to six in Norwegian **C, K, M**. The increase is, of course, a later exaggeration, and very detrimental to the effect. In those English copies in which the instrument speaks but once,[‡] **D, F, K, O**, and we may add **P**, it expresses a desire for vengeance: Hang my sister, **D, F, K**; Ye'll drown my sister, as she's dune me, **O**; Tell him to burn my sister, **P**. This is found in no Norse ballad, neither is it found in the earliest English versions. These, and the better forms of the Norse, reveal the awful secret, directly or indirectly, and, in the latter case, sometimes note the effect on the bride. Thus, in Icelandic **B**, the first string

sounds, The bride is our sister; the second, The bride is our murderer. In Danish **B** the first fiddle plays, The bride is my sister; the second, The bridegroom is my true-love; in **C, H**, the first strain is, The bride has drowned her sister, the second, Thy sister is driven [blown] to land. Färöe **A, B**, have: (1) The bride was my sister; (2) The bride was my murderer; (3) The bridegroom was my true-love. The bride then says that the harp disturbs her much, and that she lists to hear it no more. Most impressive of all, with its terse, short lines, is Icelandic **A**:

The first string made response:
'The bride was my sister once.'

The bride on the bench, she spake:
'The harp much trouble doth make.'

The second string answered the other:
'She is parting me and my lover.'

Answered the bride, red as gore:
'The harp is vexing us sore.'

The canny third string replied:
'I owe my death to the bride.'

He made all the harp-strings clang;
The bride's heart burst with the pang.

This is the wicked sister's end in both of the Icelandic ballads and in Färöe **A, B**. In Swedish **A, G**, at the first stroke on the harp she laughs; at the second she grows pale [has to be undressed]; upon the third she lay dead in her bed [falls dead on the floor]. She is burned in Danish **A, B, C, F, G**, Swedish **B**, Norwegian **A, B, C, I, M**. In Norwegian **K, L**, the younger sister (who is restored to life) begs that the elder may not be burned, but sent out of the country (cf. English **R b c**); nevertheless, she is buried alive in **L**, which is her fate also in **E**, and in other unprinted versions. A prose comment upon Danish **I** has her stabbed by the bridegroom.

Norwegian **B** 21 makes the bride, in her confusion at the revelations of the harp, ask the bridegroom to drive the fiddler out of the house. So far from complying, the bridegroom orders him mead and wine, and the bride to the

‡   Some of the unprinted Norwegian ballads are not completely described, but a departure from the rule of the major part would probably have been alluded to.
*   The stanza, 9, in which this is said is no doubt as to its form entirely modern, but not so the idea. **I** has "the first spring that he playd, *it* said," etc.
†   The fourth string is *said* to speak in Färöe **A** 30, but no utterance is recorded, and this is likely to be a mistake. In many of the versions, and in this, after the strings have spoken individually, they unite in a powerful but inarticulate concord.
‡   **I** has lost the terminal stanzas.

pile. In Norwegian **C** the bride treads on the harper's foot, then orders the playing to stop; but the bridegroom springs from the table, and cries, Let the harp have its song out, pays no regard to the lady's alleging that she has so bad a head that she cannot bear it, and finally sends her to the pile. So, nearly, Norwegian **A**. In Danish **A, C, D, H, L**, vainly in the first two, the bride tries to hush the fiddler with a bribe. He endeavors to take back what he has said in **D, L**, declaring himself a drunken fool (the passage is borrowed from another ballad): still in **L**, though successful for the nonce, she comes to the stake and wheel some months after. In **H** the fiddler dashes the instrument against a stone, seemingly to earn his bribe, but this trait belongs to versions which take the turn of the Norwegian. In **C** 15 the bride springs from the table, and says, Give the fiddlers a trifle, and let them go. This explains the last stanza of English **A** (cf., Norwegian **B** 21):

> Now pay the miller for his payne,
> And let him bee gone in the divel's name.

Swedish **F** has an entirely perverted and feeble conclusion. "A good man" takes the younger sister from the water, carries her to his house, revives her, and nurses her till the morrow, and then restores her to her father, who asks why she is so pale, and why she had not come back with her sister. She explains that she had been pushed into the water, "and we may thank this good man that I came home at all." The father tells the elder that she is a disgrace to her country, and condemns her to the "blue tower." But her sister intercedes, and a cheerful and handsome wedding follows.

Swedish **C** and nearly all the Norwegian ballads* restore the drowned girl to life, but not by those processes of the Humane Society which are successfully adopted by the "arlig man" in Swedish **F**. The harp is dashed against a stone, or upon the floor, and the girl stands forth "as good as ever." As Landstad conceives the matter (484, note 7), the elder sister is a witch, and is in the end burned *as such*. The

white body of the younger is made to take on the appearance of a crooked log, which the fishermen (who, by the way, are angels in **C, E**) innocently shape into a harp, and the music, vibrating from her hair "through all her limbs, marrow and bone," acts as a disenchantment. However this may be, the restoration of the younger sister, like all good endings foisted on tragedies, emasculates the story.

English **F** 9 has the peculiarity, not noticed elsewhere, that the drowning girl catches at a broom-root, and the elder sister forces her to let go her hold.† In Swedish **G** she is simply said to swim to an alder-root. In English **G** 8 the elder drives the younger from the land with a switch, in **I** 8 pushes her off with a silver wand.

English **O** introduces the *ghost* of the drowned sister as instructing her father's fiddler to make a string of her hair and a peg of her little finger bone, which done, the first spring the fiddle plays, it says,

> 'Ye'll drown my sister as she's dune me.'

P, which is disordered at the end, seems to have agreed with **O**. In **Q** the ghost sends, by the medium of the miller and his daughter, respects to father, mother, and true-love, adding a lock of yellow hair for the last. The ghost is found in **N**, Pinkerton's copy, as well, but there appears to the lover at dead of night, two days after the drowning. It informs him of the murder, and he makes search for the body. This is a wide departure from the original story, and plainly a modern perversion. Another variation, entirely wanting in ancient authority, [124] appears in **R, S**. The girl is not dead when she has floated down to the mill-dam, and, being drawn out of the water by the miller, offers him a handsome reward to take her back to her father [**S**, to throw her in again!]. The miller takes the reward, and pushes the girl in again, for which he is hanged.‡

Q has a burden partly Gaelic,

---

* Not **M**, and apparently not **D**, which ends:
When he kissed the harp upon the mouth, his heart broke.

† So the traitor John pushes away Catherine's hands in 'Lady Isabel and the Elf Knight,' Polish **Q** 25 (see p. 58). In the French versions **A, C, E** of the same, the knight catches at a branch to save himself, and the lady cuts it off with his sword.

.... ohone and aree (alack and O Lord),
On the banks of the Banna (White River),
    ohone and aree,

which may raise a question whether the Scotch burden Binnorie (pronounced Bínnorie, as well as Binnórie) is corrupted from it, or the corruption is on the other side. Mr Campbell notices as quaint the reply in stanza 9:

'I did not put you in with the design
Just for to pull you out again.'

We have had a similar reply, made under like circumstances, in Polish versions of No 4: see p. 58, note.

All the Norse versions of this ballad are in two-line stanzas, and all the English, except **L b** and in part **L a**.

Some of the traits of the English and Norse story are presented by an Esthonian ballad, 'The Harp,' Neus, *Ehstnische Volkslieder*, No 13, p. 56. Another version is given in Rosenplänter's *Beiträge zur genauern Kenntniss der ehstnischen Sprache*, Heft 4, 142, and a third, says Neus, in Ch. H. J. Schlegel's *Reisen in mehrere russische Gouvernements*, v, 140.* A young woman, who tells her own story, is murdered by her sisters-in-law and buried in a moor. She comes up as a birch, from which, with the jawbone of a salmon, the teeth of a pike, and her own hair (the account is somewhat confused) a harp is made. The harp is taken to the hall by the murdered girl's brother, and responds to his playing with tones of sorrow like those of the bride who leaves father and mother for the house of a husband.†

A drowned girl grows up on the sea-strand as a linden with nine branches: from the ninth her brother carves a harp. "Sweet the tone," he says, as he plays. The mother calls out through her tears, So sang my youngest daughter. G. Tielemann, in *Livona, ein historisch-poetisches Taschenbuch*, Riga u. Dorpat, 1812, p. 187, *Ueber die Volkslieder der Letten*. Dr R. Köhler points out to me a version of this ballad given with a translation by Bishop Carl Chr. Ulmann in the *Dorpater Jahrbücher*, II, 404, 1834, 'Die Lindenharfe,' and another by Pastor Karl Ulmann in his *Lettische Volkslieder, übertragen*, 1874, p. 199, No 18, 'Das Lied von der Jüngsten.' In the former of these the brother says, Sweet sounds my linden harp! The mother, weeping, It is not the linden harp; it is thy sister's soul that has swum through the water to us; it is the voice of my youngest daughter.

A Slovak ballad often translated (Talvj, *Historical View*, etc., p. 392; Wenzig's *Slawische Volkslieder*, p. 110, *Westslawischer Märchenschatz*, 273, and *Bibliothek Slavischer Poesien*, p. 134; Lewestam, *Polnische Volksagen und Märchen*, p. 151; In Bohemian, 'Zakletá dcera,' 'The Daughter Cursed,' Erben, 1864, p. 466 (with other references), Waldau, *Böhmische Granaten*, II, 97, No 137; Moravian, Sušil, p. 143, No 146; Dr R. Köhler further refers to Peter, *Volksthümliches aus Österreichisch-Schlesien*, I, 209, 'Die drei Spielleute;' Meinert, p. 122, 'Die Erle;' Vernaleken, *Alpensagen*, p. 289, No 207, 'Der Ahornbaum;' Waldau, *Böhmische Granaten*, II, 97.) comes nearer in some respects. A daughter is cursed by her mother for not succeeding in drawing water in frosty weather. Her bucket turns to stone, but she to a maple. Two fiddlers come by, and, seeing a remarkably fine tree, propose to make of it fiddles and fiddle-sticks. When they cut into the tree, blood spirts out. The tree bids them go on, and when they have done, play before the mother's door, and sing, Here is your daughter, that you cursed to stone. At the first notes the mother runs to the window, and begs them to desist, for she has suffered much since she lost her daughter.

The soul of a dead girl speaks through a tree, again, in a Lithuanian ballad, Nesselmann, *Littauische Volkslieder*, No 378, p. 320. The girl is drowned while attempting to cross a stream, carried down to the sea, and finally thrown ashore, where she grows up a linden. Her brother makes a pipe from a branch, and the

---

‡   The miller begins to lose character in **H**:

14 He dragged her out unto the shore,
    And stripped her of all she wore.

*   The ballad in Schlegel's *Reisen* is simply a threnody in Esthonian marriage ceremonies over the carrying away of the bride to her husband's house, and is not to the point.
†   Neus also refers to an Esthonian saga of Rögutaja's wife, and to 'Die Pfeiferin,' a tale, in *Das Inland*, 1846, No 48, Beilage, col. 1246ff, 1851, No 14, col. 230ff.

pipe gives out sweet, sad tones. The mother says, That tone comes not from the linden; it is thy sister's soul, that hovers over the water. A like idea is met with in another Lithuanian ballad, Rhesa, *Dainos*, ed. Kurschat, No 85, p. 231. A sister plucks a bud from a rose-bush growing over the grave of her brother, who had died from disappointed love. How fragrant! she exclaims. But her mother answers, with tears, It is not the rosebud, but the soul of the youth that died of grief.

Though the range of the ballad proper is somewhat limited, popular tales equivalent as to the characteristic circumstances are very widely diffused.

A Polish popular tale, which is, indeed, half song, Wojcicki, *Klechdy*, ed. 1851, II, 15 (Lewestam, p. 105), Kolberg, *Pieśni ludu Polskiego*, p. 292, No 40 **a, b, c**, approaches very close to the English-Norse ballad. There were three sisters, all pretty, but the youngest far surpassing the others. A young man from the far-off Ukraine fell in with them while they were making garlands. The youngest pleased him best, and he chose her for his wife. This excited the jealousy of the eldest, and a few days after, when they were gathering berries in a wood, she killed the youngest, notwithstanding the resistance of the second sister, buried her, and gave out that she had been torn to pieces by wolves. When the youth came to ask after his love, the murderess told him this tale, and so won him by her devoted consolations that he offered her his hand. A willow grew out of the grave of the youngest, and a herdsman made a pipe from one of its boughs. Blow as he would, he could get no sound from the pipe but this:

> 'Blow on, herdsman, blow! God shall bless thee so.
> The eldest was my slayer, the second tried to stay her.'

The herdsman took the pipe to the house of the murdered girl. The mother, the father, and the second sister successively tried it, and the pipe always sang a like song, Blow, mother, blow, etc. The father then put the pipe into the eldest sister's hands. She had hardly touched it, when blood spattered her cheeks, and the pipe sang:

> 'Blow on, sister, blow: God shall wreak me now.
> Thou, sister, 't was didst slay me, the younger tried to stay thee,' etc.

The murderess was torn by wild horses.[*]

In Rudchenko, *South Russian Popular Tales*, I, No 55, the murder of a brother is revealed by a flute made from a reed that grows from his grave (No 56, flute from a willow); II, No 14, the murder of a boy killed and eaten by his parents is revealed by a bird that rises from his bones. (W. W.)

In a Flemish tale reported in the *Revue des Traditions populaires*, II, 125, Janneken is killed by Milken for the sake of a golden basket. The murder is disclosed by a singing rose. In 'Les Roseaux qui chantent' a sister kills her brother in a dispute over a bush covered with *painprunelle*. Roses grow from his grave. A shepherd, hearing them sing, cuts a stem of the rosebush and whistles in it. The usual words follow. *Revue des Traditions populaires*, II, 365ff; cf. Sébillot's long note, p. 366ff. Das Flötenrohr (two prose versions), U. Jahn, *Volkssagen aus Pommern und Rügen*, No 510, pp. 399–401. (G.L.K.)

Professor Bugge reports a Norwegian tale, Grundtvig, III, 878, which resembles the ballad at the beginning. There were in a family two daughters and a son. One sister was wasteful, the other saving. The second complained of the first to her parents, and was killed and buried by the other. Foliage covered the grave, so that it could not be seen, but on the trees under which the body lay, there grew "strings." These the brother cut off and adapted to his fiddle, and when he played, the fiddle said, My sister is killed. The father, having heard the fiddle's revelation, brought his daughter to confess her act.

There is a series of tales which represent a king, or other personage, as being afflicted with a severe malady, and as promising that whichever of his children, commonly three sons, should bring him something necessary for his

---

[*] 'Siffle, berger, de mon haleine!
   Mon frère m'a tué sous les bois d' Altumène,
   Pour la rose de ma mère, que j'avais trouvée,' etc.

Poésies pop. de la France, MS., VI, 193 *bis*; popular in Champagne: *Mélusine*, I, col. 424.

cure or comfort should be his heir: (1) 'La Flor del Lililá,' Fernan Caballero, *Lágrimas*, cap. 4; (2) 'La caña del riu de arenas,' Milá, *Observaciones sobre la poesia popular*, p. 178, No 3; (3) 'Es kommt doch einmal an den Tag,' Müllenhoff, *Sagen, u. s. w.*, p. 495, No 49; (4) 'Vom singenden Dudelsack,' Gonzenbach, *Sicilianische Märchen*, I, 329, No 51. Or the inheritance is promised to whichever of the children finds something lost, or rich and rare, a griffin's feather, a golden branch, a flower: (5) 'Die Greifenfeder,' Schneller, *Märchen und Sagen aus Wälschtirol*, p. 143, No 51; (6) 'La Flauuto,' Bladé, *Contes et proverbes populaires recueillis en Armagnac*, p. 3, No 1; (7) Wackernagel, in Haupt's *Zeitschrift*, III, 35, No 3, = 'Das Todtebeindli,' Colshorn, C. u. Th., *Märchen u. Sagen*, p. 193, No 71, = Sutermeister, *Kinder- und Hausmärchen aus der Schweiz*, p. 119, No 39 = Rochholz, *Schweizersagen aus dem Aargau*, II, 126, No 353. Or a king promises his daughter to the man who shall capture a dangerous wild beast, and the exploit is undertaken by three brothers [or two]: (8) 'Der Singende Knochen,' Grimms, *K. u. H. märchen*, I, 149, No 28 (1857); (9) 'Die drei Brüder,' Curtze, *Volksüberlieferungen aus dem Fürstenthum Waldeck*, p. 53, No 11; (10) 'Der Rohrstengel,' Haltrich, *Deutsche Volksmärchen aus dem Sachsenlande, u. s. w.*, p. 225, No 42. With these we may group, though divergent in some respects, (11) 'Der goldene Apfel,' Toeppen, *Aberglauben aus Masuren*, p. 139.[*] In all these tales the youngest child is successful, and is killed, out of envy, by the eldest or by the two elder. [There are only two children in (6), (7), (8); in (4) the second is innocent, as in the Polish tale.] Reeds grow over the spot where the body is buried (1), (2), [126] (10), (11), or an elder bush (3), out of which a herdsman makes a pipe or flute; or a white bone is found by a herdsman, and he makes a pipe or horn of it (5–9); or a bag-pipe is made of the bones and skin of the murdered youth (4). The instrument, whenever it is played, attests the murder.[†]

Among the tales of the South African Bechuana, there is one of a younger brother, who has been killed by an older, immediately appearing as a bird, and announcing what has occurred. The bird is twice killed, and the last

time burnt and its ashes scattered to the winds, but still reappears, and proclaims that his body lies by a spring in the desert. Grimms, *K. u. H. märchen*, III, 361. Liebrecht has noted that the fundamental idea is found in a Chinese drama, 'The Talking Dish,' said to be based on a popular tale. An innkeeper and his wife kill one of their guests for his money, and burn the body. The innkeeper collects the ashes and pounds the bones, and makes a sort of mortar and a dish. This dish speaks very distinctly, and denounces the murderers. *Journal Asiatique*, 1851, 4th Series, vol. 18, p. 523. For a parallel to this tale see Jacottet, *Contes pop. des Bassoutos*, p. 52.

Danish **A, E** are translated by Prior, I, 381, 384. English **B**, with use of **C**, is translated by Grundtvig, *Engelske og skotske Folkeviser*, p. 104, No 15; **C**, by Afzelius, III, 22. **C**, by Talvj, *Versuch, u. s. w.*, p. 532; by Schubart, p. 133; by Gerhard, p. 143; by Doenniges, p. 81; Arndt, p.

---

[*] All these are cited in Köhler's note, Gonzenbach, II, 235.

    Add to the citations: 'Le Sifflet enchanté,' E. Cosquin, *Contes populaires lorrains*, No 26, *Romania*, VI, 565, with annotations, pp 567f; Köhler's *Nachträge in Zeitschrift für romanische Philologie*, II, 350f; Engelien u. Lahn, *Der Volksmund in der Mark Brandenburg*, I, 105, 'Diä 3 Brüder;' Sébillot, *Littérature orale de la Haute-Bretagne*, p. 220, *Les Trois Frères*, p. 226, 'Le Sifflet qui parle.' (Köhler.) 'La Flute,' Bladé, *Contes pop. de la Gascogne*, II, 100–102. (G. L. K.) 'Les roseaux qui chantent,' *Revue des Traditions Populaires*, IV, 463, V, 178; 'La rose de Pimperlé,' Meyrac, *Traditions, etc., des Ardennes*, p. 486ff; 'Los qui chante,' seven Walloon versions, E. Monseur, *Bulletin de Folklore Wallon*, I, 39ff. 'Les roseaux qui chantent,' *Revue des Traditions Populaires*, VII, 223 (blue flower); 'L'os qui chante,' discussion of the tale by M. Charles Ploix, *Rev. des Trad. Pop.*, VIII, 129ff. M. Eugène Monseur has continued his study of this tale in *Bulletin de Folklore*, I, 39–51, 89–149, II, 219–41, 245–51. See also Bugiel in Wisła, VII, 339–61, 557–80, 665–85.

    See also 'Die Geschichte von zwei Freunden,' Socin u. Stumme, *Dialekt der Houwāra des Wād Sūs in Marokko*, pp. 53, 115, *Abhandlungen der Phil.-hist. Classe der K. Sächs. Gesellschaft der Wissenschaften*, XV.

[†] On disclosure by musical instruments see *Revue Celtique*, II, 199; Hartland, *Legend of Perseus*, I, 193. F. N. Robinson. De Gubernatis, *Zoölogical Mythology*, I, 195, cites other similar stories: Afanasief, *Skazki*, v, 71, No 17, and two varieties, vi, 138, No 25; the twentieth story of Santo Stefano di Calcinaia, 325. (G. L. K.)

238; by H. Schubart in Arnim's *Tröst Ein-*
samkeit, 1808, p. 146. **C**, with use of Aytoun's
compounded version, by R. Warrens, *Schottische*

V. l. *der Vorzeit*, p. 65; Allingham's version by
Knortz, *Lieder u. Romanzen Alt-Englands*, p.
180.

A

A. a. Broadside "printed for Francis Grove, 1656,"
reprinted in *Notes and Queries*, 1st S., v, 591. b. *Wit
Restor'd*, 1658, "p. 51," p. 153 of the reprint of 1817. c.
Wit and Drollery, ed. 1682, p. 87, = Dryden's *Miscellany*,
Part 3, p. 316, ed. 1716. d. Jamieson's *Popular Ballads*, I,
315.

1 THERE were two sisters, they went playing,
  With a hie downe downe a downe-a
To see their father's ships come sayling in.
  With a hy downe downe a downe-a

2 And when they came unto the sea-brym,
  The elder did push the younger in.

3 'O sister, O sister, take me by the gowne,
  And drawe me up upon the dry ground.'

4 'O sister, O sister, that may not bee,
  Till salt and oatmeale grow both of a tree.'

5 Somtymes she sanke, somtymes she swam,
  Until she came unto the mill-dam.

6 The miller runne hastily downe the cliffe,
  And up he betook her withouten her life.

7 What did he doe with her brest-bone?
  He made him a violl to play thereupon.

8 What did he doe with her fingers so small?
  He made him peggs to his violl withall.

9 What did he doe with her nose-ridge?
  Unto his violl he made him a bridge.

10 What did he doe with her veynes so blew?
   He made him strings to his violl thereto.

11 What did he doe with her eyes so bright?
   Upon his violl he played at first sight.

12 What did he doe with her tongue so rough?
   Unto the violl it spake enough.

13 What did he doe with her two shinnes?
   Unto the violl they danc'd Moll Syms.

14 Then bespake the treble string,
   'O yonder is my father the king.'

15 Then bespake the second string,
   'O yonder sits my mother the queen.'

16 And then bespake the strings all three,
   'O yonder is my sister that drowned mee.'

17 'Now pay the miller for his payne,
   And let him bee gone in the divel's name.'

B

a. Jamieson-Brown MS., p. 39. b. Wm. Tytler's
Brown MS., No 15. c. Abbotsford MS., "Scottish
Songs," fol. 21. d. Jamieson's *Popular Ballads*, 1, 48.

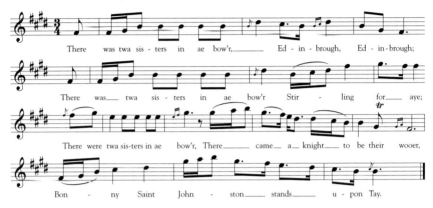

There   was twa sis - ters   in   ae bow'r,_____   Ed - in - brough,   Ed - in - brough;

There   was___   twa   sis - ters   in   ae   bow'r   Stir   -   ling   for___   aye;

There were twa sis-ters in ae   bow'r, There_____ came___ a_ knight___ to be their   wooer,

Bon   -   ny   Saint   John   -   ston____ stands_____   u - pon Tay.

B. b. Ritson-Tytler-Brown MS., No. 15; text, pp. 99–102. Sung by Mrs Brown, Falkland, Aberdeenshire. The text
underlay, from Child, V, p. 411, is very unsatisfactory. See Bronson, I, p. 177, for a conjectural reading.

1 THERE was twa sisters in a bowr,
   Edinburgh, Edinburgh
There was twa sisters in a bowr,
   Stirling for ay
There was twa sisters in a bowr,
   There came a knight to be their wooer.
   Bonny Saint Johnston stands upon Tay

2 He courted the eldest wi glove an ring,
   But he lovd the youngest above a' thing.

3 He courted the eldest wi brotch an knife,
   But lovd the youngest as his life.

4 The eldest she was vexed sair,
   An much envi'd her sister fair.

5 Into her bowr she could not rest,
   Wi grief an spite she almos brast.

6 Upon a morning fair an clear,
   She cried upon her sister dear:

7 'O sister, come to yon sea stran,
   An see our father's ships come to lan.'

8 She's taen her by the milk-white han,
   An led her down to yon sea stran.

9 The younges[t] stood upon a stane,
   The eldest came an threw her in.

10 She tooke her by the middle sma,
   An dashd her bonny back to the jaw.

11 'O sister, sister, tak my han,
   An Ise mack you heir to a' my lan.

12 'O sister, sister, tak my middle,
   An yes get my goud and my gouden girdle.

13 'O sister, sister, save my life,
   An I swear Ise never be nae man's wife.'

14 'Foul fa the ban that I should tacke,
   It twin'd me an my wardles make.

15 'Your cherry cheeks an yellow hair
   Gars me gae maiden for evermair.'

16 Sometimes she sank, an sometimes she swam,
   Till she came down yon bonny mill-dam.

17 O out it came the miller's son,
   An saw the fair maid swimmin in.

18 'O father, father, draw your dam,
   Here's either a mermaid or a swan.'

19 The miller quickly drew the dam,
   An there he found a drownd woman.

20 You coudna see her yallow hair
   For gold and pearle that were so rare.

21 You coudna see her middle sma
   For gouden girdle that was sae braw.

22 You coudna see her fingers white,
   For gouden rings that was sae gryte.

23 An by there came a harper fine,
   That harped to the king at dine.

24 When he did look that lady upon,
   He sighd and made a heavy moan.

25 He's taen three locks o her yallow hair,
   An wi them strung his harp sae fair.

26 The first tune he did play and sing,
   Was, 'Farewell to my father the king.'

27 The nextin tune that he playd syne,
   Was, 'Farewell to my mother the queen.'

28 The lasten tune that he playd then,
   Was, 'Wae to my sister, fair Ellen.'

C

Scott's *Minstrelsy*, 1802, II, 143. Compounded from
B b and a fragment of fourteen stanzas transcribed from
the recitation of an old woman by Miss Charlotte
Brooke.

1 THERE were two sisters sat in a bour;
   Binnorie, O Binnorie
There came a knight to be their wooer.
   By the bonny mill-dams of Binnorie

2 He courted the eldest with glove and ring,
   But he loed the youngest aboon a' thing.

3 He courted the eldest with broach and knife,
   But he loed the youngest aboon his life.

4 The eldest she was vexed sair,
   And sore envied her sister fair.

5 The eldest said to the youngest ane,
   'Will ye go and see our father's ships come in?'

6 She's taen her by the lilly hand,
   And led her down to the river strand.

7 The youngest stude upon a stane,
   The eldest came and pushed her in.

8 She took her by the middle sma,
   And dashed her bonnie back to the jaw.

9 'O sister, sister, reach your hand,
   And ye shall be heir of half my land.'

10 'O sister, I'll not reach my hand,
   And I'll be heir of all your land.

11 'Shame fa the hand that I should take,
   It's twin'd me and my world's make.'

12 'O sister, reach me but your glove,
   And sweet William shall be your love.'

13 'Sink on, nor hope for hand or glove,
   And sweet William shall better be my love.

14 'Your cherry cheeks and your yellow hair
   Garrd me gang maiden evermair.'

15 Sometimes she sunk, and sometimes she swam,
   Until she came to the miller's dam.

16 'O father, father, draw your dam,
   There's either a mermaid or a milk-white swan.'

17 The miller hasted and drew his dam,
   And there he found a drowned woman.

18 You could not see her yellow hair,
   For gowd and pearls that were sae rare.

19 You could na see her middle sma,
   Her gowden girdle was sae bra.

20 A famous harper passing by,
　　The sweet pale face he chanced to spy.

21 And when he looked that ladye on,
　　He sighed and made a heavy moan.

22 He made a harp of her breast-bone,
　　Whose sounds would melt a heart of stone.

23 The strings he framed of her yellow hair,
　　Whose notes made sad the listening ear.

24 He brought it to her father's hall,
　　And there was the court assembled all.

25 He laid this harp upon a stone,
　　And straight it began to play alone.

26 'O yonder sits my father, the king,
　　And yonder sits my mother, the queen.

27 'And yonder stands my brother Hugh,
　　And by him my William, sweet and true.'

28 But the last tune that the harp playd then,
　　Was 'Woe to my sister, false Helen!'

D

Kinloch's MSS, ii, 49. From the recitation of Mrs
Johnston, a North-country lady.

1 THERE lived three sisters in a bouer,
　　Edinbruch, Edinbruch
　There lived three sisters in a bouer,
　　Stirling for aye
　There lived three sisters in a bouer,
　The youngest was the sweetest flowr.
　　Bonnie St Johnston stands upon Tay

2 There cam a knicht to see them a',
　　And on the youngest his love did fa.

3 He brought the eldest ring and glove,
　　But the youngest was his ain true-love.

4 He brought the second sheath and knife,
　　But the youngest was to be his wife.

5 The eldest sister said to the youngest ane,
　　'Will ye go and see our father's ships come in?'

6 And as they walked by the linn,
　　The eldest dang the youngest in.

7 'O sister, sister, tak my hand,
　　And ye'll be heir to a' my land.'

8 'Foul fa the hand that I wad take,
　　To twin me o my warld's make.'

9 'O sister, sister, tak my glove,
　　And yese get Willie, my true-love.'

10 'Sister, sister, I'll na tak your glove,
　　For I'll get Willie, your true-love.'

11 Aye she swittert, and aye she swam,
　　Till she cam to yon bonnie mill-dam.

12 The miller's dochter cam out wi speed,
　　It was for water, to bake her bread.

13 'O father, father, gae slack your dam;
　　There's in't a lady or a milk-white swan.'
　* 　 　* 　 　* 　 　* 　 　*

14 They could na see her coal-black eyes
　　For her yellow locks hang oure her brees.

15 They could na see her weel-made middle
　　For her braid gowden girdle.
　* 　 　* 　 　* 　 　* 　 　*

16 And by there cam an auld blind fiddler,
　　And took three tets o her bonnie yellow hair.
　* 　 　* 　 　* 　 　* 　 　*

17 The first spring that the bonnie fiddle playd,
　　'Hang my cruel sister, Alison,' it said.

E

Sharpe's *Ballad Book*, No 10, p. 30.

There liv'd twa sis - ters in a bower, Hey Ed - in - bruch, how Ed - in - bruch,

There liv'd twa sis - ters in a bower, Stir - ling for___ aye;

The young - est o'___ them, O___ she was a flow - er!

Bon - ny Sanct John - stoune that stands up - on Tay.

Lady John Scott's Sharpe MS., NL Scotland MS. 843, fol. 11ᵛ. Sung by Sharpe's mother.

1 THERE livd twa sisters in a bower,
   Hey Edinbruch, how Edinbruch!
 There lived twa sisters in a bower,
   Stirling for aye!
 The youngest o them O she was a flower!
   Bonny Sanct Johnstoune that stands upon
     Tay!

2 There cam a squire frae the west,
   He loed them baith, but the youngest best.

3 He gied the eldest a gay gold ring,
   But he loed the youngest aboon a' thing.

4 'O sister, sister, will ye go to the sea?
   Our father's ships sail bonnilie.'

5 The youngest sat down upon a stane;
   The eldest shot the youngest in.

6 'O sister, sister, lend me your hand,
   And you shall hae my gouden fan.

7 'O sister, sister, save my life,
   And ye shall be the squire's wife.'

8 First she sank, and then she swam,
   Untill she cam to Tweed mill-dam.

9 The millar's daughter was baking bread,
   She went for water, as she had need.

10 'O father, father, in our mill-dam
   There's either a lady, or a milk-white swan.'

11 They could nae see her fingers small,   [130]
   Wi diamond rings they were coverd all.

12 They could nae see her yellow hair,
   Sae mony knots and platts were there.

13 They could nae see her lilly feet,
   Her gowden fringes war sae deep.

14 Bye there cam a fiddler fair,
   And he's taen three taits o her yellow hair.

F

Motherwell's MS., p. 383. From the recitation of
Agnes Lyle, Kilbarchan, 27th July, 1825.

1 THERE was two ladies livd in a bower,
  Hey with a gay and a grinding O
The youngest o them was the fairest flower
  About a' the bonny bows o London.

2 There was two ladies livd in a bower,
  An wooer unto the youngest did go.

3 The oldest one to the youngest did say,
  'Will ye take a walk with me today,
    And we'll view the bonny bows o London.

4 'Thou'll set thy foot whare I set mine,
  Thou'll set thy foot upon this stane.'

5 'I'll set my foot where thou sets thine:'
  The old sister dang the youngest in,
    At, etc.

6 'O sister dear, come tak my hand,
  Take my life safe to dry land,'
    At, etc.

7 'It's neer by my hand thy hand sall come in,
  It's neer by my hand thy hand sall come in,
    At, etc.

8 'It's thy cherry cheeks and thy white briest bane
  Gars me set a maid owre lang at hame.'

9 She clasped her hand[s] about a brume rute,
  But her cruel sister she lowsed them out.

10 Sometimes she sank, and sometimes she swam,
  Till she cam to the miller's dam.

11 The miller's bairns has muckle need,
  They were bearing in water to bake some breid.

12 Says, 'Father, dear father, in our mill-dam,
  It's either a fair maid or a milk-white swan.'

13 The miller he's spared nae his hose nor his
      shoon
  Till he brocht this lady till dry land.

14 I wad he saw na a bit o her feet,
  Her silver slippers were made so neat.

15 I wad he saw na a bit o her skin,
  For ribbons there was mony a ane.

16 He laid her on a brume buss to dry,
  To see wha was the first wad pass her by.

17 Her ain father's herd was the first man
  That by this lady gay did gang.

18 He's taen three links of her yellow hair,
  And made it a string to his fiddle there.

19 He's cut her fingers long and small
  To be fiddle-pins that neer might fail.

20 The very first spring that the fiddle did play,
  'Hang my auld sister,' I wad it did say.

21 'For she drowned me in yonder sea,
  God neer let her rest till she shall die,'
    At the bonny bows o London.

G

Motherwell's MS., p. 104. From Mrs King, Kilbarchan.

1 THERE were three sisters lived in a bouir,
  Hech, hey, my Nannie O
And the youngest was the fairest flouir.
  And the swan swims bonnie O

2 'O sister, sister, gang down to yon sand,
  And see your father's ships coming to dry land.'

3 O they have gane down to yonder sand,
  To see their father's ships coming to dry land.

4 'Gae set your fit on yonder stane,
  Till I tye up your silken goun.'

5 She set her fit on yonder stane,
   And the auldest drave the youngest in.

6 'O sister, sister, tak me by the hand,
   And ye'll get a' my father's land.

7 'O sister, sister, tak me by the gluve,
   An ye'll get Willy, my true luve.'

8 She had a switch into her hand,
   And ay she drave her frae the land.

9 O whiles she sunk, and whiles she swam,
   Until she swam to the miller's dam.

10 The miller's daughter gade doun to Tweed,
   To carry water to bake her bread.

11 'O father, O father, what's yon in the dam?
   It's either a maid or a milk-white swan.'

12 They have tane her out till yonder thorn,
   And she has lain till Monday morn.

13 She hadna, hadna twa days lain,
   Till by there came a harper fine.

14 He made a harp o her breast-bane,
   That he might play forever thereon.

H

Motherwell's MS., p. 147. From I. Goldie, March, 1825.

1 THERE were three sisters lived in a hall,
      Hey with the gay and the grandeur O
   And there came a lord to court them all.
      At the bonnie bows o London town

2 He courted the eldest with a penknife,
   And he vowed that he would take her life.

3 He courted the youngest with a glove,
   And he said that he'd be her true love.

4 'O sister, O sister, will you go and take a walk,
   And see our father's ships how they float?'

5 'O lean your foot upon the stone,
   And wash your hand in that sea-foam.'

6 She leaned her foot upon the stone,
   But her eldest sister has tumbled her down.

7 'O sister, sister, give me your hand,
   And I'll make you lady of all my land.'

8 'O I'll not lend to you my hand,
   But I'll be lady of your land.'

9 'O sister, sister, give me your glove,
   And I'll make you lady of my true love.'

10 'It's I'll not lend to you my glove,
   But I'll be lady of your true love.'

11 Sometimes she sank, and sometimes she swam,
   Until she came to a miller's dam.

12 The miller's daughter was coming out wi speed,
   For water for to bake some bread.

13 'O father, father, stop the dam,
   For it's either a lady or a milk-white swan.'

14 He dragged her out unto the shore,
   And stripped her of all she wore.

15 By cam a fiddler, and he was fair,
   And he buskit his bow in her bonnie yellow
      hair.

16 By cam her father's harper, and he was fine,   [132]
   And he made a harp o her bonny breast-bone.

17 When they came to her father's court,
   The harp [and fiddle these words] spoke:

18 'O God bless my father the king,
   And I wish the same to my mother the queen,

19 'My sister Jane she tumbled me in,
   .   .   .   .   .   .

      *   *   *   *   *

I

Kinloch MSS, v, 425. From the recitation of M.
Kinnear, 23d August, 1826.

1 THERE war twa sisters lived in a bouer,
    Binnorie and Binnorie
There cam a squire to court them baith.
    At the bonnie mill-streams o Binnorie

2 He courted the eldest with jewels and rings,
    But he lovd the youngest the best of all things.

3 He courted the eldest with a penknife,
    He lovd the youngest as dear as his life.

4 It fell ance upon a day
    That these twa sisters hae gane astray.

5 It was for to meet their father[s] ships that had
      come in.
   .   .   .   .   .

6 As they walked up the linn,
    The eldest dang the youngest in.

7 'O sister, sister, tak my hand,
    And ye'll hae Lord John and aw his land.'

8 With a silver wand she pushd her in,
   .   .   .   .   .

9 'O sister, sister, tak my glove,
    And ye sall hae my ain true love.'

10 The miller's dochter cam out wi speed,
    It was for a water to bake her bread.

11 'O father, father, gae slack your dam
    There's either a white fish or a swan.'
   *   *   *   *   *

12 Bye cam a blind fiddler that way,
    And he took three tets o her bonnie yellow
      hair.

13 And the first spring that he playd,
    It said, 'It was my sister threw me in.'

J

Notes and Queries, 4th S., v, 23, from the north of Ireland.

1 THERE were two ladies playing ball,
    Hey, ho, my Nannie O
A great lord came to court them all.
    The swan she does swim bonnie O

2 He gave to the first a golden ring,
    He gave to the second a far better thing.

   *   *   *   *   *
3 He made a harp of her breast-bone
   .   .   .   .   .

4 He set it down upon a stone,
    And it began to play its lone.

K

Mr G. R. Kinloch's papers, Kinloch MSS, VII, 256.
From Mrs Lindores.

1 'O SISTER, sister, gie me your hand,
    Binnorie and Binnorie
And I'll give the half of my fallow-land,
    By the bonnie mill-dams of Binnorie.'

   *   *   *   *   *
2 The first time the bonnie fiddle played, 'Hang
    my sister, Alison,' it said,
    'At the bonnie mill-dams of Binnorie.'

L

[133]

a. From oral tradition, *Notes and Queries*, 1st S., v,
316. b. *The Scouring of the White Horse*, p. 161. From
North Wales.

1 O was it eke a pheasant cock,
  Or eke a pheasant hen,
 Or was it the bodye of a fair ladye,
  Come swimming down the stream?

2 O it was not a pheasant cock,
  Nor eke a pheasant hen,
 But it was the bodye of a fair ladye
  Came swimming down the stream.

 *   *   *   *   *

3 And what did he do with her fair bodye?
  Fal the lal the lal laral lody
 He made it a case for his melodye.
  Fal, etc.

4 And what did he do with her legs so strong?
 He made them a stand for his violon.

5 And what did he do with her hair so fine?
 He made of it strings for his violine.

6 And what did he do with her arms so long?
 He made them bows for his violon.

7 And what did he do with her nose so thin?
 He made it a bridge for his violin.

8 And what did he do with her eyes so bright?
 He made them spectacles to put to his sight.

9 And what did he do with her petty toes?
 He made them a nosegay to put to his nose.

M

Taken down from recitation at Old Deer, 1876, by
Mrs A. F. Murison. MS., p. 79.

1 There lived twa sisters in yonder ha,
  Binórie O an Binórie
 They hadna but ae lad atween them twa,
  He's the bonnie miller lad o Binórie.

2 It fell oot upon a day,
  The auldest ane to the youngest did say,
  At the bonnie mill-dams o Binórie,

3 'O sister, O sister, will ye go to the dams,
  To hear the blackbird thrashin oer his songs?
  At the,' etc.

4 'O sister, O sister, will ye go to the dams,
  To see oor father's fish-boats come safe to dry
   lan?
  An the bonnie miller lad o Binorie.'

5 They hadna been an oor at the dams,
  Till they heard the blackbird thrashin oer his
   tune,
  At the, etc.

6 They hadna been an oor at the dams
  Till they saw their father's fish-boats come safe
   to dry lan,
  Bat they sawna the bonnie miller laddie.

7 They stood baith up upon a stane,
  An the eldest ane dang the youngest in,
  I the, etc.

8 She swam up, an she swam doon,
  An she swam back to her sister again,
  I the, etc.

9 'O sister, O sister, len me your han,
  An yes be heir to my true love,
  He's the bonnie miller lad o Binorie.'

10 'It was not for that love at I dang you in,
  But ye was fair and I was din,
  And yes droon i the dams o Binorie.'

11 The miller's daughter she cam oot,
    For water to wash her father's hans,
     Frae the, etc.

[134] 12 'O father, O father, ye will fish your dams,
    An ye'll get a white fish or a swan,
     I the,' etc.

13 They fished up and they fished doon,
    But they got nothing but a droonet woman,
     I the, etc.

14 Some o them kent by her skin sae fair,
    But weel kent he by her bonnie yallow hair
     She's the bonnie miller's lass o Binorie.

15 Some o them kent by her goons o silk,
    But weel kent he by her middle sae jimp, She's
     the bonnie miller's lass o Binorie.

16 Mony ane was at her oot-takin,
    But mony ane mair at her green grave makin,
     At the bonny mill-dams o Binorie.

N

[Pinkerton's] *Scottish Tragic Ballads*, p. 72.

1 THERE were twa sisters livd in a bouir,
    Binnorie, O Binnorie
  Their father was a baron of pouir.
    By the bonnie mildams of Binnorie

2 The youngest was meek, and fair as the may
  Whan she springs in the east wi the gowden day.

3 The eldest austerne as the winter cauld,
  Ferce was her saul, and her seiming was bauld.

4 A gallant squire cam sweet Isabel to wooe;
  Her sister had naething to luve I trow.

5 But filld was she wi dolour and ire,
  To see that to her the comlie squire

6 Preferd the debonair Isabel:
  Their hevin of luve of spyte was her hell.

7 Till ae ein she to her sister can say,
  'Sweit sister, cum let us wauk and play.'

8 They wauked up, and they wauked down,
  Sweit sang the birdis in the vallie loun.

9 Whan they cam to the roaring lin,
  She drave unweiting Isabel in.

10 'O sister, sister, tak my hand,
   And ye sall hae my silver fan.

11 'O sister, sister, tak my middle,
   And ye sall hae my gowden girdle.'

12 Sumtimes she sank, sumtimes she swam,
   Till she cam to the miller's dam.

13 The miller's dochtor was out that ein,
   And saw her rowing down the streim.

14 'O father deir, in your mil-dam
   There is either a lady or a milk-white swan!'

15 Twa days were gane, whan to her deir
   Her wraith at deid of nicht cold appeir.

16 'My luve, my deir, how can ye sleip,
   Whan your Isabel lyes in the deip!

17 'My deir, how can ye sleip bot pain
   Whan she by her cruel sister is slain!'

18 Up raise he sune, in frichtfu mude:
   'Busk ye, my meiny, and seik the flude.'

19 They socht her up and they socht her doun,
   And spyd at last her glisterin gown.

20 They raisd her wi richt meikle care;
   Pale was her cheik and grein was her hair.

O

a. Buchan's *Ballads of the North of Scotland*, ii, 128.
b. *Traditional Ballad Airs*, edited by W. Christie, i, 42.

1.There ___ were twa sis - ters in a bower, It's___ hey wi' the gay and the grind - ing;

And ae king's___ son has___ court - ed them baith, At the bon - ny, bon - ny bows o' Lon - don.

2.He court - ed the young - est wi' broach and___ ring, It's___ hey wi' the gay and the grind - ing;

And he court - ed the el - dest wi' mo - ny oth - er thing, At the bon - ny, bon - ny bows o' Lon - don.

O. b. Christie, I, 1876, p. 42. Sung by an old woman in Banffshire.

1 THERE were twa sisters in a bower,
   Hey wi the gay and the grinding
And ae king's son has courted them baith.
   At the bonny bonny bows o London

2 He courted the youngest wi broach and ring,
   He courted the eldest wi some other thing.

3 It fell ance upon a day
   The eldest to the youngest did say,

4 'Will ye gae to yon Tweed mill-dam,
   And see our father's ships come to land?'

5 They baith stood up upon a stane,
   The eldest dang the youngest in.

6 She swimmed up, sae did she down,
   Till she came to the Tweed mill-dam.

7 The miller's servant he came out,
   And saw the lady floating about.

8 'O master, master, set your mill,
   There is a fish, or a milk-white swan.'

9 They could not ken her yellow hair,
   [For] the scales o gowd that were laid there.

10 They could not ken her fingers sae white,
   The rings o gowd they were sae bright.

11 They could not ken her middle sae jimp,
   The stays o gowd were so well laced.

12 They could not ken her foot sae fair,
   The shoes o gowd they were so rare.

13 Her father's fiddler he came by,
   Upstarted her ghaist before his eye.

14 'Ye'll take a lock o my yellow hair,
   Ye'll make a string to your fiddle there.

15 'Ye'll take a lith O my little finger bane,
   And ye'll make a pin to your fiddle then.'

16 He's taen a lock o her yellow hair,
   And made a string to his fiddle there.

17 He's taen a lith o her little finger bane,
   And he's made a pin to his fiddle then.

18 The firstand spring the fiddle did play,
   Said, 'Ye'll drown my sister, as she's dune me.'   [135]

P

a. Motherwell's MS., p. 245. **b.** Motherwell's *Minstrelsy*, Appendix, p. xx, xx.

There liv'd twa sis - ters in a bower, Hey my bon - nie An - nie O,

There came a lo - ver them to woo, And the Swan swims bon - nie O,

And the swan swims bon - nie O.

P. b. Motherwell, Appendix 20. Collected by Andrew Blaikie, Paisley.

1 THERE were twa ladies in a bower,
   Hey my bonnie Nannie O
The old was black and the young ane fair.
   And the swan swims bonnie O

2 Once it happened on a day
   The auld ane to the young did say,

3 The auld ane to the young did say,
   'Will you gae to the green and play?'

4 'O sister, sister, I daurna gang,
   For fear I file my silver shoon.'

5 It was not to the green they gaed,
   But it was to the water of Tweed.

6 She bowed her back and she's taen her on,
   And she's tumbled her in Tweed mill-dam.

7 'O sister, O sister, O tak my hand,
   And I'll mak you heir of a' my land.'

8 'O sister, O sister, I'll no take your hand,
   And I'll be heir of a' your land.'

9 'O sister, O sister, O tak my thumb,
   And I'll give you my true-love John.'

10 'O sister, O sister, I'll no tak your thumb,
   And I will get your true-love John.'

11 Aye she swattered and aye she swam,
   Until she came to the mouth of the dam.

12 The miller's daughter went out to Tweed,
   To get some water to bake her bread.

13 In again she quickly ran:
   'There's a lady or a swan in our mill-dam.'

14 Out went the miller and his man
   And took the lady out of the dam.

15 They laid her on the brae to dry;
   Her father's fiddler then rode by.

16 When he this lady did come near,
   Her ghost to him then did appear.

17 'When you go to my father the king,
   You'll tell him to burn my sister Jean.

18 'When you go to my father's gate,
   You'll play a spring for fair Ellen's sake.

19 'You'll tak three links of my yellow hair,
   And play a spring for evermair.'

Q

Copied Oct. 26, 1861, by J. F. Campbell, Esq., from a collection made by Lady Caroline Murray; traced by her to an old nurse, and beyond the beginning of this century.

1 THERE dwelt twa sisters in a bower,
　Oh and ohone, and ohone and aree!
And the youngest she was the fairest flower.
　On the banks of the Banna, ohone and aree!

2 There cam a knight to court the twa,
　But on the youngest his love did fa.

3 He courted the eldest with ring and wi glove,
　But he gave the youngest all his love.

4 He courted the eldest with brooch and wi knife,
　But he loved the youngest as his life.

5 'O sister, O sister, will ye come to the stream,
　To see our father's ships come in?'

6 The youngest stood upon a stane,
　Her sister came and pusht her in.

7 'O sister, O sister, come reach me your hand,
　And ye shall hae all our father's land.

8 'O sister, O sister, come reach me your glove,
　And you shall hae William to be your true love.'

9 'I did not put you in with the design
　Just for to pull you out again.'

10 Some time she sank, some time she swam,
　Until she came to a miller's dam.

11 The miller's daughter dwelt on the Tweed,
　She went for water to bake her bread.

12 'O faither, faither, come drag me your dam,
　For there's aither a lady in 't, or a milk-white
　　swan.'

13 The miller went, and he dragd his dam,
　And he brought her fair body to lan.

14 They couldna see her waist sae sma
　For the goud and silk about it a'.

15 They couldna see her yellow hair
　For the pearls and jewels that were there.

16 Then up and spak her ghaist sae green,
　'Do ye no ken the king's dochter Jean?

17 'Tak my respects to my father the king,
　And likewise to my mother the queen.

18 'Tak my respects to my true love William,
　Tell him I deid for the love of him.

19 'Carry him a lock of my yallow hair,
　To bind his heart for evermair.'

R

a. *Notes and Queries*, 1st S., vi, 102, from Lanark-shire. **b.** Written down for J. F. Campbell, Esq., Nov. 7, 1861, at Wishaw House, Lancashire, by Lady Louisa Primrose. **c.** *The Scouring of the White Horse*, p. 158, from Berkshire, as heard by Mr Hughes from his father.

1 THERE was a king of the north countree,
    Bow down, bow down, bow down
  There was a king of the north countree,
[137]   And he had daughters one, two, three.
    I'll be true to my love, and my love'll be true
      to me

2 To the eldest he gave a beaver hat,
  And the youngest she thought much of that.

3 To the youngest he gave a gay gold chain,
  And the eldest she thought much of the same.

4 These sisters were walking on the bryn,
  And the elder pushed the younger in.

5 'Oh sister, oh sister, oh lend me your hand,
  And I will give you both houses and land.'

6 'I'll neither give you my hand nor glove,
  Unless you give me your true love.'

7 Away she sank, away she swam,
  Until she came to a miller's dam.

8 The miller and daughter stood at the door,
  And watched her floating down the shore.

9 'Oh father, oh father, I see a white swan,
  Or else it is a fair woman.'

10 The miller he took up his long crook,
   And the maiden up from the stream he took.

11 'I'll give to thee this gay gold chain,
   If you'll take me back to my father again.'

12 The miller he took the gay gold chain,
   And he pushed her into the water again.

13 The miller was hanged on his high gate
   For drowning our poor sister Kate.

14 The cat's behind the buttery shelf,
   If you want any more, you may sing it yourself.

S

Kinloch MSS, vi, 89, in Kinloch's hand.

*   *   *   *   *
1 'O FATHER, father, swims a swan,'
    This story I'll vent to thee
  'O father, father, swims a swan,
  Unless it be some dead woman.'
    I'll prove true to my true love,
    If my love prove true to me

2 The miller he held out his long fish hook,
  And hooked this fair maid from the brook.

3 She offered the miller a gold ring stane
  To throw her into the river again.

4 Down she sunk, and away she swam,
  Until she cam to her father's brook.

5 The miller was hung at his mill-gate,
  For drowning of my sister Kate.

T

Allingham's *Ballad Book*, p. xxxiii. From Ireland.

'SISTER, dear sister, where shall we go play
    Cold blows the wind, and the wind blows low

'We shall go to the salt sea's brim.'
    And the wind blows cheerily around us, high
        ho

U

Communicated by Mr W. W. Newell, as repeated
by an ignorant woman in her dotage, who learned it at
Huntington, Long Island, N. Y.

1 THERE was a man lived in the mist,
    Bow down, bow down
He loved his youngest daughter best.
    The bow is bent to me,
    So you be true to your own true love,
    And I'll be true to thee.

2 These two sisters went out to swim
    The oldest pushed the youngest in.

3 First she sank and then she swam,
    First she sank and then she swam.

4 The miller, with his rake and hook,
    He caught her by the petticoat.
        *   *   *   *   *

V

Campbell MS., II, 88.

1 THERE dwelt twa sisters in a bower,
    Benorie, O Benorie
The youngest o them was the fairest flower.
    In the merry milldams o Benorie

2 There cam a wooer them to woo,

.   .   .   .   .
    .   .   .   .   .

3 He's gien the eldest o them a broach and a real,
    Because that she loved her sister weel.
        At etc.

4 He's gien the eldest a gay penknife,
    He loved the youngest as dear as his life.
        At etc.

5 'O sister, O sister, will ye go oer yon glen,
    And see my father's ships coming in?'
        At etc.

6 'O sister dear, I darena gang,
    Because I'm feard ye throw me in.'
        The etc.

7 'O set your foot on yon sea stane,
    And was yeer hands in the sea foam.'
        At etc.

8 She set her foot on yon sea stane,
    To wash her hands in the sea foam.
        At etc.

9 .   .   .   .   .
    But the eldest has thrown the youngest in.
        The etc.

10 'O sister, O sister, lend me your hand,
    And ye'se get William and a' his land.'
        At etc.

11 The miller's daughter cam out clad in red,
    Seeking water to bake her bread.
        At etc.

12 'O father, O father, gae fish yeer mill-dam,
    There's either a lady or a milk-[white] swan.'
        In etc.

13 The miller cam out wi his lang cleek,
    And he cleekit the lady out by the feet.
        From the bonny milldam, etc.

14 Ye wadna kend her pretty feet,
    The American leather was sae neat.
        In etc.

15 Ye wadna kend her pretty legs,
    The silken stockings were so neat tied.
        In etc.

16 Ye wadna kend her pretty waist,
    The silken stays were sae neatly laced.
        In etc.

17 Ye wadna kend her pretty face,
    It was sae prettily preend oer wi lace.
        In etc.

18 Ye wadna kend her yellow hair,
    It was sae besmeared wi dust and glar.
        In etc.

19 By cam her father's fiddler fine,
    And that lady's spirit spake to him.
        From etc.

20 She bad him take three taits o her hair,
    And make them three strings to his fiddle sae
        rare.
        At etc.

21 'Take two of my fingers, sae lang and sae white,
    And make them pins to your fiddle sae neat.'
        At etc.

22 The ae first spring that the fiddle played
    Was, Cursed be Sir John, my ain true-love.
        At etc.

23 The next spring that the fiddle playd
    Was, Burn burd Hellen, she threw me in.
        The etc.

W

Communicated by Mr Thomas Lugton, of Kelso, as
sung by an old cotter-woman fifty years ago; learned by
her from her grandfather.

There___ were three la - dies play-ing at the ba,   Nor-ham,__ down__ by__ Nor - ham,

And__ oot__ cam a knight to___ view them a',__ By the bon - nie__ mill - dams o   Nor - ham.

1 Ther were three ladies playing at the ba,
    Norham, down by Norham.
  And there cam a knight to view them a'.
    By the bonnie mill-dams o Norham.

2 He courted the aldest wi diamonds and rings,
    But he loved the youngest abune a' things.

    *   *   *   *   *

3 'Oh sister, oh sister, lend me your hand,
    And pull my poor body unto dry land.

4 'Oh sister, oh sister, lend me your glove,
    And you shall have my own true love!'

5 Oot cam the miller's daughter upon Tweed,
    To carry in water to bake her bread.

6 'Oh father, oh father, there's a fish in your dam;
    It either is a lady or a milk-white swan.'

7 Oot cam the miller's man upon Tweed,
    And there he spied a lady lying dead.

8 He could not catch her by the waist,
  For her silken stays they were tight laced.

9 But he did catch her by the hand,
  And pulled her poor body unto dry land.

10 He took three taets o her bonnie yellow hair,
   To make harp strings they were so rare.

11 The very first tune that the bonnie harp played
   Was The aldest has cuisten the youngest away.

X

Dr Joseph Robertson's Note-Book, January 1, 1830, p. 7.

I see a lady in the dam,
  Binnorie, oh Binnorie

She shenes as sweet as ony swan.
  I the bonny milldams o Binnorie

Y

Communicated to Percy, April 7, 1770, and April
19, 1775, by the Rev. P. Parsons, of Wye, near Ashford,
Kent: "taken down from the mouth of the spinning-
wheel, if I may be allowed the expression."

1 There was a king lived in the North Country,
    Hey down down dery down
  There was a king lived in the North Country,
    And the bough it was bent to me
  There was a king lived in the North Country,
  And he had daughters one, two, three.
    I'll prove true to my love,
    If my love will prove true to me.

2 He gave the eldest a gay gold ring,
  But he gave the younger a better thing.

3 He bought the younger a beaver hat;
  The eldest she thought much of that.

4 'Oh sister, oh sister, let us go run,
  To see the ships come sailing along!'

5 And when they got to the sea-side brim,
  The eldest pushed the younger in.

6 'Oh sister, oh sister, lend me your hand,
  I'll make you heir of my house and land.'

7 'I'll neither lend you my hand nor my glove,
  Unless you grant me your true-love.'

8 Then down she sunk and away she swam,
  Untill she came to the miller's mill-dam.

9 The miller's daughter sat at the mill-door,
  As fair as never was seen before.

10 'Oh father, oh father, there swims a swan,
   Or else the body of a dead woman.'

11 The miller he ran with his fishing hook,
   To pull the fair maid out o the brook.

12 'Wee'll hang the miller upon the mill-gate,
   For drowning of my sister Kate.'

Z

'The Twa Sisters,' a variety of **R**, was derived from
ladies in New York, and by them from a cousin.

1 There was a man lived in the West,
    Sing bow down, bow down
  There was a man lived in the West,
    The bow was bent to me

There was a man lived in the West,
He loved his youngest daughter best;
  So you be true to your own true-love
  And I'll be true to thee.

2 He gave the youngest a beaver hat;
　The eldest she was mad at that.

3 He gave the youngest a gay gold ring;
　The eldest she had nothing.

4 As they stood by the river's brim,
　The eldest pushed the youngest in.

5 'Oh dear sister, hand me your hand,
　And I'll give you my house and land.

6 'Oh dear sister, hand me your glove,
　And you shall have my own true-love.'

7 First she sank and then she swam,
　She swam into the miller's dam.

8 The miller, with his line and hook,
　He caught her by the petticoat.

9 He robbed her of her gay gold ring,
　And then he threw her back again.

10 The miller, he was burnt in flame,
　The eldest sister fared the same.

———◆———

A. b. 1^1. went a-playing.
　Burden^2. a downe-o.
c. 1^1. went a-playing.
　Burden$^{1,\ 2}$. With a hey down, down, a down,
　down-a.
　4^2. Till oat-meal and salt grow both on a tree.
　6^1. ran hastily down the clift.
　6^2. And up he took her without any life.
　13^2. Moll Symns.
　$14^1, 15^1$. Then he bespake.
　17^2. And let him go i the devil's name.
d. 1^1. went a-playing. 1^2. ships sailing in.
　2^1. into.
　3^2. me up on.
　6^2. withouten life.
B. a. 26, 27, 28. An it *has been written in as a conjec-*
　tural emendation by Jamieson, he did it play, $^{it}/_{he}$
　playd; *and it is adopted by Jamieson in his printed*
　copy: see below, **d** 26, 27, 28.
b. *The first stanza only, agreeing with* **a** 1, *is given by*
　Anderson, Nichols's Illustrations, VII, 178.
c. *Evidently a copy of Mrs Brown's version, and in*
　Scott's MS. it has the air, as all the Tytler-Brown
　ballads had. Still it has but twenty-three stanzas,
　whereas Dr Anderson gives fifty-eight lines as the
　extent of the Tytler-Brown copy of 'The Cruel Sis-
　ter' (Nichols, Illus. Lit. Hist., *VII, 178). This,*
　counting the first stanza, with the burden, as four
　lines, according to the arrangement in Scott's MS.,
　would tally exactly with the Jamieson-Brown MS.,
　B a.
　It would seem that **B c** *had been altered by somebody*
　in order to remove the absurd combination of sea
　and mill-dam; the invitation to go see the ships come
　to land, **B a** 7, *is omitted, and "the deep milldam"*

substituted, in 8, for "yon sea-stran." *Stanza 17 of*
c, "They raisd her," *etc., cited below, occurs in*
Pinkerton, N 20, *and is more likely to be his than*
anybody's.
　2^1. brooch and ring. 2^2. abune a' thing.
　3^1. wooed . . . with glove and knife.
　3^2. looed the second.
　5^2. she well nigh brest.
　7. *wanting.*
　8^2. led her to the deep mill-dam.
　9^2. Her cruel sister pushd her in.
　11^2. And I'll mak ye.
　12. *wanting.*
　14^1. Shame fa the hand that I shall tak.
　15^1. gowden hair. 15^2. gar . . . maiden ever mair.
　16. *wanting.*
　17^1. Then out and cam. 17^2. swimming down.
　18^1. O father, haste and draw.
　19^1. his dam. 19^2. And then. (?)
Instead of 20–22:
　　They raisd her wi meikle dole and care,
　　Pale was her cheek and green was her hair.

　24^1. that corpse upon.
　25^2. he's strung.
　$26^1, 27^1, 28^1$, *for* tune, line, *in the copy (MS. has*
　tune).
　27^1. The next. 28^1. The last. 28^2. fause Ellen.
　"Note by Ritson. 'The fragment of a very different
　copy of this ballad has been communicated to J.
　R. by a friend at Dublin.'" *[J. C. Walker, no*
　doubt.]
d. Jamieson, Popular Ballads and Songs, I, 48, *says*
　that he gives his text verbatim as it was taken from
　the recitation of the lady in Fifeshire (Mrs Brown),

to whom both he and Scott were so much indebted. That this is not to be understood with absolute strictness will appear from the variations which are subjoined. Jamieson adds that he had received another copy from Mrs Arrott of Aberbrothick, "but as it furnished no readings by which the text could have been materially improved," it was not used. Both Jamieson and Scott substitute the "Binnorie" burden, "the most common and popular," says Scott, "for the one given by Mrs Brown, with which Mrs Arrott's agreed. It may be added that Jamieson's interpolations are stanzas 20, 21, 27, etc., and not, as he says (I, 49), 19, 20, 27, etc. These interpolations also occur as such in the manuscript.

1^1. sisters livd.
2^2 aboon.
3^2. he loved.
4^2. and sair envied.
5^1. Intill her bower she coudna.
5^2. maistly brast.
11^2. mak ye.
14^2. me o.
16^1. omits an.
16^2. came to the mouth o yon mill-dam.
18^2. There's.
20^2. that was.
22^2. that were.
26^1. it did.
27^1. it playd seen.
28^1. thirden tane that it.

A copy in Motherwell's MS., p. 239, is derived from Jamieson's printed edition. It omits the interpolated stanzas, and makes a few very slight changes.

C. Scott's account of his edition is as follows (II, 143, later ed., III, 287):
"It is compiled from a copy in Mrs Brown's MS., intermixed with a beautiful fragment, of fourteen verses, transmitted to the editor by J. C. Walker, Esq., the ingenious historian of the Irish bards. Mr Walker, at the same time, favored the editor with the following note: 'I am indebted to my departed friend, Miss Brooke, for the foregoing pathetic fragment. Her account of it was as follows: This song was transcribed, several years ago, from the memory of an old woman, who had no recollection of the concluding verses; probably the beginning may also be lost, as it seems to commence abruptly.' The first verse and burden of the fragment run thus:

"'O sister, sister, reach thy hand!
Hey ho, my Nanny, O
And you shall be heir of all my land.

While the swan swims bonny, O!'"

Out of this stanza, or the corresponding one in Mrs Brown's copy, Scott seems to have made his 9, 10.

'The Cruel Sister,' "Scotch Ballads, Materials for Border Minstrelsy," No 16; communicated to Scott by Major Henry Hutton, Royal Artillery, December 24, 1802 (Letters, I, No 77), as recollected by his father "and the family."

1 There were twa sisters in a bowr,
Binnorie, O Binnorie
The eldest was black and the youngest fair.
By the bonny milldams o Binnorie

After 13 (or as 14):
Your rosie cheeks and white hause-bane
Garrd me bide lang maiden at hame.

After 15:
The miller's daughter went out wi speed
To fetch some water to make her bread.

After 17:
He coud not see her fingers sma,
For the goud rings they glistend a'.

He coud na see her yellow hair
For pearlin and jewels that were so rare.

And when he saw her white hause-bane
Round it hung a gouden chain.

He stretched her owt-our the bra [139]
And moanëd her wi mekle wa.

"Then, at the end, introduce the following" (which, however, are not traditional).

The last tune the harp did sing,
'And yonder stands my false sister Alison.

'O listen, listen, all my kin,
'T was she wha drownd me in the lin.'

And when the harp this song had done
It brast a' o pieces oer the stane.

"Alison. The writer of these additional stanzas understands the name was Alison, and not Helen." Alison occurs in D, K.
E. "My mother used to sing this song." Sharpe's Ballad Book, ed. of 1880, note, p. 129.
F. 2^2. An wooer.

G. 2^1. strand, *with sand written above: sand in* 3^1.

I. 1^2. *var. in* MS. There was a knicht and he loved them bath.

    7. *The following stanza was subsequently written on an opposite blank page,—perhaps derived from* **D** 8:

> Foul fa the hand that I wad take,
> To twin me and my warld's make.

10^2. a *was, perhaps, meant to be expunged, but is only a little blotted.*

10^2. *Read: for water.*

11^2. *var. a lady or a milk-white swan.*

12, 13 *were written in later than the rest; at the same time, apparently, as the stanza above* (7).

K. *Found among Mr Kinloch's papers by Mr Macmath, and inserted by him as a note on p. 59, Vol.* II, *of Kinloch's MSS. The order of the stanzas is there, wrongly, inverted.*

I wad give you, *is the beginning of a new stanza (as seen above).*

1^2. *var.* I wad give you.

1^2. And I'll gie the hail o my father's land.

2. The first tune that the bonnie fiddle playd, 'Hang my sister Alison,' it said.

3. 'I wad gie you.'

L. a. *These fragments were communicated to* Notes and Queries, *April 3, 1852, by* "G. A. C.," *who had heard 'The Miller's Melody' sung by an old lady in his childhood, and who represents himself as probably the last survivor of those who had enjoyed the privilege of listening to her ballads. We may, therefore, assign this version to the latter part of the 18th century. The two four-line stanzas were sung to "a slow, quaint strain."* Two *others which followed were not remembered, "but their purport was that the body 'stopped hard by a miller's mill,' and that this 'miller chanced to come by,' and took it out of the water 'to make a melodye.'"* G. A. C. *goes on to say:* "My venerable friend's tune here became a more lively one, and the time quicker; but I can only recollect a few of the couplets, and these not correctly nor in order of sequence, in which the transformation of the lady into a viol is described."

b. *Some stanzas of this four-line version, with a ludicrous modern supplement, are given in 'The Scouring of the White Horse,' p. 161, as from the Welsh marshes. Five out of the first six verses are there said to be very old indeed, "the rest all patchwork by different hands." Mr Hughes has kindly informed me that he derived the ballad from his father, who had originally learned it at Ruthyn when a boy. What is material here follows:*

1 O it was not a pheasant cock,
    Nor yet a pheasant hen,
But O it was a lady fair
    Came swimming down the stream.

2 An ancient harper passing by
    Found this poor lady's body,
To which his pains he did apply
    To make a sweet melódy.

3 To cat-gut dried he her inside,
    He drew out her back-bone,
And made thereof a fiddle sweet
    All for to play upon.

4 And all her hair, so long and fair,
    That down her back did flow,
O he did lay it up with care,
    To string his fiddle bow.

5 And what did he with her fingers,
    Which were so straight and small?
O he did cut them into pegs,
    To screw up his fiddoll.

6 Then forth went he, as it might be,
    Upon a summer's day,
And met a goodly company,
    Who asked him in to play.

7 Then from her bones he drew such tones
    As made their bones to ache,
They sounded so like human groans
    Their hearts began to quake.

8 They ordered him in ale to swim,—
    For sorrow's mighty dry,—
And he to share their wassail fare
    Essayd right willingly.

9 He laid his fiddle on a shelf
    In that old manor-hall,
It played and sung all by itself,
    And thus sung this fiddoll:

10 'There sits the squire, my worthy sire,
    A-drinking hisself drunk,' etc., etc.

Anna Seward to Walter Scott, April 25–29, 1802: Letters addressed to Sir Walter Scott, I, No 54, *Abbotsford.* "The Binnorie of endless repetition has nothing truly pathetic, and the ludicrous use made of the drowned sister's body is well burlesqued in a ridiculous ballad, which I first heard sung, with farcial grimace, in my infancy [born 1747], thus:

1 And O was it a pheasant cock,
  Or eke a pheasant hen?
Or was it and a gay lady,
  Came swimming down the stream?

2 O it was not a pheasant cock,
  Or eke a pheasant hen,
But it was and a gay lady,
  Came swimming down the stream.

3 And when she came to the mill-dam
  The miller he took her body,
And with it he made him a fiddling thing,
  To make him sweet melody.

4 And what did he do with her fingers small?
He made of them pegs to his vial.

5 And what did he do with her nose-ridge?
Why to his fiddle he made it a bridge.
  Sing, O the damnd mill-dam, O

6 And what did he do with her veins so blue?
Why he made him strings his fiddle unto.

7 And what did he do with her two shins?
Why to his vial they dancd Moll Sims.

8 And what did he do with her two sides?
Why he made of them sides to his fiddle
  besides.

9 And what did he do with her great toes?
Why what he did with them that nobody
  knows.
  Sing, O the damnd mill-dam, O

For 4, 5, 6, 7, see **A** 8, 9, 10, 13.

N. *Pinkerton tells us, in the Preface to his* Ancient Scottish Poems, *p. cxxxi, that* "Binnorie is one half from tradition, one half by the editor." *One fourth and three fourths would have been a more exact apportionment. The remainder of his text, which is wholly of his invention, is as follows:*

'Gae saddle to me my swiftest steid;
Her fere, by my fae, for her dethe sall bleid.'
A page cam rinning out owr the lie:
'O heavie tydings I bring,' quoth he.
'My luvely lady is far awa gane;

We weit the fairy hae her tane.
Her sister gaed wood wi dule and rage;
Nocht cold we do her mind to suage.
"O Isabel, my sister," she wold cry,
"For thee will I weip, for thee will I die."
Till late yestrene, in an elric hour,
She lap frae aft the hichest touir.'
'Now sleip she in peace,' quoth the gallant
squire;
'Her dethe was the maist that I cold require.
But I'll main for the, my Isabel deir,
Fall mony a dreiry day, bot weir.'

20. *This stanza occurs also in* **B c** (17), *and was perhaps borrowed from Pinkerton by the reviser of that copy.*

O. a. *Buchan's note,* ii, 320: "I have seen four or five different versions of this ballad, but none in this dress, nor with the same chorus . . . . The old woman from whose recitation I took it down says she had heard another way of it, quite local, whose burden runs thus:

  'Ever into Buchanshire, vari vari O.'"

1^2. hae courted.

b. *Mr Christie has* "epitomized" *Buchan's copy (omitting stanzas 9–12), with these few slight alterations from the singing of a Banffshire woman, who died in 1860, at the age of nearly eighty:*
Burden: It's hey, etc.
2^2. And he courted the eldest wi mony other
  thing.
3^1. But it fell.
5^2. And the eldest.

P. b. *This stanza only:*

  There livd twa sisters in a bower,
    Hey my bonnie Annie O
  There cam a lover them to woo.
    And the swan swims bonnie O,
    And the swan swims bonnie O

Q. *The burden is given thus in* Pop. Tales of the West Highlands, iv, 125:

  Oh ochone, ochone a rie,
    On the banks of the Banna, ochone a rie.

R. a. *The title 'The Three Sisters,' and perhaps the first stanza, belongs rather to No 1* **A, B,** *p. 4f.*
b.   1. A farmer there lived in the north countree,
      Bo down
    And he had daughters one, two, three.

And I'll be true unto my love, if he'll be
        true unto me

(*The burden is given as* Bo down, ho down, *etc., in*
Popular Tales of the West Highlands, IV, 125.)
Between 1 and 2 **b** *has:*
    The eldest she had a lover come,
    And he fell in love with the younger one.

    He bought the younger a ...
    The elder she thought ...

3. *wanting.*
4[1]. The sisters they walkt by the river brim.
6[2]. my true love.

[141]

8. The miller's daughter was at the door,
        As sweet as any gillyflower.

9. O father, O father, there swims a swain,
        And he looks like a gentleman.

10. The miller he fetcht his line and hook,
        And he fisht the fair maiden out of the
brook.

11[1]. O miller, I'll give you guineas ten.

12. The miller he took her guineas ten,
        And then he popt her in again.

13[1]. . . . behind his back gate,
    [2]. the farmer's daughter Kate.

Instead of 14:

    The sister she sailed over the sea,
    And died an old maid of a hundred and three.

    The lover became a beggar man,
    And he drank out of a rusty tin can.

b   8, 11, 12, 14, 15 *are cited in* Popular Tales
of the West Highlands, IV, 127.
c.   1. A varmer he lived in the west countree,
            Hey-down, bow-down
        A varmer he lived in the west countree,
        And he had daughters one, two, and dree.
        And I'll be true to my love,
        If my love'll be true to me.

2, 3. *wanting.*
4[1]. As thay war walking by the river's brim.
5[1]. pray gee me thy hand.
7[1]. So down she sank and away she swam.
8. The miller's daughter stood by the door,
        As fair as any gilly-flower.
9.   here swims a swan,
        Very much like a drownded gentlewoman.
10.   The miller he fot his pole and hook,
        And he fished the fair maid out of the
brook.
11[1]. O miller, I'll gee thee guineas ten.
12[2]. pushed the fair maid in again.
Between 12 and 13 **c** *has,*

    But the crowner he cum and the justice too,
    With a hue and a cry and a hullaballoo.

    They hanged the miller beside his own gate
    For drowning the varmer's daughter, Kate.

Instead of 14:

    The sister she fled beyond the seas,
    And died an old maid among black savagees.

    So I've ended my tale of the west countree,
    And they calls it the Barkshire Tragedee.

S. 1[3]. MS., Orless.
T. "Sung to a peculiar and beautiful air." *Allingham,*
    p. xxxiii.
V. 2, 3. *In the* MS. *thus:*
        There came . . .
            Benorie . . .
        He's gien . . .
            At the merry . . .
        Because that . . .
            At the merry . . .

    8, 9. *In the* MS. *thus:*
        She set . . .
            Benorie . . .
        To wash . . .
            At the . . .
        But the eldest
            The bonny . . .

    From 18 on, the burden is
        O Benorie, O Benorie.

APPENDIX

Additional Copies

MS. of Thomas Wilkie, p. 1, in "Scotch Ballads, Materials for Border Minstrelsy," No 32; taken down "from a Miss Nancy Brockie, Bemerside." 1813.

1 THERE were twa sisters sat in a bower,
  By Nera and by Nora
The youngest was the fairest flower.
  Of all the mill-dams of Bennora

2 It happened upon a bonnie summer's day
The eldest to the youngest did say:
  In the bonnie mill-dams of Bennora

3 'We must go and we shall go
To see our brother's ships come to land.'
  In, etc. (and throughout).

4 'I winna go and I downa go,
For weeting the corks o my coal-black shoes.'

5 She set her foot into a rash-bush,
To see how tightly she was dressd.

6 But the youngest sat upon a stone,
But the eldest threw the youngest in.

7 'O sister, oh sister, come lend me your hand,
And draw my life into dry land!'

8 'You shall not have one bit o my hand;
Nor will I draw you to dry land.'

9 'O sister, O sister, come lend me your hand,
And you shall have Sir John and all his land.'

10 'You shall not have one bit o my hand,
And I'll have Sir John and all his land.

11 The miller's daughter, clad in red,
Came for some water to bake her bread.

12 'O father, O father, go fish your mill-dams,
For there either a swan or a drownd woman.'

13 You wad not have seen one bit o her waist,
The body was swelld, and the stays strait laced.

14 You wad not have seen one bit o her neck,
The chains of gold they hang so thick.

15 He has taen a tait of her bonnie yellow hair,
He's tied it to his fiddle-strings there.

16 The verry first spring that that fiddle playd
Was, Blest be [the] queen, my mother! [it] has said.

17 The verry next spring that that fiddle playd
Was, Blest be Sir John, my own true-love!

18 The very next spring that that fiddle playd
Was, Burn my sister for her sins!

———◆———

4^2. *Written at first* my black heeld shoes.
12^2. swain. 17^2. thy own.

11

THE CRUEL BROTHER

A. '[The] Cruel Brother, or the Bride's Testament.'
a. Alex. Fraser Tytler's Brown MS. **b.** Jamieson's
Popular Ballads, I, 66.
B. The Kinloch MSS, I, 21.
C. 'Ther waur three ladies,' Harris MS., p. 11 b.
D. a. *Notes and Queries*, 1st S., VI, 53. **b.** 2d S., V,
171.
E. *Notes and Queries*, 4th S., V, 105.
F. 'The Three Knights,' Gilbert's *Ancient Christmas
Carols*, 2d ed., p. 68.
G. 'Fine Flowers of the Valley.' **a.** Herd's MSS, I,
41. **b.** Herd's *Scottish Songs*, 1776, I, 88.

H. Fragment appended to **G**.
I. 'The Cruel Brother,' the Kinloch MSS, I, 27.
J. As current in County Meath, Ireland, about
1860.
K. *Notes and Queries*, 4th S., IV, 517.
L. 'The King of Fairies,' Campbell MSS, II, 19.
M. 'The Roses grow sweet aye,' Campbell MSS, II,
26.
N. 'The Bride's Testamen,' Dr Joseph Robertson's
Note-Book, January 1, 1830, one stanza.

[142]   **A a** was obtained directly from Mrs Brown
of Falkland, in 1800, by Alexander Fraser
Tytler. Jamieson says that he gives **b** verbatim
from the recitation of Mrs Arrott; but it would
seem that this must have been a slip of memory,
for the two agree except in half a dozen words.
B, C, I, J are now for the first time printed. **G**
only was taken down earlier than the present
century.

Aytoun remarks (1858): "This is, perhaps,
the most popular of all the Scottish ballads,
being commonly recited and sung even at the
present day." The copy which he gives, I, 232,
was "taken down from recitation," but is never-
theless a compound of **G** and **A b**, with a few
unimportant variations, proceeding, no doubt,
from imperfect recollection.[*] The copy in
Dixon's *Ancient Poems, Ballads, and Songs*, p.
56, repeated in Bell's volume of the same title,
p. 50, is Gilbert's **F**. Dixon informs us that the
ballad was (in 1846) still popular amongst the
peasantry in the west of England. Cunningham

gives us a piece called 'The Three Ladies of Lei-
than Ha,' *Songs of Scotland*, II, 87, which he
would fain have us believe that he did not
know he had written himself. "The common
copies of this tragic lyric," he truly says, "differ
very much from this; not so much in the story
itself as in the way it is told."

All versions but **K**, which has pretty nearly
lost all point, agree after the opening stanzas.
A–E have three ladies and only one knight; **F**
has three knights and one lady; **G, I, J, K** have
three ladies and three knights [lords in **G**,
"bonny boys" in **I**, the first line being caught
from 'Sir Hugh.'] Three knights are to no pur-
pose; only one knight has anything to do. The
reason for three ladies is, of course, that the
youngest may be preferred to the others,—an
intention somewhat obscured in **B**. The ladies
are in colors in **B, C, I, J**, and this seems to be
the better interpretation in the case of **G**,
though a strict construction of the language
would rather point to the other. The colors are
transferred to the knights in **F** because there is
only one lady. In **K** this is a part of the general
depravation of the ballad.

---

[*]   Aytoun, 1–8 = Herd, 1776, 1–8: 9–13 = Jamieson,
11–15: 14,15 = Herd, 11, 12: 16, 17 = Jamieson, 18, 19:
18, 19 = Herd, 13, 14: 20–24 Jamieson, 21–25.

'Rizzardo bello,' seems to be the same story, with a change of relations such as we often find in ballad poetry. The versions are **A**, Wolf, *Volkslieder aus Venetien*, No 83; **B**, 'Luggieri,' *Contado aretino*, communicated by Giulio Salvatori to the *Rassegna Settimanale*, Rome, 1879, June 22, No 77, p. 485; reprinted in *Romania*, XI, 391, note; repeated by Salvadori in *Giornale di Filologia Romanza*, II, 197; **C**, 'Rizzôl d'Amor,' Guerrini, *Alcuni Canti p. romagnoli*, p. 3, 1880. **D**, 'La Canzóne de 'Nucénzie,' Pitrè e Salomone-Marino, *Archivio per Tradizioni popolari*, I, 213, 1882; **E**, 'Ruggiero,' in Mazzatinti, *Canti p. umbri*, p. 286, Bologna, 1883; first published in *Giornale di Filologia Romanza*, IV, 69.* Rizzardo is conducting his bride home, and on the way kisses her arm, neck, and mouth. Her brother witnesses "questo onore," and thrusts his sword into the happy bridegroom's heart. Rizzardo tells his bride to come on slowly; he will go before to make preparation. He begs his mother to open the doors, for his bride is without, and he is wounded to death. They try to make the bride eat. She says she can neither eat nor drink: she must put her husband to bed. He gives her a ring, saying, Your brother has been the death of me; then another ring, in sign that she is to be wife of two brothers. She answers him as Guldborg answers Ribold, that she would die rather: "Rather die between two knives than be wife of two brothers." This ballad was obtained from a peasant woman of Castagnero. Another version, which unfortunately is not printed, was sung by a woman at Ostiglia on the Po.

Dr Prior remarks that the offence given by not asking a brother's assent to his sister's marriage was in ballad-times regarded as unpardonable. Other cases which show the importance of this preliminary, and the sometimes fatal consequences of omitting it, are: 'Hr. Peder og Mettelille,' Grundtvig, No 78, II, 325, sts 4, 6; 'Jornfruen i Skoven,' *Danske Viser*, III, 99, st. 15; 'Jomfru Ellensborg og Hr. Olof,' *ib.*, III, 316, st. 16; 'Iver Lang og hans Søster,' *ib.*, IV, 87, st. 116; 'Herr Helmer Blaa,' *ib.*, IV, 251, st. 8; 'Jom-

fru Giselmaar,' *ib.*, IV, 309, st. 13. See Prior's *Ancient Danish Ballads*, III, 112, 232f, 416.

There is a very common **German** ballad, 'Graf Friedrich,' in which a bride receives a mortal wound during the bringing-home, but accidentally, and from the bridegroom's hand. The marriage train is going up a hill; the way is narrow; they are crowded; Graf Friedrich's sword shoots from its sheath and wounds the bride. The bridegroom is exceedingly distressed; he tries to stop the bleeding with his shirt; she [143] begs that they may ride slowly. When they reach the house there is a splendid feast, and everything is set before the bride; but she can neither eat nor drink, and only wishes to lie down. She dies in the night. Her father comes in the morning, and, learning what has happened, runs Graf Friedrich through, then drags his body at a horse's heels, and buries it in a bog. Three lilies sprang from the spot, with an inscription announcing that Graf Friedrich was in heaven, and a voice came from the sky commanding that the body should be disinterred. The bridegroom was then buried with his bride, and this act of reparation was attended with other miraculous manifestations. As the ballads stand now, the kinship of 'Graf Friedrich' with 'The Cruel Brother' is not close and cannot be insisted on; still an early connection is not improbable.

The versions of 'Graf Friedrich' are somewhat numerous, and there is a general agreement as to all essentials. They are: **A**, a Nuremberg broadside "of about 1535," which has not been made accessible by a reprint. **B**, a Swiss broadside of 1647, without place, "printed in Seckendorf's *Musenalmanach für* 1808, p. 19;" Uhland, No 122, p. 277; Mittler, No 108; *Wunderhorn*, II, 293 (1857); Erk's *Liederhort*, No 15[a], p. 42; Böhme, No 79, p. 166: also, in *Wunderhorn*, 1808, II, 289, with omission of five stanzas and with many changes; Simrock, No 11, p. 28, omitting four stanzas and with changes; as written down by Goethe for Herder, Düntzer u. Herder, *Briefe Goethes, u. s. w.*, *Aus Herder's Nachlass*, I, 167, with the omission of eight stanzas and with some variations. **C**, *Wunderhorn* (1857), II, 299, from the Schwarzwald, = Erlach, IV, 291, Mittler, No 113. **D**, *Taschenbuch für Dichter, u. s. w.*, Theil

---

* Add a ballad of Rissiäld, Canti popolari Emiliani, Maria Carmi, *Archivio*, XII, 185, No 7.

VIII, 122, from Upper Lusatia, = Erlach, III, 448, Talvj, *Charakteristik*, p. 421. **E**, from the Kuhländchen, Meinert, p. 23, = Mittler, No 109. **F**, Hoffmann u. Richter, *Schlesische V. L.*, No 19, p. 35, = Mittler, No 112, Erk's *Liederhort*, No 15, p. 40. **G**, Zingerle, in Wolf's *Zeitschrift für deutsche Mythologie*, I, 341, from Meran. **H**, from Uckermark, Brandenburg, Mittler, No 114. **I**, Hesse, from oral tradition, Mittler, No 111. **J**, Erk u. Irmer, II, 54, No 54, from the neighborhood of Halle, = Mittler, No 110. **K**, from Estedt, district of Magdeburg, Parisius, p. 31, No 9. An additional variety of 'Graf Friedrich' is in Hruschka u. Toischer, *Deutsche Volkslieder aus Böhmen*, p. 101, No 25.

A pallikar, who is bringing home his bride, is detained on the way in consequence of his whole train leaving him to go after a stag. The young man, who has never seen his bride's face, reaches over his horse to give her a kiss; his knife disengages itself and wounds her. She begs him to staunch the blood with his handkerchief, praying only to live to see her bridegroom's house. This wish is allowed her; she withdraws the handkerchief from the wound and expires. Dozon, *Chansons p. bulgares*, 'Le baiser fatal,' p. 270, No 49.

A **Danish** ballad, 'Den saarede Jomfru,' Grundtvig, No 244, IV, 474, has this slight resemblance with 'Graf Friedrich:' While a knight is dancing with a princess, his sword glides from the scabbard and cuts her hand. To save her partner from blame, she represents to her father that she had cut herself with her brother's sword. This considerateness so touches the knight (who is, of course, her equal in rank) that he offers her his hand. The Danish story is found also in Norwegian and in Färöe ballads.

Several Slavic ballads bear characteristics resembling 'Graf Friedrich.' **Moravian**, Sušil, 'Nešt'astna svatba,' 'The Unhappy Wedding,' No 89, c, d, pp 85f. A bridegroom is bringing home his bride; his sword slips from the sheath and wounds the bride in the side. He binds up the wound, and begs her to hold out till she comes to the house. The bride can eat nothing, and dies in the night. Her mother comes in the morning with loads of cloth and feathers, is put off when she asks for her daughter, reproaches

the bridegroom for having killed her; he pleads his innocence.

Servian. Karadshitch, I, 309, No 421, 'Jani and Milenko,' belongs to this class, though mixed with portions of at least one other ballad ('Earl Brand'). Milenko wooes the fair Jani, and is favored by her mother and by all her brothers but the youngest. This brother goes hunting, and bids Jani open to nobody while he is away, but Milenko carries her off on his horse. As they are riding over a green hill, a branch of a tree catches in Jani's dress. Milenko attempts to cut the branch off with his knife, but in so doing wounds Jani in the head. Jani binds up the wound, and they go on, and presently meet the youngest brother, who hails Milenko, asks where he got the fair maid, discovers the maid to be his sister, but bids her Godspeed. On reaching his mother's house, Milenko asks that a bed may be prepared for Jani, who is in need of repose. Jani dies in the night, Milenko in the morning. They are buried in one grave; a rose is planted over her, a grape-vine over him, and these intertwine, "as it were Jani with Milenko."

The peculiar testament made by the bride in 'The Cruel Brother,' by which she bequeaths good things to her friends, but ill things to the author of her death, is highly characteristic of ballad poetry. It will be found again in 'Lord Randal,' 'Edward,' and their analogues. Still other ballads with this kind of testament are: 'Frillens Hævn,' Grundtvig, No 208 **C**, 16–18, IV, 207, **D** 3, and the Swedish ballad at p. 208, stanzas 14–17; a young man, stabbed by his leman, whom he was about to give up in order to marry, leaves his lands to his father, his bride-bed to his sister, his gilded couch to his mother, and his knife to his leman, wishing it in her body. 'Møen paa Baalet,' Grundtvig, No 109 **A**, 18–21, II, 587; Ole, falsely accused by her brother, and condemned to be burned, gives her mother her silken sark, her sister her shoes, her father her horse, and her brother her knife, with the same wish. 'Kong Valdemar og hans Søster,' Grundtvig, No 126, III, 97, has a testament in **A–E** and **I**; in **I**, 14–19 (III, 912), Liden Kirsten bequeaths her knife, with the same imprecation, to the queen, who, in the other copies, is her unrelenting foe: so Lillelin to Herr

Adelbrand, *Danske Viser*, III, 386, No 162, 16–18, Kristensen, I, 262, No 100, A 20–23, having been dragged at a horse's heels in resentment of a taunt. 'Hr. Adelbrand,' Kristensen, *Jyske Folkeminder*, X, 227, 232, No 54, A, 20ff, F, 10ff. = 'Herr Radibrand och lilla Lena,' 'Skön Helena och riddaren Hildebrand,' Lagus, *Nyländska Folkvisor*, I, 89, No 25, a, b.* 'Hr. Adelbrant og jomfru Lindelil' with a testament, again in *Skattegraveren*, I, 5, No I, and V, 17, No 12. 'Hustru og Mands Moder,' Grundtvig, No. 84, II, 404, has a testament in A, B, D, H, and [4] in the last three a bequest of shoes or sark to a cruel mother-in-law or foster-mother, with the wish that she may have no peace or much pain in the wearing. 'Catarina de Lió,' Briz y Candi, *Cansons de la Terra*, I, 209; Milá, *Romancerillo Catalan*, 2d ed., No 307, p. 291, 'Trato feroz,' seven versions. Catherine has been beaten by her mother-in-law while in a delicate state. When she is at the point of death, the mother-in-law asks what doctor she will have and what will she will make. "My will," says Catherine, "will not please you much. Send back my velvet dress to my father's; my gala dress give my sister; give my working dress to the maid, my jewels to the Virgin." "And what will you leave to me?" "What I leave you will not please you much: my husband to be hanged, my mother-in-law to be quartered, and my sister-in-law to be burned."[†] In 'Testamento della Moglie,' Nigra, No 25, p. 159, a wife who has been gone from home in pursuit of her pleasure is so beaten by her husband on her return that she dies. She leaves valuable legacies to her children and a rope to him. 'Le Testament de Marion,' another version of this story from the south of France, Uchaud, Gard, *Poésies pop. de la France*, MS., IV, fol. 283, bequeaths "my laces to my sister Marioun, my prettiest gowns to my sister Jeanneton; to my rascal of a husband three fine cords, and, if that is not enough (to hang him), the hem of his shirt." Another version, 'La belo Marioun,' in Laroche, *Folklore du Lauraguais*, p. 247. The

Portuguese ballad of 'Dona Helena' rather implies than expresses the imprecation: Braga, *C. P. do Archipelago Açoriano*, p. 225, No 15, p. 227, No 16; Almeida-Garrett, III, 56; Hartung, I, 233–43, No 18. Helena leaves her husband's house when near childbirth, out of fear of his mother. Her husband, who does not know her reason, goes after her, and compels her to return on horseback, though she has just borne a son. The consequences are what might be expected, and Helena desires to make her shrift and her will. She leaves one thing to her oldest sister, another to her youngest. "And your boy?" "To your bitch of a mother, cause of my woes." "Rather to yours," says the husband, "for I shall have to kill mine" (so Braga; Garrett differs somewhat). 'Die Frau zur Weissenburg'[‡] (A), Uhland, p. 287, No 123 B, Scherer's *Jungbrunnen*, p. 94, No 29; 'Das Lied von der Löwenburg' (B), Simrock, p. 65, No 27; 'Hans Steutlinger' (C), *Wunderhorn*, II, 168 (1857), all one story, have a bitterly sarcastic testament. A lady instigates her paramour to kill her husband. The betrayed man is asked to whom he will leave his children [commit, A, bequeath, B, C]. "To God Almighty, for he knows who they are." "Your property?" "To the poor, for the rich have enough." "Your wife?" "To young Count Frederic, whom she always liked more than me (A)." "Your castle?" "To the flames." Sušil, 'Matka travička,' pp 154, 155, No 157, two versions: A mother, not liking her son's wife, puts before him a glass of mead, and poison before the wife. God exchanges them, and the son drinks the poison. The son makes his will. To his brother he leaves four black horses, to his sister four cows and four calves, to his wife a house. "And to me?" the mother asks. "To you that big stone and the deep Danube, because you have poisoned me and parted me from my beloved."

In some cases there is no trace of animosity towards the person who has caused the testator's death; as in 'El testamento de Amelia' (who has been poisoned by her mother), Milá, *Observaciones*, p. 103, No 5, Briz y Saltó, *Can-*

---

* 'Adelbrand' is No 311 of *Danmarks gamle Folkeviser*, V, II, 297, ed. Olrik, of which the versions that have been cited in this book are B, K e, G e, F, K b, I. There is a testament in other copies of the same. Also in No 320, not yet published.

† Cf. Bladé, *Poésies pop. de la Gascogne*, II, 51.

‡ For 'Frau von Weissenburg,' 'Frau von der Löwenburg,' 'Junker Hans Steutlinger,' see Erk, ed. Böhme, Nos. 102, 103, I, 360ff.

sons de la Terra, II, 197 (two copies), No 220, p. 185, of the second edition of *Romancerillo Catalan*, with readings of eleven other copies, A–F, A_1–F_1. In B_1 only have we an ill bequest to the mother. After leaving her mother a rosary, upon the mother's asking again, What for me? the dying lady says, I will leave you my chopines, clogs, so that when you come downstairs they may break your neck. Also 'Herren Båld,' Afzelius, I, 76, No 16 (new ed. I, 59, No 15); a Swedish form of 'Frillens Hævn,' Grundtvig, IV, 203; 'Renée le Glaz' and 'Ervoanik Le Lintier,' Luzel, C. P. de la Basse Bretagne, I, 405, 539, 553; 'Elveskud,' Grundtvig, No 47, IV, 836ff, L 14, 15, M 17, O 17–19; 'Rævens Arvegods,' Kristensen, *Skattegraveren*, II, 192ff, Nos 774–78, and VIII, 209, No 810. There are also simple testaments where there is no occasion for an ill remembrance, as in 'Ribold og Guldborg,' Grundtvig, No 82, I, K, L, U, X, Æ, Kristensen, II, No 84 B; 'Pontplancoat,' Luzel, I, 383, 391. And, again, there are parodies of these wills. Thus the fox makes his will: Grundtvig, *Gamle danske Minder*, 1854, 'Mikkels Arveg-ods,' p. 24, and p. 25 a copy from a manuscript three hundred years old; Kristensen, *Jyske Folkeviser*, II, 324, No 90; 'Reven og Bjönnen,' 'Reven og Nils fiskar,' Landstad, Nos 85, 86, p. 637, 639: the robin, 'Robin's Tesment,' Buchan, I, 273, Herd's MSS, I, 154, *Scottish Songs* (1776), II, 166, Chambers' *Popular Rhymes*, p. 38, "new edition," 'Le Testament du Chien,' Bédier, *Les Fabliaux*, 2d ed., p. 473; 'Testament de la vieille Jument,' 'de la vieille Truie,' 'de la Chèvre,' Luzel, *Chansons pop. de la Basse–Bretagne*, II, 88–97. 'The Robin's Last Will,' Miss M. H. Mason's *Nursery Rhymes and Country Songs*, p. 41: and the (she) ass, Testament de l'Âne, Buchon, *Noels et Chants pop. de la Franche-Comté*, p. 89, No 28; and elsewhere.

Translated in Grundtvig's *Engelske og skotske Folkeviser*, No 33, p. 212, F, with use of A and G b; Aytoun's copy, with omissions, by Rosa Warrens, *Schottische Volkslieder der Vorzeit*, No 17, p. 80; after Allingham and others, by Knortz, *Lieder und Romanzen Alt-Englands*, No 5, p. 16.

A

a. Alex. Fraser Tytler's Brown MS. b. Jamieson's *Popular Ballads*, I, 66, purporting to be from the recitation of Mrs Arrot of Aberbrothick.

1 THERE was three ladies playd at the ba,
    With a hey ho and a lillie gay
There came a knight and played oer them a'.
    As the primrose spreads so sweetly

2 The eldest was baith tall and fair,
    But the youngest was beyond compare.

3 The midmost had a graceful mien,
    But the youngest lookd like beautie's queen.

4 The knight bowd low to a' the three,
    But to the youngest he bent his knee.

5 The ladie turned her head aside,
    The knight he woo'd her to be his bride.

6 The ladie blushd a rosy red,
    And sayd, 'Sir knight, I'm too young to wed.'

7 'O ladie fair, give me your hand,
    And I'll make you ladie of a' my land.'

8 'Sir knight, ere ye my favor win,
    You maun get consent frae a' my kin.'

9 He's got consent frae her parents dear,
    And likewise frae her sisters fair.

10 He's got consent frae her kin each one,
    But forgot to spiek to her brother John.

11 Now, when the wedding day was come,
    The knight would take his bonny bride home.

12 And many a lord and many a knight
    Came to behold that ladie bright.

13 And there was nae man that did her see,
    But wishd himself bridegroom to be.

14 Her father dear led her down the stair,
   And her sisters twain they kissd her there.

15 Her mother dear led her thro the closs,
   And her brother John set her on her horse.

16 She leand her oer the saddle-bow,
   To give him a kiss ere she did go.

17 He has taen a knife, baith lang and sharp,
   And stabbd that bonny bride to the heart.

18 She hadno ridden half thro the town,
   Until her heart's blude staind her gown.

19 'Ride softly on,' says the best young man,
   'For I think our bonny bride looks pale and wan.'

20 'O lead me gently up yon hill,
   And I'll there sit down, and make my will.'

21 'O what will you leave to your father dear?'
   'The silver-shode steed that brought me here.'

22 'What will you leave to your mother dear?'
   'My velvet pall and my silken gear.'

23 'What will you leave to your sister Anne?'
   'My silken scarf and my gowden fan.'

24 'What will you leave to your sister Grace?'
   'My bloody cloaths to wash and dress.'

25 'What will you leave to your brother John?'
   'The gallows-tree to hang him on.'

26 'What will you leave to your brother John's
   wife?'
   'The wilderness to end her life.'

27 This ladie fair in her grave was laid,
   And many a mass was oer her said.

28 But it would have made your heart right sair,
   To see the bridegroom rive his haire.

B

Kinloch's MSS, i, 21, from Mary Barr, May, 1827,
Clydesdale.

1 A GENTLEMAN cam oure the sea,
   Fine flowers in the valley
 And he has courted ladies three.
   With the light green and the yellow

2 One o them was clad in red:
   He asked if she wad be his bride.

3 One o them was clad in green:
   He asked if she wad be his queen.

4 The last o them was clad in white
   He asked if she wad be his heart's delight.

5 'Ye may ga ask my father, the king:
   Sae maun ye ask my mither, the queen.

6 'Sae maun ye ask my sister Anne:
   And dinna forget my brither John.'

7 He has asked her father, the king:
   And sae did he her mither, the queen.

8 And he has asked her sister Anne:
   But he has forgot her brother John.

9 Her father led her through the ha,
   Her mither danced afore them a'.

10 Her sister Anne led her through the closs,
   Her brither John set her on her horse.

11 It's then he drew a little penknife,
   And he reft the fair maid o her life.

12 'Ride up, ride up,' said the foremost man;
   'I think our bride comes hooly on.'

13 'Ride up, ride up,' said the second man;
   'I think our bride looks pale and wan.'

14 Up than cam the gay bridegroom,
   And straucht unto the bride he cam.

15 'Does your side-saddle sit awry?
   Or does your steed . . .

16 'Or does the rain run in your glove?
 Or wad ye chuse anither love?'

17 'The rain runs not in my glove,
 Nor will I e'er chuse anither love.

18 'But O an I war at Saint Evron's well,
 There I wad licht, and drink my fill!

19 'Oh an I war at Saint Evron's closs,
 There I wad licht, and bait my horse!'

20 Whan she cam to Saint Evron's well,
 She dought na licht to drink her fill.

21 Whan she cam to Saint Evron's closs,
 The bonny bride fell aff her horse.

22 'What will ye leave to your father, the king?'
 'The milk-white steed that I ride on.'

23 'What will ye leave to your mother, the queen?'
 'The bluidy robes that I have on.'

24 'What will ye leave to your sister Anne?'
 'My gude lord, to be wedded on.'

25 'What will ye leave to your brither John?'
 'The gallows pin to hang him on.'

26 'What will ye leave to your brither's wife?'
 'Grief and sorrow a' the days o her life.'

27 'What will ye leave to your brither's bairns?'
 'The meal-pock to hang oure the arms.'

28 Now does she neither sigh nor groan:
 She lies aneath yon marble stone.

C

Harris MS., p. 11 b, No 7.

There waur three la - dies in a ha, Hech hey___ an the lil - y gey,
By cam a knicht, an he wooed them a.___ An the rose is aye the red - der aye.

1 THERE waur three ladies in a ha,
 Hech hey an the lily gey
By cam a knicht, an he wooed them a'.
 An the rose is aye the redder aye

2 The first ane she was cled in green;
 'Will you fancy me, an be my queen?'

3 'You may seek me frae my father dear,
 An frae my mither, wha did me bear.

4 'You may seek me frae my sister Anne,
 But no, no, no frae my brither John.'

5 The niest ane she was cled in yellow;
 'Will you fancy me, an be my marrow?'

6 'Ye may seek me frae my father dear,
 An frae my mither, wha did me bear.

7 'Ye may seek me frae my sister Anne,
 But no, no, no frae my brither John.'

8 The niest ane she was cled in red:
 'Will ye fancy me, an be my bride?'

9 'Ye may seek me frae my father dear,
 An frae my mither wha did me bear.

10 'Ye may seek me frae my sister Anne,
 An dinna forget my brither John.'

11 He socht her frae her father, the king,
 An he socht her frae her mither, the queen.

12 He socht her frae her sister Anne,
 But he forgot her brither John.

13 Her mither she put on her goun,
 An her sister Anne preened the ribbons doun.

14 Her father led her doon the close,
   An her brither John set her on her horse.
   * * * * *

15 Up an spak our foremost man:
   'I think our bonnie bride's pale an wan.'
   * * * * *

16 'What will ye leave to your father dear?'
   'My . . . . . an my . . . . . chair.'

17 'What will ye leave to your mither dear?'
   'My silken screen I was wont to wear.'

18 'What will ye leave to your sister Anne?'
   'My silken snood an my golden fan.'

19 'What will you leave to your brither John?'
   'The gallows tree to hang him on.'

D

Notes and Queries, 1st S., vi, 53, 2d S., v, 171. As sung by a lady who was a native of County Kerry, Ireland.

1 THERE were three ladies playing at ball,
   Farin-dan-dan and farin-dan-dee
   There came a white knight, and he wooed
      them all.
   With adieu, sweet honey, wherever you be

2 He courted the eldest with golden rings, And
      the others with many fine things.
   And adieu, etc.

E

Notes and Queries, 4th S., v, 105. From Forfarshire, W. F.

THERE were three sisters playin at the ba,
   Wi a hech hey an a lillie gay
There cam a knicht an lookt ower the wa'.
   An the primrose springs sae sweetly.
      Sing Annet, an Marret, an fair Maisrie,
      An the dew hangs i the wood, gay ladie.

F

Gilbert's *Ancient Christmas Carols*, 2d ed., p. 68, as
remembered by the editor. West of England.

There did three Knights come___ from the West, With the high and the lil-y oh!

And these three knights___ court-ed one La-dy,___ As the rose was so sweet-ly blown.

1 THERE did three knights come from the west,
  With the high and the lily oh
And these three knights courted one lady.
  As the rose was so sweetly blown

2 The first knight came was all in white,
  And asked of her, if she'd be his delight.

3 The next knight came was all in green,
  And asked of her, if she'd be his queen.

4 The third knight came was all in red,
  And asked of her, if she would wed.

5 'Then have you asked of my father dear,
  Likewise of her who did me bear?

6 'And have you asked of my brother John?
  And also of my sister Anne?'

7 'Yes, I have asked of your father dear,
  Likewise of her who did you bear.

8 'And I have asked of your sister Anne,
  But I've not asked of your brother John.'

9 Far on the road as they rode along,
  There did they meet with her brother John.

10 She stooped low to kiss him sweet,
  He to her heart did a dagger meet.

11 'Ride on, ride on,' cried the serving man,
  'Methinks your bride she looks wondrous wan.'

12 'I wish I were on yonder stile,
  For there I would sit and bleed awhile.

13 'I wish I were on yonder hill,
  There I'd alight and make my will.'

14 'What would you give to your father dear?'
  'The gallant steed which doth me bear.'

15 'What would you give to your mother dear?'
  'My wedding shift which I do wear.

16 'But she must wash it very clean,
  For my heart's blood sticks in evry seam.'

17 'What would you give to your sister Anne?'
  'My gay gold ring and my feathered fan.'

18 'What would you give to your brother John?'
  'A rope and gallows to hang him on.'

19 'What would you give to your brother John's
    wife?'
  'A widow's weeds, and a quiet life.'

G

a. Herd's MSS, i, 41. **b.** Herd's *Scottish Songs*, 1776, i, 88.

1 THERE was three ladys in a ha,
　　Fine flowers i the valley
　There came three lords amang them a',
　　Wi the red, green, and the yellow

2 The first of them was clad in red:
　'O lady fair, will you be my bride?'

3 The second of them was clad in green:
　'O lady fair, will you be my queen?'

4 The third of them was clad in yellow:
　'O lady fair, will you be my marrow?'

5 'You must ask my father dear,
　Likewise the mother that did me bear.'

6 'You must ask my sister Ann,
　And not forget my brother John.'

7 'I have askt thy father dear,
　Likewise thy mother that did thee bear.

8 'I have askt thy sister Ann,
　But I forgot thy brother John.'

9 Her father led her through the ha,
　Her mother dancd before them a'.

10 Her sister Ann led her through the closs,
　Her brother John put her on her horse.

11 'You are high and I am low;　　　　　　[149]
　　Let me have a kiss before you go.'

12 She was louting down to kiss him sweet,
　　Wi his penknife he wounded her deep.
　　　*　　*　　*　　*　　*

13 'O lead me over into yon stile,
　　That I may stop and breath a while.

14 'O lead me over to yon stair,
　　For there I'll ly and bleed ne mair.'

15 'O what will you leave your father dear?'
　　'That milk-white steed that brought me here.'

16 'O what will you leave your mother dear?'
　　'The silken gown that I did wear.'

17 'What will you leave your sister Ann?'
　　'My silken snood and golden fan.'

18 'What will you leave your brother John?'
　　'The highest gallows to hang him on.'

19 'What will you leave your brother John's wife?'
　　'Grief and sorrow to end her life.'

20 'What will ye leave your brother John's bairns?'
　　'The world wide for them to range.'

H

Herd's MSS, I, 44, II, 75; *Scottish Songs*, 1776, I, 90
appended to **G**.

　　　　SHE louted down to gie a kiss,
　　　　　　With a hey and a lilly gay
　　　　He stuck his penknife in her hass.
　　　　　　And the rose it smells so sweetly

　　　　'Ride up, ride up,' cry'd the foremost man;
　　　　'I think our bride looks pale and wan.'

I

Kinloch's MSS, I, 21. From Mrs Bouchart, an old
lady native of Forfarshire.

1 THERE war three bonnie boys playing at the ba,
　Hech hey and a lily gay
There cam three ladies to view them a'.
　And the rose it smells sae sweetlie

2 The first ane was clad in red:
　'O,' says he, 'ye maun be my bride.'

3 The next o them was clad in green:
　'O,' says he, 'ye maun be my queen.'

4 The tither o them was clad in yellow:
　'O,' says he, 'ye maun be my marrow.'

5 'Ye maun gang to my father's bouer,
　To see gin your bride he'll let me be.'

6 Her father led her doun the stair,
　Her mither at her back did bear.

7 Her sister Jess led her out the closs,
　Her brother John set her on the horse.

8 She loutit doun to gie him a kiss;
　He struck his penknife thro her breist.

9 'Ride on, ride on,' says the foremaist man
　I think our bride looks pale and wan.'

10 'Ride on, ride on,' says the merry bridegroom;
　'I think my bride's blude is rinnin doun.'

11 'O gin I war at yon bonnie hill,
　I wad lie doun and bleed my fill!

12 'O gin I war at yon bonnie kirk-yard,
　I wad mak my testament there!'

13 'What will ye leave to your father dear?'
　'The milk-white steed that brocht me here.'

14 'What will ye leave to your mother dear?'
　'The bluidy robes that I do wear.'

15 'What will ye leave to your sister Ann?'
　'My silken snood and gowden fan.'

16 'What will ye leave to your sister Jess?'
　'The bonnie lad that I loe best.'

17 'What will ye leave to your brother John?'
　'The gallows pin to hang him on.'

18 'What will ye leave to your brother John's
　wife?'
　'Sorrow and trouble a' her life.'

19 'What will ye leave to your brother's bairns?'
　'The warld's wide, and let them beg.'

J

From Miss Margaret Reburn, as current in County
Meath, Ireland, about 1860.

1 THERE were three sisters playing ball,
　With the high and the lily O
And there came three knights to court them all.
　With the rosey sweet, heigh ho

2 The eldest of them was drest in green:
　'I wish I had you to be my queen.'

3 The second of them was drest in red
　'I wish I had you to grace my bed.'

4 The youngest of them was drest in white:
　'I wish I had you to be my wife.'

5 'Did ye ask my father brave?
　Or did ye ask my mother fair?

6 'Or did ye ask my brother John?
　For without his will I dare not move on.'

7 'I did ask your parents dear,
　But I did not see your brother John.'

* * * * *

8 'Ride on, ride on,' said the first man,
'For I fear the bride comes slowly on.'

9 'Ride on, ride on,' said the next man,
'For lo! the bride she comes bleeding on.'

* * * * *

10 'What will you leave your mother dear?'
'My heart's best love for ever and aye.'

11 'What will ye leave your sister Anne?'
'This wedding garment that I have on.'

12 'What will ye leave your brother John's wife?'
'Grief and sorrow all the days of her life.'

13 'What will ye leave your brother John?'
'The highest gallows to hang him on.'

14 'What will ye leave your brother John's son?'
'The grace of God to make him a man.'

K

Notes and Queries, 4th S., IV, 517, as "sung in Cheshire amongst the people" in the last century. T. W.

1 THERE were three ladies playing at ball,
    Gilliver, Gentle, and Rosemary
There came three knights and looked over the
        wall.
    Sing O the red rose and the white lilly

2 The first young knight, he was clothed in red,
And he said, 'Gentle lady, with me will you
        wed?'

3 The second young knight, he was clothed in
        blue,
And he said, 'To my love I shall ever be true.'

4 The third young knight, he was clothed in
        green,
And he said, 'Fairest maiden, will you be my
        queen?'

5 The lady thus spoke to the knight in red,
'With you, sir knight, I never can wed.'

6 The lady then spoke to the knight in blue,
And she said, 'Little faith I can have in you.'

7 The lady then spoke to the knight in green,
And she said, ' 'T is at court you must seek for a
        queen.'

8 The three young knights then rode away,
And the ladies they laughed, and went back to
        their play.
    Singing, etc.

L

Campbell MSS, II, 19.

1 THERE were three ladies playing at the ba,
    With a hey and a lilly gay
When the King o Fairies rode by them a'.
    And the roses they grow sweetlie

2 The foremost one was clad in blue;
He askd at her if she'd be his doo.

3 The second of them was clad in red;
He askd at her if she'd be his bride.

4 The next of them was clad in green;
He askd at her if she'd be his queen.

5 'Go you ask at my father then,
And you may ask at my mother then.

6 'You may ask at my sister Ann,
And not forget my brother John.'

7 'O I have askd at your father then,
And I have askd at your mother then.

8 'And I have askd at your sister Ann,
  But I've quite forgot your brother John.'

9 Her father led her down the stair,
  Her mother combd down her yellow hair.

10 Her sister Ann led her to the cross,
  And her brother John set her on her horse.

11 'Now you are high and I am low,
  Give me a kiss before ye go.'

12 She's lootit down to gie him a kiss,
  He gave her a deep wound and didna miss.

13 And with a penknife as sharp as a dart,
  And he has stabbit her to the heart.

14 'Ride up, ride up,' says the foremost man,
  'I think our bride looks pale an wan.'

15 'Ride up, ride up,' says the middle man,
  'I see her heart's blude trinkling down.'

16 'Ride on, ride,' says the Fairy King,
  'She will be dead lang ere we win hame.'

17 'O I wish I was at yonder cross,
  Where my brother John put me on my horse.

18 'I wish I was at yonder thorn,
  I wad curse the day that ere I was born.

19 'I wish I was at yon green hill,
  Then I wad sit and bleed my fill.'

20 'What will you leave your father then?'
  'The milk-white steed that I ride on.'

21 'What will you leave your mother then?'
  'My silver Bible and my golden fan.'

22 'What will ye leave your sister Ann?'
  'My good lord, to be married on.'

23 'What will ye leave your sister Pegg?'
  'The world wide to go and beg.'

24 'What will you leave your brother John?'
  'The gallows-tree to hang him on.'

25 'What will you leave your brother's wife?'
  'Grief and sorrow to end her life.'

M

Campbell MSS, II, 26.

1 THERE was three ladies playing at the ba,
    With a hay and a lilly gay
  A gentleman cam amang them a'.
    And the roses grow sweet aye

2 The first of them was clad in yellow,
  And he askd at her gin she'd be his marrow.

3 The next o them was clad in green;
  He askd at her gin she'd be his queen.

4 The last o them [was] clad in red;
  He askd at her gin she'd be his bride.

5 'Have ye asked at my father dear?
  Or have ye asked my mother dear?

6 'Have ye asked my sister Ann?
  Or have ye asked my brother John?'

7 'I have asked yer father dear,
  And I have asked yer mother dear.

8 'I have asked yer sister Ann,
  But I've quite forgot your brother John.'

9 Her father dear led her thro them a',
  Her mother dear led her thro the ha.

10 Her sister Ann led her thro the closs,
  And her brother John stabbed her on her horse.

11 'Ride up, ride up,' says the foremost man,
  'I think our bride looks pale and wan.'

12 'Ride up,' cries the bonny bridegroom,
  'I think the bride be bleeding.'

13 'This is the bludy month of May,
  Me and my horse bleeds night and day.

14 'O an I were at yon green hill,
I wad ly down and bleed a while.

15 'O gin I was at yon red cross,
I wad light down and corn my horse.

16 'O an I were at yon kirk-style,
I wad lye down and soon be weel.'

17 When she cam to yon green hill,
Then she lay down and bled a while.

18 And when she cam to yon red cross,
Then she lighted and corned her horse.

19 'What will ye leave your father dear?'
'My milk-white steed, which cost me dear.'

20 'What will ye leave your mother dear?'
'The bludy clothes that I do wear.'

21 'What will ye leave your sister Ann?'
'My silver bridle and my golden fan.'

22 'What will ye leave your brother John?'
'The gallows-tree to hang him on.'

23 'What will ye leave to your sister Pegg?'
'The wide world for to go and beg.'

24 When she came to yon kirk-style,
Then she lay down, and soon was weel.

N

Dr Joseph Robertson's Note-Book, January 1, 1830, No 4.

THEN out bespak the foremost priest:
Wi a heigh ho and a lilly gay
I think she's bleedin at the breast.
The flowers they spring so sweetly

---◆---

1] **A b.** 6². Oer young.
  10². spear at.
  17². the bonny.
  19¹. said.
  23¹. And what will ye.
  25¹. This fair lady. ². And a mass.
  Variations of Aytoun's copy, sts. 9–13, 16, 17, 20–24: 11¹ *omits* And; 12¹, 13¹ *omit* dear; 13² *omits* And; 16¹, through half *for* half thro; 17² *omits* For, bonny; 21², pearlin *for* silken; 22¹ *omits* And; 22², My silken gown that stands its lane; 23², shirt *for* cloaths; 24¹, And what; 24², The gates o hell to let him in.
B. "I have seen a fragment of another copy in which [the burden is]

  The red rose and the lily
  And the roses spring fu sweetly." *Kinloch, p.* 19.

E. *For this stanza we find, whatever may be the explanation, the following in Findlay MSS, I, 146.* "From Miss Butchart, Arbroath."

There were three sisters livd in a bouer,
  With a hech hey an a lillie gay
There cam a knicht to be their wooer.
  An the primrose springs sae sweetly
Sing Annet, an Marrot, an fair Maisrie,
  An the dew hangs in the wood, gay ladie.

F. 9¹. For on the road.
G. a.1. *Burden²*. The red, green, *etc.*: *afterwards,* Wi the red, *etc.*
  2². *MS. also,* He askt of me if I'd be his bride.
  3². *MS. also,* He askt of me if I'd be his queen.
  4². *MS. also,* He askt me if I'd be his marrow.
  15². *MS. also,* The gold and silver that I have here.
  16². *MS. also,* The silken garment.
  17². *MS. also,* My satine hat.
  20². *MS. also,* The world wide, let them go beg.
b. 7². the mother.
b. 14¹. into yon stair.
  Variations of Aytoun's copy, sts. 1–8, 14, 15, 18, 19 *from Herd,* 1776: 11, three sisters; 2², 3², 4² *omit* fair; 5¹, O ye maun; 6¹, And ye; 7¹, O I have;

8^1, And I have ask'd your sister; 8^2, your brother; 14^2, Give me a kiss; 15^2, When wi his knife.

H. "I have heard this song, to a very good tune not in any collection, with the above variations—the chorus, of the whole as in the above two verses." *Herd's note in his MSS.*

L. *Burden in all but* 1, 2, 13, lilly hey; *in* 16, 17, 18, spring sweetlie; *in* 22, smell sweetlie.

M. 15^1. green cross.
    17^2. bleed.

———◆———

APPENDIX

Additional Copies

"Scotch Ballads, Materials for Border Minstrelsy,"
No 22 a. In the handwriting of William Laidlaw; "from
Jean Scott."

THERE was three ladies playd at the ba,
  With a hey hey an a lilly gay
Bye cam three lords an woo'd them a'.
  Whan the roses smelld sae sweetly

The first o them was clad in yellow:
'O fair may, will ye be my marrow?'
  Whan the roses smell, etc.

The niest o them was clad i ried:
'O fair may, will ye be my bride?'

The thrid o them was clad i green:
He said, O fair may, will ye be my queen?

12

LORD RANDAL

A. From a manuscript copy, probably of the beginning of this century.

B. 'Lord Donald,' Kinloch's *Ancient Scottish Ballads*, p. 110; Kinloch MSS, VII, 89.

C. Motherwell's MS., p. 69.

D. a. 'Lord Randal,' *Minstrelsy of the Scottish Border*, 1803, III, 292. **b.** 'Lord Rannal,' Campbell MSS, II, 269.

E. Halliwell's *Popular Rhymes and Nursery Tales*, p. 261.

F. 'Lord Ronald, my Son,' Johnson's *Museum*, No 327, p. 337.

G. *Illustrations of Northern Antiquities*, p. 319.

H. From recitation, 1881.

I. 'Tiranti, my Son.' **a.** Communicated by a lady of Boston. **b.** By an aunt of the same. **c.** By a lady of New Bedford. **d.** By a lady of Cambridge. **e, f, g.** By ladies of Boston. **h.** Communicated by Mr George M. Richardson. **i.** Communicated by Mr George L. Kittredge.

J. 'The Bonnie Wee Croodlin Dow,' Motherwell's MS., p. 238.

K. a. 'The Croodlin Doo,' Chambers, *Scottish Ballads*, p. 324. **b.** 'The Wee Croodlen Doo,' Chambers, *Popular Rhymes*, 1826, p. 295, 1842, p. 53. **c.** Johnson's *Museum*, by Stenhouse and Laing, IV, 364*. **d.** 'The Crowdin Dou,' Kinloch MSS, I, 184.

L. 'Willie Doo,' Buchan's MSS, II, 322, and *Ballads*, II, 179.

M. 'The Croodin Doo,' Chambers, *Popular Rhymes*, 1870, p. 51.

N. Kinloch MSS, v, 347.

O. 'The Croodlin Doo.' From a manuscript belonging to the Fraser-Tytler family.

P. 'Lord Ronald, my son,' communicated by Mr Macmath, of Edinburgh.

Q. 'Lord Randal,' Pitcairn's MSS, III, 19.

R. 'Little wee toorin dow,' Pitcairn's MSS, III, 13, from tradition.

S. Communicated to Percy by Rev. P. Parsons, of Wye, near Ashford, Kent, April 19, 1775.

T. "Scotch Ballads, Materials for Border Minstrelsy," No 22 g.

U. Letters addressed to Sir Walter Scott, XX, No 77, Abbotsford;

2] THE title 'Lord Randal' is selected for this ballad because that name occurs in one of the better versions, and because it has become familiar through Scott's *Minstrelsy*. Scott says that the hero was more generally termed Lord Ronald: but in the versions that have come down to us this is not so. None of these can be traced back further than a century. F and D were the earliest published. Jamieson remarks with respect to G (1814): "An English gentleman, who had never paid any attention to ballads, nor ever read a collection of such things, told me that when a child he learnt from a playmate of his own age, the daughter of a clergyman in Suffolk, the following imperfect ditty."

I, a version current in eastern Massachusetts, may be carried as far back as any. **a, b** derive from Elizabeth Foster, whose parents, both natives of eastern Massachusetts, settled, after their marriage, in Maine, where she was born in 1789. Elizabeth Foster's mother is remembered to have sung the ballad, and I am informed that the daughter must have learned it not long after 1789, since she was removed in her childhood from Maine to Massachusetts, and continued there till her death. 'Tiranti' ['Taranti'] may not improbably be a corruption of Lord Randal.

The copy in Smith's *Scottish Minstrel*, III, 58, is Scott's altered. The first four stanzas are from the *Border Minstrelsy*, except the last line of the fourth, which is from Johnson's *Museum*. The last two stanzas are a poor modern invention.

Three stanzas which are found in A. Cunningham's *Scottish Songs*, I, 286f, may be given for what they are worth. 'The house of Marr,' in the first, is not to be accepted on the simple ground of its appearance in his pages. The second is inserted in his beautified edition of Scott's ballad, and has its burden accordingly; but there is, besides this, no internal evidence against the second, and none against the third.[*]

'O where have you been, Lord Ronald, my son?
O where have you been, my handsome young man?'
'At the house of Marr, mother, so make my bed soon,
For I'm wearied with hunting, and fain would lie
          down.'

'O where did she find them, Lord Randal, my son?
O where did she catch them, my handsome young
          man?'
'Neath the bush of brown bracken, so make my bed
          soon,
For I'm wae and I'm weary, and fain would lie down.'

'O what got your bloodhounds, Lord Ronald, my
          son?
O what got your bloodhounds, my handsome young
          man?'
'They lapt the broo, mother, so make my bed soon,
I am wearied with hunting, and fain would lie down.'

A pot-pourri or quodlibet, reprinted in Wolff's *Egeria*, p. 53, from a Veronese broadside of the date 1629, shows that this ballad was popular in **Italy** more than 250 years ago; for the last but one of the fragments which make up the medley happens to be the first three lines of 'L'Avvelenato,' very nearly as they are sung at the present day, and these are introduced by a summary of the story:

"Io vo' finire con questa *d'un amante*
Tradito dall' amata.
Oh che l'è sì garbata
A cantarla in ischiera:
'*Dov' andastu iersera,*
Figliuol mio ricco, savio e gentile?
Dov' andastu iersera'?"[†]

The ballad was first recovered in 1865, by Dr G. B. Bolza, who took it down from the singing of very young girls at Loveno. Since then good copies have been found at Venice. **A**, 'L'Avvelenato,' Bolza, *Canzoni popolari comasche*, No 49, *Sitzungsberichte of the Vienna Academy (philos. histor. class)*, LIII, 668, trans- [t lated in the Countess Evelyn Martinengo-Cesaresco's *Essays in the Study of Folk-Songs*, p. 219, is of seventeen stanzas, of seven short lines, all of which repeat but two: the 8th and 10th stanzas are imperfect.[‡] A mother inquires of her son where he has been. He has been at his mistress's, where he has eaten part of an eel; the rest was given to a dog, that died in the street. The mother declares that he has been poisoned. He bids her send for the doctor to see him, for the curate to shrive him, for the notary to make his will. He leaves his mother his palace, his brothers his carriage and horses, his sisters a dowry, his servants a free passage to mass ("la strada d'andà a messa" = nothing), a hundred and fifty masses for his soul; for his mistress the gallows to hang her. **B**, **C**, 'L'Avvelenato,' Bernoni, *Nuovi Canti popolari veneziani*, 1874, No 1, p. 5, p. 3, have twelve and eighteen four-line stanzas, the questions and answers in successive stanzas, and the last three lines of the first pair repeated respectively throughout.[§]

---

[*]   Compare, for dialogue and repetition, the Catalan ballad 'El Conde Arnau,' Milà, *Romancerillo*, No 78, p. 67; where, however, the first half of the third line is also regularly repeated in the fourth.

'¿Tota sola feu la vetlla, muller lleyal?
¿Tota sola feu la vetlla, viudeta, igual?'

'No la faig yo, tota sola, Comte l'Arnau,
No la faig yo tota sola, valga 'm Deu, val!'

[†]   *Opera nuova, nella quale si contiene una incatenatura di più villanelle ed altre cose ridiculose. . . . Data in luce per me Camillo, detto il Bianchino, cieco Fiorentino. Fliegendes Blatt von Verona*, 1629. *Egeria*, p. 53; p. 260, note 31.—With the above (*Egeria*, p. 59) compare especially the beginning of Italian **B**, further on.

[‡]   It begins:

"Dôve sî stâ jersira,
    Figliuol mio caro, fiorito e gentil?
Dôve sî stâ jersira?"

"Sôn stâ dalla mia dama;
    Signôra Mama, mio core sta mal!
Son stâ dalla mia dama;
    Ohimè! ch'io moro, ohimè!"

Three versions are cited by Professor D'Ancona in his *Poesia popolare Italiana*, pp 106ff. **D.** The Canon Lorenzo Panciatichi refers to the ballad in a 'Cicalata in lode della Padella e della Frittura,' recited at the Crusca, September 24, 1656, and in such manner as shows that it was well known. He quotes the first question of the mother, "Dove andastù a cena," etc. To this the son answered, he says, that he had been poisoned with a roast eel: and the mother asking what the lady had cooked it in, the reply was, In the oil pot. **E.** A version obtained by D'Ancona from the singing of a young fellow from near Pisa, of which the first four stanzas are given. Some verses after these are lost, for the testament is said to supervene immediately. **F.** A version from Lecco, which has the title, derived from its burden, 'De lu cavalieri e figliu de re,' A. Trifone Nutricati Briganti, *Intorno ai Canti e Racconti popolari del Leccese*, p. 17. The first four stanzas are cited, and it appears from these that the prince had cooked the eel himself, and, appropriately, in a gold pan. **G, H, I**, Nigra, No 26, **A, B, C**, 'Testamento dell' Avvelenato.' **J.** 'L'Amante avvelenato,' Giannini, No 27, p. 199. **K.** 'Mamma e Figghiolo,' Nerucci, in *Archivio*, II, 526. **L,** ''U Cavalieru Traditu;' communicated to *La Calabria*, October 15, 1888, p. 5, 'Storie popolari Acresi,' by Antonio Julia. Three imperfect versions (Sardinian) are in Ferraro, *C. p. in dialetto logudorese*, 1891, pp. 3–5.

B, which is given as a variant of **C**, agrees with **A** as to the agent in the young man's death. It is his mistress in **B**, but in **C** it is his mother. In both, as in **A**, he has eaten of an eel.

§   E.g. (**B**):
  1 "E dove xestu stà gieri sera,
     Figlio mio rico, sapio e gentil?
     E dove xesta stà gieri sera,
     Gentil mio cavalier?"

  2 "E mi so' stato da la mia bela;
     Signora madre, el mio cuor stà mal!
     E mi so' stato da la mia bela;
     Oh Dio, che moro, ohimè!"

  3 "E cossa t'àla dato da çena,
     Figlio mio?" etc.

  4 "E la m'à dato 'n'anguila rostita;
     Signora madre," etc.

The head he gave to the dogs, the tail to the cats (**C**). He leaves to his stewards (castaldi) his carriages and horses (**C**); to his herdsmen his cows and fields; to the maids his chamber furnishings; to his sister the bare privilege of going to mass (**C**, as in **A**); to his mother [wife, **C**] the keys of his treasure. "La forca per picarla" is in **B** as in **A** the bequest to his false love, instead of whom we have his mother in **C**.

The corresponding **German** ballad has been known to the English for two generations through Jamieson's translation. The several versions, all from oral tradition of this century, show the same resemblances and differences as the English.

A, B, 'Schlangenköchin,' eight stanzas of six lines, four of which are burden, **A**, *Liederhort*, p. 6, No 2[a], from the neighborhood of Wilsnack, Brandenburg, **B**, Peter, 1, 187, No 6, from Weidenau, Austrian Silesia, run thus: Henry tells his mother that he has been at his sweetheart's (but not a-hunting); has had a speckled fish to eat, part of which was given to the dog [eat, **B**], which burst. Henry wishes his father and mother all blessings, and hell-pains to his love, **A** 6–8. His mother, **B** 8, asks where she shall make his bed: he replies, In the churchyard. **C**, 'Grossmutter Schlangenköchin,' first published in 1802, in Maria's (Clemens Brentano's) romance *Godwi*, II, 113, afterward in the *Wunderhorn*, I, 19 (ed. 1819, I, 20, ed. 1857), has fourteen two-line stanzas, or seven of four lines, one half burden. The copy in Zuccalmaglio, p. 217, No 104, "from Hesse and North Germany," is the same thing with another line of burden intercalated and two or three slight changes. Maria has been at her grandmother's, who gave her a fish to eat which she had caught in her kitchen garden; the dog ate the leavings, and his belly burst. The conclusion agrees with **B**, neither having the testament. **D**, 'Stiefmutter,' seven stanzas of four short lines, two being burden, Uhland, No 120, p. 272; excepting one slight variation, the same as *Liederhort*, p. 5, No 2, from the vicinity of Bückeburg, Lippe-Schaumburg. A child has been at her mother's sister's house, where she has had a well-peppered broth and a glass of red wine. The dogs [and cats] had some broth too, and died on the spot. The child wishes its father a seat in

[154] heaven, for its mother one in hell. **E**, 'Kind, wo bist du denn henne west?' Reifferscheid, p. 8, No 4, from Bökendorf, Westphalia, four stanzas of six lines, combining question and answer, two of the six burden. A child has been at its step-aunt's, and has had a bit of a fish caught in the nettles along the wall. The child gives all its goods to its brother, its clothes to its sister, but three devils to its [step-]mother. **F**, 'Das vergiftete kind,' seven four-line stanzas, two burden, Schuster, *Siebenbürgisch-sächsische V. L.*, p. 62, No 58, from Mühlbach; given by Meltzl, *Acta Comparationis*, 1880, columns 143f, in another dialect. A child tells its father that its heart is bursting; it has eaten of a fish, given it by its mother, which the father declares to be an adder. The child wishes its father a seat in heaven, its mother one in hell. Two other copies are found in Böhme's Erk, No 190 b, I, 582.

A, **B** are nearer to 'Lord Randal,' and have even the name Henry which we find in English **C**. **C–F** are like **J–O**, 'The Croodlin Doo.'

Dutch. 'Isabelle,' Snellaert, p. 73, No 67, seven four-line stanzas, the first and fourth lines repeated in each. Isabel has been sewing at her aunt's, and has eaten of a fish with yellow stripes that had been caught with tongs in the cellar. The broth, poured into the street, caused the dogs to burst. She wishes her aunt a red-hot furnace, herself a spade to bury her, her brother a wife like his mother.

Swedish. **A**, 'Den lillas Testamente,' ten five-line stanzas, three lines burden, Afzelius, III, 13, No 68; ed. Bergström, I, 291, No 55. A girl, interrogated by her step-mother, says she has been at her aunt's, and has eaten two wee striped fishes. The bones she gave the dog; the stanza which should describe the effect is wanting. She wishes heaven for her father and mother, a ship for her brother, a jewel-box and chests for her sister, and hell for her step-mother and her nurse. **B**, Arwidsson, II, 90, No 88, nine five-line stanzas, two lines burden. In the first stanza, evidently corrupt, the girl says she has been at her brother's. She has had eels cooked with pepper, and the bones, given to the dogs, made them burst. She gives her father good corn in his barns, her brother and sister a ship, etc., hell to her step-mother and nurse.

Danish. 'Den forgivne Datter,' Grundtvig-Olrik, No 341, *Ridderviser*, I, 146ff,[*] two versions: **A** = Kristensen, *Jyske Folkeminder*, No 92, X, 358; **B**, communicated by Prof. Grundtvig, as obtained for the first time from tradition in 1877; five stanzas of five lines, three lines repeating. 'Den forgivne Søster' (with testament), Kristensen, *Jyske Folkeminder*, X, 358, No 92. Elselille, in answer to her mother, says she has been in the meadow, where she got twelve small snakes. She wishes heavenly joy to her father, a grave to her brother, hell torment to her sister.

Magyar. **A**. 'Der vergiftete Knabe,' Aigner, *Ungarische Volksdichtungen*, 2[e] Auflage, p. 127, in nine six-line stanzas, four being a burden. Johnnie, in answer to his mother, says he has been at his sister-in-law's, and has eaten a speckled toad, served on her handsomest plate, of which he is dying. He bequeaths to his father his best carriage, to his brothers his finest horses, to his sister his house furniture, to his sister-in-law everlasting damnation, to his mother pain and sorrow. The original of this ballad, 'A megétett János,' 'Poisoned John' (as would appear, in the Szekler idiom), was discovered by the Unitarian bishop Kriza, of Klausenburg, and was published by him in J. Arany's 'Koszoru,' in 1864. It is more exactly translated by Meltzl in the *Acta Comparationis Litterarum Universarum*, 1880, VII, columns 30f, the original immediately preceding. Aigner has omitted the second stanza, and made the third into two, in his translation. The Szekler has ten two-line stanzas, with the burden, Ah, my bowels are on fire! Ah, make ready my bed! In the second stanza John says he has eaten a four-footed crab; in the sixth he leaves his elder brother his yoke of oxen; in the seventh he leaves his team of four horses to his younger brother. Also translated in *Ungarische Revue*, 1883, p. 139, by G. Heinrich. **B**, another Szekler version, taken down by Meltzl from the mouth of a girl, is in seven two-line stanzas, with the burden, Make my bed, sweet mother! 'János,' *Acta*, cols 140f, with a German translation. John has been at his sister-in-law's, and

---

[*] Olrik mentions 7 **Swedish** copies, 5 of them unprinted.

had a stuffed chicken and a big cake. At his elder sister's they gave him the back of the axe, bloody stripes. He bequeaths to his elder sister remorse and sickness; to his sister-in-law six oxen and his wagon; to his father illness and poverty; to his mother blindness and beggary.

Wendish. 'Der vergiftete Knabe,' Haupt u. Schmaler, I, 110, No 77, twelve four-line stanzas, combining question and answer, the first and last line repeating. Henry has been at the neighbor's, has eaten part of a fish caught in the stable with a dung-fork; his dog ate the rest, and burst. There is no testament. His mother asks him where she shall make his bed; he replies, In the churchyard; turn my head westward, and cover me with green turf.

The numerous forms of this story show a general agreement, with but little difference except as to the persons who are the object and the agent of the crime. These are, according to the Italian tradition,—which is 250 years old, while no other goes back more than a hundred years, and far the larger part have been obtained in recent years,—a young man and his true-love; and in this account unite two of the three modern Italian versions, English A–G, German A, B. Scott suggests that the handsome young sportsman (whom we find in English A, C, D, E, F, H) may have been exchanged for a little child poisoned by a step-mother, to excite greater interest in the nursery. This seems very reasonable. What girl with a lover, singing the ballad, would not be tempted to put off the treacherous act on so popular, though most unjustly popular, an object of aversion? A mother, again, would scarcely allow "mother" to stand, as is the case in Italian C and German F, and a singer who considered that all blood relations should be treated as sacred would ascribe the wickedness to somebody beyond that pale, say a neighbor, as the Wendish ballad does, and Zuccalmaglio's reading of German C. The step-mother is expressly named only in English J, K c, L, M, N, O, and in four of these, J, K c, M, O, the child has a mammie,[*] which certainly proves an *alibi* for the step-mother, and confirms what Scott says.

There is a step-aunt in German E and Swedish A, and the aunt in German D and the Dutch ballad, and the grandmother in English I, K a, b, German C, are perhaps meant (as the brother in Swedish B certainly is) to be step-relations and accommodating instruments.

The poisoning is shifted to a wife in English H, to an uncle in English I d, and to a sister-in-law in the Magyar version.

There is all but universal consent that the poisoning was done by serving up snakes for fish. The Magyar says a toad, English M a four-footed fish,[†] German D a well-peppered broth and a glass of red wine. English L adds a drink of hemlock stocks to the speckled trout; F, H have simply poison. The fish are distinctively eels in the Italian versions, and in English A, D, E, G, I, Swedish B. English A, J, K, M, N, O, German A–D, the Italian, Swedish, Dutch, Wendish versions, and by implication English C, D, E also, concur in saying that a part of the fish was given to a dog [dogs, cat, cats], and that death was the consequence. Bursting or swelling is characteristic of this kind of poisoning: German A, B, C, F, English D, E, and the Dutch and Wendish versions.

The dying youth or child in many cases makes a nuncupative will, or declares his last wishes, upon a suggestion proceeding from the person who is by him, commonly from the mother: English A, B, C, H, I: German A, D, E, F: the Italian, Dutch, Swedish, Danish, Magyar versions. The bequest to the poisoner is the gallows in English B, C, H, I, Italian A, B, C; hell, English A, German A, D, F, Swedish A, B, Danish; and an equivalent in German E, the Dutch and the Magyar copy. 'The Cruel Brother,' No 11, and 'Edward,' No 13, have a will of this same fashion.

In all the English versions the burden has the entreaty "Make my bed," and this is addressed to the mother in all but L, N. In H, an Irish copy, and I, an American one, the mother asks where the bed shall be made; and

---

[*]   Grundtvig notices this absurdity, Eng. og skotske F. v., p. 286, note **.

[†]   "The nurse or nursery maid who sang these verses (to a very plaintive air) always informed the juvenile audience that the step-mother was a rank witch, and that the fish was an ask (newt), which was in Scotland formerly deemed a most poisonous reptile." C. K. Sharpe, in the *Musical Museum*, Laing-Stenhouse, IV, 364*.

the answer is, In the churchyard. This feature is found again in German **B**, **C** and in the Wendish version.

The resemblance in the form of the stanza in all the versions deserves a word of remark. For the most part, the narrative proceeds in sections of two short lines, or rather half lines, which are a question and an answer, the rest of the stanza being regularly repeated. English **L**, **N**, as written (**L** not always), separate the question and answer; this is done, too, in Italian **B**, **C**. German **E**, on the contrary, has two questions and the answers in each stanza, and is altogether peculiar. Swedish **B** varies the burden in part, imagining father, brother, sister, etc., to ask what the little girl will give to each, and adapting the reply accordingly, "Faderen min," "Broderen min."

A Bohemian and a Catalan ballad which have two of the three principal traits of the foregoing, the poisoning and the testament, do not exhibit, perhaps have lost, the third, the employment of snakes.

The story of the first is that a mother who dislikes the wife her son has chosen attempts to poison her at the wedding feast. She sets a glass of honey before the son, a glass of poison before the bride. They exchange cups. The poison is swift. The young man leaves four horses to his brother, eight cows to his sister, his fine house [156] to his wife. "And what to me, my son?" asks the mother. A broad mill-stone and the deep Moldau is the bequest to her. Waldau, *Böhmische Granaten*, II, 109, cited by Reifferscheid, p. 137 f.

The Catalan ballad seems to have been softened at the end. Here again a mother hates her daughter-in-law. She comes to the sick woman, "com qui no 'n sabès res," and asks What is the matter? The daughter says, You have poisoned me. The mother exhorts her to confess and receive the sacrament, and then make her will. She gives her castles in France to the poor and the pilgrims [and the friars], and to her brother Don Carlos [who, in one version is her husband]. Two of the versions remember the Virgin. "And to me?" "To you, my husband [my cloak, rosary], that when you go to mass you may remember me." In one version the mother asks the dying woman where she will be buried.

She says At Saint Mary's. Milá, *Observaciones*, p. 103 f, No 5, two versions: Briz y Saltó, II, 197 f, two also, the first nearly the same as Milà's first.

Poisoning by giving a snake as food, or by infusing the venom in drink, is an incident in several other popular ballads.

Donna Lombarda attempts, at the instigation of a lover, to rid herself of her husband by pounding a serpent, or its head, in a mortar, and mixing the juice with his wine [in one version simply killing the snake and putting it in a cask]: Nigra, *Canzoni del Piemonti*, in *Rivista Contemporanea*, XII, 32 ff, four versions;[*] Marcoaldi, p. 177, No 20; Wolf, *Volkslieder aus Venetien*, p. 46, No 72; Righi, *Canti popolari veronesi*, p. 37, No 100*; Ferraro, *C. p. monferrini*, p. 1, No 1; Bernoni, *C. p. veneziani*, Puntata V, No 1. In three of Nigra's versions and in Ferraro's the drink is offered when the husband returns from hunting. The husband, rendered suspicious by the look of the wine, or warned of his danger, forces his wife to drink first. So in a northern ballad, a mother who attempts to destroy her sons [step-sons] with a brewage of this description is obliged to drink first, and bursts with the poison: 'Eiturbyrlunar kvæði,' *Íslenzk Fornkvæði*, II, 79, No 43 A; 'Fru Gundela,' Arwidsson, II, 92, No 89; 'Signelill aa hennes synir,' Bugge, p. 95, No XX, the last half; 'Den onde svigermoder,' Kristensen, *Jyske Folkeviser*, I, 332, No 122; *Skattegraveren*, V, 84, No 635.[†]

In one of the commonest Slavic ballads, a girl, who finds her brother an obstacle to her desires, poisons him, at the instigation and under the instruction of the man she fancies, or of her own motion, by giving him a snake to eat, or the virus in drink. The object of her passion, on being informed of what she has done, casts her off, for fear of her doing the like to him. **Bohemian:** 'Sestra travička,' Erben, *P. n. w Čechách*, 1842, I, 9, No 2, *Prostonárodni české P.*, 1864, p. 477, No 13; Swoboda, *Sbírka č. n. P.*, p. 19; German translations by Swoboda, by Wenzig, *W. s. Märchenschatz*, p. 263, I. v. Düringsfeld, *Böhmische Rosen*, p. 176, etc.

---

[*]   'Donna Lombarda' is now No 1 of Nigra's collection, where it is given in sixteen versions.

Moravian: Sušil, p. 167, No 168. **Slovak:** Čelakowsky, *Slowanské n. P.*, iii, 76. **Polish:** Kolberg, *P. L. p.*, i, 115, No 8, some twenty versions; Wojcicki, *P. L. bialochrobatow, etc.*, i, 71, 73, 232, 289; Pauli, *P. L. polskiego*, p. 81, 82: Konopka, *P. L. krakowskiego*, p. 125; Roger, p. 66, No 119. **Servian:** Vuk, i, 215, No 302, translated by Talvj, ii, 192, by Kapper, *Gesänge der Serben*, ii, 177, and by Bowring, p. 143; Rajković, No 251. Compare, **Bulgarian**, Miladinof, No 262; **Croat:** Mažuřanie, p. 152, *Sammlung der Zeitschrift,* 'Naša Sloga,' II, No 158; **Slovenian:** Koritko, Part III, p. 47. **Russian:** Čelakowsky, as above, iii, 108 = Sacharof, IV, 7; Trudy, V, 482, No 822; p. 915, No 481. **Little Russian:** Golovatsky, Part I, pp 206, 207, 209, Nos 32, 33, 35. **Masovian:** Kozłowski, No 14, p. 52, p. 53. Etc. The attempt is made, but unsuccessfully, in Sacharof, *P. russkago N.*, iv, 7. **Lithuanian:** Bartsch, *Dainu Balsai*, I, 172ff, No 123 a, b. More ballads of poisoning, sister poisoning brother at the instance of her lover, girl poisoning her lover, and at col. 306 one resembling Lord Randal, Herrmann, *Ethnologische Mitteilungen aus Ungarn*, I, cols 292–308 (with an extensive bibliography). Herrmann's collections upon this theme are continued from cols 89–95, 203–11.*

In Golovatsky, II, 584, a mother asks her son whether he supped with the widow. He supped with her, the witch. What did she cook for him?

A small fish. Where did she catch it, dress it? Did she eat any of it? No, her head ached. Did the children? No, they went to bed.—In Verković, No 317, p. 350, the fair Stana is poisoned by her husband's parents with a snake given as a fish. (W. W.)

A version given by De Rada, *Rapsodie d'un poema albanese*, p. 78, canto x, resembles the Slavic, with a touch of the Italian. A man incites a girl to poison her brother by pounding the poison out of a serpent's head and tail and mixing it with wine.

In a widely spread Romaic ballad, a mother poisons the bride whom her son has just brought home,—an orphan girl in some versions, but in one a king's daughter wedding a king's son. The cooks who are preparing the feast are made to cook for the bride the heads of three snakes [nine snakes' heads, a three-headed snake, winged snakes and two-headed adders]. In two Epirote versions the poisoned girl bursts with the effects. "Τὰ κακὰ πεθερικά," Passow, p. 335, No 456, nearly = Zambelios, p. 753, No 41; Passow, p. 337, No 457; Tommaseo, *Canti popolari*, iii, 135; Jeannaraki, p. 127, No [157] 130[†]; Chasiotis (Epirote), p. 51, No 40, "Ἡ βουργαροποῦλα καὶ ἡ κακὴ πεθερά;" p. 103, No 22, "Ὁ Διονὺς καὶ ἡ κακὴ πεθερά." (Liebrecht, *Volkskunde*, p. 214.)

An Italian mother-in-law undertakes to poison her son's wife with a snake-potion. The wife, on her husband's return from the chase, innocently proposes to share the drink with him. Her husband no sooner has tasted than he falls dead. (Kaden, *Italiens Wunderhorn*, p. 85, translating Nannarelli, p. 52).

A Ruthenian ballad of a mother attempting to poison her son's wife, and poisoning the pair appears in Herrmann, in *Ethnologische Mittheilungen*, col. 205f.

A Slovak ballad of this sort in Kollár, *Narodnie Zpiewanky*, II, 32, translated by Herrmann, 91f, No 3; and another version of the same col. 204f, No 7. Roumanian versions, cols 206, 207f, 209f, Nos 9, 10, 12, the last with another story prefixed. See also Herrmann, col.

---

† See *Archivio*, X, 380. [See also 'Utro Fæstemø vil forgive sin Fæstemand,' in the Grundtvig-Olrik collection, No 345, *Ridderviser* I, 165ff, 3 versions A–C (A, B, from MS. sources going back in part to the 16th century; C, from oral tradition, printed by Kristensen, *Jyske Folkeminder*, No 19, I, 49, No 56, X, 234). Olrik, in an elaborate introduction, studies the relations of the Danish ballad (which is found also in Norse, Bugge's MS. collections, No. 221) to 'Donna Lombarda' and to the history of the sixth century Lombard queen Rosemunda. He opposes the views of Gaston Paris, *Journal des Savants*, 1889, pp. 616ff, and holds that 'Donna Lombarda,' 'Utro Fæstemø,' (his No 345), 'Giftblandersken' (his No 344), 'Fru Gundela,' and the Slavic ballads of the sister who poisons her brother at the instigation of her lover, are all derived from the *saga* of Rosemunda. He even regards 'Old Robin of Portingale,' No 80 in this collection, as related to the 'Utro Fæstemø.'

* Cf. the Danish ballad 'Tule Slet, Ove Knar og Fru Magnild,' Grundtvig-Olrik, No. 350, *Ridderviser*, I, 186, where, however, the murderess uses a knife.

---

† A golden bird sitting on the bride's hand, sings, "You had better not go there; you will have a bad mother-in-law and a bad father-in-law." There are ill omens also in Passow, No 457.

90, No 1, 92f, Nos 4, 5, 208f, No 11, for poi-
soning-ballads, and his references at the top of
col. 211.

Scott cites in his preface to 'Lord Randal' a
passage from a MS. chronicle of England, in
which the death of King John is described as
being brought about by administering to him
the venom of a toad (cf. the Magyar ballad).
The symptoms—swelling and rupture—are
found in the Scandinavian and Epirote ballads
referred to above, besides those previously
noticed (p. 213). King John had asked a monk
at the abbey of Swinshed how much a loaf on
the table was worth. The monk answered a
half-penny. The king said that if he could bring
it about, such a loaf should be worth twenty
pence ere half a year. The monk thought he
would rather die than that this should come to
pass. "And anon the monk went unto his abbot
and was shrived of him, and told the abbot all
that the king said, and prayed his abbot to
assoil him, for he would give the king such a
wassail that all England should be glad and joy-
ful thereof. Then went the monk into a garden,
and found a toad therein, and took her up, and
put her in a cup, and filled it with good ale, and
pricked her in every place, in the cup, till the
venom came out in every place, and brought it
before the king, and kneeled, and said: 'Sir,
wassail: for never in your life drank ye of such a
cup.' 'Begin, monk,' said the king: and the
monk drank a great draught, and took the king
the cup, and the king also drank a great

draught, and set down the cup. The monk anon
went to the firmary, and there died anon, on
whose soul God have mercy, amen. And five
monks sing for his soul especially, and shall
while the abbey standeth. The king was anon
full evil at ease, and commanded to remove the
table, and asked after the monk; and men told
him that he was dead, for his womb was broke
in sunder. When the king heard this tiding, he
commanded for to truss: but all it was for
nought, for his belly began to swell from the
drink that he drank, that he died within two
days, the morrow after Saint Luke's day." *Min-
strelsy*, III, 287f. The same story in *Eulogium
Historiarum*, ed. Haydon, III, 109f.

A is translated by Professor Emilio Teza,
'L'Avvelenatrice, Canzone Boema,' Padova,
1891, p. 12. [*Atti e Memorie della R. Accademia
di Scienze, Lettere ed Arti in Padova*, Nuova
Serie, VII, 234.] B and K c are translated by
Grundtvig, *Engelske og skotske Folkeviser*, p. 284,
286. D, by W. Grimm, 3 *Altschottische Lieder*, p.
3; by Schubart, p. 177; Arndt, p. 229; Doenni-
ges, p. 79; Gerhardt, p. 83; Knortz, *L. u. R. Alt-
Englands*, p. 174. K a by Fiedler, *Geschichte der
volksthümlichen schottischen Liederdichtung*, II,
268. German C is translated by Jamieson, *Illus-
trations*, p. 320: Swedish A by W. and M. How-
itt, *Literature and Romance of Northern Europe*, I,
265. Italian A is translated by Evelyn Car-
rington in *The Antiquary*, III, 156f. D also by
Freiligrath, II, 226, ed. Stuttggart, 1877.

A

From a small manuscript volume lent me by Mr William Macmath, of Edinburgh, containing four pieces written in or about 1710, and this ballad in a later hand. Charles Mackie, August, 1808, is scratched upon the binding.

1 'O WHERE ha you been, Lord Randal, my son?
And where ha you been, my handsome young man?'
'I ha been at the greenwood; mother, mak my bed soon,
For I'm wearied wi hunting, and fain wad lie down.'

2 'An wha met ye there, Lord Randal, my son?
An wha met you there, my handsome young man?'
'O I met wi my true-love; mother, mak my bed soon,
For I'm wearied wi huntin, an fain wad lie down.'

3 'And what did she give you, Lord Randal, my son?
And what did she give you, my handsome young man?'
'Eels fried in a pan; mother, mak my bed soon,
For I'm wearied wi huntin, and fain wad lie down.'

4 'And wha gat your leavins, Lord Randal, my son?
And wha gat your leavins, my handsom young man?'
'My hawks and my hounds; mother, mak my bed soon,
For I'm wearied wi hunting, and fain wad lie down.'

5 'And what becam of them, Lord Randal, my son?
And what becam of them, my handsome young man?'
'They stretched their legs out an died; mother, mak my bed soon,
For I'm wearied wi huntin, and fain wad lie down.'

6 'O I fear you are poisoned, Lord Randal, my son!
I fear you are poisoned, my handsome young man!'
'O yes, I am poisoned; mother, mak my bed soon,
For I'm sick at the heart, and I fain wad lie down.'

7 'What d' ye leave to your mother, Lord Randal, my son?
What d'ye leave to your mother, my handsome young man?'
'Four and twenty milk kye; mother, mak my bed soon,
For I'm sick at the heart, and I fain wad lie down.'

8 'What d' ye leave to your sister, Lord Randal, my son?
What d' ye leave to your sister, my handsome young man?'
'My gold and my silver; mother, mak my bed soon,
For I'm sick at the heart, an I fain wad lie down.'

9 'What d' ye leave to your brother, Lord Randal, my son?
What d' ye leave to your brother, my handsome young man?'
'My houses and my lands; mother, mak my bed soon,
For I'm sick at the heart, and I fain wad lie down.'

10 'What d' ye leave to your true-love, Lord Randal, my son?
What d' ye leave to your true-love, my handsome young man?'
'I leave her hell and fire; mother, mak my bed soon,
For I'm sick at the heart, and I fain wad lie down.'

B

Kinloch's *Ancient Scottish Ballads*, p. 110. From Mrs
Comie, Aberdeen.

1 'O WHARE hae ye been a' day, Lord Donald, my
son?
O whare hae ye been a' day, my jollie young
man?'
'I've been awa courtin; mither, mak my bed
sune,
For I'm sick at the heart, and I fain wad lie
doun.'

2 'What wad ye hae for your supper, Lord
Donald, my son?
What wad ye hae for your supper, my jollie
young man?'
[159] 'I've gotten my supper; mither, mak my bed
sune,
For I'm sick at the heart, and I fain wad lie
doun.'

3 'What did ye get to your supper, Lord Donald,
my son?
What did ye get to your supper, my jollie young
man?'
'A dish of sma fishes; mither mak my bed sune,
For I'm sick at the heart, and I fain wad lie
doun.'

4 'Whare gat ye the fishes, Lord Donald, my son?
Whare gat ye the fishes, my jollie young man?'
'In my father's black ditches; mither, mak my
bed sune,
For I'm sick at the heart, and I fain wad lie
doun.'

5 'What like were your fishes, Lord Donald, my
son?
What like were your fishes, my jollie young
man?'
'Black backs and spreckld bellies; mither, mak
my bed sune,
For I'm sick at the heart, and I fain wad lie
doun.'

6 'O I fear ye are poisond, Lord Donald, my son!
O I fear ye are poisond, my jollie young man!'
'O yes! I am poisond; mither mak my bed sune,
For I'm sick at the heart, and I fain wad lie
doun.'

7 'What will ye leave to your father, Lord Donald
my son?
What will ye leave to your father, my jollie
young man?'
'Baith my houses and land; mither, mak my bed
sune,
For I'm sick at the heart, and I fain wad lie
doun.'

8 'What will ye leave to your brither, Lord
Donald, my son?
What will ye leave to your brither, my jollie
young man?'
'My horse and the saddle; mither, mak my bed
sune,
For I'm sick at the heart, and I fain wad lie
doun.'

9 'What will ye leave to your sister, Lord Donald,
my son?
What will ye leave to your sister, my jollie
young man?'
'Baith my gold box and rings; mither, mak my
bed sune,
For I'm sick at the heart, and I fain wad lie
doun.'

10 'What will ye leave to your true-love, Lord
Donald, my son?
What will ye leave to your true-love, my jollie
young man?'
'The tow and the halter, for to hang on yon
tree,
And lat her hang there for the poysoning o
me.'

C

Motherwell's MS., p. 69. From the recitation of
Margaret Bain, in the parish of Blackford, Perthshire.

1 'WHAT's become of your hounds, King Henrie,
  my son?
  What's become of your hounds, my pretty little
    one?'
  'They all died on the way; mother, make my
    bed soon,
  For I'm sick to the heart, and I fain wald lie
    down.'

2 'What gat ye to your supper, King Henry, my
    son?
  What gat ye to your supper, my pretty little
    one?'
  'I gat fish boiled in broo; mother, mak my bed
    soon,
  For I'm sick to the heart, and I fain wald lie
    down.'

3 'What like were the fish, King Henry, my son?
  What like were the fish, my pretty little one?'
  'They were spreckled on the back and white on
    the belly; mother, make my bed soon,
  For I'm sick to the heart, and I fain wald lie
    down.'

4 'What leave ye to your father, King Henry, my
    son?
  What leave ye to your father, my pretty little
    one?'
  'The keys of Old Ireland, and all that's therein;
    mother, make my bed soon,
  For I'm sick to the heart, and I fain wald lie
    down.'

5 'What leave ye to your brother, King Henry,
    my son?
  What leave ye to your brother, my pretty little
    one?'
  'The keys of my coffers and all that's therein;
    mother, mak my bed soon,
  For I'm sick to the heart, and I fain wald lie
    down.'

6 'What leave ye to your sister, King Henry, my
    son?
  What leave ye to your sister, my pretty little
    one?'
  'The world's wide, she may go beg; mother,
    mak my bed soon,
  For I'm sick to the heart, and I fain wald lie
    down.'

7 'What leave ye to your trew-love, King Henry,
    my son?
  What leave ye to your trew-love, my pretty lit-
    tle one?'
  'The highest hill to hang her on, for she's poi-
    soned me and my hounds all; mother,
    make my bed soon,
  Oh I'm sick to the heart, and I fain wald lie
    down.'

D

a. *Minstrelsy of the Scottish Border,* 1803, III, 292. **b.**
Campbell MSS, II, 269.

"O where hae ye been, Lord Ran - dal, my son?

O where hae ye been, my hand - some young man?"

"I hae been to the wild wood; moth - er make my bed soon,

For I'm wear - y wi hunt - ing, and fain wald lie down."

D. b. Campbell, 1818, p. 45. Sung by Sophia Scott, the daughter of Sir Walter Scott.

1 'O WHERE hae ye been, Lord Randal, my son?
  O where hae ye been, my handsome young
      man?'
  'I hae been to the wild wood; mother, make my
      bed soon,
  For I'm weary wi hunting, and fain wald lie
      down.'

2 'Where gat ye your dinner, Lord Randal, my
      son?
  Where gat ye your dinner, my handsome young
      man?'
  'I din'd wi my true-love; mother, make my bed
      soon,
  For I'm weary wi hunting, and fain wald lie
      down.'

3 'What gat ye to your dinner, Lord Randal, my
      son?
  What gat ye to your dinner, my handsome
      young man?'
  'I gat eels boild in broo; mother, make my bed
      soon,
  For I'm weary wi hunting, and fain wald lie
      down.'

4 'What became of your bloodhounds, Lord Ran-
      dal, my son?
  What became of your bloodhounds, my hand-
      some young man?'
  'O they swelld and they died; mother, make my
      bed soon,
  For I'm weary wi hunting, and fain wald lie
      down.'

5 'O I fear ye are poisond, Lord Randal, my son!
  O I fear ye are poisond, my handsome young
      man!'
  'O yes! I am poisond; mother, make my bed
      soon,
  For I'm sick at the heart, and I fain wald lie
      down.'

E

Halliwell's *Popular Rhymes and Nursery Tales*, p. 261. "A version still popular in Scotland," 1849.

1 'Ah where have you been, Lairde Rowlande,
    my son?
  Ah where have you been, Lairde Rowlande, my
    son?'
  'I've been in the wild woods; mither, mak my
    bed soon,
  For I'm weary wi hunting, and faine would lie
    down.'

2 'Oh you've been at your true love's, Lairde
    Rowlande, my son!
  Oh you've been at your true-love's, Lairde
    Rowlande, my son!'
  'I've been at my true-love's; mither, mak my
    bed soon,
  For I'm weary wi hunting, and faine would lie
    down.'

3 'What got you to dinner, Lairde Rowlande, my
    son?
  What got you to dinner, Lairde Rowlande, my
    son?'
  'I got eels boild in brae; mither, mak my bed
    soon,
  For I'm weary wi hunting, and faine would lie
    down.'

4 'What's become of your warden, Lairde Row-
    lande, my son?
  What's become of your warden, Lairde Row-
    lande, my son?'
  'He died in the muirlands; mither, mak my bed
    soon,
  For I'm weary wi hunting, and faine would lie
    down.'

5 'What's become of your stag-hounds, Lairde
    Rowlande, my son?
  What's become of your stag-hounds, Lairde
    Rowlande, my son?'
  'They swelled and they died; mither, mak my
    bed soon,
  For I'm weary wi hunting, and faine would lie
    down.'

F

Johnson's *Museum*, No 327, p. 337. Communicated by Burns.

O___ where___ hae ye been___ Lord___ Ron - ald my___ son?___

O___ where hae ye___ been___ Lord___ Ron - ald___ my___ son?

I hae been wi' my___ sweet - heart, moth - er, make my bed___ soon,___

For I'm wear - y wi' the hunt - ing and___ fain wad___ lie___ down.

Collected by Robert Burns, as sung in Ayrshire.

1 'O WHERE hae ye been, Lord Ronald, my son?
O where hae ye been, Lord Ronald, my son?'
'I hae been wi my sweetheart; mother, make my
bed soon,
For I'm weary wi the hunting, and fain wad lie
down.'

2 'What got ye frae your sweetheart, Lord
Ronald, my son?
What got ye frae your sweetheart, Lord Ronald,
my son?'
'I hae got deadly poison; mother, make my bed
soon,
For life is a burden that soon I'll lay down.'

G

Illustrations of Northern Antiquities, p. 319. Origi-
nally from a clergyman's daughter, in Suffolk.

1 'WHERE have you been today, Billy, my son?
Where have you been today, my only man?'
'I've been a wooing; mother, make my bed
soon,
For I'm sick at heart, and fain would lay down.'

2 'What have you ate today, Billy, my son?
What have you ate today, my only man?'
'I've ate eel-pie; mother, make my bed soon,
For I'm sick at heart, and shall die before
noon.'

H

Taken down by me, February, 1881, from the reci-
tation of Ellen Healy, as repeated to her by a young girl
at "Lackabairn," Kerry, Ireland, about 1868.

1 'WHERE was you all day, my own pretty boy?
Where was you all day, my comfort and joy?'
'I was fishing and fowling; mother, make my
bed soon,
There's a pain in my heart, and I mean to lie
down.'

2 'What did you have for your breakfast, my own
pretty boy?
What did you have for your breakfast, my com-
fort and joy?'
'A cup of strong poison; mother, make my bed
soon,
There's a pain in my heart, and I mean to lie
down.'

3 'I fear you are poisoned, my own pretty boy,
I fear you are poisoned, my comfort and joy!'
'O yes, I am poisoned; mother, make my bed
soon,
There's a pain in my heart, and I mean to lie
down.'

4 'What will you leave to your father, my own
pretty boy?
What will you leave to your father, my comfort
and joy?'
'I'll leave him my house and my property;
mother, make my bed soon,
There's a pain in my heart, and I mean to lie
down.'

5 'What will you leave to your mother, my own
pretty boy?
What will you leave to your mother, my com-
fort and joy?'
'I'll leave her my coach and four horses;
mother, make my bed soon,
There's a pain in my heart, and I mean to lie
down.'

6 'What will you leave to your brother, my own
pretty boy?
What will you leave to your brother, my com-
fort and joy?'
'I'll leave him my bow and my fiddle mother,
make my bed soon,
There's a pain in my heart, and I mean to lie
down.'

7 'What will you leave to your sister, my own
pretty boy?
What will you leave to your sister, my comfort
and joy?'
'I'll leave her my gold and my silver; mother,
make my bed soon,
There's a pain in my heart, and I mean to lie
down.'

8 'What will you leave to your servant, my own
pretty boy?
What will you leave to your servant, my com-
fort and joy?'
'I'll leave him the key of my small silver box;
mother, make my bed soon,
There's a pain in my heart, and I mean to lie
down.'

9 'What will you leave to your children, my own
pretty boy?
What will you leave to your children, my com-
fort and joy?'
'The world is wide all round for to beg; mother,
make my bed soon,
There's a pain in my heart, and I mean to lie
down.'

10 'What will you leave to your wife, my own
pretty boy?
What will you leave to your wife, my comfort
and joy?'
'I'll leave her the gallows, and plenty to hang
her; mother, make my bed soon,
There's a pain in my heart, and I mean to lie
down.'

11 'Where shall I make it, my own pretty boy?
Where shall I make it, my comfort and joy?'
'Above in the churchyard, and dig it down
deep,
Put a stone to my head and a flag to my feet,
And leave me down easy until I'll take a long
sleep.'

I

a. Communicated by Mrs L. F. Wesselhoeft, of Boston, as sung to her when a child by her grandmother, Elizabeth Foster, born in Maine, who appears to have learned the ballad of her mother about 1800. **b.** By a daughter of Elizabeth Foster, as learned about 1820. **c.** By Miss Ellen Marston, of New Bedford, as learned from her mother, born 1778. **d.** By Mrs Cushing, of Cambridge, Mass., as learned in 1838 from a schoolmate, who is thought to have derived it from an old nurse. **e.** By Mrs Augustus Lowell, of Boston. **f.** By Mrs Edward Atkinson, of Boston, learned of Mrs A. Lowell, in girlhood. **g.** By Mrs A. Lowell, as derived from a friend. **h.** By Mr George M. Richardson, as learned by a lady in Southern New Hampshire, about fifty years ago, from an aged aunt. **i.** By Mr George L. Kittredge, obtained from a lady in Exeter, N. H.

1 'O WHERE have you been, Tiranti, my son?
　O where have you been, my sweet little one?'
　'I have been to my grandmother's; mother,
　　　make my bed soon,
　For I'm sick to my heart, and I'm faint to lie
　　　down.'

2 'What did you have for your supper, Tiranti, my
　　　son?
　What did you have for your supper, my sweet
　　　little one?'
　'I had eels fried in butter; mother, make my bed
　　　soon,
　For I'm sick to my heart, and I'm faint to lie
　　　down.'

3 'Where did the eels come from, Tiranti, my
　　　son?
　Where did the eels come from, my sweet little
　　　one?'
　'From the corner of the haystack; mother, make
　　　my bed soon,
　For I'm sick to my heart, and I'm faint to lie
　　　down.'

4 'What color were the eels, Tiranti, my son?
　What color were the eels, my sweet little one?'
　'They were streakëd and stripëd; mother, make
　　　my bed soon,
　For I'm sick to my heart, and I'm faint to lie
　　　down.'

5 'What'll you give to your father, Tiranti, my son?
　What'll you give to your father, my sweet little
　　　one?'
　'All my gold and my silver; mother, make my
　　　bed soon,
　For I'm sick to my heart, and I'm faint to lie
　　　down.'

6 'What'll you give to your mother, Tiranti, my
　　　son?
　What'll you give to your mother, my sweet little
　　　tle one?'
　'A coach and six horses; mother, make my bed
　　　soon,
　For I'm sick to my heart, and I'm faint to lie
　　　down.'

7 'What'll you give to your grandmother, Tiranti,
　　　my son?
　What'll you give to your grandmother, my
　　　sweet little one?'
　'A halter to hang her; mother, make my bed
　　　soon,
　For I'm sick to my heart, and I'm faint to lie
　　　down.'

8 'Where'll you have your bed made, Tiranti, my
　　　son?
　Where'll you have your bed made, my sweet
　　　little one?'
　'In the corner of the churchyard; mother, make
　　　my bed soon,
　For I'm sick to my heart, and I'm faint to lie
　　　down.'

J

Motherwell's MS., p. 238. From the recitation of
Miss Maxwell, of Brediland.

1 'O WHARE hae ye been a' day, my bonnie wee
   croodlin dow?
   O whare hae ye, been a' day, my bonnie wee
   croodlin dow?'
   'I've been at my step-mother's; oh mak my bed,
   mammie, now!
   I've been at my step-mother's; oh mak my bed,
   mammie, now!'

2 'O what did ye get at your step-mother's, my
   bonnie wee croodlin dow?' [*Twice.*]
   'I gat a wee wee fishie; oh mak my bed. mam-
   mie, now!' [*Twice.*]

3 'O whare gat she the wee fishie, my bonnie wee
   croodlin dow?'
   'In a dub before the door; oh mak my bed,
   mammie, now!'

4 'What did ye wi the wee fishie, my bonnie wee
   croodlin dow?'
   'I boild it in a wee pannie; oh mak my bed,
   mammy, now!'

5 'Wha gied ye the banes o the fishie till, my
   bonnie wee croodlin dow?'
   'I gied them till a wee doggie; oh mak my bed,
   mammie, now!'

6 'O whare is the little wee doggie, my bonnie
   wee croodlin dow?
   O whare is the little wee doggie, my bonnie
   wee croodlin doo?'
   'It shot out its fit and died, and sae maun I do
   too;
   Oh mak my bed, mammy, now, now, oh mak
   my bed, mammy, now!'

K

a. Chambers' *Scottish Ballads*, p. 324. **b.** Chambers'
Popular Rhymes of Scotland, 1826, p. 295, 1842, p. 53. **c.**
The Stenhouse-Laing ed. of Johnson's *Museum*, IV,
364*, communicated by Charles Kirkpatrick Sharpe. **d.**
Kinloch MSS, I, 184.

1 'O WHAUR hae ye been a' the day, my little wee
   croodlin doo?'
   'O I've been at my grandmother's; mak my bed,
   mammie, now!'

2 'O what gat ye at your grandmother's, my little
   wee croodlin doo?'
   'I got a bonnie wee fishie; mak my bed, mam-
   mie, now!'

3 'O whaur did she catch the fishie, my bonnie
   wee croodlin doo?'
   'She catchd it in the gutter hole: mak my bed,
   mammie, now!'

4 'And what did she do wi the fish, my little wee
   croodlin doo?'
   'She boiled it in a brass pan; O mak my bed,
   mammie, now!'

5 'And what did ye do wi the banes o't, my bon-
   nie wee croodlin doo?'
   'I gied them to my little dog; mak my bed,
   mammie, now!'

6 'And what did your little doggie do, my bonnie
   wee croodlin doo?'
   'He stretched out his head, his feet, and deed;
   and so will I, mammie, now!'

L

Buchan's MSS, II, 322; *Ballads of the North of Scotland*, II, 179.

1 'WHAR hae ye been a' the day, Willie doo,
    Willie doo?
  Whar hae ye been a' the day, Willie, my doo?'

2 'I've been to see my step-mother; make my bed,
    lay me down;
  Make my bed, lay me down, die shall I now!'

3 'What got ye frae your step-mother, Willie doo,
    Willie doo?
  What got ye frae your step-mother, Willie, my
    doo?'

4 'She gae me a speckled trout; make my bed, lay
    me down;
  She gae me a speckled trout, die shall I now!'

5 'Whar got she the speckled trout, Willie doo,
    Willie doo?
  'She got it amang the heather hills; die shall I
    now!'

6 'What did she boil it in, Willie doo, Willie
    doo?'
  'She boild it in the billy-pot; die shall I now!'

7 'What gaed she you for to drink, Willie doo,
    Willie doo?
  What gaed she you for to drink, Willie, my
    doo?'

8 'She gaed me hemlock stocks; make my bed,
    lay me down;
  Made in the brewing pot; die shall I now!'

9 They made his bed, laid him down, poor Willie
    doo, Willie doo;
  He turnd his face to the wa; he's dead now!

M

Popular Rhymes of Scotland, 1870, p. 51. "Mrs Lockhart's copy."

1 'WHERE hae ye been a' the day, my bonny wee
    croodin doo?'
  'O I hae been at my stepmother's house; make
    my bed, mammie, now, now, now,
  Make my bed, mammie, now!'

2 'Where did ye get your dinner?' my, etc.
  'I got it at my stepmother's;' make, etc.

3 'What did she gie ye to your dinner?'
  'She gae me a little four-footed fish.'

4 'Where got she the four-footed fish?'
  'She got it down in yon well strand;' O make,
    etc.

5 'What did she do with the banes o't?'
  'She gae them to the little dog.'

6 'O what became o the little dog?'
  'O it shot out its feet and died;' O make, etc.

N

Kinloch's MSS, v, 347. in Dr John Hill Burton's hand.

1 'FARE hae ye been a' day, a' day, a' day,
Fare hae ye been a' day, my little wee croudlin
doo?'

2 'I've been at my step-mammie's, my step-mam-
mie's, my step-mammie's,
I've been at my step-mammie's; come mack my
beddy now!'

3 'What got ye at yer step-mammie's,
My little wee croudlin doo?'

4 'She gied me a spreckled fishie;
Come mack my beddy now!'

5 'What did ye wi the baenies oet,
My little wee croudlin doo?'

6 'I gaed them till her little dogie;
Come mack my beddy now!'

7 'What did her little dogie syne,
My little wee croudlin doo?'

8 'He laid down his heed and feet;
And sae shall I dee now!'

O

From a manuscript collection, copied out in 1840
or 1850, by a granddaughter of Alexander Fraser-Tytler,
p. 67.

1 'O WHERE hae ye been a' the day, my wee wee
croodlin doo doo?
O where hae ye been a' the day, my bonnie wee
croodlin doo?'
'O I hae been to my step-mammie's; mak my
bed, mammy, noo, noo,
Mak my bed, mammy, noo!'

2 'O what did yere step-mammie gie to you?' etc.
'She gied to me a wee wee fish,' etc.

3 '[O] what did she boil the wee fishie in?'
'O she boiled it in a wee wee pan; it turned
baith black an blue, blue,
It turned baith black an blue.'

4 'An what did she gie the banes o't to?'
'O she gied them to a wee wee dog;' mak, etc.

5 'An what did the wee wee doggie do then?'
'O it put out its tongue and its feet, an it deed;
an sae maun I do noo, noo,
An sae maun I do noo!'

P

Communicated by Mr Macmath, of Edinburgh, as
derived from his aunt, Miss Jane Webster, formerly of
Airds of Kells, now (January, 1883) of Dalry, Kirkcud-
brightshire, who learned it more than fifty years ago
from Mary Williamson, then a nurse-maid at Airds.

1 'WHERE hae ye been a' day, Lord Ronald, my son?
Where hae ye been a' day, my handsome young
    one?'
'I've been in the wood hunting; mother, make
    my bed soon,
For I am weary, weary hunting, and fain would
    lie doun.'

2 'O where did you dine, Lord Ronald, my son?
O where did you dine, my handsome young one?'
'I dined with my sweetheart; mother, make my
    bed soon,
For I am weary, weary hunting, and fain would
    lie doun.'

3 'What got you to dine on, Lord Ronald, my son?
What got you to dine on, my handsome young
    one?'
'I got eels boiled in water that in heather doth
    run,
And I am weary, weary hunting, and fain would
    lie doun.'

4 'What did she wi the broo o them, Lord
    Ronald, my son?
What did she wi the broo o them, my hand-
    some young one?'
'She gave it to my hounds for to live upon,
And I am weary, weary hunting, and fain would
    lie doun.'

5 'Where are your hounds now, Lord Ronald, my
    son?
Where are your hounds now, my handsome
    young one?'
'They are a' swelled and bursted, and sae will I
    soon,
And I am weary, weary hunting, and fain would
    lie doun.'

6 'What will you leave your father, Lord Ronald,
    my son?
What will you leave your father, my handsome
    young one?'
'I'll leave him my lands for to live upon,
And I am weary, weary hunting, and fain would
    lie doun.'

7 'What will you leave your brother, Lord
    Ronald, my son?
What will you leave your brother, my hand-
    some young one?'
'I'll leave him my gallant steed for to ride upon,
And I am weary, weary hunting, and fain would
    lie doun.'

8 'What will you leave your sister, Lord Ronald,
    my son?
What will you leave your sister, my handsome
    young one?'
'I'll leave her my gold watch for to look upon,
And I am weary, weary hunting, and fain would
    lie doun.'

9 'What will you leave your mother, Lord
      Ronald, my son?
What will you leave your mother, my hand-
      some young one?'
'I'll leave her my Bible for to read upon,
And I am weary, weary hunting, and fain would
      lie doun.'

10 'What will you leave your sweetheart, Lord
      Ronald, my son?
What will you leave your sweetheart, my hand-
      some young one?'
'I'll leave her the gallows-tree for to hang upon,
It was her that poisoned me;' and so he fell
      down.

Q

Pitcairn's MSS, III, 19. "This was communicated to
me by my friend Patrick Robertson, Esq., Advocate,[*]
who heard it sung by an old lady in the North Country;
and though by no means enthusiastic about popular
poetry, it struck him so forcibly that he requested her to
repeat it slowly, so as he might write it down." Stanzas
2–5 "were very much similar to the set in Scott's *Min-
strelsy*," and were not taken down.

1 'O WHARE hae ye been, Lord Randal, my son?
O whare hae ye been, my handsome young
      man?'
'Oer the peat moss mang the heather, mother,
      mak my bed soon,
For I'm weary, weary hunting, and fain wad lie
      down.'

6 'What leave ye to your father, Lord Randal, my
      son?
What leave ye to your father, my handsome
      young man?'
'I leave my houses and land, mother, mak my
      bed soon,
For I'm weary, weary hunting, and fain wad lie
      down.'

7 'What leave ye to your brother, Lord Randal,
      my son?
What leave ye to your brother, my handsome
      young man?'
'O the guid milk-white steed that I rode upon,
For I'm weary, weary hunting, and fain wad lie
      down.'

8 'What leave ye to your true-love, Lord Randal,
      my son?
What leave ye to your true-love, my handsome
      young man?'
'O a high, high gallows, to hang her upon,
For I'm weary, weary hunting, and fain wad lie
      down.'

---

[*]   Afterwards a judge, with the name of Lord Robertson, but universally known as Peter Robertson, celebrated for his
wit and good fellowship as well as his law, friend of Scott, Christopher North, and Lockhart; "the Paper Lord, Lord
Peter, who broke the laws of God, of man, and metre." Mr Macmath's note.

R

Pitcairn's MSS, III, 11. "From tradition: widow Stevenson."

1 'WHARE hae ye been a' day, my little wee toorin
  dow?'
  'It's I've been at my grandmammy's; mak my
  bed, mammy, now.'

2 'And what did ye get frae your grandmammy,
  my little wee toorin dow?'
  'It's I got a wee bit fishy to eat; mak my bed,
  mammy, now.'

3 'An what did ye do wi the banes o it, my little
  wee toorin dow?'
  'I gied it to my black doggy to eat; mak my bed,
  mammy, now.'

4 'An what did your little black doggy do syne,
  my little wee toorin dow?'
  'He shot out his head, and his feet, and he died;
  as I do, mammy, now.'

S

Communicated to Percy by Rev. P. Parsons, of
Wye, near Ashford, Kent, April 19, 1775: taken down
by a friend of Mr Parsons "from the spinning-wheel, in
Suffolk."

1 'WHERE have you been today, Randall, my son?
  Where have you been today, my only man?'
  'I have been a hunting, mother, make my bed
  soon,
  For I'm sick at the heart, fain woud lie down.
  Dear sister, hold my head, dear mother, make
  my bed,
  I am sick at the heart, fain woud lie down.'

2 'What have you eat today, Randal, my son?
  What have you eat today, my only man?'
  'I have eat an eel; mother, make,' etc.

3 'What was the colour of it, Randal, my son?
  What was the colour of it, my only man?'
  'It was neither green, grey, blue nor black,
  But speckled on the back; make,' etc.

4 'Who gave you eels today, Randal, my son?
  Who gave you eels today, my only man?'
  'My own sweetheart; mother, make,' etc.

5 'Where shall I make your bed, Randal, my son?
  Where shall I make your bed, my only man?'
  'In the churchyard; mother, make,' etc.

6 'What will you leave her then, Randall, my
  son?
  What will you leave her then, my only man?'
  'A halter to hang herself; make,' etc.

T

"Scotch Ballads, Materials for Border Minstrelsy,"
No 22 g, in the handwriting of William Laidlaw.

1 'WHERE ha ye been, Lord Randal, my son?'
  'I been at the huntin, mother, mak my bed soon;
  I'm weariet wi huntin, I fain wad lie down.'

2 'What gat ye to yer supper, Lord Randal, my
  son?'
  'An eel boild i broo, mother, mak my bed soon;
  I'm,' etc.

3 'What gat yer dogs, Earl Randal, my son?'
  'The broo o the eel, mother,' etc.

4 'What leave [ye] yer false love, Lord Randal,
  my son?'
  'My goud silken garters, to hang hersel on;
  I'm,' etc.

U

Letters addressed to Sir Walter Scott, XX, No 77, Abbotsford; from Joseph Jamieson Archibald, Largs, 18th February, 1830.

"By the bye! How does your copy of 'Willie Doo' go? Or is it the same as our 'Auld Nursery Lilt,' better known by the name of 'My Wee Croodling Doo'? To give you every justice, I shall copy a stanza or two."

1 'Whare were ye the lea lang day,
    My wee crooding doo, doo?'
  'I hae been at my step-dame's;
    Mammy, mak my bed noo, noo!'

2 'Whare gat she the wee, wee fish?'
  'She gat it neist the edder-flowe.'

3 'What did she wi the fishie's banes?'
  'The wee black dog gat them to eat.'

4 'What did the wee black doggie then?'
  'He shot out his fittie an deed;
    An sae maun I now too, too.' Etc.

"The wee crooding doo next received a fatal drink, and syne a lullaby, when his bed was made 'baith saft an fine,' while his lang fareweel and dying lamentation was certainly both trying and afflicting to the loving parents." *The drink after the fish was a senseless interpolation; the 'lang fareweel' was probably the testament of the longer ballad.*

B. *Found in Kinloch MSS, VII, 89. The sixth stanza is not there, and was probably taken from Scott,* **D.**

C. 4^2. your father, King Henry, my son.

D. b. *Disordered:* **b** $1 = $ **a** 1; **b** $2 = $ **a** 4; **b** $3 = $ **a** $5^{1,2}$ $+ $ **a** $2^{3,4}$; **b** $4 = $ **a** 3; **a** $2^{1,2}$, $5^{3,4}$, *are wanting.*

b. 1^3. been at the hunting.
  3^2. I fear ye've drunk poison.
  $3^3 = $ **a** 2^3. I supd wi my auntie.
  $4^{1,2} = $ **a** $3^{1,2}$. your supper.
  This copy may be an imperfect recollection of **a.**

E. Lt.-Col. W. F. Prideaux, of Calcutta, has kindly informed me that **E** was printed in *The Universal Magazine*, 1804. It is there said to have been sung, to a very simple and very ancient Scotch tune, by a peasant-girl at the village of Randcallas, Perthshire. See, also, *Notes and Queries*, Sixth Series, XII, 134.

I. a. 1^4. faint to, *an obvious corruption of* fain to, *is found also in* **b, c;** **d** *has* fain wad; **e**, faint *or* fain; **f**, fain; **g**, **I** faint to.
  N. B. 8 *stands* 5 *in the MS. copy, but is the last stanza in all others which have it.*

b. 2^1. for your dinner.
  After 2 follows:

  Who cooked you the eels, Tiranti, my son? etc.
  O 't was my grandmother; mother, make my bed
    soon, etc.

  b $5 = $ **a** 3:^{1}.Where did she get the, eels? etc.

^{3}.By the side of the haystack, etc.
b $6 = $ **a** 7: $7 = $ **a** 8: $8 = $ **a** 5. 8^4. and die to lie down.
  a 6 is wanting in **b**.

c. 1^4. at my heart (*and always*).
  2^1. O what did she give you? *etc.* ^{8}. Striped eels fried, *etc.*
  $3 = $ **a** 4.^{1}. O how did they look? *etc.*
  ^{3}. Ringed, streaked, and speckled, *etc.*
  $4 = $ **a** 3.^{1}. O where did they come from?
  5^1. O what will you give your father, my son?
  ^{2}. O what will you give him?
  ^{3}. A coach and six horses.
  6^1. O what will you give your mother, my son? *as in 5.*
  8. All my gold and my silver.
  7^1. O what will you give your granny? *as in 5.*
  8^1. O where'll, etc.
  c *adds, as 9:*

  So this is the end of Tiranti my son,
  So this is the end of my sweet little one
  His grandmother poisoned him with an old
    dead snake,
  And he left her a halter to hang by the neck.

d. 1^1, *etc.* Tyrante.
  ^{3}. O I've been to my uncle's, *etc.*
  ^{4}. and fain wad lie doun.
  2^3. eels and fresh butter.

3 = a 4. ^{3}. black stripëd with yellow.

4 = a 7. ^{1}. What'll ye will to your mither?

^{3}. My gold and my silver.

5 = a 6. ^{1}. What'll ye will to your father?

^{3}. My coach and my horses.

6 = a 8. ^{1}. What'll you will to your uncle?

3, 5 *of a are wanting.*

e. 1^4. For I'm sick at heart, and faint [fain] to lie down.

3 = a 7. ^{1}. What will you leave your mother?

^{3}. A box full of jewels.

4^1. What will you leave your sister?

^{3}. A box of fine clothing.

5 = a 8. ^{3}. A rope to hang her with.

6 = a 5. ^{1}. Where shall I make it?

3, 4 *of a are wanting.*

f. *This copy was derived from the singing of the lady who communicated* e, *and they naturally agree closely.*

1^4. fain to lie down. f 3 = e 4: f 4 = e 3.

g. 1^4. For I'm sick at the heart, and I faint to lie down.

2^1. What did you get at your grandmother's?

^{3}. I got eels stewed in butter.

3 = a 8. ^{1}. What will you leave . . . .

4^1. What will you leave to your brother?

^{3}. A full suit of mourning.

5 = a 7. ^{1}. leave to your mother.

^{3}. A carriage and fine horses.

6 = a 5.

3, 4 *of a are wanting.*

h. *Four stanzas only,* 1, 2, 6, 7.

1^2. my own little one.

1^4. at the heart . . . and fain.

6^1. will you leave mother.

7^1. will you leave grandma. 7^3. a rope.

k. *Seven stanzas.*

1^3. to see grandmother.

1^4. sick at heart, and fain.

2^3. Stripëd eels fried.

3 = a 6, d 5, h 3.

3^{1,2}. Your grandmother has poisoned you.

3^3. I know it, I know it.

4 = a 6. 4^{1,2}. would you leave mother.

5 = a 8, b 9, h 7.

5^{1,2}. would you leave sister.

5^3. A box full of jewels.

6 = a 7; 7 = a 8.

6^{1,2}. would you leave grandmother.

6^3. A rope for to hang her.

7^{1,2}. O where shall I make it.

K. a, b, c *are printed, in the publications in which they occur, in four-line stanzas.*

b. *Omits* 4.

6^1. the little doggie. ^{2}. as I do, mammie, noo.

6^2. *Read:* head and his feet.

c. 1^1. my bonnie wee. crooden doo: *and always.*

^{2}. at my step-mither's.

2. And what did scho gie you to eat . . . .

Scho gied to me a wee fishie . . . .

3^1. An what did she catch the fishie in . . . .

4 *is wanting.*

d. 1^1. my bonnie wee crowdin, *and always.*

2^1. frae your stepmither.

2^2. She gied me a bonnie wee fish, it was baith black and blue.

5^1. my ain wee dog.

6^1. And whare is your ain wee dog.

6^2. It laid down its wee headie and deed,

And sae maun I do nou.

L. *Written in the MS., and printed by Buchan, in stanzas of 4 lines.*

M. *Printed by Chambers in stanzas of 4 lines, the last repeated.*

N. *The second line of each stanza is written as two in the MS.*

O. *The stanza, being written with short lines in the manuscript, is of seven lines, including the repetitions.*

Q. "The second, third, fourth, and fifth stanzas were very much similar to the set Lord Ronald, in Scott's *Border Minstrelsy,* and as Mr Robertson was hurried he did not take down the precise words." *MS., p.* 21.

Ronald *is changed to* Randal *in* 6, 7, *but is left in* 8.

R. *Written in four-line stanzas.*

T. 4^1. leave year.

Among C. K. Sharpe's papers, and in his handwriting, is a piece in dialogue between Mother and Son headed, Death of Lord Roñal, a Gaelic ballad founded on a tradition of his receiving poison by treachery at the castle of his mistress' father, and dying on his return home. This is the familiar Scottish ballad made over in English and mildly sentimental phraseology. All the Celtic in it is "dark Dungael, the chief of meikle guile," the father.

APPENDIX

Additional Copies

'Lairde Rowlande, or Ronalde,' *The Sporting Magazine*, XXV, 209, January, 1805; communicated by Philodice, as recited by a "peasant's girl" at Randcallas, Perthshire. (Reprinted by Mr Edward Peacock in *The Athenæum*, August 27, 1892, p. 288.)

1 'Aн, where have you been, Lairde Rowlande,
    my son?
  Ah, where have you been, Lairde Rowlande,
    my son?'
'I've been in the wild woods; mither, mak my
    bed soon,
  For I'm weary wi hunting and faine would lie
    down.'

2 Oh, you've been at your true-love's, Lairde
    Rowlande, my son,' etc.
'I've been at my true-love's; mither,' etc.

3 'What got you to dinner?' etc.
  'I got eels boild in brue; mither,' etc.

4 'What's become of your warden?' etc.
  'He died in the muirlands; mither,' etc.

5 'What's become of your stag-hounds?' etc.
  'They swelled and they died; mither,' etc.

'Jacky, my son,' written out by Miss F. J. Adams, a Devonshire lady, and derived by her from her Devonshire nurse, sixty or seventy years ago. (Baring-Gould.)

1 'Where hast thou been to-day, Jacky, my son?
  Where hast thou been to-day, my honey man?'
'Oh, I've been a courting, mother, make my
    bed soon,
For I am sick to the heart, fain would lie down.'

2 'Where shall I make it to?' etc.
'Oh, in the churchyard, mother,' etc.

3 'What wilt thou leave thy mother?' etc.
'Oh, I'll leave her my money, mother,' etc.

4 'What wilt thou leave thy father?' etc.
'Oh, I'll leave him my 'state, mother,' etc.

5 'What wilt thou leave thy sweetheart?' etc.
'A rope for to hang her, mother,' etc.

'The Croodin Doo.' Findlay MSS, I, 192.

1 'Whare did ye get your dinner the day,
  My wee, wee croodin doo?' (*Twice.*)

2 'I got it in my step-mither's ha,
  Oh, granny, mak my bed noo.' (*Twice.*)

3 'What did ye get to your dinner the day,
  My wee, wee croodin doo?' (*Twice.*)

4 'I got a wee fishie wi four wee feeties,
  Oh, granny, mak my bed noo.' (*Twice.*)

5 'Did ony body eat it but yoursel,
  My wee, wee croodin doo?' (*Twice.*)

6 'I gied the banes to my wee, wee dogie,
  Oh, granny, mak my bed noo;
  He streekit out his head an died at my feet,
  O, granny, een as I do noo.'

13

EDWARD

A. a. Motherwell's MS., p. 139. **b.** Motherwell's *Minstrelsy*, p. 339. From recitation.

B. Percy's *Reliques*, 1765, I, 53. Communicated by Sir David Dalrymple.

C. MS. of A. Laing, one stanza.

A **b**, "given from the recitation of an old woman," is evidently **A a** slightly regulated by Motherwell. **B**, we are informed in the 4th edition of the *Reliques*, p. 61, was sent Percy by Sir David Dalrymple, Lord Hailes. Motherwell thought there was reason to believe "that his lordship made a few slight verbal improvements on the copy he transmitted, and altered the hero's name to Edward,—a name which, by the bye, never occurs in a Scottish ballad, except where allusion is made to an English king."[*] Dalrymple, at least, would not be likely to change a Scotch for an English name. The Bishop might doubtless prefer Edward to Wat, or Jock, or even Davie. But as there is no evidence that any change of name was made, the point need not be discussed. As for other changes, the word "brand," in the first stanza, is possibly more literary than popular; further than this the language is entirely fit. The affectedly antique spelling[†] in Percy's copy has given rise to vague suspicions concerning the authenticity of the ballad, or of the language: but as spelling will not make an old ballad, so it will not unmake one. We have, but do not need, the later traditional copy to prove the other genuine. 'Edward' is not only unimpeachable, but has ever been regarded as one of the noblest and most sterling specimens of the popular ballad.

Motherwell seems to incline to regard 'Edward' rather as a detached portion of a bal-

lad than as complete in itself. "The verses of which it consists," he says, "generally conclude the ballad of 'The Twa Brothers,' and also some versions of 'Lizie Wan:'" *Minstrelsy*, LXVII, 12. The Finnish parallel which Motherwell refers to, might have convinced him that the ballad is complete as it is; and he knew as well as anybody that one ballad is often appended to another by reciters, to lengthen the story or improve the conclusion.[‡] More or less of 'Edward' will be found in four versions of 'The Twa Brothers' and two of 'Lizie Wan,' further on in this volume.

This ballad has been familiarly known to have an exact counterpart in **Swedish**. There are seven versions, differing only as to length: 'Sven i Rosengård,' **A**, Afzelius, No 67, III, 4, eleven two-line stanzas, with three more lines of burden; **B**, III, 3, six stanzas (Bergström's ed.,

---

[*] An eager "Englishman" might turn Motherwell's objection to the name into an argument for 'Edward' being an "English" ballad.

[†] That is to say, initial *quh* and *ʒ* for modern *wh* and *y*, for nothing else would have excited attention. Perhaps a transcriber thought he ought to give the language a look at least as old as Gavin Douglas, who spells *quhy, dois, ʒour*. The *quh* would serve a purpose, if understood as indicating that the aspirate was not to be dropped, as it often is in English *why*. The *ʒ* is the successor of *ʒ*, and was meant to be pronounced *y*, as *ʒ* is, or was, pronounced in *gaberlunʒie* and other Scottish words. See Dr J. A. H. Murray's *Dialect of the Southern Counties of Scotland*, pp. 118, 129. Since *quh* and *ʒ* serve rather as rocks of offence than landmarks, I have thought it best to use *wh* and *y*.

[‡] Motherwell also speaks of a ballad of the same nature as quoted in Werner's 'Twenty-Fourth of February.' The stanza cited (in Act I Scene 1) seems to be Herder's translation of 'Edward' given from memory.

No 54, 1, 2); C, Arwidsson, No 87 **A**, ii, 83, eighteen stanzas; **D**, No 87 **B**, ii, 86, sixteen stanzas; **E**, Aminson, *Bidrag till Södermanlands Kulturhistoria*, iii, 37, eight stanzas; **F**, Aminson, *Bidrag till Södermanlands äldere Kulturhistoria*, No V, p. 12, eleven stanzas; **G**, Thomasson, *Visor från Bleking, Nyare Bidrag*, etc., VII, No 6, p. 16, No 9.* The same in **Danish**: **A**, Grundtvig, *Engelske og skotske Folkeviser*, p. 175, nine stanzas; **B**, Boisen, *Nye og gamle Viser*, 10th ed., No 95, p. 185, 'Brodermordet.' Four concluding stanzas (When?) in Kristensen's *Skattegraveren*, II, 100, No 459. And in **Finnish**, probably derived from the Swedish, but with traits of its own: **A**, Schröter's *Finnische Runen*, p. 124, 'Werinen Pojka,' The Bloodstained Son, fifteen two-line stanzas, with two lines of refrain; **B**, 'Velisurmaaja,' Brother-Murderer, *Kanteletar*, p. x, twenty stanzas. Nine stanzas are translated by Schott, *Acta Comparationis*, 1878, IV, cols 132, 133. The murder here is for wife-seduction, a peculiar and assuredly not original variation.

All these are a dialogue between mother and son, with a question and answer in each stanza. The mother asks, Where have you been? The son replies that he has been in the stable [Danish, grove, fields; Finnish **A**, on the sea-strand]. "How is it that your foot is bloody?"[†] [clothes, shirt; Finnish, "How came your jerkin muddy?" etc.] A horse has kicked or trod on him. "How came your sword so bloody?" He then confesses that he has killed his brother. [Swedish **D** and the Danish copies have no question about the foot, etc.] Then follows a series of questions as to what the son will do with himself, and what shall become of his wife, children, etc., which are answered much as in the English ballad. Finally, in all, the mother asks when he will come back, and he replies (with some variations), When crows are white. And that will be? When swans are black. And that? When stones float. And that? When feathers sink, etc.[‡] This last feature, stupidly exaggerated in some copies, and even approaching burlesque, is one of the common-places of ballad poetry, and may or may not have been, from the beginning, a part of the ballads in which it occurs. Such a conclusion could not be made to adhere to 'Edward,' the last stanza of which is peculiar in implicating the mother in the guilt of the murder. Several versions of 'The Twa Brothers' preserve this trait, and 'Lizie Wan' also.

The stanza of this ballad was originally, in all probability, one of two lines—a question and an answer—with refrains, as we find it in **A** 10, 11, 12, and the corresponding Swedish and Finnish ballad; and in 'Lord Randal,' **J**, **K**, etc., and also the corresponding Swedish and German ballad. **A** 1, 2, 3, 5, 6, 8, 9 are now essentially stanzas of one line, with refrains; that is, the story advances in these at that rate. **A** 4, 7 (= **C**) are entirely irregular, substituting narrative or descriptive circumstances for the last line of the refrain, and so far forth departing from primitive simplicity.[§] The stanza in **B** embraces always a question and a reply, but for what is refrain in other forms of the ballad we have epical matter in many cases. **A** 1, 2, substantially, = **B** 1; **A** 3, 4 = **B** 2; **A** 5, 6 = **B** 3; **A** 8, 9 = **B** 4; **A** 11 = 6; **A** 12 = 7.

Testaments such as this ballad ends with have been spoken of under No 11.

A is translated by Grundtvig, *Engelske og skotske Folkeviser*, No 26, p. 172; by Rosa War-rens, *Schottische V. l.*, No 21, p. 96; by Wolff, *Halle der Völker*, I, 22, and Hausschatz, p. 223. **B**, in Afzelius, iii, 10; "often in Danish," Grundtvig; by Herder, *Volksliedet*, ii, 207; by

---

* 'Svend i Rosensgaard' is No 340 in the Grundtvig-Olrik collection of Danish ballads, *Ridderviser*, I, 142. Danish versions are limited to three, of which the second is a fragment and the third a copy from Norway in all but pure Danish. Of Swedish versions eleven are enumerated, besides a half-comic copy from a manuscript of 1640, or older, which is spun out to 33 stanzas. As before remarked, a palpable tendency to parody is visible in some of the Scandinavian specimens.

† We have a similar passage in most of the copies of the third class of the German ballads corresponding to No 4. A brother asks the man who has killed his sister why his shoes [sword, hands] are bloody. See p. 53, p. 56. So in Herr Axel,' Arwidsson, No 46, i, 308.

‡ Compare Sir John Mandeville, as to the Dead Sea, ch. 9 (of the Cotton MS.): "And zif a man caste iren therein, it wole flete aboven, and zif men caste a fedre therein, it wol synke to the botme."

§ These have perhaps been adapted to the stanza of 'The Twa Brothers,' with some versions of which, as already remarked, the present ballad is blended.

Döring, p. 217; Gerhard, p. 88; Knortz, *Schottische Balladen*, No 27; Adolph von Marées, p. 27; by Graf von Platen, II, 329, Stuttgart, 1847; after Herder into Magyar, by Dr Karl von Szász; in Seckendorf's *Musenalmanach für das Jahr 1808*, p. 7; and by Du Méril, *Histoire de la Poésie scandinave*, p. 467. Swedish **A**, by W. and M.

Howitt, *Literature and Romance of Northern Europe*, I, 263.[*]

---

[*] With regard to translations, I may say now, what might well have said earlier, that I do not aim at making a complete list, but give such as have fallen under my notice.

A

[16

a. Motherwell's MS., p. 139. From Mrs King, Kilbarchan. b. Motherwell's *Minstrelsy*, p. 339.

1 'WHAT bluid's that on thy coat lap,
    Son Davie, son Davie?
  What bluid's that on thy coat lap?
    And the truth come tell to me.'

2 'It is the bluid of my great hawk,
    Mother lady, mother lady:
  It is the bluid of my great hawk,
    And the truth I have told to thee.'

3 'Hawk's bluid was neer sae red,
    Son Davie, son Davie:
  Hawk's bluid was neer sae red,
    And the truth come tell to me.'

4 'It is the bluid of my greyhound,
    Mother lady, mother lady:
  It is the bluid of my greyhound,
    And it wadna rin for me.'

5 'Hound's bluid was neer sae red,
    Son Davie, son Davie:
  Hound's bluid was neer sae red,
    And the truth come tell to me.'

6 'It is the bluid o my brither John,
    Mother lady, mother lady:
  It is the bluid o my brither John,
    And the truth I have told to thee.'

7 'What about did the plea begin,
    Son Davie, son Davie?'
  'It began about the cutting of a willow wand
    That would never been a tree.'

8 'What death dost thou desire to die,
    Son Davie, son Davie?
  What death dost thou desire to die?
    And the truth come tell to me.'

9 'I'll set my foot in a bottomless ship,
    Mother lady, mother lady:
  I'll set my foot in a bottomless ship,
    And ye'll never see mair o me.'

10 'What wilt thou leave to thy poor wife,
    Son Davie, son Davie?'
  'Grief and sorrow all her life,
    And she'll never see mair o me.'

11 'What wilt thou leave to thy old son,
    Son Davie, son Davie?'
  'I'll leave him the weary world to wander up
    and down,
    And he'll never get mair o me.'

12 'What wilt thou leave to thy mother dear,
    Son Davie, son Davie?'
  'A fire o coals to burn her, wi hearty cheer,
    And she'll never get mair o me.'

B

Percy's *Reliques*, 1765, I, 53. Communicated by Sir David Dalrymple.

1 'WHY dois your brand sae drap wi bluid,
    Edward, Edward,
  Why dois your brand sae drap wi bluid,
    And why sae sad gang yee O?'

'O I hae killed my hauke sae guid,
    Mither, mither,
  O I hae killed my hauke sae guid,
    And I had nae mair bot hee O.'

2 'Your haukis bluid was nevir sae reid,
    Edward, Edward,
Your haukis bluid was nevir sae reid,
    My deir son I tell thee O.'
'O I hae killed my reid-roan steid,
    Mither, mither,
O I hae killed my reid-roan steid,
    That erst was sae fair and frie O.'

3 'Your steid was auld, and ye hae gat mair,
    Edward, Edward,
Your steid was auld, and ye hae gat mair,
    Sum other dule ye drie O.'
'O I hae killed my fadir deir,
    Mither, mither,
O I hae killed my fadir deir,
    Alas, and wae is mee O!'

4 'And whatten penance wul ye drie, for that,
    Edward, Edward?
And whatten penance will ye drie for that?
    My deir son, now tell me O.'
'Ile set my feit in yonder boat,
    Mither, mither,
Ile set my feit in yonder boat,
    And Ile fare ovir the sea O.'

5 'And what wul ye doe wi your towirs and your
    ha,
        Edward, Edward?
And what wul ye doe wi your towirs and your
    ha,
    That were sae fair to see O?'
'Ile let thame stand tul they doun fa,
    Mither, mither,
Ile let thame stand tul they doun fa,
    For here nevir mair maun I bee O,'

6 'And what wul ye leive to your bairns and your
    wife,
        Edward, Edward?
And what wul ye leive to your bairns and your
    wife,
    Whan ye gang ovir the sea O?'
'The warldis room, late them beg thrae life,
    Mither, mither,
The warldis room, late them beg thrae life,
    For thame nevir mair wul I see O.'

7 'And what wul ye leive to your ain mither deir,
        Edward, Edward?
And what wul ye leive to your ain mither deir?
    My deir son, now tell me O.'
'The curse of hell frae me sall ye beir,
    Mither, mither,
The curse of hell frae me sall ye beir,
    Sic counseils ye gave to me O.'

C

MS. of Alexander Laing, 1829, p. 25.

'O what did the fray begin about?
    My son, come tell to me:'
'It began about the breaking o the bonny hazel wand,
    And a penny wad hae bought the tree.'

◆

A. b. 1^4. tell to me O. *And so every fourth line*.
    7^4. That would never hae been a tree O.
    10^4. And she'll never get mair frae me O.
    11^3. The weary warld to wander up and down.

B. *Initial* qu *for* w *and* z *for* y *have been changed throughout to* w *and* y.
    6^7. let.

14

BABYLON; OR, THE BONNIE BANKS O FORDIE

A. a, b. 'Babylon; or, The Bonnie Banks o Fordie,' Motherwell's *Minstrelsy*, p. 88. **c.** The same, Appendix, p. xxii, No XXVI.
B. a. Herd's MSS, I, 38, II, 76. **b.** 'The Banishd Man,' *The Scots Magazine*, October, 1803, p. 699, evidently derived from Herd.

C. Motherwell's MS., p. 172.
D. Motherwell's MS., p. 174.
E. 'Duke of Perth's Three Daughters,' Kinloch's *Ancient Scottish Ballads*, p. 212.
F. "In Gipsy Tents," by Francis Hindes Groome, p. 143.

[171] **B a** is from tradition of the latter half of the eighteenth century; the other copies from the earlier part of this.

Three sisters go out (together, **A, B, C,** successively, **D, E**) to gather flowers (**A, B, E**). A banished man (outlyer bold, **D,** Loudon lord, **E**) starts up from a hiding-place, and offers them one after the other the choice of being his wife or dying by his hand.

> (**A.**) 'It's whether will ye be a rank robber's wife,
>   Or will ye die by my wee penknife?'

> (**D.**) 'Wiltow twinn with thy maidenhead, or thy
>   sweet life?'

The first and the second express a simple preference for death, and are killed and laid by, "to bear the red rose company" (**A**). The youngest, in **A**, says she has a brother in the wood, who will kill him if he kills her. The outlaw asks the brother's name, finds that he himself is the man, and takes his own life with the same weapon that had shed the blood of his sisters. **B, C, D** have three brothers, the youngest of whom is the banished lord (**C**), the outlyer bold (**D**). The story is defective in **B, C.** In **D** the outlaw, on finding what he has done, takes a long race, and falls on his knife. The conclusion of **E** is not so finely tragic. A brother John comes riding by just as the robber is about to kill the third sister, apprehends him by the agency of his three pages, and reserves him to be hanged on a tree,

> Or thrown into the poisond lake,
> To feed the toads and rattle-snake.

According to the account given by Herd, and repeated by Jamieson, the story of the lost conclusion of **B** made the banished man discover that he had killed his two brothers as well as his two sisters.

This ballad, with additional circumstances, is familiar to all branches of the Scandinavian race.

Danish. There are many versions from oral tradition, as yet unprinted, besides these two: **A,** 'Hr. Truels's Døttre,' *Danske Viser*, III, 392, No 164, there reprinted from Sandvig, *Beskrivelse over Øen Møen*, 1776: **B,** 'Herr Thors Børn,' from recent tradition of North Sleswig, Berggreen, *Danske Folke-Sange*, 3d ed., p. 88, No 42. Also 'Herr Tures Døtre,' Kristensen, *Jyske Folkeminder*, X, 294, No 72; Hr. Tures Døtre, Kristensen, *Folkeminder*, XI, 145, No 56.

A. Herr Truels' three daughters oversleep their matins one morning, and are roused by their mother. If we have overslept our matins, they say, we will make up at high mass. They set out for church, and in a wood fall in with three robbers, who say:

'Whether will ye be three robbers' wives,
Or will ye rather lose your lives?'

Much rather death, say they. The two elder sis-
ters submitted to their fate without a word; the
third made a hard resistance. With her last
breath she adjured the robbers to seek a lodging
at Herr Truels' that night. This they did. They
drank so long that they drank Herr Truels to
bed. Then they asked his wife to promise herself
to all three. First, she said, she must look into
their bags. In their bags she saw her daughters'
trinkets. She excused herself for a moment,
barred the door strongly, roused her husband,
and made it known to him that these guests had
killed his three daughters. Herr Truels called on
all his men to arm. He asked the robbers who
was their father. They said that they had been
stolen by robbers, on their way to school, one
day; had had a hard life for fourteen years; and
the first crime they had committed was killing
three maids yesterday. Herr Truels revealed to
them that they had murdered their sisters, and
offered them new clothes, in which they might
go away. "Nay," they said, "not so; life for life is
meet." They were taken out of the town, and
their heads struck off. B differs from A in only a
few points. The robbers ask lodging at Herr
Thor's, as being pilgrims. When he discovers
their true character, he threatens them with the
wheel. They say, Shall we come to the wheel?
Our father drinks Yule with the king. They tell
him their story, and their father offers them sad-
dle and horse to make their best way off. They
reply, "We will give blood for blood," spread
their cloaks on the floor, and let their blood run.

'Hr. Truelses Døtre' is No 338 of the Danish
ballads in the continuation of Grundtvig's col-
lection by Dr Axel Olrik, *Danske Ridderviser*,
1895, I, 114, where the ballad is subjected to a
minute study. The existence of a ballad is men-
tioned in 1624, and indicated as early as 1598.
There are Danish, Swedish, and Icelandic ver-
sions of the 17th century, and numerous later
copies, Danish, Swedish, Norwegian, and
Färöe: Danish, in all, 10, one of the 17th cen-
tury; Swedish 12, 4 of the 17th century; Norwe-
gian 6; Färöe 4. Five of the Norwegian copies
take the direction of the Icelandic and Färöe in
the treatment of the story. Two varieties of the

ballad may be specially distinguished: one in
which we have the miracle of a light burning or
a fountain (fountains) springing over the place
where the maids were murdered (Called by
Olrik the legendary form), the other in which
the career and fate of the sons are made promi-
nent. The "legendary" versions are the older. In
these the maids are regarded as martyrs, and
popular religious observances in connection
with the miraculous fountains and in commem-
oration of the murdered maids have been kept
up into the present century. The story is local-
ized in not less than thirteen Danish accounts
and others in Sweden.

Swedish. 'Pehr Tyrsons Döttrar i Wänge.'
A, Arwidsson, II, 413, No 166. **B**, Afzelius, III,
193, No 98: ed. Bergström, I, 380, No 84, 1. **C**,
Afzelius, III, 197: ed. Bergström, I, 382, No 84,
2, as old as the last half of the seventeenth cen-
tury. **D**, Afzelius, III, 202: ed. Bergström, I, 384,
No 84, 3. **E**, "C. J. Wessén, De paroecia Kärna
(an academical dissertation), Upsala, 1836,"
Arwidsson, as above, who mentions another
unprinted copy in the Royal Library.[*]

A. Herr Töres' daughters overslept matins,
dressed themselves handsomely, and set off for
mass. All on the heath they were met by three
wood-robbers, who demanded, Will ye be our
wives, or lose your lives? The first answered:
God save us from trying either! the second,
Rather let us range the world! the third, Better
death with honor! But

First were they the three wood-robbers' wives,
And after that they lost their young lives.

The robbers strip them; then go and ask to be
taken in by Herr Töres. He serves them with
mead and wine, but presently begins to wish his
daughters were at home. His wife sees him to
bed; then returns to her guests, who offer her a
silken sark to pass the night with them. "Give
me a sight of the silken sark," she cries, with
prophetic soul: "God have mercy on my daugh-
ters!" She rouses her husband, and tells him
that the robbers have slain his bairns. He puts

---

[*]   Professor George Stephens points me to two local-
ized prose outlines of the story, one from Småland, the
other from Skåne; 'Truls och hans barn,' in the *Svenska
Fornminnesföreningens Tidskrift*, II, 77f.

on his armor and kills two of them: the third begs to be spared till he can say who were his kin; his father's name is Töres! Father and mother resolve to build a church for penance, and it shall be called Kerna. **B, C, D**. The girls meet three "vallare," strolling men, and none of them good (**C**). The robbers cut off the girls' heads on the trunk of a birch (cf. English **C** 5: "It's lean your head upon my staff," and with his pen-knife he has cutted it aff): three springs burst forth immediately. They go to the house, and ask the mother if she will buy silken sarks that nine maids have stitched (**B**). She says:

'Open your sacks, and let me see:
Mayhap I shall know them all three.'

The father, in **B**, when he discovers that he has slain his own sons, goes to the smith, and has an iron hand fastened round his middle. The parents vow to build a church as an expiation, and it shall be called Kerna (**B, C**).

Färöe. Four versions are known; 'Torkilds Riim, eller St. Catharinæ Vise,' Lyngbye, *Færøiske Qvæder*, p. $534/_{535}$, repeated in Hammershaimb's *Færøsk Anthologi*, No 13, p. 45, 'Torkils døtur.' In this form of the story, as in the Icelandic versions which follow, the robbers are not the brothers of the maids. Torkild's two daughters sleep till the sun shines on their beds. Their father wakens them, and tells Katrine she is waited for at church. Katrine dresses herself splendidly, but does not disdain to saddle her own horse.

And since no knave was ready to help,
Katrine bridled the horse herself.

And since no knave was standing about,
Herself put the bit in her horse's mouth.

First she came upon three strollers (vadlarar[*]), then two, then one, and the last asked her

---

[*]   Lyngbye insists on translating *vadlarar* pilgrims, though his people understood the word to mean robbers. He refers to the Icelandic vallari, which, originally a pilgrim, came to mean a tramp. No one can fail to recognize the character who has become the terror of our rural districts, and to whom, in our preposterous regard for the rights of "man," we sacrifice the peace, and often the lives, of women.

whether she would pass the night with him (vera qvöldar vujv) or die. He cut off her head, and wherever her blood ran a light kindled; where her head fell a spring welled forth: where her body lay a church was [afterwards] built. The rover came to Torkild's house, and the father asked if he had seen Katrine. He said she had been at Mary kirk the day before, and asked for a lodging, feigning to be sick. This was readily granted. He went to bed, and Aasa, the other sister, waited upon him. He offered her a silken sark to sleep with him. Aasa asked to see the sark first, and found on it her sister's mark. The fellow went on to offer her a blue cloak [17] and gold crown successively, and on both of these she saw her sister's mark. Aasa bade him good-night, went to her father, and told him that the man they had housed had killed his daughter. Torkild ordered his swains to light a pile in the wood: early the next morning they burned the murderer on it.

Icelandic. Five Icelandic versions, and the first stanza of two more, are given in *Íslenzk Fornkvæði*, I, 108 ff, No 15, 'Vallara kvæði.'

The story is nearly the same as in the Färöe ballad. Two of Thorkell's daughters sleep till after the sun is up (**B, C**). They wash and dress; they set out for church (**C**). On the heath they encounter a strolling man, **A**; a tall, large man, **C, E**; a horseman or knight, **D**. He greets them: "Why will ye not speak? Are ye come of elves, or of kings themselves?" **A** [Are ye come of earls, or of beggar-churls? **B**]. They answer, We are not come of elves, nor of kings themselves; we are Thorkell's daughters, and serve Mary kirk. He asks, Will ye choose to lose your life, or shall I rather take you to wife? The choice, they say, is hard: they would rather die. He kills them and buries them. At night he goes to Thorkell's house, where Asa is alone. He knocks to be let in; Asa refuses; he draws the latch with his deft fingers (**A, C, D**). He offers Asa a silken sark to sleep with him [and a blue cloak to say nothing, **A**]. She asked to see the sark, and knew her sisters' work, begged him to wait a moment, went to her father, and told him that the murderer of his daughters was there. Thorkell dashed his harp to the floor [and kicked over the table, **D, E**]. The murderer in the morning was hanged like a dog, **A, B**.

[Thorkell tore at his hair and cut him down with an elder-stock, **C**; they fought three days, and on the fourth the villain was hanged in a strap, **E**, the knight was hanging like a dog, **D**]. A miraculous light burned over the place where the maids had been buried, **A** 16, **C** 27, **D** 24, **E** 12. When their bodies were taken into the church, the bells rang of themselves, **D**.

Norwegian versions of this ballad have been obtained from tradition, but none as yet have been published.

French. 'La Fille d'un Cabaretier,' Guillon, *Chansons pop. de l'Ain*, p. 165, has some of the circumstances of No 14. A girl is stopped by three "libertins" in a wood. She gives them her ring and her chain, to ransom her person. They say they will have that too, and kill her when she resists. They then go for breakfast to her father's tavern, and while they are paying their scot the ring falls and is recognized by her mother. The youngest confesses, and they are taken to the forest and burned. Other versions include 'Le Passage du Bois,' V. Smith, *Chants p. du Velay et du Forez*, *Romania*, X, 205; 'La Doulento,' Arbaud, I, 120; *Poésies pop. de la France*, MS., IV, fol. 442, printed in Rolland, III, 55. With these belong 'La Raggazza assassinata,' Nigra, No 12, three versions, p. 85ff; 'La Vergine uccisa,' Ferraro, *Canti p. monferrini*, p. 17; 'C'est trois garçons dépaysés,' Pineau, *Le Folk-Lore du Poitou*, p. 281; 'Les Coumpagnons,' Laroche, *Folklore du Lauraguais*, p. 245. A copy which has lost still more of the characteristic traits, was obtained by M. Couraye du Parc in Basse-Normandie: *Études romanes dédiées à Gaston Paris*, 1891, p. 47, No 10.

In a Russian ballad the only sister of nine [seven] brothers is given in marriage to a rich merchant, who lives at a distance from her home. After three years the married pair undertake a journey to her native place. On their way they are attacked by nine robbers, who kill her husband, throw her child into the sea, and act their pleasure with her. One of the nine, entering into talk with the woman, discovers that she is his sister. Sakharof, translated in Ralston's *Songs of the Russian People*, p. 49f; Ruibnikof, Part III, p. 340, No 62, Part IV, p. 99, No 19; Hilferding, col. 149, No 28, col. 844, No 167, col. 1154, No 248, col. 1265, No 294; Trudy, V, 910, No 479, **A–H**. A similar Ruthenian story in Kolberg, *Pokucie*, II, 30, No 33.

"The mains and burn of Fordie, the banks of which are very beautiful," says Aytoun (I, 159), "lie about six miles to the east of Dunkeld." Tradition has connected the story with half a dozen localities in Sweden, and, as Professor Grundtvig informs me, with at least eight places in the different provinces of Denmark. The Kerna church of the Swedish ballads, not far from Linköping (Afzelius), has been popularly supposed to derive its name from a Catharina, Karin, or Karna, killed by her own brother, a wood-robber, near its site. See Afzelius, ed. Bergström, II, 329ff: *Danske Viser*, III, 444f.

A is translated by Grundtvig, *Engelske og skotske Folkeviser*, No 34, p. 216, and, with some slight use of Aytoun, I, 160, by Rosa Warrens, *Schottische Volkslieder der Vorzeit*, No 18, p. 85. Danish **A**, by Prior, III, 252.

A

a. Motherwell's *Minstrelsy,* p. 88. **b.** The same. **c.**
The same, Appendix, p. xxii, No xxvi, apparently from
South Perthshire.

There were three sis - ters liv'd in a bower, Fair An - net, and Mar - garet, and Mar - jo - rie,

And they went out to pu' a flower, And the dew draps off the hynd - ber - ry tree.

A. c. Collected by Andrew Blaikie, Paisley.

1 THERE were three ladies lived in a bower,
       Eh vow bonnie
   And they went out to pull a flower.
       On the bonnie banks o Fordie

2 They hadna pu'ed a flower but ane,
   When up started to them a banisht man.

3 He's taen the first sister by her hand,
   And he's turned her round and made her stand.

4 'It's whether will ye be a rank robber's wife,
   Or will ye die by my wee pen-knife?'

5 'It's I'll not be a rank robber's wife,
   But I'll rather die by your wee pen-knife.'

6 He's killed this may, and he's laid her by,
   For to bear the red rose company.

[174] 7 He's taken the second ane by the hand,
   And he's turned her round and made her stand.

8 'It's whether will ye be a rank robber's wife,
   Or will ye die by my wee pen-knife?'

9 'I'll not be a rank robber's wife,
   But I'll rather die by your wee pen-knife.'

10 He's killed this may, and he's laid her by,
    For to bear the red rose company.

11 He's taken the youngest ane by the hand,
    And he's turned her round and made her stand.

12 Says, 'Will ye be a rank robber's wife,
    Or will ye die by my wee pen-knife?'

13 'I'll not be a rank robber's wife,
    Nor will I die by your wee pen-knife.

14 'For I hae a brother in this wood,
    And gin ye kill me, it's he'll kill thee.'

15 'What's thy brother's name? come tell to me.'
    'My brother's name is Baby Lon.'

16 'O sister, sister, what have I done!
    O have I done this ill to thee!

17 'O since I've done this evil deed,
    Good sall never be seen o me.'

18 He's taken out his wee pen-knife,
    And he's twyned himsel o his ain sweet life.

B

a. Herd's MSS, I, 38, II, 76. **b.** *The Scots Magazine,*
Oct., 1803, p. 699, communicated by Jamieson, and
evidently from Herd's copy.

1 THERE wond three ladies in a bower,
       Annet and Margret and Marjorie
   And they have gane out to pu a flower.
       And the dew it lyes on the wood, gay ladie

2 They had nae pu'd a flower but ane,
   When up has started a banished man.

3 He has taen the eldest by the hand,
   He has turned her about and bade her stand.

4 'Now whether will ye be a banisht man's wife,
   Or will ye be sticked wi my pen-knife?'

5 'I will na be ca'd a banished man's wife,
   I'll rather be sticked wi your pen-knife.'

6 And he has taen out his little pen-knife,
   And frae this lady he has taen the life.

7 He has taen the second by the hand,
   He has turned her about and he bad her stand.

8 'Now whether will ye be a banisht man's wife,
   Or will ye be sticked wi my pen-knife?'

9 'I will na be ca'd a banished man's wife;
   I'll rather be sticked wi your pen-knife.'

10 And he has taen out his little pen-knife,
   And frae this lady he has taen the life.

11 He has taen the youngest by the hand,
   He has turned her about and he bad her stand.

12 'Now whether will ye be a banished man's wife,
   Or will ye be sticked wi my pen-knife?'

13 'I winnae be called a banished man's wife,
   Nor yet will I be sticked wi your pen-knife.

14 'But gin my three brethren had been here,
   Ye had nae slain my sisters dear.'

*   *   *   *   *

C

Motherwell's MS., p. 172. From J. Goldie, March, 1825.

1 THERE were three sisters on a road,
   Gilly flower gentle rosemary
 And there they met a banished lord.
   And the dew it hings over the mulberry tree

2 The eldest sister was on the road,
   And there she met with the banished lord.

3 'O will ye consent to lose your life,
   Or will ye be a banished lord's wife?'

4 'I'll rather consent to lose my life
   Before I'll be a banished lord's wife.'

5 'It's lean your head upon my staff,'
   And with his pen-knife he has cutted it aff.

6 He flang her in amang the broom,
   Saying, 'Lye ye there till another ane come.'

7 The second sister was on the road,
   And there she met with the banished lord.

8 'O will ye consent to lose your life,
   Or will ye be a banished lord's wife?'

9 'I'll rather consent to lose my life
   Before I'll be a banished lord's wife.'

10 'It's lean your head upon my staff,'
   And with his pen-knife he has cutted it aff.

11 He flang her in amang the broom,
   Saying, 'Lie ye there till another ane come.'

12 The youngest sister was on the road,
   And there she met with the banished lord.

13 'O will ye consent to lose your life,
   Or will ye be a banished lord's wife?'

14 'O if my three brothers were here,
   Ye durstna put me in such a fear.'

15 'What are your three brothers, altho they were
      here,
   That I durstna put you in such a fear?'

16 'My eldest brother's a belted knight,
   The second, he's a . . .

17 'My youngest brother's a banished lord,
   And oftentimes he walks on this road.'

D

Motherwell's MS., p. 174. From the recitation of
Agnes Lyle, Kilbarchan, July 27, 1825.

1 THERE were three sisters, they lived in a bower,
    Sing Anna, sing Margaret, sing Marjorie
The youngest o them was the fairest flower.
    And the dew goes thro the wood, gay ladie

2 The oldest of them she's to the wood gane,
    To seek a braw leaf and to bring it hame.

3 There she met with an outlyer bold,
    Lies many long nights in the woods so cold.

4 'Istow a maid, or istow a wife?
    Wiltow twinn with thy maidenhead, or thy
        sweet life?'

5 'O kind sir, if I hae 't at my will,
    I'll twinn with my life, keep my maidenhead
        still.'

6 He's taen out his we pen-knife,
    He's twinned this young lady of her sweet life.

7 He wiped his knife along the dew;
    But the more he wiped, the redder it grew.

8 The second of them she's to the wood gane,
    To seek her old sister, and to bring her hame.

9 There she met with an outlyer bold,
    Lies many long nights in the woods so cold.

10 'Istow a maid, or istow a wife?
    Wiltow twinn with thy maidenhead, or thy
        sweet life?'

11 'O kind sir, if I hae 't at my will,
    I'll twinn with my life, keep my maidenhead
        still.'

12 He's taen out his we pen-knife,
    He's twinned this young lady of her sweet life.

13 He wiped his knife along the dew;
    But the more he wiped, the redder it grew.

14 The youngest of them she's to the wood gane,
    To seek her two sisters, and to bring them
        hame.

15 There she met with an outlyer bold,
    Lies many long nights in the woods so cold.

16 'Istow a maid, or istow a wife?
    Wiltow twinn with thy maidenhead, or thy
        sweet life?'

17 'If my three brethren they were here,
    Such questions as these thou durst nae speer.'

18 'Pray, what may thy three brethren be,
    That I durst na mak so bold with thee?'

19 'The eldest o them is a minister bred,
    He teaches the people from evil to good.

20 'The second o them is a ploughman good,
    He ploughs the land for his livelihood.

21 'The youngest of them is an outlyer bold,
    Lies many a long night in the woods so cold.'

22 He stuck his knife then into the ground,
    He took a long race, let himself fall on.

E

Kinloch's *Ancient Scottish Ballads*, p. 212. From Mearnsshire.

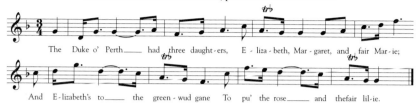

The Duke o' Perth___ had three daught-ers,   E - liza - beth, Mar - garet, and fair Mar - ie;

And E - lizabeth's to___ the green - wud gane   To pu' the rose___ and the fair lil - ie.

1 THE Duke o Perth had three daughters,
    Elizabeth, Margaret, and fair Marie;
And Elizabeth's to the greenwud gane,
    To pu the rose and the fair lilie.

2 But she hadna pu'd a rose, a rose,
    A double rose, but barely three,
Whan up and started a Loudon lord,
    Wi Loudon hose, and Loudon sheen.

3 'Will ye be called a robber's wife?
    Or will ye be stickit wi my bloody knife?
For pu'in the rose and the fair lilie,
    For pu'in them sae fair and free.'

4 'Before I'll be called a robber's wife,
    I'll rather be stickit wi your bloody knife,
For pu'in,' etc.

5 Then out he's tane his little pen-knife,
    And he's parted her and her sweet life,
And thrown her oer a bank o brume,
    There never more for to be found.

6 The Duke o Perth had three daughters,
    Elizabeth, Margaret, and fair Marie
And Margaret's to the greenwud gane,
    To pu the rose and the fair lilie.

7 She hadna pu'd a rose, a rose,
    A double rose, but barely three,
When up and started a Loudon lord,
    Wi Loudon hose, and Loudon sheen.

8 'Will ye be called a robber's wife?
    Or will ye be stickit wi my bloody knife?
For pu'in,' etc.

9 'Before I'll be called a robber's wife,
    I'll rather be stickit wi your bloody knife,
For pu'in,' etc.

10 Then out he's tane his little pen-knife,
    And he's parted her and her sweet life,
For pu'in,' etc.

11 The Duke o Perth had three daughters,
    Elizabeth, Margaret, and fair Marie
And Mary's to the greenwud gane,
    To pu the rose and the fair lilie.

12 She hadna pu'd a rose, a rose,
    A double rose, but barely three,
When up and started a Loudon lord,
    Wi Loudon hose, and Loudon sheen.

13 'O will ye be called a robber's wife?
    Or will ye be stickit wi my bloody knife?
For pu'in,' etc.

14 'Before I'll be called a robber's wife,
    I'll rather be stickit wi your bloody knife,
For pu'in,' etc.

15 But just as he took out his knife,   [177]
    To tak frae her her ain sweet life,
Her brother John cam ryding bye,
    And this bloody robber he did espy.

16 But when he saw his sister fair,
    He kennd her by her yellow hair;
He calld upon his pages three,
    To find this robber speedilie.

17 'My sisters twa that are dead and gane,
    For whom we made a heavy maene,
It's you that's twinnd them o their life,
    And wi your cruel bloody knife.

18 'Then for their life ye sair shall dree;
    Ye sall be hangit on a tree,
Or thrown into the poisond lake,
    To feed the toads and rattle-snake.'

F

"In Gipsy Tents," by Francis Hindes Groome, p. 143.

1 THERE were three sisters going from home,
  All in a lea and alony, oh
They met a man, and he made them stand,
  Down by the bonny banks of Airdrie, oh.

2 He took the first one by the hand,
He turned her round, and he made her stand.

3 Saying, Will you be a robber's wife?
Or will you die by my penknife?

4 'Oh, I wont be a robber's wife,
But I will die by your penknife.'

5 Then he took the second by her hand,
He turned her round, and he made her stand.

6 Saying, Will you be a robber's wife?
Or will you die by my penknife?

7 'Oh, I wont be a robber's wife,
But I will die by your penknife.'

8 He took the third one by the hand,
He turned her round, and he made her stand.

9 Saying, Will you be a robber's wife?
Or will you die by my penknife?

10 'Oh, I wont be a robber's wife,
And I wont die by your penknife.

11 'If my two brothers had been here,
You would not have killed my sisters two.'

12 'What was your two brothers' names?'
'One was John, and the other was James.'

13 'Oh, what did your two brothers do?'
'One was a minister, the other such as you.'

14 'Oh, what is this that I have done?
I have killed my sisters, all but one.

15 'And now I'll take out my penknife,
And here I'll end my own sweet life.'

A. a. "Given from two copies obtained from recitation, which differ but little from each other. Indeed, the only variation is in the verse where the outlawed brother unweetingly slays his sister." [19.] *Motherwell.*

b.   19. He's taken out his wee penknife,
      Hey how bonnie
   And he's twined her o her ain sweet life.
      On the, etc.

c. *The first stanza only:*

   There were three sisters livd in a bower,
      Fair Annet and Margaret and Marjorie
   And they went out to pu a flower.
      And the dew draps oft the hyndberry tree

B. a. "To a wild melancholy old tune not in any collection."
   "N. B. There are a great many other verses which I could not recover. Upon describing her brothers, the banished man finds that he has killed his two brothers and two sisters,—upon which he kills himself." *Herd.*
   2^2. MS. Quhen. 4^1, 4^2, 5^2, 12^1,12^2, 13^2, 14^2. ye, your, yet, MS. ze, zour, zet. 8, 9, 10 *are not written out.*

b. "Of this I have got only 14 stanzas, but there are many more. It is a horrid story. The banished man discovers that he has killed two of his brothers and his three (?) sisters, upon which he kills himself." *Jamieson.*
   The first two stanzas only are cited by Jamieson.
   1^1. three sisters. 2^2. up there started.

C. 7–11 *and* 12^2 *are not written out in the MS.*
   "Repeat as to the second sister, mutatis mutandis." *Motherwell.*

D. 9–13 *are not written out in the MS.* "Same as 1st sister." *Motherwell.*
   14^2. bring her.
   15, 16 *are not written out.* "Same as 1st and 2d sisters, but this additional, vizt." M.
   22^2. longe, *or* large?

15

LEESOME BRAND

A. 'Leesome Brand.' **a.** Buchan's *Ballads of the North of Scotland*, I, 38. **b.** Motherwell's MS., p. 626.

B. 'The Broom blooms bonnie,' etc., Motherwell's MS., p. 365.

THIS is one of the cases in which a remarkably fine ballad has been worse preserved in Scotland than anywhere else. Without light from abroad we cannot fully understand even so much as we have saved, and *with* this light comes a keen regret for what we have lost.

A, from Buchan's *Ballads of the North of Scotland*, is found also in Motherwell's MS., but without doubt was derived from Buchan. Though injured by the commixture of foreign elements, A has still much of the original story. B has, on the contrary, so little that distinctively and exclusively belongs to this story that it might almost as well have been put with the following ballad, 'Sheath and Knife,' as here. A third ballad, 'The Birth of Robin Hood,' preserves as much of the story as A, but in an utterly incongruous and very modern setting, being, like 'Erlinton,' C, forced into an absurd Robin Hood framework.

The mixture of four-line with two-line stanzas in A of course comes from different ballads having been blended, but for all that, these ballads might have had the same theme. Stanzas 33–35, however, are such as we meet with in ballads of the 'Earl Brand' class, but not in those of the class to which 'Leesome Brand' belongs. In the English ballads, and nearly all the Danish, of the former class, there is at least a conversation between son and mother [father], whereas in the other the catastrophe excludes such a possibility. Again, the "unco land" in the first stanza, "where winds never blew nor cocks ever crew," is at least a reminis-

cence of the paradise depicted in the beginning of many of the versions of 'Ribold and Guldborg,' and stanza 4 of 'Leesome Brand' closely resembles stanza 2 of 'Earl Brand,' A.[*] Still, the first and fourth stanzas suit one ballad as well as the other, which is not true of 33–35.

The name Leesome Brand may possibly be a corruption of Hildebrand, as Earl Brand almost certainly is; but a more likely origin is the Gysellannd of one of the kindred Danish ballads.

The white hind, stanzas 28, 30, is met with in no other ballad of this class,[†] and, besides this, the last four stanzas are in no kind of keeping with what goes before, for the "young son" is spoken of as having been first brought home at some previous period. Grundtvig has suggested that the hind and the blood came from a lost Scottish ballad resembling 'The Maid Transformed into a Hind,' 'Jomfru i Hindeham,' *D. g. F.*, No 58, Kristensen, *Jyske Folkeminder*,

---

[*]   And also stanza 3 of Buchan's 'Fairy Knight,' 'The Elfin Knight,' **D**, p. 23 of this volume, which runs:

> I hae a sister eleven years auld,
> And she to the young men's bed has made bauld.

[†]   Compare with **A**, stanzas 27, 28:

> Modhren lärde sonnenn sinn:
> 'Skiuter tu diur och skiuter ta råå;

> 'Skiuter tu diur och skiuter tu råå,
> Then salige hindenn lätt tu gå!'

'Den förtrollade Jungfrun,' Arwidsson, II, 260, No 136, **A** 1, 2.

XI 14, No 7. In this ballad a girl begs her brother, who is going hunting, to spare the little hind that "plays before his foot." The brother nevertheless shoots the hind, though not mortally, and sets to work to flay it, in which process he discovers his sister under the hind's hide. His sister tells him that she had been successively changed into a pair of scissors, a sword, a hare, a hind, by her step-mother, and that she was not to be free of the spell until she had drunk of her brother's blood. Her brother at once cuts his fingers, gives her some of his blood, and the girl is permanently restored to her natural shape, and afterwards is happily married. Stanzas similar to 36–41 of A and 12–16 of B will be found in the ballad which follows this, to which they are especially well suited by their riddling character; and I believe that they belong there, and not here. It is worthy of remark, too, that there is a *hind* in another ballad, closely related to No 16 ('The Bonny Hind'), and that the hind in 'Leesome Brand' may, in some way not now explicable, have come from this. The confounding of 'Leesome Brand' with a ballad of the 'Bonny Hind' class would be paralleled in Danish, for in 'Redselille og Medelvold' T (and perhaps I, see Grundtvig's note, v, 237), the knight is the lady's brother.

The "auld son" in B, like the first bringing home of the *young* son in A 45, 47, shows how completely the proper story has been lost sight of. There should be no son of any description at the point at which this stanza comes in, and *auld* son should everywhere be *young* son. The best we can do, to make sense of stanza 3, is to put it after 8, with the understanding that woman and child are carried off for burial; though really there is no need to move them on that account. The shooting of the child is unintelligible in the mutilated state of the ballad. It is apparently meant to be an accident. Nothing of the kind occurs in other ballads of the class, and the divergence is probably a simple corruption.

The ballad which 'Leesome Brand' represents is preserved among the Scandinavian races under four forms.

[179] **Danish.** I. 'Bolde Hr. Nilaus' Løn,' a single copy from a manuscript of the beginning of the 17th century: Grundtvig, v, 231, No 270. II.

'Redselille og Medelvold,' in an all but unexampled number of versions, of which some sixty are collated, and some twenty-five printed, by Grundtvig, most of them recently obtained from tradition, and the oldest a broadside of about the year 1770: Grundtvig, v, 234, No 271. 'Barnefødsel i Lunden,' six copies and a fragment, in Kristensen's *Skattegraveren*, X, 145ff, Nos 416–22, 1888. ('Sadlen for trang, vejen for lang,' 416, 17, 20; man's help, 416, 419; children buried alive, 417, 18, 22; sister and brother, 418; lilies from grave, 416, 17.) "Skjøn Medler,' Kristensen, *Jyske Folkeminder*, X, 182, No 46, **A–H**. Kristensen, *Folkeminder*, XI, 102, No 45, **A–I**, 9 copies. (Saddle, way, **A**; man's help, **A, B, E, F, H**; children buried alive, **A, B, C, E, F.**) III. 'Sönnens Sorg,' Grundtvig, v, 289, No 272, two versions only: **A** from the middle of the 16th century; **B** three hundred years later, previously printed in Berggreen's *Danske Folkesange*, I, No 83 (3d ed.). IV. 'Stalbroders Kvide,' Grundtvig, v, 301, No 273, two versions: **A** from the beginning of the 17th century, **B** from about 1570.

Swedish. II. **A**, broadside of 1776, reprinted in Grundtvig, No 271, v, 281, Bilag 1, and in Jamieson's *Illustrations*, p. 373ff, with a translation. **B**, 'Herr Redevall,' Afzelius, II, 189, No 58, new ed. No 51; 'Herr Riddervall,' Lagus, *Nyländska Folkvisor*, I, 75, No 20. **C**, 'Krist' Lilla och Herr Tideman,' Arwidsson, I, 352, No 54 **A**. **D, E, F, G**, from Cavallius and Stephens' manuscript collection, first printed by Grundtvig, No 271, v, 282ff, Bilag 2–5. **H**, 'Rosa lilla,' Eva Wigström, *Folkvisor från Skåne*, in *Ur de nordiska, Folkens Lif, af Artur Hazelius*, p. 133, No 8. III. A single version, of date about 1650, 'Moder och Son,' Arwidsson, II, 15, No 70. A copy of 'Lilla Lisa och Herr Nedervall' is printed by Aminson, *Bidrag, o. s. v.*, No 5, p. 17. I, 'Risa lill,' Wigström, *Folkdiktning*, II, 28.

Norwegian. II. Six versions and a fragment, from recent tradition: **A–E, G**, first printed by Grundtvig, No 271, v, 284ff, Bilag 6–11; **F**, 'Grivilja,' in Lindeman's *Norske Fjeldmelodier*, No 121. III. Six versions from recent tradition, **A–F**, first printed by Grundtvig, No 272, v, 297ff, Bilag 1–6.

Icelandic. III. 'Sonar harmur,' *Íslenzk Fornkvæði*, I, 140ff, No 17, three versions, **A, B, C,**

the last, which is the oldest, being from late in the 17th century; also the first stanza of a fourth, **D**.

All the Scandinavian versions are in two-line stanzas save Danish 272 **B**, and **A** in part, and Icelandic 17 **C**, which are in four; the last, however, in stanzas of two couplets.

It will be most convenient to give first a summary of the story of 'Redselille og Medel-vold,' and to notice the chief divergences of the other ballads afterwards. A mother and her daughter are engaged in weaving gold tissue. The mother sees milk running from the girl's breasts, and asks an explanation. After a slight attempt at evasion, the daughter confesses that she has been beguiled by a knight. The mother threatens both with punishment: he shall be hanged [burned, broken on the wheel, sent out of the country, i.e., sold into servitude], and she sent away [broiled on a gridiron, burned, drowned]. Some copies begin further back, with a stanza or two in which we are told that the knight has served in the king's court, and gained the favor of the king's daughter. Alarmed by her mother's threats, the maid goes to her lover's house at night, and after some difficulty in effecting an entrance (a common-place, like the ill-boding milk above) informs him of the fate that awaits them. The knight is sufficiently prompt now, and bids her get her gold together while he saddles his horse. They ride away, with [or without] precautions against discovery, and come to a wood. Four Norwegian versions, **A**, **B**, **C**, **G**, and also two Icelandic versions, **A**, **B**, of 'Sønnens Sorg,' interpose a piece of water, and a difficulty in crossing, owing to the ferryman's refusing help or the want of oars; but this passage is clearly an infil-tration from a different story. Arriving at the wood, the maid desires to rest a while. The cus-tomary interrogation does not fail,—whether the way is too long or the saddle too small. The knight lifts her off the horse, spreads his cloak for her on the grass, and she gives way to her anguish in such exclamations as "My mother had nine women: would that I had the worst of them!" "My mother would never have been so angry with me but she would have helped me in this strait!" Most of the Danish versions make the knight offer to bandage his eyes and render

such service as a man may; but she replies that she would rather die than that man should know of woman's pangs. So Swedish **H**, nearly. Partly to secure privacy, and partly from thirst, she expresses a wish for water, and her lover goes in search of some. (This in nearly all the [180] Danish ballads, and many of the others. But in four of the Norwegian versions of 'Sønnens Sorg' the lover is told to go and amuse himself, much as in our ballads.) When he comes to the spring or the brook, there sits a nightingale and sings. *Two* nightingales, a small bird, a voice from heaven, a small dwarf, an old man, replace the nightingale in certain copies, and in others there is nothing at all; but the great majority has a single nightingale, and, as Grundtvig points out, the single bird is right, for the bird is really a vehicle for the soul of the dead Redse-lille. The nightingale sings, "Redselille lies dead in the wood, with two sons [son and daughter] in her bosom." All that the nightingale has said is found to be true. According to Danish **O** and Swedish **C**, the knight finds the lady and a child, according to Swedish **B** and Norwegian **A**, **B**, **C**, the lady and two sons, dead. In Danish **B**, **L** (as also the Icelandic 'Sonar Harmur,' **A**, **B**, and Danish 'Stalbroders Kvide,' **A**) the knight digs a grave, and lays mother and chil-dren in it; he lays himself with them in **A**, **G**, **M**, **X**. It is not said whether the children are dead or living, and the point would hardly be raised but for what follows. In Danish **D**, **P** and Swedish **F**, it is expressly mentioned that the children are *alive*, and in **Q**, **R**, **S**, **T**, **U**, six cop-ies of **V**, and **Y**, and also in 'Bolde Hr. Nilaus' Løn,' and in 'Sønnens Sorg,' Danish **A**, Norwe-gian **A**, **C**, **D**, **E**, the children are heard, or seem to be heard, shrieking from under the ground. Nearly all the versions make the knight run himself through with his sword, either immedi-ately after the others are laid in the grave, or after he has ridden far and wide, because he cannot endure the cries of the children from under the earth. This would seem to be the original conclusion of the story; the horrible circumstance of the children being buried alive is much more likely to be slurred over or omit-ted at a later day than to be added.

We may pass over in silence the less impor-tant variations in the very numerous versions of

'Redselille and Medelvold,' nor need we be detained long by the other three Scandinavian forms of the ballad. 'Sønnens Sorg' stands in the same relation to 'Redselille and Medelvold' as 'Hildebrand and Hilde,' does to 'Ribold and Guldborg' (see p. 118 of this volume); that is, the story is told in the first person instead of the third. A father asks his son why he is so sad, Norwegian **A, B, C, D**, Icelandic **A, B, C, D**. Five years has he sat at his father's board, and never uttered a merry word. The son relates the tragedy of his life. He had lived in his early youth at the house of a nobleman, who had three daughters. He was on very familiar terms with all of them, and the youngest loved him. When the time came for him to leave the family, she proposed that he should take her with him, Danish **B**, Icelandic **A, B, C** [he makes the proposal in Norwegian **C**]. From this point the narrative is much the same as in 'Redselille and Medelvold,' and at the conclusion he falls dead in his father's arms [at the table], Norwegian **A, B, D**, Icelandic **A**. The mother takes the place of the father in Danish **B** and Swedish, and perhaps it is the mother who tells the story in English **A**, but the bad condition of the text scarcely enables us to say. Danish **B** and the Swedish copy have lost the middle and end of the proper story: there is no wood, no childbirth, no burial. The superfluous boat of some Norwegian versions of 'Redselille' reappears in these, and also in Icelandic **A, B**; it is overturned in a storm, and the lady is drowned.

'Stalbroders Kvide' differs from 'Sønnens Sorg' only in this: that the story is related to a comrade instead of father or mother.

'Bolde Hr. Nilaus' Løn,' which exists but in a single copy, has a peculiar beginning. Sir Nilaus has served eight years in the king's court without recompense. He has, however, gained the favor of the king's daughter, who tells him that she is suffering much on his account. If this be so, says Nilaus, I will quit the land with speed. He is told to wait till she has spoken to her mother. She goes to her mother and says: Sir Nilaus has served eight years, and had no reward; he desires the best that it is in your power to give. The queen exclaims, He shall [181] never have my only daughter's hand! The young lady immediately bids Nilaus saddle his

horse while she collects her gold, and from this point we have the story of Redselille.

Dutch. Willems, *Oude vlæmsche Liederen*, p. 482, No 231, 'De Ruiter en Mooi Elsje;' Hoffmann v. Fallersleben, *Niederländische Volkslieder*, 2d ed., p. 170, No 75: broadside of the date 1780.

A mother inquires into her daughter's condition, and learns that she is going with child by a trooper (he is called both 'ruiter' and 'landsknecht'). The conversation is overheard by the other party, who asks the girl whether she will ride with him or bide with her mother. She chooses to go with him, and as they ride is overtaken with pains. She asks whether there is not a house where she can rest. The soldier builds her a hut of thistles, thorns, and high stakes, and hangs his cloak over the aperture. She asks him to go away, and to come back when he hears a cry: but the maid was dead ere she cried. The trooper laid his head on a stone, and his heart brake with grief.

German. A, Simrock, No 40, p. 92, 'Von Farbe so bleich,' from Bonn and Rheindorf, repeated in Mittler, No 194. The mother, on learning her daughter's plight, imprecates a curse on her. The maid betakes herself to her lover, a trooper, who rides off with her. They come to a cool spring, and she begs for a fresh drink, but, feeling very ill, asks if there is no hamlet near, from which she could have woman's help. The aid of the trooper is rejected in the usual phrase, and he is asked to go aside, and answer when called. If there should be no call, she will be dead. There was no call, and she was found to be dead, with two sons in her bosom. The trooper wrapped the children in her apron, and dug her grave with his sword. **B**, Reifferscheid, *Westfälische Volkslieder*, p. 106, 'Ach Wunder über Wunder,' from Bökendorf: much the same as to the story. **C**, Mittler, No 195, p. 175, 'Von Farbe so bleich,' a fragment of a copy from Hesse; Zuccalmaglio, p. 187, No 90, 'Die Waisen,' an entire copy, ostensibly from the Lower Rhine, but clearly owing its last fourteen stanzas to the editor. The trooper, in this supplement, leaves the boys with his mother, and goes over seas. The boys grow up, and set out to find their father. In the course of their quest, they pass a night in a hut in a wood, and are overheard saying a prayer for their father and dead mother, by a person who announces herself as their maternal grandmother! After this it is not surprising that the father himself should turn up early the next morning. The same editor, under the name of Montanus,* gives in Die deutschen Volksfeste, p. 45f, a part of this ballad again, with variations which show his hand beyond a doubt. We are here informed that the ballad has above a hundred stanzas, and that the conclusion is that the grandmother repents her curse, makes her peace with the boys, and builds a convent. D, 'Der Ritter und seine Geliebte,' Ditfurth, Deutsche Volks- und Gesellschaftslieder des 17. und 18. Jahrhunderts, p. 14, No 13. (Köhler.) To these should be added Böhme, Erk's Liederhort, I, 592f, 'Der Reiter und seine Geliebte,' No 194 b, from Erk's papers, c, from oral tradition (fragments). Böckel, 'Das Begräbniss im Walde,' p. 33, No 47. 'Es gingen zwei Liebchen durch einen grünen Wald,' Wolfram, p. 89, No 63.

French. Bujeaud, Chants et Chansons populaires des Provinces de l'Ouest, A, I, 198, B, I, 200, 'J'entends le rossignolet;' 'La-bas, sus ces grands champs,' Pineau, Le Folk-Lore du Poitou, p. 315. A. This ballad has suffered injury at the beginning and the end, but still preserves very well the chief points of the story. A lover has promised his mistress that after returning from a long absence he would take her to see his country. While traversing a wood she is seized with her pains. The aid of her companion is declined: "Cela n'est point votre métier." She begs for water. The lover goes for some, and meets a lark, who tells him that he will find his love dead, with a child in her arms. Two stanzas follow which are to no purpose. B. Another copy of this ballad has a perverted instead of a meaningless conclusion, but this keeps some traits that are wanting in A. It is a two-line ballad, with the nightingale in the refrain: "J'entends le rossignolet." A fair maid, walking with her lover, falls ill, and lies down under a thorn. The lover asks if he shall go for her mother. "She would not come: she has a cruel heart." Shall I go for mine? "Go, like the swal-

low!" He comes back and finds his love dead, and says he will die with his mistress. The absurd conclusion follows that she was feigning death to test his love. **C.** Decombe, No 96, p. 275, 'Le fils du roi d'Espagne.' A still more corrupted copy in Poésies populaires de la France, III, fol. 143, 'La fausse morte.' **D.** Fol. 215 of the same volume, a very pretty ballad from Périgord, which has lost most of the characteristic incidents, but not the tragic conclusion.

The names in the Scandinavian ballads, it is [182] remarked by Grundtvig, v, 242, 291, are not Norse, but probably of German derivation, and, if such, would indicate a like origin for the story. The man's name, for instance, in the Danish 'Sønnens Sorg,' **A**, Gysellannd, seems to point to Gisalbrand or Gisalbald, German names of the 8th or 9th century. There is some doubt whether this Gysellannd is not due to a corruption arising in the course of tradition (see Grundtvig, v, 302); but if the name may stand, it will account for our Leesome Brand almost as satisfactorily as Hildebrand does for Earl Brand in No 7.

The passage in which the lady refuses male assistance during her travail—found as well in almost all the Danish versions of 'Redselille and Medelvold,' in the German and French, and imperfectly in Swedish **D**—occurs in several other English ballads, viz., No 102, 'Willie and Earl Richard's Daughter;' No 103, 'Rose the Red and White Lily;' No 64, 'Fair Janet,' **C** 7, **D** 1; No 63, 'Child Waters,' **J** 39; No 24, 'Bonnie Annie,' **A** 10, **B** 6, 7. A similar scene is found in Sir Beues of Hamtoun, p. 132, v. 3449ff (Maitland Club).

> Beues is seruise gan hire bede,
> To helpe hire at that nede.
> 'For Godes loue,' she seide, 'nai!
> Leue sire, thow go the wai;
> For forbede, for is pite,
> That no wimmanis priuite
> To no man thourgh me be kouthe.'

Nearly the whole of the scene in the wood is in 'Wolfdietrich.' Wolfdietrich finds a dead man and a woman naked to the girdle, who is clasping the stem of a tree. The man, who was her husband, was taking her to her mother's

---

* Montanus is Vincenz von Zuccalmaglio; the ballad-editor is Wilhelm.

house, where her first child was to be born, when he was attacked by the dragon Schadesam. She was now in the third day of her travail. Wolfdietrich, having first wrapped her in his cloak, offers his help, requesting her to tear a strip from her shift and bind it round his eyes. She rejects his assistance in this form, but sends him for water, which he brings in his helmet, but only to find the woman dead, with a lifeless child at her breast. He wraps mother and child in his mantle, carries them to a chapel, and lays them on the altar; then digs a grave with his sword, goes for the body of the man, and buries all three in the grave he has made. Grimm, *Altdänische Heldenlieder*, p. 508; Holtzmann, *Der grosse Wolfdietrich*, st. 1587–1611; Amelung u.

Jänicke,[*] *Ortnit u. die Wolfdietriche*, II, 146, **D**, st. 51–75; with differences, I, 289, **B**, st. 842–848; mother and child surviving, I, 146, **A**, st. 562–578; Weber's abstract of the Heldenbuch, in *Illustrations of Northern Antiquities*, p. 119, 120; a similar scene, ending happily, in *I Complementi della Chanson d'Huon de Bordeaux*, publicati da A. Graf, pp 26ff. (Köhler.)

'Herr Medelvold,' a mixed text of Danish II, *Danske Viser*, No 156, is translated by Jamieson, *Illustrations*, p. 377; by Borrow, *Romantic Ballads*, p. 28 (very ill); and by Prior, No 101. Swedish, II, **A**, is translated by Jamieson, *ib.*, p. 373.

---

[*]   Who suggests, II, xlv, somewhat oddly, that the passage may have been taken from Revelation, xii, 2f, 13f.

A

a. Buchan's *Ballads of the North of Scotland*, I, 38. **b.**
Motherwell's MS., p. 626.

1 My boy was scarcely ten years auld,
　　Whan he went to an unco land,
　　Where wind never blew, nor cocks ever crew,
　　Ohon for my son, Leesome Brand!

2 Awa to that king's court he went,
　　It was to serve for meat an fee
　　Gude red gowd it was his hire,
　　And lang in that king's court stayd he.

3 He hadna been in that unco land
　　But only twallmonths twa or three,
　　Till by the glancing o his ee,
　　He gaind the love o a gay ladye.

4 This ladye was scarce eleven years auld,
　　When on her love she was right bauld;
　　She was scarce up to my right knee,
　　When oft in bed wi men I'm tauld.

5 But when nine months were come and gane,
　　This ladye's face turnd pale and wane.

6 To Leesome Brand she then did say,
　　'In this place I can nae mair stay.

7 'Ye do you to my father's stable,
　　Where steeds do stand baith wight and able.

8 'Strike ane o them upo the back,
　　The swiftest will gie his head a wap.

9 'Ye take him out upo the green,   [183
　　And get him saddled and bridled seen.

10 'Get ane for you, anither for me,
　　And lat us ride out ower the lee.

11 'Ye do you to my mother's coffer,
　　And out of it ye'll take my tocher.

12 'Therein are sixty thousand pounds,
　　Which all to me by right belongs.'

13 He's done him to her father's stable,
　　Where steeds stood baith wicht and able.

14 Then he strake ane upon the back,
　　The swiftest gae his head a wap.

15 He's taen him out upo the green,
　　And got him saddled and bridled seen.

16 Ane for him, and another for her,
　　To carry them baith wi might and virr.

17 He's done him to her mother's coffer,
　　And there he's taen his lover's tocher;

18 Wherein were sixty thousand pound,
  Which all to her by right belongd.

19 When they had ridden about six mile,
  His true love then began to fail.

20 'O wae's me,' said that gay ladye,
  'I fear my back will gang in three!

21 'O gin I had but a gade midwife,
  Here this day to save my life,

22 'And ease me o my misery,
  O dear, how happy I woud be!

23 'My love, we're far frae ony town,
  There is nae midwife to be foun.

24 'But if ye'll be content wi me,
  I'll do for you what man can dee.'

25 'For no, for no, this maunna be,'
  Wi a sigh, replied this gay ladye.

26 'When I endure my grief and pain,
  My companie ye maun refrain.

27 'Ye'll take your arrow and your bow,
  And ye will hunt the deer and roe.

28 'Be sure ye touch not the white hynde,
  For she is o the woman kind.'

29 He took sic pleasure in deer and roe,
  Till he forgot his gay ladye.

30 Till by it came that milk-white hynde,
  And then he mind on his ladye syne.

31 He hasted him to yon greenwood tree,
  For to relieve his gay ladye;

32 But found his ladye lying dead,
  Likeways her young son at her head.

33 His mother lay ower her castle wa,
  And she beheld baith dale and down;
  And she beheld young Leesome Brand,
  As he came riding to the town.

34 'Get minstrels for to play,' she said,
  'And dancers to dance in my room;
  For here comes my son, Leesome Brand,
  And he comes merrilie to the town.'

35 'Seek nae minstrels to play, mother,
  Nor dancers to dance in your room;
  But tho your son comes, Leesome Brand,
  Yet he comes sorry to the town.

36 'O I hae lost my gowden knife;
  I rather had lost my ain sweet life!

37 'And I hae lost a better thing,
  The gilded sheath that it was in.'

38 'Are there nae gowdsmiths here in Fife,
  Can make to you anither knife?

39 'Are there nae sheath-makers in the land,
  Can make a sheath to Leesome Brand?'

40 'There are nae gowdsmiths here in Fife,
  Can make me sic a gowden knife;

41 'Nor nae sheath-makers in the land,
  Can make to me a sheath again.

42 'There ne'er was man in Scotland born,
  Ordaind to be so much forlorn.

43 'I've lost my ladye I lovd sae dear,   [184]
  Likeways the son she did me bear.'

44 'Put in your hand at my bed head,
  There ye'll find a gude grey horn;
  In it three draps o' Saint Paul's ain blude,
  That hae been there sin he was born.

45 'Drap twa o them o your ladye,
  And ane upo your little young son;
  Then as lively they will be
  As the first night ye brought them hame.'

46 He put his hand at her bed head,
  And there he found a gude grey horn,
  Wi three draps o' Saint Paul's ain blude,
  That had been there sin he was born.

47 Then he drappd twa on his ladye,
  And ane o them on his young son,
  And now they do as lively be,
  As the first day he brought them hame.

B

Motherwell's MS., p. 365. From the recitation of
Agnes Lyle, Kilbarchan.

1 'THERE is a feast in your father's house,
   The broom blooms bonnie and so is it fair
It becomes you and me to be very douce.
   And we'll never gang up to the broom nae
      mair

2 'You will go to yon hill so hie
   Take your bow and your arrow wi thee.'

3 He's tane his lady on his back,
   And his auld son in his coat lap.

4 'When ye hear me give a cry,
   Ye'll shoot your bow and let me lye.

5 'When ye see me lying still,
   Throw away your bow and come running me
      till.'

6 When he heard her gie the cry,
   He shot his bow and he let her lye.

7 When he saw she was lying still,
   He threw away his bow and came running her
      till.

8 It was nae wonder his heart was sad
   When he shot his auld son at her head.

9 He houkit a grave, long, large and wide,
   He buried his auld son doun by her side.

10 It was nae wonder his heart was sair
   When he shooled the mools on her yellow hair.

11 'Oh,' said his father, 'son, but thou 'rt sad!
   At our braw meeting you micht be glad.'

12 'Oh,' said he, 'Father, I've lost my knife
   I loved as dear almost as my own life.

13 'But I have lost a far better thing,
   I lost the sheath that the knife was in.'

14 'Hold thy tongue, and mak nae din;
   I'll buy thee a sheath and a knife therein.'

15 'A' the ships eer sailed the sea
   Neer'll bring such a sheath and a knife to me.

16 'A' the smiths that lives on land
   Will neer bring such a sheath and knife to my
      hand.'

———◆———

A. b. 1². he came to. ³. For wind . . . . and cock never.
     4⁴. bed wi him.
   5². His lady's.
   22². would I be.
   29¹. deer and doe.
   30². And then on his lady he did mind.
   31¹. to greenwood tree.

33¹. the castle wa.
34¹. Go, minstrels.
43¹. lady I've loved.
44³. draps Saint Paul's. ⁴. That has.
45². little wee son.
B. 2¹. Will you.

16

SHEATH AND KNIFE

A. a. Motherwell's MS., p. 286. **b.** 'The broom blooms bonnie and says it is fair,' Motherwell's *Minstrelsy*, p. 189.
B. Sharpe's *Ballad Book*, ed. by D. Laing, p. 159.
C. 'The broom blooms bonie,' Johnson's *Museum*, No 461.

D. *Notes and Queries*, First Series, v, 345, one stanza.
E. a. A half-sheet in Motherwell's handwriting. **b.** *Notes and Queries*, Eighth Series, I, 372.
F. 'The Broom blooms bonnie,' from the recitation of Agnes Lyle, Kilbarchan.

THE three stanzas of this ballad which are found in the *Musical Museum* (**C**) were furnished, it is said, by Burns. It was first printed in full (**A b**) in Motherwell's *Minstrelsy*. Motherwell retouched a verse here and there slightly, to regulate the metre. **A a** is here given as it stands in his manuscript. **B** consists of some scattered verses as remembered by Sir W. Scott.

The directions in 3, 4 receive light from a passage in 'Robin Hood's Death and Burial:'

'But give me my bent bow in my hand,
    And a broad arrow I'll let flee,
And where this arrow is taken up
    There shall my grave diggd be.

'Lay me a green sod under my head,' etc.

Other ballads with a like theme are 'The Bonny Hind,' further on in this volume, and the two which follow it.

As an arrow-shot is to fix the place for a grave here and in 'Robin Hood's Death,' so, in many popular tales, arrows are shot to determine where a wife is to be sought; see a Hindoo tale, *Asiatic Journal*, 1833, XI, 207, Benfey, *Pantschatantra*, I, 261; Hahn, *Griechische Märchen*, No 67, II, 31, 285; Afanasief, I, 346, No 23, cited by Ralston, *The Nineteenth Century*, IV, 1004, 1878; Jagić, in *Archiv für slavische Philologie*, II, 619, and R. Köhler's notes at p. 620.

Translated in Grundtvig's *E. og s. Folkeviser*, No 49, p. 308; Wolff's *Halle der Völker*, I, 64.

A

a. Motherwell's MS., p. 286. From the recitation of
Mrs King, Kilbarchan Parish, February 9, 1825. **b.** 'The
broom blooms bonnie and says it is fair,' Motherwell's
Minstrelsy, p. 189.

1 Iᴛ is talked the warld all over,
  The brume blooms bonnie and says it is fair
That the king's dochter gaes wi child to her
  brither.
And we'll never gang doun to the brume onie
  mair

2 He's taen his sister doun to her father's deer
  park,
Wi his yew-tree bow and arrows fast slung to
  his back.

3 'Now when that ye hear me gie a loud cry,
Shoot frae thy bow an arrow and there let me
  lye.

4 'And when that ye see I am lying dead,
Then ye'll put me in a grave, wi a turf at my
  head.'

5 Now when he heard her gie a loud cry,
His silver arrow frae his bow he suddenly let fly.
  Now they'll never, etc.

6 He has made a grave that was lang and was
  deep,
And he has buried his sister, wi her babe at her
  feet.
  And they'll never, etc.

7 And when he came to his father's court hall,
There was music and minstrels and dancing
  and all.
  But they'll never, etc.

8 'O Willie, O Willie, what makes thee in pain?'
'I have lost a sheath and knife that I'll never
  see again.'
  For we'll never, etc.

9 'There is ships o your father's sailing on the sea
That will bring as good a sheath and a knife
  unto thee.'

10 'There is ships o my father's sailing on the sea,
But sic a sheath and a knife they can never
  bring to me.'
  Now we'll never, etc.

B

Sharpe's *Ballad Book*, ed. by D. Laing, p. 159: Sir
Walter Scott, from his recollection of a nursery-maid's
singing.

1 Aᴇ lady has whispered the other,
  The broom grows bonnie, the broom grows
  fair
Lady Margaret's wi bairn to Sir Richard, her
  brother.
And we daur na gae doun to the broom nae
  mair

    *   *   *   *   *

2 'And when ye hear me loud, loud cry,
O bend your bow, let your arrow fly.
  And I daur na, etc.

3 'But when ye see me lying still,
O then you may come and greet your fill.'

    *   *   *   *   *

4 'It's I hae broken my little pen-knife
That I loed dearer than my life.'
  And I daur na, etc.

    *   *   *   *   *

5 'It's no for the knife that my tears doun run,
But it's a' for the case that my knife was kept
  in.'

C

Johnson's *Museum*, No 461.

It's whisper'd in par-lour, it's whisp - er'd in ha', The—broom blooms— bon-nie, the— broom blooms fair;

La-dy Mar-gret's wi' child a - mang our la-dies a', And she dare na gae down to— the broom— nae mair.

1 Iᴛ's whispered in parlour, it's whispered in ha,
   The broom blooms bonie, the broom blooms
      fair
   Lady Marget's wi child amang our ladies a'.
   And she dare na gae down to the broom nae
      mair

2 One lady whisperd unto another
   Lady Marget's wi child to Sir Richard, her
      brother.

*   *   *   *   *

3 'O when that you hear my loud loud cry,
   Then bend your bow and let your arrows fly.
   For I dare na,' etc.

D

Notes and Queries, 1st Series, v, 345, communicated
by E. F. Rimbault.

1 Aᴇ king's dochter said to anither,
   Broom blooms bonnie an grows sae fair
   We'll gae ride like sister and brither.
   But we'll never gae down to the broom nae mair

E

a. Found by Mr Macmath on a half-sheet of paper
in Motherwell's handwriting. It is not completely intel-
ligible (why should Lady Ann be left in the death-
throe, to bury herself?), but undoubtedly belongs here.
b. Colonel W. F. Prideaux has printed this piece, from a
manuscript of Motherwell's in his possession, in *Notes
and Queries*, Eighth Series, I, 372.

1 Oɴᴇ king's daughter said to anither,
   Brume blumes bonnie and grows sae fair
   'We'll gae ride like sister and brither.'
   And we'll neer gae down to the brume nae
      mair

2 'We'll ride doun into yonder valley,
   Whare the greene green trees are budding sae
      gaily.

3 'Wi hawke and hounde we will hunt sae rarely,
   And we'll come back in the morning early.'

4 They rade on like sister and brither,
   And they hunted and hawket in the valley the-
      gether.

5 'Now, lady, hauld my horse and my hawk,
   For I maun na ride, and I downa walk.

6 'But set me doun be the rute o this tree,
   For there hae I dreamt that my bed sall be.'

7 The ae king's dochter did lift doun the ither,
   And she was licht in her armis like ony fether.

8 Bonnie Lady Ann sat doun be the tree,
  And a wide grave was houkit whare nane suld
      be.

9 The hawk had nae lure, and the horse had nae
      master,
  And the faithless hounds thro the woods ran
      faster.

10 The one king's dochter has ridden awa,
   But bonnie Lady Ann lay in the deed-thraw.

F

'The Broom blooms bonnie,' from the recitation of
Agnes Lyle, Kilbarchan. Sent by Motherwell to C. K.
Sharpe with a letter dated Paisley, 8th October, 1825.

1 'THERE is a feast in your father's house,
     The broom blooms bonnie, and so is it fair
   It becomes you and me to be very douce.'
     And we'll never gang up to the broom nae
         mair

2 'Will you go to yon hill so hie,
   Take your bow and your arrow wi thee.'

3 He's tane his lady on his back,
   And his auld son in his coat-lap.

4 'When ye hear me give a cry,
   Ye'll shoot your bow and let me ly.

5 'When ye see me lying still,
   Throw awa your bow and come running me
       till.'

6 When he heard her gie a cry,
   He shot his bow and he let her lye.

7 When he saw she was lying still,
   He threw awa his bow and came running her
       till.

8 It was nae wonder his heart was sad,
   When he shot his auld son at her head.

9 He howkit a grave lang, large and wide,
   He buried his auld son down by her side.

10 It was nae wonder his heart was sair,
   When he shooled the mools on her yellow hair.

11 'Oh,' said his father, 'son, but thou'rt sad,
   At our braw meeting you micht be glad.'

12 'Oh,' said he, 'father, I've lost my knife,
   I loved as dear almost as my own life.

13 'But I have lost a far better thing,
   I lost the sheathe that the knife was in.'

14 'Hold thy tongue and mak nae din,
   I'll buy thee a sheath and a knife therein.'

15 'A' the ships ere sailed the sea
   Neer'll bring such a sheathe and knife to me.

16 'A' the smiths that lives on land
   Will neer bring such a sheath and knife to my
       hand.'

———◆———

A. b. *Motherwell's printed copy has these variations:*
    1[1]. It is talked, it is talked; *a variation found in the*
       MS.
    2[2]. slung at.
    3[1]. O when . . . loud, loud cry.
    3[2]. an arrow frae thy bow.

4[1]. cauld and dead.
5[1]. loud, loud cry.
6[1]. has houkit.
6[2]. babie.
7[1]. came hame.

7^2. dancing mang them a': *this variation also in the* MS.

9^1, 10^1. There are.

B. "I have heard the 'Broom blooms bonnie' sung by our poor old nursery-maid as often as I have teeth in my head, but after cudgelling my memory I can make no more than the following stanzas." Scott, *Sharpe's* Ballad Book, 1880, *p.* 159.

Scott makes Effie Deans, in The Heart of Mid-Lothian, *vol.* I, *ch.* 10, *sing this stanza, probably of his own making:*

> The elfin knight sat on the brae,
>> The broom grows bonny, the broom grows fair
> And by there came lilting a lady so gay.
>> And we daurna gang down to the broom nae mair

D *is in or from T. Lyle's* Ancient Ballads and Songs, *1827, p.* 241. *Scott, as Lyle says, has nearly the same burden in a stanza (of his own?) which he makes E. Deans sing, in* The Heart of Mid-Lothian.

E. a. *Some words are difficult to read.*

2. sae *wanting in burden* 1.

3^1. hunt? growis fair *in burden* 1.

5^1. *Originally* Oh hauld my bridle and stirrup. Ann, *or* come, *is written over* Oh.

9^2. faithless?

b. 1^1 Ane. 3^1. we'll hunt

6^1. let me doun by the rute o the.

7^2. And *wanting: as* ony.

9^2. faithless. 10^1. The ae.

17

HIND HORN

A. 'Hindhorn,' Motherwell's MS., p. 106.
B. 'Young Hyndhorn,' Motherwell's MS., p. 418.
C. a. 'Young Hyn Horn,' Motherwell's Note-Book, p. 42. **b.** Motherwell's MS., p. 413.
D. 'Young Hynhorn,' Cromek's *Select Scotish Songs*, II, 204.
E. 'Hynd Horn,' Motherwell's MS., p. 91.
F. 'Young Hyndhorn,' *Lowran Castle, or the Wild Boar of Curridoo: with other Tales*. By R. Trotter, Dumfries, 1822.

G. 'Hynde Horn,' Kinloch's *Ancient Scottish Ballads*, p. 135; Kinloch MSS, VII, 117.
H. a. 'Hynd Horn,' Buchan's *Ballads of the North of Scotland*, II, 268. **b.** From Mr Walker, of Aberdeen.
I. a. "Hynd Horn,' from the recitation of Miss Jane Webster. **b.** From Miss Jessie Jane Macmath and Miss Agnes Macmath, 1882.

A DEFECTIVE copy of this ballad was printed in Cromek's *Select Scottish Songs, Ancient and Modern*, 1810 (**D**). A fragment, comprising the first half of the story, was inserted in "Lowran Castle, or the Wild Boar of Curridoo: with other Tales," etc., by Robert Trotter, Dumfries, 1822[*] (**F**). A complete copy was first given in Kinloch's *Ancient Scottish Ballads*, 1827 (**G**); another, described by the editor as made up from Cromek's fragment and two copies from recitation, in Motherwell's *Minstrelsy*, p. 36,[†] later in the same year; and a third, closely resembling Kinloch's, in Buchan's *Ballads of the North of Scotland*, in 1828 (**H**). Three versions complete, or nearly so, and a fragment of a fourth are now printed for the first time, all from Motherwell's manuscripts (**A, B, C, E**).

The stanza about the auger bore [wimble bore], **B** 1, **F** 3, **H** 4, is manifestly out of place.

It is found in 'The Whummil Bore' (see further on), and may have slipped into 'Hind Horn' by reason of its following, in its proper place, a stanza beginning, "Seven lang years I hae served the king:" cf. **F** 2, **H** 3.

G 17, 18, 21, 22, which are not intelligible in their present connection, are perhaps, as well as **G** 16, **H** 18–20, borrowed from some Robin Hood ballad, in which a change is made with a beggar.

The noteworthy points in the story of Hind Horn are these. Hind Horn has served the king seven years (**D, F**), and has fallen in love with his daughter. She gives Hind Horn a jewelled ring: as long as the stone keeps its color, he may know that she is faithful; but if it changes hue, he may ken she loves another man. The king is angry (**D**), and Hind Horn goes to sea [is sent, **D**]. He has been gone seven years, **E, F** [seven years and a day, **B**], when, looking on his ring, he sees that the stone is pale and wan, **A–H**. He makes for the land at once, and, meeting an old beggar, asks him for news. No news but the king's daughter's wedding: it has lasted nine days [two and forty, **A**], and she will not go into the bride-bed till she hears of Hind Horn, **E**. Hind Horn changed cloaks and other gear with

[*] This I should have missed but for the kindness of Mr Macmath.
[†] Motherwell's printed copy, *Minstrelsy*, p. 36, is thus made up: stanzas 1, 2, 3, 8, 15, from Cromek (**D**); 4–7, 9, 11, 13,14, 16, 19, 20, 24–28,30–37, from **B**; 12, 17, 18 from **E**. 23 = **A** 14. 10, 21, 22, 29, have not been found in his manuscripts. The first line of the burden is from **B**, the second from **E**. Motherwell alters his texts slightly, now and then.

the beggar, and when he came to the king's gate asked for a drink in Horn's name,[*] **A, B, D.** The bride herself came down, and gave him a drink out of her own hand, **A, B, C, G, H.** He drank out the drink and dropped in the ring.

> 'O gat ye 't by sea, or gat ye 't by lan,
> Or gat ye 't aff a dead man's han?'

So she asked; and he answered:

> 'I gat na 't by sea, I gat na 't by lan,
> But I gat it out of your own han.' **D** 14.

> 'I got na 't by sea, I got na 't by land,
> Nor got I it aff a drownd man's hand;

> 'But I got it at my wooing,
> And I'll gie it at your wedding.' **G** 29, 30.

The bride, who had said,

> 'I'll go through nine fires so hot,
> But I'll give him a drink for Young Hynhorn's
>   sake,' **B** 16,

is no less ready now:

> 'I'll tak the red gowd frae my head,
> And follow you and beg my bread.

> 'I'll tak the red gowd frae my hair,
> And follow you for evermair.' **H** 31, 32.

But Hind Horn let his cloutie cloak fall, **G, H,** and told her,

> 'Ye need na leave your bridal gown,
> For I'll make ye ladie o many a town.'

The story of Horn, of which this ballad gives little more than the catastrophe, is related at full in:

I. 'King Horn,' a *gest* in about 1550 short verses, preserved in three manuscripts: the oldest regarded as of the second half of the 13th

century, or older; the others put at 1300 and a little later. All three have been printed: (1.) By Michel, *Horn et Rimenhild*, p. 259 ff, Bannatyne Club, 1845; J. R. Lumby, Early English Text Society, 1866; and in editions founded on Lumby's text, by Mätzner, *Altenglische Sprachproben*, p. 207 ff, and later by Wissmann, *Quellen u. Forschungen*, No 45. (2.) By Horstmann, *Archiv für das Studium der neueren Sprachen*, 1872, I, 39 ff. (3.) By Ritson, A. E. Metrical Romanceës, II, 91 ff.

II. 'Horn et Rymenhild,' a romance in about 5250 heroic verses, preserved likewise in three manuscripts; the best in the Public Library of the University of Cambridge, and of the 14th century.

III. 'Horn Childe and Maiden Rimnild,' from a manuscript of the 14th century, in not quite 100 twelve-line stanzas: Ritson, *Metrical Romanceës*, III, 282 ff; Michel, p. 341 ff.[†]

Horn, in the old English *gest*, is son of Murry [Allof], king of Suddenne. He is a youth of extraordinary beauty, and has twelve comrades, of whom Athulf and Fikenild are his favorites. One day, as Murry was out riding, he came upon fifteen ships of Saracens, just arrived. The pagans slew the king, and insured themselves, as they thought, against Horn's future revenge by putting him and his twelve aboard a vessel without sail or rudder; but "the children" drove to shore, unhurt, on the coast of Westerness. The king, Ailmar, gave them a kind reception, and committed them to Athelbrus, his steward, to be properly brought up. Rymenhild, the king's daughter, fell in love with Horn, and [189] having, with some difficulty, prevailed upon Athelbrus to bring him to her bower, offered herself to him as his wife. It were no fair wedding, Horn told her, between a thrall and a king,—a speech which hurt Rymenhild greatly; and Horn was so moved by her grief that he promised to do all she required, if she would induce the king to knight him. This was done the next day, and Horn at once knighted all his comrades. Rymenhild again sent for Horn, and urged him now to make her his wife. But Horn said he must first prove his knighthood: if he

---

[*] C 16,17 are corrupted, and also **F** 19, 23, **G** 21; all three in a way which allows of easy emendation. Hymen [high, man] in **C** should of course be Hyn Horn. The injunction in **G, H** should be to ask nothing for Peter or Paul's sake, but all for Horn's.

[†] See the edition by J. Caro, in *Englische Studien*, XII, 323 ff.

came back alive, he would then marry her. Upon this Rymenhild gave him a ring, set with stones of such virtue that he could never be slain if he looked on it and thought of his leman. The young knight had the good fortune to fall in immediately with a ship full of heathen hounds, and by the aid of his ring killed a hundred of the best of them. The next day he paid Rymenhild a visit, and found her drowned in grief on account of a bad dream. She had cast her net in the sea, and a great fish had broken it: she weened she should lose the fish that she would choose. Horn strove to comfort her, but could not conceal his apprehension that trouble was brewing. The fish proved to be Fikenild, Horn's much cherished friend. He told Ailmar of the intimacy with Rymenhild, and asserted that Horn meant to kill the king as well as marry the princess. Ailmar was very angry (v. 724, Wissmann), and much grieved, too. He found the youth in his daughter's bower, and ordered him to quit the land anon. Horn saddled his horse and armed himself, then went back to Rymenhild, and told her that he was going to a strange land for seven years: if, after that, he neither came nor sent word, she might take a husband. He sailed a good way eastward (v. 799) to Ireland, and, landing, met two princes, who invited him to take service with their father. The king, Thurston, welcomed him, and had soon occasion to employ him; for at Christmas came into court a giant, with a message from pagans newly arrived. They proposed that one of them should fight three Christians:

'If your three slay our one,
Let all this land be your own;
If our one oercomes your three,
All this land then ours shall be.'

Horn scorned to fight on such terms; he alone would undertake three of the hounds; and so he did. In the course of a hard fight it came out that these were the very heathen that had slain King Murry. Horn looked on his ring and thought on Rymenhild, then fell on his foes. Not a man of them escaped; but King Thurston lost many men in the fight, among them his two sons. Having now no heir, he offered Horn his daughter Reynild and the succession. Horn replied that he had not earned such a reward yet. He would serve the king further; and when he asked for his daughter, he hoped the king would not refuse her.

Seven years Horn stayed with King Thurston, and to Rymenhild neither sent nor went. A sorry time it was for her, and worst at the end, for King Modi of Reynis asked her in marriage, and her father consented. The wedding was to be in a few days. Rymenhild despatched messengers to every land, but Horn heard nothing, till one day, when he was going out to shoot, he encountered one of these, and learned how things stood. He sent word to his love not to be troubled; he would be there betimes. But, alas, the messenger was drowned on his way back, and Rymenhild, peering out of her door for a ray of hope, saw his body washed up by the waves. Horn now made a clean breast to Thurston, and asked for help. This was generously accorded, and Horn set sail for Westerness. He arrived not too early on the day of the wedding,—"ne might he come no later!"—left his men in a wood, and set off for Ailmar's court alone. He met a palmer, and asked his news. The palmer had come from a bridal; a wedding of maid Rymenhild, who wept and would not be married, because she had a husband, though he was out of the land. Horn changed clothes with the palmer, put on the sclavin, took scrip and staff, blackened his skin and twisted his lip, and presented himself at the king's gate. The porter would not let him in; Horn kicked open the wicket, threw the porter over the bridge, made his way into the hall, and sat down in the beggars' row. Rymenhild was weeping as if she were out of her wits, but after meat she rose to give all the knights and squires drink from a horn which she bare: such was the custom. Horn called to her

'Skink us with the first,
The beggars ben athirst.'

She laid down her horn and filled him a gallon bowl; but Horn would not drink of that.[*] He

---

[*] Hereward will not drink unless the princess presents the cup: very like Horn here. Michel, *Chroniques Anglo-Normandes*, II, 18f.

said, mysteriously, "Thou thinkest I am a beggar, but I am a fisher, come far from the East, to fish at thy feast. My net lies near at hand, and hath full seven year. I am come to see if it has taken any fish.

'I am come to fish;
Drink to me from thy dish,
Drink to Horn from horn!'"

Rymenhild looked at him, a chill creeping over her heart. What he meant by his fishing she did not see. She filled her horn and drank to him, handed it to the pilgrim, and said, "Drink thy fill, and tell me if ever thou saw Horn." Horn drank, and threw the ring into the vessel. When the princess went to bower, she found the ring she had given Horn. She feared he was dead, and sent for the palmer. The palmer said Horn had died on the voyage to Westerness, and had begged him to go with the ring to Rymenhild. Rymenhild could bear no more. She threw herself on her bed, where she had hid a knife, to kill both King Modi and herself if Horn should not come; she set the knife to her heart, and there Horn stopped her. He wiped off the black, and cried, "I am Horn!" Great was their bliss, but it was not a time to indulge themselves fully.

Horn sprang out of hall,
And let his sclavin fall, (1246)

and went to summon his knights. Rymenhild sent after him the faithful Athulf, who all the while had been watching for Horn in the tower. They slew all that were in the castle, except King Ailmar and Horn's old comrades. Horn spared even Fikenild, taking an oath of fidelity from him and the rest. Then he made himself known to Ailmar, denied what he had been charged with, and would not marry Rymenhild even now, not till he had won back Suddenne. This he went immediately about; but while he was engaged in clearing the land of Saracens and rebuilding churches, the false Fikenild bribed young and old to side with him, built a strong castle, "married" Rymenhild, carried her into his fortress, and began a feast. Horn, warned in a dream, again set sail for Wester-

ness, and came in by Fikenild's new castle. Athulf's cousin was on the shore, to tell him what had happened; how Fikenild had wedded Rymenhild that very day; he had beguiled Horn twice. Force would not avail now. Horn disguised himself and some of his knights as harpers and fiddlers, and their music gained them admittance. Horn began a lay which threw Rymenhild into a swoon. This smote him to the heart; he looked on his ring and thought of her. Fikenild and his men were soon disposed of. Horn was in a condition to reward all his faithful adherents. He married Athulf to Thurston's daughter, and made Rymenhild queen of Suddenne.

The French romance contains very nearly the same story, extended, by expansions of various sorts, to about six times the length of King Horn. It would be out of place to notice other variations than those which relate to the story preserved in the ballads. Rimild offers Horn a ring when she first avows her love. He will not take it then, but accepts a second tender, after his first fight. When he is accused to the king, he offers to clear himself by combat with heavy odds, but will not submit, king's son as he is, to purgation by oath. The king says, then he may quit the land and go—to Norway, if he will. Horn begs Rimild to maintain her love for him seven years. If he does not come then, he will send her word to act thereafter at her pleasure. Rimild exchanges the ring she had previously given him for one set with a sapphire, wearing [191] which faithfully he need not fear death by water nor fire, battle nor tourney (vv 2051–8). He looks at this ring when he fights with the pagan that had killed his father, and it fires his heart to extraordinary exploits (3166ff). Having learned through a friend, who had long been seeking him, that Rimild's father is about to marry her to a young king (Modun), Horn returns to Brittany with a large force. He leaves his men in a woody place, and goes out alone on horseback for news; meets a palmer, who tells him that the marriage is to take place that very day; gives the palmer his fine clothes in exchange for sclavin, staff and scrip, forces his way into the city, and is admitted to the banquet hall with the beggars. After the guests had eaten (4152ff), Rimild filled a splendid cup

with piment, presented it first *a sun dru*, and
then, with her maids, served the whole com-
pany. As she was making her fifth round, Horn
pulled her by the sleeve, and reproached her
with attending only to the rich. "Your credit
would be greater should you serve *us*." She set a
handsome cup before him, but he would not
drink. "Corn apelent Horn li Engleis," he said.
"If, for the love of him who bore that name, you
would give me the same horn that you offered
your *ami*, I would share it with you." All but
fainting, Rimild gave him the horn. He threw
in his ring, even that which she had given him
at parting, drank out half, and begged her to
drink by the love of him whom he had named.
In drinking, she sipped the ring into her mouth,
and she saw at once what it was (4234). "I have
found a ring," said she. "If it is yours, take it.
Blest be he to whom I gave it: if you know
aught of him, conceal it not. If you are Horn, it
were a great sin not to reveal yourself." Horn
owned that the ring was his, but denied knowl-
edge of the man she spake of. For himself, he
had been reared in that land, and by service
had come into possession of a hawk, which,
before taming it, he had put in a cage: that was
nigh seven years since: he had come now to see
what it amounted to. If it should prove to be as
good as when he left it, he would carry it away
with him; but if its feathers were ruffled and
broken, he would have nothing to do with it.
At this, Rimild broke into a laugh, and cried,
"Horn, 't is you, and your hawk has been safely
kept!"* She would go with him or kill herself.
Horn saw that she had spoken truth, but, to try
her yet further, said he was indeed Horn, whom
she had loved, but he had come back with
nothing: why should she follow a poor wretch
who could not give her a gown to her back?
"Little do you know me," was her reply. "I can
bear what you bear, and there is no king in the
East for whom I would quit you."

'Horn Childe and Maiden Rimnild,' with
many diversities of its own as to details, is more
[192] like the French than the English romance as to
the story, and, on the other hand, has one or
two resemblances to the ballads which they
both lack. Rimnild's father, maddened by the
traitor Wikel's false information, beats her till
she bleeds, and threatens to slay Horn. Rim-

nild, expecting her lover to be at least exiled,
assures Horn that she will marry no other man
for seven years. The king, who had shut himself
up till his first wrath was past, tells Horn, when
he next comes into his presence, that if he is
found in the land on the morrow, he shall be
drawn with horses and hanged. Rimnild, at
parting, gives him a ring, with these words:

'Loke thou forsake it for no thing,
It schal ben our tokening;
    The ston it is wele trewe.
When the ston wexeth wan,
Than chaungeth the thou3t of thi leman,
    Take than a newe;
When the ston wexeth rede,

---

*   When Horn was near the city, he stopped to see how
things would go. King Modun passed, with Wikel, in gay
discourse of the charms of Rimild. Horn called out to
them insultingly, and Modun asked who he was. Horn
said he had formerly served a man of consequence as his
fisherman: he had thrown a net almost seven years ago,
and had now come to give it a look. If it had taken any
fish, he would love it no more; if it should still be as he
left it, he would carry it away. Modun thinks him a fool.
(3984–4057, and nearly the same in 'Horn Childe and
Maiden Ritnild,' 77–79). This is part of a story in the
Gesta Romanorum, of a soldier who loved the emperor's
daughter, and went to the holy land for seven years, after
a mutual exchange of fidelity for that time. A king comes
to woo the princess, but is put off for seven years, upon
her alleging that she has made a vow of virginity for so
long. At the expiration of this term, the king and the sol-
dier meet as they are on the way to the princess. The
king, from certain passages between them, thinks the sol-
dier a fool. The soldier takes leave of the king under pre-
tence of looking after a net which he had laid in a certain
place seven years before, rides on ahead, and slips away
with the princess. *Gest. Rom.*, Oesterley, p. 597, No 193;
Grässe, II, 159; Madden, p. 32; Swan, I, p. lxv. A similar
story in Campbell's *Tales of the West Highlands*, I, 281,
'Baillie Lunnain.' (Simrock, *Deutsche Märchen*, No 47, is
apparently a translation from the *Gesta*.) The riddle of
the hawk, slightly varied, is met with in the romance of
Blonde of Oxford and Jehan of Dammartin, v. 2811 ff,
3143 ff, 3288 ff (ed. Le Roux de Lincy, pp. 98, 109, 114),
and, still further modified, in *Le Romant de Jehan de Paris*,
ed. Montaiglon, pp. 55, 63, 111. (Le Roux de Lincy,
Köhler, Mussafia, G. Paris). See also Suchier's edition,
Œuvres poétiques de Philippe de Remi, Sire de Beaumanoir,
II, 89, 99, 103. 'Horn et Rimenhild,' it will be observed,
has both riddles, and that of the net is introduced under
circumstances entirely like those in the *Gesta Romano-
rum*. The French romance is certainly independent of the
English in this passage.

Than have Y lorn mi maidenhed,
　Oȝaines the untrewe.' (Michel, st. 48.)

Horn, for his part, bids her every day look into a spring in her arbor: should she see his shadow, then he is about to marry another; till then his thought will not have changed (sts 48, 49). Though loved, as before, by another princess, Horn kept his faith; but when seven years were gone, on looking at the stone he saw that its hue was changed (st. 71). He immediately gathered a force, and set sail for Rimnild. On landing he saw a beggar, who turned out to be one of his old friends, and had been looking for him a long time. That day Moging the king was to marry Rimnild. They changed weeds (76); Horn forced his way into the castle. While Rimnild was serving the guests, Horn, who had tried to pass for a fool, called to her to attend to God's men. She fetched him drink, and he said, "For Horn's love, if ever he was dear to thee, go not ere this be drunk." He threw the ring into the cup: she brought him another drink (something is wrong here, for nothing is said of her seeing and recognizing the ring), and asked if Horn were there. She fainted when she learned that he was, but on recovering sent Hatherof (= Athulf) to bid the king make merry, and then to gather periwinkle and ivy, "grasses that ben of main" (to stain her face with, no doubt), and then to tell Horn to wait for her under a woodside.

'When al this folk is gon to play,
He and Y schal steal oway,
Bituene the day and the niȝt.'　(87)

Hatherof did his message. Of true love Horn was sure. He said he would come into the field with a hundred knights. A tournament follows, as in the French romance; the royal bridegroom is unhorsed, but spared; treachery is punished and forced to confession.[*]

Now is Rimnild tuiis wedde,
Horn brouȝt hir to his bedde.　(94)

That the lay or gest of King Horn is a far more primitive poem than the French romance, and could not possibly be derived from it, will probably be plain to any one who will make even a hasty comparison of the two; and that the contrary opinion should have been held by such men as Warton and Tyrwhitt must have been the result of a general theory, not of a particular examination.[†] There is, on the other hand, no sufficient reason for supposing that the English lay is the source of the other two poems. Nor do the special approximations of the ballads to the romance of Horn Child oblige us to conclude that these, or any of them, are derived from that poem. The particular resemblances are the discoloration of the ring, the elopement with the bride, in **C, G, H** (which is only prepared for, but not carried out, in Horn Child), and the agreement between the couplet just cited from Horn Child,

---

[*]　Dr Davidson informs me that many years ago he heard a version of 'Hind Horn,' in four-line stanzas, in which, as in 'Horn et Rymenhild' and 'Horn Childe and Maiden Rimnild,' Horn took part in a joust at the king's court,

An young Hind Horn was abune them a'.

He remembers further only these stanzas:

'O got ye this o the sea sailin,
　Or got ye 't o the lan?
Or got ye 't o the bloody shores o Spain,
　On a droont man's han?'

'I got na 't o the sea sailin,
　I got na 't o the lan,
Nor yet upo the bloody shores o Spain,
　On a droont man's han.'

There can hardly be a doubt that these two stanzas belong to 'The Kitchie-Boy,' 'Bonny Foot-Boy,' No 252. Cf. **A** 34, 35, **B** 47, **D** 7, 8, of that ballad.
[†]　See the excellent studies of King Horn by Wissmann, in *Quellen und Forschungen*, No 16, and *Anglia*, IV, 342 ff.
　That Horn Child, though much more modern in its present form than the Gest, "would seem to have been formed on a still older model" was suggested by T. Wright in 1835, and was the opinion of J. Grimm and of Ferdinand Wolf. Wolf maintains that Horn Child was the work of a popular jongleur, or vagrant minstrel, and that for this reason Chaucer put it among the "romances of prys," which are mentioned in Sir Thopas. Anyway, this must have been the form of the story which was known to Chaucer. Wolf, *Ueber die Lais*, p. 217f.

Now is Rimnild tuiis wedde,
Horn brouȝt hir to his bedde,

and the last stanza of **A, B, C**:

The bridegroom he had wedded the bride,
But Young Hind Horn he took her to bed. (**A**)

[193] The bridegroom thought he had the bonnie
          bride wed,
But Young Hyn Horn took the bride to bed.
(**B**)

Her ain bridegroom had her first wed,
But Young Hyn Horn had her first to bed. (**C**)

The likeness evinces a closer affinity of the
oral traditions with the later English romance
than with the earlier English or the French, but
no filiation. And were filiation to be accepted,
there would remain the question of priority. It is
often assumed, without a misgiving, that oral
tradition must needs be younger than anything
that was committed to writing some centuries
ago; but this requires in each case to be made
out; there is certainly no antecedent probability
of that kind.*

Two Scandinavian ballads, as Dr Prior has
remarked, seem to have been at least suggested
by the romances of Horn.

(1.) 'Unge Hr. Tor og Jomfru Tore,' Grundt-
vig, No 72, II, 263, translated by Prior, III, 151.
Of this there are two traditional versions: **A**
from a manuscript of the sixteenth century, **B**
from one of the seventeenth. They agree in
story. In **A**, Tor asks Sølffuermord how long she
will wait for him. Nine years, she answers, if she
can do so without angering her friends. He will
be satisfied with eight. Eight have passed: a

---

* **A, B**, and **E**, which had not been printed at the time
of his writing, will convince Professor Stimming, whose
valuable review in *Englische Studien*, I, 351 ff, supple-
ments, and in the matter of *derivation*, I think, rectifies,
Wissmann's *Untersuchungen*, that the king's daughter in
the ballads was faithful to Horn, and that they were mar-
rying her against her will, as in the romances. This con-
tingency seems not to have been foreseen when the ring
was given: but it must be admitted that it was better for
the ring to change, to the temporary clouding of the
lady's character, than to have Horn stay away and the
forced marriage go on.

family council is held, and it is decided that she
shall not have Young Tor, but a certain rich
count. Her father "gives her away" that same
day. The lady goes up to a balcony and looks
seaward. Everybody seems to be coming home
but her lover. She begs her brother to ride down
to the shore for her. Tor is just coming in, hails
the horseman, and eagerly asks how are the
maids in the isle. The brother tells him that *his*
maid has waited eight years, and is even now
drinking her bridal, but with tears. Tor takes his
harp and chess-board, and plays outside the
bridal hall till the bride hears and knows him.
He then enters the hall, and asks if there is any-
body that can win a game of chess. The father
replies, Nobody but Sølffuermord, and she sits a
bride at the board. The mother indulgently sug-
gests that the midsummer day is long, and the
bride might well try a game. The bride seeks an
express sanction of her father, who lessons her
the livelong day, being suspicious of Tor, but
towards evening consents to her playing a little
while,—not long. Tor wins the first game, and
must needs unpack his heart in a gibing para-
ble, ending

'Full hard is gold to win,
And so is a trothless quean.'

She wins the next game, takes up the parable,
and says

'Many were glad their faith to hold,
Were their lot to be controlled.'

They are soon at one, and resolve to fly. They
slip away, go aboard Tor's ship, and put off. The
bride's parents get information, and the mother,
who is a professor of the black art, raises a storm
which she means shall sink them both. No one
can steer the ship but the bride. She stands at
the helm, with her gold crown on, while her
lover is lying seasick on the deck, and she
brings the craft safe into Norway, where a sec-
ond wedding is celebrated.

(2.) The other ballad is 'Herr Lovmand og
Herr Thor,' Syv, IV, No 68, *Danske Viser*, IV,
180, No 199, translated by Prior, II, 442; Kris-
tensen, I, 136, No 52; *Skattegraveren*, VIII, 49,
No 115; *Jyske Folkeminder*, X, 252, No 62, **A–D**.

Lovmand, having betrothed Ingelil, asks how long she will be his maid. "Eight years, if I may," she says. This term has elapsed; her brothers consult, and give her to rich Herr Thor. They drink the bridal for five days; for nine days; she will not go to bed. On the evening of the tenth they begin to use force. She begs that she may first go to the look-out up-stairs. From there she sees ships, great and small, and the sails which her own hands have made for her lover. Her brother goes down to the sea, as in the other ballad, and has a similar interview. Lovmand has the excuse of having been sick seven years. He borrows the brother's horse, flies faster than a bird, and the torch is burning at the door of the bride's house when he arrives. Thor is reasonable enough to give up the bride, and to accept Lovmand's sister.

The ballad is extremely common in Sweden, and at least six versions have been published. **A**, 'Herr Lagman och Herr Thor,' from a manuscript of the end of the sixteenth century, Arwidsson, I, 165, No 24; **B**, from a manuscript, *ib.*, p. 168; **C**, from oral tradition, p. 171; **D**, 'Lageman och hans Brud,' Eva Wigström, *Folkdiktning samlad och upptecknad i Skåne*, p. 29, No 12; **E**, 'Stolt Ingrid,' *Folkvisor från Skåne*, upptecknade af E. Wigström, in Hazelius, *Ur de nordiska Folkens Lif*, p. 121, No 3; **F**, 'Deielill och Lageman,' Fagerlund, *Anteckningar om Korpo och Houtskärs Socknar*, p. 192, No 3. In **A**, **D** the bride goes off in her lover's ship; in **C** he carries her off on his horse, when the dancing is at its best, and subsequently, upon the king's requisition, settles matters with his rival by killing him in single fight. The stolid bridegroom, in the others, consents to a peaceable arrangement.

Certain points in the story of Horn—the long absence, the sudden return, the appearance under disguise at the wedding feast, and the dropping of the ring into a cup of wine obtained from the bride—repeat themselves in a great number of romantic tales. More commonly it is a husband who leaves his wife for seven years, is miraculously informed on the last day that she is to be remarried on the morrow, and is restored to his home in the nick of time, also by superhuman means. Horn is warned to go back, in the ballads and in Horn

Child, by the discoloration of his ring, but gets home as he can; this part of the story is slurred over in a way that indicates a purpose to avoid a supernatural expedient.

Very prominent among the stories referred to is that of Henry of Brunswick [Henry the Lion, Reinfrid of Brunswick], and this may well be put first, because it is preserved in Scandinavian popular ballads.[*]

(1.) The latest of these, a Swedish ballad, from a collection made at the end of the last century, 'Hertig Henrik,' Arwidsson, No 168, II, 422, represents Duke Henry as telling his wife that he is minded to go off for seven years (he says not whither, but it is of course to the East); should he stay eight or nine, she may marry the man she fancies. He cuts a ring in two; gives her one half and keeps the other. He is made captive, and serves a heathen lord and lady seven years, drawing half the plough, "like another horse." His liberation is not accounted for, but he was probably set free by his mistress, as in the ballad which follows. He gets possession of an excellent sword, and uses it on an elephant who is fighting with a lion. The grateful lion transports the duke to his own country while he is asleep. A herdsman, of whom he asks food, recommends him to go to the Brunswick mansion, where there is a wedding, and Duke Henry's former spouse is the bride. When Henry comes to the house, his daughter is standing without; he asks food for a poor pilgrim. She replies that she has never heard of a pilgrim taking a lion about with him. But they give him drink, and the bride, *pro more*, drinks out of the same bowl, and finds the half ring in the bottom. The bride feels in her pocket and finds her half,[†] and the two, when thrown upon a table, run together and make one ring.

---

[*]   See the ample introduction to 'Henrik af Brunsvig,' in Grundtvig, No 114, II, 608 ff.

[†]   It appears that these half rings are often dug up. "Neuere Ausgrabungen haben vielfach auf solche Ringstücke geführt, die, als Zeichen unverbrüchlicher Treue, einst mit dem Geliebten gebrochen, ja wie der Augenschein beweist, entzwei geschnitten, und so ins Grab mitgenommen wurden, zum Zeichen dass die Liebe über den Tod hinaus daure." Rochholz, *Schweizersagen aus dem Aargau*, II, 116.

[195]   (2.) The Danish ballad* (Grundtvig, No 114, **B**, from a 17th century manuscript), relates that Duke Henry, in consequence of a dream, took leave of his wife, enjoining her to wait to the eighth year, and, if then he did not return, marry whom she liked. In the course of his fights with the heathen, Henry was made captive, and had to draw the harrow and plough, like a beast. One day (during his lord's absence, as we learn from **A**) the heathen lady whom he served set him free. He had many adventures, and in one of them killed a panther who was pressing a lion hard, for which service the lion followed him like a dog. The duke then happened upon a hermit, who told him that his wife was to be married the next day, but he was to go to sleep, and not be concerned. He laid his head on a stone in the heathen land, and woke in a trice to hear German speech from a herdsman's mouth. The herdsman confirmed what the hermit had said: the duchess was to be married on the morrow. The duke went to the kitchen as a pilgrim, and sent word to the lady that he wished to drink to her. The duchess, surprised at this freedom, summoned him into her presence. The verses are lost in which the cup should be given the pilgrim and returned to the lady. When she drank off the wine that was left, a half ring lay in the glass.

Danish **A**, though of the 16th century, does not mention the ring.

(3.) A Flemish broadside, which may originally have been of the 15th century, relates the adventures of the Duke of Brunswick in sixty-five stanzas of four long lines: reprinted in von der Hagen's *Germania*, VIII, 359, and *Oude Liedekens in Bladeren*, L. van Paemel, No 28 = Hoffmann's *Niederländische Volkslieder*, No 2, p. 6; Coussemaker, No 47, p. 152; abridged and made over, in Willems, *O. v. L.*, p. 251, No 107. The duke, going to war, tells his wife to marry again if he stays away seven years. She gives him half of her ring. Seven years pass, and the duke, being then in desperate plight in a wilderness, is taken off by a ship; by providential direction, no doubt, though at first it does not so appear. For the fiend is aboard, who tells

him that his wife is to be married to-morrow, and offers, for his soul, to carry him to his palace in his sleep before day. The duke, relying on heaven and his lion, professes to accept the terms: he is to be taken to his palace *in his sleep.* The lion rouses his master at the right time, and the fiend is baffled. The duke goes to the marriage feast, and sends a message to the bride that he desires a drink from her in memory of her lord. They take him for a beggar, but the lady orders him wine in a gold cup. The cup goes back to her with the duke's half ring in it. She cries, "It is my husband!" joins her half to the one in the cup, and the two adhere firmly.

(4.) A German poem of the 15th century, by Michel Wyssenhere, in ninety-eight stanzas of seven lines, first printed by Massmann, *Denkmæler deutscher Sprache und Literatur*, p. 122, and afterwards by Erlach, II, 290, and elsewhere. The Lord of Brunswick receives an impression in a dream that he ought to go to the Holy Sepulchre. He cuts a ring in two, and gives his wife one half for a souvenir, but fixes no time for his absence, and so naturally says nothing about her taking another husband. He has the adventures which are usual in other versions of the story, and at last finds himself among the Wild Hunt (das wöden her), and obliges one of the company, by conjurations, to tell him how it is with his wife and children. The spirit informs him that his wife is about to marry another man. He then constrains the spirit to transport him and his lion to his castle. This is done on the same terms as in the Flemish poem, and the lion wakes his master. His wife offers him drink; he lets his half ring drop in the glass, and, upon the glass being returned to the lady, she takes out the token, finds it like her half, and cries out that she has recovered her dear husband and lord.

(5.) Henry the Lion, a chap-book printed in the 16th century, in one hundred and four stanzas of eight short verses, now known to have been composed by the painter Heinrich Götting, Dresden, 1585 (*Germania*, XXVI, 453, No 527); reprinted in Büsching's *Volkssagen, Märchen und Legenden*, p. 213 ff, and (modernized) by Simrock in the first volume of *Die deut-* [*schen Volksbücher.* The hero goes out simply in quest of adventures, and, having lost his ship

---

*   Translated, with introduction of verses from **A**, by Prior, *Ancient Danish Ballads*, II, 71.

and all his companions, is floating on a raft with his lion, when the devil comes to him and tells him that his wife is to remarry. A compact is made, and the devil balked, as before. Though we were not so informed at the beginning, it now turns out that the duke had given a half ring to the duchess seven years before, and had bidden her take a second husband if he did not come back in that time. The duke sends a servant to beg a drink of wine of his wife, and returns the cup, as in (3), (4).

(6.) A ballad in nine seven-line stanzas, supposed to be by a Meistersinger, preserved in broadsides of about 1550 and 1603, Böhme, No 5, p. 30, Erk's *Wunderhorn*, iv, 111. (7.) Hans Sachs's 'Historia,' 1562, in two hundred and four verses, *Works*, ed. 1578, Buch iv, Theil ii, Blatt lvii[b]–lviii[b];[*] *Historia: Hertzog Heinrich der löw*, XVI, 221, of the edition of the Litt. Verein in Stuttgart, ed. Goetze, 228vv. (8.) A Meistersingerlied of the end of the 16th century, in three twenty-line stanzas, printed in *Idunna u. Hermode* for March 27, 1813 (appended to p. 64), and after this, with changes, in Kretzschmer, ii, 17, No 5.—These three agree with the foregoing as to the ring.

(9.) Reinfrid von Braunschweig, c. 1300, ed. Bartsch, 1871. Reinfrid is promised by the Virgin, who appears to him thrice in vision, that he shall have issue if he will go over sea to fight the heathen. He breaks a ring which his wife had given him, and gives her one half, vv 14,906–11. If he dies, she is to marry, for public reasons, vv 14,398–407; but she is not to believe a report of his death unless she receives his half of the ring back, vv 14,782–816, 15,040–049. The latter part of the romance not being extant, we do not know the conclusion, but a variation as to the use made of the ring is probable.[†]

The story of Reinfrit is also preserved in a Bohemian prose chap-book printed before 1565. This prose is clearly a poem broken up, and it is believed that the original should be placed in the first half of the 14th century, or possibly at the end of the 13th. The hero returns, in pilgrim's garb, after seven years' absence, to find his wife about to be handed over by her father to another prince. He lets his ring fall into a cup, and goes away; his wife recognizes the ring, and is reunited to him. The story has passed from the Bohemian into Russian and Magyar. Feifalik, *Sitzungsberichte der phil.-hist. Classe der Wiener Akademie*, xxix, 83ff, the ring at p. 92; xxxii, 322ff.

Similar use is made of the ring in other German romances.[‡] (1.) 'Der edle Moringer' (MS. of 14th century) asks his wife to wait seven years for him, while he visits the land of St Thomas. He is warned by an angel, at the expiration of that period, that he will lose her if he does not go back, bewails himself to his patron, and is conveyed home in a sleep. He begs an alms at his castle-gate in the name of God, St Thomas, and the noble Moringer; is admitted to his wife's presence; sings a lay describing his own case, which moves the lady much; throws into a beaker of wine, which she sets before him, the ring by which she was married to him, sends the cup back to her, and is recognized. Böhme, No 6, p. 32; Uhland, No 298, p. 773. (2.) In the older Hildebrandslied, which is of the 14th century, or earlier, the hero, returning after an absence of thirty-two years, drops his ring into a cup of wine presented to him by his wife. Böhme, No 1, p. 1; Uhland, No 132, p. 330. (3.) Wolfdietrich drops Ortnit's ring into a cup of wine sent him by Liebgart, who has been adjudged to the Graf von Biterne in consideration of his having, as he pretended, slain the dragon. The cup is returned to the empress, the ring identified, the pretension refuted, and Liebgart given to Ortnit's avenger. Wolfdietrich B, ed. Jänicke, i, 280ff, stanzas 767–785. (4.) King Rother (whose history has passages of the strongest resemblance to Horn's), coming to retrieve his wife, who has been kidnapped and carried [197]

---

[*]   I have not seen this, and depend upon others here.

[†]   Gödeke, 'Reinfrit von Braunschweig,' p. 89, conjectures that the half ring was, or would have been, employed in the sequel by some impostor (the story may never have been finished) as evidence of Brunswick's death. A ring is so used in a Silesian tradition, of the general character of that of Henry the Lion, with the difference that the knight is awakened by a cock's crowing: 'Die Hahnkrähe bei Breslau,' in Kern's *Schlesische Sagen-Chronik*, p. 151. There is a variation of this last, without the deception by means of the ring, in Goedsche's *Schlesischer Sagenschatz*, p. 37, No 16.

[‡]   See Nigra, *Romania*, XIV, 255f, note 2.

back to her father, lands below Constantinople, at a woody and hilly place, and assumes a pilgrim's disguise. On his way to the city he meets a man who tells him that Ymelot of Babylon has invaded Greece, and taken Constantin, his wife's father, prisoner; and that Constantin, to save his life, has consented to give his daughter to the heathen king's son. Rother steals into the hall, and even under the table at which the royal party are sitting, and contrives to slip his ring into the hand of his distressed young queen, who, thus assured of his presence, immediately recovers her spirits. Massmann, *Deutsche Gedichte des zwœlften Jahrhunderts*, Theil ii, p. 213, vv 3687–3878.

A corrupt fragment of a ballad, 'Der Bettler,' in Schröer's *Ausflug nach Gottschee*, p. 210f (Köhler), retains features like 'Hind Horn.' The beggar comes to a wedding, and sits by the stove. The bride kindly says, Nobody is thinking of the beggar, and hands him a glass of wine. He says, Thanks, fair bride; thou wast my first wife. Upon this the *bridegroom* jumps over the table, crying, Bachelor I came, and bachelor will go.

One of the best and oldest stories of the kind we are engaged with is transmitted by Cæsarius of Heisterbach in his *Dialogus Miraculorum*, of the first quarter of the 13th century. Gerard, a soldier living in Holenbach ("his grandchildren are still alive, and there is hardly a man in the town who does not know about this"), being, like Moringer, devoted to St Thomas of India, was impelled to visit his shrine. He broke a ring and gave one half to his wife, saying, Expect me back in five years, and marry whom you wish if I do not come then. The journey, which would be long enough any way, was providentially protracted. He reached the shrine at last, and said his prayers, and then remembered that that was the last day of his fifth year. Alas, my wife will marry again, he thought; and quite right he was, for the wedding was even then preparing. A devil, acting under the orders of St Thomas, set Gerard down at his own door. He found his wife supping with her second partner, and dropped his half ring into her cup. She took it out, fitted it to the half which had been given her, rushed

into his arms, and bade good-by to the new bridegroom. Ed. Strange, II, 131.

A tradition closely resembling this has been found in Switzerland, Gerard and St Thomas being exchanged for Wernhart von Strättlingen[*] and St Michael. Menzel's *Odin*, p. 96.

According to a Devonshire tradition given by Mrs Bray, *Traditions of Devonshire*, II, 172 (II, 32 of the new ed. of 1879, which has a fresh title, *The Borders of the Tamar and the Tavy*), Sir Francis Drake, having been abroad seven years, was apprised by one of his devils that his wife was about to marry again. He immediately discharged one of his great guns up through the earth. The cannon-ball "fell with a loud explosion between the lady and her intended bridegroom," who were before the altar. In another version, known to Southey and communicated by him to Mrs Bray (as above, II, 174; new ed., II, 33, 34), the marriage is broken off by a large stone (no doubt a gun-stone) which falls on the lady's train as she is on her way to church. Drake, in this version, returns in disguise, but is recognized by his smile. See for various stories of the same kind, 'Iouenn Kerménou,' Luzel, *Contes pop. de Basse-Bretagne*, I, 416; 'Der todte Schuldner,' Zingerle, *Zeitschrift für deutsche Mythologie*, II, 367; 'De witte Swâne,' Woeste, the same, III, 46, translated from the Markish dialect by Simrock, 'Der gute Gerhard,' u. s. w., p. 75; Vernaleken, *Mythen u. Bräuche des Volkes in Oesterreich*, p. 372; Vernaleken, *Kinder- und Hausmärchen*, No 54, p. 315f; J. H. Knowles, *Folk-Tales of Kashmir*, p. 184f; Prym u. Socin, *Syrische Sagen u. Märchen*, No 20, II, 72. (G. L. K.)

Another of the most remarkable tales of this class is exquisitely told by Boccaccio in the *Decamerone*, G. x, N. ix. Messer Torello, going to the crusade, begs his wife to wait a year, a month, and a day before she marries again. The lady assures him that she will never be another man's wife; but he replies that a woman young, beautiful, and of high family, as she is, will not be allowed to have her way. With her parting embrace she gives him a ring from her finger, saying, If I die before I see you again, remember me when you look on this. The Christians were

[*] See the note to I, 350, of Birlinger and Buck, *Volksthümliches aus Schwaben*.

wasted by an excessive mortality, and those who escaped the ravages of disease fell into the hands of Saladin, and were imprisoned by him in various cities, Torello in Alexandria. Here he was recognized by Saladin, whom he had entertained with the most delicate and splendid hospitality a few months before, when the soldan was travelling through Italy in disguise. Saladin's return for this courtesy was so magnificent as almost to put Lombardy out of Torello's head,[*] and besides he trusted that his wife had been informed of his safety by a letter which he had sent. This was not so, however, and the death of another Torello was reported in Italy as his, in consequence of which his supposed widow was solicited in marriage, and was obliged to consent to take another husband after the time should have expired which she had promised to wait. A week before the last day, Torello learned that the ship which carried his letter had been wrecked, and the thought that his wife would now marry again drove him almost mad. Saladin extracted from him the cause of his distress, and promised that he should yet be at home before the time was out, which Torello, who had heard that such things had often been done, was ready to believe. And in fact, by means of one of his necromancers, Saladin caused Torello to be transported to Pavia in one night—the night before the new nuptials.[†] Torello appeared at the banquet the next day in the guise of a Saracen, under the escort of an uncle of his, a churchman, and at the right moment sent word to the lady that it was a custom in his country for a bride to send her cup filled with wine to any stranger who might be present, and for him to drink half and cover the cup, and for her to drink the rest. To this the lady graciously assented. Torello drank out most of the wine, dropped in the ring which his wife had given him when they parted, and covered the cup. The lady, upon lifting the cover, saw the ring, knew her husband, and, upsetting the table in her ecstasy, threw herself into Torello's arms.

Tales of this description still maintain themselves in popular tradition. 'Der Ring ehelicher Treue,' Gottschalk, *Deutsche Volksmärchen*, II, 135, relates how Kuno von Falkenstein, going on a crusade, breaks his ring and gives one half to his wife, begging her to wait seven years before she marries again. He has the adventures of Henry of Brunswick, with differences, and, like Moringer, sings a lay describing his own case. The new bridegroom hands him a cup; he drops in his half ring, and passes the cup to the bride. The two halves join of themselves.[‡] Other examples, not without variations and deficiencies, in details, are afforded by 'Der getheilte Trauring,' Schmitz, *Sagen u. Legenden des Eifler Volkes*, p. 82; 'Bodman,' Uhland, in Pfeiffer's *Germania*, IV, 73–76; 'Graf Hubert von Kalw,' Meier, *Deutsche Sagen, u. s. w., aus Schwaben*, p. 332, No 369, Grimms, *Deutsche Sagen*, No 524; 'Der Bärenhäuter,' Grimms, *K. u. H. märchen*, No 101; 'Berthold von Neuhaus,' in Kern's *Schlesische Sagen-Chronik*, p. 93; Stier, *Ungarische Volksmärchen*, p. 53.

A story of the same kind is interwoven with an exceedingly impressive adventure related of Richard Sans-Peur in *Les Chroniques de Normandie*, Rouen, 1487, chap. lvii, cited in Michel, *Chronique des Ducs de Normandie par Benoit*, II, 336ff. A second is told of Guillaume Martel, seigneur de Bacqueville; still others of a seigneur Gilbert de Lomblon, a comrade of St. Louis in his first crusade. Amélie de Bosquet, *La Normandie romanesque et merveilleuse*, pp. 465–68, 470.

---

[*] There are marked correspondences between Boccaccio's story and the veritable history of Henry the Lion as given by Bartsch, *Herzog Ernst*, cxxvi f: e.g., the presents of clothes by the empress (transferred to Torello's wife), and the handsome behavior of two soldans, here attributed to Saladin.

[†] For the marvellous transportation in these stories, see a note by Liebrecht in *Jahrbüch für rom. u. eng. Literatur*, III, 147. In the same, IV, 110, Liebrecht refers to the legend of Hugh of Halton, recounted by Dugdale in his *Antiquities of Warwickshire*, II, 646, ed. of 1730, and *Monasticon Anglicanum*, IV, 90f, ed. 1823 (and perhaps in Dugdale's *Baronage of England*, but I have not found it there). Hugo is another Gerard: the two half-rings miraculously unite. (Köhler.) See, also, Landau on Torello, 'Der Wunderritt,' *Quellen des Dekameron* 1884, pp 193–218; and Leskien u. Brugman, *Litauische Volkslieder und Märchen*, No 22, p. 437f: Wollner's notes, p. 571. (G.L.K.)

[‡] Without the conclusion, also in Binder's *Schwäbische Volkssagen*, II, 173. These Volksmärchen, by the way, are "erzählt" by Gottschalk. It is not made quite so clear as could be wished, whether they are merely re-told.

The warning by a dream, the preternaturally rapid transportation, and the arrival in time to prevent a second marriage taking effect are found in the story of Aboulfaouaris, *Cabinet des Fées*, XV, 336ff, *Les Mille et un Jours*, Paris, 1840, 228ff. Rohde, *Der griechische Roman*, p. 182: F. Liebrecht.

In a Bulgarian ballad, Stojan is married on Sunday; on Monday he is ordered to join the army. His wife gives him a posy, which will remain fresh until she marries another man. He serves nine years; the tenth the queen discovers from his talk that he has a wife, and gives him permission to go home. He arrives the very day on which his wife is to be remarried, goes to the wedding, and asks her to kiss his hand and accept a gift from him. She recognizes him by the ring on his hand, sends off the guests, and goes home with him. *Collection of the Ministry of Instruction*, I, 39. In a variant, Verković, p. 329, No 301, the man is gone three years, and arrives just as the wedding procession comes for the bride. Other Slavic versions include: Servian, Vuk, III, No 25; Bulgarian, Miladinof, Nos 65, 66, 111, 572, Kačanovskij, Nos 68–73, 112 (W. W.)

A Picard ballad, existing in two versions, partly cited by Rathery in the *Moniteur Universel* for August 26, 1853, tells of a Sire de Créqui, who, going beyond seas with his sovereign, breaks his ring and gives half to his young wife; is gone ten years, and made captive by the Turks, who condemn him to death on account of his adhesion to Christ; and is transported to his chateau on the eve of the day of his doom. This very day his wife is to take another husband, sorely against her will. Créqui appears in the rags of a beggar, and legitimates himself by producing his half of the ring (which, in a way not explained by Rathery, has been brought back by a swan).

'Le Retour du Mari,' Puymaigre, *Chants populaires messins*, p. 20; Fleury, *Littérature Orale de la Basse-Normandie*, p. 268; E. Legrand, *Romania*, X, 374, also from Normandy, has also some traits of ballads of this class. A bridegroom has to go on a campaign the very day of his nuptials. The campaign lasts seven years, and the day of his return his wife is about to remarry. He is invited to the wedding supper, and towards the close of it proposes to play cards to see who shall have the bride. The guests are surprised. The soldier says he will have the bride without winning her at cards or dice, and, turning to the lady, asks, Where are the rings I gave you at your wedding seven years ago? She will go for them; and here the story breaks off.* Additional versions include Victor Smith, 'Le Retour du Mari,' *Chants pop. du Velay et du Forez*, in *Romania*, IX, 289; Tarbé, *Romancero de Champagne*, II, 122. "E. Muller, Chansons de mon village, journal Le Mémorial de la Loire du 19 septembre, 1867; Daymard, Collection de vieilles chansons, p. 220 *du Bulletin de la Société des études du Lot*, 1879" (V. Smith); 'Un Retour de Guerre' (cards), Daymard, pp. 203, 4. Imperfect copies of this ballad in Guillon, *Chansons pop. de l'Ain*, p. 95, 'Les deux Maris,' p. 39, 'Ma pauvre Elise.'

An Italian form of 'Le Retour du Mari' is 'Il Ritorno del Soldato,' Nigra, No 28[b], p. 174. Another Italian ballad has some of the points in the story of Horn. A man goes off for seven years immediately after marriage; the woman looking out towards the sea perceives a pilgrim approaching; he asks for charity, and makes what seems an impudent suggestion, for which she threatens him with punishment. But how if I were your husband? Then you would give me some token. He pulls out his wedding-ring from under his cloak. 'Il finto [falso] Pellegrino,' Bernoni, ix, no 7, Ferraro, C. *p. monferrini*, p. 33, Giannini, p. 151 (nearly the same in *Archivio*, VI, 361); 'La Moglie fedele,' Wolf, p. 59, No 81, Ive, p. 334; 'Bennardo,' Nerucci, in *Archivio*, III, 44.

A ballad of the nature of 'Le Retour du Mari' is very popular in Poland: Kolberg, No 22, pp 224ff, some dozen copies; Wojcicki, I,

---

* Germaine's husband, after an absence of seven years, overcomes his wife's doubts of his identity by exhibiting half of her ring, which *happened* to break the day of their wedding, or the day after: Puymaigre, p. 11, Champfleury, *Chansons des Provinces*, p. 77. The conclusion to Sir Tristrem, which Scott supplied, "abridged from the French metrical romance, in the style of Tomas of Erceldoune," makes Ganhardin lay a ring in a cup which Brengwain hands Ysonde, who recognizes the ring as Tristrem's token. The cup was one of the presents made to King Mark by Tristrem's envoy, and is transferred to Ysonde by Scott. The passage has been cited as ancient and genuine.

287; Wojcicki, II, 311 = Kolberg's c; Lipinski, p. 159 = Kolberg's i; Konopka, p. 121, No 20; Kozłowski, No 5, p. 35, p. 36, two copies; Kolberg, Lud, IV, 23, No 146; VI, 166f, No 332; XII, 115–118, Nos 221–224 (jumps seven tables and touches the eighth); XVI, 271, No 438; XVI, 272, No 440; Valjavec, p. 300, No 17; Kolberg, Mazowsze, II, 109, No 251; Roger, p. 13, Nos 25, 26. A soldier comes back after seven years' absence to his "widow;" drops ring into cup, and is recognized as her husband. Lud, XXI, 61, No 123. In Moravian, 'První milejší,' 'The First Love,' Sušil, No 135, p. 131. The general course of the story is that a young man has to go to the war the day of his wedding or the day after. He commits his bride to her mother, saying, Keep her for me seven years; and if I do not then come back, give her to whom you please. He is gone seven years, and, returning then, asks for his wife. She has just been given to another. He asks for a fiddle [pipe], and says he will go to the wedding. They advise him to stay away, for there will be a disturbance. No, he will only stand at the door and play. The bride jumps over four tables, and makes a courtesy to him on a fifth, welcomes him and dismisses the new bridegroom.

The same hard fortune is that of Costantino, a young Albanian,[*] who is called to the service of his king three days after his marriage. He gives back her ring to his wife, and tells her he must go to the wars for nine years. Should he not return in nine years and nine days, he bids her marry. The young wife says nothing, waits her nine years and nine days, and then, since she is much sought for, her father wishes her to marry. She says nothing, again, and they prepare for the bridal. Costantino, sleeping in the king's palace, has a bad dream, which makes him heave a sigh that comes to his sovereign's ear. The king summons all his soldiers, and inquires who heaved that sigh. Costantino con-

fesses it was he, and says it was because his wife was marrying. The king orders him to take the swiftest horse and make for his home. Costantino meets his father, and learns that his dream is true, presses on to the church, arrives at the door at the same time as the bridal procession, and offers himself for a bride's-man. When they come to the exchange of rings, Costantino contrives that his ring shall remain on the bride's finger. She knows the ring; her tears burst forth. Costantino declares himself as having been already crowned with the lady.[†] Camarda, Appendice al Saggio di Grammatologia, etc., 90–97, a Calabrian-Albanian copy. See also De Grazie, Canti p. albanesi, p. 118. There is a Sicilian, but incomplete, in Vigo, Canti popolari siciliani, p. 342ff, ed. 1857, p. 695ff, ed. 1870–74. Another version, agreeing closely with Camarda's, appears in De Rada, Rapsodie d'un poema albanese raccolte nelle colonie del Napoletano, pp 61–64.

With this belongs a ballad, very common in Greece, which, however, has for the most part lost even more of what was in all probability the original catastrophe. "Αναγνωρισμός,' Chasiotis, Popular Songs of Epirus, p. 88, No 27, comes nearer the common story than other versions.[‡] A man who had been twelve years a slave after being a bridegroom of three days, dreams that his wife is marrying, runs to the cellar, and begins to sing dirges. The king hears, and is moved. "If it is one of the servants, increase his pay; if a slave, set him free." The slave tells his story (in three lines); the king bids him take a swift gray. The slave asks the horses, which is a swift gray. Only one answers, an old steed with forty wounds. "I am a swift gray; tie two or three handkerchiefs around your head, and tie yourself to my back!"[§] He comes upon his father pruning the vineyard.

---

[*] The Epirots and Albanians have a custom of betrothing or marrying, commonly in early youth, and of then parting for a long period. A woman was lately (1875) buried at Iannina who, as the archbishop boasted in the funeral discourse, had preserved her fidelity to a husband who had been separated from her thirty years. This unhappy usage has given rise to a distinct class of songs. Dozon, Chansons populaires bulgares, p. 294, note.

[†] In the Greek rite rings are used in the betrothal, which as a rule immediately precedes the marriage. The rings are exchanged by the priest and sponsors (Camarda says three times). So in Twelfth Night, iv, 3, as Prior remarks, II, 277, apropos of 'Axel and Walborg', st. 44. Crowns, of vine twigs, etc., are the emblems in the nuptial ceremony, and these are also changed from one head to the other.

[‡] I was guided to nearly all these Greek ballads by Professor Liebrecht's notes, Zur Volkskunde, p. 207.

"Whose sheep are those feeding in the mead- ows?" "My lost son's." He comes to his mother. "What bride are they marrying?" "My lost son's." "Shall I get to them in church while they are crowning?" "If you have a fast horse, you will find them crowning; if you have a bad horse, you will find them at table." He finds them at church, and calls out, A bad way ye have: why do ye not bring out the bride, so that strangers may give her the cup? A good way we have, they answer, we who bring out the bride, and strangers give her the cup. Then he takes out his ring, while he is about to present the cup to the bride. The bride can read; she stands and reads (his name), and bids the company begone, for her mate has come, the first crowned.

In other cases we find the hero in prison. He was put in for thirty days; the keys are lost, and he stays thirty years. Legrand, p. 326, No 145; Νεοελληνικὰ Ἀνάλεκτα, I, 85, No 19. More fre- quently he is a galley slave: Zambelios, p. 678, No 103 = Passow, No 448; Tommaseo, III, 152 = Passow, No 449; Sakellarios, Κυπριακά, III, 37, No 13; Νεοελληνικὰ Ἀνάλεκτα, I, 86, No 20; Jeannaraki, Ἄσματα κρητικά, p. 203, No 265. His bad dream [a letter from home] makes him heave a sigh which shakes the prison, or [200] stops [splits] the galley.[*] In Tommaseo, III, 152, on reaching the church, he cries, "Stand aside, gentlemen, stand aside, my masters; let the bride pour for me." She pours him one cup and two, and exclaims (the ring which was dropped into the cup having dropped out of the story), My John has come back! Then they both "go out like candles." In Sakellarios they embrace

and fall dead, and when laid in the grave come up as a cypress and a citron tree. In the Cretan ballad John does not dismount, but takes the bride on to the horse and is off with her; so in the beautiful ballad in Fauriel, II, 140, No 11, "Ἡ Ἁρπαγη," "peut-être la plus distinguée de ee recueil," which belongs with this group, but seems to be later at the beginning and the end. Even here the bride takes a cup to pour a draught for the horseman. To these should be added Manousos, II, 103 (also cited II, 215, where it more properly belongs); Ζωγραφεῖος Ἀγών, p. 76, No 26.

In Russia the ring story is told of Dobrynya and Nastasya. Dobrynya, sent out shortly after his marriage to collect tribute for Vladimir, requests Nastasya to wait for him twelve years:[†] then she may wed again, so it be not with Aly- osha. Twelve years pass. Alyosha avows that he has seen Dobrynya's corpse lying on the steppe, and sues for her hand. Vladimir supports the suit, and Nastasya is constrained to accept this prohibited husband. Dobrynya's horse [two doves, a pilgrim] reveals to his master what is going on, and carries him home with marvel- lous speed. Dobrynya gains admittance to the wedding-feast in the guise of a merry-maker, and so pleases Vladimir with his singing that he is allowed to sit where he likes. He places him- self opposite Nastasya, drops his ring in a cup, and asks her to drink to him. She finds the ring in the bottom, falls at his feet and implores par- don.[‡] Wollner, Volksepik der Grossrussen, p. 122f; Rambaud, La Russie Épique, p. 86f.

We have the ring employed somewhat after the fashion of these western tales in Somadeva's story of Vidúshaka. The Vidyádharí Bhadrá, having to part for a while with Vidúshaka, for whom she had conceived a passion, gives him her ring. Subsequently, Vidúshaka obliges a rak- shas whom he has subdued to convey him to the foot of a mountain on which Bhadrá had taken refuge. Many beautiful girls come to fetch water in golden pitchers from a lake, and, on inquiring, Vidúshaka finds that the water is for

§   This high-mettled horse is a capital figure in most of the versions. In one of them the caution is given, "Do not feel safe in spurring him: he will scatter thy brains ten ells below the ground." The gray (otherwise the black) is of the same breed as the Russian Dobrynya's, a little way on; or the foal that took Charles the Great, under similar circumstances, from Passau to Aachen between morn and eve, ('Karl der Grosse,' from Enenkels Weltbuch, c. 1250, in von der Hagen's Gesammtabenteuer, II, 619ff); or the black in the poem and tale of Thedel von Walmoden.

*   In Jeannaraki the bey says, "My slave, give us a song, and I will free you." John sings of his love, whom he was to lose that day. So Zambelios, as above, Tommaseo, p. 152, and Νεο. Ἀνάλ. No. 20. Compare Brunswick, in Wyssenhere, and Moringer.

†   Three, six, or twelve, Dobrynya and Nastasya in Hil- ferding, Nos 23, 26, 33, 38, 43, columns 131, 144, 160, 176, 211, and twenty other places; Ruibnikof, I, 169, No 27, III, 90, No 18; Miss Hapgood's Epic Songs of Russia, Dobrynya and Alyosha, p. 253.

Bhadrá. One of the girls asks him to lift her pitcher on to her shoulder, and while doing this he drops into the pitcher Bhadrá's ring. When the water is poured on Bhadrá's hands, the ring falls out. Bhadrá asks her maids if they have seen a stranger. They say they have seen a mortal, and that he had helped one of them with her pitcher. They are ordered to go for the youth at once, for he is Bhadrá's consort.[*]

According to the letter of the ballads, should the ring given Horn by his lady turn wan or blue, this would signify that she loved another man: but though accuracy would be very desirable in such a case, these words are rather loose, since she never faltered in her love, and submitted to marry another, so far as she submitted, only under constraint. 'Horn Child,' sts 48, 71, agrees with the ballads as to this point. We meet a ring of similar virtue in 'Bonny Bee-Hom,' Jamieson's *Popular Ballads*, I, 187, and Buchan's *Ballads of the North of Scotland*, I, 169.

J   'But gin this ring should fade or fail,
    Or the stone should change its hue,
    Be sure your love is dead and gone,
    Or she has proved untrue.'
                  Jamieson, p. 191.

[‡]   Otherwise: Nastasya waits six years, as desired; is told that Dobrynya is dead and is urged to marry Alyosha; will not hear of marriage for six years more; Vladimir then interposes. Dobrynya is furious, as these absentees are sometimes pleased to be. He complains that women have long hair and short wits, and so does Brunswick in Wyssenhere's poem, st. 89. Numerous as are the instances of these long absences, the woman is rarely, if ever, represented as in the least to blame. The behavior of the man, on the other hand, is in some cases trying. Thus, the Conde Dirlos tells his young wife to wait for him seven years, and if he does not come in eight to marry the ninth. He accomplishes the object of his expedition in three years, but stays fifteen, never writes,—he had taken an unnecessary oath not to do that before he started,—and forbids anybody else to write, on pain of death. Such is his humor; but he is very much provoked at being reported dead. Wolf and Hofmann, *Primavera y Flor de Romances*, II, 129, No 164.

[*]   *Kathā sarit sāgara* (of the early part of the 12th century), Tawney's translation, I, 136ff. The story is cited by Rajna, in *Romania*, VI, 359. Herr v. Bodman leaves his marriage ring in a wash-bowl! Meier, *Deutsche V. m. aus Schwaben*, 214f.

In the Roumanian ballad, 'Ring and Handkerchief,' a prince going to war gives his wife a ring: if it should rust, he is dead. She gives him a gold-embroidered handkerchief: if the gold melts, she is dead. Alecsandri, *Poesiĕ populare ale Românilor*, p. 20, No 7; Stanley, *Rouman Anthology*, p. 16, p. 193. In Gonzenbach's *Sicilianische Märchen*, I, 39, No 7, a prince, on parting with his sister, gives her a ring, saying, So long as the stone is clear, I am well: if it is dimmed, that is a sign that I am dead. So No 5, at p. 23. A young man, in a Silesian story, receives a ring from his sweetheart, with the assurance that he can count upon her faith as long as the ring holds; and after twenty years' detention in the mines of Siberia, is warned of trouble by the ring's breaking: Goedsche, *Schlesischer Sagen- Historien- u. Legendenschatz*, I, 37, No 16. So in some copies of 'Lamkin,' the lord has a foreboding that some ill has happened to his lady from the rings on his fingers bursting in twain: Motherwell, p. 291, st. 23; Finlay, II, 47, st. 30.[†]

In Miklosich, Ueber die Mundarten der Zigeuner, IV, *Märchen u. Lieder*, 15th Tale, pp 52–55, at the end of a story of the class referred to at p. 531f, a maid, parting from her lover for three years, divides her ring with him. He forgets, and prepares to marry another woman. She comes to the nuptials, and is not known. She throws the half ring into a cup, drinks, and hands the cup to him. He sees the half ring, and joins it to his own. This is my wife, he says. She delivered me from death. He annuls his marriage, and espouses the right woman. (Köhler.)

A personage appeared at Magdeburg in 1348 in the disguise of a pilgrim, asked for a cup of wine from the archbishop's table, and, in drinking, dropped into the cup from his mouth the seal ring of the margrave Waldemar, supposed to have been long dead, but whom he confessed or avowed himself to be. Klöden, *Diplomatische Geschichte des für falsch erklärten Markgrafen Waldemar*, p. 189f. (Köhler.)

A wife who long pursues her husband, lost to her through spells, drops a ring into his broth at the feast for his second marriage, is recognized, and they are happily reunited: The Tale of the Hoodie, Campbell, *West Highland Tales*, I, 63–66.

In a pretty Portuguese ballad, which has numerous parallels in other languages, a long-absent husband, after tormenting his wife by telling her that she is a widow, legitimates himself by saying Where is your half of the ring which we parted? Here is mine: 'Bella Infanta,' Almeida-Garrett, II, 11, 14, Braga, *Cantos p. do*

---

† The ring given Horn by Rymenhild, in 'King Horn,' 579ff (Wissmann), and in the French romance, 2056ff, protects him against material harm or mishap, or assures him superiority in fight, as long as he is faithful. So in Buchan's version of 'Bonny Bee-Ho'm,' st. 8:

> 'As lang's this ring's your body on,
> Your blood shall neer be drawn.'

"The king's daughter of Linne" gives her champion two rings, one of which renders him invulnerable, and the other will staunch the blood of any of his men who may be wounded: Motherwell's *Minstrelsy*, Introduction, p. lvii. Eglamore's ring, Percy MS., II, 363, st. 51, will preserve his life on water or land. A ring given Wolfdietrich by the empress, D VIII, st. 42, ed. Jänicke, doubles his strength and makes him fire-proof in his fight with the dragon. The ring lent Ywaine by his lady will keep him from prison, sickness, loss of blood, or being made captive in battle, and give him superiority to all antagonists, so long as he is true in love: Ritson, *Met. Rom.* I, 65, vv 1533ff. These talismans are also known in India: Tawney's *Kathā sarit sāgara*, II, 161. But an Indian ring which Reinfrît receives from his wife before he departs for the crusade, 15,066ff, has no equal, after all; for, besides doing as much as the best of these, it imparts perpetual good spirits. It is interesting to know that this matchless jewel had once been the property of a Scottish king, and was given by him to his daughter when she was sent to Norway to be married: under convoy of Sir Patrick Spens?

Archipelago Açoriano, p. 300; 'Dona Infanta,' 'Dona Catherina,' Braga, *Romanceiro Geral*, pp 3f, 7; 'A bella Infanta,' Bellermann, p. 100, No 12.

The cases in which a simple ring is the means of recognition or confirmation need, of course, not be multiplied.*

The three singing laverocks in **B** 3, **F** 4, (cf. **A** 3,) are to be taken as curiosities of art. Artificial singing-birds are often mentioned in the earlier times, (by Sir John Mandeville for instance): see Liebrecht, *Volkskunde*, p. 89f, No 5. Such birds, and artificially hissing snakes, occur in the Great-Russian bylina of Djuk Stepanović; cf. Wollner, *Untersuchungen ü. d. grossr. Volksepik*, p. 134f. (W. W.) For more of these curiosities (in Salman u. Morolf, Orendel, Virginal, Laurin, etc.), see Vogt's note, p. 181 (248ff.), to Salman u. Morolf.

Hind Horn is translated by Grundtvig, *Eng. og sk. Folkeviser*, p. 274, No 42, mainly after the copy in Motherwell's *Minstrelsy*; by Rosa Warrens, *Schottische V. l. der Vorzeit*, p. 161, No 37, after Buchan (**H**); by Knortz, *L. u. R. Alt-Englands*, p. 184, No 52, after Allingham.

---

* See, further, for ring stories, Wesselofsky, Neue Beiträge zur Geschichte der Salomonsage, in *Archiv für Slavische Philologie*, VI, 397f; Hahn, *Neugriechische Märchen*, No 25; W. Freiherr von Tettau, *Ueber einige bis jetzt unbekannte Erfurter Drucke, u. s. w., Jahrbücher der königlichen Akademie zu Erfurt*, Neue Folge, Heft VI, S. 291 at the end of an excellent article on Ritter Morgeners Wallfahrt. (Köhler.)

A

Motherwell's MS., p. 106. From Mrs King, Kilbarchan.

1 In Scotland there was a babie born,
   Lill lal, etc.
And his name it was called young Hind Horn.
   With a fal lal, etc.

2 He sent a letter to our king
That he was in love with his daughter Jean.

3 He's gien to her a silver wand,
With seven living lavrocks sitting thereon.

4 She's gien to him a diamond ring,
With seven bright diamonds set therein.

5 'When this ring grows pale and wan,
You may know by it my love is gane.'

6 One day as he looked his ring upon,
He saw the diamonds pale and wan.

7 He left the sea and came to land,
And the first that he met was an old beggar man.

8 'What news, what news?' said young Hind Horn;
'No news, no news,' said the old beggar man.

9 'No news,' said the beggar, 'no news at a',
But there is a wedding in the king's ha.

2] 10 'But there is a wedding in the king's ha,
That has halden these forty days and twa.'

11 'Will ye lend me your begging coat?
And I'll lend you my scarlet cloak.

12 'Will you lend me your beggar's rung?
And I'll gie you my steed to ride upon.

13 'Will you lend me your wig o hair,
To cover mine, because it is fair?'

14 The auld beggar man was bound for the mill,
But young Hind Horn for the king's hall.

15 The auld beggar man was bound for to ride,
But young Hind Horn was bound for the bride.

16 When he came to the king's gate,
He sought a drink for Hind Horn's sake.

17 The bride came down with a glass of wine,
When he drank out the glass, and dropt in the
   ring.

18 'O got ye this by sea or land?
Or got ye it off a dead man's hand?'

19 'I got not it by sea, I got it by land,
And I got it, madam, out of your own hand.'

20 'O I'll cast off my gowns of brown,
And beg wi you frae town to town.

21 'O I'll cast off my gowns of red,
And I'll beg wi you to win my bread.'

22 'Ye needna cast off your gowns of brown,
For I'll make you lady o many a town.

23 'Ye needna cast off your gowns of red,
It's only a sham, the begging o my bread.'

24 The bridegroom he had wedded the bride,
But young Hind Horn he took her to bed.

B

Motherwell's MS., p. 418. From the singing of a
servant-girl at Halkhead.

1 I NEVER saw my love before,
　With a hey lillelu and a ho lo lan
Till I saw her thro an oger bore.
　With a hey down and a hey diddle downie

2 She gave to me a gay gold ring,
　With three shining diamonds set therein.

3 And I gave to her a silver wand,
　With three singing lavrocks set thereon.

4 'What if these diamonds lose their hue,
　Just when your love begins for to rew?'

5 He's left the land, and he's gone to sea,
　And he's stayd there seven years and a day.

6 But when he looked this ring upon,
　The shining diamonds were both pale and wan.

7 He's left the seas and he's come to the land,
　And there he met with an auld beggar man.

8 'What news, what news, thou auld beggar man
　For it is seven years sin I've seen lan.'

9 'No news,' said the old beggar man, 'at all,
　But there is a wedding in the king's hall.'

10 'Wilt thou give to me thy begging coat?
　And I'll give to thee my scarlet cloak.

11 'Wilt thou give to me thy begging staff?
　And I'll give to thee my good gray steed.'

12 The old beggar man was bound for to ride,
　But Young Hynd Horn was bound for the bride.

13 When he came to the king's gate,
　He asked a drink for Young Hynd Horn's sake.

14 The news unto the bonnie bride came
　That at the yett there stands an auld man.

15 'There stands an auld man at the king's gate; [20
　He asketh a drink for young Hyn Horn's sake.'

16 'I'll go thro nine fires so hot,
　But I'll give him a drink for Young Hyn Horn's
　sake.'

17 She gave him a drink out of her own hand;
　He drank out the drink and he dropt in the
　ring.

18 'Got thou 't by sea, or got thou 't by land?
　Or got thou 't out of any dead man's hand?'

19 'I got it not by sea, but I got it by land,
　For I got it out of thine own hand.'

20 'I'll cast off my gowns of brown,
　And I'll follow thee from town to town.

21 'I'll cast off my gowns of red,
　And along with thee I'll beg my bread.'

22 'Thou need not cast off thy gowns of brown,
　For I can make thee lady of many a town.

23 'Thou need not cast off thy gowns of red,
　For I can maintain thee with both wine and
　bread.'

24 The bridegroom thought he had the bonnie
　bride wed,
　But Young Hyn Horn took the bride to bed.

C

a. Motherwell's Note-Book, p. 42: from Agnes Lyle.
b. Motherwell's MS., p. 413: from the singing of Agnes
Lyle, Kilbarchan, August 24, 1825.

1 Young Hyn Horn's to the king's court gone,
   Hoch hey and an ney O
He's fallen in love with his little daughter Jean.
   Let my love alone, I pray you

2 He's bocht to her a little gown,
   With seven broad flowers spread it along.

3 She's given to him a gay gold ring.
   The posie upon it was richt plain.

4 'When you see it losing its comely hue,
   So will I my love to you.'

5 Then within a little wee,
   Hyn Horn left land and went to sea.

6 When he lookt his ring upon,
   He saw it growing pale and wan.

7 Then within a little [wee] again,
   Hyn Horn left sea and came to the land.

8 As he was riding along the way,
   There he met with a jovial beggar.

9 'What news, what news, old man?' he did say:
   'This is the king's young dochter's wedding day.'

10 'If this be true you tell to me,
   You must niffer clothes with me.

11 'You'll gie me your cloutit coat,
   I'll gie you my fine velvet coat.

12 'You'll gie me your cloutit pock,
   I'll gie you my purse; it'll be no joke.'

13 'Perhaps there['s] nothing in it, not one bawbee;'
   'Yes, there's gold and silver both,' said he.

14 'You'll gie me your bags of bread,
   And I'll gie you my milk-white steed.'

15 When they had niffered all, he said,
   'You maun learn me how I'll beg.'

16 'When you come before the gate,
   You'll ask for a drink for the highman's sake.'

17 When that he came before the gate,
   He calld for a drink for the highman's sake.

18 The bride cam tripping down the stair,
   To see whaten a bold beggar was there.

19 She gave him a drink with her own hand;   [204]
   He loot the ring drop in the can.

20 'Got ye this by sea or land?
   Or took ye 't aff a dead man's hand?'

21 'I got na it by sea nor land,
   But I got it aff your own hand.'

22 The bridegroom cam tripping down the stair,
   But there was neither bride nor beggar there.

23 Her ain bridegroom had her first wed,
   But Young Hyn Horn had her first to bed.

D

Cromek's *Select Scotish Songs*, ii, 204.

1 Near Edinburgh was a young son born, Hey
   lilelu an a how low lan
An his name it was called young Hyn Horn.
   An it's hey down down deedle airo

2 Seven long years he served the king,
   An it's a' for the sake of his daughter Jean.

3 The king an angry man was he;
   He send young Hyn Horn to the sea.

   *   *   *   *   *

4 An on his finger she put a ring.

   .   .   .   .   .

   *   *   *   *   *

5 'When your ring turns pale and wan,
   Then I'm in love wi another man.'
      *   *   *   *   *

6 Upon a day he lookd at his ring,
   It was as pale as anything.

7 He's left the sea, an he's come to the lan,
   An there he met an auld beggar man.

8 'What news, what news, my auld beggar man?
   What news, what news, by sea or by lan?'

9 'Nae news, nae news,' the auld beggar said,
   'But the king's dochter Jean is going to be wed.'

10 'Cast off, cast off thy auld beggar-weed,
    An I'll gie thee my gude gray steed.'
      *   *   *   *   *

11 When he cam to our guid king's yet,
    He sought a glass o wine for young Hyn Horn's
      sake.

12 He drank out the wine, an he put in the ring,
    An he bade them carry't to the king's dochter
      Jean.
      *   *   *   *   *

13 'O gat ye 't by sea, or gat ye 't by lan?
    Or gat ye 't aff a dead man's han?'

14 'I gat na 't by sea, I gat na 't by lan,
    But I gat it out of your own han.'
      *   *   *   *   *

15 'Go take away my bridal gown,
    For I'll follow him frae town to town.'

16 'Ye need na leave your bridal gown,
    For I'll make ye ladie o' mony a town.'

E

Motherwell's MS., p. 91. From the recitation of Mrs Wilson.

1 Hynd Horn he has lookt on his ring,
      Hey ninny ninny, how ninny nanny
   And it was baith black and blue,
   And she is either dead or she's married.
      And the barck and the broom blooms bonnie

2 Hynd Horn he has shuped to land,
   And the first he met was an auld beggar man.

3 'What news, what news, my silly auld man?
   For it is seven years syne I have seen land.

4 'What news, what news, my auld beggar man?
   What news, what news, by sea or by land?'

5 'There is a king's dochter in the east,
   And she has been marryed these nine nights
      past.

6 'Intil the bride's bed she winna gang   [2
   Till she hears tell of her Hynd Horn.'

7 'Cast aff, cast aff thy auld beggar weed,
   And I will gie thee my gude gray steed.'

F

Lowran Castle, or the Wild Boar of Curridoo: with
other Tales. By Robert Trotter, Dumfries, 1822, p. 6.
From the recitation of a young friend.

1 In Newport town this knight was born,
      Hey lily loo, hey loo lan
   And they've called him Young Hynd Horn.
      Fal lal la, fal the dal the dady

2 Seven long years he served the king,
   For the love of his daughter Jean.

3 He courted her through a wimble bore,
   The way never woman was courted before.

4 He gave her through a silver wand,
   With three singing laverocks there upon.

5 She gave him back a gay gold ring,
   With three bright diamonds glittering.

6 'When this ring grows pale and blue,
     Fair Jeanie's love is lost to you.'

7 Young Hynd Horn is gone to sea,
     And there seven long years staid he.

8 When he lookd his ring upon,
     It grew pale and it grew wan.

9 Young Hynd Horn is come to land,
     When he met an old beggar man.

10 'What news, what news doth thee betide?'
     'No news, but Princess Jeanie's a bride.'

11 'Will ye give me your old brown cap?
     And I'll give you my gold-laced hat.

12 'Will ye give me your begging weed?
     And I'll give you my good grey steed.'

13 The beggar has got on to ride,
     But Young Hynd Horn's bound for the bride.

            *   *   *   *   *

G

Kinloch's *Ancient Scottish Ballads*, p. 135. "From the
recitation of my niece, M. Kinnear, 23 Aug, 1826:" the
north of Scotland.

1 'HYNDE HORN's bound love, and Hynde Horn's
          free,
     Whare was ye born, or in what countrie?'

2 'In gude greenwud whare I was born,
     And all my friends left me forlorn.

3 'I gave my love a silver wand;
     That was to rule oure all Scotland.

4 'My love gave me a gay gowd ring;
     That was to rule abune a' thing.'

5 'As lang as that ring keeps new in hue,
     Ye may ken that your love loves you.

6 'But whan that ring turns pale and wan,
     Ye may ken that your love loves anither man.'

7 He hoisted up his sails, and away sailed he,
     Till that he cam to a foreign countrie.

8 He looked at his ring; it was turnd pale and wan;
     He said, 'I wish I war at hame again.'

9 He hoisted up his sails, and hame sailed he,
     Until that he came to his ain countrie.

10 The first ane that he met wi
     Was wi a pair auld beggar man.

11 'What news, what news, my silly old man?
     What news hae ye got to tell to me?'

12 'Na news, na news,' the puir man did say,
     'But this is our queen's wedding day.'

13 'Ye'll lend me your begging weed,
     And I'll gie you my riding steed.'

14 'My begging weed is na for thee,   [206]
     Your riding steed is na for me.'

15 But he has changed wi the beggar man,
     .   .   .   .   .

16 'Which is the gate that ye used to gae?
     And what are the words ye beg wi?'

17 'Whan ye come to yon high hill,
     Ye'll draw your bent bow nigh until.

18 'Whan ye come to yonder town,
     Ye'll let your bent bow low fall down.

19 'Ye'll seek meat for St Peter, ask for St Paul,
     And seek for the sake of Hynde Horn all.

20 'But tak ye frae nane of them a',
     Till ye get frae the bonnie bride hersel O.'

21 Whan he cam to yon high hill,
     He drew his bent bow nigh until.

22 And whan he cam to yonder town,
     He lute his bent bow low fall down.

23 He saught meat for St Peter, he askd for St Paul,
　　And he sought for the sake of Hynde Horn all.

24 But he would tak frae nane o them a',
　　Till he got frae the bonnie bride hersel O.

25 The bride cam tripping doun the stair,
　　Wi the scales o red gowd on her hair.

26 Wi a glass of red wine in her hand,
　　To gie to the puir auld beggar man.

27 It's out he drank the glass o wine,
　　And into the glass he dropt the ring.

28 'Got ye 't by sea, or got ye 't by land,
　　Or got ye 't aff a drownd man's hand?'

29 'I got na 't by sea, I got na 't by land,
　　Nor got I it aff a drownd man's hand.

30 'But I got it at my wooing,
　　And I'll gie it at your wedding.'

31 'I'll tak the scales o gowd frae my head,
　　I'll follow you, and beg my bread.

32 'I'll tak the scales of gowd frae my hair,
　　I'll follow you for evermair.'

33 She has tane the scales o gowd frae her head,
　　She has followed him to beg her bread.

34 She has tane the scales o gowd frae her hair,
　　And she has followed him for evermair.

35 But atween the kitchen and the ha,
　　There he lute his cloutie cloak fa.

36 And the red gowd shined oure him a',
　　And the bride frae the bridegroom was stown
　　awa.

H

a. Buchan's *Ballads of the North of Scotland*, II, 268.
b. From Mr Walker, of Aberdeen, author of 'The Bards
of Bonaccord,' taken down by a correspondent of his on
lower Deeside about 1880.

1 'HYND HORN fair, and Hynd Horn free,
　　O where were you born, in what countrie?'

2 'In gude greenwood, there I was born,
　　And all my forbears me beforn.

3 'O seven years I served the king,
　　And as for wages, I never gat nane;

4 'But ae sight o his ae daughter,
　　And that was thro an augre bore.

5 'My love gae me a siller wand,
　　'T was to rule ower a' Scotland.

6 'And she gae me a gay gowd ring,
　　The virtue o 't was above a' thing.'

7 'As lang's this ring it keeps the hue,
　　Ye'll know I am a lover true:

8 'But when the ring turns pale and wan,
　　Ye'll know I love another man.'

9 He hoist up sails, and awa saild he,
　　And saild into a far countrie.

10 And when he lookd upon his ring,
　　He knew she loved another man.

11 He hoist up sails and home came he,
　　Home unto his ain countrie.

12 The first he met on his own land,
　　It chancd to be a beggar man.

13 'What news, what news, my gade auld man?
　　What news, what news, hae ye to me?'

14 'Nae news, nae news,' said the auld man,
　　'The morn's our queen's wedding day.'

15 'Will ye lend me your begging weed?
　　And I'll lend you my riding steed.'

16 'My begging weed will ill suit thee,
　　And your riding steed will ill suit me.'

17 But part be right, and part be wrang,
    Frae the beggar man the cloak he wan.

18 'Auld man, come tell to me your leed;
    What news ye gie when ye beg your bread.'

19 'As ye walk up unto the hill,
    Your pike staff ye lend ye till.

20 'But whan ye come near by the yett,
    Straight to them ye will upstep.

21 'Take nane frae Peter, nor frae Paul,
    Nane frae high or low o them all.

22 'And frae them all ye will take nane,
    Until it comes frae the bride's ain hand.'

23 He took nane frae Peter nor frae Paul,
    Nane frae the high nor low o them all.

24 And frae them all he would take nane,
    Until it came frae the bride's ain hand.

25 The bride came tripping down the stair,
    The combs o red gowd in her hair.

26 A cup o red wine in her hand,
    And that she gae to the beggar man.

27 Out o the cup he drank the wine,
    And into the cup he dropt the ring.

28 'O got ye 't by sea, or got ye 't by land,
    Or got ye 't on a drownd man's hand?'

29 'I got it not by sea, nor got it by land,
    Nor got I it on a drownd man's hand.

30 'But I got it at my wooing gay,
    And I'll gie 't you on your wedding day.'

31 'I'll take the red gowd frae my head,
    And follow you, and beg my bread.

32 'I'll take the red gowd frae my hair,
    And follow you for evermair.'

33 Atween the kitchen and the ha,
    He loot his cloutie cloak down fa.

34 And wi red gowd shone ower them a,
    And frae the bridegroom the bride he sta.

I

a. "Hynd Horn,' from the recitation of Miss Jane Webster, formerly of Airds of Kells, now of Dalry, both in the Stewartry of Kirkcudbright, December 12, 1882. **b.** From Miss Jessie Jane Macmath and Miss Agnes Macmath, nieces of Miss Webster, December 11, 1882: originally derived from an old nurse. Communicated by Mr Macmath, of Edinburgh.

She gave him a gay gold ring, Hey li-le-lu and how lo lan, But he gave her a far bet-ter thing, With my hey down and a hey did-dle down-ie.

*   *   *   *   *

1 She gave him a gay gold ring,
    Hey lillelu and how lo lan
But he gave her a far better thing.
    With my hey down and a hey diddle downie

2 He gave her a silver wan,
    With nine bright laverocks thereupon.

    *   *   *   *   *

3 Young Hynd Horn is come to the lan,
  There he met a beggar man.

4 'What news, what news do ye betide?'
  'Na news but Jeanie's the prince's bride.'

5 'Wilt thou give me thy begging weed?
  And I'll give thee my good grey steed.

6 'Wilt thou give me thy auld grey hair?
  And I'll give ye mine that is thrice as fair.'

7 The beggar he got on for to ride,
  But young Hynd Horn is bound for the bride.

8 First the news came to the ha,
  Then to the room mang the gentles a'.

9 'There stands a beggar at our gate,
  Asking a drink for young Hynd Horn's sake.'

10 'I'll ga through nine fires hot
  To give him a drink for young Hynd Horn's
  sake.'

11 She gave him the drink, and he dropt in the
  ring;
  The lady turned baith pale an wan.

12 'Oh got ye it by sea, or got ye it by lan?
  Or got ye it off some dead man's han?'

13 'I got it not by sea, nor I got it not by lan,
  But I got it off thy milk-white han.'

14 'I'll cast off my dress of red,
  And I'll go with thee and beg my bread.

15 'I'll cast off my dress of brown,
  And follow you from city to town.

16 'I'll cast off my dress of green,
  For I am not ashamed with you to be seen.'

17 'You need not cast off your dress of red,
  For I can support thee on both wine and bread.

18 'You need not cast off your dress of brown,
  For I can keep you a lady in any town.

19 'You need not cast off your dress of green,
  For I can maintain you as gay as a queen.'

A. 1^2, 8^1,14^2, 15^2, 16^2, 24^2. Hindhorn.
B. *The burden is given in Motherwell, Appendix, p. xviii, thus:*

  With a hey lilloo and a how lo lan
  And the birk and the brume blooms bonnie.

12^2, 13^2. Hyndhorn. 15^2, 16^2, 24^2. Hynhorn.
C. a. 5^2. to see. 5^2, 7^2. Hynhorn. 23^2. H. horn.
11^1. clouted. 11^1, 14^1. give.
14^2. white milk. **b.** milk-white.
16^2. hymen's. **b.** highman's.
22^1. can.
b. 5^2, 7^2, 23^2. Hynhorn.
7^1. little wee.
13^1. there's.
D. 1^2, 3^2, 11^2. Hynhorn.
E. *The second line of the burden stands after st. 2 in MS.*
2^1. *The MS reading may be* sheeped.
2^1, 6^2. Hyndhorn.
F. 1^2, 7^1, 9^1, 13^2, Hyndhorn.

G. In Kinloch MSS, VII, 117. *After* "from the recita- [208
tion of my niece, M. Kinnear, 23 August, 1826,"
is written in pencil "Christy Smith," *who may have
been the person from whom Miss Kinnear derived
the ballad, or another reciter. Changes are made in
pencil, some of which are written over in ink, some
not. The printed copy, as usual with Kinloch, dif-
fers in some slight respects from the manuscript.*
15. *On the opposite page, over against this stanza, is
written:*

  But part by richt, or part be wrang,
  The auldman's duddie cloak he's on.

G *would have been printed as it stands in Kinloch MSS
VII, 117, had the volume been in my possession.
The copy principally used in Kinloch's* Ancient
Scottish Ballads, *p. 138, was derived from the edi-
tor's niece, M. Kinnear. Readings of another copy
are written in pencil over the transcript of the first in
places, and as the name* "Christy Smith" *is also*

written at the beginning in pencil, it may be sup-
posed that these readings were furnished by this
Christy Smith. Kinloch adopted some of these read-
ings into the copy which appears in his book, and he
introduced others which seem to be his own. The
readings of the Kinnear copy not retained by Kin-
loch will now be given under **a**, and those supplied
(as may be supposed) by Christy Smith under **b**.

a. 1^2. Whare was ye born? or frae what cuntrie?
3^1. a gay gowd wand. 4^1. a silver ring.
5^1. Whan that ring. 6^1. Whan that ring.
7^2. Till he cam. 8^1. Whan he lookit to.
8^2. Says, I wish. 9^2. Until he cam till.
10^1. met with. 10^2. It was with.
11^1. my puir auld man. 13^1. to me.
13^2. I'll lend you.
15^1. He has changed wi the puir auld.
16^1. What is the way that ye use. 16^2. words that.
18^1, 22^1. to yon town end.
19^2. your Hynde (your *struck out*).
23^2. his Hynde (his *struck out*).
24^1. he took na frae ane.
27^1. But he drank his glass. 27^2. Into it he dropt.
30^2. to your. 34^2. him evermair.
36^1. The red: oure them aw.

b. 1^2. in what. 2^1. greenwud's. 2^2. have left.
3^1. a silver wand.
4^1. And my love gave me a gay gowd ring.
5^1. As lang as that ring. 7^2. Till that he cam.
9^2. Until that. 10^2. a jolly beggar man.
15^1. *struck out in pencil.*
18^1. And whan: yonder down.
20^2. Unless it be frae. 22^1. yonder down.
24^1. But he wad tak frae nane. 34^2. for evermair.

G and H are printed by Kinloch and by Buchan in four-
line stanzas.
The stanzas printed by Motherwell, which have
not been found in his manuscripts, are:

10 Seven lang years he has been on the sea,
And Hynd Horn has looked how his ring
may be.

21 The auld beggar man cast off his coat,
And he's taen up the scarlet cloak.

22 The auld beggar man threw down his staff,
And he has mounted the good gray steed.

29 She went to the gate where the auld man
did stand,
And she gave him a drink out of her own
hand.

H. b. 1^1. Hey how, bound, lovie, hey how, free.
6^2. An the glintin o't was aboon.
10. An when he looked the ring upon, O but it
was pale an wan!
13^2. What news, what news is in this lan?
19. Ye'll ging up to yon high hill,
An ye'll blaw yer trumpet loud an shrill.
20. Doun at yon gate ye will enter in,
And at yon stair ye will stan still.
21. Ye'll seek meat frae ane, ye'll seek meat frae
twa,
Ye'll seek meat fra the highest to the lowest
o them a'.
22. But it's out o their hans an ye will tak nane
Till it comes out o the bride's ain han.
26^2. Wi the links o the yellow gowd in her hair.
After 27: An when she looked the ring upon, O
but she grew pale an wan!
After 28: Or got ye it frae ane that is far, far away,
To gie unto me upon my weddin-day?
30. But I got it frae you when I gaed away, To gie
unto you on your weddin-day.
32. It's I'll gang wi you for evermore, An beg my
bread frae door to door.

I. b. 1–3, 6, 8, 10, 14, 16–19, *wanting.*
Burden 2: Wi my hey-dey an my hey deedle
downie.

5^1. O gie to me your aul beggar weed.

11. She gave him the cup, and he dropped in
the ring:
O but she turned pale an wan!

Between 11 and 12:

O whaur got e that gay gold ring?

.   .   .   .

13^2. your ain fair han.

15. O bring to me my dress o broun,
An I'll beg wi you frae toun tae toun.

APPENDIX

Additional Copies

G. a. Kinloch has made numerous small changes. The ballad will now be given as first written down, Kinloch MSS, VII, 117. It appears to have been derived by Miss Kinnear from Christy Smith.

1 'HYNDE Horn's bound, love, and Hynde Horn's
   free;
   Whare was ye born? or frae what cuntrie?'

2 'In gude greenwud whare I was born,
   And all my friends left me forlorn.

3 'I gave my love a gay gowd wand,
   That was to rule oure all Scotland.

4 'My love gave me a silver ring,
   That was to rule abune aw thing.

5 'Whan that ring keeps new in hue,
   Ye may ken that your love loves you.

6 'Whan that ring turns pale and wan,
   Ye may ken that your love loves anither man.'

7 He hoisted up his sails, and away sailed he
   Till he cam to a foreign cuntree.

8 Whan he lookit to his ring, it was turnd pale
       and wan;
   Says, I wish I war at hame again.

9 He hoisted up his sails, and hame sailed he
   Until he cam till his ain cuntree.

10 The first ane that he met with,
    It was with a puir auld beggar-man.

11 'What news? what news, my puir auld man?
    What news hae ye got to tell to me?'

12 'Na news, na news,' the puirman did say,
    'But this is our queen's wedding-day.'

13 'Ye'll lend me your begging-weed,
    And I'll lend you my riding-steed.'

14 'My begging-weed is na for thee,
    Your riding-steed is na for me.'

15 He has changed wi the puir auld beggar-man.

16 'What is the way that ye use to gae?
    And what are the words that ye beg wi?'

17 'Whan ye come to yon high hill,
    Ye'll draw your bent bow nigh until.

18 'Whan ye come to yon town-end,
    Ye'll lat your bent bow low fall doun.

19 'Ye'll seek meat for St Peter, ask for St Paul,
    And seek for the sake of your Hynde Horn all.

20 'But tak ye frae nane o them aw
    Till ye get frae the bonnie bride hersel O.'

21 Whan he cam to yon high hill,
    He drew his bent bow nigh until.

22 And when he cam to yon toun-end,
    He loot his bent bow low fall doun.

23 He sought for St Peter, he askd for St Paul,
    And he sought for the sake of his Hynde Horn
       all.

24 But he took na frae ane o them aw
    Till he got frae the bonnie bride hersel O.

25 The bride cam tripping doun the stair,
    Wi the scales o red gowd on her hair.

26 Wi a glass o red wine in her hand,
    To gie to the puir beggar-man,

27 Out he drank his glass o wine,
    Into it he dropt the ring.

28 'Got ye 't by sea, or got ye 't by land,
    Or got ye 't aff a drownd man's hand?'

29 'I got na 't by sea, I got na 't by land,
 Nor gat I it aff a drownd man's hand;

30 'But I got it at my wooing,
 And I'll gie it to your wedding.'

31 'I'll tak the scales o gowd frae my head,
 I'll follow you, and beg my bread.

32 'I'll tak the scales o gowd frae my hair,
 I'll follow you for evermair.'

33 She has tane the scales o gowd frae her head,
 She's followed him, to beg her bread.

34 She has tane the scales o gowd frae her hair,
 And she has followd him evermair.

35 Atween the kitchen and the ha,
 There he loot his cloutie cloak fa.

36 The red gowd shined oure them aw,
 And the bride frae the bridegroom was stown
  awa.

18

SIR LIONEL

A. 'Sir Lionell,' Percy MS., p. 32, Hales and Furnivall, I, 75.

B. 'Isaac-a-Bell and Hugh the Græme,' Christie, Traditional Ballad Airs, I, 110.

C. a. 'The Jovial Hunter of Bromsgrove,' Allies, The British, Roman, and Saxon Antiquities and Folk-Lore of Worcestershire, 2d ed., p. 116. b. Bell's

Ancient Poems, Ballads and Songs of the Peasantry of England, p. 124.

D. Allies, as above, p. 118.

E. a. 'The Old Man and his Three Sons,' Bell, as above, p. 250. b. Mr Robert White's papers.

F. Allies, as above, p. 120.

B can be traced in Banffshire, according to Christie, for more than a hundred years, through the old woman that sang it, and her forbears. C a, D were originally published by Allies in the year 1845, in a pamphlet bearing the title *The Jovial Hunter of Bromsgrove, Horne the Hunter, and Robin Hood*. No intimation as to the source of his copy, C b, is given by Bell, i.e., Dixon. Apparently all the variations from Allies, C a, are of the nature of editorial improvements. E a is said (1857) to be current in the north of England as a nursery song.

One half of A, the oldest and fullest copy of this ballad (the second and fourth quarters), is wanting in the Percy MS. What we can gather of the story is this. A knight finds a lady sitting in a tree, A, C, D [under a tree, E], who tells him that a wild boar has slain Sir Broning, A [killed her lord and thirty of his men, C; worried her lord and wounded thirty, E]. The knight kills the boar, B–D, and seems to have received bad wounds in the process, A, B; the boar belonged to a giant, B; or a wild woman, C, D. The knight is required to forfeit his hawks and leash, and the little finger of his right hand, A [his horse, his hound, and his lady, C]. He refuses to submit to such disgrace, though in no condition to resist, A; the giant allows him time to heal his wounds, forty days, A; thirty-three, B; and he is to leave his lady as

security for his return, A. At the end of this time the knight comes back sound and well, A, B, and kills the giant as he had killed the boar, B. C and D say nothing of the knight having been wounded. The wild woman, to revenge her "pretty spotted pig," flies fiercely at him, and he cleaves her in two. The last quarter of the Percy copy would, no doubt, reveal what became of the lady who was sitting in the tree, as to which the traditional copies give no light.

Our ballad has much in common with the romance of 'Sir Eglamour of Artois,' Percy MS., Hales and Furnivall, II, 338; *Thornton Romances*, Camden Society, ed. Halliwell, p. 121; Ellis, *Metrical Romances*, from an early printed copy, Bohn's ed., p. 527. Eglamour, simple knight, loving Christabel, an earl's daughter, is required by the father, who does not wish him well, to do three deeds of arms, the second being to kill a boar in the kingdom of Sattin or Sydon, which had been known to slay forty armed knights in one day (Percy, st. 37).[*] This Eglamour does, after a very severe fight. The boar belonged to a giant, who had kept him fifteen years to slay Christian men (Thornton, st. 42, Percy, 40). This giant had demanded the king of Sydon's daughter's hand, and comes to

---

* A king's daughter is to be given to the man that rids the country of a boar: Diarmaid and the Magic Boar, Campbell, *Tales of the West Highlands*, III, 81.

carry her off, by force, if necessary, the day following the boar-fight. Eglamour, who had been found by the king in the forest, in a state of exhaustion, after a contest which had lasted to the third or fourth day, and had been taken home by him and kindly cared for, is now ready for action again. He goes to the castle walls with a squire, who carries the boar's head on a spear. The giant, seeing the head, exclaims,

'Alas, art thou dead!
  My trust was all in thee!
Now by the law that I lieve in,
My little speckled hoglin,
  Dear bought shall thy death be.'
                              Percy, st. 44.

Eglamour kills the giant, and returns to Artois with both heads. The earl has another adventure ready for him, and hopes the third chance may quit all. Eglamour asks for twelve weeks to rest his weary body.

B comes nearest the romance, and possibly even the wood of Tore is a reminiscence of Artois. The colloquy with the giant in **B** is also, perhaps, suggested by one which had previously taken place between Eglamour and another giant, brother of this, after the knight had killed one of his harts (Percy, st. 25). **C** 11, **D** 9 strikingly resemble the passage of the romance cited above (Percy, 44, Thornton, 47).

The ballad has also taken up something from the romance of 'Eger and Grime,' Percy MS., Hales and Furnivall, I, 341; Laing, *Early Metrical Tales*, p. 1; 'Sir Eger, Sir Grahame, and Sir Gray-Steel,' Ellis's *Specimens*, p. 546. Sir Egrabell (Rackabello, Isaac-a-Bell), Lionel's father, recalls Sir Eger, and Hugh the Græme in **B** is of course the Grahame or Grime of the romance, the Hugh being derived from a later ballad. Gray-Steel, a man of proof, although not quite a giant, cuts off the little finger of Eger's right hand, as the giant proposes to do to Lionel in **A** 21.

The friar in **E** 1³, 4¹, may be a corruption of Ryalas, or some like name, as the first line of the burden of **E**, 'Wind well, *Lion*, good hunter,' seems to be a perversion of 'Wind well *thy horn*, good hunter,' in **C**, **D**.* This part of the burden, especially as it occurs in **A**, is found, nearly, in a

fragment of a song of the time of Henry VIII, given by Mr Chappell in his *Popular Music of the Olden Time*, I, 58, as copied from "MSS Reg., Append. 58."†

'Blow thy horne, hunter,
  Cum, blow thy horne on hye!
In yonder wode there lyeth a doo,
  In fayth she woll not dye.
Cum, blow thy horne, hunter,
Cum, blow thy horne, joly hunter!'

A terrible swine is a somewhat favorite figure in romantic tales. A worthy peer of the boar of Sydon is killed by King Arthur in 'The Avowynge of King Arthur,' etc., Robson, *Three Early English Metrical Romances* (see st. xii). But both of these, and even the Erymanthian, must lower their bristles before the boar in 'Kilhwch [210] and Olwen,' *Mabinogion*, Part iv, pp. 309-16. Compared with any of these, the "felon sow" presented by Ralph Rokeby to the friars of Richmond (Evans, *Old Ballads*, II, 270, ed. 1810, Scott, Appendix to Rokeby, note M) is a tame villatic pig: the old mettle is bred out.

Professor Grundtvig has communicated to me a curious Danish ballad of this class, 'Limgrises Vise,' from a manuscript of the latter part of the 16th century. A very intractable damsel, after rejecting a multitude of aspirants, at last marries, with the boast that her progeny shall be fairer than Christ in heaven. She has a litter of nine pups, a pig, and a boy. The pig grows to be a monster, and a scourge to the whole region.

He drank up the water from dike and from dam,
And ate up, besides, both goose, gris and lamb.

The beast is at last disposed of by baiting him with the nine congenerate dogs, who jump down his throat, rend liver and lights, and find their death there, too. This ballad smacks of the broadside, and is assigned to the 16th century.

---

* The friar might also be borrowed from 'The Felon Sow and the Friars of Richmond,' but this piece does not appear to have been extensively known.
† Found, with slight variations, in Add. MS. 31922, British Museum, 39, b (Henry VIII): Ewald, in *Anglia*, XII, 238.

A fragment of a Swedish swine-ballad, in the popular tone, is given by Dybeck, *Runa*, 1845, p. 23; another, very similar, in Axelson's *Vesterdalarne*, p. 179, 'Koloregris,' and Professor Sophus Bugge has recovered some Norwegian verses. The Danish story of the monstrous birth of the pig has become localized: the Liimfiord is related to have been made by the grubbing of the Limgris: Thiele, *Danmarks Folkesagn*, II. 19, two forms.

There can hardly be anything but the name in common between the Lionel of this ballad and Lancelot's cousin-german.

A

Percy MS., p. 32, Hales and Furnivall, I, 75.

1 Sir Egrabell had sonnes three,
  Blow thy horne, good hunter
Sir Lyonell was one of these.
  As I am a gentle hunter

2 Sir Lyonell wold on hunting ryde,
  Vntill the forrest him beside.

3 And as he rode thorrow the wood,
  Where trees and harts and all were good,

4 And as he rode over the plaine,
  There he saw a knight lay slaine.

5 And as he rode still on the plaine,
  He saw a lady sitt in a graine.

6 'Say thou, lady, and tell thou me,
  What blood shedd heere has bee.'

7 'Of this blood shedd we may all rew,
  Both wife and childe and man alsoe.

8 'For it is not past 3 days right
  Since Sir Broninge was mad a knight.

9 'Nor it is not more than 3 dayes agoe
  Since the wild bore did him sloe.'

10 'Say thou, lady, and tell thou mee,
   How long thou wilt sitt in that tree.'

11 She said, 'I will sitt in this tree
   Till my friends doe feitch me.'

12 'Tell me, lady, and doe not misse,
   Where that your friends dwellings is.'

13 'Downe,' shee said, 'in yonder towne,
   There dwells my freinds of great renowne.'

14 Says, 'Lady, Ile ryde into yonder towne
   And see wether your friends beene bowne.

15 'I my self wilbe the formost man
   That shall come, lady, to feitch you home.'

16 But as he rode then by the way,
   He thought it shame to goe away;

17 And vmbethought him of a wile,
   How he might that wilde bore beguile.

18 'Sir Egrabell,' he said, 'my father was
   He neuer left lady in such a case;

19 'Noe more will I' . . .

       *   *   *   *   *

20 'And a[fter] that thou shalt doe mee
   Thy hawkes and thy lease alsoe.

21 'Soe shalt thou doe at my command
   The litle fingar on thy right hand.'

22 'Ere I wold leaue all this with thee,
   Vpoon this ground I rather dyee.'

23 The gyant gane Sir Lyonell such a blow,
   The fyer out of his eyen did throw.

24 He said then, 'if I were saffe and sound,
   As with-in this bower I was in this ground,

25 'It shold be in the next towne told
   How deare thy buffett it was sold;

26 'And it shold haue beene in the next towne said
   How well thy buffett it were paid.'

27 'Take 40 daies into spite,
   To heale thy wounds that beene soe wide.

28 'When 40 dayes beene at an end,
   Heere meete thou me both safe and sound.

29 'And till thou come to me againe,
   With me thoust leaue thy lady alone.'

30 When 40 dayes was at an end,
   Sir Lyonell of his wounds was healed sound.

31 He tooke with him a litle page,
   He gane to him good yeomans wage.

32 And as he rode by one hawthorne,
   Even there did hang his hunting horne.

33 He sett his bugle to his mouth,
   And blew his bugle still full south.

34 He blew his bugle lowde and shrill;
   The lady heard, and came him till.

35 Sayes, 'the gyant lyes vnder yond low,
   And well he heares your bugle blow.

36 'And bidds me of good cheere be,
   This night heele supp with you and me.'

37 Hee sett that lady vppon a steede,
   And a litle boy before her yeede.

38 And said, 'lady, if you see that I must dye,
   As euer you loued me, from me flye.

39 'But, lady, if you see *that* I must liue,'

*   *   *   *   *

B

Christie, *Traditional Ballad Airs*, I, 110. From the
singing of an old woman in Buckie, Enzie, Banffshire.

1 A KNICHT had two sons o sma fame,
   Hey nien nanny
 Isaac-a-Bell and Hugh the Graeme.
   And the norlan flowers spring bonny

2 And to the youngest he did say,
   'What occupation will you hae?
   When the, etc.

3 'Will you gae fee to pick a mill?
   Or will you keep hogs on yon hill?'
   While the, etc.

4 'I winna fee to pick a mill,
   Nor will I keep hogs on yon hill.
   While the, etc.

5 'But it is said, as I do hear,
   That war will last for seven year,
   And the, etc.

6 'With a giant and a boar
   That range into the wood o Tore.
   And the, etc.

7 'You'll horse and armour to me provide,
  That through Tore wood I may safely ride.'
    When the, etc.

[212] 8 The knicht did horse and armour provide,
  That through Tore wood Graeme micht safely
          ride.
    When the, etc.

9 Then he rode through the wood o Tore,
  And up it started the grisly boar.
    When the, etc.

10 The firsten bout that he did ride,
  The boar he wounded in the left side.
    When the, etc.

11 The nexten bout at the boar he gaed,
  He from the boar took aff his head.
    And the, etc.

12 As he rode back through the wood o Tore,
  Up started the giant him before.
    And the, etc.

13 'O cam you through the wood o Tore,
  Or did you see my good wild boar?'
    And the, etc.

14 'I cam now through the wood o Tore,
  But woe be to your grisly boar.
    And the, etc.

15 'The firsten bout that I did ride,
  I wounded your wild boar in the side.
    And the, etc.

16 'The nexten bout at him I gaed,
  From your wild boar I took aff his head.'
    And the, etc.

17 'Gin you have cut aff the head o my boar,
  It's your head shall be taen therfore.
    And the, etc.

18 'I'll gie you thirty days and three,
  To heal your wounds, then come to me.'
    While the, etc.

19 'It's after thirty days and three,
  When my wounds heal, I'll come to thee.'
    When the, etc.

20 So Græme is back to the wood o Tore,
  And he's killd the giant, as he killd the boar.
    And the, etc.

C

a. Allies, *The British, Roman, and Saxon Antiquities
and Folk-Lore of Worcestershire*, 2d ed., p. 116. From the
recitation of Benjamin Brown, of Upper Wick, about
1845. b. *Ancient Poems, Ballads and Songs of the Peas-
antry of England*, edited by Robert Bell, p. 124.

1 SIR ROBERT BOLTON had three sons,
    Wind well thy horn, good hunter
  And one of them was called Sir Ryalas.
    For he was a jovial hunter

2 He rang'd all round down by the woodside,
  Till up in the top of a tree a gay lady he spy'd.
    For he was, etc.

3 'O what dost thou mean, fair lady?' said he;
  'O the wild boar has killed my lord and his men
        thirty.'
    As thou beest, etc.

4 'O what shall I do this wild boar to see?'
  'O thee blow a blast, and he'll come unto thee.'
    As thou beest, etc.

5 [Then he put his horn unto his mouth],
  Then he blowd a blast full north, east, west and
        south.
    As he was, etc.

6 And the wild boar heard him full into his den;
  Then he made the best of his speed unto him.
    To Sir Ryalas, etc.

7 Then the wild boar, being so stout and so strong,
  He thrashd down the trees as he came along.
    To Sir Ryalas, etc.

13] 8 'O what dost thou want of me?' the wild boar
          said he;
        'O I think in my heart I can do enough for thee.'
          For I am, etc.

9 Then they fought four hours in a long summer's
          day,
    Till the wild boar fain would have gotten away.
      From Sir Ryalas, etc.

10 Then Sir Ryalas drawd his broad sword with might,
   And he fairly cut his head off quite.
     For he was, etc.

11 Then out of the wood the wild woman flew:
   'Oh thou hast killed my pretty spotted pig!
     As thou beest, etc.

12 'There are three things I do demand of thee,
     It's thy horn, and thy hound, and thy gay lady.'
       As thou beest, etc.

13 'If these three things thou dost demand of me,
     It's just as my sword and thy neck can agree.'
       For I am, etc.

14 Then into his locks the wild woman flew,
     Till she thought in her heart she had torn him
         through.
       As he was, etc.

15 Then Sir Ryalas drawd his broad sword again,
     And he fairly split her head in twain.
       For he was, etc.

16 In Bromsgrove church they both do lie;
     There the wild boar's head is picturd by
       Sir Ryalas, etc.

D

Allies, *Antiquities and Folk-Lore of Worcestershire*, p.
118. From the recitation of —— Oseman, Hartlebury.

1 As I went up one brook, one brook,
    Well wind the horn, good hunter
  I saw a fair maiden sit on a tree top.
    As thou art the jovial hunter

2 I said, 'Fair maiden, what brings you here?'
  'It is the wild boar that has drove me here.'
    As thou art, etc.

3 'I wish I could that wild boar see;'
  'Well wind the horn, good hunter,
  And the wild boar soon will come to thee.'
    As thou art, etc.

4 Then he put his horn unto his mouth,
  And he blowd both east, west, north and south.
    As he was, etc.

5 The wild boar hearing it into his den,
  [Then he made the best of his speed unto him].

6 He whetted his tusks for to make them strong,
  And he cut down the oak and the ash as he
        came along.
    For to meet with, etc.

7 They fought five hours one long summer's day,
    Till the wild boar he yelld, and he'd fain run
        away.
      And away from, etc.

8 O then he cut his head clean off,
  .   .   .   .   .

9 Then there came an old lady running out of
        the wood,
    Saying, 'You have killed my pretty, my pretty
        spotted pig.'
      As thou art, etc.

10 Then at him this old lady she did go,
     And he clove her from the top of her head to
         her toe.
       As he was, etc.

11 In Bromsgrove churchyard this old lady lies,
     And the face of the boar's head there is drawn
         by,
       That was killed by, etc.

E

[214]

a. *Ancient Poems, Ballads and Songs of the Peasantry of England*, edited by Robert Bell, p. 250. **b.** Mr Robert White's papers.

1 THERE was an old man and sons he had three;
　Wind well, Lion, good hunter
　A friar he being one of the three,
　With pleasure he ranged the north country.
　　For he was a jovial hunter

2 As he went to the woods some pastime to see,
　He spied a fair lady under a tree,
　Sighing and moaning mournfully.
　　He was, etc.

3 'What are you doing, my fair lady?'
　'I'm frightened the wild boar he will kill me;
　He has worried my lord and wounded thirty.'
　　As thou art, etc.

4 Then the friar he put his horn to his mouth,
　And he blew a blast, east, west, north and
　　south,
　And the wild boar from his den he came forth.
　　Unto the, etc.

F

Allies, *Antiquities of Worcestershire*, p. 120.

SIR RACKABELLO had three sons,
　Wind well your horn, brave hunter
Sir Ryalash was one of these.
　And he was a jovial hunter

———◆———

A. 3¹. MS. And as thé.
　6². MS. had bee.
　11¹. MS. I wilt.
　12¹. MS. miste.
　16². MS. awaw.
　17¹. MS. vnbethought while.
　19. *Between 19 and 20 half a page of the MS. is wanting.* 20¹. a[fter]: *MS. blotted.*
　36¹. MS. bidds eue.
　39. *Half a page of the MS. is wanting.*
B. *The stanzas are doubled in Christie, to suit the air.*
C. a. 3¹, 4², 7². **D.** 2¹, 3², 6. *John Cole, who had heard an old man sing the ballad fifty years before (Allies, p. 115), could recollect only so much:*

　　'Oh! lady, Oh! lady, what bringst thou
　　　here?'
　　Wind went his horn, as a hunter
　　'Thee blow another blast, and he'll soon
　　　come to thee.'
　　As thou art a jovial hunter

　　He whetted his tusks as he came along,
　　Wind went his horn, as a hunter

a　5, 6 *stand thus in Allies:*

　v Then he blowd a blast full north, east, west
　　and south,
　　For he was, etc.
　And the wild boar heard him full into his
　　den,
　　As he was, etc.

　vi Then he made the best of his speed unto
　　him.
　　(*Two lines wrongly supplied from another
　　source.*)
　　To Sir Ryalas, etc.

　5 *has been completed from the corresponding stanza in*
　D, *and the two verses of 6, separated above, are put
　together.*
b. 1¹. Old Sir Robert. 1². was Sir Ryalas.
　2². Till in a tree-top.
　3¹. dost thee. 3². The wild boar's killed my lord
　　and has thirty men gored.
　Burden². And thou beest.
　4¹. for to see.

5^1. As in *Allies* (see above), except full *in* his den.

5^2. then heard him full in his den.

215] 6^1. As in *Allies* (see above), but 6^2 supplied by Bell.

7^2. Thrashed down the trees as he ramped him along.

8^1. 'Oh, what dost thee want of me, wild boar.'

Burden^2. the jovial.

9^1. summer. 9^2. have got him.

10^2. cut the boar's head off quite.

11^2. Oh, my pretty spotted pig thou hast slew.

Burden^2. for thou beest.

12^1. I demand them of thee.

13^1. dost ask.

14^1. long locks. 14^2. to tear him through.

Burden^2. Though he was.

15^2. into twain.

16^1. the knight he doth lie. 16^2. And the wild boar's head is pictured thereby.

D. 5, 6. *In Allies thus:*

> v The wild boar hearing it into his den,
>   Well wind, etc.
> He whetted his tusks, for to make them
>   strong,
> And he cut down the oak and the ash as he
>   came along.
> For to meet with, etc.

Stanza 5 has been completed from stanza vi of Allies' other ballad, and 6 duly separated from the first line of 5.

8^2, 9. *In Allies' copy thus:*

> vii Oh! then he cut his head clean off!
>   Well wind, etc.
> Then there came an old lady running out of
>   the wood
> Saying, 'You have killed my pretty, my
>   pretty spotted pig.'
> As thou art, etc.

What stanza 8 should be is easily seen from **C** 10.

C 16, **D** 11. *As imperfectly remembered by Allies* (p. 114):

> In Bromsgrove church his corpse doth lie,
>   Why winded his horn the hunter?
> Because there was a wild boar nigh,
>   And as he was a jovial hunter.

E. b. "Fragment found on the fly-leaf of an old book." *Mr R. White's papers.*

1^2. one of these three. 1^1. wide countrie.

Burden^2. He was.

2^1. was in woods. 2^3. With a bloody river running near she.

3^1. He said, 'Fair lady what are you doing there?'

3^3. killed my lord.

4. *wanting.*

19

KING ORFEO

The Leisure Hour, February 14, 1880, No 1468: Folk-
Lore from Unst, Shetland, by Mrs Saxby, p. 109.

MR EDMONDSTON, from whose memory this ballad was derived, notes that though stanzas are probably lost after the first which would give some account of the king in the east wooing the lady in the west, no such verses were sung to him. He had forgotten some stanzas after the fourth, of which the substance was that the lady was carried off by fairies; that the king went in quest of her, and one day saw a company passing along a hillside, among whom he recognized his lost wife. The troop went to what seemed a great "ha-house," or castle, on the hillside. Stanzas after the eighth were also forgotten, the purport being that a messenger from behind the grey stane appeared and invited the king in.

[216]   We have here in traditional song the story of the justly admired mediæval romance of Orpheus, in which fairy-land supplants Tartarus, faithful love is rewarded, and Eurydice (Heurodis, Erodys, Eroudys) is retrieved. This tale has come down to us in three versions: **A**, in the Auchinleck MS., dating from the beginning of the fourteenth century, Advocates Library, Edinburgh, printed in Laing's *Select Remains of the Ancient Popular Poetry of Scotland*, 'Orfeo and Heurodis,' No 3; **B**, Ashmole MS., 61, Bodleian Library, of the first half of the fifteenth century, printed in Halliwell's *Illustrations of Fairy Mythology*, 'Kyng Orfew,' p. 37;[*] **C**, Harleian MS., 3810, British Museum, printed by Ritson, *Metrical Romanceës*, II, 248, 'Sir Orpheo;' lately edited by Dr Oscar Zielke: *Sir Orfeo, ein englisches Feenmärchen aus dem Mittelalter, mit Einleitung und Anmerkungen,*

Breslau, 1880. At the end of the Auchinleck copy we are told that harpers in Britain heard this marvel, and made a lay thereof, which they called, after the king, 'Lay Orfeo.' The other two copies also, but in verses which are a repetition of the introduction to 'Lay le Freine,' call this a Breton lay.[†]

The story is this (**A**). Orfeo was a king [and so good a harper never none was, **B**]. One day in May his queen went out to a garden with two maidens, and fell asleep under an "ympe" tree. When she waked she shrieked, tore her clothes, and acted very wildly. Her maidens ran to the palace and called for help, for the queen would go mad. Knights and ladies went to the queen, took her away, and put her to bed; but still the excitement continued. The king, in great affliction, besought her to tell him what was the matter, and what he could do. Alas! she said, I have loved thee as my life, and thou me, but now we must part. As she slept knights had come to her and had bidden her come speak with their king. Upon her refusal, the king himself came, with a company of knights and damsels, all on snow-white steeds, and made her ride on a palfrey by his side, and, after he had shown her his palace, brought her back and

---

*   The Bodleian copy also refers to the lay of Orpheus at the end. (G. L. K.) So the Lai de l'Espine, Roquefort, *Poésies de Marie de France*, I, 556, V. 185, and *Floire et Blanceflor*, ed. Du Méril, p. 231, v. 71: Zielke, *Sir Orfeo*, p. 131.

†   For correspondences between Sir Orfeo and the Irish epic tale of the Wooing of Etain, see Kittredge, in *The American Journal of Philology*, VII, 191 ff.

said: Look thou be under this ympe tree tomorrow, to go with us; and if thou makest us any let, we will take thee by force, wherever thou be. The next day Orfeo took the queen to the tree under guard of a thousand knights, all resolved to die before they would give her up: but she was spirited away right from the midst of them, no one knew whither.

The king all but died of grief, but it was no boot. He gave his kingdom in charge to his high steward, told his barons to choose a new king when they should learn that he was dead, put on a sclavin and nothing else, took his harp, and went barefoot out at the gate. Ten years he lived in the woods and on the heath; his body wasted away, his beard grew to his girdle. His only solace was in his harp, and, when the weather was bright, he would play, and all the beasts and birds would flock to him. Often at hot noonday he would see the king of fairy hunting with his rout, or an armed host would go by him with banners displayed, or knights and ladies would come dancing; but whither they went he could not tell. One day he descried sixty ladies who were hawking. He went towards them and saw that one of them was Heurodis. He looked at her wistfully, and she at him; neither spoke a word, but tears fell from her eyes, and the ladies hurried her away. He followed, and spared neither stub nor stem. They went in at a rock, and he after. They alighted at a superb castle; he knocked at the gate, told the porter he was a minstrel, and was let in. There he saw Heurodis, sleeping under an ympe tree.

Orfeo went into the hall, and saw a king and queen, sitting in a tabernacle. He kneeled down before the king. What man art thou? said the king. I never sent for thee, and never found I man so bold as to come here unbidden. Lord, quoth Orfeo, I am but a poor minstrel, and it is a way of ours to seek many a lord's house, though we be not welcome. Without more words he took his harp and began to play. All the palace came to listen, and lay down at his feet. The king sat still and was glad to hear, and, when the harping was done, said, Minstrel, ask of me whatever it be; I will pay thee largely.

"Sir," said Orfeo, "I beseech thee give me the lady that sleepeth under the ympe tree." "Nay," quoth the king, "ye were a sorry couple; for [217] thou art lean and rough and black, and she is lovely and has no lack. A lothly thing were it to see her in thy company." "Gentle king," replied the harper, "it were a fouler thing to hear a lie from thy mouth." "Take her, then, and be blithe of her," said the king.

Orfeo now turned homewards, but first presented himself to the steward alone, and in beggar's clothes, as a harper from heathendom, to see if he were a true man. The loyal steward was ready to welcome every good harper for love of his lord. King Orfeo made himself known; the steward threw over the table, and fell down at his feet, and so did all the lords. They brought the queen to the town. Orfeo and Heurodis were crowned anew, and lived long afterward.

The Scandinavian burden was, perhaps, no more intelligible to the singer than "Hey non nonny" is to us. The first line seems to be Unst for Danish

> Skoven årle grön
> > (Early green's the wood).

The sense of the other line is not so obvious. Professor Grundtvig has suggested to me,

> Hvor hjorten han går årlig
> > (Where the hart goes early).[*]

The relations of the Danish 'Harpens Kraft,' and incidentally those of this ballad, to the English romance are discussed, with his usual acuteness, by Professor Sophus Bugge in *Arkiv för nordisk Filologi*, VII, 97ff, 1891. See 'Glasgerion,' No 67 of this collection.

---

[*]   The first half of the Norse burden is more likely to have been, originally, what would correspond to the Danish Skoven [er] herlig grön, or, Skoven herlig grönnes. In the other half, grün forbids us to look for hjort in giorten, where we are rather to see Danish urt (English wort), Icelandic jurt: so that this would be, in Danish, Hvor urten hun grönnes herlig. (Note of Mr Axel Olrik.)

A

The Leisure Hour, February 14, 1880, No 1468, p.
109. Obtained from the singing of Andrew Coutts, an
old man in Unst, Shetland, by Mr Biot Edmondston.

1 DER lived a king inta da aste,
    Scowan ürla grün
  Der lived a lady in da wast.
    Whar giorten han grün oarlac

2 Dis king he has a huntin gaen,
  He's left his Lady Isabel alane.

3 'Oh I wis ye'd never gaen away,
  For at your hame is döl an wae.

4 'For da king o Ferrie we his daert,
  Has pierced your lady to da hert.'
  *   *   *   *   *
5 And aifter dem da king has gaen,
  But whan he cam it was a grey stane.

6 Dan he took oot his pipes ta play,
  Bit sair his hert wi döl an wae.

7 And first he played da notes o noy,
  An dan he played da notes o joy.

8 An dan he played da göd gabber reel,
  Dat meicht ha made a sick hert hale.
  *   *   *   *   *

9 'Noo come ye in inta wir ha,
  An come ye in among wis a'.'

10 Now he's gaen in inta der ha,
   An he's gaen in among dem a'.

11 Dan he took out his pipes to play,
   Bit sair his hert wi döl an wae.

12 An first he played da notes o noy,
   An dan he played da notes o joy.

13 An dan he played da göd gabber reel,
   Dat meicht ha made a sick hert hale.

14 'Noo tell to us what ye will hae:
   What sall we gie you for your play?

15 'What I will hae I will you tell,
   An dat's me Lady Isabel.'

16 'Yees tak your lady, an yees gaeng hame,
   An yees be king ower a' your ain.'

17 He's taen his lady, an he's gaen hame,
   An noo he's king ower a' his ain.

20

THE CRUEL MOTHER

A. Herd's MSS, I, 132, II, 191. Herd's *Ancient and Modern Scottish Songs*, 1776, II, 237.

B. a. 'Fine Flowers in the Valley,' Johnson's *Museum*, p. 331. **b.** Scott's *Minstrelsy*, III, 259 (1803).

C. 'The Cruel Mother,' Motherwell's *Minstrelsy*, p. 161.

D. a. Kinloch MSS, V, 103. **b.** 'The Cruel Mother,' Kinloch, *Ancient Scottish Ballads*, p. 46; Kinloch MSS, VII, 23.

E. 'The Cruel Mother.' **a.** Motherwell's MS., p. 390. **b.** Motherwell's Note-Book, p. 33.

F. 'The Cruel Mother.' **a.** Buchan's MSS, II, 98; Motherwell's MS., p. 514. **b.** Buchan's *Ballads of the North of Scotland*, II, 222.

G. *Notes and Queries*, 1st S., VIII, 358.

H. 'The Cruel Mother,' Motherwell's MS., p. 402

I. 'The Minister's Daughter of New York.' **a.** Buchan's MSS, II, 111; Motherwell's MS., p. 475. **b.** Buchan's *Ballads of the North of Scotland*, II, 217.

c. 'Hey wi the rose and the lindie O,' Christie, *Traditional Ballad Airs*, I, 106.

J. a. 'The Rose o Malindie O,' Harris MS., f. 10. **b.** Fragment communicated by Dr T. Davidson.

K. Motherwell's MS., p. 186.

L. 'Fine Flowers in the Valley,' Smith's *Scottish Minstrel*, IV, 33.

M. From Miss M. Reburn, as learned in County Meath, Ireland, one stanza.

N. 'The Loch o the Loanie,' Campbell MSS, II, 264.

O. Percy Papers.

P. Pepys Ballads, V, 4, No 2, from a transcript in the Percy Papers.

Q. 'The Cruel Mother,' *Shropshire Folk-Lore*, edited by Charlotte Sophia Burne, 1883–86, p. 540.

R. a. MS. of Thomas Wilkie, p. 4, in "Scotch Ballads, Materials for Border Minstrelsy," No 33. **b.** "Scotch Ballads, Materials," etc., No 113.

S. Findlay's MSS, I, 58f, derived from his mother.

Two fragments of this ballad, **A, B,** were printed in the last quarter of the eighteenth century; **C–L** were committed to writing after 1800; and, of these, **E, H, J, K** are now printed for the first time.

A–H differ only slightly, but several of these versions are very imperfect. A young woman, who passes for a leal maiden, gives birth to two babes [**A, B,** one, **H,** three], puts them to death with a penknife, **B–F,** and buries them, or, **H,** ties them hand and feet and buries them alive. She afterwards sees two pretty boys, and exclaims that if they were hers she would treat them most tenderly. They make answer that when they were hers they were very differently treated, rehearse what she had done, and inform or threaten her that hell shall be her

portion, **C, D, E, F, H.** In **I** the children are buried alive, as in **H,** in **J a** strangled, in **J b** and **L** killed with the penknife, but the story is the same down to the termination, where, instead of simple hell-fire, there are various seven-year penances, properly belonging to the ballad of 'The Maid and the Palmer,' which follows this.

All the English ballads are in two-line stanzas.[*]

Until 1870 no corresponding ballad had been found in Denmark, though none was more likely to occur in **Danish.** That year Kristensen,

---

[*] All the genuine ones. 'Lady Anne,' in Scott's *Minstrelsy*, III, 259, 1803, is on the face of it a modern composition, with extensive variations, on the theme of the popular ballad. It is here given in an Appendix, with a companion piece from Cromek's *Remains of Nithsdale and Galloway Song*.

in the course of his very remarkable ballad-quest in Jutland, recovered two versions which approach surprisingly near to Scottish tradition, and especially to E: *Jyske Folkeviser*, I, 329, No 121 A, B, 'Barnemordersken.' Two other Danish versions have been obtained since then, but have not been published.[*] A and B are much [219] the same, and a close translation of A will not take much more space than would be required for a sufficient abstract.

Little Kirsten took with her the bower-women five,
And with them she went to the wood belive.

She spread her cloak down on the earth,
And on it to two little twins gave birth.

She laid them under a turf so green,
Nor suffered for them a sorrow unseen.

She laid them under so broad a stone,
Suffered sorrow nor harm for what she had done.

Eight years it was, and the children twain
Would fain go home to their mother again.

They went and before Our Lord they stood:
'Might we go home to our mother, we would.'

'Ye may go to your mother, if ye will,
But ye may not contrive any ill.'

They knocked at the door, they made no din:
'Rise up, our mother, and let us in.'

By life and by death hath she cursed and sworn,
That never a child in the world had she borne.

'Stop, stop, dear mother, and swear not so fast,
We shall recount to you what has passed.

'You took with you the bower-women five,
And with them went to the wood belive.

'You spread your cloak down on the earth,
And on it to two little twins gave birth.

'You laid us under a turf so green,
Nor suffered for us a sorrow unseen.

'You laid us under so broad a stone,
Suffered sorrow nor harm for what you had done.'

'Nay my dear bairns, but stay with me;
And four barrels of gold shall be your fee.'

'You may give us four, or five, if you choose,
But not for all that, heaven will we lose.

'You may give us eight, you may give us nine,
But not for all these, heaven will we tine.

'Our seat is made ready in heavenly light,
But for you a seat in hell is dight.'

A ballad is spread all over Germany which is probably a variation of 'The Cruel Mother,' though the resemblance is rather in the general character than in the details. **A**, 'Höllisches Recht,' *Wunderhorn*, II, 202, ed. of 1808, II, 205, ed. 1857. Mittler, No 489, p. 383, seems to be this regulated and filled out. **B**, Erlach, 'Die Rabenmutter,' IV, 148; repeated, with the addition of one stanza, by Zuccalmaglio, p. 203, No 97. **C**, 'Die Kindsmörderinn,' Meinert, p. 164, from the Kuhländchen; turned into current German, Erk's *Liederhort*, p. 144, No 41[c]. **D**, Simrock, p. 87, No 37[a], from the Aargau. **E**, 'Das falsche Mutterherz,' Erk u. Irmer, Heft 5, No 7, and 'Die Kindesmörderin,' Erk's *Liederhort*, p. 140, No 41, Brandenburg. **F**, *Liederhort*, p. 142, No 41[a], Silesia. **G**, *Liederhort*, p. 143, 41[b], from the Rhein, very near to **B**. **H**, Hoffmann u. Richter, No 31, p. 54, and **I**, No 32, p. 57, Silesia. **J**, Ditfurth, *Fränkische Volkslieder*, II, 12, No 13. **K**, 'Die Rabenmutter,' Peter, *Volksthümliches aus Österreichisch-Schlesien*, I, 210, No 21. **L**, 'Der Teufel u. die Müllerstochter,' Pröhle, *Weltliche u. geistliche V. l.*, p. 15, No 9, Hanoverian Harz. **M**. Pater Amand Baumgarten, *Aus der volksmässigen Ueberlieferung der Heimat*: IX, Geburt, Heirat, Tod, mit einem Anhang von Liedern, p. 140. ['Das ausgesetzte Kind.'] **N**. A. Schlossar, *Deutsche Volkslieder aus Steiermark*, p. 336, No 306, 'Der alte Halter und das Kind' (not yet seen by me). (Köhler.) **O**, O. Knoop, *Volkssagen, Erzählungen, u. s. w., aus dem östlichen Hinterpommern*, Posen, 1885, pp.

---

[*]   To these should be added 'I dølgsmål,' Kristensen, *Skattegraveren*, V 98, No 644 corrupted; 'Barnemordersken,' Kristensen, *Jyske Folkeminder*, X, 356, No 90, **A**, **B**.

x, xi: 'Es trieb ein Schäfer mit Lämmlein raus.'
Fr. Schönwerth, *Aus der Oberpfalz*, I, 234, gives
a prose tale which is evidently founded on the
ballad of 'The Cruel Mother' (three children,
one in the water, one in dung, one in the
wood). (Köhler.) **P**, 'Die Schäferstochter,' as
sung in the neighborhood of Köslin, Ulrich
Jahn, *Volkssagen aus Pommern u. Rügen*, No
393, p. 310f. (G.L.K.) **Q**, **R**, Hruschka u.
Toischer, *Deutsche Volkslieder aus Böhmen*, p.
129, No 40 a, b. **S**, Deutsche Volksballaden aus
Südungarn, Grünn und Baróti, in *Ethnologische
Mitteilungen aus Ungarn*, II, 201, No 4, 1892. **T**,
Wolfram, p. 90, No 64, 'Es hütet ein Schäfer an
jenem Rain,' 'Die Rabenmutter;' Böhme's edi-
tion of Erk's *Liederhort*, I, 636, No 212 e; and to
the literature several items at p. 637. Repeti-
tions and compounded copies are not noticed.

The story is nearly this in all. A herdsman,
passing through a wood, hears the cry of a child,
but cannot make out whence the sound comes.
The child announces that it is hidden in a hol-
low tree, and asks to be taken to the house
where its mother is to be married that day.
There arrived, the child proclaims before all
the company that the bride is its mother. The
bride, or some one of the party, calls attention
to the fact that she is still wearing her maiden-
wreath. Nevertheless, says the child, she has
had three children: one she drowned, one she
buried in a dung-heap [the sand], and one she
hid in a hollow tree. The bride wishes that the
devil may come for her if this is true, and, upon

the word, Satan appears and takes her off; in **B**,
G, J, with words like these:

'Komm her, komm her, meine schönste Braut,
Dein Sessel ist dir in der Hölle gebaut.' **J** 9.

A **Wendish** version, 'Der Höllentanz,' in
Haupt and Schmaler, I, 290, No 292, differs
from the German ballads only in this, that the
bride has already borne nine children, and
going with the tenth.

A ballad of Slavic origin in Nesselmann's
Littauische Volkslieder, No 380, p. 322, resembles
the German and Wendish versions of 'The
Cruel Mother,' with a touch of 'The Maid and
the Palmer.' (G. L. K.) Similar Slavic ballads
include: **Polish**, Kolberg, *Lud*, IV, 52, No 220;
XII, 308f, Nos 611, 612; XVII, 9, No 17; XVIII,
188, No 346; XXI, 85, No 179; XXII, 160, No
284; Kolberg, *Mazowsze*, II, 160, No 352; IV,
366, No 436.

A **Magyar-Croat** ballad of the same tenor as
the German is found in Kurelac, p. 150, No
451. (W. W.)

A combination of **B, C, D, F** is translated by
Grundtvig, *Engelske og skotske Folkeviser*, No 48,
p. 279, and **I**, from the eighth stanza on, p. 282.
C is translated by Wolff, *Halle der Völker*, I, 11,
and Hausschatz, p. 223; Allingham's version
(nearly **B a**) by Knortz, *L. u. R. Alt-Englands*, p.
178, No 48.

A

Herd's MSS, I, 132, II, 191: *Ancient and Modern
Scottish Songs*, 1776, II, 237.

*   *   *   *   *

1 And there she's leand her back to a thorn,
   Oh and alelladay, oh and alelladay
And there she has her baby born.
   Ten thousand times good night and be wi
      thee

2 She has houked a grave ayont the sun,
   And there she has buried the sweet babe in.

3 And she's gane back to her father's ha,
   She's counted the leelest maid o them a'.

*   *   *   *   *

4 'O look not sae sweet, my bonie babe,
   Gin ye smyle sae, ye'll smyle me dead.'

*   *   *   *   *

B

a. Johnson's *Museum*, p. 331. **b.** Scott's *Minstrelsy*,
1803, III, 259, preface.

1 SHE sat down below a thorn,
  Fine flowers in the valley
And there she has her sweet babe born.
  And the green leaves they grow rarely

2 'Smile na sae sweet, my bonie babe,
  And ye smile sae sweet, ye'll smile me dead.'

3 She's taen out her little pen-knife,
  And twinnd the sweet babe o its life.

4 She's howket a grave by the light o the moon
  And there she's buried her sweet babe in.

5 As she was going to the church,
  She saw a sweet babe in the porch.

6 'O sweet babe, and thou were mine,
  I wad cleed thee in the silk so fine.'

7 'O mother dear, when I was thine,
  You did na prove to me sae kind.'

*   *   *   *   *

C

Motherwell's *Minstrelsy*, p. 161.

1 SHE leaned her back unto a thorn,
  Three, three, and three by three
And there she has her two babes born.
  Three, three, and thirty-three

2 She took frae 'bout her ribbon-belt,
  And there she bound them hand and foot.

3 She has taen out her wee pen-knife,
  And there she ended baith their life.

4 She has howked a hole baith deep and wide,
  She has put them in baith side by side.

[221] 5 She has covered them oer wi a marble stane,
  Thinking she would gang maiden hame.

6 As she was walking by her father's castle wa,
  She saw twa pretty babes playing at the ba.

7 'O bonnie babes, gin ye were mine,
  I would dress you up in satin fine.

8 'O I would dress you in the silk,
  And wash you ay in morning milk.'

9 'O cruel mother, we were thine,
  And thou made us to wear the twine.

10 'O cursed mother, heaven's high,
  And that's where thou will neer win nigh.

11 'O cursed mother, hell is deep,
  And there thou'll enter step by step.'

D

a. Kinloch's MSS, v, 103, in the handwriting of
James Beattie. **b.** Kinloch's *Ancient Scottish Ballads*, p.
46: from the recitation of Miss C. Beattie; Kinloch
MSS, VII, 23.

There lives a la - dy__ in Lon - don __ All a - lone and a - lon - ie

She's gane wi' bairn to__ the clerk's son __ Doun by the green - wud sae bon - nie.

1 THERE lives a lady in London,
 All alone and alone ee
She's gane wi bairn to the clerk's son.
 Down by the green wood sae bonnie

2 She's taen her mantle her about,
 She's gane aff to the gude green wood.

3 She's set her back untill an oak,
 First it bowed and then it broke.

4 She's set her back untill a tree,
 Bonny were the twa boys she did bear.

5 But she took out a little pen-knife,
 And she parted them and their sweet life.

6 She's aff untill her father's ha;
 She was the lealest maiden that was amang
 them a'.

7 As she lookit oure the castle wa,
 She spied twa bonnie boys playing at the ba.

8 'O if these two babes were mine,
 They should wear the silk and the sabelline!'

9 'O mother dear, when we were thine,
 We neither wore the silks nor the sabelline.

10 'But out ye took a little pen-knife,
 And ye parted us and our sweet life.

11 'But now we're in the heavens hie,
 And ye've the pains o hell to drie.'

E

a. Motherwell's MS., p. 390. **b.** Motherwell's Note-
book, p. 33. From the recitation of Agnes Lyle, Kil-
barchan, August 24, 1825.

1 THERE was a lady, she lived in Lurk,
 Sing hey alone and alonie O
She fell in love with her father's clerk.
 Down by yon greenwood sidie O

2 She loved him seven years and a day,
 Till her big belly did her betray.

3 She leaned her back unto a tree,
 And there began her sad misery.

4 She set her foot unto a thorn,
 And there she got her two babes born.

5 She took out her wee pen-knife,
 She twind them both of their sweet life.

6 She took the sattins was on her head,
 She rolled them in both when they were dead.

7 She howkit a grave forenent the sun,
 And there she buried her twa babes in.

8 As she was walking thro her father's ha,
 She spied twa boys playing at the ba.

9 'O pretty boys, if ye were mine, [222]
 I would dress ye both in the silks so fine.'

10 'O mother dear, when we were thine,
    Thou neer dressed us in silks so fine.

11 'For thou was a lady, thou livd in Lurk,
    And thou fell in love with thy father's clerk.

12 'Thou loved him seven years and a day,
    Till thy big belly did thee betray.

13 'Thou leaned thy back unto a tree,
    And there began thy sad misery.

14 'Thou set thy foot unto a thorn,
    And there thou got thy two babes born.

15 'Thou took out thy wee pen-knife,
    And twind us both of our sweet life.

16 'Thou took the sattins was on thy head,
    Thou rolled us both in when we were dead.

17 'Thou howkit a grave forenent the sun,
    And there thou buried thy twa babes in.

18 'But now we're both in [the] heavens hie,
    There is pardon for us, but none for thee.'

19 'My pretty boys, beg pardon for me!'
    'There is pardon for us, but none for thee.'

F

a. Buchan's MSS, II, 98; Motherwell's MS., p. 514.
b. Buchan's *Ballads of the North of Scotland*, II, 222.

1 IT fell ance upon a day,
    Edinburgh, Edinburgh
  It fell ance upon a day,
    Stirling for aye
  It fell ance upon a day
  The clerk and lady went to play.
    So proper Saint Johnston stands fair upon
      Tay

2 'If my baby be a son,
    I'll make him a lord of high renown.'

3 She's leand her back to the wa,
    Prayd that her pains might fa.

4 She's leand her back to the thorn,
    There was her baby born.

5 'O bonny baby, if ye suck sair,
    You'll never suck by my side mair.'

6 She's riven the muslin frae her head,
    Tied the baby hand and feet.

7 Out she took her little pen-knife,
    Twind the young thing o its sweet life.

8 She's howked a hole anent the meen,
    There laid her sweet baby in.

9 She had her to her father's ha,
    She was the meekest maid amang them a'.

10 It fell ance upon a day,
    She saw twa babies at their play.

11 'O bonny babies, gin ye were mine,
    I'd cleathe you in the silks sae fine.'

12 'O wild mother, when we were thine,
    You cleathd us not in silks so fine.

13 'But now we're in the heavens high,
    And you've the pains o hell to try.'

14 She threw hersell oer the castle-wa,
    There I wat she got a fa.

G

Notes and Queries, 1st S., VIII, 358. From Warwick-
shire, communicated by C. Clifton Barry.

1 THERE was a lady lived on [a] lea,
    All alone, alone O
Down by the greenwood side went she.
    Down the greenwood side O

2 She set her foot all on a thorn,
    There she had two babies born.

3 O she had nothing to lap them in,
    But a white appurn, and that was thin.

H

Motherwell's MS., p. 402. From Agnes Laird, Kil-
barchan, August 24, 1825.

1 THERE was a lady brisk and smart,
    All in a lone and a lonie O
And she goes with child to her father's clark.
    Down by the greenwood sidie O

2 Big, big oh she went away,
    And then she set her foot to a tree.

3 Big she set her foot to a stone,
    Till her three bonnie babes were borne.

4 She took the ribbons off her head,
    She tied the little babes hand and feet.

5 She howkit a hole before the sun,
    She's laid these three bonnie babes in.

6 She covered them over with marble stone,
    For dukes and lords to walk upon.

7 She lookit over her father's castle wa,
    She saw three bonnie boys playing at the ba.

8 The first o them was clad in red,
    To shew the innocence of their blood.

9 The neist o them was clad in green,
    To shew that death they had been in.

10 The next was naked to the skin,
    To shew they were murderd when they were
      born.

11 'O bonnie babes, an ye were mine,
    I wad dress you in the satins so fine.'

12 'O mother dear, when we were thine,
    Thou did not use us half so kind.'

13 'O bonnie babes, an ye be mine,
    Whare hae ye been a' this time?'

14 'We were at our father's house,
    Preparing a place for thee and us.'

15 'Whaten a place hae ye prepar'd for me?'
    'Heaven's for us, but hell's for thee.

16 'O mother dear, but heaven's high;
    That is the place thou'll ne'er come nigh.

17 'O mother dear, but hell is deep;
    'T will cause thee bitterlie to weep.'

I

a. Buchan's MS., II, 111; Motherwell's MS., p. 475. b. Buchan's *Ballads of the North of Scotland*, II, 217.
c. Christie, *Traditional Ballad Airs*, I, 106.

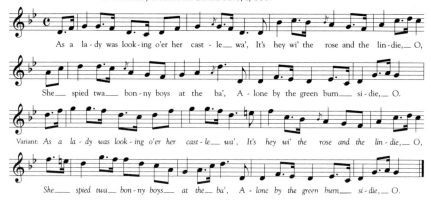

I. c. Christie, I, 1876, p. 106. Sung in Banffshire.

1 THE minister's daughter of New York,
   Hey wi the rose and the lindie, O
Has faen in love wi her father's clerk.
   Alone by the green burn sidie, O

2 She courted him six years and a day,
   At length her belly did her betray.

3 She did her down to the greenwood gang,
   To spend awa a while o her time.

4 She lent her back unto a thorn,
   And she's got her twa bonny boys born.

[224] 5 She's taen the ribbons frae her hair,
   Bound their bodyes fast and sair.

6 She's put them aneath a marble stane,
   Thinking a maiden to gae hame.

7 Looking oer her castle wa,
   She spied her bonny boys at the ba.

8 'O bonny babies, if ye were mine,
   I woud feed you with the white bread and wine.

9 'I woud feed you wi the ferra cow's milk,
   And dress you in the finest silk.'

10 'O cruel mother, when we were thine,
   We saw none of your bread and wine.

11 'We saw none of your ferra cow's milk,
   Nor wore we of your finest silk.'

12 'O bonny babies, can ye tell me,
   What sort of death for you I must die?'

13 'Yes, cruel mother, we'll tell to thee,
   What sort of death for us you must die.

14 'Seven years a fowl in the woods,
   Seven years a fish in the floods.

15 'Seven years to be a church bell,
   Seven years a porter in hell.'

16 'Welcome, welcome, fowl in the wood[s],
   Welcome, welcome, fish in the flood[s].

17 'Welcome, welcome, to be a church bell,
   But heavens keep me out of hell.'

J

a. Harris MS., fol. 10, "Mrs Harris and others." b.
Fragment communicated by Dr T. Davidson.

She leant her back a - gainst a thorn, Hey for the Rose o' Ma - lin - die O,

And there she has__ twa__ bon - nie babes born, A - doon by the green wood sid - ie O.

1 SHE leant her back against a thorn,
   Hey for the Rose o' Malindie O
 And there she has twa bonnie babes born.
   Adoon by the green wood sidie O

2 She's taen the ribbon frae her head,
   An hankit their necks till they waur dead.

3 She luikit outowre her castle wa,
   An saw twa nakit boys, playin at the ba.

4 'O bonnie boys, waur ye but mine,
   I wald feed ye wi flour-bread an wine.'

5 'O fause mother, whan we waur thine,
   Ye didna feed us wi flour-bread an wine.'

6 'O bonnie boys, gif ye waur mine,
   I wald clied ye wi silk sae fine.'

7 'O fause mother, whan we waur thine,
   You didna clied us in silk sae fine.

8 'Ye tuik the ribbon aff your head,
   An' hankit our necks till we waur dead.

       *   *   *   *   *

9 'Ye sall be seven years bird on the tree,
   Ye sall be seven years fish i the sea.

10 'Ye sall be seven years eel i the pule,
   An ye sall be seven years doon into hell.'

11 'Welcome, welcome, bird on the tree,
   Welcome, welcome, fish i the sea.

12 'Welcome, welcome, eel i the pule,
   But oh for gudesake, keep me frae hell!'

K

Motherwell's MS., p. 186,

1 LADY MARGARET looked oer the castle wa,
   Hey and a lo and a lilly O
 And she saw twa bonnie babes playing at the ba.
   Down by the green wood sidy O

2 'O pretty babes, an ye were mine,
   I would dress you in the silks so fine.'

3 'O false mother, when we were thine,
   Ye did not dress us in silks so fine.'

4 'O bonnie babes, an ye were mine,
   I would feed you on the bread and wine.'

5 'O false mother, when we were thine,
   Ye did not feed us on the bread and the wine.'

6 'Seven years a fish in the sea,
   And seven years a bird in the tree.

7 'Seven years to ring a bell,
   And seven years porter in hell.'

L

Smith's *Scottish Minstrel*, IV, 33, 2d ed.

(Variant phrases)

1 A LADY lookd out at a castle wa
    Fine flowers in the valley
  She saw twa bonnie babes playing at the ba.
    And the green leaves they grow rarely

2 'O my bonnie babes, an ye were mine,
    I would cleed ye i the scarlet sae fine.

3 'I'd lay ye saft in beds o down,
    And watch ye morning, night and noon.'

4 'O mither dear, when we were thine,
    Ye didna cleed us i the scarlet sae fine.

5 'But ye took out yere little pen-knife,
    And parted us frae our sweet life.

6 'Ye howkit a hole aneath the moon,
    And there ye laid our bodies down.

7 'Ye happit the hole wi mossy stanes,
    And there ye left our wee bit banes.

8 'But ye ken weel, O mither dear,
    Ye never cam that gate for fear.'

      *   *   *   *   *

9 'Seven lang years ye'll ring the bell,

M

Communicated by Miss Margaret Reburn, as
learned in County Meath, Ireland, about 1860.

'O MOTHER dear, when we were thine,
    All a lee and aloney O
You neither dressed us in coarse or fine.'
    Down by the greenwood sidy O

N

Campbell MSS, II, 264.

1 As I lookit oer my father's castle wa,
    All alone and alone O
  I saw two pretty babes playing at the ba.
    Down by yon green-wood sidie

2 'O pretty babes, gin ye were mine,'
    Hey the loch o the Loanie
  'I would clead ye o the silk sae fine.'
    Down by that green-wood sidie

3 'O sweet darlings, gin ye were mine,'
    Hey the loch o the Loanie
  'I would feed ye on the morning's milk.'
    Down by that green-wood sidie

4 'O mither dear, when we were thine,'
    By the loch o the Loanie
  'Ye neither dressd us wi silk nor twine.'
    Down by this green-wood sidie

5 'But ye tuke out your little pen-knife,'
   By, etc.
  'And there ye tuke yer little babes' life.'
   Down by the, etc.

6 'O mither dear, when this ye had done,'
   Alone by, etc.
  'Ye unkirtled yersel, and ye wrapt us in't.'
   Down by the, etc.

7 'Neist ye houkit a hole fornent the seen.'
   All alone and alone O
  'And tearless ye stappit your little babes in.'
   Down by the, etc.

8 'But we are in the heavens high,'
   And far frae the loch o the Loanie
  'But ye hae the pains o hell to d[r]ie.'
   Before ye leave the green-wood sidie

O

Percy Papers, with no account of the derivation.

1 THERE was a duke's daughter lived at York,
   All alone and alone a
  And she fell in love with her father's clarke.
   Down by the greenwood side a, side a,
   Down, etc.

2 She loved him seven long years and a day,
  Till at last she came big-bellied away.

3 She set her back against a thorn,
  And there she had two pretty babes born.

4 She took out a penknife long and short,
  And she pierc'd these pretty babes to the ten-
   der heart.

5 So as she was walking in her father's hall,
  She saw three pretty babes playing at ball.

6 The one was clothed in purple, the other in
   pall,
  And the other was cloathed in no cloths at all.

7 'O pretty babes, pretty babes, will you be mine?
  You shall be clothed in scarlet so fine,
   And ye shall drink ale, beer, and wine.'

8 'We are three angels, as other angels be,
  And the hotest place in hell is reserved for
   thee.'

P

Pepys Ballads, V, 4, No 2, from a transcript in the Percy Papers.

1 THERE was a duke's daughter lived in York,
   Come bend and bear away the bows of yew
  So secretly she loved her father's clark.
   Gentle hearts, be to me true.

2 She loved him long and many a day,
  Till big with child she went away.

3 She went into the wide wilderness;
  Poor she was to be pitied for heaviness.

4 She leant her back against a tree,
  And there she endurd much misery.

5 She leant her back against an oak,
  With bitter sighs these words she spoke.

6 She set her foot against a thorne,
  And there she had two pretty babes born.

7 She took her filliting off her head,
  And there she ty'd them hand and leg.

8 She had a penknife long [and] sharp,
  And there she stuck them to the heart.

9 She dug a grave, it was long and deep,
  And there she laid them in to sleep.

10 The coldest earth it was their bed,
   The green grass was their coverlid.

11 As she was a going by her father's hall,
   She see three children a playing at ball.

12 One was drest in scarlet fine,
   And the other[s was naked] as ere they was
    born.

13 'O mother, O mother, if these children was mine,
   I wold dress them [in] scarlet fine.'

14 'O mother, O mother, when we was thine,
   You did not dress [us] in scarlet fine.

15 'You set your back against a tree,
   And there you endured great misery.

16 'You set your foot against a thorne,
   And there you had us pritty babes born.

17 'You took your filliting off your head,
   And there you bound us, hand to leg.

18 'You had a penknife long and sharp,
   And there you stuck us to the heart.

19 'You dug a grave, it was long and deep,
   And there you laid us in to sleep.

20 The coldest earth it was our bed,
   The green grass was our coverlid.

21 'O mother, mother, for your sin
   Heaven-gate you shall not enter in.

22 'O mother, mother, for your sin
   Hell-gates stands open to let you in.'

23 The lady's cheeks lookd pale and wan,
   'Alass I,' said she, 'what have I done!'

24 She tore her silken locks of hair,
   And dy'd away in sad despair.

25 Young ladies all, of beauty bright,
   Take warning by her last good-night.

Q

'The Cruel Mother,' *Shropshire Folk-Lore*, edited by
Charlotte Sophia Burne, 1883–86, p. 540; "sung by
Eliza Wharton and brothers, children of gipsies, habitu-
ally travelling in North Shropshire and Staffordshire,
13th July, 1885."

There was a la-dy, a lady of York, Ri fol i did-dle i gee wo!
She fell a-court-ing in her own fath-er's park, Down by the green-wood side, O!

1 THERE was a lady, a lady of York,
   Ri fol i diddle i gee wo
She fell a-courting in her own father's park.
   Down by the greenwood side, O

2 She leaned her back against the stile,
   There she had two pretty babes born.

3 And she had nothing to lap 'em in,
   But she had a penknife sharp and keen.

4 .   .   .   .   .
   There she stabbed them right through the
      heart.

5 She wiped the penknife in the sludge;
   The more she wiped it, the more the blood
      showed.

6 As she was walking in her own father's park,
   She saw two pretty babes playing with a ball.

7 'Pretty babes, pretty babes, if you were mine,
   I'd dress you up in silks so fine.'

8 'Dear mother, dear mother, [when we were
      thine,]
   You dressed us not in silks so fine.

9 'Here we go to the heavens so high,
   You'll go to bad when you do die.'

R

a. MS. of Thomas Wilkie, p. 4, in "Scotch Ballads, Materials for Border Minstrelsy," No 33. "Taken down from Mrs Hislope, Gattonside. The air is plaintive and very wild." 1813. b. "Scotch Ballads, Materials," etc., No 113; in the hand of T. Wilkie.

1 As I looked over my father's castle-wa,
　　All alone and alone, O
　I saw two pretty babes playing at the ba.
　　Down by yone greenwood side, O

2 'O pretty babes, if ye were mine,'
　　All alone, etc.,
　'I would clead you o the silk so fine.'
　　Alone by the, etc.

3 'O mother dear, when we were thine,
　Ye houket a hole fornent the sun,'
　　And laid yer two babes in, O

4 'O pretty babes, if ye were mine,
　　I would feed you wi the morning's milk.'
　　Alone by, etc.

5 'O mother dear, when we were thine,
　　Ye houket a hole fornent the sun.
　　And laid yer two babes in, O.

6 'But we are in the heavens high,
　　And ye hae the pains of hell to dri.'
　　Alone by, etc.

7 'O pretty babes, pray weel for me!'
　'Aye, mother, as ye did for we.'
　　Down by, etc.

S

Findlay's MSS, I, 58f, derived from his mother.

1 I LOOKĔD ower the castle-wa,
　　Hey rose, ma lindie, O
　Saw twa bonnie babies playin at the ba.
　　Doon in the green wood-sidie, O

2 'O bonnie babies, an ye were mine,
　I wad feid ye wi flour-breid an wine.'

3 'O cruel mother, when we were thine,
　You did not prove to us sae kin.'

4 'O bonnie babies, an ye were mine
　I wad cleid ye wi scarlet sae fine.'

5 'O cruel mother, when we were thine,
　You did not prove to us sae fine.

6 'For wi a penknife ye took our life
　And threw us ower the castle-wa.'

7 'O bonnie babies, what wad ye hae dune to me
　For my bein sae cruel to thee?'

8 'Seven yeare a fish in the flood,
　Seven yeare a bird in the wood.

9 'Seven yeare a tinglin bell,
　Seventeen yeare in the deepest hell.'
　　Under the green wood-sidie, O

A. *Superscribed*, "Fragment to its own tune. Melancholy." *Against the first line of the burden is written in the margin*, "perhaps alas-a-day," *and this change is adopted in Herd's printed copy. Scott suggested* well-a-day.
　4^2. *MSS and ed.* 1776 *have* ze . . . ze'll.

B. b. "A fragment [*of 5 stanzas*] containing the following verses, which I have often heard sung in my childhood." Scott, iii. 259. *No burden is given.*
　1^1. She set her back against. 1^2. young son born.
　2^1. O smile nae sae.

3, 4, *wanting*.

5^1. An when that lady went. 5^2. She spied a naked boy.

6^1. O bonnie boy, an ye. 6^2. I'd cleed ye in the silks.

7^2. To me ye were na half.

Cunningham, Songs of Scotland, *i*, 340, *says:* "I remember a verse, and but a verse, of an old ballad which records a horrible instance of barbarity," *and quotes the first two stanzas of Scott's fragment literally; from which we may infer that it was Scott's fragment that he partly remembered. But he goes on:* "At this moment a hunter came—one whose suit the lady had long rejected with scorn the brother of her lover:

He took the babe on his spear point,
    And threw it upon a thorn:
'Let the wind blow east, the wind blow west,
    The cradle will rock alone.'

Cunningham's recollection was evidently much confused. This last stanza, which is not in the metre of the others, is perhaps from some copy of 'Edom o Gordon.'*

C. 9, 10, 11 *are in Motherwell's MS., p.* 183, *written in pencil.*

D. a. 6^2. I was.

b. *Kinloch makes slight changes in his printed copy, as usual.*

4^1. until a brier.

5^1. out she's tane.

6^2. She seemd the lealest maiden amang.

8^1. O an thae.

E. 1^1, 11^1. Lurk *may be a corruption of* York, *which is written in pencil (by way of suggestion?) in the MSS.*

a. 16^1. on your.

b. 4^1, 14^1. upon a thorn.

5^2. twind *wanting*. 6^1. sattins *wanting*.

13, 14, 15, 16, 17 *are not written out in the notebook.*

18^1. the heavens.

19^2. but there is none.

F. a. 9 *stands last but one in the MS.*

14^2. Here.

b. 4^2. has her.

7^2. sweet *is omitted*.

Printed as from the MS. in Dixon's Scottish Traditional Versions, etc., *p.* 46. *Dixon has changed*

baby *to* babies *in* 4, 5, 6, 8, *and indulges in other variations*.

H. *The ballad had been heard with two different burdens; besides the one given in the text, this:*

Three and three, and three by three
Ah me, some forty three

7 'Lady Mary Ann,' Johnson's Museum, *No* 377, *begins:*

O Lady Mary Ann looks oer the castle wa,
She saw three bonie boys playing at the ba.

I. a, b. 14^1, 16^1. fool, *i.e.* fowl *spelt phonetically*.

a. 3^1. greenwoods

b. 2^2. it did.

8^2. with white.

11^2. wear'd.

13^2. maun die.

c. "Epitomized" *from Buchan, ii,* 217, "and somewhat changed for this work, some of the changes being made according to the way the Editor has heard it sung." *Note by Christie, p.* 106.

Burden, It's hey with the rose, *etc.*

7^1. As a lady was looking. 7^2. She spied twa.

11^2. Nor wore we a.

12^2. What sort of pain for you I must drie.

13^2. What sort of pain for us you must drie.

14^2. And seven.

Printed as from the MS. in Dixon's Scottish Traditional Versions of Ancient Ballads, *p.* 50, 'The Minister's Dochter o Newarke,' *with a few arbitrary changes*.

J. a. 9^1. You.

b *has stanzas corresponding to* **a** 1, 3, 4, 6, *and, in place of* 2,

She's taen oot a little pen-knife,
And she's robbit them o their sweet life.

Burden^1. Hey i the rose o Mylindsay O.

1^1. until a thorn. 1^2. An syne her twa bonnie boys was born.

3^1. As she leukit oer her father's. 3^2. bonnie boys.

4^1. an ye were mine. 4^2. bread.

6^2. claithe ye in.

L. 8 *looks like an interpolation, and very probably the ballad was docked at the beginning in order to suit the parlor better*.

P. The Duke's Daughter's Cruelty, or, The Wonderful Apparition of two Infants who she murtherd and buried in a Forrest for to hide her Shame. Printed for J. Deacon at the Sign of the Angel in Guil[t]-spur Street.

---

*   Cunningham, as Mr Macmath has reminded me, has made this stanza a part of another ballad, in Cromek's *Remains*, p. 223.

[226]

Either the printer or the transcriber was careless.

5². sights. 11¹. gowing.
12². was naked *inserted by Percy.*
16¹. you foot; throne, *and perhaps also in* 6¹.
20¹. coldeth. 23¹. wand. 25¹. waring.

After 10 *is introduced, absurdly, this stanza, derived from* 'The Famous Flower of Serving-Men:'

She cut her hair, changed her name
From Fair Elinor to Sweet William.

The copy in Pepys, V, 4 No 2 is also in the Crawford collection, No 1127, and in that from the Osterley Park library, British Museum, C. 39. k. 6 (60). It is dated 1688–95 in the Crawford catalogue, and 1690? in the Museum catalogue.
The text is here corrected according to the Museum copy.
2¹. lovd. 3². for her heaviness. 6². pritty.

8¹. long and sharp. 12². other as naked as.
13². would. 14². dress us.
21¹, 22¹. O mother, O mother.
23¹. Alass! said. *After* 10, *etc.*: hair and.
Title: Infants whom.
Imprint: London: Printed, *etc.*: Guiltspur.
(9², 19². have into, *wrongly.*)

R. a. 3¹. when that ye had done *is written above* we were thine.

b. 1. *Burden, second line,* by the. 2². with the.

After 2:

'O mother dear, when we were thine,
Ye stabd us wi your little penknife.'
Down by the, etc.

3¹. when that ye had done. 4, 5. *Wanting.*
6. *Burden, second line,* Down by the, etc.

———◆———

APPENDIX

Lady Anne

"This ballad was communicated to me by Mr Kirkpatrick Sharpe of Hoddom, who mentions having copied it from an old magazine. Although it has probably received some modern corrections, the general turn seems to be ancient, and corresponds with that of a fragment [B b], which I have often heard sung in my childhood." *Minstrelsy of the Scottish Border,* iii, 259, ed. 1803.

Buchan, *Gleanings,* p. 90, has an additional stanza between 8 and 9 of Scott's, whether from the old magazine or not, it would not be worth the while to ascertain.

Cunningham, *Songs of Scotland,* i, 339, has rewritten even 'Lady Anne.'

Translated by Schubart, p. 170, and by Gerhard, p. 92.

1 Fair Lady Anne sate in her bower,
   Down by the greenwood side,
   And the flowers did spring, and the birds did sing,
   'T was the pleasant May-day tide.

2 But fair Lady Anne on Sir William calld,
   With the tear grit in her ee,
   'O though thou be fause, may Heaven thee guard,
   In the wars ayont the sea!'

3 Out of the wood came three bonnie boys,
   Upon the simmer's morn,
   And they did sing and play at the ba',
   As naked as they were born.

4 'O seven lang years wad I sit here,
   Amang the frost and snaw,
   A' to hae but ane o these bonnie boys,
   A playing at the ba.'

5 Then up and spake the eldest boy,
    'Now listen, thou fair ladie,
And ponder well the rede that I tell,
    Then make ye a choice of the three.

6 ' 'T is I am Peter, and this is Paul,
    And that ane, sae fair to see,
But a twelve-month sinsyne to paradise came,
    To join with our companie.'

7 'O I will hae the snaw-white boy,
    The bonniest of the three:'
'And if I were thine, and in thy propine,
    O what wad ye do to me?'

8 ' 'T is I wad clead thee in silk and gowd,
    And nourice thee on my knee:'
'O mither, mither, when I was thine,
    Sic kindness I couldna see.

9 'Beneath the turf, where now I stand,
    The fause nurse buried me;
The cruel pen-knife sticks still in my heart,
    And I come not back to thee.'

———◆———

"There are many variations of this affecting tale. One of them appears in the *Musical Museum*, and is there called 'Fine Flowers of the Valley,' of which the present is either the original or a parallel song. I am inclined to think it is the original." Cromek's *Remains of Nithsdale and Galloway Song*, p. 267.

This is translated by Talvj, *Versuch*, p. 571.

1 There sat 'mang the flowers a fair ladie,
    Sing ohon, ohon, and ohon O
And there she has born a sweet babie.
    Adown by the greenwode side O

2 An strait she rowed its swaddling band,
An O! nae mother grips took her hand.

3 O twice it lifted its bonnie wee ee:
'Thae looks gae through the saul o me!'

4 She buried the bonnie babe neath the brier,
And washed her hands wi mony a tear.

5 And as she kneelt to her God in prayer,
The sweet wee babe was smiling there.

6 'O ay, my God, as I look to thee,
My babe's atween my God and me.

7 'Ay, ay, it lifts its bonnie wee ee:
' "Sic kindness get as ye shawed me," '

8 'An O its smiles wad win me in,
But I'm borne down by deadly sin.'

21

THE MAID AND THE PALMER

A. Percy MS., p. 461. 'Lillumwham,' Hales and Furnivall, IV, 96.

B. Sharpe's *Ballad Book*, ed. Laing, p. 157.

THE only English copy of this ballad that approaches completeness is furnished by the Percy manuscript, **A**. Sir Walter Scott remembered, and communicated to Kirkpatrick Sharpe, three stanzas, and half of the burden, of another version, **B**.

There are three versions in **Danish**, no one of them very well preserved. **A**, 'Maria Magdalena,' is a broadside of about 1700, existing in two identical editions: Grundtvig, No 98, II, 530; **B**, 'Mariu vísa,' No 9 of Hammershaimb's *Færøsk Anthologi*, p. 35, was written down in the Färöe isles in 1848; **C** was obtained from recitation by Kristensen in Jutland in 1869, *Jyske Folkeviser*, I, 197, No 72, 'Synderinden,' *Skattegraveren*, VII, 81, No 505, and *Jyske Folkeminder*, X, 71, No 20.

A **Färöe** version, from the end of the last century or the beginning of this, is given in Grundtvig's notes, p. 533ff.

Versions recently obtained from recitation in **Norway** are: 'Maria,' Bugge's *Gamle Norske Folkeviser*, No 18; **A**, p. 88; **B**, p. 90, a fragment, which has since been completed, but only two more stanzas printed, Grundtvig, III, 889; **C**, Bugge, p. 91. **D**, **E** are reported, but only a stanza or two printed, Grundtvig, III, 889f; **F**, printed 890f, and **G**, as obtained by Lindeman, 891: all these, **D–G**, communicated by Bugge. **C**, and one or two others, are rather Danish than Norwegian.

This is, according to Afzelius, one of the commonest of **Swedish** ballads. These versions are known: **A**, "a broadside of 1798 and 1802," Grundtvig, II, 531, Bergström's Afzelius, I, 335;

B, 'Magdalena,' Atterbom's *Poetisk Kalender for 1816*, p. 20; **C**, Afzelius, II, 229; **D**, Arwidsson, I, 377, No 60; **E**, Dybeck's *Svenska Visor*, Häfte 2, No 6, only two stanzas; **F**, **G**, "in Wiede's collection, in the Swedish Historical and Antiquarian Academy;" **H**, "in Cavallius and Stephens' collection, where also **A**, **F**, **G** are found;" **I**, Maximilian Axelson's *Vesterdalarne*, p. 171; **J**, 'Jungfru Adelin,' **E**. Wigström's *Folkdiktning*, No 38, p. 76; **K**, 'Jungfru Maja,' *Album utgifvet af Nyländingar*, VI, 227, repeated in Lagus, *Nyländska Folkvisor*, I, 105, No 32. **A–F** are printed in Grundtvig's notes, II, 533ff, and also some verses of **G**, **H**.

The ballad is known to have existed in **Icelandic** from a minute of Arne Magnusson, who cites the line, "Swear not, swear not, wretched woman," but it has not been recovered (Grundtvig, III, 891, note d).

Finnish, 'Mataleenan vesimatka,' *Kanteletar*, ed. 1864, p. 240, first printed by C. A. Gottlund, *Otava*, 1832, II, 9 (Rolland, *Chansons Populaires*, VI, 47–50, with a translation).

The story of the woman of Samaria, John, iv, is in all these blended with mediæval traditions concerning Mary Magdalen, who is assumed to be the same with the woman "which was a sinner," in Luke, vii, 37, and also with Mary, sister of Lazarus.[*] This is the view of the larger part of the Latin ecclesiastical writers, while most of the Greeks distinguish the three (Butler, 'Lives of the Saints,' VII, 290,

---

[*] M. G. Doncieux has attempted to arrange "Le cycle de Sainte Marie-Madelaine," in *Revue des Traditions Populaires*, VI, 257.

note). It was reserved for ballads, as Grundtvig remarks, to confound the Magdalen with the Samaritan woman.

The traditional Mary Magdalen was a beautiful woman of royal descent, who derived her surname from Magdalum, her portion of the great family estate. For some of her earlier years entirely given over to carnal delights, "unde jam, proprio nomine perdito, peccatrix consueverat appellari," she was, by the preaching of Jesus, converted to a passionate repentance and devotedness. In the course of the persecution of the church at Jerusalem, when Stephen was [229] slain and the Christians widely dispersed, Mary, with Lazarus, her brother, Martha, and many more, were set afloat on the Mediterranean in a rudderless ship, with the expectation that they would find a watery grave. But the malice of the unbelieving was overruled, and the vessel came safe into port at Marseilles. Having labored some time for the christianizing of the people, and founded churches and bishoprics, Mary retired to a solitude where there was neither water, tree, nor plant, and passed the last thirty years of her life in heavenly contemplation. The cave in which she secluded herself is still shown at La Sainte Baume. The absence of material comforts was, in her case, not so great a deprivation, since every day at the canonical hours she was carried by angels to the skies, and heard, with ears of the flesh, the performances of the heavenly choirs, whereby she was so thoroughly refected that when the angels restored her to her cave she was in need of no bodily aliment. (*Golden Legend*, Græsse, c. 96.) It is the practical Martha that performs real austerities, and those which are ascribed to her correspond too closely with the penance in the Scandinavian ballads not to be the original of it: "Nam in primis *septem* annis, glandibus et radicibus herbisque crudis et *pomis** silvestribus corpusculum sustentans potius quam reficiens, victitavit .... Extensis solo ramis arboreis aut viteis, lapide pro cervicali capiti superposito subjecto, ... incumbebat." (Vincent of Beauvais, *Spec. Hist.*, ix, 100.)

The best-preserved Scandinavian ballads concur nearly in this account. A woman at a

well, or a stream, is approached by Jesus, who asks for drink. She says she has no vessel to serve him with. He replies that if she were pure, he would drink from her hands. She protests innocence with oaths, but is silenced by his telling her that she has had three children, one with her father, one with her brother, one with her parish priest: Danish **A, B, C**; Färöe; Swedish **C, D, F, I, J, K**; Norwegian **A, C, F, G**. She falls at his feet, and begs him to shrive her. Jesus appoints her a seven years' penance in the wood. Her food shall be the buds or the leaves of the tree [grass, worts, berries, bark], her drink the dew [brook, juice of plants], her bed the hard ground [linden-roots, thorns and prickles, rocks, straw and sticks]; all the while she shall be harassed by bears and lions [wolves], or snakes and drakes (this last in Swedish **B, C, D, I, K**, Norwegian **A**). The time expired, Jesus returns and asks how she has liked her penance. She answers, as if she had eaten daintily, drunk wine, slept on silk or swan's-down, and had angelic company [had been listening to music].[†] Jesus then tells her that a place is ready for her in heaven.

The penance lasts eight years in Swedish **C, F, J**, Norwegian **A**; Nine in the Färöe ballad; fifteen in Danish **B**; and six weeks in Danish **C**. It is to range the field in Danish **A**, Swedish **F**; to walk the snows barefoot in the Färöe ballad and Norwegian **B**; in Norwegian **D** to stand nine

---

* The Magdalen's food is to be dry apple in Danish **B** 9.

† Swedish **F**:

14 'And tell me how has it been with thy meat?'
'O I have eaten of almonds sweet.'

15 'And tell me how it has been with thy drink?'
'I have drunk both mead and wine, I think.'

16 'And tell me how was that bed of thine?'
'Oh I have rested on ermeline.'

Norwegian **G**:

13 'I have fed as well on herbage wild
As others have fed on roast and broiled.

14 'I have rested as well on the hard, hard stone
As others have rested on beds of down.

15 'I have drunk as well from the rippling rill
As others that drank both wine and ale.'

years in a rough stream and eight years naked in the church-paths.

The names Maria, or Magdalena, Jesus, or Christ, are found in most of the Scandinavian ballads. Swedish **E** has 'Lena (Lilla Lena); Swedish **H** He-lena; **J**, Adelin; **K**, Maja. Norwegian **A** gives no name to the woman, and Danish **A** a name only in the burden; Norwegian **B** has, corruptly, Margjit. In Danish **C**, Norwegian **B, G**, Jesus is called an *old* man, correspondingly with the "old palmer" of English **A**, but the old man is afterwards called Jesus in Norwegian **G** (**B** is not printed in full), and in the burden of Danish **C**. The Son is exchanged for the Father in Swedish **D**.

Stanzas 4, 5 of Swedish **A, G**, approach singularly near to English **A** 6, 7:

Swedish **A**:

4 'Would thy leman now but come,
   Thou wouldst give him to drink out of thy hand.'

5 By all the worlds Magdalen swore,
   That leman she never had.

Swedish **G**:

4 'Yes, but if I thy leman were,
   I should get drink from thy snow-white hand.'

5 Maria swore by the Holy Ghost,
   She neer had to do with any man.

The woman is said to have taken the lives of her three children in Danish **A, B, C**, and of two in Swedish **C, D, F, I, J, K** (**B** also, where there are but two in all), a trait probably borrowed from 'The Cruel Mother.'

The seven years' penance of the Scandinavian ballads is multiplied three times in English **A**, and four times in **B** and in those versions of 'The Cruel Mother' which have been affected by the present ballad (20, **I, J, K**; **L** is defective). What is more important, the penance in the English ballads is completely different in kind, consisting not in exaggerated austerities, but partly, at least, in transmigration or metensomatosis: seven years to be a fish, 20, **I, J, K**; seven years a bird, 20, **I, J, K**; seven years a

stone, 21, **A, B**; seven years an eel, 20, **J**; seven years a bell, or bellclapper, 20, **I**, 21, **A** (to ring a bell, 20, **K, L**). Seven years in hell seems to have been part of the penance or penalty in every case: seven years a porter in hell, 21, **B**, 20, **I, K**; seven years down in hell, 20, **J**; seven years to "ring the bell and see sic sights as ye darna tell, 20, **L**;" "other seven to lead an ape in hell," **A**, a burlesque variation of the portership.

The Finnish Mataleena, going to the well for water, sees the reflection of her face, and bewails her lost charms. Jesus begs a drink: she says she has no can, no glass. He bids her confess. "Where are your three boys? One you threw into the fire, one into the water, and one you buried in the wilderness." She fills a pail with her tears, washes his feet, and wipes them with her hair: then asks for penance. "Put me, Lord Jesus, where you will. Make me a ladder-bridge over the sea, a brand in the fire, a coal in the furnace."

There are several Slavic ballads which blend the story of the Samaritan woman and that of 'The Cruel Mother,' without admixture of the Magdalen. **Wendish A**, 'Aria' (M-aria?), Haupt and Schmaler, 1, 287, No 290, has a maid who goes for water on Sunday morning, and is joined by an old man who asks for a drink. She says the water is not clean; it is dusty and covered with leaves. He says, The water is clean, but you are unclean. She demands proof, and he bids her go to church in her maiden wreath. This she does. The grass withers before her, a track of blood follows her, and in the church-yard there come to her nine headless boys, who say, Nine sons hast thou killed, chopt off their heads, and meanest to do the same for a tenth. She entreats their forgiveness, enters the church, sprinkles herself with holy water, kneels at the altar and crosses herself, then suddenly sinks into the ground, so that nothing is to be seen but her yellow hair. **B**, 'Die Kindesmörderin,' *ib.*, ii, 149, No 197, begins like **A**. As the maid proceeds to the church, nine graves open before her, and nine souls follow her into the church. The oldest of her children springs upon her and breaks her neck, saying, "Mother, here is thy reward. Nine of us didst thou kill."

There are two **Moravian** ballads of the same tenor: **A**, *Deutsches Museum*, 1855, I, 282, translated by M. Klapp: **B**, communicated to the *Zeitschrift des böhmischen Museums*, 1842, p. 401, by A. W. Šembera, as sung by the "mährisch sprechenden Slawen" in Prussian Silesia; the first seven stanzas translated in Haupt u. Schmaler, II, 314, note to No 197. The Lord God goes out one Sunday morning, and meets a maid, whom he asks for water. She says the water is not clean. He replies that it is [231] cleaner than she: for (**A**) she has seduced fifteen men and had children with all of them, has filled hell with the men and the sea with the children. He sends her to church; but, as she enters the church-yard, the bells begin to ring (of themselves), and when she enters the church, all the images turn their backs. As she falls on her knees, she is changed into a pillar of salt. Sušil, No 3, p. 2, closely resembles Moravian **A**; the woman is turned to stone. In a variant, p. 3, she has had fifty paramours, and again in a Little-Russian ballad, Golovatsky, I, 235, No 68, seventy. In this last, after shrift, the sinner is dissipated in dust. (W. W.) A Bohemian ballad, to the same effect, appears in Waldau's *Böhmische Granaten*, II, 210, No 299.

Several **White Russian** versions are recorded in Šejn, II, 607ff, Nos 12–16, 'Pesn' o grěšnoj děvě, Song of the sinful girl,' five copies, the third imperfect. Jesus sends the girl to church, in the first the earth comes up seven cubits, the lights go out, etc.; she shrives herself, and things are as before. In the other copies she crumbles to dust.

Polish (with variations): Kolberg, *Lud*; XII, 309, No 613; XIX, 187, No 658; XX, 101, No 37; XXI, 86, No 180; XXII, 161f, Nos 285, 286; Kolberg, *Mazowsze*, I, 142, No 46; IV, 367, No 437; Siarkowski, in *Zbiór wiadomości*, IV, 94, No 18.

The popular ballads of some of the southern nations give us the legend of the Magdalen without mixture.

French. A, *Poésies populaires de la France*, I (not paged), from Sermoyer, Ain, thirty lines, made stanzas by repetition. Printed by Rolland, *Chansons Populaires*, VI, 22, *o* (it is folio 60 of the MS.). Two other before imprinted versions *p*, *q*, at pp. 25, 26, of Rolland. Mary goes from door to door seeking Jesus. He asks what she wants: she answers, To be shriven. Her sins have been such, she says, that the earth ought not to bear her up, the trees that see her can but tremble. For penance she is to stay seven years in the woods of Baume, eat the roots of the trees, drink the dew, and sleep under a juniper. Jesus comes to inquire about her when this space has expired. She says she is well, but her hands, once white as flower-de-luce, are now black as leather. For this Jesus requires her to stay seven years longer, and then, being thoroughly cured of her old vanities, she is told,

'Marie Magdeleine, allez au paradis;
La porte en est ouverte depuis hier à midi.'

B is nearly the same legend in Provençal: Damase Arbaud, I, 64. The penance is seven years in a cave, at the end of which Jesus passes, and asks Mary what she has had to eat and drink. "Wild roots, and not always them; muddy water, and not always that." The conclusion is peculiar. Mary expresses a wish to wash her hands. Jesus pricks the rock, and water gushes out. She bewails the lost beauty of her hands, and is remanded to the cavern for another seven years. Upon her exclaiming at the hardship, Jesus tells her that Martha shall come to console her, the wood-dove fetch her food, the birds drink. But Mary is not reconciled:

'Lord God, my good father,
    Make me not go back again!
With the tears from my eyes
    I will wash my hands clean.

'With the tears from my eyes
    I will wash your feet,
And then I will dry them
    With the hair of my head.'

C, *Poésies populaires de la Gascogne*, Bladé, 1881, p. 339, 'La pauvre Madeleine,' seventeen stanzas of four short lines, resembles **B** till the close. When Jesus comes back after the second penance, and Mary says, as she had before, that she has lived like the beasts, only she has lacked water, Jesus again causes water to spring from the rock. But Mary says, I want no water. I should have to go back to the cave for another seven years. She is conducted straightway to paradise.

D, Bladé, as before, p. 183, 'Marie-Madeleine,' six stanzas of five short lines. Mary is sent to the mountains for seven years' penance; at the end of that time washes her hands in a brook, and is guilty of admiring them; is sent back to the mountains for seven years, and is then taken to heaven.

A **Catalan** ballad combines the legend of the Magdalen's penance with that of her conversion: Milá, *Observaciones*, p. 128, No 27, 'Santa Magdalena,' and Briz y Saltó, *Cansons de la Terra*, ii, 99. The *Romancerillo Catalan*, in the new edition, p. 10, No 12, 'Magdalena,' gives another version, with the variations of eight more copies, that of the *Observaciones* being now **C**. Martha, returning from church, asks Magdalen, who is combing her hair with a gold comb, if she has been at mass. Magdalen says no, nor had she thought of going. Martha advises her to go, for she certainly will fall in love with the preacher, a young man; pity that he ever was a friar. Magdalen attires herself with the utmost splendor, and, to hear the sermon better, takes a place immediately under the pulpit. The first word of the sermon touched her; at the middle she fainted. She stripped off all her ornaments, and laid them at the preacher's feet. At the door of the church she inquired of a penitent where Jesus was to be found. She sought him out at the house of Simon, washed his feet with her tears, and wiped them with her hair, picked up from the floor the bones which he had thrown away. Jesus at last noticed her, and asked what she wished. She wished to confess. He imposed the penance of seven years on a mountain, "eating herbs and fennels, eating bitter herbs." Magdalen turned homewards after the seven years, and found on the way a spring, where she washed her hands, with a sigh over their disfigurement. She heard a voice that said, Magdalen, thou hast sinned. She asked for new penance, and was sent back to the mountain for seven years more. At the end of this second term she died, and was borne to the skies with every honor from the Virgin, saints, and angels.

Italian. A, Ive, *Canti popolari istriani*, p. 366, No 14, 'S. Maria Maddalena;' *Archivio*, VIII, 323, *Canti Parmigiani*, No 2, three stanzas only. Mary's father, dying, left her a castle of gold and silver, from which one day she saw Jesus pass. She wept a fountain of tears to wash his feet, and dried his feet with her tresses. Then she asked for a penance. She wished to go into a cave without door or windows, sleep on the bare ground, eat raw herbs, and drink a *little* salt water; and this she did. In 'La Maddalena,' Guerrini, *Alcuni C. p. romagnoli*, p. 7, there is no penance.

B, *Archivio*, XIV, 211f, 'Maria Maddalena,' two copies, fragmentary. In the second, Maria asks the master of a vessel to take her in; a tempest arises; the dona pecatrice, lest the vessel should founder on her account, with many people aboard, throws herself into the sea, is swallowed by a whale, and not disgorged for three-and-thirty years.

Danish **A** is translated by Prior, ii, 25, No 44: Swedish **C** by William and Mary Howitt. *Literature and Romance of Northern Europe*, i, 282.

A

Percy MS., p. 461. Furnivall, iv, 96.

1 THE maid shee went to the well to washe,
  Lillumwham, lillumwham!
The mayd shee went to the well to washe,
  Whatt then? what then?
The maid shee went to the well to washe,

Dew ffell of her lilly white fleshe.
  Grandam boy, grandam boy, heye!
Leg a derry, leg a merry, mett, mer, whoope, whir!
Driuance, larumben, grandam boy, heye!

2 While shee washte and while shee ronge,
  While shee hangd o the hazle wand.

3 There came an old palmer by the way,
  Sais, 'God speed thee well, thou faire maid!'

4 'Hast either cupp, or can,
  To giue an old palmer drinke therin?'

5 Sayes, 'I have neither cupp nor cann,
  To giue an old palmer drinke therin.'

6 'But an thy lemman came from Roome,
  Cupps and canns thou wold ffind soone.'

7 Shee sware by God & good St. John,
  Lemman had shee neuer none.

8 Saies, 'Peace, ffaire mayd, you are fforsworne!
  Nine children you haue borne.

9 'Three were buryed vnder thy bed's head,
  Other three vnder thy brewing leade.

10 'Other three on yon play greene;
   Count, maid, and there be 9.'

11 'But I hope you are the good old man
   That all the world beleeues vpon.

12 'Old palmer, I pray thee,
   Pennaunce *that* thou wilt giue to me.'

13 'Penance I can giue thee none,
   But 7 yeere to be a stepping-stone.

14 'Other seaven a clapper in a bell,
   Other 7 to lead an ape in hell.

15 'When thou hast thy penance done,
   Then thoust come a mayden home.'

B

A *Ballad Book*, by Charles Kirkpatrick Sharpe,
edited by David Laing, p. 157f, VII; from Sir W. Scott's
recollection.

1 'SEVEN years ye shall be a stone,

        .   .   .   .   .

  For many a poor palmer to rest him upon.
    And you the fair maiden of Gowden-gane

2 'Seven years ye'll be porter of hell,
  And then I'll take you to mysell.'

        *   *   *   *   *

3 'Weel may I be a' the other three,
  But porter of hell I never will be.'
    And I, etc.

———————◆———————

[233] **A.** 2^1. White shee washee & white. 2^2. White.
        9^1. They were.
        10^1. on won. 10^2. maids.
   B. *Note by* Scott: "There is or was a curious song with
        this burthen to the verse,

        'And I the fair maiden of Gowden-gane.'

Said maiden is, I think, courted by the devil in
human shape, but I only recollect imperfectly
the concluding stanzas [1, 2]:

        'Seven years ye shall be a stone,'

(here a chorus line which I have forgot), etc. The
lady answers, in allusion to a former word which
I have forgotten,

        Weel may I be [etc., st. 3]."

22

ST STEPHEN AND HEROD

Sloane MS., 2593, fol. 22 b; British Museum.

THE manuscript which preserves this delightful little legend has been judged by the handwriting to be of the age of Henry VI. It was printed entire by Mr T. Wright, in 1856, for the Warton Club, under the title, *Songs and Carols*, from a manuscript in the British Museum of the fifteenth century, the ballad at p. 63. Ritson gave the piece as 'A Carol for St Stephen's Day,' in *Ancient Songs*, 1790, p. 83, and it has often been repeated; e.g., in Sandys' *Christmas Carols*, p. 4, Sylvester's, p. 1.[*]

The story, with the Wise Men replacing Stephen, is also found in the carol, still current, of 'The Carnal and the Crane,' Sandys, p. 152, in conjunction with other legends and in this order: the Nativity, the Wise Men's passage with Herod, the Massacre of the Innocents, the Flight into Egypt, Herod and the Sower.

The legend of Stephen and Herod occurs, and is even still living, in Scandinavian tradition, combined, as in English, with others relating to the infancy of Jesus.

Danish. 'Jesusbarnet, Stefan og Herodes:' **A**, Grundtvig, No 96, II, 525. First printed in Erik Pontoppidan's little book on the reliques of Paganism and Papistry among the Danish People, 1736, p. 70, as taken down from the singing of an old beggar-woman before the author's door.[†] Syv alludes to the ballad in 1695, and cites one stanza. The first five of eleven stanzas are devoted to the beauty of the Virgin, the Annunciation, and the birth of the Saviour. The song then goes on thus:

6 Saint Stephen leads the foals to water,
　　All by the star so gleaming:
　　'Of a truth the prophet now is born
　　　That all the world shall ransom.'

7 King Herod answered thus to him:
　　'I'll not believe this story,
　　Till the roasted cock that is on the board
　　　Claps his wings and crows before me.'

8 The cock he clapped his wings and crew,
　　'Our Lord, this is his birthday!'
　　Herod fell off from his kingly seat,
　　　For grief he fell a swooning.

9 King Herod bade saddle his courser gray,
　　He listed to ride to Bethlem;
　　Fain would he slay the little child   [234]
　　　That to cope with him pretended.

10 Mary took the child in her arms,
　　And Joseph the ass took also,
　　So they traversed the Jewish land,
　　　To Egypt, as God them guided.

11 The little children whose blood was shed,
　　They were full fourteen thousand,
　　But Jesus was thirty miles away
　　　Before the sun was setting.

---

[*]　Prof. Child specifies the following addition for this page, but I am at a loss to identify the referent: (M.F.H.) 'Stjærnevisen,' Kristensen, XI, 207, No 76 A, B, has nothing about Stephen, but is confined to the scripture-history, piety, and New Year's wishes.

[†]　Everriculum fermenti veteris, seu residuæ in Danico orbe cum paganismi tum papismi reliquiæ in apricum prolatæ. "Rogata anus num vera esse crederet quæ canebat, respondit: Me illa in dubium vocaturam averruncet Deus!" Grundtvig, II, 518.

B. A broadside of fourteen four-line stanzas, in two copies, **a** of the middle, **b** from the latter part, of the last century. **b** was printed "in the *Dansk Kirketidende* for 1862, No 43," by Professor George Stephens: **a** is given by Grundtvig, III, 881. The first three stanzas correspond to **A** 1–5, the next three to **A** 6–8: the visit of the Wise Men to Herod is then intercalated, 7–10, and the story concludes as in **A** 9–11.

C. 'Sankt Steffan,' Kristensen, II, 123, No 36, from recitation about 1870, eight four-line stanzas, 1–3 agreeing with **A** 3–6, 4–6 with **A** 6–9, 7, 8 with **A** 9, 11. The verbal resemblance with the copy sung by the old beggar-woman more than a hundred and thirty years before is often close.

A **Färöe** version, 'Rudisar vísa,' was communicated to the *Dansk Kirketidende* for 1852, p. 293, by Hammershaimb, twenty-six two-line stanzas (Grundtvig, II, 519); No 11 of Hammershaimb's *Færøsk Anthologi*, p. 39. Three copies are now known. Stephen is in Herod's service. He goes out and sees the star in the east, whereby he knows that the Saviour of the world, "the great king," is born. He comes in and makes this announcement. Herod orders his eyes to be put out: so, he says, it will appear whether this "king" will help him. They put out Stephen's eyes, but now he sees as well by night as before by day. At this moment a cock, roast and carved, is put on the board before Herod, who cries out:

'If this cock would stand up and crow,
Then in Stephen's tale should I trow.'

Herod he stood, and Herod did wait,
The cock came together that lay in the plate.

The cock flew up on the red gold chair,
He clapped his wings, and he crew so fair.

Herod orders his horse and rides to Bethlehem, to find the new-born king. As he comes in, Mary greets him, and tells him there is still mead and wine. He answers that she need not be so mild with him: he will have her son and nail him on the cross. "Then you must go to heaven for him," says Mary. Herod makes an attempt on Jesus, but is seized by twelve angels and thrown into the Jordan, where the Evil One takes charge of him.

Swedish. A single stanza, corresponding to Danish **A** 6, **B** 4, **C** 4, is preserved in a carol, 'Staffans Visa,' which was wont to be sung all over Sweden on St Stephen's day, in the Christmas sport, not yet given up, called Staffansskede; which consisted in young fellows riding about from house to house early in the morning of the second day of Yule, and levying refreshments.[*] One of the party carried at the end of a pole a lighted lantern, made of hoops and oiled paper, which was sometimes in the shape of a six-cornered star. Much of the chant was improvised, and both the good wishes and the suggestions as to the expected treat would naturally be suited to particular cases; but the first stanza, with but slight variations, was (Afzelius, III, 208, 210):

Stephen was a stable-groom,
    We thank you now so kindly!
He watered the five foals all and some,
    Ere the morning star was shining.
    No daylight's to be seen,
        The stars in the sky
            Are gleaming.

or,

---

[*] "Staffans-skede, lusus, vel, ut rectius dicam, licentia puerorum agrestium, qui in Festo S. Stephani, equis vecti per villas discurrunt, et cerevisiam in lagenis, ad hoc ipsum præparatis, mendicando ostiatim colligunt:" a dissertation, Upsala, 1734, cited by Bergström in his edition of Afzelius, II, 358, note 28. Skede is gallop, or run, Icelandic skeið (Bergström), Norwegian skeid, skjei. Many copies of the Staffansvisa have been collected: see Bergström's Afzelius, II, 356: and for a description of the custom as practised among Swedes in Finland, with links and lanterns, but no foals, Fagerlund, *Anteckningar om Korpo och Houtskärs Socknar*, p. 39ff. Something very similar was known in Holstein: see Schütze, *Holsteinsches Idioticon*, III, 200, as quoted by Grundtvig, II, 521, note **. From Chambers' *Book of Days*, II, 763f, it appears that a custom, called a Stephening, was still existing at the beginning of this century, of the inhabitants of the parish of Drayton Beauchamp, Bucks, paying a visit to the rector on December 26, and lightening his stores of all the bread, cheese and ale they wanted. Chambers, again, in his *Popular Rhymes of Scotland*, p. 168f, gives a song closely resembling the Staffansvisa, which was sung before every house on New Year's eve, in Deerness, Orkney, with the same object of stimulating hospitality. Similar practices are known in the Scottish Highlands: see Campbell, *Tales of the West Highlands*, III, 19, and Chambers, at p. 167 of the *Popular Rhymes*.

Stephen was a stable-groom,
  Bear thee well my foal!
He watered the five foals all and some,
  God help us and Saint Stephen!
The sun is not a-shining,
But the stars in the sky
  Are gleaming.

There is also a Swedish ballad which has the substance of the story of Danish **A** 6–8, but without any allusion to Stephen. It occurs as a broadside, in two copies, dated 1848, 1851, and was communicated by Professor Stephens to the *Dansk Kirketidende*, 1861, Nos 3, 4, and is reprinted by Grundtvig, III, 882f, and in Bergström's Afzelius, II, 360f. There are eleven four-line stanzas, of which the last six relate how Mary was saved from Herod by the miracle of the Sower (see 'The Carnal and the Crane,' stanzas 18–28). The first five cover the matter of our ballad. The first runs:

In Bethlem of Judah a star there rose,
  At the time of the birth of Christ Jesus:
'Now a child is born into the world
  That shall suffer for us death and torment.'

Herod then calls his court and council, and says to them, as he says to Stephen in the Danish ballad, "I cannot believe your story unless the cock on this table claps his wings and crows." This comes to pass, and Herod exclaims that he can never thrive till he has made that child feel the effects of his wrath. He then steeps his hands in the blood of the Innocents, and falls off his throne in a marvellous swoon. Mary is warned to fly to Egypt. It is altogether likely that the person who speaks in the first stanza was originally the same as the one who says nearly the same thing in the three Danish ballads, that is, Stephen, and altogether unlikely that Herod's words, which are addressed to Stephen in the Danish ballads, were addressed to his court and council rather than to Stephen here.

Norwegian. Two stanzas, much corrupted, of what may have been a ballad like the foregoing, have been recovered by Professor Bugge, and are given by Grundtvig, III, 883.

St Stephen's appearance as a stable-groom, expressly in the Swedish carol and by implication in the Danish ballads, is to be explained by his being the patron of horses among the northern nations.[*] On his day, December 26, which is even called in Germany the great Horse Day, it was the custom for horses to be let blood to keep them well during the year following, or raced to protect them from witches. In Sweden they were watered "ad alienos fontes" (which, perhaps, is what Stephen is engaged in in the carol), and treated to the ale which had been left in the cups on St Stephen's eve; etc., etc.[†] This way of observing St Stephen's day is presumed to be confined to the north of Europe, or at least to be derived from that quarter. Other saints are patrons of horses in the south, as St Eloi, St Antony, and we must seek the explanation of St Stephen's having that office in Scandinavia, Germany, and England in the earlier history of these regions. It was suggested as long ago as the middle of the sixteenth century by the Archbishop Olaus Magnus, that the horseracing, which was universal in Sweden on December 26, was a remnant of heathen customs. The horse was sacred to Frey, and Yule was Frey's festival. There can hardly be a doubt that the customs connected with St Stephen's day are a continuation, under Christian auspices, of old rites and habits which, as in so many other cases, the church found it easier to consecrate than to abolish.[‡]

The miracle of the cock is met with in other ballads,[§] which, for the most part, relate the wide-spread legend of the Pilgrims of St James.

[236]

---

[*]   Stephen in all the ballads can be none other than the first martyr, though Ihre, and other Swedes since his day, choose, for their part, to understand a "Stephanum primum Helsingorum apostolum," who certainly did not see the star in the east. The peasantry in Helsingland, we are told, make their saints' day December 26, too, and their St Stephen is a great patron of horses. The misappropriation of the glories of the protomartyr is somewhat transparent.

[†]   Grundtvig, whom I chiefly follow here, II, 521–24. In a note on page 521, supplemented at III, 883 e, Grundtvig has collected much interesting evidence of December 26 being the great Horse Day. J. W. Wolf, cited by Grundtvig, II, 524, had said previously: "Nichts im leben des ersten christlichen blutzeugen erinnert auch nur fern an pferde; trotzdem machte das volk ihn zum patron der pferde, und setzte ihn also an die stelle des Fro, dem im Norden, und nicht weniger bei uns, die pferde heilig waren." *Beiträge zur deutschen Mythologie*, I, 124.

French. In three versions, Chants de Pauvres en Forez et en Velay, collected by M. Victor Smith, *Romania*, II, 473 ff; 'Trois Pelerins de Dieu,' Meyrac, *Traditions, etc., des Ardennes*, p. 280. Three pilgrims, father, mother, and son, on their way to St James, stop at an inn, at St Dominic. A maid-servant, enamored of the youth (qui ressemble une image, que semblavoz-un ange) is repelled by him, and in revenge puts a silver cup [cups] belonging to the house into his knapsack. The party is pursued and brought back, and the young pilgrim is hanged. He exhorts his father to accomplish his vow, and to come that way when he returns. When the father returns, after three [six] months, the boy is found to be alive; his feet have been supported, and he has been nourished, by God and the saints. The father tells the judge that his son is alive; the judge replies, I will believe that when this roast fowl crows. The bird crows: **A**, le poulet se mit a chanter sur la table; **B**, le poulet vole au ciel, trois fois n'a battu l'aile; **C**, trois fois il a chanté, trois fois l'a battu l'aile. The boy is taken down and the maid hanged.

To these we may add an imperfect French ballad in *Mélusine*, VI, 24, from a wood-cut "at least three centuries old," and a Piedmontese popular tale communicated by Count Nigra to the editor of *Mélusine*, VI, 25 f. M. Gaidoz, at the same place, 26 f, cites two versions of the resuscitation of the cock, from example-books. The first, from Erythræus (i.e. Rossi), ch. CLV, p. 187, is essentially the same as the legend of St Gunther given from *Acta Sanctorum* (p. 327). The other, from the Giardino d' Essempi of Razzi, is the story told by Vincentius (p. 321, note †).

Catalan. **A**, Milá, *Observaciones sobre la poesia popular*, p. 106, No 7, 'El Romero;' **B**, Briz, *Cansons de la Terra*, I, 71, 'S. Jaume de Galicia,'

two copies essentially agreeing.[*] The course of the story is nearly as in the French. The son does not ask his father to come back. It is a touch of nature that the mother cannot be prevented from going back by all that her husband can say. The boy is more than well. St James has been sustaining his feet, the Virgin his head.[†] He directs his mother to go to the alcalde (Milá), who will be dining on a cock and a hen, and to request him politely to release her son, who is still alive. The alcalde replies: "Off with you! Your son is as much alive as this cock and hen." The cock began to crow, the hen laid an egg in the dish!

Dutch. 'Een liedeken van sint Jacob,' *Antwerpener Liederbuch*, 1544, No 20, Hoffmann, p. 26; Uhland, p. 803, No 303; Willems, p. 318, No 133. The pilgrims here are only father and son. The host's daughter avows her love to her father, and desires to detain the young pilgrim. The older pilgrim, hearing of this, says, My son with me and I with him. We will seek St James, as pilgrims good and true. The girl puts the cup in the father's sack. The son offers himself in his father's place, and is hanged. The father finds that St James and the Virgin have not been unmindful of the pious, and tells the host that his son is alive. The host, in a rage, exclaims, "That's as true as that these roast fowls shall fly out at the door!"

> But ere the host could utter the words,
> One by one from the spit brake the birds,
>   And into the street went flitting;
> They flew on the roof of St Dominic's house,
> Where all the brothers were sitting.

The brothers resolve unanimously to go to the judicial authority in procession; the innocent youth is taken down, the host hanged, and his daughter buried alive.

Wendish. Haupt und Schmaler, I, 285, No 289, 'Der gehenkte Schenkwirth.' There are two pilgrims, father and son. The host himself

---

‡   Jean Baptiste Thiers, *Traité des Superstitions, etc.*, 2d ed., Paris, 1697, as cited by Liebrecht, Gervasius von Tilbury, Otia Imperialia, p. 233, No 169, condemns the belief, "qu'il vaut bien mieux . . . . saigner des chevaux le jour de la fête de S. Estienne qu'à tout autre jour." This may be one of the practices which Thiers had learned of from his reading (see Liebrecht's preface, p. xvii f), but might also have migrated from the east or north into France. Superstitions, like new fashions, are always sure of a hospitable reception, even though they impose a servitude.

§   A roast pheasant gets feathers and flies away in attestation of a tale: M. Wardrop, *Georgian Folktales*, p. 10 f, No 2. (G. L. K.)

---

*   Milá's new edition, *Romancerillo Catalan*, No 31, 'El romero acusado de robo,' pp 36–38, adds six copies, not differing in anything important. In **C**, the youth, un estudiant, n'era ros com un fil d'or, blanch com Santa Catarina.

†   I may note that Thomas Becket stands by his votaries when brought to the gallows as effectually as St James. See Robertson, *Materials, etc.*, I, 369, 471, 515, 524.

puts his gold key into the boy's basket. The boy is hanged: the father bids him hang a year and a day, till he returns. The Virgin has put a stool under the boy's feet, and the angels have fed him. The father announces to the host that his son is living. The host will not believe this till three dry staves which he has in the house shall put out green shoots. This comes to pass. The host will not believe till three fowls that are roasting shall recover their feathers and fly out of the window. This also comes to pass. The host is hanged.

A **Breton** ballad, 'Marguerite Laurent,' Luzel, I, **A**, p. 211, **B**, p. 215, inverts a principal circumstance in the story of the pilgrims: a maid is hanged on a false accusation of having stolen a piece of plate. This may be an independent tradition or a corrupt form of the other. Marguerite has, by the grace of St Anne and of the Virgin, suffered no harm. A young clerk, her lover, having ascertained this, reports the case to the seneschal, who will not believe till the roasted capon on the dish crows. The capon crows. Marguerite goes on her bare knees to St Anne and to Notre-Dame du Folgoat, and dies in the church of the latter (first version).

'Notre-Dame du Folgoat,' Villemarqué, *Barzaz Breiz*, p. 272, No 38, 6th ed., is of a different tenor. Marie Fanchonik, wrongly condemned to be executed for child murder, though hanged, does not die. The executioner reports to the seneschal. "Burn her," says the seneschal. "Though in fire up to her breast," says the executioner, "she is laughing heartily." "Sooner shall this capon crow than I will believe you." The capon crows: a roast capon on the dish, all eaten but the feet. 'Skuin over de groenelands heide,' Dykstra en van der Meulen, p. 121, resembles the Breton stories, but lacks the miracle of the capon. See also Böhme's Erk, I, 637ff, No 213 a, 'Die Weismutter,' b, 'Die unschuldig gehangene und gerettete Dienstmagd,' and note to b; Wolfram, p. 38, No 10, 'Zu Frankfurt steht ein Wirtshaus.'

Religious writers of the 13th century have their version of the story of the pilgrims, but without the prodigy of the cock. Vincent of Beauvais, *Speculum Historiale*, l. 26, c. 33, who bases his narrative on a collection of the miracles of St James incorrectly attributed to Pope Callixtus II,[*] has but two pilgrims, Germans, father and son. On their way to Compostella they pass a night in an inn at Toulouse. The host, having an eye to the forfeiture of their effects, makes them drunk and hides a silver cup in their wallet. Son wishes to die for father, and father for son. The son is hanged, and St James interposes to preserve his life.[†] With Vincent agree the author of the *Golden Legend*, following Callixtus, Graesse, 2d ed., p. 426, c. 99 (94), § 5,[‡] and Cæsarius Heisterbacensis, *Dialogus Miraculorum*, c. 58, II, 130, ed. Strange, who, however, does not profess to remember every particular, and omits to specify Toulouse as the place. Nicolas Bertrand, who published in 1515 a history of Toulouse, places the miracle there.[§] He has three pilgrims, like the French and Spanish ballads, and the roast fowl

---

[*]   From a copy of this collection the story is given in *Acta Sanctorum*, VI Julii, p. 50, § 202ff.

[†]   Vincent, as pointed out by Professor George Stephens, knew of the miracle of the cock, and tells it at l. 25, c. 64, on the authority of Pietro Damiani. Two Bolognese dining together, one of them carved a cock and dressed it with pepper and sauce. "Gossip," says the other, "you have 'fixed' that cock so that Peter himself could not put him on his legs again." "Peter? No, not Christ himself." At this the cock jumped up, in all his feathers, clapped his wings, crew, and threw the sauce all over the blasphemous pair, whereby they were smitten with leprosy.

[‡]   So, naturally, the *Fornsvenskt Legendarium*, I, 170, and the *Catalan Recull de Eximplis e Miracles*, etc., Barcelona, 1880, I, 298. (R. Köhler.)

[§]   Opus de Tholosanorum. gestis, fol. 49 verso, according to *Acta S.*, p. 46, of the volume last cited. Toulouse rivalled with Compostella in the possession of relics of St James, and was amply entitled to the honor of the miracle. Dr Andrew Borde, in his *First Book of the Introduction of Knowledge*, says that an ancient doctor of divinity at Compostella told him, "We have not one hair nor bone of St. James; for St James the More and St James the Less, St Bartholomew and St Philip, St Simon and Jude, St Bernard and St George, with divers other saints, Carolus Magnus brought them to Toulouse." Ed. Furnivall, p. 204f. I do not know where the splenetic old divine got his information, but certainly from no source so trustworthy as the chronicle of Turpin. Besides other places in France, the body, or at least the head, of St James was claimed by churches in Italy, Germany, and the Low Countries. But the author of an old Itinerary of the Pilgrims to Compostella asserts that James the Greater is one of four saints who never changed his burial-place. See Victor Le Clerc in *Hist. Litt. de la France*, xxi, 283.

flying from the spit to convince a doubting offi-
cial, like the Dutch and Wendish ballads.

[238]   But, much earlier than the last date, this
miracle of St James had become connected
with the town of San Domingo de la Calzada,
one of the stations on the way to Compostella,[*]
some hours east of Burgos. Roig, the Valencian
poet, on arriving there in the course of his pil-
grimage, tells the tale briefly, with two roasted
fowls, cock and hen: *Lo Libre do les Dones e de
Conçells*, 1460, as printed by Briz from the edi-
tion of 1735, p. 42, Book 2, vv 135–183. Lucio
Marineo, whose work, *De las cosas memorables
de España*, appeared in 1530, had been at San
Domingo, and is able to make some addition to
the miracle of the cock. Up to the revivifica-
tion, his account agrees very well with the
Spanish ballad. A roast cock and hen are lying
before the mayor, and when he expresses his
incredulity, they jump from the dish on to the
table, in feathers whiter than snow. After the
pilgrims had set out a second time on their way
to Compostella, to return thanks to St James,
the mayor returned to his house with the priests
and all the people, and took the cock and hen
to the church, where they lived seven years,
and then died, leaving behind them a pair of
the same snowy whiteness, who in turn, after
seven years, left their successors, and so on to
Marineo's day; and though of the infinite num-
ber of pilgrims who resorted to the tomb each
took away a feather, the plumage was always
full, and Marineo speaks as an eye-witness.
(Edition of 1539, fol. xliii.) Dr Andrew Borde
gives nearly the same account as Marineo, in
the *First Book of the Introduction of Knowledge*,
1544, p. 202 ff, ed. Furnivall.[†] A description of
San Domingo de la Calzada, with a narration of
the miracle of St James, is cited by Birlinger
from a manuscript of travels by a young Ger-
man, 1587–93, in *Alemannia*, XIII, 42–44. The
traveller had heard "the fable" in Italy, too, and
had seen a painting of it at Savona (R. Köhler).
De Gubernatis, *Zoölogical Mythology* II, 283f,

note 2, after citing the legend of San Domingo
de la Calzada, adds: A similar wonder is said, by
Sigonio, to have taken place in the eleventh
century in the Bolognese; but instead of St
James, Christ and St Peter appear to perform
miracles (G. L. K.).

Early in the sixteenth century the subject
was treated in at least two miracle-plays, for
which it is very well adapted: Un miracolo di
tre Pellegrini, printed at Florence early in the
sixteenth century, D'Ancona, *Sacre Rappresen-
tazioni*, III, 465; *Ludus Sancti Jacobi, fragment de
mystère provençale*, Camille Arnaud, 1858.[‡]

Nicolas Bertrand, before referred to, speaks
of the miracle as depicted in churches and
chapels of St James. It was, for example,
painted by Pietro Antonio of Foligno, in the fif-
teenth century, in SS. Antonio e Jacopo at
Assisi, and by Pisanello in the old church of the
Tempio at Florence, and, in the next century,
by Palmezzano in S. Biagio di S. Girolamo at
Forlì, and by Lo Spagna in a small chapel or tri-
bune dedicated to St James, about four miles
from Spoleto, on the way to Foligno. The same
legend is painted on one of the lower windows
of St Ouen, and again on a window of St Vin-
cent, at Rouen. Professor George Stephens
informs me that the miracle of the cock is
depicted, among scenes from the life of Jesus,
on an *antependium* of an altar, derived from an
old church in Slesvig, and now in the Danish
Museum. Behind a large table sits a crowned
woman, and at her left stands a crowned man,
who points to a dish from which a cock has
started up, with beak wide open. At the queen's
right stands an old woman, simply clad and
leaning on a staff. This picture comes between
the Magi announcing Christ's Birth and the
Massacre of the Innocents, and the crowned
figures are judged by Professor Stephens to be
Herod and Herodias. Who the old woman
should be it is not easy to say, but there can be
no connection with St James. The work is
assigned to the last part of the fourteenth cen-
tury. Many more cases might, no doubt, be eas-
ily collected.[§]

---

*   See 'La grande Chanson des Pélerins de Saint-
Jacques,' in Socard, *Noëls et Cantiques, etc.*, p. 76, last
stanza, p. 80, third stanza, p. 89, fifth stanza; the last =
Romancero de Champagne, I, 165, stanza 5.
†   Southey follows Marineo in his Christmas Tale of
"The Pilgrim to Compostella."

‡   "Auch eine deutsche Jesuitenkomödie, Peregrinus
Compostellanus, Innsbruck, 1624, behandelt diesen
Stoff. F. Liebrecht, in *Serapeum*, 1864, S. 235."

It is not at all surprising that a miracle performed at San Domingo de la Calzada should, in the course of time, be at that place attributed to the patron of the locality; and we actually find Luis de la Vega, in a life of this San Domingo published at Burgos in 1606, repeating Marineo's story, very nearly, with a substitution of Dominic for James.[*] More than this, this author claims for this saint, who, saving reverence, is decidedly *minorum gentium*, the merit and glory of delivering a captive from the Moors, wherein he, or tradition, makes free again with St James's rightful honors. The Moor, when told that the captive will some day be missing, rejoins, If you keep him as close as when I last saw him, he will as soon escape as this roast cock will fly and crow. It is obvious that this anecdote is a simple jumble of two miracles of St James, the freeing of the captives, recounted in *Acta Sanctorum*, vi Julii, p. 47, § 190f, and the saving the life of the young pilgrim.[†]

The restoration of a roasted fowl to life is also narrated in *Acta Sanctorum*, i Septembris, p. 529, § 289, as occurring early in the eleventh century (the date assigned to the story of the pilgrims), at the table of St Stephen, the first king of Hungary. St Gunther was sitting with the king while he was dining. The king pressed Gunther to partake of a roast peacock, but Gunther, as he was bound by his rule to do, declined. The king then ordered him to eat. Gunther bent his head and implored the divine mercy; the bird flew up from the dish; the king no longer persisted. The author of the article, without questioning the reality of the miracle, well remarks that there seems to be something

wrong in the story, since it is impossible that the holy king should have commanded the saint to break his vow.

[†] For Luis de la Vega, see *Acta Sanctorum*, iii Maii; p. 171f, §§ 6, 7, 8, vi Julii, p. 46, § 187. The Spanish and the Dutch ballad give due glory to St James and the Virgin; French C to God and St James. The Wendish ballad can hardly he expected to celebrate St James, and refers the justification and saving of the boy to the Virgin and the saints. French A has St Michas; **B**, God and the Virgin.

Luis de la Vega, with what seems an excess of caution, says, p. 172, as above, § 8: appositique erant ad comedendum, gallus et gallina, *assati nescio an elixi*. Of boiled fowl we have not heard so far. But we find in a song in Fletcher's Play of 'The Spanish Curate,' this stanza:

The stewd cock shall crow, cock-a-loodle-loo,
A loud cock-a-loodle shall he crow;
The duck and the drake shall swim in a lake
Of onions and claret below.
Act III, Sc. 2; Dyce, viii, 436.

In Father Merolla's *Voyage to Congo*, 1682, a reference to which I owe to Liebrecht, there is a story of a stewed cock, which, on the whole, justifies Luis de la Vega's scruple. This must have been introduced into Africa by some missioner, and, when so introduced, the miracle must have had an object, which it had lost before the tale came to Father Merolla.

One of two parties at feud having marched upon the chief city of his antagonist, and found all the inhabitants fled, the soldiers fell to rifling the houses and killing all the living creatures they met, to satisfy their hunger. "Amongst the rest they found a cock of a larger size than ordinary, with a great ring of iron about one of his legs, which occasioned one of the wisest among them to cry out, Surely this cock must be bewitched, and it is not at all proper for us to meddle with. To which the rest answered, Be it what it will, we are resolved to eat it. For this end they immediately killed and tore it to pieces after the manner of the negroes, and afterwards put it into a pot to boil. When it was enough, they took it out into a platter, and two, according to the custom, having said grace, five of them sat down to it with great greediness. But before they had touched a bit, to their great wonder and amazement, the boiled pieces of the cock, though sodden, and near dissolved, began to move about and unite into the form they were in before, and, being so united, the restored cock immediately raised himself up, and jumped out of the platter upon the ground, where he walked about as well as when he was first taken. Afterwards he leaped upon an adjoining wall, where he became new feathered all of a sudden, and then took his flight to a tree hard by, where fixing himself, he, after three claps of his wings, made a most hideous noise, and then disappeared. Every one may easily imagine what a terrible fright the spectators were in at this sight, who, leaping with a thousand Ave Marias in their mouths from the place where this had happened, were contented to observe most of the particulars at a distance." It appears that the brother of one of the two contending parties was said to have had a very large cock, from whose crowing he took auguries, but whether this was the same as the one restored to life is not known. Churchill's *Collection of Voyages and Travels*, 1704, i, 682, Pinkerton's *Collection*, xvi, 229.

---

§ Vasari, v, 184, Milan, 1809; Crowe and Cavalcaselle, iii, 124, ii, 566ff, ed. 1866; Mrs Jameson's *Sacred and Legendary Art*, i, 241, ed. 1857. Professor N. Høyen indicated to Grundtvig the picture of Pietro Antonio, and d'Ancona refers to Pisanello's.

[*] He denies the perpetual multiplication of the feathers, and adds that the very gallows on which the pilgrim was hanged is erected in the upper part of the church, where everybody can see it. It is diverting to find Grossenhain, in Saxony, claiming the miracle on the ground of a big cock in an altar picture in a chapel of St James: Grässe, *Sagenschatz des Königreichs Sachsen*, 2d ed., i, 80, No 82, from Chladenius, *Materilien zu Grossenhayner Stadtchronik*, i, 2, Pirna, 1788; in verse by Ziehnert, *Volkssagen*, p. 99, No 14, ed. 1851.

Three stone partridges on a buttress of a church at Mühlhausen are thus accounted for. In the early days of the Reformation a couple of orthodox divines, while waiting dinner, were discussing the prospect of the infection spreading to their good city. One of them, growing warm, declared that there was as much chance of that as of the three partridges that were roasting in the kitchen taking flight from the spit. Immediately there was heard a fluttering and a cooing in the region of the kitchen, the three birds winged their way from the house, and, lighting on the buttress of Mary Kirk, were instantly turned to stone, and there they are. *Thüringen und der Harz, mit ihren Merkwürdigkeiten, u. s. w.*, VI, 20f. (Köhler.)

An ox stands in place of the cock in Ioannis Vastovii Vitis Aquilonia, *sive Vitæ Sanctorum regni Sveo-goth-ici, emend. et illustr.* Er. Benzelius filius, Upsiliæ, 1708, p. 59. A heathen in West Gothland (Vestrogothia) had killed his herdsman, Torsten, a Christian, and was reproached for it by Torsten's wife. Pointing to an ox that had been slaughtered, the heathen answered: Tam Torstenum tuum, quem sanctum et in cœlis vivere existimas, plane ita vivum credo prout hunc bovem quem in frusta cædendum conspicis. Mirum dictu, vix verba finiverat, cum e vestigio bos in pedes se erexit vivus, stupore omnibus qui adstabant attonitis. Quare sacellum in loco eodem erectum, multaque miracula, præsertim in pecorum curatione, patrata. (Köhler.)

But the prime circumstance in the legend, the resuscitation of the cock, does not belong in the eleventh century, where Vincent and others have put it, but in the first, where it is put by the English and Scandinavian ballads. A French romance somewhat older than Vincent, Ogier le Danois, agrees with the later English ballad in making the occasion to be the visit of the Wise Men to Herod. Herod will not believe what they say,

'Se cis capon que ci m'est en présant
N'en est plumeus com il estoit devant,
Et se redrece it la perche en cantant.'

vv 11621–23.

And what he exacts is performed for his conviction.[*] Nevertheless, as we shall now see, the

true epoch of the event is not the Nativity, but the Passion.[†]

The ultimate source of the miracle of the reanimated cock is an interpolation in two late Greek manuscripts of the so-called Gospel of Nicodemus: Thilo, *Codex Apocryphus Novi Testamenti*, p. cxxix f; Tischendorf, *Evangelia Apocrypha*, p. 269, note 3. After Judas had tried to induce the Jews to take back the thirty pieces, he went to his house to hang himself, and found his wife sitting there, and a cock roasting on a spit before the coals. He said to his wife, Get me a rope, for I mean to hang myself, as I deserve. His wife said to him, Why do you say such things? And Judas said to her, Know in truth that I have betrayed my master Jesus to evil-doers, who will put him to death. But he will rise on the third day, and woe to us. His wife said, Do not talk so nor believe it; for this cock that is roasting before the coals will as soon crow as Jesus rise again as you say. And even while she was speaking the words, the cock flapped his wings and crew thrice. Then Judas was still more persuaded, and straightway made a noose of the rope and hanged himself.[‡]

The Cursor Mundi gives its own turn to this relation, with the intent to blacken Judas a little more.[§] When Judas had betrayed Jesus, he went to his mother with his pence, boasting of the act. "Hast thou sold thy master?" said she. "Shame shall be thy lot, for they will put him to

---

[*]   *La Chevalerie Ogier de Danemarche, par Raimbert de Paris, Poëme du xii siècle, etc.*, II, 485, vv 11606–627.

[†]   Most of the literature on the topic of the restoration of the roasted cock to life is collected by Dr R. Köhler and by Ferdinand Wolf, in *Jahrbüch für romanische u. englische Literatur*, III, 58ff, 67f. Dr Köhler now adds these notes: The miracle of St James, in Hermann von Fritslar's *Heiligenleben*, Pfeiffer's *Deutsche Mystiker des vierzehnten Jahrhunderts*, I, 168f; Hahn, *Das alte Passional* (from the Golden Legend), p. 223, v. 47–p. 225, v. 85; Lütolf, *Sagen, Bräuche und Legenden aus Lucern, u. s. w.*, p. 367, No 334; von Alpenburg, *Deutsche Alpensagen*, p. 137, No 135; Sepp, *Altbayerischer Sagenschatz*, pp 652ff, 656f.

[‡]   The gospel of Nicodemus was introduced into the French and the Italian romance of Perceforest, but unfortunately this "narratio ab inepto Græculo pessime interpolata" (Thilo) seems to be lacking.

[§]   Cursor Mundi, a Northumbrian poem of the 14th century, in four versions, ed. by R. Morris, p. 912f, vv 15961–998. This passage was kindly pointed out to me by Professor George Stephens.

death; but he shall rise again." "Rise, mother?" said Judas, "sooner shall this cock rise up that was scalded yesternight."

Hardly had he said the word,
  The cock leapt up and flew,
Feathered fairer than before,
  And by God's grace he crew;
The traitor false began to fear,
  His peril well he knew.
This cock it was the self-same cock
  Which Peter made to rue,
When he had thrice denied his lord
And proved to him untrue.

The monk Andrius has the scene between Judas and his mother as in Cursor Mundi, and attributes to Greek writers the opinion that the roasted cock was the same that caused Peter's compunction. Mussafia, *Sulla legenda del legno della Croce, Sitz. Ber. der phil.-hist. Classe der Wiener Akad.*, LXIII, 206, note. (Köhler.)

An Irish reference to the story is related in *Notes and Queries*, 5th series, IX, 412 a: "About the year 1850 I was on a visit to the rector of Kilmeen, near Clonakilty, in the county of Cork. My friend brought me to visit the ruins of an old castle. Over the open fireplace, in the great hall there was a stone, about two or three feet square, carved in the rudest fashion, and evidently representing our Lord's sufferings. There were the cross, the nails, the hammer, the scourge; but there was one piece of sculpture which I could not understand. It was a sort of rude semi-circle, the curve below and the diameter above, and at the junction a figure intended to represent a bird. My friend asked me what it meant. I confessed my ignorance. 'That,' said he, 'is the cock. The servants were boiling him for supper, but when the moment came to convict the *apostle* he started up, perched on the side of the pot, and astonished the assembly by his salutation of the morning.'" (Kohler.)

In *The Ely Volume*, or, *The Contributions of our Foreign Missions to Science, etc.*, 2d ed., Boston, 1885, the editor, Dr Laurie, discoursing of the Yezidees, says they speak of Satan as Melek Taoos, King Peacock, and the cawals (a sort of circuit-riders), "carry round with them brazen

images of a bird on a sort of Oriental candlestick, as vouchers for their mission, and a means of blessing to their followers. One of them gave Dr Lobdell the following account of the origin of this name [Melek Taoos]. In the absence of his disciples, Satan, in the form of a dervish, took Christ down from the cross and carried him to heaven. Soon after the Marys came and asked the dervish where Christ was. They would not believe his reply, but promised to do so if he would restore the chicken he was eating to life. He did so, and when he told them who he was they adored him. When he left them he promised always to appear to them as a beautiful bird, and so the peacock became his symbol." P. 315. (G. L. K.)

A further version appears in a Russian tale: Jesus visits a Jew on Easter Sunday and reproaches him with not believing in the resurrection. The Jew replies that Jesus having been put to death it was as impossible for him to come to life again as it would be for a roast chicken which lies before them. Faith can do anything, says Jesus. The fowl comes to life and lays eggs; the Jew has himself baptized. Kostomarof, *Monuments of the older Russian Literature*, I, 217. In a note, a Red-Russian ballad is mentioned which seems to be identical with Golovatsky, II, 6, No 8. A young Jewess, who was carrying water, was the first to see Jesus after his resurrection. She tells her father, as he sits at meat, that the God of the Russians is risen from the dead. "If you were not my daughter, I would have you drowned," says the father. "The God of the Russians will not rise again in till that capon flies up and crows." The capon does both; the Jew is turned to stone. (W. W.)

A still different version existed among the Copts, who had their copies of the apocryphal writings, and among them the gospel of Nicodemus.

The Copts say, according to Thévenot, "that on the day of the Supper a roasted cock was served to our Lord, and that when Judas went out to sell Jesus to the Jews, the Saviour commanded the cock to get up and follow him; which the cock did, and brought back his report to our Lord that Judas had sold him, for which service this cock shall be admitted to paradise."[*]

The herald of the morn is described in other carols as making known the birth of the Saviour to the animal creation, or the more familiar members of it.

"There is a sheet of carols headed thus: 'CHRISTUS NATUS EST, Christ is born,' with a wood-cut ten inches high by eight and one half inches wide, representing the stable at Bethlehem; Christ in the crib, watched by the Virgin and Joseph; shepherds kneeling; angels attending; a man playing on the bagpipes; a woman with a basket of fruit on her head; a sheep bleating and an ox lowing on the ground; a raven croaking and a crow cawing on the hayrack; a cock crowing above them; and angels singing in the sky. The animals have labels from their mouths, bearing Latin inscriptions. Down the side of the woodcut is the following account and explanation: 'A religious man, inventing the conceits of both birds and beasts, drawn in the picture of our Saviour's birth, doth thus express them. The cock croweth *Christus natus est*, Christ is born. The raven asked *Quando*, When? The crow replied, *Hac nocte*, This night. The ox cryeth out, *Ubi, ubi?* Where, where? The sheep bleated out, *Bethlehem*, Bethlehem. A voice from heaven sounded, *Gloria in excelsis*, Glory be on high!'" London, 1701. Hone's *Every-Day Book*, I, col. 1600f.

[241]   So in Vieux Noëls français, in *Les Noëls Bressans*, etc., par Philibert Le Due, p. 145; Marin, *Cantos Populares*, I, 61, No 124; Iglesia, *El Idioma Gallego* ('a maldicion d' a ovella'), cf. II, 8, note †, III, 174, both cited by Munthe.

Joie des Bestes
à la nouvelle de la naissance du Sauveur.

Comme les Bestes autrefois
Parloient mieux latin que françois,
Le Coq, de loin voyant le faict,

---

* *Rélation d'un Voyage fait an Levant* par Monsieur De Thévenot, Paris, 1665, I, 502. Cited by Thilo, p. xxxvii, and by Victor Smith, *Romania*, II, 474, who adds: "Parmi les manuscrits rapportés d'Éthiopie par M. d'Abbadie, il se trouve un volume dont le titre a pour équivalent, Actes de la passion. Un chapitre de ce volume, intitulé Le livre du coq, développe la légende indiquée par Thévenot. Catalogue raisonné des manuscrits éthiopiens, appartenant à M. A. T. d'Abbadie, in 4°, imp. impériale, Paris, 1859."

S'écria: *Christus natus est;*
Le Bœuf, d'un air tout ébaubi,
Demande: *Ubi, ubi, ubi?*
La Chèvre, ae torchant le groin,
Respond que c'est à *Bethleem;*
Maistre Baudet, *curiosus*
De l'aller voir, dit: *Eamus;*
Et, droit sur ses pattes, le Veau
Beugle deux fois: *Volo, volo.*[*]

Also: "Quando Christo nasceu, disse o gallo: Jesus-Christo é ná . . . á . . . á . . . do." Leite de Vasconcellos, *Tradições pop. de Portugal*, p. 148, No 285 *b*.

Again in Munthe, *Folkpoesi från Asturien*, III, No 24, cited by Pitrè in *Archivio*, VIII, 141:

Cantou il gatsu:
¡Cristu naciú!
Dixu il buey:
¡Agú?
Dixu la ubecha:
¡En Bilén!
Dixu la cabra:
¡Catsa, cascarra,
Que nació en Grenada!

And again, in Italian, Bolza, *Canzoni popolari comasche*, p. 654, No 30:

Il Gallo.   È nato Gesù
Il Bue.   In dôva?
La Pecora.   Betlèm! Betlèm!
L'Asino.   Andèm! Andèm! Andèm!

Azevedo, *Romanceiro do Archipelago da Madeira*, p. 3 (R. Köhler):

Em dezembro, vintecinco,
Meio da noite chegado,
Uni anjo ia no ar
A dizer: Elle é já nado.
Pergunta lo boi: Aonde?
La mula pergunta: Qaem?
Canta lo gallo: Jesus.
Diz la ovelha: Bethlem.

---

* "Ce couplet se débite en imitant successivement le chant du coq, le mugissement du bœuf, le cri de la chèvre, le braiment de l'âne, et le beuglement du veau." Bolza makes a similar explanation with regard to the Italian colloquy.

Several German versions follow a similar pattern: Wer sind die ersten Vorbothen Gottes? Der Hahn, weil er kräht, "Christ ist geboren." Der Tauber, weil er ruft, "Wo? "Und der Ziegenbock, weil er schreit, "Z' Bethlehem." Pater Amand Baumgarten, Aus der volksmässigen Ueberlieferung der Heimat, I, Zur volksthümlichen Naturkunde, p. 94. (Köhler.) Simrock, Das deutsche Kinderbuch, 2d ed., p. 173, No 719; 3d ed., p. 192, No 787:

Hahn: Kikeriki! Gott der Herr lebt!
Ochs: Wo? Wo?
Geiss: Mäh! zu Bethlehem!*

A little Greek ballad, 'The Taking of Constantinople,' only seven lines long, relates a miracle entirely like that of the cock, which was operated for the conviction of incredulity. A nun, frying fish, hears a voice from above, saying, Cease your frying, the city will fall into the hands of the Turks. "When the fish fly out of the pan alive," she says, "then shall the Turks take the city." The fish fly out of the pan alive,† and the Turkish admiraud comes riding into the city. Zambelios, p. 600, No 2; Passow, p. 147, No 197. (Liebrecht, Volkskunde, p. 179.) The Taking of Stamboul, in Bezsonof, Kalyeki Perekhozhie, I, 617, No 138.

In a Bulgarian version of this ballad, a roasted cock crows and fried fish come to life:

Sbornik of the Ministry of Public Instruction, II, 82. In other ballads the same incident is transferred to the downfall of Bulgaria: Kačanovskij, p. 235, No 116; Sbornik, II, 129, 2, and II, 131, 2. (W. W.)

With Herod's questions and Stephen's answers in stanzas 5–8, we may compare a passage in some of the Greek ballads cited under No 17, p. 273.

Σκλάβε, πανᾷς; σκλάβε, διψᾷς; μὴ τὸ ψωμὶ σνῦ
    λείπει;
Σκλάβε, πανᾷς; σκλάβε, διψᾷς; σκλάβε κρασὶν σνῦ
    λείπει;
Lakkyt þe eyþer mete or drynk?
Μήτε πεινῶ, μήτε διψῶ, μήτε ψωμὶ [κρασὶν] μοῦ
    λείπει.
Lakit me neyþer mete ne drynk.
    Jeannaraki, p. 203, No 265:
    Sakellarios, p. 37, No 13.
Σκλάβε, πεινᾷς; σκλάβε, διψᾷς; σκλάβε, ῥόγα σοῦ
    λείπει.
Σκλάβε, πεινᾷς; σκλάβε, διψᾷς; σκλάβε μου ροῦχα
    θέλεις;
Lakkyt þe eyþer gold or fe,
    Or ony ryche wede?
Οὔτε πεινῶ, οὔτε διψῶ, οὔτε ῥόγα μοῦ λείπει.
Μήτε πεινῶ, μήτε διψῶ, μήτε καὶ ροῦχα θέλω.
Lakyt me neyþer gold ne fe,
    Ne non ryche wede.
Tommaseo, III, 154; Passow, p. 330, No 449:
Tommaseo, III, 152; Zambelios, p. 678, No 103;
    Passow, No 448.‡

A Danish translation of the English ballad is printed in Dansk Kirketidende for 1852, p. 254 (Grundtvig). Danish A is translated by Dr Prior, I, 398.

---

* Man begegnet auf alten Holzschnitten einer Abbildung von Christi Geburt, welche durch die dabei stehenden Thiere erklärt werden soll. Der Hahn auf der Stange krähet da: Christus natus est! und das Lämmlein überschnappender Stimme drein: Ubi? und das Lämmlein bläheret die Antwort: Bethlehem! Rochholz, Alemannisches Kinderlied und Kinderspiel aus der Schweiz, p. 69f. (Köhler.)

† See Wesselofsky, Archiv f. slavische Philologie, VI, 574.

‡ Compare Bergström and Nordlander, 98, 3; Pidal, p. 128.

Sloane MS., 2593, fol. 22 b, British Museum.

1 SEYNT Steuene was a clerk in kyng Herowdes
   halle,
   And seruyd him of bred and cloþ, as euery kyng
   befalle.

2 Steuyn out of kechone cam, wyth boris hed on
   honde;
   He saw a sterre was fayr and bryȝt ouer Bedlem
   stonde.

3 He kyst adoun þe boris hed and went in to þe
   halle:
   'I forsak þe, kyng Herowdes, and þi werkes alle.

4 'I forsak þe, kyng Herowdes, and þi werkes alle;
   Þer is a chyld in Bedlem born is beter þan we
   alle.'

5 'Quat eylyt þe, Steuene? quat is þe befalle?
[242]   Lakkyt þe eyþer mete or drynk in kyng
   Herowdes halle?'

6 'Lakit me neyþer mete ne drynk in kyng
   Herowdes halle
   Þer is a chyld in Bedlem born is beter þan we
   alle.'

7 Quat eylyt þe, Steuyn? art þu wod, or þu gyn-
   nyst to brede?
   Lakkyt þe eyþer gold or fe, or ony ryche wede?'

8 'Lakyt me neyþer gold ne fe, ne non ryche
   wede;
   Þer is a chyld in Bedlem born xal helpyn vs at
   our nede.'

9 'Þat is al so soþ, Steuyn, al so soþ, iwys,
   As þis capoun crowe xal þat lyþ here in myn
   dysh.'

10 Þat word was not so sone seyd, þat word in þat
   halle,
   Þe capoun crew Cristus natus est! among þe
   lordes alle.

11 Rysyt vp, myn turmentowres, be to and al be on,
   And ledyt Steuyn out of þis town, and stonyt
   hym wyth ston!'

12 Tokyn he Steuene, and stonyd hym in the way,
   And þerfore is his euyn on Crystes owyn day

———◆———

1², 5¹. be falle.
3¹. a doun. 3², 4¹. for sak.
5². There is room only for the h at the end of the line.

9¹. also . . . also . . . I wys. 9². dych.
10². a mong.

23

JUDAS

MS. B. 14, 39, of the thirteenth century, library of Trinity College, Cambridge, as printed in Wright & Halliwell's *Reliquiæ Antiquæ*, I, 144.

This legend, which has not been heretofore recognized as a ballad, is, so far as is known, unique in several particulars. The common tradition gives Judas an extraordinary domestic history,[*] but does not endow him with a sister as perfidious as himself. Neither is his selling his Master for thirty pieces accounted for elsewhere as it is here, if it may be strictly said to be accounted for here.

A popular explanation, founded upon John xii, 3–6, and current for six centuries and more, is that Judas, bearing the bag, was accustomed to take tithes of all moneys that came into his hands, and that he considered he had lost thirty pence on the precious ointment which had not been sold for three hundred pence, and took this way of indemnifying himself.

A Wendish ballad, Haupt und Schmaler, I, 276, No 284, has the following story. Jesus besought hospitality for himself and his disciples of a poor widow. She could give a lodging, but had no bread. Jesus said he would care for that, and asked which of his disciples would go and buy bread for thirty pieces of silver. Judas offered himself eagerly, and went to the Jews' street to do his errand. Jews were gaming, under

a tub, and they challenged Judas to play. The first time he won the stake, and the second. The third time he lost everything. "Why so sad, Judas?" they say: "go sell your Master for thirty pieces." We are to suppose Judas to have rejoined his company. Jesus then asks who has sold him. John says, Is it I? and Peter, and then Judas, to whom Jesus replies, Thou knowest best. Judas, in remorse, runs to hang himself. The Lord bids him turn, for his sin is forgiven. But Judas keeps on till he comes to a fir: "Soft wood, thou fir, thou wilt not bear me." Further on, till he comes to an aspen. "Hard wood, thou aspen, thou wilt bear me." So he hanged himself on the aspen; and still the aspen shakes and trembles for fear of the judgment day.

According to the ballads, then, Judas lost the thirty pieces at play, or was robbed of them, with collusion of his sister. But his passionate behavior in the English ballad, st. 9, goes beyond all apparent occasion. Surely it was not for his tithe of the thirty pieces. And why does he insist to Pilate on the very thirty pieces he had lost, rejecting every other form of payment? The ballad-singer might answer, So it was, and rest contented. Or perhaps he might have heard, and might tell us by way of comment, that these pieces had for long ages been destined to be "the price of him that was valued, whom they of the children of Israel did value;" had been coined by Abraham's father for Ninus, and been given by Terah to his son; had passed through various hands to the Ishmaelites, had been paid by them as the price of

---

[*] *Legenda Aurea*, Grässe, 2d ed., p. 184ff; Mone's *Anzeiger*, VII, col. 532f, and Du Méril, *Poésies populaires latines do Moyen Age*, p. 326ff; Furnivall, *Early English Poems and Lives of Saints*, p. 107ff; Douhet, *Dictionnaire des Légendes*, col. 714ff; *Das alte Passional*, ed. K. A. Hahn, p. 312ff; Bäckström, *Svenska Folkböcker*, II, 198ff; W. Creizenach, *Judas Ischarioth in Legende und Sage des Mittelalters*, in Paul and Braune's *Beiträge*, II, 177ff, etc.

Joseph, and been repaid to Joseph by his breth-
ren for corn in Egypt; thence were transferred
to Sheba, and in the course of events were
brought by the Queen of the South as an offer-
ing to Solomon's temple; when the temple was
despoiled by Nebuchadnezzar, were given by
him to the king of Godolia, and after the king-
dom of Godolia had been fused in that of
Nubia, were brought as his tribute to the infant
Jesus by Melchior, king of the same, etc.[*]

It is much to be regretted that the manu-
script from which this piece was taken has been
for some years lost from Trinity College Library,
so that a collation of Wright's text has not been
possible.

---

[*]   See Fabricius, *Codex Pseudepigraphus Veteris Testa-
menti*, ii, 79; Godfrey of Viterbo (who derives his infor-
mation from a lost writing of the apostle Bartholomew)
in his *Pantheon*, Pistorius, *German. Script.*, ed. Struve, ii,
243, or E. Du Méril, *Poésies pop. latines du Moyen Age*, p.
321; Genesi de Scriptura, *Biblioteca Catalana*, p. 20, etc.

1 Hit wes upon a Scere-thorsday that ure loverd
      aros;
   Ful milde were the wordes he spec to Judas.

2 'Judas, thou most to Jurselem, oure mete for to
      bugge;
   Thritti platen of selver thou here up othi rugge.

3 'Thou comest fer ithe brode stret, fer ithe brode
      strete;
   Summe of thine tunesmen ther thou meiht
      imete.'

4 .   .   .   .   .
   Imette wid is soster, the swikele wimon.

5 'Judas, thou were wrthe me stende the wid
      ston,
   For the false prophete that tou bilevest upon.'

6 'Be stille, leve soster, thin herte the tobreke!
   Wiste min loverd Crist, ful wel he wolde be
      wreke.'

7 'Judas, go thou on the roc, heie upon the ston;
   Lei thin heved imy barm, slep thou the anon.'

8 Sone so Judas of slepe was awake,
   Thritti platen of selver from hym weren itake.

[244] 9 He drou hymselve bi the cop, that al it lavede a
      blode;
   The Jewes out of Jurselem awenden he were
      wode.

10 Foret hym com the riche Jeu that heihte Pila-
      tus:
   'Wolte sulle thi loverd, that hette Jesus?'

11 'I nul sulle my loverd [for] nones cunnes eihte,
   Bote hit be for the thritti platen that he me
      bitaihte.'

12 'Wolte sulle thi lord Crist for enes cunnes
      golde?'
   'Nay, bote hit be for the platen that he habben
      wolde.'

13 In him com ur lord Crist gon, as is postles seten
      at mete:
   'Wou sitte ye, postles, ant wi nule ye ete?

14 ['Wou sitte ye, postles, ant wi nule ye ete?]
   Ic am ibouht ant isold today for oure mete.'

15 Up stod him Judas: 'Lord, am I that . . .?
   'I nas never othe stude ther me the evel spec.'

16 Up him stod Peter, and spec wid al is mihte,
      .   .   .   .   .

17 'Thau Pilatus him come wid ten hundred
      cnihtes,
   Yet ic wolde, loverd, for thi love fihte.'

18 'Still thou be, Peter, wel I the icnowe;
   Thou wolt fursake me thrien ar the coc him
      crowe.'

———◆———

Not divided into stanzas in Reliquiæ Antiquæ.
3^2. meist.
10^1. heiste.
11^1. eiste. 11^2. bitaiste.
14^2. i-boust.
16^1. miste.

17^1. cnistes. 17^2. fiste.
*In the absence of the original manuscript, I have
thought it better to change Wright's s in the above
instances (3–17) to h. In this substitution I follow
Mätzner's* Altenglische Sprachproben, *i*, 114.

———◆———

APPENDIX

Trinity College MS. B, 14, 39, has been recovered,
and Professor Skeat has had the kindness to furnish a
copy of the ballad. Wright's text proves to be in all
essentials accurate; but, on account of the age and great
interest of the poem, Professor Skeat's copy is here
reproduced. The ballad has no title in the MS.

Hit wes upon a scereþorsday þat vre louerd aros.
    ful milde were þe wordes he spec to iudas.
iudas þou most to iurselem oure mete for to bugge.
    þritti platen of seluer þou bere up oþi rugge.
Þou comest fer iþe brode stret fer iþe brode strete.   5
    summe of þine tunesmen þer þou meist i mete.
imette wid is soster þe swikele wimon.
    iudas þou were wrþe me stende the wid ston.   .íí.
for the false prophete þat tou bileuest upon.
Be stille leue soster þin herte þe to breke.   10
    wiste min louerd crist ful wel he wolde be wreke.
Iudas go þou on þe roc heie up on þe ston.
    lei þin heued i my barm slep þou þe anon.
Sone so iudas of slepe was awake.
    þritti platen of seluer from hym weren itake.   15
He drou hym selue bi þe cop þat al it lauede ablode.
    þe iewes out of iurselem awenden he were wode.
Foret hym com þe riche ieu þat heiste pilatus.
    wolte sulle þi louerd þat hette iesus.
I nul sulle my louerd for nones cunnes eiste.   20
bote hit be for þe þritti platen. þat he me bi taiste.
Wolte stille þi lord crist for enes cunnes golde.
Nay bote hit be for þe platen. þat he habben wolde.
In him com ur lord* gon as is postles seten at mete.
    Wou sitte ye postles ant wi nule ye ete.   .íí.   25
    ic am iboust ant isold to day for oure mete.
Vp stod him iudas lord am i þat
    I nas neuer oþe stude þer me þe euel spec.
Vp him stod peter ant spec wid al is miste.
þau pilatus him come wid ten hundred cnistes. .íí.   30
yet ic wolde louerd for þi loue fiste.
Still þou be peter. wel i þe i cnowe.
tou wolt fur sake me trien. ar te coc him crowe.   33

V. 24, *. The word *c'st* has here been erased, and
    should *not* be inserted. Skeat.

V. 27. Blank space. Read 'frek' (= man). Skeat.

    The MS. has íí at end of ll. 8, 25, 30. This means
    that there are here *two* second lines, i.e., that
    three lines rime together. Skeat. The long f's of
    the MS. are printed s.

24

BONNIE ANNIE

A. 'Bonnie Annie,' Kinloch's *Ancient Scottish Ballads*, p. 123.
B. 'The High Banks o Yarrow,' Motherwell's MS., p. 652.

C. Collected by Rev. S. Baring-Gould in South Devon. **a.** From an old man at Bradstone. **b.** From a young man at Dartmoor. **c.** From an old man at Holne.

HAD an old copy of this still pretty and touching, but much disordered, ballad been saved, we should perhaps have had a story like this. Bonnie Annie, having stolen her father's gold and her mother's fee, and fled with her paramour (like the maid in No **4**), the ship in which she is sailing encounters a storm and cannot get on. Annie is seized with the pangs of travail, and deplores the absence of women (**B** 6, 7, **A** 9, 10; compare No **15**, 21–26). The sailors say there is somebody on board who is marked for death, or flying from a just doom. They cast lots, and the lot falls on Annie,—a result which strikes us as having more semblance of the "corrupted currents of this world" than of a pure judgment of God. Annie, conscious only of her own guilt, asks to be thrown [245] overboard. Her paramour offers great sums to the crew to save her, but their efforts prove useless, and Annie again begs, or they now insist, that she shall be cast into the sea with her babe. This done, the ship is able to sail on; Annie floats to shore and is buried there.

The captain of the ship is the guilty man in **A**, in **B** a rich squire. **A** may exhibit the original plot, but it is just as likely that the captain was substituted for a passenger, under the influence of another ballad, in which there is no Annie, but a ship-master stained with many crimes, whom the lot points out as endangering or obstructing the vessel. See 'Brown Robyn's Confession,' further on.

If the narrative in Jonah, i, is the ultimate source of this and similar stories, it must be owned that the tradition has maintained its principal traits in this ballad remarkably well. Jonah flies from the presence of the Lord in a ship; the ship is overtaken by a tempest;[*] the sailors cast lots to know who is the guilty cause, and the lot falls on Jonah; he bids the sailors take him up and cast him into the sea; nevertheless the men row hard to bring the ship to land, but cannot succeed; they throw Jonah into the water, and the storm ceases.[†]

Translated in Grundtvig's *Engelske og skotske Folkeviser*, p. 199, No 31.

---

[*]   Jonah is asleep below. This trait we find in several Norse ballads: see 'Brown Robyn's Confession.'
[†]   A singular episode in the life of Saint Mary Magdalen in the *Golden Legend*, Grässe, c. xcvi, 2, p. 409ff, indicates a belief that even a dead body might prejudice the safety of a ship. The princess of Marseilles, in the course of a storm, has given birth to a boy and expired. The sailors demand that the body shall be thrown into the sea (and apparently the boy, too), for, they say, as long as it shall be with us this thumping will not cease. They presently see a hill, and think it better to put off the corpse, and the boy, there, than that these should be devoured by sea-monsters. Fear will fasten upon anything in such a case.
   The *Digby Mystery of Mary Magdalene* has this scene, at p. 122 of the New Shakspere Society edition, ed. Furnivall.

A

Kinloch's *Ancient Scottish Ballads*, p. 123.

1 THERE was a rich lord, and he lived in Forfar,
  He had a fair lady, and one only dochter.

2 O she was fair, O dear, she was bonnie!
  A ship's captain courted her to be his honey.

3 There cam a ship's captain out owre the sea
      sailing,
  He courted this young thing till he got her wi
      bairn.

4 'Ye'll steal your father's gowd, and your
      mother's money,
  And I'll mak ye a lady in Ireland bonnie.'

5 She's stown her father's gowd, and her mother's
      money,
  But she was never a lady in Ireland bonnie.
      *   *   *   *   *

6 'There's fey fowk in our ship, she winna sail for
      me,
  There's fey fowk in our ship, she winna sail for
      me.'

7 They've casten black bullets twice six and
      forty,
  And ae the black bullet fell on bonnie Annie.

8 'Ye'll tak me in your arms twa, lo, lift me cannie,
  Throw me out owre board, your ain dear Annie.'

9 He has tane her in his arms twa, lo, lifted her
      cannie,
  He has laid her on a bed of down, his ain dear
      Annie.

10 'What can a woman do, love, I'll do for ye;'
   'Muckle can a woman do, ye canna do for me.'

11 'Lay about, steer about, lay our ship cannie,
   Do all ye can to save my dear Annie.'

12 'I've laid about, steerd about, laid about cannie,
   But all I can do, she winna sail for me.

13 'Ye'll tak her in your arms twa, lo, lift her cannie, [246]
   And throw her out owre board, your ain dear
      Annie.'

14 He has tane her in his arms twa, lo, lifted her
      cannie,
   He has thrown her out owre board, his ain dear
      Annie.

15 As the ship sailed, bonnie Annie she swam,
   And she was at Ireland as soon as them.

16 He made his love a coffin of the gowd sae yellow,
   And buried his bonnie love doun in a sea valley.

B

Motherwell's MS., p. 652. From the singing of a
boy, Henry French, Ayr.

1 Down in Dumbarton there wonnd a rich mer-
      chant,
  Down in Dumbarton there wond a rich mer-
      chant,
  And he had nae family but ae only dochter.
  Sing fal lal de deedle, fal lal de deedle lair, O a
      day

2 There cam a rich squire, intending to woo her,
  He wooed her until he had got her wi babie.

3 'Oh what shall I do! oh what shall come o me!
  Baith father and mither will think naething o
      me.'

4 'Gae up to your father, bring down gowd and
      money,
  And I'll take ye ower to a braw Irish ladie.'

5 She gade to her father, brought down gowd and
      money,
  And she's awa ower to a braw Irish ladie.

6 She hadna sailed far till the young thing cried
        'Women!'
    'What women can do, my dear, I'll do for you.'

7 'O haud your tongue, foolish man, dinna talk
        vainly,
    For ye never kent what a woman driet for you.

8 'Gae wash your hands in the cauld spring
        water,
    And dry them on a towel a' giltit wi silver.

9 'And tak me by the middle, and lift me up saft-
        lie,
    And throw me ower shipboard, baith me and
        my babie.'

10 He took her by the middle, and lifted her saftly,
    And threw her ower shipboard, baith her and
        her babie.

11 Sometimes she did sink, sometimes she did
        float it,
    Until that she cam to the high banks o Yarrow.

12 'O captain tak gowd, O sailors tak money,
    And launch out your sma boat till I sail for my
        honey.'

13 'How can I tak gowd, how can I tak money?
    My ship's on a sand bank, she winna sail for
        me.'

14 The captain took gowd, the sailors took money,
    And they launchd out their sma boat till he
        sailed for his honey.

15 'Mak my love a coffin o the gowd sae yellow,
    Whar the wood it is dear, and the planks they
        are narrow,
    And bury my love on the high banks o Yarrow.'

16 They made her a coffin o the gowd sae yellow,
    And buried her deep on the high banks o Yar-
        row.

C

The Rev. S. Baring-Gould has recently found this
ballad in South Devon. **a.** Taken down from a man of
above eighty years at Bradstone. **b.** From a young man
at Dartmoor. **c.** From an old man at Holne.

'Twas of a sea-captain came o'er the salt billow
He courted a maiden down by the green willow.
"O take of your father his gold and his treasure,
O take of your mother her fee without measure."

1 'T WAS of a sea-captain came oer the salt bil-
        low,
    He courted a maiden down by the green wil-
        low:
    'O take of your father his gold and his treasure,
    O take of your mother her fee without mea-
        sure.'

2 'I'll take of my father his gold and his treasure,
    I'll take of my mother her fee without mea-
        sure:'
    She has come with the captain unto the sea-
        side, O,
    'We'll sail to lands foreign upon the blue
        tide, O!'

3 And when she had sailed today and tomorrow,
    She was beating her hands, she was crying in
        sorrow;
  And when she had sailed the days were not
        many,
    The sails were outspread, but of miles made
        not any.

4 And when she had sailed today and tomorrow,
    She was beating her hands, she was crying in
        sorrow;
  And when she had sailed not many a mile, O,
    The maid was delivered of a beautiful child,
        O.

5 .   .   .   .   .   .

6 'O take a white napkin, about my head bind it!
    O take a white napkin, about my feet wind
        it!
  Alack! I must sink, both me and my baby,
    Alack! I must sink in the deep salten water.

7 'O captain, O captain, here's fifty gold crown,
        O,
    I pray thee to bear me and turn the ship
        round, O;
  O captain, O captain, here's fifty gold pound,
        O,
    If thou wilt but set me upon the green
        ground, O.'

8 'O never, O never! the wind it blows stronger,
    O never, O never! the time it grows longer;
  And better it were that thy baby and thou, O,
    Should drown than the crew of the vessel, I
        vow, O.'

9 'O get me a boat that is narrow and thin, O,
    And set me and my little baby therein, O:'
  'O no, it were better that thy baby and thou, O,
    Should drown than the crew of the vessel, I
        vow, O.'

10 They got a white napkin, about her head
        bound it,
    They got a white napkin, about her feet
        wound it;
  They cast her then overboard, baby and she, O,
    Together to sink in the cruel salt sea, O.

11 The moon it was shining, the tide it was run-
        ning;
    O what in the wake of the vessel was swim-
        ming?
  'O see, boys! O see how she floats on the water!
    O see, boys! O see! the undutiful daughter!

12 'Why swim in the moonlight, upon the sea
        swaying?
    O what art thou seeking? for what art thou
        praying?'
  'O captain, O captain, I float on the water;
    For the sea giveth up the undutiful daughter.

13 'O take of my father the gold and the treasure,
    O take of my mother her fee without mea-
        sure;
  O make me a coffin of gold that is yellow,
    And bury me under the banks of green wil-
        low!'

14 'I will make thee a coffin of gold that is yellow,
    I'll bury thee under the banks of green wil-
        low;
  I'll bury thee there as becometh a lady,
    I'll bury thee there, both thou and thy baby.'

15 The sails they were spread, and the wind it was
        blowing,
    The sea was so salt, and the tide it was flow-
        ing;
  They steered for the land, and they reachd the
        shore, O,
    But the corpse of the maiden had reachd
        there before, O.

---

*7] **A.** *Printed by Kinloch in four-line stanzas.*
      16¹. coffin off the Goats of Yerrow.
    B. 16. *Motherwell, Minstrelsy, p. xcix, 146, gives the
      stanza thus:*

They made his love a coffin of the gowd sae yel-
    low,
They made his love a coffin of the gowd sae yel-
    low,

And they buried her deep on the high banks of Yarrow.

Sing fal lal, de deedle, fal lal, de deedle lair, Oh a Day!

C. b. $1^{1,2}$. There was a sea-captain came to the sea-side, O,

He courted a damsel and got her in trouble.

13^3. coffin of the deepest stoll yellow.

15^4. But the mother and baby had got there before, O.

c.   1 'T is of a sea-captain, down by the green willow,

He courted a damsel and brought her in trouble;

When gone her mother's good will and all her father's money,

She fled across the wide sea along with her Johnny.

2 They had not been sailing the miles they were many

Before she was delivered of a beautiful baby:

'O tie up my head! O and tie it up easy,

And throw me overboard, both me and my baby!'

3 She floated on the waves, and she floated so easy,

That they took her on board again, both she and her baby.

(*The rest forgotten.*)

25

WILLIE'S LYKE-WAKE

A. 'Willie, Willie,' Kinloch's MSS, I, 53.
B. a. 'Blue Flowers and Yellow,' Buchan's *Ballads of the North of Scotland*, I, 185. b. 'The Blue Flowers and the Yellow,' Christie, *Traditional Ballad Airs*, I, 120.
C. Motherwell's MS., p. 187.

D. 'Amang the blue flowers and yellow,' Motherwell's *Minstrelsy*, Appendix, p. xix, No xvii, one stanza.
E. 'Willie's Lyke-Wake.' a. Buchan's *Ballads of the North of Scotland*, II, 51. b. Christie, *Traditional Ballad Airs*, I, 122.

THIS piece was first printed by Buchan, in 1828, and all the copies which have been recovered are of about that date. The device of a lover's feigning death as a means of winning a shy mistress enjoys a considerable popularity in European ballads. Even more favorite is a ballad in which the *woman* adopts this expedient, in order to escape from the control of her relations: see 'The Gay Goshawk,' No 96 in this collection.

A **Danish** ballad answering to our Feigned Lyke-Wake is preserved, as I am informed by Professor Grundtvig, in no less than fourteen manuscripts, some of them of the 16th century, and is still living in tradition. Five versions, as yet unprinted, A–E, have been furnished me by the editor of the *Ballads of Denmark*.

A, from a manuscript of the sixteenth century. Young Herre Karl asks his mother's rede how he may get the maid his heart is set upon. She advises him to feign sickness, and be laid on his bier, no one to know his counsel but the page who is to do his errands. The page bids the lady to the wake that night. Little Kirstin asks her mother's leave to keep wake over Karl. The wake is to be in the upper room of Karl's house. The mother says, Be on your guard; he means to cheat you; but Kirstin, neither listening to her mother nor asking her father, goes to keep wake in the upper room. When she went in she could not see the lights for her tears. She begged all

the good people to pray for Karl's soul, sat down by his head and made her own prayer, and murmured, While thou livedst I loved thee. She lifted the cloths, and there lay Karl wide awake and laughing. "All the devils in hell receive thy soul!" she cried. "If thou livedst a hundred years, thou shouldst never have my good will!" Karl proposed that she should pass the night with him. "Why would you deceive me!" Kirstin exclaimed. "Why did you not go to my father and betroth me honorably?" Karl immediately rode to her father's to do this, and they were married.

B. a, from MSS of 1610 and later, almost identical with b, 'Den forstilte Vaagestue,' [248] Levninger, Part II, 1784, p. 34, No 7.* This version gives us some rather unnecessary previous history. Karl has sued for Ingerlille three years, and had an ill answer. He follows her to church one fine day, and, after mass, squeezes her fingers and asks, Will you take pity on me? She replies, You must ask my father and friends; and he, I have, and can get no good answer. If you will give me your troth, we can see to that best ourselves. "Never," she says. "Farewell, then; but Christ may change your mind." Karl meets his mother on his way from church, who asks why he is so pale. He tells her his plight, and is

---

* But **a** has two stanzas more: the first a stev-stamme, or lyrical introduction (see p. 7), the other, 31, nearly a repetition of Sandvig's 29.

advised, as before, to use craft. The wake is held
on Karl's premises.* Ingerlille, in scarlet mantle,
goes with her maids. She avows her love, but
adds that it was a fixed idea in her mind that he
would deceive her. She lifts up the white cloth
that covers the face. Karl laughs, and says, We
were good friends before, so are we still. Bear
out the bier, and follow me to bed with the fair
maid. She hopes he will have respect for her
honor. Karl reassures her, leaves her with his
mother, rides to Ingerlille's house, obtains her
parents' approbation, and buys wine for his
wedding.

C, from manuscripts of the sixteenth cen-
tury; 'Hr. Mortens Klosterrov,' Kristensen, *Jyske
Folkeminder*, X, 264, No 64. Karl is given out for
dead, and his pages ride to the convent to ask
that his body may be laid in the cloister. The
bier is borne in; the prioress comes to meet it,
with much respect. The pages go about bidding
maids to the wake. Ellin asks her mother if she
may go. (This looks as if there had originally
been no convent in the ballad.) Her mother
tells her to put on red gold and be wary of Karl,
he is so very tricky. When Ellin owns her
attachment, Karl whispers softly, Do not weep,
but follow me. Horses were ready at the
portal—*black* horses all! Karl sprang from the
bier, took Ellin, and made for the door. The
nuns, who stood reading in the choir, thought it
was an angel that had translated her, and
wished one would come for them. Karl, with fif-
teen men who were in waiting, carried Ellin
home, and drank his bridal with her.

D, from recent oral tradition. As Karl lay in
his bed, he said, How shall I get the fair maid
out of the convent? His foster-mother heard
him, and recommended him to feign death and
bid the fair maid to his wake. The maid asked
her father's leave to go, but he said, Nay, the
moment you are inside the door he will seize
you by the foot. But when the page, who had

* After the page has bidden Ingerlille to the wake, we
are told, **a** 27, 28, **b** 26, 27: all the convent bells were
going, and the tidings spreading that the knight was
dead; all the ladies of the convent sat sewing, except
Ingerlille, who wept. But Ingerlille, in the next stanza,
puts on her scarlet cloak and goes to the höjeloft to see
her father and mother. The two stanzas quoted signify
nothing in this version.

first come in blue, comes back in scarlet, she
goes. She stands at Karl's head and says, I never
shall forget thee; at his feet, "I wished thee
well;" at his side, "Thou wast my dearest." Then
she turns and bids everybody good-night, but
Karl seizes her, and calls to his friends to come
drink his bridal. We hear nothing of the con-
vent after the first stanza.

E, from oral tradition of another quarter.
Karl consults his mother how he shall get little
Kirstin out of the convent, and receives the
same counsel. A page is sent to the convent,
and asks who will come to the wake now Herr
Karl is dead? Little Kirstin, without application
to the prioress, goes to her mother, who does
not forbid her, but warns her that Karl will cap-
ture her as sure as she goes into the room.

The maid has the door by the handle,
    And is wishing them all good-night
Young Karl, that lay a corpse on the bier,
    Sprang up and held her tight.

'Why here's a board and benches,
    And there's no dead body here;
This eve I'll drink my mead and wine,
    All with my Kirstin dear.

'Why here's a board and beds too,
    And here there's nobody dead;
To-morrow will I go to the priest,
    All with my plighted maid.'

F, another copy from recent tradition, was
published in 1875, in Kristensen's *Jyske Folke-
viser*, II, 213, No 62, 'Vaagestuen;' 'Vågestuen,'
in Kristensen's *Skattegraveren*, II, 17, No 17; IV,
17, 115, Nos 26, 285. There is no word of a
convent here. The story is made very short.
Kirsten's mother says she will be fooled if she
goes to the wake. The last stanza, departing
from all other copies, says that when Kirsten
woke in the morning Karl was off.

G. 'Klosterranet,' *Levninger*, I, 23, No 4
(1780), *Danske Viser*, IV, 261, No 212, a very
second-rate ballad, may have the praise of pre-
serving consistency and conventual discipline.
The young lady does not slip out to see her
mother without leave asked and had. It is my
persuasion that the convent, with its little jest

about the poor nuns, is a later invention, and that C is a blending of two different stories. In G, Herr Morten betroths Proud Adeluds, who is more virtuous than rich. His friends object; her friends do not want spirit, and swear that she shall never be his. Morten's father sends him out of the country, and Adeluds is put into a convent. After nine years Morten returns, and, having rejected an advantageous match proposed by his father, advises with his brother, Herr Nilaus, how to get his true love out of the cloister. The brother's plan is that of the mother and foster-mother in the other versions. Herr Nilaus promises a rich gift if Morten's body may be buried within the cloister. From this point the story is materially the same as in C.

H. A copy, which I have not yet seen, in Rahbek's *Læsning i blandede Æmner* (or Hesperus), III, 151, 1822 (Bergström).

'Hertugen af Skage,' *Danske Viser*, II, 191, No 88, has this slight agreement with the foregoing ballads. Voldemar, the king's youngest son, hearing that the duke has a daughter, Hildegerd, that surpasses all maids, seeks her out in a convent in which she has taken refuge, and gets a cold reception. He feigns death, desiring that his bones may repose in the cloister. His bier is carried into the convent church. Hildegerd lights nine candles for him, and expresses compassion for his early death. While she is standing before the altar of the Virgin, Voldemar carries her out of the church by force.

This, says Afzelius, 1814, is one of the commonest ballads in **Sweden**, and is often represented as a drama by young people in country places. **A a**, 'Herr Carl, eller Klosterrofvet,' Afzelius, I, 179, No 26, new ed. No 24; **b**, Afzelius, *Sago-Häfder*, ed. 1851, IV, 106; **c**. Lagus, *Nyländska Folkvisor*, I, 51, No 12. **B**. Atterbom, *Poetisk Kalender* for 1816, p. 63, 'Det lefvande Liket.' **C**. Rancken, *Några. Prof af Folksång, o. s. v.*, p. 13, No 4. **D**. Aminson, *Bidrag till Södermanlands Kulturhistoria*, II, 18. These differ but slightly from Danish **D**, **E**. All four conclude with the humorous verses about the nuns, which in Rancken's copy take this rollicking turn:

And all the nuns in the convent they all
    danced in a ring;
'Christ send another such angel, to take us all
    under his wing!'

And all the nuns in the convent, they all
    danced each her lone;
'Christ send another such angel, to take us off
    every one!'

Bergström, new Afzelius, II, 131, refers to another version in Gyllenmärs' visbok, p. 191, and to a good copy obtained by himself.[*]

An Icelandic version for the 17th century, which is after the fashion of Danish C, G, is given in *Íslenzk Fornkvæði*, II, 59, No 40, 'Marteins kviða.' The lover has in all three a troop of armed men in waiting outside of the convent.

Professor Bugge has obtained a version in Norway, which, however, is as to language essentially Danish. (Bergström, as above.)

French. 'Le Soldat au Convent,' Victor Smith, *Vielles Chansons recueillies en Velay et en Forez*, p. 24, No 21, or *Romania*, VII, 73; Fleury, *Littérature Orale de la Basse-Normandie*, p. 310, 'La Religieuse;' *Poésies populaires de la France*, III, fol. 289, fol. 297. A soldier who has been absent some years in the wars returns to find his mistress in a convent; obtains permission to see her for a last time, puts a ring on her finger, and then "falls dead." His love insists on conducting his funeral; the lover returns to life and carries her off.

There is a very gay and pretty south-European ballad, in which the artifice of feigning death is successfully tried by a lover after the failure of other measures.

A. Magyar. Arany and Gyulai, I, 172, No 18, 'Pálbeli Szép Antal;' translated by Aigner, [250] *Ungarische Volksdichtungen*, p. 80, 'Schön Anton,' and by G. Heinrich, in *Ungarische Revue*, 1883, p. 155. Handsome Tony tells his mother that he shall die for Helen. The mother says, Not yet. I will build a marvellous mill. The first wheel shall grind out pearls, the middle stone discharge kisses, the third wheel distrib-

---

[*] Bröms Gyllenmärs' visbok has been printed in *Nyare Bidrag, o. s. v.*, 1887, and the ballad of Herr Carl is No 77, p. 252. There is an imperfect copy in Bergström ock Nordlander, *Nyare Bidrag*, p. 102, No 9.

ute small change. The pretty maids will come to see, and Helen among them. Helen asks her mother's leave to see the mill. "Go not," the mother replies. "They are throwing the net, and a fox will be caught." Tony again says he must die. His mother says, not yet; for she will build an iron bridge; the girls will come to see it, and Helen among them. Helen asks to see the bridge; her mother answers as before. Tony says once more that he shall die for Helen. His mother again rejoins, Not yet. Make believe to be dead; the girls will come to see you, and Helen among them. Helen entreats to be allowed to go to see the handsome young man that has died. Her mother tells her she will never come back. Tony's mother calls to him to get up; the girl he was dying for is even now before the gate, in the court, standing at his feet. "Never," says Helen, "saw I so handsome a dead man,—eyes smiling, mouth tempting kisses, and his feet all ready for a spring." Up he jumped and embraced her. The same story, perverted to tragedy at the end, appears in Golovatsky, II, 710, No 13, a ballad of the Carpathian Russians in Hungary.

B. Italian. Ferraro, *Canti popolari monferrini*, p. 59, No 40, 'Il Genovese;' given in eight versions, one a fragment, by Nigra, No 41, p. 257; Canti pop. Emiliani, Maria Carmi, *Archivio*, XII, 187, No 9.[*] The Genoese, not obtaining the beautiful daughter of a rich merchant on demand, plants a garden. All the girls come for flowers, except the one desired. He then gives a ball, with thirty-two musicians. All the girls are there, but not the merchant's daughter. He then builds a church, very richly adorned. All the girls come to mass, all but one. Next he sets the bells a ringing, in token of his death. The fair one goes to the window to ask who is dead. The good people ("ra bun-ha gent," in the Danish ballad "det gode folk") tell her that it is her first love, and suggest that she should attend the funeral. She asks her father, who consents if she will not cry. As she was leaving the church, the lover came to life, and called to the priests and friars to stop singing. They went to the

high altar to be married. A similar story is found in a tale, 'La Furnarella,' A. de Nino, *Usi e Costumi abruzzesi*, III, 198, No 37. (R. Köhler.)

C. Slovenian. Vraz, *Narodne pešni ilirske*, p. 93, 'Čudna bolezen' ('Strange Sickness'); translated by Anastasius Grün, *Volkslieder aus Krain*, p. 36, 'Der Scheintodte.' "Build a church, mother," cries the love-sick youth, "that all who will may hear mass; perhaps my love among them." The mother built a church, one and another came, but not his love. "Dig a well, mother, that those who will may fetch water; perhaps my love among them." The well was dug, one and another came for water, but not his love. "Say I am dead, mother, that those who will may come to pray." Those who wished came, his love first of all. The youth was peeping through the window. "What kind of dead man is this, that stretches his arms for an embrace, and puts out his mouth for a kiss?" A Russian form of this story is found in Trudy, V, 113, No 249.[†]

Bulgarian. Verković, p. 334, No 304. Stojan, who wants to carry off Bojana, does, at his mother's advice, everything to bring her within his reach. He builds a church, digs a well, plants a garden. All the maids come but her. He then feigns death; she comes with flowers and mourns over him; he seizes her; the priest blesses their union. Miladinof, p. 294, No 185. An old woman, in a like case, advises a young man to feign death, and brings Bojana to see the body. "Why," asks Bojana, "do his eyes look as if they had sight, his arms as if they would lay hold of me, his feet as if ready to jump up?"

---

† The story of **A**, **B**, **C** in a tale, 'La Furnarella,' A. de Nino, *Usi e Costumi abruzzesi*, III, 198, No 37. (R. Köhler.)

Dr R. Köhler points out to me a German copy of **A, B, C**, which I had overlooked, in Schröer, *Ein Ausflug nach Gottschee*, p. 266ff, 'Hansel junc.' The mother builds a mill and a church, and then the young man feigns death, as before. But a very cheap tragic turn is given to the conclusion when the young man springs up and kisses his love. She falls dead with fright, and he declares that since she has died for him he will die for her. So they are buried severally at one and the other side of the church, and two lily stocks are planted, which embrace "like two real married people;" or, a vine grows from one and a flower from the other.

---

* A fragment in Dalmedico, *Canti del popolo veneziano*, p. 109, seems, as Maria Carmi suggests, to belong to this ballad.

"That is because he died so suddenly," says the beldam. The youth springs up and embraces Bojana. A Magyar-Croat version begins like this last, but has suffered corruption: Kurelac, p. 148, No. 447. (W. W.)

Danish **G** translated by the Rev. J. Johnstone, 'The Robbery of the Nunnery, or,

The Abbess Outwitted,' Copenhagen, 1786 (*Danske Viser*, II, 366); by Prior, III, 400. Swedish **A**, by G. Stephens, *Foreign Quarterly Review*, 1841, XXVI, 49, and by the Howitts, *Lit. and Rom. of Northern Europe*, I, 292. English **C**, by Rosa Warrens, *Schottische V. l.*, p. 144, No 33.

A

Kinloch's MSS, I, 53, from the recitation of Mary
Barr, Lesmahagow, aged upwards of seventy. May, 1827.

1 'WILLIE, Willie, I'll learn you a wile,'
  And the sun shines over the valleys and a'
'How this pretty fair maid ye may beguile.'
  Amang the blue flowrs and the yellow and a'

2 'Ye maun lie doun just as ye were dead,
  And tak your winding-sheet around your head.

3 'Ye maun gie the bellman his bell-groat,
  To ring your dead-bell at your lover's yett.'

4 He lay doun just as he war dead,
  And took his winding-sheet round his head.

5 He gied the bellman his bell-groat,
  To ring his dead-bell at his lover's yett.

6 'O wha is this that is dead, I hear?'
'O wha but Willie that loed ye sae dear.'

7 She is to her father's chamber gone,
  And on her knees she's fallen down.

8 'O father, O father, ye maun grant me this;
  I hope that ye will na tak it amiss.

9 'That I to Willie's burial should go;
  For he is dead, full well I do know.'

10 'Ye'll tak your seven bauld brethren wi thee,
  And to Willie's burial straucht go ye.'

11 It's whan she cam to the outmost yett,
  She made the silver fly round for his sake.

12 It's whan she cam to the inmost yett,
  She made the red gowd fly round for his sake.

13 As she walked frae the court to the parlour there,
  The pretty corpse syne began for to steer.

14 He took her by the waist sae neat and sae sma,
  And throw her atween him and the wa.

15 'O Willie, O Willie, let me alane this nicht,
  O let me alane till we're wedded richt.'

16 'Ye cam unto me baith sae meek and mild,
  But I'll mak ye gae hame a wedded wife wi child.'

B

a. Buchan's *Ballads of the North of Scotland*, 1, 185. **b.**
Christie, *Traditional Ballad Airs*, 1, 120.

"O__ Wil-lie my son, what makes__ you sae sad? As the sun shines ov-er the val-ley."

"I am sare-ly__ sick for the love__ of a maid, A-mang the blue flow-ers and the yel-low."

"Is__ she an heir-ess or la-dy sae free, As the sun shines o-ver the val-ley;

That __ she will__ take no__ pi-ty on thee, A-mang the blue flow-ers and the yel-low?"

B. b. W. Christie. Sung by an old woman in Banffshire.

1 'O WILLIE my son, what makes you sae sad?'
   As the sun shines over the valley
  'I lye sarely sick for the love of a maid.'
   Amang the blue flowers and the yellow

2 'Were she an heiress or lady sae free,
   That she will take no pity on thee?'

3 'O Willie, my son, I'll learn you a wile,
   How this fair maid ye may beguile.

4 'Ye'll gie the principal bellman a groat,
   And ye'll gar him cry your dead lyke-wake.'

5 Then he gae the principal bellman a groat,
   He bade him cry his dead lyke-wake.

6 This maiden she stood till she heard it a',
   And down frae her cheeks the tears did fa.

7 She is hame to her father's ain bower:
   'I'll gang to yon lyke-wake ae single hour.'

8 'Ye must take with you your ain brither John;
   It's not meet for maidens to venture alone.'

9 'I'll not take with me my brither John,
   But I'll gang along, myself all alone.'

10 When she came to young Willie's yate,
   His seven brithers were standing thereat.

11 Then they did conduct her into the ha,
   Amang the weepers and merry mourners a'.

12 When she lifted up the covering sae red,
   With melancholy countenance to look on the
   dead,

13 He's taen her in his arms, laid her gainst the wa,
   Says, 'Lye ye here, fair maid, till day.'

14 'O spare me, O spare me, but this single night,
   And let me gang hame a maiden sae bright.'

15 'Tho all your kin were about your bower,
   Ye shall not be a maiden ae single hour.

16 'Fair maid, ye came here without a convoy,
   But ye shall return wi a horse and a boy.

17 'Ye came here a maiden sae mild,
   But ye shall gae hame a wedded wife with child.'

C

Motherwell's MS., p. 187.

1 'O WILLIE, Willie, what makes thee so sad?
   And the sun shines over the valley
  'I have loved a lady these seven years and mair.'
   Down amang the blue flowers and the yellow

2 'O Willie, lie down as thou were dead,
   And lay thy winding-sheet down at thy head.

3 'And gie to the bellman a belling-great,
   To ring the dead-bell at thy love's bower-yett.'

4 He laid him down as he were dead,
   And he drew the winding-sheet oer his head.

5 He gied to the bellman a belling-great,
   To ring the dead-bell at his love's bower-yett.
      *   *   *   *   *

6 When that she came to her true lover's gate,
   She dealt the red gold and all for his sake.

7 And when that she came to her true lover's
     bower,
   She had not been there for the space of half an
     hour,

8 Till that she cam to her true lover's bed,
   And she lifted the winding-sheet to look at the
     dead.

9 He took her by the hand so meek and sma,
   And he cast her over between him and the wa.

10 'Tho all your friends were in the bower,
   I would not let you go for the space of half an
     hour.

11 'You came to me without either horse or boy,
   But I will send you home with a merry convoy.'

D

Motherwell's *Minstrelsy*, Appendix, p. xix, No XVII.

O John-ie, dear John-ie what makes ye sae sad, As the sun shines ow-er the val-ley;
I think nae mu-sic will mak ye___ glad, A-mang the blue flowers and the___ yel-low.

'O JOHNIE, dear Johnie, what makes ye sae sad?'
   As the sun shines ower the valley
'I think nae music will mak ye glad.'
   Amang the blue flowers and the yellow

E

a. Buchan's *Ballads of the North of Scotland*, II, 51. **b.**
Christie, *Traditional Ballad Airs*, I, 122.

1 'IF MY love loves me, she lets me not know,
   That is a dowie chance;
  I wish that I the same could do,
   Tho my love were in France, France,
   Tho my love were in France.

2 'O lang think I, and very lang,
   And lang think I, I true;
  But lang and langer will I think
   Or my love o me rue.

3 'I will write a broad letter,
   And write it sae perfite,
  That an she winna o me rue,
   I'll bid her come to my lyke.'

4 Then he has written a broad letter,
   And seald it wi his hand,
  And sent it on to his true love,
   As fast as boy could gang.

5 When she looked the letter upon,
   A light laugh then gae she;
  But ere she read it to an end,
   The tear blinded her ee.

6 'O saddle to me a steed, father,
   O saddle to me a steed;
  For word is come to me this night,
   That my true love is dead.'

7 'The steeds are in the stable, daughter,
   The keys are casten by;
  Ye cannot won to-night, daughter,
   To-morrow ye'se won away.'

8 She has cut aff her yellow locks,
   A little aboon her ee,
  And she is on to Willie's lyke,
   As fast as gang could she.

9 As she gaed ower yon high hill head,
   She saw a dowie light;
  It was the candles at Willie's lyke,
   And torches burning bright.

10 Three o Willie's eldest brothers
    Were making for him a bier;
   One half o it was gude red gowd,
    The other siller clear.

11 Three o Willie's eldest sisters
    Were making for him a sark;
   The one half o it was cambric fine,
    The other needle wark.

12 Out spake the youngest o his sisters,
    As she stood on the fleer:
   How happy would our brother been,
    If ye'd been sooner here!

13 She lifted up the green covering,
    And gae him kisses three;
    Then he lookd up into her face,
    The blythe blink in his ee.

14 O then he started to his feet,
    And thus to her said he:
    Fair Annie, since we're met again,
    Parted nae mair we'se be.

B. b *is a with stanzas 3, 12–15 omitted, and* "a few alterations, some of them given from the recitation of an old woman." "Buchan's version differs little from the way the old woman sang the ballad." *The old woman's variations, so far as adopted, are certainly of the most trifling.*
1^2. I am. 2^1. Is she. 7^1. And she.
16^1. Ye've come. 16^2. And ye.
17. *Evidently by Christie:*
    'Fair maid, I love thee as my life,

But ye shall gae hame a lovd wedded wife.'
C. *Burden. The lines are transposed in the second stanza, but are given in the third in the order of the first.*
3^1, 5^1. MS. belling great.
11^2. you come.
E. b."Given with some changes from the way the editor has heard it sung."
2^2. I trow. 3^1. But I. 3^3. That gin.
7^3. the night.

APPENDIX
Additional Copies

'The Blue Flowers and the Yellow,' Greenock, printed by W. Scott [1810].

1 'THIS seven long years I've courted a maid,'
    As the sun shines over the valley
    'And she neer would consent for to be my bride.'
    Among the blue flowers and the yellow

2 'O Jamie, O Jamie, I'll learn you the way
    How your innocent love you'll betray.

3 'If you will give to the bell-man a groat,
    And he'll toll you down a merry night-wake.'

4 Now he has given the bell-man a groat,
    And he has tolld him down a merry nightwake.

5 'It's I must go to my true-love's wake,
    For late last night I heard he was dead.'

6 'Take with you your horse and boy,
    And give your true lover his last convoy.'

7 'I'll have neither horse nor boy,
    But I'll go alone, and I'll mourn and cry.'

8 When that she came to her true-love's hall,
    Then the tears they did down fall.

9 She lifted up the sheets so small,
    He took her in his arms and he threw her to the wa.

10 'It's let me go a maid, young Jamie,' she said,
    'And I will be your bride, and to-morrow we'll be wed.'

11 'If all your friends were in this bower,
    You should not be a maid one quarter of an hour.

12 'You came here a maid meek and mild,
    But you shall go home both marryd and with child.'

13 He gave to her a gay gold ring,
    And the next day they had a gay wedding.

The unfortunate Weaver. To which are added The Farmer's Daughter and The Blue Flowers and the Yellow. Greenock. Printed by W. Scott. [1810.] British Museum, 11621. b. 7 (43).

26

THE THREE RAVENS

a. *Melismata. Musicall Phansies. Fitting the Court, Cittie, and Countrey Humours.* London, 1611, No 20 [Misprinted 22]. [T. Ravenscroft.]

b. 'The Three Ravens,' Motherwell's *Minstrelsy,* Appendix, p. xviii, No XII.

a was printed from *Melismata*, by Ritson, in his *Ancient Songs*, 1790, p. 155. Mr Chappell remarked, about 1855, *Popular Music of the Olden Time*, I, 59, that this ballad was still so popular in some parts of the country that he had "been favored with a variety of copies of it, written down from memory, and all differing in some respects, both as to words and tune, but with sufficient resemblance to prove a similar origin." Motherwell, *Minstrelsy*, Introduction, p. lxxvii, note 49, says he had met with several copies almost the same as **a**. **b** is the first stanza of one of these (traditional) versions, "very popular in Scotland."

The following verses, first printed in the *Minstrelsy of the Scottish Border*, and known in several versions in Scotland, are treated by Motherwell and others as a traditionary form of 'The Three Ravens.' They are, however, as Scott says, "rather a counterpart than a copy of the other," and sound something like a cynical variation of the tender little English ballad. Dr Rimbault (*Notes and Queries*, Ser. v, III, 518) speaks of unprinted copies taken down by Mr Blaikie and by Mr Thomas Lyle of Airth.

THE TWA CORBIES.

a. *Minstrelsy of the Scottish Border*, III, 239, ed. 1803, communicated by C. K. Sharpe, as written down from tradition by a lady. **b.** *Albyn's Anthology*, II, 27, 1818, "from the singing of Mr Thomas Shortreed, of Jedburgh, as sung and recited by his mother." **c.** Chambers's *Scottish Ballads*, p. 283, partly from recitation and partly from the *Border Minstrelsy*. **d.** Fraser-Tytler MS., p. 70.

(b) As I cam' by yon auld house end, I saw twa cor-bies sit-tin there-on,

The tane un-to the t'oth-er did say, "O whare sall we gae dine the⸻ day?"

O⸻ whare sall we gae dine the⸻ day?

b. Campbell, *Albyn's Anthology*, II, p. 26–27, 1818.

1 As I was walking all alane,
 I heard twa corbies making a mane;
 The tane unto the t'other say,
 'Where sall we gang and dine to-day?'

2 'In behint yon auld fail dyke,
 I wot there lies a new slain knight;
 And naebody kens that he lies there,
 But his hawk, his hound, and lady fair.

3 'His hound is to the hunting gane,
 His hawk to fetch the wild-fowl hame,
 His lady's ta'en another mate,
 So we may mak our dinner sweet.

4 'Ye'll sit on his white hause-bane,
 And I'll pike out his bonny blue een;
 Wi ae lock o his gowden hair
 We'll theek our nest when it grows bare.

5 'Mony a one for him makes mane,
 But nane sall ken where he is gane;
 Oer his white banes, when they are bare,
 The wind sall blaw for evermair.'

"The song of 'The Twa Corbies' was given to
me by Miss Erskine of Alva (now Mrs Kerr),
who, I think, said that she had written it down

from the recitation of an old woman at Alva."
C. K. Sharpe to Scott, August 8, 1802, Letters,
I, 70, Abbotsford; printed in Sharpe's Letters, ed.
Allardyce, I, 136.

J. Haslewood made an entry in his copy of
Ritson's Scotish Songs of a MS. Lute-Book (pre-
sented to Dr C. Burney by Dr Skene, of
Marischal College, in 1781), which contained
airs "noted and collected by Robert Gordon, at
Aberdeen, in the year of our Lord 1627."
Among some ninety titles of tunes mentioned,
there occur 'Ther wer three ravens,' and 'God
be with the, Geordie.' (W. Macmath.)

'The Three Ravens' is translated by Grundt-
vig, Engelske og skotske Folkeviser, p. 145, No 23;
by Henrietta Schubart, p. 155; Gerhard, p. 95;
Rosa Warrens, Schottische V. l. der Vorzeit, p.
198; Wolff, Halle der Völker, I, 12, Hausschatz,
p. 205.

'The Twa Corbies' (Scott), by Grundtvig, p.
143, No 22; Arndt, p. 224; Gerhard, p. 94;
Schubart, p. 157; Knortz, L. u. R. Alt-Englands,
p. 194; Rosa Warrens, p. 89. The three first
stanzas, a little freely rendered into four, pass for
Pushkin's: Works, 1856, II, 462, xxiv.

a. Ravenscroft, 1611, No 20.

1 THERE were three rauens sat on a tree,
 Downe a downe, hay down, hay downe
 There were three rauens sat on a tree;
  With a downe
 There were three rauens sat on a tree,
 They were as blacke as they might be.
  With a downe derrie, derrie, derrie, downe,
  downe

2 The one of them said to his mate,
 'Where shall we our breakfast take?'

3 'Downe in yonder greene field,
 There lies a knight slain vnder his shield.

4 'His hounds they lie downe at his feete,
 So well they can their master keepe.

5 'His haukes they flie so eagerly,
    There's no fowle dare him come nie.'

6 Downe there comes a fallow doe,
    As great with yong as she might goe.

7 She lift vp his bloudy hed,
    And kist his wounds that were so red.

8 She got him vp vpon her backe,
    And carried him to earthen lake.

9 She buried him before the prime,
    She was dead herselfe ere euen-song time.

10 God send euery gentleman,
    Such haukes, such hounds, and such a leman.

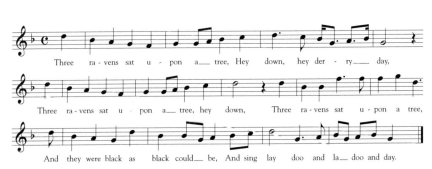

Three ra-vens sat u-pon a tree, Hey down, hey der-ry day,

Three ra-vens sat u-pon a tree, hey down, Three ra-vens sat u-pon a tree,

And they were black as black could be, And sing lay doo and la doo and day.

b. Motherwell, 1827, Appendix No. 12. Collected by Andrew Blaikie, Paisley.

b. THREE ravens sat upon a tree,
    Hey down, hey derry day
Three ravens sat upon a tree,
    Hey down

Three ravens sat upon a tree,
And they were black as black could be.
And sing lay doo and la doo and day

Variations of The Twa Corbies.

b. 1. As I cam by yon auld house end,
        I saw twa corbies sittin thereon.

   2^1. Whare but by yon new fa'en birk.

   3. We'll sit upon his bonny breast-bane,
       And we'll pick out his bonny gray een;
       We'll set our claws intil his yellow hair,
       And big our bowr, it's a' blawn bare.

   4. My mother clekit me o an egg,
       And brought me up i the feathers gray,
       And bade me flee whereer I wad,
       For winter wad be my dying day.

5. Now winter it is come and past,
    And a' the birds are biggin their nests,
    But I'll flee high aboon them a',
    And sing a sang for summer's sake.

c. 1.   As I gaed doun by yon hous-en,
            Twa corbies there were sittand their lane.

   2^1. O down beside yon new-faun birk.
   3^1. His horse.
   3^2. His hounds to bring the wild deer hame.
   4.   O we'll sit on his bonnie breist-bane,
            And we'll pyke out his bonnie grey een.

d. 1^1. walking forth. 1^2. the ither. 1^3. we twa dine.
   3^2. wild bird.
   5^2. naebody kens.
   5^3. when we've laid them bare. 5^4. win may blaw.

APPENDIX

It has already been noted that traditional copies of 'The Three Ravens' have been far from infrequent. When a ballad has been nearly three hundred years in print, and in a very impressive form, the chance that traditional copies, differing principally by what they lack, should be coeval and independent amounts at most to a bare possibility. Traditional copies have, however, sometimes been given in this collection on the ground of a very slight chance; and not unreasonably, I think, considering the scope of the undertaking.

The copy which follows was communicated by E. L. K. to *Notes and Queries*, Eighth Series, II, 437, 1892, and has been sent me lately in MS. by Mr R. Brimley Johnson, of Cambridge, England, with this note:

"From E. Peacock, Esq., F. S. A., of Dunstan House, Kirton-in-Lindsay, Lincolnshire, whose father, born in 1793, heard it as a boy at harvest-suppers and sheep-shearings, and took down a copy from the recitation of Harry Richard, a laborer, who could not read, and had learnt it 'from his fore-elders.' He lived at Northorpe, where a grass-field joining a little stream, called Ea, Ee, and Hay, is pointed out as the scene of the tragedy."

1 There was three ravens in a tree,
　As black as any jet could be.
　　A down a derry down

2 Says the middlemost raven to his mate,
　Where shall we go to get ought to eat?

3 'It's down in yonder grass-green field
　There lies a squire dead and killd.

4 'His horse all standing by his side,
　Thinking he'll get up and ride.

5 'His hounds all standing at his feet,
　Licking his wounds that run so deep.'

6 Then comes a lady, full of woe,
　As big wi bairn as she can go.

7 She lifted up his bloody head,
　And kissd his lips that were so red.

8 She laid her down all by his side,
　And for the love of him she died.

———◆———

6^2. *Var.* child.

27

THE WHUMMIL BORE

a. Motherwell's MS., p. 191. b. Motherwell's *Min-strelsy*, Appendix, p. xvi, No iii.

THIS ballad, if it ever were one, seems not to have been met with, or at least to have been thought worth notice, by anybody but Mother-well. As already observed in the preface to 'Hind Horn,' stanza 2 seems to have slipped into that ballad, in consequence of the resem-blance of stanza 1 to **F** 2, **H** 3 of 'Hind Horn.' This first stanza is, however, a commonplace in English and elsewhere: e.g., 'The Squire of Low Degree:'

He served the kyng, her father dere,
Fully the tyme of seven yere. vv 5, 6.

He loved her more then seven yere,
Yet was he of her love never the nere.
vv 17, 18.

Ritson, *Met. Rom.* iii, 145 f.

Prof. Wollner notes that this trait of serving the king long without sight of his daughter is rather frequently found in Slavic. For example, in Karadžič, II, 617, No 96, Yakšič Mitar serves the vojvode Yanko nine years and never sees his sister.

b. Motherwell, 1827. Collected by Andrew Blaikie, Paisley.

1 SEVEN lang years I hae served the king,
  Fa fa fa fa lilly
And I never got a sight of his daughter but ane.
  With my glimpy, glimpy, glimpy eedle,
  Lillum too tee a ta too a tee a ta a tally

2 I saw her thro a whummil bore,
  And I neer got a sight of her no more.

3 Twa was putting on her gown,
  And ten was putting pins therein.

4 Twa was putting on her shoon,
  And twa was buckling them again.

5 Five was combing down her hair,
  And I never got a sight of her nae mair.

6 Her neck and breast was like the snow,
  Then from the bore I was forced to go.

———◆———

a. 2^2. *Variation:* And she was washing in a pond.
   6^2. *Variation:* Ye might have tied me with a strae.

b. *Burden:* Fa, fa, falilly
   With my glimpy, glimpy, glimpy eedle,
   Lillum too a tee too a tally.

28

BURD ELLEN AND YOUNG TAMLANE

Maidment's *North Countrie Garland*, 1824, p. 21. Communicated by R. Pitcairn, "from the recitation of a female relative, who had heard it frequently sung in her childhood," about sixty years before the above date. In Pitcairn's MSS, III, 49, from the tradition of Mrs Gammel.

MOTHERWELL informs us, *Minstrelsy*, p. xciv of Introduction, note to 141, that 'Burd Helen and Young Tamlene' is very popular, and that various sets of it are to be found traditionally current (1827).

I cannot connect this fragment with what is elsewhere handed down concerning Tamlane, or with the story of any other ballad.

1 BURD ELLEN sits in her bower windowe,
   With a double laddy double, and for the double dow
 Twisting the red silk and the blue.
   With the double rose and the Machey

2 And whiles she twisted, and whiles she twan,
 And whiles the tears fell down amang.

3 Till once there by cam Young Tamlane:
 'Come light, O light, and rock your young son.'

4 'If you winna rock him, you may let him rair,
 For I hae rocked my share and mair.'
    *   *   *   *   *
5 Young Tamlane to the seas he's gane,
 And a' women's curse in his company's gane.

7

29

THE BOY AND THE MANTLE

Percy MS., p. 284. Hales & Furnivall, II, 304.

THIS ballad and the two which follow it are clearly not of the same rise, and not meant for the same ears, as those which go before. They would come down by professional rather than by domestic tradition, through minstrels rather than knitters and weavers. They suit the hall better than the bower, the tavern or public square better than the cottage, and would not go to the spinning-wheel at all. An exceedingly good piece of minstrelsy 'The Boy and the Mantle' is, too; much livelier than most of the numerous variations on the somewhat overhandled theme.[*]

Of these, as nearest related, the fabliau or "romance" of Le Mantel Mautaillié, 'Cort Mantel,' must be put first: Montaiglon et Raynaud, *Recueil Général des Fabliaux*, III, 1, from four manuscripts, three of the thirteenth century, one of the fourteenth; and previously by Michel, from the three older manuscripts, in Wolf, *Ueber die Lais*, p. 324. A rendering of the fabliau in prose, existing in a single manuscript, was several times printed in the sixteenth century: given in Legrand, ed. Renouard, I, 126, and before, somewhat modernized, by Caylus, 'Les Manteaux,' *Œuvres Badines*, VI, 435.[†]

The story in 'Cort Mantel' goes thus. Arthur was holding full court at Pentecost, never more splendidly. Not only kings, dukes, and counts were there, but the attendance of all young bachelors had been commanded, and he that had a *bele amie* was to bring her. The court assembled on Saturday, and on Sunday all the world went to church. After service the queen took the ladies to her apartments, till dinner should be ready. But it was Arthur's wont not to dine that day until he had had or heard-of some adventure;[‡] dinner was kept waiting; and it was therefore with great satisfaction that the [258] knights saw a handsome and courteous varlet arrive, who must certainly bring news; news that was not to be good to all, though some would be pleased (cf. stanza 5 of the ballad). A maid had sent him from a very distant country to ask a boon of the king. He was not to name the boon or the lady till he had had the king's promise; but what he asked was no harm. The king having said that he would grant what was asked, the varlet took from a bag a beautiful mantle, of fairy workmanship. This mantle would fit no dame or damsel who had in any way misbehaved towards husband or lover; it would be too short or too long; and the boon was that the king should require all the ladies of the court to put it on.

---

[*] After I had finished what I had to say in the way of introduction to this ballad, there appeared the study of the Trinkhorn- and Mantelsage, by Otto Warnatsch: *Der Mantel, Bruchstück eines Lanzeletromans, etc.*, Breslau, 1883. To this very thorough piece of work, in which the relations of the multiform versions of the double-branched story are investigated with a care that had never before been attempted, I naturally have frequent occasion to refer, and by its help I have supplied some of my deficiencies, indicating always the place by the author's name.

[†] The *Bibliothèque des Romans*, 1777, Février, pp. 112–115, gives an abstract of a small printed piece in prose, there assigned to the beginning of the sixteenth century, which, as Warnatsch observes, p. 72, must have been a different thing from the tale given by Legrand, inasmuch as it brings in Lancelot and Gawain as suppressing the jests of Kay and Dinadam.

The ladies were still waiting dinner, unconscious of what was coming. Gawain was sent to require their presence, and he simply told them that the magnificent mantle was to be given to the one it best fitted. The king repeated the assurance, and the queen, who wished much to win the mantle, was the first to try it on. It proved too short. Ywain suggested that a young lady who stood near the queen should try. This she readily did, and what was short before was shorter still. Kay, who had been making his comments unguardedly, now divulged the secret, and after that nobody cared to have to do with the mantle. The king said, We may as well give it back; but the varlet insisted on having the king's promise. There was general consternation and bad humor.

Kay called his mistress, and very confidently urged her to put on the mantle. She demurred, on the ground that she might give offence by forwardness; but this roused suspicion in Kay, and she had no resource but to go on. The mantle was again lamentably short. Bruns and Ydier let loose some gibes. Kay bade them wait; he had hopes for them. Gawain's *amie* next underwent the test, then Ywain's, then Perceval's. Still a sad disappointment. Many were the curses on the mantle that would fit nobody, and on him that brought it. Kay takes the unlucky ladies, one after the other, to sit with his mistress.

At this juncture Kay proposes that they shall have dinner, and continue the experiment by and by. The varlet is relentless; but Kay has the pleasure of seeing Ydier discomfited. And so they go on through the whole court, till the varlet says that he fears he shall be obliged to carry his mantle away with him. But first let the chambers be searched; some one may be in hiding who may save the credit of the court. The king orders a search, and they find one lady, not in hiding, but in her bed, because she is not well. Being told that she must come, she presents herself as soon as she can dress, greatly to the vexation of her lover, whose name is Carados Briebras. The varlet explains to her the quality of the mantle, and Carados, in verses very honorable to his heart, begs that she will not put it on if she has any misgivings.[*] The lady says very meekly that she dare not boast being better than other people, but, if it so please her lord, she will willingly don the mantle. This she does, and in sight of all the barons it is neither too short nor too long. "It was well we sent for her," says the varlet. "Lady, your lover ought to be delighted. I have carried this mantle to many courts, and of more than a thousand who have put it on you are the only one that has escaped disgrace. I give it to you, and well you deserve it." The king confirms the gift, and no one can gainsay.

A Norse prose translation of the French fabliau was executed by order of the Norwegian king, Hákon Hákonarson, whose reign covers the years 1217-63. Of this translation, 'Möttuls

---

‡ The custom of Arthur not to eat till he had heard of some adventure or strange news was confined to those days when he held full court, according to Perceval le Gallois, II, 217, 15,664-71, and the Roman de Perceval, fol. lxxviii. It is mentioned, with the same limitations, I suppose, in the Roman de Lancelot, III, fol. lxxxii, and we learn from this last romance, I, fol. xxxvi, that Arthur was accustomed to hold a court and wear his crown five times in the year, at Easter, Ascension-day, Pentecost, All Saints, and Christmas. The Roman de Merlin, II, lvi[b], or, as cited by Southey, II, 48, 49, says that "King Arthur, after his first dinner at Logres, when he brought home his bride, made a vow that while he wore a crown he never would seat himself at table till some adventure had occurred." In Malory's *King Arthur*, Kay reminds the king that this had been the old custom of his court at Pentecost. Arthur is said to observe this custom on Christmas, "vpon such a dere day," in Sir Gawayn and the Green Knight, Madden, p. 6, vv 90-99. Messire Gauvain says "à feste ne mangast, devant," etc., p. 2, vv 18-21. Wolfram von Eschenbach's Parzival does not limit the custom to high holidays, ed. Bartsch, I, 331, vv 875-79; and see Riddarasögur, Parcevals Saga, etc., ed. Kölbing, p. 26. Neither does Wigalois, vv 247-51, or a fragment of Daniel von Blühenthal, *Symbolæ ad literaturam Teutonicam*, p. 465, cited by Benecke, *Wigalois*, p. 436f, or the Färöe Galians kvæði, Kölbing, in *Germania*, XX, 397. See Madden's *Syr Gawayne*, which has furnished much of this note, pp 310-12; Southey's *King Arthur*, II, 203, 462. Robin Hood imitates Arthur: see the beginning of the Little Gest.

---

* 'Quar je vous aim tant bonement,
  Que je ne voudroie savoir
  Vostre mesfet por nul avoir.
  Miex en veuil je estre en doutance.
  Por tot le royaume de France,
  N'en voudroie je estre cert;
  Quar qui sa bone amie pert
  Molt a perdu, ce m'est avis.' 818-25.

Saga,' a fragment has come down which is as old as 1300; there are also portions of a manuscript which is assigned to about 1400, and two transcripts of this latter, made when it was com-
9] plete, besides other less important copies. This translation, which is reasonably close and was made from a good exemplar, has been most excellently edited by Messrs Cederschiöld and Wulff, *Versions nordiques du Fabliau Le Mantel Mautaillié,* Lund, 1877, p. 1.* It presents no divergences from the story as just given which are material here.

Not so with the 'Skikkju Rímur,' or Mantle Rhymes, an Icelandic composition of the fifteenth century, in three parts, embracing in all one hundred and eighty-five four-line stanzas: Cederschiöld and Wulff, p. 51. In these the story is told with additions, which occur partially in our ballad. The mantle is of white velvet. Three elf-women had been not less than fifteen years in weaving it, and it seemed both yellow and gray, green and black, red and blue: 11, 22, 23, 26. Our English minstrel describes these variations of color as occurring after Guenever had put the mantle on: stanzas 11, 12. Again, there are among the Pentecostal guests a king and queen of Dwarf Land; a beardless king of Small-Maids Land, with a queen eight years old; and a King Felix, three hundred years old, with a beard to the crotch, and a wife, tall and fat, to whom he has been two centuries married,—all these severally attended by generous retinues of pigmies, juveniles, and seniors: I, 28–35; III, 41. Felix is of course the prototype of the old knight pattering over a creed in stanzas 21–24 of the ballad, and he will have his representative in several other pieces presently to be spoken of. In the end Arthur sends all the ladies from his court in disgrace, and his knights to the wars; we will get better wives, he says: III, 74, 75.

The land of Small-Maids and the long-lived race are mentioned in a brief geographical chapter (the thirteenth) of that singular gallimaufry the saga of Samson the Fair, but not in

connection with a probation by the mantle, though this saga has appropriated portions of the story. Here the mantle is one which four fairies have worked at for eighteen years, as a penalty for stealing from the fleece of a very remarkable ram; and it is of this same fleece, described as being of all hues, gold, silk, *ok kolors,* that the mantle is woven. It would hold off from an unchaste woman and fall off from a thief. Quintalin, to ransom his life, undertakes to get the mantle for Samson. Its virtue is tried at two weddings, the second being Samson's; and on this last occasion Valentina, Samson's bride, is the only woman who can put it on. The mantle is given to Valentina, as in the fabliau to Carados's wife, but nevertheless we hear later of its being presented by Samson to another lady, who, a good while after, was robbed of the same by a pirate, and the mantle carried to Africa. From Africa it was sent to our Arthur by a lady named Elida, "and hence the saga of the mantle."† Björner, *Nordiska Kämpa Dater,* cc 12, 14, 15, 21, 22, 24.

There is also an incomplete German version of the fabliau, now credibly shown to be the work of Heinrich von dem Türlin, dating from the earliest years of the thirteenth century.‡ Though the author has dealt freely with his original, there are indications that this, like the [260] Möttulssaga, was founded upon some version of the fabliau which is not now extant. One of these is an agreement between vv 574–6 and the sixth stanza of our ballad. The mantle, in English, is enclosed between two nut-shells;§ in German, the bag from which it is taken is hardly a span wide. In the Möttulssaga, p. 9, l. 6, the mantle comes from a *púss,* a small bag hanging on the belt; in Ulrich von Zatzikhoven's Lanzelet, from ein mæzigez teschelîn, and in the latter case the mantle instantaneously expands to full size (Warnatsch); it is also of all colors known to man, vv 5807–19. Again, when Guenever had put on the mantle,

---

* See also Brynjúlfsson, *Saga af Tristram ok Ísönd, samt Möttuls Saga, Udtog,* pp 318–26, Copenhagen, 1878. There is a general presumption that the larger part of the works translated for King Hákon were derived from England. C. & W., p. 47.

† That is, the current one. The Samson saga professes to supply the earlier history. Samson's father is another Arthur, king of England. An abstract of so much of the saga as pertains to the Mantle is given by Cederschiöld and Wulff, p. 90f. Warnatsch, p. 73f, shows that the Rímur and Samson had probably a common source, independent of the Möttulssaga.

st. 10 of our ballad, "it was from the top to the toe as sheeres had itt shread." So in 'Der Mantel,' vv 732, 733:

Unde [= unten] het man in zerizzen,
Oder mit mezzern zesnitten.*

The Lanzelet of Ulrich von Zatzikhoven, dating from the first years of the thirteenth century, with peculiarities of detail and a partially new set of names, presents the outline of the same story. A sea-fairy sends a maid to Arthur with a magnificent gift, which is, however, conditioned upon his granting a boon. Arthur assents, and the maid takes, from a small bag which she wears at her girdle, a mantle, which is of all colors that man ever saw or heard of, and is worked with every manner of beast, fowl, and strange fish. The king's promise obliges him to make all the court ladies don the mantle, she to have it whom it perfectly fits. More than two hundred try, and there is no absolute fit.[†] But Iblis, Lanzelet's wife, is not present: she is languishing on account of his absence on a dangerous adventure. She is sent for, and by general agreement the mantle is, on her, the best-fitting garment woman ever wore. Ed. Hahn, vv 5746–6135.

---

‡ By Warnatsch, who gives the text with the corresponding passages of the fabliau in a parallel column, pp 8–54: the argument for Heinrich's authorship, pp 85–105. 'Der Mantel' had been previously printed in Haupt and Hoffmann's *Altdeutsche Blätter*, II, 27, and by Müllenhoff in his *Altdeutsche Sprachproben*, p. 125. Of this poem, which Warnatsch, pp 105–110, holds to be a fragment of a lost romance of Lanzelet, written before the 'Crône,' only 994 verses are left. Deducting about a hundred of introduction, there are some 782 German against some 314 French verses, an excess which is owing, no doubt, largely to insertions and expansions on the part of Heinrich, but in some measure to the existing texts of the fabliau having suffered abridgment. The whole matter of the church service, with the going and coming, is dispatched in less than a dozen verses in the French, but occupies more than seventy in German, and just here we read in the French:

Ci ne vueil je plus demorer,
Ni de noient fere lone conte,
Si con l'estoire le raconte.

But possibly the last verse should be taken with what follows.
§ In Hahn, *Griechische Märchen*, No 70, II, 60f, a walnut contains a dress with the earth and its flowers displayed on it, an almond one with the heaven and its stars, a hazel-nut one with the sea and its fishes. No 7, I, 99, a walnut contains a complete costume exhibiting heaven with its stars, a hazel-nut another with the sea and its waves. No 67, II, 33, an almond encloses a woman's dress with heaven and its stars on it, a hazel-nut a suit for her husband. In the Grimms' No 113, three walnuts contain successively each a finer dress than the other, II, 142f, ed. 1857. There are three similar nuts in Haltrich, No 43, and in *Volksmärchen aus Venetien, Jahrbuch für r. u. e. Lit.*, VII, 249, No 12. Ulrich's mantle is worked with all manner of beasts, birds, and sea monsters, on earth or under, and betwixt earth and heaven: Lanzelet, 5820–27.

---

* I cite the text according to Warnatsch. Warnatsch thinks it worth noticing that it is the queen only, in Mantel 771f, as in our ballad, st. 14, that curses the maker of the mantle; not, as in the fabliau, the gentlemen whose feelings were so much tried. These, like the queen in the ballad, ont maudit le mantel, et celui qui li aporta.

† Not even for Ginovere hübsch unde guot, or Enîte diu reine. The queen has always been heedful of her acts, and has never done anything wrong: doch ist siu an den gedenken missevarn, Heaven knows how. Ulrich is very feeble here.

A remark is here in place which will be still more applicable to some of the tests that are to be spoken of further on. Both the French fabliau and the English ballad give to the mantle the power of detecting the woman that has once done amiss, a de rien messerré. We naturally suppose that we understand what is meant. The trial in the fabliau is so conducted as to confirm our original conception of the nature of the inquest, and so it is, in the case of Arthur's queen, Kay's lady, and the old knight's wife, in the ballad. But when we come to the charmingly pretty passage about Cradock's wife, what are we to think? Is the mantle in a teasing mood, or is it exhibiting its real quality? If once to have kissed Cradock's mouth before marriage is once to have done amiss, Heaven keep our Mirandas and our Perditas, and Heaven forgive our Juliets and our Rosalinds! ("Les dames et demoiselles, pour être baisées devant leur noces, il n'est pas la coutume de France," we know, but this nice custom could hardly have had sway in England. Is then this passage rendered from something in French that is lost?) But the mantle, in the ballad, after indulging its humor or its captiousness for a moment, does Cradock's wife full justice. The mantle, if uncompromising as to acts, at least does not assume to bring thoughts under its jurisdiction. Many of the probations allow themselves this range, and as no definite idea is given of what is charged, no one need be shocked, or perhaps disturbed, by the number of convictions. The satire loses zest, and the moral effect is not improved.

The adventure of the Mantle is very briefly reported to Gawain, when on his way with Ydain to Arthur, by a youth who had just come from the court, in terms entirely according with the French fabliau, in Messire Gauvain, ou La Vengeance de Raguidel, by the trouvère Raoul, ed. Hippeau, p. 135ff, vv 3906–55, and in the Dutch Lancelot, ed. Jonckbloet, Part II, p. 85, vv 12,500–527, poems of the thirteenth century. The one lady whom the mantle fits is in the latter Carados vrindinne, in the other l'amie Caraduel Briefbras.

The Scalachronica, by Sir Thomas Gray of Heton, a chronicle of England and Scotland, 1066–1362, begun in 1355, gives the analysis of many romances, and that of the adventure of the Mantle in this form. There was sent to Arthur's court the mantle of Karodes, which was of such virtue that it would fit no woman who was not willing that her husband should know both her act and her thought.[*] This was the occasion of much mirth, for the mantle was either too short, or too long, or too tight, for all the ladies except Karodes' wife. And it was said that this mantle was sent by the father of Karodes, a magician, to prove the goodness of his son's wife.[†]

Two fifteenth-century German versions of the Mantle story give it a shape of their own. In Fastnachtspiele aus dem fünfzehnten Jahrhundert, II, 665, No 81, 'Der Luneten Mantel,' the amiable Lunet, so well and favorably known in romances, takes the place of the English boy

and French varlet. The story has the usual course. The mantle is unsuccessfully tried by Arthur's queen, by the wife of the Greek emperor, and by the queen of Lorraine. The king of Spain, who announces himself as the oldest man present, is willing to excuse his wife, who is the youngest of the royal ladies. She says, If we lack lands and gold, "so sei wir doch an eren reich," offers herself to the test with the fearlessness of innocence, and comes off clear, to the delight of her aged spouse. A meistergesang, Bruns, Beiträge zur kritischen Bearbeitung alter Handschriften, p. 143,[‡] 'Lanethen Mantel,' again awards the prize to the young wife of a very old knight. Laneth, a clean maid, who is Arthur's niece, having made herself poor by her bounty, is cast off by her uncle's wife and accused of loose behavior. She makes her trouble known to a dwarf, a good friend of her father's, and receives from him a mantle to take to Arthur's court: if anybody huffs her, she is to put it to use. The queen opens upon Laneth, as soon as she appears, with language not unlike that which she employs of Cradock's wife in stanzas 33, 34 of the ballad. The mantle is offered to any lady that it will fit. In front it comes to the queen's knee, and it drags on the ground behind. Three hundred and fifty knights' ladies fare as ill as the sovereign.[§]

The Dean of Lismore's collection of Gaelic poetry, made in the early part of the sixteenth century, contains a ballad, obscure in places, but clearly presenting the outlines of the English ballad or French fabliau.[**] Finn, Diarmaid, and four other heroes are drinking, with their six wives. The women take too much, and fall to boasting of their chastity. While they are so engaged, a maid approaches who is clad in a seamless robe of pure white. She sits down by Finn, and he asks her what is the virtue of the garment. She replies that her seamless robe will completely cover none but the spotless wife.

* Nul femme que [ne] vouloit lesser sauoir à soun marry soun fet et pensé. T. Wright, in Archæologia Cambrensis, January, 1863, p. 10. Mr Wright gives one of the texts of Cort Mantel, with an English translation. We are further told, in Scalachronica, that this mantle was afterwards made into a chasuble, and that it is "to this day" preserved at Glastonbury. Three versions of the fabliau testify that Carados and his amie deposited the mantle in a Welsh abbey. The Skikkju Rímur say that the lady presented it to the cloister of Cologne; the Möttulssaga says simply a monastery (and, indeed, the mantle, as described by some, must have had a vocation that way from the beginning). "Item, in the castel of Douer ye may see Gauwayn's skull and Cradok's mantel:" Caxton, in his preface to Kyng Arthur, 1485, I, ii, in Southey's ed.; cited by Michel, Tristan, II, 181, and from him by Warnatsch.
† For this enchanter see Le Livre de Karados in Perceval le Gallois, ed. Potvin, II, 118ff. It is not said in the printed copy that he sent the mantle [horn].

‡ Another copy, assigned to the end of the 14th century, from the Kolmar MS., Bartsch, p. 373, No LXIX (Warnatsch).
§ Warnatsch shows, p. 75f, that the fastnachtspiel must have been made up in part from some version of the Mantle story which was also the source of the meisterlied, and in part from a meisterlied of the Horn, which will be mentioned further on.

Conan, a sort of Kay, says, Give it to my wife at once, that we may learn the truth of what they [262] have been saying. The robe shrinks into folds, and Conan is so angry that he seizes his spear and kills his wife.* Diarmaid's wife tries, and the robe clings about her hair; Oscar's, and it does not reach to her middle; Maighinis, Finn's wife, and it folds around her ears. MacRea's wife only is completely covered. The 'daughter of Deirg,' certainly a wife of Finn, and here seemingly to be identified with Maighinis, claims the robe: she has done nothing to be ashamed of; she has erred only with Finn. Finn curses her and womankind, "because of her who came that day."

The probation by the Horn runs parallel with that by the Mantle, with which it is combined in the English ballad. Whether this or that is the anterior creation it is not possible to say, though the 'Lai du Corn' is, beyond question, as Ferdinand Wolf held, of a more original

---

** The Dean of Lismore's Book, edited by Rev. Thomas M'Lauchan, p. 72 of the translation, ⁵⁹/₅₁ of the original. Repeated in Campbell's *Heroic Gaelic Ballads*, p. 138f, 'The Maid of the White Mantle.' Mr Campbell remarks: "This ballad, or the story of it, is known in Irish writings, it is not remembered in Scotland now." Mr Wright cites this poem, *Archæologia Cambrensis*, p. 14f, 39f. See the elaborate article by Professor Ludw, Chr. Stern, Die gälische Ballade vom Mantel in *Macgregors Liederbuche*, *Zeitschrift für celtische Philologie*, I, 294ff. The text is given according to the edition of Alexander Cameron, *Reliquiae Celticae*, I, 76, with another copy from a 1628 MS. in the Franciscan Convent at Dublin. Stern's translation clears up some points, and brings out one striking similarity between the Gaelic and the English ballad. When MacReith's wife tried on the mantle, "er passte ihr, beides an Fuss und Hand, bis auf die Gabel ihrer kleinen Finger und Zehen." She explains this failure of the mantel to cover her completely: "'Einen Kuss bekam ich verstohlen von O'Duibhnes Sohne Diarmaid; der Mantel würde bis auf den Boden reichen, wenn es nicht der allein wäre.'" Compare sts 28–30 of 'The Boy and the Mantle.' This similarity, in a feature unknown to other versions of the story, coupled with the form 'Craddocke' in the English ballad (a form which "nur aus dem welschen Caradawc entstanden sein kann") convinces Stern that 'The Boy and the Mantle,' and probably also the Gaelic ballad, are derived directly from Welsh tradition, independently of the Old French versions, which, however, he thinks also go back ultimately to Wales (p. 310). I am indebted to Dr F. N. Robinson for calling my attention to Stern's article. (G.L.K.)
* Cf. Arthur in the Lai du Corn and Fraw Tristerat Horn, a little further on.

stamp, fresher and more in the popular vein than the fabliau of the Mantle, as we have it.† The 'Lai du Corn,' preserved in a single not very early manuscript (Digby 86, Bodleian Library, "of the second half of the thirteenth or beginning of the fourteenth century"), may well belong, where Wolf puts it, in the middle of the twelfth. Robert Bikez, the jongleur who composed it, attributes the first authorship to "Garadue," the hero, and says that he himself derived the story from the oral communication of an abbé. Arthur has assembled thirty thousand knights at a feast at Pentecost, and each of them is paired with a lady. Before dinner there arrives a donzel, with an ivory horn adorned with four gold bands and rich jewels. This horn has been sent Arthur by Mangounz, king of Moraine. The youth is told to take his place before the king, who promises to knight him after dinner and give him a handsome present the next day; but he laughingly excuses himself, on the ground that it is not proper for a squire to eat at a knight's table, and retires. Arthur sees that there is an inscription on the horn, and desires that his "chapelein" may read it. Everybody is eager to hear, but some repent afterwards. The horn was made by a fairy, who endued it with this quality, that no man should drink of it without spilling, if his wife had not been true in act and thought. Even the queen hung her head, and so did all the barons that had wives. The maids jested, and looked at their lovers with "Now we shall see." Arthur

---

† Wolf at first speaks of the lai as being made over into the fabliau, in regular court style, ganz nach höfischer Weise, about the middle of the 13th century; then goes on to say that even if the author of the fabliau followed another version of the story, he must have known the jongleur's poem, because he has repeated some of the introductory lines of the lai. This excellent scholar happened, for once, not to observe that the first fourteen lines of the lai, excepting the fourth, which is questionable, are in a longer metre than the rest of the poem, in eights and sevens, not sixes, and the first three of the lai, which agree with the first three of the fabliau, in the eight-syllable verse of the latter; so that it was not the author of the fabliau that borrowed. Warnatsch (who has also made this last remark) has noted other agreements between lai and fabliau, p. 61. Both of these acknowledge their derivation from an earlier *dit, estoire*, not having which we shall find it hard to determine by which and from what the borrowing was done.

was offended, but ordered Kay to fill. The king drank and spilled; seized a knife, and was about to strike the queen, but was withheld by his knights. Gawain gallantly came to the queen's vindication. "Be not such a churl," he said, "for there is no married woman but has her foolish thought." The queen demanded an ordeal by fire: if a hair of her were burned, she would be torn by horses. She confessed that the horn was in so far right that she had once given a ring to a youth who had killed a giant that had accused Gawain of treason, etc. She thought this youth would be a desirable addition to the court. Arthur was not convinced: he would make everybody try the horn now, king, duke, and count, for he would not be the only one to be shamed. Eleven kings, thirty counts, all who essay, spill: they are very angry, and bid the devil take him who brought and him who sent the horn. When Arthur saw this, he began to laugh: he regarded the horn as a great present, he said, and he would part with it to nobody except the man that could drink out of it. The queen blushed so prettily that he kissed her three times, and asked her pardon for his bad humor. The queen said, Let everybody take the horn, small and great. There was a knight who was the happiest man in all the court, the least a braggart, the most mannerly, and the most redoubtable after Gawain. His name was Garadue, and he had a wife, *mout leal*, who was a fairy for beauty, and surpassed by none but the queen. Garadue looked at her. She did not change color. "Drink," she said; "indeed, you are at fault to hesitate." She would never have husband but him: for a woman should be a dove, and accept no second mate. Garadue was naturally very much pleased: he sprang to his feet, took the horn, and, crying Wassail! to the king, drank out every drop. Arthur presented him with Cirencester, and, for his wife's sake, with the horn, which was exhibited there on great days.

The romance of Perceval le Gallois, by Chrestien de Troyes and others (second half of the twelfth century), describes Arthur, like the fabliau, as putting off dinner till he should hear of some strange news or adventure. A knight rides into the hall, with an ivory horn, gold-banded and richly jewelled, hanging from his

neck, and presents it to the king. Have it filled with pure water, says the bearer, and the water will turn to the best wine in the world, enough for all who are present. "A rich present!" exclaims Kay. But no knight whose wife or love has betrayed him shall drink without spilling. "Or empire vostre présens," says Kay. The king has the horn filled, and does not heed Guenever, who begs him not to drink, for it is some enchantment, to shame honest folk. "Then I pray God," says the queen, "that if you try to drink you may be wet." The king essays to drink, and Guenever has her prayer. Kay has the same luck, and all the knights,[*] till the horn comes to Carados (Brisié-Bras). Carados, as in the lai, hesitates; his wife (Guinon, Guimer) looks at him, and says, Drink! He spills not a drop. Guenever and many a dame hate nothing so much as her. Perceval le Gallois, ed. Potvin, II, 216ff, vv 15,640–767.[†]

The story of 'Le Livre de Carados,' in Perceval, is given in abridgment by the author of Le Roman du Renard contrefait, writing in the second half of the fourteenth century: Tarbé, *Poètes de Champagne antérieurs au siècle de François I*[er], Histoire de Quarados Brun-Bras, p. 79ff. The horn here becomes a cup.

A meistergesang, entitled 'Dis ist Frauw Tristerat Horn von Saphoien,' and found in the same fifteenth-century manuscript as Der Lanethen Mantel, Bruns, as before, p. 139, preserves many features of the lai. While Arthur is at table with seven other kings and their wives, a damsel comes, bringing an ivory horn, with gold letters about the rim, a present from Frau Tristerat of Savoy. The king sends for a clerk to read the inscription, and declares he will begin the experiment. The damsel prudently retires. Arthur is thoroughly wet, and on the point of striking the queen, but is prevented by a knight. The seven kings then take the horn, one after the other. Six of them fare like Arthur. The king of Spain looks at his wife, fearing shame. She encourages him to drink, saying, as in the

---

[*]   Montpellier MS.

[†]   Perceval exhibits agreements, both as to phrase and matter, now with the lai, now with the fabliau, and this phenomenon will occur again and again. This suggests the likelihood of a source which combined traits of both lai and fabliau: Warnatsch, pp 62–64.

other meistergesang, If we are poor in goods, we are rich in honor. Arthur presents him with the horn, and adds cities and lands. Another copy of this piece was printed by Zingerle, in *Germania*, V, 101, 'Das goldene Horn.' The queen is aus der Syrenen lant.[*]

A fastnachtspiel gives substantially the same form to the story: Keller, *Nachlese*, No 127, p. 183. Arthur invites seven kings and queens to his court. His wife wishes him to ask his sister, the Queen of Cyprus, also; but she has offended him, and he cannot be prevailed upon to do it. The Queen of Cyprus sends the horn to Arthur [264] by her maid as a gift from a queen who is to be nameless, and in fulfilling her charge the messenger describes her lady simply as a sea princess. The inscription is read aloud by one of Arthur's knights. The King of Spain carries off the honors, and receives in gift, besides the horn, a ducal crown, and gold to boot. Arthur resolves that the horn shall be forgotten, and no grudge borne against the women, and proposes a dance, which he leads off with his wife.[†]

We have Arthur joining in a dance under nearly the same circumstances in an English "bowrd" found in a MS. of about the middle of the fifteenth century (Ashmolean Museum, No

61) The king has a bugle horn, which always stands before him, and often amuses himself by experimenting with it. Those who cannot drink without spilling are set at a table by themselves, with willow garlands on their heads, and served with the best. Upon the occasion of a visit from the Duke of Gloucester, the king, wishing to entertain his guest with an exhibition of the property of the horn, says he will try all who are present. He begins himself, as he was wont to do, but this time spills. He takes the mishap merrily, and says he may now join in a dance which the "freyry" were to have after meat. 'The Cokwolds Daunce,' Hartshorne's *Ancient Metrical Tales*, p. 209; Karajan, *Frühlingsgabe* [Schatzgräber], p. 17; Hazlitt, *Remains of Early Popular Poetry*, I, 38.[‡]

Heinrich von dem Türlîn narrates the episode of the probation by the Horn with variations of his own, among them the important one of subjecting the women to the test as well as the men.[§] In his Crône, put at 1200–10, a misshapen, dwarfish knight, whose skin is overgrown with scales, riding on a monster who is fish before and dolphin behind, with wings on its legs, presents himself to Arthur on Christmas Day as an envoy from a sea king, who offers the British monarch a gift on condition of his first granting a boon. The gift is a cup, made by a necromancer of Toledo, of which no man or woman can drink who has been false to love, and it is to be the king's if there shall be anybody at the court who can stand the test. The ladies are sent for, and the messenger gives the cup first to them. They all spill. The knights follow, Arthur first; and he, to the general astonishment, bears the proof, which no one else does except the sea king's messenger. Caraduz[**] von Caz fails with the rest. Diu Crône, ed. Scholl, vv 466–3189.

---

[*]   So amended by Zingerle from Syrneyer lant. A third copy is cited as in the Kolmar MS., No 806, Bartsch, *Meisterlieder der Kolmarer Handschrift*, p. 74 (Warnatsch). A remarkable agreement between the French lai, 94, 97, 99–102, and Wigamur 2623–30 convinces Warnatsch that the source of this meisterlied must have been a Middle High German rendering of some form of the Drinking-horn Test closely resembling the lai. See Warnatsch, p. 66.

[†]   The king of *Spain*, who is again the poorest of all the kings, p. 206, line 32, p. 214, line 22, is addressed by Arthur as his nephew, p. 207, line 11, and p. 193, line 30. Carados is called Arthur's nephew in Perceval (he is son of Arthur's niece), e.g. 15,782, and Carados, his father, is Carados de *Vaigne*, II, 117. It is said of Kalegras's *amie* in the 'Mantle Rhymes,' III, 59, that many a lady looked down upon her. This may be a chance expression, or possibly point to the poverty which is attributed to the royal pair of Spain in *Fastnachtspiele*, Nos 81, 127, and in Frau Tristerat Horn. In Der Lanethen Mantel, Laneth is Arthur's niece, and poor: see p. 361.

The fastnachtspiel has points in common with the fabliau, and the assumption of a source which combined features of both lai and fabliau is warrantable: Warnatsch, pp 66–68.

[‡]   This is a thoroughly dissolute piece, but not ambiguous. It is also the most humorous of the whole series.

[§]   Warnatsch shows that Heinrich cannot have derived any part of his Trinkhornprobe from the Perceval of Chrestien, characteristic agreements with Perceval being entirely wanting. There are agreements with the lai, many more with the fabliau; and Heinrich's poem, so far as it is not of his own invention, he believes to be compounded from his own version of the fabliau and some lost version of the Horntest: pp 111–114.

The prose Tristan confines the proof to the women, and transfers the scene to King Mark's court. Morgan the Fay having sent the enchanted horn to Arthur's court by the hands of a damsel, to avenge herself on Guenever, two knights who had a spite against Mark and Tristan intercept it, and cause the horn to be taken to King Mark, who is informed that no lady that has been false to her lord can drink of it without spilling. Yseult spills, and the king says she deserves to die. But, fortunately or unfortunately, all the rest of the ladies save four are found to be in the same plight as the queen. The courtiers, resolved to make the best of a bad matter, declare that they have no confidence in the probation, and the king consents to treat the horn as a deception, and acquits his wife.*

Ariosto has introduced the magical vessel made by Morgan the Fay for Arthur's behoof† into Orlando Furioso. A gentleman tries it on his guests for ten years, and they all spill but Rinaldo, who declines il periglioso saggio: canto XLII, 70–73, 97–104; XLIII, 6–44. Upon Ariosto's narrative La Fontaine founded the tale and the comedy of 'La Coupe Enchantée,' Works ed. Moland, IV, 37, V, 361.

In a piece in the Wunderhorn, I, 389, ed. 1819, called 'Die Ausgleichung,' and purporting to be from oral tradition, but reading like an imitation, or at most a reconstruction, of a meistergesang, the cup and mantle are made to operate conjointly: the former to convict a king and his knights, the other a queen and her ladies, of unfaithfulness in love. Only the youngest of the ladies can wear the mantle, and only the oldest of the knights, to whom she is espoused, can drink from the cup. This knight, on being presented with the cup, turns into a dwarf; the lady, on receiving the gift of the mantle, into a fay. They pour a drop of wine from the cup upon the mantle, and give the mantle to the queen, and the cup, empty, to the king. After this, the king and all the world can drink without inconvenience, and the mantle fits every woman. But the stain on the mantle grows bigger every year, and the cup gives out a hollow sound like tin! An allegory, we may suppose, and, so far as it is intelligible, of the weakest sort.

Tegau Eurvron is spoken of in Welsh triads as one of the three chaste ladies, and again as one of the three fair ladies, of Arthur's court.‡ She is called the wife of Caradawc Vreichvras by various Welsh writers, and by her surname of "Gold-breasted" she should be so.§ If we may trust the author of The Welsh Bards, Tegau was the possessor of three treasures or rarities "which befitted none but herself," a mantle, a

---

** The principal variations of this name, of which the Welsh Caradoc assumed to be the original, are: Craddocke (English ballad) Carados, Cradox (Cort Mantel); Karodes (Scalachronica) Caraduz (Crône, 2309, elsewhere) Karadas; Carigras, Kaligras (Rímur); Karodeus, Caraduel (Perceval, 12,466, 12,457, 12,491, but generally), Carados, -ot, or; Caraduel (Messire Gauvain, 3943); Garadue (Lai du Corn); Karadin (Möttuls Saga). Garadue probably = Caraduel, which, in Percival twice, and once in Messire Gauvain, is used for Carados, through confusion with Arthur's residence, Carduel, Cardoil. So Karadas is twice put in the Crône, 16,726, 16,743, for Karidol = Cardoil. Might not Karadin have been written for Karadiu?

* Tristan of Hélie de Borron, I, 73 verso, in Rajna, Fonti dell' Orlando Furioso, p. 498ff. So in Malory's King Arthur, Southey, I, 297, Wright, II, 64. The Italian Tristan, La Tavola Ritonda, ed. Polidori, XLIII, pp 157–160, makes 686 try, of whom only 13 prove to be innocent, and those in spite of themselves. Another account exempts 2 out of 365: Nannucci, Manuale, II, 168–171.

† Un vasello fatto da ber, qual già, per fare accorto il suo fratello del fallo di Ginevra, fe Morgana: XLIII, 28; un bel nappo d'or, di fuor di gemme, XLII, 98. The Orlando concurs with the prose Tristan as to the malice of Morgan, but does not, with the Tristan, depart from prescription in making the women drink. Warnatsch observes that the Orlando agrees with the Horn Fastnachtspiel, and may with it follow some lost version of the story: p. 69.

Before leaving these drinking-tests, mention may be made of Oberon's gold cup, which, upon his passing his right hand three times round it and making the sign of the cross, fills with wine enough for all the living and the dead; but no one an drink s'il n'est preudom, et nes et purs et sans pecié mortel: Huon de Bordeaux, ed. Guessard et Grandmaison, p. 109f, vv 3652–60.

‡ The Myvyrian Archæology of Wales, II, 13, triad 54 = triad 103, p. 73; p. 17, triad 78 = triad 108, p. 73.

§ See the story in Le Livre de Carados, Perceval le Gallois, Potvin, especially II, 214–16, vv 15,577–638. "The Rev. Evan Evans," says Percy, Reliques, III, 349, ed. 1794, "affirmed that the story of the Boy and the Mantle is taken from what is related in some of the old Welsh MSS of Tegan Earfron, one of King Arthur's mistresses." This aspersion, which is even absurd, must have arisen from a misunderstanding on the part of the Bishop: no Welshman could so err.

goblet, and a knife. The mantle is mentioned in a triad, [*] and is referred to as having the variable hue attributed to it in our ballad and elsewhere. There are three things, says the triad, of which no man knows the color; the peacock's expanded tail, the mantle of Tegau Eurvron, and the miser's pence. Of this mantle, Jones, in whose list of "Thirteen Rarities of Kingly Regalia" of the Island of Britain it stands eleventh, says, No one could put it on who had dishonored marriage, nor a young damsel who had committed incontinence; but it would cover a chaste woman from top to toe: *Welsh Bards,* II, 49. The mantle certainly seems to be identified by what is said of its color in the (not very ancient) triad, and so must have the property attributed to it by Jones, but one would be glad to have had Jones cite chapter and verse for his description.

[266]

There is a drinking-horn among the Thirteen Precious Things of the Island of Britain, which, like the conjurer's bottle of our day, will furnish any liquor that is called for, and a knife which will serve four-and-twenty men at meat "all at once." How this horn and this knife should befit none but the chaste and lovely Tegau, it is not easy to comprehend. Meanwhile the horn and the knife are not the property of Cradock's wife, in the English ballad: the horn falls to Cradock of right, and the knife was his from the beginning. Instead of Tegau's mantle we have in another account a mantle of Arthur, which is the familiar cloak that allows the wearer to see everything without himself being seen. Not much light, therefore, but rather considerable mist, comes from these Welsh traditions, of very uncertain date and significance. It may be that somebody who had heard of the three Welsh rarities, and of the mantle and horn as being two of them, supposed that the knife must have similar virtues with the horn and mantle, whence its appearance in our ballad; but no proof has yet been given that the

Welsh horn and knife had ever a power of testing chastity. [†]

Heinrich von dem Türlin, not satisfied with testing Arthur's court first with the mantle, and again with the horn, renews the experiment with a Glove, in a couple of thousand lines more of tedious imitation of 'Cort Mantel,' [‡] Crône, 22,990–24,719. This glove renders the right side of the body invisible, when put on by man or woman free of blame, but leaves in the other case some portion of that side visible and bare. A great many ladies and knights don the glove, and all have reason to regret the trial except Arthur and Gawain. [§]

There is another German imitation of the fabliau of the mantle, in the form (1) of farce of the fifteenth century and (2) of meistergesang printed in the sixteenth. In these there is substituted for the mantle a Crown that exposes the infidelity of husbands.

---

[*]   *Myvyrian Archæology,* III, 247[a], No 10, pointed out to me by Professor Evans. The story of the 'Boy and the Mantle,' says Warton, "is recorded in many manuscript Welsh chronicles, as I learn from original letters of Llwyd, in the Ashmolean Museum:" *History of English Poetry,* ed. 1871, I, 97, note 1.

[†]   The horn is No 4 in Jones's list, and No 3 in a manuscript of Justice Bosanquet; the knife is 13th in Jones and 6th in the other; the mantle of invisibility is 13th in the Bosanquet series, and, under the title of Arthur's veil or mask, 1st in Jones. The mantle of Tegau Eurvron does not occur in the Bosanquet MS. Jones says, "The original Welsh account of the above regalia was transcribed from a transcript of Mr Edward Llwyd, the antiquary, who informs me that he copied it from an old parchment MS. I have collated this with two other MSS." Not a word of dates. Jones's *Welsh Bards,* II, 47–49; Lady Charlotte Guest's *Mabinogion,* III, 353–55.

Lady Charlotte Guest remarks that a boar's head in some form appears as the armorial bearing of all of Caradawc's name. Though most anxious to believe all that is said of Caradawc, I am compelled to doubt whether this goes far to prove that he owned the knife celebrated in the ballad.

[‡]   Heinrich seeks to put his wearisome invention off on Chrestien de Troyes. Warnatsch argues with force against any authorship but Heinrich's, pp 116ff.

[§]   Gawain had failed in the earlier trial, though he had no fault in mind or body, except that he rated his favor with women too high: 1996–2000.

In the first two probations a false heart is the corpus delicti; something is said of carnal offences, but not very distinctly.

The scope of the glove is of the widest. It takes cognizance of *rede und gedanc* in maids, *werc und gedanc* in wives, *tugent und manheit, unzuht und zageheit,* in men. One must have known as little what one was convicted of as if one had been in the hands of the Holy Office.

1. "Das Vasnachtspil mit der Kron."[*] A "master" has been sent to Arthur's court with a rich crown, which the King of Abian wishes to present to whichever king or lord it shall fit, and it will fit only those who have not "lost their honor." The King of Orient begins the trial, very much against his will: the crown turns to ram's horns. The King of Cyprus is obliged to follow, though he says the devil is in the crown: the crown hangs about his neck. Appeals are made to Arthur that the trial may now stop, so that the knights may devote themselves to the object for which they had come together, the service and honor of the ladies. But here Lanet, Arthur's sister (so she is styled), interposes, and expresses a hope that no honors are intended the queen, for she is not worthy of them, having broken her faith. Arthur is very angry, and says that Lanet has by her injurious language forfeited all her lands, and shall be expelled from court. (Cf. Der Lanethen Mantel, p. 361.) A knight begs the king to desist, for he who heeds every tale that is told of his wife shall never be easy.

2. The meistergesang 'Die Krone der Königin von Afion.'[†] While his majesty of Afion is holding a great feast, a youth enters the hall bearing a splendid crown, which has such chaste things in it that no king can wear it who haunts false love. The crown had been secretly made by order of the queen. The king wishes to buy the crown at any price, but the youth informs him that it is to be given free to the man who can wear it. The king asks the favor of being the first to try the crown: when put on his head it falls down to his back. The King of Portugal is eager to be next: the crown falls upon his shoulder. The King of Holland at first refuses to put on the crown, for there was magic in it, and it was only meant to shame them: but he is obliged to yield, and the crown goes to his girdle. The King of Cyprus offers himself to the

adventure: the crown falls to his loins. And so with eleven. But there was a "Young Philips," King of England, who thought he might carry off the prize. His wife was gray and old and ugly, and quite willing, on this account, to overlook e bisserle Falschheit, and told him that he might spare himself. But he would not be prevented; so they put the crown on him, and it fitted to a hair. This makes an edifying pendant to 'Der Luneten Mantel,' p. 361.

Still another imitation is the Magical Bridge in the younger Titurel which Klingsor throws over the Sibra. Knights and ladies assembled at Arthur's court, if less than perfect,[‡] on attempting to ride over it are thrown off into the water, or stumble and fall on the bridge: ed. Hahn, p. 232ff, st. 2337ff. Hans Sachs has told this story twice, with Virgil for the magician: ed. Keller, *Historia, König Artus mit der ehbrecher-brugk*, II, 262; Goedeke, *Dichtungen von Hans Sachs*, I, 175. Kirchhof follows Hans Sachs in a story in *Wendunmuth*, ed. Österley, II, 38.

Florimel's Girdle, in the fourth book of the 'Fairy Queen,' canto v, once more, is formed on the same pattern.[§]

There might be further included in imitations of the horn or mantle test several other inventions which are clearly, as to form, modelled on this original, but which have a different object: the valley from which no false lover could escape till it had been entered by one "qui de nulle chose auroit vers s'amie fausé ne mespris, nè d'euvre nè de pensée nè de talent," the prose Lancelot in Jonckbloet, II, lxix (Warnatsch), Ferrario, *Storia ed Analisi, Lancilotto del*

---

[*] *Fastnachtspiele aus dem fünfzehnten Jahrhundert*, Zweiter Theil, p. 654, No 80.

[†] From Vulpius's *Curiositäten*, II, 463, in Erlach, I, 132, after a printed copy of the beginning of the 16th century: Wolff, *Halle der Völker*, II, 243, from a Fliegendes Blatt of the 16th century. Two copies are cited by title in Mone's *Anzeiger*, VIII, 354 b, No 1; 378, No 165. Wolff prints Asion.

[‡] A man must be "clear as beryl." One of the knights is tumbled into the water for having kissed a lady; but this is according to the code, for he had done it without leave. We learn from Perceval that kissing is permissible; marry, not without the lady be willing. 'Die bruck zu Karidol' is alluded to in 'Der Spiegel,' Meister Altswert, ed. Holland u. Keller, p. 179, vv 10–13. (Goedeke.) A man who has transferred his devotion from an earlier love to the image of a lady shown him in a mirror says the bridge would have thrown him over.

[§] Florimel's girdle is a poor contrivance every way, and most of all for practical purposes; for we are told in stanza 3 that it *gives* the virtue of chaste love to all who wear it, and then that whosoever contrary doth prove cannot keep it on. But what could one expect from a cast-off girdle of Venus?

Lago, III, 372, Legrand, Fabliaux, I, 156; the arch in Amadis, which no man or woman can pass who has been unfaithful to a first love, and again, the sword which only the knight who loves his lady best can draw, and the partly withered garland which becomes completely fresh on the head of the lady who best loves her husband or lover, Amadís de Gaula, l. ii, introduccion, c. 1, c. 14, and ballad 1890 in Duran, II, 665; the cup of congealed tears in Palmerin of England, which liquefies in the hand of the best knight and faithfulest lover, chapters 87–89, II, 322ff, ed. of London, 1807.

[268]   Besides those which have been spoken of, not a few other criterions of chastity occur in romantic tales.

Bed clothes and bed. 'Gil Brenton,' **A, B**; the corresponding Swedish ballad, **A, B, E**; Danish, Grundtvig, No 275: [*] see pp 91 f of this volume.

A **stepping-stone** by the bed-side. 'Vesle Aase Gaasepige,' Asbjørnsen og Moe, No 29: see p. 93.

A **chair** in which no leal maiden can sit, or will sit till bidden (?). 'Gil Brenton,' **D, C**.

Flowers [foliage]. 1. In the Sanskrit story of Guhasena, the merchant's son, and Devasmitá, this married pair, who are to be separated for a time, receive from Shiva each a **red lotus**: if either should be unfaithful, the lotus in the hand of the other would fade, but not otherwise: Kathā sarit sāgara, ch. 13, Tawney, I, 86, Brockhaus, I, 137. 2. In the Tales of a Parrot, a soldier, going into service, receives from his wife a **rose** [flower, nosegay, garland], which will keep fresh as long as she remains true: Rosen, Tuti-nameh, from the Turkish version, I, 109; Wickerhauser, also from the Turkish, p. 57; Iken, p. 30,[†] from the Persian of Kadiri; Kathá Sarit Ságara, Tawney's translation, II, 601. 3. So

---

the knight Margon in the French romance of Perceforest, vol. IV, ch. 16 and 17. 4. In a Turkish tale found in a manuscript collection called 'Joy after Sorrow,' an architect or housewright, having to leave home for want of employment, is presented by his wife with a bunch of evergreen of the same property. 5. An English story of a wright reverts to the rose. A widow, having nothing else to give with her daughter, presents the bridegroom with a rose-garland, which will hold its hue while his wife is "stable:" 'The Wright's Chaste Wife,' by Adam of Cobsam, from a manuscript of about 1462, ed. Furnivall. 6. On going to war a king gives each of his two daughters a rose. "Si vous tombez en faute, quoi que ce soit," says he, "vos roses flétriont." Both princesses yield to the solicitations of their lovers, so that the king, on returning, finds both roses withered, and is grieved thereat. Vinson, Folk-Lore du Pays Basque, p. 102.[‡]

A **shirt** [mantle]. 1. In connection with the same incidents there is substituted for the unfading flower, in Gesta Romanorum, 69, a shirt. This a knight's wife gives to a carpenter or housewright who has married her daughter, and it will not need washing, will not tear, wear, or change color, as long as both husband and wife are faithful, but will lose all is its virtues if either is untrue. The shirt given by a wife to a husband in several versions of an otherwise different story. 2. In the German meistergesang and the Flemish tale Alexander of Metz: Körner, Historische Volkslieder, p. 49, No 8; Goedeke, Deutsche Dichtung im Mittelalter, 2d ed., p. 569ff; 'De Historia van Florentina,' etc., Van den Bergh, De nederlandsche Volksromans, p. 52f. 3. In the story 'Von dem König von Spanien[§] und seiner Frau,' Müllenhoff, Sagen, u. s. w., p. 586, No 607, a wife gives the shirt to her husband the morning after the wedding: it will always be white until she dies, when it will turn black, or unless she misbehaves, in which case it will be spotted. 4. 'Die getreue Frau,'

---

[*]   Nightingales in Grundtvig, No 274, **A, B**: see p. 91. See, also, Uhland, Zur Geschichte der Dichtung, III, 121 f.

[†]   Neither the Sanskrit Shukasaptati nor Nakshabi's Persian version, made early in the fourteenth century, has been published. The Turkish version is said to have been made in the second half of the next century, for Bajazet II. Kadiri's is probably of the seventeenth century. An English and Persian version (Kadiri's), 1801, has the tale at p. 43; Small's English, from a Hindustani version of Kadiri, 1875, at p. 40.

[‡]   In the Contes à rire, p. 89, a sylph who loves a prince gives him a flower and a vase which will blacken upon his wife's proving unfaithful: Legrand, 1779, I, 78. I have not seen this edition of the book, but presume that this tale is entirely akin with the above.

[§]   Cf. the King of Spain, at pp. 361, 363. The agreement may, or may not, be accidental.

Plönnies, in Wolf's *Zeitschrift für deutsche Mythologie*, II, 377. An English princess gives her consort, a Spanish prince, at parting, a white shirt which will not spot as long as she is faithful. 5. 'Die treue Frau,' Curtze, *Volksüberlieferungen aus Waldeck*, p. 146. A merchant's son, married to a princess, goes away for a voyage; they change rings and shirts, and neither shirt will soil until one of the two shall be untrue. 6. 'Die getreue Frau,' J. W. Wolf, *Deutsche Hausmärchen*, at p. 102. A prince, going on a voyage, gives his sword to his wife; as long as the blade is not spotted, he is faithful. He receives from the princess a mantle; as long as it is white, her faith is inviolate.

A **picture**. For the rose, as in Perceforest, there is substituted, in a story otherwise essentially the same, a picture. A knight, compelled to leave his wife, receives from a magician a picture of her, small enough to carry in a box about his person, which will turn yellow if she is tempted, pale if she wavers, black if she yields, but will otherwise preserve its fresh hues: Bandello, Part I, nov. 21. This tale, translated in Painter's *Palace of Pleasure*, 1567 (ed. Haslewood, II, 471, nov. 28), furnished the plot for Massinger's 'Picture,' 1630. The miniature will keep its color as long as the woman is innocent and unattempted, will grow yellow if she is solicited but unconquered, and black if she surrenders: Act I, Scene 1. Bandello's story is also the foundation of Sénecé's tale, 'Filer le parfait amour,' with a wax image taking the place of the picture: *Œuvres Choisies*, ed. Charles et Cap, p. 95.*

A **ring**. The picture is exchanged for a ring in a French tale derived, and in parts almost translated, from Bandello's: the sixth in 'Les Faveurs et les Disgraces de l'Amour,' etc., said to have appeared in 1696.† A white stone set in the ring may become yellow or black under circumstances. Such a ring Rimnild gave Horn Child: when the stone should grow wan, her

thoughts would have changed; should it grow red, she is no more a maid: see p. 264. A father, being required to leave three daughters, gives them each such a ring in Basile, *Pentamerone*, III, 4. The rings are changed into glass distaffs in 'L'Adroite Princesse,' an imitation of this story by Mlle. Lhéritier de Villaudon, which has sometimes been printed with Perrault's tales: Perrault, *Contes des Fées*, ed. Giraud, p. 239; Dunlop, ch. 13.‡

A **mirror**, in the History of Prince Zeyn Alasnam, reflecting the image of a chaste maid, will remain unblurred: *Arabian Nights*, Scott, IV, 120, 124; *1001 Nacht*, Habicht, VI, 146, 150; etc. Virgil made a mirror of like property; it exposed the woman that was "new-fangle," *wandelmüetic*, by the ignition of a "worm" in the glass: *Meisterlieder der Kolmarer Handschrift*, Bartsch, p. 605 (Warnatsch). There is also one of these mirrors in Primaleon, l. ii, cap. 27; Rajna, *Le Fonti dell' Orlando Furioso*, p. 504, note 3. Alfred de Musset, in 'Barberine,' substitutes a pocket-mirror for the picture in Bandello, Part I, nov. 21: *Œuvres Complètes*, III, 378ff.

A **harp**, in the hands of an image, upon the approach of a *despucellée*, plays out of tune and breaks a string: Perceval le Gallois, II, 149, vv 13,365–72 (Rajna, as above).

A **chessboard** in the *English Prose Merlin*, ed. Wheatley, ch. 21, vol. i, part II, p. 363, can be "mated" only by one that has never been false in love: (G. L. K.)

A crystal **brook**, in the amiral's garden in Flor and Blancheflor, when crossed by a virgin remains pellucid, but in the other case becomes red, or turbid: ed. Du Méril, p. 75, vv 1811–14; Bekker, *Berlin Academy*, XLIV, 26, vv 2069–72; Fleck, ed. Sommer, p. 148, vv 4472–82; Swedish, ed. Klemming, p. 38, 1122–25; Lower

---

* All these examples of the probation by flowers, shirt, or picture are noticed in Loiseleur Deslongchamps, *Essai sur les fables indiennes*, p. 107ff; or in Von der Hagen's *Gesammtabenteuer*, III, lxxxiv ff; or in an article by Reinhold Köhler, of his usual excellence, in *Jahrbuch für romanische und englische Literatur*, VIII, 44ff.

† Köhler, as above, p. 60f.

‡ "The jacinth stone will not be worne on the finger of an adulterer, nor the olive grow if planted by one that leadeth his life in unlawful lusts." Greene, Never too late, Pt. II, 1590, *Works*, ed. Grosart, VIII, 141. A note on the general subject in G. Rua, *Novelle del "Mambriano,"* pp. 66f, 73–83. G. L. K. [See also Zupitza, Herrig's *Archiv f. das Studium der neueren Sprachen*, LXXXII, 201; Nyrop, *Dania*, I, 13, n. 2; Feilberg, *Dania*, I, 154; 'La Mensuration du Cou,' Perdrizet and Gaidoz, *Mélusine*, VI, 225ff.]

Rhine, Haupt's *Zeitschrift*, XXI, 321, vv 57–62; Middle Greek, Bekker, *Berlin Academy*, 1845, p. 165, Wagner, *Mediæval Greek Texts*, p. 40f, vv 1339–48; English, ed. Hausknecht, 1885, p. 189, vv 715–20; etc.* In the English poem, Hartshorne's *Ancient Metrical Tales*, p. 93, if a clean maid wash her hands in the water, it remains quiet and clear; but if one who has lost her purity do this, the water will yell like mad and become red as blood.

A **spring** in Apollonius Heinrichs von Neustadt blackens the hand of the more serious offender, but in a milder case only the ring-finger, "der die geringste Befleckung, nicht erträgt." W. Grimm's *Kleinere Schriften*, III, 446. (C. R. Lanman.)

The **stone** Aptor, in Wigamur, vv 1100–21, is red to the sight of clean man or woman, but misty to others: Von der Hagen und Büsching, *Deutsche Gedichte des Mittelalters*, p. 12 (Warnatsch).†

[270] A **statue**, in an Italian ballad, moved its eyes when young women who had sacrificed their honor were presented to it: Ferraro, *Canti popolari di Ferrara, Cento e Pontelagoscuro*, p. 84, 'Il Conte Cagnolino.' There was said to be a statue of Venus in Constantinople which could not be approached by an incontinent woman without a very shameful exposure; and again, a pillar surmounted by four horns, which turned round three times if any κερατᾶς came up to it.‡ Virgil, 'Filius,' made a brass statue which no misbehaving woman might touch, and a vicious one

received violent blows from it: *Meisterlieder der Kolmarer Handschrift*, Bartsch, p. 604, 14th century. This statue would bite off the fingers of an adulteress if they were put in its mouth, according to a poem of the same century published by Bartsch in *Germania*, IV, 237; and a third version makes the statue do this to *all* perjurers, agreeing in other respects with the second: *Kolmarer Meisterlieder*, as before, p. 338. In the two last the offence of the wife causes a horn to grow out of the husband's forehead. Much of the story in these poems is derived from the fifteenth tale of the Shukasaptati, where a woman offers to pass between the legs of a statue of a Yaksha, which only an innocent one can do: Benfey, *Pantschatantra*, I, 457; R. Schmidt's translation, p. 29f.§

---

* The chaste Sítá clears herself of unjust suspicion by passing safely over a certain lake: *Kathā sarit sāgara*, Tawney's translation, I, 486f.

† There is a stone in the Danish Vigoleis with the Gold Wheel which no one could approach "who was not as clean as when he came from his mother's body." Gawain could touch it with his hand, Arthur often sat upon it, and Vigoleis was found sitting on it. Nyerup, *Almindelig Morskabslæsning i Danmark og Norge*, p. 129, a chap-book of 1732. The stone is not quite so strict in the German *Volksbuch*, Marbach, No 18, p. 13f, Simrock, III, 432f. In the German romance no man less than immaculate in all respects can touch it: *Wigalois*, ed. Benecke, p. 57, vv 1485–88.

See also the Magnet, *Orpheus de Lapidibus*, Leipsic, 1764, Hamberger, p. 318, translated by Evax, *De Gemmis*, cap. 25; and the Agate, "Albertus Magnus, *De Mineralibus*, l. II, sect. ii, c. 7:" cited by Du Méril, *Floire et Blanceflor*, p. clxvi. (G. L. K.)

‡ Georgii Codini Excerpta de antiquitatibus Constantinopolitanis, in *Corpus Scriptorum Historiæ Byzantinæ*, XLV, 50f, cited by Liebrecht, *Germania*, I, 264; De Originibus Constantinopolitanis, cited by Lütcke, Von der Hagen's *Germania*, I, 152, referred to by Liebrecht: both anecdotes in Banduri, *Imperium Orientale, Anonymus de Ant. Const.* p. 35, 96, p. 57, 162. The statue again in a note of Nic. Alemannus to Procopius, *Arcana*, 1623, p. 83: cited by Mr Wright, *Archæologia Cambrensis*, as above, p. 17. Mr Wright also makes mention, p. 16, of the blind dog that quidam Andreas (evidently a merry one) was exhibiting in the seventeenth year of Justinian, which, among other clever performances, ostendebat in utero habentes et fornicarios et adulteros et avaros et magnanimos—omnes cum veritate: *Historia Miscella*, Eyssenhardt, p. 377f, l. 18, c. 23; Cedrenus, in the *Byzantine Corpus*, XXXIII, 657, Theophanes, in XXXVIII, 347f.

§ The *Meisterlieder* and the Indian tale are cited by Warnatsch. Virgil's statue was circumvented by an artifice which is employed in this tale of the Shukasaptati, and in other oriental stories presumably derived from it; and so was the well-known Bocca della Verità, *Kaiserchronik*, Massmann, pp 448f. The Bocca della Verità bit off the fingers of perjurers, but took no particular cognizance of the unchaste. In the English 'Virgilius' it is a brass serpent with the same property: Thoms, *A Collection of Early Prose Romances*, II, p. 34 of Virgilius, ed. 1827: cited by Sir Walter Scott, 'Sir Tristrem,' p. 432, ed. 1833, apropos of the trick of the shameless Ysonde. (G. L. K.) A barleycorn [grain of wheat], again, which stood on end when *any* false oath was sworn over it, Jülg, *Mongolische Märchensammlung, Die Geschichte des Ardschi-Bordschi Chan*, pp 250–52, cited by Benfey, *Pantschatantra*, I, 458, and referred to by Warnatsch, does not belong with special tests of chastity.

There is a **shield** in Perceval le Gallois which no knight can wear with safety in a tournament if he is not all that a knight should be, and if he has not, also, "bele amie qui soit loiaus sans trecerie." Several of Arthur's knights try the shield with disastrous results; Perceval is more fortunate. (See 31805–31, 31865, 32023–48, 32410ff, Potvin, IV, 45ff.)

According to a popular belief in Austria, says J. Grimm, you may know a clean maid by her being able to blow out a **candle** with one puff and to light it again with another. The phrase was known in Spain: "Matar un candil con un soplo y encenderlo con otro."[*] Grimm adds that it is an article of popular faith in India that a virgin can make a ball of **water**, or carry water in a sieve: *Rechtsalterthümer*, p. 932; Grimm, *Deutsche Mythologie*, p. 931, ed. 1876. "Ebenso trägt die indische Mariatale, so lang ihre Gedanken rein sind, ohne Gefäss das zu Kugeln geballte Wasser:" *Kinderund Hausmärchen*, III, 264, 9, ed. 1856. See Benfey, *Orient und Occident*, I, 719ff, II, 97. (F. Liebrecht.) For the Mariatale story (from P. Sonnerat, *Voyage aux Indes Orientales, etc.*), see 'Paria,' in *Goethes lyrische Gedichte*, erläutert von H. Düntzer, II, 449ff, ed. 1875.

The carrying of water in a sieve is also found in Valerius Maximus, viii, 1, 5: Eodem auxilii genere, Tucciae virginis Vestalis, incesti criminis reae, castitas infamiae nube obscurata emersit. Quae conscientia certae sinceritatis suae spem salutis ancipiti argumento ausa petere est. Arrepto enim cribro, 'Vesta,' inquit, 'si sacris tuis castas semper admovi manus, effice ut hoc hauriam. e Tiberi aquam et in aedem tuam perferam.' Audaciter et temere iactis votis sacerdotis rerum ipsa natura cessit. Cf. also Pliny, *Hist. Nat.*, xxviii, 2 (3), and the commentators.

---

[*] The phrase looks more malicious than *naïf*, whether Austrian or Spanish, and implies, I fear, an exsufflicate and blown surmise about female virtue; and so of the Indian 'Volksglaube.' The candle-test is said to be in use for men in Silesia: Warnatsch, citing Weinhold, p. 58.

Similarly, Wer ein ausgelöschtes Licht wieder anblasen kann ist noch Jungfrau oder Junggeselle. Wer ein ganz volles Glas zum. Munde führen kann, ohne einen Tropfen su verschütten, ist Junggeselle. Zingerle, *Sitten der Tiroler*, p. 35.

If a girl takes a pot of boiling water off the fire, and the pot ceases to boil, this is a sign of lost modesty. Lammert, *Volksmedizin und medizinischer Aberglaube in Bayern, u. s. w.*, p. 146.

A stunned white **elephant** will be resusciated if touched by the hand of a chaste woman. A king's eighty thousand wives, and subsequently all the women in his capital, touch the elephant without effect. A serving-woman, devoted to her husband, touches the elephant, and it rises in sound health and begins to eat. *Kathā sarit sāgara*, Book VII, ch. 36, Tawney's translation, p. 329f: H. H. Wilson's *Essays*, II, 129f. ("In the 115th Tale of the *Gesta Romanorum*, we read that two chaste virgins were able to lull to sleep and kill an elephant that no one else could approach." Tawney's note.) (C. R. Lanman.)

An ordeal for chastity is a feature in several of the Greek romances. In Heliodorus's *Æthiopica*, x, 8, 9, victims to be offered to the sun and moon, who must be pure, are obliged to mount a **brazier** covered with a golden grating. The soles of those who are less than perfect are burned. Theagenes and Chariclea experience no inconvenience. The *Clitophon and Leucippe* of Achilles Tatius, VIII, 6, 13, 14, has a **cave** in the grove of Diana of Ephesus, in which they shut up a woman. If it is a virgin, a delicious melody is presently heard from a syrinx, the doors open of themselves, and the woman comes out crowned with pine leaves; if not a virgin, a wail is heard, and the woman is never seen again. There is also a not perfectly convincing trial, by the Stygian **water**, in § 12, which seems to be imitated in the *Hysmine and Hysminias* of Eustathius [Eumathius], VIII, 7, XI, 17. In the temple of Diana, at Artycomis, stands a statue of the goddess, with bow in hand, and from about her feet flows water like a roaring river. A woman, crowned with laurel, being put in, she will float quietly, if all is right; but should she not have kept her allegiance to Dian, the goddess bends her bow as if to shoot at her head, which causes the culprit to duck, and the water carries off her wreath.[†]

The **dragon** kept by the priests of Lanuvian Juno ate honey-cakes from the hands of pure maids who went down into its cave, but twined round the unchaste and bit them: Aelian, *Hist.*

An., XI, 6, Propertius, IV (v), 8. See Die Jung-
fernprobe in der Drachenhöhle zu Lanuvium, C.
A. Böttiger's *Kleine Schriften*, I, 178ff. (G. L. K.)

[271]   It is prescribed in Numbers V, 11–31, that
any man jealous of his wife may bring her to the
priest, who shall, with and after various ceremo-
nies, give her a bitter drink of holy water in
which dust from the floor of the tabernacle has
been infused. If she have trespassed, her body
shall swell and rot. In the Pseudo-Matthew's
Gospel, ch. xii, Joseph and Mary successively
take this aquam potationis domini.* No pre-
tender to innocence could taste this and then
make seven turns round the altar, without some
sign of sin appearing in the face. The experi-
ment shows both to be faultless. So, with some
variation, the sixteenth chapter of the Prote-
vangelium of James. This trial is the subject of
one of the *Coventry Mysteries*, No 14, p. 137ff,
ed. Halliwell, and no doubt of other scripture
plays. It is naturally introduced into Wernher's
Maria, Hoffmann, *Fundgruben*, II, 188, line 26ff,
and probably into other lives of the Virgin.

There was a (qualified) test of priestesses of
Ge at Ægæ by drinking bull's blood, according
to Pausanias, VIII, xxv, 8; cited by H. C. Lea,
Superstition and Force, 3d ed., 1878, p. 236f.
(G.L.K.)

Herodotus relates, II, 111, that Pheron, son
of Sesostris, after a blindness of ten years' dura-
tion, received an intimation from an oracle
that he would recover his sight upon following
a certain prescription, such as we are assured is
still thought well of in Egypt in cases of oph-
thalmia. For this the coöperation of a chaste
woman was indispensable. Repeatedly balked,
the king finally regained his vision, and collect-
ing in a town many women of whom he had
vainly hoped aid, in which number his queen
was included, he set fire to the place and
burned both it and them, and then married the
woman to whom he was so much indebted.
(First cited in the *Gentleman's Magazine*, 1795,
vol. 65, I, 114.) The coincidence with forego-
ing tales is certainly curious, but to all appear-
ance accidental.[†]

The 'Boy and the Mantle' was printed "ver-
batim" from his manuscript by Percy in the *Rel-
iques*, III, 3, ed. 1765. The copy at p. 314 is of
course the same "revised and altered" by Percy,
but has been sometimes mistaken for an inde-
pendent one.

Translated by Herder, I, 219; Bodmer, I, 18;
Bothe, p. 59.

---

† These are all noted in Liebrecht's *Dunlop*, pp 11, 16,
33. The spring, says the author of *Hysmine*, served as
good a purpose for Artycomis as the Rhine did for the
Celts; referring to a test of the legitimacy of children by
swinging or dipping them in the Rhine, which the
"Celts" practiced, according to a poem in the *Anthology*:
Jacobs, II, 42f, No 125; Grimm, *Deutsche
Rechtsalterthümer*, p. 935 (Warnatsch).
* See, also, Konrad von Fussesbrunnen, Die Kindheit
Jesu, ed. Kochendörffer, *Quellen u. Forschungen*, XLIII, p.
81f, vv 573–88, 617–21, 673ff. (G.L.K.)

† Besides sources specially referred to, there may be
mentioned, as particularly useful for the history of these
tests. Legrand, *Fabliaux*, 1779, I, 60, 76–78; Dunlop's *His-
tory of Fiction*, 1814, in many places, with Liebrecht's
notes, 1851; Grässe, *Sagenkreise*, 1842, pp 185–87; Von
der Hagen's *Gesammtabenteuer*, 1850, III, lxxxiv–xc,
cxxxv f.

On the Herodotean story, see E. Lefébure, *Mélusine*,
IV, 37–39.—St Wilfred's Needle, in Ripon Minster. 'In
ipso templo, avorum memoria Wilfridi acus celeberrima
fuit. Id erat augustum in cryptoporticu foramen quo
mulierum pudicitia explorabatur; quæ enim castæ erant
facile transibant, quæ dubia fama nescio quo miraculo
constrictæ detinebantur.' Camden, *Britannia*, ed. 1607, p.
570; see *Folk-Lore Journal*, II, 286. (G. L. K.)

Percy MS., p. 284: Hales and Furnivall, II, 304.

1 IN the third day of May
   to Carleile did come
A kind curteous child,
   that cold much of wisdome.

2 A kirtle and a mantle
   this child had vppon,
With brauches and ringes
   full richelye bedone.

3 He had a sute of silke,
   about his middle drawne;
Without he cold of curtesye,
   he thought itt much shame.

4 'God speed thee, King Arthur,
   sitting att thy meate!
And the goodly Queene Gueneuer!
   I canott her fforgett.

5 'I tell you lords in this hall,
   I hett you all heede,
Except you be the more surer,
   is you for to dread.'

6 He plucked out of his potewer,
   and longer wold not dwell,
He pulled forth a pretty mantle,
   betweene two nut-shells.

7 'Haue thou here, King Arthure,
   haue thou heere of mee;
Giue itt to thy comely queene,
   shapen as itt is alreadye.

8 'Itt shall neuer become that wiffe
   that hath once done amisse:'
Then euery knight in the kings court
   began to care for his.

9 Forth came dame Gueneuer,
   to the mantle shee her bed;
The ladye shee was new-fangle,
   but yett shee was affrayd.

10 When shee had taken the mantle,
   shee stoode as she had beene madd;
It was from the top to the toe
   as sheeres had itt shread.

11 One while was itt gaule,
   another while was itt greene;
Another while was itt wadded;
   ill itt did her beseeme.

12 Another while was it blacke,
   and bore the worst hue;
'By my troth,' quoth King Arthur,
   'I thinke thou be not true.'

13 Shee threw downe the mantle,
   that bright was of blee,
Fast with a rudd redd
   to her chamber can shee flee.

14 Shee curst the weauer and the walker
   that clothe that had wrought,
And bade a vengeance on his crowne
   that hither hath itt brought.

15 'I had rather be in a wood,
   vnder a greene tree,
Then in King Arthurs court
   shamed for to bee.'

16 Kay called forth his ladye,
   and bade her come neere;
Saies, 'Madam, and thou be guiltye,
   I pray thee hold thee there.'

17 Forth came his ladye
   shortlye and anon,
Boldlye to the mantle
   then is shee gone.

18 When she had tane the mantle,
   and cast it her about,
Then was shee bare
   all aboue the buttocckes.

19 Then euery knight
   that was in the kings court
Talked, laughed, and showted,
   full oft att that sport.

20 Shee threw downe the mantle,
   that bright was of blee,
Ffast with a red rudd
   to her chamber can shee flee.

21 Forth came an old knight,
   pattering ore a creede,
   And he proferred to this little boy
   twenty markes to his meede,

22 And all the time of the Christmasse
   willinglye to ffeede;
   For why, this mantle might
   doe his wiffe some need.

23 When shee had tane the mantle,
   of cloth that was made,
   Shee had no more left on her
   but a tassell and a threed:
   Then euery knight in the kings court
   bade euill might shee speed.

24 Shee threw downe the mantle,
   that bright was of blee,
   And fast with a redd rudd
   to her chamber can shee flee.

25 Craddocke called forth his ladye,
   and bade her come in;
   Saith, 'Winne this mantle, ladye,
   with a litle dinne.

26 'Winne this mantle, ladye,
   and it shalbe thine
   If thou neuer did amisse
   since thou wast mine.'

27 Forth came Craddockes ladye
   shortlye and anon,
   But boldlye to the mantle
   then is shee gone.

[273] 28 When shee had tane the mantle,
   and cast itt her about,
   Vpp att her great toe
   itt began to crinkle and crowt;
   Shee said, 'Bowe downe, mantle,
   and shame me not for nought.

29 'Once I did amisse,
   I tell you certainlye,
   When I kist Craddockes mouth
   vnder a greene tree,
   When I kist Craddockes mouth
   before he marryed mee.'

30 When shee had her shreeuen,
   and her sines shee had tolde,
   The mantle stoode about her
   right as shee wold;

31 Seemelye of coulour,
   glittering like gold
   Then euery knight in Arthurs court
   did her behold.

32 Then spake dame Gueneuer
   to Arthur our king:
   'She hath tane yonder mantle,
   not with wright but with wronge!

33 'See you not yonder woman
   that maketh her selfe soe clene
   I haue seene tane out of her bedd
   of men fiueteene;

34 'Preists, clarkes, and wedded men,
   from her by-deene;
   Yett shee taketh the mantle,
   and maketh her-selfe cleane!'

35 Then spake the litle boy
   that kept the mantle in hold;
   Sayes 'King, chasten thy wiffe;
   of her words shee is to bold.

36 'Shee is a bitch and a witch,
   and a whore bold;
   King, in thine owne hall
   thou art a cuchold.'

37 The litle boy stoode
   looking ouer a dore;
   He was ware of a wyld bore,
   wold haue werryed a man.

38 He pulld forth a wood kniffe,
   fast thither that he ran;
   He brought in the bores head,
   and quitted him like a man.

39 He brought in the bores head,
   and was wonderous bold;
   He said there was neuer a cucholds kniffe
   carue itt that cold.

40 Some rubbed their kniues
    vppon a whetstone;
Some threw them vnder the table,
    and said they had none.

41 King Arthur and the child
    stood looking them vpon;
All their kniues edges
    turned backe againe.

42 Craddoccke had a litle kniue
    of iron and of steele;
He birtled the bores head
    wonderous weele,
That euery knight in the kings court
    had a morssell.

43 The litle boy had a horne,
    of red gold that ronge;
He said, 'there was noe cuckolde
    shall drinke of my horne,
But he shold itt sheede,
    either behind or beforne.'

44 Some shedd on their shoulder,
    and some on their knee;
He that cold not hitt his mouth
    put it in his eye;
And he that was a cuckold,
    euery man might him see.

45 Craddoccke wan the horne
    and the bores head;
His ladye wan the mantle
    vnto her meede;
Euerye such a lonely ladye,
    God send her well to speede!

4] & is printed and, wherever it occurs.
2^3. MS. might be read branches.
5^2. all heate. 6^4. 2 nut-shells.
8^4. his wiffe.
9^2. biled. "Query the le in the MS." Furnivall.
18^4. Perhaps the last word was originally tout, as Mr
    T. Wright has suggested.
19^3. lauged. 21^4. 20 markes.
22^2. willinglye.

33^2. MS. perhaps has cleare altered to clene.
33^4. fiueteeene.
37^1. A litle.
37^2. Perhaps, as Percy suggested, two lines have
    dropped out after this, and the two which follow
    belong with the next stanza.
40^1, 41^3. kiues.
41^1. Arthus.
44^2. sone on.

30

KING ARTHUR AND KING CORNWALL

Percy MS., p. 24. Hales & Furnivall, I, 61; Madden's
Syr Gawayne, p. 275.

THE mutilation of the earlier pages of the Percy manuscript leaves us in possession of only one half of this ballad, and that half in eight fragments, so that even the outline of the story cannot be fully made out.[*] We have, to be sure, the whole of a French poem which must be regarded as the probable source of the ballad, and, in view of the recklessness of the destroyer Time, may take comfort; for there are few things in this kind that the Middle Ages have bequeathed which we could not better spare. But the losses from the English ballad are still very regrettable, since from what is in our hands we can see that the story was treated in an original way, and so much so that comparison does not stead us materially.

'King Arthur and King Cornwall' is apparently an imitation, or a traditional variation, of Charlemagne's Journey to Jerusalem and Constantinople, a *chanson de geste* of complete individuality and of remarkable interest.[†] This all but incomparable relic exists in only a single manuscript,[‡] and that ill written and not older than the end of the thirteenth century, while the poem itself may be assigned to the beginning of the twelfth, if not to the latter part of the eleventh.[§] Subsequently, the story, with modifications, was introduced into the romance of Galien, and in this setting it occurs in three forms, two manuscript of the fifteenth century, and the third a printed edition of the date 1500. These are all in prose, but betray by metrical remains imbedded in them their descent from a romance in verse, which there are reasons for putting at least as early as the beginning of the fourteenth century.[**]

[†]   That this ballad is a traditional variation of Charlemagne's Journey to Jerusalem and Constantinople, was, I am convinced, too hastily said. See M. Gaston Paris's remarks at p. 110f. of his paper, Les romans en vers du cycle de la Table Ronde (Extrait du tome xxx de *l'Histoire Littéraire de la France*). The king who thinks himself best king in the world, etc., occurs (it is Arthur) also in the romance of Rigomer: the same, p. 92.

[‡]   British Museum (but now missing), King's Library, 16, E, VIII, fol. 131, recto: "Ci comence le liuere cumment charels de fraunce voiet in ierhusalem Et par parols sa feme a constantinnoble pur vere roy hugon." First published by Michel, London, 1836, and lately reëdited, with due care, by Koschwitz: *Karls des Grossen Reise nach Jerusalem and Constantinopel*, Heilbronn, 1880; 2d ed., 1883.

[§]   See the argument of Gaston Paris, *Romania*, IX, 7ff; and of Koschwitz, *Karl des Grossen Reise*, 2te Auflage, Einleitung, pp. xiv–xxxii.

[**]   Printed by Koschwitz in *Sechs Bearbeitungen von Karls des Grossen Reise*, the last from a somewhat later edition, pp. 40–133. In the view of Gaston Paris, the Pilgrimage was made over (renouvelé) at the end of the twelfth or the beginning of the thirteenth century, and this *rifacimento* intercalated in Galien by some rhymer of the fourteenth. See his 'Galien,' in *Hist. Litt. de la France*, XXVIII, 221–239, for all that concerns the subject.

A Galien in verse has been found in the library of Sir Thomas Phillipps, at Cheltenham. *Romania*, XII, 5.

---

[*]   Half a page is gone in the manuscript between 'Robin Hood's Death' and the beginning of this ballad, and again between the end of this ballad and the beginning of 'Sir Lionel.' 'Robin Hood's Death,' judging by another copy, is complete within two or three stanzas, and 'Sir Lionel' appears to lack nothing. We may suppose that quite half a dozen stanzas are lost from both the beginning and the end of 'King Arthur and King Cornwall.'

A very little of the story, and this little *75]* much changed, is found in Italian romances of Charles's Journey to Spain and of Ogier the Dane. The derivation from Galien is patent.[*]

The Journey of Charlemagne achieved great popularity, as it needs must. It forms a section of the Karlamagnus Saga, a prose translation into Norse of *gestes* of Charles and his peers, made in the thirteenth century, and probably for King Hákon the Old, though this is not expressly said, as in the case of the 'Mantle.' Through the Norwegian version the story of Charles's journey passed into the other Scandinavian dialects. There is a Swedish version, slightly defective, existing in a manuscript earlier than 1450, and known to be older than the manuscript, and a Danish abridgment, thought to have been made from the Swedish version, is preserved in a manuscript dated 1480, which again is probably derived from an elder. Like the 'Mantle,' the Journey of Charlemagne is treated in Icelandic Rímur, the oldest manuscript being put at about 1500. These Rhymes (Geiplur, Gabs, Japes), though their basis is the Norwegian Saga, present variations from the existing manuscripts of this saga. There is also a Färöe traditional ballad upon this theme, 'Geipa-táttur.' This ballad has much that is peculiar to itself.[†]

Charlemagne's Journey was also turned into Welsh in the thirteenth century. Three versions are known, of which the best is in the Red Book of Hergest.[‡]

Let us now see what is narrated in the French poem.

One day when Charlemagne was at St Denis he had put on his crown and sword, and his wife had on a most beautiful crown, too. Charles took her by the hand, under an olive-tree, and asked her if she had ever seen a king to whom crown and sword were so becoming. The empress was so unwise as to reply that pos-sibly he thought too well of himself: she knew of a king who appeared to even better advantage when he wore his crown. Charles angrily demanded where this king was to be found: they would wear their crowns together, and if the French sided with her, well; but if she had not spoken truth, he would cut off her head. The empress endeavored to explain away what she had said: the other king was simply richer, but not so good a knight, etc. Charles bade her name him, on her head. There being no escape, the empress said she had heard much of Hugo, the emperor of Greece and Constantinople. "By my faith," said Charles, "you have made me angry and lost my love, and are in a fair way to lose your head, too. I will never rest till I have seen this king."

The emperor, having made his offering at St *[276]* Denis, returned to Paris, taking with him his twelve peers and some thousand of knights. To

---

[*] *Il Viaggio di Carlo Magno in Ispagna,* pubblicato per cure di Antonio Ceruti, C. LI, II, 170: Rajna, Uggeri il Danese nella letteratura romanzesca degl' Italiani, *Romania,* IV, 414ff. A king of Portugal, of the faith of Apollo and Mahound, takes the place of the king of Constantinople in the former, and one Saracen or another in the several versions of the second. G. Paris, in *Romania,* IX, 3, 10, notes.

[†] The Norwegian version in *Karlamagnus Saga ok Kappa hans,* ed. Unger, p. 466, the Seventh Part. Both the Swedish and Danish are given in Storm's *Sagnkredsene om Karl den Store, etc.,* Kristiania, 1874, pp. 228–245. For the sources, see p. 160ff. The whole of the Danish Chronicle of Charlemagne is printed in Brandt's *Romantisk Digtning fra Middelalderen,* Copenhagen, 1877, the Journey to the Holy Land, p. 146ff. Brandt does not admit that the Danish chronicle was translated from Swedish: p. 347. The 'Geiplur,' 968 vv, and one version of 'Geipa-táttur,' 340 vv, are included in Koschwitz's *Sechs Bearbeitungen,* p. 139ff, p. 174ff. For a discussion of them see Kölbing in *Germania,* XX, 233–239, and as to the relations of the several versions, etc., Koschwitz, in *Romanische Studien,* II, 1ff, his *Ueberlieferung und Sprache der Chanson du Voyage de Charlemagne,* and *Sechs Bearbeitungen,* Einleitung. The Färöe ballad is thought to show traces in some places of Christiern Pedersen's edition of the Danish chronicle, 1534 (Kölbing, as above, 238, 239), or of stall prints founded on that. This does not, however, necessarily put the ballad into the sixteenth century. Might not Pedersen have had ballad authority for such changes and additions as he made? It may well be supposed that he had, and if what is peculiar to Pedersen may have come from ballads, we must hesitate to derive the ballads from Pedersen. It is, moreover, neither strange nor unexampled that popular ballads should be affected by tradition committed to print as well as by tradition still floating in memory. The Färöe copies of 'Greve Genselin,' for example, as Grundtvig remarks, I, 223, note, though undoubtedly original and independent of Danish, evince acquaintance with Vedel's printed text.

[‡] Given, with an English translation by Professor Rhys, in *Sechs Bearbeitungen,* p. 1, p. 19.

these he announced that they were to accompany him to Jerusalem, to adore the cross and the sepulchre, and that he would incidentally look up a king that he had heard of. They were to take with them seven hundred camels, laden with gold and silver, and be prepared for an absence of seven years.

Charlemagne gave his people a handsome equipment, but not of arms. They left behind them their lances and swords, and took the pilgrim's staff and scrip. When they came to a great plain it appeared that the number was not less than eighty thousand: but we do not have to drag this host through the story, which concerns itself only with Charles and his peers. They arrived at Jerusalem one fine day, selected their inns, and went to the minster. Here Jesus and his apostles had sung mass, and the chairs which they had occupied were still there. Charles seated himself in the middle one, his peers on either side. A Jew came in, and, seeing Charles, fell to trembling; so fierce was the countenance of the emperor that he dared not look at it, but fled from the church to the patriarch, and begged to be baptized, for God himself and the twelve apostles were come. The patriarch went to the church, in procession, with his clergy. Charles rose and made a profound salutation, the priest and the monarch embraced, and the patriarch inquired who it was that had assumed to enter that church as he had done. "Charles is my name," was the answer. "Twelve kings have I conquered, and I am seeking a thirteenth whom I have heard of. I have come to Jerusalem to adore the cross and the sepulchre." The patriarch proving gracious, Charles went on to ask for relics to take home with him. "A plentet en avrez," says the patriarch; "St Simeon's arm, St Lazarus's head, St Stephen's—" "Thanks!" "The sudarium, one of the nails, the crown of thorns, the cup, the dish, the knife, some of St Peter's beard, some hairs from his head—" "Thanks!" "Some of Mary's milk, of the holy shift—" And all these Charles received.[*] He stayed four months in Jerusalem, and began the church of St Mary. He presented the patriarch with a hundred mule-

loads of gold and silver, and asked "his leave and pardon" to return to France: but first he would find out the king whom his wife had praised. They take the way through Jericho to gather palms. The relics are so strong that every stream they come to divides before them, every blind man receives sight, the crooked are made straight, and the dumb speak.[†] On reaching Constantinople they have ample reason to be impressed with the magnificence of the place. Passing twenty thousand knights, who are playing at chess and tables, dressed in pall and ermine, with fur cloaks training at their feet, and three thousand damsels in equally sumptuous attire, who are disporting with their lovers, they come to the king, who is at that moment taking his day at the plough, not on foot, goad in hand, but seated most splendidly in a chair drawn by mules, and holding a gold wand, the plough all gold, too; none of this elegance, however, impairing the straightness of his majesty's furrow. The kings exchange greetings. Charles tells Hugo that he is last from Jerusalem, and should be glad to see him and his knights. Hugo makes him free to stay a year, if he likes, unyokes the oxen, and conducts his guests to the palace.

The palace is gorgeous in the extreme, and, omitting other architectural details, it is circular, and so constructed as to turn like a wheel when the wind strikes it from the west. Charles thinks his own wealth not worth a glove in comparison, and remembers how he had threatened his wife. "Lordings," he says, "many a palace have I seen, but none like this had even Alexander, Constantine, or Cæsar." At that moment a strong wind arose which set the palace in lively motion; the emperor was fain to sit down on the floor; the twelve peers were all upset, and as they lay on their backs, with faces covered, said one to the other, "This is a bad

---

[*] There are some variations in the list of relics in the other versions. The Rímur say "many," without specifying.

[†] On the way from Jerusalem to Constantinople the French, according to Galien, were waylaid by several thousand Saracens. Three or four of the peers prepared for a fight, though armed only with swords ("which they never or only most reluctantly put off," Arsenal MS.), but Charles and the rest felt a better confidence in the relics, and through the prayers of the more prudent and pious of the company their foes were turned into rocks and stones.

business: the doors are open, and yet we can't get out!" But as evening approached the wind subsided; the Franks recovered their legs, and went to supper. At the table they saw the queen and the princess, a beautiful blonde, of whom Oliver became at once enamored. After a most royal repast, the king conducted Charles and the twelve to a bed-chamber, in which there were thirteen beds. It is doubtful whether modern luxury can vie with the appointments in any respect, and certain that we are hopelessly behind in one, for this room was lighted by a carbuncle. But, again, there was one luxury which Hugo did not allow them, and this was privacy, even so much privacy as thirteen can have. He had put a man in a hollow place under a marble stair, to watch them through a little hole.

The Franks, as it appears later, had drunk heavily at supper, and this must be their excuse for giving themselves over, when in a foreign country, to a usage or propensity which they had no doubt indulged in at home, and which is familiar in northern poetry and saga, that of making brags (gabs, Anglo-Saxon beót, gilp*). Charles began: Let Hugo arm his best man in two hauberks and two helms, and set him on a charger: then, if he will lend me his sword, I will with a blow cut through helms, hauberks, and saddle, and if I let it have its course, the blade shall never be recovered but by digging a spear's depth in the ground. "Perdy," says the man in hiding, "what a fool King Hugo was when he gave you lodging!"

Roland followed: Tell Hugo to lend me his horn, and I will go into yon plain and blow such a blast that not a gate or a door in all the city shall be left standing, and a good man Hugo will be, if he faces me, not to have his beard burned from his face and his fur robe car-

ried away. Again said the man under the stair, "What a fool was King Hugo!"

The emperor next called upon Oliver, whose gab was:

'Prenget li reis sit fille qui tant at bloi le peil,
En sa chambre nos metet en un lit en requeit;
Se jo n'ai testimoigne de li anuit cent feiz,
Demain perde la teste, par covent li otrei.'

"You will stop before that," said the spy; "great shame have you spoken."

Archbishop Turpin's brag was next in order: it would have been more in keeping for Turpin of Hounslow Heath, and we have all seen it performed in the travelling circus. While three of the king's best horses are running at full speed on the plain, he will overtake and mount the foremost, passing the others, and will keep four big apples in constant motion from one hand to the other; if he lets one fall, put out his eyes.† "A good brag this," is the comment of the simple scout (l'escolte), "and no shame to my lord."

William of Orange will take in one hand a metal ball which thirty men have never been able to stir, and will hurl it at the palace wall and bring down more than forty toises of it. "The king is a knave if he does not make you try," says l'escolte.

The other eight gabs may be passed over, save one. Bernard de Brusban says, "You see [278] that roaring stream? To-morrow I will make it leave its bed, cover the fields, fill the cellars of the city, drench the people, and drive King Hugo into his highest tower, from which he shall never come down without my leave." "The man is mad," says the spy. "What a fool King Hugo was! As soon as morning dawns they shall all pack."

---

* The heir of a Scandinavian king, or earl, at the feast which solemnized his accession, drank a bragur-full, a chief's cup or king's toast, to the memory of his father, and then made some important vow. This he did before he took his father's seat. The guests then made vows. The custom seems not to have been confined to these funeral banquets. See Vigfusson, at the word B r a g r. Charles and his peers show their blood. See, also, Miss Hapgood's *Epic Songs of Russia*, p. 300; also pp. 48, 50, 61, 65, 161, etc.

† Excepting the Welsh translation, which conforms to the original, all other versions give Bernard's gab to Turpin, and most others Turpin's to Bernard. The Danish chronicle assigns the "grand three-horse act" to Gerard; the Färöe ballad omits it; the two manuscript Galiens attribute it to Bernard [Berart] de Mondidier, the printed Galien to Berenger. In these last the feat is, though enormously weighted with armor, to leap over two horses and come down on the back of the third so heavily as to break his bones. There are, in one version or another, other differences as to the feats.

The spy carries his report to his master without a moment's delay. Hugo swears that if the brags are not accomplished as made, his guests shall lose their heads, and orders out a hundred thousand men-at-arms to enforce his resolution.

When the devout emperor of the west came from mass the next morning (Hugo was evidently not in a state of mind to go), he advanced to meet his brother of Constantinople, olive branch in hand; but Hugo called out from far off, "Charles, why did you make me the butt of your brags and your scorns?" and repeated that all must be done, or thirteen heads would fall. Charles replied that they had drunk a good deal of wine the night before, and that it was the custom for the French when they had gone to bed to allow themselves in jesting. He desired to speak with his knights. When they were together, the emperor said that they had drunk too much, and had uttered what they ought not. He caused the relics to be brought, and they all fell to praying and beating their breasts, that they might be saved from Hugo's wrath, when lo, an angel appeared, who bade them not be afraid; they had committed a great folly yesterday, and must never brag again, but for this time, "Go, begin, not one of them shall fail." *

Charles returned to Hugo master of the situation. He repeated that they had drunk too much wine the night before, and went on to say that it was an outrage on Hugo's part to set a spy in the room, and that they knew a land where such an act would be accounted villainy: "but all shall be carried out; choose who shall begin." Hugo said, Oliver; and let him not fall short of his boast, or I will cut off his head, and the other twelve shall share his fate. The next morning, in pursuance of an arrangement made between Oliver and the princess, the king was

informed that what had been undertaken had been precisely discharged. "The first has saved himself," says Hugo; "by magic, I believe; now I wish to know about the rest." "What next?" says Charlemagne. William of Orange was called for, threw off his furs, lifted the huge ball with one hand, hurled it at the wall, and threw down more than forty toises. "They are enchanters," said the king to his men. "Now I should like to see if the rest will do as much. If one of them fails, I will hang them all to-morrow." "Do you want any more of the gabs?" asked Charles. Hugo called upon Bernard to do what he had threatened. Bernard asked the prayers of the emperor, ran down to the water, and made the sign of the cross. All the water left its bed, spread over the fields, came into the city, filled the cellars, drenched the people, and drove King Hugo into his highest tower; Charles and the peers being the while ensconced in an old pine-tree, all praying for God's pity.

Charles in the tree heard Hugo in the tower making his moan: he would give the emperor all his treasure, would become his man and hold his kingdom of him. The emperor was moved, and prayed that the flood might stop, and at once the water began to ebb. Hugo was able to descend from his tower, and he came to Charles, under an "ympe tree," and repeated what he had uttered in the moment of extremity. "Do you want the rest of the gabs?" asked Charles. "Ne de ceste semaine," replied Hugo. "Then, since you are my man," said the emperor, "we will make a holiday and wear our crowns together." When the French saw the two monarchs walking together, and Charles overtopping Hugo by fifteen inches, they said the queen was a fool to compare anybody with him. [2]

After this promenade there was mass, at which Turpin officiated, and then a grand dinner. Hugo once more proffered all his treasures to Charles, but Charles would not take a denier. "We must be going," he said. The French mounted their mules, and went off in high spirits. Very happy was Charles to have conquered such a king without a battle. Charles went directly to St Denis, and performed his devotions. The nail and the crown he deposited on the altar, distributed the other relies over the

---

* In Galien, Hugo is exceedingly frightened by Charlemagne's fierce demeanor and by what he is told by a recreant Frenchman who is living in exile at his court, and rouses the city for an assault on his guests, in which he loses two thousand of his people. A parley ensues. Hugo will hear of no accommodation unless the gabs are performed. "Content," says Charles, angrily, "they shall be, if you wish;" but he feels how great the peril is, and goes to church to invoke the aid of heaven, which is vouchsafed.

kingdom, and for the love of the sepulchre he gave up his anger against the queen.

The story in the English ballad, so far as it is to be collected from our eight fragments, is that Arthur, represented as King of Little Britain, while boasting to Gawain of his round table, is told by Guenever that she knows of one immeasurably finer; the very trestle is worth his halls and his gold, and the palace it stands in is worth all Little Britain besides; but not a word will she say as to where this table and this goodly building may be. Arthur makes a vow never to sleep two nights in one place till he sees that round table; and, taking for companions Gawain, Tristram, Sir Bredbeddle, and an otherwise unknown Sir Marramiles, sets out on the quest.

The pilgrimage which, to save his dignity, Charles makes a cover for his visit to the rival king forms no part of Arthur's programme.[*] The five assume a palmer's weed simply for disguise, and travel east and west, in many a strange country, only to arrive at Cornwall, so very little a way from home.

The proud porter of Cornwall's gate, a minion swain, befittingly clad in a suit of gold, for his master is the richest king in Christendom, or yet in heathenness, is evidently impressed with Arthur's bearing, as is quite the rule in such cases:[†] he has been porter thirty years and three, but [has never seen the like]. Cornwall would naturally ask the pilgrims some questions. From their mentioning some shrine of Our Lady he infers that they have been in Britain,—Little Britain we must suppose to be meant. Cornwall asks if they ever knew King Arthur, and boasts that he had lived seven years in Little Britain, and had had a daughter by Arthur's wife, now a lady of radiant beauty, and Arthur has none such.[‡] He then sends for his steed, which he can ride three times as far in a day as Arthur can any of his, and we may sup-

pose that he also exhibits to his guests a horn and a sword of remarkable properties, and a Burlow-Beanie, or Billy-Blin, a seven-headed, fire-breathing fiend whom he has in his service. Arthur is then conducted to bed, and the Billy-Blin, shut up, as far as we can make out, in some sort of barrel, or other vessel,[§] is set by [280] Arthur's bed-side to hear and report the talk of the pilgrims. Now, it would seem, the knights make each their vow or brag. Arthur's is that he will be the death of Cornwall King before he sees Little Britain. Gawain, who represents Oliver, will have Cornwall's daughter home

‡   In Heinrich vom Türlin's Crône we have the following passage, vv 3313–4888, very possibly to be found in some French predecessor, which recalls the relations of Cornwall King and Guenever. The queen's demeanor may be an imitation of Charlemagne's (Arthur's) wife's bluntness, but the liaison of which Cornwall boasts appears to be vouched by no other tradition, and must be regarded as the invention of the author of this ballad.

Arthur and three comrades return half frozen from a hunt. Arthur sits down at the fire to warm himself. The queen taunts him: she knows a knight who rides, winter and summer alike, in a simple shirt, chanting love-songs the while. Arthur resolves to go out with the three the next night to overhaul this hardy chevalier. The three attendants of the king have an encounter with him and fare hard at his hands, but Arthur has the advantage of the stranger, who reveals himself to the king as Guenever's first love, by name Gasozein, and shows a token which he had received from her.

§   Under thrub chadler closed was hee. 31².
     The bunge of the trubchandler he burst in three. 43².

Being unable to make anything of thrub, trub, I am compelled to conjecture *the rub-chadler, that rub-chandler.* The fiend is certainly closed under a barrel or tub, and I suppose a rubbish barrel or tub. Rubb, however derived, occurs in Icelandic in the sense of rubbish, and chalder, however derived, is a Scottish form of the familiar chaldron. Professor Skeat, with great probability, suggests that chalder = chaudeler, chaudière. Caldaria *lignea* are cited by Ducange. Cad or kad is well known in the sense barrel, and cadiolus, cadulus, are found in Ducange. Cadler, chadler, however, cannot be called a likely derivative from cad.

In stanza 48 the fiend, after he has been ousted from the "trubchandler," is told to "lie still in that wall of stone," which is perhaps his ordinary lair. The spy is concealed under a flight of stone steps in the French poem; in "a large hollow stone in the door outside" in the Welsh story; in a hollow pillar in Galien and the Rímur; in a stone vault in the Färöe ballad: Koschwitz, *Karls Reise*, p. 64; *Sechs Bearbeitungen*, pp 29, 52, 85, 117, 153, 179.

---

*   Arthur is said to have "socht to the ciete of Criste," in 'Golagros and Gawane,' Madden's 'Syr Gawayne,' p. 143, v. 302. The author probably followed the so-called Nennius, c. 63.

†   Cf. 'Young Beichan,' where the porter has also served thirty years and three; 'The Grene Knight,' Percy MS., Hales and Furnivall, II, 62; the porter in Kilhwch and Olwen, *Mabinogion*, II, 255f.

with him. Here there is an unlucky gap. Tristram should undertake to carry off the horn, Marramiles the steed, and Sir Bredbeddle the sword. But first it would be necessary to subdue the loathly fiend. Bredbeddle goes to work without dallying, bursts open the rub-chadler with his sword, and fights the fire-breathing monster in a style that is a joy to see; but sword, knife, and axe all break, and he is left without a weapon. Yet he had something better to fall back on, and that was a little book which he had found by the seaside, no doubt in the course of those long travels which conducted the pilgrims from Little Britain to Cornwall. It was probably a book of Evangiles; our Lord had written it with his hands and sealed it with his blood. With this little book, which in a manner takes the place of the relics in the French tale, for the safety of the pilgrims and the accomplishment of their vows are secured through it, Bredbeddle conjures the Burlow-beanie, and shuts him up till wanted in a "wall of stone," which reminds us of the place in which Hugo's spy is concealed. He then reports to Arthur, who has a great desire to see the fiend in all his terrors, and, upon the king's promising to stand firm, Bredbeddle makes the fiend start out again, with his seven heads and the fire flying out of his mouth. The Billy-Blin is now entirely amenable to command: Bredbeddle has only to "conjure" him to do a thing, and it is done. First he fetches down the steed. Marramiles, who perhaps had vowed to bring off the horse, considers that he is the man to ride him, but finds he can do nothing with him, and has to call on Bredbeddle for help. The Billy-Blin is required to tell how the steed is to be ridden, and reveals that three strokes of a gold wand which stands in Cornwall's study-window will make him spring like spark from brand. And so it comes out that Cornwall is a magician. Next the horn has to be fetched, but, when brought, it cannot be sounded. For this a certain powder is required. This the fiend procures, and Tristram blows a blast which rends the horn up to the midst.* Finally the Billy-Blin is conjured to fetch the sword, and with this sword Arthur

goes and strikes off Cornwall's head. So Arthur keeps his vow, and, so far as we can see, all the rest are in a condition to keep theirs.

The English ballad retains too little of the French story to enable us to say what form of it this little was derived from. The poem of Galien would cover all that is borrowed as well as the Journey of Charlemagne. It may be regarded as an indication of late origin that in this ballad Arthur is king of Little Britain, that Bredbeddle and Marramiles are made the fellows of Gawain and Tristram, Bredbeddle carrying off all the honors, and that Cornwall has had an intrigue with Arthur's queen. The name Bredbeddle is found elsewhere only in the late Percy version of the romance of the Green Knight, Hales and Furnivall, II, 56, which version alludes to a custom of the Knights of the Bath, an order said to have been instituted by Henry IV at his coronation, in 1399.

The Färöe ballad, 'Geipa-táttur,' exists in four versions: A, Svabo's manuscript collection, 1782, III, 1, 85 stanzas; printed by Hammershaimb in Færøsk Anthologi, p. 139, No 20; B, Sandøbog, 1822, p. 49, 140 stanzas; C, Flugløbog, c. 1840, p. 9, 120 stanzas; D, Syderø version, obtained by Hammershaimb, 1848, 103 stanzas.† It repeats the story of the Norse saga, with a moderate number of traditional accretions and changes. The emperor, from his throne, asks his champions where is his superior [equal]. They all drop their heads; no one ventures to answer but the queen, who better had been silent. "The emperor of Constantinople" (Hákin, D), she says, "is thy superior." "If he is not," answers Karl, "thou shalt burn on bale." In B, when they have already started for Constantinople, Turpin persuades them to go rather to Jerusalem: in the other versions it must be assumed that the holy city was on the route. As Karl enters the church the bells ring and the candles light of themselves, C, D. There are thirteen seats in the choir: Karl takes the one

---

*   Roland's last blast splits his horn. See the citations by G. Paris, in *Romania*, XI, 506f.

†   The first has been printed by Kölbing in Koschwitz's *Sechs Bearbeitungen*, as already said. The four texts were most kindly communicated to me by Professor Grundtvig, a short time before his lamentable death, copied by his own hand in parallel columns, with a restoration of the order of the stanzas, which is considerably disturbed in all, and a few necessary emendations.

that Jesus had occupied, and the peers those of the apostles. A heathen tells the patriarch* that the Lord is come down from heaven, **C, D**. The patriarch proceeds to the church, with no attendance but his altar-book [singing from his altar-book]; he asks Karl what he has come for, and Karl replies, to see the halidoms, **A, C, D**. In **B** the patriarch presents himself to the emperor at his lodging, and inquires his purpose; and, learning that he is on his way to Constantinople, for glory, advises him first to go to the church, where the ways and means of success are to be found. The patriarch gives Karl some of the relics: the napkin on which Jesus had wiped his hands, cups from which he had drunk, etc. Karl, in **A, C**, now announces that he is on his way to Constantinople; the patriarch begs him not to go, for he will have much to suffer. At the exterior gate of the palace will be twelve white bears, ready to go at him; the sight of his sword [of the holy napkin, **B**] will cause them to fall stone-dead, or at least harmless, **B**. At the gate next within there will be twelve wolf-dogs† [and further on twelve toads, **B**], which must be disposed of in like wise: etc. The castle stands on a hundred pillars, **A**, and is full of ingenious contrivances: the floor goes up to the sky, and the roof comes down to the ground, **B**. Karl now sets out, with the patriarch's blessing and escort. Before they reach the palace they come upon three hundred knights and ladies dancing, which also had been foretold, and at the portals of the palace they find and vanquish the formidable beasts. The palace is to the full as splendid and as artfully constructed as they had been informed: the floor goes up and the roof comes down, **B**; there are monstrous figures (?), with horns at

their mouths, and upon a wind rising the horns all sound, the building begins to revolve, and the Frenchmen jump up, each clinging to the other, **B, C, D**. Karl remembers what his wife had said, **A, D**.

Of the reception by the monarch of Constantinople nothing further is said. We are immediately taken to the bedroom, in which there are twelve beds, with a thirteenth in the middle, and also a stone arch, or vault, inside of which is a man with a candle. Karl proposes that they shall choose feats, make boasts, rouses [*skemtan*, jests, **C**]. These would inevitably be more or less deranged and corrupted in the course of tradition. **A** and **C** have lost many. Karl's boast, dropped in **B, C**, is that he will smite King Hákin, so that the sword's point shall stick in the ground, **D**; hit the emperor on the neck and knock him off his horse, **A**. Roland, in all, will blow the emperor's hair off his head with the blast of his horn. Oliver's remains as in the French poem. William of Orange's ball is changed to a bolt. The exploit with the horses and apples is assigned to Bernard in **D**, the only version which preserves it, as in the Norse saga; and, as in the saga again, it is Turpin, and not Bernard, who brings in the [282] river upon the town, and forces the king to take refuge in the tower.

Early in the morning the spy reports in writing, and King Hákin, **D**, says that Karl and his twelve peers shall burn on the bale, **A, C, D**, if they cannot make good their boasts, **B**. Karl's queen appears to him in his sleep, **A**, and bids him think of last night's words. It is the queen of Constantinople in **B, C, D** who rouses Karl to a sense of his plight; in **B** she tells him that the brags have been reported, and that burning will be the penalty unless they be achieved. Karl then sees that his wife knew what she was saying, and vows to give her Hildarheim and a scarlet cloak if he gets home alive. He hastens to church; a dove descends from heaven and sits on his arm [in **B** a voice comes from heaven]; he is assured that the boasts shall all be performed, but never let such a thing be done again. In **A** three of the feats are executed, in **D** four, in **C** seven, Oliver's in each case strictly, and Turpin's, naturally, last. The king in **C** does the feat which is proposed by

* Pól, **A, C**, Kortunatus, **B**, i.e. Koronatus (Grundtvig). Coronatus = clericus, tonsura seu corona clericali donatus: Ducange.
† The white bears and the wolf-dogs are found in another Färöe ballad, as yet unprinted, 'Ásmundur skeinkjari,' where they are subdued by an arm-ring and "rune-gold:" the white bears in a kindred ballad, Grundtvig, No 71, **A** 4, 5, 8, 9, **C** 6, 7, 13, quelled with a lily-twig; **E** 12, 13, with runes; and in No 70, **A** 28, **B** 27, 30. The source of this ballad is Fjölsvinnsmál, which has two watch-dogs in 13, 14. 'Kilhwch and Olwen,' *Mabinogion*, II, has a similar story, and there are nine watch-dogs, at p. 277. (Grundtvig.)

Eimer in the saga. **A** and **C** end abruptly with Turpin's exploit. In **D** Karl falls on his knees and prays, and the water retires; Karl rides out of Constantinople, followed three days on the road by Koronatus, as Hákin is now called, stanza 103: it is Karlamagnús that wears his crown higher. **B** takes a turn of its own. Roland, Olger and Oliver are called upon to do their brags. Roland blows so that nobody in Constantinople can keep his legs, and the emperor falls into the mud, but he blows not a hair off the emperor's head; Olger slings the gold-bolt over the wall, but breaks off none; Oliver gives a hundred kisses, as in the saga. The emperor remarks each time, I hold him no champion that performs his rouse that way. But Turpin's brag is thoroughly done; the emperor is driven to the tower, and begs Karl to turn off the water; no more feats shall be exacted. Now the two kaisers walk in the hall, conferring about tribute, which Karl takes and rides away. When he reaches home his queen welcomes him, and asks what happened at Constantinople: "Hvat gekk af?" "This," says Karl; "I know the truth now; you shall be queen as before, and shall have a voice in the rule."

It is manifest that Charlemagne's pilgrimage to Jerusalem and the visit to the king of Constantinople, though somewhat intimately combined in the old French *geste*, were originally distinct narratives. As far as we can judge, nothing of the pilgrimage was retained by the English ballad. We are not certain, even, that it is Charlemagne's visit to Hugo upon which the ballad was formed, though the great popularity of the French poem makes this altogether likely. As M. Gaston Paris has said and shown,[*] the visit to Hugo is one of a cycle of tales of which the framework is this: that a king who regards himself as the richest or most magnificent in the world is told that there is somebody that outstrips him, and undertakes a visit to his rival to determine which surpasses the other, threatening death to the person who has disturbed his self-complacency, in case the rival

should turn out to be his inferior. A familiar example is afforded by the tale of Aboulcassem, the first of the Mille et un Jours. Haroun Alraschid was incessantly boasting that no prince in the world was so generous as he.[†] The vizier Giafar humbly exhorted the caliph not to praise himself, but to leave that to others. The caliph, much piqued, demanded, Do you then know anybody who compares with me? Giafar felt compelled to reply that there was a young man [2 at Basra, who, though in a private station, was not inferior even to the caliph in point of generosity. Haroun was very angry, and, on Giafar's persisting in what he had said, had the vizier arrested, and finally resolved to go to Basra to see with his own eyes: if Giafar should have spoken the truth, he should be rewarded, but in the other event he should forfeit his life.[‡]

This story, it is true, shows no trace of the gabs which Charlemagne and the peers make, and which Hugo requires to be accomplished on pain of death. The gabs are a well-known North-European custom, and need not be sought for further; but the requiring by one king of certain feats to be executed by another under a heavy penalty is a feature of a large class of Eastern tales of which there has already been occasion to speak: see 'The Elfin Knight,' p. 16. The demand in these, however, is made not in person, but through an ambassador. The combination of a personal visit with a task to be performed under penalty of death is seen in the Vafþrúðnismál, where Odin, disguised as a trav-

---

[*] *Romania*, IX, 8 ff. The English ballad has also combined two stories: that of the gabs with another in which a magical horse, horn, and sword are made prize of by a favored hero.

[†] The particular for which superiority is claimed will naturally vary. The author of Charlemagne's Journey has the good taste not to give prominence to simple riches, but in Galion riches is from the beginning the point. So none hath so much gold as Cornwall King. Solomon's fame is to exceed all the kings of the earth "for riches and for wisdom;" and although the queen of Sheba came to prove him with hard questions, she must have had the other matter also in view, for she says, The half was not told me; thy wisdom and prosperity exceedeth the fame which I heard: 1 Kings, x. Coming down to very late times, we observe that it is the wealth of the Abbot of Canterbury which exposes him to a visit from the king.

[‡] The tale in the Mille et un Jours is directly from the Persian, but the Persian is in the preface said to be a version from Indian, that is, Sanskrit. There are two Tatar traditional versions in Radloff, IV, 120, 310, which are cited by G. Paris.

eller, seeks a contest in knowledge with the wisest of the giants.[*]

The story of the gabs has been retold in two modern imitations: very indifferently by Nivelle de la Chaussée, 'Le Roi Hugon,' *Œuvres*, t. V, supplément, p. 66, ed. 1778, and well by M. J. Chénier, 'Les Miracles,' III, 259, ed. 1824.[†] Uhland treated the subject dramatically in a composition which has not been published: Keller, *Altfranzösische Sagen*, 1876, Inhalt (Koschwitz).

For the "ghesting" referenced in sts 17, 18, compare Carle of Carlile, vv 143ff, Percy MS., Hales and Furnivall, III, 282.

---

[*] Cited by G. Paris, who refers also to King Gylfi's expedition to Asgard (an imitation of Odin's to Vafþrúðnir), and sees some resemblance to the revolving palace of King Hugo in the vanishing mansion in which Gylfi is received in Gylfaginning; and again to Thor's visit to the giant Geirröðr, Skáldskaparmál, 18, which terminates by the giant's flinging a red-hot iron bar at Thor, who catches it and sends it back through an iron pillar, through Geirröðr skulking behind the pillar, through the wall of the house, and into the ground, a fair matching of Charlemagne's gab. (The giant Geirröðr, like Cornwall King, is skilled in magic.) The beginning of Biterolf and Dietleib also recalls that of Charlemagne's Journey. Biterolf, a Spanish king, hears from an old palmer, who has seen many a hero among Christians and heathens, that none is the equal of Attila. Biterolf had thought that he himself had no superior, and sets out with eleven chosen knights to see Etzel's court with his own eyes. *Romania*, IX, 9f.

Játmundr [Hlöðver], a haughty emperor in Saxonland, sitting on his throne one day, in the best humor with himself, asks Sigurðr, his prime minister, where is the monarch that is his match. Sigurðr demurs a little; the emperor specifies his hawk, horse, and sword as quite incomparable. That may be, says the counsellor, but his master's glory, to be complete, requires a queen that is his peer. The suggestion of a possible equal rouses the emperor's ire. "But since you talk such folly, name one," he says. Sigurðr names the daughter of Hrólfr [Hugo] of Constantinople, and is sent to demand her in marriage. *Magus saga jarls*, ed. Cederschiöld, c. i: Wulff, *Recherches sur les Sagas de Mágus et de Geirard*, p. 14f.

[†] G. Paris, *Histoire Poétique de Charlemagne*, p. 344.

Percy MS., p. 24. Hales and Furnivall, I, 61; Madden's *Syr Gawayne*, p. 275.

*   *   *   *   *

1 [Saies, 'Come here, cuzen Gawaine so gay,]
    My sisters sonne be yee;
    Ffor you shall see one of the fairest round tables
    That euer you see with your eye.'

2 Then bespake Lady Queen Gueneuer,
    And these were the words said shee:
    'I know where a round table is, thou noble king,
    Is worth thy round table and other such
        three

3 'The trestle that stands vnder this round table,'
        she said,
    'Lowe downe to the mould,
    It is worth thy round table, thou worthy king,
    Thy halls, and all thy gold.

4 'The place where this round table stands in,
    .   .   .   .   .
[284]   It is worth thy castle, thy gold, thy fee,
    And all good Litle Britaine.'

5 'Where may that table be, lady?' quoth hee,
    'Or where may all that goodly building be?'
    'You shall it seeke,' shee says, 'till you it find,
    For you shall neuer gett more of me.'

6 Then bespake him noble King Arthur,
    These were the words said hee:
    'Ile make mine avow to God,
    And alsoe to the Trinity,

7 'Ile never sleepe one night there as I doe
        another,
    Till that round table I see:
    Sir Marramiles and Sir Tristeram,
    Fellowes that ye shall bee.

8 .   .   .   .   .
    .   .   .   .   .
    'Weele be clad in palmers weede,
    Fiue palmers we will bee;

9 'There is noe outlandish man will vs abide,
    Nor will vs come nye.'
    Then they riued east and thé riued west,
    In many a strange country.

10 Then they tranckled a litle further,
    They saw a battle new sett:
    'Now, by my faith,' saies noble King Arthur,
    .   .   .   well   .   .

*   *   *   *   *

11 But when he cam to this . . c . .
    And to the palace gate,
    Soe ready was ther a proud porter,
    And met him soone therat.

12 Shooes of gold the porter had on,
    And all his other rayment was vnto the
        same:
    'Now, by my faith,' saies noble King Arthur,
    'Yonder is a minion swaine.'

13 Then bespake noble King Arthur,
    These were the words says hee:
    'Come hither, thou proud porter,
    I pray thee come hither to me.

14 'I haue two poore rings of my finger,
    The better of them Ile giue to thee;
    Tell who may be lord of this castle,' he says,
    'Or who is lord in this cuntry?'

15 'Cornewall King,' the porter sayes,
    'There is none soe rich as hee;
    Neither in christendome, nor yet in heathen-
        nest,
    None hath soe much gold as he.'

16 And then bespake him noble King Arthur,
    These were the words sayes hee:
    'I haue two poore rings of my finger,
    The better of them Ile giue thee,
    If thou wilt greete him well, Cornewall King,
    And greete him well from me.

17 'Pray him for one nights lodging and two
        meales meate,
    For his love that dyed vppon a tree
    Of one ghesting and two meales meate,
    For his loue that dyed vppon a tree.

18 'Of one ghesting, of two meales meate,
   For his love that was of virgin borne,
   And in the morning *that* we may scape away,
   Either *w*ithout scath or scorne.'

19 Then forth is gone this proud porter,
   As fast as he cold hye,
   And when he came befor Cornewall K*ing*,
   He kneeled downe on his knee.

20 Sayes, 'I haue beene porter-man, at thy gate,
   This thirty winter and three . .

   .   .   .   .   .

   *   *   *   *   *

21 .   .   .   .   .

   .   .   .   .   .

   Our Lady was borne; then thought Cornewall K*ing*
   These palmers had beene in Britt*aine*.

22 Then bespake him Cornwall King,
   These were the words he said there
   'Did you euer know a comely k*ing*,
   His name was King Arthur?'

23 And then bespake him noble K*ing* Arthur,
   These were the words said hee:
   'I doe not know that comly k*ing*,
   But once my selfe I did him see.'
   Then bespake Cornwall K*ing* againe,
   These were the words said he:

24 Sayes, 'Seuen yeere I was clad and fed,
   In Litle Brittaine, in a bower;
   I had a daughter by K*ing* Arthurs wife,
   That now is called my flower;
   For K*ing* Arthur, that kindly cockward,
   Hath none such in his bower.

25 'For I durst sweare, and saue my othe,
   That same lady soe bright,
   That a man *that* were laid on his death bed
   Wold open his eyes on her to haue sight.'
   'Now, by my faith,' sayes noble K*ing* Arthur,
   'And that's a full faire wight!'

26 And then bespake Cornwall [King] againe,
   And these were the words he said:
   'Come hither, fiue or three of my knights,
   And feitch me downe my steed;
   King Arthur, that foule cockeward,
   Hath none such, if he had need.

27 'For I can ryde him as far on a day
   As King Arthur can doe any of his on three;
   And is it not a pleasure for a k*ing*
   When he shall ryde forth on his iourney?

28 'For the eyes that beene in his head,
   Th*é* glister as doth the gleed.'
   'Now, by my faith,' says noble King Arthur,
   '*That* is a well faire steed.'

   *   *   *   *   *

29 .   .   .   .   .

   .   .   .   .   .

   'Nobody say . . . .
   But one *that*'s learned to speake.'

30 Then K*ing* Arthur to his bed was brought,
   A greeiued man was hee;
   And soe were all his fellowes with him,
   From him th*é* thought neuer to flee.

31 Then take they did that lodly groome,
   And under the rub-chadler closed was hee,
   And he was set by K*ing* Arthurs bed-side,
   To heere theire talke and theire comunye;

32 *That* he might come forth, and make proclama-
       tion,
   Long before it was day;
   It was more for K*ing* Cornwalls pleasure,
   Then it was for K*ing* Arthurs pay.

33 And when K*ing* Arthur in his bed was laid,
   These were the words said hee:
   'Ile make mine avow to God,
   And alsoe to the Trinity,
   That Ile be the bane of Cornwall Kinge,
   Litle Brittaine or euer I see!'

34 'It is an vnaduised vow,' saies Gawaine the gay,
   'As ever k*ing* hard make I;
   But wee *that* beene fiue christian men,
   Of the christen faith are wee,
   And we shall fight against anoynted k*ing*
   And all his armorie.'

35 And then bespake him noble Arthur,
   And these were the words said he:
   'Why, if thou be afraid, S*ir* Gawaine the gay,
   Goe home, and drinke wine in thine owne
       country.'

36 And then bespake Sir Gawaine the gay,
    And these were the words said hee:
'Nay, seeing you have made such a hearty vow,
    Heere another vow make will I.

37 'Ile make mine avow to God,
    And alsoe to the Trinity,
That I will haue yonder faire lady
    To Litle Brittaine with mee.

38 'Ile hose her hourly to my heart,
    And with her Ile worke my will;'

.   .   .   .   .
    .   .   .   .   .

*   *   *   *   *

39 .   .   .   .   .
    These were the words sayd hee:
'Befor I wold wrestle with yonder feend,
    It is better be drowned in the sea.'

[286] 40 And then bespake Sir Bredbeddle,
    And these were the words said he:
'Why, I will wrestle with yon lodly feend,
    God, my gouernor thou wilt bee!'

41 Then bespake him noble Arthur,
    And these were the words said he:
'What weapons wilt thou haue, thou gentle
        knight?
    I pray thee tell to me.'

42 He says, 'Collen brand Ile haue in my hand,
    And a Millaine knife fast by me knee,
And a Danish axe fast in my hands,
    That a sure weapon I thinke wilbe.'

43 Then with his Collen brand that he had in his
        hand
    The bunge of that rub-chandler he burst in
        three;
With that start out a lodly feend,
    With seuen heads, and one body.

44 The fyer towards the element flew,
    Out of his mouth, where was great plentie;
The knight stoode in the middle and fought,
    That it was great ioy to see.

45 Till his Collaine brand brake in his hand,
    And his Millaine knife burst on his knee,
And then the Danish axe burst in his hand first,
    That a sur weapon he thought shold be.

46 But now is the knight left without any weapons,
    And alacke! it was the more pitty;
But a surer weapon then he had one,
    Had neuer lord in Christentye
And all was but one litle booke,
    He found it by the side of the sea.

47 He found it at the sea-side,
    Wrucked upp in a floode;
Our Lord had written it with his hands,
    And sealed it with his bloode.

*   *   *   *   *

48 'That thou doe not s . . . .
    But ly still in that wall of stone,
Till I haue beene with noble King Arthur,
    And told him what I haue done.'

49 And when he came to the kings chamber,
    He cold of his curtesie:
Says, 'Sleepe you, wake you, noble King
        Arthur?
    And euer Iesus waken yee!'

50 'Nay, I am not sleeping, I am waking,'
    These were the words said hee;
'Ffor thee I haue card; how hast thou fared?
    O gentle knight, let me see.'

51 The knight wrought the king his booke,
    Bad him behold, reede and see;
And euer he found it on the backside of the
        leafe
    As noble Arthur wold wish it to be.

52 And then bespake him King Arthur,
    'Alas! thow gentle knight, how may this be,
That I might see him in the same licknesse
    That he stood vnto thee?'

53 And then bespake him the Greene Knight,
    These were the words said hee:
'If youle stand stifly in the battell stronge,
    For I haue won all the victory.'

54 Then bespake him the king againe,
    And these were the words said hee:
'If wee stand not stifly in this battell strong,
    Wee are worthy to be hanged all on a tree.'

55 Then bespake him the Greene Knight,
  These were the words said he:
  Saies, 'I doe coniure thee, thou fowle feend,
  In the same licknesse thou stood vnto me.'

56 With that start out a lodly feend,
  With seuen heads, and one body;
  The fier towards the element flaugh,
  Out of his mouth, where was great plenty.

57 The knight stood in the middle p . . .
    .   .   .   .   .
    .   .   .   .   .
  *   *   *   *   *

58 .   .   .   .   .
  7] . . . they stood the space of an houre,
  I know not what they did.

59 And then bespake him the Greene Knight,
  And these were the words said he:
  Saith, 'I coniure thee, thou fowle feend,
  That thou feitch downe the steed that we
    see.'

60 And then forth is gone Burlow-beanie,
  As fast as he cold hie,
  And feitch he did that faire steed,
  And came againe by and by.

61 Then bespake him Sir Marramiles,
  And these were the words said hee:
  'Riding of this steed, brother Bredbeddle,
  The mastery belongs to me.'

62 Marramiles tooke the steed to his hand,
  To ryd him he was full bold;
  He cold noe more make him goe
  Then a child of three yeere old.

63 He laid vppon him with heele and hand,
  With yard that was soe fell;
  'Helpe! brother Bredbeddle,' says Marramile,
  'For I thinke he be the devill of hell.

64 'Helpe! brother Bredbeddle,' says Marramile,
  'Helpe! for Christs pittye;
  Ffor without thy help, brother Bredbeddle,
  He will neuer be rydden for me.'

65 Then bespake him Sir Bredbeddle,
  These were the words said he:
  'I coniure thee, thou Burlow-beane,
  Thou tell me how this steed was riddin in his
    country.'

66 He saith, 'there is a gold wand
  Stands in King Cornwalls study windowe;
    .   .   .   .   .
    .   .   .   .   .

67 'Let him take that wand in that window,
  And strike three strokes on that steed;
  And then he will spring forth of his hand
  As sparke doth out of gleede.'

68 And then bespake him the Greene Knight,
    .   .   .   .   .
    .   .   .   .   .
  *   *   *   *   *

69 .   .   .   .   .
    .   .   .   .   .
  A lowd blast he may blow then.

70 And then bespake Sir Bredebeddle,
  To the ffeend these words said hee:
  Says, 'I coniure thee, thou Burlow-beanie,
  The powder-box thou feitch me.'

71 Then forth is gone Burlow-beanie,
  As fast as he cold hie,
  And feich he did the powder-box,
  And came againe by and by.

72 Then Sir Tristeram tooke powder forth of that
    box,
  And blent it with warme sweet milke,
  And there put it vnto that horne,
  And swilled it about in that ilke.

73 Then he tooke the horne in his hand,
  And a lowd blast he blew;
  He rent the horne vp to the midst,
  All his ffellowes this thé knew.

74 Then bespake him the Greene Knight,
  These were the words said he:
  Saies, 'I coniure thee, thou Burlow-beanie,
  That thou feitch me the sword that I see.'

75 Then forth is gone Burlow-beanie,
    As fast as he cold hie,
    And feitch he did that faire sword,
    And came againe by and by.

76 Then bespake him Sir Bredbeddle,
    To the king these words said he:
    'Take this sword in thy hand, thou noble King
      Arthur,
    For the vowes sake that thou made Ile giue it
      th[ee,]
    And goe strike off King Cornewalls head,
    In bed were he doth lye.'

77 Then forth is gone noble King Arthur,   [2
    As fast as he cold hye,
    And strucken he hath off King Cornwalls head,
    And came againe by and by.

78 He put the head vpon a swords point,

    .   .   .   .

    .   .   .   .

    .   .   .   .

  *   *   *   *   *

1[1]. *The tops of the letters of this line were cut off in binding. Percy thought it had stood previously,*

come here Cuzen Gawaine so gay.

Furnivall says "the bottoms of the letters left suit better those in the text" *as given.*
4 *and* 5, 8 *and* 9, *are joined in the MS.*
10[4]. *Half a page is gone from the MS., or about* 38 *or* 40 *lines; and so after* 20[2], 28[4] 38[2], 47[4], 57[1], 68[1], 78[1].
14[2]. *they* better.
17[3], 18[1]. *The first two words are hard to make out, and look like* A vne.
18[2]. *boirne.*
19[1]. *his* gone.
20[2]. *The lower half of the letters is gone.*

21. *In MS.:*
    our Lady was borne
    then thought cornewall King these Palmers had
    beene in Brittanie.

28[4].? *MS. Only the upper part of the letters is left.*
31[2]. under thrub chadler.
35. *After this stanza is written, in the left margin of the MS.,* The 3d Part.
38[1]. homly to my hurt. *Madden read* hourly.
39[1]. *The top line is pared away.*
41[2]. they words.
43[2]. of the trubchandler.
46[1]. then had he.
64. p', *i.e.* pro *or* per, me. *Madden.*
66. *Attached to* 65 *in MS.*
69[4]. ? *MS.*
76[5,6]. *Joined with* 77 *in MS.*
& *and Arabic numerals have been frequently written out.*

31

THE MARRIAGE OF SIR GAWAIN

Percy MS., p. 46. Hales & Furnivall, I, 105; Madden's *Syr Gawayne*, p. 288; Percy's *Reliques*, ed. l 794, III, 350.

WE have here again half a ballad, in seven fragments, but the essentials of the story, which is well known from other versions, happen to be preserved, or may be inferred.

Arthur, apparently some day after Christmas, had been encountered at Tarn Wadling,[*] in the forest of Inglewood, by a bold baron armed with a club, who offered him the choice of fighting, or ransoming himself by coming back on New Year's day and bringing word what women most desire. Arthur puts this question in all quarters, and having collected many answers, in which, possibly, he had little confidence, he rides to keep his day. On the way he meets a frightfully ugly woman; she intimates that she could help him. Arthur promises her Gawain in marriage, if she will, and she imparts to him the right answer. Arthur finds the baron waiting for him at the tarn, and presents first the answers which he had collected and written down. These are contemptuously rejected. Arthur then says that he had met a lady on a moor, who had told him that a woman would have her will. The baron says that the misshapen lady on the moor was his sister, and he will burn her if he can get hold of her. Upon Arthur's return he tells his knights that he has a wife for one of them, and they ride with the king to see her, or perhaps for her to make her choice. When they see the bride, they decline the match in vehement terms, all but Gawain, who is somehow led to waive "a little foul sight

and misliking." She is bedded in all her repulsiveness, and turns to a beautiful young woman. To try Gawain's compliance further, she asks him whether he will have her in this likeness by night only or only by day. Putting aside his own preference, Gawain leaves the choice to her, and this is all that is needed to keep her perpetually beautiful. For a stepmother had witched her to go on the wild moor in that fiendly shape until she should meet some knight who would let her have all her will. Her brother, under a like spell, was to challenge men either to fight with him at odds or to answer his hard question.

These incidents, with the variation that Arthur (who does not show all his customary chivalry in this ballad) waits for Gawain's consent before he promises him in marriage, are found in a romance, probably of the fifteenth century, printed in Madden's *Syr Gawayne*, and somewhat hastily pronounced by the editor to be "unquestionably the original of the mutilated poem in the Percy folio." [†]

Arthur while hunting in Ingleswood, stalked and finally shot a great hart, which fell in a fern-brake. While the king, alone and far from his men, was engaged in making the assay, there appeared a groom, bearing the quaint name of Gromer Somer Joure,[‡] who grimly told him that he meant now to requite him for hav-

[*] Still so called: near Aiketgate, Hesket. Lysons, *Cumberland*, p. 112.

[†] 'The Weddynge of Sʳ Gawen and Dame Ragnell,' Rawlinson MS., C 86, Bodleian Library, the portion containing the poem being paper, and indicating the close of Henry VII's reign. The poem is in six-line stanzas, and, with a leaf that is wanting, would amount to about 925 lines. Madden's *Syr Gawayne*, lxiv, lxvii, 26, 298ᵃ–298y.

ing taken away his lands. Arthur represented that it would be a shame to knighthood for an armed man to kill a man in green, and offered him any satisfaction. The only terms Gromer would grant were that Arthur should come back alone to that place that day twelvemonth, and then tell him what women love best; not bringing the right answer, he was to lose his head. The king gave his oath, and they parted. The knights, summoned by the king's bugle, found him in heavy cheer, and the reason he would at first tell no man, but after a while took Gawain into confidence. Gawain advised that they two should ride into strange country in different directions, put the question to every man and woman they met, and write the answers in a book. This they did, and each made a large collection. Gawain thought they could not fail, but the king was anxious, and considered that it would be prudent to spend the only month that was left in prosecuting the inquiry in the region of Ingleswood. Gawain agreed that it was good to be speering, and bade the king doubt not that some of his saws should help at need.

Arthur rode to Ingleswood, and met a lady, riding on a richly-caparisoned palfrey, but herself of a hideousness which beggars words; nevertheless the items are not spared.[*] She came up to Arthur and told him that she knew his counsel; none of his answers would help. If he would grant her one thing, she would warrant his life; otherwise, he must lose his head. This one thing was that she should be Gawain's wife. The king said this lay with Gawain; he would do what he could, but it were a pity to make Gawain wed so foul a lady. "No matter," she rejoined, "though I be foul: choice for a mate

hath an owl. When thou comest to thine [2] answer, I shall meet thee; else art thou lost."

The king returned to Carlisle with a heart no lighter, and the first man he saw was Gawain, who asked how he had sped. Never so ill: he had met a lady who had offered to save his life, but she was the foulest he had ever seen, and the condition was that Gawain should be her husband. "Is that all?" said Gawain. "I will wed her once and again, though she were the devil; else were I no friend." Well might the king exclaim, "Of all knights thou bearest the flower!"

After five or six days more the time came for the answer. The king had hardly ridden a mile into the forest when he met the lady, by name Dame Ragnell. He told her Gawain should wed her, and demanded *her* answer. "Some say this and some say that, but above all things women desire to have the sovereignty; tell this to the knight; he will curse her that told thee, for his labor is lost." Arthur, thus equipped, rode on as fast as he could go, through mire and fen. Gromer was waiting, and sternly demanded the answer. Arthur offered his two books, for Dame Ragnell had told him to save himself by any of those answers if he could. "Nay, nay, king," said Gromer, "thou art but a dead man." "Abide, Sir Gromer, I have an answer shall make all sure. Women desire sovereignty." "She that told thee that was my sister, Dame Ragnell; I pray I may see her burn on a fire." And so they parted.

Dame Ragnell was waiting for Arthur, too, and would hear of nothing but immediate fulfillment of her bargain. She followed the king to his court, and required him to produce Gawain instantly, who came and plighted his troth. The queen begged her to be married privately, and early in the morning. Dame Ragnell would consent to no such arrangement. She would not go to church till high-mass time, and she would dine in the open hall. At her wedding she was dressed more splendidly than the queen, and she sat at the head of the table at the dinner afterwards. There her appetite was all but as horrible as her person: she ate three capons, three curlews, and great bake meats, all that was set before her, less and more.[†]

‡   Sir Gromer occurs in "The Turke and Gowin," Percy MS., Hales and Furnivall, I, 102; Sir Grummore Grammorsum, "a good knight of Scotland," in *Morte d'Arthur* ed. Wright, I, 286 and elsewhere (Madden); Gromere Gromorson (Grummore Gummursum) and Gromore somyr Ioure, in Malory's *Morte D'arthur*, ed. Sommer, 256, 258, 799.
*   Miss Martha Carey Thomas, in her *Dissertation on Sir Gawain and the Green Knight, etc.*, Zürich, 1883, pp. 62–64, has shown that the ugly woman in the English romances is probably derived from 'La damoisele hydeuse,' in the Perceval of Chrestien de Troyes, vv 5996–6015. See, also, *The Academy*, October 19, 1889, p. 255. (G. L. K.)

†   See 'King Henry,' the next ballad.

A leaf is wanting now, but what followed is easily imagined. She chided Gawain for his off-ishness, and begged him to kiss her, at least. "I will do more," said Gawain, and, turning, beheld the fairest creature he ever saw. But the transformed lady told him that her beauty would not hold: he must choose whether she should be fair by night and foul by day, or fair by day and foul by night.* Gawain said the choice was hard, and left all to her. "Gramercy," said the lady, "thou shalt have me fair both day and night." Then she told him that her step-dame had turned her into that monstrous shape by necromancy, not to recover her own till the best knight in England had wedded her and given her sovereignty in all points.† A charming little scene follows, vv 715–99, in which Arthur visits Gawain in the morning, fearing

* The Gaelic tale of 'The Hoodie' offers a similar choice. The hoodie, a species of crow, having married the youngest of a farmer's three daughters, says to her, "Whether wouldst thou rather that I should be a hoodie by day and a man at night, or be a hoodie at night and a man by day?" The woman maintains her proper sovereignty, and does not leave the decision to him: "'I would rather that thou wert a man by day and a hoodie at night,' says she. After this he was a splendid fellow by day, and a hoodie at night." Campbell, *Popular Tales of the West Highlands*, I, 63.
The having one shape by day and another by night is a common feature in popular tales: as, to be a bear by day and a man by night, Hrólfr Kraki's Saga, c. 26, Asbjørnsen og Moe, *Norske Folke-Eventyr*, No 41; a lion by day and a man by night, Grimms, *K. u. H. märchen*, No 88; a crab by day and a man by night, B. Schmidt, *Griechische Märchen, u. s. w.*, No 10; a snake by day and a mair by night, Karadshitch, *Volksmärchen der Serben*, Nos 9, 10; a pumpkin by day and a man by night, A. & A. Schott, *Walachische Mährchen*, No 23; a ring by day, a man by night, Müllenhoff, No 27, p. 466, Karadshitch, No 6, Afanasief, VI, 189; Curtin, *Myths and Folk-Lore of Ireland*, 1890, pp. 51, 68, 69, 71, 136; "La nuit si jolie fille, le jour si jolie biche:" Pineau, *Le Folk-Lore du Poitou*, p. 391; A raven by day, a woman by night: von Wlislocki, *M. u. S. der Bukowinaer u. Siebenbürger Armenier*, p. 75. On transformations of all kinds, see S. Prato, *Bulletin de Folklore*, 1892, p. 316ff. Three princes in 'Kung Lindorm,' Nicolovius, *Folklifwet*, p. 48ff, are cranes by day and men by night, the king himself being man by day and worm by night. The double shape is sometimes implied though not mentioned.
† The brother, Gromer Somer Joure, was a victim of the same necromancy; so the Carl of Carlile, Percy MS,, Hales & Furnivall, III, 291.

lest the fiend may have slain him. Something of this may very likely have been in that half page [291] of the ballad which is lost after stanza 48.

Gower and Chaucer both have this tale, though with a different setting, and with the variation, beyond doubt original in the story, that the man whose life is saved by rightly answering the question has himself to marry the monstrous woman in return for her prompting him.

Gower relates, *Confessio Amantis*, Book First, I, 89–104, ed. Pauli, that Florent, nephew of the emperor, as Gawain is of Arthur, slew Branchus, a man of high rank. Branchus's kin refrained from vengeance, out of fear of the emperor; but a shrewd lady, grandmother to Branchus, undertook to compass Florent's death in a way that should bring blame upon nobody. She sent for Florent, and told him that she would engage that he should not be molested by the family of Branchus if he could answer a question she would ask. He was to have a proper allowance of time to find the answer, but he was also to agree that his life should be for-feited unless his answer were right. Florent made oath to this agreement, and sought the opinions of the wisest people upon the subject, but their opinions were in no accord. Consider-ing, therefore, that he must default, he took leave of the emperor, adjuring him to allow no revenge to be taken if he lost his life, and went to meet his fate. But on his way through a forest he saw an ugly old woman, who called to him to stop. This woman told him that he was going to certain death, and asked what he would give her to save him. He said, anything she should ask, and she required of him a promise of mar-riage. That he would not give. "Ride on to your death, then," said she. Florent began to reflect that the woman was very old, and might be hid-den away somewhere till she died, and that there was no other chance of deliverance, and at last pledged his word that he would marry her if it should turn out that his life could be saved only through the answer that she should teach him. She was perfectly willing that he should try all other shifts first, but if they failed, then let him say that women cared most to be sovereign in love. Florent kept back this answer as long as he could. None of his own replies availed, and the lady who presided in judgment at last told him that he could be allowed but one more. Then he gave the old woman's answer, and was discharged, with a curse on her that told.[*]

The old woman was waiting for Florent, and he now had full leisure to inspect all her points; but he was a knight, and would hold his troth. He set her on his horse before him, rode by night and lay close by day, till he came to his castle. There the ladies made an attempt to attire her for the wedding, and she was the fouler for their pains. They were married that night. He turned away from the bride; she prayed him not to be so discourteous. He turned toward her, with a great moral effort, and saw (for the chamber was full of light) a lady of eighteen, of unequalled beauty. As he would have drawn her to him she forbade, and said he must make his choice, to have her such by day or by night. "Choose for us both," was his reply. "Thanks," quoth she, "for since you have made me sovereign, I shall be both night and day as I am now." She explained that, having been daughter of the king of Sicily, her stepmother had forshapen her, the spell to hold till she had won the love and the sovereignty of what knight passed all others in good name.

The scene of Chaucer's tale, The Wife of Bath, returns to Arthur's court. One of the bachelors of the household, when returning from hawking, commits a rape, for which he is condemned to death. But the queen and other ladies intercede for him, and the king leaves his life at the disposal of the queen. The queen, like the shrewd lady in Gower, but with no intent to trapan the young man, says that his [292] life shall depend upon his being able to tell her what women most desire, and gives him a year and a day to seek an answer. He makes extensive inquiries, but there is no region in which

two creatures can be found to be of the same mind, and he turns homeward very downcast.

On his way through a wood he saw a company of ladies dancing, and moved towards them, in the hope that he might learn something. But ere he came the dancers had vanished, and all he found was the ugliest woman conceivable sitting on the green. She asked the knight what he wanted, and he told her it was to know what women most desire. "Plight me thy troth to do the next thing I ask of thee, and I will tell thee." He gave his word, and she whispered the secret in his ear.

The court assembled, the queen herself sitting as justice, and the knight was commanded to say what thing women love best. He made his response triumphantly; there was no dissenting voice. But as soon as he was declared to have ransomed his life, up sprang the old woman he had met in the wood. She had taught the man his answer, he had plighted his word to do the first thing she asked of him, and now she asked him to make her his wife. The promise was not disputed, but the poor youth begged her to make some other request; to take all he had in the world, and let him go. She would not yield, and they were married the next day. When they have gone to bed, the old wife, "smiling ever mo," rallies her husband for his indifference, and lectures him for objecting to ugliness, age, and vulgar birth, which things, she says, are a great security for him, and then gives him his election, to have her ugly and old as she is, but true, or young and fair, with the possible contingencies. The knight has the grace to leave the decision to her. "Then I have the sovereignty," she says, "and I will be both fair and good; throw up the curtain and see." Fair and young she was, and they lived to their lives' end in perfect joy.

Chaucer has left out the step-mother and her bewitchment, and saves, humbles, and rewards the young knight by the agency of a good fairy; for the ugly old woman is evidently such by her own will and for her own purposes. She is "smiling ever mo," and has the power, as she says, to set all right whenever she pleases. Her fate is not dependent on the knight's compliance, though his is.

---

[*]   And whan that this matrons herde
    The maner how this knight answerde,
    She saide, Ha, treson, wo the be!
    That hast thus told the privete
    Which alle women most desire:
    I wolde that thou were a-fire!

So Sir Gawen and Dame Ragnell, vv 474f, and our ballad, stanzas 29, 30.

The Wife of Bath's Tale is made into a ballad, or what is called a sonnet, 'Of a Knight and a Fair Virgin,' in *The Crown Garland of Golden Roses*, compiled by Richard Johnson, not far from 1600: see the Percy Society reprint, edited by W. Chappell, vol. vi of the, series, p. 68. Upon Chaucer's story is founded Voltaire's tale, admirable in its way, of Ce qui plaît aux Dames, 1762; of which the author writes, 1765, November 4, that it had had great success at Fontainebleau in the form of a comic opera, entitled La Fée Urgèle.[*] The amusing ballad of The Knight and Shepherd's Daughter has much in common with the Wife of Bath's Tale, and might, if we could trace its pedigree, go back to a common original.[†]

Tales resembling the Marriage of Gawain must have been widely spread during the Middle Ages. The ballad of 'King Henry' has much in common with the one now under consideration, and Norse and Gaelic connections, and is probably much earlier. Parallels out of English include this, from an Icelandic saga:

Grímr was on the verge of marriage with Lopthæna, but a week before the appointed day the bride was gone, and nobody knew what had become of her. Her father had given her a step-mother five years before, and the step-mother had been far from kind; but what then? Grímr was restless and unhappy, and got no tidings. A year of scarcity coming, he left home with two of his people. After an adventure with four trolls, he had a fight with twelve men, in which, though they were all slain, he lost his comrades and was very badly wounded. As he lay on the ground, looking only for death, a woman passed, if so she might be called; for she was not taller than a child of seven years, so stout that Grímr's arms would not go round her,

misshapen, bald, black, ugly, and disgusting in every particular. She came up to Grímr, and asked him if he would accept his life from her. "Hardly," said he, "you are so loathsome." But life was precious, and he presently consented. She took him up and ran with him, as if he were a babe, till she came to a large cave; there she set him down, and it seemed to Grímr that she was uglier than before. "Now pay me for saving your life," she said, "and kiss me." "I cannot," said Grimr, "you look so diabolical." "Expect no help, then, from me," said she, "and I see that it will soon be all over with you." "Since it must be, loath as I am," said Grímr, and went and kissed her; she seemed not so bad to kiss as to look at. When night came she made up a bed, and asked Grímr whether he would lie alone or with her. "Alone," he answered. "Then," said she, "I shall take no pains about healing your wounds." Grímr said he would rather lie with her, if he had no other chance, and she bound up his wounds, so that he seemed to feel no more of them. No sooner was Grímr abed than he fell asleep, and when he woke, he saw lying by him almost the fairest woman he had ever laid eyes on, and marvellously like his true-love, Lopthæna. At the bedside he saw lying the troll-casing which she had worn; he jumped up and burned this. The woman was very faint; he sprinkled her with water, and she came to, and said, It is well for both of us; I saved thy life first, and thou hast freed me from bondage. It was indeed Lopthæna, whom the step-mother had transformed into a horrible shape, odious to men and trolls, which she should never come out of till a man should consent to three things,— which no man ever would,—to accept his life at her hands, to kiss her, and to share her bed. Gríms saga loðinkinna, Rafn, *Fornaldar Sögur*, II, 143–52.

Gorvömb, a monstrous creature, in reward for great services, asks to have the king's brother for husband, and in bed turns into a beautiful princess. She had been suffering under the spells of a step-mother. 'Gorvömb,' Arnason, II, 375, Powell, *Icelandic Legends*, Second Series, 366, 'The Paunch.'

Mr Whitley Stokes has pointed out that the incident of a hag turning into a beautiful

---

[*] This was a melodrama by Favart, in four acts: reduced in 1821 to one act, at the Gymnase.

[†] Chaucer's tale is commonly said to be derived from Gower's, but without sufficient reason. Vv 6507–14, ed. Tyrwhitt, are close to Dame Ragnell, 409–420. Gower may have got his from some Example-book. I have not seen it remarked, and therefore will note, that Example-books may have been known in England as early as 1000, for Aelfric seems to speak slightingly of them in his treatise on the Old Testament. The Proverbs, he says, is a "bigspellbóc, *ná swilce gé secgað*, ac wísdómes bigspell and warnung wið dysig," etc.

woman after a man has bedded with her occurs in the Book of Ballymote, an Irish MS. of about 1400, and elsewhere and earlier in Irish story, as in the Book of Leinster, a MS. of the middle of the twelfth century. *The Academy*, XLI, 399 (1892). It is singular that the sovereignty in the first tale is the sovereignty of Erin, with which the disenchanted hag rewards her deliverer, and not the sovereignty over woman's will which is the solution of the riddle in the ballad. See also the remarks of Mr Alfred Nutt in the same volume, p. 425 (and, again, *Academy*, October 19, 1889, p. 255), who, while denying the necessity for any continental derivation of the hideous woman, suggests that Rosette in Gautier's Conte du Graal, vv 25380–744, furnishes a more likely origin for her than Chrétien's damoisele, since it does not appear that the latter is under spells, and spells which are loosed by the action of a hero.[*]

Mr Clouston, *Originals and Analogues of some of Chaucer's Canterbury Tales*, p. 520 cites a pretty story from a modern Turkish author, in

which, as so often happens, parts are reversed. A young king of the fairies of a certain realm is cursed by his mother to appear old and ugly until a fair mortal girl shall love him enough to miss his company. This comes to pass after forty years, and the ugly old man becomes a beautiful youth of seventeen. *Phantasms from the Presence of God*, written in 1796–97 by 'Ali 'Aziz Efendi, the Cretan.

Sir Frederic Madden, in his annotations upon this ballad, 'Syr Gawayne,' p. 359, remarks that Sir Steven, stanza 31, does not occur in the Round Table romances; that Sir Banier, 32, is probably a mistake for Beduer, the king's constable; and that Sir Bore and Sir Garrett, in the same stanza, are Sir Bors de Gauves, brother of Lionel, and Gareth, or Gaheriet, the younger brother of Gawain.

'The Marriage of Sir Gawaine,' as filled out by Percy from the fragments in his manuscript, *Reliques*, 1765, III, 11, is translated by Bodmer, I, 110; by Bothe, p. 75; by Knortz, *Lieder u. Romanzen Alt-Englands*, p. 135.

---

[*]   See also O'Grady, *Silva Gadelica*, p. 328 ff; translation, p. 370 ff. F. N. Robinson.

1 KINGE ARTHUR liues in merry Carleile,
    And seemely is to see,
And there he hath with him Queene Genever,
    That bride soe bright of blee.

2 And there he hath with [him] Queene Gen-
        ever,
    That bride soe bright in bower,
And all his barons about him stoode,
    That were both stiffe and stowre.

3 The king kept a royall Christmasse,
    Of mirth and great honor,
    And when . . . .

      .   .   .   .

   *   *   *   *   *

4 'And bring me word what thing it is
    That a woman [will] most desire;
This shalbe thy ransome, Arthur,' he sayes,
    'For Ile haue noe other hier.'

5 *King* Arthur then held vp his hand,
    According thene as was the law;
He tooke his leaue of the baron there,
    And homward can he draw.

6 And when he came to merry Carlile,
    To his chamber he is gone,
And ther came to him his cozen Sir Gawaine,
    As he did make his mone.

7 And there came to him his cozen Sir Gawaine,
    That was a curteous knight;
'Why sigh you soe sore, vnckle Arthur,' he said,
    'Or who hath done thee vnright?'

8 'O peace, O peace, thou gentle Gawaine,
    That faire may thee beffall!
For if thou knew my sighing soe deepe,
    Thou wold not meruaile att all.'

9 'Ffor when I came to Tearne Wadling,
  A bold barron there I fand,
With a great club vpon his backe,
  Standing stiffe and strong.

10 'And he asked me wether I wold fight
  Or from him I shold begone,
O[r] else I must him a ransome pay,
  And soe depart him from.

11 'To fight with him I saw noe cause;
  Methought it was not meet;
For he was stiffe and strong with-all,
  His strokes were nothing sweete.

12 'Therefor this is my ransome, Gawaine,
  I ought to him to pay;
I must come againe, as I am sworne,
  Vpon the New Yeers day;

13 'And I must bring him word what thing it is

  .   .   .   .   .

    .   .   .   .   .

  .   .   .   .   .

*   *   *   *   *

14 Then king Arthur drest him for to ryde,
  In one soe rich array,
Toward the fore-said Tearne Wadling,
  That he might keepe his day.

15 And as he rode over a more,
  Hee see a lady where shee sate
Betwixt an oke and a greene hollen;
  She was cladd in red scarlett.

16 Then there as shold haue stood her mouth,
  Then there was sett her eye;
The other was in her forhead fast,
  The way that she might see.

17 Her nose was crooked and turnd outward,
  Her mouth stood foule a-wry;
A worse formed lady than shee was,
  Neuer man saw with his eye.

18 To halch vpon him, King Arthur,
  This lady was full faine,
But King Arthur had forgott his lesson,
  What he shold say againe.

19 'What knight art thou,' the lady sayd,
  'That will not speak to me?
Of me be thou nothing dismayd,
  Tho I be vgly to see.

20 'For I haue halched you curteouslye,
  And you will not me againe;
Yett I may happen Sir Knight,' shee said,
  'To ease thee of thy paine.'

21 'Giue thou ease me, lady,' he said,
  'Or helpe me any thing,
Thou shalt have gentle Gawaine, my cozen,
  And marry him with a ring.'

22 'Why, if I help thee not, thou noble King
    Arthur,
  Of thy owne hearts desiringe,
Of gentle Gawaine . . . . .

  .   .   .   .   .

*   *   *   *   *

23 And when he came to the Tearne Wadling,
  The baron there cold he finde,
With a great weapon on his backe,
  Standing stiffe and stronge.

24 And then he tooke King Arthurs letters in his
    hands,
  And away he cold them fling,
And then be puld out a good browne sword,
  And cryd himselfe a king.

25 And he sayd, I have thee and thy land, Arthur, [295]
  To doe as it pleaseth me,
For this is not thy ransome sure,
  Therfore yeeld thee to me.

26 And then bespoke him noble Arthur,
  And bad him hold his hand:
'And giue me leaue to speake my mind
  In defence of all my land.'

27 He said, As I came over a more,
  I see a lady where shee sate
Betweene an oke and a green hollen;
  Shee was clad in red scarlett.

28 And she says a woman will haue her will,
  And this is all her cheef desire:
Doe me right, as thou art a baron of sckill,
  This is thy ransome and all thy hyer.

29 He sayes, An early vengeance light on her!
　　She walkes on yonder more;
　　It was my sister that told thee this,
　　And she is a misshappen hore.

30 But heer Ile make mine avow to God
　　To doe her an euill turne,
　　For an euer I may thate fowle theefe get,
　　In a fyer I will her burne.

　　*　　*　　*　　*　　*

31 Sir Lancelott and Sir Steven bold,
　　They rode with them that day,
　　And the formost of the company
　　There rode the steward Kay.

32 Soe did Sir Banier and Sir Bore,
　　Sir Garrett with them soe gay,
　　Soe did Sir Tristeram *that* gentle knight,
　　To the forrest fresh and gay.

33 And when he came to the greene forrest,
　　Vnderneath a greene holly tree,
　　Their sate that lady in red scarlet
　　That vnseemly was to see.

34 Sir Kay beheld this ladys face,
　　And looked vppon her swire;
　　'Whosoeuer kisses this lady,' he sayes,
　　'Of his kisse he stands in feare.'

35 Sir Kay beheld the lady againe,
　　And looked vpon her snout;
　　'Whosoeuer kisses this lady,' he saies,
　　'Of his kisse he stands in doubt.'

36 'Peace, cozen Kay,' then said Sir Gawaine,
　　'Amend thee of thy life;
　　For there is a knight amongst vs all
　　That must marry her to his wife.'

37 'What! wedd her to wiffe!' then said Sir Kay,
　　'In the diuells name anon!
　　Gett me a wiffe where-ere I may,
　　For I had rather be slaine!'

38 Then some tooke vp their hawkes in hast,
　　And some tooke vp their hounds,
　　And some sware they wold not marry her
　　For citty nor for towne.

39 And then be-spake him noble *King* Arthur,
　　And sware there by this day,
　　'For a litle foule sight and mmisliking
　　　.　　　.　　　.　　　.　　　.

　　*　　*　　*　　*　　*

40 Then shee said, Choose thee, gentle Gawaine,
　　Truth as I doe say,
　　Wether thou wilt haue me in this liknesse
　　In the night or else in the day.

41 And then bespake him gentle Gawaine,
　　Was one soe mild of moode,
　　Sayes, Well I know what I wold say,
　　God grant it may be good!

42 To haue thee fowle in the night
　　When I with thee shold play—
　　Yet I had rather, if I might,
　　Haue thee fowle in the day.

43 'What! when lords goe with ther feires,' shee
　　　said,
　　'Both to the ale and wine,
　　Alas! then I must hyde my selfe,
　　I must not goe withinne.'

44 And then bespake him gentle Gawaine,
　　Said, Lady, that's but skill;
　　And because thou art my own lady,
　　Thou shalt haue all thy will.

45 Then she said 'Blesed be thou, gentle Gawain, *l.*
　　This day *that* I thee see,
　　For as thou seest me att this time,
　　From hencforth I wilbe.

46 My father was an old knight,
　　And yett it chanced soe
　　That he marryed a younge lady
　　That brought me to this woe.

47 Shee witched me, being a faire young lady,
　　To the greene forrest to dwell,
　　And there I must walke in womans liknesse,
　　Most like a feend of hell.

48 She witched my brother to a carlish b . . .
　　　.　　　.　　　.　　　.　　　.
　　.　　　.　　　.　　　.　　　.
　　　.　　　.　　　.　　　.　　　.

* * * * *
49 . . . .

'That looked soe foule, and that was wont
On the wild more to goe.'

50 'Come kisse her, brother Kay,' then said Sir
Gawaine,
'And amend thé of thy liffe;
I sweare this is the same lady
That I marryed to my wiffe.'

51 Sir Kay kissed that lady bright,
Standing vpon his ffeete;
He swore, as he was trew knight,
The spice was neuer soe sweete.

52 'Well, cozen Gawaine,' sayes Sir Kay,
'Thy chance is fallen arright,
For thou hast gotten one of the fairest maids
I euer saw with my sight.'

53 'It is my fortune,' said Sir Gawaine;
'For my vnckle Arthurs sake
I am glad as grasse wold be of raine,
Great ioy that I may take.'

54 Sir Gawaine tooke the lady by the one arme,
Sir Kay tooke her by the tother,
They led her straight to King Arthur,
As they were brother and brother.

55 King Arthur welcomed them there all,
And soe did Lady Geneuer his queene,
With all the knights of the Round Table,
Most seemly to be seene.

56 King Arthur beheld that lady faire
That was soe faire and bright,
He thanked Christ in Trinity
For Sir Gawaine that gentle knight.

57 Soe did the knights, both more and lesse,
Reioyced all that day
For the good chance that hapened was
To Sir Gawaine and his lady gay.

-----◆-----

1[1.] Qqueene.
3[3]. *Half a page gone from the MS., about 9 stanzas; and so after* 13[1], 22[3], 30[4], 39[3], 48[1].
19[1]. *Perhaps* sayes.
23[2]. he fimde.
25[1]. *Perhaps* sayes. 26[2]. *Perhaps* hands.
27[1]. He *altered from* the *in MS.*
31. "The 2d Part" *is written here in the left margin of the MS.* Furnivall.

34[2]. her smire.
37[4]. shaine.
41[2]. with one.
43[1]. seires.
44[2]. a skill. 45[3]. thou see
48[1]. Carlist B . . .
& *is printed* and.

32

KING HENRY

'King Henry.' **a.** The Jamieson-Brown MS., p. 31. **b.**
Minstrelsy of the Scottish Border, 1802, II, 132.

Scott describes his copy of 'King Henry' as "edited from the MS. of Mrs Brown, corrected by a recited fragment." This MS. of Mrs Brown was William Tytler's, in which, as we learn from Anderson's communication to Percy (see p. 89, above), this ballad was No 11. Anderson notes that it extended to twenty-two stanzas, the number in Scott's copy. No account is given of the recited fragment. As published by Jamieson, II, 194, the ballad is increased by interpolation to thirty-four stanzas. "The interpolations will be found inclosed in brackets," but a painful contrast of style of itself distinguishes them. They were entered by Jamieson in his manuscript as well.

The fourteenth stanza, as now printed, the eighteenth in Jamieson's copy, is not there bracketed as an interpolation, and yet it is not in the manuscript. This stanza, however, with some verbal variation, is found in Scott's version, and as it may have been obtained by Jamieson in one of his visits to Mrs Brown, it has been allowed to stand.

Lewis rewrote the William Tytler version for his *Tales of Wonder*, 'Courteous King Jamie,' II, 453, No 57, and it was in this shape that the ballad first came out, 1801.

The story is a variety of that which is found in 'The Marriage of Sir Gawain,' and has its parallel, as Scott observed, in an episode in Hrólfr Kraki's saga; A, Torfæus, *Historia Hrolfi Krakii*, c. vii, Havniæ, 1705; B, *Fornaldar Sögur*, Rafn, I, 30f, c. 15.

King Helgi, father of Hrólfr Kraki, in consequence of a lamentable misadventure, was liv-

ing in a solitary way in a retired lodge. One stormy Yule-night there was a loud wail at the door, after he had gone to bed. Helgi bethought himself that it was unkingly of him to leave anything to suffer outside, and got up and unlocked the door. There he saw a poor tattered creature of a woman, hideously misshapen, filthy, starved, and frozen (**A**), who begged that she might come in. The king took her in, and bade her get under straw and bearskin to warm herself. She entreated him to let her come into his bed, and said that her life depended on his conceding this boon. "It is not what I wish," replied Helgi, "but if it is as thou sayest, lie here at the stock, in thy clothes, and it will do me no harm." She got into the bed, and the king turned to the wall. A light was burning, and after a while the king took a look over his shoulder; never had he seen a fairer woman than was lying there, and not in rags, but in a silk kirtle. The king turned towards her now, and she informed him that his kindness had freed her from a weird imposed by her stepmother, which she was to be subject to till some king had admitted her to his bed, **A**. She had asked this grace of many, but no one before had been moved to grant it.

Every point of the Norse saga, except the stepmother's weird, is found in the Gaelic tale 'Nighean Righ fo Thuinn,' 'The Daughter of King Under-waves,' Campbell's *Popular Tales of the West Highlands*, No lxxxvi, III, 403f.

The Finn were together one wild night, when there was rain and snow. An uncouth woman knocked at Fionn's door about midnight, and cried to him to let her in under cover. "Thou strange, ugly creature, with thy hair down to thy heels, how canst thou ask me to let thee in!" he answered. She went away, with a scream, and the whole scene was repeated with Oisean. Then she came to Diarmaid. "Thou art hideous," he said, "and thy hair is down to thy heels, but come in." When she had come in, she told Diarmaid that she had been travelling over ocean and sea for seven years, without being housed, till he had admitted her. She asked that she might come near the fire. "Come," said Diarmaid; but when she approached everybody retreated, because she was so hideous. She had not been long at the fire, when she wished to be under Diarmaid's blanket. "Thou art growing too bold," said he, "but come." She came under the blanket, and he turned a fold of it between them. "She was not long thus, when he gave a start, and he gazed at her, and he saw the finest drop of blood that ever was, from the beginning of the universe till the end of the world, at his side."

Mr Campbell has a fragment of a Gaelic ballad upon this story, vol. xvii., p. 212 of his manuscript collection, 'Collun gun Cheann,' or 'The Headless Trunk,' twenty-two lines. In this case, as the title imports, a body without a head replaces the hideous, dirty, and unkempt draggle-tail who begs shelter of the Finn successively and obtains her boon only from Diarmaid. See Campbell's *Gaelic Ballads*, p. ix.

The monstrous deformity of the woman is a trait in the ballad of 'The Marriage of Sir Gawain,' and related stories, and is described in these with revolting details. Her exaggerated appetite also is found in the romance of The Wedding of Sir Gawen and Dame Ragnell, see p. 392. The occasion on which she exhibits it is there the wedding feast, and the scene consequently resembles, even more closely there than here, what we meet with in the Danish ballads of 'Greve Genselin,' Grundtvig, No 16, I, 222, and 'Tord af Havsgaard,' Grundtvig, No 1, I, 1, IV, 580 (= Kristensen, 'Thors Hammer,' I, 85, No 85) the latter founded on the Þrymskviða, or Hamarsheimt of the older Edda. In a Norwegian version of 'Greve Genselin,' Grundtvig, IV, 732, the feats of eating and drinking are performed not by the bride, but by an old woman who acts as bridesmaid, brúrekvinne.[*]

A maid who submits, at a linden-worm's entreaty, to lie in the same bed with him, finds a king's son by her side in the morning: Grundtvig, 'Lindormen,' No 65, **B**, **C**, II, 213, III, 839; Kristensen, I, 195, No 71; Afzelius, III, 121, No 88; Arwidsson, II, 270, No 139; Hazelius, *Ur de nordiska Folkens Lif*, p. 117, and p. 149; Kristensen, *Jyske Folkeminder*, X, 20, No 9, Lagus, *Nyländska Folkvisor*, I, 97, No 29, *a*, *b*. (Lindworm asks for a kiss in *a* 4, *b* 2); Brüder Zingerle, *Tirols Volksdichtungen*, II, 173 ff; cf. II, 317. (G. L. K.) In 'Ode und de Slang',' Müllenhoff, *Sagen u. s. w.*, p. 383, a maid, without much reluctance, lets a snake successively come into the house, into her chamber, and finally into her bed, upon which the snake changes immediately into a prince. In J. Krainz, *Mythen u. Sagen aus dem steirischen Hochlande*. No. 147, p. 194, a man marries a snake. At midnight it becomes a woman, and it keeps that form thereafter

"In an unpublished story of the Monferrato, communicated to me by Dr Ferraro, a beautiful girl, when plucking up a cabbage, sees under its roots a large room, goes down into it, and finds a serpent there, who promises to make her fortune if she will kiss him and sleep with him. The girl consents. After three months the serpent begins to assume the legs of a man, then a man's body, and finally the face of a handsome youth, the son of a king, and marries his young deliverer." De Gubernatis, *Zoölogical Mythology*, II, 418. (G. L. K.)

Scott's copy is translated by Schubart, p. 127, and by Gerhard, p. 129; Jamieson's, without the interpolations, after Aytoun, II, 22, by Knortz, *Schottische Balladen*, No 36.

---

[*]   The like by a carlin at a birth-feast, 'Kællingen til Barsel,' Kristensen, II, 341, No 100, Landstad, p. 666, No 96; known also in Sweden. Again, by a fighting friar, 'Den stridbare Munken,' Arwidsson, I, 417. 'Greve Genselin' is translated by Prior, I, 173, and by Jamieson, *Illustrations of Northern Antiquities*, p. 310; 'Tord af Havsgaard' by Prior, I, 3. So of a frog, Colshorns, p. 139, No 42.

Lat nev-er a man a woo - ing wend, That lack-eth thing - is three,

A___ routh o' gold, and o - pen heart,___ An' fu' o' char - i - ty.

a. Ritson-Tytler-Brown MS. Sung by Mrs Brown, Falkland, Aberdeenshire.

1 LAT never a man a wooing wend
   That lacketh thingis three;
   A routh o gold, an open heart,
   Ay fu o charity.

2 As this I speak of King Henry,
   For he lay burd-alone;
   An he's doen him to a jelly hunt's ha,
   Was seven miles frac a town.

3 He chas'd the deer now him before,
   An the roe down by the den,
   Till the fattest buck in a' the flock
   King Henry he has slain.

4 O he has doen him to his ha,
   To make him beerly cheer;
   An in it came a griesly ghost,
   Steed stappin i the fleer.

[299] 5 Her head hat the reef-tree o the house,
   Her middle ye mot wel span;
   He's thrown to her his gay mantle,
   Says, 'Lady, hap your lingcan.'

6 Her teeth was a' like teather stakes,
   Her nose like club or mell;
   An I ken naething she 'peard to be,
   But the fiend that wons in hell.

7 'Some meat, some meat, ye King Henry,
   Some meat ye gie to me!'
   'An what meat's in this house, lady,
   An what ha I to gie?'
   'O ye do kill your berry-brown steed,
   An you bring him here to me.'

8 O whan he slew his berry-brown steed,
   Wow but his heart was sair!
   Shee eat him [a'] up, skin an bane,
   Left naething but hide an hair.

9 'Mair meat, mair meat, ye King Henry,
   Mair meat ye gi to me!'
   'An what meat's in this house, lady,
   An what ha I to gi?'
   'O ye do kill your good gray-hounds,
   An ye bring them a' to me.'

10 O whan he slew his good gray-hounds,
   Wow but his heart was sair!
   She eat them a' up, skin an bane,
   Left naething but hide an hair.

11 'Mair meat, mair meat, ye King Henry,
   Mair meat ye gi to me!'
   'An what meat's i this house, lady,
   An what ha I to gi?'
   'O ye do kill your gay gos-hawks,
   An ye bring them here to me.'

12 O whan he slew his gay gos-hawks,
   Wow but his heart was sair!
   She eat them a' up, skin an bane,
   Left naething but feathers bare.

13 'Some drink, some drink, now, King Henry,
   Some drink ye bring to me!'
   'O what drink's i this house, lady,
   That you're nae welcome ti?'
   'O ye sew up your horse's hide,
   An bring in a drink to me.'

14 And he's sewd up the bloody hide,
   A puncheon o wine put in;
   She drank it a' up at a waught,
   Left na ae drap ahin.

15 'A bed, a bed, now, King Henry,
   A bed you mak to me!
   For ye maun pu the heather green,
   An mak a bed to me.'

16 O pu'd has he the heather green,
 An made to her a bed,
An up has he taen his gay mantle,
 An oer it has he spread.

17 'Tak aff your claiths, now, King Henry,
 An lye down by my side!'
'O God forbid,' says King Henry,
 'That ever the like betide;
That ever the fiend that wons in hell
 Shoud streak down by my side.'

 * * * * *

18 Whan night was gane, and day was come,
 An the sun shone throw the ha,
The fairest lady that ever was seen
 Lay atween him an the wa.

19 'O well is me!' says King Henry,
 'How lang'll this last wi me?'
Then out it spake that fair lady,
 'Even till the day you dee.

20 'For I've met wi mony a gentle knight
 That's gien me sic a fill,
But never before wi a courteous knight
 That ga me a' my will.'

---

a. 13⁵. shew. 19¹. will.
b. 1. *The first stanza of the original of this copy, as cited by Anderson, is:*

 Let never a man a wooing wend
  That lacketh things three,
 A routh of gold, and open heart,
  An fu o charity.

1⁴. And fu o courtesey.
2¹. And this was seen o.
2³. And he has taen him to a haunted hunt's ha.
3¹. He's chaced the dun deer thro the wood.
3³. in a' the herd.
4. He's taen him to his hunting ha,
  For to make burly cheir;
  When loud the wind was heard to sound,
  And an earthquake rocked the floor.

 And darkness coverd a' the hall,
  Where they sat at their meat;
 The gray dogs, youling, left their food,
  And crept to Henrie's feet.

 And louder houled the rising wind
  And burst the fastned door;
 And in there came a griesly ghost,
  Stood stamping on the floor.

The wind and darkness are not of Scott's invention, for nearly all that is not in **a** *is found in Lewis, too.*

5³,⁴. Each frighted huntsman fled the ha,
  And left the king alone.

7⁴⁻⁶. That ye're nae wellcum tee?'
 'O ye's gae kill your berry brown steed,
  And serve him up to me.'

9⁴. That ye're na wellcum tee
10³. a' up, ane by ane.

11⁴⁻⁶. That I hae left to gie?'
 'O ye do fell your gay goss-hawks,
  And bring them a' to me.'

12¹. he felled. 12³. bane by bane.
14². And put in a pipe of wine.
14³. up a' at ae draught. 14⁴. drap therein.
15. *Between* ² *and* ³:

 And what's the bed i this house, ladye,
  That ye're nae wellcum tee?

15³. O ye maun pu the green heather.

17¹,². Now swear, now swear, ye king Henrie,
 To take me for your bride.

18¹. When day was come, and night was gane.
19³. And out and spak that ladye fair.
20. For I was witched to a ghastly shape,
  All by my stepdame's skill,
 Till I should meet wi a courteous knight
  Wad gie me a' my will.

33

KEMPY KAY

A. 'Kempy Kay.' Pitcairn's MSS, II, 125. *Scottish Ballads and Songs* [James Maidment], Edinb. 1859, p. 35; Sharpe's *Ballad Book*, p. 81.
B. 'Kempy Kaye.' **a.** Kinloch MSS, I, 65. **b.** Kinloch's *Ballad Book*, p. 41.
C. 'Kempy Kay,' or 'Kempy Kane,' Motherwell's MS., p. 193. The first stanza in Motherwell's *Minstrelsy*, Appendix, p. xxiv, No XXX.

D. 'Kempy Kay,' Motherwell's MS., p. 192.
E. 'Drowsy Lane.' Campbell MSS, II, 122.
F. 'Bar aye your bower door weel.' Campbell MSS, II, 101.
G. 'King Knapperty.' Buchan's MSS, I, 133.

ALL these versions of 'Kempy Kay' are known, or may be presumed, to have been taken down within the first three decades of this century; **A** is traced as many years back into the last. The fourth stanza of **A** clearly belongs to some other ballad. Both **A** and **B** appear to have undergone some slight changes when published by Sharpe and Kinloch respectively. Some verses from this ballad have been [301] adopted into one form of a still more unpleasant piece in the Campbell collection, concerning a wife who was "the queen of all sluts."[*]

[*] MSS, II, 294, "What a had luck had I" = The Queen of all Sluts, the same, p. 297. Stanzas 2, 3, 4, of the former are:

> Then een in her head are like two rotten plumbs;
> Turn her about and see how she glooms.
>
> The teeth in her head were like harrow-pins;
> Turn her about, and see how she girns.
>
> The hair in her head was like heathercrows,
> The l. . . s were in 't thick as linseed bows.

A comparatively inoffensive version, 'The Queen of Sluts,' in Chambers' *Scottish Songs*, p. 454.
I have serious doubts whether this offensive ballad has not been made too important; whether, notwithstanding the points noted below, it is anything more than a variety of 'The Queen of all Sluts.'

Sharpe remarks: "This song my learned readers will perceive to be of Scandinavian origin, and that the wooer's name was probably suggested by Sir Kaye's of the Round Table. . . . The description of Bengoleer's daughter resembles that of the enchanted damsel who appeared to courteous King Henrie." It is among possibilities that the ballad was an outgrowth from some form of the story of The Marriage of Sir Gawain, in the Percy version of which the "unseemly" lady is so rudely commented on and rejected by Kay. This unseemly lady, in The Wedding of Gawen and Dame Ragnell, and her counterpart in 'King Henry,' who is of superhuman height, show an extravagant voracity which recalls the giantess in 'Greve Genselin.' In 'Greve Genselin,' a burlesque form of an heroic ballad which is preserved in a pure shape in three Färöe versions (Grundtvig, IV, 737–42), there are many kemps invited to the wedding, and in a little dance which is had the smallest kemp is fifteen ells to [below] the knee, Grundtvig, No 16, **A** 26, **B** 29, **C** 29. Kempy Kay has gigantic dimensions in **A** 7, **C** 9, **E** 7: teeth like tether-stakes, a nose three [nine, five] feet long, three ells [nine yards] between his shoulders, a span between his eyne.[†] Of the bride it is said in **A** 12 that her finger nails were like the teeth of a rake and her teeth like tether-stakes. This is not decisive; it is her ugliness, filthiness, and laziness that are made most of. We may assume that she would be in dimension and the shape of nature a

---

† The Carl of Carlile has the space of a large span between his brows, three yards over his shoulders, fingers like tether-stakes, and fifty cubits of height. Percy MS., Hales & Furnivall, III, 283f, vv 179–187.

match for the kemp, but she does not comport herself especially like a giantess.

If Kempy Kay be the original name of the wooer, Knapperty and Chickmakin might easily be derived from corrupt pronunciations like Kampeky, Kimpaky.

A

Pitcairn's MSS, II, 125, as taken down by Mr Pitcairn from the singing of his aunt, Mrs Gammell, who had learned it in the neighborhood of Kincaid, Stirlingshire, when a child, or about 1770. *Scotish Ballads and Songs* [James Maidment], Edinburgh, 1859, p. 35; Sharpe's *Ballad Book*, p. 81.

1 Kempy Kaye's a wooing gane,
    Far, far ayont the sea,
And he has met with an auld, auld man,
    His gudefaythir to be.

2 'It's I'm coming to court your daughter dear,
    And some part of your gear:'
'And by my sooth,' quoth Bengoleer,
    'She'll sare a man a wear.

3 'My dochter she's a thrifty lass,
    She span seven year to me,
And if it were weel counted up,
    Full three heire it would be.

4 'What's the matter wi you, my fair creature,
    You look so pale and wan?
I'm sure you was once the fairest creature
    That ever the sun shined on.

5 'Gae scrape yoursel, and gae scart yoursel,
    And mak your brucket face clean,
For the wooers are to be here to nighte,
    And your body's to be seen.'

6 Sae they scrapit her, and they scartit her,
    Like the face of an aussy pan;
Syne in cam Kempy Kay himself,
    A clever and tall young man.

7 His teeth they were like tether-sticks,
    His nose was three fit lang,
Between his shouthers was ells three,
    And tween his eyne a span.

8 He led his dochter by the hand,
    His dochter ben brought he:
'O is she not the fairest lass
    That's in great Christendye?'

9 Ilka hair intil her head
    Was like a heather-cowe,
And ilka louse anunder it
    Was like a bruckit ewe.

10 She had tauchy teeth and kaily lips,
    And wide lugs, fou o hair;
Her pouches fou o peasemeal-daighe
    A' hinging down her spare.

11 Ilka eye intil her head
    Was like a rotten plumbe,
And down browed was the queyne,
    And sairly did she gloom.

12 Ilka nail upon her hand
    Was like an iron rake,
And ilka tooth intil her head
    Was like a tether-stake.

*   *   *   *   *

13 She gied to him a gravat,
    O the auld horse's sheet,
And he gied her a gay gold ring,
    O the auld couple-root.

B

a. Kinloch MSS, I, 65. b. Kinloch's *Ballad Book*, p. 41. From the recitation of Mary Barr.

1 KEMPY KAY is a wooing gane,
    Far ayont the sea,
And there he met wi auld Goling,
    His gudefather to be, be,
    His gudefather to be.

2 'Whare are ye gaun, O Kempy Kaye,
    Whare are ye gaun sae sune?'
'O I am gaun to court a wife,
    And think na ye that's weel dune?'

3 'An ye be gaun to court a wife,
    As ye do tell to me,
'T is ye sall hae my Fusome Fug,
    Your ae wife for to be.'

4 Whan auld Goling cam to the house,
    He lookit thro a hole,
And there he saw the dirty drab
    Just whisking oure the coal.

5 'Rise up, rise up my Fusome Fug,
    And mak your foul face clean,
For the brawest wooer that ere ye saw
    Is come develling doun the green.'

6 Up then rose the Fusome Fug,
    To mak her foul face clean;
And aye she cursed her mither
    She had na water in.

7 She rampit out, and she rampit in,
    She rampit but and ben;
The tittles and tattles that hang frae her tail
    Wad muck an acre o land.

8 She had a neis upon her face
    Was like an auld pat-fit;
Atween her neis bot an her mou
    Was inch thick deep wi dirt.

9 She had twa een intil her head
    War like twa rotten plums;
The heavy brows hung doun her face,
    And O I vow she glooms!

10 He gied to her a braw silk napkin,
    Was made o' an auld horse-brat:
'I ne'er wore a silk napkin a' my life,
    But weel I wat Ise wear that.'

11 He gied to her a braw gowd ring,
    Was made frae an auld brass pan:
'I neer wore a gowd ring in a' my life,
    But now I wat Ise wear ane.'

12 Whan thir twa lovers had met thegither,
    O kissing to get their fill,
The slaver that hang atween their twa gabs
    Wad hae tetherd a ten year auld bill.

C

Motherwell's MS., p. 193. Motherwell's *Minstrelsy*,
Appendix, p. xxiv, No XXX, the first stanza.

Kem - py Kane's a woo - in' gane, And far ay - ont the sea a - wee;

And there he met wi' Drear - y - lane, His gay gude father to be a - wee.

1 KEMPY KAYE's a wooing gane,
   And far beyond the sea,   a wee
 And there he met wi Drearylane,
   His gay gudefather to be.   a wee

2 'Gude een, gude een,' quo Drearylane,
   'Gude een, gude een,' quo he,   a wee
 'I've come your dochter's love to win,
   I kenna how it will do.'   a wee

3 'My dochter she's a thrifty lass,
   She's spun this gay seven year,
 And if it come to gude guiding,
   It will be half a heer.'

4 'Rise up, rise up, ye dirty slut,
   And wash your foul face clean;
 The wooers will be here the night
   That suld been here yestreen.'

5 They took him ben to the fire en,
   And set him on a chair;
 He looked on the lass that he loved best,
   And thought she was wondrous fair.

6 The een that was in our bride's head
   Was like twa rotten plooms;
 She was a chaunler-chaftit quean,
   And O but she did gloom!

7 The skin that was on our bride's breast
   Was like a saffron bag,
 And aye her hand was at her neek,
   And riving up the scabs.

8 The hair that was on our bride's head
   Was like a heather-cow,
 And every louse that lookit out
   Was like a brockit ewe.

9 Betwixd Kempy's shouthers was three ells,
   His nose was nine feet lang,
 His teeth they were like tether sticks,
   Between his eyne a span.

10 So aye they kissed, and aye they clapped,
   I wat they kissed weel;
 The slaver that hang between their mouths
   Wad hae tethered a twa year auld bill.

D

Motherwell's MS., p. 192.

*   *   *   *   *

1 THE father came unto the door,
   And keeked thro the key-hole,   a wee
 And there he saw his dochter Jean,
   Sitting on a coal.   a wee

2 They scartit her, and scrapit her,
   Wi the hand o a rusty pan,   a wee
 Her father he did all his best
   For to get her a man.   a wee

3 She is to the stoups gane,
   There is nae water in;
 She's cursed the hands and ban'd the feet
   That did na bring it in.

4 Out then spak her auld mither,
   In her bed whare she lay:
 'If there is nae water in the house,
   Gae harl her thro the lin.'

5 O she is to the saipy-sapples gane,
   That stood for seven year,
And there she washed her foul face clean,
   And dried it wi a huggar.

6 He's gien her a gay gold ring,
   Just like a cable-rope,
And she's gien him a gay gravat,
   Made out o the tail o a sark.

E

Campbell MSS, II, 122.

1 'Gud een, gud een,' says Chickmakin,
   'Ye're welcome here,' says Drowsy Lane;
   'I'm comd to court your daughter Jean,
   And marry her wi yer will, a wee.'

2 'My daughter Jean's a thrifty lass,
   She's spun these seven lang years to me,
   And gin she spin another seven
   She'll munt a half an heir, a wee.'

[304]

3 Drowsy Lane, it's he's gane hame,
   And keekit through the hole,   a wee
And there he saw his daughter Jean
   A reeking oer the coal.   a wee

4 'Get up, get up, ye dirty bitch,
   And wash yer foul face clean,
For they are to be here the night
   That should hae been here yestreen.'

5 Up she rose, pat on her clothes,
   She's washen her foul face clean;
She cursd the hands, she ban'd the feet,
   That wadna bring the water in.

6 She rubbit hersel, she scrubbit hersel,
   Wi the side of a rustit pan, a wee,
And in a little came Chickmakin,
   A braw young lad indeed was he.

7 His teeth they were like tether-steeks,
   His nose was five feet lang;
Between his shoulders was nine yards broad,
   And between his een a span.

8 Ilka hair into his head
   Was like a heather-cowe,
And ilka louse that lookit out
   Was like a brookit ewe.

9 Thae twa kissd and thae twa clapt,
   And thae twa kissd their fill,
And aye the slaver between them hang
   Wad tetherd a ten-pund bull.

10 They twa kissd and they twa clapt,
   And they gaed to their bed, a wee,
And at their head a knocking stane
   And at their feet a mell, a wee.

11 The auld wife she lay in her bed:
   'And gin ye'll do my bidding a wee,
And gin ye'll do my bidding,' quoth she,
   'Yees whirl her oer the lea, a wee.'

F

Campbell MSS, II, 101.

1 As I cam oer yon misty muir,
   And oer yon grass-green hill,
There I saw a campy carle
   Going to the mill.
And bar aye yer bower door weel weel,
And bar aye yer bower door weel.

2 I lookit in at her window,
   And in at her hove hole,
And there I saw a fousome fag,
   Cowering oer a coal.

3 'Get up, get up, ye fousome fag,
   And make yer face fou clean;
For the wooers will be here the night,
   And your body will be seen.'

4 He gave her a gay cravat,
   'T was of an auld horse-sheet;
He gave her a gay goud ring,
   'T was of an auld tree root.

5 He laid his arms about her neck,
  They were like kipple-roots;
  And aye he kissd her wi his lips,
  They were like meller's hoops.

6 When they were laid in marriage bed,
  And covered oer wi fail,
  The knocking mell below their heads
  Did serve them wondrous weel.

7 Ilka pap into her breasts
  Was like a saffron bag,
  And aye his hand at her a . . e
  Was tearing up the scabs.

8 Ilka hair into her head
  Was like a heather-cow,
  And ilka louse that lookit out
  Was like a brookit ewe.

G

Buchan's MSS, I, 133.

1 KING KNAPPERTY he's a hunting gane,
  Oer hills and mountains high, high, high,
  A gude pike-staff intill his hand,
  And dulgets anew forbye, I, I, I,
  And dulgets anew forbye.

2 Then he met in wi an auld woman,
  Was feeding her flocks near by, I, I, I:
  'I'm come a wooing to your daughter,
  And a very gude bargain am I, I, I.'

3 And she's awa to her wee hole house,
  Lookd in a wee chip hole,
  And there she saw her filthy wee flag,
  Was sitting athort the coal.

4 'Get up, get up, ye filthy foul flag,
  And make your foul face clean;
  There are wooers coming to the town,
  And your foul face mauna be seen.'

5 Then up she raise, an awa she gaes,
  And in at the back o the door,
  And there a pig o water she saw,
  'T was seven years auld an mair.

6 Aye she rubbed, an aye she scrubbed,
  To make her foul face clean,
  And aye she bannd the auld wife, her mither,
  For nae bringing clean water in.

7 King Knapperty he came in at the door,
  Stood even up in the floor;
  Altho that she had neer seen him before,
  She kent him to be her dear.

8 He has taen her in his arms twa,
  And kissd her, cheek and chin:
  'I neer was kissd afore in my life,
  But this night got mony ane.'

9 He has put his hand in his pocket,
  And he's taen out a ring:
  Says, 'Take ye that, my dearest dear,
  It is made o the brazen pan.'

10 She thankd him ance, she thankd him twice,
   She thankd him oer again:
   'I neer got a ring before in my life,
   But this night hae gotten ane.'

11 These lovers bed it was well made,
   And at their hearts' desire;
   These lovers bed it was well made,
   At the side o the kitchen fire.

12 The bolster that these lovers had
   Was the mattock an the mell,
   And the covring that these lovers had
   Was the clouted cloak an pale.

13 The draps that fell frae her twa een
   Woud have gard a froth-mill gang,
   An [the] clunkerts that hung at their heels
   Woud hae muckd an acre o land.

14 An ilka hair that was in their head
   Was like a heather-cow,
   And ilka tenant that it containd
   Was like a lintseed-bow.

———————◆———————

A. $5^{3,4}$. *Var.* For Kempy Kay will be here the night
        Or else the morn at een.

9^4. *Var.* Was like a lintseed bow.

These variations are found in Sharpe's copy.
The first seven stanzas are put in the order 1, 6, 7, 3,
2, 4, 5.
2^1. I'm coming.
3^4. Full ten wobs it would be.
$4^{1,3}$. fair maiden, fairest maiden.
5^2. bruchty. 6^3. And in.
7^4. Between his een.
10^4. War hinging.
11^3. An down down.
12^3. teeth, *no doubt to indicate the pronunciation.*

A was communicated to C. K. Sharpe by Robert
Pitcairn with the stanzas in the order printed by
Sharpe. The arrangement in **A** would seem,
therefore, to have been an afterthought of
Pitcairn's. There is some slight difference of
reading, also, in Pitcairn's MS., and one defect
is supplied. Since we have Pitcairn's copy only
in Sharpe's handwriting, we cannot determine
which of the two made the changes. The varia-
tions in the copy sent Sharpe are (besides the
order, as aforesaid) as follows:

2^1. I'm coming. 2^4. o weir.
3^4. three heire *wanting.* 4^4. Shone. 5^2. A bruchty.
5^3. the night. 6^3. And in. 7^4. Between.
9^4. a lintseed bow (*with the variant* a bruchtit ewe).
10^1. lauchty *in Sharpe with a line drawn in ink
through* l (*probably by the editor, as this is a presen-
tation copy*).
10^4. A' *wanting.* 12^3. teeth into.
13^2. sheets (*no doubt erroneously*). A *stanza
between* 8 *and* 9 *is noted as deficient, and some-
thing after* 13.
B. a. 4^1. Whan Kempy Kaye. *Other copies show that it
must be the father, and not the wooer.*
6^3. ae, *with* ay *in the margin: qu.* aye as?

b. *The variations of the* Ballad Book *are apparently
arbitrary.*
1^2. Far far. 8^4. o dirt.
After 9 *follows:*   [3c

        Ilka hair that was on her head
            Was like a heather cow,
        And ilka louse that lookit out
            Was like a lintseed bow.

a^4 *succeeds, with* Kempy Kaye *for* auld Goling, *and is
necessarily transferred if the reading* Kempy Kaye
is retained.
C. *The order of the first five stanzas in the MS is* 1, 2, 5,
4, 3.
    A wee *is the burden after every second and fourth
    verse, and so with* **D.**
    $1^{1,2}$. *In* Motherwell's Minstrelsy, *Appendix, p. xxiv,
    No xxx,*

        Kempy Kane's a wooin gane,
            And far ayont the sea awee.

    3^2. years. 5^2. on a stool.

    In a copy of **C** *sent Sharpe by Motherwell in a letter of
    December* 6, 1824, *the fourth stanza is lacking, the
    fifth is third.*

    3^2. span : years. 5^2. stool.

D. *The first stanza is numbered* 3 *in the MS., the second
5, and there is space left, as if for another, between
2 and* 3.
E. A wee, *originally a burden at the middle and the end
of the stanza, as in* **C, D,** *has been adopted into the
verse in* 1, 2, 6, 10(?), 11, *in which stanzas the
even lines are of four accents instead of three.* 2, 6
can be easily restored, on the model of **C** 3, **A** 6.
    5^4. in the water.
G. I, I, I *is added as burden to every second and fourth
line; except* 1^2, *which adds* high, high, *and* 2^4, *only*
I, I.

———————◆———————

APPENDIX

Additional Copies

'Knip Knap,' taken down in the summer of 1893 by
Mr Walker, of Aberdeen, at Portlethen, from the sing-
ing of an old man, as learned more than fifty years
before from an old blacksmith at Dyce, near Aberdeen.

1 KNIP KNAP a hunting went,
  Out-ower the head o yon hill, aye, aye
Wi a lust o pig-staves out-oer his shouther,
  An mony a dulchach forby, aye, aye

2 There he met an old woman,
  Was herdin at her kye;
'I'm come yer ae dochter to woo,'
  'She's a very good servant,' said I.

3 The wife gaed hame to her ain hole-house,
  Lookit in at her ain spunk-hole,
An there she saw her ain foul flag,
  Loupin across the coal.

4 'Win up, win up, my ae foul flag,
  An mak yer foul face clean,
For yer wooer is comin here the nicht,
  But yer foul face canna be seen. na, na'

5 She's taen the sheave-wisps out o her sheen,
  An in behint the door,
An she has faen to the stale strang,
  Seven year auld an more.

6 An aye she scrubbit, an aye she weesh,
  Out-ower the pint o her chin,
Till a knip-knap cam to the door,
  She kent it was her wooer.

7 He's taen her in his airms twa,
  Kissd her cheek an chin:
'An I hae gotten kisses twa,
  Whaur I never thocht to get ane.'

8 The verra hair was in her head
  Was like the heather-cowe,
An ilka louse at the reet o that
  Was like a brockit ewe.

9 The verra ee was in her head
  Was like a muckle pan,
The hunkers and clunkers that hang frae her
    sheen
  Wad hae covered an acre o lan.

10 The verra teeth was in her head
   Was like a tether's cheek,
An the sneeters and snotters that hang frae her
    nose
   Wad a gart a frozen mill gang.

11 The verra tongue was in her head
   Wad been a guid mill-clap,

12 .

An ye may know very weel by that
  She was a comely woman.

34

KEMP OWYNE

A. 'Kemp Owyne.' Buchan's *Ballads of the North of Scotland*, II, 78; Motherwell's *Minstrelsy*, p. 373; 'Kemp Owayne,' Motherwell's MS., p. 448.

B. 'Kempion.' **a.** Jamieson-Brown MS., p. 29. **b.** Scott's *Minstrelsy*, 1802, II, 93, from William Tytler's Brown MS., No 9, "with corrections from a recited fragment."

It is not, perhaps, material to explain how Owain, "the king's son Urien," happens to be awarded the adventure which here follows. It is enough that his right is as good as that of other knights to whom the same achievement has been assigned, though the romance, or, as the phrase used to be, "the book," says nothing upon the subject. Owain's slaying the fire-drake who was getting the better of the lion may have led to his name becoming associated with the still more gallant exploit of thrice kissing a fire-drake to effect a disenchantment. The ring in **A** 9 might more plausibly be regarded as being a repetition of that which Owain's lady gave him on leaving her for a twelvemonth's outing, a ring which would keep him from loss of blood, and also from prison, sickness, and defeat in battle—in short, preserve him against all the accidents which the knight suggested might prevent his holding his day—provided that he had it by him and thought on her. Ritson, *Ywaine and Gawin*, vv 1514–38.

But an Icelandic saga comes near enough to the story of the ballad as given in **A** to show where its connections lie. Álsól and a brother and sister are all transformed by a stepmother, a handsome woman, much younger than her husband. Álsól's heavy weird is to be a nondescript monster with a horse's tail, hoofs, and mane, white eyes, big mouth, and huge hands, and never to be released from the spell till a king's son shall consent to kiss her. One night when Hjálmtèr had landed on a woody island, and it

had fallen to him to keep watch, he heard a great din and crashing in the woods, so that the oaks trembled. Presently this monster came out of the thicket with a fine sword in her hand, such as he had not seen the like of. They had a colloquy, and he asked her to let him have the sword. She said he should not have it unless he would kiss her. "I will not kiss thy snout," said Hjálmtèr, "for mayhap I should stick to it." But something came into his mind which made him think better of her offer, and he said he was ready. "You must leap upon my neck, then," she said, "when I throw up the sword, and if you then hesitate, it will be your death." She threw up the sword, he leaped on her neck and kissed her, and she gave him the sword, with an augury of victory and good luck for him all his days. The retransformation does not occur on the spot, but further on Hjálmtèr meets Álsól as a young lady at the court of her brother, who has also been restored to his proper form and station; everything is explained; Hjálmtèr marries her, and his foster-brother her sister. Hjálmtèrs ok Ölvers Saga, cc 10, 22, Rafn, *Fornaldar Sögur*, III, 473ff, 514ff.

In many tales of the sort a single kiss suffices to undo the spell and reverse the transformation; in others, as in the ballad, three are required. The triplication of the kiss has led in **A** to a triplication of the talisman against wounds. The popular genius was inventive enough to vary the properties of the several gifts, and we may believe that belt, ring, and sword had originally each its peculiar quality. The peril of touching fin or tail in **A** seems to correspond to that in the saga of hesitating when the sword is thrown up.

The **Danish** ballad, 'Jomfruen i Ormeham,' from MSS of the sixteenth and the seventeenth century, Grundtvig, No 59, II, 177, resembles both the first version of the Scottish ballad and the Icelandic saga in the points that the maid offers gifts and is rehabilitated by a kiss. The maid in her proper shape, which, it appears, she may resume for a portion of the day, stands at Sir Jenus's bedside and offers him gifts—five silver-bowls, all the gold in her kist, twelve foals, twelve boats—and ends with saying, "Were I a swain, as you are, I would betroth a maid." It is now close upon midnight, and she hints that he must be quick. But Jenus is fast asleep the while; twelve strikes, and the maid instantly turns into a little snake. The page, however, has been awake, and he repeats to his master all that has occurred.* Sir Jenus orders his horse, rides along a hillside, and sees the little snake in the grass. He bends over and kisses it, and it turns to a courteous maid, who thanks him, and offers him any boon he may ask. He asks her to be his, and as she has loved him before this, she has no difficulty in plighting him her troth.

A maid transformed by a step-mother into a tree is freed by being kissed by a man, in 'Jomfruen i Linden,' Grundtvig, II, 214, No 66, Kristensen, II, 90, No 31; 'Linden,' Afzelius, III, 114, 118, No 87; 'Linden,' Kristensen's Skattegraveren, V, 50, No 455; 'Jomfruen i Linden,' Kristensen, Jyske Folkeminder, X, 22, No 10. In 'Linden,' Kristensen, I, 13, No 5, a combination of two ballads, a prince cuts down the linden, which changes to a linden-worm; he kisses the worm, and a young maid stands before him.

A knight bewitched into the shape of a troll is restored by being kissed by a peasant's wife thrice [once], 'Trolden og Bondens Hustru,' Grundtvig, II, 142, No 52, **A, B**; a prince by a kiss from a maid, 'Lindormen,' Grundtvig, *D. g. F.*, II, 211, No 65 **A**, 'Slangen og den lille Pige,' *Danske Folkeminder*, 1861, p. 15. A princess in the form of a toad is kissed three times and so disenchanted: *Revue des Traditions populaires*, III, 475–6. A princess in the form of a black wolf must be kissed thrice to be disenchanted: Vernaleken, *Alpensagen*, p. 123. A princess persuades a man to attempt her release from enchantment. Three successive kisses are necessary. On the first occasion she appears as a serpent; he can kiss her but once. The second attempt is also unsuccessful; she appears as a salamander and is kissed twice. The third time she takes the form of a toad, and the three kisses are happily given. Luzel, in the *Annuaire de la Soc. des Traditions populaires*, II, 53. (G. L. K.)

The removal of a spell which compels man or woman to appear continuously or alternately as a monster, commonly a snake, by three kisses or by one, is a regular feature in the numerous **German** tales of Schlangenjungfrauen, Weissefrauen. Often the man is afraid to venture the third kiss, or even a single one. See Grimm, *Deutsche Sagen*, No 13, No 222; Dobeneck, *Des deutschen Mittelalters Volksglauben*, I, 18 = Grimm, No 13; Mone's *Anzeiger*, III, 89, VII, 476; Panzer, *Bayerische Sagen u. Bräuche*, I, 196, [308] No 214; Schönhuth, *Die Burgen u. s. w. Badens u. der Pfalz*, I, 105; Stöber, *Die Sagen des Elsasses*, p. 346, No 277, p. 248, No 190; Curtze, *Volksüberlieferungen aus Waldeck*, p. 198; Sommer, *Sagen, Märchen u. Gebräuche aus Sachsen u. Thüringen*, p. 21, No 16; Schambach u. Müller, p. 104, No 132; Müllenhoff, p. 580, No 597; Wolf, *Hessische Sagen*, No 46; etc., etc.: also, Kreutzwald, *Ehstnische Märchen*, by Löwe, No 19, p. 270f. So in some forms of 'Beauty and the Beast:' Töppen, *Aberglauben aus Masuren*, p. 142; Mikuličić, *Narodne Pripovietke*, p. 1, No 1; Afanasief, VII, 153, No 15; Coelho, *Contos populares portuguezes*, p. 69, No 29.†

---

* The incident of a woman trying to move a man who all the while is in a deep sleep, and of his servant reporting what has been going on, can hardly have belonged to this ballad from the beginning. It is exceedingly common in popular tales: see 'The Red Bull of Norroway,' in Chambers's *Popular Rhymes of Scotland*, 3d ed., p. 99; Grimms, 'Das singende springende Löweneckerchen,' No 88, 'Der Eisenhofen,' No 127, and the notes in vol. iii; Leskien u. Brugman, *Litauische Volkslieder und Märchen*, 'Vom weissen Wolf,' No 23, p. 438, and Wollner's note, p. 571.

† But not in Mme Villeneuve's or in Mme de Beaumont's 'La Belle et la Bête.'

Caspar Decurtins, Märchen aus dem Bündner Oberlande, nach dem Räto-Romanischen erzählt, Jecklin, *Volksthümliches aus Graubünden*, Zürich, 1874, p. 126, has a tale of a Schlangenjungfrau who is a maid by day and a serpent by night, and is disenchanted by three kisses. (G. L. K.)*

Rivals or peers of Owain among romantic knights are, first, Lanzelet, in Ulrich von Zatzikhoven's poem, who kisses a serpent on the mouth once, which, *after bathing in a spring* (see 'Tam Lin'), becomes the finest woman ever seen: vv 7836–7939. Brandimarte, again, in Orlando Innamorato, lib. II., c. XXVI, stanzas 7–15; and Carduino, I Cantari di Carduino, Rajna, stanzas 49, 54f, 61–64, pp 35–41. Le Bel Inconnu is an involuntary instrument in such a disenchantment, for the snake fascinates him first and kisses him without his knowledge; he afterwards goes to sleep, and finds a beautiful woman standing at his head when he wakes: ed. Hippeau, p. 110ff, v. 3101ff. The English Libius Disconius is kist or he it wist, and the dragon at once turns to a beautiful woman: Percy MS., Hales & Furnivall, II, 493f; Ritson, *Romances*, II, 84f. Espertius, in *Tiran le Blanc*, is so overcome with fear that he cannot kiss the dragon,—a daughter of Hippocrates, transformed by Diana, in the island of Lango,—but Espertius not running away, as two men before him had done, the dragon kisses him with equally good effect: Caylus, *Tiran le Blanc*, II, 334–39. This particular disenchantment had not been accomplished down to Sir John Mandeville's time, for he mentions only the failures: *Voyage and Travel*, c. iv, pp 28–31, ed. 1725. Amadis d'Astra touches two dragons on

the face and breast, and restores them to young-ladyhood: *Historia del Principe Sferamundi*, the 13th book of Amadis of Gaul, P. II, c. xcvii, pp 458–462, Venice, 1610. This feat is shown by the details to be only a variation of the story in *Tiran le Blanc*.[†]

The Rev. Mr Lamb, of Norham, communicated to Hutchinson, author of 'A View of Northumberland,' a ballad entitled 'The Laidley Worm of Spindleston Heughs,' with this harmless preamble: "A song 500 years old, made by the old Mountain Bard, Duncan Frasier, living on Cheviot, A. D. 1270. From an ancient manuscript." This composition of Mr Lamb's—for nearly every line of it is his—is not only based on popular tradition, but evidently preserves some small fragments of a popular ballad, and for this reason is given in an Appendix. There is a copy deviating but very little from the print in Kinloch's MSS, I, 187. It was obtained from the recitation of an old woman in Berwickshire.[‡] In this recited version the Child of Wynd, or Childy Wynd (Child Owyne), has become Child o Wane (Child Owayn).

Mr R. H. Evans, in his preface to this ballad, *Old Ballads*, 1810, IV, 241, says that Mr Turner had informed him "that a lady upwards of seventy had heard her mother repeat an older and nearly similar ballad."

A is translated by Rosa Warrens, *Schottische Volkslieder*, p. 19; **B b** by Gerhard, p. 171, by Schubart, p. 110, by Knortz, *Lieder u. Romanzen Alt-Englands*, p. 201. 'Jomfruen i Ormeham' by Prior, III, 135.

---

* A remarkable case alleged to have occurred at Cesena in 1464: Angelo do Tummulillis, *Notabilia Temporum*, ed. Corvisieri, 1890, p. 124ff; Giornale Storico della Letteratura Italiana, XVII, 161. (G. L. K.) On the whole subject see R. Köhler's notes in Mennung, *Der Bel Inconnu*, p. 20; S. Prato's notes, *Bulletin de Folklore*, 1892, p. 333f. W. H. Schofield, Studies on the Libeaus Desconus, in *Studies and Notes in Philology and Literature published under the direction of the Modern Language Departments of Harvard University*, IV, 199ff.

† Lanzelet is cited by J. Grimm; Brandimarte by Walter Scott; Carduino by G. Paris; Espertius by Dunlop; Amadis d'Astra by Valentin Schmidt. Dunlop refers to a similar story in the sixth tale of the *Contes Amoureux de Jean Flore*, written towards the end of the fifteenth century.

‡ "The Childe of Wane, as a protector of disconsolate damsels, is still remembered by young girls at school in the neighborhood of Bamborough, who apply the title to any boy who protects them from the assaults of their school-fellows." (Kinloch.)

A

Buchan, *Ballads of the North of Scotland*, II, 78, from
Mr Nicol of Strichen, as learned in his youth from old
people; Motherwell's *Minstrelsy*, p. 374; Motherwell's
MS., p. 448.

1 HER mother died when she was young,
   Which gave her cause to make great moan;
   Her father married the warst woman
   That ever lived in Christendom.

2 She served her with foot and hand,
   In every thing that she could dee,
   Till once, in an unlucky time,
   She threw her in ower Craigy's sea.

3 Says, 'Lie you there, dove Isabel,
   And all my sorrows lie with thee;
   Till Kemp Owyne come ower the sea,
   And borrow you with kisses three,
   Let all the warld do what they will,
   Oh borrowed shall you never be!'

4 Her breath grew strang, her hair grew lang,
   And twisted thrice about the tree,
   And all the people, far and near,
   Thought that a savage beast was she.

5 These news did come to Kemp Owyne,
   Where he lived, far beyond the sea;
   He hasted him to Craigy's sea,
   And on the savage beast lookd he.

6 Her breath was strang, her hair was lang,
   And twisted was about the tree,
   And with a swing she came about:
   'Come to Craigy's sea, and kiss with me.

7 'Here is a royal belt,' she cried,
   'That I have found in the green sea;
   And while your body it is on,
   Drawn shall your blood never be;
   But if you touch me, tail or fin,
   I vow my belt your death shall be.'

8 He stepped in, gave her a kiss,
   The royal belt he brought him wi;
   Her breath was strang, her hair was lang,
   And twisted twice about the tree,
   And with a swing she came about:
   'Come to Craigy's sea, and kiss with me.

9 'Here is a royal ring,' she said,
   'That I have found in the green sea;
   And while your finger it is on,
   Drawn shall your blood never be;
   But if you touch me, tail or fin,
   I swear my ring your death shall be.'

10 He stepped in, gave her a kiss,
   The royal ring he brought him wi;
   Her breath was strang, her hair was lang,
   And twisted ance about the tree,
   And with a swing she came about:
   'Come to Craigy's sea, and kiss with me.

11 'Here is a royal brand,' she said,
   'That I have found in the green sea;
   And while your body it is on,
   Drawn shall your blood never be;
   But if you touch me, tail or fin,
   I swear my brand your death shall be.'

12 He stepped in, gave her a kiss,
   The royal brand he brought him wi;
   Her breath was sweet, her hair grew short,
   And twisted nane about the tree,
   And smilingly she came about,
   As fair a woman as fair could be.

B

a. Jamieson-Brown MS., p. 29. **b.** Scott's *Minstrelsy*,
II, 93, 1802, from William Tytler's Brown MS., No 9,
"with corrections from a recited fragment."

"Come here, come here, ye free-ly feed, An' lay your head low on my knee,

The heav-iest wierd i will you read, That ever was read til a la-dy.

1 'COME here, come here, you freely feed,
 An lay your head low on my knee;
 The hardest weird I will you read
  That eer war read to a lady.

2 'O meikle dollour sall you dree,
 An ay the sat seas oer ye ['s] swim;
 An far mair dollour sall ye dree
  On Eastmuir craigs, or ye them clim.

3 'I wot ye's be a weary wight,
 An releived sall ye never be
 Till Kempion, the kingis son,
  Come to the craig and thrice kiss thee.'

[310] 4 O meickle dollour did she dree,
 An ay the sat seas oer she swam;
 An far mair dollour did she dree
  On Eastmuir craigs, or them she clam;
 An ay she cried for Kempion,
  Gin he would come till her han.

5 Now word has gane to Kempion
 That sich a beast was in his lan,
 An ay be sure she would gae mad
  Gin she gat nae help frae his han.

6 'Now by my sooth,' says Kempion,
 'This fiery beast I ['ll] gang to see;'
 'An by my sooth,' says Segramour,
  'My ae brother, I'll gang you wi.'

7 O biggit ha they a bonny boat,
 An they hae set her to the sea,
 An Kempion an Segramour
  The fiery beast ha gane to see:
 A mile afore they reachd the shore,
  I wot she gard the red fire flee.

8 'O Segramour, keep my boat afloat,
 An lat her no the lan so near;
 For the wicked beast she'll sure gae mad,
  An set fire to the land an mair.'

9 'O out o my stye I winna rise —
 An it is na for the fear o thee —
 Till Kempion, the kingis son,
  Come to the craig an thrice kiss me.'

10 He's louted him oer the Eastmuir craig,
 An he has gien her kisses ane;
 Awa she gid, an again she came,
  The fieryest beast that ever was seen.

11 'O out o my stye I winna rise —
 An it is na for fear o thee —
 Till Kempion, the kingis son,
  Come to the craig an thrice kiss me.'

12 He louted him oer the Eastmuir craig,
 An he has gien her kisses twa;
 Awa she gid, an again she came,
  The fieryest beast that ever you saw.

13 'O out o my stye I winna rise —
 An it is na for fear o ye —
 Till Kempion, the kingis son,
  Come to the craig an thrice kiss me.'

14 He's louted him oer the Eastmuir craig,
 An he has gien her kisses three;
 Awa she gid, an again she came,
  The fairest lady that ever coud be.

15 'An by my sooth,' say[s] Kempion,
    'My ain true love—for this is she—
O was it wolf into the wood,
    Or was it fish intill the sea,
Or was it man, or wile woman,
    My true love, that misshapit thee?'

16 'It was na wolf into the wood,
    Nor was it fish into the sea,
But it was my stepmother,
    An wae an weary mot she be.

17 'O a heavier weird light her upon
    Than ever fell on wile woman;
Her hair's grow rough, an her teeth's grow lang,
    An on her four feet sal she gang.

18 'Nane sall tack pitty her upon,
    But in Wormie's Wood she sall ay won,
An relieved sall she never be,
    Till St Mungo come oer the sea.'

A. *Buchan gives 4–6 in two six-line stanzas. There are a*
   few trivial diversities between Motherwell's manu-
   script, or my copy of it, and his printed text, which
   conforms to Buchan's.

B. a.*Written in long or double lines in the manuscript.*

2^2, 4^2. or.

5^3. a besure.

8^4. landy mair

11^4. twice.

16^3. wicked *is inserted before* stepmother, *seemingly*
   by Jamieson.

b. *The first stanza, as given by Anderson, Nichols, Lit-*
   erary Illustrations, VII, 177, *is:*

   'Come here, come here, ye freely feed,
       And lay your head low on my knee;
   The heaviest weird I will you read
       That ever was read till a lady.'

1^3. heaviest. 1^4. gaye ladye.

2^2. ye'se. 2^4. when ye.

3^1. I weird ye to a fiery beast.

$5 =$ a $4^{5,6} +$ a $5^{1,2}$: a $5^{3,4}$ *omitted:*

   And aye she cried for Kempion,
       Gin he would but cum to her hand;
   Now word has gane to Kempion
       That sicken a beast was in his land.

6^4. wi thee.

7 *omits* a^{3,4}. 7^5. But a mile before.

7^6. Around them she.

8^2. oer near. 8^3. will sure.

8^4. to a' the land and mair.

After 8 is inserted:

   Syne has he bent an arblast bow,
       And aimd an arrow at her head,
   And swore if she didna quit the land,
       Wi that same shaft to shoot her dead.

9^1. stythe. 9^2. awe o thee.

10^1. dizzy crag. 10^2. gien the monster.

11^1. stythe. 11^2. And not for a' thy bow nor thee.

12^1. Estmere craigs.

13^1. my den. 13^2. Nor flee it for the feir o thee.

13^1. Kempion, that courteous knight.

14^1. lofty craig. 14^4. loveliest lady eer.

$15^{1,2}$. *After this is inserted:*

   They surely had a heart o stane,
       Could put thee to such misery.

15^{3-6} *make a separate stanza.*

15^3, 16^1. warwolf in the wood.

15^4, 16^2. mermaid in the sea.

15^1. my ain true.

17^1. weird shall light her on.

17^3. Her hair shall grow . . . teeth grow.

18^2. In Wormeswood she aye shall won.

$18^{5,6}$. And sighing said that weary wight,
    I doubt that day I'll never see.

APPENDIX

The Laidley Worm of Spindleston Heughs

A *View of Northumberland*, by W. Hutchinson,
Anno 1776, Newcastle, 1778, II, 162–64. Communi-
cated by the Rev. Mr Lamb, of Norham.

Kinloch's account of the tradition in relation to the queen, as it maintains itself in Berwickshire, is quite in accord with German *sagen* about enchanted ladies, innocent or guilty, and as such may be worth giving: Kinloch MSS, I, 187.

"Though the ballad mentions that the queen was transformed into 'a spiteful toad of monstrous size,' and was doomed in that form to wend on the earth until the end of the world, yet the tradition of the country gives another account of the endurance of her enchantment. It is said that in form of a toad as big as a 'clockin hen' she is doomed to expiate her guilt by confinement in a cavern in Bamborough castle, in which she is to remain in her enchanted shape until some one shall have the hardihood to break the spell by penetrating the cavern, whose 'invisible' door only opens every seven years, on Christmas eve. The adventurer, after entering the cavern, must take the sword and horn of the Childe of Wane, which hang on the wall, and having unsheathed and resheathed the sword thrice, and wound three blasts on the horn, he must kiss the toad three times; upon which the enchantment will be dissolved, and the queen will recover her human form.

"Many adventurers, it is said, have attempted to disenchant the queen, but have all failed, having immediately fallen into a trance, something similar to the princes in the Arabian tale who went in search of the Talking Bird, Singing Tree, and Yellow Water. The last one, it is said, who made the attempt was a countryman, about sixty years ago, who, having watched on Christmas eve the opening of the door, entered the cavern, took the sword and horn from the wall, unsheathed and resheathed the sword thrice, blew three blasts on the horn, and was proceeding to the final disenchantment by kissing the toad, which he had saluted twice, when, perceiving the various strange sleepers to arise from the floor, his courage failed, and he fled from the cavern, having just attained the outside of the door when it suddenly shut with a loud clap, catching hold of the skirt of his coat, which was torn off and left in the door.

And none since that time
To enter the cavern presume."

[312] 1 THE king is gone from Bambrough castle,
Long may the princess mourn;
Long may she stand on the castle wall,
Looking for his return.

2 She has knotted the keys upon a string,
And with her she has them taen,
She has cast them oer her left shoulder,
And to the gate she is gane.

3 She tripped out, she tripped in,
She tript into the yard;
But it was more for the king's sake,
Than for the queen's regard.

4 It fell out on a day the king
Brought the queen with him home,
And all the lords in our country
To welcome them did come.

5 'O welcome, father,' the lady cries,
'Unto your halls and bowers;
And so are you, my stepmother,
For all that is here is yours.'

6 A lord said, wondering while she spake,
This princess of the North
Surpasses all of female kind
In beauty and in worth.

7 The envious queen replied: At least,
    You might have excepted me;
    In a few hours I will her bring
    Down to a low degree.

8 I will her liken to a laidley worm,
    That warps about the stone,
    And not till Childy Wynd comes back
    Shall she again be won.

9 The princess stood at the bower door,
    Laughing, who could her blame?
    But eer the next day's sun went down,
    A long worm she became.

10 For seven miles east, and seven miles west,
    And seven miles north and south,
    No blade of grass or corn could grow,
    So venomous was her mouth.

11 The milk of seven stately cows—
    It was costly her to keep—
    Was brought her daily, which she drank
    Before she went to sleep.

12 At this day may be seen the cave
    Which held her folded up,
    And the stone trough, the very same
    Out of which she did sup.

13 Word went east, and word went west,
    And word is gone over the sea,
    That a laidley worm in Spindleston Heughs
    Would ruin the north country.

14 Word went east, and word went west,
    And over the sea did go;
    The Child of Wynd got wit of it,
    Which filled his heart with woe.

15 He called straight his merry men all,
    They thirty were and three:
    'I wish I were at Spindleston,
    This desperate worm to see.

16 'We have no time now here to waste,
    Hence quickly let us sail;
    My only sister Margaret,
    Something, I fear, doth ail.'

17 They built a ship without delay,
    With masts of the rown tree,
    With fluttering sails of silk so fine,
    And set her on the sea.

18 They went aboard; the wind with speed
    Blew them along the deep;
    At length they spied an huge square tower,
    On a rock high and steep.

19 The sea was smooth, the weather clear;
    When they approached nigher,
    King Ida's castle they well knew,
    And the banks of Bambroughshire.

20 The queen looked out at her bower-window,
    To see what she could see;
    There she espied a gallant ship,
    Sailing upon the sea.

21 When she beheld the silken sails,
    Full glancing in the sun,
    To sink the ship she sent away
    Her witch-wives every one.

22 Their spells were vain; the hags returned
    To the queen in sorrowful mood,
    Crying that witches have no power
    Where there is rown-tree wood.

23 Her last effort, she sent a boat,
    Which in the haven lay,
    With armed men to board the ship,
    But they were driven away.

24 The worm leapt up, the worm leapt down,
    She plaited round the stane;
    And ay as the ship came to the land
    She banged it off again.

25 The Child then ran out of her reach   [313]
    The ship on Budle sand,
    And jumping into the shallow sea,
    Securely got to land.

26 And now he drew his berry-brown sword,
    And laid it on her head,
    And swore, if she did harm to him,
    That he would strike her dead.

27 'O quit thy sword, and bend thy bow,
    And give me kisses three;
    For though I am a poisonous worm,
    No hurt I will do to thee.

28 'O quit thy sword, and bend thy bow,
    And give me kisses three;
    If I am not won eer the sun go down,
    Won I shall never be.'

29 He quitted his sword, he bent his bow,
    He gave her kisses three;
  She crept into a hole a worm,
    But stept out a lady.

30 No cloathing had this lady fine,
    To keep her from the cold;
  He took his mantle from him about,
    And round her did it fold.

31 He has taken his mantle from him about,
    And it he wrapt her in,
  And they are up to Bambrough castle,
    As fast as they can win.

32 His absence and her serpent shape
    The king had long deplored;
  He now rejoiced to see them both
    Again to him restored.

33 The queen they wanted, whom they found
    All pale, and sore afraid,
  Because she knew her power must yield
    To Childy Wynd's, who said:

34 'Woe be to thee, thou wicked witch,
    An ill death mayest thou dee;
  As thou my sister hast likened,
    So likened shalt thou be.

35 'I will turn you into a toad,
    That on the ground doth wend,
  And won, won shalt thou never be,
    Till this world hath an end.'

36 Now on the sand near Ida's tower,
    She crawls a loathsome toad,
  And venom spits on every maid
    She meets upon her road.

37 The virgins all of Bambrough town
    Will swear that they have seen
  This spiteful toad, of monstrous size,
    Whilst walking they have been.

38 All folks believe within the shire
    This story to be true,
  And they all run to Spindleston,
    The cave and trough to view.

39 This fact now Duncan Frasier,
    Of Cheviot, sings in rhime,
  Lest Bambroughshire men should forget
    Some part of it in time.

————◆————

28³. son.

————◆————

Additional Copies

From a manuscript collection of Charles Kirk-
patrick Sharpe's, p. 2; "Second Collection," see Sharpe's
Ballad Book, ed. 1880, p. 144. This copy closely resem-
bles **A**.

1 HER mother died when she was young,
    And was laid in the silent tomb;
  The father weded the weel worst woman
    This day that lives in Christiendom.

2 She served her with hands and feet,
    In every way that well could be,
  Yet she did once upon a day
    Throw her in over a craig of sea.

3 Says, Ly you there, you dove Isabeal,
    And let you never borrowed be
  Till Kempenwine come ower the sea
    And borrow you with kisses three;
  Whatever any may do or say,
    O borrowed may you never be!

4 Her breath grew strong, and her hair grew long,
    And twisted thrice about a tree,
  And so hideous-like she did apear
    That all who saw her from her did flee.

5 Now Kempenwine gat word of this
    Where he was living beyond the sea;
    He hied him straight unto that shoar,
    The monstrous creature for to se.

6 Her breath was strong, and her hair was long,
    And twisted was around the tree,
    And with a swing she cried aloud,
    Come to craig of sea and kiss with me.

7 'Here is a royal ring,' she cried,
    'That I have found in the green sea,
    And while your finger it is on
    Drawn shall your blood never be;
    But if you touch me, tail or fin,
    I vow this brand your death shall be.'

8 He steppëd in, gave her a kiss,
    The royal ring he brought him wi;
    Her breath was strong, and [her] hair was long,
    Yet twisted twice about the tree,
    And with a swing she came about,
    'Come to craig of sea and kiss with me.

9 'Here is a royal belt,' she cried,
    'That I have found in the green sea,
    And while your body it is on
    Drawn shall your blood never be;
    But if you touch me, tail or fin,
    I vow this brand your death shall be.'

10 He steppëd in, gave her a kiss,
    The royal belt he brought him wee;
    Her breath yet strong, her hair yet long,
    Yet twisted once about the tree,
    And with a swing she came about,
    'Come to craig of sea and kiss with me.

11 'Here is a royal brand,' she cried,
    'That I have found in the green sea,
    And while your body it is on
    Drawn shall your blood never be;
    But if you touch me, tail or fin,
    I vow my brand your death shall be.'

12 He steppëd in, gave her a kiss,
    The royal brand he brought him wee;
    Her breath now soft, her hair now short,
    And disengagëd from the tree,
    She fell into his arms two,
    As fair a woman as ever could be.

———◆———

Written in long lines, and not divided into stanzas.
8². him with. 6⁴, 8⁶, 10⁶. Craig of sea.

———◆———

The Rev. Robert Lambe sent Percy, under date of January 29, 1768, "the best copy of 'The Laidley Worm' that he could procure from many incorrect, imperfect, and nonsensical ones." There are differences between this and the copy printed in Hutchinson [Not for the first time. A stall-copy among the Percy papers is of the date 1772, and an edition of 1771, from Lambe's manuscript, is transcribed for Percy by Bulman], but one is about as good as the other. In this earlier copy 2 follows 3 and 37 is wanting. 6 and 7 read

O up then spake the queen herself:
    Who's this that welcoms me?
A lord replied, The king's daughter,
    The flower of the North Country.

'Wo be to thee, thou gray-haird man,
    Thou mightst have excepted me;
Before the morn at this same time
    I'll bring her to low degree.'

And 17, 22:

He straightway built a bonny ship,
    And set her on the sea;
Her sails were made of silk so fine,
    Her masts of rowan-tree.

The hags came back, finding their charms
    Most powerfully withstood;
For warlocks, witches, cannot work
    Where there is rowan-tree wood.

Duncan Frasier does not appear in the last stanza:

> Now this fact, as it happened, is
>   For their good sung in rhime,
> Lest they should some important part
>   Forget of it in time.

Along with this earlier copy of Lambe's is found another, undescribed, which shows both agreements and variations: 2 follows 3, and 6, 7

and the final stanza are the same. 17 and 22 are wanting, and there are, therefore, no witches and no rowan-tree. Instead of 21–23, we have this very bad stanza:

> 'Run, run, my men, my sailors send
>   Aboard yon ship so tall,
> And bid them drown the Child of Wind;
>   But he soon slew them all.'

In the same parcel there is a copy of 'The Laidley Worm' which is somewhat more in the popular tone than the one already printed. It was sent in an undated letter [1775?] to J. Balman, Esq., of Sheepwash, Morpeth, by E. G., that is, Captain E. Grow. "The above," says E. G., "is the Haggworm as I collected it from an old woman. I wrote to the Revrd Mr Lamb for his ballad, and directed him to send to you. . . . I think the inclosed more original then his, for

Mr Lamb, tho a good antiquarian, is but a bad poet, and above the one half is his own composing." Mr J. Bulman appears to have transmitted this version to Percy, to whom, upon another occasion, May 25, 1775, he sends "a bold imitation of the song, now lost, of the Laidler Worm (written by Duncan Frazier, the monk on Cheviot, in 1270), by a lady, Miss Graham of Gloriorum, in Northumberland;" of which nothing need be said.

'The Hagg Worm,' obtained from an old woman by Captain E. Grow.

1 BAMBROUGH Castle's a bouny place,
    Built on a marble stone,
  But long, long did the lady look
    Eer her father came home.

2 She knotted the keys upon a string,
    And with her she has them taen;
  She cast them oer her left shoulder,
    And to the gates she is gaen.

3 It fell out on a day the king
    Brought his new lady home,
  And all the lordling[s] in his realm
    To welcome them did come.

4 'You'r welcome, father,' the lady cries,
    'To your halls and your towers,
  And so are you, good queen,' said she,
    'For all that's here is yours.'

5 'O who is this,' said the queen,
    'That welcomes me so high?'
  Up then spake a greyhaird man,
    An ill dead may he dee!
  'T is the kinges aie daughter,
    The flower of the North Country.

6 'O woe betyde the[e], greyhaired man,
    An ill dead may thou dee!
  Had she been fairer then she is,
    You might have excepted me.

7 'I'll liken her to a laidley worm,
    That warps about the stone,
  And not till Child of Wynd comes back
    Shall she again be wonne.'

8 The lady stood at her bower-door,
    A loud laughter took she:
  'I hope your prayers will have no pith;
    You took not God with ye.'

9 She calld on her waiting-maid—
  They calld her Dorothy—
'The coffer that my gold lies in,
  I leave to thee the key.

10 'Her hellish spells seize on my heart,
   And quick will alter me;
For eer the seting sun is down
   A laidler worm I'll be.'

11 Word's gone east, and word's gone west,
   And word's gone oer the sea,
There's a laidler worm in Spindlestone Heughs
   Will destroy the North Countree.

12 For seven miles east and seven miles west,
   And seven miles north and south,
Nea blade of grass or corn will grow,
   For the venom of her mouth.

13 To this day may be seen the cave
   This monsterous worm embowered,
And the stone trough where seven cows' milk
   She every day devoured.

14 Word's gone east and word's gone west,
   Word oer the sea did go;
The Child of Wynd got wit of it,
   Which filld his heart with woe.

15 'I have no sister but barely one,
   I fear fair Margery!
I wish I was at Spindlestone Heughs,
   This laidler worm to see.'

16 Up then spoke his eldest brother,
   An angry man was he:
O thou art young, far over young,
   To sail the stormy sea.

17 'Peace, brother,' said the Child of Wynd,
   'Dear brother, let me be;
For when we come to danger dire,
   I must fight when you will flee.

18 'O let us build a bonny ship,
   And set her in the sea;
The sails shall be of silken twine,
   The masts of rowon-tree.'

19 They built a ship, the wind and tyde
   Drave them along the deep;
At last they saw a stately tower,
   On the rock high and steep.

20 The sea was smooth, the sky was clear;
   As they approached nigher,
King Ida's castle well they knew,
   And the banks of Balmburghshire.

21 The queen lookd thro her bower-window,
   To see what she coud see,
And she espied a gallant ship
   Come sailing along the sea.

22 She calld on her witch-women
   To sink them in the main;
They hoisted up their silken sails,
   And to Warren bridge they gane.

23 The worm lept up, the worm lept down,
   She plaited round the stane,
And as the ship came to the land
   She banged them off again.

24 The Child leapd in the shallow water
   That flows oer Budle sand,
And when he drew his berry-brown sword
   She suffered them to land.

25 When they came to Bamburg castle
   They tirled at the ring;
'Who's that,' said the proud porter,
   'That woud so fain be in?'

26 ''Tis the king's son and Child of Wynd,
   Who have long been oer the sea;
We come to see our sister dear,
   The peirless Margery.'

27 'Heigh a ween, and Oh a ween!
   A ween, a woe-ses me!
She's a laidler worm at Spindlestone Heughs,
   These seven years and three.'

28 They highed them stright to Spindleston
   Heughs—
   Grief added to their speed—
Where out she came a laidler worm,
   And strack their hearts with dread.

29 The Child drew out his berry-brown sword,
   And waved it oer her head,
   And cried, If thou   .   .
     .   .   .   .   .

30 'O quit thy sword, and bend thy bow,
   And give me kisses three;
   For if I am not wonne eer the sun goes down,
   Wonne will I never be.'

31 He quit his sword, he bent his bow,
   He gave her kisses three;
   She threw out her fireballs,
   And fiercely made them flee.

32 In she went, and out she came,
   A laidley ask was she:
   'Oh, tho I am a laidley ask,
   No harm I'll do to thee.

33 'Oh quit thy sword, and bend thy bow,
   And give me kisses three;
   For if I am not wonne eer the sun goes down,
   Wonne will I never be.'

34 He quit his sword, be bent his bow,
   And gave her kisses three;
   But she threw out her fireballs,
   And fiercely made them flee.

35 In she went, and out she came,
   A laidley adder was she;
   ['Oh, tho I am a laidley adder,
   No harm I'll do to thee.]

36 'Oh quit thy sword, and bend thy bow,
   And give me kisses three;
   [For if I am not wonne eer the sun goes down,
   Wonne will I never be.']

37 He quit his sword, he bent his bow,
   He gave her kisses three;
   She crept into the cave a snake,
   But stept out a lady.

38 'O quit thy sword, unbend thy bow,
   And give me kisses three;
   For tho I am a lady fair,
   I am   .   .   to modesty?

39 He took his mantle from his back,
   And wrapd his sister in,
   And thei'r away to Bainburg Castle,
   As fast as they coud winne.

40 His absence and her reptile form
   The king had long deplored,
   But now rejoiced to see them both
   Again to him restored.

41 The queen he sought, who when he found
   All quailed and sore affraid,
   Because she knew her power must yield
   To Child of Wynd, who said:

42 'O woe be to the[e], wicked woman,
   An ill deed may thou dee!
   As thou my sister likened,
   So likened thou shalt be.

43 'I change thy body to a toad,
   That on the earth doth wend,
   And wonne, wonne shalt thou never be
   Untill the world doth end!'

44 Now on the ground, near Ida's tower,
   She crawls a loathsome toad,
   And venom spits on every maid
   She meets upon the road.

8^3. with have.
27^2. *The correction to* woe *is is obvious, but, not knowing that there may not have been some such popular interjection as* woe-ses, *I leave it.*
32^4. to three.
35.   In she went, and out she came,
     A laidley adder was she:
     Oh quit thy sword, and bend thy bow,

           And give me kisses three.'

She t[h]rew out her fire-balls, etc., *is written between the second and third lines. There seems to be no occasion for a third discharge of fireballs; but indeed the fireballs should come before the kisses, anyway.*
42^2. deed did thou.

35

ALLISON GROSS

'Allison Gross,' Jamieson-Brown MS., p. 40.

'ALLISON GROSS' was printed by Jamieson, *Popular Ballads*, II, 187, without deviation from the manuscript save in spelling.

In a Greek tale, a nereid, that is elf or fairy, turns a youth who had refused to espouse her into a snake, the curse to continue till he finds another love who is as fair as she: 'Die Schönste,' B. Schmidt, *Griechische Märchen, etc.*, No 10. This tale is a variety of 'Beauty and the Beast,' one of the numerous wild growths from that ever charming French story.[*]

An elf, a hill-troll, a mermaid, make a young man offers of splendid gifts, to obtain his love or the promise of his faith, in 'Elveskud,' Grundtvig, No 47, many of the Danish and two of the Norwegian copies; 'Hertig Magnus och Elfvorna,' Afzelius, III, 172; 'Hr. Magnus og Bjærgtrolden,' Grundtvig, No 48, Arwidsson, No 147 B; 'Herr Magnus och Hafstrollet,' Afzelius, No 95, Bugge, No 11; a lind-worm, similarly, to a young woman, 'Lindormen,' Grundtvig, No 65; 'Bjærgjomfruens frieri,' Kristensen's *Skattegraveren*, II, 100, No 460; XII, 22ff, Nos 16, 17; *Folkeminder*, XI, 20ff, No 18, A–E. Magnus answers the hill-troll that he should be glad to plight faith with her were she like other women, but she is the ugliest troll that could be found: Grundtvig, II, 121, **A** 6, **B** 7; Arwidsson, II, 303, **B** 5; Afzelius, III, 169, st. 5, 173, st. 6. This is like what we read in stanza 7 of our ballad, but the answer is inevitable in any such case. Magnus comes off scot-free.

The queen of the fairies undoing the spell of the witch is a remarkable feature, not paralleled, so far as I know, in English or northern tradition. The Greek nereids, however, who do pretty much everything, good or bad, that is ascribed to northern elves or fairies, and even bear an appellation resembling that by which fairies are spoken of in Scotland and Ireland, "the good damsels," "the good ladies," have a queen who is described as taking no part in the unfriendly acts of her subjects, but as being kindly disposed towards mankind, and even as repairing the mischief which subordinate sprites have done against her will. If now the fairy queen might interpose in behalf of men against her own kith and kin, much more likely would she be to exert herself to thwart the malignity of a witch.[†]

The object of the witch's blowing thrice on a grass-green horn in 8^2 is not clear, for nothing comes of it. In the closely related ballad which follows this, a witch uses a horn to summon the sea-fishes, among whom there is one who has been the victim of her spells. The horn is appropriate. Witches were supposed to blow horns when they joined the wild hunt, and horn-blower, "hornblåse," is twice cited by Grimm as an equivalent to witch: *Deutsche Mythologie*, p. 886.

[†] B. Schmidt, *Das Volksleben der Neugriechen*, pp 100f, 107, 123. Euphemistically the nereids are called ἡ καλαὶς ἀρχόντισσαις, ἡ καλαὶς κυράδες, ἡ καλόκαρδαις, ἡ καλότυχαις; their sovereign is ἡ μεγάλη κυρά, ἡ πρώτη, etc.

---

[*] Of these Dr Reinhold Köhler has given me a note of more than twenty. The French tale itself had, in all likelihood, a popular foundation.

Translated by Grundtvig, *Engelske og skotske Folkeviser*, No 19; by Rosa Warrens, *Schottische Volkslieder*, No 7; Knortz, *Lieder und Romanzen* *Alt-Englands*, No 9; Loève-Veimars, *Ballades de l'Angleterre*, p. 353.

1 O ALLISON GROSS, that lives in yon towr,
  The ugliest witch i the north country,
  Has trysted me ae day up till her bowr,
  An monny fair speech she made to me.

2 She stroaked my head, an she kembed my hair,
  An she set me down saftly on her knee;
  Says, Gin ye will be my lemman so true,
  Sae monny braw things as I woud you gi.

3 She showd me a mantle o red scarlet,
  Wi gouden flowrs an fringes fine;
  Says, Gin ye will be my lemman so true,
  This goodly gift it sal be thine.

4 'Awa, awa, ye ugly witch,
  Haud far awa, an lat me be;
  I never will be your lemman sae true,
  An I wish I were out o your company.'

5 She neist brought a sark o the saftest silk,
  Well wrought wi pearles about the ban;
  Says, Gin you will be my ain true love,
  This goodly gift you sal comman.

6 She showd me a cup of the good red gold,
  Well set wi jewls sae fair to see;
  Says, Gin you will be my lemman sae true,
  This goodly gift I will you gi.

[315] 7 'Awa, awa, ye ugly witch,
  Had far awa, and lat me be;
  For I woudna ance kiss your ugly mouth
  For a' the gifts that ye coud gi.'

8 She's turnd her right and roun about,
  An thrice she blaw on a grass-green horn,
  An she sware by the meen and the stars abeen,
  That she'd gar me rue the day I was born.

9 Then out has she taen a silver wand,
  An she's turnd her three times roun an roun;
  She's mutterd sich words till my strength it faild,
  An I fell down senceless upon the groun.

10 She's turnd me into an ugly worm,
  And gard me toddle about the tree;
  An ay, on ilka Saturdays night,
  My sister Maisry came to me,

11 Wi silver bason an silver kemb,
  To kemb my heady upon her knee;
  But or I had kissd her ugly mouth,
  I'd rather a toddled about the tree.

12 But as it fell out on last Hallow-even,
  When the seely court was ridin by,
  The queen lighted down on a gowany bank,
  Nae far frae the tree where I wont to lye.

13 She took me up in her milk-white han,
  An she's stroakd me three times oer her knee;
  She chang'd me again to my ain proper shape,
  An I nae mair maun toddle about the tree.

36

THE LAILY WORM
AND THE MACHREL OF THE SEA

Skene MS., p. 30: taken down from recitation in the
north of Scotland, in 1802 or 1803.

SOMEWHAT mutilated, and also defaced, though it be, this ballad has certainly never been retouched by a pen, but is pure tradition. It has the first stanza in common with 'Kemp Owyne,' and shares more than that with 'Allison Gross.' But it is independent of 'Allison Gross,' and has a far more original sound.

Maisry's services in washing and combing are more conceivable when rendered by a maid in her proper shape, as in 'Allison Gross,' than when attributed to a machrel of the sea; and it is likely that the machrel returned to her own figure every Saturday, and that this is one of the points lost from the story. It is said, here as in 'Allison Gross,' that Maisry kames the laily head on her knee.[*] It would be a mere cavil to raise a difficulty about combing a laily worm's head. The fiery beast in 'Kemp Owyne,' **A**, has long hair, and the laily worm may have had enough to be better for combing.[†]

It is only natural that the transformed maid should not wish to trust herself again in the hands of the stepmother, but it is not according to poetical justice that she should remain a machrel of the sea, and here again we may suppose something to have dropped out.

We have had a double transformation, of sister and brother, in the 'Marriage of Gawain' and in the 'Wedding of Gawen and Dame Ragnell,' and again, with a second sister added, in the story of Álsól. Brother and sister are trans- [316] formed in the Danish 'Nattergalen,' Grundtvig, No 57; Kristensen, *Folkeminder*, XI, 25, No 20, A–C; Näktergalsvisan, Bohlin, in *Nyare Bidrag till Kännedom om de Svenska Landsmålen*, II, 10, *Folktoner från Jämtland*, pp. 5, 6. It is an aggravation of stepmother malice that the victim of enchantment, however amiable and inoffensive before, should become truculent and destructive; so with the brother of Gawain's bride, and with the Carl of Carlile. The stepmother is satisfactorily disposed of, as she is in 'Kemp Owyne,' **B**, and the 'Laidly Worm of Spindleston Heughs.'

---

[*] Dives, in one version of a well-known carol, has "a place prepared in hell, to sit upon a *serpent's knee*." The pious chanson in question is a very different thing from an old ballad, which, it is hoped, no one will think capable of fatuity.

[†] As, for example, a dragon has in Hahn's *Griechische Märchen*, No 26, I, 187, and elsewhere.

In a Kaffir tale a girl marries a crocodile. The crocodile bids her lick his face. Upon her doing so, the crocodile casts his skin and turns into a strong and handsome man. He had been transformed by the enemies of his father's house. Theal, *Kaffir Folk-Lore*, 1882, p. 37, cited by Mr Clouston.

1 'I WAS but seven year auld
   When my mither she did die;
My father married the ae warst woman
   The warld did ever see.

2 'For she has made me the laily worm,
   That lies at the fit o the tree,
An my sister Masery she's made
   The machrel of the sea.

3 'An every Saturday at noon
   The machrel comes to me,
An she takes my laily head
   An lays it on her knee,
She kaims it wi a siller kaim,
   An washes 't in the sea.

4 'Seven knights hae I slain,
   Sin I lay at the fit of the tree,
An ye war na my ain father,
   The eight ane ye should be.'

5 'Sing on your song, ye laily worm,
   That ye did sing to me:'
'I never sung that song but what
   I would it sing to thee.

6 'I was but seven year auld,
   When my mither she did die;
My father married the ae warst woman
   The warld did ever see.

7 'For she changed me to the laily worm,
   That lies at the fit o the tree,
And my sister Masery
   To the machrel of the sea.

8 'And every Saturday at noon
   The machrel comes to me,
An she takes my laily head
   An lays it on her knee,
An kames it wi a siller kame,
   An washes it i the sea.

9 'Seven knights hae I slain,
   Sin I lay at the fit o the tree,
An ye war na my ain father,
   The eighth ane ye shoud be.'

10 He sent for his lady,
   As fast as send could he:
'Whar is my son that ye sent frae me,
   And my daughter, Lady Masery?'

11 'Your son is at our king's court,
   Serving for meat an fee,
An your daughter's at our queen's court,
   .   .   .   .   .

12 'Ye lie, ye ill woman,
   Sae loud as I hear ye lie;
My son's the laily worm,
   That lies at the fit o the tree,
And my daughter, Lady Masery,
   Is the machrel of the sea!

13 She has tane a siller wan,
   An gien him strokes three,
And he has started up the bravest knight
   That ever your eyes did see.

14 She has taen a small horn,
   An loud an shrill blew she,
An a' the fish came her untill
   But the proud machrel of the sea:
'Ye shapeit me ance an unseemly shape,
   An ye's never mare shape me.'

15 He has sent to the wood
   For whins and for hawthorn,
An he has taen that gay lady,
   An there he did her burn.

———◆———

2^2, 7^2. lays: *but* lies, 12^4.
3^3. ducks, *but compare* 8^3.

———◆———

APPENDIX
Additional Copies

Though Skene has rendered this ballad with reasonable fidelity, for an editor, it shall, on account of its interest, be given as it stands in the old lady's MS., where it is No 2. It proves not absolutely true, as I have said, that the Skene ballad has "never been retouched by a pen."

1 'I was bat seven year alld
    Fan my mider she did dee,
My father marrëd the ae warst woman
    The wardle did ever see.

2 'For she has made me the lailly worm
    That lays att the fitt of the tree,
An o my sister Meassry
    The machrel of the sea.

3 'An every Saterday att noon
    The machrl comes to me,
An she takes my laylë head,
    An lays it on her knee,
An keames it we a silver kemm,
    An washes it in the sea.

4 'Seven knights ha I slain
    Sane I lay att the fitt of the tree;
An ye war na my ain father,
    The eight an ye sud be.'

5 'Sing on your song, ye l[a]ily worm,
    That ye sung to me;'
'I never sung that song
    But fatt I wad sing to ye.

6 'I was but seven year aull
    Fan my mider she [did] dee,
My father marrëd the a warst woman
    The wardle did ever see.

7 'She changed me to the layel[y] worm
    That layes att the fitt of the tree,
An my sister Messry
    [To] the makrell of the sea.

8 'And every Saterday att noon
    The machrell comes to me,
An she takes my layly head,
    An layes it on her knee,
An kames it weth a siller kame,
    An washes it in the sea.

9 'Seven knights ha I slain
    San I lay att the fitt of the tree;
An ye war na my ain father,
    The eight ye sud be.'

10 He sent for his lady
    As fast as sen cod he:
'Far is my son,
    That ye sent fra me,
And my daughter,
    Lady Messry?'

11 'Yer son is att our king's court,
    Sarving for meatt an fee,
And yer daugh[t]er is att our quin's court,
    A mary suit an free.'

12 'Ye lee, ye ill woman,
    Sa loud as I hear ye lea,
For my son is the layelly worm
    That lays at the fitt of the tree,
An my daughter Messry
    The machrell of the sea.'

13 She has tain a silver wan
    An gine him stroks three,
An he started up the bravest knight
    Your eyes did ever see.

14 She has tane a small horn
    An loud an shill blue she,
An a' the fish came her tell but the proud machrell,
    An she stood by the sea:
'Ye shaped me ance an unshemly shape,
    An ye's never mare shape me.'

15 He has sent to the wood
    For hathorn an fun,
An he has tane that gay lady,
    An ther he did her burne.

———◆———

Written without division into stanzas or verses.
3^2. comes ea (aye); *but, on repetition in* 8^2, *comes simply, with better metre.*
15^1. hes has. 15^3. that that.

THOMAS RYMER

A. 'Thomas Rymer and Queen of Elfland,' Alexander Fraser Tytler's Brown MS., No 1.
B. 'Thomas the Rhymer,' Campbell MSS, II, 83.

C. 'Thomas the Rhymer,' *Minstrelsy of the Scottish Border*, II, 251, 1802, "from a copy obtained from a lady residing not far from Erceldoune, corrected and enlarged by one in Mrs Brown's MS."

A is one of the nine ballads transmitted to Alexander Fraser Tytler by Mrs Brown in April, 1800, as written down from her recollection.[*] This copy was printed by Jamieson, II, 7, in his preface to 'True Thomas and the Queen of Elfland.' **B**, never published as yet, has been corrupted here and there, but only by tradition. **C** being compounded of **A** and another version, that portion which is found in **A** is put in smaller type.

Thomas of Erceldoune, otherwise Thomas the Rhymer, and in the popular style True Thomas, has had a fame as a seer, which, though progressively narrowed, is, after the lapse of nearly or quite six centuries, far from being extinguished. The common people throughout the whole of Scotland, according to Mr Robert Chambers (1870), continue to regard him with veneration, and to preserve a great number of his prophetic sayings, which they habitually seek to connect with "dear years" and other notable public events.[†] A prediction of Thomas of Erceldoune's is recorded in a manuscript which is put at a date before 1320, and he is referred to with other soothsayers in the

Scalachronica, a French chronicle of English history begun in 1355. Erceldoune is spoken of as a poet in Robert Mannyng's translation of Langtoft's chronicle, finished in 1338; and in the Auchinleck copy of 'Sir Tristrem,' said to have been made about 1350, a Thomas is said to have been consulted at Erþeldoun touching the history of Tristrem. So that we seem safe in holding that Thomas of Erceldoune had a reputation both as prophet and poet in the earlier part of the fourteenth century. The vaticinations of Thomas are cited by various later chroniclers, and had as much credit in England as in Scotland. "During the fourteenth, fifteenth, and sixteenth centuries," says Chambers, "to fabricate a prophecy in the name of Thomas the Rhymer appears to have been found a good stroke of policy on many occasions. Thus was his authority employed to countenance the views of Edward III against Scottish independence, to favor the ambitious views of the Duke of Albany in the minority of James V, and to sustain the spirits of the nation under the harassing invasions of Henry VIII." During the Jacobite rising of 1745 the accomplishment of Thomas's as then unfulfilled predictions was looked for by many. His prophecies, and those of other Scotch soothsayers, were consulted, says Lord Hailes, "with a weak if not criminal curiosity." Even as late as the French revolutionary war a rhyme of Thomas's caused much distress and consternation in the border counties of Scotland, where people were fearing an

---

* See the letter of Dr Anderson to Bishop Percy, December 29, 1800, in Nichols's *Illustrations of the Literary History of the Eighteenth Century*, VII, 178f.

† Chambers' *Popular Rhymes of Scotland*, 1870, pp. 211–224. See, also, Scott's *Minstrelsy*, IV, 110–116, 129–151, ed. 1833. But, above all, Dr J. A. H. Murray's Introduction to *The Romance and Prophecies of Thomas of Erceldoune*, 1875.

invasion. The 'Whole Prophecie' of Merlin, Thomas Rymour, and others, collected and issued as early as 1603, continued to be printed as a chap-book down to the beginning of this century, when, says Dr Murray, few farm-houses in Scotland were without a copy of it.

18] All this might have been if Thomas of Erceldoune had been not more historical than Merlin. But the name is known to have belonged to a real person. Thomas Rymor de Ercildune is witness to a deed whereby one Petrus de Haga obliges himself to make a certain payment to the Abbey of Melrose. Petrus de Haga is, in turn, witness to a charter made by Richard de Moreville. Unluckily, neither of these deeds is dated. But Moreville was constable of Scotland from 1162 to 1189. If we suppose Moreville's charter to have been given towards 1189, and Haga to have been then about twenty years old, and so born about 1170, and further suppose Haga to have made his grant to Melrose towards the end of a life of threescore, or three score and ten, the time of Thomas Rymer's signature would be about 1230 or 1240. If Thomas Rymer was then twenty years of age, his birth would have been at 1210 or 1220. In the year 1294 Thomas de Ercildoun, son and heir of Thomas Rymour de Ercildoun, conveyed to a religious house his inheritance of lands in Ercildoun. With Thomas Rhymer in mind, one naturally interprets Thomas Rymour as the prophet and Thomas de Ercildoun as his son. If Rymour was the surname of this family,[*] it would have been better, for us at least, if the surname had been subjoined to the first Thomas also. As the language stands, we are left to choose among several possibilities. Thomas the Rhymer may have been dead in 1294; Thomas Rymour, meaning the same person, may have made this cession of lands in 1294, and have survived still some years. Thomas, the father, may, as Dr Murray suggests, have retired from the world, but still be living, and it may be his son who resigns the lands. Blind Harry's *Life of Wallace* makes Thomas Rimour to be alive down to 1296 or 1297. A story reported by

Bower in his continuation of Fordun, c. 1430, makes Thomas to have predicted the death of Alexander III in 1286, when, according to the previous (necessarily very loose) calculation, the seer would have been between sixty-six and seventy-six. Neither of these last dates is established by the strongest evidence, but there is no reason for refusing to admit, at least, that Thomas of Erceldoune may have been alive at the latter epoch.

Thomas of Erceldoune's prophetic power was a gift of the queen of the elves; the modern elves, equally those of northern Europe and of Greece, resembling in respect to this attribute the nymphs of the ancient Hellenic mythology. How Thomas attained this grace is set forth in the first of three fits of a poem which bears his name. This poem has come down in four somewhat defective copies: the earliest written a little before the middle of the fifteenth century, two others about 1450, the fourth later. There is a still later manuscript copy of the second and third fits.[†] All the manuscripts are English, but it is manifest from the nature of the topics that the original poem was the work of a Scotsman. All four of the complete versions speak of an older story: 'gyff it be als the storye sayes,' v. 83, 'als the storye tellis full ryghte,' v. 123. The older story, if any, must be the work of Thomas. The circumstance that the poem, as we have it, begins in the first person, and after a long passage returns for a moment to the first person, though most of the tale is told in the third, is of no importance; nor would it have been important if the whole narrative had been put into Thomas's mouth, since that is the simplest of literary artifices.

Thomas, having found favor with the queen of Elfland, was taken with her to that country, and there he remained more than three [seven] years. Then the time came round when a tribute had to be paid to hell, and as Thomas was too likely to be chosen by the fiend, the elf queen conducted him back to the world of men. At the moment of parting Thomas desires

---

[*] Hector Boece (1527) says the surname was Leirmont, but there is no evidence for this that is of value. See Murray, p. xiii.

[†] The five copies have been edited by Dr J. A. H. Murray, and printed by the Early English Text Society. A reconstructed text by Dr Alois Brandl makes the second volume of *a Sammlung englischer Denkmäler in kritischen Ausgaben*, Berlin, 1880.

some token which may authenticate his having
[319] spoken with her. She gives him the gift of
soothsaying. He presses her to stay and tell him
some ferly. Upon this she begins a train of pre-
dictions, which Thomas more than once
importunes her to continue. The first two of
these, the failure of Baliol's party and the battle
of Halidon Hill, 1333, stand by themselves, but
they are followed by a series in chronological
order, extending from the battle of Falkirk to
the battle of Otterbourn, 1298–1388. The third
fit, excepting, perhaps, a reference to Henry
IV's invasion of Scotland in 1401, seems to
consist, not of predictions made after the event,
but of "adaptations of legendary prophecies, tra-
ditionally preserved from far earlier times, and
furbished up anew at each period of national
trouble and distress, in expectation of their ful-
filment being at length at hand."*

The older "story," which is twice referred to
in the prologue to the prophecies of Thomas of
Erceldoune, was undoubtedly a romance which
narrated the adventure of Thomas with the elf
queen *simply*, without specification of his
prophecies. In all probability it concluded, in
accordance with the ordinary popular tradition,
with Thomas's return to fairy-land after a cer-
tain time passed in this world.† For the story of
Thomas and the Elf-queen is but another ver-
sion of what is related of Ogier le Danois and
Morgan the Fay. Six fairies made gifts to Ogier
at his birth. By the favor of five he was to be the
strongest, the bravest, the most successful, the
handsomest, the most susceptible, of knights:

Morgan's gift was that, after a long and fatiguing
career of glory, he should live with her at her
castle of Avalon, in the enjoyment of a still
longer youth and never wearying pleasures.
When Ogier had passed his hundredth year,
Morgan took measures to carry out her promise.
She had him wrecked, while he was on a voyage
to France, on a loadstone rock conveniently
near to Avalon, which Avalon is a little way
this side of the terrestrial paradise. In due course
he comes to an orchard, and there he eats an
apple, which affects him so peculiarly that he
looks for nothing but death. He turns to the
east, and sees a beautiful lady, magnificently
attired. He takes her for the Virgin; she corrects
his error, and announces herself as Morgan the
Fay. She puts a ring on his finger which restores
his youth, and then places a crown on his head
which makes him forget all the past. For two
hundred years Ogier lived in such delights as no
worldly being can imagine, and the two hun-
dred years seemed to him but twenty. Christen-
dom was then in danger, and even Morgan
thought his presence was required in the world.
The crown being taken from his head, the
memory of the past revived, and with it the
desire to return to France. He was sent back by
the fairy, properly provided, vanquished the foes
of Christianity in a short space, and after a time
was brought back by Morgan the Fay to Avalon.

The fairy adventures of Thomas and of Ogier
have the essential points in common, and even
the particular trait that the fairy is taken to be
the Virgin.‡ The occurrence of this trait again
in the ballad, viewed in connection with the
general similarity of the two, will leave no doubt
that the ballad had its source in the romance. [3
Yet it is an entirely popular ballad as to style,§
and must be of considerable age, though the ear-

---

* Murray, pp xxiv–xxvii. As might be expected, the
later texts corrupt the names of persons and of places,
and alter the results of battles. Dr Murray remarks "The
oldest text makes the Scots win Halidon hill, with the
slaughter of six thousand Englishmen, while the other
texts, wise after the fact, makes the Scots lose, as they
actually did." This, and the consideration that a question
about the conflict between the families of Bruce and
Baliol would not be put after 1400, when the Baliol line
was extinct, disposes Dr Murray to think that verses 326–
56 of the second fit, with perhaps the first fit, the conclu-
sion of the poem, and an indefinite portion of fit third,
may have been written on the eve of Halidon Hill, with a
view to encourage the Scots.
† The poem, vv 675–80, says only that Thomas and
the lady did not part for ever and aye, but that she was to
visit him at Huntley banks.

‡ In a Breton story, 'La Fleur du Rocher,' Sébillot,
Contes pop. de la Haute-Bretagne, II, 31, Jean Cate
addresses the fairy, when he first sees her, as the Virgin
Mary. (G. L. K.)
§ Excepting the two satirical stanzas with which
Scott's version (C) concludes. "The repugnance of Tho-
mas to be debarred the use of falsehood when he should
find it convenient," may have, as Scott says, "a comic
effect," but is, for a ballad, a miserable conceit. Both bal-
lad and romance are serious.

liest version (**A**) can be traced at farthest only into the first half of the last century.

The scene of the meeting of Thomas with the elf queen is Huntly Banks and the Eildon Tree in versions **B**, **C** of the ballad, as in the romance.* Neither of these is mentioned in **A**, the reciter of which was an Aberdeen woman. The elf-lady's costume and equipment, minutely given in the romance (henceforth referred to as **R**), are reduced in the ballad to a skirt of grass-green silk and a velvet mantle, **A**, and a dapple-gray horse, **B** 2 (**R** 5), with nine and fifty bells on each tett of its mane, **A** 2 (three bells on either side of the bridle, **R** 9).† Thomas salutes the fairy as queen of heaven, **A** 8, **R** 11. **B** 3 has suffered a Protestant alteration which makes nonsense of the following stanza. She corrects his mistake in all, and in **B** 4 tells him she is out hunting, as in **R** 16. As **C** 5 stands, she challenges Thomas to kiss her, warning him at the same time, unnaturally, and of course in consequence of a corrupt reading, of the danger which Thomas defies, **C** 6. These two stanzas in **C** represent the passage in the romance 17–21, in which Thomas embraces

the fairy queen, and are wanting in **A**, **B**, though not to be spared. It is contact with the fairy that gives her the power to carry her paramour off, for carry him off she does, and he is in great fright at having to go. The ballad is no worse, and the romance would have been much better, for the omission of another passage, impressive in itself, but incompatible with the proper and original story. The elf-queen had told Thomas that he would ruin her beauty, if he had his will, and so it came to pass: her eyes seemed out, her rich clothing was away, her body was like the lead; and it is while thus disfigured that she bids Thomas take leave of sun and moon, so that his alarm is not without reason.‡ He must go with her for seven years, **A**, **B**; only for a twelvemonth, **R**. She takes him up behind her, **A**; she rides and he runs, **B**; she leads him in at Eldon hill, **R**; they cross a water, [321] he wading up to the knee, **B**, **R**. The water is subterranean in **R**, and for three days naught is heard but the soughing of the flood. Then they come to an orchard, **A**, **B**, **R**, and Thomas, like to tyne for lack of food, is about to pull fruit, but is told that the fruit is cursed, **A** 9, **B** 8;§ if he plucks it, his soul goes to the fire of hell, **R** 35. The fairy has made a provision of safe bread

---

* Eildon Tree, the site of which is supposed now to be marked by the Eildon Tree Stone, stood, or should have stood, on the slope of the eastern of the three Eildon Hills. Huntly Banks are about half a mile to the west of the Eildon Stone, on the same hill-slope. Erceldoun, a village on the Leader, two miles above its junction with the Tweed, is all but visible from the Eildon Stone. Murray, pp l–lii.

† In **B** 2, absurdly, the lady holds nine bells in her hand. Ringing or jingling bridles are ascribed to fairies, Tam Lin, **A** 37, Cromek's *Remains of Nithsdale and Galloway Song*, p. 298 ("manes hung wi whustles that the win played on," p. 299). The fairy's saddle has a bordure of bells in the English Launfal, Halliwell's *Illustrations of Fairy Mythology*, p. 31, but not in Marie's lai. The dwarf-king Antiloie, in Ulrich Von Eschenbach's *Alexander*, has bells on his bridle: Grimm, *Deutsche Mythologie*, I, 385. These bells, however, are not at all distinctive of fairies, but are the ordinary decoration of elegant "outriders" in the Middle Ages, especially of women. In the romance of Richard Cœur de Lion, a messenger's trappings ring with five hundred bells. Besides the bridle, bells were sometimes attached to the horse's breastplate, to the saddle-bow, crupper, and stirrups. Conde Claros's steed has three hundred around his breastplate. See Weber's *Metrical Romances*, R. C. de Lion, vv 1514–17, 5712–14, cited by T. Wright, *History of Domestic Manners in England*, 214f; Liebrecht, Gervasius, p. 122; Kölbing, *Englische Studien*, III, 105; Zupitza and Varnhagen, *Anglia*, III, 371, IV, 417; and particularly A. Schultz, *Das höfische Leben zur Zeit der Minnesinger*, I, 235, 388–91; R. Köhler, *Zeitschr. des Vereins f. Volkskunde*, VI, 60.

‡ The original I suppose to be the very cheerful tale of Ogier, with which the author of Thomas of Erceldoune has blended a very serious one, without any regard to the irreconcilableness of the two. He is presently forced to undo this melancholy transformation of the fairy, as we shall see. Brandl, 'Thomas of Erceldoune,' p. 20, cites from Giraldus Cambrensis, *Itinerarium Cambriæ*, I, 5, a story about one Meilyr, a Welshman, the like of which our poet had in mind. This Meilyr was a great soothsayer, and "owed his skill to the following adventure:" Being in company one evening with a girl for whom he had long had a passion, desideratis amplexibus atque deliciis cum indulsisset, statim loco puellæ formosæ formam quamdam villosam, hispidam et hirsutam, adeoque enormiter deformem invenit, quod in ipso ejusdem aspectu dementire, cœpit et insanire. Meilyr recovered his reason after several years, through the merits of the saints, but always kept up an intimacy with unclean spirits, and by their help foretold the future. It is not said that they gave him the tongue that never could lie, but no other tongue could be successfully in his presence: he always saw a little devil capering on it. He was able, by similar indications, to point out the lies and errors of books. The experiment being once tried of laying the Gospel of John in his lap, every devil instantly decamped. Geoffrey of Monmouth's history was substituted, and imps swarmed all over the book and him, too.

§ **B** 8³,⁴ "It was a' that cursed fruit o thine beggared man and woman in your countrie:" the fruit of the Forbidden Tree.

and wine for him in the ballad, **A** 10, **B** 9, but he has still to fast a while in the romance. **C**, which lacks this passage, makes them ride till they reach a wide desert, and leave living land behind, 9; and here (but in **A**, **B**, and **R** in the vicinity of the orchard) the fairy bids Thomas lay his head on her knee, and she will show him rare sights. These are the way to heaven, **A** 12, **B** 11, **R** 38; the way to hell, **A** 13, **B** 10, **R** 41; the road to Elfland, whither they are going, **A** 14. **R** does not point out the road to Elfland, but the elf-queen's castle on a high hill; and there are two additional ferlies, the way to paradise and the way to purgatory,[*] 39, 40. Thomas, in **A** 15, is now admonished that he must hold his tongue, for if he speaks a word he will never get back to his own country; in **R** 44 he is told to answer none but the elf-queen, whatever may be said to him, and this course he takes in **B** 12. But before they proceed to the castle the lady resumes all the beauty and splendor which she had lost, and no explanation is offered save the naive one in the Lansdowne copy, that if she had not, the king, her consort, would have known that she had been in fault. Now follows in **A** 15 (as recited, here 7), **C** 15, 16, the passage through the subterranean water, which should come before they reach the orchard, as in **B** 6, **R** 30, 31. There is much exaggeration in the ballad: they wade through rivers in darkness and hear the sea roaring, **C** 15, **A** 7, as in **R**, but they also wade through red blood to the knee, **A** 7, **C** 16, and the crossing occupies not three days, as in **R** 31, but forty days, **A** 7. In **C** they *now* come to the garden. Stanzas 15, 16 are out of place in **C**, as just remarked, and 17 is entirely perverted. The cursed fruit which Thomas is not to touch in **A** 9, **B** 8, **R** 35, is offered him by the elf-queen as his wages, and will give him the tongue that can never lie, a gift which is made him in the romance at the beginning of the second fit, when the fairy is preparing to part with him. Stanzas 18, 19 of **C** are certainly a modern, and as certainly an ill-devised, interpolation. **B** has lost the conclusion. In **A**, **C**, Thomas gets a fairy costume, and is not seen on earth again for seven years.

---

[*]   Purgatory is omitted in the Cotton MS. of the romance, as in the ballad.

The romance, after some description of the life at the elf-castle, informs us that Thomas lived there more than three years [Cambridge MS., seven], and thought the time but a space of three days, an almost moderate illusion compared with the experience of other mortals under analogous circumstances.[†] The fairy queen then hurried him away, on the eve of the day when the foul fiend was to come to fetch his tribute. He was a mickle man and hend, and there was every reason to fear that he would be chosen. She brought him again to Eldon Tree, and was bidding him farewell. Thomas begged of her a token of his conversation with her, and she gave him the gift of true speaking. He urged her further to tell him some ferly, and she made him several predictions, but he would not let her go without more and more. Finally, with a promise to meet him on Huntly Banks when she might, she left him under the tree.

Popular tradition, as Sir Walter Scott represents, held that, though Thomas was allowed to revisit the earth after a seven years' sojourn in fairy-land, he was under an obligation to go back to the elf-queen whenever she should summon him. One day while he "was making

---

[†]   Ogier le Danois hardly exceeded the proportion of the ordinary hyperbole of lovers: two hundred years seemed but twenty. The British king Herla lived with the king of the dwarfs more than two hundred years, and thought the time but three days: Walter Mapes, *Nugæ Curialium*, ed. Wright, p. 16f (Liebrecht). The strongest case, I believe, is the exquisite legend, versified by Trench, of the monk, with whom three hundred years passed, while he was listening to a bird's song—as he thought, less than three hours. For some of the countless repetitions of the idea, see Pauli's *Schimpf und Ernst*, ed. Oesterley, No 562, and notes, p. 537; Liebrecht's *Gervasius*, p. 89, W. Hertz, *Deutsche Sage im Elsass*, pp 115–18, 263; A. Graf, *La Leggenda del Paradiso Terrestre*, pp 26–29, 31–33, and notes; J. Koch, *Die Siebenschläferlegende*, kap. ii.
   The duration of paradisiac bliss exceeds three hundred years in some accounts. Three hundred years seem but three days in the Italian legend of three monks, Graf, *Miti, Leggende, etc.*, 1892, I, 87f, and in that of the young prince who invites an angel to his wedding, Graf, 90ff, after the Latin text published by Schwarzer, *Zeitschrift für deutsche Philologie*, XIII, 338–51, 1881. (R. Köhler pointed out in the same journal, XIV, 96ff, that an abstract of the story had been given in Vulpius's *Curiositäten*, I, 179ff, as early as 1811.) In the lai of Guingamor, printed by M. Gaston Paris in *Romania*, VIII, 50ff, 1879, three hundred years pass as three days. In both the last, the eating of earthly food brings an immediate decrepitude, followed by speedy death in the case of the prince. [See also W. Hertz, *Spielmannsbuch*, p. 318f.]

merry with his friends in the town of Ercel-
doune, a person came running in, and told,
with marks of fear and astonishment, that a
hart and hind had left the neighboring forest,
and were composedly and slowly parading the
street of the village. The prophet instantly
arose, left his habitation, and followed the won-
derful animals to the forest, whence he was
never seen to return." He is, however, expected
to come back again at some future time.

What we learn from the adventures of Tho-
mas concerning the perils of dealing with fair-
ies, and the precautions to be observed, agrees
with the general teaching of tradition upon the
subject. In this matter there is pretty much one
rule for all "unco" folk, be they fairies, dwarfs,
water-sprites, devils, or departed spirits, and, in
a limited way, for witches, too. Thomas, having
kissed the elf-queen's lips, must go with her.
When the dead Willy comes to ask back his
faith and troth of Margaret, and she says he
must first kiss her, cheek and chin, he replies,
"If I should kiss your red, red lips, Your days
would not be long."[*] When Thomas is about to
pull fruit in the subterranean garden, or para-
dise, the elf bids him let be: all the plagues of
hell light on the fruit of this country; "if thou
pluck it, thy soul goes to the fire of hell."[†] The
queen had taken the precaution of bringing
some honest bread and wine with her for Tho-

mas's behoof. So when Burd Ellen's brother sets
out to rescue his sister, who had been carried off
by the king of Elfland, his sage adviser enjoins
him to eat and drink nothing in fairy-land,
whatever his hunger or thirst; "for if he tasted
or touched in Elfland, he must remain in the
power of the elves, and never see middle-eard
again."[‡] Abstinence from speech is equally
advisable, according to our ballad and to other
authority: Gin ae word you should chance to
speak, you will neer get back to your ain coun-
trie, **A** 15. They've asked him questions, one
and all, but he answered none but that fair
ladie, **B** 12. What so any man to thee say, look
thou answer none but me, **R** 44.

That eating and drinking, personal contact,
exchange of speech, receiving of gifts, in any
abode of unearthly beings, including the dead,
will reduce a man to their fellowship and condi-
tion might be enforced by a great number of
examples, and has already been abundantly
shown by Professor Wilhelm Müller in his
beautiful essay, Zur Symbolik der deutschen
Volkssage.[§] The popular belief of the northern
nations in this matter is more completely
shown than anywhere else in Saxo's account of [323]
King Gormo's visit to Guthmund, and it will be
enough to cite that. The Danish King Gormo,
having heard extraordinary things of the riches
of Geruth (the giant Geirröðr), determines to
verify the reports with his own eyes, under the
guidance of Thorkill, from whom he has
received them. The land of Geruth is far to the
northeast, beyond the sun and stars, and within
the realm of Chaos and Old Night. It is, in fact,
a very dismal and terrific sort of Hades. The
way to it lies through the dominion of Guth-
mund, Geruth's brother, which is described as a
paradise, but a paradise of the same dubious
attractions as that in Thomas of Erceldoune.
Guthmund, himself a giant, receives the travel-

---

[*] In an exquisite little ballad obtained by Tommaseo
from a peasant-girl of Empoli, I, 26, a lover who had vis-
ited hell, and there met and kissed his mistress, is told by
her that he must not hope ever to go thence. How the
lover escaped in this instance is not explained. Such
things happen sometimes, but not often enough to
encourage one to take the risk.

Sono stato all' inferno, e son tornato:
Misericordia, la gente che c'era!
V'era una stanza tutta illuminata,
E dentro v'era la speranza mia.
Quando mi vedde, gran festa mi fece,
E poi mi disse: Dolce anima mia,
Non ti arricordi del tempo passato,
Quando tu mi dicevi, "anima mia?"
Ora, mio caro ben, baciami in bocca,
Baciami tanto ch'io contenta sia.
È tanto saporita la tua bocca!
Di grazia saporisci anco la mia.
Ora, mio caro ben, che m'hai baciata,
Di qui non isperar d'andarne via.

[†] **A** 8, 9, **R** 34, 35. It was not that Thomas was about
to pluck fruit from the Forbidden Tree, though **B** under-
stands it so: cf. **R** 32, 33. The curse of this tree seems,
however, to have affected all Paradise. In modern Greek
popular poetry Paradise occurs sometimes entirely in the
sense of Hades. See B. Schmidt, Volksleben der Neu-
griechen, p. 249.

[‡] Jamieson, in Illustrations of Northern Antiquities, p.
398: 'Child Rowland and Burd Ellen.'

lers, a band of about three hundred, very graciously, and conducts them to his palace. Thorkill takes his comrades apart, and puts them on their guard: they must eat and drink nothing that is offered them, but live on the

§   *Niedersächsische Sagen und Märchen*, Schambach and Muller, p. 373. Shakspere has this: "They are fairies; he that speaks to them shall die;" Falstaff, in *Merry Wives of Windsor*, V, 5. Ancient Greek tradition is not without traces of the same ideas. It was Persephone's eating of the pomegranate kernel that consigned her to the lower world, in spite of Zeus and Demeter's opposition. The drinking of Circe's brewage and the eating of lotus had an effect on the companions of Ulysses such as is sometimes ascribed to the food and drink of fairies, or other demons, that of producing forgetfulness of home: *Odyssey*, x, 236, IX, 97. But it would not be safe to build much on this. A Hebrew tale makes the human wife of a demon charge a man who has come to perform a certain service for the family not to eat or drink in the house, or to take any present of her husband, exactly repeating the precautions observed in Grimm, *Deutsche Sagen*, Nos 41, 49: Tendlau, *Das Buch der Sagen und Legenden jüdischer Vorzeit*, p. 141. The children of Shem may probably have derived this trait in the story from the children of Japhet. Aladdin, in the Arabian Nights, is to have a care, above all things, that he does not touch the walls of the subterranean chamber so much as with his clothes, or he will die instantly. This again, by itself, is not very conclusive. In The Turke and Gowin, Percy MS., ed. Hales and Furnivall, I, 93 f, vv 83–101, the Turk will not let Gawain touch any of the viands set forth in the underground castle, but brings in safe victual for him. (G. L. K.)

provisions which they have brought, must keep off from the people of the place and not touch them; if they partake of any of the food, they will forget everything, and have to pass their lives in this foul society. Guthmund complains that they slight his hospitality, but Thorkill, now and always, has an excuse ready. The genial monarch offers Gormo one of his twelve beautiful daughters in marriage, and their choice of wives to all the rest of the train. Most of the Danes like the proposition, but Thorkill renews his warnings. Four take the bait, and lose all recollection of the past. Guthmund now commends the delicious fruits of his garden, and tries every art to make the king taste them. But he is again foiled by Thorkill, and clearly perceiving that he has met his match, transports the travellers over the river which separates him and his brother, and allows them to continue their journey.[*]

C is translated by Talvj, *Versuch, etc.*, p. 552; by Doenniges, p. 64; by Arndt, *Blütenlese*, p. 246; by Rosa Warrens, *Schottische Volkslieder*, p. 14; by Knortz, *Lieder u. Romanzen*, p. 1; by Edward Barry, *Cycle populaire de Robin Hood*, p. 92; and by F. H. Bothe, *Janus*, p. 122, after Barry.

[*]   *Historia Danica*, l. viii: Müller et Velschow, I, 420–25.

A

Alexander Fraser Tytler's Brown MS., No 1: Jamieson's *Popular Ballads*, II, 7.

1   TRUE THOMAS lay oer yond grassy bank,
    And he beheld a ladie gay,
  A ladie that was brisk and bold,
    Come riding oer the fernie brae.

2   Her skirt was of the grass-green silk,
    Her mantel of the velvet fine,
  At ilka tett of her horse's mane
    Hung fifty silver bells and nine.

3   True Thomas he took off his hat,
    And bowed him low down till his knee:
  'All hail, thou mighty Queen of Heaven!
    For your peer on earth I never did see.'

4   'O no, O no, True Thomas,' she says,
    'That name does not belong to me;
  I am but the queen of fair Elfland,
    And I'm come here for to visit thee.

    *   *   *   *   *

5   'But ye maun go wi me now, Thomas,
    True Thomas, ye maun go wi me,
  For ye maun serve me seven years,
    Thro weel or wae as may chance to be.'

6   She turned about her milk-white steed,
    And took True Thomas up behind,
  And aye wheneer her bridle rang,
    The steed flew swifter than the wind.

7 For forty days and forty nights
  He wade thro red blude to the knee,
And he saw neither sun nor moon,
  But heard the roaring of the sea.

8 O they rade on, and further on,
  Until they came to a garden green
'Light down, light down, ye ladie free,
  Some of that fruit let me pull to thee.'

9 'O no, O no, True Thomas,' she says,
  'That fruit maun not be touched by thee,
For a' the plagues that are in hell
  Light on the fruit of this countrie.

10 'But I have a loaf here in my lap,
  Likewise a bottle of claret wine,
And now ere we go farther on,
  We'll rest a while, and ye may dine.'

11 When he had eaten and drunk his fill,
  'Lay down your head upon my knee,'
The lady sayd, 'ere we climb yon hill,
  And I will show you fairlies three.

12 'O see not ye yon narrow road,
  So thick beset wi thorns and briers?
That is the path of righteousness,
  Tho after it but few enquires.

13 'And see not ye that braid braid road,
  That lies across yon lillie leven?
That is the path of wickedness,
  Tho some call it the road to heaven.

14 'And see not ye that bonny road,
  Which winds about the fernie brae?
That is the road to fair Elfland,
  Whe[re] you and I this night maun gae.

15 'But Thomas, ye maun hold your tongue,
  Whatever you may hear or see,
For gin ae word you should chance to speak,
  You will neer get back to your ain countrie.'

16 He has gotten a coat of the even cloth,
  And a pair of shoes of velvet green,
And till seven years were past and gone
  True Thomas on earth was never seen.

B

Campbell MSS, II, 83.

1 As Thomas lay on Huntlie banks—
  A wat a weel bred man was he—
And there he spied a lady fair,
  Coming riding down by the Eildon tree.

2 The horse she rode on was dapple gray,
  And in her hand she held bells nine;
I thought I heard this fair lady say
  These fair siller bells they should a' be mine.

3 It's Thomas even forward went,
  And lootit low down on his knee:
'Weel met thee save, my lady fair,
  For thou 'rt the flower o this countrie.'

4 'O no, O no, Thomas,' she says,
  'O no, O no, that can never be,
For I'm but a lady of an unco land,
  Comd out a hunting, as ye may see.

5 'O harp and carp, Thomas,' she says,
  'O harp and carp, and go wi me;
It's be seven years, Thomas, and a day,
  Or you see man or woman in your ain coun-
    trie.'

6 It's she has rode, and Thomas ran,
  Until they cam to yon water clear;
He's coosten off his hose and shon,
  And he's wooden the water up to the knee.

7 It's she has rode, and Thomas ran,
  Until they cam to yon garden green;
He's put up his hand for to pull down ane,
  For the lack o food he was like to tyne.

8 'Hold your hand, Thomas,' she says,
  'Hold your hand, that must not be;
It was a' that cursed fruit o thine
  Beggared man and woman in your countrie.

9 'But I have a loaf and a soup o wine,
  And ye shall go and dine wi me;
[325] And lay yer head down in my lap,
  And I will tell ye farlies three.

10 'It's dont ye see yon broad broad way,
  That leadeth down by yon skerry fell?
  It's ill's the man that dothe thereon gang,
  For it leadeth him straight to the gates o hell.

11 'It's dont ye see yon narrow way,
  That leadeth down by yon lillie lea?
  It's weel's the man that doth therein gang,
  For it leads him straight to the heaven hie.'

 *   *   *   *   *

12 It's when she cam into the hall
  I wat a weel bred man was he—
  They've asked him question[s], one and all,
  But he answered none but that fair ladie.

13 O they speerd at her where she did him get,
  And she told them at the Eildon tree;

  .   .   .   .   .
  .   .   .   .   .

C

Minstrelsy of the Scottish Border, II, 251, ed. 1802.

True Thomas lay on Huntlie bank; A ferlie he spied wi' his ee;

And there he spied a ladye bright, Come riding down by the Eildon Tree.

1 TRUE Thomas lay on Huntlie bank,
  A ferlie he spied wi' his ee,
  And there he saw a lady bright,
  Come riding down by the Eildon Tree.

2 Her shirt was o the grass-green silk,
  Her mantle o the velvet fyne,
  At ilka tett of her horse's mane
  Hang fifty siller bells and nine.

3 True Thomas, he pulld aff his cap,
  And louted low down to his knee:
  'All hail, thou mighty Queen of Heavn!
  For thy peer on earth I never did see.'

4 'O no, O no, Thomas,' she said,
  'That name does not belang to me;
  I am but the queen of fair Elfland,
  That am hither come to visit thee.

5 'Harp and carp, Thomas,' she said,
  'Harp and carp along wi me,
  And if ye dare to kiss my lips,
  Sure of your bodie I will be.'

6 'Betide me weal, betide me woe,
  That weird shall never danton me;'
  Syne be has kissed her rosy lips,
  All underneath the Eildon Tree.

7 'Now, ye maun go wi me,' she said,
  'True Thomas, ye maun go wi me,
  And ye maun serve me seven years,
  Thro weal or woe, as may chance to be.'

8 She mounted on her milk-white steed,
  She's taen True Thomas up behind,
  And aye wheneer her bridle rung,
  The steed flew swifter than the wind.

9 O they rade on, and farther on—
  The steed gaed swifter than the wind—
  Untill they reached a desart wide,
  And living land was left behind.

10 'Light down, light down, now, True Thomas,
  And lean your head upon my knee;
  Abide and rest a little space,
  And I will shew you ferlies three.

11 'O see ye not yon narrow road,
    So thick beset with thorns and briers?
  That is the path of righteousness,
    Tho after it but few enquires.

12 'And see not ye that braid braid road,
    That lies across that lily leven?
  That is the path of wickedness,
    Tho some call it the road to heaven.

13 'And see not ye that bonny road,
    That winds about the fernie brae?
  That is the road to fair Elfland,
    Where thou and I this night maun gae.

14 'But, Thomas, ye maun hold your tongue,
    Whatever ye may hear or see,
  For, if you speak word in Elflyn land,
    Ye'll neer get back to your ain countrie.'

15 O they rade on, and farther on,
    And they waded thro rivers aboon the knee,
  And they saw neither sun nor moon,
    But they heard the roaring of the sea.

16 It was mirk mirk night, and there was nae stern light,
    And they waded thro red blude to the knee
  For a' the blude that's shed on earth
    Rins thro the springs o that countrie.

17 Syne they came on to a garden green,
    And she pu'd an apple frae a tree:
  'Take this for thy wages, True Thomas,
    It will give the tongue that can never lie.'

18 'My tongue is mine ain,' True Thomas said;
    'A gudely gift ye wad gie to me!
  I neither dought to buy nor sell,
    At fair or tryst where I may be.

19 'I dought neither speak to prince or peer,
    Nor ask of grace from fair ladye:'
  'Now hold thy peace,' the lady said,
    'For as I say, so must it be.'

20 He has gotten a coat of the even cloth,
    And a pair of shoes of velvet green,
  And till seven years were gane and past
    True Thomas on earth was never seen.

———◆———

A. 7 *stands* 15 *in the MS.*
  8^2. golden green, *if my copy is right.*
  $11^{2,3}$ *are* $11^{3,2}$ *in the MS.: the order of words is still not simple enough for a ballad.*
  14^4. goe.

Jamieson has a few variations, which I suppose to be his own.

1^1. oer yonder bank. 3^4. your like. 4^4. And I am come here to. 6^4. Her steed. 8^2. garden, *rightly.*
10^2. clarry. 11^2. Lay your head. 12^1. see you not. 12^4. there's few. 13. see ye not yon. 14^1. see ye not. 14^2. Which winds.
B. 3^2. her knee. 3^3. thou save.
12^1. MS. *perhaps* unto.
$13^{1,2}$ *follow st.* 12 *without separation.*
C. 20^1. a cloth.

———◆———

APPENDIX

Thomas off Ersseldoune

Thornton MS., leaf 149, back, as printed by Dr J.
A. H. Murray.

[A prologue of six stanzas, found only in the
Thornton MS., is omitted, as being, even if genuine,
not to the present purpose.]

1 Als I me wente þis endres daye,
    Ffull faste in mynd makand my mone,
  In a mery mornynge of Maye,
    By Huntle bankkes my selfe allone,

2 I herde þe jaye and þe throstelle,
    The mawys menyde of hir songe,
  Þe wodewale beryde als a belle,
    That alle þe wode a-bowte me ronge.

3 Allonne in longynge thus als I laye,
    Vndyre-nethe a semely tre,
  [Saw] I whare a lady gaye
    [Came ridand] ouer a longe lee.

4 If I solde sytt to domesdaye,
    With my tonge to wrobbe and wrye,
  Certanely þat lady gaye
    Neuer bese scho askryede for mee.

5 Hir palfraye was a dappill graye,
    Swylke one ne saghe I neuer none;
  Als dose þe sonne on someres daye,
    Þat faire lady hir selfe scho schone.

6 Hir selle it was of roelle bone,
    Ffull semely was þat syghte to see;
  Stefly sett with precyous stones,
    And compaste all with crapotee;

7 Stones of oryente, grete plente.
    Hir hare abowte hir hede it hange;
  Scho rade ouer þat lange lee;
    A whylle scho blewe, a-noþer scho sange.

8 Hir garthes of nobyll sylke þay were,
    The bukylls were of berelle stone,
  Hir steraps were of crystalle clere,
    And all with perelle ouer-by-gone.

9 Hir payetrelle was of irale fyne,
    Hir cropoure was of orpharë,
  And als clere golde hir brydill it schone;
    One aythir syde hange bellys three.

10 [Scho led *three* grehoundis in a leesshe,]
    And seuene raches by hir þay rone;
  Seho bare an horne abowte hir halse,
    And vndir hir belte full many a flone.

11 Thomas laye and sawe þat syghte,
    Vndir-nethe ane semly tree;
  He sayd, 3one es Marye, moste of myghte,
    Þat bare þat childe þat dyede for mee.

12 Bot if I speke with 3one lady bryghte,
    I hope myne herte will bryste in three;
  Now sall I go with all my myghte,
    Hir for to mete at Eldoune tree.

13 Thomas rathely vpe he rase,
    And he rane ouer þat mountayne hye;
  Gyff it be als the storye sayes,
    He hir mette at Eldone tree.

14 He knelyde downe appone his knee,
    Vndir-nethe þat grenwode spraye,
  And sayd, Lufly ladye, rewe one mee,
    Qwene of heuene, als þou wele maye!

15 Then spake þat lady milde of thoghte:
    Thomas, late swylke wordes bee;
  Qwene of heuene ne am I noghte,
    Ffor I tuke neuer so heghe degre.

16 Bote I ame of ane oþer countree,
    If I be payrelde moste of pryse;
  I ryde aftyre this wylde fee;
    My raches rynnys at my devyse.'

17 'If þou be parelde moste of pryse,
 And here rydis thus in thy folye,
 Of lufe, lady, als þou erte wyse,
 Þon gyffe me leue to lye the bye.'

18 Scho sayde, þou mane, þat ware folye;
 I praye þe, Thomas, þou late me bee;
 Ffor I saye þe full sekirlye,
 Þat synne will for-doo all my beaute.

19 'Now, lufly ladye, rewe one mee,
 And I will euer more with the duelle;
 Here my trouthe I will the plyghte,
 Whethir þou will in heuene or helle.'

20 'Mane of molde, þou will me marre,
 But ȝitt þou sall hafe all thy will;
 And trowe it wele, þou chewys þe werre,
 Ffor alle my beaute will þou spylle.'

21 Downe þane lyghte þat lady bryghte,
 Vndir-nethe þat grenewode sprayȝe;
 And, als the storye tellis full ryghte,
 Seuene sythis by hir he laye.

22 Scho sayd, Mane, the lykes thy playe:
 Whate byrde in boure maye delle with the?
 Thou merrys me all þis longe daye;
 I pray the, Thomas, late me bee.

23 Thomas stode vpe in þat stede,
 And he by-helde þat lady gaye;
 Hir hare it hange all ouer hir hede,
 Hir eghne semede owte, þat are were graye.

24 And alle þe riche clothynge was a-waye,
 Þat he by-fore sawe in þat stede;
 Hir a schanke blake, hir oþer graye,
 And all hir body lyke the lede.

25 Thomas laye, and sawe þat syghte,
 Vndir-nethe þat grenewod tree.
 .   .   .   .   .   .
 .   .   .   .   .   .

26 Þan said Thomas, Allas! allas!
 In faythe þis es a dullfull syghte;
 How arte þou fadyde þus in þe face,
 Þat schane by-fore als þe sonne so bryght[e]!

27 Scho sayd, Thomas, take leue at sone and mon[e],
 And als at lefe þat grewes on tree;
 This twelmoneth sall þou with me gone,
 And medill-erthe sall þou none see.'

28 He knelyd downe appone his knee,
 Vndir-nethe þat grenewod sprayȝe,
 And sayd, Lufly lady, rewe on mee,
 Mylde qwene of heuene, als þou beste maye!

29 'Allas!' he sayd, 'and wa es mee!
 I trowe my dedis wyll wirke me care;
 My saulle, Jhesu, by-teche I the,
 Whedir-some þat euer my banes sall fare.'

30 Scho ledde hym in at Eldone hill,
 Vndir-nethe a derne lee,
 Whare it was dirke as mydnyght myrke,
 And euer þe water till his knee.

31 The montenans of dayes three,
 He herd bot swoghynge of þe flode
 At þe laste he sayde, Full wa es mee!
 Almaste I dye, for fawte of f[ode.]

32 Scho lede hym in-till a faire herbere,
 Whare frwte was g[ro]wan[d gret plentee]
 Pere and appill, bothe ryppe þay were,
 The date, and als the damasee.

33 Þe fygge, and alsso þe wyneberye,
 The nyghtgales byggande on þair neste;
 Þe papeioyes faste abowte gane flye,
 And throstylls sange, wolde hafe no reste.   [328]

34 He pressede to pulle frowte with his hande,
 Als mane for fude þat was nere faynt;
 Scho sayd, Thomas, þou late þame stande,
 Or ells þe fende the will atteynt.

35 If þou it plokk, sothely to saye,
 Thi saul, gose to þe fyre of helle;
 It commes neuer owte or domesdaye,
 Bot þer in payne ay for to duelle.

36 Thomas, sothely I the hyghte,
 Come lygge thyne hede downe on my knee,
 And [þou] sall se þe fayreste syghte
 Þat euer sawe mane of thi contree.

37 He did in hye als scho hym badde;
    Appone hir knee his hede he layde,
Ffor hir to paye he was full glade;
    And þane þat lady to hym sayde:

38 Seese þou nowe ȝone faire waye,
    Þat lygges ouer ȝone heghe mountayne?
ȝone es þe waye to heuene for aye,
    Whene synfull sawles are passed þer payne.

39 Seese þou nowe ȝone oþer waye,
    Þat lygges lawe by-nethe ȝone rysse?
ȝone es þe waye, þe sothe to saye,
    Vn-to þe joye of paradyse.

40 Seese þou ȝitt ȝone thirde waye,
    Þat ligges vndir ȝone grene playne?
ȝone es þe waye, with tene and traye,
    Whare synfull saulis suffirris þaire payne.

41 Bot seese þou nowe ȝone ferthe waye,
    Þat lygges ouer ȝone depe delle?
ȝone es þe waye, so waylawaye!
    Vn-to þe birnande fyre of helle.

42 Seese þou ȝitt ȝone faire castelle,
    [Þat standis ouer] ȝone heghe hill?
Of towne and towre it beris þe belle;
    In erthe es none lyke it vn-till.

41 Ffor sothe, Thomas, ȝone es myne awenne,
    And þe kynges of this countree;
Bot me ware leuer be hanged and drawene,
    Or þat he wyste þou laye by me.

44 When þou commes to ȝone castelle gay,
    I pray þe curtase mane to bee:
And whate so any mane to þe saye,
    Luke þou answere none bott mee.

45 My lorde es seruede at ylk a mese
    With thritty knyghttis faire and free;
I sall saye, syttande at the desse,
    I tuke thi speche by-ȝonde the see

46 Thomas still als stane he stude,
    And he by-helde þat lady gaye;
Scho come agayne als faire and gude,
    And also ryche one hir palfraye.

47 Hir grewehundis fillide with dere blode,
    Hir raches couplede, by my faye;
Scho blewe hir horne with mayne and mode,
    Vn-to þe castelle scho tuke þe waye.

48 In-to þe haulle sothely scho went,
    Thomas foloued at hir hande;
Than ladyes come, bothe faire and gent,
    With curtassye to hir knelande.

49 Harpe and fethill bothe þay fande,
    Getterne, and als so þe sawtrye;
Lutte and rybybe bothe gangande,
    And all manere of mynstralsye.

50 Þe most meruelle þat Thomas thoghte,
    Whene þat he stode appone the flore;
Ffor feftty hertis in were broghte,
    Þat were bothe grete and store.

51 Raches laye lapande in þe blode,
    Cokes come, with dryssynge knyfe;
Thay brittened þame als þay were wode;
    Reuelle amanges þame was full ryfe.

52 Knyghtis dawnesede by three and three,
    There was revelle, gamene and playe;
Lufly ladyes, faire and free,
    That satte and sange one riche araye.

53 Thomas duellide in that solace
    More þane I ȝowe saye, parde,
Till one a daye, so hafe I grace,
    My lufly lady sayde to mee:

54 'Do buske the, Thomas, þe buse agayne,
    Ffor þou may here no lengare be;
Hye the faste, with myghte and mayne,
    I sall the brynge till Eldone tree.

55 Thomas sayde þane, with heuy chere,
    Lufly lady, nowe late me bee;
Ffor certis, lady, I hafe bene here
    Noghte bot þe space of dayes three.

56 'Ffor sothe, Thomas, als I þe telle,
    Þou base bene here thre ȝere and more;
Bot langere here þou may noghte duelle;
    The skylle I sall þe telle whare-fore.

57 'To morne of belle þe foulle fende
    Amange this folke will feche his fee;
29] And þou arte mekill mane and hende;
    I trowe full wele he wolde chese the.

58 'Ffor alle þe gold þat euer may bee,
    Ffro hethyne vn-to þe worldis ende,
    Þou bese neuer be-trayede for mee;
    Þerefore with me I rede thou wende.'

59 Scho broghte hym agayne to Eldone tree,
    Vndir-nethe þat grenewode spraye;
    In Huntlee bannkes es mery to bee,
    Whare fowles synges bothe nyght and daye.

60 'Fferre owtt in ȝone mountane graye,
    Thomas, my fawkone bygges a neste;
    A fawconne es an erlis praye;
    Ffor-thi in na place may he reste.

61 'Ffare well, Thomas, I wend my waye,
    Ffor me by-houys ouer thir benttis browne:'
    Loo here a fytt: more es to saye,
    All of Thomas of Erselldowne.

FYTT II.

1 'Fare wele, Thomas, I wend my waye,
    I may no lengare stande with the:'
    'Gyff me a tokynynge, lady gaye,
    That I may saye I spake with the.'

2 'To harpe or carpe, whare-so þou gose,
    Thomas, þou sall hafe þe chose sothely:'
    And he saide, Harpynge kepe I none,
    Ffor tonge es chefe of mynstralsye.

3 'If þou will spelle, or tales telle,
    Thomas, þou sall neuer lesynge lye;
    Whare euer þou fare, by frythe or felle,
    I praye the speke none euyll of me.

4 'Ffare wele, Thomas, with-owttyne gyle,
    I may no lengare duelle with the:'
    'Lufly lady, habyde a while,
    And telle þou me of some ferly.'

5 'Thomas, herkyne what I the saye: etc.

Here begin the prophecies.

———◆———

& *and* j *are replaced by* and *and* I.
2¹. throstyll cokke: throstell, *Cambridge MS.*
2². menyde hir.
10¹. *Wanting.* She led, etc., *Cambridge.*
12⁴, 13⁴. *Lansdowne,* elden; *Cambridge,* eldryn,
    eldryne.
16². prysse.

17¹. prysee. 17³. wysse.
43⁴. me by. *Cambridge,* be me.
46⁴. also.

FYTT 2.
2¹. þou gose. *Cambridge,* ȝe gon.

———◆———

Additional Copies

"Thomas the Rhymer. Variations. J. Ormiston,
Kelso." "Scotch Ballads, Materials for Border Min-
strelsy," No 96, Abbotsford; in the handwriting of John
Leyden.

HER horse was o the dapple-gray,
  And in her hands she held bells nine:
'Harp and carp, Thomas,' she said,
  For a' thae bonny bells shall be thine.'

It was a night without delight,

And they rade on and on, I wiss,
    (amiss)
  Till they came to a garden green;
He reached his hand to pu an apple,
  For lack o fruit he was like to tyne.

'Now had your hand, Thomas,' she said,
  'Had your hand, and go wi me;
That is the evil fruit o hell,
  Beguiled man and women in your countrie.

'O see you not that road, Thomas,
  That lies down by that little hill?
Curst is the man has that road to gang,
  For it takes him to the lowest hell.

'O see you not that road, Thomas,
  That lies across yon lily lea?
Blest is the man has that road to gang,
  For it takes him to the heavens hie.

'When ye come to my father's ha,
    To see what a learned man you be
They will you question, one and a',
  But you must answer none but me,
And I will answer them again
  I gat you at the Eildon tree.'

And when, etc.
  He answered none but that gay ladie.

'Harp and carp, gin ye gang wi me,
  It shall be seven year and day
Or ye return to your countrie.

'Wherever ye gang, or wherever ye be,
  Ye'se bear the tongue that can never lie.

'Gin ere ye want to see me again,
  Gang to the bonny banks o Farnalie.'

———————◆———————

'Thomas the Rhymer,' "Scotch Ballads, Materials
for Border Minstrelsy," No 97, Abbotsford; communi-
cated to Sir Walter Scott by Mrs Christiana Green-
wood, London, May 27, 1806 (Letters, I, 189), from the
recitation of her mother and of her aunt, both then
above sixty, who learned it in their childhood from
Kirstan Scot, a very old woman, at Longnewton, near
Jedburgh.

1 THOMAS lay on the Huntlie bank,
    A spying ferlies wi his eee,
  And he did spy a lady gay,
    Come riding down by the lang lee.

2 Her steed was o the dapple grey,
    And at its mane there hung bells nine;
  He thought he heard that lady say,
    'They gowden bells sall a' be thine.'

3 Her mantle was o velvet green,
    And a' set round wi jewels fine;
  Her hawk and hounds were at her side,
    And her bugle-horn wi gowd did shine.

4 Thomas took aff baith cloak and cap,
    For to salute this gay lady:
  'O save ye, save ye, fair Queen o Heavn,
    And ay weel met ye save and see!'

5 'I'm no the Queen o Heavn, Thomas;
　　I never carried my head sae hee;
　For I am but a lady gay,
　　Come out to hunt in my follee.

6 'Now gin ye kiss my mouth, Thomas,
　　Ye mauna miss my fair bodee;
　Then ye may een gang hame and tell
　　That ye've lain wi a gay ladee.'

7 'O gin I loe a lady fair,
　　Nae ill tales o her wad I tell,
　And it's wi thee I fain wad gae,
　　Tho it were een to heavn or hell.'

8 'Then harp and carp, Thomas,' she said,
　　'Then harp and carp alang wi me;
　But it will be seven years and a day
　　Till ye win back to yere ain countrie.'

9 The lady rade, True Thomas ran,
　　Untill they cam to a water wan;
　O it was night, and nae delight,
　　And Thomas wade aboon the knee.

10 It was dark night, and nae starn-light,
　　And on they waded lang days three,
　And they heard the roaring o a flood,
　　And Thomas a waefou man was he.

11 Then they rade on, and farther on,
　　Untill they came to a garden green;
　To pu an apple he put up his hand,
　　For the lack o food he was like to tyne.

12 'O haud yere hand, Thomas,' she cried,
　　'And let that green flourishing be;
　For it's the very fruit o hell,
　　Beguiles baith man and woman o yere coun-
　　　trie.

13 'But look afore ye, True Thomas,
　　And I shall show ye ferlies three;
　Yon is the gate leads to our land,
　　Where thou and I sae soon shall be.

14 'And dinna ye see yon road, Thomas,
　　That lies out-owr yon lilly lee?
　Weel is the man yon gate may gang,
　　For it leads him straight to the heavens hie.

15 'But do you see yon road, Thomas,
　　That lies out-owr yon frosty fell?
　Ill is the man yon gate may gang,
　　For it leads him straight to the pit o hell.

16 'Now when ye come to our court, Thomas,
　　See that a weel-learnd man ye be;
　For they will ask ye, one and all,
　　But ye maun answer nane but me.

17 'And when nae answer they obtain,
　　Then will they come and question me,
　And I will answer them again
　　That I gat yere aith at the Eildon tree.

*　　　*　　　*　　　*　　　*

18 'Ilka seven years, Thomas,
　　We pay our teindings unto hell,
　And ye're sae leesome and sae strang
　　That I fear, Thomas, it will be yeresell.'

———•———

1¹. the Lang-lee. 12². flour is hing.

38

THE WEE WEE MAN

A. a. 'The Wee Wee Man,' Herd's MSS, I, 153; Herd's *Scottish Songs*, 1776, I, 95.
B. Caw's *Poetical Museum*, p. 348.
C. 'The Wee Wee Man,' Scott's *Minstrelsy*, II, 234, ed. 1802.
D. 'The Wee Wee Man,' Kinloch MSS, VII, 253.

E. a. 'The Wee Wee Man,' Motherwell's Note-Book, fol. 40; Motherwell's MS., p. 195. b. Motherwell's *Minstrelsy*, p. 343.
F. 'The Wee Wee Man,' Motherwell's MS., p. 68.
G. 'The Little Man,' Buchan's *Ballads of the North of Scotland*, I, 263.

THIS extremely airy and sparkling little ballad varies but slightly in the half dozen known copies. The one in the *Musical Museum*, No 870, p. 382, and that in Ritson's *Scotish Songs*, II, 139, are reprinted from Herd.

Singularly enough, there is a poem in eight-line stanzas, in a fourteenth-century manuscript, [330] which stands in somewhat the same relation to this ballad as the poem of Thomas of Erceldoune does to the ballad of Thomas Rymer, but with the important difference that there is no reason for deriving the ballad from the poem in this instance. There seems to have been an intention to make it, like Thomas of Erceldoune, an introduction to a string of prophecies which follows, but no junction has been effected. This poem is given in an appendix.

A is translated by Arndt, *Blütenlese*, p. 210; B, with a few improvements from E b, by Rosa Warrens, *Schottische Volkslieder*, p. 12.

A

Herd's MSS, I, 153, Herd's *Ancient and Modern Scottish Songs*, 1776, I, 95.

1 As I was wa'king all alone,
    Between a water and a wa,
  And there I spy'd a wee wee man,
    And he was the least that ere I saw.

2 His legs were scarce a shathmont's length,
    And thick and thimber was his thigh;
  Between his brows there was a span,
    And between his shoulders there was three.

3 He took up a meikle stane,
    And he flang 't as far as I could see;
  Though I had been a Wallace wight,
    I couldna liften 't to my knee.

4 'O wee wee man, but thou be strang!
    O tell me where thy dwelling be?'
  'My dwelling's down at yon bonny bower;
    O will you go with me and see?'

5 On we lap, and awa we rade,
  Till we came to yon bonny green;
  We lighted down for to bait our horse,
  And out there came a lady fine.

6 Four and twenty at her back,
  And they were a' clad out in green;
  Though the King of Scotland had been there,
  The warst o them might hae been his queen.

7 On we lap, and awa we rade,
  Till we came to yon bonny ha,
  Whare the roof was o the beaten gould,
  And the floor was o the cristal a'.

8 When we came to the stair-foot,
  Ladies were dancing, jimp and sma,
  But in the twinkling of an eye,
  My wee wee man was clean awa.

B

Caw's *Poetical Museum*, p. 348.

1 As I was walking by my lane,
  Atween a water and a wa,
  There sune I spied a wee wee man,
  He was the least that eir I saw.

2 His legs were scant a shathmont's length,
  And sma and limber was his thie;
  Atween his shoulders was ae span,
  About his middle war but three.

3 He has tane up a meikle stane,
  And flang 't as far as I cold see;
  Ein thouch I had been Wallace wicht,
  I dought na lift it to my knie.

4 'O wee wee man, but ye be strang!
  Tell me whar may thy dwelling be?'
  'I dwell beneth that bonnie bouir
  O will ye gae wi me and see?'

5 On we lap, and awa we rade,
  Till we cam to a bonny green;
  We lichted syne to bait our steid,
  And out there cam a lady sheen.

6 Wi four and twentie at her back,
  A' comely cled in glistering green;
  Thouch there the King of Scots had stude,
  The warst micht weil hae been his queen.

7 On syne we past wi wondering cheir,
  Till we cam to a bonny ha;
  The roof was o the beaten gowd,   [331]
  The flure was o the crystal a'.

8 When we cam there, wi wee wee knichts
  War ladies dancing, jimp and sma,
  But in the twinkling of an eie,
  Baith green and ha war clein awa.

C

Scott's *Minstrelsy*, II, 234, ed. 1802, incorporated
with 'The Young Tamlane.' From recitation.

1 'T was down by Carterhaugh, father,
  I walked beside the wa,
  And there I saw a wee wee man,
  The least that eer I saw.

2 His legs were skant a shathmont lang,
  Yet umber was his thie;
  Between his brows there was ae span,
  And between his shoulders thrie.

3 He's taen and flung a meikle stane,
  As far as I could see;
  I could na, had I been Wallace wight,
  Hae lifted it to my knee.

4 'O wee wee man, but ye be strang!
  Where may thy dwelling be?'
  'It's down beside yon bonny bower;
  Fair lady, come and see.'

5 On we lap, and away we rade,
  Down to a bonny green;
  We lighted down to bait our steed,
  And we saw the fairy queen.

6 With four and twenty at her back,
  Of ladies clad in green;
  Tho the King of Scotland had been there,
  The worst might hae been his queen.

7 On we lap, and away we rade,
    Down to a bonny ha;
  The roof was o the beaten goud,
    The floor was of chrystal a'.

8 And there were dancing on the floor,
    Fair ladies jimp and sma;
  But in the twinkling o an eye,
    They sainted clean awa.

D

Kinloch MSS, VII, 253. From Mrs Elder.

1 As I gaed out to tak a walk,
    Atween the water and the wa,
  There I met wi a wee wee man,
    The weest man that ere I saw.

2 Thick and short was his legs,
    And sma and thin was his thie,
  And atween his een a flee micht gae,
    And atween his shouthers were inches three.

3 And he has tane up a muckle stane,
    And thrown it farther than I coud see;
  If I had been as strong as ere Wallace was,
    I coud na lift it to my knie.

4 'O,' quo I, 'but ye be strong!
    And O where may your dwelling be?'
  'It's down in to yon bonnie glen;
    Gin ye dinna believe, ye can come and see.'

5 And we rade on, and we sped on,
    Till we cam to yon bonny glen,
  And there we lichted and louted in,
    And there we saw a dainty dame.

6 There was four and twenty wating on her,
    And ilka ane was clad in green,
  And he had been the king of fair Scotland,
    The warst o them micht hae been his queen.

7 There war pipers playing on ilka stair,
    And ladies dancing in ilka ha,
  But before ye coud hae sadd what was that,
    The house and wee manie was awa.

E

    a. Motherwell's Note-Book, fol. 40, "from Agnes Lyle;"
Motherwell's MS., p. 195, "from the recitation of Agnes
Laird, Kilbarchan." **b.** Motherwell's Minstrelsy, p. 343.

1 As I was walking mine alone,
    Betwext the water and the wa,
  There I spied a wee wee man,
    He was the least ane that eer I saw.

2 His leg was scarse a shaftmont lang,
    Both thick and nimble was his knee;
  Between his eyes there was a span,
    Betwixt his shoulders were ells three.

3 This wee wee man pulled up a stone,
    He flang 't as far as I could see;
  Tho I had been like Wallace strong,
    I wadna gotn 't up to my knee.

4 I said, Wee man, oh, but you're strong!
    Where is your dwelling, or where may 't be?
  'My dwelling's at yon bonnie green;
    Fair lady, will ye go and see?'

5 On we lap, and awa we rade,
    Until we came to yonder green;
  We lichtit down to rest our steed,
    And there cam out a lady soon.

6 Four and twenty at her back,
    And every one of them was clad in green;
  Altho he had been the King of Scotland,
    The warst o them a' micht hae been his queen.

7 There were pipers playing in every neuk,
    And ladies dancing, jimp and sma,
  And aye the owre-turn o their tune
    Was 'Our wee wee man has been lang awa.'

F

Motherwell's MS., p. 68, "from the recitation of Mrs Wilson, of the Renfrewshire Tontine; now of the Caledonian Hotel, Inverness."

1 As I was walking mine alane,
    Between the water and the wa,
And oh there I spy'd a wee wee mannie,
    The weeest mannie that ere I saw.

2 His legs they were na a gude inch lang,
    And thick and nimble was his thie;
Between his een there was a span,
    And between his shouthers there were ells
      three.

3 I asked at this wee wee mannie
    Whare his dwelling place might be;
The answer that he gied to me
    Was, Cum alang, and ye shall see.

4 So we 'll awa, and on we rade,
    Till we cam to yon bonnie green;
We lichted down to bait our horse,
    And up and started a lady syne.

5 Wi four and twenty at her back,
    And they were a' weell clad in green;
Tho I had been a crowned king,
    The warst o them might ha been my queen.

6 So we 'll awa, and on we rade,
    Till we cam to yon bonnie hall;
The rafters were o the beaten gold,
    And silver wire were the kebars all.

7 And there was mirth in every end,
    And ladies dancing, ane and a,
And aye the owre-turn o their sang
    Was 'The wee wee mannie's been lang awa.'

G

Buchan's *Ballads of the North of Scotland*, I, 263.

1 As I gaed out to tak the air,
    Between Midmar and bonny Craigha,
There I met a little wee man,
    The less o him I never saw.

2 His legs were but a finger lang,
    And thick and nimle was his knee;
Between his brows there was a span,
    Between his shoulders ells three.

3 He lifted a stane sax feet in hight,
    He lifted it up till his right knee,
And fifty yards and mair, I'm sure,
    I wyte he made the stane to flee.

4 'O little wee man, but ye be wight!
    Tell me whar your dwelling be;'
'I hae a bower, compactly built,
    Madam, gin ye'll cum and see.'

5 Sae on we lap, and awa we rade,
    Till we come to yon little ha;
The kipples ware o the gude red gowd,
    The reef was o the proseyla.

6 Pipers were playing, ladies dancing,
    The ladies dancing, jimp and sma;
At ilka turning o the spring,
    The little man was wearin 's wa.

7 Out gat the lights, on cam the mist,
    Ladies nor mannie mair coud see
I turnd about, and gae a look,
    Just at the foot o' Benachie.

A. 2^2. *The printed copy has* thighs.
4^3. dwelling down.

There is a copy of this ballad in Cunningham's Songs
of Scotland, *I, 303. Though no confidence can be
felt in the genuineness of the* "several variations
from recitation and singing," *with which Cun-
ningham says he sought to improve Herd's version,
the more considerable ones are here noted.*
1^3. O there I met. 2^1. a shathmont lang.
3^3. been a giant born. 4^1. ye're wonder strong.
4^4. O ladie, gang wi me. 5^1. away we flew.
5^2. to a valley green.
5^3. down and he stamped his foot.
5^4. And up there rose.
6^1. Wi four. 6^2. the glossy green.
7^2. stately ha.

8.   And there were harpings loud and sweet,
       And ladies dancing, jimp and sma;
       He clapped his hands, and ere I wist,
       He sank and saunted clean awa.

E. a. 4^1. your.
Motherwell has made one or two slight changes in
    copying from his Note-Book into his MS.
b. *Besides some alterations of his own, Motherwell has
    introduced readings from* **F**.
2^4. there were.
3^3. as Wallace.
5^4. lady sheen. 6^1. Wi four.
6^2. And they were a' weel clad.
After 6 is inserted **F** 6, *with the first line changed to*

So on we lap, and awa we rade.

APPENDIX

This piece is found in Cotton MS., Julius, A, V, the
ninth article in the manuscript, fol. 175, r°, (otherwise
180, r°). It is here given nearly as printed by Mr Tho-
mas Wright in his edition of the *Chronicle of Pierre de
Langtoft*, II, 452. It had been previously printed in Rit-
son's *Ancient Songs*, ed. 1829, I, 40; Finlay's *Scottish Bal-
lads*, II, 168; the *Retrospective Review*, Second Series, II,
326. The prophecies, omitted here, are given by all the
above.

1 ALS y yod on ay Mounday
    Bytwene Wyltinden and Walle,
  Me ane aftere brade waye,
    Ay litel man y mette withalle;
  The leste that ever I sathe, [sothe] to say,
    Oithere in boure, oithere in halle;
  His robe was noithere grene na gray,
    Bot alle yt was of riche palle.

2 On me he cald, and bad me bide;
    Well stille y stode ay litel space;
  Fra Lanchestre the parke syde
    Yeen he come, wel fair his pase.
  He hailsed me with mikel pride;
    Ic haved wel mykel ferly wat he was;
  I saide, Wel mote the bityde!
    That litel man with large face.

3 I biheld that litel man
    Bi the stretes als we gon gae;
  His berd was syde ay large span,
    And glided als the fethere of pae;
  His heved was wyte als any swan,
    His hegehen ware gret and grai alsso;
  Brues lange, wel I the can
    Merke it to five inches and mae.

4 Armes scort, for sothe I saye,
    Ay span seemed thaem to bee;
  Handes brade, vytouten nay,
    And fingeres lange, he scheued me.
  Ay stan he toke op thate it lay,
    And castid forth that I mothe see
  Ay merke-soote of large way
    Bifor me strides he castid three.

5 Wel stille I stod als did the stane,
    To loke him on thouth me nouthe lange;
His robe was alle golde bigane,
    Wel craftlike maked, I underestande;
Botones asurd, everlke ane,
    Fra his elbouthe on til his hande;
Eldelike man was he nane,
    That in myn herte icke onderestande.

6 Til him I sayde ful sone on ane,
    For forthirmare I wald him fraine,
Glalli wild I wit thi name,
    And I wist wat me mouthe gaine;
Thou ert so litel of flesse and bane,
    And so mikel of mithe and mayne;
Ware vones thou, litel man, at hame?
    Wit of the I walde ful faine.

7 'Thoth I be litel and lith,
    Am y nothe wytouten wane;
Fferli frained thou wat I hith,
    Yat thou salt noth with my name.
My wonige stede ful wel es dyth,
    Nou sone thou salt se at hame.'
Til him I sayde, For Godes mith,
    Lat me forth myn erand gane.

8 'The thar noth of thin errand lette,
    Thouth thou come ay stende wit me;
Forthere salt thou noth bisette
    Bi miles twa noythere bi three.'
Na linger durste I for him lette,
    But forth ij fundid wyt that free;
Stintid vs broke no becke;
    Ferlicke me thouth ho so mouth bee.

9 He vent forth, als ij you say,
    In at ay yate, ij understande;
Intil ay yate, wundouten nay;
    It to se thouth me nouth lange.
The bankers on the binkes lay,
    And fair lordes sette ij fonde
In ilka ay hirn ij herd ay lay,
    And levedys south meloude sange.

The meeting with the little man was on Monday. We are now invited to listen to a tale told on Wednesday by "a moody barn," who is presently addressed, in language which, to be sure, fits the elf well enough, as "merry man, that is so wight:" but things do not fay at all here.

10 Lithe, bothe yonge and alde:
    Of ay worde ij will you saye,
A litel tale that me was told
    Erli on ay Wedenesdaye.
A mody barn, that was ful bald,
    My frend that ij frained aye,
Al my yerning he me tald,
    And yatid me als we went bi waye.

11 'Miri man, that es so wythe,
    Of ay thinge gif me answere:
For him that mensked man wyt mith,
    Wat sal worth of this were?' &c.

The orthography of this piece, if rightly rendered, is peculiar, and it is certainly not consistent.
    1⁵. saith *for* saw *occurs in* 23⁸.
    2⁴. *Wright*, Y cen: *Retrosp. Rev.*, Yeen.
    3⁸. *W.*, Merkes: *R. R.*, Merke. fize.
    5⁵. *W.*, everlkes: *R. R.*, euerelke.
6⁸. *W.*, of their: *R. R.*, of ye (þe). i. wald.
7⁴. *W.*, That thou: *R. R.*, yat.
7⁵. dygh. 9⁴. south me.
9⁸. me loude.
10⁷. *W.*, thering: *R. R.*, yering.
10⁸. *W.*, y atid: *R. R.*, yatid.

13

39

TAM LIN

A. 'Tam Lin,' Johnson's *Museum*, p. 423, 1792. Communicated by Burns.

B. 'Young Tom Line,' Glenriddell MS., vol. xi, No 17, 1791.

C. 'Kertonha, or, The Fairy Court,' Herd, *The Ancient and Modern Scots Songs*, 1769, p. 300.

D. 'Tom Linn.' a. Motherwell's MS., p. 532. b. Maidment's *New Book of Old Ballads*, p. 54. c. 'Tom o Linn,' Pitcairn's MSS, III, fol. 67.

E. 'Young Tamlin,' Motherwell's Note-Book, fol. 13.

F. 'Tomaline,' Motherwell's MS., p. 64.

G. 'Tam-a-line, the Elfin Knight,' Buchan's MSS, I, 8; 'Tam a-Lin, or The Knight of Faerylande,' Motherwell's MS., p. 595. Dixon, *Scottish Traditionary Versions of Ancient Ballads*, Percy Society, XVII, 11.

H. 'Young Tam Lane,' Campbell MSS, II, 129.

I. 'The Young Tamlane.' *Minstrelsy of the Scottish Border*: a, II, 337, ed. 1833, II, 245, ed. 1803; b, II, 228, ed. 1802.

J. 'Young Tamlane,' Kinloch MSS, V, 391.

K. Communicated to Scott November 11, 1812, by Hugh Irvine, Drum, Aberdeenshire.

L. "Scotch Ballads, Materials for Border Minstrelsy," No 27, Abbotsford.

M. "Scotch Ballads, Materials for Border Minstrelsy," No 15.

N. 'Tamlane,' "Scotch Ballads, Materials for Border Minstrelsy," No 96 a.

O. 'The Queen of the Fairies,' Macmath MS., p. 57.

THE first twenty-two stanzas of **B** differ from the corresponding ones in **A**, 1–23, omitting 16, by only a few words, and there are other agreements in the second half of these versions. Burns's intimacy with Robert Riddell would naturally lead to a communication from one to the other; but both may have derived the verses that are common from the same third party. Herd's fragment, **C**, was the earliest printed. Scott's version, **I**, as he himself states, was compounded of the *Museum* copy, Riddell's, Herd's, and "several recitals from tradition." **I** b, the edition of 1802, contained fragments of 'The Bromfield Hill' and of 'The Wee Wee Man,' which were dropped from the later edition; but unfortunately this later edition was corrupted with eleven new stanzas, which are not simply somewhat of a modern cast as to diction, as Scott remarks, but of a grossly modern invention, and as unlike popular verse as anything can be. **I** is given according to the later edition,

with those stanzas omitted; and all that is peculiar to this version, and not taken from the *Museum*, Glenriddell, or Herd, is distinguished from the rest by the larger type. This, it will be immediately seen, is very little.

The copy in *Tales of Wonder*, II, 459, is **A**, altered by Lewis. Mr Joseph Robertson notes, Kinloch MSS, VI, 10, that his mother had communicated to him some fragments of this ballad slightly differing from Scott's version, with a substitution of the name True Tammas for Tam Lane.

The *Scots Magazine* for October, 1818, LXXXII, 327–29, has a "fragment" of more than sixty stanzas, composed in an abominable artificial lingo, on the subject of this ballad, and alleged to have been taken from the mouth of a good old peasant, who, not having heard the ballad for thirty years, could remember no more. Thomas the Rhymer appears in the last lines with very great distinction, but it is not clear what part he has in the story.*

6] A copy printed in Aberdeen, 1862, and said to have been edited by the Rev. John Burnett Pratt, of Cruden, Aberdeenshire, is made up from Aytoun and Scott, with a number of slight changes.†

'The Tayl of the 3ong Tamlene' is spoken of as told among a company of shepherds, in Vedderburn's *Complaint of Scotland*, 1549, p. 63 of Dr James A. H. Murray's edition for the Early English Text Society. 'Thom of Lyn' is mentioned as a dance of the same party, a little further on, Murray, p. 66, and 'Young Thomlin' is the name of an air in a medley in "Wood's MS.," inserted, as David Laing thought, between 1600 and 1620, and printed in Forbes's *Cantus*, 1666: Stenhouse's ed. of *The Scots Musical Museum*, 1853, IV, 440. "A ballett of Thomalyn" is licensed to Master John Wallye and Mistress Toye in 1558: Arber, *Transcript of the Registers of the Company of Stationers*, I, 22; cited by Furnivall, Captain Cox, &c., *Ballad Society*, p. clxiv.

Sir Walter Scott relates a tradition of an attempt to rescue a woman from fairydom which recalls the ill success of many of the

efforts to disenchant White Ladies in Germany: "The wife of a farmer in Lothian had been carried off by the fairies, and, during the year of probation, repeatedly appeared on Sunday, in the midst of her children, combing their hair. On one of these occasions she was accosted by her husband; when she related to him the unfortunate event which had separated them, instructed him by what means he might win her, and exhorted him to exert all his courage, since her temporal and eternal happiness depended on the success of his attempt. The farmer, who ardently loved his wife, set out at Halloween, and, in the midst of a plot of furze, waited impatiently for the procession of the fairies. At the ringing of the fairy bridles, and the wild, unearthly sound which accompanied the cavalcade, his heart failed him, and he suffered the ghostly train to pass by without interruption. When the last had rode past, the whole troop vanished, with loud shouts of laughter and exultation, among which he plainly discovered the voice of his wife, lamenting that he had lost her forever." The same author proceeds to recount a real incident, which took place at the town of North Berwick, within memory, of a man who was prevented from undertaking, or at least meditating, a similar rescue only by shrewd and prompt practical measures on the part of his minister.‡

This fine ballad stands by itself, and is not, as might have been expected, found in possession of any people but the Scottish. Yet it has connections, through the principal feature in the story, the retransformation of Tam Lin, with Greek popular tradition older than Homer.

Something of the successive changes of shape is met with in a Scandinavian ballad: 'Nattergalen,' Grundtvig, II, 168, No 57; 'Den förtrollade Prinsessan,' Afzelius, II, 67, No 41; Atterbom, *Poetisk Kalender*, 1816, p. 44; Dybeck, *Runa*, 1844, p. 94, No 2; Axelson, *Vandring i Wermlands Elfdal*, p. 21, No 3; Lindeman, *Norske Fjeldmelodier*, Tekstbilag til 1ste Bind, p. 3, No 10; Aminson, *Bidrag, etc.*, IV, 6, No 27; Aminson, IV, 6, No 27; 'Den förtrollade

---

* These are the concluding verses, coming much nearer to the language of this world than the rest. They may have a basis of tradition:

> Whar they war aware o the Fairy King,
>   A huntan wi his train.
>
> Four an twenty gentlemen
>   Cam by on steeds o brown
> In his hand ilk bore a siller wand,
>   On his head a siller crown.
>
> Four an twenty beltit knichts
>   On daiplit greys cam by;
> Gowden their wands an crowns, whilk scanct
>   Like streamers in the sky.
>
> Four an twenty noble kings
>   Cam by on steeds o snaw,
> But True Thomas, the gude Rhymer,
>   Was king outower them a'.

† "Tamlane: an old Scottish Border Ballad. Aberdeen, Lewis and James Smith, 1862." I am indebted for a sight of this copy, and for the information as to the editor, to Mr Macmath.

‡   *Minstrelsy of the Scottish Border*, II, 221–24, ed. 1802.

prinsessan,' Lagus, *Nyländska Folkvisor*, I, 67, No 17.

Though many copies of this ballad have been obtained from the mouth of the people, all that are known are derived from flying sheets, of which there is a Danish one dated 1721 and a Swedish of the year 1738. What is of more account, the style of the piece, as we have it, is not quite popular. Nevertheless, the story is entirely of the popular stamp, and so is the feature in it which alone concerns us mate-
[337] rially. A nightingale relates to a knight how she had once had a lover, but a stepmother soon upset all that, and turned her into a bird and her brother into a wolf. The curse was not to be taken off the brother till he drank of his step-dame's blood, and after seven years he caught her, when she was taking a walk in a wood, tore out her heart, and regained his human shape. The knight proposes to the bird that she shall come and pass the winter in his bower, and go back to the wood in the summer: this, the nightingale says, the step-mother had forbid-den, as long as she wore feathers. The knight seizes the bird by the foot, takes her home to his bower, and fastens the windows and doors. She turns to all the marvellous beasts one ever heard of,—to a lion, a bear, a variety of small snakes, and at last to a loathsome lind-worm. The knight makes a sufficient incision for blood to come, and a maid stands on the floor as fair as a flower. He now asks after her origin, and she answers, Egypt's king was my father, and its queen my mother; my brother was doomed to rove the woods as a wolf. "If Egypt's king," he rejoins, "was your father, and its queen your mother, then for sure you are my sister's daugh-ter, who was doomed to be a nightingale."*

We come much nearer, and indeed surpris-ingly near, to the principal event of the Scot-tish ballad in a Cretan fairy-tale, cited from Chourmouzis by Bernhard Schmidt.† A young peasant of the village Sgourokepháli, who was a good player on the rote, used to be taken by the nereids into their grotto for the sake of his music. He fell in love with one of them, and, not knowing how to help himself, had recourse to an old woman of his village. She gave him this advice: that just before cock-crow he should seize his beloved by the hair, and hold on, unterrified, till the cock crew, whatever forms she should assume. The peasant gave good heed, and the next time he was taken into the cave fell to playing, as usual, and the nere-ids to dancing. But as cock-crow drew nigh, he put down his instrument, sprang upon the object of his passion, and grasped her by her locks. She instantly changed shape; became a dog, a snake, a camel, fire. But he kept his cour-age and held on, and presently the cock crew, and the nereids vanished all but one. His love returned to her proper beauty, and went with him to his home. After the lapse of a year she bore a son, but in all this time never uttered a word. The young husband was fain to ask coun-sel of the old woman again, who told him to heat the oven hot, and say to his wife that if she would not speak he would throw the boy into the oven. He acted upon this prescription; the nereid cried out, Let go my child, dog! tore the infant from his arms, and vanished.

This Cretan tale, recovered from tradition even later than our ballad, repeats all the important circumstances of the forced marriage of Thetis with Peleus. Chiron, like the old woman, suggested to his protégé that he should lay hands on the nereid, and keep his hold through whatever metamorphosis she might make. He looked out for his opportunity and seized her; she turned to fire, water, and a wild beast, but he did not let go till she resumed her primitive shape. Thetis, having borne a son, wished to make him immortal; to which end she buried him in fire by night, to burn out his human elements, and anointed him with ambrosia by day. Peleus was not taken into counsel, but watched her, and saw the boy gasp-ing in the fire, which made him call out; and Thetis, thus thwarted, abandoned the child and went back to the nereids. Apollodorus, *Biblioth-eca*, III, 13, 5, 6.

---

* Restoration from enchantment is effected by drink-ing blood, in other ballads, as Grundtvig, No 55, II, 156, No 58, II, 174; in No 56, II, 158, by a maid in falcon shape eating of a bit of flesh which her lover had cut from his breast.

† *Volksleben der Neugriechen*, pp 115–17, "from Chour-mouzis, κρητικά, p. 69f, Athens, 1842." Chourmouzis heard this story, about 1820 or 1830, from an old Cretan peasant, who had heard it from his grandfather.

The Cretan tale does not differ from the one repeated by Apollodorus from earlier writers a couple of thousand years ago more than two versions of a story gathered from oral tradition in these days are apt to do. Whether it has come down to our time from mouth to mouth through twenty-five centuries or more, or whether, having died out of the popular memory, it was reintroduced through literature, is a question that cannot be decided with certainty; but there will be nothing unlikely in the former supposition to those who bear in mind the tenacity of tradition among people who have never known books.[*]

B 34,

First dip me in a stand of milk,
And then in a stand of water;
Haud me fast, let me na gae,
I'll be your bairnie's father,

has an occult and very important significance which has only very lately been pointed out, and which modern reciters had completely lost knowledge of, as appears by the disorder into which the stanzas have fallen.[†] Immersion in a liquid, generally water, but sometimes milk, is a process requisite for passing from a non-human shape, produced by enchantment, back into the human, and also for returning from the human to a non-human state, whether produced by enchantment or original. We have seen that

the serpent which Lanzelet kisses, in Ulrich's romance, is not by that simple though essential act instantly turned into a woman. It is still necessary that she should bathe in a spring (p. 414). In an Albanian tale, 'Taubenliebe,' Hahn, No 102, II, 130, a dove flies into a princess's window, and, receiving her caresses, asks, Do you love me? The princess answering Yes, the dove says, Then have a dish of milk ready tomorrow, and you shall see what a handsome man I am. A dish of milk is ready the next morning; the dove flies into the window, dips himself in the milk, drops his feathers, and steps out a beautiful youth. When it is time to go, the youth dips in the milk, and flies off a dove. This goes on every day for two years.

A king transformed into a nightingale being plunged three times into water resumes his shape in Vernaleken, *K. u. H. märchen*, No 15, p. 79. In Guillaume de Palerne, ed. Michelant, v. 7770ff, pp. 225, 226, the queen who changes the werewolf back into a man takes care that he shall have a warm bath as soon as the transformation is over; but this may be merely the bath preliminary to his being dubbed knight (as in Li Chevaliers as Deus Espees, ed. Förster, vv 1547–49, p. 50, and L'Ordene de Chevalerie, vv 111–124, Barbazan-Méon, I, 63, 64). A fairy maiden is turned into a wooden statue. This is burned and the ashes thrown into a pond, whence she immediately emerges in her proper shape. She is next doomed to take the form of a snake. Her lover, acting under advice, cuts up a good part of the snake into little bits, and throws these into a pond. She emerges again. J. H. Knowles, *Folk-Tales of Kashmir*, p. 468ff. (G. L. K.) An old woman is rejuvenated by being burnt to bones, and the bones being thrown into a tub of milk: Ralston, *Russian Folk-Tales*, p. 59, 'The Smith and the Demon;' Afanasief, *Legendui*, No 31, from Dahl's manuscript collection.

---

[*]   The silence of the Cretan fairy, as **B.** Schmidt has remarked, even seems to explain Sophocles calling the nuptials of Peleus and Thetis "speechless," ἀφθόγγους γάμους. Sophocles gives the transformations as being lion, snake, fire, water: Scholia in *Pindari Nemea*, III, 60; Schmidt, as before, p. 116, note. That a firm grip and a fearless one would make any sea-god do your will would appear from the additional instances of Menelaus and Proteus, in *Odyssey*, IV, and of Hercules and Nereus, Apollodorus, II, 5, 11, 4, Scholia in *Apollonii Argonaut.*, IV, 1396. Proteus masks as lion, snake, panther, boar, running water, tree; Nereus as water, fire, or, as Apollodorus says, in all sorts of shapes. Bacchus was accustomed to transform himself when violence was done him, but it is not recorded that he was ever brought to terms like the watery divinities. See Mannhardt, *Wald- und Feldkulte*, II, 60–64, who also well remarks that the tales of the White Ladies, who, to be released from a ban, must be kissed three times in various shapes, as toad, wolf, snake, etc., have relation to these Greek traditions.

[†]   The significance of the immersion in water is shown by Mannhardt, *Wald- und Feldkulte*, II, 64ff. The disorder in the stanzas of **A** at this place has of course been rectified. In Scott's version, I, transformations are added at random from C, *after* the dipping in milk and in water, which seems indeed to have been regarded by the reciters only as a measure for cooling red-hot iron or the burning gleed, and not as the act essential for restoration to the human nature.

King Bean, in the form of a flying thing, turns into a handsome youth after bathing in three vessels successively, one of milk and water, one of milk, one of rose-water: Bernoni, *Fiabe pop. veneziane*, p. 87, No 17, translated by Crane, *Italian Popular Tales*, p. 12. A green bird bathes in a pan of milk, and becomes a handsome youth, and, bathing in gold basins full of water, this youth turns into a bird again: Pitrè, *Fiabe, Novelle e Racconti*, I, 163, No 18, translated by Crane, p. 2, and note, p. 321. A prince and his two servants, transformed into pigeons, resume their proper shape on plunging into basins of gold, silver, and bronze respectively: a Tuscan story in De Gubernatis, *Zoölogical Mythology*, II, 299f, note. (G. L. K.)

A Greek tale, 'Goldgerte,' Hahn, No 7, I, 97, has the same transformation, with water for milk. Our **B** 34 has well-water only.* Perhaps the bath of milk occurred in one earlier version of our ballad, the water-bath in another, and the two accounts became blended in time.

The end of the mutations, in **F** 11, **G** 43, is a naked man, and a mother-naked man in **B** 33, under the presumed right arrangement; meaning by right arrangement, however, not the original arrangement, but the most consistent one for the actual form of the tradition. Judging by analogy, the naked man should issue from the bath of milk or of water; into which he should have gone in one of his non-human shapes, a dove, swan, or snake (for which, too, a "stand" of milk or of water is a more practicable bath than for a man). The fragment **C** adds some slight probability to this supposition. The last change there is into "a dove but and a swan;" then Tam Lin bids the maiden to let go, for he'll "be a perfect man:" this, nevertheless, he could not well become without some further ceremony. **A** is the only version which has preserved an essentially correct process: Tam Lin, when a burning gleed, is to be thrown into well-water, from which he will step forth a naked knight.[†]

[339]   At stated periods, which the ballads make to be seven years, the fiend of hell is entitled to take his teind, tithe, or kane from the people of

fairy-land: **A** 24, **B** 23, **C** 5, **D** 15, **G** 28, **H** 15. The fiend prefers those that are fair and fu o flesh, according to **A**, **G**; ane o flesh and blood, **D**. **H** makes the queen fear for herself; "the koors they hae gane round about, and I fear it will be mysel." **H** is not discordant with popular tradition elsewhere, which attributes to fairies the practice of abstracting young children to serve as substitutes for themselves in this tribute: Scott's *Minstrelsy*, II, 220, 1802. **D** 15 says "the last here goes to hell," which would certainly not be equitable, and **C** "we're a' dung down to hell," where "all" must be meant only

[†]   In the MS. of **B** also the transformation into a het gad of iron comes just before the direction to dip the object into a stand of milk; but we have the turning into a mother-naked man several stanzas earlier. By reading, in 33¹, I'll turn, and putting 33 after 34, we should have the order of events which we find in **A**.

That Tam Lin should go into water or milk as a dove or snake, or in some other of his temporary forms, and *come out* a man, is the only disposition which is consistent with the order of the world to which he belongs. Mannhardt gives us a most curious and interesting insight into some of the laws of that world in *Wald- und Feldkulte*, II, 64–70. The wife of a Cashmere king, in a story there cited from Benfey's *Pantschatantra*, I, 254, § 92, is delivered of a serpent, but is reported to have borne a son. Another king offers his daughter in marriage, and the Cashmere king, to keep his secret, accepts the proposal. In due time the princess claims her bridegroom, and they give her the snake. Though greatly distressed, she accepts her lot, and takes the snake about to the holy places, at the last of which she receives a command to put the snake into the water-tank. As soon as this is done the snake takes the form of a man. A woman's giving birth to a snake was by no means a rare thing in Karst in the seventeenth century, and it was the rule in one noble family that all the offspring should be in serpent form, or at least have a serpent's head; but a bath in water turned them into human shape. For elves and water nymphs who have entered into connections with men in the form of women, bathing in water is equally necessary for resuming their previous shape, as appears from an ancient version of the story of Melusina: Gervasius, ed. Liebrecht, p. 4f, and Vincentius Bellovacensis, *Speculum Naturale*, 2,127 (from Helinandus), cited by Liebrecht, at p. 66.

A lad who had been changed into an ass by a couple of witches recovers his shape merely by jumping into water and rolling about in it: William of Malmesbury's *Kings of England*, c. 10, cited by Vincent of Beauvais, *Speculum Naturale*, iii, 109; Düntzer, Liebrecht's *Dunlop*, p. 538. Simple illusions of magic, such as clods and wisps made to appear swine to our eyes, are inevitably dissolved when the unrealities touch water. Liebrecht's *Gervasius*, p. 65.

---

*   Possibly the holy water in **D** 17, **G** 32, is a relic of the water-bath.

of the naturalized members of the community. Poor Alison Pearson, who lost her life in 1586 for believing these things, testified that the tribute was annual. Mr William Sympson, who had been taken away by the fairies, "bidd her sign herself that she be not taken away, for the teind of them are tane to hell everie year:" Scott, as above, p. 208. See Isabel Gowdie's case, in the *Scottish Journal*, I, 256, and compare Pitcairn's *Criminal Trials*. The kindly queen of the fairies[*] will not allow Thomas of Erceldoune to be exposed to this peril, and hurries him back to earth the day before the fiend comes for his due. Thomas is in peculiar danger, for the reason given in **A, G, R**.

> To morne of helle þe foulle fende
> Amange this folke will feche his fee;
> And þou art mekill man and hende;
> I trowe full wele he wolde chese the.

The elf-queen, **A** 42, **B** 40, would have taken out Tam's twa gray een, had she known he was to be borrowed, and have put in twa een of tree, **B** 41, **D** 34, **E** 21, **H** 14; she would have taken out his heart of flesh, and have put in, **B, D, E**, a heart of stane, **H** of tree. The taking out of the eyes would probably be to deprive Tam of the faculty of recognizing fairy folk thereafter. Mortals whose eyes have been touched with fairies' salve can see them when they are to others invisible, and such persons, upon distinguishing and saluting fairies, have often had not simply this power but their ordinary eyesight taken away: see Cromek's *Remains of Nithsdale and Galloway Song*, p. 304; Thiele, *Danmarks Folkesagn*, 1843, II, 202, IV; J. O'Hanlon, Irish Folk-Lore, *Gentleman's Magazine*, 1865, Pt II, in the *Gentleman's Magazine Library*, ed. Gomme; English, *Traditional Lore*, p. 12; Sébillot, *Contes pop. de la Haute-Bretagne*, II, 41, 42, cf. I, 122–3; the same, *Traditions et Superstitions de la Haute-Bretagne*, I, 89, 109; the same, *Littérature orale de la Haute-Bretagne*, pp. 19–23, 24–27, and note; Mrs Bray, *Traditions of Devonshire*, 1838, I, 184–188, I, 175ff. of the new ed. called *The Borders of the Tamar and the Tavy*; "Lageniesis" [J. O'Hanlon], *Irish Folk-Lore*, Glasgow, n. d., pp.

48–49; Kirk's *Invisible Commonwealth*, ed. Lang pp. 13, 34; *Denham Tracts*, II, 138f. In a Breton story a fairy gives a one-eyed woman an eye of crystal, warning her not to speak of what she may see with it. Disregarding this injunction, the woman is deprived of the gift. Sébillot, *Contes pop. de la Haute-Bretagne*, II, 24–25. This feature, in one form or another, occurs in nearly all the stories of mortal women who have helped elf-women in travail that are reported by Arnason, *Íslenzkar Þjóðsögur*, I, 15ff. (G. L. K.) Grimm has given instances of witches, Slavic, German, Norse and Italian, taking out the heart of man (which they are wont to devour), and replacing it in some instances with straw, wood, or something of the kind; nor do the Roman witches appear to have been behind later ones in this dealing: *Deutsche Mythologie*, 904f, and the note III, 312.

The fairy in the Lai de Lanval, v. 547, rides on a white palfrey, and also two damsels, her harbingers, v. 471; so the fairy princess in the English Launfal, Halliwell, *Fairy Mythology*, p. 30. The fairy king and all his knights and ladies ride on white steeds in King Orfeo, Halliwell, as above, p. 41. The queen of Elfland rides a milk-white steed in Thomas Rymer, **A, C**; in **B**, and [340] all copies of Thomas of Erceldoune, her palfrey is dapple gray. Tam Lin, **A** 28, **B** 27, etc., is distinguished from all the rest of his "court" by being thus mounted; all the other horses are black or brown.

Tam Lane was taken by the fairies, according to **G** 26, 27, **K** 14, while sleeping under an apple-tree. In Sir Orfeo (ed. Zielke, v. 68, vv 399–405) it was the queen's sleeping under an ympe-tree that led to her being carried off by the fairy king, and the ympe-tree we may suppose to be some kind of fruit tree, if not exclusively the apple.[†] Thomas of Erceldoune is lying under a semely [derne, cumly] tree, when he sees the fairy queen. The derivation of that poem from Ogier le Danois shows that this must have been an apple-tree. Special trees are considered in Greece dangerous to lie under in

---

[*] Cf. 'Allison Gross.'

[†] In the lay de Tydorel, published by Gaston Paris in *Romania*, VIII, 67, a queen goes to sleep, v. 30, soz une ente, with strange results. (G. L. K.) Bugge, *Arkiv för nordisk Filologi*, VII, 104, refers to Liebrecht, Gervasius von Tilbury, p. 117, and to W. Hertz, *Spielmannsbuch*, p. 322.

summer and at noon,[*] as exposing one to be taken by the nereids or fairies, especially plane, poplar, fig, nut, and St John's bread: Schmidt, *Volksleben der Neugriechen*, p. 119. The elder and the linden are favorites of the elves in Denmark. So Lancelot goes to sleep about noon under an apple-tree, and is enchanted by Morgan the Fay. Malory's *Morte Darthur*, bk. vi, ch. I, ch. 3, ed. Sommer, I, 188, 186. (G. L. K.)

The rencounter at the beginning between Tam Lin and Janet (in the wood, **D, F, G**) is repeated between Hind Etin [Young Akin] and Margaret in 'Hind Etin,' further on. Some Slavic ballads open in a similar way, but there is nothing noteworthy in that: see p. 60. "First they did call me Jack," etc., **D** 9, is a commonplace of frequent occurrence: see, e.g., 'The Knight and Shepherd's Daughter.'

Some humorous verses, excellent in their way, about one Tam o Lin are very well known: as Tam o the Linn, Chambers, *Scottish Songs*, p. 455, *Popular Rhymes of Scotland*, p. 33, ed. 1870; Sharpe's *Ballads*, new ed., p. 44, p. 137, No XVI; Tommy Linn, *North Country Chorister*, ed. Ritson, p. 3; Halliwell's *Popular Rhymes and Nursery Tales*, p. 271, ed. 1849; Thomas o Linn, Kinloch MSS, III, 45, V, 81; Tam o Lin, Campbell MSS., II, 107. (Miss Joanna Baillie tried her hand at an imitation, but the jocosity of the

real thing is not feminine.) A fool sings this stanza from such a song in Wager's comedy, 'The longer thou livest, the more fool thou art,' put at about 1568; see Furnivall, *Captain Cox, his Ballads and Books*, p. cxxvii; Robert Mylne's MS. Collection of Scots Poems, Part I, 8, 1707:

Tom a Lin and his wife, and his wiues mother,
They went ouer a bridge all three together;
The bridge was broken, and they fell in:
'The deuil go with all!' quoth Tom a Lin.

Mr Halliwell-Phillips (as above) says that "an immense variety of songs and catches relating to Tommy Linn are known throughout the country." Brian o Lynn seems to be popular in Ireland: *Lover's Legends and Stories of Ireland*, p. 260f. There is no connection between the song and the ballad beyond the name: the song is no parody, no burlesque, of the ballad, as it has been called.

"Carterhaugh is a plain at the confluence of the Ettrick with the Yarrow, scarcely an English mile above the town of Selkirk, and on this plain they show two or three rings on the ground, where, they say, the stands of milk and water stood, and upon which grass never grows." Glenriddell MS.

Translated, after Scott, by Schubart, p. 139, and Büsching's *Wöchentliche Nachrichten*, I, 247; by Arndt, *Blütenlese*, p. 212; after Aytoun, I, 7, by Rosa Warrens, *Schottische Volkslieder*, No 8; by Knortz, *Schottische Balladen*, No 17, apparently after Aytoun and Allingham. The Danish 'Nattergalen' is translated by Prior, III, 118, No 116.

---

[*]   "Is not this connected with the belief in a δαιμόνιον μεσημβρινον (LXX, Psalm xci, 6)? as to which see Rochholz, *Deutscher Unsterblichkeitsglaube*, pp. 62ff, 67ff, and cf. Lobeck, *Aglaophamus*, pp. 1092–3." Kittredge, Sir Orfeo, in the *American Journal of Philology*, VII, 190, where also there is something about the dangerous character of orchards. Of processions of fairy knights, see p. 189 of the same.

A

Johnson's *Museum*, p. 423, No 411. Communicated
by Robert Burns.

O___ I for-bid you, maid-ens a' That wear gowd o[n] your hair,

To come or gae by Cart-er-haugh, For young Tam Lin is there.

1 O I FORBID you, maidens a',
   That wear gowd on your hair,
To come or gae by Carterhaugh,
   For young Tam Lin is there.

2 There's nane that gaes by Carterhaugh
   But they leave him a wad,
Either their rings, or green mantles,
   Or else their maidenhead.

3 Janet has kilted her green kirtle
   A little aboon her knee,
And she has broded her yellow hair
   A little aboon her bree,
And she's awa to Carterhaugh,
   As fast as she can hie.

4 When she came to Carterhaugh
   Tam Lin was at the well,
And there she fand his steed standing,
   But away was himsel.

5 She had na pu'd a double rose,
   A rose but only twa,
Till up then started young Tam Lin,
   Says, Lady, thou's pu nae mae.

6 Why pu's thou the rose, Janet,
   And why breaks thou the wand?
Or why comes thou to Carterhaugh
   Withoutten my command?

7 'Carterhaugh, it is my ain,
   My daddie gave it me;
I'll come and gang by Carterhaugh,
   And ask nae leave at thee.'

*   *   *   *   *

8 Janet has kilted her green kirtle
   A little aboon her knee,
And she has snooded her yellow hair
   A little aboon her bree,
And she is to her father's ha,
   As fast as she can hie.

9 Four and twenty ladies fair
   Were playing at the ba,
And out then cam the fair Janet,
   Ance the flower amang them a'.

10 Four and twenty ladies fair
   Were playing at the chess,
And out then cam the fair Janet,
   As green as onie glass.

11 Out then spak an auld grey knight,
   Lay oer the castle wa,
And says, Alas, fair Janet, for thee
   But we'll be blamed a'.

12 'Haud your tongue, ye auld fac'd knight,
   Some ill death may ye die!
Father my bairn on whom I will,
   I'll father nane on thee.'

13 Out then spak her father dear,
   And he spak meek and mild;
'And ever alas, sweet Janet,' he says,
   'I think thou gaes wi child.'

14 'If that I gae wi child, father,
   Mysel maun bear the blame;
There's neer a laird about your ha
   Shall get the bairn's name.

15 'If my love were an earthly knight,
   As he's an elfin grey,
I wad na gie my ain true-love
   For nae lord that ye hae.

16 'The steed that my true-love rides on
      Is lighter than the wind;
   Wi siller he is shod before,
      Wi burning gowd behind.'

17 Janet has kilted her green kirtle
      A little aboon her knee,
   And she has snooded her yellow hair
      A little aboon her bree,
   And she's awa to Carterhaugh,
      As fast as she can hie.

18 When she cam to Carterhaugh,
      Tam Lin was at the well,
   And there she fand his steed standing,
      But away was himsel.

19 She had na pu'd a double rose,
      A rose but only twa,
   Till up then started young Tam Lin,
      Says Lady, thou pu's nae mae.

20 Why pu's thou the rose, Janet,
      Amang the groves sae green,
   And a' to kill the bonie babe
      That we gat us between?

21 'O tell me, tell me, Tam Lin,' she says,
      'For 's sake that died on tree,
   If eer ye was in holy chapel,
      Or christendom did see?'

22 'Roxbrugh he was my grandfather,
      Took me with him to bide,
[342] And ance it fell upon a day
      That wae did me betide.

23 'And ance it fell upon a day,
      A cauld day and a snell,
   When we were frae the hunting come,
      That frae my horse I fell;
   The Queen o Fairies she caught me,
      In yon green hill to dwell.

24 'And pleasant is the fairy land,
      But, an eerie tale to tell,
   Ay at the end of seven years
      We pay a tiend to hell;
   I am sae fair and fu o flesh,
      I'm feard it be mysel.

25 'But the night is Halloween, lady,
      The morn is Hallowday;
   Then win me, win me, an ye will,
      For weel I wat ye may.

26 'Just at the mirk and midnight hour
      The fairy folk will ride,
   And they that wad their true-love win,
      At Miles Cross they maun bide.'

27 'But how shall I thee ken, Tam Lin,
      Or how my true-love know,
   Amang sae mony unco knights
      The like I never saw?'

28 'O first let pass the black, lady,
      And syne let pass the brown,
   But quickly run to the milk-white steed,
      Pu ye his rider down.

29 'For I'll ride on the milk-white steed,
      And ay nearest the town;
   Because I was an earthly knight
      They gie me that renown.

30 'My right hand will be glovd, lady,
      My left hand will be bare,
   Cockt up shall my bonnet be,
      And kaimd down shall my hair,
   And thae's the takens I gie thee,
      Nae doubt I will be there.

31 'They'll turn me in your arms, lady,
      Into an esk and adder;
   But hold me fast, and fear me not,
      I am your bairn's father.

32 'They'll turn me to a bear sae grim,
      And then a lion bold;
   But hold me fast, and fear me not,
      As ye shall love your child.

33 'Again they'll turn me in your arms
      To a red het gaud of airn;
   But hold me fast, and fear me not,
      I'll do to you nae harm.

34 'And last they'll turn me in your arms
      Into the burning gleed;
   Then throw me into well water,
      O throw me in wi speed.

35 'And then I'll be your ain true-love,
    I'll turn a naked knight;
  Then cover me wi your green mantle,
    And cover me out o sight.'

36 Gloomy, gloomy was the night,
    And eerie was the way,
  As fair Jenny in her green mantle
    To Miles Cross she did gae.

37 About the middle o the night
    She heard the bridles ring;
  This lady was as glad at that
    As any earthly thing.

38 First she let the black pass by,
    And syne she let the brown;
  But quickly she ran to the milk-white steed,
    And pu'd the rider down.

39 Sae weel she minded what he did say,
    And young Tam Lin did win;
  Syne coverd him wi her green mantle,
    As blythe's a bird in spring.

40 Out then spak the Queen o Fairies,
    Out of a bush o broom:
  'Them that has gotten young Tam Lin
    Has gotten a stately groom.'

41 Out then spak the Queen o Fairies,
    And an angry woman was she:
  'Shame betide her ill-far'd face,
    And an ill death may she die,
  For she's taen awa the boniest knight
    In a' my companie.

42 'But had I kend, Tam Lin,' she says,   [343]
    'What now this night I see,
  I wad hae taen out thy twa grey een,
    And put in twa een o tree.'

B

Glenriddell's MSS, vol. xi, No 17.

1 I FORBID ye, maidens a',
    That wear goud on your gear,
  To come and gae by Carterhaugh,
    For young Tom Line is there.

2 There's nane that gaes by Carterhaugh
    But they leave him a wad,
  Either their things or green mantles,
    Or else their maidenhead.

3 But Janet has kilted her green kirtle
    A little above her knee,
  And she has broded her yellow hair
    A little above her bree,
  And she has gaen for Carterhaugh,
    As fast as she can hie.

4 When she came to Carterhaugh
    Tom Line was at the well,
  And there she fand his steed standing,
    But away was himsell.

5 She hadna pu'd a double rose,
    A rose but only twae,
  Till up then started young Tom Line,
    Says, Lady, thou's pu nae mae.

6 Why pu's thou the rose, Janet?
    Why breaks thou the wand?
  Why comest thou to Carterhaugh
    Withouthen my command?

7 'Fair Carterhaugh it is my ain,
    My daddy gave it me;
  I'll come and gae by Carterhaugh,
    And ask nae leave at thee.'

*   *   *   *   *

8 Janet has kilted her green kirtle
    A little aboon her knee,
  And she has snooded her yellow hair
    A little aboon her bree,
  And she is on to her father's ha,
    As fast as she can hie.

9 Four and twenty ladies fair
    Were playing at the ba,
  And out then came fair Janet,
    The flowr amang them a'.

10 Four and twenty ladies fair
    Were playing at the chess,
  Out then came fair Janet,
    As green as ony glass.

11 Out spak an auld grey-headed knight,
   Lay owre the castle wa,
   And says, Alas, fair Janet,
   For thee we'll be blam'd a'.

12 'Had your tongue, you auld grey knight,
   Some ill dead may ye die!
   Father my bairn on whom I will,
   I'll father nane on thee.'

13 Out then spak her father dear,
   He spak baith thick and milde;
   'And ever alas, sweet Janet,' he says,
   'I think ye gae wi childe.'

14 'If that I gae wi child, father,
   Mysell bears a' the blame;
   There's not a laird about your ha
   Shall get the bairnie's name.

15 'If my lord were an earthly knight,
   As he's an elfish grey,
   I wad na gie my ain true-love
   For nae lord that ye hae.'

16 Janet has kilted her green kirtle
   A little aboon her knee,
   And she has snooded her yellow hair
   A little aboon her bree,
   And she's away to Carterhaugh,
   As fast as she can hie.

17 When she came to Carterhaugh,
   Tom Line was at the well,
   And there she faund his steed standing,
   But away was himsell.

18 She hadna pu'd a double rose,
   A rose but only twae,
   [344] Till up then started young Tom Line,
   Says, Lady, thou's pu na mae.

19 Why pu's thou the rose Janet,
   Out owr yon groves sae green,
   And a' to kill your bonny babe,
   That we gat us between?

20 'O tell me, tell me, Tom,' she says,
   'For 's sake who died on tree,
   If eer ye were in holy chapel,
   Or christendom did see.'

21 'Roxburgh he was my grandfather,
   Took me with him to bide,
   And ance it fell upon a day
   That wae did me betide.

22 'Ance it fell upon a day,
   A cauld day and a snell,
   When we were frae the hunting come,
   That from my horse I fell.

23 'The Queen of Fairies she came by,
   Took me wi her to dwell,
   Evn where she has a pleasant land
   For those that in it dwell,
   But at the end o seven years,
   They pay their teind to hell.

24 'The night it is gude Halloween,
   The fairie folk do ride,
   And they that wad their true-love win,
   At Miles Cross they maun bide.'

25 'But how shall I thee ken, Thomas,
   Or how shall I thee knaw,
   Amang a pack o uncouth knights
   The like I never saw?'

26 'The first company that passes by,
   Say na, and let them gae;
   The next company that passes by,
   Say na, and do right sae;
   The third company that passes by,
   Then I'll be ane o thae.

27 'Some ride upon a black, lady,
   And some ride on a brown,
   But I ride on a milk-white steed,
   And ay nearest the town:
   Because I was an earthly knight
   They gae me that renown.

28 'My right hand will be glovd, lady,
   My left hand will be bare,
   And thae's the tokens I gie thee,
   Nae doubt I will be there.

29 'Then hie thee to the milk-white steed,
   And pu me quickly down,
   Cast thy green kirtle owr me,
   And keep me frae the rain.

30 'They'll turn me in thy arms, lady,
  An adder and a snake;
  But hold me fast, let me na gae,
  To be your warldly mate.

31 'They'll turn me in your arms, lady,
  A grey greyhound to girn;
  But hald me fast, let me na gae,
  The father o your bairn.

32 'They'll turn me in your arms, lady,
  A red het gad o iron;
  Then haud me fast, and be na feard
  I'll do to you nae harm.

33 'They'll turn me in your arms, lady,
  A mother-naked man;
  Cast your green kirtle owr me,
  To keep me frae the rain.

34 'First dip me in a stand o milk,
  And then a stand o water;
  Haud me fast, let me na gae,
  I'll be your bairnie's father.'

35 Janet has kilted her green kirtle
  A little aboon her knee,
  And she has snooded her yellow hair
  A little aboon her bree,
  And she is on to Miles Cross,
  As fast as she can hie.

36 The first company that passd by,
  She said na, and let them gae;
  The next company that passed by,
  She said na, and did right sae;
  The third company that passed by,
  Then he was ane o thae.

37 She hied her to the milk-white steed,
  And pu'd him quickly down;
  She cast her green kirtle owr him,
  To keep him frae the rain;
  Then she did all was orderd her,   [345]
  And sae recoverd him.

38 Then out then spak the Queen o Fairies,
  Out o a bush o broom:
  'They that hae gotten young Tom Line
  Hae got a stately groom.'

39 Out than spak the Queen o Fairies,
  Out o a bush of rye:
  'Them that has gotten young Tom Line
  Has the best knight in my company.

40 'Had I kend, Thomas,' she says,
  'A lady wad hae borrowd thee,
  I wad hae taen out thy twa grey een,
  Put in twa een o tree.

41 'Had I but kend, Thomas,' she says,
  'Before I came frae hame,
  I had taen out that heart o flesh,
  Put in a heart o stane.'

C

Herd, *The Ancient and Modern Scots Songs*, 1769, p. 300.

*   *   *   *   *

1 She's prickt hersell and prind hersell,
  By the ae light o the moon,
  And she's awa to Kertonha,
  As fast as she can gang.

2 'What gars ye pu the rose, Jennet?
  What gars ye break the tree?
  What gars you gang to Kertonha
  Without the leave of me?'

3 'Yes, I will pu the rose, Thomas,
  And I will break the tree;
  For Kertonha shoud be my ain,
  Nor ask I leave of thee.'

4 'Full pleasant is the fairy land,
  And happy there to dwell;
  I am a fairy, lyth and limb,
  Fair maiden, view me well.

5 'O pleasant is the fairy land,
  How happy there to dwell!
  But ay at every seven years end
  We're a' dung down to hell.

6 'The morn is good Halloween,
  And our court a' will ride;
  If ony maiden wins her man,
  Then she may be his bride.

7 'But first ye'll let the black gae by,
   And then ye'll let the brown;
Then I'll ride on a milk-white steed,
   You'll pu me to the ground.

8 'And first, I'll grow into your arms
   An esk but and an edder;
Had me fast, let me not gang,
   I'll be your bairn's father.

9 'Next, I'll grow into your arms
   A toad but and an eel;
Had me fast, let me not gang,
   If you do love me leel.

10 'Last, I'll grow into your arms
   A dove but and a swan;
Then, maiden fair, you'll let me go,
   I'll be a perfect man.'

D

a. Motherwell's MS., p. 532, a North Country ver-
sion. **b.** Maidment's *New Book of Old Ballads*, 1844, p.
54, from the recitation of an old woman. **c.** Pitcairn's
MSS, 1817–25, III, p. 67: "procured by David Webster,
Bookseller, from tradition."

1 O ALL you ladies young and gay,
   Who are so sweet and fair,
Do not go into Chaster's wood,
   For Tomlin will be there.

2 Fair Margret sat in her bonny bower,
   Sewing her silken seam,
And wished to be in Chaster's wood,
   Among the leaves so green.

[346] 3 She let her seam fall to her foot,
   The needle to her toe,
And she has gone to Chaster's wood,
   As fast as she could go.

4 When she began to pull the flowers,
   She pulld both red and green;
Then by did come, and by did go,
   Said, Fair maid, let aleene.

5 'O why pluck you the flowers, lady,
   Or why climb you the tree?
Or why come ye to Chaster's wood
   Without the leave of me?'

6 'O I will pull the flowers,' she said,
   'Or I will break the tree,
For Chaster's wood it is my own,
   I'll no ask leave at thee.'

7 He took her by the milk-white hand,
   And by the grass green sleeve,
And laid her low down on the flowers,
   At her he asked no leave.

8 The lady blushed, and sourly frowned,
   And she did think great shame;
Says, 'If you are a gentleman,
   You will tell me your name.'

9 'First they did call me Jack,' he said,
   'And then they called me John,
But since I lived in the fairy court
   Tomlin has always been my name.

10 'So do not pluck that flower, lady,
   That has these pimples gray;
They would destroy the bonny babe
   That we've got in our play.'

11 'O tell me, Tomlin,' she said,
   'And tell it to me soon,
Was you ever at good church-door,
   Or got you christendoom?'

12 'O I have been at good church-door,
   And aff her yetts within;
I was the Laird of Foulis's son,
   The heir of all this land.

13 'But it fell once upon a day,
   As hunting I did ride,
As I rode east and west yon hill
   There woe did me betide.

14 'O drowsy, drowsy as I was!
   Dead sleep upon me fell;
The Queen of Fairies she was there,
   And took me to hersell.

15 'The Elfins is a pretty place,
   In which I love to dwell,
   But yet at every seven years' end
   The last here goes to hell;
   And as I am ane o flesh and blood,
   I fear the next be mysell.

16 'The morn at even is Halloween;
   Our fairy court will ride,
   Throw England and Scotland both,
   Throw al the world wide;
   And if ye would me borrow,
   At Rides Cross ye may bide.

17 'You may go into the Miles Moss,
   Between twelve hours and one;
   Take holy water in your hand,
   And cast a compass round.

18 'The first court that comes along,
   You'll let them all pass by;
   The next court that comes along,
   Salute them reverently.

19 'The next court that comes along
   Is clad in robes of green,
   And it's the head court of them all,
   For in it rides the queen.

20 'And I upon a milk-white steed,
   With a gold star in my crown;
   Because I am an earthly man
   I'm next to the queen in renown.

21 'Then seize upon me with a spring,
   Then to the ground I'll fa,
   And then you'll hear a rueful cry
   That Tomlin is awa.

22 'Then I'll grow in your arms two
   Like to a savage wild;
   But hold me fast, let me not go,
   I'm father of your child.

23 'I'll grow into your arms two
   Like an adder or a snake;
   But hold me fast, let me not go,
   I'll be your earthly maick.

24 'I'll grow into your arms two
   Like iron in strong fire;
   But hold me fast, let me not go,
   Then you'll have your desire.'

25 She rid down to Miles Cross,
   Between twelve hours and one,
   Took holy water in her hand,
   And cast a compass round.

26 The first court that came along,
   She let them all pass by;
   The next court that came along
   Saluted reverently.

27 The next court that came along
   Were clad in robes of green,
   When Tomlin, on a milk-white steed,
   She saw ride with the queen.

28 She seized him in her arms two,
   He to the ground did fa,
   And then she heard a ruefull cry
   'Tomlin is now awa.'

29 He grew into her arms two
   Like to a savage wild;
   She held him fast, let him not go,
   The father of her child.

30 He grew into her arms two
   Like an adder or a snake;
   She held him fast, let him not go,
   He was her earthly maick.

31 He grew into her arms two
   Like iron in hot fire;
   She held him fast, let him not go,
   He was her heart's desire.

32 Then sounded out throw elphin court,
   With a loud shout and a cry,
   That the pretty maid of Chaster's wood
   That day had caught her prey.

33 'O stay, Tomlin,' cried Elphin Queen,
   'Till I pay you your fee;'
   'His father has lands and rents enough,
   He wants no fee from thee.'

34 'O had I known at early morn
   Tomlin would from me gone,
   I would have taken out his heart of flesh
   Put in a heart of stone.'

E

Motherwell's Note-book, p. 13.

1 LADY MARGARET is over gravel green,
   And over gravel grey,
   And she's awa to Charteris ha,
   Lang lang three hour or day.

2 She hadna pu'd a flower, a flower,
   A flower but only ane,
   Till up and started young Tamlin,
   Says, Lady, let alane.

3 She hadna pu'd a flower, a flower,
   A flower but only twa,
   Till up and started young Tamlene,
   Atween her and the wa.

4 'How daur you pu my flower, madam?
   How daur ye break my tree?
   How daur ye come to Charter's ha,
   Without the leave of me?'

5 'Weel I may pu the rose,' she said,
   'But I daurna break the tree;
   And Charter's ha is my father's,
   And I'm his heir to be.'

6 'If Charteris ha be thy father's,
   I was ance as gude mysell;
   But as I came in by Lady Kirk,
   And in by Lady Well,

7 'Deep and drowsy was the sleep
   On my poor body fell;
   By came the Queen of Faery,
   Made me with her to dwell.

8 'But the morn at een is Halloween,
   Our fairy foks a' do ride;
   And she that will her true-love win,
   At Blackstock she must bide.

9 'First let by the black,' he said,
   'And syne let by the brown;
[348] But when you see the milk-white steed,
   You'll pull his rider down.

10 'You'll pull him into thy arms,
   Let his bricht bridle fa,
   And he'll fa low into your arms
   Like stone in castle's wa.

11 'They'll first shape him into your arms
   An adder or a snake;
   But hold him fast, let him not go,
   He'll be your world's make.

12 'They'll next shape him into your arms
   Like a wood black dog to bite;
   Hold him fast, let him not go,
   For he'll be your heart's delight.

13 'They'll next shape [him] into your arms
   Like a red-het gaud o airn;
   But hold him fast, let him not go,
   He's the father o your bairn.

14 'They'll next shape him into your arms
   Like the laidliest worm of Ind;
   But hold him fast, let him not go,
   And cry aye "Young Tamlin."'

     *   *   *   *   *

15 Lady Margaret first let by the black,
   And syne let by the brown,
   But when she saw the milk-white steed
   She pulled the rider down.

16 She pulled him into her arms,
   Let his bright bridle fa',
   And he fell low into her arms,
   Like stone in castle's wa.

17 They first shaped him into arms
   An adder or a snake;
   But she held him fast, let him not go,
   For he'd be her warld's make.

18 They next shaped him into her arms
   Like a wood black dog to bite;
   But she held him fast, let him not go,
   For he'd be her heart's delight.

19 They next shaped him into her arms
   Like a red-het gaud o airn;
   But she held him fast, let him not go,
   He'd be father o her bairn.

20 They next shaped him into her arms
   Like the laidliest worm of Ind;
   But she held him fast, let him not go,
   And cried aye 'Young Tamlin.'

21 The Queen of Faery turned her horse about,
   Says, Adieu to thee, Tamlene!
   For if I had kent what I ken this night,
   If I had kent it yestreen,
   I wad hae taen out thy heart o flesh,
   And put in a heart o stane.

F

Motherwell's MS., p. 64, from the recitation of widow McCormick, February, 1825. Learned by widow McCormick from an old woman in Dumbarton: Motherwell's Note-Book, p. 4.

*   *   *   *   *

1 SHE's taen her petticoat by the band,
   Her mantle owre her arm,
And she's awa to Chester wood,
   As fast as she could run.

2 She scarsely pulled a rose, a rose,
   She scarse pulled two or three,
Till up there starts Thomas
   On the Lady Margaret's knee.

3 She's taen her petticoat by the band,
   Her mantle owre her arm,
And Lady Margaret's gane hame agen,
   As fast as she could run.

4 Up starts Lady Margaret's sister,
   An angry woman was she:
'If there ever was a woman wi child,
   Margaret, you are wi!'

5 Up starts Lady Margaret's mother,
   An angry woman was she:
'There grows ane herb in yon kirk-yard
   That will scathe the babe away.'

6 She took her petticoats by the band,
   Her mantle owre her arm,
And she's gane to yon kirk-yard
   As fast as she could run.

7 She scarcely pulled an herb, an herb,
   She scarse pulled two or three,
Till up starts there Thomas
   Upon this Lady Margret's knee.

8 'How dare ye pull a rose?' he says,
   'How dare ye break the tree?
How dare ye pull this herb,' he says,
   'To scathe my babe away?

9 'This night is Halloweve,' he said,
   'Our court is going to waste,
And them that loves their true-love best
   At Chester bridge they'll meet.

10 'First let pass the black,' he says,
   'And then let pass the brown,
But when ye meet the milk-white steed,
   Pull ye the rider down.

11 'They'll turn me to an eagle,' he says,
   'And then into an ass;
Come, hold me fast, and fear me not,
   The man that you love best.

12 'They'll turn me to a flash of fire,
   And then to a naked man;
Come, wrap you your mantle me about,
   And then you'll have me won.'

13 She took her petticoats by the band,
   Her mantle owre her arm,
And she's awa to Chester bridge,
   As fast as she could run.

14 And first she did let pass the black,
   And then let pass the brown,
But when she met the milk-white steed,
   She pulled the rider down.

15 They turned him in her arms an eagle,
   And then into an ass;
But she held him fast, and feared him not,
   The man that she loved best.

16 They turned him into a flash of fire,
   And then into a naked man;
But she wrapped her mantle him about,
   And then she had him won.

17 'O wae be to ye, Lady Margaret,
   And an ill death may you die,
For you've robbed me of the bravest knight
   That eer rode in our company.'

G

Buchan's MSS, I, 8; Motherwell's MS., p. 595.

1 TAKE warning, a' ye ladies fair,
  That wear gowd on your hair,
Come never unto Charter's woods,
  For Tam-a-line he's there.

2 Even about that knight's middle
  O' siller bells are nine;
Nae ane comes to Charter wood,
  And a maid returns again.

3 Lady Margaret sits in her bower door,
  Sewing at her silken seam;
And she langd to gang to Charter woods,
  To pou the roses green.

4 She hadna poud a rose, a rose,
  Nor broken a branch but ane,
Till by it came him true Tam-a-line,
  Says, Ladye, lat alane.

5 O why pou ye the rose, the rose?
  Or why brake ye the tree?
Or why come ye to Charter woods,
  Without leave askd of me?

6 'I will pou the rose, the rose,
  And I will brake the tree;
Charter woods are a' my ain,
  I'll ask nae leave o thee.'

7 He's taen her by the milk-white hand,
  And by the grass-green sleeve,
And laid her low on gude green wood,
  At her he spierd nae leave.

8 When he had got his wills of her,
  His wills as he had taen,
He's taen her by the middle sma,
  Set her to feet again.

9 She turnd her right and round about,
  To spier her true-love's name,
[350] But naething heard she, nor naething saw,
  As a' the woods grew dim.

10 Seven days she tarried there,
  Saw neither sun nor meen;
At length, by a sma glimmering light,
  Came thro the wood her lane.

11 When she came to her father's court,
  As fine as ony queen;
But when eight months were past and gane,
  Got on the gown o' green.

12 Then out it speaks an eldren knight,
  As he stood at the yett:
'Our king's daughter, she gaes wi bairn,
  And we'll get a' the wyte.'

13 'O had your tongue, ye eldren man,
  And bring me not to shame;
Although that I do gang wi bairn,
  Yese naeways get the blame.

14 'Were my love but an earthly man,
  As he's an elfin knight,
I woudna gie my ain true love
  For a' that's in my sight.'

15 Then out it speaks her brither dear,
  He meant to do her harm:
'There is an herb in Charter wood
  Will twine you an the bairn.'

16 She's taen her mantle her about,
  Her coffer by the band,
And she is on to Charter wood,
  As fast as she coud gang.

17 She hadna poud a rose, a rose,
  Nor braken a branch but ane,
Till by it came him Tam-a-Line,
  Says, Ladye, lat alane.

18 O why pou ye the pile, Margaret,
  The pile o the gravil green,
For to destroy the bonny bairn
  That we got us between?

19 O why pou ye the pile, Margaret,
  The pile o the gravil gray,
For to destroy the bonny bairn
  That we got in our play?

20 For if it be a knave-bairn,
  He's heir o a' my land;
But if it be a lass-bairn,
  In red gowd she shall gang.

21 'If my luve were an earthly man,
    As he's an elfin rae,
  I coud gang bound, love, for your sake,
    A twalmonth and a day.'

22 'Indeed your love's an earthly man,
    The same as well as thee,
  And lang I've haunted Charter woods,
    A' for your fair bodie.'

23 'O tell me, tell me, Tam-a-Line,
    O tell, an tell me true,
  Tell me this night, an mak nae lie,
    What pedigree are you?'

24 'O I hae been at gade church-door,
    An I've got christendom;
  I'm the Earl o' Forbes' eldest son,
    An heir ower a' his land.

25 'When I was young, o three years old,
    Muckle was made o me;
  My step-mother put on my claithes,
    An ill, ill sained she me.

26 'Ae fatal morning I went out,
    Dreading nae injury,
  And thinking lang, fell soun asleep,
    Beneath an apple tree.

27 'Then by it came the Elfin Queen,
    And laid her hand on me;
  And from that time since ever I mind,
    I've been in her companie.

28 'O Elfin it's a bonny place,
    In it fain woud I dwell;
  But ay at ilka seven years' end
    They pay a tiend to hell,
  And I'm sae fou o flesh an blude,
    I'm sair feard for mysell.'

29 'O tell me, tell me, Tam-a-Line,
    O tell, an tell me true;
  Tell me this night, an mak nae lie,
    What way I'll borrow you?'

30 'The morn is Halloween night,
    The elfin court will ride,
  Through England, and thro a' Scotland,
    And through the world wide.

31 'O they begin at sky setting,
    Rides a' the evening tide;
  And she that will her true-love borrow,
    [At] Miles-corse will him bide.

32 'Ye'll do you down to Miles-corse,
    Between twall hours and ane,
  And full your hands o holy water,
    And cast your compass roun.

33 'Then the first an court that comes you till
    Is published king and queen;
  The next an court that comes you till,
    It is maidens mony ane.

34 'The next an court that comes you till
    Is footmen, grooms and squires;
  The next an court that comes you till
    Is knights, and I'll be there.

35 'I Tam-a-Line, on milk-white steed,
    A goud star on my crown;
  Because I was an earthly knight,
    Got that for a renown.

36 'And out at my steed's right nostril,
    He'll breathe a fiery flame;
  Ye'll loot you low, and sain yoursel,
    And ye'll be busy then.

37 'Ye'll take my horse then by the head,
    And lat the bridal fa;
  The Queen o' Elfin she'll cry out,
    True Tam-a-Line's awa.

38 'Then I'll appear in your arms
    Like the wolf that neer woud tame;
  Ye'll had me fast, lat me not go,
    Case we neer meet again.

39 'Then I'll appear in your arms
    Like the fire that burns sae bauld;
  Ye'll had me fast, lat me not go,
    I'll be as iron cauld.

40 'Then I'll appear in your arms
    Like the adder an the snake;
  Ye'll had me fast, lat me not go,
    I am your warld's make.

41 'Then I'll appear in your arms
    Like to the deer sae wild;
    Ye'll had me fast, lat me not go,
    And I'll father your child.

42 'And I'll appear in your arms
    Like to a silken string;
    Ye'll had me fast, lat me not go,
    Till ye see the fair morning.

43 'And I'll appear in your arms
    Like to a naked man;
    Ye'll had me fast, lat me not go,
    And wi you I'll gae hame.'

44 Then she has done her to Miles-corse,
    Between twall hours an ane,
    And filled her hands o holy water,
    And kiest her compass roun.

45 The first an court that came her till
    Was published king and queen;
    The niest an court that came her till
    Was maidens mony ane.

46 The niest an court that came her till
    Was footmen, grooms and squires;
    The niest an court that came her till
    Was knights, and he was there.

47 True Tam-a-Line, on milk-white steed,
    A gowd star on his crown;
    Because he was an earthly man,
    Got that for a renown.

48 And out at the steed's right nostril,
    He breathd a fiery flame;
    She loots her low, an sains hersell,
    And she was busy then.

49 She's taen the horse then by the head,
    And loot the bridle fa;
    The Queen o Elfin she cried out,
    'True Tam-a-Line's awa.'

50 'Stay still, true Tam-a-Line,' she says,
    'Till I pay you your fee:'
    'His father wants not lands nor rents,
    He'll ask nae fee frae thee.'

51 'Gin I had kent yestreen, yestreen,   l3
    What I ken weel the day,
    I shoud taen your fu fause heart,
    Gien you a heart o clay.'

52 Then he appeared in her arms
    Like the wolf that neer woud tame;
    She held him fast, let him not go,
    Case they neer meet again.

53 Then he appeared in her arms
    Like the fire burning bauld;
    She held him fast, let him not go,
    He was as iron cauld.

51 And he appeared in her arms
    Like the adder an the snake;
    She held him fast, let him not go,
    He was her warld's make.

55 And he appeared in her arms
    Like to the deer sae wild;
    She held him fast, let him not go,
    He's father o her child.

56 And he appeared in her arms
    Like to a silken string;
    She held him fast, let him not go,
    Till she saw fair morning.

57 And he appeared in her arms
    Like to a naked man;
    She held him fast, let him not go,
    And wi her he's gane hame.

58 These news hae reachd thro a' Scotland,
    And far ayont the Tay,
    That Lady Margaret, our king's daughter,
    That night had gaind her prey.

59 She borrowed her love at mirk midnight,
    Bare her young son ere day,
    And though ye'd search the warld wide,
    Ye'll nae find sic a may.

H

Campbell MSS, II, 129.

1 I FORBID ye, maidens a',
    That wears gowd in your hair,
  To come or gang by Carterhaugh,
    For young Tam Lane is there.

2 I forbid ye, maidens a',
    That wears gowd in your green,
  To come or gang by Carterhaugh,
    For fear of young Tam Lane.

3 'Go saddle for me the black,' says Janet,
    'Go saddle for me the brown,
  And I'll away to Carterhaugh,
    And flower mysell the gown.

4 'Go saddle for me the brown,' says Janet,
    'Go saddle for me the black,
  And I'll away to Carterhaugh,
    And flower mysel a hat.'

   *   *   *   *   *

5 She had not pulld a flowr, a flowr,
    A flower but only three,
  Till up there startit young Tam Lane,
    Just at bird Janet's knee.

6 'Why pullst thou the herb, Janet,
    And why breaks thou the tree?
  Why put you back the bonny babe
    That's between you and me?'

7 'If my child was to an earthly man,
    As it is to a wild buck rae,
  I would wake him the length of the winter's
      night,
    And the lea lang simmer's day.'

8 'The night is Halloween, Janet,
    When our gude neighbours will ride,
  And them that would their true-love won
    At Blackning Cross maun bide.

9 'Many will the black ride by,
    And many will the brown,
  But I ride on a milk-white steed,
    And ride nearest the town:
  Because I was a christened knight
    They gie me that renown.

10 'Many will the black ride by,
    But far mae will the brown;
  But when ye see the milk-white stead,   [353]
    Grip fast and pull me down.

11 'Take me in yer arms, Janet,
    An ask, an adder lang;
  The grip ye get ye maun haud fast,
    I'll be father to your bairn.

12 'Take me in your arms, Janet,
    An adder and a snake;
  The grip ye get ye maun haud fast,
    I'll be your warld's make.'

   *   *   *   *   *

13 Up bespak the Queen of Fairies,
    She spak baith loud and high:
  'Had I kend the day at noon
    Tam Lane had been won from me,

14 'I wad hae taen out his heart o flesh,
    Put in a heart o tree,
  That a' the maids o Middle Middle Mist
    Should neer hae taen Tam Lane frae me.'

15 Up bespack the Queen of Fairies,
    And she spak wi a loud yell:
  'Aye at every seven year's end
    We pay the kane to hell,
  And the koors they hae gane round about,
    And I fear it will be mysel.'

I

a. *Minstrelsy of the Scottish Border*, II, 337, ed. 1833;
II, 245, ed. 1803. b. II, 228, ed. 1802.

1 'O I forbid ye, maidens a',
    That wear gowd on your hair,
  To come or gae by Carterhaugh,
    For young Tamlane is there.

2 'There's nane that gaes by Carterhaugh
    But maun leave him a wad,
  Either gowd rings, or green mantles,
    Or else their maidenheid.

3 'Now gowd rings ye may buy, maidens,
    Green mantles ye may spin,
  But, gin ye lose your maidenheid,
    Ye'll neer get that agen.'

4 But up then spak her, fair Janet,
    The fairest o' a' her kin:
  'I'll cum and gang to Carterhaugh,
    And ask nae leave o him.'

5 Janet has kilted her green kirtle
    A little abune her knee,
  And she has braided her yellow hair
    A little abune her bree.

6 And when she came to Carterhaugh,
    She gaed beside the well,
  And there she fand his steed standing,
    But away was himsell.

7 She hadna pu'd a red red rose,
    A rose but barely three,
  Till up and starts a wee wee man,
    At lady Janet's knee.

8 Says, Why pu ye the rose, Janet?
    What gars ye break the tree?
  Or why come ye to Carterhaugh,
    Withouten leave o me?

9 Says, Carterhaugh it is mine ain,
    My daddie gave it me;
  I'll come and gang to Carterhaugh,
    And ask nae leave o thee.

10 He's taen her by the milk-white hand,
    Among the leaves sae green,
  And what they did I cannot tell,
    The green leaves were between.

11 He's taen her by the milk-white hand,
    Among the roses red,
  And what they did I cannot say,
    She neer returnd a maid.

12 When she cam to her father's ha,
    She looked pale and wan;
  They thought she'd dreed some sair sickness,
    Or been with some leman.

13 She didna comb her yellow hair
    Nor make meikle o her head,
  And ilka thing that lady took
    Was like to be her deid.

14 It's four and twenty ladies fair
    Were playing at the ba;
  Janet, the wightest of them anes,
    Was faintest o them a'.

15 Four and twenty ladies fair
    Were playing at the chess;
  And out there came the fair Janet,
    As green as any grass.

16 Out and spak an auld grey-headed knight,
    Lay oer the castle wa:
  'And ever, alas! for thee, Janet,
    But we'll be blamed a'!'

17 'Now haud your tongue, ye auld grey knight,
    And an ill deid may ye die!
  Father my bairn on whom I will,
    I'll father nane on thee.'

18 Out then spak her father dear,
    And be spak meik and mild:
  'And ever, alas! my sweet Janet,
    I fear ye gae with child.'

19 'And if I be with child, father,
    Mysell maun bear the blame;
  There's neer a knight about your ha
    Shall hae the bairnie's name.

20 'And if I be with child, father,
    'T will prove a wondrous birth,
  For weel I swear I'm not wi bairn
    To any man on earth.

21 'If my love were an earthly knight,
  As he's an elfin grey,
  I wadna gie my ain true love
  For nae lord that ye hae.'

22 She prinkd hersell and prinnd hersell,
  By the ae light of the moon,
  And she's away to Carterhaugh,
  To speak wi young Tamlane.

23 And when she cam to Carterhaugh,
  She gaed beside the well,
  And there she saw the steed standing,
  But away was himsell.

24 She hadna pu'd a double rose,
  A rose but only twae,
  When up and started young Tamlane,
  Says, Lady, thou pu's nae mae.

25 Why pu ye the rose, Janet,
  Within this garden grene,
  And a' to kill the bonny babe
  That we got us between?

26 'The truth ye'll tell to me, Tamlane,
  A word ye mauna lie;
  Gin eer ye was in haly chapel,
  Or sained in Christentie?'

27 'The truth I'll tell to thee, Janet,
  A word I winna lie;
  A knight me got, and a lady me bore,
  As well as they did thee.

28 'Randolph, Earl Murray, was my sire,
  Dunbar, Earl March, is thine;
  We loved when we were children small,
  Which yet you well may mind.

29 'When I was a boy just turnd of nine,
  My uncle sent for me,
  To hunt and hawk, and ride with him,
  And keep him companie.

30 'There came a wind out of the north,
  A sharp wind and a snell,
  And a deep sleep came over me,
  And frae my horse I fell.

31 'The Queen of Fairies keppit me
  In yon green hill to dwell,
  And I'm a fairy, lyth and limb,
  Fair ladye, view me well.

32 'Then would I never tire, Janet,
  In Elfish land to dwell,
  But aye, at every seven years,
  They pay the teind to hell;
  And I am sae fat and fair of flesh,
  I fear 't will be mysell.

33 'This night is Halloween, Janet,
  The morn is Hallowday,
  And gin ye dare your true love win,
  Ye hae nae time to stay.

34 'The night it is good Halloween,
  When fairy folk will ride,
  And they that wad their true-love win,
  At Miles Cross they maun bide.'   [355]

35 'But how shall I thee ken, Tamlane?
  Or how shall I thee knaw,
  Amang so many unearthly knights,
  The like I never saw?'

36 'The first company that passes by,
  Say na, and let them gae;
  The next company that passes by,
  Say na, and do right sae;
  The third company that passes by,
  Then I'll be ane o thae.

37 'First let pass the black, Janet,
  And syne let pass the brown,
  But grip ye to the milk-white steed,
  And pu the rider down.

38 'For I ride on the milk-white steed,
  And aye nearest the town;
  Because I was a christend knight,
  They gave me that renown.

39 'My right hand will be gloved, Janet,
  My left hand will be bare;
  And these the tokens I gie thee,
  Nae doubt I will be there.

40 'They'll turn me in your arms, Janet,
  An adder and a snake;
  But had me fast, let me not pass,
  Gin ye wad be my maik.

41 'They'll turn me in your arms, Janet,
  An adder and an ask;
  They'll turn me in your arms, Janet,
  A bale that burns fast.

42 'They'll turn me in your arms, Janet,
        A red-hot gad o airn;
    But haud me fast, let me not pass,
        For I'll do you no harm.

43 'First dip me in a stand o milk,
        And then in a stand o water;
    But had me fast, let me not pass,
        I'll be your bairn's father.

44 'And next they'll shape me in your arms
        A tod but and an eel;
    But had me fast, nor let me gang,
        As you do love me weel.

45 'They'll shape me in your arms, Janet,
        A dove but and a swan,
    And last they'll shape me in your arms
        A mother-naked man;
    Cast your green mantle over me,
        I'll be myself again.'

46 Gloomy, gloomy, was the night,
        And eiry was the way,
    As fair Janet, in her green mantle,
        To Miles Cross she did gae.

47 About the dead hour o the night
        She heard the bridles ring
    And Janet was as glad o that
        As any earthly thing.

48 And first gaed by the black black steed,
        And then gaed by the brown;
    But fast she gript the milk-white steed,
        And pu'd the rider down.

49 She pu'd him frae the milk-white steed,
        And loot the bridle fa,
    And up there raise an erlish cry,
        'He's won amang us a'!'

50 They shaped him in fair Janet's arms
        An esk but and an adder;
    She held him fast in every shape,
        To be her bairn's father.

51 They shaped him in her arms at last
        A mother-naked man,
    She wrapt him in her green mantle,
        And sae her true love wan.

52 Up then spake the Queen o Fairies,
        Out o a bush o broom:
    'She that has borrowd young Tamlane
        Has gotten a stately groom.'

53 Up then spake the Queen o Fairies,
        Out o a bush o rye:
    'She's taen awa the bonniest knight
        In a' my cumpanie.

54 'But had I kennd, Tamlane,' she says,
        'A lady wad borrowd thee
    I wad taen out thy twa grey een,
        Put in twa een o tree.

55 'Had I but kennd, Tamlane,' she says,
        'Before ye came frae hame,
    I wad taen out your heart o flesh,
        Put in a heart o stane.

56 'Had I but had the wit yestreen
        That I hae coft the day,
    I'd paid my kane seven times to hell
        Ere you'd been won away.'

J

"A fragment of Young Tamlane," Kinloch MSS, V,
391. In Dr John Hill Burton's handwriting, and perhaps
from the recitation of Mrs Robertson (Christian Leslie),
mother of Dr Joseph Robertson.

    *   *   *   *   *
1 'The night, the night is Halloween,
        Tomorrow's Hallowday,

    .   .   .   .   .

    .   .   .   .   .

2 'The night, the night is Halloween,
        Our seely court maun ride,
    Thro England and thro Ireland both,
        And a' the warld wide.
    *   *   *   *   *

3 'The firsten court that comes ye bye,
   You'll lout, and let them gae;
   The seconden court that comes you bye,
   You'll hail them reverently.

4 'The thirden court that comes you by,
   Sae weel's ye will me ken,
   For some will be on a black, a black,
   And some will be on a brown,
   But I will be on a bluid-red steed,
   And will ride neist the queen.

5 'The thirden court that comes you bye,
   Sae weel's ye will me ken,
   For I'll be on a bluid-red steed,
   Wi three stars on his crown.

6 'Ye'll tak the horse head in yer hand,
   And grip the bridle fast;
   The Queen o Elfin will gie a cry,
   "True Tamas is stown awa!"

7 'And I will grow in your twa hands
   An adder and an eel;
   But the grip ye get ye'll hold it fast,
   I'll by father to yer chiel.

8 'I will wax in your twa hans
   As hot as any coal;
   But if you love me as you say,
   You'll think of me and thole.

9 'O I will grow in your twa hands
   An adder and a snake;
   The grip ye get now hold it fast,
   And I'll be your world's mait.

10 'O I'll gae in at your gown sleeve,
    And out at your gown hem,
    And I'll stand up before thee then
    A freely naked man.

11 'O I'll gae in at your gown sleeve,
    And out at your gown hem,
    And I'll stand before you then,
    But claithing I'll hae nane.

12 'Ye'll do you down to Carden's Ha,
    And down to Carden's stream,
    And there you'll see our seely court,
    As they come riding hame.'

        *   *   *   *   *

13 'It's nae wonder, my daughter Janet,
    True Tammas ye thought on;
    An he were a woman as he's a man,
    My bedfellow he should be.'

                ———•———

1 The night, the night is Halloween,
   Tomorrow's Hallowday, our seely court maun
      ride,
   Thro England and thro Ireland both,
   And a' the warld wide.

K

Communicated to Scott November 11, 1812, by
Hugh Irvine, Drum, Aberdeenshire, as procured from
the recitation of an old woman in Buchan: Letters, V,
No 137, Abbotsford. (Not in Irvine's hand.)

1 LEADY MARGAT stands in her boor-door,
   Clead in the robs of green;
   She longed to go to Charters Woods,
   To pull the flowers her lean.

2 She had not puld a rose, a rose,
   O not a rose but one,
   Till up it starts True Thomas,
   Said, Leady, let alone.

3 'Why pull ye the rose, Marget?
   Or why break ye the tree?
   Or why come ye to Charters Woods
   Without the leave of me?'

4 'I will pull the rose,' she said,
   'And I will break the tree,
   For Charters Woods is all my own,
   And I'l ask no leave of the.'

5 He's tean her by the milk-white hand,
    And by the grass-green sleeve,
  And laid her lo at the foot of the tree,
    At her he askt no leave.

6 It fell once upon a day
    They wer a pleaying at the ba,
  And every one was reed and whyte,
    Leady Marget's culler was all awa.

7 Out it speaks an elder man,
    As he stood in the gate,
  'Our king's daughter she gos we bern,
    And we will get the wait.'

8 'If I be we bern,' she said,
    'My own self beer the blame!
  There is not a man in my father's court
    Will get my bern's name.'

9 'There grows a flower in Charters Woods,
    It grows on gravel greay,
  It ould destroy the boney young bern
    That ye got in your pley.'

10 She's tean her mantle her about,
    Her green glove on her hand,
  And she's awa to Charters Woods,
    As fest as she could gang.

11 She had no puld a pile, a pile,
    O not a pile but one,
  Up it startid True Thomas,
    Said, Leady, lat alean.

12 'Why pull ye the pile, Marget,
    That grows on gravel green,
  For to destroy the boney young bern
    That we got us between?'

13 'If it were to an earthly man,
    As [it is] to an elphan knight,
  I ould walk for my true-love's sake
    All the long winter's night.'

14 'When I was a boy of eleven years old,
    And much was made of me,
  I went out to my father's garden,
    Fell asleep at yon aple tree:
  The queen of Elphan [she] came by,
    And laid on her hands on me.

15 'Elphan it's a boney place,
    In it fain wid I dwall;
  But ey at every seven years end
    We pay the teene to hell:
  I'm so full of flesh and blood
    I'm sear feart for mysel.

16 'The morn's Hallow Even's night,
    When a' our courts do ride,
  Through England and through Irland,
    Through a' the world wide:
  And she that would her true-love borrow
    At Miles Corse she may bide.

17 'The first an court that ye come till,
    Ye let them a' pass by;
  The next an court that ye come till,
    Ye hile them reverendly.

18 'The next an court that ye come till,
    An therein rides the queen,
  Me upon a milk-whyte steed,
    And a gold star in my croun;
  Because I am a erle's soon,
    I get that for my renoun.

19 'Ye take me in your armes,
    Give me a right sear fa;
  The queen of Elphan she'l cry out,
    True Thomas is awa!

20 'First I'l be in your armes
    The fire burning so bold;
  Ye hold me fast, let me no pass
    Till I be like iron cold.

21 'Next I'l be in your armes
    The fire burning so wild;
  Ye hold me fast, let me no pass,
    I'm the father of your child.'

22 The first court that came her till,
    She let them a' pass by;
  The nex an court that came her till,
    She helt them reverendly.

23 The nex an court that came her till,
    And therein read the queen,
  True Thomas on a milk-whyte steed,
    A gold star in his croun;
  Because he was a earl's soon,
    He got that for his renoun.

24 She's tean him in her arms,
      Geen him a right sore fa;
   The queen of Elphan she cried out,
      True Thomas is awa!

25 He was into her arms
      The fire burning so bold;
   She held him fast, let him no pass
      Till he was like iron cold.

26 He was into her arms
      The fire burning so wild;
   She held him fast, let him no pass,
      He was the father of her child.

27 The queen of Elphan she cried out,
      An angry woman was she,
   'Let Leady Marget an her true-love be,
      She's bought him dearer than me.'

L

"Scotch Ballads, Materials for Border Minstrelsy," No
27, Abbotsford; in the handwriting of William Laidlaw.

1 I CHARGE ye, a' ye ladies fair,
      That wear goud in your hair,
   To come an gang bye Carterhaugh,
      For young Tam Lien is there.

      *   *   *   *   *

2 Then Janet kiltit her green cleadin
      A wee aboon her knee,
   An she's gane away to Carterhaugh,
      As fast as she can dree.

3 When Janet cam to Carterhaugh,
      Tam Lien was at the wall,
   An there he left his steed stannin,
      But away he gaed his sell.

4 She had na pu'd a red, red rose,
      A rose but only thre,
   Till up then startit young Tam Lien,
      Just at young Jenet's knee.

5 'What gars ye pu the rose, Janet,
      Briek branches frae the tree,
   An come an gang by Carterhaugh,
      An speir nae leave of me?'

6 'What need I speir leave o thee, Tam?
      What need I speir leave o thee,
   When Carterhaugh is a' mine ain,
      My father gae it me?'

      *   *   *   *   *

7 She's kiltit up her green cleadin
      A wee aboon her knee,
   An she's away to her ain bower-door,
      As fast as she can dree.

      *   *   *   *   *

8 There war four-an-twentie fair ladies
      A' dancin in a chess,
   An some war blue an some war green,
      But Janet was like the gress.

9 There war four-an-twentie fair ladies
      A' playin at the ba,
   An some war red an som wer white,
      But Jennet was like the snaw.

M

"Scotch Ballads, Materials for Border Minstrelsy," No
15. Communicated to Scott by Major Henry Hutton, Royal
Artillery, 24th December, 1802, as recollected by his father
"and the family:" Letters I, No 77. Major Hutton intimates
that stanzas 46–49 of the first edition of 'Tamlane' ('Rox-
burgh was my grandfather,' ff, corresponding to I 28–32)
should be struck out, and his verses inserted. But 4–12 of
Hutton's stanzas belong to 'Thomas Rymer.'

1 My FATHER was a noble knight,
　　And was much gi'n to play,
　And I myself a bonny boy,
　　And followed him away.

2 He rowd me in his hunting-coat
　　And layd me down to sleep,
　And by the queen of fairies came,
　　And took me up to keep.

3 She set me on a milk-white steed;
　　'Twas o the elfin kind;
　His feet were shot wi beaten goud,
　　And fleeter than the wind.

4 Then we raid on and on'ard mair,
　　Oer mountain, hill and lee,
　Till we came to a hie, hie wa,
　　Upon a mountain's bree.

5 The apples hung like stars of goud
　　Out-our that wa sa fine;
　I put my hand to pu down ane,
　　For want of food I thought to tine.

6 'O had your hand, Tamas!' she said,
　　'O let that evil fruit now be!
　It was that apple ye see there
　　Beguil'd man and woman in your country.

7 'O dinna ye see yon road, Tamas,
　　Down by yon lilie lee?
　Blessd is the man who yon gate gaes,
　　It leads him to the heavens hie.

8 'And dinna ye see yon road, Tamas,
　　Down by yon frosty fell?
　Curst is the man that yon gate gaes,
　　For it leads to the gates of hell.

9 'O dinna ye see yon castle, Tamas,
　　That's biggit between the twa,
　And theekit wi the beaten goud?
　　O that's the fairies' ha.

10 'O when ye come to the ha, Tamas,
　　See that a weel-learnd boy ye be;
　They'll ask ye questions ane and a',
　　But see ye answer nane but me.

11 'If ye speak to ain but me, Tamas,
　　A fairie ye maun ever bide;
　But if ye speak to nane but me, Tamas,
　　Ye may come to be your country's pride.'

12 And when he came to Fairie Ha,
　　I wot a weel-learnd boy was he;
　They askd him questions ane and a',
　　But he answerd nane but his ladie.

13 There was four-and-twenty gude knights'-sons
　　In fairie land obliged to bide,
　And of a' the pages that were there
　　Fair Tamas was his ladie's pride.

14 There was four-and-twenty earthly boys,
　　Wha all played at the ba,
　But Tamas was the bonniest boy,
　　And playd the best amang them a'.

15 There was four-and-twenty earthly maids,
　　Wha a' playd at the chess,
　Their colour rosy-red and white,
　　Their gowns were green as grass.

16 'And pleasant are our fairie sports,
　　We flie o'er hill and dale;
　But at the end of seven years
　　They pay the teen to hell.

17 'And now's the time, at Hallowmess,
　　Late on the morrow's even,
　And if ye miss me then, Janet,
　　I'm lost for yearis seven.'

N

'Tamlane,' "Scotch Ballads, Materials for Border Minstrelsy," No 96 a; in the handwriting of John Leyden.

'GOWD RINGS I can buy, Thomas,
  Green mantles I can spin,
But gin ye take my maidenheid
  I'll neer get that again.'

Out and spak the queen o fairies,
  Out o a shot o wheat,
'She that has gotten young Tamlane
  Has gotten my heart's delight!

O

'The Queen of the Fairies,' Macmath MS., p. 57. "Taken down by me 14th October, 1886, from the recitation of Mr Alexander Kirk, Inspector of Poor, Dalry, in the Stewartry of Kirkcudbright, who learned it about fifty years ago from the singing of David Rae, Barlay, Balmaclellan."

This copy has been considerably made over, and was very likely learned from print. The cane in the maid's hand, already sufficiently occupied, either with the Bible or with holy water, is an imbecility such as only the "makers" of latter days are capable of. (There is a cane in another ballad which I cannot at this moment recall.)

1 THE MAID that sits in Katherine's Hall,
    Clad in her robes so black,
  She has to yon garden gone,
    For flowers to flower her hat.

2 She had not pulled the red, red rose,
    A double rose but three,
  When up there starts a gentleman,
    Just at this lady's knee.

3 Says, Who's this pulls the red, red rose?
    Breaks branches off the tree?
  Or who's this treads my garden-grass,
    Without the leave of me?

4 'Yes, I will pull the red, red rose,
    Break branches off the tree,
  This garden in Moorcartney wood,
    Without the leave o thee.'

5 He took her by the milk-white hand
    And gently laid her down,
  Just in below some shady trees
    Where the green leaves hung down.

6 'Come tell to me, kind sir,' she said,
    'What before you never told;
  Are you an earthly man?' said she,
    'A knight or a baron bold?'

7 'I'll tell to you, fair lady,' he said,
    'What before I neer did tell;
  I'm Earl Douglas's second son,
    With the queen of the fairies I dwell.

8 'When riding through yon forest-wood,
    And by yon grass-green well,
  A sudden sleep me overtook,
    And off my steed I fell.

9 'The queen of the fairies, being there,
    Made me with her to dwell,
  And still once in the seven years
    We pay a teind to hell.

10 'And because I am an earthly man,
    Myself doth greatly fear,
  For the cleverest man in all our train
    To Pluto must go this year.

11 'This night is Halloween, lady,
       And the fairies they will ride;
   The maid that will her true-love win
       At Miles Cross she may bide.'

12 'But how shall I thee ken, though, sir?
       Or how shall I thee know,
   Amang a pack o hellish wraiths,
       Before I never saw?'

13 'Some rides upon a black horse, lady,
       And some upon a brown,
   But I myself on a milk-white steed,
       And aye nearest the toun.

14 'My right hand shall be covered, lady,
       My left hand shall be bare,
   And that's a token good enough
       That you will find me there.

15 'Take the Bible in your right hand,
       With God for to be your guide,
   Take holy water in thy left hand,
       And throw it on every side.'

16 She's taen her mantle her about,
       A cane into her hand,
   And she has unto Miles Cross gone,
       As hard as she can gang.

17 First she has letten the black pass by,
       And then she has letten the brown,
   But she's taen a fast hold o the milk-white
           steed,
       And she's pulled Earl Thomas doun.

18 The queen o the fairies being there,
       Sae loud she's letten a cry,
   'The maid that sits in Katherine's Hall
       This night has gotten her prey.

19 'But hadst thou waited, fair lady,
       Till about this time the morn,
   He would hae been as far from thee or me
       As the wind that blew when he was born.'

20 They turned him in this lady's arms
       Like the adder and the snake;
   She held him fast; why should she not?
       Though her poor heart was like to break.

21 They turned him in this lady's arms
       Like two red gads of airn;
   She held him fast; why should she not?
       She knew they could do her no harm.

22 They turned him in this lady's arms
       Like to all things that was vile;
   She held him fast; why should she not?
       The father of her child.

23 They turned him in this lady's arms
       Like to a naked knight;
   She's taen him hame to her ain bower,
       And clothed him in armour bright.

---◆---

A. *Divided in the* Museum *into* $45\frac{1}{2}$ *four-line stanzas,*
     without heed to rhyme or reason, $3^{5,6}$ *making a*
     stanza with $4^{1,2}$, *etc.*
   3^1. has belted. 4^2. Tom, *elsewhere* Tam.
   17^4. brie. 34^2. burning lead.
B. "An Old Song called Young Tom Line."
   Written in twenty-six stanzas of four [three, two]
   long, or double, lines.
   19^3. yon bonny babes.
   26^2. and do right sae.
   26^4. and let them gae. *See* 36.
   26, 27, 28, 29, 30, 31, 32, 33 *stand in MS.* 31, 26,
   27, 32, 28, 29, 33, 30.

Mr Macmath *has found an earlier transcript of* **B** *in*
Glenriddel's MSS, VIII, 106, 1789. *The variations*
(except those of spelling, which are numerous) are
as follows:

   1^2. that wears. 1^3. go. 3^3. has snoded.
   3^5. is gaen. 5^1. had not. 6^3. comes. 7^2. give.
   $8^{2,4}$, $16^{2,4}$, $35^{2,4}$. above.
   11^1. Out then: gray-head.
   11^3. And ever alas, fair Janet, he says.
   13^3. fair Janet. 13^4. thow gaes. 14^1. If I.
   14^3. Ther'e not. 14^4, 34^4. bairns.
   15^4. Ye nae, *wrongly.* 16^5. she is on.
   19^2. groves green. 20^1. Thomas. 20^2. for his.

20^3. Whether ever. 22^3. from the.

22^4. Then from. 23^3. The Queen o Fairies has.

23^4. do dwell. 23^6. Fiend, *wrongly.*

24^1. is a Hallow-een. 24^3. And them.

25^3. Amongst. 27^1. ride on. 27^6. gave.

30^4. wardly. 31^3. Hald me. 34^2. then in.

37^4. And there. 38^3. Them that hes. 38^4. Has.

$40^{3,4}$. eyes. 41^1. kend. 41^3. I'd.

D a, *excepting the title and the first stanza, is in a hand not Motherwell's.*

   b *has 26 stanzas,* **c** *has 12. The first 12 stanzas, of* **a** *and* **b** *and the 12 of* **c,** *and again the first 22 stanzas of* **a** *and* **b,** *are almost verbally the same, and* **a** *23 =* **b** *24.* **b** *has but 26 stanzas.*

a. 15 *stands* 24 *in MS.*

   17^1. Miles Cross: **b,** Moss.

   17^3. the holy.

   19^2. So (?) clad: **b,** is clad.

   22^1. twa. 25^1. ride.

b. 4^4. let abeene. 6^4. I'll ask no.

   7^3. her down. 10^4. gotten in.

   11^1. to me. 11^3. at a.

   12^4. his land. 15^3. and through.

   16^5. if that. 16^6. Rides Cross, *as in* **a.**

   17^3. Take holy. 20^4. next the.

After 23:

> 'I'll grow into your arms two
> Like ice on frozen lake;
> But hold me fast, let me not go,
> Or from your goupen break.'

> 25 And it's next night into Miles Moss
> Fair Margaret has gone,
> When lo she stands beside Rides Cross,
> Between twelve hours and one.

> 26 There's holy water in her hand,
> She casts a compass round,
> And presently a fairy band
> Comes riding oer the mound.

c. 1^3. O go not. 1^3, *and always,* Chester's wood.

   3^1. the seam.

   4^4. let alane.

   6^1. will pluck. 6^4. ask no.

   9^4. has been.

   11^1. me, Tom o Lin.

   12^4. his land.

D a. *This copy occurs in* "the second collection" *of Charles Kirkpatrick Sharpe, p. 3, with a few variations, as follows. (See Sharpe's Ballad Book, ed. 1880, p. 145.)*

1^3. Charters wood, *and always.* 3^1. the seam.

3^3. is gone. 5^2. ye. 6^4. ask no. 10^4. we have.

11^1. to me. 12^2. aft her gates. 12^3. the Lord of Forbes.

12^4. all his. 15 *occurs after* 24. 15^1. Tho Elfin.

15^4. the tenth one goes. 15^5. I am an, *or,* I a man.

16^5. if that. 16^6. miles Cross.

17^1. go unto the Miles cross. 20^4. next the.

23^1, 24^1. int. 25^1. She did her down.

27^2. so green. 27^3. Where. 27^4. ride next.

28^4. he is. 29^4. He. 32^2. and cry.

34^1. I thought.

D c. 12^2. aft.

E. 18, 19, 20 *are not written out. We are directed to understand them to be* "as in preceding stanzas, making the necessary grammatical changes."

F. 11^2, 15^2. ass, *somebody's blunder for* ask.

G. 21^2. elfin gray, *Motherwell, but see* **H,** 7^2.

   26^1. Ay. 31^1. began.

   58^2. *Motherwell:* far's the river Tay.

   58^4. *Motherwell:* she gained.

Motherwell, as usual, seems to have made some slight changes in copying.

I. *Scott's copy having been* "prepared from a collation of the printed copies," *namely, those in Johnson's Museum and Herd's Scottish Songs,* "with a very accurate one in Glenriddell's MS., and with several recitals from tradition," *what was not derived from tradition, but from the Museum, Glenriddell, and Herd, is printed in smaller type.*

"The variations in the tale of Tamlane" *were derived* "from the recitation of an old woman residing near Kirkhill, in West Lothian:" *Scott's Minstrelsy,* II, 102, 1802.

a. 3, 20, *not in* **b.**

After 31 *are omitted five stanzas of the copy obtained by Scott* "from a gentleman residing near Langholm," *and others, of the same origin, after* 46 *and* 47. *The stanzas introduced into* **I a** *were from* "Mr Beattie of Meikledale's Tamlane," *as appears from a letter of Scott to Laidlaw, January 21, 1803. (W. Macmath.)*

The "gentleman residing near Langholm," *from whom Scott derived the stanzas of a modern cast, was a Mr Beattie, of Meikledale, and Scott suspected that they might be the work of some poetical clergyman or schoolmaster: letter to W. Laidlaw, January 21, 1803, cited by Carruthers, Abbotsford Notanda, appended to R. Chambers's Life of Scott, 1871, p. 121 f.*

> 32 'But we that live in Fairy-land
> No sickness know nor pain;
> I quit my body when I will,
> And take to it again.

33 'I quit my body when I please,
   Or unto it repair;
   We can inhabit at our ease
   In either earth or air.

[357]   34 'Our shapes and size we can convert
      To either large or small;
      An old nut-shell's the same to us
      As is the lofty hall.

35 'We sleep in rose-buds soft and sweet,
   We revel in the stream;
   We wanton lightly on the wind
   Or glide on a sunbeam.

36 'And all our wants are well supplied
   From every rich man's store,
   Who thankless sins the gifts he gets,
   And vainly grasps, for more.'

40⁴. buy me maik, *a plain misprint for the* be my
maik *of* **b** 57.

46. *After this stanza are omitted:*

52 The heavens were black, the night was
      dark,
   And dreary was the place,
   But Janet stood with eager wish
   Her lover to embrace.

53 Betwixt the hours of twelve and one
   A north wind tore the bent,
   And straight she heard strange elritch
      sounds
   Upon that wind which went.

47. *After this stanza are omitted:*

55 Their oaten pipes blew wondrous shrill,
   The hemlock small blew clear,
   And louder notes from hemlock large,
   And bog-reed, struck the ear;
   But solemn sounds, or sober thoughts,
   The fairies cannot bear.

56 They sing, inspired with love and joy,
   Like skylarks in the air;
   Of solid sense, or thought that's grave,
   You'll find no traces there.

57 Fair Janet stood, with mind unmoved,
   The dreary heath upon,
   And louder, louder waxd the sound
   As they came riding on.

58 Will o Wisp before them went,
   Sent forth a twinkling light,
   And soon she saw the fairy bands
   All riding in her sight.

b 6–12 *is a fragment of* 'The Broomfield-Hill,' *intro-
duced by a stanza formed on the sixth, as here
given:*

5 And she's away to Carterhaugh,
   And gaed beside the wood,
   And there was sleeping young Tamlane,
   And his steed beside him stood.

After the fragment of 'The Broomfield-Hill' *follows:*

13 Fair Janet, in her green cleiding,
   Returned upon the morn,
   And she met her father's ae brother,
   The laird of Abercorn.

*And then these two stanzas, the first altered from
Herd's fragment of* 'The Broomfield Hill,' 'I'll
wager, I'll wager,' *p.* 310, *ed.* 1769, *and the sec-
ond from Herd's fragment,* 'Kertonha,' *or version*
C *of this ballad:*

14 I'll wager, I'll wager, I'll wager wi you
   Five hunder merk and ten,
   I'll maiden gang to Carterhaugh,
   And maiden come again.

15 She princked hersell, and prin'd hersell,
   By the ae light of the moon,
   And she's away to Carterhaugh
   As fast as she could win.

Instead of **a** 10, 11, **b** *has:*

He's taen her by the milk-white hand,
   And by the grass-green sleeve,
He's led her to the fairy ground,
   And spierd at her nae leave.

Instead of 14 *of* **a**, **b** *has something nearer to* **A, B** 9:

23 It's four and twenty ladies fair
   Were in her father's ha,
   Whan in there came the fair Janet,
   The flower amang them a'.

After 21 *of* **a** *follows in* **b** *a copy of* 'The Wee Wee
Man,' 32–39, *attached by these two stanzas, which
had been* "introduced in one recital only:"

30 'Is it to a man of might, Janet,
  Or is it to a man o mean?
  Or is it unto young Tamlane,
  That's wi the fairies gane?'

31 ''Twas down by Carterhaugh, father,
  I walked beside the wa,
  And there I saw a wee, wee man,
  The least that eer I saw.'

Instead of 22, which had been used before, we have in
b:

40 Janet's put on her green cleiding,
  Whan near nine months were gane,
  And she's awa to Carterhaugh,
  To speak wi young Tamlane.

b *has in place of* **a** *28–30*:

46 Roxburgh was my grandfather,
  Took me with him to bide,
  And as we frae the hunting came
  This harm did me betide.

47 Roxburgh was a hunting knight,
  And loved hunting well,
  And on a cauld and frosty day
  Down frae my horse I fell.

b 49 *has* **A** 24 *instead of* **a** 37, **I** 32.
b $61^2 =$ **a** $49^2 =$ **I** 44^2 *has* toad, *and so has* **C** 9^2,
from which the stanza is taken. Tod *is an improve-*
ment, but probably an editorial improvement.

J. Cf. **A** 25, 26; **D** 16; **G** 30; **I** 33, 34.
  8^4. think and of me thole.
K. 3^2. breat. 15^4. tune (?). 16^1. Thee.
  27^2. woman *is struck out.*

L. *This fragment does not appear to have been among the*
  "several recitals from tradition" used by Scott in
  making up his ballad. Some lines which it might be
  supposed to have furnished occur in the edition of
  1802, issued before Scott's acquaintance with Laid-
  law began.
  1^3. To *is doubtful; almost* bound *in.*
  6^4. gae *written over* left *struck out.*
  8^2, 9^2. A' *in the MS.*

40

THE QUEEN OF ELFAN'S NOURICE

Skene MSS, No 8, p. 25. Sharpe's *Ballad Book*, ed. Laing, p. 169.

WE see from this pretty fragment, which, after the nature of the best popular ballad, forces you to chant and will not be read, that a woman had been carried off, four days after bearing a son, to serve as nurse in the elf-queen's family. She is promised that she shall be permitted to return home if she will tend the fairy's bairn till he has got the use of his legs. We could well have spared stanzas 10–12, which belong to 'Thomas Rymer,' to know a little more of the proper story.

That elves and water-spirits have frequently solicited the help of mortal women at lying-in time is well known: see Stewart's *Popular Superstitions of the Highlands*, p. 104; Grimm, *Deutsche Sagen*, Nos 41, 49, 68, 69, 304; Müllenhoff, Nos 443, 444; Thiele, *Danmarks Folkesagen*, 1843, II, 200, Nos 1–4; Asbjørnsen, *Norske Huldre-Eventyr*, 2d ed., I, 16; Maurer, *Isländische Volkssagen*, p. 6f; Keightley's *Fairy Mythology*, pp 122, 261, 275, 301, 311, 388, 488; Hunt, *Popular Romances of the West of England* ed. 1881, p. 83; P. I. Begbie, *Supernatural Illusions*, London, 1851, I, 44–47; Bartsch, *Sagen, u. s. w., aus Meklenburg*, I, 85, No 95; Kuhn, *Märkische Sagen*, p. 82, No 81, and *Sagen, u. s. w., aus Westfalen*, I, 285f, No 331, and note; Grässe, *Sagen des Königreichs Sachsen*, 2d ed., I, 73, No 69, I, 395, No 455; Peter, *Volksthümliches aus Österreichisch-Schlesien*, II, 16; Lütolf, *Sagen, u. s. w., aus Lucern, u. s. w.*, p. 476, No 478; Rochholz, *Naturmythen*, p. 113f, No 9, and note, and especially the same author's *Schweizersagen aus dem Aargau*, I, 339: Wolf, *Niederländische Sagen*, p. 501, No 417; Árnason, *Íslenzkar Þjóðsögur*, I, 13–22 (eight); Sébillot, *Littérature orale de la Haute-Bretagne*, pp. 19–23; the same, *Traditions et Superstitions de la Haute-Bretagne*, I, 89, 109; Vinson, *Folk-Lore du Pays Basque*, pp. 40, 41; Meier, *Deutsche Sagen, u. s. w., aus Schwaben*, pp. 16–18, 59, 62; Mrs Bray, *Traditions of Devonshire*, 1838, I, 184–188 (in the new ed., which is called *The Borders of the Tamar and the Tavy*, I, 174ff.); "Lageniensis" [J. O'Hanlon], *Irish Folk-Lore*, Glasgow, n. d.; pp. 48, 49; U. Jahn, *Volkssagen aus Pommern und Rügen*, pp. 50, 72; Vonbun, *Die Sagen Vorarlbergs*, p. 16, cf. p. 6; Vernaleken, *Alpensagen*, p. 183; E. S. Hartland, *The Archæological Review*, IV, 328ff; Göngu-Hrólfs Saga, c. 15, Rafn, *Fornaldar Sögur*, III, 276, Ásmundarson, *Fornaldarsögur Norðrlanda*, III, 174, 175; 'La Sage-femme et la Fée,' R. Basset, *Contes pop. berbères*, 1887, No 26, p. 55 (and see notes, pp. 162, 163); Wucke, *Sagen der mittleren Werra*, II, 25; Gebhart, *Oesterreichisches Sagenbuch*, p. 208; Baader, *Neugesammelte Volkssagen*, No 95, p. 68; Kirk's *Secret Commonwealth*, ed. Lang, p. 13; *Denham Tracts*, II, 138.[*] They also like to have their offspring suckled by earthly women: Sébillot, *Contes populaires de la Haute-Bretagne*, I, 121. It is

---

[*] Many of these instances are cited by Grimm, *Deutsche Mythologie*, 1875, I, 378. In Thiele's first example the necessity of having Christian aid comes from the lying-in woman being a Christian who had been carried off by an elf. In Asbjørnsen's tale, the woman who is sent for to act as midwife finds that her own serving-maid is forced, without being aware of it, to work all night in the elfin establishment, and is very tired with double duty. In Göngu-Hrólfs Saga, the elf-woman's daughter has lain on the floor nineteen days in travail, for she cannot be delivered unless a mortal man lay hands upon her. Hrólfr is lured to the elf-woman's hall for this purpose.

said, writes Gervase of Tilbury, that nobody is more exposed to being carried off by water-sprites than a woman in milk, and that they *59]* sometimes restore such a woman, with pay for her services, after she has nursed their wretched fry seven years. He had himself seen a woman who had been abducted for this purpose, while washing clothes on the bank of the Rhone. She had to nurse the nix's son under the water for that term, and then was sent back unhurt. *Otia Imperialia*, III, 85, Liebrecht, p. 38. Choice is naturally made of the healthiest and handsomest mothers for this office. "A fine young woman of Nithsdale, when first made a mother, was sitting singing and rocking her child, when a pretty lady came into her cottage, covered with a fairy mantle. She carried a beautiful child in her arms, swaddled in green silk. 'Gie my bonnie thing a suck,' said the fairy. The young woman, conscious to whom the child belonged, took it kindly in her arms, and laid it to her breast. The lady instantly disappeared, saying, 'Nurse kin', an ne'er want.' The young mother nurtured the two babes, and was astonished, whenever she awoke, at finding the richest suits of apparel for both children, with meat of most delicious flavor. This food tasted, says tradition, like loaf mixed with wine and honey," etc. Cromek, *Remains of Nithsdale and Galloway Song*, p. 302.

I____ heard a cow low, a bonnie cow low, An a cow low down in glen;

Lang,____ lang____ will my____ young son greet Or his mith‑er bid____ him come ben.

W. Walker, Aberdeen. "Perhaps an improvised adaptation of a pibroch tune."

1 I HEARD a cow low, a bonnie cow low,
 An a cow low down in yon glen;
 Lang, lang will my young son greet
 Or his mither bid him come ben.

2 I heard a cow low, a bonnie cow low,
 An a cow low down in yon fauld;
 Lang, lang will my young son greet
 Or his mither take him frae cauld.

  * * * * *

3 .   . .   .

 Waken, Queen of Elfan,
  An hear your nourice moan.'

4 'O moan ye for your meat,
 Or moan ye for your fee,
 Or moan ye for the ither bounties
 That ladies are wont to gie?'

5 'I moan na for my meat,
 Nor moan I for my fee,
 Nor moan I for the ither bounties
 That ladies are wont to gie.

6 .   .   .   .

 But I moan for my young son
 I left in four nights auld.

7 'I moan na for my meat,
 Nor yet for my fee,
 But I mourn for Christen land,
 It's there I fain would be.'

8 'O nurse my bairn, nourice,' she says,
 'Till he stan at your knee,
 An ye 's win hame to Christen land,
 Whar fain it's ye wad be.

9 'O keep my bairn, nourice,
 Till he gang by the hauld,
 An ye 's win hame to your young son
 Ye left in four nights auld.'

*   *   *   *   *

10 'O nourice lay your head
  Upo my knee:
 See ye na that narrow road
  Up by yon tree?

11 . . . . .

  . . . .

 That's the road the righteous goes,
  And that's the road to heaven.

12 'An see na ye that braid road,
  Down by yon sunny fell?
 Yon's the road the wicked gae,
  An that's the road to hell.'

*   *   *   *   *

———◆———

1^1. an a bonnie cow low, *with an* crossed out.
2^2. yon fall: fauld *in margin*.
6^4. auld *not in MS., supplied from* 9^4.
7^3. Christend.
8^1. she says *is probably the comment of the singer or reciter*.

41

HIND ETIN

A. 'Young Akin,' Buchan's *Ballads of the North of Scotland*, I, 6. Motherwell's MS., p. 554.
B. 'Hynde Etin,' Kinloch's *Ancient Scottish Ballads*, p. 228.

C. 'Young Hastings,' Buchan, *Ballads of the North of Scotland*, II, 67. 'Young Hastings the Groom,' Motherwell's MS., p. 450; Motherwell's *Minstrelsy*, p. 287.

It is scarcely necessary to remark that this ballad, like too many others, has suffered severely by the accidents of tradition. **A** has been not simply damaged by passing through low mouths, but has been worked over by low hands. Something considerable has been lost from the story, and fine romantic features, preserved in Norse and German ballads, have been quite effaced.

Margaret, a king's daughter, **A**, an earl's daughter, **B**, a lady of noble birth, **C**, as she sits sewing in her bower door, hears a note in Elmond's wood and wishes herself there, **A**. The wood is Amon-shaw in **C**, Mulberry in **B**: the Elmond (Amond, Elfman?) is probably significant. So far the heroine resembles Lady Isabel in No 4, who, sewing in her bower, bears an elf-horn, and cannot resist the enchanted tone. Margaret makes for the wood as fast as she can go. The note that is heard in **A** is mistaken in **B** for *nuts*: Margaret, as she stands in her bower door, spies some nuts growing in the wood, and wishes herself there. Arrived at the wood, Margaret, in **A** as well as **B**, immediately takes to pulling nuts.[*] The lady is carried off in **C** under cover of a magical mist, and the hero in all is no ordinary hind.

Margaret has hardly pulled a nut, when she is confronted by young Akin, **A**, otherwise, and correctly, called Etin in **B**, a hind of giant strength in both, who accuses her of trespassing, and stops her. Akin pulls up the highest tree in the wood and builds a bower, invisible to passers-by, for their habitation. **B**, which recognizes no influence of enchantment upon the lady's will, as found in **A**, and no prepossession on her part, as in **C**, makes Hind Etin pull up the biggest tree in the forest as well, but it is to scoop out a cave many fathoms deep, in which he confines Margaret till she comes to terms, and consents to *go home* with him, wherever that may be. Hastings, another corruption of Etin, carries off the lady on his horse to the wood, "where again their loves are sworn," and there they take up their abode in a cave of stone, **C** 9. Lady Margaret lives with the etin seven years, and bears him seven sons, **A** 9; many years, and bears seven sons, **B**; ten years, and bears seven bairns, **C** 6, 8, 9.[†]

Once upon a time the etin goes hunting, and takes his eldest boy with him. The boy asks [361] his father why his mother is so often in tears, and the father says it is because she was born of high degree, but had been stolen by him; "is wife of Hynde Etin, wha ne'er got christendame," **B** 15. The etin, who could pull the

---

[*] This reading, *nuts*, may have subsequently made its way into **A** instead of *rose*, which it would be more ballad-like for Margaret to be plucking, as the maid does in 'Tam Lin,' where also the passage **A** 3–6, **B** 2–4 occurs. Grimm suggests a parallel to Tam Lin in the dwarf Laurin, who does not allow trespassing in his rose-garden: *Deutsche Mythologie*, III, 130. But the resemblance seems not material, there being no woman in the case. The pretence of trespass in Tam Lin and Hind Etin is a simple commonplace, and we have it in some Slavic forms of No 4, as at p. 60.

highest tree in the wood up by the roots, adds in **A** 15 that when he stole his wife he was her father's cup-bearer! and that he caught her "on a misty night," which reminds us of the mist which Young Hastings, "the groom," cast before the lady's attendants when he carried her off.

The next time Akin goes hunting he leaves his young comrade behind, and the boy tells his mother that he heard "fine music ring" when he was coming home, on the other occasion. She wishes she had been there. He takes his mother and six brothers, and they make their way through the wood at their best speed, not knowing in what direction they are going. But luckily they come to the gate of the king, the father and grandfather of the band. The mother sends her eldest boy in with three rings, to propitiate the porter, the butler-boy, who acts as usher in this particular palace, and the minstrel who plays before the king. His majesty is so struck with the resemblance of the boy to his daughter that he is blinded with tears. The boy informs his grandfather that his mother is standing at the gates, with six more brothers, and the king orders that she be admitted. He asks her to dine, but she can touch nothing till she has seen her mother and sister. Admitted to her mother, the queen in turn says, You will dine with me; but she can touch nothing till she has seen her sister. Her sister, again, invites her to dine, but now she can touch nothing till

she has seen her "dear husband." Rangers are sent into the wood to fetch Young Akin, under promise of a full pardon. He is found tearing his yellow hair. The king now asks Akin to dine with him, and there appears to have been a family dinner. While this is going on the boy expresses a wish to be christened, "to get christendoun;" in all his eight years he had never been in a church. The king promises that he shall go that very day with his mother, and all seven of the boys seem to have got their christendoun; and so, we may hope, did Hind Etin, who was, if possible, more in want of it than they; **B** 15, 19.

In this story **A** and **B** pretty nearly agree. **C** has nothing of the restoration of the lady to her parents and home. The mother, in this version, having harped her seven bairns asleep, sits down and weeps bitterly. She wishes, like Fair Annie, that they were rats, and she a cat, to eat them one and all. She has lived ten years in a stone cave, and has never had a churching. The eldest boy suggests that they shall all go to some church: they be christened and she be churched. This is accomplished without any difficulty, and, as the tale stands, we can only wonder that it had not been attempted before.

The etin of the Scottish story is in Norse and German a dwarf-king, elf-king, hill-king, or even a merman. The ballad is still sung in Scandinavia and Germany, but only the Danes have versions taken down before the present century.

Danish. 'Jomfruen og Dværgekongen,' Grundtvig, No 37, **A–C** from manuscripts of the sixteenth century. **A–G**, Grundtvig, II, 39–46; **H, I, III**, 806–808; **K–T**, IV, 795–800, **P–S** being short fragments. **K** previously in "Fylla," a weekly newspaper, 1870, Nos 23, 30; **L–O, Q, R**, 'Agnete i Bjærget,' in Kristensen's *Jyske Folkeviser*, II, 72, 77, 349, 74, I, xxxi, II, 79; **U**, a short fragment, *Danske Viser*, V, x, xi; **V**, 'Jomfruen og dværgen,' Kristensen, *Skattegraveren*, III, 98, No 393; **W**, a fragment of four stanzas, IV, 193, No 570; **X**, 'Agnete i Bjærget,' Kristensen, *Jyske Folkeminder*, X, 3, No 2; **Y**, 'Jomfruen i Bjærget,' fragment, in Kristensen, *Folkeminder*, XI, 6, No 12.

Swedish. 'Den Bergtagna,' **A, B**, Afzelius, I, 1, No 1, II, 201. **C**, 'Bergkonungen,' Afzelius, II,

† **B** is defective in the middle and the end. "The reciter, unfortunately, could not remember more of the ballad, although the story was strongly impressed on her memory. She related that the lady, after having been taken home by Hynde Etin, lived with him many years, and bore him seven sons, the eldest of whom, after the inquiries at his parents detailed in the ballad, determines to go in search of the earl, his grandfather. At his departure his mother instructs him how to proceed, giving him a ring to bribe the porter at her father's gate, and a silken vest, wrought by her own hand, to be worn in presence of her father. The son sets out, and arrives at the castle, where, by bribing the porter, he gets admission to the earl, who, struck with the resemblance of the youth to his lost daughter, and the similarity of the vest to one she had wrought for himself, examines the young man, from whom he discovers the fate of his daughter. He gladly receives his grandson, and goes to his daughter's residence, where he meets her and Hynde Etin, who is pardoned by the earl, through the intercession of his daughter." Kinloch, *Ancient Scottish Ballads*, p. 226f.

22, No 35. **D, E,** 'Herr Elver, Bergakonungen,' Arwidsson, II, 277, No 141 B, II, 275, No 141 A. **F,** 'Jungfrun och Bergakonungen,' Arwidsson, II, 280, No 142. **G,** 'Agneta och Bergamannen,' Wigström, *Folkdiktning,* p. 13. **H,** 'Jungfrun och Bergamannen,' the same, p. 21. **I, K, L,** in Cavallius and Stephens' manuscript collection (**K, L,** fragments), given by Grundtvig, IV, 803. **M,** F. L. Borgströms *Folkvisor,* No 11, described by Grundtvig, IV, 802. **N,** Werner's *Westergötlands Fornminnen,* p. 93f, two stanzas.

Norwegian. A, B,^{*} **C,** 'Liti Kersti, som vart inkvervd,' Landstad, p. 431, No 42, p. 442, No 44, p. 446, No 45. **D,** 'Margit Hjuxe, som vart inkvervd,' the same, p. 451, No 46. **E, F,** 'Målfri,' 'Antonetta,' Grundtvig, IV, 801f, the last evidently derived from Denmark. **G–P,** nine versions communicated to Grundtvig by Professor Sophus Bugge, and partially described in *Danmarks gamle Folkeviser,* III, 808–10. Lindeman gives the first stanza of **A** with airs No 214, No 262 of his *Fjeldmelodier,* and perhaps had different copies. Nos 323, 320 may also have been versions of this ballad. **C,** rewritten, occurs in J. M. Moe og Ivar Mortensen's *Norske Fornkvæde og Folkevisur,* p. 16. Mixed forms, in which the ballad proper is blended with another, Landstad, No 43 = Swedish, Arwidsson, No 145; eight, communicated by Bugge, Grundtvig, III, 810–13; two others, IV, 483f.†

Färöe. A, B, Grundtvig, IV, 803f.

Icelandic. 'Rika álfs kvæði,' *Íslenzk Fornkvæði,* No 4.

Danish **A,** one of the three sixteenth-century versions, tells how a knight, expressing a strong desire to obtain a king's daughter, is overheard by a dwarf, who says this shall never be. The dwarf pretends to bargain with the knight for his services in forwarding the knight's object, but consults meanwhile with his mother how he may get the lady for himself.‡ The mother tells him that the princess will go to even-song, and the dwarf writes runes on the way she must go by, which compel her to come to the hill. The dwarf holds out his hand and asks, How came ye to this strange land? to which the lady answers mournfully, I wot never how. The dwarf says, You have pledged yourself to a knight, and he has betrayed you with runes: this eve you shall be the dwarf's guest. She stayed there the night, and was taken back to her mother in the morning. Eight years went by; her hand was sought by five kings, nine counts, but no one of them could get a good answer. One day her mother asked, Why are thy cheeks so faded? Why can no one get thee? She then revealed that she had been beguiled by the dwarf, and had seven sons and a daughter in the hill, none of whom she ever saw. She thought she was alone, but the dwarf-king was listening. He strikes her with an elf-rod, and bids her hie to the hill after him. Late in the evening the poor thing dons her cloak, knocks at her father's door, and says goodnight to the friends that never will see her again, then sadly turns to the hill. Her seven sons advance to meet her, and ask why she told of their father. Her tears run sore; she gives no answer; she is dead ere midnight.

With **A** agrees another of the three old Danish copies, **B,** and three modern ones, **D, M, N,** have something of the opening scene which characterizes **A.** So also Swedish **C, I,** and the Icelandic ballad. In Swedish **C,** Proud Margaret, who is daughter of a king of seven kingdoms, will have none of her suitors (this circumstance comes too soon). A hill-king asks [363] his mother how he may get her. She asks in return, What will you give me to make her come of herself to the hill? He promises red gold and chestfuls of pence; and one Sunday morning Margaret, who has set out to go to church, is made—by magical operations, of course—to take the way to the hill.

A second form begins a stage later: Danish **C, G, K,** Swedish **D, E, K,** Norwegian **A, C, E,**

---

*   **B,** Landstad 44 (which has only this in common with the Scottish ballad, that a hill-man carries a maid to his cave), has much resemblance at the beginning to 'Kvindemorderen,' Grundtvig, No 183, our No 4. See Grundtvig's note ** at III, 810. This is only what might be looked for, since both ballads deal with abductions.

†   It is not necessary, for purposes of the English ballad, to notice these mixed forms.

‡   In 'Nøkkens Svig,' **C,** Grundtvig, No 39, the merman consults with his mother, and then, as also in other copies of the ballad, transforms himself into a knight. See the translation by Prior, III, 269; Jamieson, *Popular Ballads,* I, 210; Lewis, *Tales of Wonder,* I, 60.

G, H, I (?), K, L, M (?) N (?), Färöe A, B. We learn nothing of the device by which the maid has been entrapped. Mother and daughter are sitting in their bower, and the mother asks her child why her cheeks are pale, why milk is running from her breasts. She answers that she has been working too hard; that what is taken for milk is mead. The mother retorts that other women do not suffer from their industry; that mead is brown, and milk is white. Hereupon the daughter reveals that she has been beguiled by an elf, and, though living under her mother's roof, has had eight or nine children (seven or eight sons and a daughter; fifteen children, Färöe A, B), none of whom she ever saw, since after birth they were always transferred to the hill (see, especially, Danish C, G, also A; Norwegian H, I; Färöe A, B). The mother (who disowns her, Danish C, G, Swedish D, E, Norwegian K), in several versions, asks what gifts she got for her honor. Among these was a harp [horn, Norwegian L], which she was to play when she was unhappy. The mother asks for a piece, and the first tones bring the elf, who reproaches the daughter for betraying him: had she concealed their connection she might still have lived at home, C; but now she must go with him. She is kindly received by her children. They give her a drink which makes her forget father and mother, heaven and earth, moon and sun, and even makes her think she was born in the hill, Danish C, G, Swedish D, Norwegian A, C.*

Danish G, K, Färöe A, B, take a tragic turn: the woman dies in the first two the night she comes to the hill. Danish C, one of the sixteenth-century versions, goes as far as possible in the other direction. The elfking pats Maldfred's cheek, takes her in his arms, gives her a queen's crown and name.

> And this he did for the lily-wand,
> He had himself christened and all his land!

A third series of versions offers the probable type of the much-corrupted Scottish ballads, and under this head come Danish E, F, H, I, L–R, T; Swedish A, B, F–I, and also C, after an introduction which belongs to the first class; Norwegian D, F. The characteristic feature is

that the woman has been living eight or nine years in the hill, and has there borne her children, commonly seven sons and a daughter. She sets out to go to matins, and whether under the influence of runes, or accidentally, or purposely, takes the way to the hill. In a few cases it is clear that she does not seek the hill-man or put herself in his way, e.g., Danish N, Swedish G, but Swedish A, H, N make her apply for admission at the hill-door. In Danish I, N–R, T, Norwegian F, it is not said that she was on her way to church; she is in a field or in the hill. In Swedish F she has been two years in the cave, and it seems to her as if she had come yesterday. After her eight or nine years with the hill-man the woman longs to go home, Danish E, F, I, Swedish A, F, I, Norwegian D; to go to church, Danish L, M, N, P, T, Norwegian F; for she had heard Denmark's bells, church bells, Danish L–P, T, Swedish G, Norwegian D, F. She had [³ heard these bells as she watched the cradle, Danish T, P, Swedish G; sat by the cradle and sang, T 4; compare English C 7. She asks the hill-man's permission, and it is granted on certain terms: she is not to talk of him and her life in the hill, Danish E, I, Swedish A, F, I, is to come back, Danish F, must not stay longer than an hour or two, Norwegian D; she is not to wear her gold, her best clothes, not to let out her hair, not to go into her mother's pew at the church, not to bow when the priest pronounces the holy name, or make an offering, or go home

---

* The beauty of the Norse ballads should make an Englishman's heart wring for his loss. They are particularly pretty here, where the forgetful draught is administered; as Norwegian C, A:

> Forth came her daughter, as jimp as a wand,
> She dances a dance, with silver can in hand.
> 'O where wast thou bred, and where wast thou born?
> And where were thy maiden-garments shorn?'
> 'In Norway was I bred, in Norway was I born,
> And in Norway were my maiden-garments shorn.'
> The ae first drink from the silver can she drank,
> What stock she was come of she clean forgat.
> 'O where wast thou bred, and where wast thou born?
> And where were thy maiden-garments shorn?'
> 'In the hill was I bred, and there was I born,
> In the hill were my maiden-garments shorn.'

Compare, for style, the beginning of 'Hind Horn' G, H, pp 281, 282.

after service, etc., Danish **I, L–P, T**, Norwegian **F**. All these last conditions she violates, nor does she in the least heed the injunction not to speak of the hill-man. The consequence is that he summarily presents himself, whether at the church or the paternal mansion, and orders her back to the hill, sometimes striking her on the ear or cheek so that blood runs, or beating her with a rod, Danish **E, I, L, M, S, T**, Swedish **A, B, C, H, I**, Norwegian **F**. In a few versions, the hill-man tells her that her children are crying for her, and she replies, Let them cry; I will never go back to the hill; Danish **M, N, O**, Norwegian **F**. In Danish **E**, Swedish **G**, a gold apple thrown into her lap seems to compel her to return; more commonly main force is used. She is carried dead into the hill, or dies immediately on her arrival, in Norwegian **F**, Danish **T**; she dies of grief, according to traditional comment, in Norwegian **D**. They give her a drink, and her heart breaks, Swedish **A, G, H, M**; but elsewhere the drink only induces forgetfulness, Danish **L, M**, Swedish **B, C, F**.

Much of the story of 'Jomfruen og Dværgekongen' recurs in the ballad of 'Agnete og Havmanden,' which, for our purposes, may be treated as a simple variation of the other. The Norse forms are again numerous, but all from broadsides dating, at most, a century back, or from recent tradition.

Danish. 'Agnete og Havmanden,' Grundtvig, No 38, **A–D**, II, 51ff, 656ff, III, 813ff. Copies of **A** are numerous, and two had been previously printed; in *Danske Viser*, I, 313, No 50, and "in Barfod's Brage og Idun, II, 264." **E**, Rask's *Morskabslæsning*, III, 81, Grundtvig, II, 659. **F**, one stanza, Grundtvig, p. 660. **G, H**, the same, III, 816. **I**, Kristensen, II, 75, No 28 C, Grundtvig, IV, 807. **K**, Grundtvig, IV, 808;* **L**, 'Angenede og havmanden,' Kristensen, *Skattegraveren*, III, 17, No 34; **M–O**, 'Agnete i Havet,' Kristensen, *Jyske Folkeminder*, X, 6, No 3, A–C; **P**, 'Agnete og Havmanden,' Kristensen, *Skatte-*

graveren, III, p. 17, No 34, XII, 65ff, Nos 136, 137; **Q**, Efterslæt, p. 2, No 2, p. 174, No 126; **R**, *Folkeminder*, XI, 7, No 13, A–D.

Swedish. A, B, C, in Cavallius and Stephens' unprinted collection, described by Grundtvig, II, 661. **D**, 'Agneta och Hafsmannen,' Eva Wigström's *Folkdiktning*, p. 9. **E**, Bergström's Afzelius, II, 308. **F**, 'Skön Anna och Hafskungen,' Aminson, *Bidrag till Södermanlands äldre Kulturhistoria*, III, 43. **G**, 'Helena och Hafsmannen,' the same, p. 46.

Norwegian. A, Grundtvig, III, 817, properly Danish rather than Norwegian. **B**, a version partly described at p. 818. **C**, Grundtvig, IV, 809, also more Danish than Norwegian. All these communicated by Bugge.

Danish **C, G**, Norwegian **A**, have a hill-man instead of a merman, and might as well have been put with the other ballad. On the other hand, the Danish versions **M, N, O** of 'The Maid and the Dwarf-King' call the maid Agenet, and give the hill-man a name, Nek, Netmand, Mekmand, which implies a watery origin for him, and the fragments **P, Q, R** have similar names, Nekmand, Negen, Lækkemand, as also Agenete, and might as well have been ranked with 'Agnes and the Merman.' In 'The Maid and the Dwarf-King,' Swedish **L** (one stanza) the maid is taken by "Pel Elfven" to the sea.

Agnes goes willingly with the merman to the sea-bottom, Danish **A, D, E, K**, Swedish **A, D, E**, Norwegian **A, C**. She lives there, according to many versions, eight years, and has seven children. As she is sitting and singing by the cradle one day, she hears the bells of England, Danish **A, C, D, E, H, I, K**, Swedish **D** [church bells, bells, **F, G**], Norwegian **A, C**. She asks if she may go to church, go home, and receives [365] permission on the same terms as in the other ballad. Her mother asks her what gifts she had received, Danish **A, D, E, H, I**, Swedish **E, F**, Norwegian **C**. When the merman comes into the church all the images turn their backs, Danish **A, D, K**, Swedish **D, F, G**, Norwegian **A, C**; and, in some cases, for Agnes, too. He tells her that the children are crying for her; she refuses to go back, Danish **A, C, D, I, K**, Swedish **D, F, G** (and apparently **A, B, C**), Norwegian **C**. In Norwegian **A** the merman strikes her

---

* For reasons, doubtless sufficient, but to me unknown, Grundtvig has not noticed two copies in Boisen's *Nye og gamle Viser*, 10th edition, p. 192, p. 194. The former of these is like **A**, with more resemblance here and there to other versions, and may be a made-up copy; the other, 'Agnete og Bjærgmanden, fra Sønderjylland,' consists of stanzas 1–5 of **C**.

on the cheek, and she returns; in Danish **I** she is taken back quietly; in Danish **C** he gives her so sore an ail that she dies presently; in Danish **H** she is taken away by force, and poisoned by her children; in Danish **K** the merman says that if she stays with her mother they must divide the children (five). He takes two, she two, and each has to take half of the odd one.

The Norse forms of 'Agnes and the Merman' are conceded to have been derived from Germany: see Grundtvig, IV, 812. Of the **German** ballad, which is somewhat nearer to the English, the following versions have been noted:

A. 'Die schöne Agniese,' Fiedler, *Volksreime und Volkslieder in Anhalt-Dessau*, p. 140, No 1 = Mittler, No 553. **B.** 'Die schöne Agnese,' Parisius, *Deutsche Volkslieder in der Altmark und im Magdeburgischen gesammelt*, p. 29, No 8 **B**, from nearly the same region as **A**. **C.** Parisius, p. 28, No 8 A, Pechau on the Elbe. **D.** 'Die schöne Angnina,' Erk's *Neue Sammlung*, ii, 40, No 26 = Mittler, No 552, from the neighborhood of Magdeburg. **E.** 'Die Schöne Agnete,' Erk's *Liederhort*, No 16[a], p. 47, Erk's *Wunderhorn*, IV, 91, from the neighborhood of Guben. **F.** 'Die schöne Dorothea,' *Liederhort*, No 16[b], p. 48, Gramzow in der Ukermark. **G.** 'Die schöne Hannăle,' *Liederhort*, No 16, p. 44, Erk's *Wunderhorn*, IV, 87, Silesia. **H.** 'Die schöne Hannele,' Hoffmann u. Richter, *Schlesische Volkslieder*, p. 3, No 1 = Mittler, No 551, Böhme, No 90 A, Breslau. 'Der Wassermann,' Simrock, No 1, is a compounded copy. **I**, Birlinger u. Crecelius, *Deutsche Lieder*, Festgruss an L. Erk, No 1, 3 stanzas. (R. Köhler.) **J.** 'Die schöne Dorothea,' Gadde-Gloddow, *V. l. aus Hinterpommern, Zeitschrift hir Volkskunde*, III, 227.

A wild merman has become enamored of the King of England's daughter, **A, B, C, D**. He plates a bridge with gold; she often walks over the bridge; it sinks with her into the water [the merman drags her down into the water, **H**]. She stays below seven years, and bears seven sons. One day [by the cradle, **C, G**] she hears the bells of England, **A** 6, **B, C, D, F** [bells, **E, G, H**], and longs to go to church. She expresses this wish to the merman, **C, D, G, H**. The merman says she must take her seven sons with her, **B, C, D**; she must come back, **G, H**. She takes

her seven sons by the hand, and goes with them to England, **A** 5, **B** 7; cf. Scottish **C** 13, 14, **A** 22, 50. When she enters the church everything in it bows, **A, B, F**. Her parents are there, **C, D**; her father opens the pew, her mother lays a cushion for her, **G, H**. As she goes out of the church, there stands the merman, **A, B, E, F**. Her parents take her home in **D, G, H**. They seat her at the table, and while she is eating, a gold apple falls into her lap (cf. 'The Maid and the Dwarf-King,' Danish **E**, Swedish **G**), which she begs her mother to throw into the fire; the merman appears, and asks if she wishes him burnt, **G, H**. The merman, when he presents himself at the church, asks whether the woman will go back with him, or die where she is, and she prefers death on the spot, **A, B, E**. In the other case, he says that if she will not return, the children must be divided,—three and three, and half of the seventh to each; the mother prefers the water to this. **D** has a peculiar and not very happy trait. The merman fastens a chain to his wife's foot before she goes up, and, having been kept long waiting, draws it in. But the people at the church have taken off the chain, and he finds nothing at the end of it. He asks whether she does not wish to live with him; she replies, I will no longer torment you, or fret myself to death.

The story of Agnes and the Merman occurs in a Wendish ballad, with an introductory seene found in the beautiful German ballad, 'Wassermanns Brant:'[*] Haupt und Schmaler, I, 62, No 34. A maid begs that she may be left to herself for a year, but her father says it is time for her to be married. She goes to her chamber, weeps and wrings her hands. The merman comes and asks, Where is my bride? They tell him that she is in her chamber, weeping and wringing her hands. The merman asks her the reason, and she answers, They all say that you are the merwoman's son. He says he will build her a bridge of pure silver and gold, and have her driven over it with thirty carriages and forty horses; but ere she has half passed the bridge it goes down to the bottom. She is seven years

---

[*]   See five versions in Mittler, Nos 546–550. As Grundtvig remarks, what is one ballad in Wendish is two in German and three in Norse: *D. g. F.*, IV, 810.

below, has seven sons in as many years, and is going with the eighth. She implores her husband to permit her to go to church in the upper world, and he consents, with the proviso that she shall not stay for the benediction. At church she sees her brother and sister, who receive her kindly. She tells them that she cannot stay till the benediction;* they beg her to come home to dine with them. She does wait till the benediction; the merman rushes frantically about. As she leaves the church and is saying good-by to her sister, she meets the merman, who snatches the youngest child from her (she appears to have all seven with her), tears it in pieces, strangles the rest, scatters their limbs on the road, and hangs himself, asking, Does not your heart grieve for your children? She answers, I grieve for none but the youngest.†

A Slovenian ballad has the story with modifications, Achacel and Korytko, Şlovénşke Péşmi krajnskiga Naróda, I, 30,‡ 'Povodnji mósh;' given in abstract by Haupt and Schmaler, I, 339, note to No. 34. Mizika goes to a dance, in spite of her mother's forbidding. Her mother, in a rage, wishes that the merman may fetch her. A young man who dances with her whirls her round so furiously that she complains, but he becomes still more violent. Mizika sees how it is, and exclaims, The merman has come for me! The merman flies out of the window with her, and plunges into the water. She bears a son, and asks leave to pay a visit to her mother; and this is allowed on conditions,

one of which is that she shall not expose herself to a benediction. She does not conform, and the merman comes and says that her son is crying for her. She refuses to go with him, and he tears the boy in two, that each may have a half.

Two or three of the minuter correspondences between the Scottish and the Norse or German ballads, which have not been referred to, may be indicated in conclusion. The hillman, in several Norwegian copies, as **B, M**, carries off the lady on horseback, and so Hastings in **C**. In **A** 34–39, the returned sister, being invited to dine, cannot eat a bit or drink a drop. So, in 'The Maid and the Dwarf-King,' Swedish **G** 15, 16, they set before Agnes dishes four and five, dishes eight and nine, but she can take nothing:

Agneta ej smakte en endaste bit.

Young Akin, in **A** 43, is found in the wood, "tearing his yellow hair." The merman has golden hair in Danish **A** 16, Swedish **D** 2, 19, Norwegian **A** 17 (nothing very remarkable, certainly), and in Danish **D** 31 wrings his hands and is very unhappy, because Agnes refuses to return. It is much more important that in one of the Swedish copies of the merman ballad, Grundtvig, II, 661a, we find a trace of the 'christendom' which is made such an object in the Scottish ballads:

'Nay,' said the mother, 'now thou art mine,'
And christened her with water and with wine.

'The Maid and the Dwarf-King,' Danish **E**, is translated by Prior, III, 338; Swedish **A** by Stephens, *Foreign Quarterly Review*, XXV, 35; Swedish **C** by Keightley, *Fairy Mythology*, p. 103. [367] 'Agnes and the Merman,' Danish **A, C**, by Prior, III, 332, 335; some copy of **A** by Borrow, p. 120; Øhlenschlæger's ballad by Buchanan, p. 76.

Scottish **B** is translated, after Allingham, by Knortz, *Lieder u. Romanzen*, No 30; **A** 1–8, **C** 6–14, by Rosa Warrens, *Schottische Volkslieder*, No 2; a compounded version by Roberts into German by Podhorszki, *Acta Comparationis, etc.*, VIII, 69–73.

---

* This trait, corresponding to the prohibition in the Norse ballads of bowing when the holy name is pronounced, occurs frequently in tradition, as might be expected. In a Swedish merman-ballad, 'Necken,' Afzelius, III, 133, the nix, who has attended to church the lady whom he is about to kidnap, makes off with his best speed when the priest reads the benediction. See, further, Árnason's *Íslenzkar Þjóðsögur*, I, 73f; Maurer's *Isländische Volkssagen*, 19f; Liebrecht, Gervasius, p. 26, LVII, and p. 126, note (Grundtvig).

† The merfolk are apt to be ferocious, as compared with hill-people, elves, etc. See Grimm, *Deutsche Mythologie*, I, 409f.

‡ I 79, of a second edition, which, says Vraz, has an objectionable fantastic spelling due to the publisher.

A

Buchan's *Ballads of the North of Scotland*, I, 6; Moth-
erwell's MS., p. 554.

1 LADY MARGARET sits in her bower door,
  Sewing at her silken seam;
She heard a note in Elmond's wood,
  And wishd she there had been.

2 She loot the seam fa frae her side,
  And the needle to her tae,
And she is on to Elmond's wood
  As fast as she coud gae.

3 She hadna pu'd a nut, a nut,
  Nor broken a branch but ane,
Till by it came a young hind chiel,
  Says, Lady, lat alane.

4 O why pu ye the nut, the nut,
  Or why brake ye the tree?
For I am forester o this wood:
  Ye shoud spier leave at me.

5 'I'll ask leave at no living man,
  Nor yet will I at thee;
My father is king oer a' this realm,
  This wood belongs to me.'

6 She hadna pu'd a nut, a nut,
  Nor broken a branch but three,
Till by it came him Young Akin,
  And gard her lat them be.

7 The highest tree in Elmond's wood,
  He's pu'd it by the reet,
And he has built for her a bower,
  Near by a hallow seat.

8 He's built a bower, made it secure
  Wi carbuncle and stane;
Tho travellers were never sae nigh,
  Appearance it had nane.

9 He's kept her there in Elmond's wood,
  For six lang years and one,
Till six pretty sons to him she bear,
  And the seventh she's brought home.

10 It fell ance upon a day,
  This guid lord went from home,
And he is to the hunting gane,
  Took wi him his eldest son.

11 And when they were on a guid way,
  Wi slowly pace did walk,
The boy's heart being something wae,
  He thus began to talk:

12 'A question I woud ask, father,
  Gin ye woudna angry be:'
'Say on, say on, my bonny boy,
  Ye 'se nae be quarrelld by me.'

13 'I see my mither's cheeks aye weet,
  I never can see them dry;
And I wonder what aileth my mither,
  To mourn continually.'

14 'Your mither was a king's daughter,
  Sprung frae a high degree,
And she might hae wed some worthy prince,
  Had she nae been stown by me.

15 'I was her father's cup-bearer,
  Just at that fatal time;
I catchd her on a misty night,
  Whan summer was in prime.

16 'My luve to her was most sincere,
  Her luve was great for me,
But when she hardships doth endure,
  Her folly she does see.'

17 'I'll shoot the huntin o the bush,
  The linnet o the tree,
And bring them to my dear mither,
  See if she'll merrier be.'

18 It fell upo another day,
  This guid lord he thought lang,
And he is to the hunting gane,
  Took wi him his dog and gun.

19 Wi bow and arrow by his side,
  He's aff, single, alane,
  And left his seven children to stay
  Wi their mither at hame.

20 'O I will tell to you, mither,
  Gin ye wadna angry be:'
  'Speak on, speak on, my little wee boy,
  Ye 'se nae be quarrelld by me.'

21 'As we came frae the hynd-hunting,
  We heard fine music ring:'
  'My blessings on you, my bonny boy,
  I wish I'd been there my lane.'

22 He's taen his mither by the hand,
  His six brithers also,
  And they are on thro Elmond's wood,
  As fast as they coud go.

23 They wistna weel where they were gaen,
  Wi the stratlins o their feet;
  They wistna weel where they were gaen,
  Till at her father's yate.

24 'I hae nae money in my pocket,
  But royal rings hae three;
  I'll gie them you, my little young son,
  And ye'll walk there for me.

25 'Ye'll gie the first to the proud porter,
  And he will lat you in;
  Ye'll gie the next to the butler-boy,
  And he will show you ben;

26 'Ye'll gie the third to the minstrel
  That plays before the king;
  He'll play success to the bonny boy
  Came thro the wood him lane.'

27 He gae the first to the proud porter,
  And he opend an let him in;
  He gae the next to the butler-boy,
  And he has shown him ben;

28 He gae the third to the minstrel
  That playd before the king;
  And he playd success to the bonny boy
  Came thro the wood him lane.

29 Now when he came before the king,
  Fell low down on his knee;
  The king he turned round about
  And the saut tear blinded his ee.

30 'Win up, win up, my bonny boy,
  Gang frae my companie;
  Ye look sae like my dear daughter,
  My heart will birst in three.'

31 'If I look like your dear daughter,
  A wonder it is none;
  If I look like your dear daughter,
  I am her eldest son.'

32 'Will ye tell me, ye little wee boy,
  Where may my Margaret be?'
  'She's just now standing at your yates,
  And my six brithers her wi.'

33 'O where are all my porter-boys
  That I pay meat and fee,
  To open my yates baith wide and braid?
  Let her come in to me.'

34 When she came in before the king,
  Fell low down on her knee;
  'Win up, win up, my daughter dear,
  This day ye'll dine wi me.'

35 'Ae bit I canno eat, father,
  Nor ae drop can I drink,
  Till I see my mither and sister dear,
  For lang for them I think.'

36 When she came before the queen,
  Fell low down on her knee;
  'Win up, win up, my daughter dear
  This day ye 'se dine wi me.'

37 'Ae bit I canno eat, mither,
  Nor ae drop can I drink,
  Until I see my dear sister,
  For lang for her I think.'

38 When that these two sisters met,
  She haild her courteouslie;
  'Come ben, come ben, my sister dear,
  This day ye 'se dine wi me.'

[369] 39 'Ae bit I canno eat, sister,
  Nor ae drop can I drink,
  Until I see my dear husband,
  For lang for him I think.'

40 'O where are all my rangers bold
  That I pay meat and fee,
  To search the forest far an wide,
  And bring Akin to me?'

41 Out it speaks the little wee boy:
  Na, na, this maunna be;
  Without ye grant a free pardon,
  I hope ye'll nae him see.

42 'O here I grant a free pardon,
  Well seald by my own han;
  Ye may make search for Young Akin,
  As soon as ever you can.'

43 They searchd the country wide and braid,
  The forests far and near,
  And found him into Elmond's wood,
  Tearing his yellow hair.

44 'Win up, win up now, Young Akin,
  Win up, and boun wi me;
  We're messengers come from the court,
  The king wants you to see.'

45 'O lat him take frae me my head,
  Or hang me on a tree;
  For since I've lost my dear lady,
  Life's no pleasure to me.'

46 'Your head will nae be touchd, Akin,
  Nor hangd upon a tree;
  Your lady's in her father's court,
  And all he wants is thee.'

47 When he came in before the king,
  Fell low down on his knee;
  'Win up, win up now, Young Akin,
  This day ye 'se dine wi me.'

48 But as they were at dinner set,
  The boy asked a boun:
  'I wish we were in the good church,
  For to get christendoun.

49 'We hae lived in guid green wood
  This seven years and ane;
  But a' this time, since eer I mind,
  Was never a church within.'

50 'Your asking's nae sae great, my boy,
  But granted it shall be;
  This day to guid church ye shall gang,
  And your mither shall gang you wi.'

51 When unto the guid church she came,
  She at the door did stan;
  She was sae sair sunk down wi shame,
  She coudna come farer ben.

52 Then out it speaks the parish priest,
  And a sweet smile gae he:
  'Come ben, come ben, my lily flower,
  Present your babes to me.'

53 Charles, Vincent, Sam and Dick,
  And likewise James and John;
  They calld the eldest Young Akin,
  Which was his father's name.

54 Then they staid in the royal court,
  And livd wi mirth and glee,
  And when her father was deceasd,
  Heir of the crown was she.

B

Kinloch's *Ancient Scottish Ballads*, p. 228.

1 MAY MARGRET stood in her bouer door,
    Kaiming doun her yellow hair;
    She spied some nuts growin in the wud,
    And wishd that she was there.

2 She has plaited her yellow locks
    A little abune her bree,
    And she has kilted her petticoats
    A little below her knee,
    And she's aff to Mulberry wud,
    As fast as she could gae.

3 She had na pu'd a nut, a nut,
    A nut but barely ane,
    Till up started the Hynde Etin,
    Says, Lady, let thae alane!

4 'Mulberry wuds are a' my ain;
    My father gied them me,
    To sport and play when I thought lang;
    And they sall na be tane by thee.'

5 And ae she pu'd the tither berrie,
    Na thinking o' the skaith,
    And said, To wrang ye, Hynde Etin,
    I wad be unco laith.

6 But he has tane her by the yellow locks,
    And tied her till a tree,
    And said, For slichting my commands,
    An ill death sall ye dree.

7 He pu'd a tree out o the wud,
    The biggest that was there,
    And he howkit a cave monie fathoms deep,
    And put May Margret there.

8 'Now rest ye there, ye saucie may;
    My wuds are free for thee;
    And gif I tak ye to mysell,
    The better ye'll like me.'

9 Na rest, na rest May Margret took,
    Sleep she got never nane;
    Her back lay on the cauld, cauld floor,
    Her head upon a stane.

10 'O tak me out,' May Margret cried,
    'O tak me hame to thee,
    And I sall be your bounden page
    Until the day I dee.'

11 He took her out o the dungeon deep,
    And awa wi him she's gane;
    But sad was the day an earl's dochter
    Gaed hame wi Hynde Etin.

*   *   *   *   *

12 It fell out ance upon a day
    Hynde Etin's to the hunting gane,
    And he has tane wi him his eldest son,
    For to carry his game.

13 'O I wad ask ye something, father,
    An ye wadna angry be;'
    'Ask on, ask on, my eldest son,
    Ask onie thing at me.'

14 'My mother's cheeks are aft times weet,
    Alas! they are seldom dry;'
    'Na wonder, na wonder, my eldest son,
    Tho she should brast and die.

15 'For your mother was an earl's dochter,
    Of noble birth and fame,
    And now she's wife o Hynde Etin,
    Wha neer got christendame.

16 'But we'll shoot the laverock in the lift,
    The buntlin on the tree,
    And ye'll tak them hame to your mother,
    And see if she'll comforted be.'

*   *   *   *   *

17 'I wad ask ye something, mother,
    An ye wadna angry be;'
    'Ask on, ask on, my eldest son,
    Ask onie thing at me.'

18 'Your cheeks they are aft times weet,
    Alas! they're seldom dry;'
    'Na wonder, na wonder, my eldest son,
    Tho I should brast and die.

19 'For I was ance an earl's dochter,
    Of noble birth and fame,
    And now I am the wife of Hynde Etin,
    Wha neer got christendame.'

*   *   *   *   *

C

Buchan's *Ballads of the North of Scotland*, II, 67,
communicated by Mr James Nicol, of Strichen; Moth-
erwell's *Minstrelsy*, p. 287; Motherwell's MS., p. 450.

1 'O WELL like I to ride in a mist,
    And shoot in a northern win,
  And far better a lady to steal,
    That's come of a noble kin.'

2 Four an twenty fair ladies
    Put on this lady's sheen,
  And as mony young gentlemen
    Did lead her ower the green.

[371] 3 Yet she preferred before them all
    Him, young Hastings the Groom;
  He's coosten a mist before them all,
    And away this lady has taen.

4 He's taken the lady on him behind,
    Spared neither grass nor corn,
  Till they came to the wood o Amonshaw,
    Where again their loves were sworn.

5 And they hae lived in that wood
    Full mony a year and day,
  And were supported from time to time
    By what he made of prey.

6 And seven bairns, fair and fine,
    There she has born to him,
  And never was in gude church-door,
    Nor ever got gade kirking.

7 Ance she took harp into her hand,
    And harped them a' asleep,
  Then she sat down at their couch-side,
    And bitterly did weep.

8 Said, Seven bairns hae I born now
    To my lord in the ha;
  I wish they were seven greedy rats,
    To run upon the wa,
  And I mysel a great grey cat,
    To eat them ane and a'.

9 For ten lang years now I hae lived
    Within this cave of stane,
  And never was at gude church-door,
    Nor got no gude churching.

10 O then out spake her eldest child,
    And a fine boy was he:
  O hold your tongue, my mother dear;
    I'll tell you what to dee.

11 Take you the youngest in your lap,
    The next youngest by the hand,
  Put all the rest of us you before,
    As you learnt us to gang.

12 And go with us unto some kirk—
    You say they are built of stane—
  And let us all be christened,
    And you get gude kirking.

13 She took the youngest in her lap,
    The next youngest by the hand,
  Set all the rest of them her before,
    As she learnt them to gang.

14 And she has left the wood with them,
    And to the kirk has gane,
  Where the gude priest them christened,
    And gave her gude kirking.

———◆———

C. *Motherwell's copies exhibit five or six slight variations from Buchan.*

42

CLERK COLVILL

A. 'Clark Colven,' from a transcript of No 13 of William Tytler's Brown MS.

B. 'Clerk Colvill, or, The Mermaid,' Herd's *Ancient and Modern Scots Songs*, 1769, p. 302.

C. W. F. in *Notes and Queries*, Fourth Series, VIII, 510, from the recitation of a lady in Forfarshire.

ALTHOUGH, as has been already said, William Tytler's Brown manuscript is now not to be found, a copy of two of its fifteen ballads has been preserved in the Fraser Tytler family, and 'Clerk Colvill,' **A** ('Clark Colven') is one of the two.[*] This ballad is not in Jamieson's Brown manuscript. Rewritten by Lewis, **A** was published in *Tales of Wonder*, 1801, II, 445, No 56. **B**, 1769, is the earliest printed English copy, but a corresponding Danish ballad antedates its publication by seventy-five years. Of **C**, W. F., who communicated it to *Notes and Queries*, says: "I have reason to believe that it is originally from the same source as that from which Scott, and especially Jamieson, derived many of their best ballads." This source should be no other than Mrs Brown, who certainly may have known two versions of Clerk Colvill; but **C** is markedly different from **A**. An Abbotsford manuscript, entitled "Scottish Songs," has, at fol. 3, a version which appears to have been made up from Lewis's copy, its original, **A**, and Herd's, **B**.

All the English versions are deplorably imperfect, and **C** is corrupted, besides. The story which they afford is this. Clerk Colvill, newly married as we may infer, is solemnly entreated by his gay lady never to go near a well-fared may who haunts a certain spring or water. It is clear that before his marriage he had been in the habit of resorting to this mermaid, as she is afterwards called, and equally clear, from the impatient answer which he renders his dame, that he means to visit her again. His coming is hailed with pleasure by the mermaid, who, in the course of their interview, does something which gives him a strange pain in the head,—a pain only increased by a prescription which she pretends will cure it, and, as she then exultingly tells him, sure to grow worse until he is dead. He draws his sword on her, but she merrily springs into the water. He mounts his horse, rides home tristful, alights heavily, and bids his mother make his bed, for all is over with him.

C is at the beginning blended with verses which belong to 'Willie and May Margaret,' Jamieson, I, 135 (from Mrs Brown's recitation), or 'The Drowned Lovers,' Buchan, I, 140. In this ballad a mother adjures her son not to go wooing, under pain of her curse. He goes, nevertheless, and is drowned. It is obvious, without remark, that the band and belt in **C** 1 do not suit the mother; neither does the phrase 'love Colin' in the second stanza.[†] **C** 9–11 afford an important variation from the other versions. The mermaid appears at the foot of the young man's bed, and offers him a choice between

---

[*] "From a MS. in my grandfather's writing, with the following note: Copied from an old MS. in the possession of Alexander Fraser Tytler." Note of Miss Mary Fraser Tytler. The first stanza agrees with that which is cited from the original by Dr Anderson in Nichols's *Illustrations*, VII, 177, and the number of stanzas is the same.

Colvill, which has become familiar from Herd's copy, is the correct form, and Colven, Colvin, a vulgarized one, which in **C** lapses into Colin.

dying then and living with her in the water. (See the Norwegian ballads at p. 504.)

Clerk Colvill is not, as his representative is or may be in other ballads, the guiltless and guileless object of the love or envy of a water-sprite or elf. His relations with the mermaid began before his marriage with his gay lady, and his death is the natural penalty of his desertion of the water-nymph; for no point is better established than the fatal consequences of inconstancy in such connections.* His history, were it fully told, would closely resemble that of the Knight of Staufenberg, as narrated in a German poem of about the year 1300.[†]

[373] The already very distinguished chevalier, Peter Diemringer, of Staufenberg (in the Ortenau, Baden, four leagues from Strassburg), when riding to mass one Whitsunday, saw a lady of surpassing beauty, dressed with equal magnificence, sitting on a rock by the wayside. He became instantaneously enamored, and, greeting the lady in terms expressive of his admiration, received no discouraging reply. The

† Still, though these *particular verses* appear to have come from 'The Drowned Lovers,' they may represent other original ones which were to the same effect. See, further on, the beginning of some Färöe versions.

* Hoc equidem a viris omni exceptione majoribus quotidie scimus probatum, quod quosdam hujusmodi larvarum quas fadas nominant amatores audivimus, et cum ad aliarum foeminarum matrimonia se transtulerunt, ante mortuos quam cum superinductis carnali se copula immiscuerunt. Des Gervasius von Tilbury Otia Imperialia (of about 1211), Liebrecht, p. 41.

† Der Ritter von Stauffenberg, from a MS. of perhaps 1437, C. M. Engelhardt, Strassburg, 1823. Edited by Oskar Jänicke, in *Altdeutsche Studien* von O. Jänicke, E. Steinmeyer, W. Wilmanns, Berlin, 1871. *Die Legende vom Ritter Herrn Peter Diemringer von Staufenberg in der Ortenau*, reprint by F. Culemann of the Strassburg edition of Martin Schott, 1480–82. The old printed copy was made by Fischart in 1588 (Jobin, Strassburg, in that year), this 'ernewerte Beschreibung der alten Geschicht' is rehashed in seven 'Romanzen' in *Wunderhorn*, I, 407–18, ed. 1806, 401–12, ed. 1853. Simrock, *Die deutschen Volksbücher*, III, 1–48. See the edition by Edward Schröder: *Zwei altdeutsche Rittermåren*, Moriz von Craon, Peter von Staufenberg. Berlin, 1894. Schröder dates the composition of the poem about 1310 (p. LI). He shows that Schott's edition, which Culemann followed, was a reprint of one printed by Prüss in 1483 at the earliest, but thinks that it followed that of Prüss at no long interval (p. XXXIV). Cf. also Schorbach, *Zeitschr. f. deutsches Altertum*, XL, 123ff.

lady rose; the knight sprang from his horse, took a hand which she offered, helped her from the rock, and they sat down on the grass. The knight asked how she came to be there alone. The lady replied that she had been waiting for him: ever since he could bestride a horse she had been devoted to him; she had been his help and protection in tourneys and fights, in all climes and regions, though he had never seen her. The knight wished he might ever be hers. He could have his wish, she said, and never know trouble or sickness, on one condition, and that was that he never should marry: if he did this, he would die in three days. He vowed to be hers as long as he lived; they exchanged kisses, and then she bade him mount his horse and go to mass. After the benediction he was to return home, and when he was alone in his chamber, and wished for her, she would come, and so always; that privilege God had given her: "swâ ich wil, dâ bin ich." They had their meeting when he returned from church: he redoubled his vows, she promised him all good things, and the bounties which he received from her overflowed upon all his friends and comrades.

The knight now undertook a chivalrous tour, to see such parts of the world as he had not visited before. Wherever he went, the fair lady had only to be wished for and she was by him: there was no bound to her love or her gifts. Upon his return he was beset by relatives and friends, and urged to marry. He put them off with excuses: he was too young to sacrifice his freedom, and what not. They returned to the charge before long, and set a wise man of his kindred at him to beg a boon of him. "Anything," he said, "but marrying: rather cut me into strips than that." Having silenced his advisers by this reply, he went to his closet and wished for his lady. She was full of sympathy, and thought it might make his position a little easier if he should tell his officious friends something of the real case, how he had a wife who attended him wherever he went and was the source of all his prosperity; but he must not let them persuade him, or what she had predicted would surely come to pass.

At this time a king was to be chosen at Frankfurt, and all the nobility flocked thither, and among them Staufenberg, with a splendid train. He, as usual, was first in all tourneys, and made himself remarked for his liberal gifts and his generous consideration of youthful antagonists: his praise was in everybody's mouth. The king sent for him, and offered him an orphan niece of eighteen, with a rich dowry. The knight excused himself as unworthy of such a match. The king said his niece must accept such a husband as he pleased to give, and many swore that Staufenberg was a fool. Bishops, who were there in plenty, asked him if he had a wife already. Staufenberg availed himself of the leave which had been given him, and told his whole story, not omitting that he was sure to die in three days if he married. "Let me see the woman," said one of the bishops. "She lets nobody see her but me," answered Staufenberg. "Then it is a devil," said another of the clergy, "and your soul is lost forever." Staufenberg yielded, and said he would do the king's will. He was betrothed that very hour, and set out for Ortenau, where he had appointed the celebration of the nuptials. When night came he wished for the invisible lady. She appeared, and told him with all gentleness that he must prepare for the fate of which she had forewarned him, a fate seemingly inevitable, and not the consequence of her resentment. At the wedding feast she would display her foot in sight of all the guests: when he saw that, let him send for the priest. The knight thought of what the clergy had said, and that this might be a cheat of the devil. The bride was brought to Staufenberg, the feast was held, but at the very beginning of it a foot whiter than ivory was seen through the ceiling. Staufenberg tore his hair and cried, Friends, ye have ruined yourselves and me! He begged his bride and all who had come with her to the wedding to stay for his funeral, ordered a bed to be prepared for him and a priest to be sent for. He asked his brothers to give his bride all that he had promised her. But she said no; his friends should rather have all that she had brought; she would have no other husband, and since she had been the cause of his death she would go into a cloister, where no eye should see her: which she did after she had returned to her own country.

A superscription to the old poem denominates Staufenberg's amphibious consort a merfey, sea-fairy; but that description is not to be strictly interpreted, no more than mer-fey, or fata morgana, is in some other romantic tales. There is nothing of the water-sprite in her, nor is she spoken of by any such name in the poem itself. The local legends of sixty years ago,[*] and perhaps still, make her to have been a proper water-nymph. She is first met with by the young knight near a spring or a brook, and it is in a piece of water that he finds his death, and that on the evening of his wedding day.

Clerk Colvill and the mermaid are represented by Sir Oluf and an elf in Scandinavian ballads to the number of about seventy. The oldest of these is derived from a Danish manuscript of 1550, two centuries and a half later than the Staufenberg poem, but two earlier than Clerk Colvill, the oldest ballad outside of the Scandinavian series. Five other versions are of the date 1700, or earlier, the rest from tradition of this century. No ballad has received more attention from the heroic Danish editor, whose study of 'Elveskud' presents an admirably ordered synoptic view of all the versions known up to 1881: Grundtvig, No 47, II, 109–19, 663–66; III, 824–25; IV, 835–74.[†]

The Scandinavian versions are:

Färöe, four: **A**, 39 sts, **B**, 24 sts, **C**, 18 sts, **D**, 23 sts, Grundtvig, IV, 849–52.

Icelandic, twelve, differing slightly except at the very end; **A**, 'Kvæði af Ólafi Liljurós,' 24 sts, MS. of 1665; **B**, **C**, MS. of about 1700, 20 sts, 1 st.; **D**, 18 sts; **E**, 17 sts; **F**, **G**, 16 sts; **H**, 'Ólafs kvæði,' 22 sts; **I a**, 18 sts; **I b**, 20 sts; **K**, 22 sts; **L**, 24 sts; **M**, 25 sts. These in *Íslenzk Fornkvæði*, pp 4–10, **A a** in full, but only the variations of the other versions. **I b**, previously, 'Ólafur og álfamær,' Berggreen, *Danske Folke-Sange og Melodier*, 2d ed., pp 56, 57, No 20 d; and **M**, "Snót, p. 200."

Danish, twenty-six: 'Elveskud' **A**, 54 sts, MS. of 1550, Grundtvig, II, 112; **B**, 25 sts, Syv

---

[*] Engelhardt, pp 6, 13f: *Sagen aus Baden und der Umgegend*, Carlsruhe, 1834, pp 107–122.

[†] Separately printed, under the title, *Elveskud, dansk, svensk, norsk, færøsk, islandsk, skotsk, vendisk, bømisk, tysk, fransk, italiensk, katalonsk, spansk, bretonsk Folkevise, i overblik ved Svend Grundtvig*. Kjøbenhavn, 1881.

No 87 (1695), *Danske Viser*, I, 237, Grundtvig, II, 114; **C**, 29 sts, the same, II, 115; **D a, D b**, 31, 15 sts, II, 116, 665; **E–G**, 20, 16, 8 sts, II, 117–19; **H, I**, 32, 25 sts, II, 663–64; **K**, 29 sts, **L**, 15 sts, **M**, 27 sts, **N**, 16 sts, **O**, 83 sts, **P**, 22 sts, **Q**, 7 sts, **R**, 22 sts, **S**, 32 sts, **T**, 27 sts, **U**, 25 sts, **V**, 18 sts, **X**, 11 sts, **Y**, 11 sts, **Z**, 8 sts, **Æ**, 23 sts, IV, 835–47; **Ø**, 10 sts, Boisen, *Nye og gamle Viser*, 1875, p. 191, No 98; **AA**, 'Elvedansen,' Kristensen, *Jyske Folkeminder*, X, 10, 372, No 5, A, B, C; **BB**, 'Elveskud,' Kristensen, *Skattegraveren*, XII, 54, No 125; **CC**, 'Elvedansen,' *Folkeminder*, XI, 15, No 17, **A–C**.

Swedish, eight: **A**, 15 sts, 'Elf-Qvinnan och Herr Olof,' MS. of seventeenth century, Afzelius, III, 165; **B**, 12 sts, 'Herr Olof i Elfvornas dans,' Afzelius, III, 160; **C**, 18 sts, Afzelius, III, 162; **D**, 21 sts, 'Herr Olof och Elfvorna,' Arwidsson, II, 304; **E**, 20 sts, Arwidsson, II, 307; **F**, 19 sts, Grundtvig, IV, 848; **G**, 12 sts, 'Herr Olof och Elffrun,' Djurklou, p. 94; **H**, 8 sts, Afzelius, *Sago-Häfder*, ed. 1844, ii, 157. **I**, 'Prins Olof,' Wigström, *Folkdiktning*, II, 16, is rationalized; the elf is simply a *frilla*, mistress.

Norwegian, eighteen: **A**, 39 sts, 'Olaf Liljukrans,' Landstad, p. 355; **B**, 15 sts, Landstad, p. 843; **C–S**, collections of Professor Bugge, used in manuscript by Grundtvig; **C**, 36 sts, partly printed in Grundtvig, III, 824; **D**, 23 sts, Grundtvig, III, 824–25, partly; **E**, 22 sts; **F**, 11 sts; **G**, 27 sts; **H**, 13 sts; **I**, 7 sts; **K**, 4 sts, two printed, *ib.*, p. 824.[*]

Of these the Färöe versions are nearest to the English. Olaf's mother asks him whither he [375] means to ride; his corselet is hanging in the loft; **A, C, D**. "I am going to the heath, to course the hind," he says. "You are not going to course the hind; you are going to your leman. White is your shirt, well is it washed, but bloody shalt it be when it is taken off," **A, D**. "God grant it be not as she bodes!" exclaims Olaf, as he turns from his mother, **A**. He rides to the hills and comes to an elf-house. An elf comes out, braiding her hair, and invites him to dance. "You need not braid your hair for me; I have not come a-wooing," he says. "I must quit the company of elves, for to-morrow is my bridal." "If you will have no more to do with elves, a sick

bridegroom shall you be! Would you rather lie seven years in a sick-bed, or go to the mould to-morrow?" He would rather go to the mould to-morrow. The elf brought him a drink, with an atter-corn, a poison grain, floating in it: at the first draught his belt burst **A, B**[*]. "Kiss me," she said, "before you ride." He leaned over and kissed her, though little mind had he to it: she was beguiling him, him so sick a man. His mother came out to meet him: "Why are you so pale, as if you had been in an elf-dance?" "I have been in an elf-dance," he said,[†] went to bed, turned his face to the wall, and was dead before midnight. His mother and his love (*moy, vív*) died thereupon.

Distinct evidence of previous converse with elves is lacking in the Icelandic versions. Olaf rides along the cliffs, and comes upon an elf-house. One elf comes out with her hair twined with gold, another with a silver tankard, a third in a silver belt, and a fourth welcomes him by name. "Come into the booth and drink with us." "I will not live with elves," says Olaf; "rather will I believe in God." The elf answers that he might do both, excuses herself for a moment, and comes back in a cloak, which hides a sword. "You shall not go without giving us a kiss," she says. Olaf leans over his saddle-bow and kisses her, with but half a heart, and she thrusts the sword under his shoulder-blade into the roots of his heart. He sees his heart's blood under his horse's feet, and spurs home to his mother. "Whence comest thou, my son, and why so pale, as if thou hadst been in an elf-dance (*leik*)?" "It boots not to hide it from thee: an elf has beguiled me. Make my bed, mother; bandage my side, sister." He dies presently: there was more mourning than mirth; three were borne to the grave together.

Nearly all the Danish and Swedish versions, and a good number of the Norwegian, interpose

---

[*] All the Norse versions are in two-line stanzas.

[†] In 'Jomfruen og Dværgekongen,' **C** 25, 26, Grundtvig, No 37, the woman who has been carried off to the hill, wishing to die, asks that atter-corns may be put into her drink. She evidently gets, however, only the villarkonn, elvar-konn, of Landstad, Nos 42–45, which are of lethean property. But in *J. og D.* **F**, we may infer an atter-corn, though none is mentioned, from the effect of the draughts, which is that belt, stays, and sark successively burst. See p. 490f.

an affecting scene between the death of the hero and that of his bride and his mother. The bride, on her way to Olaf's house, and on her arrival, is disconcerted and alarmed by several ominous proceedings or circumstances. She hears bells tolling; sees people weeping; sees men come and go, but not the bridegroom. She is put off for a time with false explanations, but in the end discovers the awful fact. Such a passage occurs in the oldest Danish copy, which is also the oldest known copy of the ballad. The importance of this version is such that the story requires to be given with some detail.

Oluf rode out before dawn, but it seemed to him bright as day.[*] He rode to a hill where dwarfs were dancing. A maid stepped out from the dance, put her arm round his neck, and asked him whither he would ride. "To talk with my true-love," said he. "But first," said she, "you must dance with us." She then went on to make him great offers if he would plight himself to her: a horse that would go to Rome and back in an hour, and a gold saddle for it; a new corselet, having which he never need fly from man; a sword such as never was used in war. Such were all her benches as if gold were laid in links, and *76]* such were all her drawbridges as the gold on his hands. "Keep your gold," he answered; "I will go home to my true-love." She struck him on the cheek, so that the blood spattered his coat; she struck him midshoulders, so that he fell to the ground: "Stand up, Oluf, and ride home; you shall not live more than a day." He turned his horse, and rode home a shattered man. His mother was at the gate: "Why comest thou home so sad?" "Dear mother, take my horse; dear brother, fetch a priest." "Say not so, Oluf; many a sick man does not die. To whom do you give your betrothed?" "Rise, my seven brothers, and ride to meet my young bride."

As the bride's train came near the town, they heard the bells going. "Why is this?" she asked, her heart already heavy with pain; "I know of no one having been sick." They told

her it was a custom there to receive a bride so. But when she entered the house, all the women were weeping. "Why are these ladies weeping?" No one durst answer a word. The bride went on into the hall, and took her place on the bride-bench. "I see," she said, "knights go and come, but I see not my lord Oluf." The mother answered, Oluf is gone to the wood with hawk and hound. "Does he care more for hawk and hound than for his young bride?"

At evening they lighted the torches as if to conduct the bride to the bride-bed; but Oluf's page, who followed his lady, revealed the truth on the way. "My lord," he said, "lies on his bier above, and you are to give your troth to his brother." "Never shalt thou see that day that I shall give my troth to two brothers." She begged the ladies that she might see the dead. They opened the door; she ran to the bier, threw back the cloth, kissed the body precipitately; her heart broke in pieces; grievous was it to see.

The mother's attempt to conceal the death of her son from his wife occurs also in 'Ebbe Tygesøns Dødsridt' and 'Hr. Magnuses Dødsridt,' Olrik, *Danske Ridderviser*, Nos 320, 321, and Swedish copies of the former; borrowed no doubt from 'Elveskud.'

Danish **B**, printed by Syv in 1695, is the copy by which the ballad of the Elf-shot has become so extensively known since Herder's time, through his translation and others.[†]

The principal variations of the Scandinavian ballads, so far as they have not been given, now remain to be noted.

The hero's name is mostly Oluf, Ole, or a modification of this, Wolle, Rolig, Volder; sometimes with an appendage, as Färöe Ólavur Riddararós, Rósinkrans, Icelandic Ólafur Lil-

---

[*] So, also, Swedish **A**, **F**, Norwegian **A**, **C**. This is a cantrip sleight of the elves. The Icelandic burden supposes this illumination, "The low was burning red;" and when Olaf seeks to escape, in Norwegian **A**, **C**, **E**, **G**, **I**, **K**, he has to make his way through the elf-flame, elvelogi.

[†] Grundtvig remarks that Herder's translation, 'Erlkönigs Tochter,' *Volkslieder*, II, 158, took so well with the Germans that at last it came to pass for an original German ballad. The *Wunderhorn*, I, 261, ed. 1806, gives it with the title, 'Herr Olof,' as from a flying sheet (= Scherer's *Deutsche Volkslieder*, 1851, p. 371). It appears, with some little changes, in Zarnack's *Deutsche Volkslieder*, 1819, I, 29, whence it passed into Erlach, IV, 6, and Richter und Marschner, p. 60. Kretzschmer has the translation, again, with a variation here and there, set to a "North German" and to a "Westphalian" air, p. 8, p. 9.

jurós, Norwegian Olaf Liljukrans, etc. It is Peder in Danish **H, I, O, P, Q, R, Æ**.

Excepting the Färöe ballads, Oluf is not distinctly represented as having had previous acquaintance with the elves. In Swedish **A** 5 he says, I cannot dance with you, my betrothed has forbidden me; in Danish **C**, I should be very glad if I could; to-morrow is my wedding-day.

The object of his riding out is to hunt, or the like, in Danish **D b, E, F, I, R, T, X, Y**; to bid guests to his wedding, Danish **B, C, D a, G, H, K–N, P, S, U, V, Ø**, Norwegian **A, B**.

He falls in with dwarfs, Danish **A, H**, Norwegian **A**; trolds, Danish **I**; elves and dwarfs, Norwegian **B**, and a variation of **A**: elsewhere it is elves.

There is naturally some diversity in the gifts which the elf offers Oluf in order to induce him to dance with her. He more commonly replies that the offer is a handsome one, 'kan jeg vel få,' but dance with her he cannot; sometimes that his true-love has already given him that, or two, three, seven such, Danish **D a, I, T, X, Y**.

If he will not dance with her, the elf threatens him with sore sickness, Danish **B, E, H, Z, Ø**, Norwegian **A**, Swedish **E, F**; a great misfortune, Danish **F**, Swedish **A**; sharp knives, Danish **P**; it shall cost him his young life, Danish **D a, b, T, Y**.

Oluf dances with the elves, obviously under compulsion, in Danish **C, D, G–N, S, T, U, X, Y**, Swedish **F**, and only in these. He dances till [377] both his boots are full of blood, **D a** 15, **D b** 4, **G** 5, **I** 11, **K** 5, **L** 5, **M** 6, **N** 7, **S** 6 [shoes], **T** 10, **U** 5, **X** 8, **Y** 7; he dances so long that he is nigh dead, **I** 12.

The hard choice between dying at once or lying sick seven years is found, out of the Färöe ballads, only in Danish **H** 8, **M** 8, **O** 4, **Q** 2, **S** 8. Norwegian ballads, like English **C**, present an option between living with elves and dying, essentially a repetition of the terms under which Peter of Staufenberg weds the fairy, that he shall forfeit his life if he takes a mortal wife. So Norwegian

A 12   Whether wilt thou rather live with the elves,
     Or leave the elves, a sick man

  13   Whether wilt thou be with the elves,
     Or bid thy guests and be sick?

B 9   Whether wilt thou stay with the elves,
     Or, a sick man, flit [bring home] thy true-
     love?

  10   Whether wilt thou be with elves,
     Or, a sick man, flit thy bride?

There is no answer.
Norwegian **C, E, G, I** resemble **A**. **H** is more definite.

  6   Whether wilt thou go off sick, "under isle,"
     Or wilt thou marry an elf-maid?

  7   Whether wilt thou go off sick, under hill,
     Or wilt thou marry an elf-wife?

To which Olaf answers that he lists not to go off a sick man, and he cannot marry an elf.

The two last stanzas of English **C**, which correspond to these,

    'Will ye lie there an die, Clerk Colin,
     Will ye lie there an die?
    Or will ye gang to Clyde's water,
     To fish in flood wi me?'

    'I will lie here an die,' he said,
     'I will lie here an die;
    In spite o a' the deils in hell,
     I will lie here an die,'

may originally have come in before the mermaid and the clerk parted; but her visit to him as he lies in bed is paralleled by that of the fairy to Staufenberg after he has been persuaded to give up what he had been brought to regard as an infernal liaison; and certainly Clerk Colin's language might lead us to think that some priest had been with him, too.

Upon Oluf's now seeking to make his escape through the elves' flame, ring, dance, etc., Norwegian **A, B, C, E, G, I, H, K**, the elf-woman strikes at him with a gold band, her wand, hand, a branch or twig; gives him a blow on the cheek, between the shoulders, over his white neck; stabs him in the heart, gives him knife-strokes five, nine; sickness follows the stroke, or blood: Danish **A, B, F, N, O, R, V, Z, Æ, Ø**, Swedish **D, G**, Norwegian **A–E, H, I**, Icelandic. The knife-stabs are delayed till the elves have put him on his horse in Danish **D**, **G**, **X**; as he sprang to his horse the knives rang after him, **H**. "Ride home," they say, "you shall not live more than a day" [five hours, two hours], Danish **A**, **C**, **K–N**, **S**, **U**, **V**. His hair fades, Danish **E**; his cheek pales, Danish **E**, Norwegian **A**; sickness follows him home, Swedish **A**, **C**, **D**, **E**; the blood is running out of the wound in his heart, Swedish **G**; when he reaches his father's house both his boots are full of blood, Danish **R**, **Æ**.

His mother [father] is standing without, and asks, Why so pale? Why runs the blood from thy saddle? Oluf, in some instances, pretends that his horse, not being sure-footed, had stumbled, and thrown him against a tree, but is told, or of himself adds, that he has been among the elves. He asks one or the other of his family to take his horse, bring a priest, make his bed, put on a bandage. He says he shall never rise from his bed, Swedish **C**, Danish **F**; fears he shall not live till the priest comes, Danish **O**, **P**.

The important passage which relates the arrival of the bride, the ominous circumstances at the bridegroom's house, the attempts to keep the bride in ignorance of his death, and her final discovery that she is widowed before mar-riage, occupies some thirty stanzas in Danish **A**, the oldest of all copies; in Danish **B** it is reduced to six; in other Danish versions it has a range of from fifteen to two; but, shorter or longer, it is found in all versions but **R**, **Ø**, and the frag-ments **G**, **L**, **Q**, **X**, **Z**. All the Swedish versions have a similar scene, extending from three to nine stanzas, with the exception of **G** and of **A**, which latter should perhaps be treated as a frag-ment. In Norwegian **A**, again, this part of the story fills ten stanzas; **B** lacks it, but **C–H** (which have not been published in full) have it, and probably other unpublished copies.

The bride is expected the next day, Danish **D**, **F**, **I**, **K**, **N**, **O**, **S**, **T**, **U**, Swedish **A**, **D**. In Danish **A** Oluf begs his brothers, shortly after his reaching home, to set out to meet her; he fears she may arrive that very night, Danish **Æ**. "What shall I answer your young bride?" asks the mother, Danish **B**, **C**, **D**, etc., Swedish **H**. "Tell her that I have gone to the wood, to hunt and shoot, to try my horse and my dogs," Dan-ish **B**, **C**, **D**, **F**, **H**, **I**, **K**, **O**, **S**, **T**, **U**, Swedish **D**,

H, Norwegian **A**, **L**; in Danish **N** only, "Say I died in the night." Oluf now makes his will; he wishes to assign his bride to his brother, Danish **L**, **O**, **R**, Norwegian **C**, **F**; he dies before the bride can come to him. (Norwegian **F** seems to have gone wrong here.)

The bride, with her train, comes in the morning, Danish **B**, **D**, **E**, **I**, **M**, **T**, Swedish **D**, Norwegian **D**; Swedish **C** makes her wait for her bridegroom several days. As she passes through the town the bells are tolling, and she anxiously asks why, Danish **A**, **K**, **O**, **S**, **U**; she is told that it is a custom there to ring when the bride comes, Danish **A**, Swedish **B**. In Danish **H**, though it is day, she sees a light burning in Oluf's chamber, and this alarms her. When she comes to the house, Oluf's mother is weeping, all the ladies are weeping, or there are other signs of grief, Danish **A**, **C**, **H**, **U**, **Æ**. When she asks the reason, no one can answer, or she is told that a woman, a fair knight, is dead, **A**, **C**, **H**. Now she asks, Where is Oluf, who should have come to meet me, should have been here to receive me? Danish **K**, **O**, **S**, **U**, **D**, **E**, **I**, **T**, etc. They conduct the bride into the hall and seat her on the bride bench; knights come and go; they pour out mead and wine. "Where is Oluf," she asks again; the mother replies, as best she can, that Oluf is gone to the wood, Danish **B**, **H**, Norwegian **A**, **D**, Swedish **H**, etc. "Does he then care more for that than for his bride?" Danish **A**, **D**, **I**, **M**, etc., Swedish **C**, **D**, Norwe-gian **A**, **E**, **G**.

The truth is now avowed that Oluf is dead, Danish **A**, **D**, **I**, **T**, **Y**, **Æ**, Swedish **B**, Norwe-gian **G**. The bride begs that she may see the dead, Danish **A**, **C**, **P**, **Æ**, Swedish **F**, Norwe-gian **D**, **E**, and makes her way to the room where Oluf is lying. She puts aside the cloths that cover him, or the curtains, or the flowers, Danish **A**, **B**, **K**, **V**, etc., Swedish **C**, **D**, Norwe-gian **C**, **D**, **E**, **G**; says a word or two to her lover, Danish **A**, **C**, **E**, **H**, Swedish **E**, **F**, Norwegian **G**; kisses him, Danish **A**, **C**, **H**; her heart breaks, Danish **A**, **C**; she swoons dead at his feet, Dan-ish **K**, **M**, **S**, **U**. In Norwegian **A**, **C**, **D**, she kills herself with Olaf's sword; in Swedish **E**, with her own knife. In Danish **R** she dies in Oluf's mother's arms. On the morrow, when it was day, in Oluf's house three corpses lay: the first was

Oluf, the second his maid, the third his mother, of grief was she dead: Danish, Swedish, Norwegian, *passim.*[*]

Breton ballads preserve the story in a form closely akin to the Scandinavian, and particularly to the oldest Danish version. I have seen the following, all from recent tradition: **A, C,** [379] 'Ann Aotro ar C'hont,' 'Le Seigneur Comte,' Luzel, I, $\frac{4}{5}$, $\frac{16}{17}$, fifty-seven and fifty-nine two-line stanzas. **B,** 'Ann Aotro Nann,' 'Le Seigneur Nann,' Luzel, I, $\frac{10}{11}$, fifty-seven stanzas.[†] **D,** 'Aotrou Nann hag ar Gorrigan,' 'Le Seigneur Nann et la Fée,' Villemarqué, p. 25, ed. 1867, thirty-nine stanzas. **E,** 'Monsieur Nann,' *Poésies populaires de la France*, MS., V, fol. 381, fifty-three verses. **F,** 'Sonen Gertrud guet bi Vam,' 'Chant de Gertrude et de sa Mère,' L. Kérardven [= Dufilhol], Guionvac'h, *Études sur la Bretagne*, 2d ed., Paris, 1835, p. 362, p. 13, eleven four-line stanzas; printed entire (twenty-one stanzas instead of eleven) by Gaidoz, in *Mélusine*, IV, 301 ff. (The language appears to be Cornish.) **G,** Rolland in *Romania*, XII, 117, a somewhat abridged literal translation, in French; 'Le Sône de la Fiancée,' *Revue des Provinces*, III, 3e livraison; Bladé, not seen by me.

The count [Nann] and his wife were married at the respective ages of thirteen and twelve. The next year a son was born [a boy and girl, **D**]. The young husband asked the countess if she had a fancy for anything. She owned that she should like a bit of game, and he took his gun [lance] and went to the wood. At the

entrance of the wood he met a fairy [a dwarf, **E**; a hind, **G**; saw a white hind, which he pursued hotly till evening, when he dismounted near a grotto to drink, and there was a korrigan, sitting by the spring, combing her hair with a gold comb, **D**]. The fairy [dwarf, hind] said that she had long been looking for him, **A, B, C, E, G.** "Now that I have met you, you must marry me."[‡] "Marry you? Not I. I am married already." "Choose either to die in three days or to lie sick in bed seven [three] years" [and then die, **C**]. He would rather die in three days, for his wife is very young, and would suffer greatly [he would rather die that instant than wed a korrigan, **D**].

On reaching home the young man called to his mother to make his bed; he should never get up again. [His mother, in **C** 21, says, Do not weep so: it is not every sick man that dies, as in Danish **A** 22.] He recounted his meeting with the fairy, and begged that his wife might not be informed of his death.

The countess asked, What has happened to my husband, that he does not come to see me? She was told that he had gone to the wood to get her something, **A** [to Paris, **C**; to the city, **D**]. Why were the men-servants weeping? The best horse had been drowned in bathing him, **A, E**; had been eaten by the wolves, **B**; had broken his neck, **C**; had died, **F**. They were not to weep; others should be bought. And why were the maids weeping? Linen had been lost in washing, **A, C, E, F**; the best silver cover had been stolen, **F**. They must not weep; the loss would be supplied. Why were the priests chanting? [the bells tolling, **E, F**]. A poor person whom they had lodged had died in the night, **A–E** [a young prince had died, **F**]. What dress should she wear for her churching,—red or blue? **D, F**.[§] The custom had come in of wearing black [she asks for red, they give her black, **F**]. On arriving at the church, or cemetery, she saw that the earth had been disturbed; her pew was hung with black, **B**; why was this? "I can no

---

[*] Owing to a close resemblance of circumstances in 'The Elf-shot,' in 'Frillens Hævn' ('The Leman's Wreak'), Grundtvig, No 208, and in 'Ribold og Guldborg,' Grundtvig, No 82, these ballads naturally have details in common. The pretence that the horse was not surefooted and hurtled his rider against a tree; the request to mother, father, etc., to make the bed, take care of the horse, apply a bandage, send for a priest, etc.; the testament, the assignment of the bride by the dying man to his brother, and her declaration that she will never give her troth to two brothers; and the nearly simultaneous death of hero, bride, and mother, occur in many versions of both Elveskud and Ribold, and most of them in Frillens Hævn. A little Danish ballad, 'Hr. Olufs Død,' cited by Grundtvig, IV, 847, seems to be Elveskud with the elf-shot omitted.

[†] Luzel was in possession of other versions, but he assures us that every detail is contained in one or the other of these three.

[‡] **B** 13, "You must marry me straightway, or give me my weight in silver;" *then*, "or die in three days," etc. It is not impossible that this stanza, entirely out of place in this ballad, was derived from 'Le Comte des Chapelles,' Luzel, p. 457, from which certain French versions have taken a part of their story. See Luzel, the eighth and ninth stanzas, on p. 461.

longer conceal it," said her mother-in-law: "your husband is dead." She died upon the spot, **A**, **D**. "Take my keys, take care of my son; I will stay with his father," **B**, **C**. "Your son is dead, your daughter is dead," **F**.*

This ballad has spread, apparently from Brittany, over all France. No distinct trace of the fairy remains, however, except in a single case.
380] The versions that have been made public, so far as they have come to my knowledge, are as follows, resemblance to the Breton ballad principally directing the arrangement.

A. 'Le fils Louis,' Vendée, pays de Retz, *Poésies populaires de la France*, MS., III, fol. 118, printed in *Romania*, XI, 100, 44 verses, printed by Rolland, III, 39. **B**. Normandy, 1876, communicated by Legrand to *Romania*, X, 372, 61 verses. **C**. 'Le Fils Arnaud,' Noëlas, *Essai d'un Romancero forézien*, 68 verses. **D**. Victor Smith, Chants populaires du Velay et du Forez, *Romania*, X, 583, 68 verses. **E**. The same, p. 581, 64 verses. **F**. Saint-Denis, *Poés. pop. de la France*, III, fol. 103, *Romania*, XI, 98, 74 verses, as sung by a young girl, her mother and grandmother. **G**. Poitou et Vendée, *Études historiques et artistiques par B. Fillon et O. De Rochbrune*, 7ᵉ–10ᵉ livraisons, Fontenay-le-Comte, 1865, article Nalliers, pp 17, 18, nineteen four-line stanzas and a couplet; before by B. Fillon in "L'Histoire véridique des fraudes et exécrables voleries et subtilités de Guillery, depuis sa naissance jusqu'à la juste punition de ses crimes, Fontenay, 1848," extracted in *Poés. pop.*, III, fol. 112; other copies at fol. 108 and at fol. 116; *Romania*, XI, 101, 78 verses. **H**. Bourbonnais, *Poés. pop.* III, fol. 91, *Romania*, XI, 103, 38

verses, sung by a woman seventy-two years old. **I**. Bretagne, Loudéac, *Poés. pop.*, III, fol. 121, *Romania*, XI, 103f, 61 verses. **J**. *Poés. pop.*, III, fol. 285, *Romania*, XII, 115 (I), 50 verses. **K**. Bretagne (?), *Romania*, XII, 115f, 36 verses. **L**. V. Smith, Chants pop. du Velay et du Forez, *Romania*, X, 582, 57 verses. **M**. 'Le roi Renaud,' Flévy, *Puymaigre*, I, 39, 78 verses. **N**. Touraine, Bléré, Brachet in *Revue Critique*, II, 125, 60 verses. **O**. The same, variations of a later version. **P**. 'L'Arnaud l'Infant,' Limoges, *Laforest, Limoges au XVIIᵉ siècle*, 1862, p. 300, *Poés. pop.*, III, fol. 95, *Romania*, XI, 104, 82 verses, printed by Rolland, III, p. 41, p. 37. **Q**. Charente, *Poés. pop.*, III, fol. 107, *Romania*, XI, 99, 60 verses. **R**. Cambes, Lot-et-Garonne, *Romania*, XII, 116, 46 verses. **S**. Jura, *Revue des Deux Mondes*, 1854, Août, p. 486, 50 verses. **T**. Rouen, *Poés. pop.* III, fol. 100, *Romania*, XI, 102, 60 verses, communicated by a gentleman who at the beginning of the century had learned the ballad from an aunt, who had received it from an aged nun. Printed by Rolland, III, p. 32, and in *Revue des Traditions pop.*, I, 33. **U**. a, Buchon, *Noëls et Chants populaires de la Franche-Comté*, p. 85, 34 verses; b, Tarbé, Romancero de Champagne, Vol. II, *Chants Populaires*, p. 125, 32 verses; c, G. de Nerval, *La Bohème Galante*, ed. 1866, p. 77, *Les Filles du Feu*, ed. 1868, p. 130, 30 verses; d, 'Jean Renaud,' Bujeaud, *Chants et Chansons populaires des Provinces de l'Ouest*, II, 213, 32 verses. **V**. *Poés. pop.*, III, fol. 122, *Romania*, XI, 100f, 32 verses. **W**. Le Blésois, Ampère, *Instructions, etc.*, p. 37, 36 verses. **X**. Provence, *Poés. pop.*, III, fol. 114, *Romania*, XI, 105, 44 verses, printed by Rolland, III, 45. **Y**. 'Lou Counte Arnaud,' Bivès, Gers, Bladé, *Poés. pop. de la Gascogne*, II, 134/135, 48 verses. **Z**. Vagney, Vosges, *Mélusine*, p. 75, 44 verses. **AA**. Cambes, Lot-et-Garonne, *Romania*, XII, 116f, 40 verses. **BB**. Quercy, Sérignac, *Poés. pop.*, *Romania*, XI, 106, 34 verses. **CC**. Quercy, *Poés. pop.*, *Romania*, XI, 107, 26 verses. **DD**. Bretagne, Villemarqué, *Barzaz-Breiz*, ed. 1846, I, 46, 12 verses. **EE**. Orléans, *Poés. pop.*, III, fol. 102, *Romania*, XI, 107, 10 verses. **FF**. Auvergne, *Poés. pop.*, III, fol. 89, *Romania*, XI, 107f, 6 verses. **GG**. Boulonnais, 'La Ballade du Roi Renaud,' E. Hamy, in *Almanach de Boulogne-sur-Mer* pour 1863, p.

§   **B** 50, "A white gown, or *broget*, or my violet petticoat?" Luzel says he does not understand *broget*, and in his Observations, prefixed to the volume, expresses a conjecture that it must have been altered from *droged*, robe d'enfant, robe doe femme, but we evidently want a color. Grundtvig remarks that *broget* would make sense in Danish, where it means party-colored. Scotch *broakit* is black and white. Icelandic *brók*, tartan, party-colored cloth, is said to be from Gaelic *breac*, versicolor (Vigfusson). This points to a suitable meaning for Breton *broget*.
*   **D** adds: "It was a marvel to see, the night after husband and wife had been buried, two oaks rise from the common tomb, and on their branches two white doves, which sang there at daybreak, and then took flight for the skies."

110 (compounded from several versions), 16 four-line stanzas; in *Revue des T. p.*, III, 195.* **HH**, **II**. 'Jean Renaud,' Decombe, *Chansons pop. d'Ille-et-Vilaine*, Nos 89, 90, pp. 253, 256; **JJ**. Le Limousin. **KK**. Le Loiret. **LL**. La Vendée, in *Mélusine*, II, cols 302–305: the last from "Revue de la Province de l'Ouest, 1856–57, IV, 50." The first stanza, and four of the concluding, in *Poésies pop. de la France*, MS., VI, 491 and 491 *bis*. **MM**. Five stanzas in *Poés. pop. de la F.*, MS., VI, 491, printed by Rolland, III, 36. **NN**. 38 verses, without indication of place, by C. de Sivry in *Rev. des T. p.*, II, 24. **OO**. 'Le roi Léouis,' Haute-Bretagne, 60 verses, P. Sébillot, in the same, III, 196. **PP**, **QQ**. 'Arnaud,' Quercy, Daymard, p. 167f, 34 verses, 26 verses. **RR**. 'Lou Counte Arnaud,' Bas-Quercy, Soleville, *Chants p. du Bas-Quercy*, 1889, p. 13, 10 stanzas. **SS**. Limousine, *La Tradition*, V, 184. **TT**. 'La chanson de Renaud,' Pineau, *Le Folk-Lore du Poitou*, p. 399; **UU**. 'La Mort de Jean Raynaud,' *Wallonia*, I, 22. **VV**, **WW**. Versions de la Bresse, one, and a fragment, J. Tiersot, *Revue des Traditions Populaires*, VII, 654ff. **XX**. 'La Mort de Jean Renaud,' Beauquier, *Chansons p. recueillies en Franche-Comté*, p. 152. A Basque version, with a translation, appears in *Rev. des Trad. pop.*, III, 198.

The name of the hero in the French ballad is mostly Renaud, or some modification of Renaud: Jean Renaud, **G**, **H**, **U**; Renom, **AA**; Arnaud, **C**, **E**, **L**, **Y**, **BB**; L'Arnaud l'Infant, **P**; [381] Louis Renaud, brother of Jean, **F**. It is Louis in **A**, **I**, **J**, **V**. He is king, or of the royal family, **F**, **M**, **N**, **O**, **Q**, **W**, **BB**, **CC**, **GG**; count, **Y**; Renaud le grand, **H**, **Z**. In **A**, while he is walking in his meadows, he meets Death, who asks him, peremptorily, Would you rather die this very night, or languish seven years? and he answers that he prefers to die at once. Here there is a very plain trace of the older fairy. He

is mortally hurt, while hunting, by a wolf, **B**; by a boar, **DD**. But in more than twenty versions he returns from war, often with a horrible wound, "apportant son cœur dans sa main," **C**; "tenant ses tripes dans ses mains," **N**; "oque ses tripes sur sa main, sen estoumac on sen chapea, sen cûr covert de sen mentea," **G**; etc. In **F**, **I**, **J** he comes home in a dying state from prison (to which he was consigned, according to **I**, for robbing a church!). In these versions the story is confused with that of another ballad, existing in Breton, and very likely in French, 'Komt ar Chapel,' 'Le Comte des Chapelles,' Luzel, I, $^{456}/_{457}$, or 'Le Page de Louis XIII,' Villemarqué, *Barzaz-Breiz*, p. 301. A fragment of a corresponding Italian ballad is given by Nigra, *Romania*, XI, 397, No 9.

Renaud, as it will be convenient to call the hero, coming home triste et chagrin, **F**, **P**, **U** b, c, triste et bien malau, **Y**, receives on his arriving felicitations from his mother on account of the birth of a son. He has no heart to respond to these: "Ni de ma femme, ni de mon fils, je ne saurais me réjoui." He asks that his bed may be made, with precautions against his wife's hearing. At midnight he is dead.

The wife, hearing the men-servants weeping, asks her mother-in-law the cause. The best horse [horses] has been found dead in the stable, has strayed away, etc., **B**, **D–S**, **GG**. "No matter for that," says the wife; "when Renaud comes he will bring better," **B**, **D–G**, **L–Q**, **GG**. The maids are heard weeping; why is that? They have lost, or injured, sheets in the washing, **B**, **D**, **E**, **G**, **J**. When Renaud comes we shall have better, **B**, **D**, **E**, **G**. Or a piece of plate has been lost or broken, **A**, **F**, **H**, **I**, **K**, **O**. [It is children with the toothache, **F**, **U** a, b, c, d]. "What is this chanting which I hear?" It is a procession, making the tour of the house: **B**, **D–F**, **L**, **P–X**, **GG**. "What gown shall I wear when I go to church?" Black is the color for women at their churching, **B**, **F**, **I**, **L**, **M**, **O**, **P**, **V**, **Y**; black is more becoming, plus joli, plus convenant, plus conséquent, **A**, **D**, **H**, **K**, **N**, **R**, **X**, **BB**, **DD**, **GG**; "quittez le ros', quittez le gris, prenez le noir, pour mieux choisir," etc., **Q**, **W**, **U**, **E**, **S**, **T**.

Besides these four questions, all of which occur in Breton ballads, there are two which are met with in many versions, always coming

---

*   It will be observed that some of the Renaud ballads in the *Poésies populaires de la France* were derived from earlier publications: such as were communicated by collectors appear to have been sent in in 1852 or 1853. The versions cited by Rathery, *Revue Critique*, II, 287ff, are all from the MS. *Poésies populaires*. **BB**, **CC** have either been overlooked by me in turning over the first five volumes, or occur in vol. vi, which has not yet been received. **GG** came to hand too late to be ranked at its proper place.

before the last. "What is this pounding (frapper, cogner, taper) which I hear?" It is carpenters, or masons, repairing some part of the house, **D, E, K, L, N, P–U, W; A, V, X, AA; GG.** "Why are the bells ringing?" For a procession, or because a distinguished personage has come, has died, etc., **A, B, F–L, Q, R, W, Y, AA, DD, GG.** On the way to church [or cemetery] herdboys or others say to one another, as the lady goes by, That is the wife of the king, the seigneur, that was buried last night, or the like; and the mother-in-law has again to put aside the lady's question as to what they were saying, **D, E, G, H, L–P, S, T, X, Y, FF, GG.**

Flambeaux or candles are burning at the church, **E, V**; a taper is presented to the widow, **M,** or holy water, **N, T, Z, GG**; the church is hung with black, **D, O, FF**; the funeral is going on, **AA, CC.** "Whose is this new monument?" "What a fine tomb!" **M, N, R, T, Z, GG.** The scene in other cases is transferred to the cemetery. "Why has the earth been disturbed?" "What new monument is this?" **A, DD; C, F, I, J, P.** In **B** the tomb is in the garden; in **L, S, X, BB** the place is not defined.

The young wife utters a piercing shriek, **C, D, K, L, N.** Open earth, split tomb, split tiles! **A, B, Q, R, V, W, X, Y;** I will stay with my husband, will die with my husband, will not go back, **A, C, D, M, N, Q, R, S, X, Y, Z, BB, CC, GG.** She bids her mother take her keys, **B, C, G, L, M, P, Y, BB, CC, GG,** and commits her son [children] to her kinsfolk, to bring up piously, **B, G, I, J, L, M, O, Z, BB, CC.** In **H, P, Q, W, X, Y** the earth opens, and in the last four it encloses her. In **K** heaven is rent by her shriek, and she sees her husband in light (who says, strangely, that his mouth smacks of rot); he bids her bring up the children as Christians. Heaven opens to her prayer in **AA**, and a voice cries, Wife, come up hither! In **GG** the voice from heaven says, Go to your child: I will keep your husband safe. There are other variations.[*]

G, T, I say expressly that Renaud's wife died the next day, or after hearing three masses, or soon after. **M, O,** by a feeble modern perversion, make her go into a convent.

Italian ballads cover very much the same ground as the French. The versions hitherto published are:

A. 'La Lavandaia,' Cento, Ferraro, *Canti popolari di Ferrara, Cento e Pontelagoscuro*, p. 52, 16 verses, *Romania*, XI, 397, amended. **B.** 'Il Cavaliere della bella Spada,' Pontelagoscuro, Ferraro, p. 107, previously in *Rivista di Filologia romanza*, II, 205, 28 verses, *Romania*, XI, 398, *Rivista di letteratura popolare*, p. 56, 1877. **C.** Piedmont, communicated by Nigra, with other versions, to *Romania*, XI, 394, No 4, 48 verses. **D.** *Romania*, XI, 393f, No 3, 34 verses. **E.** *Ib.* p. 395, No 6, 42 verses. **F.** *Ib.* p. 392f, No 2, 46 verses. **G.** 'Conte Anzolin,' Wolf, *Volkslieder aus Venetien*, p. 61, 57 verses. **H.** *Romania*, XI, 396, No 7, 38 verses. **I.** *Ib.* p. 394f, No 5, 26 verses. **J.** 'Il re Carlino,' Ferraro, *Canti popolari monferrini*, p. 34, 42 verses. **K.** *Romania*, XI, 392, No 1, 20 verses. **L.** 'Il Conte Angiolino,' Rovigno, Ive, *Canti popolari istriani*, p. 344, 34 verses. **M.** 'Il Conte Cagnolino,' Pontelagoscuro, Ferraro, as above, p. 84, *Rivista di Filologia romanza*, II, 196, 36 verses. All these are from recent tradition. **N.** 'El conte Anzolin,' Villanis, Canzoni pop. Zaratine, *Archivio*, XI, 32. A burlesque form in Canti pop. Emiliani, Maria Carmi, *Archivio*, XII, 186, and a Venetian rispetto of the same character (noted by Maria Carmi) in Bernoni, *Canti pop. Veneziani*, 1873, Puntata 7, p. 12, No 62.[†]

---

[*]   In C the mother-in-law tells her daughter, austerely:

Vous aurez plutôt trouvé un mari
Que moi je n'aurai trouvé un fils.

So **E**, nearly. A mother makes a like remark to the betrothed of a dead son in the Danish ballad of 'Ebbe Tygesen,' Grundtvig, *Danske Kæmpeviser og Folkesange, fornyede i gammel Stil*, 1867, p. 122, st. 14. **F** and **T** conclude with these words of the wife:

'Ma mère, dites au fossoyeur
Qu'il creuse une fosse pour deux;
'Et que l'espace y soit si grand
Que l'on y mette aussi l'enfant.'

The burial of father, mother, and child in a common grave is found elsewhere in ballads, as in 'Redselille og Medelvold,' Grundtvig, No 271, **A** 37, **G** 20, **M** 26, **X** 27.
[†]   C–F, H–K now in Nigra's collection, 'Morte Occulta,' A–G, No 21, p. 142, in a different order. C, D, E, F, H, I, K are in Nigra now A, C, D, E, G, F, B. The fragment spoken of p. 511 is now Nigra's No 22, p. 149 'Mal ferito.' The tale which follows this is given p. 148f.

The name Rinaldo, Rinald, is found only in I, C, and the latter has also Lüis. Lüis is the name in E; Carlino, Carlin, in J, H; Angiolino, Anzolin, L, G; Cagnolino, M. The rank is king in C, E, H–K; prince, D; count, G, L, M.

A and B, corrupted fragments though they be, retain clear traces of the ancient form of the story, and of the English variety of that form. Under the bridge of the Rella [Diamantina] a woman is washing clothes, gh' è 'na lavandera. A knight passes, B, and apparently accosts the laundress. She moves into the water, and the knight after her; the knight embraces her, A. Dowy rade he hame, el va a cà tüto mojà, A. In B (passing over some verses which have intruded) he has many knife-stabs, and his horse many also.[*] He asks his mother to put him to bed and his horse into the stable, and gives directions about his funeral.

All of the story which precedes the hero's return home is either omitted, D, F, J, K, L, or abridged to a single stanza: ven da la cassa lo re Rinald, ven da la cassa, l'è tüt ferì, C; ven da la guerra re Rinaldo, ven da la guerra, l'è tüt ferì, I, E, H; save that G, which like C makes him to have been hunting (and to have been bitten by a mad dog), adds that, while he was hunting, his wife had given birth to a boy. M has an entirely false beginning: Count Cagnolino was disposed to marry, but wished to be secure about his wife's previous life. He had a marble statue in his garden which moved its eyes when any girl that had gone astray presented herself [383] before it. The daughter of Captain Tartaglia having been declined, for reason, and another young woman espoused, Tartaglia killed the count while they were hunting.

The wounded man, already feeling the approach of death, F, G, L, asks that his bed may be made; he shall die before the morrow, D, F, J; let not his wife know, F, G. The wife asks why the men-servants, coachmen, are weeping, and is told that they have drowned [lost] some of the horses, C–J, M [have burned the king's carriage, K]. We will get others when

the king comes, she answers, C, D, H [when I get up, F, as in Breton A]. Why are the maids weeping? The maids have lost sheets or towels in washing, F, I, K; have scorched the shirts in ironing, C, D, H. When the king comes, he will buy or bring better, C, D, H [when I get up, F, as in Breton A]. Why are the priests chanting? For a great feast to-morrow, F. Why are the carpenters at work? They are making a cradle for your boy, C–E, H–K. Why do the bells ring? A great lord is dead; in honor of somebody or something; C, E–L. Why does not Anzolin come to see me? He has gone a-hunting, G, L. What dress shall I put on to go to church? [When I get up I shall put on red, F, I.] You in black and I in gray, as in our country is the way, C–F, H, I [H moda a Paris, by corruption of dël pais]; I white, you gray, J; you will look well in black, M; put on red, or put on white, or put on black for custom's sake, G.

The children in the street say, That is the wife of the lord who was buried, or the people look at the lady in a marked way, C, J, G, M; and why is this? For the last time the mother-in-law puts off the question. At the church, under the family bench, there is a grave new made, and now it has to be said that the husband is buried there, C–K, M.

A conclusion is wanting in half of the ballads, and what there is is corrupted in others. The widow commends her boy to her husband's mother, G, M, and says she will die with her dear one, D, E, J, M. In C, as in French V, she wishes to speak to her husband. If the dead ever spake to the quick, she would speak once to her dear Lüis; if the quick ever spake to the dead, she would speak once to her dear husband. In G she bids the grave unlock, that she may come into the arms of her beloved, and then bids it close, that in his arms she may stay: cf. French Y, Q, X, R, AA.

The story of the Italian ballad, under the title of 'Il Conte Angiolino,' was given in epitome by Luigi Carrer, in his Prose e Poesie, Venice, 1838, IV, 81 f, before any copy had been published (omitted in later editions). According to Carrer's version, the lady, hearing bells, and seeing from her windows the church lighted up as for some office, extracts the fact from her mother-in-law on the spot, and then,

---

[*]   Shutting our eyes to other Romance versions, or, we may say, opening them to Scandinavian ones, we might see in these stabs the wounds made by the elf-knives in Danish D, G, H, N, O, R, X, Swedish G, Norwegian H, I. See 'Don Joan y Don Ramon,' further on.

going to the church and seeing her husband's tomb, prays that it would open and receive her.

A fragment of an Italian ballad given by Nigra, *Romania*, XI, 396, No 8, describes three card players, quarrelling over their game, as passing from words to knives, and from knives to pistols, and one of the party, the king of Spain, as being wounded in the fray. He rides home with a depressed air, and asks his mother to make his bed, for he shall be dead at midnight and his horse at dawn. There is a confusion of two stories here, as will be seen from Spanish ballads which are to be spoken of. Both stories are mixed with the original adventure of the mermaid in 'Il Cavaliere della bella spada,' already referred to as **B**. In this last the knight has a hundred and fifty stabs, and his horse ninety.[*]

Nigra has added to the valuable and beautiful ballads furnished to *Romania*, XI, a tale (p. 398) from the province of Turin, which preserves the earlier portion of the Breton story. A hunter comes upon a beautiful woman under a rock. She requires him to marry her, and is told by the hunter that he is already married. The beautiful woman, who is of course a fairy, presents the hunter with a box for his wife, which he is not to open. This box contains an explosive girdle, intended to be her death; and the hunter's curiosity impelling him to examine the gift, he is so much injured by a detonation which follows that he can just drag himself home to die.

Catalan. This ballad is very common in Catalonia, and has been found in Asturias. Since it is also known in Portugal, we may presume that it might be recovered in other parts of the peninsula. **A.** 'La bona viuda,' Briz, *Cansons de la Terra*, III, 155, 32 verses. **D.** 'La Viuda,' 33 verses' Milá y Fontanals, *Romancerillo Catalan*, 2d. ed., p. 155, No 204. **C–I.** *Ib.* p. 156f. **J.** *Ib.* p. 157f, No 204₁, 36 verses. There are two good Asturian versions in Pidal, 'Doña

Alda,' Nos 46, 47, pp. 181, 183. The editor mentions a copy in the second number of *Folk-Lore Betico-Extremeño*, much injured by tradition, which is more like the Catalan than the Asturian versions.

The name of the husband is Don Joan de Sevilla, **D**, Don Joan, **F**, Don Olalbo, **I**, Don Francisco, **J**, Don Pedro, **K**. His wife, a princess, **A, G**, has given birth to a child, or is on the eve of so doing. The gentleman is away from home, or is about to leave home on a pilgrimage of a year and a day, **A, G**; has gone to war, **D**; to a hunt, **I, K**. He dies just as he returns home or is leaving home, or away from home, in other versions, but in **K** comes back in a dying condition, and begs that his state may be concealed from his wife. The lady, hearing a commotion in the house, and asking the cause, is told that it is the noisy mirth of the servants, **A–D**. There is music, chanting, tolling of bells; and this is said to be for a great person who has died, **B, D, A**. In **B, D**, the wife asks, Can it be for my husband? In **J** the mother-in-law explains her own sorrowful demeanor as occasioned by the death of an uncle, and we are informed that the burial was without bells, in order that the new mother might not hear. In **J** only do we have the question, Where is my husband? He has been summoned to court, says the mother-in-law, where, as a favorite, he will stay a year and ten days. When should the young mother go to mass? Peasants go after a fortnight, tradesfolk after forty days, etc.; she, as a great lady, will wait a year and a day, **A, D, I**, a year, **B**, a year and ten days, **J**. What dress should she wear, silk, gold tissue, silver? etc. Black would become her best, **A, J, K**. [Doña Ana, in **K**, like the lady in Italian **G**, resists the suggestion of mourning, as proper only for a widow, and appears in a costume de Pascua florida: in some other copies also she seems to wear a gay dress.] The people, the children, point to her, and say, There is the widow, and her mother-in-law parries the inquiry why she is the object of remark; but the truth is avowed when they see a grave digging, and the wife asks for whom it is, **A**. In **J** the lady sees a monument in the church, hung with black, reads her husband's name, and swoons. **B, C** make the mother's explanation follow upon the children's talk. In **K** the announcement is made first by a shepherd, then confirmed by gaping spectators and by a rejected lover. The widow commends her child to its grandmother, and says she will go to her husband in heaven, **A–D**; dies on the spot, **K**; Don Francisco dies in March, Doña Ana in May, **J**.

'Don Joan y Don Ramon' is a ballad in which a young man returns to his mother mortally wounded, and therefore would be likely to blend in the memory of reciters with any other ballad in which the same incident occurred. A version from the Balearic Islands may be put first, which has not yet taken up any characteristic part of the story of Renaud: *Recuerdos y Bellezas de España*, Mallorca, p. 336, 1842 = Milá, 1853, p. 114, No 15, Briz, III, 172; *Die Balearen in Wort und Bild geschildert*, by the Archduke Ludwig Salvator, Leipzig, 1871, II, 556.*

[385] Don Joan and Don Ramon are returning from the chase. Don Ramon falls from his horse; Don Joan rides off. Don Ramon's mother sees her son coming through a field, gathering plants to heal his wounds. "What is the matter?" she asks; "you are pale." "I have been bled, and they made a mistake." "Ill luck to the barber!" "Curse him not; it is the last time. Between me and my horse we have nine and twenty lance thrusts; the horse has nine and I the rest. The horse will die tonight and I in the morning. Bury him in the best place in the stable, and me in St Eulalia; lay a sword crosswise over my grave, and if it is asked who killed me, let the answer be, Don Joan de la cassada."

There are numerous Catalan versions, and most of them add something to this story: Milá, 2d ed., 'El guerrero mal herido,' p. 171, No 210, **A–F**, A_1–G_1, A_{11}; Briz, III, 171f, two copies. These disagree considerably as to the cause of the hero's death, and the names are not constant. In A_1 of Milá, as in the Balearic ballad, Don Joan and Don Ramon are coming from the chase, and have a passage at lances; Don Joan is left dead, and Don Ramon is little short of it. **A, B**, of Milá, tell us that Don Pedro died on

the field of battle and Don Joan came home mortally wounded. **E** says that Don Joan and Don Ramon come from the chase, but Don Joan immediately says that he comes from a great battle. It is battle in F_1, in E_1 (with Gastó returning), and in both the Catalan copies of Briz, the hero being Don Joan in the first of these last, and in the other nameless. The wounded man says he has been badly bled, Milá, **A, B,** A_1, C_1, Briz 2; he and his horse have lance wounds fifty-nine, thirty-nine, twenty-nine, etc., the horse nine and he the rest, Milá, **A, B, E,** A_1, Briz 1. His mother informs him that his wife has borne a child, "a boy like the morning star," Briz 1, and says that if he will go to the best chamber he will find her surrounded by dames and ladies. This gives him no pleasure; he docs not care for wife, nor dames, nor ladies, nor boys, nor morning stars: Briz 1, Milá, A_1–G_1. He asks to have his bed made, Milá, **A–D,** B_1, C_1, Briz 1, 2, for he shall die at midnight and his horse at dawn, **A–D,** A_1, Briz 2, and gives directions for his burial and that of his horse. Let the bells toll when he is dead, and when people ask for whom it is, the answer will be, For Don Joan, Briz 1, Gastó, Milá, E_1, who was killed in battle. Let his arms be put over the place where his horse is buried, and when people ask whose arms they are his mother will say, My son's, who died in battle, Milá **A,** B_1. Let a drawn sword be laid across his grave, and let those that ask who killed him be told, Don Joan, at the chase, Milá, A_1.†

We have, probably, to do with two different ballads here, versions **A–F** of Milá's 'Guerrero mal herido,' and Briz's second, belonging with 'Don Joan y Don Ramon,' while A_1–G_1 of Milá, and Briz's first, represent a ballad of the Renaud class. It is, however, possible that the first series may be imperfect copies of the second.

'Don Joan y Don Ramon' has agreements with Italian **B, A**: in **B**, particularly, we note the hundred and fifty stabs of the knight and the ninety of his horse.

Spanish. 'Don Pedro,' *El Folk-Lore Frexnense y Bético-Extremeño*, Fregenal, 1883–84; (1) p.

---

* The version in the *Recuerdos* was obtained in Majorca by Don J. M. Quadrado. The editor remarks that the employment of the articles Il and La instead of Es and Sa proves it to be as old as the sixteenth century. *Die Balearen, etc.*, is cited after Grundtvig.

† I do not entirely understand Professor Milá's arrangement of those texts which he has not printed in full, and it is very likely that more of his copies than I have cited exhibit some of the traits specified.

129 (and 180), Zafra, Badajoz, D. Sergio Her-
nandez; (2) p. 182, Badajoz; (3) p. 183, Mon-
tanchez, provincia de Cácares; (4)
Constantina, provincia de Sevilla, D. Antonio
Machado y Alvarez.

Portuguese. A good Portuguese version, 'D.
Pedro e D. Leonarda,' in fifty short verses,
unfortunately lacking the conclusion, has been
lately communicated to *Romania* (XI, 585) by
Leite de Vasconcellos. Dom Pedro went hunt-
ing, to be gone a year and a day, but was com-
pelled to return home owing to a malady which
seized him. His mother greets him with the
information that his wife has given birth to a
son. "Comfort and cheer her," he says, "and for
me make a bed, which I shall never rise from."
The wife asks, Where is my husband, that he
does not come to see me? "He has gone a-hunt-
ing for a year and a day," replies the mother.
What is this commotion in the house? "Only
visitors." But the bells are tolling! Could it be
for my husband? "No, no; it is for a feast-day."
When do women go to mass after child-birth?
"Some in three weeks and some in two, but a
lady of your rank after a year and a day." And
6] what color do they wear? "Some light blue and
some a thousand wonders, but you, as a lady of
rank, will go in mourning." The ballad stops
abruptly with a half-pettish, half-humorous
imprecation from the daughter-in-law against
the mother for keeping her shut up so long.

There is a Slavic ballad, which, like the ver-
sions that are so popular with the Romance
nations, abridges the first part of the story, and
makes the interest turn upon the gradual dis-
covery of the hero's death, but in other respects
agrees with northern tradition.

Bohemian. A a. Erben, p. 473, No 9, Heř-
man a Dornička = Waldau, *Böhmische Granaten,*
I, 73, No 100 = Wenzig, *Slawische V. l.*, 1830,
p. 47; **b.** Čelakowsky, I, 26 = Haupt u.
Schmaler, I, 327. **B.** Erben, p. 475. **C.** Mora-
vian, Sušil, p. 82, No 89a, 'Nešťastná svatba,'
'The Doleful Wedding.' **D.** Sušil, p. 83, No 89b.
E. Slovak, Čelakowsky, I, 80.

Wendish. A. Haupt und Schmaler, I, 31, No
3, 'Zrudny kwas,' 'The Doleful Wedding.' **B.** II,
131, No 182, 'Plakajuen ńeẃesta,' 'The Weep-
ing Bride' (the last eight stanzas, the ten before
being in no connection).

The hero on his wedding day is making
ready his horse to fetch the bride; for he is, as in
the Scandinavian ballads, not yet a married
man. His mother, Bohemian **A**, ascertaining his
intention, begs him not to go himself with the
bridal escort. Obviously she has a premonition
of misfortune. Herman will never invite guests,
and not go for them. The mother, in an access
of passion, exclaims, If you go, may you break
your neck, and never come back! Here we are
reminded of the Färöe ballad. Bohemian **C, D**
make the forebodings to rise in Herman's mind,
not in his mother's. The mother opposes the
match in Bohemian **E**, and the sister wishes
that he may break his neck. Wendish **A** has
nothing of opposition or bodement before the
start, but the crows go winging about the young
men who are going for the bride, and caw a hor-
rible song, how the bridegroom shall fall from
his horse and break his neck. The train sets off
with a band of trumpets, drums, and stringed
instruments, or, Bohemian **D**, with a discharge
of a hundred muskets, and when they come to a
linden in a meadow Herman's horse "breaks his
foot," and the rider his neck; Bohemian **D**,
when they come to a copse in a meadow the
hundred pieces are again discharged, and Her-
man is mortally wounded. His friends stand
debating what they shall do. The dying man
bids them keep on: since the bride cannot be
his, she shall be his youngest brother's, Bohe-
mian **A, C**; cf. Danish **L, O, R**, Norwegian **C, F**.
The train arrives at the bride's house; the bride
comes out to greet them, but, not seeing the
bridegroom, inquires affrightedly what has
become of him. They pretend that he has
remained at home to see to the tables. The
mother is reluctant to give them the bride, but
finally yields. When the train comes again to
the linden in the mead, Dorothy sees blood. It
is Herman's! she cries; but they assure her that
it is the blood of a deer that Herman had killed
for the feast. They reach Herman's house,
where the bride has an appalling reception,
which need not be particularized.

In Bohemian **A**, while they are at supper (or
at half-eve = three in the afternoon), a death-
bell is heard. Dorothy turns pale. For whom are
they tolling? Surely it is for Herman. They tell
her that Herman is lying in his room with a bad

headache, and that the bell is ringing for a child. But she guesses the truth, sinks down and dies, **a**. She wears two knives in her hair, and thrusts one of them into her heart, **b**. The two are buried in one grave. In Bohemian **B** the bell sounds for the first time as the first course is brought on, and a second time when the second course comes. The bride is told in each case that the knell is for a child. Upon the third sounding, when the third course is brought in, they tell her that it is for Herman. She seizes two knives and runs to the graveyard: with one she digs herself a grave, and with the other stabs herself. In the Wendish fragment **B**, at the first and second course (there is no bell) the bride asks where the bridegroom is, and at the third repeats the question with tears. She is told that he is ranging the woods, killing game for his wedding. In Bohemian **C** the bell tolls while they are getting the table ready. The bride asks if it is for Herman, and is told that it is for a child. When they sit down to table, the bells toll again. For whom should this be? For whom but Herman? She springs out of the window, and the catastrophe is the same as in Bohemian **B**. In **D** the bride hears the bell as the train is approaching the house, and they say it is for a child. On entering the court she asks where Herman is. He is in the cellar drawing wine for his guests. She asks again for Herman as the company sits down to table, and the answer is, In the chamber, lying in a coffin. She springs from the table and rushes to the chamber, seizing two golden knives, one of which she plunges into her heart. In Bohemian **E**, when the bride arrives at John the bridegroom's house, and asks where he is, they tell her she had better go to bed till midnight. The moment she touches John he springs out of bed, and cries, Dear people, why have ye laid a living

[387]

woman with a dead man? They stand, saying, What shall we give her, a white cap or a green chaplet? "I have not deserved the white (widow's) cap," she says; "I have deserved a green chaplet." In Wendish **A**, when the bell first knolls, the bride asks, Where is the bridegroom? and they answer, In the new chamber, putting on his fine clothes. A second toll evokes a second inquiry; and they say he is in the new room, putting on his sword. The third time they conceal nothing: He fell off his horse and broke his neck. "Then tear off my fine clothes and dress me in white, that I may mourn a year and a day, and go to church in a green chaplet, and never forget him that loved me!" It will be remembered that the bride takes her own life in Norwegian **A**, **C**, **D**, and in Swedish **E**, as she does in Bohemian **A b**, **B**, **C**, **D**.

B is translated by Grundtvig, *Engelske og skotske Folkeviser*, p. 305, No 48; by Doenniges, p. 25.

'Der Ritter von Staufenberg' is translated by Jamieson, from the "Romanzen" in the *Wunderhorn*, in *Illustrations of Northern Antiquities*, p. 257. Danish **A** by Prior, II, 301; **B** by Jamieson, *Popular Ballads*, I, 219, and by Prior, II, 306, Buchanan, p. 52. 'The Erl-King's Daughter,' "Danish," in Lewis's *Tales of Wonder*, I, 53, No 10, is rendered from Herder. Swedish **A** by Keightley, *Fairy Mythology*, p. 84; **B** by Keightley, p. 82, and by William and Mary Howitt, *Literature and Romance of Northern Europe*, I, 269. There is a version from Swedish by J. H. Dixon, in *Notes and Queries*, 4th Series, I, 168. Breton **D** by Keightley, as above, p. 433, and by Tom Taylor, *Ballads and Songs of Brittany*, 'Lord Nann and the Fairy,' p. 9. Bohemian **A b** by Bowring, *Cheskian Anthology*, p. 69.

A

From a transcript from William Tytler's Brown MS.

Clark Colven and his gay___ la - die,   As they walked to yon gar - den green,
A belt about her mid - dle_ gimp,   Which cost Clark Col - ven crowns___ fif - teen:

(Oh, the birk and the row an,___ and the brume it blows bon - nie.)

Ritson-Tytler-Brown MS., pp. 6–9. Sung by Mrs Brown, Falkland, Aberdeenshire.
Text underlay based on Bronson's conjectural reading, I, p. 334.

1 CLARK COLVEN and his gay ladie,
   As they walked to yon garden green,
  A belt about her middle gimp,
   Which cost Clark Colven crowns fifteen:

2 'O hearken weel now, my good lord,
   O hearken weel to what I say;
  When ye gang to the wall o Stream,
   O gang nae neer the well-fared may.'

3 'O haud your tongue, my gay ladie,
   Tak nae sic care o me;
  For I nae saw a fair woman
   I like so well as thee.'

4 He mounted on his berry-brown steed,
   And merry, merry rade he on,
  Till he came to the wall o Stream,
   And there he saw the mermaiden.

5 'Ye wash, ye wash, ye bonny may,
   And ay 's ye wash your sark o silk:'
  'It's a' for you, ye gentle knight,
   My skin is whiter than the milk.'

6 He's taen her by the milk-white hand,
   He's taen her by the sleeve sae green,
  And he's forgotten his gay ladie,
   And away with the fair maiden.

   *   *   *   *   *

7 'Ohon, alas!' says Clark Colven,
   'And aye sae sair's I mean my head!'
  And merrily leugh the mermaiden,
   'O win on till you be dead.

8 'But out ye tak your little pen-knife,
   And frae my sark ye shear a gare;
  Row that about your lovely head,
   And the pain ye'll never feel nae mair.'

9 Out he has taen his little pen-knife,
   And frae her sark he's shorn a gare,
  Rowed that about his lovely head,
   But the pain increased mair and mair.

10 'Ohon, alas!' says Clark Colven,
   'An aye sae sair's I mean my head!'
  And merrily laughd the mermaiden,
   'It will ay be war till ye be dead.'

11 Then out he drew his trusty blade,
   And thought wi it to be her dead,
  But she's become a fish again,
   And merrily sprang into the fleed.

12 He's mounted on his berry-brown steed,
   And dowy, dowy rade he home,
  And heavily, heavily lighted down
   When to his ladie's bower-door he came.

13 'Oh, mither, mither, mak my bed,
   And, gentle ladie, lay me down;
  Oh, brither, brither, unbend my bow,
   'T will never be bent by me again.'

14 His mither she has made his bed,
   His gentle ladie laid him down,
  His brither he has unbent his bow,
   'T was never bent by him again.

B

Herd's *Ancient and Modern Scots Songs*, 1769, p.
302: ed. 1776, I, 161.

1 CLERK COLVILL and his lusty dame
    Were walking in the garden green;
  The belt around her stately waist
    Cost Clerk Colvill of pounds fifteen.

2 'O promise me now, Clerk Colvill,
    Or it will cost ye muckle strife,
  Ride never by the wells of Slane,
    If ye wad live and brook your life.'

3 'Now speak nae mair, my lusty dame,
    Now speak nae mair of that to me;
  Did I neer see a fair woman,
    But I wad sin with her body?'

4 He's taen leave o his gay lady,
    Nought minding what his lady said,
  And he's rode by the wells of Slane,
    Where washing was a bonny maid.

5 'Wash on, wash on, my bonny maid,
    That wash sae clean your sark of silk;'
  'And weel fa you, fair gentleman,
    Your body whiter than the milk.'

*   *   *   *   *

6 Then loud, loud cry'd the Clerk Colvill,
    'O my head it pains me sair;'
  'Then take, then take,' the maiden said,
    'And frae my sark you'll cut a gare.'

7 Then she's gied him a little bane-knife,
    And frae her sark he cut a share;
  She's ty'd it round his whey-white face,
    But ay his head it aked mair.

8 Then louder cry'd the Clerk Colvill,
    'O sairer, sairer akes my head;'
  'And sairer, sairer ever will,'
    The maiden crys, 'till you be dead.'

9 Out then he drew his shining blade,
    Thinking to stick her where she stood,
  But she was vanishd to a fish,
    And swam far off, a fair mermaid.

10 'O mother, mother, braid my hair;
    My lusty lady, make my bed;
  O brother, take my sword and spear,
    For I have seen the false mermaid.'

C

Notes and Queries, 4th Series, VIII, 510, from the
recitation of a lady in Forfarshire.

1 CLERK COLIN and his mother dear
    Were in the garden green;
  The band that was about her neck
    Cost Colin pounds fifteen;
  The belt about her middle sae sma
    Cost twice as much again.

2 'Forbidden gin ye wad be, love Colin,
    Forbidden gin ye wad be,
  And gang nae mair to Clyde's water,
    To court yon gay ladie.'

3 'Forbid me frae your ha, mother,
    Forbid me frae your hour,
  But forbid me not frae yon ladie
    She's fair as ony flour.

4 'Forbidden I winna be, mother,
    Forbidden I winna be,
  For I maun gang to Clyde's water,
    To court yon gay ladie.'

5 An he is on his saddle set,
    As fast as he could win,
  An he is on to Clyde's water,
    By the lee licht o the moon.

6 An when he cam to the Clyde's water
    He lichted lowly down,
  An there he saw the mermaiden,
    Washin silk upon a stane.

l3

7 'Come down, come down, now, Clerk Colin,
  Come down an [fish] wi me;
  I'll row ye in my arms twa,
  An a foot I sanna jee.'

    *   *   *   *   *

8 'O mother, mother, mak my bed,
  And, sister, lay me doun,
  An brother, tak my bow an shoot,
  For my shooting is done.'

9 He wasna weel laid in his bed,
  Nor yet weel fa'en asleep,
  When up an started the mermaiden,
  Just at Clerk Colin's feet.

10 'Will ye lie there an die, Clerk Colin,
   Will ye lie there an die?
   Or will ye gang to Clyde's water,
   To fish in flood wi me?'

11 'I will lie here an die,' he said,
   'I will lie here an die;
   In spite o a' the deils in hell
   I will lie here an die.'

———◆———

A. 7³. laugh; *but we have* laughd *in* 10³.
  9³. Rowed *seems to be written* Round, *possibly* Rowad.
  14³. brother.
B. 5⁴. *The edition of* 1776 *has* body's.
C. 7. When they part he returns home, and on the way his head becomes "wondrous sair:" *seemingly a comment of the reciter.*

  The Abbotsford copy in "Scottish Songs," *fol. 3, has these readings, not found in Lewis, the Brown MS., or Herd.*
  3². And dinna deave me wi your din: *Lewis,*
    And haud, my Lady gay, your din.

6³. He's laid her on the flowery green.

A copy in the Findlay MSS, I, 141: 'Clerk Colin,' *from Miss Butchart, Arbroath, 1868: Miss Butchart, who died about 1890, aged above ninety years, was the daughter of the Mrs Butchart from whom Kinloch got certain ballads, and niece to the Mrs Arrot who was one of Jamieson's contributors. In the MS. there are these readings:*

2³. To gang. 4³. maun gae. 5². could gang.
6¹. To Clyde's.

43

THE BROOMFIELD HILL

A. 'The Broomfield Hill.' **a**. Scott's *Minstrelsy*, III, 271, 1803. **b**. The same, II, 229, 1802.
B. 'I'll wager, I'll wager,' etc., Herd's *Ancient and Modern Scots Songs*, 1769, p. 310.
C. 'Broomfield Hills,' Buchan's *Ballads of the North of Scotland*, II, 291.

D. 'Lord John,' Kinloch's *Ancient Scottish Ballads*, p. 195.
E. Joseph Robertson's Note-Book, January, 1830, p. 7.
F. 'The Merry Broomfield, or The West Country Wager.' **a**. *Douce Ballads*, III, fol. 64[b]. **b**. The same, IV, fol. 10.

A SONG of 'Brume, brume on hil' is one of those named in *The Complaint of Scotland*, 1549, p. 64 of Dr J. A. H. Murray's edition. "The foot of the song" is sung, with others, by Moros in Wager's "very merry and pithy Comedy called The longer thou livest the more fool thou art," c. 1568. 'Broom, broom on hil' is also one of Captain Cox's "bunch of ballets and songs, all auncient," No 53 of the collection, 1575.[*] The lines that Moros sings are:

Brome, brome on hill,
The gentle brome on hill, hill,
Brome, brome on Hive hill,
The gentle brome on Hive hill,
The brome stands on Hive hill a.

"A more sanguine antiquary than the editor," says Scott, "might perhaps endeavor to identify this poem, which is of undoubted antiquity, with the 'Broom, broom on hill' mentioned . . . as forming part of Captain Cox's collection." Assuredly "Broom, broom on hill," if that were all, would justify no such identification, but the occurrence of Hive hill, both in the burden which Moros sings and in the eighth stanza of Scott's ballad, is a circumstance

that would embolden even a very cautious antiquary, if he had received Hive hill from tradition, and was therefore unaffected by a suspicion that this locality had been introduced by an editor from the old song.[†]

Most of the versions give no explicit account of the knight's prolonged sleep. He must needs be asleep when the lady comes to him, else there would be no story; but his heavy slumber, not broken by all the efforts of his

[*] Furnivall, *Captain Cox, his Ballads and Books*, pp cxxvii f. Ritson cited the comedy in the dissertation prefixed to his *Ancient Songs*, 1790, p. lx.

[†] Motherwell remarks, at page 42 of his Introduction, "The song is popular still, and is often to be met with." It was printed in a cheap American song-book, which I have not been able to recover, under the title of 'The Green Broomfield,' and with some cis-atlantic variations. *Graham's Illustrated Magazine*, September, 1858, gives these stanzas:

"Then when she went to the green broom field,
    Where her love was fast asleep,
With a gray *goose*-hawk and a green laurel bough,
    And a green broom under his feet.

"And when he awoke from out his sleep,
    An angry man was he;
He looked to the East, and he looked to the West,
    And he wept for his sweetheart to see.

"Oh! where was you, my gray *goose*-hawk,
    The hawk that I loved so dear,
That you did not awake me from out my sleep,
    When my sweetheart was so near?"

horse and his hawk, is as a matter of course not natural; es geht nicht zu mit rechten dingen; the witch-wife of **A** 4 is at the bottom of that. And yet the broom-flowers strewed on his hals-bane in **A** 8, **B** 3, and the roses in **D** 6, are only to be a sign that the maid had been there and was gone. Considering the character of many of Buchan's versions, we cannot feel sure that **C** has not borrowed the second and third stanzas from **B**, and the witch-wife, in the sixth, from **A**; but it would be extravagant to call in question the genuineness of **C** as a whole. The eighth stanza gives us the light which we require.

'Ye'll pu the bloom frae aff the broom,
   Strew 't at his head and feet,
And aye the thicker that ye do strew,
   The sounder he will sleep.'

The silver belt about the knight's head in **A** 5 can hardly have to do with his sleeping, and to me seems meaningless. It is possible that roses are not used at random in **D** 6, though, like the posie of pleasant perfume in **F** 9, they serve only to prove that the lady had been there. An excrescence on the dogrose, rosen-schwamm, schlafkunz, kunz, schlafapfel, it is believed in Germany, if laid under a man's pillow, will make him sleep till it is taken away. Grimm, *Deutsche Mythologie*, p. 1008, and *Deutsches Wörterbuch* (Hildebrand), V, 2753 e.

C makes the lady hide in the broom to hear what the knight will say when he wakes, and in this point agrees with the broadside **F**, as also in the comment made by the men on their master in stanza 24; cf. **F** 16.

Mr J. W. Dixon has reprinted an Aldermary Churchyard copy of the broadside, differing as to four or five words only from **F**, in *Ancient Poems, Ballads, and Songs of the Peasantry of England*, p. 116, Percy Society, Volume XVII. The editor remarks that **A** is evidently taken from **F**; from which it is clear that the pungent buckishness of the broadside does not necessarily make an impression. **A** smells of the broom; **F** suggests the groom.[*]

_____
[*]   The broadside is also copied into Buchan's MSS, II, 197.

The sleep which is produced in **A** by strewing the flower of the broom on a man's head and feet, according to a witch's advice, is brought about in two Norse ballads by means not simply occult, but altogether preternatural; that is, by the power of runes. One of these, 'Sömnrunorna,' Arwidsson, II, 249, No 133, is preserved in a manuscript of the end of the seventeenth, or the beginning of the eighteenth, century. The other, 'Sövnerunerne,' Grundtvig, II, 337, No 81, was taken down in 1847 from the singing of a woman seventy-five years of age.

The Swedish ballad runs thus. There is a damsel in our land who every night will sleep with a man, and dance a maid in the morning. The fame of this comes to the ears of the son of the king of England, who orders his horse, thinking to catch this damsel. When he arrives at the castle gate, there stands the lady, and asks him what is his haste. He frankly answers that he expects to get a fair maid's honor for his pains, and she bids him follow her to the upper room. She lays sheets on the bed, and writes strong runes on them. The youth sits down on the bed, and is asleep before he can stretch himself out. He sleeps through that day, and the next, and into the third. Then the lady rouses him. "Wake up; you are sleeping your two eyes out." He is still so heavy that he can hardly stir. He offers her his horse and saddle to report the matter as he wishes. "Keep your horse," she says; "shame fa such liars."

The Danish story is much the same. One of a king's five sons goes to make trial of the maid. She tells him to fasten his horse while she goes before and unlocks; calls to her maid to bring five feather-beds, feather-beds nine, and write a sleep on each of them. He sleeps through three days, and is roused the fourth, with "Wake up, wake up; you have slept away your pluck." He offers her a bribe, as before, which she scornfully rejects, assuring him that he will not be spared when she comes among maids and knights.

A sleep produced by runes or gramarye is one of the two main incidents of a tale in the *Gesta Romanorum*, better known through the other, which is the forfeit of flesh for money not forthcoming at the day set, as in the *Merchant of Venice*: Latin, Oesterley, No 195, p. 603;[†] English, Harleian MS. 7333, No 40, printed by

Douce, *Illustrations of Shakspere*, I, 281, Madden, p. 130, Herrtage, p. 158; German, No 68, of the printed edition of 1489 (which I have [392] not seen). A knight, who has a passion for an emperor's daughter, engages to give a thousand [hundred] marks for being once admitted to her bed. He instantly falls asleep, and has to be roused in the morning. Like terms are made for a second night, and the man's lands have to be pledged to raise the money. He sleeps as before, but stipulates for a third night at the same price. A merchant lends him the thousand marks, on condition that, if he breaks his day, his creditor may take the money's weight of flesh from his body. Feeling what a risk he is now running, the knight consults a philosopher, Virgil, in the English version. The philosopher (who in the Latin version says he ought to know, for he had helped the lady to her trick) tells the knight that between the sheet and coverlet of the bed there is a letter, which causes the sleep; this he must find, and, when found, cast far from the bed. The knight follows these directions, and gets the better of the lady, who conceives a reciprocal passion for him, and delivers him, in the sequel, from the fearful penalty of his bond by pleading that the flesh must be taken without shedding of blood.

Josyan, in Sir Bevis of Hamptoun, preserves her chastity by the use of a rune:

'I shall go make me a writ,
Thorough a clerk wise of wit,
That there shall no man have grace,
While that letter is in place,
Against my will to lie me by,
Nor do me shame nor villany.'
She did that letter soon be wrought
On the manner as she had thought;
About her neck she hanged it.

Ellis's *English Metrical Romances*, London, 1848, p. 256.

The romance of Dolopathos, a variety of the Seven Wise Masters, written about 1185, considerably before the earliest date which has hitherto been proposed for the compilation of the *Gesta*, has this story, with variations, of which only these require to be noted. The lady has herself been a student in magic. She is wooed of many; all comers are received, and pay a hundred marks; any one who accomplishes his will may wed her the next day. An enchanted feather of a screech-owl, laid under the pillow, makes all who enter the bed fall asleep at once, and many have been baffled by this charm. At last a youth of high birth, but small means, tries his fortune, and, failing at the first essay, tries once more. Thinking that the softness of his couch was the cause of his falling asleep, he puts away the pillow, and in this process the feather is thrown out: *Iohannis de Alta Silva Dolopathos*, ed. Oesterley, pp 57–59; Herbers, *Li Romans de Dolopathos*, Brunet et Montaiglon, vv 7096–7498, pp 244–59; Le Roux de Lincy, in a sequel to Loiseleur-Deslongchamps's *Essai sur les fables indiennes*, pp 211ff. This form of the tale is found in German, in a fifteenth-century manuscript, from which it was printed by Haupt in *Altdeutsche Blätter*, I, 143–49; but here the sleep is produced by the use of *both* the means employed in the *Gesta* and in Dolopathos, letter (runes) and feather, "the wild man's feather."[*]

Magic is dropped, and a sleeping draught administered, just as the man is going to bed, in a version of the story in the *Pecorone of Ser Giovanni Fiorentino*, Giornata, IV^a, Nov. 1_a (last quarter of the fourteenth century). Upon the third trial the man, warned by a friendly chambermaid not to drink, pours the medicated wine into his bosom. The account of Ser Giovanni is adopted in *Les Adventures d'Abdalla, fils d'Hanif, etc.*, La Haye, 1713, *Bibliothèque des Romans*, 1778, Janvier, I, 112–14, 143f.

† The Anglo-Latin text in Harleian MS. 2270, No 48. The text of Harleian MS., 2270, compared with another copy in Harleian MS., No 5259, is given in Wright's *Latin Stories*, p. 114, No 126, Percy Society, vol. viii. (R. Köhler.)

In the Lai de Doon, ed. G. Paris, *Romania*, VIII, 61ff, those who sleep in the bed are found dead in the morning, and Doon simply sits up all night. (R. Köhler.)

* Sy . . . bereytte keyn abende das bette met der czöberye met der schryft und met des wylden mannes veddere, p. 145, lines 8, 10–12; das quam alles von der czoyberye, das die jungfrowe dy knaben alle beczobert hatte met schryft und met bryven, dy sy en under dy höbt leyte under dy kussen, und met den veddern von den wylden ruchen lüten, lines 1–5. Only *one* letter and one feather is employed in each case.

Ellin writes sleep-runes on the cushions on which her husband's sons are to sleep, in the Danish ballad 'Frændehævn,' Grundtvig, No 4, A 33 [C 45].

In Icelandic tales a sleep-thorn* is employed, probably a thorn inscribed with runes. The thorn is stuck into the clothes or into the head (the ears, according to the popular notion, Vigfusson), and the sleep lasts till the thorn is taken out. Odin stuck such a thorn into Brynhild's garments: Fáfnismál, 43; Sigrdrífumál, 7; Völsúnga Saga, Fornaldar Sögur, I, 166. The thorn is put into the clothes also in the Icelandic fairy-tale, Mærþöll, Maurer, Isländische Volkssagen, p. 286. Ólöf, to save herself from Helgi's violence, and to punish his insolence, sticks him with a sleep-thorn after he is dead drunk: Hrólfs Saga Kraka, Fornaldar Sögur I, 18f, Torfæus, p. 32. Vilhjálmr sticks a sleep-thorn into Hrólfr, and he lies as if dead so long as the thorn is in him: Gaungu-Hrólfs Saga, Forn. S., III, 303, 306.

Sleep-thorns, or something similar, occur in the West Highland tales. In a story partly reported by Campbell, I, xci, "the sister put gath nimh, a poisonous sting or thorn, into the bed, and the prince was as though he were dead for three days, and he was buried. But Knowledge told the other two dogs what to do, and they scraped up the prince and took out the thorn, and he came alive again and went home." So in "The Widow's Son," Campbell, II, 296: "On the morrow he went, but the carlin stuck a bior nimh, spike of hurt, in the outside of the door post, and when he came to the church he fell asleep." In another version of The Widow's Son, II, 297, a "big pin" serves as the "spike of hurt." Cf. the needle in Haltrich, Deutsche Volksmärchen aus dem Sachsenlande in Siebenbürgen, 3d ed., p. 141, No 32; Curtin, Myths and Folk-Lore of Ireland, 1890, pp. 40, 130ff, 200; Hyde, Beside the Fire, Irish-Gaelic Folk-Stories, p. 43; MacInnes, Folk and Hero Tales, 1890, p. 141 (cf. p. 459). (G. L. K.)†

---

* Svefnþorn, Danish søvntorn, or søvnpreen: blundstafir, sleep-staves, rods (if not letters, runes) in Sigdrífumál, 2.

† Sleep-pin, Wlislocki, M. u. S. der transylvanischen Zigeuner, p. 46. Compare the wand in J. H. Knowles's Folk-Tales of Kashmir, p. 199. (G. L. K.)

In Gongu-Rólvs kvæði, Hammershaimb, Færøiske Qvæder, No 16, p. 140, sts 99–105, Lindin remains a maid for two nights, and loses the name the third, but the sleep-rune or thorn which should explain this does not occur.

A pillow of soporific quality, which Kamele, by Isot's direction, puts under Kaedin's head, assures her safety though she lies all night by his side: Ulrich's continuation of Gottfried's Tristan, vv 1668–99, 1744–85; and Heinrich's continuation, omitting the last circumstance, vv 4861–4960 (J. Grimm).

The witch-woman, in the English ballad, A 4, represents the philosopher in the Gesta, and the wager in the other versions the fee or fine exacted by the lady in the Gesta and elsewhere.

An Italian ballad, a slight and unmeritable thing, follows the story of Ser Giovanni, or agrees with it, in respect to the sleeping-draught. A man falls in with a girl at a spring, and offers her a hundred ducats, or scudi, per una nottina. The girl says that she must consult her mother. The mother advises her to accept the offer: she will give the man a drug, and the money will serve for a dowry. The man, roused in the morning, counts out the money with one hand and wipes his eyes with the other. When asked why he is crying, he replies that the money is not the loss he weeps for, and makes a second offer of the same amount. The girl wishes to refer the matter to her mother again, but the gallant says the mother shall not take him in a second time. One version (A) ends somewhat more respectably: the girl declares that, having come off with her honor once, she will not again expose herself to shame. A. Ferraro, Canti popolari monferrini, 'La Ragazza onesta,' p. 66, No 47. B. Ferraro, C. p. di Ferrara, Cento e Pontelagoscuro, p. 53 (Cento) No 4, 'La Ragazza onesta.' C. The same, p. 94 (Pontelagoscuro) No 8, 'La Brunetta,' previously in Rivista di Filologia Romanza, II, 200. D. Wolf, Volkslieder aus Venetien, p. 74, 'La Contadina alla Fonte.' E. Bernoni, C. p. veneziani, Puntata V, No 4, p. 6, 'La bella Brunetta.' F. Bolza, Canzoni p. comasche, p. 677, No 57, 'L'Amante deluso.' G. Ive, C. p. istriani, p. 324, No 4, 'La Contadina alla Fonte.' H. Gianandria, C. p. marchigiani, p. 277, No 12, 'La Madre indegna.' I. Ferraro, C. p. della Bassa Romagna, Rivista di

Letteratura popolare, p. 57, 'La Ragazza onesta.' J. Casetti e Imbriani, C. *p. delle Provincie merid- ionali*, p. 1, No 1 (Chieti), the first sixteen verses. **K**. *Archivio per Tradizioni popolari*, I, 89, No 4, 'La Fandéll e lu Cavalére,' the first thir- teen lines. To these may be added Righi, p. 33, No 96; Nigra, No 77, p. 393, 'La Bevanda son- nifera,' **A–H**; Giannini, 'Il Cavaliere ingan- nato,' p. 157; Ferrari, *Biblioteca di Lett. pop. italiana*, I, 218, 'La bella Brunetta;' Finamore, in *Archivio*, I, 89, La Fandell' e lu Cavaljiere (mixed); Nerucci, in *Archivio*, II, 524, 'La Raga- zza Fantina;' Julia, in *Archivio*, VI, 244, 'La 'nfantina e lu Cavalieri;' Rondini, in *Archivio*, VII, 189; 'La bella Brunetta,' Ferrari, *C. p. in San Pietro Capofiume*; 'La Bevanda sonnifera,' Giannini, Canzoni del Contado di Massa Lun- ense, *Archivio*, VIII, 109, No 11, 279, No 7; 'Quarante ans j'ai travaillé,' Georgeakis et Pineau, *Folk-lore de Lesbos*, p. 246. Ricordi, *Canti p. Lombardi*, No 9, 'La Moraschina,' gives the first half of the story, with a slight alteration for propriety's sake.

'The Sleepy Merchant,' a modern ballad, in Kinloch's MSS, V, 26, was perhaps fashioned on some traditional report of the story in Il Pecor- one. The girl gives the merchant a drink, and when the sun is up starts to her feet, crying, "I'm a leal maiden yet!" The merchant comes back, and gets another dram, but "tooms it a' between the bolster and the wa," and then sits up and sings.

A ballad found everywhere in Germany, but always in what appears to be an extremely defective form, must originally, one would think, have had some connection with those which we are considering. A hunter meets a girl on the heath, and takes her with him to his hut, where they pass the night. She rouses him in

the morning, and proclaims herself still a maid. The hunter is so chagrined that he is of a mind to kill her, but spares her life. 'Der Jäger,' 'Der ernsthafte Jäger,' 'Des Jägers Verdruss,' 'Der Jäger und die reine Jungfrau,' 'Der verschlafene Jäger:' Meinert, p. 203; *Wunderhorn*, 1857, I, 274, Birlinger u. Crecelius, I, 190; Büsching u. von der Hagen, p. 134, No 51; Nicolai, *Alma- nach*, I, 77 (fragment); Erk u. Irmer, ii, 12, No 15; Meier, p. 305, No 170; Pröhle, No 54, p. 81; Fiedler, p. 175; Erk, *Liederhort*, pp 377f, Nos 174, 174[a]; Hoffmann u. Richter, p. 202, No 176; Ditfurth, *Fränkische Volkslieder*, II, 26f, Nos 30, 31; Norrenberg, *Des Dülkener Fiedlers Lied- erbuch*, No 20, p. 16; J. A. E. Köhler, *Volks- brauch im Voigtlande*, p. 307; Jeitteles, Volkslied in Steiermark, *Archiv für Lit. gesch.*, IX, 861, etc.; Uhland, No 104, Niederdeutsches Lieder- buch, in *Niederdeutsche Volkslieder, herausgege- ben vom Verein für niederdeutsche Sprachforschung*, p. 40, No 63, No 59, 'vermuth- lich vom Eingang des 17. Jhd.' Jäger-Romanze in Böhme, *Altdeutsches Liederbuch*, No 437, from Melchior Franck, *Fasciculus Quodlibeticus*, Nürnberg, 1611, No 6: slightly different, no dis- position to kill the maid. Three copies of this all but inevitable ballad in *Blätter für Pommer- sche Volkskunde*, II. Jahrgang, p. 77f, 'Jägerslied;' and more might be added. Cf. *Die Mâeget*, Flemish, Büsching u. von der Hagen, p. 311; Willems, p. 160, No 61; 'Kurz gefasst,' Alfred Müller, *Volkslieder aus dem Erzgebirge*, p. 90.*

A a is translated by Doenniges, p. 3; by Ger- hard, p. 146; by Arndt, *Blütenlese*, p. 226.

---

* The first stanza of the German ballad occurs in a music-book of 1622: Hoffmann u. Richter, p. 202, who add that the ballad is extant in Dutch and Flemish.

A

a. Scott's *Minstrelsy*, III, 271, ed. 1803. **b.** Sts. 8–14
the same, II, 229, ed. 1802.

1 THERE was a knight and a lady bright,
　　Had a true tryste at the broom;
　The ane gaed early in the morning,
　　The other in the afternoon.

2 And ay she sat in her mother's bower door,
　　And ay she made her mane:
　'O whether should I gang to the Broomfield
　　　Hill,
　　Or should I stay at hame?

3 'For if I gang to the Broomfield Hill,
　　My maidenhead is gone;
　And if I chance to stay at hame,
　　My love will ca me mansworn.'

4 Up then spake a witch-woman,
　　Ay from the room aboon:
　'O ye may gang to the Broomfield Hill,
　　And yet come maiden hame.

5 'For when ye gang to the Broomfield Hill,
　　Ye'll find your love asleep,
　With a silver belt about his head,
　　And a broom-cow at his feet.

6 'Take ye the blossom of the broom,
　　The blossom it smells sweet,
　And strew it at your true-love's head,
　　And likewise at his feet.

7 'Take ye the rings off your fingers,
　　Put them on his right hand,
　To let him know, when he doth awake,
　　His love was at his command.'

8 She pu'd the broom flower on Hive Hill,
　　And strewd on 's white hals-bane,
　And that was to be wittering true
　　That maiden she had gane.

9 'O where were ye, my milk-white steed,
　　That I hae coft sae dear,
　That wadna watch and waken me
　　When there was maiden here?'

10 'I stamped wi my foot, master,
　　And gard my bridle ring,
　But na kin thing wald waken ye,
　　Till she was past and gane.'

11 'And wae betide ye, my gay goss-hawk,
　　That I did love sae dear,
　That wadna watch and waken me
　　When there was maiden here.'

12 'I clapped wi my wings, master,
　　And aye my bells I rang,
　And aye cry'd, Waken, waken, master,
　　Before the ladye gang.'

13 'But haste and haste, my gude white steed,
　　To come the maiden till,
　Or a' the birds of gude green wood
　　Of your flesh shall have their fill.'

14 'Ye need na burst your gude white steed
　　Wi racing oer the howm;
　Nae bird flies faster through the wood,
　　Than she fled through the broom.'

B

Herd, *Ancient and Modern Scots Songs*, 1769, p. 310.

1 'I'LL wager, I'll wager, I'll wager with you
　　Five hundred merks and ten,
　That a maid shanae go to yon bonny green
　　　wood,
　　And a maiden return agen.'

2 'I'll wager, I'll wager, I'll wager with you
　　Five hundred merks and ten,
　That a maid shall go to yon bonny green wood,
　　And a maiden return agen.'

＊　　＊　　＊　　＊　　＊

3 She's pu'd the blooms aff the broom-bush,
　　And strewd them on 's white hass-bane:
　　'This is a sign whereby you may know
　　That a maiden was here, but she's gane.'

4 'O where was you, my good gray steed,
　　That I hae loed sae dear?
　　O why did you not awaken me
　　When my true love was here?'

5 'I stamped with my foot, master,
　　And gard my bridle ring,
　　But you wadnae waken from your sleep
　　Till your love was past and gane.'

6 'Now I may sing as dreary a sang
　　As the bird sung on the brier,
　　For my true love is far removd,
　　And I'll neer see her mair.'

C

Buchan's *Ballads of the North of Scotland*, II, 291.

1 THERE was a knight and lady bright
　　Set trysts amo the broom,
　　The one to come at morning ear,
　　The other at afternoon.

2 'I'll wager a wager wi you,' he said,
　　'An hundred merks and ten,
　　That ye shall not go to Broomfield Hills,
　　Return a maiden again.'

3 'I'll wager a wager wi you,' she said,
　　'A hundred pounds and ten,
　　That I will gang to Broomfield Hills,
　　A maiden return again.'

4 The lady stands in her bower door,
　　And thus she made her mane:
　　'O shall I gang to Broomfield Hills,
　　Or shall I stay at hame?

5 'If I do gang to Broomfield Hills,
　　A maid I'll not return;
　　But if I stay from Broomfield Hills,
　　I'll be a maid mis-sworn.'

6 Then out it speaks an auld witch-wife,
　　Sat in the bower aboon:
　　'O ye shall gang to Broomfield Hills,
　　Ye shall not stay at hame.

7 'But when ye gang to Broomfield Hills,
　　Walk nine times round and round;
　　Down below a bonny burn bank,
　　Ye'll find your love sleeping sound.

8 'Ye'll pu the bloom frae aff the broom,
　　Strew 't at his head and feet,
　　And aye the thicker that ye do strew,
　　The sounder he will sleep.

9 'The broach that is on your napkin,
　　Put it on his breast bane,
　　To let him know, when he does wake,
　　That 's true love 's come and gane.

10 'The rings that are on your fingers,
　　Lay them down on a stane,
　　To let him know, when he does wake,
　　That 's true love 's come and gane.

11 'And when ye hae your work all done,
　　Ye'll gang to a bush o' broom,
　　And then you'll hear what he will say,
　　When he sees ye are gane.'

12 When she came to Broomfield Hills,
　　She walkd it nine times round,
　　And down below yon burn bank,
　　She found him sleeping sound.

13 She pu'd the bloom frae aff the broom,
　　Strew'd it at 's head and feet,
　　And aye the thicker that she strewd,
　　The sounder he did sleep.

14 The broach that was on her napkin,
　　She put on his breast bane,
　　To let him know, when he did wake,
　　His love was come and gane.

15 The rings that were on her fingers,
   She laid upon a stane,
   To let him know, when he did wake,
   His love was come and gane.

16 Now when she had her work all dune,
   She went to a bush o broom,
   That she might hear what he did say,
   When he saw she was gane.

17 'O where were ye, my guid grey hound,
   That I paid for sae dear,
   Ye didna waken me frae my sleep
   When my true love was sae near?'

18 'I scraped wi my foot, master,
   Till a' my collars rang,
   But still the mair that I did scrape,
   Waken woud ye nane.'

19 'Where were ye, my berry-brown steed,
   That I paid for sae dear,
   That ye woudna waken me out o my sleep
   When my love was sae near?'

20 'I patted wi my foot, master,
   Till a' my bridles rang,
   But still the mair that I did patt,
   Waken woud ye nane.'

21 'O where were ye, my gay goss-hawk,
   That I paid for sae dear,
   That ye woudna waken me out o my sleep
   When ye saw my love near?'

22 'I flapped wi my wings, master,
   Till a' my bells they rang,
   But still the mair that I did flap,
   Waken woud ye nane.'

23 'O where were ye, my merry young men,
   That I pay meat and fee,
   Ye woudna waken me out o' my sleep
   When my love ye did see?'

24 'Ye'll sleep mair on the night, master,
   And wake mair on the day;
   Gae sooner down to Broomfield Hills
   When ye've sic pranks to play.

25 'If I had seen any armed men
   Come riding over the hill—
   But I saw but a fair lady
   Come quietly you until.'

26 'O wae mat worth you, my young men,
   That I pay meat and fee,
   That ye woudna waken me frae sleep
   When ye my love did see.

27 'O had I waked when she was nigh,
   And o her got my will,
   I shoudna cared upon the morn
   Tho sma birds o her were fill.'

28 When she went out, right bitter wept,
   But singing came she hame;
   Says, I hae been at Broomfield Hills,
   And maid returnd again.

D

Kinloch's *Ancient Scottish Ballads*, p. 195.

'I'll wager, I'll wa - ger says Lord John, 'A hund - red merks and ten, That ye win-na gae to the bonnie broom - fields, Anda maid re - turn a - gain.'

1 'I'LL wager, I'll wager,' says Lord John,
   'A hundred merks and ten,
   That ye winna gae to the bonnie broom-fields,
   And a maid return again.'

2 'But I'll lay a wager wi you, Lord John,
   A' your merks oure again,
   That I'll gae alane to the bonnie broom-fields,
   And a maid return again.'

3 Then Lord John mounted his grey steed,
   And his hound wi his bells sae bricht,
   And swiftly he rade to the bonny broom-fields,
   Wi his hawks, like a lord or knicht.

4 'Now rest, now rest, my bonnie grey steed,
   My lady will soon be here,
   And I'll lay my head aneath this rose sae red,
   And the bonnie burn sae near.'

5 But sound, sound was the sleep he took,
   For he slept till it was noon,
   And his lady cam at day, left a taiken and away,
   Gaed as licht as a glint o the moon.

6 She strawed the roses on the ground,
   Threw her mantle on the brier,
   And the belt around her middle sae jimp,
   As a taiken that she'd been there.

7 The rustling leaves flew round his head,
   And rousd him frae his dream;
   He saw by the roses, and mantle sae green,
   That his love had been there and was gane.

[397]

8 'O whare was ye, my gude grey steed,
   That I coft ye sae dear,
   That ye didna waken your master,
   Whan ye kend that his love was here?'

9 'I pautit wi my foot, master,
   Garrd a' my bridles ring,
   And still I cried, Waken, gude master,
   For now is the hour and time.'

10 'Then whare was ye, my bonnie grey hound,
    That I coft ye sae dear,
    That ye didna waken your master,
    Whan ye kend that his love was here?'

11 'I pautit wi my foot, master,
    Garrd a' my bells to ring,
    And still I cried, Waken, gude master,
    For now is the hour and time.'

12 'But whare was ye, my hawks, my hawks,
    That I coft ye sae dear,
    That ye didna waken your master,
    Whan ye kend that his love was here?'

13 'O wyte na me, now, my master dear,
    I garrd a' my young hawks sing,
    And still I cried, Waken, gude master,
    For now is the hour and time.'

14 'Then be it sae, my wager gane,
    'Twill skaith frae meikle ill,
    For gif I had found her in bonnie broom-fields,
    O her heart's blude ye'd drunken your fill.'

E

Joseph Robertson's Note-Book, January 1, 1830, p. 7.

1 'I'LL wager, I'll wager wi you, fair maid,
   Five hunder punds and ten,
   That a maid winna gae to the bonnie green
      bower,
   An a maid return back agen.'

2 'I'll wager, I'll wager wi you, kin' sir,
   Five hunder punds and ten,
   That a maid I'll gang to the bonnie green bower,
   An a maid return again.'

3 But when she cam to the bonnie green bower,
   Her true-love was fast asleep;
   Sumtimes she kist his rosie, rosie lips,
   An his breath was wondrous sweet.

4 Sometimes she went to the crown o his head,
   Sometimes to the soles o his feet,
   Sometimes she kist his rosie, rosie lips,
   An his breath was wondrous sweet.

5 She's taen a ring frae her finger,
   Laid it upon his breast-bane;
   It was for a token that she had been there,
   That she had been there, but was gane.

6 'Where was you, where was ye, my merrymen a',
   That I do luve sae dear,
   That ye didna waken me out o my sleep
   When my true love was here?

7 'Where was ye, where was ye, my gay goshawk,
   That I do luve sae dear,
That ye didna waken me out o my sleep
   Whan my true love was here?'

8 'Wi my wings I flaw, kin' sir,
   An wi my bill I sang,
But ye woudna waken out o yer sleep
   Till your true love was gane.'

9 'Where was ye, my bonnie grey steed,
   That I do luve sae dear,
That ye didna waken me out o my sleep
   When my true love was here?'

10 'I stampit wi my fit, maister,
   And made my bridle ring,
But ye wadna waken out o yer sleep,
   Till your true love was gane.'

F

a. *Douce Ballads*, III, fol. 64b: Newcastle, printed and sold by John White, in Pilgrim Street. b. *Douce Ballads*, IV, fol. 10.

98]

1 A NOBLE young squire that livd in the west,
   He courted a young lady gay,
And as he was merry, he put forth a jest,
   A wager with her he would lay.

2 'A wager with me?' the young lady reply'd,
   'I pray, about what must it be?
If I like the humour you shan't be deny'd;
   I love to be merry and free.'

3 Quoth he, 'I will lay yon an hundred pounds,
   A hundred pounds, aye, and ten,
That a maid if you go to the merry broom-field,
   That a maid you return not again.'

4 'I'll lay you that wager,' the lady she said,
   Then the money she flung down amain;
'To the merry broomfield I'll go a pure maid,
   The same I'll return home again.'

5 He coverd her bett in the midst of the hall
   With an hundred and ten jolly pounds,
And then to his servant straightway he did call,
   For to bring forth his hawk and his hounds.

6 A ready obedience the servant did yield,
   And all was made ready oer night;
Next morning he went to the merry broom-field,
   To meet with his love and delight.

7 Now when he came there, having waited a
      while,
   Among the green broom down he lies;
The lady came to him, and coud not but smile,
   For sleep then had closed his eyes.

8 Upon his right hand a gold ring she secur'd,
   Down from her own finger so fair,
That when he awaked he might be assur'd
   His lady and love had been there.

9 She left him a posie of pleasant perfume,
   Then stept from the place where he lay;
Then hid herself close in the besom of the
      broom,
   To hear what her true-love would say.

10 He wakend and found the gold ring on his hand,
   Then sorrow of heart he was in:
'My love has been here, I do well understand,
   And this wager I now shall not win.

11 'O where was you, my goodly gawshawk,
   The which I have purchasd so dear?
Why did you not waken me out of my sleep
   When the lady, my lover, was here?'

12 'O with my bells did I ring, master,
   And eke with my feet did I run;
And still did I cry, Pray awake, master,
   She's here now, and soon will be gone.'

13 'O where was you, my gallant greyhound,
   Whose collar is flourishd with gold?
Why hadst thou not wakend me out of my sleep
   When thou didst my lady behold?'

14 'Dear master, I barkd with my mouth when she
      came,
   And likewise my coller I shook,
And told you that here was the beautiful dame,
   But no notice of me then you took.'

15 'O where was thou, my serving-man,
    Whom I have cloathed so fine?
If you had wak'd me when she was here,
    The wager then had been mine.'

16 'In the night ye should have slept, master,
    And kept awake in the day;
Had you not been sleeping when hither she
    came,
Then a maid she had not gone away.'

17 Then home he returnd, when the wager was
    lost,
    With sorrow of heart, I may say;
The lady she laughd to find her love crost,—
    This was upon midsummer-day.

18 'O squire, I laid in the bushes conceald,
    And heard you when you did complain;
And thus I have been to the merry broom-field,
    And a maid returnd back again.

19 'Be chearful, be chearful, and do not repine,   [39
    For now 't is as clear as the sun,
The money, the money, the money is mine,
    The wager I fairly have won.'

A. b. 8^1. flower frae the bush. 8^3. a witter true.
    9^2. I did love.
    11^1. gray goshawk. 11^2. sae well.
    11^3. When my love was here hersell.
    12^4. Afore your true love gang.
    13^3. in good.
    14$^{2-4}$. By running oer the howm;
        Nae hare runs swifter oer the lea
        Nor your love ran thro the broom.

E *concludes with these stanzas, which do not belong to
    this ballad:*

11   'Rise up, rise up, my bonnie grey cock,
            And craw when it is day,
        An your neck sall be o the beaten gowd,
            And your wings o the silver lay.'

12   But the cock provd fauss, and untrue he
            was,
            And he crew three hour ower seen,
        The lassie thocht it day, and sent her love
            away,
            An it was but a blink o the meen.

13   'If I had him but agen,' she says,
            'O if I but had him agen,
        The best grey cock that ever crew at morn
            Should never bereave me o 's charms.'

F. a. 8^2. fingers. 11^1, 13^1. Oh. 15^2. I am.
b. 2^2. I pray you now, what.
    3^1. Said he. 3^4. *omits* That.
    4^3. *omits* pure. 4^4. And the . . . back again.
    5^2. ten good. 5^3. he strait. 5^4. *omits* For.
    6^1. his servants. 6^2. *omits* made.
    6^4. his joy.
    7^4. sleep had fast. 8^2. finger.
    9^3. in the midst. 9^4. what her lover.
    10^1. Awaking he found. 10^2. of bearst.
    10^3. *omits* do. 11^3. wake. 11^4. and lover.
    12^{1,2}. I did. 12^3. wake. 12^4. here and she.
    13^3. Why did you not wake.
    14^1. I barked aloud when. 14^3. that there was my.
    15^2. 1 have. 15^3. when she had been here.
    15^4. had been surely mine.
    16^1. *omits* should. 17^3. to see.
    18^1. lay. 18^3. So I. 18^4. have returnd.
    b *has no imprint.*

44

THE TWA MAGICIANS

Buchan's *Ballads of the North of Scotland*, I, 24; Motherwell's MS., p. 570.

A BASE-BORN cousin of a pretty ballad known over all Southern Europe, and elsewhere, and in especially graceful forms in France.

The **French** ballad generally begins with a young man's announcing that he has won a mistress, and intends to pay her a visit on Sunday, or to give her an *aubade*. She declines his visit, or his music. To avoid him she will turn, e.g., into a rose; then he will turn bee, and kiss her. She will turn quail; he sportsman, and bag her. She will turn carp; he angler, and catch her. She will turn hare; and he hound. She will turn nun; he priest, and confess her day and night. She will fall sick; he will watch with her, or be her doctor. She will become a star; he a cloud, and muffle her. She will die; he will turn earth, into which they will put her, or St Peter, and receive her into Paradise. In the end she says, Since you are inevitable, you may as well have me as another; or more complaisantly, Je me donnerai à toi, puisque tu m'aimes tant.

This ballad might probably be found anywhere in France, but most of the known versions are from south of the Loire. **A**. *Romania*, X, 390, E. Legrand, from Normandy; also known in Champagne. **B**. 'Les Transformations,' V. Smith, Vielles Chansons du Velay et du Forez, *Romania*, VII, 61ff. **C**. *Poésies populaires de la France*, MS., III, fol. 233, Vienne. **D**. The same, II, fol. 39, Guéret, Creuse. **E, F**. The same volume, fol. 41, fol. 42; partly, in *Revue des Traditions populaires*, I, 104f. **E** is printed by Rolland, IV, 30, *b*. **G**. 'La maitresse gagnée,' the same volume, fol. 38: "on chante cette chanson stir les confines du département de l'Ain qui le

séparent de la Savoie."[*] **H**. 'J'ai fait une maitresse,' Champfleury, *Chansons populaires des Provinces*, p. 90, Bourbonnais. **I**. 'Adiu, Margaridoto,' Bladé, *Poésies pop. de la Gascogne*, II, 360. **J**. *Mélusine*, col. 338f, Carcasonne. **K**. Montel et Lambert, *Chansons pop. du Languedoc*, p. 544–51, and *Revue des Langues romanes*, XII, 261–67, four copies. **L**. 'Les Transfourmatiens,' Arbaud, II, 128. The Provençal ballad is introduced by Mistral into *Mirèio*, Chant III, as the song of Magali. **M**. 'La Poursuite d'Amour,' Marelle, in *Archiv für das Studium der neueren Sprachen*, LVI, 191. **N**. 'J'ai fait une maitresse,' Gagnon, *Chansons populaires du Canada*, p. 137, and Lovell, *Recueil de Chansons canadiennes*, 'Chanson de Voyageur,' p. 68. **O**. Gagnon, p. 78. **P**. 'Mignonne,' Guillon, p. 248, Ain. **Q**. 'Les Transformations,' Avenay, Marne, Gaston Paris, in *Rev. des Trad. pop.*, I, 98. **R**. Haute-Bretagne, Sébillot, the same, p. 100. **S**. Le Morvan, Tiersot, p. 102. **T**. Tarn-et-Garonne, the same, II, 208. **U**. 'Les Métamorphoses,' Finistère, Rolland, IV, 32, *c*. **V**. Environs de Brest, the same, p. 33, *d*. **W**. 'J'ai fait une maîtresse,' Daymard, p. 51, Quercy. **X**. 'Margarideto,' Soleville, *Chants p. du Bas-Quercy*, p. 94. **Y**. 'Les Transformations,' Wallonia, I, 50.

Catalan. Closely resembling the French: **A**. 'La Esquerpa,' Briz, Cansons de la Terra, I, 125. **B, C, D**. 'Las Transformaciones,' Milá, *Romancerillo Catalan*, p. 393, No 513.

Italian. Reduced to a *rispetto*, Tigri, *Canti popolari toscani*, ed. 1860, p. 241, No 861; Vigo,

[*] There are two other versions in this great collection besides the five cited, but either I have overlooked these, or they are in Volume VI, not yet received.

Canti p. siciliani, 1870–74, No 1711, Pitrè, *Studj di Poesia pop.*, p. 76; Casetti e Imbriani, C. p. *delle Provincie meridionali*, p. 187: all cited by D'Ancona, *Poesia pop.*, p. 341. A ballad in Nigra, No 59, p. 329, 'Amore inevitabile.'

Roumanian. 'Cucul şi Turturica,' Alecsandri, *Poesiĕ populare ale Românilor*, p. 7, No 3; French version, by the same, *Ballades et Chants populaires*, p. 35, No 7; Schuller, *Romänische Volkslieder*, p. 47. The cuckoo, or the lover under that style, asks the dove to be his mistress till Sunday. The dove, for his sake, would not say No, but because of his mother, who is a witch, if not let alone will change into a roll, and hide under the ashes. Then he will turn into a shovel, and get her out. She will turn into a reed, and hide in the pond. He will come as shepherd to find a reed for a flute, put her to his lips, and cover her with kisses. She will change to an image, and hide in the depths of the church. He will come every day in the week, as deacon or chorister, to kiss the images (a pious usage in those parts), and she will not thus escape him. Schuller refers to another version, in Schuster's unprinted collection, in which youth and maid carry on this contest in their proper persons, and not under figure.

Ladin. Flugi, *Die Volkslieder des Engadin*, p. 83, No 12. "Who is the younker that goes a-field ere dawn? Who is his love?" "A maid all too fair, with dowry small enough." "Maid, wilt give me a rose?" "No; my father has forbidden." "Wilt be my love?" "Rather a seed, and hide in the earth." "Then I will be a bird, and pick thee out," etc.

Greek. Tommaseo, III, 61, Passow, p. 431, No 574a. A girl tells her mother she will kill herself rather than accept the Turk: she will turn swallow, and take to the woods. The mother replies, Turn what you will, he will turn hunter, and take you from me. The same kernel of this ballad of transformations in Comparetti, *Saggi dei Dialetti greci dell' Italia meridionale*, p. 38, No 36, as M. Paul Meyer has remarked, *Revue Critique*, II, 302. Cf. 'Les Transformations,' Georgeakis et Pineau, *Folk-lore de Lesbos*, p. 210ff. (no mention of the Turk's transforming himself).

The ballad is well known to the Slavic nations.

Moravian. Čelakowský, p. 75, No 6, Wenzig, *Slawische Volkslieder*, p. 72, *Bibliothek slavischer Poesien*, p. 92. A youth threatens to carry off a maid for his wife. She will fly to the wood as a dove. He has a rifle that will bring her down. She will jump into the water as a fish. He has a net that will take the fish. She will turn to a hare; he to a dog; she cannot escape him.

Bohemian. Waldau, *Böhmische Granaten*, II, 75, No 107, dove, gun; fish, hook; hare, dog.

Polish. Very common. **A a.** Wacław z Oleska, p. 417, No 287; Konopka, p. 124. A young man says, though he should ride night and day for it, ride his horse's eyes out, the maid must be his. She will turn to a bird, and take to the thicket. But carpenters have axes which can fell a wood. Then she will be a fish, and take to the water. But fishermen have nets which will find her. Then she will become a wild duck, and swim on the lake. Sportsmen have rifles to shoot ducks. Then she will be a star in the sky, and give light to the people. He has a feeling for the poor, and will bring the star down to the earth by his prayers. "I see," she says, "it's God's ordinance; whithersoever I betake myself, you are up with me; I will be yours after all." Nearly the same mutations in other versions, with some variety of introduction and arrangement. **A b.** Kolberg, *Lud*, VI, 129, No 257. **A c.** "Przyjaciel ludu, 1836, rok 2, No 34;" Lipiński, p. 135; Kolberg, *Lud* XII, 98, No 193. **B.** Pauli, *Pieśni ludu Polskiego*, I, 135. **C.** The same, p. 133. **D.** Kolberg, *Lud*, XII, 99, No 194. **E.** *Lud*, IV, 19, No 137. **F.** *Lud*, XII, 97, No 192. **G.** *Lud*, II, 134, No 161. **H.** *Lud*, VI, 130, No 258. **I.** Woicicki, I, 141, Waldbrühl, *Slawische Balalaika*, p. 433. **J. a, b.** Roger, p. 147, No 285, p. 148, No 286. **K–O.** Kolberg, *Lud*, XXI, 27, No 50; XXII, 102, No 157; Kolberg, *Mazowsze*, II, 54f, Nos 131, 132; III, 247, 321; IV, 274, No 240.

Servian. Karadshitch, I, 434, No 602, translated in Bowring's *Servian Popular Poetry*, p. 195; Talvj, II, 100; Kapper, II, 208; Pellegrini, p. 93. Rather than be her lover's, the maid will turn into a gold-jug in a drinking-house; he will be mine host. She will change into a cup in a coffee-house; he will be *cafetier*. She will become a quail, he a sportsman; a fish, he a net. Pellegrini has still another form, 'La fanciulla assediata,' p. 37. An old man desires a maid. She will rather turn into a lamb; he will turn into a wolf. She will become a quail; he a hawk. She will change into a rose; he into a goat, and tear off the rose from the tree.

Magyar-Croat. In a ballad the lover advises the maid, who has been chidden by her mother on his account, if her mother repeats the scolding, to turn herself into a fish, then he will be a fisherman, etc. Kurelac, p. 309, XV, 2. (W. W.)

Persian. Chodzko, *Specimens of the Popular Poetry of Persia*, p. 487, No 61, Songs of the Ghilanis. This and French **Q** are noted by Hasdek in the Roumanian periodical *Columna lui Traian*, 1876, p. 44, 1877, p. 301, apropos of 'Cuicul şi Turturica.'

Dalmatian. Francesco Carrara, *Canti del popolo dalmata*, Zara, 1849, p. ix.

Finnish. In the *Kalevala*, Ilmarinen, after the death of his first wife, steals her younger sister, who is very unwilling to accompany him. She threatens to break his sledge to pieces, but it is made of iron. She will turn into a salmon (Schnäpel) in the sea; he will give chase in the form of a pike. She will become an ermine; he an otter, and pursue her. She will fly off as a lark; he will follow as an eagle. Here the talk of transformation ends: Rune 37, vv 148–178. The next morning Ilmarinen in his wrath turns the maid into a gull. *Kalewala*, übertragen von Schiefner, pp. 226–228. (G. L. K.)

There can be little doubt that these ballads are derived, or take their hint, from popular tales, in which (1) a youth and maid, pursued by a sorcerer, fiend, giant, ogre, are transformed by the magical powers of one or the other into such shapes as enable them to elude, and finally to escape, apprehension; or (2) a young fellow, who has been apprenticed to a sorcerer, fiend, etc., and has acquired the black art by surreptitious reading in his master's books, being pursued, as before, assumes a variety of forms, and his master others, adapted to the destruction of his intended victim, until the tables are turned by the fugitive's taking on the stronger figure and despatching his adversary.

Specimens of the first kind are afforded by Gonzenbach, *Sicilianische Märchen*, Nos 14, 15, 54, 55; Grimms, Nos 51, 56, 113; Schneller, No 27; Pitrè, *Fiabe, Novelle e Racconti siciliani*, No 15; Imbriani, *Novellaja milanese*, No 27, N.

fiorentana, No 29; Maspons y Labrós, *Rondallayre*, I, 85, II, 30; Cosquin, *Contes lorrains*, I, 103, No 9, and notes, in *Romania*, V, 354; Ralston's *Russian Folk-Tales*, p. 129f, from Afanasief, V, No 23; Bechstein, *Märchenbuch*, p. 75, ed. 1879, which combines both. Others in Köhler's note to Gonzenbach, No 14, at II, 214. Other specimens of this kind include Luzel, *Annuaire de la Société des Traditions populaires*, II, 56; Baissac, *Folk-Lore de l'Île Maurice*, p. 88ff; Wigström, *Sagor och Äfventyr uppttecknad i Skåne*, p. 37; Luzel, *Revue des Traditions populaires*, I, 287, 288; Luzel, *Contes pop. de Basse-Bretagne*, II, 13, 41ff, cf. 64–66; Vernaleken, *Kinder- und Hausmärchen*, No 49, p. 277; Bladé, *Contes pop. de la Gascogne*, II, 26–36; Carnoy, *Contes populaires picards*, *Romania*, VIII, 227. Cf. also Ortoli, *Contes pop. de l'Île de Corse*, pp. 27–29, and Cosquin's notes (which do not cite any of the above-mentioned places), *Contes pop. de Lorraine*, I, 105ff; R. Köhler's notes to L. Gonzenbach's *Sicilianische Märchen*, now published by J. Bolte, *Zeitschrift des Vereins für Volkskunde*, VI, 65; Tale in Curtin's *Myths and Folk-Lore of Ireland*, pp. 152–6. Cf. also *Notes and Queries*, 7th Series, IX, 101, 295; Clouston, *Popular Tales and Fictions*, I, 413ff. (G. L. K.)*

Of the second kind, among very many, are Straparola, viii, 5, see Grimms, III, 288, Louveau et Larivey, II, 152; Grimms, No 68, III, 117; Müllenhoff, No 27, p. 466; Pröhle, *Märchen für die Jugend*, No 26; Asbjørnsen og Moe, No 57; Grundtvig, *Gamle danske Minder*, 1854, Nos 255, 256; Hahn, *Griechische Märchen*, No 68; the Breton tale Koadalan, Luzel, in *Revue Celtique*, I, $^{106}/_{197}$; the Schotts, *Walachische Mährchen*, No 18;† Woicicki, *Klechdy*, II, 26, No

---

* The incidents of the flight of the girl and her lover, the pursuit and the transformations, and of the Devil outwitted by his pupil are discussed by G. Rua, *Novelle del "Mambriano" del Cieco da Ferrara*, p. 95. See also M. Wardrop, *Georgian Tales*, p. 4, No. 1. (G. L. K.)

† The Schotts are reminded by their story that Wade puts his son Weland in apprenticeship to Mimir Smith, and to the dwarfs. They might have noted that the devil, in the Wallachian tale, wishes to keep his prentice a second year, as the dwarfs wish to do in the case of Weland. That little trait comes, no doubt, from Weland's story; but we will not, therefore, conclude that our smith is Weland Smith, and his adventure with the lady founded upon that of Weland with Nidung's daughter.

4; Karadshitch, No 6; Afanasief, V, 95f, No 22, [402] VI, 189ff, No 45 a, b, and other Russian and Little Russian versions, VIII, 340; Luzel, *Contes pop. de Basse-Bretagne*, II, 92–95, and note; Haltrich, *Deutsche Volksmärchen aus dem Sachsenlande, u. s. w.*, 3d ed., 1882, No 14, p. 52f. Köhler adds several examples of one kind or the other in a note to Koadalan, *Revue Celtique*, I, 132, and Wollner Slavic parallels in a note to Leskien und Brugman, *Litauische Volkslieder und Märchen*, p. 537f.

The usual course of events in these last is that the prentice takes refuge in one of many pomegranate kernels, barley-corns, poppy-seeds, millet-grains, pearls; the master becomes a cock, hen, sparrow, and picks up all of these but one, which turns into a fox, dog, weasel, crow, cat, hawk, vulture, that kills the bird.

The same story occurs in the Turkish *Forty Viziers*, Behrnauer, p. 195ff, the last transformations being millet, cock, man, who tears off the cock's head. Also in the introduction to *Siddhi-Kür*, Jülg, pp 1–3, where there are seven masters instead of one, and the final changes are worms, instead of seeds, seven hens, a man with a cane who kills the hens.[*]

The pomegranate and cock (found in Straparola) are among the metamorphoses in the contest between the afrite and the princess in the tale of the Second Calender in the *Arabian Nights*.

Entirely similar is the pursuit of Gwion the pigmy by the goddess Koridgwen, cited by Villemarqué, *Barzaz Breiz*, p. lvi, ed. 1867, from the *Myvyrian Archaiology of Wales*, I, 17. Gwion

having, by an accident, come to the knowledge of superhuman mysteries, Koridgwen wishes to take his life. He flees, and turns successively into a hare, fish, bird; she follows, in the form of hound, otter, hawk; finally he becomes a wheaten grain, she a hen, and swallows the grain. The Welsh text, with an English translation, is given by Stephens, *Literature of the Kymry*, p. 170: cf. pp. 174, 175. (G. L. K.) See, also, the mabinogi of Taliesin in Lady Charlotte Guest's *Mabinogion*, Part VII, p. 358f.

The ordinary tale has found its way into rhyme in a German broadside ballad, Longard, *Altrheinländische Mährlein und Liedlein*, p. 76, No 40, 'Von einem gottlosen Zauberer und seiner unschuldigen Kindlein wunderbarer Erlösung.' The two children of an ungodly magician, a boy and a girl, are devoted by him to the devil. The boy had read in his father's books while his father was away. They flee, and are pursued: the girl becomes a pond, the boy a fish. The wicked wizard goes for a net. The boy pronounces a spell, by which the girl is turned into a chapel, and he into an image on the altar. The wizard, unable to get at the image, goes for fire. The boy changes the girl into a threshing-floor, himself into a barley-corn. The wizard becomes a hen, and is about to swallow the grain of barley. By another spell the boy changes himself into a fox, and then twists the hen's neck.[†]

Translated by Gerhard, p. 18.

[†] "The pursuit in various forms by the witch lady has an exact counterpart in a story of which I have many versions and which I had intended to give if I had room. It is called 'The Fuller's Son,' 'The Cotter's Son,' and other names, and it bears a strong resemblance to the end of the Norse tale of 'Farmer Weathersky.'" Campbell, *Popular Tales of the West Highlands*, IV, 297. (G. L. K.)

[*] See Benfey, *Pantschatantra*, I, 410f, who maintains the Mongol tale to be of Indian origin, and thinks the story to have been derived from the contests in magic between Buddhist and Brahman saints, of which many are related in Buddhist legends.

Buchan's *Ballads of the North of Scotland*, I, 24;
Motherwell's MS., p. 570.

1 THE LADY stands in her bower door,
   As straight as willow wand;
   The blacksmith stood a little forebye,
   Wi hammer in his hand.

2 'Weel may ye dress ye, lady fair,
   Into your robes o red;
   Before the morn at this same time,
   I'll gain your maidenhead.'

3 'Awa, awa, ye coal-black smith,
   Woud ye do me the wrang
   To think to gain my maidenhead,
   That I hae kept sae lang!'

4 Then she has hadden up her hand,
   And she sware by the mold,
   'I wudna be a blacksmith's wife
   For the full o a chest o gold.

5 'I'd rather I were dead and gone,
   And my body laid in grave,
   Ere a rusty stock o coal-black smith
   My maidenhead shoud have.'

6 But he has hadden up his hand,
   And he sware by the mass,
   'I'll cause ye be my light leman
   For the hauf o that and less.'
      O bide, lady, bide,
         And aye he bade her bide;
      The rusty smith your leman shall be,
         For a' your muckle pride.

7 Then she became a turtle dow,
   To fly up in the air,
   And he became another dow,
   And they flew pair and pair.
      O bide, lady, bide, &c.

8 She turnd hersell into an eel,
   To swim into yon burn,
   And he became a speckled trout,
   To gie the eel a turn.
      O bide, lady, bide, &c.

9 Then she became a duck, a duck,
   To puddle in a peel,
   And he became a rose-kaimd drake,
   To gie the duck a dreel.
      O bide, lady, bide, &c.

10 She turnd hersell into a hare,
   To rin upon yon hill,
   And he became a gude grey-hound,
   And boldly he did fill.
      O bide, lady, bide, &c.

11 Then she became a gay grey mare,
   And stood in yonder slack,
   And he became a gilt saddle.
   And sat upon her back.
      Was she wae, he held her sae,
         And still he bade her bide;
      The rusty smith her leman was,
         For a' her muckle pride.

12 Then she became a het girdle,
   And he became a cake,
   And a' the ways she turnd hersell,
   The blacksmith was her make.
      Was she wae, &c.

13 She turnd hersell into a ship,
   To sail out ower the flood;
   He ca'ed a nail intill her tail,
   And syne the ship she stood.
      Was she wae, &c.

14 Then she became a silken plaid,
   And stretchd upon a bed,
   And he became a green covering,
   And gaind her maidenhead.
      Was she wae, &c.

45

KING JOHN AND THE BISHOP

A. 'Kinge John and Bishoppe,' Percy MS., p. 184; Hales and Furnivall, I, 508.

B. 'King John and the Abbot of Canterbury,' broadside printed for P. Brooksby.

THE broadside **B** was printed, with trifling variations, or corrections, in *Pills to Purge Melancholy*, IV, 29 (1719), and in *Old Ballads*, II, 49 (1723). It is found in several of the collections: Pepys, II, 128, No 112; *Roxburghe*, III, 883; Ouvry, No 47; the Bagford; and it was among Heber's ballads. Brooksby published from 1672 to 1695, and **B** was "allowed" by Roger l'Estrange, who was licenser from 1663 to 1685: Chappell, *The Roxburghe Ballads*, I, xviii, xxiii. *Roxburghe*, III, 883, is **B**. *Roxburghe*, III, 494 was printed and sold by John White, Newcastle-upon-Tyne, "circa 1777:" Ebsworth, *Roxburghe Ballads*, VI, 749. 'The King and the Bishop,' *Roxburghe*, III, 170, is printed in the same volume, p. 751, and 'The Old Abbot and King Olfrey,' Pepys, II, 127, at p. 753. The title of **B** is A *new* ballad of King John and the Abbot of Canterbury, to the tune of 'The King and the Lord Abbot.'* This older ballad seems not to have come down.

There are at least two other broadsides [404] extant upon the same subject, both mentioned by Percy, and both inferior even to **B**, and in a far less popular style: 'The King and the Bishop,' Pepys, I, 472, No 243, *Roxburghe*, III, 170, *Douce*, fol. 110; and 'The Old Abbot and King Olfrey,' *Douce*, II, fol. 169, Pepys, II, 127, No 111, printed in *Old Ballads*, II, 55.[†] In both of these the Shepherd is the Bishop's brother, which he is not in **B**; in **A** he is half-brother.

Pepys's *Penny Merriments* contain, I, 14, 'The pleasant History of King Henry the Eighth and the Abbot of Reading.'[‡] This last may, without rashness, be assumed to be a variation of 'King John and the Abbot.'

Percy admitted 'King John and the Abbot' to his *Reliques*, II, 302, introducing many lines from **A** "worth reviving," and many improvements of his own,[§] and thus making undeniably a very good ballad out of a very poor one.

The story of this ballad was told in Scotland, some fifty years ago, of the Gudeman of Ballengeigh, James the V, the hero of not a few other tales. Once on a time, falling in with the priest of Markinch (near Falkland), and finding him a dullard, he gave the poor man four questions to think of till they next met, with an intimation that his benefice would be lost were

---

* A New Ballad of King John and the Abbot of Canterbury. To the Tune of The King and the Lord Abbot. With allowance. Ro. L'Estrange. Printed for P. Brooksby at the Golden Ball in Pye-corner.

† The King and the Bishop, or,

Unlearned Men hard matters out can find
When Learned Bishops Princes eyes do blind.

To the Tune of Chievy Chase. Printed for F. Coles, T. Vere, and J. Wright (1655–80). Printed for J. Wright, Clarke, W. Thackeray, and T. Passenver.

The Old Abbot and King Olfrey. To the tune of the Shaking of the Sheets. Printed by and for A. M., and sold by the booksellers of London.

J. Wright's date is 1650–82, T. Passinger's, 1670–82. Chappell.

‡ Printed by J. M. for C. D., at the Stationers Armes within Aldgate. C. D. is, no doubt, C. Dennison, who published 1685–89. See Chappell, *The Roxburghe Ballads*, I, xix.

§ Among these, St Bittel for St Andrew of **A** 26, with the note, "meaning probably St Botolph:" why "probably"?

they not rightly answered. The questions were those of our ballad, preceded by Where is the middle of the earth? The parson could make nothing of them, and was forced to resort to a miller of the neighborhood, who was reputed a clever fellow. When called to answer the first question, the miller put out his staff, and said, There, as your majesty will find by measuring. The others were dealt with as in the ballad. The king said that the miller should have the parson's place, but the miller begged off from this in favor of the incumbent. Small, *Interesting Roman Antiquities recently discovered in Fife*, p. 289 ff.

Riddle stories in which a forfeit is to be paid by a vanquished party have incidentally been referred to under No 1 and No 2. They are a very extensive class. The oldest example is that of Samson's riddle, with a stake of thirty sheets (or shirts) and thirty change of garments: Judges, xiv, 12 ff. Another from Semitic tradition is what is related of Solomon and Hiram of Tyre, in *Josephus against Apion*, i, 17, 18, and *Antiquities*, viii, 5. After the manner of Amasis and the Æthiopian king in Plutarch (see p. 18), they send one another riddles, with a heavy fine for failure,—in this case a pecuniary one. Solomon at first poses Hiram; then Hiram guesses Solomon's riddles, by the aid of Abdemon (or the son of Abdemon), and in turn poses Solomon with riddles devised by Abdemon.*

Of this kind is the Russian tale, How Fraud made entrance into Russia. Ivan the Terrible demands tribute of neighboring princes. They propose to him three riddles: if he guesses them, they are to pay twelve casks of gold and tribute; if he fails, they take his kingdom. A marvellous old man helps the Tsar out. He has been promised a cask of gold, but the Tsar fills one of the casks two thirds with sand, and offers that. The old man tells him that he, the Tsar, has brought

Fraud into the land, never to be eradicated. Ivan begs him to take one of the other casks, but in vain. The old man vanishes; it was God. Rybnikof, II, 232, No 39. (W. W.)

'Pá grönaliðheiði,' Landstad, p. 369, is a contest in riddles between two brothers (refreshingly original in some parts), introduced by three stanzas, in which it is agreed that the defeated party shall forfeit his share of their inheritance: and this the editor seems to take quite seriously.

Death is the penalty attending defeat in many of these wit-contests.† Odin (Vafþrúðnismál), jealous of the giant Vafþrúðnir's wisdom, wishes to put it to the test. He enters the giant's hall, assuming the name of Gagnráðr, [405] and announces the object of his visit. The giant tells him he shall never go out again unless he prove the wiser, asks a few questions to see whether he be worth contending with, and, finding him so, proposes a decisive trial, with their heads for the stake. Odin now propounds, first, twelve questions, mostly in cosmogony, and then five relating to the future of the universe; and all these the giant is perfectly competent to answer. The very unfair question is then put, What did Odin say in his son's ear ere Balder mounted the funeral pile? Upon this Vafþrûðnir owns himself vanquished, and we may be sure he was not spared by his antagonist.

The Hervarar saga contains a story which, in its outlines, approximates to that of our ballad until we come to the conclusion, where there is no likeness. King Heiðrekr, after a long career of blood, gave up war and took to law-making. He chose his twelve wisest men for judges, and swore, with one hand on the head and the other on the bristles of a huge hog

---

* This story serves as a gloss on 2 Chronicles, ii, 13, 14, where Hiram sends Solomon a cunning Tyrian, skilful to find out every device which shall be put to him by the cunning men of Jerusalem. The Queen of Sheba's hard questions to Solomon, not specified in 1 Kings, x, 1–13, were, according to tradition, of the same general character as the Indian ones spoken of at p. 17. See Hertz, *Die Rätsel der Königin von Saba*, Zeitschrift für deutsches Altertum, XXVII, 1 ff.

† There is no occasion to accumulate examples, but this Oriental one is worth mentioning. In the tale of Gôsht-i Fryânô, Akht, the sorcerer, will give three and thirty riddles to Gôsht, and if Gôsht shall give no answer, or say, I know not, he will slay him. After answering all the riddles, Gôsht says he will give Akht three on the same terms, and the sorcerer, failing to solve them, is slain. Arḍâ-Virâf, Pahlavî text, etc., Haug and West, Bombay and London, 1872, pp. 250, 263f. This tale Köhler has shown to be one with that of the fine Kirghish lay 'Die Lerche,' in Radloff, *Proben der Volkslitteratur der türkischen Stämme Süd-Sibiriens*, III, 780: see *Zeitschrift der deutschen morgenländischen Gesellschaft*, XIX, 633 ff.

which he had reared, that no man should do such things that he should not get justice from these twelve, while any one who preferred might clear himself by giving the king riddles which he could not guess. There was a man named Gestr, and surnamed the Blind, a very bad and troublesome fellow, who had withheld from Heiðrekr tribute that was due. The king sent him word to come to him and submit to the judgment of the twelve: if he did not, the case would be tried with arms. Neither of these courses pleased Gestr, who was conscious of being very guilty: he took the resolution of making offerings to Odin for help. One night there was a knock. Gestr went to the door, and saw a man, who announced his name as Gestr. After mutual inquiries about the news, the stranger asked whether Gestr the Blind was not in trouble about something. Gestr the Blind explained his plight fully, and the stranger said, "I will go to the king and try what I can effect: we will exchange looks and clothes." The stranger, in the guise of Gestr, entered the king's hall, and said, Sire, I am come to make my peace. "Will you abide by the judgment of my men of law?" asked the king. "Are there not other ways?" inquired Gestr. "Yes: you shall give me riddles which I cannot guess, and so purchase your peace." Gestr assented, with feigned hesitation; chairs were brought, and everybody looked to hear something fine. Gestr gave, and Heiðrekr promptly answered, some thirty riddles.[*] Then said Gestr: Tell thou me this only, since thou thinkest to be wiser than all kings: What said Odin in Balder's ear before he was borne to the pile? "Shame and cowardice," exclaimed Heiðrekr, "and all manner of poltroonery, jugglery, goblinry! no one knows those words of thine save thou thyself, evil and wretched wight!" So saying, Heiðrekr drew Tyrfing, that never was bared but somebody must fall, to cut down Gestr. The disguised Odin changed to a hawk, and made for the window, but did not escape before Heiðrekr's sword had docked the bird's tail. For breaking his own

truce Odin said Heiðrekr should die by the hand of a slave, which came to pass. *Fornaldar Sögur*, Rafn, I, 462 ff.

The same story has come down in a Färöe ballad, 'Gátu ríma,' Hammershaimb, *Færøiske Qvæder*, No 4, p. 26 (and previously published in the *Antiquarisk Tidsskrift*, 1849–51, pp 75–78), translated by Dr Prior, I, 336 ff. Gest promises Odin twelve gold marks to take his place. The riddles are announced as thirteen in number, but the ballad is slightly defective, and among others the last question, What were Odin's words to Balder? is lost. Odin flies off in the shape of a falcon; Hejdrek and all his men are burned up.

A tale presenting the essential traits of our ballad is cited in Vincent of Beauvais's *Speculum Morale*, i, 4, 10, at the end, and told by Étienne de Bourbon, A. Lecoy de la Marche, *Anecdotes historiques, légendes et apologues, tirés du recueil inédit d'Étienne de Bourbon*, No 86. We read, he says, of a king, who, seeking a handle for wrenching money out of a wealthy and wise man, put him three questions, apparently insoluble, intending to make him pay a large sum for not answering them: 1, Where is the middle point of the earth? 2, How much water is there in the sea? 3, How great is the mercy of God? On the appointed day, having been brought from prison into the presence to ransom himself if he could, the respondent, by the *advice of a certain philosopher*, proceeded thus. He planted his staff where he stood, and said, Here is the centre; disprove it if you can. If you wish me to measure the sea, stop the rivers, so that nothing may flow in till I have done; then I will give you the contents. To answer your third question, I must borrow your robes and your throne. Then mounting the throne, clothed with the royal insignia, "Behold," said he, "the height of the mercy of God: but now I was a slave, now I am a king; but now poor, and now rich; but now in prison and in chains, and now at liberty," etc.

In Von Wlislocki, M. u. S. der Bukowinaer u. Siebenbürger Armenier, 'Der weise Mann,' No 30, p. 83 ff, a Christian ascetic has taken up his abode in a hogshead, on which he has written, "If thou art wise, live as I live!" The sultan puts three questions to him; How far is it to heaven? At how much do you value me? Which is the

---

[*] These are proper riddles, and of a kind still current in popular tradition. See, e.g., Svend Vonved, Grundtvig, I, 237 f. There are thirty-five, before the last, in the oldest text, given, with a translation, by Vigfusson and Powell, *Corpus Poeticum Boreale*, 'King Heidrek's Riddles,' I, 86 ff.

best religion? The penalty for failure to solve them is to be dragged at the tail of the sultan's horse. The answers are: A day's journey; twenty-nine silver pieces; neither of the two religions is the better, for the two are God's eyes, one of which is as dear to him as the other.

In an as yet unprinted fifteenth-century Low German poem on the Seven Deadly Sins (Josefs Gedicht von den sieben Todsünden . . . nach der Handschrift bekannt gemacht von Dr Babucke, *Oster-Programm des Progymnasiums zu Norden*, 1874, p. 18), a king puts an abbot four questions:

De erste vraghe was, wor dat ertrike wende
Unn were hoghest, eft he dat kende;
De ander, wor dat unghelucke queme
Unn bleve, wan dat eyn ende neme;
Dat drudde, wo gud de konig were na rade
Wan he stunde in synem besten wade;
De verde, we syner eldermoder beneme
Den maghedom unn dar wedder in queme.

The abbot's swineherd, named Reyneke, answers:

De erste vraghe, wor de erde hoghest were,
Reyneke sede: In deme hemmel kommet, here,
By deme vadere Cristus syn vordere hant,
Dar is de hoghe unn keret de erde bekant.
De andere, wor dat lucke ghinghe an,
Dar moste dat ungelucke wenden unn stan,
Unn konde nerghen vorder komen.
Dat hebbe ik by my sulven vornomen:
Ghisterne was ik eyn sweyn, nu bin ik bes-
    choren,
Unde byn to eyneme heren koren.

The replies to the third and fourth questions are wanting through the loss of some leaves of the MS. As to the first question, compare the legend of St Andrew, *Legenda Aurea*, ed. Grässe, p. 21, ubi terra sit altior omni coelo; to which the answer is made, in coelo empyreo, ubi residet corpus Christi. See, also, Gering, *Íslendzk Æventýri*, No 24, I, 95, II, 77, and note. For the fourth question see Kemble's *Salomon and Saturn*, p. 295, and Köhler in *Germania*, VII, 476.

Of the same stamp is a story in the English *Gesta Romanorum*, Madden, p. 55, No 19. A

knight was accused to the emperor by his enemies, but not so as to give a plausible ground for steps against him. The emperor could hit upon no way but to put him questions, on pain of life and death. The questions were seven; the third and the sixth will suffice: How many gallons of salt water been in the sea? Answer: Let all the outpassings of fresh water be stopped, and I shall tell thee. How many days' journey beth in the circle of the world? Answer: Only the space of one day.[*]

Much nearer to the ballad, and earlier than the preceding, is the Stricker's tale of Âmîs and the Bishop, in the *Pfaffe Âmîs*, dated at about 1236. Âmîs, a learned and bountiful priest in England, excited the envy of his bishop, who sent for him, told him that he lived in better style than his superior, and demanded a subvention. The priest flatly refused to give the bishop anything but a good dinner. "Then you shall lose your church," said the bishop in wrath. But the priest, strong in a good conscience, felt small concern about that: he said the bishop might test his fitness with any examination he pleased. That I will do, said the bishop, and gave him five questions. "How much is there in the sea?" "One tun," answered Âmîs; "and if you think I am not right, stop all the rivers that flow in, and I will measure it and convince you." "Let the rivers run," said the bishop. "How many days from Adam to our time?" "Seven," said the parson; "for as soon as seven are gone, they begin again." The bishop, fast losing his temper, next demanded "What is the exact middle of the earth? Tell me, or lose your church." "Why, my church stands on it," replied Âmîs. "Let your men measure, and take the church if it prove not so." The bishop declined the task, and asked once more: How far is it from earth to sky? and then: What is the width of the sky? to which Âmîs replied after the same fashion.

In this tale of the Stricker the parson answers for himself, and not by deputy, and

---

[*] *The Two Noble Kinsmen*, V, ii, 67, 68,

Daughter. How far is 't now to the end o the world, my masters?
Doctor. Why, a day's journey, wench.

(G. L. K.)

none of the questions are those of our ballad. But in a tale of Franco Sacchetti,[*] given in two forms, Novella iv[a], we have both the abbot and his humble representative, and an agreement as to one of the questions. Bernabò Visconti († 1385) was offended with a rich abbot, who had neglected some dogs that had been entrusted to his care, and was minded to make the abbot pay him a fine; but so far yielded to the abbot's protest as to promise to release him from all penalties if he could answer four questions: How far is it from here to heaven? How much water is there in the sea? What is going on in hell? What is the value of my person? A day was given to get up the answers. The abbot went home, in the depths of melancholy, and met on the way one of his millers, who inquired what was the matter, and, after receiving an explanation, offered to take the abbot's place, disguising himself as well as he could. The answers to the two first questions are not the usual ones: huge numbers are given, and the seigneur is told to measure for himself, if not willing to accept them. The answer to the fourth is twenty-nine deniers; for our Lord was sold for [407] thirty, and you must be worth one less than he. Messer Bernabò said the miller should be abbot, and the abbot miller, from that time forth. Sacchetti says that others tell the story of a pope and an abbot, adding one question. The gardener of the monastery presents the abbot, makes the usual answer to the second question as to the water in the sea, and prizes Christ's vicar at twenty-eight deniers.

The excellent old farce, "Ein Spil von einem Kaiser und eim Apt," *Fastnachtspiele aus dem fünfzehnten Jahrhundert*, I, 199, No 22, obliges the abbot to answer three questions, or pay for all the damages done in the course of a calamitous invasion. The abbot has a week's grace allowed him. The questions are three: How much water in the sea? How much is the emperor worth? Whose luck came quickest? The miller answers for the abbot: Three tubs, if they are big enough; eight and twenty pence; and *he* is the man whose luck came quickest, for just before he was a miller, now he is an abbot.

---

[*] Sacchetti's life extended beyond 1400, or perhaps beyond 1410.

The emperor says that, since the miller has acted for the abbot, abbot he shall be.

Very like this, as to the form of the story, is the anecdote in Pauli's *Schimpf und Ernst*, LV, p. 46, ed. Oesterley (c. 1522). A nobleman, who is seeking an occasion to quarrel with an abbot, tells him that he must answer these questions in three days, or be deposed: What do you value me at? Where is the middle of the world? How far apart are good and bad luck? A swineherd answers for him: Since Christ was sold for thirty pence, I rate the emperor at twenty-nine and you at twenty-eight; my church is the midpoint of the world, and, if you will not believe me, measure for yourself; good and bad luck are but one night apart, for yesterday I was a swineherd, to-day I am an abbot. Then, says the nobleman, an abbot shall you stay. With this agrees, say the Grimms, the tale in Eyring's *Proverbiorum Copia* (1601), I, 165–168, III, 23–25.

Waldis, *Esopus* (1548), B. 3, Fabel 92, Kurz, I, 382, agrees in general with Pauli: but in place of the first two questions has these three: How far is to heaven? How deep is the sea? How many tubs will hold all the sea-water? The answers are: A short day's journey, for Christ ascended in the morning and was in heaven before night; a stone's cast; one tub, if large enough.

Teofilo Folengo (1491–1544), as pointed out by Köhler, has the story in the 8th canto of his *Orlandino*; and here we find the third question of our ballad. There are three besides: How far from earth to heaven? From the east to the west?—a modification of the second question in the ballad; How many drops of water in the seas about Italy? The abbot's cook, Marcolf, answers to the first, One leap, as proved by Satan's fall; to the second, One day's journey, if the sun is to be trusted; and insists that, for a correct count under the third, all the rivers shall first be stopped. To the fourth he makes the never-stale reply, You *think* I am the abbot, but I am the cook. Rainero says he shall remain abbot, and the abbot be cook. (Stanzas 38, 39, 64–69, pp 186f, 195ff, London edition of 1775.)

A capital Spanish story, 'Gramatica Parda,' Trueba, *Cuentos Populares*, p. 287, has all three of the questions asked and answered as in our ballad. There is a curate who sets up to know everything, and the king, "el rey que rabió," has found him out, and gives him a month to make his three answers, with a premium and a penalty. The curate is forced to call in a despised goatherd, who also had all along seen through the shallowness of the priest. The king makes the goatherd "archipámpano" of Seville, and condemns the curate to wear the herdsman's garb and tend his goats for a month.[*]

The first and third questions of the ballad are found in the thirty-eighth tale of *Le Grand Parangon des Nouvelles Nouvelles* of Nicolas de Troyes, 1536 (ed. Mabille, p. 155ff); in the *Patrañuelo* of Juan de Timoneda, 1576, Pat. 14, Novelistas anteriores á Cervantes, in the *Rivadeneyra Biblioteca*, p. 154f; and in the Herzog Heinrich Julius von Braunschweig's comedy, *Von einem Edelman welcher einem Abt drey Fragen auffgegeben*, 1594, ed. Holland, p. 500ff. The other question is as to the centre of the earth, and the usual answers are given by the abbot's miller, cook, servant, except that in Timoneda the cook is so rational as to say that the centre must be under the king's feet, seeing that the world is as round as a ball.[†] The question Where is the middle of the earth? is replaced by How many stars are there in the sky? the other two remaining, in Balthasar Schupp, *Schriften*, Franckfurt, 1701, I, 91f

[*] The form of the third question is slightly varied at first ¿Cuál es el error en que yo estoy pensando? But when put to the herdsman the question is simply ¿En qué estoy yo pensando? I was pointed to this story by Seidemann, in *Archiv für Litteraturgeschichte*, IX, 423. Trueba's C. P. forms vol. 19 of Brockhaus's *Coleccion de Autores Españoles*.

[†] The editor of the *Grand Parangon*, at p. xiii, cites from an older source an anecdote of a king insisting upon being told how much he ought to bring if offered for sale. While his courtiers are giving flattering replies, a fool leaps forward and says, Twenty-nine deniers, and no more; for if you were worth thirty, that would be autant que le tout-puissant Dieu valut, quant il fut vendu. The king took this answer to heart, and repented of his vanities. So an emperor is converted by this reply from a man-at-arms, Van den verwenden Keyser, Jan van Hollant, c. 1400, Willems, *Belgisch Museum*, X, 57; Thijm, p. 145. The like question and answer, as a riddle, in a German MS. of the fifteenth century, and in *Questions énigmatiques*, Lyon, 1619; Köhler, in *Weimarisches Jahrbuch*, V, 354ff. To these should be added the Æsopian tale, P. Syrku, Zur mittelalterlichen Erzählungsliteratur aus dem Bulgarischen, *Archiv für slavische Philologie*, VII, 94–97.

(Köhler), and in Gottlieb Cober († 1717), *Cabinet-prediger*, 2[r] Theil, No 65, p. 323 (Gräter, *Idunna u. Hermode*, 1814, No 33, p. 131, and p. 87). The abbot's miller gives a huge number, and bids the king (of France) verify it, if he wishes. This last is no doubt the version of the story referred to by the Grimms in their note to *K. u. H. märchen*, No 152.

We encounter a slight variation, not for the better, in *L'Élite des Contes du Sieur d'Ouville* († 1656 or 1657), Rouen, 1699, I, 241; à la Haye, 1703, I, 296; ed. Ristelhuber, 1876, p. 46 (Köhler); *Nouveaux Contes à Rire*, Cologne, 1709, p. 266; *Contes à Rire*, Paris, 1781, I, 184. An ignorant and violent nobleman threatens a parson, who plumes himself on a little astrology, that he will expose him as an impostor if he does not answer four questions: Where is the middle of the world? What am I worth? What am I thinking? What do I believe? The village miller answers for the curé. The reply to the third question is, You are thinking more of your own interest than of mine; the others as before. This story is retold, after tradition, by Cénac Moncaut, *Contes populaires de la Gascogne*, p. 50, of a marquis, archiprêtre, and miller. The query, What am I thinking of? with the answer, More of your interest than of mine (which is not exactly in the popular manner), is replaced by a logical puzzle, not found elsewhere: Quel est le nombre qui se trouve renfermé dans deux œufs?

The King and the Abbot is preserved, in modern German tradition, in this form. An emperor, riding by a cloister, reads the inscription, We are two farthings poorer than the emperor, and live free of cares. Wait a bit, says the emperor, and I will give you some cares. He sends for the abbot, and says, Answer these three questions in three days, or I will depose you. The questions are, How deep is the sea? How many stars in the sky? How far from good luck to bad? The shepherd of the monastery gives the answers, and is told, as in several cases before, If you are the abbot, abbot you shall be. J. W. Wolf, *Hessische Sagen*, p. 166, No 262, II. 'Gustav Adolf und der Abt von Benediktbeuern,' in Sepp's *Altbayerischer Sagenschatz*, p. 554, No 153, is another form of the same story, with a substitution of How far is it to heaven? for the first question, and the answers are given by a kitchie-boy.[*] In 'Hans ohne Sorgen,' Meier, *Deutsche Volksmärchen aus Schwaben*, p. 305, the questions are, How far is it to heaven? How deep is the sea? How many leaves has a linden? and the shepherd again undertakes the [409] answers.[†] 'Der Miller ohne Sorgen,' Müllenhoff, p. 153, 208, is a mutilated variation of these. The abbot disappears, and the questions are put to the miller, who answers for himself. The second question is How much does the moon weigh? and the answer, Four quarters; if you don't believe it, you must weigh for yourself.

We meet the miller *sans souci* again in a Danish tale, which otherwise agrees entirely with our ballad. The questions are answered by the rich miller's herdsman: Grundtvig, *Gamle danske Minder*, 1854, p. 112, No 111.

Other repetitions of the popular tale, many of them with the monk or miller *sans souci*. Bartsch, *Sagen, Märchen u. Gebräuche aus Meklenburg*, I, 496 (Pater ohne Sorgen); Asbjørnsen, *Norske Folke-Eventyr*, Ny Samling, 1876, p. 128, No 26; Bondeson, *Halländske Sagor*, p. 103, No 27; the same, *Svenska Folksagor*, p. 24, No 7 (utan all sorg), cf. p. 22, No 6; Wigström, *Sagor och Äfventyr upptecknade i Skåne*, p. 109, in *Nyare bidrag till kännedom om de svenska landsmålen och svenskt folklif*, V, 1; Lespy, *Prover-*

---

[*]   In Prussia Frederick the Great plays the part of Gustavus. Sepp, p. 558.

[†]   Another Swabian story, in Meier, No 28, p. 99, is a mixed form. The Duke of Swabia reads "Hans sans cares" over a miller's house-door, and says, "Bide a wee: if you have no cares, I will give you some." The duke, to give the miller a taste of what care is, says he must solve this riddle or lose his mill: Come to me neither by day nor by night, neither naked nor clothed, neither on foot nor on horseback. The miller promises his man his daughter in marriage and the mill in succession, if he will help him out of his dilemma. The man at once says, Go on Mid-week, for Mid-week is no day (Mitt-woch ist ja gar kein Tag, wie Sonn-tag, Mon-tag), neither is it night; and if you are to be neither clothed nor bare, put on a fishing-net; and if you are to go neither on foot nor on horseback, ride to him on an ass. All but the beginning of this is derived from the cycle of 'The Clever Wench:' see No 2. Haltrich, *Deutsche Volksmärchen in Siebenbürgen*, No 45, which is also of this cycle, has taken up a little of 'Hans ohne Sorgen.' A church has an inscription, Wir leben ohne Sorgen. This vexes the king, who says as before, Just wait, and I will give you reason for cares, p. 244, ed. 1856.

bes du Pays de Béarn, p. 102; Bladé, *Contes pop. de la Gascogne*, III, 297; Moisant de Brieux, *Origines de quelques coutumes anciennes, etc.*, Caen, 1874, I, 147, II, 100; *Armana prouvençau*, 1874, p. 33 (parson, bishop, gardener, middle of the earth, weight of the moon, what is my valuation? what am I thinking?); Pitrè, *Fiabe, Novelle, etc.*, II, 323, No 97 (senza, pinseri); Imbriani, *La novellaja fiorentina, etc.*, p. 621, V (Milanese, senza pensà); Braga, *Contos tradicionaes do povo portuguez*, I, 157, No 71, previously in *Era Nova*, 1881, p. 244 (sem cuidados), and No 160; Krauss, *Sagen u. Märchen der Südslaven*, II, 252, No 112 (ohne Sorgen); Erman, *Archiv für die wissenschaftliche Kunde von Russland*, XXIV, 146 (Czar Peter, kummerloses Kloster); Vinson, *Le Folk-Lore du Pays basque*, p. 106; Cerquand, *Légendes et recits pop. du Pays basque*, No 108. An Armenian, a Slovak, and a Hungarian version, by H. v. Wlisłocki, *Zs. f. vergleichende Litteraturgeschichte, u. s. w.*, N. F., IV, 106ff, 1891.

Unterhaltende Räthsel-Spiele in Fragen u. Antworten, gesammelt von C. H. W., Merseburg, 1824, has the story of king, abbot, and shepherd, with the three riddles, How far is it to heaven? How deep is the sea? What is better than a gold coach? The shepherd prompts the abbot, and the abbot answers the king in person. The answer to the third is, the rain that falls between Whitsuntide and St John's. For this reply compare *Archiv für slavische Philologie*, V, 56, lines 25–36.

A Croatian version of the story is given by Valyavets, 'Frater i turski car,' p. 262. The Turkish tsar is disposed to expel all monks from his dominions, but determines first to send for an abbot to try his calibre. The abbot is too much frightened to go, and his cook, as in Foligno and Timoneda, takes his place. The questions are, Where is the centre of the world? What is God doing now? What am I thinking? The first and third are disposed of in the usual way. When called to answer the second, the cook said, You can't see through the ceiling: we must go out into the field. When they came to the field, the cook said again, How can I see when I am on such a small ass? Let me have your horse. The sultan consented to exchange beasts, and then the cook said, God is wondering that a sultan should be sitting on an ass and a monk on a horse. The sultan was pleased with the answers, and reasoning, If the cook is so clever, what must the abbot be, decided to let the monks alone. Afanasief, who cites this story from Valyavets (*Narodnuiya russkiya Skazki*, VIII, 460), says that he heard in the government of Voroneje a story of a soldier who dressed himself as a monk and presented himself before a tsar who was in the habit of puzzling people with riddles. The questions are, How many drops in the sea? How many stars in the sky? What do I think? And the answer to the last is, Thou thinkest, gosudar, that I am a monk, but I am merely a soldier.[*] Another Magyar version appears in *Zs. f. vergleichende Literaturgeschichte*, N. F. V, 467.

A few tales, out of many remaining, may be now briefly mentioned, on account of variations in the setting.

A prisoner is to be released if he can tell a queen how much she is worth, the centre of the world, and what she thinks. A peasant changes clothes with the prisoner, and answers *pro more*. *Kurtzweiliger Zeitvertreiber* durch C. A. M. von W., 1668, p. 70f, in Köhler, *Orient und Occident*, I, 43.

A scholar has done learning. His master says he must now answer three questions, or have his head taken off. The master's brother, a miller, comes to his aid. The questions are, How many ladders would reach to the sky? Where is the middle of the world? What is the world worth? Or, according to another tradition, the two last are, How long will it take to go round the world? What is my thought? Campbell, *Popular Tales of the West Highlands*, II, 391 f.

Eulenspiegel went to Prague, and advertised himself on the doors of the churches and lecture-rooms as a great master, capable of answering questions that nobody else could solve. To put him down, the rector and his colleagues summoned Eulenspiegel to an examination before the university. Five questions were given him: How much water is there in the sea? How many days from Adam to now? Where is the middle of the world? How far from earth to heaven? What is the breadth of the sky? Lap-

penberg, *Dr Thomas Murners Ulenspiegel*, p. 38, No 28; Howleglas, ed. Ouvry, p. 28.

A herdboy had a great fame for his shrewd answers. The king did not believe in him, but sent for him, and said, If you can answer three questions that I shall put, I will regard you as my own child, and you shall live in my palace. [410] The questions are, How many drops of water are there in the ocean? How many stars in the sky? How many seconds in eternity? The Grimms, K. u. H. märchen, No 152, 'Das Hirtenbüblein.'

Three questions are put to a counsellor of the king's, of which the first two are, Where does the sun rise? How far from heaven to earth? The answers, by a shepherd, are extraordinarily feeble. *Jüdisches Maasäbuch*, cap. 126, cited from *Helwigs Jüdische Historien*, No 39, in the Grimms' note to *Das Hirtenbüblein*. Also given in Grünbaum's *Jüdischdeutsche Chrestomathie*, 1882, pp. 440–43. The third question is, What am I thinking? with the usual answer.

Three monks, who know everything, in the course of their travels come to a sultan's dominions, and he invites them to turn Mussulmans. This they agree to do if he will answer their questions. All the sultan's doctors are convened, but can do nothing with the monks' questions. The hodja (the court-fool) is sent for. The first question, Where is the middle of the earth? is answered as usual. The second monk asks, How many stars are there in the sky? The answer is, As many as there are hairs on my ass. Have you counted? ask the monks. Have *you* counted? rejoins the fool. Answer me this, says the same monk, and we shall see if your number is right: How many hairs are there in my beard? "As many as in my ass's tail." "Prove it." "My dear man, if you don't believe me, count yourself; or we will pull all the hairs out of both, count them, and settle the matter." The monks submit, and become Mussulmans. *Les plaisanteries de Nasr-eddin Hodja, traduites du turc* par J. A. Decourdemanche, No 70, p. 59ff.

The Turkish emperor sends word to Kaiser Leopold that unless the emperor can answer three questions he shall come down upon him with all his Turks. The counsellors are summoned, but there is no help in them. The court-fool offers to get his master out of the difficulty, if he may have the loan of crown and sceptre. When the fool comes to Constantinople, there lies the sultan in the window, and calls out, Are you the emperor, and will you answer my questions? Where does the world end? "Here, where my horse is standing." How far is it to heaven? "One day's journey, and no inn on the road." What is God thinking of now? "He is thinking that I am one fool and you another." J. W. Wolf, *Hessische Sagen*, p. 165, No 262 I.[*]

---

[*]   In the beginning there is a clear trace of the Oriental tales of 'The Clever Lass' cycle.

For the literature, see especially the Grimms' *Kinder- und Hausmärchen*, notes to No 152; R. Köhler in *Orient und Occident*, I, 439–41; Oesterley's note to Pauli's *Schimpf und Ernst*, No 55, p. 479; Keller, *Fastnachtspiele*, Nachlese, p. 338, note to 199.

Translated, after Percy's *Reliques*, II, 302, 1765, by Bodmer, II, 111; by Doenniges, p. 152; by Ritter, *Archiv für das Studium der neueren Sprachen*, XXII, 222; by von Marées, p. 7, No 2. Retold by Bürger, 'Der Kaiser und der Abt,' *Göttinger Musenalmanach für 1785*, p. 177.

A

Percy MS., p. 184. Hales and Furnivall, I, 508.

1 OFF an ancient story Ile tell you anon,
   Of a notable prince *that* was called King Iohn,
   In England was borne, with maine and with
      might;
   Hee did much wrong and mainteined litle right.

2 This noble prince was vexed in veretye,
   For he was angry with the Bishopp of Canter-
      bury;
   Ffor his house-keeping and his good cheere,
   Thé rode post for him, as you shall heare.

3 They rode post for him verry hastilye;
   The king sayd the bishopp kept a better house
      then hee:
   A hundred men euen, as I [have heard] say,
   The bishopp kept in his house euerye day,
   And fifty gold chaines, without any doubt,
   In veluett coates waited the bishopp about.

[411]   4 The bishopp, he came to the court anon,
   Before his prince *that* was called King Iohn.
   As soone as the bishopp the king did see,
   'O,' quoth the king, 'bishopp, thow art welcome
      to mee.
   There is noe man soe welcome to towne
   As thou *that* workes treason against my crowne.'

5 'My leege,' quoth the bishopp, 'I wold it were
      knowne
   I spend, your grace, nothing but *that* that's my
      owne;
   I trust your grace will doe me noe deare
   For spending my owne trew gotten geere.'

6 'Yes,' quoth the king, 'bishopp, thou must needs
      dye,
   Eccept thou can answere mee questions three;
   Thy head shalbe smitten quite from thy bodye,
   And all thy liuing remayne vnto mee.

7 'First,' quoth the king, 'tell me in this steade,
   With this crowne of gold heere vpon my head,
   Amongst my nobilitye, with ioy and much
      mirth,
   Lett me know within one pennye what I am
      worth.

8 'Secondlye, tell me without any dowbt
   How soone I may goe the whole world about;
   And thirdly, tell mee or euer I stinte,
   What is the thing, bishopp, *that* I doe thinke.
   Twenty dayes pardon thoust haue trulye,
   And come againe and answere mee.'

9 The bishopp bade the king god night att a word;
   He rode betwixt Cambridge and Oxenford,
   But neuer a doctor there was soe wise
   Cold shew him these questions or enterprise.

10 Wherewith the bishopp was nothing gladd,
   But in his hart was heauy and sadd,
   And hyed him home to a house in the countrye,
   To ease some part of his melanchollye.

11 His halfe-brother dwelt there, was feirce and fell,
   Noe better but a shepard to the bishoppe himself;
   The shepard came to the bishopp anon,
   Saying, My Lord, you are welcome home!

12 'What ayles you,' quoth the shepard, 'that you
     are soe sadd,
  And had wonte to haue beene soe merry and gladd?'
  'Nothing,' quoth the bishopp, 'I ayle att this time;
  Will not thee availe to know, brother mine.'

13 'Brother,' quoth the shepeard, 'you haue heard itt,
  That a ffoole may teach a wisemane witt;
  Say me therfore whatsoeuer you will,
  And if I doe you noe good, Ile doe you noe ill.'

14 Quoth the bishop: I haue beene att the court anon,
  Before my prince is called King Iohn,
  And there he hath charged mee
  Against his crowne with traitorye.

15 If I cannott answer his misterye,
  Three questions hee hath propounded to mee,
  He will haue my land soe faire and free,
  And alsoe the head from my bodye.

16 The first question was, to tell him in that stead,
  With the crowne of gold vpon his head,
  Amongst his nobilitye, with ioy and much mirth,
  To lett him know within one penye what hee is
     worth.

17 And secondlye, to tell him with-out any doubt
  How soone he may goe the whole world about;
  And thirdlye, to tell him, or ere I stint,
  What is the thinge that he does thinke.

18 'Brother,' quoth the shepard, 'you are a man of
     learninge;
  What neede you stand in doubt of soe small a
     thinge?
  Lend me,' quoth the shepard, 'your ministers
     apparrell,
  Ile ryde to the court and answere your quarrell.

19 'Lend me your serving men, say me not nay,
  With all your best horsses that ryd on the way;
  Ile to the court, this matter to stay;
  Ile speake with King Iohn and heare what heele
     say.'

20 The bishopp with speed prepared then
  To sett forth the shepard with horsse and man;
  The shepard was liuely without any doubt;
  I wott a royall companye came to the court.

21 The shepard hee came to the court anon
  Before [his] prince that was called King Iohn.
  As soone as the king the shepard did see,
  'O,' quoth the king, 'bishopp, thou art welcome
    to me.'
  The shepard was soe like the bishopp his brother,
  The king cold not know the one from the other.

22 Quoth the king, Bishopp, thou art welcome to me
  If thou can answer me my questions three.
  Said the shepard, If it please your grace,
  Show mee what the first quest[i]on was.

23 'First,' quoth the king, 'tell mee in this stead,
  With the crowne of gold vpon my head,
  Amongst my nobilitye, with ioy and much mirth,
  Within one pennye what I am worth.'

24 Quoth the shepard, To make your grace noe offence,
  I thinke you are worth nine and twenty pence;
  For our Lord Iesus, that bought vs all,
  For thirty pence was sold into thrall
  Amongst the cursed Iewes, as I to you doe showe;
  But I know Christ was one penye better then you.

25 Then the king laught, and swore by St Andrew
  He was not thought to bee of such a small value.
  'Secondlye, tell mee with-out any doubt
  How soone I may goe the world round about.'

26 Saies the shepard, It is noe time with your grace
    to scorne,
  But rise betime with the sun in the morne,
  And follow his course till his vprising,
  And then you may know without any leasing.

27 And this [to] your grace shall proue the same,
  You are come to the same place from whence
    you came;
  [In] twenty-four houres, with-out any doubt,
  Your grace may the world goe round about;
  The world round about, euen as I doe say,
  If with the sun you can goe the next way.

28 'And thirdlye tell me or euer I stint,
  What is the thing, bishoppe, that I doe thinke.'
  'That shall I doe,' quoth the shepeard; 'for veretye,
  You thinke I am the bishopp of Canterburye.'

29 'Why, art not thou? the truth tell to me;
  For I doe thinke soe,' quoth the king, 'by St Marye.'
  'Not soe,' quoth the shepeard; 'the truth shalbe
    knowne,
  I am his poore shepeard; my brother is att home.'

30 'Why,' quoth the king, 'if itt soe bee,
   Ile make thee bishopp here to mee.'
   'Noe, Sir,' quoth the shepard, 'I pray you be still,
   For Ile not bee bishop but against my will;
   For I am not fitt for any such deede,
   For I can neither write nor reede.'

31 'Why then,' quoth the king, 'Ile giue thee cleere
   A pattent of three hundred pound a yeere;
   That I will giue thee franke and free;
   Take thee that, shepard, for coming to me.

32 'Free pardon Ile giue,' the kings grace said,
   'To saue the bishopp, his land and his head;
   With him nor thee Ile be nothing wrath;
   Here is the pardon for him and thee both.'

33 Then the shepard he had noe more to say,
   But tooke the pardon and rode his way:
   When he came to the bishopps place,
   The bishopp asket anon how all things was.

34 'Brother,' quoth the shepard, 'I haue well sped,
   For I haue saued both your land and your head;
   The king with you is nothing wrath,
   For heere is the pardon for you and mee both.'

35 Then the bishopes hart was of a merry cheere: [⌐
   'Brother, thy paines Ile quitt them cleare;
   For I will giue thee a patent to thee and to thine
   Of fifty pound a yeere, land good and fine.'

36 .   .   .   .   .

   'I will to thee noe longer croche nor creepe,
   Nor Ile serue thee noe more to keepe thy
      sheepe.'

37 Whereeuer wist you shepard before,
   That had in his head witt such store
   To pleasure a bishopp in such a like case,
   To answer three questions to the kings grace?
   Whereeuer wist you shepard gett cleare
   Three hundred and fifty pound a yeere?

38 I neuer hard of his fellow before.
   Nor I neuer shall: now I need to say noe more.
   I neuer knew shepeard that gott such a liuinge
   But David, the shepeard, that was a king.

B

Broadside, printed for P. Brooksby, at the Golden
Ball in Pye-corner (1672–95).

1 I'LL tell you a story, a story anon,
   Of a noble prince, and his name was King John;
   For he was a prince, and a prince of great might,
   He held up great wrongs, he put down great
      right.
   Derry down, down hey, derry down

2 I'll tell you a story, a story so merry,
   Concerning the Abbot of Canterbury,
   And of his house-keeping and high renown,
   Which made him resort to fair London town.

3 'How now, father abbot? 'T is told unto me
   That thou keepest a far better house than I;
   And for [thy] house-keeping and high renown,
   I fear thou has treason against my crown.'

4 'I hope, my liege, that you owe me no grudge
   For spending of my true-gotten goods:'
   'If thou dost not answer me questions three,
   Thy head shall be taken from thy body.

5 'When I am set so high on my steed,
   With my crown of gold upon my head,
   Amongst all my nobility, with joy and much
      mirth,
   Thou must tell me to one penny what I am worth.

6 'And the next question you must not flout,
   How long I shall be riding the world about;
   And the third question thou must not shrink,
   But tell to me truly what I do think.'

7 'O these are hard questions for my shallow wit,
   For I cannot answer your grace as yet;
   But if you will give me but three days space,
   I'll do my endeavor to answer your grace.'

8 'O three days space I will thee give,
   For that is the longest day thou hast to live.
   And if thou dost not answer these questions
      right,
   Thy head shall be taken from thy body quite.'

9 And as the shepherd was going to his fold,
  He spy'd the old abbot come riding along:
  'How now, master abbot? You'r welcome home;
  What news have you brought from good King
      John?'

10 'Sad news, sad news I have thee to give,
   For I have but three days space for to live;
   If I do not answer him questions three,
   My head will be taken from my body.

11 'When he is set so high on his steed,
   With his crown of gold upon his head,
   Amongst all his nobility, with joy and much
      mirth,
   I must tell him to one penny what he is worth.

12 'And the next question I must not flout,
   How long he shall be riding the world about;
   And the third question I must not shrink
   But tell him truly what he does think.'

13 'O master, did you never hear it yet,
   That a fool may learn a wiseman wit?
   Lend me but your horse and your apparel,
   I'll ride to fair London and answer the quarrel.'

14 'Now I am set so high on my steed,
   With my crown of gold upon my head,
   Amongst all my nobility, with joy and much
      mirth,
   Now tell me to one penny what I am worth.'

15 'For thirty pence our Saviour was sold,
   Amongst the false Jews, as you have been told,
   And nine and twenty's the worth of thee,
   For I think thou are one penny worser than he.'

16 'And the next question thou mayst not flout;
   How long I shall be riding the world about.'
   'You must rise with the sun, and ride with the
      same,
   Until the next morning he rises again,
   And then I am sure you will make no doubt
   But in twenty-four hours you'l ride it about.'

17 'And the third question you must not shrink,
   But tell me truly what I do think.'
   'All that I can do, and 't will make you merry;
   For you think I'm the Abbot of Canterbury,
   But I'm his poor shepherd, as you may see,
   And am come to beg pardon for he and for me.'

18 The king he turned him about and did smile,
   Saying, Thou shalt be the abbot the other
      while:
   'O no, my grace, there is no such need,
   For I can neither write nor read.'

19 'Then four pounds a week will I give unto thee
   For this merry jest thou hast told unto me;
   And tell the old abbot, when thou comest
      home,
   Thou hast brought him a pardon from good
      King John.'

———◆———

A. *Not divided into stanzas in the MS.*
  3^3, 3^5, 6^2, 8^5, 15^2, 22^2, 24^4, 27^3, 31^2, 37^4. *Arabic*
     numerals are expressed in letters.
  14^1. thy court.
  24^2. worth 29 pence.

31^2. patten. 31^4. Caming.
35^4. 50^{1}i. 37^6. 35^{1}i.
B. 5^1, 11^1, 14^1. on my [his] steed so high.
  7^1. my sh ow.
  11^1. sat. 12^3. thou must. 19^4. K. John.

46

CAPTAIN WEDDERBURN'S COURTSHIP

A. a. 'I'll no ly neist the wa,' Herd's MS., I, 161. b. 'She'll no ly neist [the] wa,' the same, II, 100.
B. a. 'The Earl of Rosslyn's Daughter,' Kinloch MSS, I, 83. b. 'Lord Roslin's Daughter,' *Lord Roslin's Daughter's Garland*, p. 4. c. 'Lord Roslin's Daughter,' Buchan's MSS, II, 34. d. 'Captain Wed- derburn's Courtship,' Jamieson's *Popular Ballads*, II, 159. e. Harris MS., fol. 19 b, No 14. f. *Notes and Queries*, 2d S., IV, 170. g. 'Captian Wederburn,' "The Old Lady's Collection," No 38.
C. 'The Laird of Roslin's Daughter,' Sheldon's *Minstrelsy of the English Border*, p. 232.

A COPY of this ballad was printed in *The New British Songster, a Collection of Songs, Scots and English, with Toasts and Sentiments for the Bottle*, Falkirk, 1785: see Motherwell, p. lxxiv.[*] Few were more popular, says Motherwell, and [415] Jamieson remarks that 'Captain Wedderburn' was equally in vogue in the north and the south of Scotland.

Jamieson writes to the *Scots Magazine*, 1803, p. 701: "Of this ballad I have got one whole copy and part of another, and I remember a good deal of it as I have heard it sung in Moray-shire when I was a child." In his *Popular Ballads*, II, 154, 1806, he says that the copy which he prints was furnished him from Mr Herd's MS. by the editor of the *Border Minstrelsy*, and that he had himself supplied a few readings of small importance from his own recollection. There is some inaccuracy here. The version given by Jamieson is rather **B**, with readings from **A**.

We have had of the questions six, **A** 11, 12, What is greener than the grass? in No 1, **A** 15, **C** 13, **D** 5; What's higher than the tree? in **C** 9, **D** 1; What's war than a woman's wiss? ("than a woman was") **A** 15, **C** 13, **D** 5; What's deeper than the sea? **A** 13, **B** 8, **C** 9, **D** 1. Of the three dishes, **A** 8, 9, we have the bird without a gall in Ein Spil von den Freiheit, *Fastnachtspiele* aus dem 15ⁿ Jhdt, II, 558, v. 23,[†] and the two oth-ers in the following song, from a manuscript assigned to the fifteenth century, and also pre-served in several forms by oral tradition:[‡] Sloane MS., No 2593, British Museum; Wright's *Songs and Carols*, 1836, No 8; as printed for the Warton Club, No xxix, p. 33.

I have a зong suster fer beзondyn the se,
Many be the drowryis that che sente me.

Che sente me the cherye, withoutyn ony ston,
And so che dede [the] dowe, withoutyn ony bon.

Sche sente mé the brere, withoutyn ony rynde,
Sche bad me love my lemman withoute longgyng.

How xuld ony cherye be withoute ston?
And how xuld ony dowe ben withoute bon?

How xuld any brere ben withoute rynde?
How xuld y love myn lemman without longyng?

Quan the cherye was a flour, than hadde it non ston;
Quan the dowe was an ey, than hadde it non bon.

Quan the brere was onbred, than hadde it non rynd;
Quan the mayden haзt that che lovit, che is with-out longyng

---

[*] This book has been pursued by me for years, with the coöperation of many friends and agents, but in vain.

[†] Followed by Virgil's riddle, *Ecl.* iii, 104–5, Where is the sky but three spans broad?

Rev. J. Baring-Gould informs me that there is an Irish version of this piece in Ulster Ballads, British Museum, 1162. k. 6, entitled 'The Lover's Riddle.' The lady, who in **B**, **C** is walking through the wood 'her lane,' is in the Ulster copy walking 'down a narrow lane,' and she meets 'with William Dicken, a keeper of the game.' The only important difference as to the riddles and the answers is that the young lady remembers her Bible to good purpose, and gives Melchisedec as an example of a priest unborn (Hebrews vii, 3).

'Captain Wedderburn's Courtship,' or 'Lord Roslin's Daughter,'[*] is a counterpart of the ballad in which a maid wins a husband by guessing riddles. (See Nos 1 and 2, and also the following ballad, for a lady who *gives* riddles.) The [416] ingenious suitor, though not so favorite a subject as the clever maid, may boast that he is of an old and celebrated family. We find him in the *Gesta Romanorum*, No 70; Oesterley, p. 383, Madden's English Versions, No 35, p. 384. A king had a beautiful daughter, whom he wished to dispose of in marriage; but she had made a vow that she would accept no husband who had not achieved three tasks: to tell her how many feet long, broad, and deep were the four elements; to change the wind from the north; to take fire into his bosom, next the flesh, without harm. The king issued a proclamation in accordance with these terms. Many tried and failed, but at last there came a soldier who succeeded. To answer the first question he made his servant lie down, and measured him from head to foot. Every living being is composed of the four elements, he said, and I find not more than seven feet in them. A very easy way was hit on for performing the second task: the soldier simply turned his horse's head to the east, and, since wind is the life of every animal, maintained that he had changed the wind. The king was evidently not inclined to be strict, and said, Clear enough. Let us go on to the third. Then, by the aid of a stone which he always carried about him, the soldier put handfuls of burning coals into his bosom without injury. The king gave his daughter to the soldier.

An extraordinary ballad in Sakellarios's Κυπριακά, III, 15, No 6, 'The Hundred Sayings,' subjects a lover to a severe probation of riddles. (Liebrecht has given a full abstract of the story in Gosche's *Archiv*, II, 29, repeated in Liebrecht, *Zur Volkskunde*, p. 162 ff.) A youth is madly enamored of a king's daughter, but, though his devotion knows no bound, cannot for a long time get a word from her mouth, and

---

‡ Halliwell's *Popular Rhymes and Nursery Tales*, p. 150; Halliwell's *Nursery Rhymes*, No 375; *Notes and Queries*, 3d Ser., IX, 401; 4th Ser., III, 501, 604; *Macmillan's Magazine*, V, 248, by T. Hughes; Miss M. H. Mason gives two copies in her *Nursery Rhymes and Country Songs*, pp. 23, 24, 'A Paradox.' A version from Scotland has been printed in the *Folk-Lore Journal*, III, 272, 'I had six lovers over the sea.' The first of these runs:

I have four sisters beyond the sea,
  Para-mara, dictum, domine
And they did send four presents to me.
  Partum, quartum, paradise, tempum,
  Para-mara, dictum, domine

The first it was a bird without eer a bone,
The second was a cherry without eer a stone.

The third it was a blanket without eer a thread,
The fourth it was a book which no man could read.

How can there be a bird without eer a bone?
How can there be a cherry without eer a stone?

How can there be a blanket without eer a thread?
How can there be a book which no man can read?

When the bird's in the shell, there is no bone;
When the cherry's in the bud, there is no stone.

When the blanket's in the fleece, there is no thread;
When the book's in the press, no man can read.

The Minnesinger dames went far beyond our laird's daughter in the way of requiring "ferlies" from their lovers. Der Tanhuser and Boppe represent that their ladies would be satisfied with nothing short of their turning the course of rivers; bringing them the salamander, the basilisk, the graal, Paris's apple; giving them a sight of Enoch and Elijah in the body, a hearing of the sirens, etc. Von der Hagen, *Minnesinger*, II, 91 f, 385 f.

---

* There were, no doubt, Grissels enough in the very distinguished family of the Sinclairs of Roslin to furnish one for this ballad. I see two mentioned among the Sinclairs of Herdmanstoun. Even a Wedderburn connection, as I am informed, is not absolutely lacking. George Home of Wedderburn († 1497), married the eldest daughter of John Sinclair of Herdmanstoun: Douglas's *Peerage of Scotland*, ed. Wood, 1813, II, 174.

then only disdain. She shuts herself up in a
tower. He prays for a heat that may force her to
come to the window, and that she may drop her
spindle, and he be the only one to bring it to
her. The heavens are kind: all this comes to
pass, and she is fain to beg him to bring her the
spindle. She asks, Can you do what I say?
Shoulder a tower? make a stack of eggs? trim a
date-tree, standing in a great river?[*] All this he
can do. She sends him away once and again to
learn various things; last of all, the hundred say-
ings that lovers use. He presents himself for
examination. "One?" "There is one only God:
may he help me!" "Two?" "Two doves with sil-
ver wings are sporting together: I saw how they
kissed," etc. "Three?" "Holy Trinity, help me to
love the maid!" "Four?" "There is a four-pointed
cross on thy smock, and it implores God I may
be thy mate:" and so he is catechised through
all the units and tens.[†] Then the lady suddenly
turns about, concedes everything, and proposes
that they shall go to church: but the man says,
If I am to marry all my loves, I have one in
every town, and wife and children in Constan-
tinople. They part with reciprocal scurrilities.

Usually when the hand of a princess is to be
won by the performance of tasks, whether
requiring wit, courage, the overcoming of magic
arts, or what not, the loss of your head is the
penalty of failure. (See the preface to the fol-
lowing ballad.) Apollonius of Tyre, of Greek

* The difficulty here is the want of a ποῦ στῶ, from
which to climb the tree.
† These number-riddles or songs are known to every
nation of Europe. E.g., Chambers' Popular Rhymes of Scot-
land, p. 44, ed. 1870, from Buchan's MSS, I, 280:

O what will be our ane, boys?
O what will be our ane, boys?
My only ane, she walks alane,
And evermair has dune, boys, etc.

See Köhler in Orient und Occident, II, 558–9. A dragon,
in Hahn's Griechische u. Albanesische Märchen, II, 210,
gives Penteklimas ten of these number-riddles: if he
answers them he is to have a fine castle; if not, he is to be
eaten. An old woman answers for him: "One is God, two
are the righteous, etc.; ten is your own word, and now
burst, dragon!" The dragon bursts, and Penteklimas
inherits his possessions. See R. Köhler, Die Pehlevi-
Erzählung von Gôsht-i Fryânô, etc., in Zeitschrift der deut-
sche; morgenländischen Gesellschaft, XXIX, 634–36.

original, but first found in a Latin form, is per-
haps the oldest riddle-story of this description.
Though its age has not been determined, the
tale has been carried back even to the end of
the third or the beginning of the fourth century,
was a great favorite with the Middle Ages, and
is kept only too familiar by the play of Pericles.

More deserving of perpetuation is the
charming Persian story of Prince Calaf, in Pétis
de La Croix's 1001 Days (45e–82e jour), upon
which Carlo Gozzi founded his play of "La
Turandot," now best known through Schiller's
translation. Tourandocte's riddles are such as
we should call legitimate, and are three in num-
ber. "What is the being that is found in every
land, is dear to all the world, and cannot endure
a fellow?" Calaf answers, The sun. "What
mother swallows the children she has given
birth to, as soon as they have attained their
growth?" The sea, says Calaf, for the rivers that
flow into it all came from it. "What is the tree
that has all its leaves white on one side and
black on the other?" This tree, Calaf answers, is
the year, which is made up of days and nights.[‡]

A third example of this hazardous wooing is
the story of The Fair One of the Castle, the
fourth in the Persian poem of The Seven Fig-
ures (or Beauties), by Nisami of Gendsch (†
1180). A Russian princess is shut up in a castle
made inaccessible by a talisman, and every
suitor must satisfy four conditions: he must be a
man of honor, vanquish the enchanted guards,
take away the talisman, and obtain the consent
of her father. Many had essayed their fortune,
and their heads were now arrayed on the pinna-
cles of the castle.[§] A young prince had fulfilled
the first three conditions, but the father would
not approve his suit until he had solved the
princess's riddles. These are expressed symboli-
cally, and answered in the same way. The prin-
cess sends the prince two pearls from her
earring: he at once takes her meaning,—life is
like two drops of water,—and returns the pearls
with three diamonds, to signify that joy—faith,
hope, and love—can prolong life. The princess

‡ Gozzi retains the first and third riddles, Schiller only
the third. By a happy idea, new riddles were introduced
at the successive performances of Schiller's play. Turan-
dot appears as a traditional tale in Schneller's Märchen u.
Sagen aus Wälschtirol, No 49, p. 132, "I tre Indovinelli."

now sends him three jewels in a box, with sugar. The prince seizes the idea,—life is blended with sensuous desire,—and pours milk on the sugar, to intimate that as milk dissolves sugar, so sensuous desire is quenched by true love. After four such interchanges, the princess seals her

§   The castle with walls and gate thus equipped, or a palisade of stakes each crowned with a head, is all but a commonplace in such adventures. This grim stroke of fancy is best in 'La mule sanz frain,' where there are four hundred stakes, *all but one* surmounted with a bloody head: Méon, *Nouveau Recueil*, I, 15, vv 429–37. For these parlous princesses, of all sorts, see Grundtvig, 'Den farlige Jomfru,' IV, 43 ff, No 184. The *one* stake with no head on it occurs in the *Kalevala*. Lemminkäinen, going to the Northland, is warned by his mother that he will find a courtyard planted with stakes, with a head on every stake but one, on which his head will be stuck. Schiefner, Rune 26, vv 315–22, p. 163. (G. L. K.)

The *one* stake with no head on it occurs also in Wolfdietrich B. The heathen, whom Wolfdietrich afterwards overcomes at knife-throwing, threatens him thus:

"Sihstu dort an den zinnen fünf hundert houbet stân,
Diu ich mit mînen henden alle verderbet hân
Noch stât ein zinne lære an mînem türnlin:
Dâ muoz dîn werdez houbet ze einem phande sîn."
(St. 595, Jänicke, *Deutsches Heldenbuch*, III, 256.)

Two cases in Campbell's *Popular Tales of the West Highlands.* "Many a leech has come, said the porter. There is not a spike on the town without a leech's head but one, and may be it is for thy head that one is." (The Ceabharnach, I, 312.) Conall "saw the very finest castle that ever was seen from the beginning of the universe till the end of eternity, and a great wall at the back of the fortress, and iron spikes within a foot of each other, about and around it; and a man's head upon every spike but the one spike. Fear struck him and he fell a-shaking. He thought that it was his own head that would go on the headless spike." (The Story of Conall Gulban, III, 202.) In Crestien's *Erec et Enide*, Erec overcomes a knight in an orchard. There are many stakes crowned with heads, but one stake is empty. Erec is informed that this is for *his* head, and that it is customary thus to keep a stake waiting for a newcomer, a fresh one being set up as often as a head is taken. Ed. by Bekker in Haupt's *Ztschr.*, X, 520, 521, vv 5732–66. (G.L.K.) In 'The Lad with the Skin Covering,' "They were told that in front of the king's house there were twenty-score poles, with a head on each pole with the exception of three." J. G. Campbell, *The Fians*, p. 261. (There are three adventurers in this case.) Cf. Curtin, *Myths and Folk-Lore of Ireland*, 1890, pp. 37, 114f, 193; MacInnes, *Folk and Hero Tales*, Folk-Lore Society, 1890, pp. 79, 453; W. H. Schofield, in the (Harvard) *Studies and Notes in Philology and Literature*, IV, 175ff.

consent with a device not less elegant than the others.[*]

A popular tale of this class is current in Russia, with this variation: that the hard-hearted princess requires her lovers to give her riddles, and those who cannot pose her lose their heads. Foolish Iván, the youngest of three brothers, adventures after many have failed. On his way to the trial he sees a horse in a cornfield and drives it out with a whip, and further on kills a snake with a lance, saying in each case, Here's a riddle! Confronted with the princess, he says to her, As I came to you, I saw by the roadside what was good; and in the good was good; so I set to work, and with what was good I drove the good from the good. The good fled from the good out of the good. The princess pleads a headache, and puts off her answer till the next day, when Iván gives her his second enigma: As I came to you, I saw on the way what was bad, and I struck the bad with a bad thing, and of what was bad the bad died. The princess, unable to solve these puzzles, is obliged to accept foolish Iván. (Afanasief, *Skazki*, II, 225 ff, No 20, in Ralston's *Songs of the Russian People*, p. 354 f.) Closely related to this tale, and still nearer to one another, are the Grimms' No 22, 'Das Räthsel' (see, also, the note in their third volume), and the West Highland story, 'The Ridere (Knight) of Riddles,' Campbell, No 22, II, 27. In the former, as in the Russian tale, it is the princess that must be puzzled before she will yield her hand; in the latter, an unmatchable beauty is to be had by no man who does not put a question which her father cannot solve. Similar yet are 'Las tres adivinanzas,' Marin, *Cantos pop. españoles*, I, 395; ' Soldatino,' Archivio, per *Tradizioni popolari*, I, 57.

Here may be put three drolleries, all clearly [418] of the same origin, in which a fool wins a princess by nonplussing her: 'The Three Questions,' Halliwell's *Popular Rhymes and Nursery Tales*, p. 32; a "schwank" of the fourteenth century, by Heinz der Kellner, Von der Hagen's *Gesammtabenteuer*, No 63, III, 179 (there very improperly called Turandot); 'Spurningen,' Asbjørnsen og

[*]   Von Hammer, *Geschichte der schönen Redekünste Persiens*, p. 116, previously cited by Von der Hagen, *Gesammtabenteuer*, III, lxii.

Moe, *Norske Folke-Eventyr*, No 4, Dasent, *Popular Tales from the Norse*, p. 148.[*] According to the first of these, the king of the East Angles promises his clever daughter to any one who can answer three of her questions (in the other versions, more correctly, *silence* her). Three brothers, one of them a natural, set out for the court, and, on the way, Jack finds successively an egg, a crooked hazel-stick, and a nut, and each time explodes with laughter. When they are ushered into the presence, Jack bawls out, What a troop of fair ladies! "Yes," says the princess, "we are fair ladies, for we carry fire in our bosoms." "Then roast me an egg," says Jack, pulling out the egg from his pocket. "How will you get it out again?" asks the princess? "With a crooked stick," says Jack, producing the same. "Where did that come from?" says the princess. "From a nut," answers Jack, pulling out the nut. And so, as the princess is silenced, the fool gets her in marriage.[†]

Even nowadays riddles play a noteworthy part in the marriages of Russian peasants. In the government Pskof, as we are informed by Khudyakof, the bridegroom's party is not admitted into the bride's house until all the riddles given by the party of the bride have been answered; whence the saying or proverb, to the behoof of bridegrooms, Choose comrades that can guess riddles. In the village of Davshina, in the Yaroslav government, the bridegroom's best man presents himself at the bride's house on the wedding-day, and finding a man, called the bride-seller, sitting by the bride, asks him to surrender the bride and vacate his place. "Fair and softly," answers the seller; "you will not get the bride for nothing; make us a bid, if you will. And how will you trade? will you pay in riddles or in gold?" If the best man is prepared for the emergency, as we must suppose he always would

be, he answers, I will pay in riddles. Half a dozen or more riddles are now put by the seller, of which these are favorable specimens: Give me the sea, full to the brim, and with a bottom of silver. The best man makes no answer in words, but fills a bowl with beer and lays a coin at the bottom. Tell me the thing, naked itself, which has a shift over its bosom. The best man hands the seller a candle. Finally the seller says, Give me something which the master of this house lacks. The best man then brings in the bridegroom. The seller gives up his seat, and hands the best man a plate, saying, Put in this what all pretty girls like. The best man puts in what money he thinks proper, the bridesmaids take it and quit the house, and the bridegroom's friends carry off the bride.

So, apparently in some ballad, a maid gives riddles, and will marry only the man who will guess them.

> By day like a hoop,
>   By night like a snake;
> Who reads my riddle,
>   I take him for mate.   (A belt.)
>   No 1103 of Khudyakof.[‡]

In Radloff's *Songs and Tales of the Turkish tribes in East Siberia*, I, 60, a father, wanting a wife for his son, applies to another man, who has a marriageable daughter. The latter will not make a match unless the young man's father will come to him with pelt and sans pelt, by the road and not by the road, on a horse and yet not on a horse: see 13ff of this volume. The young man gives his father proper instructions, and wins his wife.

A Lithuanian mother sends her daughter to the wood to fetch "winter May and summer snow." She meets a herdsman, and asks where she can find these. The herdsman offers to teach her these riddles in return for his love, and she complying with these terms, gives her the answers: The evergreen tree is winter May, and sea-foam is summer snow. *Beiträge zur*

---

[*]   See R. Köhler's article on Hagen, No 63, in *Germania*, XIV, 269, written in 1868, to which, Dr K. informs me, he could now make numerous additions. See, also, Stiefel, *Ueber die Quelle der Turandot-Dichtung Heinz des Kellners*, in *Zeitschr. f. vergleichende Litteraturgeschichte*, N. F., VIII, 257 ff.

[†]   The German schwank affixes the forfeit of the head to failure. In the Norwegian the unsuccessful brothers get off with a thrashing. The fire in the English, found also in the German, recalls the third task in the *Gesta Romanorum*.

[‡]   Khudyakof, in the Ethnographical Collection of the Russian Geographical Society, *Etnografitcheskiy Sbornik*, etc., VI, 9, 10, 8. Ralston, *The Songs of the Russian People*, p. 353.

Kunde Preussens, I, 515 (Rhesa), and Ausland, 1839, p. 1230.

The European tales, excepting the three drolleries (and even they are perhaps to be regarded only as parodies of the others), must be of Oriental derivation; but the far north presents us with a similar story in the lay of Alvíss, in the elder Edda. The dwarf Alvíss comes to claim Freya for his bride by virtue of a promise from the gods. Thor* says that the bride is in his charge, and that he was from home when the

* Vigfusson objects to Thor being the interlocutor, though that is the name in the MS., because cunning does not suit Thor's blunt character, and proposes Odin instead. "May be the dwarf first met Thor (Wingthor), whereupon Woden (Wingi) came up." *Corpus Poeticum Boreale,* I, 81.

promise was made: at any rate, Alvíss shall not have the maid unless he can answer all the questions that shall be put him. Thor then requires Alvíss to give him the names of earth, heaven, moon, sun, etc., ending with barley and the poor creature small beer, in all the worlds; that is, in the dialect of the gods, of mankind, giants, elves, dwarfs, etc. Alvíss does this with such completeness as to extort Thor's admiration, but is craftily detained in so doing till after sunrise, when Thor cries, You are taken in! Above ground at dawn! and the dwarf turns to stone.

Translated, in part, after Aytoun, by Knortz, *Schottische Balladen,* p. 107.

A

a. Herd's MS., I, 161. **b.** The same, II, 100.

1 THE laird of Bristoll's daughter was in the
woods walking,
And by came Captain Wetherbourn, a servant
to the king;
And he said to his livery man, Wer 't not
against the law,
I would tak her to mine ain bed, and lay her
neist the wa.

2 'I'm into my father's woods, amongst my
father's trees,
O kind sir, let mee walk alane, O kind sir, if you
please;
The butler's bell it will be rung, and I'll be mist
awa;
I'll lye into mine ain bed, neither at stock nor
wa.'

3 'O my bonny lady, the bed it's not be mine,
For I'll command my servants for to call it
thine;
The hangings are silk satin, the sheets are hol-
land sma,
And we 's baith lye in ae bed, but you 's lye
neist the wa.'

4 'And so, my bonny lady,—I do not know your
name,—
But my name's Captain Wetherburn, and I'm a
man of fame;
Tho your father and a' his men were here, I
would na stand in awe
To tak you to mine ain bed, and lay you neist
the wa.

5 'Oh my bonny, bonny lady, if you'll gie me your
hand,
You shall hae drums and trumpets to sound at
your command;
Wi fifty men to guard you, sae weel their swords
can dra,
And wee 's baith lye in ae bed, but you 's lye
neist the wa.'

6 He's mounted her upon a steid, behind his gen-
tleman,
And he himself did walk afoot, to had his lady
on,
With his hand about her midle sae jimp, for
fear that she should fa;
She man lye in his bed, but she'll not lye neist
the wa.

[420] 7 He's taen her into Edinburgh, his landlady cam
        ben:
        'And monny bonny ladys in Edinburgh hae I
            seen,
        But the like of this fine creature my eyes they
            never sa;'
        'O dame bring ben a down-bed, for she 's lye
            neist the wa.'

8 'Hold your tongue, young man,' she said, 'and
        dinna trouble me,
    Unless you get to my supper, and that is dishes
        three;
    Dishes three to my supper, tho I eat nane at a',
    Before I lye in your bed, but I winna lye neist
        the wa.

9 'You maun get to my supper a cherry but a
        stane,
    And you man get to my supper a capon but a
        bane,
    And you man get a gentle bird that flies want-
        ing the ga,
    Before I lye in your bed, but I'll not lye neist
        the wa.'

10 'A cherry whan in blossom is a cherry but a
        stane;
    A capon when he's in the egg canna hae a
        bane;
    The dow it is a gentle bird that flies wanting
        the ga;
    And ye man lye in my bed, between me and
        the wa.'

11 'Hold your tongue, young man,' she said, 'and
        dinna me perplex,
    Unless you tell me questions, and that is ques-
        tions six;
    Tell me them as I shall ask them, and that is
        twa by twa,
    Before I lye in your bed, but I'll not lye neist
        the wa.

12 'What is greener than the grass, what's higher
        than the tree?
    What's war than a woman's wiss, what's deeper
        than the sea?
    What bird sings first, and whereupon the dew
        down first does fa?
    Before I lye in your bed, but I'll not lye neist
        the wa.'

13 'Virgus is greener than the grass, heaven's
        higher than the tree;
    The deil's war than a woman's wish, hell's
        deeper than the sea;
    The cock sings first, on the Sugar Loaf the dew
        down first does fa;
    And ye man lye in my bed, betweest me and
        the wa.'

14 'Hold your tongue, young man,' she said, 'I pray
        you give it oer,
    Unless you tell me questions, and that is ques-
        tions four;
    Tell me them as I shall ask them, and that is
        twa by twa,
    Before I lye in your bed, but I winna lye neist
        the wa.

15 'You man get to me a plumb that does in winter
        grow;
    And likewise a silk mantle that never waft gaed
        thro;
    A sparrow's horn, a priest unborn, this night to
        join us twa,
    Before I lye in your bed, but I winna lye neist
        the wa.'

16 'There is a plumb in my father's yeard that does
        in winter grow;
    Likewise he has a silk mantle that never waft
        gaed thro;
    A sparrow's horn, it may be found, there's ane
        in every tae,
    There's ane upo the mouth of him, perhaps
        there may be twa.

17 'The priest is standing at the door, just ready to
        come in;
    Nae man could sae that he was born, to lie it is
        a sin;
    For a wild boar bored his mother's side, he out
        of it did fa;
    And you man lye in my bed, between me and
        the wa.'

18 Little kent Grizey Sinclair, that morning when
        she raise,
    'T was to be the hindermost of a' her single days;
    For now she's Captain Wetherburn's wife, a
        man she never saw,
    And she man lye in his bed, but she'll not lye
        neist the wa.

[21]

B

a. Kinloch MSS, I, 83, from Mary Barr's recitation.
b. *Lord Roslin's Daughter's Garland.* **c.** Buchan's MSS, II,
34. **d.** Jamieson's *Popular Ballads,* II, 159. **e.** Harris MS.,
fol. 19 b, No 14, from Mrs Harris's recitation. **f.** *Notes
and Queries,* 2d S., IV, 170, "as sung among the peas-
antry of the Mearns," 1857. **g.** 'Captian Wederburn,'
"The Old Lady's Collection," No 38.

(3)"I maun hae to my sup - per a__ bird with - out a bone;__

And I maun hae to my sup - per a cher-ry with - out a stone;

An I maun hae a gen - tle bird that flies with - out__ a gaw,

Be - fore that I gae with you,_____ I tell you, aye or na."

B. e. Harris MS.

1 THE Lord of Rosslyn's daughter gaed through
the wud her lane,
And there she met Captain Wedderburn, a ser-
vant to the king.
He said unto his livery-man, Were 't na agen
the law,
I wad tak her to my ain bed, and lay her at the
wa.

2 'I'm walking here my lane,' she says, 'amang my
father's trees;
And ye may lat me walk my lane, kind sir, now
gin ye please.
The supper-bell it will be rung, and I'll be missd
awa;
Sae I'll na lie in your bed, at neither stock nor
wa.'

3 He said, My pretty lady, I pray lend me your
hand,
And ye'll hae drums and trumpets always at
your command;
And fifty men to guard ye wi, that weel their
swords can draw;
Sae we'll baith lie in ae bed, and ye'll lie at the
wa.

4 'Haud awa frae me, kind sir, I pray let go my
hand;
The supper-bell it will be rung, nae langer
maun I stand.
My father he'll na supper tak, gif I be missd
awa;
Sae I'll na lie in your bed, at neither stock nor
wa.'

5 'O my name is Captain Wedderburn, my name
I'll neer deny,
And I command ten thousand men, upo yon
mountains high.
Tho your father and his men were here, of
them I'd stand na awe,
But should tak ye to my ain bed, and lay ye
neist the wa.'

6 Then he lap aff his milk-white steed, and set
the lady on,
And a' the way he walkd on foot, he held her
by the hand;
He held her by the middle jimp, for fear that
she should fa;
Saying, I'll tak ye to my ain bed, and lay thee at
the wa.

7 He took her to his quartering-house, his land-
lady looked ben,
Saying, Monie a pretty ladie in Edinbruch I've
seen;
But sic 'na pretty ladie is not into it a':
Gae, mak for her a fine down-bed, and lay her
at the wa.

8 'O haud awa frae me, kind sir, I pray ye lat me
be,
For I'll na lie in your bed till I get dishes three;
Dishes three maun be dressd for me, gif I
should eat them a',
Before I lie in your bed, at either stock or wa.

9 ''T is I maun hae to my supper a chicken with-
out a bane;
And I maun hae to my supper a cherry without
a stane;
And I maun hae to my supper a bird without a
gaw,
Before I lie in your bed, at either stock or wa.'

10 'Whan the chicken's in the shell, I am sure it
has na bane;
And whan the cherry's in the bloom, I wat it
has na stane;
The dove she is a genty bird, she flees without a
gaw;
Sae we'll baith lie in ae bed, and ye'll be at the
wa.'

11 'O haud awa frae me, kind sir, I pray ye give me
owre,
For I'll na lie in your bed, till I get presents
four;
Presents four ye maun gie me, and that is twa
and twa,
Before I lie in your bed, at either stock or wa.

[422] 12 ''T is I maun hae some winter fruit that in
December grew;
And I maun hae a silk mantil that waft gaed
never through;
A sparrow's horn, a priest unborn, this nicht to
join us twa,
Before I lie in your bed, at either stock or wa.'

13 'My father has some winter fruit that in
December grew;
My mither has a silk mantil the waft gaed
never through;
A sparrow's horn ye soon may find, there's ane
on evry claw,
And twa upo the gab o it, and ye shall get them
a.

14 'The priest he stands without the yett, just
ready to come in;
Nae man can say he eer was born, nae man
without he sin;
He was haill cut frae his mither's side, and frae
the same let fa;
Sae we'll baith lie in ae bed, and ye 'se lie at the
wa.'

15 'O haud awa frae me, kind sir, I pray don't me
perplex,
For I'll na lie in your bed till ye answer ques-
tions six:
Questions six ye maun answer me, and that is
four and twa,
Before I lie in your bed, at either stock or wa.

16 'O what is greener than the gress, what's higher
than thae trees?
O what is worse than women's wish, what's
deeper than the seas?
What bird craws first, what tree buds first, what
first does on them fa?
Before I lie in your bed, at either stock or wa.'

17 'Death is greener than the gress, heaven higher
than thae trees;
The devil's waur than women's wish, hell's
deeper than the seas;
The cock craws first, the cedar buds first, dew
first on them does fa;
Sae we'll baith lie in ae bed, and ye 'se lie at the
wa.'

18 Little did this lady think, that morning whan
she raise,
That this was for to be the last o a' her maiden
days.
But there's na into the king's realm to be found
a blither twa,
And now she's Mrs Wedderburn, and she lies at
the wa.

C

Sheldon's *Minstrelsy of the English Border*, p. 232, as recited "by a lady of Berwick on Tweed, who used to sing it in her childhood, and had learnt it from her nurse."

1 THE laird of Roslin's daughter walked thro the
    wood her lane,
  And by came Captain Wedderburn, a servant to
    the Queen;
  He said unto his serving man, Wer 't not agaynst
    the law,
  I would tak her to my ain house as lady o my ha.

2 He said, My pretty ladye, I pray give me your
    hand;
  You shall have drums and trumpets always at
    your command;
  With fifty men to guard you, that well their
    swords can draw,
  And I'll tak ye to my ain bed, and lay you next
    the wa.

3 'I'm walking in my feyther's shaws:' quo he, My
    charming maid,
  I am much better than I look, so be you not afraid;
  For I serve the queen of a' Scotland, and a gentil
    dame is she;
  So we 'se be married ere the morn, gin ye can
    fancy me.

4 .   .   .   .   .

  'The sparrow shall toot on his horn, gif naething
    us befa,
  And I'll mak you up a down-bed, and lay you
    next the wa.

5 'Now hold away from me, kind sir, I pray you let
    me be;
  I wont be lady of your ha till you answer ques-
    tions three;
  Questions three you must answer me, and that is
    one and twa,
  Before I gae to Woodland's house, and be lady o
    your ha.

6 'You must get me to my supper a chicken with-
    out a bone;
  You must get me to my supper a cherry without a
    stone;
  You must get me to my supper a bird without a ga,
  Before I go to Woodland's house and be lady of
    your ha.'

7 'When the cherry is in the bloom, I'm sure it has
    no stone;
  When the chicken's in the shell, I'm sure it has
    nae bone;
  The dove she is a gentil bird, and flies without a
    ga;
  So I've answered you your questions three, and
    you're lady of my ha.'

*   *   *   *   *

8 'Questions three you must answer me: What's
    higher than the trees?
  And what is worse than woman's voice? What's
    deeper than the seas?'

  .   .   .   .

    .   .   .   .

9 He answered then so readily: Heaven's higher
    than the trees;
  The devil's worse than woman's voice; hell's
    deeper than the seas;

  .   .   .   .

    .   .   .   .

10 'One question still you must answer me, or you I
    laugh to scorn;
  Go seek me out an English priest, of woman
    never born;'

  .   .   .   .

    .   .   .   .

11 'Oh then,' quo he, 'my young brother from
    mother's side was torn,
  And he's a gentil English priest, of woman never
    born;'

  .   .   .   .

    .   .   .   .

12 Little did his lady think, that morning when she
    raise,
  It was to be the very last of all her mayden days;

  .   .   .   .

A. a. 2^4. I lye. $4^{3,4}$ and $5^{3,4}$ have been interchanged. 5^4. lye you. **b.** lay. 7^1. teen. 17^1. priest was. 17^2. it was. 17^3. boned (?) **b** has bored.

b is a copy of **a**, but with the long lines broken up into two, and some slight variations.

b. 3^4. And we'll.
5^1. Omits if. 6^3. Omits sae jimp.
11^2. and they are questions. 12^2. wish.
13^4. betwixt.
B. In stanzas of four short lines.
a. 16^2, 17^2. Var. women's vice. 17^1. Var. Poison is greener.
17^2. Var. There's nathing waur.
b. Lord Roslin's Daughter's Garland. Containing three excellent new songs.
I. The Drunkard Reformed.
II. The Devil and the Grinder.
III. Lord Roslin's Daughter.
Licensed and entered according to order.
1^1. walks throw. 1^2. And by came.
1^3. servant man. 1^4, 3^4, 6^4, 7^4, 10^4, 14^4, 18^4. next the wa. 17^4. neist.
2^3, 4^3. missd you know. 3^4. And we'll . . . and thou 's ly next.
4^2. will I. 4^4. So I not.
$5^{1,2}$. Then said the pretty lady, I pray tell me your name.
    My name is Captain Wedderburn, a servant to the king.
5^3. of him I'd not stand in aw.
6^1. He lighted off.
6^2. And held her by the milk-white hand even as they rode along.
6^3. so jimp. 6^4. So I'll take. 7^1. lodging house.
7^3. But such a pretty face as thine in it I never saw.
7^4. make her up a down-bed.

[424] 8^2. will not go to your bed till you dress me.
8^3. three you must do to me.
9^1. O I must have . . . a cherry without a stone.
9^2. a chicken without a bone.

$10^{1,2}$. When the cherry is into the bloom I am sure it hath no stone,
    And when the chicken's in the shell I'm sure it hath no bone.

10^3. it is a gentle.
11^2. I will not go till . . . till you answer me questions.
11^3. Questions four you must tell me.

12^1. You must get to me. 12^2. That the wraft was neer ca'd.
$12^{3,4}$ and $16^{3,4}$ (and consequently $13^{3,4}$, $17^{3,4}$) are wrongly interchanged in **b**, mixing up ferlies and questions.
a $12^{3,4}$, $13^{3,4}$, 14, 15, $16^{1,2}$, $16^{3,4}$, $17^{1,2}$, $17^{3,4}$ = **b** $15^{3,4}$, $16^{3,4}$, 17, 14, $15^{1,2}$, $12^{3,4}$, $16^{1,2}$, $13^{3,4}$.
13^2. the wraft was neer ca'd throw.
$13^{3,4}$. A sparrow's horn you well may get, there's one on ilka pa.
14^1. standing at the door.
14^3. A hole cut in his mother's side, he from the same did fa.
16^2. And what . . . women's voice.
16^3. What bird sings best, and wood buds first, that dew does on them fa.
17^1. sky is higher. 17^2. worse than women's voice.
17^3. the dew does on them fa.
18^2. the last night. 18^3. now they both lie in one bed.

c closely resembling **b**, the variations from **b** are given.
c. 1. came omitted, v. 2; unto, v. 3.
2. into your bed, v. 4.
3. guard you . . . who well, v. 3; into . . . thou'lt, v. 4.
$5^{1,2}$. Then says, v. 1.
6. lighted from . . . this lady, v. 1; middle jimp, v. 3.
7. pretty fair, v. 2; as this, v. 3.
8. dress me, v. 3.
9. unto, vv 1, 2; O I must, v. 2.
10. in the bloom, v. 1; we both shall ly in, v. 4.
11. will give oer, v. 1; to your . . . you tell me, v. 2.
12. You must get to me . . . that waft, v. 2; bird sings first . . . on them does, v. 3.
13. sings first, v. 3.
14. in your . . . you tell me, v. 2; I'll ly in, v. 4.
15. What is . . . woman's, v. 2; I'll ly in, v. 4.
16. Death's greener than the grass, hell's deeper than the seas,
    The devil's worse than woman's voice, sky's higher than the trees, vv 1, 2; every paw, v. 3; thou shalt, v. 4.
18. the lady . . . rose, v. 1; It was to be the very last, v. 2; they ly in ae, v. 4.
d. Follows the garland (**b**, **c**) through the first nine stanzas, with changes from Jamieson's "own recollection," or invention, and one from **A**. 10 has certainly arbitrary alterations. The remaining eight stanzas are the corresponding ones of **A** treated

freely. The comparison here is with **b**, *readings from* **A** *in 11–18 not being noticed.*

1^3. serving men.

2^3. mist awa, *from* **A**; *so in* 4^3, *a stanza not in* **A**.

5^3. I'd have nae awe.

6^1. He lighted aff . . . this lady. 6^3. middle jimp. 6^4. To tak her to his ain.

7^3. sic a lovely face as thine. 7^4. Gae mak her down.

8^3. maun dress to me.

9^1. It's ye maun get. $9^{2, 3}$. And ye maun get.

10^1. It's whan the cherry is in the flirry.

10^2. in the egg.

10^3. And sin the flood o Noah the dow she had nae ga.

A, B d, 11, $12^{1, 2}$, $13^{1, 2}$, 14, $15^{1, 2}$, $16^{1, 2} =$
B b, c, 14, $15^{1, 2}$, $16^{1, 2}$, 11, $12^{1, 2}$, $13^{1, 2}$.

11^1. and gie your fleechin oer.

11^2. Unless you'll find me ferlies, and that is ferlies four.

11^3. Ferlies four ye maun find me.

11^4. Or I'll never lie.

12^2. And get to me. 12^3. doth first down.

12^4. Ye sall tell afore I lay me down between you and the wa.

13^2. has an Indian gown that waft.

13^3. on cedar top the dew.

14^2. that gait me perplex. 14^3. three times twa.

15^1. the greenest grass. 15^2. war nor an ill woman's wish.

16^3. horn is quickly found . . . on every claw.

16^4. There's ane upon the neb of him.

17^3. A wild bore tore his mither's side.

18^3. now there's nae within the realm, I think.

e *has stanzas 1, 5 (?), 9, 12, 10, 13, 14 of* **a**, *the first two imperfect. The last line of each stanza is changed, no doubt for delicacy's sake, to* I will tak you wi me, I tell you, aye or na, *or the like.*

> 1. The Earl o Roslin's dochter gaed out to tak the air;
> She met a gallant gentleman, as hame she did repair;
>
> .   .   .   .   .
>
> I win tak you wi me, I tell you, aye or no.
>
> 5(?). I am Captain Wedderburn, a servant to the king.
>
> .   .   .   .   .
>
> I will tak you wi me, I tell you, aye or no.

9^1. I maun hae to my supper a bird without a bone.

9^3. An I maun hae a gentle bird that flies.

9^4. Before that I gae with you, I tell you, aye or na.

10^1. When the bird is in the egg. 10^2. in the bud . . . I'm sure.

10^3. it is a gentle bird.

12^2, 13^2. a gey mantle . . . neer ca'ed.

13^3. sune sall get.

14^1. is standing at. 14^2. say that he was . . . a sin.

f. *Stanzas 9, 10 only.*

9^1. 'T is I maun hae to my supper a bird without a bone.

9^2. withouten stone. 9^3. withouten ga.

10^1. When the bird is in the shell, I'm sure.

10^2. I'm sure.

10^3. a gentle . . . withouten ga.

C. *Printed in stanzas of four short lines.*

———◆———

Professor Child's additions, Vol V, p. 216f contain the following extended supplement to the endnotes, provided without commentary. It is printed here as received. [M.F. H.]

B. a. 1 The lard of Roslie's doughter was walking on the green,
> An by came Captain Wederburn, a servant to our king,
> An he said to his livery-man, Wer it no agenst our laa,
> I wad take her to my ain bed an lay her neast the waa.

a.   2 'I am in my father's garden, walken among my father's trees,
> An ye dou latt me walk a whill nou, kind sir, if ye pleas;
> For the supper-beals they will be rung an I will be mised awa.'

a. 4^3. An my father will ate nae supper gine I be mised awa.'

a.   6. He lighted off his hors an sett the lady one,
> .   .   .   .   .

A. a.$6^{1,3}$. He sett her ahind his livery-man, was leath to latt her faa:

A. a.5⁴. 'We's baith lay in ae bed, an ye 's lay neast
the wa.'

B. a.   7 Fan they came to his quarter-house, his
landl[ad]y came ben:
Ther is mony bonny lady in Edenbrugh
toun,
Bat sick a bonny lady is no in it aa;'
Says, 'Lass, mak up a doun-bed, we will lay
her nist the waa.'

a.   8 'Hold yer toung, youna, man,' she says, 'an
latt yer folly be;
I winnë come to my bed till ye gett to me
things three.

.   .   .   .

.   .   .   .

a.   9 'Ye gett to my supper a cherrey without a
ston,
An ye gett to my suppeer a chiken without
a bone,
An ye gett to my super a burd that flayes
without a gaa,
Or I winnë lay in your bed, nether att stok
nor waa.'

a.   10 'The cherry when it is in the bloum, it is
without a ston;
The chiken when it is in the egg is with-
out a bon;
The dove she is a harmless burd, she flays
without a gaa;
An we 's baith lay in ae bed, an ye 's lay
nist the waa.'

a.   15 'Hold off yer hands, young man,' she says,
'an dou not me perplex;
I winnë gae to my bed till ye tell me qus-
tens six;

.   .   .   .

.   .   .   .

a.   16 'What is greaner nor the grass? what is
hig[h]er the[n] the tree?
What is war nor woman's wish? what is
deaper nor the sea?
What burd sings first? what life buds first, an
what dos on it faa?
I winnë lay in your bed, nether att stok
nor waa.'

a.   17 'Death is greaner nor the grass; heaven is
higher nor the tree;
The divell is war nor woman's wish; hell is
deaper nor the sea;
The coke crous first; the suderen wood
springs first, the due dos on it faa;
An we 's baith lay in ae bed, an ye 's lay
neast the waa.'

a.   11 'Hold off yer hands, young man,' she says,
'an yer folly gie our,
I winne come to your bed till ye gett to me
things four;

.   .   .   .

.   .   .   .

a.   12 'Ye gett to me a cherry that in December
grou;
Leguays a fine silk mantell that waft gad
never throu;
A sparrou's horn, a prist unborn, this night
to join us tua;
Or I winnë lay in your bed, nether att stok
nor waa.'

a.   13 'Ther is a hote-bed in my father's garden
wher winter chirrys grou,
Lequays a fine silk mantell in his closet
which waft never gaid throu;

.   .   .   .

.   .   .   .

a.   14 'Ther is a prist nou att the dore, just ready
to come in,
An never one could say he was born,
For ther was a holl cut out of his mother's
side, an out of it he did faa;
An we 's baith lay in ae bed, an ye 's lay
nist the waa.'

a.   18 Littel kent the lassie in the morning fan she
raise
That wad be the last of a' her maiden days;
For nou she is marrëd to Captian Weder-
burn, that afore she never saa,
An they baith lay in ae bed, an she lays
nest the waa.

7⁴. Lays, Lass. 10¹. bloun. 12¹. grous.

47

PROUD LADY MARGARET

A. 'Proud Lady Margaret,' Scott's *Minstrelsy*, III, 275, ed. 1803.
B. a. 'The Courteous Knight,' Buchan's *Ballads of the North of Scotland*, I, 91; Motherwell's MS., p. 591. b. Motherwell's *Minstrelsy*, Introduction, p. lxxxi.

C. 'The Jolly Hind Squire,' Buchan's MSS, II, 95.
D. 'The Knicht o Archerdale,' Harris MS., fol. 7, No 3.
E. 'Fair Margret,' A. Laing, *Ancient Ballads and Songs*, MS., 1829, p. 6.

A was communicated to Scott "by Mr Hamilton, music-seller, Edinburgh, with whose mother it had been a favorite." Two stanzas and one line were wanting, and were supplied by Scott "from a different ballad, having a plot somewhat similar." The stanzas were 6 and 9. C was printed from the MS., with a few changes, under the title of 'The Bonny Hind Squire,' by Dixon, in *Scottish Traditional Versions of Ancient Ballads*, p. 42, and from Dixon in Bell's *Early Ballads*, p. 183. Christie, *Traditional Ballad Airs*, I, 28, says the ballad was called 'Jolly Janet' by the old people in Aberdeenshire.

A–D are plainly compounded of two ballads, the conclusion being derived from E. The lady's looking oer her castle wa, her putting riddles, and her having gard so mony die, make the supposition far from incredible that the Proud Lady Margaret of the first part of the ballad may originally have been one of the cruel princesses spoken of in the preface to 'Captain Wedderburn's Courtship,' p. 549. But the corrupt condition of the texts of A–D forbids any confident opinion.

A dead mistress similarly admonishes her lover, in a ballad from Brittany, given in Ampère, *Instructions relatives aux Poésies populaires de la France*, p. 36.

"Non, je ne dors ni ne soumeille,
Je sis dans l'enfer à brûler.

"Auprès de moi reste une place,
C'est pour vous, Piar', qu'on l'a gardée."

"Ha! dites-moi plustot, ma Jeanne,
Comment fair' pour n'y point aller?"

"Il faut aller à la grand-messe,
Et aux vêpres, sans y manquer.

"Faut point aller aux fileries,
Comm' vous aviez d'accoutumé.

"Ne faut point embrasser les filles
Sur l' bout du coffre an pied du lect."

So Beaurepaire, *Étude*, p. 53; Puymaigre, 'La Damnée,' *Chants populaires*, I, 115; V. Smith, Chants du Velay et du Forez, *Romania*, IV, 449f, 'La Concubine;' 'La fille damnée,' Daymard, p. 178; 'La sposa morta,' *Archivio*, VIII, 274; the "romance" in Ballesteros, *Cancionero popular gallego*, III, 256; see also the "romance" 'Bernal Francez' from Algarve in *Encyclopedia Republicana*, Lisbon, 1882, p. 156; and Luzel, "Celui qui alla voir sa maitresse en enfer," I, 44, 45. In this last, a lover, whose mistress has died, goes into a monastery, where he prays continually that he may see her again. The devil presents himself in the likeness of a young man, and on condition of being something gently considered takes him to hell. He sees his mistress sitting in a fiery chair (cf. B, 30, 31), devoured by serpents night and day, and is informed that fasts and masses on his part will only make things worse. Like Dives, she sends word to her sister not to do as she has done. Some of these traits are found also in one or another of the French versions.

Translated by Doenniges, p. 6, after Scott, and by Knortz, *Schottische Balladen*, No 1, after Aytoun, II, 62.

A

Scott's *Minstrelsy*, III, 275, ed. 1803. Communicated "by Mr Hamilton, music-seller, Edinburgh, with whose mother it had been a favorite."

1 'T was on a night, an evening bright,
When the dew began to fa,
Lady Margaret was walking up and down,
Looking oer her castle wa.

2 She looked east and she looked west,
To see what she could spy,
When a gallant knight came in her sight,
And to the gate drew nigh.

3 'You seem to be no gentleman,
You wear your boots so wide;
But you seem to be some cunning hunter,
You wear the horn so syde.'

4 'I am no cunning hunter,' he said,
'Nor neer intend to be;
But I am come to this castle
To seek the love of thee.
And if you do not grant me love,
This night for thee I'll die.'

5 'If you should die for me, sir knight,
There's few for you will meane;
For mony a better has died for me,
Whose graves are growing green.

6 ['But ye maun read my riddle,' she said,
'And answer my questions three;
And but ye read them right,' she said,
'Gae stretch ye out and die.]

7 'Now what is the flower, the ae first flower,
Springs either on moor or dale?
And what is the bird, the bonnie bonnie bird,
Sings on the evening gale?'

8 'The primrose is the ae first flower
Springs either on moor or dale,
And the thristlecock is the bonniest bird
Sings on the evening gale.'

9 ['But what's the little coin,' she said,
'Wald buy my castle bound?
And what's the little boat,' she said,
'Can sail the world all round?']

10 'O hey, how mony small pennies
Make thrice three thousand pound?
Or hey, how mony salt fishes
Swim a' the salt sea round?'

11 'I think you maun be my match,' she said,
'My match and something mair;
You are the first eer got the grant
Of love frae my father's heir.

12 'My father was lord of nine castles,
My mother lady of three;
My father was lord of nine castles,
And there's nane to heir but me.

13 'And round about a' thae castles
You may baith plow and saw,
And on the fifteenth day of May
The meadows they will maw.'

14 'O hald your tongue, Lady Margaret,' he said,
'For loud I hear you lie;
Your father was lord of nine castles,
Your mother was lady of three;
Your father was lord of nine castles,
But ye fa heir to but three.

15 'And round about a' thae castles
  You may baith plow and saw,
  But on the fifteenth day of May
  The meadows will not maw.

16 'I am your brother Willie,' he said,
  'I trew ye ken na me;
  I came to humble your haughty heart,
  Has gard sae mony die.'

17 'If ye be my brother Willie,' she said,
  'As I trow weel ye be,
  This night I'll neither eat nor drink,
  But gae alang wi thee.'

18 'O hold your tongue, Lady Margaret,' he said,
  'Again I hear you lie;
  For ye've unwashen hands and ye've unwashen
    feet,
  To gae to clay wi me.'

19 'For the wee worms are my bedfellows,
  And cauld clay is my sheets,
  And when the stormy winds do blow,
  My body lies and sleeps.'

B

a. Buchan's *Ballads of the North of Scotland*, I, 91;
Motherwell's MS., p. 591. b. Motherwell's *Minstrelsy*,
Introduction, p. lxxxi.

1 THERE was a knight, in a summer's night,
  Appeard in a lady's hall,
  As she was walking up and down,
  Looking oer her castle wall.

2 'God make you safe and free, fair maid,
  God make you safe and free!'
  'O sae fa you, ye courteous knight,
  What are your wills wi me?'

3 'My wills wi you are not sma, lady,
  My wills wi you nae sma,
  And since there's nane your bower within,
  Ye 'se hae my secrets a'.

4 'For here am I a courtier,
  A courtier come to thee,
  And if ye winna grant your love,
  All for your sake I'll dee.'

5 'If that ye dee for me, sir knight,
  Few for you will make meen;
  For mony gude lord's done the same,
  Their graves are growing green.'

6 'O winna ye pity me, fair maid,
  O winna ye pity me?
  O winna ye pity a courteous knight,
  Whose love is laid on thee?'

7 'Ye say ye are a courteous knight,
  But I think ye are nane;
  I think ye're but a millar bred,
  By the colour o your claithing.

8 'You seem to be some false young man,   [428]
  You wear your hat sae wide;
  You seem to be some false young man,
  You wear your boots sae side.'

9 'Indeed I am a courteous knight,
  And of great pedigree;
  Nae knight did mair for a lady bright
  Than I will do for thee.

10 'O I'll put smiths in your smithy,
  To shoe for you a steed,
  And I'll put tailors in your bower,
  To make for you a weed.

11 'I will put cooks in your kitchen,
  And butlers in your ha,
  And on the tap o your father's castle
  I'll big gude corn and saw.'

12 'If ye be a courteous knight,
  As I trust not ye be,
  Ye'll answer some o the sma questions
  That I will ask at thee.

13 'What is the fairest flower, tell me,
     That grows in mire or dale?
   Likewise, which is the sweetest bird
     Sings next the nightingale?
   Or what's the finest thing,' she says,
     'That king or queen can wile?'

14 'The primrose is the fairest flower
     That grows in mire or dale;
   The mavis is the sweetest bird
     Next to the nightingale;
   And yellow gowd's the finest thing
     That king or queen can wale.

15 'Ye hae asked many questions, lady,
     I've you as many told;'
   'But how many pennies round
     Make a hundred pounds in gold?

16 'How many of the small fishes
     Do swim the salt seas round?
   Or what's the seemliest sight you'll see
     Into a May morning?'

        *   *   *   *   *

17 'Berry-brown ale and a birken speal,
     And wine in a horn green;
   A milk-white lace in a fair maid's dress
     Looks gay in a May morning.'

18 'Mony's the questions I've askd at thee,
     And ye've answerd them a';
   Ye are mine, and I am thine,
     Amo the sheets sae sma.

19 'You may be my match, kind sir,
     You may be my match and more;
   There neer was ane came sic a length
     Wi my father's heir before.

20 'My father's lord o nine castles,
     My mother she's lady ower three,
   And there is nane to heir them all,
     No never a ane but me;
   Unless it be Willie, my ae brother,
     But he's far ayont the sea.'

21 'If your father's laird o nine castles,
     Your mother lady ower three,
   I am Willie your ae brother,
     Was far beyond the sea.'

22 'If ye be Willie, my ae brother,
     As I doubt sair ye be,
   But if it's true ye tell me now,
     This night I'll gang wi thee.'

23 'Ye've ower ill washen feet, Janet,
     And ower ill washen hands,
   And ower coarse robes on your body,
     Alang wi me to gang.

24 'The worms they are my bed-fellows,
     And the cauld clay my sheet,
   And the higher that the wind does blaw,
     The sounder I do sleep.

25 'My body's buried in Dumfermline,
     And far beyond the sea,
   But day nor night nae rest coud get,
     All for the pride o thee.

26 'Leave aff your pride, jelly Janet,' he says,
     'Use it not ony mair;
   Or when ye come where I hae been
     You will repent it sair.

27 'Cast aff, cast aff, sister,' he says,
     'The gowd lace frae your crown;
   For if ye gang where I hae been,
     Ye'll wear it laigher down.

28 'When ye're in the gude church set,
     The gowd pins in your hair,
   Ye take mair delight in your feckless dress
     Than ye do in your morning prayer.

29 'And when ye walk in the church-yard,
     And in your dress are seen,
   There is nae lady that sees your face
     But wishes your grave were green.

30 'You're straight and tall, handsome withall,
     But your pride owergoes your wit,
   But if ye do not your ways refrain,
     In Pirie's chair ye'll sit.

31 'In Pirie's chair you'll sit, I say,
     The lowest seat o hell;
   If ye do not amend your ways,
     It's there that ye must dwell.'

32 Wi that he vanishd frae her sight,
     Wi the twinkling o an eye;
   Naething mair the lady saw
     But the gloomy clouds and sky.

C

Buchan's MSS, II, 95.

1 ONCE there was a jolly hind squire
   Appeard in a lady's ha,
And aye she walked up and down,
   Looking oer her castle wa.

2 'What is your wills wi me, kind sir?
   What is your wills wi me?'
'My wills are [not] sma wi thee, lady,
   My wills are [not] sma wi thee.

3 'For here I stand a courtier,
   And a courtier come to thee,
And if ye will not grant me your love,
   For your sake I will die.'

4 'If you die for my sake,' she says,
   'Few for you will make moan;
Many better's died for my sake,
   Their graves are growing green.

5 'You appear to be some false young man,
   You wear your hat so wide;
You appear to be some false young man,
   You wear your boots so side.

6 'An asking, asking, sir,' she said,
   'An asking ye'll grant me:'
'Ask on, ask on, lady,' he said,
   'What may your asking be?'

7 'What's the first thing in flower,' she said,
   'That springs in mire or dale?
What's the next bird that sings,' she says,
   'Unto the nightingale?
Or what is the finest thing,' she says,
   'That king or queen can wile?'

8 'The primrose is the first in flower
   That springs in mire or dale;
The thristle-throat is the next that sings
   Unto the nightingale;
And yellow gold is the finest thing
   That king or queen can wile.

9 'You have asked many questions, lady,
   I've you as many told;'
'But how many pennies round
   Make a hundred pounds in gold?

10 'How many small fishes
   Do swim the salt seas round?
Or what's the seemliest sight you'll see
   Into a May morning?'

   *   *   *   *   *

11 'There's ale into the birken scale,
   Wine in the horn green;
There's gold in the king's banner
   When he is fighting keen.'

12 'You may be my match, kind sir,' she said,
   'You may be my match and more;
There neer was one came such a length
   With my father's heir before.

13 'My father's lord of nine castles,
   No body heir but me.'
'Your father's lord of nine castles,
   Your mother's lady of three;

14 'Your father's heir of nine castles,
   And you are heir to three;
For I am William, thy ae brother,
   That died beyond the sea.'

15 'If ye be William, my ae brother,   [430]
   This night, O well is me!
If ye be William, my ae brother,
   This night I'll go with thee.'

16 'For no, for no, jelly Janet,' he says,
   'For no, that cannot be;
You've oer foul feet and ill washen hands
   To be in my company.

17 'For the wee wee worms are my bedfellows,
   And the cold clay is my sheet,
And the higher that the winds do blow,
   The sounder I do sleep.

18 'Leave off your pride, jelly Janet,' he says,
   'Use it not any more;
Or when you come where I have been
   You will repent it sore.

19 'When you go in at yon church door,
   The red gold on your hair,
More will look at your yellow locks
   Than look on the Lord's prayer.

20 'When you go in at yon church door,
      The red gold on your crown;
    When you come where I have been,
      You'll wear it laigher down.'

21 The jolly hind squire, he went away
      In the twinkling of an eye,
    Left the lady sorrowful behind,
      With many bitter cry.

D

Harris's MS., fol. 7, No 3. From Mrs Harris's recitation.

There cam a knicht to Arch-er-dale, His steed was win-der sma,

An there he spied a la-dy bricht, Luik-in owre her cast-le wa.

1 THERE cam a knicht to Archerdale,
    His steed was winder sma,
  An there he spied a lady bricht,
    Luikin owre her castle wa.

2 'Ye dinna seem a gentle knicht,
    Though on horseback ye do ride;
  Ye seem to be some sutor's son
    Your butes they are sae wide.'

3 'Ye dinna seem a lady gay,
    Though ye be bound wi pride;
  Else I'd gane bye your father's gate
    But either taunt or gibe.'

4 He turned aboot his hie horse head,
    An awa he was boun to ride,
  But neatly wi her mouth she spak:
    Oh bide, fine squire, oh bide.

5 'Bide, oh bide, ye hindy squire,
    Tell me mair o your tale;
  Tell me some o that wondrous lied
    Ye've learnt in Archerdale.

6 'What gaes in a speal?' she said,
    'What in a horn green?
  An what gaes on a lady's head,
    Whan it is washen clean?'

7 'Ale gaes in a speal,' he said,
    'Wine in a horn green;
  An silk gaes on a lady's head,
    Whan it is washen clean.'

8 Aboot he turned his hie horse head,
    An awa he was boun to ride,
  When neatly wi her mouth she spak:
    Oh bide, fine squire, oh bide.

9 'Bide, oh bide, ye hindy squire,
    Tell me mair o your tale;
  Tell me some o that unco lied
    You've learnt in Archerdale.

10 'Ye are as like my ae brither
    As ever I did see;
  But he's been buried in yon kirkyaird
    It's mair than years is three.'

11 'I am as like your ae brither
    As ever ye did see;
  But I canna get peace into my grave,
    A' for the pride o thee.

12 'Leave pride, Janet, leave pride, Janet,
    Leave pride an vanitie;
  If ye come the roads that I hae come,
    Sair warned will ye be.

13 'Ye come in by yonder kirk
    Wi the goud preens in your sleeve;
  When you're bracht hame to yon kirkyaird,
    You'll gie them a' thier leave.

14 'Ye come in to yonder kirk
    Wi the goud plaits in your hair;
  When you're bracht hame to yon kirkyaird,
    You will them a' forbear.'

15 He got her in her mither's bour,
    Puttin goud plaits in her hair;
  He left her in her father's gairden,
    Mournin her sins sae sair.

E

Alex. Laing, *Ancient Ballads and Songs*, etc., etc.,
from the recitation of old people. Never published.
1829. P. 6.

1 FAIR MARGRET was a young ladye,
   An come of high degree;
   Fair Margret was a young ladye,
   An proud as proud coud be.

2 Fair Margret was a rich ladye,
   The king's cousin was she;
   Fair Margret was a rich ladye,
   An vain as vain coud be.

3 She war'd her wealth on the gay cleedin
   That comes frae yont the sea,
   She spent her time frae morning till night
   Adorning her fair bodye.

4 Ae night she sate in her stately ha,
   Kaimin her yellow hair,
   When in there cum like a gentle knight,
   An a white scarf he did wear.

5 'O what's your will wi me, sir knight,
   O what's your will wi me?
   You're the likest to my ae brother
   That ever I did see.

6 'You're the likest to my ae brother
   That ever I hae seen,
   But he's buried in Dunfermline kirk,
   A month an mair bygane.'

7 'I'm the likest to your ae brother
   That ever ye did see,
   But I canna get rest into my grave,
   A' for the pride of thee.

8 'Leave pride, Margret, leave pride, Margret,
   Leave pride an vanity;
   Ere ye see the sights that I hae seen,
   Sair altered ye maun be.

9 'O ye come in at the kirk-door
   Wi the gowd plaits in your hair;
   But wud ye see what I hae seen,
   Ye maun them a' forbear.

10 'O ye come in at the kirk-door
   Wi the gowd prins i your sleeve;
   But wad ye see what I hae seen,
   Ye maun gie them a' their leave.

11 'Leave pride, Margret, leave pride, Margret,
   Leave pride an vanity;
   Ere ye see the sights that I hae seen,
   Sair altered ye maun be.'

12 He got her in her stately ha,
   Kaimin her yellow hair,
   He left her on her sick sick bed,
   Sheding the saut saut tear.

———◆———

A. *Two stanzas (6, 9) and a line were wanting in the
copy supplied by Hamilton. March 23, 1803,
Hamilton sent to Scott the following verses, "to
come in at the first break." There were still four
lines, which should come before these, that Hamil-
ton could not recollect.* "Scotch Ballads, Materials
for Border Minstrelsy," No 117. *See* B 17, C 11,
where also there is defect, and D 6, 7.

   'O wherein leems the beer?' she said,
      'Or wherein leems the wine?
   O wherein leems the gold?' she said,
      'Or wherein leems the twine?'

   'The beer is put in a drinking-horn,
      The wine in glasses fine,
   There's gold in store between two kings,

      When they are fighting keen,
   And the twine is between a lady's two
      hands
   When they are washen clean.'

B 15^{3,4}, 16^{1,2}, C 9^{3,4}, 10^{1,2} *are rightly answers, not
   questions: cf.* A 9, 10. D 6 *furnishes the question
   answered in* B 17.

B. b. *Motherwell begins at st.* 25.
   27^2 gowd band.
   28^1, 29^1. kirk. 30^2. owergangs.
   32^2. In the. 32^3. And naething.

C. Kind Squire *in the title, and* kind *in* 1^1, 21^1; *I sup-
   pose by mistake of my copyist.*
   16^3. You're (?).
   17^2. the clay cold.

E. 8^3, 11^3. E'er.

YOUNG ANDREW

Percy MS., p. 292. Hales and Furnivall, II, 328.

'Young Andrew' is known only from the Percy manuscript. The story recalls both 'Lady Isabel and the Elf-Knight,' No 4, and 'The Fair Flower of Northumberland,' No 9. The lady, Helen, 25^3, is bidden to take, and does take, gold with her in stanzas 5–7, as in No 4, English **E** 2, 3, **D** 7, Danish **A** 12, **E** 7, 9, 15, **L** 5, 6, and nearly all the Polish copies, and again in No 9, **A** 14. She is stripped of her clothes and headgear in 8–17, as in No 4, English **C–E**, German **G**, **H**, and many of the Polish versions. These are destined by Young Andrew for his lady ("that dwells so far in a strange country") in 10, 12, 14, as by Ulinger for his sister, and by Adelger for his mother, in German **G** 18, **H** 15. In 15 the lady entreats Young Andrew to leave her her smock; so in No 4, Polish **L** 8, "You brought me from home in a green gown; take me back in a shift of tow," and **R** 13, "You took me away in red satin; let me go back at least in a smock."

18 has the choice between dying and going home again which is presented in 'Lady Isabel,' Polish **AA** 4, **H** 10, **R** 11, and implied in 'The Fair Flower of Northumberland,' **D** 2–5; in **A** 25 of this last the choice is between dying and being a paramour. In 20, 21, the lady says, "If my father ever catches you, you're sure to flower a gallows-tree," etc.; in No 4, Polish **J** 5, "If God would grant me to reach the other bank, you know, wretch, what death you would die." The father is unrelenting in this ballad, v. 26, and receives his daughter with severity in 'The Fair Flower of Northumberland,' **B** 13, **C** 13. The conclusion of 'Young Andrew' is mutilated and hard to make out. He seems to have been pursued and caught, as John is in the Polish ballads, **O**, **P**, **T**, etc., of No 4. Why he was not promptly disposed of, and how the wolf comes into the story, will probably never be known.

1 As I was cast in my ffirst sleepe,
　　A dreadffull draught in my mind I drew,
　Ffor I was dreamed of a yong man,
　　Some men called him yonge Andrew.

2 The moone shone bright, and itt cast a ffayre light,
　　Sayes shee, Welcome, my honey, my hart, and my sweete!
　For I haue loued thee this seuen long yeere,
　　And our chance itt was wee cold neuer meete.

3 Then he tooke her in his armes two,
　　And kissed her both cheeke and chin,
　And twise or thrise he pleased this may
　　Before they tow did part in twinn.

4 Saies, Now, good sir, you haue had your will,
　　You can demand no more of mee;
　Good sir, remember what you said before,
　　And goe to the church and marry mee.

5 'Ffaire maid, I cannott doe as I wold;
　　　　·　　　·　　　·　　　·
　Goe home and fett thy fathers redd gold,
　　And I'le goe to the church and marry thee.

6 This ladye is gone to her ffathers hall,
 And well she knew where his red gold lay,
 And counted fforth five hundred pound,
 Besides all other iuells and chaines:

433) 7 And brought itt all to younge Andrew,
 Itt was well counted vpon his knee;
 Then he tooke her by the lillye white hand,
 And led her vp to an hill soe hye.

8 Shee had vpon a gowne of blacke veluett,
 (A pittyffull sight after yee shall see:)
 'Put of thy clothes, bonny wenche,' he sayes,
 'For noe ffoote further thoust gang with mee.'

9 But then shee put of her gowne of veluett,
 With many a salt teare from her eye,
 And in a kirtle of ffine breaden silke
 Shee stood beffore young Andrews eye.

10 Sais, O put off thy kirtle of silke,
 Ffor some and all shall goe with mee;
 And to my owne lady I must itt beare,
 Who I must needs loue better then thee.

11 Then shee put of her kirtle of silke,
 With many a salt teare still ffrom her eye;
 In a peticoate of scarlett redd
 Shee stood before young Andrewes eye.

12 Saies, O put of thy peticoate,
 For some and all of itt shall goe with mee;
 And to my owne lady I will itt beare,
 Which dwells soe ffarr in a strange countrye.

13 But then shee put of her peticoate,
 With many a salt teare still from her eye,
 And in a smocke of braue white silke
 Shee stood before young Andrews eye.

14 Saies, O put of thy smocke of silke,
 For some and all shall goe with mee;
 Vnto my owne ladye I will itt beare,
 That dwells soe ffarr in a strange countrye.

15 Sayes, O remember, young Andrew,
 Once of a woman you were borne;
 And ffor that birth that Marye bore,
 I pray you let my smocke be vpon!

16 'Yes, ffayre ladye, I know itt well,
 Once of a woman I was borne;
 Yett ffor noe birth that Mary bore,
 Thy smocke shall not be left here vpon.'

17 But then shee put of her head-geere ffine;
 Shee hadd billaments worth a hundred
 pound;
 The hayre that was vpon this bony wench head
 Couered her bodye downe to the ground.

18 Then he pulled forth a Scottish brand,
 And held itt there in his owne right hand;
 Saies, Whether wilt thou dye vpon my swords
 point, ladye,
 Or thow wilt goe naked home againe?

19 'Liffe is sweet,' then, 'sir,' said shee,
 'Therfore I pray you leaue mee with mine;
 Before I wold dye on your swords point,
 I had rather goe naked home againe.

20 'My ffather,' shee sayes, 'is a right good erle
 As any remaines in his countrye;
 If euer he doe your body take,
 You'r sure to fflower a gallow tree.

21 'And I haue seuen brethren,' shee sayes,
 'And they are all hardy men and bold;
 Giff euer thé doe your body take,
 You must neuer gang quicke ouer the mold.'

22 'If your ffather be a right good erle
 As any remaines in his owne countrye,
 Tush! he shall neuer my body take,
 I'le gang soe ffast ouer the sea.

23 'If you haue seuen brethren,' he sayes,
 'If they be neuer soe hardy or bold,
 Tush! they shall neuer my body take,
 I'le gang soe ffast into the Scottish mold.'

24 Now this ladye is gone to her fathers hall,
 When euery body their rest did take;
 But the Erle which was her ffather
 Lay waken for his deere daughters sake.

25 'But who is that,' her ffather can say,
 'That soe priuilye knowes the pinn?'
 'It's Hellen, your owne deere daughter, ffather,
 I pray you rise and lett me in.'

26 .   .   .   .   .

   'Noe, by my hood!' quoth her ffather then,
   'My [house] thoust neuer come within,
     Without I had my red gold againe.'

[434] 27 'Nay, your gold is gone, ffather!' said shee,

     .   .   .   .   .

   'Then naked thou came into this world,
     And naked thou shalt returne againe.'

28 'Nay! God fforgaue his death, father,' shee
     sayes,
   And soe I hope you will doe mee;'
   'Away, away, thou cursed woman,
     I pray God an ill death thou may dye!'

29 Shee stood soe long quacking on the ground
   Till her hart itt burst in three;
   And then shee ffell dead downe in a swoond,
   And this was the end of this bonny ladye.

30 Ithe morning, when her ffather gott vpp,
   A pittyfull sight there he might see;
   His owne deere daughter was dead, without
     clothes,
   The teares they trickeled fast ffrom his eye.

31 .   .   .   .   .

   Sais, Fye of gold, and ffye of ffee!
   For I sett soe much by my red gold
   That now itt hath lost both my daughter and
     mee!'

32 .   .   .   .   .

   But after this time he neere dought good day,
   But as flowers doth fade in the frost,
     Soe he did wast and weare away.

33 But let vs leaue talking of this ladye,
   And talke some more of young Andrew;
   Ffor ffalse he was to this bonny ladye,
   More pitty *that* he had not beene true.

34 He was not gone a mile into the wild forrest,
   Or halfe a mile into the hart of Wales,
   But there they cought him by such a braue wyle
   That hee must come to tell noe more tales.

   *   *   *   *   *

35 .   .   .   .   .

   Ffull soone a wolfe did of him smell,
   And shee came roaring like a beare,
     And gaping like a ffeend of hell.

36 Soe they ffought together like two lyons,
   And fire betweene them two glashet out;
   Thé raught eche other such a great rappe
   That there young Andrew was slaine, well I
     wott.

37 But now young Andrew he is dead,
   But he was neuer buryed vnder mold,
   For ther as the wolfe devoured him,
   There lyes all this great erles gold.

1^3. of one. 3^3. 2.^{se}, 3.^{se}.
7^4. to one. 17^2. 100$^{l.i.}$.
19^1. My liffe.
25^2. *that* pinn.

30^3. any *follows* without, *but is crossed out.*
30^4. they teares. 33^4. itt had.
Arabic numbers are in several cases expressed in let-
ters.

49

THE TWA BROTHERS

A. Sharpe's *Ballad Book*, p. 56, No 19.
B. 'The Cruel Brother,' Motherwell's MS., p. 259. From the recitation of Mrs McCormick.
C. 'The Twa Brithers,' Motherwell's MS., p. 649. From the recitation of Mrs Cunningham.
D. 'The Twa Brothers, or, The Wood o Warslin,' Jamieson's *Popular Ballads*, I, 59. From the recitation of Mrs Arrott.
E. 'The Twa Brothers,' Motherwell's *Minstrelsy*, p. 60.

F. 'The Two Brothers,' Buchan's MSS, I, 57; Motherwell's MS., p. 662.
G. a. 'John and William,' taken down from the singing of little girls in South Boston. **b**. From a child in New York. Both communicated by Mr W. W. Newell.
H. 'Perthshire Tredgey.' From a copy formerly in the possession of Charles Kirkpatrick Sharpe.
I. Communicated by Mr J. K. Hudson of Manchester.

ALL the Scottish versions were obtained within the first third of this century, and since then no others have been heard of. It is interesting to find the ballad still in the mouths of children in American cities, in the mouths of the poorest, whose heritage these old things are.[*] The American versions, though greatly damaged, preserve the names John and William, which all the other copies have.

B and **C** are considerably corrupted. It need hardly be mentioned that the age of the boys in the first two stanzas of **B** does not suit the story. According to **C** 8, 15, the mother had cursed John, before he left home, with a wish that he might never return; and in **C** 9, John sends word to his true-love that he is in his grave for her dear sake alone. These points seem to have been taken from some copy of 'Willie and May Margaret,' or 'The Drowned Lovers.' The conclusion of both **B** and **C** belongs to 'Sweet William's Ghost.' **C** 18 may be corrected by **B** 10, though there is an absurd jumble of pipes and harp in the latter. The harp, in a deft hand, effects like wonders in many a ballad: e.g.,

'Harpens Kraft,' Grundtvig, II, 65, No 40; even a pipe in **C** 14–16 of the same.

D, **E**, **F**, **G** supplement the story with more or less of the ballad of 'Edward:' see p. 235. There is a copy in Nimmo, *Songs and Ballads of Clydesdale*, p. 131, made from **D**, **E**, with half a dozen lines for connection.

Jamieson inquires for this ballad in the *Scots Magazine* for October, 1803, p. 701, at which time he had only the first stanza and the first half of the third. He fills out the imperfect stanza nearly as in the copy which he afterwards printed:

But out an Willie's taen his knife,
   And did his brother slay.

Of the five other Scottish versions, all except **B** make the deadly wound to be the result of accident, and this is, in Motherwell's view, a point essential. The other reading, he says, is at variance with the rest of the story, and "sweeps away the deep impression this simple ballad would otherwise have made upon the feelings: for it is almost unnecessary to mention that its touching interest is made to centre in the boundless sorrow and cureless remorse of him who had been the unintentional cause of

---

[*] Mr Newell says: "I have heard it sung at a picnic, by a whole carful of little girls. The melody is pretty. These children were of the poorest class."

his brother's death, and in the solicitude which that high-minded and generous spirit expresses, even in the last agonies of nature, for the safety and fortunes of the truly wretched and unhappy survivor," But the generosity of the dying man is plainly greater if his brother has killed him in an outburst of passion; and what is gained this [436] way will fully offset the loss, if any, which comes from the fratricide having cause for "cureless remorse" as well as boundless sorrow. Motherwell's criticism, in fact, is not quite intelligible. (*Minstrelsy*, p. 61.)

The variation in the story is the same as that between the English 'Cruel Brother' and the German 'Graf Friedrich:' in the former the bride is killed by her offended brother; in the latter it is the bridegroom's sword slipping from its sheath that inflicts the mortal hurt.

Motherwell was inclined to believe, and Kirkpatrick Sharpe was convinced, that this ballad was founded upon an event that happened near Edinburgh as late as 1589, that of one of the Somervilles having been killed by his brother's pistol accidentally going off. Sharpe afterward found a case of a boy of thirteen killing a young brother in anger at having his hair pulled. This most melancholy story, the particulars of which are given in the last edition of the *Ballad Book*, p. 130, note xix, dates nearly a hundred years later, 1682. Only the briefest mention need be made of these unusually gratuitous surmises.*

Kirkland, in **D**, was probably suggested by the kirkyard of other versions, assisted, possibly, by a reminiscence of the Kirkley in 'Robin Hood's Death and Burial;' for it will be observed that stanzas 8, 9 of **D** come pretty near to those in which Robin Hood gives direction for his grave; **F** 9, 10, **B** 5, 6 less near.†

---

* It ought to have been remarked that it was a William Somerville that killed John. The names being the same as in the ballad, "unusually gratuitous" is not warranted.

† "The house of Inchmurry, formerly called Kirkland, was built of old by the abbot of Holyrood-house for his accommodation when he came to that country, and was formerly the minister's manse." *Statistical Account of Scotland*, XIII, 506, cited by Jamieson, I, 62. There are still three or four Kirklands in Scotland and the north of England.

Cunningham has entitled a romance of his, upon the theme of 'The Two Brothers' (which, once more, he ventures to print nearly in the state in which he once had the pleasure of hearing it sung), 'Fair Annie of Kirkland:' *Songs of Scotland*, II, 16.

The very pathetic passage in which the dying youth directs that father, mother, and sister shall be kept in ignorance of his death, and then, feeling how vain the attempt to conceal the fact from his true-love will be, bids that she be informed that he is in his grave and will never come back, is too truly a touch of nature to be found only here. Something similar occurs in 'Mary Hamilton,' where, however, the circumstances are very different:

'And here's to the jolly sailor lad
    That sails upon the faeme!
And let not my father nor mother get wit
    But that I shall come again.

'And here's to the jolly sailor lad
    That sails upon the sea!
But let not my father nor mother get wit
    O the death that I maun dee.'

In one of the older Croat ballads Marko Kraljević and his brother Andrija, who have made booty of three horses, quarrel about the third when they come to dividing, and Marko fells Andrija with a stab. Andrija charges Marko not to tell their mother what took place, but to say that he is not coming home, because he has become enamored of a girl in a foreign country. Bogišić, p. 18, No 6. There is a Magyar-Croat variant of this, in which two brothers returning from war fall out about a girl, and the older (who, by the way, is a married man) stabs the younger. The dying brother wishes the mother to be told that he has stayed behind to buy presents for her and his sisters. The mother asks when her son will come home. The elder brother answers, When a crow turns white and a withered maple greens. The (simple) mother gets a crow and bathes it daily in milk, and irrigates the tree with wine; but in vain. Other Slavic examples of these hopeless eventualities: Little-Russian, Golovatsky, I, 74, No 30, 97, No 7, 164, No 12, 173, No 23, 229, No 59; II, 41,

No 61, 585, No 18, 592, No 27; III, 12, No 9, 136, No 256, 212, No 78; Bohemian, Erben, p. 182, No 340; Polish, Roger, p. 3, No 2; Servian, Vuk, I, No 364, Herzegovine, p. 209, No 176, p. 322, No 332; Bulgarian, Verković, No 226; Dozon, p. 95; Magyar-Croat, Kurelac, p. 11, No 61, p. 130, No 430, p. 156, No 457 (and note), p. 157, No 459, p. 244, No 557. (W. W.)

In a fine Norse ballad (see 'Brown Robyn's Confession,' further on) a man who is to be thrown overboard to save a ship takes his leave of the world with these words:

'If any of you should get back to land,
    And my foster-mother ask for me,
Tell her I'm serving in the king's court,
    And living right merrily.

'If any of you should get back to land,
    And my true-love ask for me,
Bid her to marry another man,
    For I am under the sea.'

A baron, who has been mortally wounded in a duel, gives this charge to his servant

'Faites mes compliments à ma femme,
Mais ne lui dites pas que j'ai été tué;
Mais dites lui que je serai allé à Paris,
Pour saluer le roi Louis.

'Dites que je serai allé à Paris,
Pour saluer le roi Louis,
Et que j'ai acheté un nouveau cheval,
Le petit cœur de mon cheval était trop gai.'
(Le Seigneur de Rosmadec, Luzel, I, $^{368}/_{369}$, $^{374}/_{375}$.)

In like manner a dying klepht: "If our comrades ask about me, tell them not that I have died: say only that I have married in strange lands; have taken the flat stone for mother-in-law, the black earth for my wife, the black worms for brothers-in-law." Zambelios, p. 606, No 11, Fauriel, I, 51, Passow, p. 118, No 152; so in the beautiful Roumanian 'Miorița,' Alecsandri, p. 3; and again, Zambelios, p. 672, No 94, Passow, p. 113, No 146. In the Danish 'Elveskud,' Grundtvig, II, 115, No 47, B 18, Ole would simply have the tragic truth kept from his bride:

'Hearken, Sir Ole, of mickle pride,
How shall I answer thy young bride?'

'You must say I am gone to the wood,
To prove horse and hounds, if they be good.'

Such questions and answers as we have in D 20, E 17, F 24, are of the commonest occurrence in popular poetry, and not unknown to the poetry of art. Ballads of the 'Edward' class end generally or always in this way: see p. 235. We have again the particular question and answer which occur here in 'Lizie Wan' and in one version of 'The Trooper and Fair Maid,' Jamieson's Popular Ballads, II, 158. The question may be: When will you come back? When shall you cease to love me? When shall we be married? etc.; and the answer: When apple-trees grow in the seas; when fishes fly and seas gang dry; when all streams run together; when all swift streams are still; when it snows roses and rains wine; when all grass is rue; when the nightingale sings on the sea and the cuckoo is heard in winter; when poplars bear cherries and oaks roses; when feathers sink and stones swim; when sand sown on a stone germinates, etc., etc. See Virgil, Ecl. i, 59–63; Ovid, Met. xiii, 324–27; Wolf, Ueber die Lais, p. 433; 'Svend Vonved,' Grundtvig, I, 240, No 18, A, D; Buchan's Ballads of the North of Scotland, 'Lord Jamie Douglas,' I, 232f, Motherwell's Minstrelsy, Appendix, p. vii, Kinloch, Finlay, etc.; Pills to Purge Melancholy, V, 37; 'Der verwundete Knabe,' 'Die verwundete Dame,' Mittler, Nos 49–53, Erk's Liederhort, pp 111–115, Wunderhorn, IV, 358–63, Longard, p. 39, No 18, Pröhle, Welt. u. geist. Volkslieder, p. 12, No 6; Meinert, pp 28, 60, 73; Uhland, p. 127, No 65; Wunderhorn (1857), II, 223, Reifferscheid, p. 23, Liederhort, p. 345, Erk, Neue Sammlung, ii, 39, Kretzschmer, I, 143; Zuccalmaglio, pp 103, 153, 595; Peter, Volksthümliches aus Österreichschlesien, I, 274; Ditfurth, II, 9, No 10; Fiedler, p. 187; Des Turcken Vassnachtspiel, Tieck's Deutsches Theater, I, 8; Uhland, Zur Geschichte der Dichtung, III, 216ff; Tigri, Canti popolari toscani (1860), pp 230–242, Nos 820, 822, 823, 832, 836–40, 857, 858, 862, 868; Visconti, Saggio dei Canti p. della Provincia di Marrittima e Campagna, p. 21, No 18; Nino, Saggio di Canti

p. sabinesi, p. 28f, p. 30f; Pitrè, Saggi di Critica letteraria, p. 25; Braga, Cantos p. do Archipelago Açoriano, p. 220; Möckesch, Romänische Dichtungen, p. 6f, No 2; Passow, p. 273f, Nos 387, 388; B. Schmidt, Griechische Märchen, etc., p. 154, No 10, and note, p. 253; Morosi, Studi sui Dialetti greci della Terra d'Otranto, p. 30, lxxv, p. 32, lxxix; Pellegrini, Canti p. dei Greci di Cargese, p. 21; De Rada, Rapsodie d'un Poema albanese, p. 29; Haupt u. Schmaler, Volkslieder der Wenden, I, 76, No 47, I, 182, No 158, I, 299, No 300; Altmann, Balalaika, Russische Volkslieder, p. 233, No 184; Golovatsky, Narodnyya Piesni galitzskoy i ugorskoy Rusi, II, 585, No 18, III, i, 12, No 9; Maximovitch, Sbornik ukrainskikh Pyesen, p. 7, No 1, p. 107, No 30; Dozon, Chansons p. bulgares, p. 283, No 57; Bodenstedt, Die poetische Ukraine, p. 46, No 14; Jordan, Ueber kleinrussische Volkspoesie, Blätter für lit. Unterhaltung, 1840, No 252, p. 1014 (Uhland); Rhesa, Ueber litthauische Volkspoesie, in Beiträge zur Kunde Preussens, I, 523; Aigner, Ungarische Volksdichtungen, pp 147, 149; Passow, p. 316, No 437, vv 37, 38; Legrand, Recueil de Chansons pop. grecques, p. 220, v. 24ff, p. 330, v. 17ff; Aravandinos, No 435, v. 7ff: etc.

D is translated by Afzelius, Grimm, Talvj, Rosa Warrens. **E** is translated by Grundtvig, Engelske og skotske Folkeviser, p. 168; Afzelius, III, 7; Grimm, Drei altschottische Lieder, p. 5; Talvj, Charakteristik, p. 567; Rosa Warrens, Schottische V. l. der Vorzeit, p. 91. Knortz, Schottische Balladen, No 4, translates Aytoun, I, 193.

A

Sharpe's Ballad Book, p. 56, No 19.

1 THERE were twa brethren in the north,
   They went to the school thegither;
   The one unto the other said,
   Will you try a warsle afore?

2 They warsled up, they warsled down,
   Till Sir John fell to the ground,
   And there was a knife in Sir Willie's pouch,
   Gied him a deadlie wound.

3 'Oh brither dear, take me on your back,
   Carry me to yon burn clear,
   And wash the blood from off my wound,
   And it will bleed nae mair.'

4 He took him up upon his back,
   Carried him to yon burn clear,
   And washd the blood from off his wound,
   But aye it bled the mair.

5 'Oh brither dear, take me on your back,
   Carry me to yon kirk-yard,
   And dig a grave baith wide and deep,
   And lay my body there.'

6 He's taen him up upon his back,
   Carried him to yon kirk-yard,
   And dug a grave baith deep and wide,
   And laid his body there.

7 'But what will I say to my father dear,
   Gin he chance to say, Willie, whar's John?'
   'Oh say that he's to England gone,
   To buy him a cask of wine.'

8 'And what will I say to my mother dear,
   Gin she chance to say, Willie, whar's John?'
   'Oh say that he's to England gone,
   To buy her a new silk gown.'

9 'And what will I say to my sister dear,
   Gin she chance to say, Willie, whar's John?'
   'Oh say that he's to England gone,
   To buy her a wedding ring.'

10 'But what will I say to her you loe dear,
   Gin she cry, Why tarries my John?'
   'Oh tell her I lie in Kirk-land fair,
   And home again will never come.'

B

Motherwell's MS., p. 259. From Widow McCor-
mick, January 19, 1825.

1 THERE was two little boys going to the school,
   And twa little boys they be,
   They met three brothers playing at the ba,
   And ladies dansing hey.

2 'It's whether will ye play at the ba, brither,
   Or else throw at the stone?'
   'I am too little, I am too young,
   O brother let me alone.'

3 He pulled out a little penknife,
   That was baith sharp and sma,
   He gave his brother a deadly wound
   That was deep, long and sair.

4 He took the holland sark off his back,
   He tore it frae breast to gare,
   He laid it to the bloody wound,
   That still bled mair and mair.

5 'It's take me on your back, brother,' he says,
   'And carry me to yon kirk-yard,
   And make me there a very fine grave,
   That will be long and large.

6 'Lay my bible at my head,' he says,
   'My chaunter at my feet,
   My bow and arrows by my side,
   And soundly I will sleep.

7 'When you go home, brother,' he says,
   'My father will ask for me;
   You may tell him I am in Saussif town,
   Learning my lesson free.

8 'When you go home, brother,' he says,
   'My mother will ask for me;
   You may tell her I am in Sausaf town,
   And I'll come home merrily.

9 'When you go home, brother,' he says,
   'Lady Margaret will ask for me;
   You may tell her I'm dead and in grave laid,
   And buried in Sausaff toun.'

10 She put the small pipes to her mouth,   [439]
   And she harped both far and near,
   Till she harped the small birds off the briers,
   And her true love out of the grave.

11 'What's this? what's this, lady Margaret?' he
       says,
   'What's this you want of me?'
   'One sweet kiss of your ruby lips,
   That's all I want of thee.'

12 'My lips they are so bitter,' he says,
   'My breath it is so strong,
   If you get one kiss of my ruby lips,
   Your days will not be long.'

C

Motherwell's MS., p. 649. From the recitation of
Mrs Cunningham, Ayr.

1 THERE were twa brithers at ae scule
   As they were coming hame,
   Then said the ane until the other
   'John, will ye throw the stane?'

2 'I will not throw the stane, brither,
   I will not play at the ba;
   But gin ye come to yonder wood
   I'll warsle you a fa.'

3 The firsten fa young Johnie got,
   It brought him to the ground;
   The wee pen-knife in Willie's pocket
   Gied him a deadly wound.

4 'Tak aff, tak aff my holland sark,
   And rive it frae gore to gore,
   And stap it in my bleeding wounds,
   They'll aiblins bleed noe more.'

5 He pouit aff his holland sark,
    And rave it frae gore to gore,
    And stapt it in his bleeding wounds,
    But ay they bled the more.

6 'O brither, tak me on your back,
    And bear me hence away,
    And carry me to Chester kirk,
    And lay me in the clay.'

7 'What will I say to your father,
    This night when I return?'
    'Tell him I'm gane to Chester scule,
    And tell him no to murn.'

8 'What will I say to your mother,
    This nicht whan I gae hame?'
    'She wishd afore I cam awa
    That I might neer gae hame.'

9 'What will I say to your true-love,
    This nicht when I gae hame?'
    'Tell her I'm dead and in my grave,
    For her dear sake alane.'

10 He took him upon his back
    And bore him hence away,
    And carried him to Chester kirk,
    And laid him in the clay.

11 He laid him in the cauld cauld clay,
    And he cuirt him wi a stane,
    And he's awa to his fathers ha,
    Sae dowilie alane.

12 'You're welcome, dear son,' he said,
    'You're welcome hame to me;
    But what's come o your brither John,
    That gade awa wi thee?'

13 'Oh he's awa to Chester scule,
    A scholar he'll return;
    He bade me tell his father dear
    About him no to murn.'

14 'You're welcome hame, dear son,' she said,
    'You're welcome hame to me;
    But what's come o your brither John,
    That gade awa wi thee?'

15 'He bade me tell his mother dear,
    This nicht when I cam hame,
    Ye wisht before he gade awa,
    That he might neer return.'

16 Then next came up his true-love dear,
    And heavy was her moan;
    'You're welcome hame, dear Will,' she said,
    'But whare's your brither John?'

17 'O lady, cease your trouble now,
    O cease your heavy moan;
    He's dead and in the cauld cauld clay,
    For your dear sake alone.'

18 She ran distraught, she wept, she sicht,
    She wept the sma brids frae the tree,
    She wept the starns adoun frae the lift,
    She wept the fish out o the sea.

19 'O cease your weeping, my ain true-love,
    Ye but disturb my rest;'
    'Is that my ain true lover John,
    The man that I loe best?'

20 ''T is naething but my ghaist,' he said,
    'That's sent to comfort thee;
    O cease your weeping, my true-love,
    And 't will gie peace to me.'

D

Jamieson's *Popular Ballads*, I, 59. From the recita-
tion of Mrs W. Arrott, of Aberbrothick.

1 'O will ye gae to the school, brother?
    Or will ye gae to the ba?
    Or will ye gae to the wood a-warslin,
    To see whilk o's maun fa?'

2 'It's I winna gae to the school, brother,
    Nor will I gae to the ba;
    But I will gae to the wood a-warslin,
    And it is you maun fa.'

3 They warstled up, they warstled down,
  The lee-lang simmer's day;

  .   .   .   .   .

        .   .   .   .   .

4 'O lift me up upon your back,
  Tak me to yon wall fair;
  You'll wash my bluidy wounds oer and oer,
  And syne they'll bleed nae mair.'

5 'And ye'll tak aff my hollin sark,
  And riv 't frae gair to gair;
  Ye'll stap it in my bluidy wounds,
  And syne they'll bleed nae mair.'

6 He's liftit his brother upon his back,
  Taen him to yon wall fair;
  He's washed his bluidy wounds oer and oer,
  But ay they bled mair and mair.

7 And he's taen aff his hollin sark,
  And riven 't frae gair to gair;
  He's stappit it in his bluidy wounds,
  But ay they bled mair and mair.

8 'Ye'll lift me up upon your back,
  Tak me to Kirkland fair;
  Ye'll mak my greaf baith braid and lang,
  And lay my body there.

9 'Ye'll lay my arrows at my head,
  My bent bow at my feet,
  My sword and buckler at my side,
  As I was wont to sleep.

10 'Whan ye gae hame to your father,
  He'll speer for his son John:
  Say, ye left him into Kirkland fair,
  Learning the school alone.

11 'When ye gae hame to my sister,
  She'll speer for her brother John:
  Ye'll say, ye left him in Kirkland fair,
  The green grass growin aboon.

12 'Whan ye gae hame to my true-love,
  She'll speer for her lord John:
  Ye'll say, ye left him in Kirkland fair,
  But hame ye fear he'll never come.'

13 He's gane hame to his father;
  He speered for his son John:
  'It's I left him into Kirkland fair,
  Learning the school alone.'

14 And whan he gaed hame to his sister,
  She speered for her brother John:
  'It's I left him into Kirkland fair,
  The green grass growin aboon.'

15 And whan he gaed home to his true-love,
  She speerd for her lord John:
  'It's I left him into Kirkland fair,
  And hame I fear he'll never come.'

16 'But whaten bluid's that on your sword, Willie?
  Sweet Willie, tell to me;'
  'O it is the bluid o my grey hounds,
  They wadna rin for me.'

17 'It's nae the bluid o your hounds, Willie,
  Their bluid was never so red;
  But it is the bluid o my true-love,   [441]
  That ye hae slain indeed.'

18 That fair may wept, that fair may mournd,
  That fair may mournd and pin'd:
  'When every lady looks for her love,
  I neer need look for mine.'

19 'O whaten a death will ye die, Willie?
  Now, Willie, tell to me;'
  'Ye'll put me in a bottomless boat,
  And I'll gae sail the sea.'

20 'Whan will ye come hame again, Willie?
  Now, Willie, tell to me;'
  'Whan the sun and moon dances on the green,
  And that will never be.'

E

Motherwell's *Minstrelsy*, p. 60.

1 THERE were twa brothers at the scule,
　　And when they got awa,
　'It's will ye play at the stane-chucking,
　　Or will ye play at the ba,
　　Or will ye gae up to yon hill head,
　　And there we'll warsell a fa?'

2 'I winna play at the stane-chucking,
　　Nor will I play at the ba;
　But I'll gae up to yon bonnie green hill,
　　And there we'll warsel a fa.'

3 They warsled up, they warsled down,
　　Till John fell to the ground;
　A dirk fell out of William's pouch,
　　And gave John a deadly wound.

4 'O lift me upon your back,
　　Take me to yon well fair,
　And wash my bloody wounds oer and oer,
　　And they'll neer bleed nae mair.'

5 He's lifted his brother upon his back,
　　Taen him to yon well fair;
　He's wash'd his bluidy wounds oer and oer,
　　But they bleed ay mair and mair.

6 'Tak ye aff my holland sark,
　　And rive it gair by gair,
　And row it in my bluidy wounds,
　　And they'll neer bleed nae mair.'

7 He's taken aff his holland sark,
　　And torn it gair by gair;
　He's rowit it in his bluidy wounds,
　　But they bleed ay mair and mair.

8 'Tak now aff my green cleiding,
　　And row me saftly in,
　And tak me up to yon kirk-style,
　　Whare the grass grows fair and green.'

9 He's taken aff the green cleiding,
　　And rowed him saftly in;
　He's laid him down by yon kirk-style,
　　Whare the grass grows fair and green.

10 'What will ye say to your father dear,
　　When ye gae hame at een?'
　'I'll say ye're lying at yon kirk-style,
　　Whare the grass grows fair and green.'

11 'O no, O no, my brother dear,
　　O you must not say so;
　But say that I'm gane to a foreign land,
　　Whare nae man does me know.'

12 When he sat in his father's chair,
　　He grew baith pale and wan:
　'O what blude's that upon your brow?
　　O dear son, tell to me;'
　'It is the blude o my gude gray steed,
　　He wadna ride wi me.'

13 'O thy steed's blude was neer sae red,
　　Nor eer sae dear to me:
　O what blude's this upon your cheek?
　　O dear son, tell to me;'
　'It is the blude of my greyhound,
　　He wadna hunt for me.'

14 'O thy hound's blude was neer sae red,
　　Nor eer sae dear to me:
　O what blude's this upon your hand?
　　O dear son, tell to me;'
　'It is the blude of my gay goss-hawk,
　　He wadna flee for me.'

15 'O thy hawk's blude was neer sae red,
　　Nor eer sae dear to me:
　O what blude's this upon your dirk?
　　Dear Willie, tell to me;'
　'It is the blude of my ae brother,
　　O dule and wae is me!'

16 'O what will ye say to your father?
　　Dear Willie, tell to me;'
　'I'll saddle my steed, and awa I'll ride,
　　To dwell in some far countrie.'

17 'O when will ye come hame again?
　　Dear Willie, tell to me;'
　'When sun and mune leap on yon hill,
　　And that will never be.'

18 She turnd hersel right round about,
　　And her heart burst into three:
　'My ae best son is deid and gane,
　　And my tother ane I'll neer see.'

F

Buchan's MSS, I, 57; Motherwell's MS., p. 662.

1 THERE were twa brothers in the east,
  Went to the school o Ayr;
  The one unto the other did say,
  Come let us wrestle here.

2 They wrestled up and wrestled down,
  Till John fell to the ground;
  There being a knife in Willie's pocket,
  Gae John his deadly wound.

3 'O is it for my gold, brother?
  Or for my white monie?
  Or is it for my lands sae braid,
  That ye hae killed me?'

4 'It is not for your gold,' he said,
  'Nor for your white monie;
  It is by the hand o accident
  That I hae killed thee.'

5 'Ye'll take the shirt that's on my back,
  Rive it frae gair to gair,
  And try to stop my bloody wounds,
  For they bleed wonderous sair.'

6 He's taen the shirt was on his back,
  Reave it frae gare to gare,
  And tried to stop his bleeding wounds,
  But still they bled the mair.

7 'Ye'll take me up upon your back,
  Carry me to yon water clear,
  And try to stop my bloody wounds,
  For they run wonderous sair.'

8 He's taen him up upon his back,
  Carried him to yon water clear,
  And tried to stop his bleeding wounds,
  But still they bled the mair.

9 'Ye'll take me up upon your back,
  Carry me to yon church-yard;
  Ye'll dig a grave baith wide and deep,
  And then ye'll lay me there.

10 'Ye'll put a head-stane at my head,
  Another at my feet,
  Likewise a sod on my breast-bane,
  The souner I may sleep.

11 'Whenever my father asks of thee,
  Saying, What's become of John?
  Ye'll tell frae me, I'm ower the sea,
  For a cargo of good wine.

12 'And when my sweetheart asks of thee,
  Saying, What's become of John?
  Ye'll tell frae me, I'm ower the sea,
  To buy a wedding gown.

13 'And when my sister asks of thee,
  Saying, William, where is John?
  Ye'll tell frae me, I'm ower the sea,
  To learn some merry sang.

14 'And when my mother asks of thee,
  Saying, William, where is John?
  Tell her I'm buried in green Fordland,
  The grass growing ower my tomb.'

15 He's taen him up upon his back,
  Carried him to yon church-yard,
  And dug a grave baith wide and deep,
  And he was buried there.

16 He laid a head-stane at his head,
  Another at his feet,
  And laid a green sod on his breast, [443]
  The souner he might sleep.

17 His father asked when he came hame,
  Saying, 'William, where is John?'
  Then John said, 'He is ower the sea,
  To bring you hame some wine.'

18 'What blood is this upon you, William,
  And looks sae red on thee?'
  'It is the blood o my grey-hound,
  He woudna run for me.'

19 'O that's nae like your grey-hound's blude,
  William, that I do see;
  I fear it is your own brother's blood
  That looks sae red on thee.'

20 'That is not my own brother's blude,
  Father, that ye do see;
  It is the blood o my good grey steed,
  He woudna carry me.'

21 'O that is nae your grey steed's blude,
      William, that I do see;
   It is the blood o your brother John,
      That looks sae red on thee.'

22 'It's nae the blood o my brother John,
      Father, that ye do see;
   It is the blude o my good grey hawk,
      Because he woudna flee.'

23 'O that is nae your grey hawk's blood,
      William, that I do see:'
   'Well, it's the blude o my brother,
      This country I maun flee.'

24 'O when will ye come back again,
      My dear son, tell to me?'
   'When sun and moon gae three times round,
      And this will never be.'

25 'Ohon, alas! now William, my son,
      This is bad news to me;
   Your brother's death I'll aye bewail,
      And the absence o thee.'

G

a. Taken down lately from the singing of little girls
in South Boston. **b.** Two stanzas, from a child in New
York, 1880. Communicated by Mr W. W. Newell.

1 As John and William were coming home one
         day,
      One Saturday afternoon,
   Says John to William, Come and try a fight,
      Or will you throw a stone?
   Or will you come down to yonder, yonder town
      Where the maids are all playing ball, ball,
         ball,
      Where the maids are all playing ball?

2 Says William to John, I will not try a fight,
      Nor will I throw a stone,
   Nor will I come down to yonder town,
      Where the maids are all playing ball.

3 So John took out of his pocket
      A knife both long and sharp,
   And stuck it through his brother's heart,
      And the blood came pouring down.

4 Says John to William, 'Take off thy shirt,
      And tear it from gore to gore,
   And wrap it round your bleeding heart,
      And the blood will pour no more.'

5 So John took off his shirt,
      And tore it from gore to gore,
   And wrapped it round his bleeding heart,
      And the blood came pouring more.

6 'What shall I tell your dear father,
      When I go home to-night?'
   'You'll tell him I'm dead and in my grave,
      For the truth must be told.'

7 'What shall I tell your dear mother,
      When I go home to-night?'
   'You'll tell her I'm dead and in my grave,
      For the truth must be told.'

8 'How came this blood upon your knife?
      My son, come tell to me;'
   'It is the blood of a rabbit I have killed,
      O mother, pardon me.'

9 'The blood of a rabbit couldnt be so pure,   [4
      My son, come tell to me:'
   'It is the blood of a squirrel I have killed,
      O mother, pardon me.'

10 'The blood of a squirrel couldnt be so pure,
      My son, come tell to me:'
   'It is the blood of a brother I have killed,
      O mother, pardon me.'

H

'Perthshire Tredgey.' From a copy formerly in the possession of Charles Kirkpatrick Sharpe. This fragment has some resemblances to **F.** "Copied 1823" is endorsed on the sheet (in the hand which made an insertion in st. 11) and crossed out.

1 Two pretty boys lived in the North,
  The went to the school so rare;
 The one unto the other said,
  We'll try some battle of war.

2 The worselaid up, the worselaid down,
  Till John lay on the ground;
 A pen-knife out of William's pocket
  Gave John a deadly wound.

3 'O is it for my gold?' he said,
  'Or for my rich monie?
 Or is it for my land sa broad,
  That you have killed me?'

4 'It's neither for your gold,' he said,
  'Or for your rich monie,
 But it is for your land sa broad
  That I have killed thee.'

5 'You'll take [me] up upon your back,
  Carry me to Wastlen kirk-yard;
 You 'ill houk a hole large and deep,
  And lay my body there.

6 'You'll put a good stone on my head,
  Another at me feet,
 A good green turf upon my breast,
  That the sounder I m[a]y sleep.

7 'And if my father chance to ask
  What's come of your brother John,

 .   .   .   .

 *   *   *   **

8 'What blood is this upon your coat?
  I pray come tell to me;'
 'It is the blood of my grey hound,
  It would not run for me.'

9 'The blood of your greyhound was near so red,
  I pray come tell to me;'
 'It is the blood of my black horse,
  It would not hunt for me.'

10 'The blood of your black horse was near so red,
  I pray come tell to me;'
 'It is the blood of my brother John,
  Since better canna be.'

 *   *   *   *   *

11 He put his foot upon a ship,
  Saying, I am gane our the sea;
 'O when will you come back again,
  I pray come tell to me.'

12 'When the sun and the moon passes over the
  broom,
  That['s] the day you'll never see.'

I

Communicated by Mr J. K. Hudson of Manchester. Sung after a St George play regularly acted on All Souls' Day at a village a few miles from Chester, and written down for Mr Hudson by one of the performers, a lad of sixteen. The play was introduced by a song called Souling (similar to a Stephening, see p. 322), and followed by two songs, of which this is the last, the whole dramatic company singing.

1 'And it's where hast thou been all this night
     long, my son?
   Come tell it unto me.'
 'I have been lying on yonder bull-rushes,
    Which lies beneath yond tree.'

2 'And it's what are the spots on this thy coat,
     my son?
   Come tell it unto me.'
 'They are the spots of my poor brother's blood,
    Which lies beneath yonder tree.'

3 'And it's what didst thou kill thy poor brother
     for, my son?
   Come tell it unto me.'
 'Because he killed two pretty little birds,
    Which flew from tree to tree.'

4 'And it's what will the father say when he
     comes, my son?
   Come tell it unto me.'
 'I will dress me up in sailor's clothes,
    And my face he will never see.'

5 'And it's what wilt thou do with thy pretty little wife, my son?
   Come tell it unto me.'
 'I will dress her up in lad[d]ie's clothes,
    And she will sail along with me.'

6 'And it's what wilt thou do with thy children
     three, my son?
   Come tell it unto me.'
 'I will leave them to my poor grandfather to
     rear,
    And comfort [to] him [to be].'

7 'And it's when shall we see thy face again, my
     son?
   Come tell it unto me.'
 'When the sun and moon shines both at once,
    And that shall never be.'

A. 1². Var. to the chase.
   10³. "As to Kirk-land, my copy has only kirk-yard, till the last verse, where land has been added from conjecture." Sharpe's Ballad-Book, p. 56.
   A was derived by Sharpe from Elizabeth Kerry. The original copy was not all written at one time, but may have been written by one person. The first and the last stanza, and some corrections, are in the same hand as a letter which accompanied the ballad. The paper has a watermark of 1817. A few trifling differences in the MS. may be noted:
   1¹. two.
   1². school (Note. "I have heard it called the Chase") : the githar.
   1⁴. a far. 2¹. wrestled. 4⁴. And. 5¹. brother.
   6³. both. 7², 8², 9². Should for Gin.

   8¹. what shall. 10¹. But wanting.
   10³. in fair Kirkland. (Letter. "I remembered a fair Kirk something, and Kirkland it must have been.")
   10⁴. again wanting.
D. 1³, 2³. o Warslin.
F. 13³. tell me free.
   Motherwell has Scotticised the spelling.
   9⁴. Motherwell has leave.
   11¹, 12¹, 13¹, 14¹. Motherwell, speirs at thee.
   23³. Motherwell has my ae brother.
G. b.   1 Jack and William was gone to school,
       One fine afternoon;
     Jack says to William, Will you try a fight?
       Do not throw no stones.

2 Jack took out his little penknife,
    The end of it was sharp,
He stuck it through his brother's heart,
And the blood was teeming down.

H. 2^1. worse laid, *misheard for* warseled.
    3^3. lands abroad *for* land sae broad (*misheard*).

4^1. After your, la *and half of an* n, lan *caught from* 3^3.

4^3. land abroad. *The reciter, or more probably the transcriber, has become confirmed in the error made in* 3^3.

11^3. come *inserted in a different hand.*

$11^{3,4}$ *should probably be the first half of stanza* 12.

APPENDIX

Additional Copies

A b. 'The Two Brothers,' *Walks near Edinburgh*, by Margaret Warrender, 1890, p. 60. Given to Lady John Scott many years ago by Campbell Riddell, brother of Sir James Riddell of Ardnamurchan.

1 THERE were two brothers in the north,
    Lord William and Lord John,
And they would try a wrestling match,
    So to the fields they've gone, gone, gone,
    So to the fields they've gone.

2 They wrestled up, they wrestled down,
    Till Lord John fell on the ground.
And a knife into Lord William's pocket
    Gave him a deadly wound.

3 'Oh take me on your back, dear William,' he
        said,
    'And carry me to the burnie clear,
And wash my wound sae deep and dark,
    Maybe 't will bleed nae mair.'

4 He took him up upon his back,
    An carried him to the burnie clear,
But aye the mair he washed his wound
    It aye did bleed the mair.

5 'Oh take me on your back, dear William,' he
        said,
    'And carry me to the kirkyard fair,
And dig a grave sae deep and dark,
    And lay my body there.'

6 'But what shall I say to my father dear
    When he says, Willie, what's become of
        John?'
'Oh tell him I am gone to Greenock town,
    To buy him a puncheon of rum.'

7 'And what shall I say to my sister dear
    When she says, Willie, what's become of
        John?'
'Oh tell her I've gone to London town
    To buy her a marriage-gown.'

8 'But what shall I say to my grandmother dear
    When she says, Willie, what's become of
        John?'
'Oh tell her I'm in the kirkyard dark,
    And that I'm dead and gone.'

50

THE BONNY HIND

'The Bonny Hyn,' Herd's MSS, I, 224; II, fol. 65, fol. 83.

THIS piece is transcribed three times in Herd's manuscripts, with a note prefixed in each instance that it was copied from the mouth of a milkmaid in 1771. An endorsement to the same effect on the last transcript gives the date as 1787, no doubt by mistake. Scott had only MS. I in his hands, which accidentally omits two stanzas (13, 14), and he printed this defective copy with the omission of still another (4): Minstrelsy, II, 298, ed. 1802; III, 309, ed. 1833. Motherwell supplies these omitted stanzas, almost in Herd's very words, in the Introduction to his collection, p. lxxxiv, note 99.[*] He remarks, p. 189, that tales of this kind abound in the traditional poetry of Scotland. The two ballads which follow, Nos 51, 52, are of the same general description.

In the first half of the story 'The Bonny Hind' comes very near to the fine Scandinavian ballad of 'Margaret,' as yet known to be preserved only in Färöe and Icelandic. The conclusions differ altogether. Margaret in the Färöe ballad, 'Margretu kvæði,' Færøiske Qvæder, Hammershaimb, No 18, is the only daughter of the Norwegian king Magnus, and has been put in a convent. After two or three months she longs to see her father's house again. On her way thither she is assaulted by a young noble with extreme violence: to whom she says,

Now you have torn off all my clothes, and done me sin and shame,
I beg you, before God most high, tell me what is your name.

Magnus, he answers, is his father, and Gertrude his mother, and he himself is Olaf, and was brought up in the woods. By this she recognizes that he is her own brother. Olaf begs her to go [144] back to the convent, and say nothing, bearing her sorrow as she may. This she does. But every autumn the king makes a feast, and invites to it all the nuns in the cloister. Margaret is missed, and asked for. Is she sick or dead? Why does she not come to the feast, like other merry dames? The wicked abbess answers, Your daughter is neither sick nor dead; she goes with child, like other merry dames. The king rides off to the cloister, encounters his daughter, and demands who is the father of her child. She replies that she will sooner die than tell. The king leaves her in wrath, but returns presently, resolved to burn the convent, and Margaret in it. Olaf comes from the wood, tired and weary, sees the cloister burning, and quenches the flames with his heart's blood.

The Icelandic ballad, 'Margrètar kvæði,' Íslenzk Fornkvæði, Grundtvig and Sigurðsson, No 14, has the same story. It is, however, the man who brings on the discovery by asking the woman's parentage. The editors inform us that the same subject is treated in an unprinted Icelandic ballad, less popular as to style and stanza, in the Arne Magnussen collection, 154.

The story of Kullervo, incorporated in what is called the national epic of the Finns, the Kal-

---

[*] Motherwell MS., p. 485, professes to copy the ballad from Herd's MS. by way of supplying the stanzas wanting in Scott. There are, however, in Motherwell's transcript considerable deviations from Herd, a fact which I am unable to understand.

evala, has striking resemblances with the ballads of the Bonny Hind class. While returning home in his sledge from a somewhat distant errand, Kullervo met three times a girl who was travelling on snow-shoes, and invited her to get in with him. She rejected his invitation with fierceness, and the third time he pulled her into the sledge by force. She angrily bade him let her go, or she would dash the sledge to pieces; but he won her over by showing her rich things. The next morning she asked what was his race and family; for it seemed to her that he must come of a great line. "No," he said, "neither of great nor small. I am Kalervo's unhappy son. Tell me of what stock art thou." "Of neither great nor small," she answered. "I am Kalervo's unhappy daughter." She was, in fact, a long-lost sister of Kullervo's, who, when a child, had gone to the wood for berries, and had never found her way home. She had wept the first day and the second; the third and fourth, the fifth and sixth, she had tried every way to kill herself. She broke out in heart-piercing lamentations:

'O that I had died then, wretched!
O that I had perished, weak one!
Had not lived to bear these horrors,
Had not lived this shame to suffer!'

So saying she sprang from the sledge into the river, and found relief under the waters.

Kullervo, mad with anguish, went home to his mother, and told her what had happened. He asked only how he might die,—by wolf or bear, by whale or sea-pike. His mother vainly sought to soothe him. He consented to live only till the wrongs of his parents had been revenged. His mother tried to dissuade him even from seeking a hero's death in fight.

'If thou die in battle, tell me,
What protection shall remain then
For the old age of thy father?'
'Let him die in any alley,
Lay his life down in the house-yard.'
'What protection shall remain then
For the old age of thy mother?'
'Let her die on any straw-truss;
Let her stifle in the stable.'

'Who shall then be left thy brother,
Who stand by him in mischances?'
'Let him pine away in the forest,
Let him drop down on the common.'
'Who shall then be left thy sister,
Who stand by her in mischances?'
'When she goes to the well for water,
Or to the washing, let her stumble.'

Kullervo had his fill of revenge. Meanwhile father, brother, sister, and mother died, and he came back to his home to find it empty and cold. A voice from his mother's grave seemed to direct him to go to the wood for food: obeying it, he came again to the polluted spot, where grass or flowers would not grow any more. He asked his sword would it like to feed on guilty flesh and drink wicked blood. The sword said, Why should I not like to feed on guilty flesh and drink wicked blood, I that feed on the flesh of the good and drink the blood of the sinless? [446] Kullervo set the sword hilt in the earth, and threw himself on the point. (*Kalewala*, übertragen von Schiefner, runes 35, 36.)

The dialogue between Kullervo and his mother is very like a passage in another Finnish rune, 'Werinen Pojka,' 'The Bloody Son,' Schröter, *Finnische Runen*, 124, ed. 1819; 150, ed. 1834. This last is a form of the ballad known in Scottish as 'Edward,' No 13, or of 'The Twa Brothers,' No 49. Something similar is found in 'Lizie Wan,' No 51.

The passage 5–7 is a commonplace that may be expected to recur under the same or analogous circumstances, as it does in 'Tam Lin,' **D**, 'The Knight and Shepherd's Daughter,' 'The Maid and the Magpie,' and in one version of 'The Broom of Cowdenknows.' These are much less serious ballads, and the tone of stanza 5, which so ill befits the distressful situation, is perhaps owing to that stanza's having been transferred from some copy of one of these. It might well change places with this, from 'The Knight and Shepherd's Daughter,' **A**:

Sith you have had your will of me,
    And put me to open shame,
Now, if you are a courteous knight,
    Tell me what is your name.

Much better with the solemn adjuration in the
Färöe 'Margaret,' or even this in 'Ebbe Galt,'
Danske Viser, No 63, 8:

Now you have had your will of me,
  To both of us small gain,
By the God that is above all things,
  I beg you tell your name.

Herd's MSS, II, fol. 65. "Copied from the mouth of
a milkmaid, by W. L, in 1771."

1 O MAY she comes, and may she goes,
    Down by yon gardens green,
  And there she spied a gallant squire
    As squire had ever been.

2 And may she comes, and may she goes,
    Down by yon hollin tree,
  And there she spied a brisk young squire,
    And a brisk young squire was he.

3 'Give me your green manteel, fair maid,
    Give me your maidenhead;
  Gif ye winna gie me your green manteel,
    Gi me your maidenhead.'

4 He has taen her by the milk-white hand,
    And softly laid her down,
  And when he's lifted her up again
    Given her a silver kaim.

5 'Perhaps there may be bairns, kind sir,
    Perhaps there may be nane;
  But if you be a courtier,
    You'll tell to me your name.'

6 'I am nae courtier, fair maid,
    But new come frae the sea;
  I am nae courtier, fair maid,
    But when I court 'ith thee.

7 'They call me Jack when I'm abroad,
    Sometimes they call me John;
  But when I'm in my father's bower
    Jock Randal is my name.'

8 'Ye lee, ye lee, ye bonny lad,
    Sae loud's I hear ye lee!
  Ffor I'm Lord Randal's yae daughter,
    He has nae mair nor me.'

9 'Ye lee, ye lee, ye bonny may,
    Sae loud's I hear ye lee!
  For I'm Lord Randal's yae yae son,
    Just now come oer the sea.'

10 She's putten her hand down by her spare,
     And out she's taen a knife,
   And she has putn 't in her heart's bluid,
     And taen away her life.

11 And he's taen up his bonny sister,
     With the big tear in his een,
   And he has buried his bonny sister
     Amang the hollins green.

12 And syne he's hyed him oer the dale,
     His father dear to see: [44
   'Sing O and O for my bonny hind,
     Beneath yon hollin tree!'

13 'What needs you care for your bonny hyn?
     For it you needna care;
   There's aught score hyns in yonder park,
     And five score hyns to spare.

14 'Four score of them are siller-shod,
     Of thae ye may get three;'
   'But O and O for my bonny hyn,
     Beneath yon hollin tree!'

15 'What needs you care for your bonny hyn?
     For it you need na care;
   Take you the best, gi me the warst,
     Since plenty is to spare.'

16 'I care na for your hyns, my lord,
     I care na for your fee;
   But O and O for my bonny hyn,
     Beneath the hollin tree!'

17 'O were ye at your sister's bower,
     Your sister fair to see,
   Ye'll think na mair o your bonny hyn
     Beneath the hollin tree.'

*   *   *   *   *

———◆———

'The Bonny Heyn,' I, 224.

3^2. *Should be* It's not for you a weed. *Motherwell.*

4^3. *The third copy omits* when.

$4^{3,4}$. he lifted, He gae her. *Motherwell.*

$5^{1,2}$. *The second copy has* they.

6^4. *All have* courteth. *Scott prints* wi' thee, with thee.

7^3. *The third copy has* tower.

$10^{3,4}$. She's soakt it in her red heart's blood,
    And twin'd herself of life. *Motherwell.*

13, 14. *The first copy omits these stanzas.*

51

LIZIE WAN

A. a. 'Lizie Wan,' Herd's MSS, I, 151; II, 78. **b.**   **B.** 'Rosie Ann,' Motherwell's MS., p. 398.
Herd's *Scottish Songs*, 1776, I, 91.

A, FIRST printed in Herd's *Scottish Songs*, ed. 1776, is here given from his manuscript copy. **B** is now printed for the first time.

A is translated by Grundtvig, *Engelske og skotske Folkeviser*, No 50, who subjoins a Danish ballad, 'Liden Ellen og hendes Broder,' of similar character. Of this the editor had three versions, differing but little, and all of slight poetical value, and he prints one which was committed to writing some sixty or seventy years ago, with some readings from the others. Liden Jensen, having killed Liden Ellen in a wood, pretends to his mother that she has gone off with some knights. He is betrayed by blood on his clothes, confesses the truth, and is condemned to be burned. 'Herr Axel,' Arwidsson's Swedish collection, No 46, I, 308, under similar circumstances, kills Stolts Kirstin's two children, is asked by his mother why his hands are bloody, pretends to have slain a hind in the wood, and has his head struck off by order of his father.

'Herr Peder og hans Söster,' an unpublished Danish ballad, of which Grundtvig obtained a single traditional version, has also a slight resemblance to 'Lizie Wan.' Kirsten invites Sir [44 Peter to her bed. He declines for various reasons, which she refutes. She discovers him to be her brother by her needle-work in his shirt. He draws his knife and stabs her. "This was also a pitiful sight, the twin children playing in the mother's bosom." Compare Kristensen, II, No 74 **A, D, E**, at the end.

The conclusion, **A** 11–12, **B** 10–17, resembles that of 'The Twa Brothers,' No 49, but is poetically much inferior.

A

Herd's MSS, I, 151; stanzas 1–6, II, p. 78. Herd's
Scottish Songs, 1776, I, 91.

1 LIZIE WAN sits at her father's bower-door,
    Weeping and making a mane,
And by there came her father dear:
    'What ails thee, Lizie Wan?'

2 'I ail, and I ail, dear father,' she said,
    'And I'll tell you a reason for why;
There is a child between my twa sides,
    Between my dear billy and I.'

3 Now Lizie Wan sits at her father's bower-door,
    Sighing and making a mane,
And by there came her brother dear
    'What ails thee, Lizie Wan?'

4 'I ail, I ail, dear brither,' she said,
    'And I'll tell you a reason for why;
There is a child between my twa sides,
    Between you, dear billy, and I.'

5 'And hast thou tald father and mother o that?
    And hast thou tald sae o me?'
And he has drawn his gude braid sword,
    That hang down by his knee.

6 And he has cutted aff Lizie Wan's head,
    And her fair body in three,
And he's awa to his mothers bower,
    And sair aghast was he.

7 'What ails thee, what ails thee, Geordy Wan?
    What ails thee sae fast to rin?
For I see by thy ill colour
    Some fallow's deed thou hast done.'

8 'Some fallow's deed I have done, mother,
    And I pray you pardon me;
For I've cutted aff my greyhound's head;
    He wadna rin for me.'

9 'Thy greyhound's bluid was never sae red,
    O my son Geordy Wan!
For I see by thy ill colour
    Some fallow's deed thou hast done.'

10 'Some fallow's deed I hae done, mother,
    And I pray you pardon me;
For I hae cutted aff Lizie Wan's head
    And her fair body in three.'

11 'O what wilt thou do when thy father comes
        hame,
    O my son Geordy Wan?'
'I'll set my foot in a bottomless boat,
    And swim to the sea-ground.'

12 'And when will thou come hame again,
    O my son Geordy Wan?'
'The sun and the moon shall dance on the
        green
    That night when I come hame.'

B

Motherwell's MS. p. 398. From the recitation of
Mrs Storie, Lochwinnich.

1 ROSIE she sat in her simmer bower,
    Greitin and making grit mane,
When down by cam her father, saying,
    What ails thee Rosie Ann?

2 'A deal, a deal, dear father,' she said,
    'Great reason hae I to mane,
For there lyes a little babe in my side,
    Between me and my brither John.'

3 Rosie she sat in her simmer bower,
    Weeping and making great mane,
And wha cam doun but her mither dear,
    Saying, What ails thee, Rosie Ann?

4 'A deal, a deal, dear mither,' she said,
    'Great reason hae I to mane,
For there lyes a little babe in my side,
    Between me and my brither John.'

5 Rosie she sat in her simmer bower,
    Greiting and making great mane,
And wha came doun but her sister dear,
    Saying, What ails thee, Rosie Ann?

6 'A deal, a deal, dear sister,' she said,
    'Great reason hae I to mane,
For there lyes a little babe in my side,
    Between me and my brither John.'

7 Rosie she sat in her simmer bower,
    Weeping and making great mane,
And wha cam doun but her fause, fause brither,
    Saying, What ails thee, Rosie Ann?

8 'A deal, a deal, dear brither,' she said,
    'Great reason hae I to cry,
For there lyes a little babe in my side,
    Between yoursell and I.'

9 'Weel ye hae tauld father, and ye hae tauld
        mither,
    And ye hae tauld sister, a' three;'
Syne he pulled out his wee penknife,
    And he cut her fair bodie in three.

10 'O what blude is that on the point o your knife,
    Dear son, come tell to me?'
'It is my horse's, that I did kill,
    Dear mother and fair ladie.'

11 'The blude o your horse was neer sae red,
    Dear son, come tell to me:'
  'It is my grandfather's, that I hae killed,
    Dear mother and fair ladie.'

12 'The blude o your grandfather was neer sae
        fresh,
    Dear son, come tell to me:'
  'It is my sister's, that I did kill,
    Dear mother and fair ladie.'

13 'What will ye do when your father comes
        hame,
    Dear son, come tell to me?'
  'I'll set my foot on yon shipboard,
    And I hope she'll sail wi me.'

14 'What will ye do wi your bonny bonny young
        wife,
    Dear son, come tell to me?'
  'I'll set her foot on some other ship,
    And I hope she'll follow me.'

15 'And what will ye do wi your wee son,
    Dear son, come tell to me?'
  'I'll leave him wi you, my dear mother,
    To keep in remembrance of me.'

16 'What will ye do wi your houses and lands,
    Dear son, come tell to me?'
  'I'll leave them wi you, my dear mother,
    To keep my own babie.'

17 'And whan will you return again,
    Dear son, come tell to me?'
  'When the sun and the mune meet on yon hill,
    And I hope that'll neer be.'

———◆———

B. *Written without division into stanzas.*

52

THE KING'S DOCHTER LADY JEAN

A. a. 'The King's Dochter Lady Jean,' Mother-well's MS., p. 657. b. 'Lady Jean,' Motherwell's *Minstrelsy*, Appendix, p. xxi.
B. Motherwell's MS., p. 275; the first six lines in Motherwell's Minstrelsy, p. 189f.

C. 'Castle Ha's Daughter,' Buchan's *Ballads of the North of Scotland*, I, 241.
D. 'Bold Burnet's Daughter.' a. Buchan's MSS, I, 120. b. The same, II, 141.

B is the ballad referred to, and partly cited, in Motherwell's preface to 'The Broom blooms bonnie and says it is fair,' *Minstrelsy*, p. 189. This copy has been extremely injured by tradition; so much so as not to be intelligible in places except by comparison with A. The act described in stanza 9 should be done by the king's daughter's own hand; stanza 12 should be addressed by her to her sister; stanza 13 is composed of fragments of two. C and D have suffered worse, for they have been corrupted and vulgarized.

At the beginning there is resemblance to 'Tam Lin' and to 'Hind Etin.'

A

a. Motherwell's MS., p. 657. From the recitation of
Mrs Storie, Lochwinnich. b. Motherwell's *Minstrelsy*,
Appendix, p. xxi, No XXIII, one stanza.

The king's daugh - ter was__ sit - ting in her win - dow, Sew - ing at her fine silk - en seam,

She luik - it out at her braw bow - er win - dow, And she saw the leaves grow - in' green, my love,

And she saw the leaves__ grow - ing green.

A. b. Motherwell, 1827, Appendix No XXIII. Noted by Andrew Blaikie, Paisley.

1 THE king's young dochter was sitting in her
window,
Sewing at her silken seam;
She lookt out o the bow-window,
And she saw the leaves growing green, my
luve,
And she saw the leaves growing green.

2 She stuck her needle into her sleeve,
Her seam down by her tae,
And she is awa to the merrie green-wood,
To pu the nit and slae.

3 She hadna pu't a nit at a',
A nit but scarcely three,
Till out and spak a braw young man,
Saying, How daur ye bow the tree?

4 'It's I will pu the nit,' she said,
    'And I will bow the tree,
    And I will come to the merrie green wud,
    And na ax leive o thee.'

5 He took her by the middle sae sma,
    And laid her on the gerss sae green,
    And he has taen his will o her,
    And he loot her up agen.

6 'Now syn ye hae got your will o me,
    Pray tell to me your name;
    For I am the king's young dochter,' she said,
    'And this nicht I daurna gang hame.'

7 'Gif ye be the king's young dochter,' he said,
    'I am his auldest son;
    I wish I had died on some frem isle,
    And never had come hame!

8 'The first time I came hame, Jeanie,
    Thou was na here nor born;
    I wish my pretty ship had sunk,
    And I had been forlorn!

9 'The neist time I came hame, Jeanie,
    Thou was sittin on the nourice knee;
    And I wish my pretty ship had sunk,
    And I had never seen thee!

10 'And the neist time I came hame, Jeanie,
    I met thee here alane;
    [451]   I wish my pretty ship had sunk,
    And I had neer come hame!'

11 She put her hand down by her side,
    And doun into her spare,
    And she pou't out a wee pen-knife,
    And she wounded hersell fu sair.

12 Hooly, hooly rase she up,
    And hooly she gade hame,
    Until she came to her father's parlour,
    And there she did sick and mane.

13 'O sister, sister, mak my bed,
    O the clean sheets and strae,
    O sister, sister, mak my bed,
    Down in the parlour below.'

14 Her father he came tripping down the stair,
    His steps they were fu slow;
    'I think, I think, Lady Jean,' he said,
    'Ye're lying far ower low.'

15 'O late yestreen, as I came hame,
    Down by yon castil wa,
    O heavy, heavy was the stane
    That on my briest did fa!'

16 Her mother she came tripping doun the stair,
    Her steps they were fu slow;
    'I think, I think, Lady Jean,' she said,
    'Ye're lying far ower low.'

17 'O late yestreen, as I cam hame,
    Down by yon castil wa,
    O heavy, heavy was the stane
    That on my breast did fa!'

18 Her sister came tripping doun the stair,
    Her steps they were fu slow;
    'I think, I think, Lady Jean,' she said,
    'Ye're lying far ower low.'

18 'O late yestreen, as I cam hame,
    Doun by yon castil wa,
    O heavy, heavy was the stane
    That on my breast did fa!'

19 Her brither he cam trippin doun the stair,
    His steps they were fa slow;
    He sank into his sister's arms,
    And they died as white as snaw.

B

Motherwell's MS., p. 275; the first six lines in
Motherwell's *Minstrelsy*, p. 189. From Margery
Johnston.

1 LADY MARGARET sits in her bow-window,
  Sewing her silken seam;
  .   .   .   .   .
    .   .   .   .   .

2 She's drapt the thimble at her tae,
  And her scissars at her heel,
  And she's awa to the merry green-wood,
  To see the leaves grow green.

3 She had scarsely bowed a branch,
  Or plucked a nut frae the tree,
  Till up and starts a fair young man,
  And a fair young man was he.

4 'How dare ye shake the leaves?' he said,
  'How dare ye break the tree?
  How dare ye pluck the nuts,' he said,
  'Without the leave of me?'

5 .   .   .   .   .
    .   .   .   .   .
  'Oh I know the merry green wood's my ain,
  And I'll ask the leave of nane.'

6 He gript her by the middle sae sma,
  He gently sat her down,
  While the grass grew up on every side,
  And the apple trees hang down.

7 She says, Young man, what is your name?
  For ye've brought me to meikle shame;
  For I am the king's youngest daughter,
  And how shall I gae hame?

8 'If you're the king's youngest daughter,
  It's I'm his auldest son,
  And heavy heavy is the deed, sister,
  That you and I have done.'

9 He had a penknife in his hand,
  Hang low down by his gair,
  And between the long rib and the short one   [452]
  He woundit her deep and sair.

10 .   .   .   .   .
     .   .   .   .   .
   And fast and fast her ruddy bright blood
   Fell drapping on the ground.

11 She took the glove off her right hand,
   And slowly slipt it in the wound,
   And slowly has she risen up,
   And slowly slipped home.

  *   *   *   *   *

12 'O sister dear, when thou gaes hame
   Unto thy father's ha,
   It's make my bed baith braid and lang,
   Wi the sheets as white as snaw.'

  *   *   *   *   *

13 'When I came by the high church-yard
   Heavy was the stain that bruised my heel,
   . . . . that bruised my heart,
   I'm afraid it shall neer heal.'

  *   *   *   *   *

C

Buchan's *Ballads and Songs of the North of Scotland*, I, 241.

1 As Annie sat into her bower,
  A thought came in her head,
  That she would gang to gude greenwood,
  Across the flowery mead.

2 She hadna pu'd a flower, a flower,
  Nor broken a branch but twa,
  Till by it came a gentle squire,
  Says, Lady, come awa.

3 There's nane that comes to gude greenwood
  But pays to me a tein,
  And I maun hae your maidenhead,
  Or than your mantle green.

4 'My mantle's o the finest silk,
  Anither I can spin;
  But gin you take my maidenhead,
  The like I'll never fin.'

5 He's taen her by the milk-white hand,
   And by the grass-green sleeve,
There laid her low in gude greenwood,
   And at her spierd nae leave.

6 When he had got his wills o her,
   His wills as he had taen,
She said, If you rightly knew my birth,
   Ye'd better letten alane.

7 'Is your father a lord o might?
   Or baron o high degree?
Or what race are ye sprung frae,
   That I should lat ye be?'

8 'O I am Castle Ha's daughter,
   O birth and high degree,
And if he knows what ye hae done,
   He'll hang you on a tree.'

9 'If ye be Castle Ha's daughter,
   This day I am undone;
If ye be Castle Ha's daughter,
   I am his only son.'

10 'Ye lie, ye lie, ye jelly hind squire,
   Sae loud as I hear you lie,
Castle Ha, he has but ae dear son,
   And he is far beyond the sea.'

11 'O I am Castle Ha's dear son,
   A word I dinna lie;
Yes, I am Castle Ha's dear son,
   And new come oer the sea.

12 ''T was yesterday, that fatal day,
   That I did cross the faem;
I wish my bonny ship had sunk,
   And I had neer come hame.'

13 Then dowie, dowie, raise she up,
   And dowie came she hame,
And stripped aff her silk mantle,
   And then to bed she's gane.

14 Then in it came her mother dear.
   And she steps in the fleer:
[453]   'Win up, win up, now fair Annie,
   What makes your lying here?'

15 'This morning fair, as I went out,
   Near by yon castle wa,
Great and heavy was the stane
   That on my foot did fa.'

16 'Hae I nae ha's, hae I nae bowers,
   Towers, or mony a town?
Will not these cure your bonny foot,
   Gar you gae hale and soun?'

17 'Ye hae ha's, and ye hae bowers,
   And towers, and mony a town,
But nought will cure my bonny foot,
   Gar me gang hale and soun.'

18 Then in it came her father dear,
   And he trips in the fleer:
'Win up, win up, now fair Annie,
   What makes your lying here?'

19 'This morning fair, as I went out,
   Near by yon castle wa,
Great and heavy was the stane
   That on my foot did fa.'

20 'Hae I nae ha's, hae I nae bowers,
   And towers, and mony a town?
Will not these cure your bonny foot,
   Gar you gang hale and soun?'

21 'O ye hae ha's, and ye hae bowers,
   And towers, and mony a town,
But nought will cure my bonny foot,
   Gar me gang hale and soun.'

22 Then in it came her sister Grace
   As she steps in the fleer,
'Win up, win up, now fair Annie,
   What makes your lying here?

23 'Win up, and see your ae brother,
   That's new come ower the sea;'
'Ohon, alas!' says fair Annie,
   'He spake ower soon wi me.'

24 To her room her brother's gane,
   Stroked back her yellow hair,
To her lips his ain did press,
   But words spake never mair.

D

a. Buchan's MSS, I, 120. **b**. The same, II, 141.

1 THE lady's taen her mantle her middle about,
    Into the woods she's gane,

   .   .   .   .   .
      .   .   .   .   .

2 She hadna poud a flower o gude green-wood,
    O never a flower but ane,
Till by he comes, an by he gangs,
    Says, Lady, lat alane.

3 For I am forester o this wood,
    And I hae power to pine
Your mantle or your maidenhead,
    Which o the twa ye'll twine.

4 'My mantle is o gude green silk,
    Another I can card an spin;
But gin ye tak my maidenhead,
    The like I'll never fin.'

5 He's taen her by the milk-white hand,
    And by the grass-green sleeve,
And laid her low at the foot o a tree,
    At her high kin spierd nae leave.

6 'I am bold Burnet's ae daughter,
    You might hae lat me be:'
'And I'm bold Burnet's ae dear son,
    Then dear! how can this dee?'

7 'Ye lie, ye lie, ye jolly hind squire,
    So loud's I hear you lie!
Bold Burnet has but ae dear son,
    He's sailing on the sea.'

8 'Yesterday, about this same time,
    My bonny ship came to land;
I wish she'd sunken in the sea,
    And never seen the strand!

9 'Heal well this deed on me, lady,
    Heal well this deed on me!'
'Although I would heal it neer sae well,
    Our God above does see.'

10 She's taen her mantle her middle about,   *[454]*
    And mourning went she hame,
And a' the way she sighd full sair,
    Crying, Am I to blame!

11 Ben it came her father dear,
    Stout stepping on the flear
'Win up, win up, my daughter Janet,
    And welcome your brother here.'

12 Up she's taen her milk-white hand,
    Streakd by his yellow hair,
Then turnd about her bonny face,
    And word spake never mair.

A. **b**. 1². fine silken.
    1³. She luikit out at her braw bower window.
B. 1^{1,2} *and* 2 *are joined in the MS.*
    5^{1,4} *joined with* 4. 5⁴. no leave of thee, *an emenda-*
    tion by Motherwell, for rhyme.
    9⁴. He struck: *an emendation.*
    10^{3,4} *are joined with* 9.
    13³. That bruised by heart.
    After 13 *is written* A stanza wanting.
D. *The first three stanzas are not properly divided in* **a**,
    and in **b** *the first fourteen lines not divided at all.*
a. 11². An stepping. 7¹. kind squire *in both copies.*

b. 5⁴. kin's.
    9¹. Heal well, heal well on me, Lady Janet.
    11². Stout stepping.
    12³. She turned.

53

YOUNG BEICHAN

A. 'Young Bicham,' Jamieson-Brown MS., p. 13, c. 1783.

B. 'Young Brechin,' Glenriddell MSS, XI, 80, 1791.

C. 'Young Bekie.' **a**. Jamieson-Brown MS., p. 11, c. 1783. **b**. Jamieson's *Popular Ballads*, II, 127.

D. 'Young Beachen,' Skene MSS, p. 70, 1802–1803.

E. 'Young Beichan and Susie Pye,' Jamieson's *Popular Ballads*, II, 117.

F. 'Susan Pye and Lord Beichan,' Pitcairn's MSS, III, 159.

G. Communicated by Mr Alex. Laing, of Newburgh-on-Tay.

H. 'Lord Beichan and Susie Pye,' Kinloch's *Ancient Scottish Ballads*, p. 260.

I. Communicated by Mr David Loudon, Morham, Haddington.

J. Dr Joseph Robertson's Note-Book, 'Adversaria,' p. 85.

K. Communicated by Mr David Loudon.

L. Miss Burne, *Shropshire Folk-Lore*, p. 547.

M. 'Young Bondwell,' Buchan's MSS, I, 18. J. H. Dixon, *Scottish Traditional Versions of Ancient Ballads*, p. 1.

N. 'Susan Py, or Young Bichen's Garland.' **a**. Falkirk, printed by T. Johnson, 1815. **b**. Stirling, M. Randall.

A, B, D, F, and the fragment G now appear for the first time in print, and the same is true of I, J, K, which are of less account. C a is here given according to the manuscript, without Jamieson's "collations." Of E and C b Jamieson [455] says: This ballad and that which succeeds it are given from copies taken from Mrs Brown's recitation,[*] collated with two other copies procured from Scotland; one in MS.; another, very good, one printed for the stalls; a third, in the possession of the late Reverend Jonathan Boucher, of Epsom, taken from recitation in the north of England; and a fourth, about one third as long as the others, which the editor picked off an old wall in Piccadilly. L, the only English copy, was derived from the singing of a London vagrant. It is, says Dixon, the common English broadsheet "turned into the dialect of Coc-

kaigne."[†] M was probably a broadside or stall copy, and is certainly of that quality, but preserves a very ancient traditional feature.

D and M, besides the name Linne, have in common a repetition of the song, a trait which we also find in one version of 'The Heir of Linne;'[‡] see Dixon's *Scottish Traditional Versions of Ancient Ballads*, p. 30, stanzas 2–6, Percy Society, vol. XVII.

'Lord Beichim,' Findlay's MSS, I, 1, from Jeanie Meldrum, Framedrum, Forfarshire, has

---

[*] Mr Macmath has ascertained that Mrs Brown was born in 1747. She learned most of her ballads before she was twelve years old, or before 1759. 1783, or a little earlier, is the date when these copies were taken down from her singing or recitation.

[†] *The Borderer's Table Book*, VII, 21. Dixon says, a little before, that the Stirling broadside of 'Lord Bateman' varies but slightly from the English printed by Hoggett, Durham, and Pitts, Catnach, and others, London. This is not true of the Stirling broadside of 'Young Bichen:' see N b. I did not notice, until too late, that I had not furnished myself with the broadside 'Lord Bateman,' and have been obliged to turn back the Cruikshank copy into ordinary orthography.

[‡] We have this repetition in two other ballads of the Skene MSS besides D; see p. 428 of this volume, sts 1–9; also in 'The Lord of Learne,' Percy MS., Hales and Furnivall, I, 192f, vv 269–304.

these verses, found in **G** and in Spanish and Italian ballads.

("She meets a shepherd and addresses him.")

> 'Whas are a' thae flocks o sheep?
>   And whas are a' thae droves o kye?
> And whas are a' thae statelie mansions,
>   That are in the way that I passd bye?'

> 'O these are a' Lord Beichim's sheep,
>   And these are a' Lord Beichim's kye,
> And these are a' Lord Beichim's castles,
>   That are in the way that ye passd bye.'

There are three or four stanzas more, but they resemble the English vulgar broadsides. There must have been a printed copy in circulation in Scotland which has not been recovered.

In Bell's *Ancient Poems, Ballads, and Songs of the Peasantry of England*, p. 68, it is remarked that **L**, "the only ancient form in which the ballad has existed in print," is one of the publications mentioned in one of Thackeray's catalogues of broadsides. The 'Bateman,' in Thackeray's list, is the title of an entirely different ballad, 'A Warning for Maidens, or Young Bateman,' reprinted from the Roxburghe collection by W. Chappell, III, 193.

"Young Beichan" is a favorite ballad, and most deservedly. There are beautiful repetitions of the story in the ballads of other nations, and it has secondary affinities with the extensive cycle of 'Hind Horn,' the parts of the principal actors in the one being inverted in the other.

The hero's name is mostly Beichan, with slight modifications like Bekie, **C**, Bicham, **A**, Brechin, **B**; in **L**, Bateman; in **M**, Bondwell. The heroine is Susan Pye in ten of the fourteen versions; Isbel in **C**; Essels, evidently a variety of Isbel, in **M**, which has peculiar relations with **C**; Sophia in **K**, **L**.

Beichan is London born in **A**, **D**, [**E**], **H**, **I**, **N**, English born in **B**; London city is his own, **A** 6, **B** 7, **F** 7, or he has a hall there, **I** 7, **N** 27f; half Northumberland belongs to him, **L**; he is lord of the towers of Line, **D** 9, **C** 5, **M** 5, which are in London, **D** 15f, but are transferred by reciters to the water of Tay, **M** 29, and to Glasgow, or the vicinity, **H** 20. **H**, though it starts

with calling him London born, speaks of him thereafter as a Scottish lord, 12, 18, 31.[*]

Beichan has an Englishman's desire strange countries for to see, **A**, **D**, [**E**], **I**, **L**, **N**. In **C**, **M** he goes abroad, Quentin Durward fashion, not to gratify his taste for travel, but to serve for meat and fee. **F** makes him go to the Holy Land, without specifying his motive, but we may fairly suppose it religious. **C** sends him no further than France, and **M** to an unnamed foreign land. He becomes the slave of a Moor or Turk, **A**, **B**, **D**, **H**, **I**, **L**, **N**, or a "Prudent," **F**, who treats him cruelly. They bore his shoulders and put in a "tree," and make him draw carts, like horse or ox, **A**, **B**, **D**, [**E**], **H**; draw plough and harrow, **F**, plough and cart, **N**; or tread the wine-press, **I**. This is because he is a staunch Christian, and would never bend a knee to [456] Mahound or Termagant, **E**, or onie of their stocks, **H**, or gods, **I**. They cast him into a dungeon, where he can neither hear nor see, and he is nigh perishing with hunger. This, also, is done in **H** 5, on account of his perseverance in Christianity; but in **C**, **M** he is imprisoned for falling in love with the king's daughter, or other lovely may.

From his prison Beichan makes his moan (not to a stock or a stone, but to the Queen of Heaven, **D** 4). His hounds go masterless, his hawks flee from tree to tree, his younger brother will heir his lands, and he shall never see home again, **E**, **H**. If a lady [earl] would borrow him, he would run at her stirrup [foot, bridle]; if a widow [auld wife] would borrow him, he would become her son; and if a maid would borrow him, he would wed her with a ring, **C**, **D**, **M**, **B**.[†] The only daughter of the, Moor, Turk, or king (of a 'Savoyen,' **B** 5, perhaps a corruption of Saracen), already interested in

---

[*] "An old woman who died in Errol, Carse of Gowrie, about twenty years ago, aged nearly ninety years, was wont invariably to sing this ballad: 'Young Lundie was in Brechin born.' Lundie is an estate now belonging to the Earl of Camperdoun, north from Dundee." A. Laing, note to **G**. That is to say, the old woman's world was Forfarshire.

Mr Logan had heard in Scotland a version in which the hero was called Lord Bangol: *A Pedlar's Pack*, p. 15.

[†] Cf. 'The Fair Flower of Northumberland,' **B** 2, **E** 2, pp 157f.

the captive, or immediately becoming so upon hearing Beichan's song, asks him if he has lands and means at home to maintain a lady that should set him free, and is told that he has ample estates, all of which he would bestow on such a lady, **A, B, E, F, H, L, N**. She steals the keys and delivers the prisoner, **C, D, E, I, J, L, M, N**; refreshes him with bread and wine [wine], **A, D, E, F, J** 4, **K** 3, **B, H, L**; supplies him with money, **C** 9, **H** 15, **M** 12, **N** 14, and with a ship, **F** 9, **H** 18, **L** 9; to which **C, M** add a horse and hounds [and hawks, **M**]. She bids him mind on the lady's love that freed him out of pine, **A** 8, **D** 12, [**E** 13], **M** 14, **N** 15, and in **E** 16 breaks a ring from her finger, and gives half of it to Beichan to assist his memory. There is a solemn vow, or at least a clear understanding, that they are to marry within seven years, **A** 9, **B** 9, **E** 12f, **H** 17, 19, **L** 8, **N** 11 [three years, **C** 11].

When seven years are at an end, or even before, Susan Pye feels a longing, or a misgiving, which impels her to go in search of the object of her affections, and she sets her foot on good shipboard, and turns her back on her own country, **A** 10, **B** 10, **D** 15, **L** 10, **N** 23.* **C** and **M** preserve here a highly important feature which is wanting in the other versions. Isbel, or Essels, is roused from her sleep by the Billy Blin, **C** 14, by a woman in green, a fairy, **M** 15, who makes known to her that that very day, or the morn, is Bekie's [Bondwell's] wedding day. She is directed to attire herself and her maids very splendidly, and go to the strand; a vessel will come sailing to her, and they are to go on board. The Billy Blin will row her over the sea, **C** 19; she will stroke the ship with a wand, and take God to be her pilot, **M** 19. Thus, by miraculous intervention, she arrives at the nick of time.

Beichan's fickleness is not accounted for in most of the versions. He soon forgot his deliverer and courted another, he was young, and thought not upon Susan Pye, say **H, N**. **C**, on the contrary, tells us that Beichan had not been a twelvemonth in his own country, when he was forced to marry a duke's daughter or lose all his land. **E** and **K** intimate that he acts under

constraint; the wedding has lasted three and thirty days, and he will not bed with his bride for love of one beyond the sea, **E** 21, **K** 1.[†]

On landing, Susan Pye falls in with a shepherd feeding his flock, **E, K** [a boy watering his steeds, **M**]. She asks, Whose are these sheep, these kye, these castles? and is told they are Lord Beichan's, **G**. She asks the news, and is informed that there is a wedding in yonder hall that has lasted thirty days and three, **E, K**, or that there is to be a wedding on the morn, **M**; it seems to be a matter generally known, **N**. In other versions she comes directly to Young Beichan's hall, and is first informed by the porter, **A, B, F, H, L**, or the fact is confirmed by the porter, **E, M, N**; she hears the music within, and divines, **C**. She bribes the porter to bid the bridegroom come and speak to her, **A, B, C, D,** [45] **J, N**; send her down bread and wine, and not forget the lady who brought him out of prison, **B, F, H, J, K, L**. In **E** 26 she sends up her half ring to the bridegroom [a ring in **N** 40, but not till Beichan has declined to come down].

The porter falls on his knee and informs his master that the fairest and richest lady that eyes ever saw is at the gate [ladies, **C, M**]. The bride, or the bride's mother more commonly, reproves the porter for his graceless speech; he might have excepted the bride, or her mother, or both: "Gin she be braw without, we's be as braw within." But the porter is compelled by truth to persist in his allegation; fair as they may be, they were never to compare with yon lady, **B, D, E, H, M**. Beichan takes the table with his foot and makes the cups and cans to flee, **B** 18, **D** 23, **F** 28, **G** 3, **H** 42, **J** 5, **N** 42;[‡] he exclaims that it can be none but Susie Pye, **A, B, D, G, H, I** [Burd Isbel, **C**], and clears the stair, fifteen steps, thirty steps, in three bounds, **A** 19, **D** 24, **N** 43. His old love reproaches him for his forgetfulness, **A, C, D, M, N**;[§] she asks back her faith and troth, **B** 21. Beichan bids the forenoon bride's mother take back her daughter: he will double her dowry, **A** 22, **D** 27, **E** 39; she came on horseback, she shall go back in chari-

---

* She does not get away without exciting the solicitude or wrath of her father, **F, M, J, N**, and in the first two has to use artifice.

† A point borrowed, it well may be, from 'Hind Horn,' **E** 5f, **A** 10.
‡ So Torello's wife upsets the table, in Boccaccio's story: see p. 270. One of her Slavic kinswomen jumps over four tables and lights on a fifth.

ots, coaches, three, **B** 22, **D** 27[*] [**H** 49, in char-
iot free]. He marries Susie Pye, having her
baptized by the name of Lady Jean, **A, B, D,**
[**E**], **F, I, J.**[†]

This story of Beichan, or Bekie, agrees in
the general outline, and also in some details,
with a well-known legend about Gilbert Beket,
father of St Thomas. The earlier and more
authentic biographies lack this particular bit of
romance, but the legend nevertheless goes back
to a date not much later than a century after
the death of the saint, being found in a poetical
narrative preserved in a manuscript of about
1300.[‡]

We learn from this legend that Gilbert
Beket, in his youth, assumed the cross and went
to the Holy Land, accompanied only by one
Richard, his servant. They "did their pilgrim-
age" in holy places, and at last, with other
Christians, were made captive by the Saracens
and put in strong prison. They suffered great
hardship and ignominy in the service of the
Saracen prince Admiraud. But Gilbert found
more grace than the rest; he was promoted to
serve the prince at meat (in his chains), and
the prince often would ask him about England
and the English faith. Admiraud's only daugh-
ter fell in love with Gilbert, and when she saw
her time, in turn asked him the like questions.
Gilbert told her that he was born in London;
told her of the belief of Christians, and of the
endless bliss that should be their meed. The
58] maid asked him if he was ready to die for his

Lord's love, and Gilbert declared that he would,
joyfully. When the maid saw that he was so
steadfast, she stood long in thought, and then
said, I will quit all for love of thee, and become
Christian, if thou wilt marry me. Gilbert feared
that this might be a wile; he replied that he was
at her disposition, but he must bethink himself.
She went on loving him, the longer the more.
After this Gilbert and the rest broke prison and
made their way to the Christians. The prince's
daughter, reduced to desperation by love and
grief, left her heritage and her kin, sparing for
no sorrow, peril, or contempt that might come
to her, not knowing whither to go or whether
he would marry her when found, and went in
quest of Gilbert. She asked the way to England,
and when she had come there had no word but
London to assist her further. She roamed
through the streets, followed by a noisy and
jeering crowd of wild boys and what not, until
one day by chance she stopped by the house in
which Gilbert lived. The man Richard, hearing
a tumult, came out to see what was the matter,
recognized the princess, and ran to tell his mas-
ter.[§] Gilbert bade Richard take the lady to the
house of a respectable woman near by, and pres-

---

§ In C 34, M 49, she is recognized by one of the
hounds which she had given him. So Bos, seigneur de
Bénac, who breaks a ring with his wife, goes to the East,
and is prisoner among the Saracens seven years, on com-
ing back is recognized only by his greyhound: *Magasin
Pittoresque*, VI, 56b. It is scarcely necessary to scent the
Odyssey here.

* Ridiculously changed in **J** 6, **K** 6, **L** 20, to a coach
and three, reminding us of that master-stroke in Thack-
eray's ballad of 'Little Billee,' "a captain of a seventy-
three." 'Little Billee,' by the way, is really like an old bal-
lad, fallen on evil days and evil tongues; whereas the seri-
ous imitations of traditional ballads are not the least like,
and yet, in their way, are often not less ludicrous.

† In **M**, to make everything pleasant, Bondwell offers
the bride five hundred pounds to marry his cousin John.
She says, Keep your money; John was my first love. So
Bondwell is married at early morn, and John in the after-
noon.

‡ Harleian MS. 2277, from which the life of Beket, in
long couplets, was printed by Mr W. H. Black for the
Percy Society, in 1845. The story of Gilbert Beket is con-
tained in the first 150vv. The style of this composition
entirely resembles that of Robert of Gloucester, and por-
tions of the life of Beket are identical with the *Chronicle*;
whence Mr Black plausibly argues that both are by the
same hand. The account of Beket's parentage is interpo-
lated into Edward Grim's *Life*, in Cotton MS. Vitellius,
C, xii, from which it is printed by Robertson, *Materials
for the History of Thomas Becket*, II, 453ff. It is found in
Bromton's *Chronicle*, Twysden, Scriptores X, columns
1052–55, and in the *First Quadrilogus*, Paris, 1495, from
which it is reprinted by Migne, *Patrologiæ Cursus Compl-
etus*, CXC, cols 346ff. The tale has been accepted by
many writers who would have been better historians for a
little reading of romances. Augustin Thierry sees in Tho-
mas Beket a Saxon contending in high place, for the
interests and with the natural hatred of his race, against
Norman Henry, just as he finds in the yeoman Robin
Hood a leader of Saxon serfs engaged in irregular war
with Norman Richard. But both of St Thomas's parents
were Norman; the father of Rotten, the mother of Caen.
The legend was introduced by Lawrence Wade, following
John of Exeter, into a metrical life of Beket of about the
year 1500: see the poem in *Englische Studien*, III, 417,
edited by Horstmann.

ently went to see her. She swooned when she saw him. Gilbert was nothing if not discreet: he "held him still," as if he had nothing in mind. But there was a conference of six bishops just then at St. Paul's, and he went and told them his story and asked advice. One of the six prophetically saw a divine indication that the two were meant to be married, and all finally recommended this if the lady would become Christian. Brought before the bishops, she said, Most gladly, if he will espouse me; else I had not left my kin. She was baptized[*] with great ceremony, and the marriage followed.

The very day after the wedding Gilbert was seized with such an overmastering desire to go back to the Holy Land that he wist not what to do. But his wife was thoroughly converted, and after a struggle with herself she consented, on condition that Beket should leave with her the man Richard, who knew her language. Gilbert was gone three years and a half, and when he came back Thomas was a fine boy.

§   Richard, the proud porter of the ballads, is perhaps most like himself in **M** 32 ff.
*   Neither her old name nor her Christian name is told us in this legend. Gilbert Beket's wife was Matilda, according to most authorities, but Roësa according to one: see Robertson, as above, IV, 81; Migne, cols 278f. Fox has made Roësa into Rose, *Acts and Monuments*, I, 267, ed. 1641.
    Gilbert and Rose (but Roësa is not Rose) recall to Hippeau, *Vie de St Thomas par Garnier de Pont Sainte Maxence*, p. xxiii, Elie de Saint Gille and Rosamonde, whose adventures have thus much resemblance with those of Beket and of Bekie. Elie de Saint Gille, after performing astounding feats of valor in fight with a horde of Saracens who have made a descent on Brittany, is carried off to their land. The amiral Macabré requires Elie to adore Mahomet; Elie refuses in the most insolent terms, and is condemned to the gallows. He effects his escape, and finds himself before Macabré's castle. Here, in another fight, he is desperately wounded, but is restored by the skill of Rosamonde, the amiral's daughter, who is Christian at heart, and loves the Frank. To save her from being forced to marry the king of Bagdad, Elie fights as her champion. In the end she is baptized, as a preparation for her union with Elie, but he, having been present at the ceremony, is adjudged by the archbishop to be gossip to her, and Elie and Rosamonde are otherwise disposed of. So the French romance, but in the Norse, which, as Kölbing maintains, is likely to preserve the original story here, there is no such splitting of cumin, and hero and heroine are united.

That our ballad has been *affected* by the legend of Gilbert Beket is altogether likely. The name Bekie is very close to Beket, and several versions, **A, D, H, I, N**, set out rather formally with the announcement that Bekie was London born, like the Latin biographies and the versified one of Garnier de Pont Sainte Maxence. Our ballad, also, in some versions, has the Moor's daughter baptized, a point which of course could not fail in the legend. More important still is it that the hero of the English ballad goes home and forgets the woman he has left in a foreign land, instead of going away from home and forgetting the love he has left there. But the ballad, for all that, is not derived from the legend. Stories and ballads of the general cast of 'Young Beichan' are extremely frequent.[†] The legend lacks some of the main [45 points of these stories, and the ballad, in one version or another, has them, as will be seen by referring to what has been said under 'Hind Horn,' pp 267ff. Bekie and Beket go to the East, like Henry and Reinfrit of Brunswick, the Noble Moringer,[‡] the good Gerhard, Messer Torello, the Sire de Créqui, Alexander of Metz, and others. Like the larger part of these, they are made prisoners by the Saracens. He will not bow the knee to Mahound; neither will the Sire de Créqui, though he die for it.[§] Beichan is made to draw cart, plough, harrow, like a beast. So Henry of Brunswick in a Swedish and a Danish ballad,[**] and Alexander von Metz, or the Graf von Rom, in his most beautiful and

†   There is one in the *Gesta Romanorum*, cap. 5, Österley, p. 278, of about the same age as the Beket legend. It is not particularly important. A young man is captured by a pirate, and his father will not send his ransom. The pirate's daughter often visits the captive, who appeals to her to exert herself for his liberation. She promises to effect his freedom if he will marry her. This he agrees to. She releases him from his chains without her father's knowledge, and flies with him to his native land.
‡   For a late German ballad on the Moringer story ('von dem Markgrafen Backenweil') see Bolte, *Zeitschrift des Vereins für Volkskunde*, III, 65–7, and for notes of dramas upon the theme, pp. 62–4. I do not observe that I have anywhere referred to the admirably comprehensive treatment of the subject by von Tettau, *Ueber einige bis jetzt unbekannte Erfurter Drucke des 15. Jahrhunderts, Ritter Morgeners Wallfahrt*, pp. 75–123. The book did not come into my hands till two years after my preface was written.

touching story.[*] Henry of Brunswick is set free by a "heathen" lady in the Danish ballad. In one version of Beichan, **E**, the lady on parting with her love breaks her ring and gives him one half, as Henry, or his wife, Reinfrit, Gerhard, Créqui, and others do. At this point in the story the woman pursues the man, and parts are inverted. Susan Pye is warned that Beichan is to be married the next day, in **C** by a Billy-Blin, in **M** by a woman in green, or fairy, and is conveyed to Beichan's castle or hall with miraculous despatch, just as Henry and others are warned, and are transported to their homes by devil, angel, or necromancer. In **E** and **N** the old love is identified by a half ring or ring, as in so many of the stories of the class of Henry the Lion.

Norse, Spanish, and Italian ballads preserve a story essentially the same as that of 'Young Beichan.'

Scandinavian.

Danish. 'Stolt Ellensborg,' Grundtvig, IV, 238, No 218, nine versions, **A–G**, from manuscripts of the sixteenth and seventeenth centuries, **H**, **I**, from recent tradition. 'Ellen henter sin Fæstemand,' Kristensen, *Jyske Folkeminder*, X, 125, No 34, **A**, **B**. **B** is previously printed (with alterations) in Levninger, 'Jomfrue Ellensborg,' I, 66, No 12, *Danske Viser*, III, 268, No 213; I, 'Stalt Ellen henter sin Fæstemand' is in Kristensen, I, 89, No 36. Of the older texts,

A, **B**, **C** are absolutely pure and true to tradition, **D–G** retouched or made over.

Icelandic, of the seventeenth century, Grundtvig, as above, p. 259, **M**.

Swedish, from Cavallius and Stephens' collection, Grundtvig, p. 255, **K**.

Färöe, taken down in 1827, Grundtvig, p. 256; printed in Hammershaimb's *Færøsk Anthologi*, p. 260, No 33, 'Harra Pætur og Elinborg' (four copies), **L**.

Norwegian, 'Herre Per i Riki,' Landstad, p. 596, No 76, **N**.

The variations of these twelve versions are insignificant. The names Herr Peder den Rige and Ellensborg [Ellen] are found in nearly all. It comes into Sir Peter's mind that he ought to go to Jerusalem to expiate his sins, and he asks his betrothed, Ellensborg, how long she will wait for him. She will wait eight years, and marry no other, though the king should woo her [seven, **L**; nine, **M**, "If I do not come then, break the engagement;" eight, and not more, **N**]. The time passes and Peter does not come back. Ellensborg goes to the strand. Traders come steering in, and she is asked to buy of their ware,—sendal, linen, and silk green as leek. She cares not for these things; have they not seen her sister's son [brother], for whom she is grieving to death? They know nothing of her sister's son, but well they know Sir Peter the rich: he has betrothed a lady in the Øster-king's [460] realm;[†] a heathen woman, "and you never came into his mind," **E** 13; he is to be married to-morrow, **K** 6. A wee swain tells her, **M** 14, 16, that he sits in Austurríki drinking the ale of forgetfulness, and will never come home; he shall not drink long, says she. Ellensborg asks her brother to undertake a voyage for her; he will go with her if she will wait till summer; rather than wait till summer she will go alone, **A**, **D**, **G**. She asks fraternal advice about going in search of her lover, **A**, **E**, the advice of her uncles, **I**; asks the loan of a ship, **B**, **C**, **F**, **H**, **N**. She is told that such a thing would be a shame; she had better

---

§ Nor Guarinos in the Spanish ballad, Duran, No 402, I, 265; Wolf and Hofmann, *Primavera*, II, 321. Guarinos is very cruelly treated, but it is his horse, not he, that has to draw carts. For the Sire de Créqui see also Dinaux, *Trouvères*, III, 161 ff (Köhler).

** And in 'Der Herr von Falkenstein,' a variety of the story, Meier, *Deutsche Sagen aus Schwaben*, p. 319, No 362. A Christian undergoes the same hardship in Schöppner, *Sagenbuch*, III, 127, No 1076. For other cases of the wonderful deliverance of captive knights, not previously mentioned by me, see Hocker, in Wolf's *Zeitschrift für deutsche Mythologie*, I, 306.

* A meisterlied of Alexander von Metz, of the second half of the fifteenth century, Körner, *Historische Volkslieder*, p. 49; the ballad 'Der Graf von Rom,' or 'Der Graf im Pfluge,' Uhland, p. 784, No 299, printed as early as 1493; *De Historie van Florentina*, Huysvrouwe van Alexander van Mets, 1621, van den Bergh, *De nederlandsche Volksromans*, p. 52. And see Goedeke, *Deutsche Dichtung im Mittelalter*, pp 569, 574; Uhland, *Schriften zur Geschichte der Dichtung*, IV, 297–309; *Danske Viser*, V, 67.

† Øster-kongens rige, Østerige, Østerland, Austrríki, understood by Grundtvig as Garðaríki, the Scandinavian-Russian kingdom of the tenth and eleventh centuries. Austrríki is used vaguely, but especially of the east of Europe, Russia, Austria, sometimes including Turkey (Vigfusson).

take another lover; the object is not worth the trouble; the voyage is bad for a man and worse for a woman. Her maids give her advice that is more to her mind, **E**, but are as prudent as the rest in the later **I**. She attires herself like a knight, clips her maids' hair, **B, H, I, L, M**, and puts them into men's clothes, **D, L**; sets herself to steer and the maids to row, **A–G, L**.[*]

The voyage is less than two months, **B, C, E**; less than three months, **I**; quite three months, **L**. It is the first day of the bridal when she lands, **B** 22, **E** 24, **N** 14; in **B** Ellensborg learns this from a boy who is walking on the sand. Sword at side, she enters the hall where Peter is drinking his bridal. Peter, can in hand, rises and says, Bless your eyes, my sister's son; welcome to this strange land. In **B** he asks, How are my father and mother? and she tells him that his father lies dead on his bier, his mother in sick-bed. In **L**, waiting for no greeting, she says, Well you sit at the board with your wife! Are all lords wont thus to keep their faith? The bride's mother, **D, G**, the heathen bride, **E**, an unnamed person, probably the bride, **A, B, F, N**, says, That is not your sister's son, but much more like a woman; her hair is like spun gold, and braided up under a silk cap.

A tells us, and so **F, G**, that it was two months before Ellensborg could speak to Peter privately. Then, on a Yule day, when he was going to church, she said, It does not occur to you that you gave me your troth. Sir Peter stood as if women had shorn his hair, and recollected all as if it had been yesterday. In **B–E, H, I, L, M, N**, this incident has, perhaps, dropped out. In these immediately, as in **A, F, G**, after this interview, Sir Peter, recalled to his senses or to his fidelity, conceives the purpose of flying with Ellensborg. Good people, he says, knights and swains, ladies and maids, follow my bride to bed, while I take my sister's son over the meads, through the wood, **B–E, H, I, N**. In **A, F**, Sir Peter asks the bride how long she will bide while he takes his nephew across the kingdom;

in **G** begs the boon that, since his sister's son is going, he may ride with him, just accompany him to the strand and take leave of him; in **L, M**, hopes she will not be angry if he convoys his nephew three days on his way. (It is at this point in **C, H, I, L**, that the bride says it is no sister's son, but a woman.) The bride remarks that there are knights and swains enow to escort his sister's son, and that he might more fitly stay where he is, but Sir Peter persists that he will see his nephew off in person.

Sir Peter and Ellensborg go aboard the ship, he crying, You will see me no more! When they are at sea Ellensborg lets out her hair, **A, B, C, H**; she wishes that the abandoned bride may now feel the grief which she herself had borne for years. The proceeding is less covert in **I, L, M** than in the other versions.

As Ellensborg and Peter are making for the ship in **D** 30, 31 (and **G** 36, 37, borrowed from **D**), she says, Tell me, Sir Peter, why would you deceive me so? Sir Peter answers that he never meant to deceive her; it was the lady of Øster-land that did it; she had changed his mind. A magical change is meant. This agrees with what [46] is said in **A** 24, 25 (also **F, G**), that when Ellensborg got Peter alone to herself, and said, You do not remember that you plighted your troth to me, everything came back to him as if it had happened yesterday. And again in the Färöe copy, **L** 49, Ellensborg, from the prow, cries to Ingibjörg on the strand, Farewell to thee with thy *elf-ways*, við títt elvargangi! I have taken to myself my true love that I lent thee so long; implying that Sir Peter had been detained by Circean arts, by a sleepy drench of óminnis öl, or ale of forgetfulness, Icelandic **M** 14, which, in the light of the other ballads, is to be understood literally, and not figuratively. The feature of a man being made, by magical or other means, to forget a first love who had done and suffered much for him, and being suddenly restored to consciousness and his original predilection, is of the commonest occurrence in traditional tales.[†]

Our English ballad affords no other positive trace of external interference with the hero's will than the far-fetched allegation in **C** that the choice before him was to accept a duke's daughter or forfeit his lands. The explanation

---

[*]   In Swedish **K**, as she pushes off from land, she exclaims:

    'Gud Fader i Himmelens rike
    Skall vara min styresman!'

Cf. **M** 28:

    And she's taen God her pilot to be.

of his inconstancy in **H, N**, that young men ever were fickle found, is vulgar, and also insufficient, for Beichan returns to his old love *per saltum*, like one from whose eyes scales have fallen and from whose back a weight has been taken, not tamely, like a facile youth that has swerved. **E** and **K**, as already said, distinctly recognize that Beichan was not acting with free mind, and, for myself, I have little doubt that, if we could go back far enough, we should find that he had all along been faithful at heart.

Spanish. A. 'El Conde Sol,' Duran, *Romancero*, I, 180, No 327, from tradition in Andalusia, by the editor; Wolf and Hofmann, *Primavera*, II, 48, No 135. In this most beautiful romance the County Sol, named general in great wars between Spain and Portugal, and leaving a young wife dissolved in tears, tells her that she is free to marry if he does not come back in six years. Six pass, and eight, and more than ten, yet the county does not return, nor does there come news of him. His wife implores and obtains leave of her father to go in search of her husband. She traverses France and Italy, land and sea, and is on the point of giving up hope, when one day she sees a herdsman pasturing cows. Whose are these cows? she asks. The County Sol's, is the answer. And whose these wheat-fields, these ewes, these gardens, and that palace? whose the horses I hear neigh? The County Sol's, is the answer in each case.[*] And who that lady that a man folds in his arms? The lady is betrothed to him and the county is to marry her. The countess changes her silken robe for the herdsman's sackcloth, and goes to ask an alms at the county's gate. Beyond all hope, the county comes out himself to bring it. "Whence comest thou, pilgrim?" he asks. She was born in Spain. "How didst thou make thy way hither?" She came to seek her husband,

footing the thorns by land, risking the perils of the sea; and when she found him he was about to marry, he had forgotten his faithful wife. "Pilgrim, thou art surely the devil, come to try me." "No devil," she said, "but thy wife indeed, and therefore come to seek thee." Upon this, without a moment's tarrying, the county ordered his horse, took up his wife, and made his best speed to his native castle. The bride he [462] would have taken remained unmarried, for those that put on others' robes are sure to be stripped naked.

B. 'Gerineldo,' taken down in Asturias by Amador de los Rios, *Jahrbuch für romanische u. englische Literatur*, III, 290, 1861, and the same year (Nigra) in *Revista Iberica*, I, 51; also in Pidal, *Asturian Romances*, p. 90f; and in Munthe, *Folkpoesi från Asturien*, No 2, second part, p. 112 b (Upsala Universitets Årsskrift); but imperfect: a version far inferior to **A**, and differing in no important respect as to the story.

Catalan. 'La boda interrumpida,' Milá, *Romancerillo Catalan*, p. 221, No 244, seven copies, **A–G**, none good. **A**, which is about one third Castilian, relates that war is declared between France and Portugal, and the son of Conde Burgos made general. The countess his wife does nothing but weep. The husband tells her to marry again if he does not come back in seven years. More than seven years are gone, and the lady's father asks why she does not marry. "How can I," she replies, "if the count is living? Give me your blessing, and let me go in search of him." She goes a hundred leagues on foot, in the disguise of a pilgrim. Arrived at a palace she sees pages pass, and asks them for whom a horse is intended. It is for Count Burgos's son, who marries that night. She asks to be directed to the young count, is told that she

---

[*] This passage leads the editors of *Primavera* to remark, II, 52, that 'El Conde Sol' shows distinct traits of 'Le Chat Botté.' Similar questions are asked in English G, the other Spanish versions, and the Italian, and in nearly all the Greek ballads referred to on p. 273f; always under the same circumstances, and to bring about the discovery which gives the turn to the story. The questions in 'Le Chat Botté' are introduced for an entirely different purpose, and cannot rationally suggest a borrowing on either side. The hasty note would certainly have been erased by the very distinguished editors upon a moment's consideration.

[†] See 'The Red Bull of Norroway,' Chambers, *Popular Rhymes of Scotland*, 1870, p. 99; 'Mestermø,' Asbjørnsen og Moe, No 46; 'Hass-Fru,' Cavallius och Stephens, No 14; Powell, *Icelandic Legends*, Second Series, p. 377; the Grimms, Nos 56, 113, 186, 193; *Pentamerone*, II, 7, III, 9; Gonzenbach, Nos 14, 54, 55, and Köhler's note; Hahn, *Griechische u. Albanesische Märchen*, No 54; Carleton, *Traits and Stories of the Irish Peasantry*, 10th ed., I, 23; Campbell, *West Highland Tales*, I, 25, No 2, and Köhler's notes in *Orient und Occident*, II, 103–114, etc., etc.

will find him in the hall, enters, and begs an alms, as coming from Italy and without a penny. The young man says, If you come from Italy, what is the news? Is Conde Bueso's wife living? The pilgrim desires some description of the lady. It seems that she wore a very costly petticoat on her wedding-day. The pilgrim takes off *her glove* and shows her ring; she also takes off and shows the expensive petticoat. There is great weeping in that palace, for first wives never can be forgotten. Don Bueso and the pilgrim clap hands and go home.

Italian: Piedmontese. A. 'Moran d'Inglulterra,' communicated to *Rivista Contemporanea*, XXXI, 3, 1862, by Nigra, who gives the variations of four other versions; 'Moran d' Inghilterra,' with a second version, in Nigra, No 42, p. 263. The daughter of the sultan is so handsome that they know not whom to give her to, but decide upon Moran of England. The first day of his marriage he did nothing but kiss her, the second he wished to leave her, and the third he went off to the war. "When shall you return?" asked his wife. "If not in seven years, marry." She waited seven years, but Moran did not come. His wife went all over England on horseback, and came upon a cowherd. "Whose cows are these?" she asked. They were Moran's. "Has Moran a wife?" This is the day when he is to marry, and if she makes haste she will be in time for the wedding. She spurs her horse, and arrives in season. They offer her to drink in a gold cup. She will drink from no cup that is not her own; she will not drink while another woman is there; she will not drink till she is mistress. Moran throws his arms round her neck, saying, Mistress you ever have been and still shall be.

B. 'Morando,' Ferraro, *Canti popolari monferrini*, p. 42, No 32, from Alessandria. Murando d'Inghilterra, of the king's household, fell in love with the princess, for which the king sent him off. The lady knocked at his door, and asked when he would come back. In seven years, was the answer, and if not she was to marry. The princess stole a hundred scudi from her father, frizzled her hair French fashion, bought a fashionable suit, and rode three days and nights without touching ground, eating, or drinking. She came upon a laundryman, and

asked who was in command there. Murando. She knocked at the door, and Murando asked, Have you come to our wedding? She would come to the dance. At the dance she was recognized by the servants. Murando asked, How came you here? "I rode three days and three nights without touching ground, eating, or drinking." This is my wife, said Murando; and the other lady he bade return to her father.

It is possible that this ballad may formerly have been known in France. Nothing is left and known that shows this conclusively, but there is an approach to the Norse form in a fragment which occurs in several widely separated localities. A lover goes off in November, promising his love to return in December, but does not. A messenger comes to bid the lady, in his name, seek another lover, for he has another love. "Is she fairer than I, or more powerful?" She is not [463] fairer, but more powerful: she makes rosemary flower on the edge of her sleeve, changes the sea into wine and fish into flesh. Bujeaud, I, 203. Another version of the French ballad ('Tout au milieu de Paris') is in Meyrac, *Traditions, etc., des Ardennes*, p. 238. In 'La Femme Abandonnée,' Puymaigre, I, 72, the lover is married to a Fleming:

Elle fait venir le soleil
A minuit dans sa chambre,
Elle fait bouiller la marmite
Sans feu et sans rente.

In a Canadian version, 'Entre Paris et Saint-Denis,' Gagnon, p. 303, the deserted woman is a king's daughter, and the new love,

Ell' fait neiger, ell' fait grêler,
Ell' fait le vent qui vente.
Ell' fait reluire le soleil
A minuit dans sa chambre.
Ell' fait pousser le romarin
Sur le bord de la manche.

Puymaigre notes that there is a version very near to the Canadian in the sixth volume of *Poésies populaires de la France*, cinquième recueil, Ardennes, No 2; printed in *Mélusine*, II, col. 44. Another copy in *Mélusine*, I, col. 123.[*]

A broadside ballad, 'The Turkish Lady,' 'The Turkish Lady and the English Slave,' printed in Logan's *Pedlar's Pack*, p. 16, Christie, I, 247, from singing, and preserved also in the Kinloch MSS, V, 53, I, 263, from Elizabeth Beattie's recitation, simply relates how a Turkish pirate's daughter fell in love with an Englishman, her slave, offered to release him if he would turn Turk, but chose the better part of flying with him to Bristol, and becoming herself a Christian brave.

Sir William Stanley, passing through Constantinople, is condemned to die for his religion. A lady, walking under the prison walls, hears his lament, and begs his life of the Turk. She would make him her husband, and bring him to adore Mahomet. She offers to set the prisoner free if he will marry her, but he has a wife and children on English ground. The lady is sorry, but generously gives Stanley five hundred pounds to carry him to his own country.

* Puymaigre finds also some resemblance in his 'Petite Rosalie,' I, 74. See his note.

Sir William Stanley's *Garland*, Halliwell's *Palatine Anthology*, pp 277f.

Two Magyars have been shut up in a dungeon by the sultan, and have not seen sun, moon, or stars for seven years. The sultan's daughter hears their moan, and offers to free them if they will take her to Hungary. This they promise to do. She gets the keys, takes money, opens the doors, and the three make off. They are followed; one of the Magyars kills all the pursuers but one, who is left to carry back the news. It is now proposed that there shall be a duel to determine who shall have the lady. She begs them rather to cut off her head than to fight about her. Szilágyi Niklas says he has a love at home, and leaves the sultan's daughter to his comrade, Hagymási László. Aigner, *Ungarische Volksdichtungen*, p. 93: see p. 145 of this volume.

C b is translated by Loève-Veimars, p. 330; E by Cesare Cantù, *Documenti alla Storia Universale*, Torino, 1858, Tomo V°, Parte III^a, p. 796; E, as retouched by Allingham, by Knortz, *L. u. R. Alt-Englands*, p. 18.

A

Jamieson-Brown MS., p. 13.

1 In London city was Bicham born,
    He longd strange countries for to see,
  But he was taen by a savage Moor,
    Who handld him right cruely.

2 For thro his shoulder he put a bore,
    An thro the bore has pitten a tree,
  An he's gard him draw the carts o wine,
    Where horse and oxen had wont to be.

3 He's casten [him] in a dungeon deep,
    Where he coud neither hear nor see;
  He's shut him up in a prison strong,
    An he's handld him right cruely.

4 O this Moor he had but ae daughter,
    I wot her name was Shusy Pye;
  She's doen her to the prison-house,
    And she's calld Young Bicham one word by.

5 'O hae ye ony lands or rents,   [464]
    Or citys in your ain country,
  Coud free you out of prison strong,
    An coud mantain a lady free?'

6 'O London city is my own,
    An other citys twa or three,
  Coud loose me out o prison strong,
    An coud mantain a lady free.'

7 O she has bribed her father's men
    Wi meikle goud and white money,
  She's gotten the key o the prison doors,
    An she has set Young Bicham free.

8 She's gi'n him a loaf o good white bread,
    But an a flask o Spanish wine,
  An she bad him mind on the ladie's love
    That sae kindly freed him out o pine.

9 'Go set your foot on good ship-board,
    An haste you back to your ain country,
An before that seven years has an end,
    Come back again, love, and marry me.'

10 It was long or seven years had an end
    She longd fu sair her love to see;
She's set her foot on good ship-board,
    An turnd her back on her ain country.

11 She's saild up, so has she doun,
    Till she came to the other side
She's landed at Young Bicham's gates,
    An I hop this day she sal be his bride.

12 'Is this Young Bicham's gates?' says she,
    'Or is that noble prince within?'
'He's up the stairs wi his bonny bride,
    An monny a lord and lady wi him.'

13 'O has he taen a bonny bride,
    An has he clean forgotten me!'
An sighing said that gay lady,
    I wish I were in my ain country!

14 But she's pitten her han in her pocket,
    An gin the porter guineas three;
Says, Take ye that, ye proud porter,
    An bid the bridegroom speak to me.

15 O whan the porter came up the stair,
    He's fa'n low down upon his knee:
Won up, won up, ye proud porter,
    An what makes a' this courtesy

16 'O I've been porter at your gates
    This mair nor seven years an three,
But there is a lady at them now
    The like of whom I never did see.

17 'For on every finger she has a ring,
    An on the mid-finger she has three,
An there's as meikle goud aboon her brow
    As woud buy an earldome o lan to me.'

18 Then up it started Young Bicham,
    An sware so loud by Our Lady,
'It can be nane but Shusy Pye,
    That has come oer the sea to me.'

19 O quickly ran he down the stair,
    O fifteen steps he has made but three
He's tane his bonny love in his arms,
    An a wot he kissd her tenderly.

20 'O hae you tane a bonny bride?
    An hae you quite forsaken me?
An hae ye quite forgotten her
    That gae you life an liberty?'

21 She's lookit oer her left shoulder
    To hide the tears stood in her ee;
'Now fare thee well, Young Bicham,' she says,
    'I'll strive to think nae mair on thee.'

22 'Take back your daughter, madam,' he says,
    'An a double dowry I'll gi her wi;
For I maun marry my first true love,
    That's done and suffered so much for me.'

23 He's take his bonny love by the han,
    And led her to yon fountain stane;
He's changd her name frae Shusy Pye,
    An he's cald her his bonny love, Lady Jane.

B

[465.

Glenriddell MSS, XI, 80.

1 In England was Young Brechin born,
    Of parents of a high degree;
The selld him to the savage Moor,
    Where they abused him maist cruellie.

2 Thro evry shoulder they bord a bore,
    And thro evry bore they pat a tree;
They made him draw the carts o wine,
    Which horse and owsn were wont to drie.

3 The pat him into prison strong,
    Where he could neither hear nor see;
They pat him in a dark dungeon,
    Where he was sick and like to die.

4 'Is there neer an auld wife in this town
    That'll borrow me to be her son?
Is there neer a young maid in this town
    Will take me for her chiefest one?'

5 A Savoyen has an only daughter,
   I wat she's called Young Brichen by;
   'O sleepst thou, wakest thou, Brichen?' she says,
   'Or who is 't that does on me cry?

6 'O hast thou any house or lands,
   Or hast thou any castles free,
   That thou wadst gi to a lady fair
   That out o prison wad bring thee?'

7 'O lady, Lundin it is mine,
   And other castles twa or three;
   These I wad gie to a lady fair
   That out of prison wad set me free.'

8 She's taen him by the milk-white hand,
   And led him to a towr sae hie,
   She's made him drink the wine sae reid,
   And sung to him like a mavosie.

9 O these two luvers made a bond,
   For seven years, and that is lang,
   That he was to marry no other wife,
   And she's to marry no other man.

10 When seven years were past and gane,
   This young lady began to lang,
   And she's awa to Lundin gane,
   To see if Brechin's got safe to land.

11 When she came to Young Brechin's yett,
   She chappit gently at the gin;
   'Is this Young Brechin's yett?' she says,
   'Or is this lusty lord within?'
   'O yes, this is Lord Brechin's yett,
   And I wat this be his bridal een.'

12 She's put her hand in her pocket,
   And thrawin the porter guineas three;
   'Gang up the stair, young man,' she says,
   'And bid your master come down to me.

13 'Bid him bring a bite o his ae best bread,
   And a bottle o his ae best wine,
   And neer forget that lady fair
   That did him out o prison bring.'

14 The porter tripped up the stair,
   And fell low down upon his knee:
   'Rise up, rise up, ye proud porter,
   What mean you by this courtesie?'

15 'O I hae been porter at your yett
   This thirty years and a' but three;
   There stands the fairest lady thereat
   That ever my twa een did see.

16 'On evry finger she has a ring,
   On her mid-finger she has three;
   She's as much gold on her horse's neck
   As wad by a earldom o land to me.

17 'She bids you send o your ae best bread,
   And a bottle o your ae best wine,
   And neer forget the lady fair
   That out o prison did you bring.'

18 He's taen the table wi his foot,
   And made the cups and cans to flee:
   'I'll wager a' the lands I hae
   That Susan Pye's come oer the sea.'

*   *   *   *   *

19 Then up and spak the bride's mother:
   'And O an ill deid may ye die!
   If ye didna except the bonny bride,
   Ye might hae ay excepted me.'

20 'O ye are fair, and fair, madam,
   And ay the fairer may ye be!
   But the fairest day that eer ye saw,
   Ye were neer sae fair as yon lady.'

21 O when these lovers two did meet, [466]
   The tear it blinded baith their ee;
   'Gie me my faith and troth,' she says,
   'For now fain hame wad I be.'

22 'Tak hame your daughter, madam,' he says,
   'She's neer a bit the war o me;
   Except a kiss o her bonny lips,
   Of her body I am free;
   She came to me on a single horse,
   Now I'll send her hame in chariots three.'

23 He's taen her by the milk-white hand,
   And he's led her to a yard o stane;
   He's changed her name frae Susan Pye,
   And calld her lusty Lady Jane.

C

a. Jamieson-Brown MS., p. 11. **b.** Jamieson's *Popular Ballads*, II, 127.

Young Bek - ie was as brave a____ knight As ev - er____ sail'd the sea,

An' he's ta'en him to____ the____ court of France____ To____ serve for meat and fee.

Ritson-Tytler-Brown MS., pp. 38–47. Sung by Mrs Brown, Aberdeen.

1 Young Bekie was as brave a knight
   As ever saild the sea;
   An he's doen him to the court of France,
   To serve for meat and fee.

2 He had nae been i the court of France
   A twelvemonth nor sae long,
   Til he fell in love with the king's daughter,
   An was thrown in prison strong.

3 The king he had but ae daughter,
   Burd Isbel was her name;
   An she has to the prison-house gane,
   To hear the prisoner's mane.

4 'O gin a lady woud borrow me,
   At her stirrup-foot I woud rin;
   Or gin a widow wad borrow me,
   I woud swear to be her son.

5 'Or gin a virgin woud borrow me,
   I woud wed her wi a ring;
   I'd gi her ha's, I'd gie her bowers,
   The bonny towrs o Linne.'

6 O barefoot, barefoot gaed she but,
   An barefoot came she ben;
   It was no for want o hose an shoone,
   Nor time to put them on.

7 But a' for fear that her father dear
   Had heard her making din:
   She's stown the keys o the prison-house dor
   An latten the prisoner gang.

8 O whan she saw him, Young Bekie,
   Her heart was wondrous sair!
   For the mice but an the bold rottons
   Had eaten his yallow hair.

9 She's gien him a shaver for his beard,
   A comber till his hair,
   Five hunder pound in his pocket,
   To spen, an nae to spair.

10 She's gien him a steed was good in need,
   An a saddle o royal bone,
   A leash o hounds o ae litter,
   An Hector called one.

11 Atween this twa a vow was made,
   'T was made full solemnly,
   That or three years was come an gane,
   Well married they shoud be.

12 He had nae been in 's ain country
   A twelvemonth till an end,
   Till he's forcd to marry a duke's daughter,
   Or than lose a' his land.

13 'Ohon, alas!' says Young Beckie,
   'I know not what to dee;
   For I canno win to Burd Isbel,
   And she kensnae to come to me.'

14 O it fell once upon a day
   Burd Isbel fell asleep,
   An up it starts the Belly Blin,
   An stood at her bed-feet.

15 'O waken, waken, Burd Isbel,
   How [can] you sleep so soun,
   Whan this is Bekie's wedding day,
   An the marriage gain on?

16 'Ye do ye to your mither's bowr,
   Think neither sin nor shame;
   An ye tak twa o your mither's marys,
   To keep ye frae thinking lang.

[462]

17 'Ye dress yoursel in the red scarlet,
　　An your marys in dainty green,
　　An ye pit girdles about your middles
　　Woud buy an earldome.

18 'O ye gang down by yon sea-side,
　　An down by yon sea-stran;
　　Sae bonny will the Hollans boats
　　Come rowin till your han.

19 'Ye set your milk-white foot abord,
　　Cry, Hail ye, Domine!
　　An I shal be the steerer o 't,
　　To row you oer the sea.'

20 She's tane her till her mither's bowr,
　　Thought neither sin nor shame,
　　An she took twa o her mither's marys,
　　To keep her frae thinking lang.

21 She dressd hersel i the red scarlet,
　　Her marys i dainty green,
　　And they pat girdles about their middles
　　Woud buy an earldome.

22 An they gid down by yon sea-side,
　　An down by yon sea-stran;
　　Sae bonny did the Hollan boats
　　Come rowin to their han.

23 She set her milk-white foot on board,
　　Cried, Hail ye, Domine!
　　An the Belly Blin was the steerer o 't,
　　To row her oer the sea.

24 Whan she came to Young Bekie's gate,
　　She heard the music play;
　　Sae well she kent frae a' she heard,
　　It was his wedding day.

25 She's pitten her han in her pocket,
　　Gin the porter guineas three;
　　'Hae, tak ye that, ye proud porter,
　　Bid the bride-groom speake to me.'

26 O whan that he cam up the stair,
　　He fell low down on his knee:
　　He haild the king, an he haild the queen,
　　An he haild him, Young Bekie.

27 'O I've been porter at your gates
　　This thirty years an three;
　　But there's three ladies at them now,
　　Their like I never did see.

28 'There's ane o them dressd in red scarlet,
　　And twa in dainty green,
　　An they hae girdles about their middles
　　Woud buy an earldome.'

29 Then out it spake the bierly bride,
　　Was a' goud to the chin;
　　'Gin she be braw without,' she says,
　　'We 's be as braw within.'

30 Then up it starts him, Young Bekie,
　　An the tears was in his ee:
　　'I'll lay my life it's Burd Isbel,
　　Come oer the sea to me.'

31 O quickly ran he down the stair,
　　An whan he saw 't was shee,
　　He kindly took her in his arms,
　　And kissd her tenderly.

32 'O hae ye forgotten, Young Bekie,
　　The vow ye made to me,
　　Whan I took you out o the prison strong,
　　Whan ye was condemnd to die?

33 'I gae you a steed was good in need,
　　An a saddle o royal bone,
　　A leash o hounds o ae litter,
　　An Hector called one.'

34 It was well kent what the lady said,
　　That it wasnae a lee,
　　For at ilka word the lady spake,
　　The hound fell at her knee.

35 'Tak hame, tak hame your daughter dear,
　　A blessing gae her wi,
　　For I maun marry my Burd Isbel,
　　That's come oer the sea to me.'

36 'Is this the custom o your house,
　　Or the fashion o your lan,
　　To marry a maid in a May mornin,
　　An send her back at even?'

D

Skene MSS, p. 70. North of Scotland, 1802–3.

1 YOUNG BEACHEN was born in fair London,
  And foreign lands he langed to see;
  He was taen by the savage Moor,
  An the used him most cruellie.

2 Through his showlder they pat a bore,
  And through the bore the pat a tree;
  They made him trail their ousen carts,
  And they used him most cruellie.

3 The savage Moor had ae daughter,
  I wat her name was Susan Pay;
  An she is to the prison house,
  To hear the prisoner's moan.

4 He made na his moan to a stock,
  He made na it to a stone,
  But it was to the Queen of Heaven
  That he made his moan.

5 'Gin a lady wad borrow me,
  I at her foot wad run;
  An a widdow wad borrow me,
  I wad become her son.

6 'But an a maid wad borrow me,
  I wad wed her wi a ring;
  I wad make her lady of haas and bowers,
  An of the high towers of Line.'

7 'Sing oer yer sang, Young Beachen,' she says,
  'Sing oer yer sang to me;'
  'I never sang that sang, lady,
  But I wad sing to thee.

8 'Gin a lady wad borrow me,
  I at her foot wad run;
  An a widdow wad borrow me,
  I wad become her son.

9 'But an a maid wad borrow me,
  I wad wed her wi a ring;
  I wad make her lady of haas and bowers,
  An of the high towers of Line.'

10 Saftly, [saftly] gaed she but,
  An saftly gaed she ben,
  It was na for want of hose nor shoon,
  Nor time to pet them on.

11 .   .   .   .   .
  .   .   .   .   .
  An she has staen the keys of the prison,
  An latten Young Beachen gang.

12 She gae him a leaf of her white bread,
  An a bottle of her wine,
  She bad him mind on the lady's love
  That freed him out of pine.

13 She gae him a steed was guid in need,
  A saddle of the bane,
  Five hundred pown in his pocket,
  Bad him gae speeding hame.

14 An a leash of guid grayhounds,
  .   .   .   .   .
  .   .   .   .   .
  .   .   .   .   .

15 Whan seven lang years were come and gane,
  Shusie Pay thought lang,
  An she is on to fair London,
  As fast as she could gang.

16 Whan she cam to Young Beachen's gate,
  .   .   .   .   .
  'Is Young Beachen at hame,
  Or is he in this countrie?'

17 'He is at hame, is hear,' they said,
  .   .   .   .   .
  An sighan says her Susie Pay,
  Has he quite forgotten me?

18 On every finger she had a ring,
  On the middle finger three;
  She gae the porter ane of them:
  'Get a word o your lord to me.'

19 He gaed up the stair,
  Fell low down on his knee:
  'Win up, my proud porter,
  What is your will wi me?'

20 'I hae been porter at yer gate
  This thirty year and three
  The fairst lady is at yer gate
  Mine eyes did ever see.'

21 Out spak the bride's mither,
   An a haghty woman was she:
   'If ye had na eccepted the bonny bride,
   Ye might well ha eccepted me.'

[469]

22 'No disparagement to you, madam,
   Nor none unto her Grace;
   The sole of your lady's foot
   Is fairer than her face.'

23 He's gaen the table wi his foot,
   And couped it wi his knee:
   'I wad my head and a' my land
   'T is Susie Pay, come oer the sea.'

24 The stair was thirty steps,
   I wat he made them three
   He took her in his arms twa:
   'Susie Pay, ye'r welcome to me.'

25 'Gie me a shive of your white bread,
   An a bottle of your wine;
   Dinna ye mind on the lady's love
   That freed ye out of pine?'

26 He took her . . . . .
   Down to yon garden green,
   An changed her name fra Susie Pay,
   An called her bonny Lady Jean.

27 'Yer daughter came here on high horse-back,
   She sal gae hame in coaches three,
   An I sall double her tocher our,
   She's nane the war o me.'

28 'It's na the fashion o our countrie,
   Nor yet o yer nane,
   To wed a maid in the morning,
   An send her hame at een.'

29 'It's na the fashion o my countrie,
   Nor is it of my nane,
   But I man mind on the lady's love
   That freed me out of pine.'

E

Jamieson's *Popular Ballads*, II, 117, compounded from **A**, a manuscript and a stall copy from Scotland, a recited copy from the north of England, and a short version picked off a Wall in London. (The parts which repeat **A** are in smaller type.)

1 In London was Young Beichan born,
   He longed strange countries for to see,
   But he was taen by a savage Moor,
   Who handled him right cruellie.

2 For he viewed the fashions of that land,
   Their way of worship viewed he,
   But to Mahound or Termagant
   Would Beichan never bend a knee.

3 So in every shoulder they've putten a bore,
   In every bore they've putten a tree,
   And they have made him trail the wine
   And spices on his fair bodie.

4 They've casten him in a dungeon deep,
   Where he could neither hear nor see,
   For seven years they kept him there,
   Till he for hunger's like to die.

5 This Moor he had but ae daughter,
   Her name was called Susie Pye,
   And every day as she took the air,
   Near Beichan's prison she passed by.

6 O so it fell upon a day
   She heard Young Beichan sadly sing;
   'My hounds they all go masterless,
   My hawks they flee from tree to tree,
   My younger brother will heir my land,
   Fair England again I'll never see!'

7 All night long no rest she got,
   Young Beichan's song for thinking on;
   She's stown the keys from her father's head,
   And to the prison strong is gone.

8 And she has opend the prison doors,
   I wot she opend two or three,
   Ere she could come Young Beichan at,
   He was locked up so curiouslie.

9 But when she came Young Beichan before,
   Sore wonderd he that may to see;
   He took her for some fair captive:
   'Fair Lady, I pray, of what countrie?'

10 'O have ye any lands,' she said,
   'Or castles in your own countrie,
   That ye could give to a lady fair,
   From prison strong to set you free?'

11 'Near London town I have a hall,
   With other castles two or three;
   I'll give them all to the lady fair
   That out of prison will set me free.'

12 'Give me the truth of your right hand,
   The truth of it give unto me,
   That for seven years ye'll no lady wed,
   Unless it be along with me.'

[470] 13 'I'll give thee the truth of my right hand,
   The truth of it I'll freely gie,
   That for seven years I'll stay unwed,
   For the kindness thou dost show to me.'

14 And she has brib'd the proud warder
   Wi mickle gold and white monie,
   She's gotten the keys of the prison strong,
   And she has set Young Beichan free.

15 She's gien him to eat the good spice-cake,
   She's gien him to drink the blood-red wine,
   She's bidden him sometimes think on her,
   That sae kindly freed him out of pine.

16 She's broken a ring from her finger,
   And to Beichan half of it gave she:
   Keep it, to mind you of that love
   The lady bore that set you free.

17 'And set your foot on good ship-board,
   And haste ye back to your own countrie,
   And before that seven years have an end,
   Come back again, love, and marry me.'

18 But long ere seven years had an end,
   She longd full sore her love to see,
   For ever a voice within her breast
   Said, 'Beichan has broke his vow to thee:'
   So she's set her foot on good ship-board,
   And turnd her back on her own countrie.

19 She sailed east, she sailed west,
   Till to fair England's shore she came,
   Where a bonny shepherd she espied,
   Feeding his sheep upon the plain.

20 'What news, what news, thou bonny shepherd?
   What news hast thou to tell to me?'
   'Such news I hear, ladie,' he says,
   'The like was never in this countrie.

21 'There is a wedding in yonder hall,
   Has lasted these thirty days and three;
   Young Beichan will not bed with his bride,
   For love of one that's yond the sea.'

22 She's put her hand in her pocket,
   Gien him the gold and white monie:
   'Hae, take ye that, my bonny boy,
   For the good news thou tellst to me.'

23 When she came to Young Beichan's gate,
   She tirled softly at the pin;
   So ready was the proud porter
   To open and let this lady in.

24 'Is this Young Beichan's hall,' she said,
   'Or is that noble lord within?'
   'Yea, he's in the hall among them all,
   And this is the day o his weddin.'

25 'And has he wed anither love?
   And has he clean forgotten me?'
   And sighin said that gay ladie,
   I wish I were in my own countrie!

26 And she has taen her gay gold ring,
   That with her love she brake so free;
   Says, Gie him that, ye proud porter,
   And bid the bridegroom speak to me.

27 When the porter came his lord before,
   He kneeled down low on his knee:
   'What aileth thee, my proud porter,
   Thou art so full of courtesie?'

28 'I've been porter at your gates,
   It's thirty long years now and three;
   But there stands a lady at them now,
   The like o her did I never see.

29 'For on every finger she has a ring,
   And on her mid-finger she has three,
   And as meickle gold aboon her brow
   As would buy an earldom to me.'

30 It's out then spak the bride's mother,
 Aye and an angry woman was shee:
 'Ye might have excepted our bonny bride,
 And twa or three of our companie.'

31 'O hold your tongue, thou bride's mother,
 Of all your folly let me be;
 She's ten times fairer nor the bride,
 And all that's in your companie.

32 'She begs one sheave of your white bread,
 But and a cup of your red wine,
 And to remember the lady's love
 That last relievd you out of pine.'

33 'O well-a-day!' said Beichan then,
 'That I so soon have married thee!
 For it can be none but Susie Pye,
 That sailed the sea for love of me.'

34 And quickly hied he down the stair;
 Of fifteen steps he made but three;
 He's taen his bonny love in his arms,
 And kist and kist her tenderlie.

35 'O hae ye taen anither bride?
 And hae ye quite forgotten me?
 And hae ye quite forgotten her
 That gave you life and libertie?'

36 She looked oer her left shoulder,
 To hide the tears stood in her ee:
 'Now fare thee well, Young Beichan,' she says,
 'I'll try to think no more on thee.'

37 'O never, never, Susie Pye,
 For surely this can never be,
 Nor ever shall I wed but her
 That's done and dreed so much for me.'

38 Then out and spak the forenoon bride: [471]
 'My lord, your love it changeth soon;
 This morning I was made your bride,
 And another chose ere it be noon.'

39 'O hold thy tongue, thou forenoon bride,
 Ye're neer a whit the worse for me,
 And whan ye return to your own countrie,
 A double dower I'll send with thee.'

40 He's taen Susie Pye by the white hand,
 And gently led her up and down,
 And ay as he kist her red rosy lips,
 'Ye're welcome, jewel, to your own.'

41 He's taen her by the milk-white hand,
 And led her to yon fountain stane;
 He's changed her name from Susie Pye,
 And he's call'd her his bonny love, Lady Jane.

F

Pitcairn's MSS, III, 159, 1817–25. From the recitation of Widow Stevenson, aged seventy-three: "East Country."

1 IN the lands where Lord Beichan was born,
 Amang the stately steps of stane,
 He wore the goud at his left shoulder,
 But to the Holy Land he's gane.

2 He was na lang in the Holy Land,
 Amang the Prudents that was black,
 He was na lang in the Holy Land,
 Till the Prudent did Lord Beichan tak.

3 The gard him draw baith pleugh and harrow,
 And horse and oxen twa or three;
 They cast him in a dark dungeon,
 Whare he coud neither hear nor see.

4 The Prudent had a fair daughter,
 I wot they ca'd her Susy Pye,
 And all the keys in that city
 Hang at that lady by and bye.

5 It once fell out upon a day
 That into the prison she did gae,
 And whan she cam to the prison door,
 She kneeled low down on her knee.

6 'O hae ye ony lands, Beichan,
 Or hae ye ony castles hie,
 Whar ye wad tak a young thing to,
 If out of prison I wad let thee?'

7 'Fair London's mine, dear lady,' he said,
  'And other places twa or three,
  Whar I wad tak a young thing to,
  If out of prison ye wad let me.'

8 O she has opened the prison door,
  And other places twa or three,
  And gien him bread, and wine to drink,
  In her own chamber privately.

9 O then she built a bonny ship,
  And she has set it on the main,
  And she has built a bonny ship,
  It's for to tak Lord Beichan hame.

10 O she's gaen murning up and down,
   And she's gaen murnin to the sea,
   Then to her father she has gane in,
   Wha spak to her right angrily.

11 'O do ye mourn for the goud, daughter,
   Or do ye mourn for the whyte monie?
   Or do ye mourn for the English squire?
   I wat I will gar hang him hie.'

12 'I neither mourn for the goud, father,
   Nor do I for the whyte monie,
   Nor do I for the English squire;
   And I care na tho ye hang him hie.

13 'But I hae promised an errand to go,
   Seven lang miles ayont the sea,
   And blythe and merry I never will be
   Untill that errand you let me.'

14 'That errand, daughter, you may gang,
   Seven long miles beyond the sea,
   Since blythe and merry you'll neer be
   Untill that errand I'll let thee.'

15 O she has built a bonny ship,
   And she has set it in the sea,
   And she has built a bonny ship,
   It's all for to tak her a long journie.

16 And she's sailed a' the summer day,
   I wat the wind blew wondrous fair;
   In sight of fair London she has come,
   And till Lord Beichan's yett she walked.

17 Whan she cam till Lord Beichan's yett,   [472]
   She rappit loudly at the pin:
   'Is Beichan lord of this bonny place?
   I pray ye open and let me in.

18 'And O is this Lord Beichan's yett,
   And is the noble lord within?'
   'O yes, it is Lord Beichan's yett,
   He's wi his bride and mony a ane.'

19 'If you'll gang up to Lord Beichan,
   Tell him the words that I tell thee;
   It will put him in mind of Susy Pye,
   And the Holy Land, whareer he be.

20 'Tell him to send one bite of bread,
   It's and a glass of his gude red wine,
   Nor to forget the lady's love.
   That loosed him out of prison strong.'

            *   *   *   *   *

21 'I hae been porter at your yett,
   I'm sure this therty lang years and three,
   But the fairest lady stands thereat
   That evir my twa eyes did see.

22 'On ilka finger she has a ring,
   And on the foremost she has three;
   As muckle goud is on her head
   As wad buy an earldom of land to thee.

23 'She bids you send a bite of bread,
   It's and a glass of your gude red wine,
   Nor to forget the lady's love
   That let you out of prison strong.'

24 It's up and spak the bride's mother,
   A weight of goud hung at her chin:
   'There is no one so fair without
   But there are, I wat, as fair within.'

25 It's up and spak the bride hersel,
   As she sat by the gude lord's knee:
   'Awa, awa, ye proud porter,
   This day ye might hae excepted me.'

            *   *   *   *   *

26 'Tak hence, tak hence your fair daughter,
   Tak hame your daughter fair frae me;
   For saving one kiss of her bonny lips,
   I'm sure of her body I am free.

27 'Awa, awa, ye proud mither,
   It's tak your daughter fair frae me;
   For I brought her home with chariots six,
   And I'll send her back wi coaches three.'

28 It's he's taen the table wi his fit,
   And syne he took it wi his knee;
   He gard the glasses and wine so red,
   He gard them all in flinders flee.

29 O he's gane down the steps of stairs,
   And a' the stately steps of stane,
   Until he cam to Susy Pye;
   I wat the tears blinded baith their eyne.

30 He led her up the steps of stairs,
   And a' the stately steps of stane,
   And changed her name from Susy Pye,
   And ca'd her lusty Lady Jane.

31 'O fye, gar cooks mak ready meat,
   O fye, gar cooks the pots supply,
   That it may be talked of in fair London,
   I've been twice married in ae day.'

G

Communicated by Mr Alexander Laing, of New-burg-on-Tay, as derived from the recitation of Miss Walker.

*   *   *   *   *   *   *   *   *   *

1 'O wha's aught a' yon flock o sheep,
   An wha's aught a' yon flock o kye?
   An wha's aught a' yon pretty castles,
   That you sae often do pass bye?'

2 'They're a' Lord Beekin's sheep,
   They're a' Lord Beekin's kye;
   They're a' Lord Beekin's castles,
   That you sae often do pass bye.'

3 He's tane [the] table wi his feet,
   Made cups an candlesticks to flee:
   'I'll lay my life 't is Susy Pie,
   Come owr the seas to marry me.'

H

731

Kinloch's *Ancient Scottish Ballads*, p. 260.

Young Beich-an was in Lon-don born, He___ was a man of___ hie de-gree;

He past thro mon-ie___ king-doms great, Un-til he cam un-to Grand Tur-kie.

1 YOUNG BEICHAN was in London born,
   He was a man of hie degree;
   He past thro monie kingdoms great,
   Until he cam unto Grand Turkie.

2 He viewd the fashions of that land,
   Their way of worship viewed he,
   But unto onie of their stocks
   He wadna sae much as bow a knee:

3 Which made him to be taken straight,
　　And brought afore their hie jurie;
　The savage Moor did speak upricht,
　　And made him meikle ill to dree.

4 In ilka shoulder they've bord a hole,
　　And in ilka hole they've put a tree;
　They've made him to draw carts and wains,
　　Till he was sick and like to dee.

5 But Young Beichan was a Christian born,
　　And still a Christian was he;
　Which made them put him in prison strang,
　　And cauld and hunger sair to dree,
　And fed on nocht but bread and water,
　　Until the day that he mot dee.

6 In this prison there grew a tree,
　　And it was unco stout and strang,
　Where he was chained by the middle,
　　Until his life was almaist gane.

7 The savage Moor had but ae dochter,
　　And her name it was Susie Pye,
　And ilka day as she took the air,
　　The prison door she passed bye.

8 But it fell ance upon a day,
　　As she was walking, she heard him sing;
　She listend to his tale of woe,
　　A happy day for Young Beichan!

9 'My hounds they all go masterless,
　　My hawks they flee frae tree to tree,
　My youngest brother will heir my lands,
　　My native land I'll never see.'

10 'O were I but the prison-keeper,
　　As I'm a ladie o hie degree,
　I soon wad set this youth at large,
　　And send him to his ain countrie.'

11 She went away into her chamber,
　　All nicht she never closd her ee;
　And when the morning begoud to dawn,
　　At the prison door alane was she.

12 She gied the keeper a piece of gowd,
　　And monie pieces o white monie,
　To tak her thro the bolts and bars,
　　The lord frae Scotland she langd to see;
　She saw young Beichan at the stake,
　　Which made her weep maist bitterlie.

13 'O hae ye got onie lands,' she says,
　　'Or castles in your ain countrie?
　It's what wad ye gie to the ladie fair
　　Wha out o prison wad set you free?'

14 'It's I hae houses, and I hae lands,
　　Wi monie castles fair to see,
　And I wad gie a' to that ladie gay,
　　Wha out o prison wad set me free.'

15 The keeper syne brak aff his chains,
　　And set Lord Beichan at libertie;
　She filld his pockets baith wi gowd,
　　To tak him till his ain countrie.

16 She took him frae her father's prison,
　　And gied to him the best o wine,
　And a brave health she drank to him:
　　'I wish, Lord Beichan, ye were mine!

17 'It's seven lang years I'll mak a vow,
　　And seven lang years I'll keep it true;
　If ye'll wed wi na ither woman,
　　It's I will wed na man but you.'

18 She's tane him to her father's port,
　　And gien to him a ship o fame:
　'Farewell, farewell, my Scottish lord,
　　I fear I'll neer see you again.'

19 Lord Beichan turnd him round about,
　　And lowly, lowly loutit he:
　'Ere seven lang years come to an end,
　　I'll tak you to mine ain countrie.'

　　*　　*　　*　　*　　*

20 Then whan he cam to Glasgow town,
　　A happy, happy man was he;
　The ladies a' around him thrangd,
　　To see him come frae slaverie.

21 His mother she had died o sorrow,
　　And a' his brothers were dead but he;
　His lands they a' were lying waste,
　　In ruins were his castles free.

22 Na porter there stood at his yett,
　　Na human creature he could see,
　Except the screeching owls and bats,
　　Had he to bear him companie.

23 But gowd will gar the castles grow,
  And he had gowd and jewels free,
  And soon the pages around him thrangd,
    To serve him on their bended knee.

24 His hall was hung wi silk and satin,
  His table rung wi mirth and glee,
  He soon forgot the lady fair
    That lowsd him out o slaverie.

25 Lord Beichan courted a lady gay,
  To heir wi him his lands sae free,
  Neer thinking that a lady fair
    Was on her way frae Grand Turkie.

26 For Susie Pye could get na rest,
  Nor day nor nicht could happy be,
  Still thinking on the Scottish lord,
    Till she was sick and like to dee.

27 But she has builded a bonnie ship,
  Weel mannd wi seamen o hie degree,
  And secretly she stept on board,
    And bid adieu to her ain countrie.

28 But whan she cam to the Scottish shore,
  The bells were ringing sae merrilie;
  It was Lord Beichan's wedding day,
    Wi a lady fair o hie degree.

29 But sic a vessel was never seen
  The very masts were tappd wi gold,
  Her sails were made o the satin fine,
    Maist beautiful for to behold.

30 But whan the lady cam on shore,
  Attended wi her pages three,
  Her shoon were of the beaten gowd,
    And she a lady of great beautie.

31 Then to the skipper she did say,
  'Can ye this answer gie to me?
  Where are Lord Beichan's lands sae braid?
    He surely lives in this countrie.'

32 Then up bespak the skipper bold,
  For he could speak the Turkish tongue:
  'Lord Beichan lives not far away;
    This is the day of his wedding.'

33 'If ye will guide me to Beichan's yetts,
  I will ye well reward,' said she;
  Then she and all her pages went,
    A very gallant companie.

34 When she cam to Lord Beichan's yetts,
  She tirld gently at the pin;
  Sae ready was the proud porter
    To let the wedding guests come in.

35 'Is this Lord Beichan's house,' she says,
  'Or is that noble lord within?'
  'Yes, he is gane into the hall,
    With his brave bride and monie ane.'

36 'Ye'll bid him send me a piece of bread,
  Bot and a cup of his best wine;
  And bid him mind the lady's love
    That ance did lowse him out o pyne.'

37 Then in and cam the porter bold,
  I wat he gae three shouts and three:
  'The fairest lady stands at your yetts
    That ever my twa een did see.'

38 Then up bespak the bride's mither,
  I wat an angry woman was she:
  'You micht hae excepted our bonnie bride,
    Tho she'd been three times as fair as she.'

39 'My dame, your daughter's fair enough,
  And aye the fairer mot she be!
  But the fairest time that eer she was,
    She'll na compare wi this ladie.

40 'She has a gowd ring on ilka finger,
  And on her mid-finger she has three;
  She has as meikle gowd upon her head
    As wad buy an earldom o land to thee.

41 'My lord, she begs some o your bread,   [475]
  Bot and a cup o your best wine,
  And bids you mind the lady's love
    That ance did lowse ye out o pyne.'

42 Then up and started Lord Beichan,
  I wat he made the table flee:
  'I wad gie a' my yearlie rent
    'T were Susie Pye come owre the sea.'

43 Syne up bespak the bride's mother,
    She was never heard to speak sae free:
'Ye'll no forsake my ae dochter,
    Tho Susie Pye has crossd the sea?'

44 'Tak hame, tak hame, your dochter, madam,
    For she is neer the waur o me;
She cam to me on horseback riding,
    And she sall gang hame in chariot free.'

45 He's tane Susie Pye by the milk-white hand,
    And led her thro his halls sae hie:
'Ye're now Lord Beichan's lawful wife,
    And thrice ye're welcome unto me.'

46 Lord Beichan prepard for another wedding,
    Wi baith their hearts sae fu o glee;
Says, 'I'll range na mair in foreign lands,
    Sin Susie Pye has crossd the sea.

47 'Fy! gar a' our cooks mak ready,
    And fy! gar a' our pipers play,
And fy! gar trumpets gae thro the toun,
    That Lord Beichan's wedded twice in a day!'

I

Communicated by Mr David Louden, as recited by
Mrs Dodds, Morham, Haddington, the reciter being
above seventy in 1873.

1 IN London was Young Bechin born,
    Foreign nations he longed to see;
He passed through many kingdoms great,
    At length he came unto Turkie.

2 He viewed the fashions of that land,
    The ways of worship viewed he,
But unto any of their gods
    He would not so much as bow the knee.

3 On every shoulder they made a bore,
    In every bore they put a tree,
Then they made him the winepress tread,
    And all in spite of his fair bodie.

4 They put him into a deep dungeon,
    Where he could neither hear nor see,
And for seven years they kept him there,
    Till for hunger he was like to die.

5 Stephen, their king, had a daughter fair,
    Yet never a man to her came nigh;
And every day she took the air,
    Near to his prison she passed by.

6 One day she heard Young Bechin sing
    A song that pleased her so well,
No rest she got till she came to him,
    All in his lonely prison cell.

7 'I have a hall in London town,
    With other buildings two or three,
And I'll give them all to the ladye fair
    That from this dungeon shall set me free.'

8 She stole the keys from her dad's head,
    And if she oped one door ay she opened
        three,
Till she Young Bechin could find out,
    He was locked up so curiouslie.

    *   *   *   *   *

9 'I've been a porter at your gate
    This thirty years now, ay and three;
There stands a ladye at your gate,
    The like of her I neer did see.

10 'On every finger she has a ring,
    On the mid-finger she has three;
She's as much gold about her brow
    As would an earldom buy to me.'

    *   *   *   *   *

11 He's taen her by the milk-white hand,
    He gently led her through the green;
He changed her name from Susie Pie,
    An he's called her lovely Ladye Jean.

J

Dr Joseph Robertson's Note-Book, "Adversaria," p. 85. From tradition.

*   *   *   *   *

1 She's taen the keys frae her fadder's coffer,
     Tho he keeps them most sacredlie,
     And she has opend the prison strong,
     And set Young Beichan at libertie.

*   *   *   *   *

2 .   .   .   .   .
     .   .   .   .   .
     'Gae up the countrie, my chile,' she says,
     'Till your fadder's wrath be turned from thee.'

*   *   *   *   *

3 She's put her han intill her purse,
     And gave the porter guineas three;
     Says, 'Tak ye that, ye proud porter,
     And tell your master to speak wi me.

4 'Ye'll bid him bring a shower o his best love,
     But and a bottle o his wine,
     And do to me as I did to him in time past,
     And brought him out o muckle pine.'

5 He's taen the table wi his foot,
     And he has keppit it wi his knee:
     'I'll wager my life and a' my lan,
     It's Susan Pie come ower the sea.

6 'Rise up, rise up, my bonnie bride,
     Ye're neither better nor waur for me;
     Ye cam to me on a horse and saddle,
     But ye may gang back in a coach and three.'

K

Communicated by Mr David Louden, as obtained from Mrs Dickson, Rentonhall.

*   *   *   *   *

1 'There is a marriage in yonder hall,
     Has lasted thirty days and three;
     The bridegroom winna bed the bride,
     For the sake of one that's owre the sea.'

*   *   *   *   *

2 'What news, what news, my brave young por-
     ter?
     What news, what news have ye for me?'
     'As beautiful a ladye stands at your gate
     As eer my two eyes yet did see.'

3 'A slice of bread to her get ready,
     And a bottle of the best of wine;
     Not to forget that fair young ladye
     Who did release thee out of close confine.'

4 Lord Bechin in a passion flew,
     And rent himself like a sword in three,
     Saying, 'I would give all my father's riches
     If my Sophia was 'cross the sea.'

5 Up spoke the young bride's mother,
     Who never was heard to speak so free,
     Saying, 'I hope you'll not forget my only
     daughter,
     Though your Sophia be 'cross the sea.'

6 'I own a bride I've wed your daughter,
     She's nothing else the worse of me;
     She came to me on a horse and saddle,
     She may go back in a coach and three.'

L

A modern street or broadside ballad given from
singing by Miss Burne, *Shropshire Folk-Lore*, p. 547.

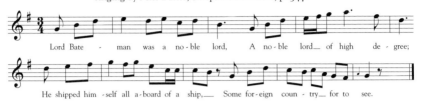

Lord Bate - man was a no-ble lord, A no-ble lord— of high de-gree;

He shipped him -self all a-board of a ship,— Some for-eign coun - try— for to see.

1 LORD BATEMAN was a noble lord,
    A noble lord of high degree;
  He shipped himself on board a ship,
    Some foreign country he would go see.

2 He sailed East, and he sailed West,
    Until he came to proud Turkey,
  When he was taken and put to prison,
    Until his life was almost gone.

3 And in this prison there grew a tree,
    It grew so stout and strong,
  Where he was chained by the middle,
    Until his life was almost gone.

[477] 4 This Turk he had one only daughter,
    The fairest creature my eyes did see;
  She stole the keys of her father's prison,
    And swore Lord Bateman she would set free.

5 'Have you got houses? Have you got lands?
    Or does Northumberland belong to thee?
  What would you give to the fair young lady
    That out of prison would set you free?'

6 'I have got houses, I have got lands,
    And half Northumberland belongs to me;
  I'll give it all to the fair young lady
    That out of prison would set me free.'

7 O then she took me to her father's hall,
    And gave to me the best of wine,
  And every health she drank unto him,
    'I wish, Lord Bateman, that you were mine!

8 'Now in seven years I'll make a vow,
    And seven years I'll keep it strong,
  If you'll wed with no other woman,
    I will wed with no other man.'

9 O then she took him to her father's harbour,
    And gave to him a ship of fame:
  'Farewell, farewell to you, Lord Bateman,
    I'm afraid I neer shall see you again.'

10 Now seven long years are gone and past,
    And fourteen days, well known to thee;
  She packed up all her gay clothing,
    And swore Lord Bateman she would go see.

11 But when she came to Lord Bateman's castle,
    So boldly she did ring the bell;
  'Who's there, who's there?' cried the proud por-
      ter,
    Who's there? come unto me tell.'

12 'O is this Lord Bateman's castle?
    Or is his Lordship here within?'
  'O yes, O yes,' cried the young porter,
    'He's just now taken his new bride in.'

13 'O tell him to send me a slice of bread,
    And a bottle of the best wine,
  And not forgetting the fair young lady
    Who did release him when close confined.'

14 Away, away, went this proud young porter,
    Away, away, and away went he,
  Until he came to Lord Bateman's chamber;
    Down on his bended knees fell he.

15 'What news, what news, my proud young porter?
    What news hast thou brought unto me?'
  'There is the fairest of all young creatures
    That eer my two eyes did see.

16 'She has got rings on every finger.
    And round one of them she has got three,
  And as much gay clothing round her
    As would buy all Northumberland free.

17 'She bids you send her a slice of bread,
   And a bottle of the best wine,
   And not forgetting the fair young lady
   Who did release you when close confined.'

18 Lord Bateman he then in a passion flew,
   And broke his sword in splinters three,
   Saying, I will give all my father's riches,
   That if Sophia has crossed the sea.

19 Then up spoke the young bride'[s] mother,
   Who never was heard to speak so free:
   You'll not forget my only daughter,
   That if Sophia has crossed the sea.

20 'I own I made a bride of your daughter;
   She's neither the better or worse for me;
   She came to me with her horse and saddle,
   She may go back in her coach and three.'

21 Lord Bateman prepared another marriage,
   With both their hearts so full of glee:
   'I'll range no more in foreign countries,
   Now since Sophia has crossed the sea.'

   Pitts, Seven Dials.

M

478]

Buchan's MSS, I, 18. J. H. Dixon, *Scottish Tradi-
tional Versions of Ancient Ballads*, p. 1.

1 YOUNG BONWELL was a squire's ae son,
   And a squire's ae son was he;
   He went abroad to a foreign land,
   To serve for meat and fee.

2 He hadna been in that country
   A twalmonth and a day,
   Till he was cast in prison strong,
   For the sake of a lovely may.

3 'O if my father get word of this,
   At hame in his ain country,
   He'll send red gowd for my relief,
   And a bag o white money.

4 'O gin an earl woud borrow me,
   At his bridle I woud rin;
   Or gin a widow woud borrow me,
   I'd swear to be her son.

5 'Or gin a may woud borrow me,
   I'd wed her wi a ring,
   Infeft her wi the ha's and bowers
   O the bonny towers o Linne.'

6 But it fell ance upon a day
   Dame Essels she thought lang,
   And she is to the jail-house door,
   To hear Young Bondwell's sang.

7 'Sing on, sing on, my bonny Bondwell,
   The sang ye sang just now:'
   'I never sang the sang, lady,
   But I woud war 't on you.

8 'O gin my father get word o this,
   At hame in his ain country,
   He'll send red gowd for my relief,
   And a bag o white money.

9 'O gin an earl woud borrow me,
   At his bridle I woud rin;
   Or gin a widow would borrow me,
   I'd swear to be her son.

10 'Or gin a may woud borrow me,
   I woud wed her wi a ring,
   Infeft her wi the ha's and bowers
   O the bonny towers o Linne.'

11 She's stole the keys o the jail-house door,
   Where under the bed they lay;
   She's opend to him the jail-house door,
   And set Young Bondwell free.

12 She gae 'm a steed was swift in need,
   A saddle o royal ben,
   A hunder pund o pennies round,
   Bade him gae roav an spend.

13 A couple o hounds o ae litter,
   And Cain they ca'd the one;
   Twa gay gos-hawks she gae likeways,
   To keep him onthought lang.

14 When mony days were past and gane,
   Dame Essels thought fell lang,
   And she is to her lonely bower,
   To shorten her wi a sang.

15 The sang has such a melody,
    It lulld her fast asleep;
    Up starts a woman, clad in green,
    And stood at her bed-feet.

16 'Win up, win up, Dame Essels,' she says,
    'This day ye sleep ower lang;
    The morn is the squire's wedding day,
    In the bonny towers o Linne.

17 'Ye'll dress yoursell in the robes o green,
    Your maids in robes sae fair,
    And ye'll put girdles about their middles,
    Sae costly, rich and rare.

18 'Ye'll take your maries alang wi you,
    Till ye come to yon strand;
    There ye'll see a ship, wi sails all up,
    Come sailing to dry land.

19 'Ye'll take a wand into your hand,
    Ye'll stroke her round about,
    And ye'll take God your pilot to be,
    To drown ye'll take nae doubt.'

20 Then up it raise her Dame Essels,
    Sought water to wash her hands,
    But aye the faster that she washd,
    The tears they trickling ran.

21 Then in it came her father dear,
    And in the floor steps he:
    'What ails Dame Essels, my daughter dear,
    Ye weep sae bitterlie?

22 'Want ye a small fish frae the flood,
    Or turtle frae the sea?
    Or is there man in a' my realm
    This day has offended thee?'

23 'I want nae small fish frae the flood,
    Nor turtle frae the sea;
    But Young Bondwell, your ain prisoner,
    This day has offended me.'

24 Her father turnd him round about,
    A solemn oath sware he:
    'If this be true ye tell me now
    High hanged he shall be.

25 'To-morrow morning he shall be
    Hung high upon a tree:'
    Dame Essels whisperd to hersel,
    'Father, ye've made a lie.'

26 She dressd hersel in robes o green,   ⌊479
    Her maids in robes sae fair,
    Wi gowden girdles round their middles,
    Sae costly, rich and rare.

27 She's taen her mantle her about,
    A maiden in every hand;
    They saw a ship, wi sails a' up,
    Come sailing to dry land.

28 She's taen a wand intill her hand,
    And stroked her round about,
    And she's taen God her pilot to be,
    To drown she took nae doubt.

29 So they saild on, and further on,
    Till to the water o Tay;
    There they spied a bonny little boy,
    Was watering his steeds sae gay.

30 'What news, what news, my little boy,
    What news hae ye to me?
    Are there any weddings in this place,
    Or any gaun to be?'

31 'There is a wedding in this place,
    A wedding very soon;
    The morn's the young squire's wedding day,
    In the bonny towers of Linne.'

32 O then she walked alang the way
    To see what coud be seen,
    And there she saw the proud porter,
    Drest in a mantle green.

33 'What news, what news, porter?' she said,
    'What news hae ye to me?
    Are there any weddings in this place,
    Or any gaun to be?'

34 'There is a wedding in this place,
    A wedding very soon;
    The morn is Young Bondwell's wedding day,
    The bonny squire o Linne.'

35 'Gae to your master, porter,' she said,
    'Gae ye right speedilie;
    Bid him come and speak wi a maid
    That wishes his face to see.'

36 The porter's up to his master gane,
    Fell low down on his knee;
    'Win up, win up, my porter,' he said,
    'Why bow ye low to me?'

37 'I hae been porter at your yetts
  These thirty years and three,
  But fairer maids than's at them now
  My eyes did never see.

38 'The foremost she is drest in green,
  The rest in fine attire,
  Wi gowden girdles round their middles,
  Well worth a sheriff's hire.'

39 Then out it speaks Bondwell's own bride,
  Was a' gowd to the chin;
  'They canno be fairer thereout,' she says,
  'Than we that are therein.'

40 'There is a difference, my dame,' he said,
  ''Tween that ladye's colour and yours;
  As much difference as you were a stock,
  She o the lily flowers.'

41 Then out it speaks him Young Bondwell,
  An angry man was he:
  'Cast up the yetts baith wide an braid,
  These ladies I may see.'

42 Quickly up stairs Dame Essel's gane,
  Her maidens next her wi;
  Then said the bride, This lady's face
  Shows the porter's tauld nae lie.

43 The lady unto Bondwell spake,
  These words pronounced she:
  O hearken, hearken, fause Bondwell,
  These words that I tell thee.

44 Is this the way ye keep your vows
  That ye did make to me,
  When your feet were in iron fetters,
  Ae foot ye coudna flee?

45 I stole the keys o the jail-house door
  Frae under the bed they lay,
  And opend up the jail-house door,
  Set you at liberty.

46 Gae you a steed was swift in need,
  A saddle o royal ben,
  A hunder pund o pennies round,
  Bade you gae rove an spend.

47 A couple o hounds o ae litter,
  Cain they ca'ed the ane,
  Twa gay gos-hawks as swift's eer flew,
  To keep you onthought lang.

48 But since this day ye've broke your vow,
  For which ye're sair to blame,
  And since nae mair I'll get o you,
  O Cain, will ye gae hame?

49 'O Cain! O Cain!' the lady cried,
  And Cain did her ken;
  They baith flappd round the lady's knee,
  Like a couple o armed men.

50 He's to his bride wi hat in hand,
  And haild her courteouslie:
  'Sit down by me, my bonny Bondwell,
  What makes this courtesie?'

51 'An asking, asking, fair lady,
  An asking ye'll grant me;'
  'Ask on, ask on, my bonny Bondwell,
  What may your askings be?'

52 'Five hundred pounds to you I'll gie,   [480]
  Of gowd an white monie,
  If ye'll wed John, my ain cousin;
  He looks as fair as me.'

53 'Keep well your monie, Bondwell,' she said,
  'Nae monie I ask o thee;
  Your cousin John was my first love,
  My husband now he 's be.'

54 Bondwell was married at morning ear,
  John in the afternoon;
  Dame Essels is lady ower a' the bowers
  And the high towers o Linne.

N

a. Falkirk, printed by T. Johnston, 1815. b. Stirling, M. Randall.

1 In London was Young Bichen born,
  He longd strange lands to see;
  He set his foot on good ship-board,
  And he sailed over the sea.

2 He had not been in a foreign land
  A day but only three,
  Till he was taken by a savage Moor,
  And they used him most cruelly.

3 In every shoulder they put a pin,
  To every pin they put a tree;
  They made him draw the plow and cart,
  Like horse and oxen in his country.

4 He had not servd the savage Moor
  A week, nay scarcely but only three,
  Till he has casten him in prison strong,
  Till he with hunger was like to die.

5 It fell out once upon a day
  That Young Bichen he made his moan,
  As he lay bound in irons strong,
  In a dark and deep dungeon.

6 'An I were again in fair England,
  As many merry day I have been,
  Then I would curb my roving youth
  No more to see a strange land.

7 'O an I were free again now,
  And my feet well set on the sea,
  I would live in peace in my own country,
  And a foreign land I no more would see.'

8 The savage Moor had but one daughter,
  I wot her name was Susan Py;
  She heard Young Bichen make his moan,
  At the prison-door as she past by.

9 'O have ye any lands,' she said,
  'Or have you any money free,
  Or have you any revenues,
  To maintain a lady like me?'

10 'O I have land in fair England,
   And I have estates two or three,
   And likewise I have revenues,
   To maintain a lady like thee.'

11 'O will you promise, Young Bichen,' she says,
   'And keep your vow faithful to me,
   That at the end of seven years
   In fair England you'll marry me?

12 'I'll steal the keys from my father dear,
   Tho he keeps them most secretly;
   I'll risk my life for to save thine,
   And set thee safe upon the sea.'

13 She's stolen the keys from her father,
   From under the bed where they lay;
   She opened the prison strong
   And set Young Bichen at liberty.

14 She's gone to her father's coffer,
   Where the gold was red and fair to see;
   She filled his pockets with good red gold,
   And she set him far upon the sea.

15 'O mind you well, Young Bichen,' she says,
   'The vows and oaths you made to me;
   When you are come to your native land,
   O then remember Susan Py!'

16 But when her father he came home
   He missd the keys there where they lay;
   He went into the prison strong,
   But he saw Young Bichen was away.

17 'Go bring your daughter, madam,' he says,
   'And bring her here unto me;
   Altho I have no more but her,
   Tomorrow I'll gar hang her high.'

18 The lady calld on the maiden fair
   To come to her most speedily;
   'Go up the country, my child,' she says,
   'Stay with my brother two years or three.

19 'I have a brother, he lives in the isles,
   He will keep thee most courteously
   And stay with him, my child,' she says,
   'Till thy father's wrath be turnd from thee.'

20 Now will we leave young Susan Py
   A while in her own country,
   And will return to Young Bichen,
   Who is safe arrived in fair England.

21 He had not been in fair England
   Above years scarcely three,
   Till he has courted another maid,
   And so forgot his Susan Py.

[481] 22 The youth being young and in his prime,
   Of Susan Py thought not upon,
   But his love was laid on another maid,
   And the marriage-day it did draw on.

23 But eer the seven years were run,
   Susan Py she thought full long;
   She set her foot on good ship-board,
   And she has saild for fair England.

24 On every finger she put a ring,
   On her mid-finger she put three;
   She filld her pockets with good red gold,
   And she has sailed oer the sea.

25 She had not been in fair England
   A day, a day, but only three,
   Till she heard Young Bichen was a bridegroom,
   And the morrow to be the wedding-day.

26 'Since it is so,' said young Susan,
   'That he has provd so false to me,
   I'll hie me to Young Bichen's gates,
   And see if he minds Susan Py.'

27 She has gone up thro London town,
   Where many a lady she there did spy;
   There was not a lady in all London
   Young Susan that could outvie.

28 She has calld upon a waiting-man,
   A waiting-man who stood near by:
   'Convey me to Young Bichen's gates,
   And well rewarded shals thou be.'

29 When she came to Young Bichen's gate
   She chapped loudly at the pin,
   Till down there came the proud porter;
   'Who's there,' he says, 'That would be in?'

30 'Open the gates, porter,' she says,
   'Open them to a lady gay,
   And tell your master, porter,' she says,
   'To speak a word or two with me.'

31 The porter he has opend the gates;
   His eyes were dazled to see
   A lady dressd in gold and jewels;
   No page nor waiting-man had she.

32 'O pardon me, madam,' he cried,
   'This day it is his wedding-day;
   He's up the stairs with his lovely bride,
   And a sight of him you cannot see.'

33 She put her hand in her pocket,
   And therefrom took out guineas three,
   And gave to him, saying, Please, kind sir,
   Bring down your master straight to me.

34 The porter up again has gone,
   And he fell low down on his knee,
   Saying, Master, you will please come down
   To a lady who wants you to see.

35 A lady gay stands at your gates,
   The like of her I neer did see;
   She has more gold above her eye
   Nor would buy a baron's land to me.

36 Out then spake the bride's mother,
   I'm sure an angry woman was she:
   'You're impudent and insolent,
   For ye might excepted the bride and me.'

37 'Ye lie, ye lie, ye proud woman,
   I'm sure sae loud as I hear you lie;
   She has more gold on her body
   Than would buy the lands, the bride, and thee!'

38 'Go down, go down, porter,' he says,
   'And tell the lady gay from me
   That I'm up-stairs wi my lovely bride,
   And a sight of her I cannot see.'

39 The porter he goes down again,
   The lady waited patiently:
   'My master's with his lovely bride,
   And he'll not win down my dame to see.'

40 From off her finger she's taen a ring;
   'Give that your master,' she says, 'From me,
   And tell him now, young man,' she says,
   'To send down a cup of wine to me.'

41 'Here's ring for you, master,' he says,
   'On her mid-finger she has three,
   And you are desird, my lord,' he says,
   'To send down a cup of wine with me.'

42 He hit the table with his foot,
   He kepd it with his right knee:
   'I'll wed my life and all my land
   That is Susan Py, come o'er the sea!'

43 He has gone unto the stair-head,
    A step he took but barely three;
He opend the gates most speedily,
    And Susan Py he there could see.

44 'Is this the way, Young Bichen,' she says,
    'Is this the way you've guided me?
I relieved you from prison strong,
    And ill have you rewarded me.

45 'O mind ye, Young Bichen,' she says,
    'The vows and oaths that ye made to me,
When ye lay bound in prison strong,
    In a deep dungeon of misery?'

46 He took her by the milk-white hand,
    And led her into the palace fine;
There was not a lady in all the palace
    But Susan Py did all outshine.

47 The day concluded with joy and mirth,
    On every side there might you see;
There was great joy in all England
    For the wedding-day of Susan Py.

---

[482] **B.** 17^1. bids me. 22^{5,6}. *Connected with* 23 *in* MS. 22^6. send he.

C. a. 15^2. How y you.

b. 3^3. *omits* house. 4^2. *omits* foot.

7^1. *omits* dear.

7^3. For she's . . . of the prison.

7^4. And gane the dungeon within.

8^1. And when.

8^2. Wow but her heart was sair.

9^1. She's gotten. 11^1. thir twa.

13^2. I kenna. 13^4. kensnae.

14^1. fell out. 15^2. How y you.

16^1. till. 16^2. As fast as ye can gang.

16^3. tak three. 16^4. To haud ye unthocht lang.

18^1. Syne ye. 18^3. And bonny.

19^3. And I will.

20^2. As fast as she could gang.

20^3. she's taen.

20^4. To haud her unthocht lang.

22^3. And sae bonny did.

22^4. till. 24^3. And her mind misgae by.

24^4. That 't was. 25^2. markis three.

25^4. Bid your master. 27^4. did never.

29^1. and spak. 29^3. be fine.

29^4. as fine. 32^3. out of.

34^3. at the first. 35^2. gang.

36^4. Send her back a maid.

D. *Written throughout without division into stanzas.*

7. *A like repetition occurs again in the Skene* MSS: *see No* 36, *p.* 428.

10^{1,2}. *One line in the* MS. *The metre, in several places where it is incomplete, was doubtless made full by repetition: see* 19^{1,3}.

13^2. bone.

14^1. *This line thus:* (an a Leash of guid gray hounds). *The reciter evidently could remember only this point in the stanza.*

16, 17. Whan she cam to Young Beachens gate
    Is Young Beachen at hame
    Or is he in this countrie
    He is at hame is hearly (?) said
    Hine an sigh an says her Susie Pay
    Has he quite forgotten me

19^{1,3}. *Probably sung, the stair, the stair; win up, win up.*

22^{3,4}. *The latter half of the stanza must be supposed to be addressed to* Young Beachen.

26^{1,2}. He took her down to yon gouden green.

27^4. Sh 's. 29^2. my name.

After 29 *a stanza belonging apparently to some other ballad:*

    Courtess kind, an generous mind,
        An winna ye answer me?
    An whan the hard their lady's word,
        Well answered was she.

E. 6$^{4-6}$ *was introduced, with other metrical passages, into a long tale of* 'Young Beichan and Susy Pye,' *which Motherwell had heard related, and of which he gives a specimen at p.* xv. *of his Introduction:* "Well, ye must know that in the Moor's castle there was a massymore, which is a dark dungeon for keeping prisoners. It was twenty feet below the ground, and into this hole they closed poor Beichan. There he stood, night and day, up to his waist in puddle water; but night or day it was all one to him, for no ae styme of light ever got in. So he lay there a lang and weary while, and thinking on his heavy weird, he made a murnfu sang to pass the time, and this was the sang that he made, and grat when he sang it, for he never thought of ever escaping from the massymore, or of seeing his ain country again:

'My hounds they all run masterless,
    My hawks they flee from tree to tree;
My youngest brother will heir my lands,
    And fair England again I'll never see.

'Oh were I free as I hae been,
    And my ship swimming once more on sea,
I'd turn my face to fair England,
    And sail no more to a strange countrie.'

"Now the cruel Moor had a beautiful daughter, called Susy Pye, who was accustomed to take a walk every morning in her garden, and as she was walking ae day she heard the sough o Beichan's sang, coming as it were from below the ground," etc., etc.

F. 3^3. dungeon (donjon). 6^1. only lands.
    6^2. only castles. 8^1. Oh.
[483] 10^3. ha she has gane in: *originally* has she gane in.
    13^2. Many, *with* Seven *written over:* Seven *in* 14^2.
    20. *After this stanza:* Then the porter gaed up the stair and said.
    25. *After this stanza:* Then Lord Beichan gat up, and was in a great wrath, and said.
    31. ae: *indistinct, but seems to have been* one *changed to* ae *or* a.

H. 4^3. carts and wains *for* carts o wine *of* **A** 2^3, **B** 2^3. *We have* wine *in* **H** 4^3, **I** 3^3, *and* wine *is in all likelihood original.*
    Christie, I, 31, abridges this version, making "a few slight alterations from the way he had heard it sung:" *these, and one or two more.*
    2^4. wadna bend nor bow.
    7^1. The Moor he had.

25^1. But Beichan courted.

I. 1^1. Bechin *was pronounced* Beekin.

K.   1. *Before this, as gloss, or remnant of a preceding stanza:* She came to a shepherd, and he replied.
    2. *After this, in explanation:* She gave Lord Bechin a slice of bread and a bottle of wine when she released him from prison, hence the following. 3^1. to him.
    4. *After this:* He had married another lady, not having heard from his Sophia for seven long years.

L.   *For the modern vulgar ballad, Catnach's is a better copy than that of Pitts. See Kidson,* Traditional Tunes, *p. 34, for Catnach.*

M. 10^3. in *for* wi(?): wi *in* 5^3.
    12^2, 46^2. bend. *Possibly, however, understood to be* bend = leather, *instead of* ben = bane, bone.
    13^4, 47^4. on thought.

N.   **a.** Susan Py, or Young Bichens Garland. Shewing how he went to a far country, and was taken by a savage Moor and cast into prison, and delivered by the Moor's daughter, on promise of marriage; and how he came to England, and was going to be wedded to another bride; with the happy arrival of Susan Py on the wedding day. Falkirk, Printed by T. Johnston, 1815.

    b. 3^4. his own.
    4^2. A week, a week, but only.
    7^3. own land.
    7^4. And foreign lands no more.
    11^1. young man. 13^2. he lay.
    24^3. her trunks. 25^4. was the.
    28^2. that stood hard by. 28^4. thou shalt.
    29^2. She knocked. 31^4. waiting-maid.
    32^2. For this is his.
    34^1. up the stairs. 34^3. will you.
    36^4. Ye might.
    37^2. Sae loud as I hear ye lie.
    39^4. And a sight of him you cannot see.
    40^4. To bring. 42^3. I'll lay.
    44^2. way that you've used me.
    47^4. wedding of.

APPENDIX
Additional Copies

'Earl Bichet,' "Scotch Ballads, Materials for Border Minstrelsy," No 83, Abbotsford. Communicated to Scott by Mrs Christiana Greenwood, London, May 27, 1806 (Letters, I, No 189), as heard by her in her youth at Longnewton, near Jedburgh, "where most of the old women could sing it."

1 EARL BICHET's sworn a mighty aith,
　　And a solemn vow made he,
　That he wad to the Holy Land,
　　To the Holy Land wad be gae.

2 When he came to the Holy Land,
　　Amang the Infidels sae black,
　They hae consulted them amang
　　The Earl Bichet for to take.

3 And when they basely him betrayd
　　They put him into fetters strang,
　And threw him in a dungeon dark,
　　To spend the weary night sae lang.

4 Then in ilka shoulder they bored a hole,
　　In his right shoulder they bored three,
　And they gard him draw the coops o wine,
　　Till he was sick and like to dee.

5 Then they took him out o their carts and wains,
　　And put him in a castle of stone;
　When the stars shone bright, and the moon
　　　gave light,
　　The sad Earl Bichet he saw none.

6 The king had only ae daughter,
　　And it was orderd sae to be
　That, as she walked up and down,
　　By the strong-prison-door cam she.

7 Then she heard Earl Bichet sad
　　Making his pityful mane,
　In doolfu sounds and moving sighs
　　Wad melt a heart o stane.

8 'When I was in my ain countrie,
　　I drank the wine sae clear;
　But now I canna get bare bread;
　　O I wis I had neer come here!

9 'When I was in my ain countrie,
　　I drank the wine sae red;
　But now I canna get a bite o bare bread;
　　O I wis that I were dead!'

*　　*　　*　　*　　*

10 'Gae bring to me the good leaven [bread],
　　To eat when I do need;
　Gae bring to me the good red wine,
　　To drink when I do dread.'

11 'Gae ask my father for his leave
　　To bring them unto me,
　And for the keys o the prison-door,
　　To set Earl Bichet free.'

*　　*　　*　　*　　*

12 Then she went into her ain chamber
　　And prayd most heartilie,
　And when that she rose up again
　　The keys fell at her knee.

*　　*　　*　　*　　*

13 Then they hae made a solemn vow
　　Between themselves alone,
　That he was to marry no other woman,
　　And she no other man.

14 And Earl Bichet's to sail to fair Scotland,
　　Far oer the roaring faem,
　And till seven years were past and gone
　　This vow was to remain.

15 Then she built him a stately ship,
　　And set it on the sea,
　Wi four-and-twenty mariners,
　　To bear him companie.

16 'My blessing gae wi ye, Earl Bichet,
　　My blessing gae wi thee;
　My blessing be wi a' the mariners
　　That are to sail wi thee.'

17 Then they saild east, and they saild wast,
　　Till they saild to Earl Bichet's yett,
　When nane was sae ready as his mother dear
　　To welcome her ain son back.

18 'Ye're welcome, welcome, Earl Bichet,
    Ye're dearly welcome hame to me!
And ye're as welcome to Lady Jean,
    For she has lang looked for thee.'

19 'What haste, what haste, O mother dear,
    To wale a wife for me?
For what will I do wi the bonny bride
    That I hae left ayont the sea?'

20 When seven years were past and gone,
    Seven years but and a day,
The Saracen lady took a crying in her sleep,
    And she has cried sair till day.

21 'O daughter, is it for a man o might?
    Or is it for a man o mine?'
'It's neither for a man o might,
    Nor is it for a man o thine.

22 'Bat if ye'll build me a ship, father,
    And set it on the sea,
I will away to some other land,
    To seek a true-love free.'

23 Then he built her a gallant ship,
    And set it on the sea,
Wi a hunder and fifty mariners,
    To bear her companie.

24 At every corner o the ship
    A siller bell did hing,
And at ilka jawing o the faem
    The siller bells did ring.

25 Then they saild east, and they saild wast,
    Till they cam to Earl Bichet's yett;
Nane was sae ready as the porter
    To open and let her in thereat.

26 'O is this Earl Bichet's castle-yett?
    Or is that noble knight within?
For I am weary, sad and wet,
    And far I've come ayont the faem.'

27 'He's up the stair at supper set,
    And mony a noble knight wi him;
He's up the stair wi his bonny bride,
    And mony a lady gay wi them.'

28 She's put her hand into her purse
    And taen out fifty merks and three:
'If this be the Earl Bichet's castle,
    Tell him to speak three words wi me.

29 'Tell him to send me a bit o his bread
    But an a bottle o his wine,
And no forget the lady's love
    That freed him out o prison strong.'

30 The porter he gaed up the stair,
    And mony bow and binge gae he;
'What means, what means,' cried Earl Bichet,
    'O what means a' this courtesie?

31 'O I hae been porter at yere yett
    These four-and-twenty years and three;
But the fairest lady now stands thereat
    That ever my two eyes did see.

32 'She has a ring on her foremost finger,
    And on her middle-finger three;
She has as much gowd about her waist
    As wad buy earldoms o land for thee.

33 'She wants to speak three words wi thee,
    And a little o yere bread and wine,
And not to forget the lady's love
    That freed ye out o prison strong.'

34 'I'll lay my life,' cried Earl Bichet,
    'It's my true love come oer the sea!'
Then up and spake the bride's mother,
    'It's a bonny time to speak wi thee!'

35 'O your doughter came here on a horse's back,
    But I'll set her hame in a chariot free;
For, except a kiss o her bonny mouth,
    Of her fair body I am free.'

36 There war thirty cups on the table set,
    He gard them a' in flinders flee;
There war thirty steps into the stair,
    And he has louped them a' but three.

37 Then he took her saftly in his arms,
    And kissed her right tenderlie:
'Ye're welcome here, my ain true love,
    Sae dearly welcome ye're to me!'

    *   *   *   *   *

    ———•———

7³. doolfu: 1 *struck out.*
At *the end:* "Some verses are wanting at the conclu-
    sion."

———◆———

The following stanza, entered by Scott in the
quarto volume "Scottish Songs," 1795, fol. 29 back,
Abbotsford library, N. 3, is much too good to be lost:

> YOUNG BECHIN was in Scotland born,
>   He longed far countries for to see,
> And he bound himself to a savage Moor,
>   Who used him but indifferently.

———◆———

D is now given as it stands in "The Old Lady's Col-
lection," from which it was copied by Skene: 'Young
Beachen,' No. 14.

1 YOUNG BEACHEN as born in fair London,
    An foiren lands he langed to see,
  An he was tean by the savage Mour,
    An they used him mast cruely.

2 Throu his shoulder they patt a bore,
    An throu the bore they patt a tree,
  An they made him tralle ther ousen-carts,
    An they used him most cruelly.

3 The savige More had ae doughter,
    I wat her name was Susan Pay,
  An she is to the prison-house
    To hear the prisenor's mone.

4 He made na his mone to a stok,
    He made it no to a ston,
  But it was to the Quin of Heaven,
    That he made his mone.

5 'Gine a lady wad borrou me,
    Att her foot I wad rune,
  An a widdou wad borrou me,
    I wad becom her sone.

6 'Bat an a maid wad borrou me,
    I wad wed her we a ring,
  I wad make her lady of haas an bours,
    An of the high tours of Line.'

7 'Sing our yer sang, Young Bichen,' she says,
    'Sing our yer sang to me;'
  'I never sang that sang, lady,
    Bat fat I wad sing to ye.

8 'An a lady wad borrou me,
    Att her foot I wad rune,
  An a widdou wad borrou me,
    I wad becom her son.

9 'Bat an a maid wad borrou me,
    I wad wed her we a ring,
  I wad mak her lady of haas an bours,
    An of the high tours of Line.'

10 Saftly gaid she but,
     An saftly gaid she ben;
   It was na for want of hose nor shone,
     Nor time to pit them on.

11   .   .   .   .   .   .
       .   .   .   .   .
     An she has stoun the kees of the prison,
       An latten Young Beachen gang.

12 She gae him a lofe of her whit bread,
     An a bottel of her wine,
   She bad him mind on the leady's love
     That fread him out of pine.

13 She gae him a stead was gued in time of nead,
     A sadle of the bone,
   Five hundred poun in his poket,
     Bad him gae speading home.

14 An a lish of gued gray honds,
       .   .   .   .   .
     .   .   .   .   .
       .   .   .   .   .

15 Fan seven lang year wer come an gane,
    Shusie Pay thought lang,
  An she is on to fair London,
    As fast as she could gang.

16 Fan she came to Young Beachen's gate,
    .   .   .   .   .
  'Is Young Beachen att home,
    Or is he in this country?'

17 'He is att home,
    [H]is bearly bride him we;'
  Sighan says her Susë Pay,
    'Has he quit forgotten me?'

18 On every finger she had a ring,
    An on the middel finger three;
  She gave the porter on of them,
    'Gett a word of your lord to me.'

19 He gaed up the stare,
    Fell lau doun on his knee:
  'Win up, my proud porter,
    What is your will we [me]?'

20 'I ha ben porter att your gate
    This therty year an three;
  The fairest lady is att yer gate
    Mine eays did ever see.'

21 Out spak the brid's mother,
    An a haghty woman was she;
  'If ye had not excepted the bonny brid,
    Ye might well ha excepted me.'

22 'No desparegment to you, madam,
    Nor non to her grace;
  The sol of yon lady's foot
    Is fairer then yer face.'

23 He's geen the table we his foot,
    An caped it we his knee:
  'I wad my head an a' my land
    It's Susie Pay come over the sea.'

24 The stare was therty steps,
    I wat he made them three;
  He toke her in his arms tua,
    'Susie Pay, y'er welcom to me!'

25 'Gie me a shive of your whit bread,
    An a bottel of your wine;
  Dinner ye mind on the lady's love
    That freed ye out of pine?'

26 He took her
    Doun to yon garden green,
  An changed her name fra Shusie Pay,
    An called her bonny Lady Jean.

27 'Yer daughter came hear on high hors-back,
    She sall gae hame in coaches three,
  An I sall dubel her tocher our,
    She is nean the war of me.'

28 'It's na the fashon of our count[r]y,
    Nor yet of our name,
  To wed a may in the morning
    An send her hame att none.'

29 'It's na the fashon of my country,
    Nor of my name,
  Bat I man mind on the lady's love
    That freed me out of pine.'

———◆———

5^2. I att her foot I: cf. 8^2. 9^3. tours: cf. 6^3.
13^4. spending. 17^3. Sigh an. 18^2. niddel.
After 29:

  Courtes kind an generse mind,
    An winne ye ansur me?
  An fan they hard ther lady's word,
    Well ansuared was she.

———◆———

[L]

The Loving Ballad of Lord Bateman. Illustrated by
George Cruikshank. 1839. This copy previously stood
as **L**, but has been replaced according to Prof. Child's
instructions, Vol II, p. 476.

1 LORD BATEMAN was a noble lord,
  A noble lord of high degree;
He shipped himself all aboard of a ship,
  Some foreign country for to see.

2 He sailed east, he sailed west,
  Until he came to famed Turkey,
Where he was taken and put to prison,
  Until his life was quite weary.

3 All in this prison there grew a tree,
  O there it grew so stout and strong!
Where he was chained all by the middle,
  Until his life was almost gone.

4 This Turk he had one only daughter,
  The fairest my two eyes eer see;
She steel the keys of her father's prison,
  And swore Lord Bateman she would let go
    free.

5 O she took him to her father's cellar,
  And gave to him the best of wine;
And every health she drank unto him
  Was, 'I wish, Lord Bateman, as you was
    mine.'

6 'O have you got houses, have you got land,
  And does Northumberland belong to thee?
And what would you give to the fair young lady
  As out of prison would let you go free?'

7 'O I've got houses and I've got land,
  And half Northumberland belongs to me;
And I will give it all to the fair young lady
  As out of prison would let me go free.'

8 'O in seven long years, I'll make a vow
  For seven long years, and keep it strong,
That if you'll wed no other woman,
  O I will wed no other man.'

9 O she took him to her father's harbor,
  And gave to him a ship of fame,
Saying, Farewell, farewell to you, Lord Bate-
    man,
  I fear I never shall see you again.

10 Now seven long years is gone and past,
  And fourteen days, well known to me;
She packed up all her gay clothing,
  And swore Lord Bateman she would go see.

11 O when she arrived at Lord Bateman's castle,
  How boldly then she rang the bell!
'Who's there? who's there?' cries the proud
    young porter,
  'O come unto me pray quickly tell.'

12 'O is this here Lord Bateman's castle,
  And is his lordship here within?'
'O yes, O yes,' cries the proud young porter,
  'He's just now taking his young bride in.'

13 'O bid him to send me a slice of bread,
  And a bottle of the very best wine,
And not forgetting the fair young lady
  As did release him when close confine.'

14 O away and away went this proud young porter,
  O away and away and away went he,
Until he come to Lord Bateman's chamber,
  When he went down on his bended knee.

15 'What news, what news, my proud young por-
    ter?
  What news, what news? Come tell to me:'
'O there is the fairest young lady
  As ever my two eyes did see.

16 'She has got rings on every finger,
  And on one finger she has got three;
With as much gay gold about her middle
  As would buy half Northumberlee.

17 'O she bids you to send her a slice of bread,
  And a bottle of the very best wine,
And not forgetting the fair young lady
  As did release you when close confine.'

18 Lord Bateman then in passion flew,
  And broke his sword in splinters three,
Saying, I will give half of my father's land,
  If so be as Sophia has crossed the sea.

19 Then up and spoke this young bride's mother,
   Who never was heard to speak so free;
   Saying, You'll not forget my only daughter,
      If so be as Sophia has crossed the sea.

20 'O it's true I made a bride of your daughter,
   But she's neither the better nor the worse for
      me;
   She came to me with a horse and saddle,
      But she may go home in a coach and three.'

21 Lord Bateman then prepared another marriage,
   With both their hearts so full of glee,
   Saying, I will roam no more to foreign coun-
      tries,
   Now that Sophia has crossed the sea.

L. "This affecting legend is given . . . precisely as I have frequently heard it sung on Saturday nights, outside a house of general refreshment (familiarly termed a wine-vaults) at Battle-bridge. The singer is a young gentleman who can scarcely have numbered nineteen summers. . . . I have taken down the words from his own mouth at different periods, and have been careful to preserve his pronunciation." [*Attributed to Charles Dickens.*] *As there is no reason for indicating pronunciation here, in this more than in other cases, the phonetic spelling is replaced by common orthography. Forms of speech have, however, been preserved, excepting two, with regard to which I may have been too nice.*

1^3. his-self. 5^2, 9^2. guv.

Prof. Child provides the following tune in the Appendix to Volume V, p. 415. It does not appear to be associated with any of the preceding texts. [M.F.H.]

Harris MS., No. "27" (=26).

Loomis
house
press

*Specializing in resources on
balladry, traditional music,
folklore and folk-life.*

*For information about additional volumes in this set,
or about related titles which might interest you, please
visit us on the web at*

http://www.loomishousepress.com/

or send a postcard to

Loomis House Press
503 Washington Street
Northfield, MN 55057